IBM® WebSphere® Application Server: The Complete Reference

About the Authors

Ron Ben-Natan is Chief Technology Officer at ViryaNet Inc.—a software provider of wireless workforce management and field service solutions. Prior to that he worked for companies including Intel, Merrill Lynch, J.P. Morgan, and AT&T Bell Laboratories. He has a Ph.D. in computer science in the field of distributed computing and has been architecting and developing distributed applications for over 15 years. His hobby is writing about how technology is used to solve real problems, and he has authored books titled *CORBA*, *Objects on the Web*, *CORBA on the Web*, *IBM SanFrancisco Developer's Guide*, *IBM WebSphere Starter Kit*, and *Integrating Service Level Agreements* as well as numerous articles and tutorials. He can be reached at rbennata@hotmail.com.

Ori Sasson is an independent software consultant involved in several global projects deployed in Switzerland, Singapore, and Israel. He has a B.S. and M.S. in computer science and mathematics from the Hebrew University of Jerusalem and is currently pursuing a Ph.D. in theoretical computer science. He has co-authored several books, including *IBM WebSphere Starter Kit* and *IBM SanFrancisco Developer's Guide*, both published by McGraw-Hill.

IBM® WebSphere® Application Server: The Complete Reference

Ron Ben-Natan
Ori Sasson

McGraw-Hill/Osborne
New York Chicago San Francisco
Lisbon London Madrid Mexico City
Milan New Delhi San Juan
Seoul Singapore Sydney Toronto

McGraw-Hill/Osborne
2600 Tenth Street
Berkeley, California 94710
U.S.A.

To arrange bulk purchase discounts for sales promotions, premiums, or fund-raisers, please contact **McGraw-Hill**/Osborne at the above address. For information on translations or book distributors outside the U.S.A., please see the International Contact Information page immediately following the index of this book.

IBM® WebSphere® Application Server: The Complete Reference

234567890 DOC DOC 0198765432

Book p/n 0-07-222395-2 and CD p/n 0-07-222396-0
parts of
ISBN 0-07-222394-4

Publisher
Brandon A. Nordin

Vice President & Associate Publisher
Scott Rogers

Editorial Director
Wendy Rinaldi

Senior Acquisitions Editor
Nany Maragiogilo

Project Editors
Jenn Tust, Madhu Prasher

Acquisitions Coordinator
Tim Madrid

Technical Editors
David Draeger, Tom Gissel
Andrew McCright, Keith McGuinnes

Copy Editors
Emily Rader, Lisa Theobald

Proofreaders
Cheryl Abel, Nancy McLaughlin
Deidre Dolce

Indexer
Valerie Robbins

Page Composition
Apollo Publishing Services
and Osborne Production Staff

Illustrators
Michael Mueller, Lyssa Wald
Melinda Moore Lytle

Series Design
Peter F. Hancik

This book was composed with Corel VENTURA™ Publisher.

Documentation Used by IBM

IBM WebSphere Application ServerPlus for Tivoli product documentation

IBM WebSphere Application Server Online Documentation Center (Part of the product distribution)

Redbooks

Java Application Development for CICS, SG24-5275-01

Revealed! Architecting Web Access of CICS, SG24-4566-00

Application Development with VisualAge for Java Enterprise, SG24-5081-00

Web Enabling System/390 Applications Using WebSphere for OS/390, Java, and MQSeries, REDP0027

Web Caching and Filtering with IBM WebSphere Performance Pack, REDP0009

Caching and Filtering to Manage Internet Traffic and Bandwidth Demand, REDP0003

IBM WebSphere Performance Pack: Caching and Filtering with IBM Web Traffic Express, SG24-5859-00

IBM WebSphere Performance Pack: Load Balancing with IBM SecureWay Network Dispatcher, SG24-5858-00

IBM WebSphere Performance Pack: Web Content Management with IBM AFS Enterprise File System, SG24-5857-00

Managing Your Java Software with IBM SecureWay On-Demand Server Release 2.0, SG24-5846-00

Java Thin Client Systems: With VisualAge Generator—In IBM WebSphere Application Server, SG24-5468-00

Developing an e-business Application for the IBM WebSphere Application Server, SG24-5423-00

IBM WebSphere and VisualAge for Java Database Integration with DB2, Oracle, and SQL Server, SG24-5471-00

WebSphere Application Server: Standard and Advanced Editions, SG24-5460-00

Using VisualAge for Java Enterprise Version 2 to Develop CORBA and EJB Applications, SG24-5276-00

IBM WebSphere Performance Pack Usage and Administration, SG24-5233-00

Dedicated to Yael and Rinat.
—Ori & Ron

Contents

Part II

WebSphere Technologies

Part IV
Core Services

Part V

Developing Servlets and JavaServer Pages

Acknowledgments

We would like to thank the IBM review team who devoted their time and attention to raising the quality of the book. Their thoroughness, knowledge, and experience have had a tremendous impact on the contents of this book. Thank you to:

- Jim Stetor, Manager WebSphere Execution Team
- David R. Draeger, WebSphere Software Engineer and member of the WebSphere Execution Team
- Thomas R. Gissel, WebSphere Software Engineer and Senior member of the WebSphere Execution Team
- Andrew McCright, WebSphere Software Engineer and member of the WebSphere Execution Team
- Keith McGuinnes, WebSphere Software Engineer, and member of the WebSphere Execution Team

We would also like to thank John E. Botsford, IBM Retail Publishing, who helped with the IBM software included on the CD.

Finally, we would like to thank the amazing team at Osborne/McGraw-Hill including:

- Lisa Bandini, Production Manager
- David Zielonka, Managing Editor
- Wendy Rinaldi, Editorial Director
- Nancy Maragioglio, Senior Acquisitions Editor
- Madhu Prasher, Project Editor
- Jenn Tust, Project Editor
- Timothy Madrid, Acquisitions Coordinator
- Emily Rader, Copy Editor
- Lisa Theobald, Copy Editor
- Nancy McLaughlin, Proofreader
- Cheryl Abel, Proofreader
- Deidre Dolce, Proofreader
- Lyssa Wald, Illustration Supervisor
- Michael Mueller, Illustrator
- Melinda Moore Lytle, DTP Composition Specialist
- Elizabeth Jang, DTP Composition Specialist
- John Patrus, DTP Composition Specialist
- Valerie Robbins, Indexer

We'd also like to thank Jan Benes and his team at Apollo Publishing Services, the lead compositors.

This is the seventh book we have authored; we have *never* worked with such a great team as this one—thank you!

—*Ori & Ron*

Part I

Getting Started

Chapter 1

What Is WebSphere?

IBM is generally considered one of the most important software vendors, and this is even more true in the e-business space. In fact, many would say that IBM is the most influential vendor and has the best vision and product scope in spaces such as Web application development, Java, middleware, and enterprise systems. This chapter gives a brief look into the IBM e-business product landscape. WebSphere is IBM's cornerstone in this blueprint and is both the application server platform on which IBM's e-business blueprint is built and the umbrella product name of a full suite of products for building applications. This chapter discusses the application server, as well as some of the products belonging to the business product family such as WebSphere Portal Server, WebSphere Studio, and WebSphere Voice Server.

WebSphere is Internet infrastructure software known as *middleware*. It enables companies to develop, deploy, and integrate next-generation e-business applications, such as those for business-to-business e-commerce; it also supports business applications from simple Web publishing to enterprise-scale transaction processing applications. WebSphere transforms the way businesses manage customer, partner, and employee relationships. For example, you can use it to create a compelling Web experience that improves the quality and quantity of site traffic, to extend applications to incorporate mobile devices so the sales force can service clients faster, or to build an electronic e-marketplace that lowers sourcing costs.

WebSphere: A Product Family or an Application Server?

WebSphere is the cornerstone of IBM's Internet strategy. In essence, it is a product line comprising a variety of tools for developing, deploying, and maintaining Internet Web sites and e-business systems. At the center of this product line is the WebSphere Application Server. WebSphere Application Server is an application deployment environment for applications implemented as Java server-side code. WebSphere Application Server comes in three different flavors, differing in their complexity and in their coverage:

- **Advanced Single Server Edition** This edition provides most of the Java 2 Platform Enterprise Edition (J2EE) functions offered in the Advanced Edition, but for an environment that comprises only a single server. This version is limited in many ways, partly in its deployment and performance options and partly in its administration features.
- **Advanced Edition, Full Configuration** This is the flagship application server offered by IBM. If you are running your applications in a production environment, you will most likely need this version. It includes support for servlets, JavaServer Pages (JSP), Extensible Markup Language (XML), Enterprise JavaBeans (EJB), messaging, and much more.

- **Advanced Edition, Developer License** This edition offers a low-priced server that is equivalent in features to the Single Server Edition but that cannot be used in a production runtime environment. It is available from the IBM site as an evaluation download. (The Full Advanced Edition is not, which is surprising.)

WebSphere Application Server was introduced to the market in the fall of 1998. Since then, several new releases have been made; at the time of this writing, the latest version is 4.0. The material in this book pertains to this version. An important aspect of version 4.0 is that it is the first version to comply with the Java 2 Enterprise Edition (J2EE) specification. Because it is based on J2EE, version 4.0 ensures compatibility and interoperability with products from other vendors, as well as conformance to a methodology that is used by a large number of developers.

WebSphere as a product suite is the central and most important element in IBM's e-business strategy. In fact, the term "IBM WebSphere family" is used by IBM-ers as a synonym for e-business, and the IBM WebSphere family includes much more than the WebSphere server itself—such products as development tools, monitoring components, configuration management utilities, and more. This framework is very broad, and it is sometimes difficult to understand, from reading IBM marketing documents, which products are truly part of WebSphere and which ones are just given the "WebSphere" name to make them appear as more complete offerings. In this book, we will focus primarily on WebSphere as an application server, but we will also provide information on closely related products in the WebSphere family—products you can use to build and deploy true e-business applications in no time. Two good examples are WebSphere Studio Advanced Developer and VisualAge for Java. Both of these products are development environments for Web applications, and both have connectors and integration points with the WebSphere server.

The remainder of this chapter offers an overview of the WebSphere line of products. It provides a nontechnical look at the various offerings from IBM under the WebSphere name. While these products are not directly related to the subject of this book, any serious WebSphere developer should be acquainted at least with their names. Furthermore, the sheer number of products that go under the WebSphere umbrella shows how serious IBM is about building the WebSphere brand name.

WebSphere Application Server

This section focuses on WebSphere Application Server and details the differences between the various editions. All of the editions provide the functionality of an *application server*. This term does not have a precise definition, but in this context it refers to a server that extends the functionality of a Web server. A traditional Web server is a server capable of responding to HTTP protocol requests. An application server provides the ability to execute Java server-side code, allowing for the generation of dynamic content and the implementation of complex enterprise applications.

WebSphere Advanced Single Server Edition

The Single Server Edition of WebSphere, new in version 4.0, is the entry-level product. Before version 4.0, WebSphere Standard Edition served this purpose, and was primarily aimed at developing and deploying relatively simple applications. Even though the Standard Edition was an entry-level product, you did get a WebSphere server, along with all the core services and supporting utilities. The main feature of the Standard Edition was the Java execution engine, which supports Java servlets and JSP. If you are not familiar with these terms, they refer to pieces of Java code that generate HTML or other content. (These concepts are explained in detail later in the book.)

The Standard Edition of WebSphere Application Server has been discontinued in version 4.0. It is available with version 3.5 and previous versions, and IBM offers easy migration from version 3.5 to 4.0. The main reason for the Standard Edition being discontinued is that it is not compliant with J2EE (a Java standard for application servers), due to its lack of EJB support. The probable other reason for this line being discontinued is that it hurt IBM's revenue stream from WebSphere—in many cases, people preferred using the Standard Edition because of its much lower price.

The Single Server Edition is similar to the Standard Edition in that it serves as the entry level to WebSphere. It is different in that it offers much more than did the Standard Edition, including support for EJB. It targets department-level applications and is useful for building complete e-business solutions that do not require much in terms of performance, throughput, 24/7 operation, and so on. It is a limited edition that is useful to get your hands around. Many of the samples that appear throughout this book are based on the Single Server Edition. Examples are based on the Full Advanced Edition only when the functionality shown is nonexistent in the Single Server Edition.

WebSphere Advanced Edition, Full Configuration

The Advanced Edition is IBM's flagship application server. It is fully J2EE-compliant, and it appears to have the widest appeal. It provides the most useful functionalities of the Enterprise Edition, but without the complexities. It is, in our opinion, a world-class Java application server that is very deep in functionality for the developer, as well as for the administrator.

The Advanced Edition includes support for Enterprise JavaBeans (EJB), transactional database connectivity, and Web services. EJB and Web services, addressed in detail later in the book, are exciting and important technologies for developing enterprise applications.

The Full Advanced Edition offers a richer deployment environment than the Single Server Edition. It allows you to run several application server instances (possibly on different hosts), while providing the illusion of a single virtual server. This means that you can bring up a set of servers that work cooperatively as one server. This feature allows you to seamlessly tie up a set of servers, boosting both the performance and the reliability of your system. While this probably is a good thing in any setting, it is critical for e-business applications, because the most basic motivation for building e-business applications is opening up the business to users on the Web. The vast number of users on the Web offers a huge potential in terms of clientele; however, from a technical standpoint, it places a heavy burden on the applications. This burden stems from the computational load and the resulting performance problems, but it is also due to the fact that the Web environment is much less controlled than a typical client/server environment. Consequently, the deployment platform on which the e-business applications run must be highly tolerant and highly scalable. The most naive yet most effective way of acheiving this is to set up a group of hosts that can support the applications together. In most cases, this is easier said than done, since a lot of effort is required in order to coordinate the different machines. In the Full Advanced Edition, you get this feature without any effort; so, apart from doing the proper configuration, it is really "plug and play."

WebSphere Enterprise Extensions

The Enterprise Edition of WebSphere was IBM's high-end solution for the server market. It was discontinued as of version 4.0 and currently exists only up to version 3.5. Originally, it targeted organizations having e-business applications that were very demanding from the aspect of distribution and transaction-related requirements. Such applications have high demands, and the way IBM attacked this problem was to enrich the Advanced Edition with additional capabilities by integrating it with a set of "power tools." These tools, shown in the following list, must now be purchased separately in a package called Enterprise Extensions.

- Component Broker
- TXSeries
- MQSeries
- WebSphere Enterprise Services

It is difficult to imagine a situation in which you would actually make use of all these products at the same time, because in some cases their capabilities overlap. But one cannot ignore the fact that Enterprise Extensions provides products and capabilities that will handle virtually any requirement for high levels of distribution, transaction support, messaging, and practically anything else.

One of the major things IBM did in version 4.0 was to take the three editions of version 3.5 (Standard, Advanced, and Enterprise) and merge them into a single code line. In version 4.0, the features that previously could only be run on Enterprise Edition can now be run on WebSphere Advanced Edition by installing Enterprise Extensions.

Component Broker

Component Broker is an object engine that supports the Common Object Request Broker Architecture (CORBA) model, as well as EJB. Since the EJB specification has been expanded to place Remote Method Invocation (RMI) over the Internet Inter-ORB Protocol (IIOP), J2EE servers have a lot of CORBA support by definition. We believe that Component Broker appeals only to organizations that have an existing investment in other programming languages, such as C++, and to those whose environment includes a mix of programming languages so that they are unable to commit to a Java environment. The reason is that most of the extra functionality provided by the Component Broker relates to supporting code and functionality in languages other than Java, and to object models other than EJB. IBM provides the C++ CORBA software development kit to facilitate a standard way of integrating C and C++ code into the J2EE environment, and of building and deploying C++ CORBA clients.

Apart from being an Object Request Broker (ORB) and supporting EJB, Component Broker also provides support for a large number of services that are useful when building business applications. These services include concurrency control, lifecycle, event, notification, object identity and naming, security, transaction, session, query (via the Object-Oriented Structured Query Language (OOSQL) standard), cache, and workload management services.

TXSeries

TXSeries is actually two different products—TXSeries CICS (Customer Information Control System) and TXSeries Encina. Both products are transaction monitors that are used by applications with extremely high transaction requirements, and both are completely unrelated to the world of Java and the Internet. With TXSeries, IBM has managed to provide developers with connectors that conveniently "glue" these products to WebSphere Application Server.

MQSeries

MQSeries is a distributed messaging solution from IBM. The appeal of this product—and the appeal of integrating it into WebSphere—is the fact that it is used by many corporate developers. MQSeries is similar to the TXSeries products, and IBM has managed to provide excellent connectors (or adapters) for using it from within Java code. MQSeries also includes support for using MQSeries within the context of the Java Messaging Service (JMS) API.

Enterprise Services

The last major component of Enterprise Extensions is WebSphere Enterprise Services, which essentially is a collection of capabilities offered by IBM that didn't make it into the J2EE standard. The services include

- **ActiveX Bridge** Allows developers to extend J2EE EJB connectivity to existing software components based on Microsoft's Component Object Model (COM) technologies.
- **Internationalization Service** Provides mechanisms for implementing J2EE applications in a manner that adapts presentation and business logic based on different client locales and time zones. Note that Java has built-in support for

internationalization, but that the requirements for this functionality become more complex in the setting of J2EE applications, where a single transaction can span several locales.

- **Extended Messaging Support** Allows the J2EE server to accept inbound asynchronous messages via a JMS listener.
- **Business Rule Beans** Enables the encapsulation of business rules outside of application code, in an external rules set.
- **Shared Work Areas** Provides an abstraction of shared memory for J2EE applications, allowing developers to share information between objects without invoking explicit methods or passing messages.
- **Business Process Beans (Technology Preview)** Provides advanced business process support via different transaction processing paradigms. This framework allows chained J2EE transactions, automatic initiation of transactions using time-based or messaged-based triggers, and concurrent invocations of J2EE components, such as EJB and connectors.

Platform Support

The whole line of WebSphere servers is currently offered on most major operating systems. It is available for Microsoft's Windows NT and Windows 2000, as well as for most flavors of UNIX, including Sun Solaris, IBM AIX, Red Hat Linux, and HP-UX. Because it is an IBM product, it is also available on IBM AS/400. You can connect to any relational database having a Java Database Connectivity (JDBC) driver by including that driver in the classpath of the Java application server. Since some elements make use of built-in WebSphere features (such as database connection pooling, automated persistence, and so on), it is not enough to plug in the driver in some cases. The primary database platform supported (besides IBM's own DB2) is Oracle 8. In this book, our examples will use DB2 and Oracle—but they can be easily implemented on any other database with JDBC support. The major databases supported are

- DB2
- Oracle
- Informix
- Sybase
- SQL Server

For more details on supported products, see the following Web site:

http://www-4.ibm.com/software/webservers/appserv/doc/v40/prereqs/ae_v401.htm

The WebSphere Family of Products

This section reviews the WebSphere family of products beyond the Application Server.

WebSphere Studio Application Developer

WebSphere Studio Application Developer (WSAD) is a new product within the WebSphere line. It is a merge of VisualAge for Java and WebSphere Studio. It therefore targets Java developers, Web site and script builders, and more.

VisualAge for Java is IBM's Java Integrated Development Environment (IDE). Apart from being a full-blown IDE for Java and being an advanced tool for developing, testing, and debugging Java applications, it includes inherent support for WebSphere. Namely, it allows you to develop servlets, JSPs, and EJBs, and run them from within VisualAge for Java. The execution environment provided by VisualAge for Java is a downsized version of the actual WebSphere server.

Realizing the scarcity of development resources in large organizations, IBM developed two variants of VisualAge for Java that allow developers with little or no Java skills to generate code and to develop applications:

- **VisualAge Application Rules** Allows you to quickly build and deploy rule-based applications. Using other IBM tools and middleware, you can build large applications relatively easily.
- **VisualAge Generator** Allows rapid development and deployment of Web-based applications, which mask the complexities of transactions, communications, and databases.

WebSphere Studio provides a powerful set of tools for building dynamic Web pages and applications. It provides a visual authoring environment for designing pure HTML pages and pages with JavaScript, Dynamic HTML (DHTML) and JSPs. As with other WebSphere-related products, WebSphere Studio works in harmony with the WebSphere server and VisualAge for Java.

Another product that provides a visual editing environment for Web pages with dynamic content is WebSphere Homepage Builder, formerly known as TopPage.

WebSphere Business Components

WebSphere Business Components is a library of components aimed at saving time for application developers. The various components have well-defined interfaces and provide rich functionality. By and large, the components provided in this package are EJBs, which increases their usability and portability, and shortens the learning curve for using them. The WebSphere Business Components product is based on a previous product named SanFrancisco.

Project SanFrancisco started out when several large IBM customers went to IBM and asked for assistance in upgrading a set of enterprise-level, mission-critical applications to new technologies. These companies had large application suites in various business domains, and were interested in replacing their old technology bases (often COBOL running on a mainframe) with object-oriented, network-centric architectures. The implications of widespread technology migration and application rewrites were so great that these companies requested guidance and assistance from their large vendor, IBM.

As the relationships with IBM around the technology migration were formulated, a few areas in which IBM could assist were defined. Technology adoption, retraining, and knowledge transfer were areas in which IBM clearly could help. Analysis and design were also targeted: skilled developers and analysts from IBM could be involved with internal development projects to bootstrap processes and make sure that designs were done correctly. As these relationships formed, however, it became clear that more was necessary. As is always the case with new technologies, they hold much promise but initially lack many infrastructure components that come with years of use and market maturity. Multitier software architectures and network-centric application infrastructure is no exception. The companies working with IBM, along with IBM itself, identified fairly early on that they would all benefit greatly if some infrastructure components were put in place that could then be reused throughout the business systems being created. And so project SanFrancisco was born.

Project SanFrancisco started with wide-scale analysis of the business systems for which it would be used. It was then constructed as a set of business process components that could be reused within multiple business systems and domains. Quite early on, the fundamental structure of the project was set to make use of the notion of object-oriented frameworks—as opposed to class libraries, for example. As such, SanFrancisco provided an infrastructure—a consistent design and programming model, along with default business logic that could be changed and extended. Reusable object-oriented software components are certainly not new to the software industry, and even in terms of frameworks, the market has already seen some excellent implementations. Nevertheless, SanFrancisco implemented the largest, most complete set of frameworks of all. In addition, it was one of the first examples of frameworks that included high-level business functionality; most frameworks used today solve only low-level system issues and user interface problems.

So what is the state of the project? SanFrancisco was a collaborative effort led by IBM, involving hundreds of international independent software vendors (ISVs) that were willing to base their system architectures on the SanFrancisco frameworks and to help stabilize and form the ultimate structure of the product.

While SanFrancisco included many frameworks, services, and utilities, the core of the environment was made up of three software layers with increasing proximity to business applications: the Foundation layer, the Common Business Objects layer, and the Core Business Processes layer. Each of these layers relied on the previous layer (see Figure 1-1).

The Foundation layer implemented the infrastructure and services available for all objects participating in the SanFrancisco environment. It supported the notion of object

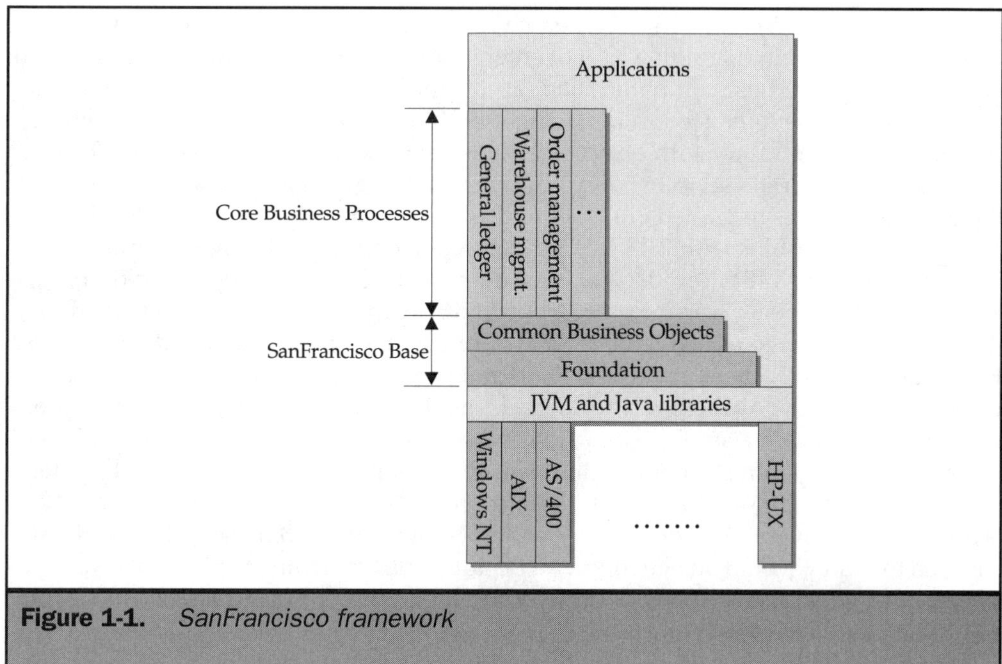

Figure 1-1. *SanFrancisco framework*

persistence, transaction processing, distribution and location transparency, naming, security, ownership, and so on. It was the largest layer, and the one that provided context-free, infrastructure-related support useful for all applications.

The Common Business Objects layer implemented a set of elementary business objects common to a very large set of business domains. These objects included addresses, money-related objects, customer and location, and more.

The final layer, Core Business Processes, provided complete sets of business objects and processes that formed sets of mini-applications and included working functionality that was useful in the relevant domains. This layer actually was not one layer, but rather a set of vertical layers, each providing support in a certain domain. Naturally, the first verticals to be selected were those most relevant to IBM customers; however, as time went on, additional verticals were added.

By understanding and using both the Core Business Processes and the Common Business Objects, one could customize the SanFrancisco frameworks either through derivation or composition (or a combination of both), making the end result extremely attractive. The simplest reuse scenario involved using business objects and processes out of the box while setting properties that were built-in parameters of the business objects. The next level of complexity allowed you to alter the way in which objects were created and to define which class would be used for instantiating a certain business concept. By supplying your own extension to the business class, you could customize behavior while remaining within the framework. Alternatively, you could fully extend a domain's class through substitution, or through derivation and modification, of functionality.

As shown in Figure 1-1, the Foundation layer and the Common Business Objects layer form the SanFrancisco Base. The base layers provided the services and the underlying object support required for building multitier, distributed, object-oriented applications, along with a fundamental set of objects that conformed to the SanFrancisco patterns. This not only allowed the application builder to be semi-oblivious to the difficulties involved with complex application architectures, it also helped to jump-start the development process.

The Core Business Processes complemented the base with rich functionality in various domains, all while building on the base. As Figure 1-1 shows, an application builder was not limited in how the frameworks could be used. Applications could be built within one or more of the Core Business Processes, in which case SanFrancisco could provide the most bang for the buck. If the domain was not covered by one of the process frameworks, or if the functionality provided was too different from the one required, the application could make use of the Common Business Objects layer as a set of reusable business objects that functioned within the SanFrancisco environment. This use saved a lot of development time and even more testing time, but still required more work than did use of the Core Business Process layer.

Finally, new business objects were sometimes created directly over the Foundation. In this case, the new business objects made use of the underlying services only, which solved the most complex issues in the system architecture. Obviously, any combination of the described alternatives was possible; an application may have used parts of the Core Business Processes or some of the Common Business Objects directly, combined with a set of objects using Foundation layer services. Once all pieces of the application used these services, the objects worked in tandem.

We mentioned that as long as objects were built over the Foundation layer, they formed a coherent application structure. Building objects that are external to the foundation to work at the application level was much more difficult and was not recommended. As long as objects used the Foundation layer services and conformed to the SanFrancisco patterns, they could participate in the SanFrancisco world and thus make use of the benefits. Objects not built in this way needed to solve many difficult problems, such as persistence, transactions, and so on. Even worse, if you decided to depart from the SanFrancisco model, you had to synchronize and maintain the two models. For example, if you had a single business transaction that included objects using the base and objects that required self-management for transactions, you somehow had to synchronize all of this into one transaction—something that really should not be attempted without serious "adult" supervision.

The SanFrancisco project was not successful. In fact, it was highly unsuccessful given the amount of investment funding that IBM poured into it (as well as into Taligent, which formed some of the roots of SanFrancisco). When WebSphere emerged as the dominant Java and e-business platform that it is, IBM quickly repositioned and rebuilt SanFrancisco on top of EJB as the base framework and on WebSphere as the deployment environment. WebSphere Business Components is still expanding, and it appears to be a promising line of products; it certainly implements a lot of business functionality!

WebSphere Transcoding Publisher

One of the challenges of developing applications for today's Internet is the multitude of devices that can access the Web. In addition to the traditional PC-based and UNIX-based browsers, there are growing numbers of personal digital assistants (PDAs) and cellular phones that provide Web access. For such devices, it is either required or helpful to produce content in a manner that matches the device capabilities. In other words, content must be reformatted to fit the screen, and possibly be presented in a different markup language altogether. For example, cellular phones might require content in Wireless Markup Language (WML), part of the WAP standard, or Compact HTML (CHTML).

Enter WebSphere Transcoding Publisher. This product provides you with the capability to reformat and adapt your data on the server side, according to your needs.

WebSphere Voice Server

A recent venue of expansion for Internet applications is the realm of voice services, via call centers and voice portals. IBM has moved into this domain with the WebSphere Voice Server. This server builds on the WebSphere server and VoiceXML (a special variant of XML for voice-based documents), and provides the tools for building Web-based voice portals and call centers.

WebSphere Portal Server

A few years back, portals were "the next big thing" in the Internet world. The glamour has now faded away, but on the other hand, any company can build its own custom portal Web site with products such as WebSphere Portal Server. It allows users to sign in and receive personalized content—and, of course, it may be built to contain any specific content required to serve the needs of customers, business partners, and employees.

WebSphere Everyplace Suite

The WebSphere Everyplace Suite is IBM's player in the mobile computing and mobile Internet arena. While some of its capabilities overlap those of the WebSphere Transcoding Publisher, this product aims to provide a complete out-of-the-box solution for building sites for mobile users accessing content from PDAs or cellular phones. WebSphere Everyplace Suite includes a client-side component called WebSphere Everyplace Embedded Edition.

WebSphere Personalization

WebSphere Personalization gives you the capability to provide users with personalized content that is customized for their individual needs and preferences.

Obviously, the same effect can be achieved with a relatively small programming effort using WebSphere Application Server itself.

WebSphere Edge Server

Previously called WebSphere Performance Pack, WebSphere Edge Server provides a multitude of performance capabilities. These include load balancing, content-based routing (which affects quality of service), content filtering, and content caching. It is important to note that this product works with various Web servers, not necessarily just IBM's.

WebSphere Site Analyzer

WebSphere Site Analyzer provides Web site visitor activity and usage capabilities. The power of this product stems from the fact that it provides all the data required for analyzing Web site visitor behavior, and at the same time is tightly integrated with other IBM products, such as the WebSphere Application Server itself and WebSphere Commerce Suite.

Tivoli Policy Director

Tivoli Policy Director is a part of the Tivoli family of products. It is aimed at managing the security policy for e-business and Web-based applications.

WebSphere Commerce Suite

WebSphere Commerce Suite provides tools for building e-commerce sites quickly and relatively easily. WebSphere Commerce Suite includes a subproduct called WebSphere Payment Manager—which, as the name implies, is used to manage payments.

WebSphere Business-to-Business Integrator

B2B is yet another buzzword that has lost its glamour with the bust of the dot-com bubble. WebSphere Business-to-Business Integrator allows you to bridge the gap between your own company's enterprise computing systems and those of customers, suppliers, and business partners. The basic technology for doing all of this is XML, but this product combines some of IBM's integration and transaction products.

WebSphere Partner Agreement Manager

WebSphere Partner Agreement Manager allows an organization to automate interactions with partners (suppliers, for example), customers, and e-markets. Such automation can help improve supply chain efficiency and effectiveness.

Summary

Because this book is a reference on the topic of developing Web applications using WebSphere tools and deploying them on WebSphere Application Server, it does not go into detail on most of the products in the WebSphere family that were mentioned in this chapter. In fact, many of these products deserve "complete references" of their own. As this book focuses on WebSphere Application Server only, it provides much detail on EJB, servlets, JSP, all aspects of J2EE, deployment topologies, and much more.

Chapter 2

Installing and Starting WebSphere

This chapter delves into WebSphere and runs through a typical installation. You will walk through a complete installation procedure for Windows (NT or 2000) and for Linux. IBM does not currently support Windows XP, and the plan is to support it formally in the version 5.0 product line only. Still, we have been running on XP for quite a long time; as long as you don't try it in a production environment, you will probably be OK. The installation procedure for UNIX platforms is quite similar to that for Linux. Some troubleshooting tips are covered later in the chapter, although in most cases, installation should go smoothly. By the end of this chapter, you should be ready to install WebSphere on your machine with no problems.

To initiate the installation process, you need to open the installation program, which is available on a CD or as a download from *www.ibm.com/websphere*. An evaluation version of WebSphere Application Server Advanced Single Server Edition is provided in the CD that accompanies this book.

Windows Installation

Once you start the installation program, the first window that pops up is the warning window. Apart from indicating that WebSphere is copyrighted, this warning window also recommends closing any open applications. This is extremely important if you are running a Web server or a previous version of WebSphere. You should shut these down prior to continuing with the installation.

WebSphere 4.0 does not require a Web server. Version 4.0 comes with a built-in, fully functional Web server, which runs on port 9080. It is not recommended for production use, but it does allow a user to test a WebSphere Application Server (WAS) installation without installing a Web server.

For a production environment, we suggest you install a Web server (or an HTTP server) to work with, such as Microsoft IIS, iPlanet, Apache, or Lotus Domino. The WebSphere installation includes the default application server, which is IBM HTTP Server. If you want to use WebSphere with a different Web server, you must install it prior to running the WebSphere installation. Web servers are discussed at length in Chapter 6.

If you already have a version of WebSphere installed, the installation program will automatically detect it and offer to either upgrade it or install a fresh new copy (see Figure 2-1). Of course, if you've never installed WebSphere, this offer will not appear.

After you've made your selection, or if you don't have WebSphere installed, the Installation Options window appears, offering two different installation methods. The first option, Typical Installation, installs IBM HTTP Server and the IBM Java Developer's Kit (JDK) 1.3.0, along with the WebSphere Application Server. The JDK used for WebSphere is the IBM JDK 1.3.0. The second option, Custom Installation, allows you to select which components to install. Specifically, it lets you select a different JDK and install other Web server plug-ins (see Figure 2-2). Note that if you use a JDK, you must

Previous Installation Detected

Previous version(s) of WebSphere have been detected. You can upgrade this version or install a new copy of WebSphere.

Perform Migration

WebSphere Application Server Version 3.5

Previous Install Directory

C:\WebSphere\AppServer

Backup and Uninstall

< Back

Next >

Cancel

Figure 2-1. *Detecting an existing version of WebSphere*

first ensure that it is works correctly with WebSphere. Obviously, JDK 1.3.0 from IBM will work perfectly.

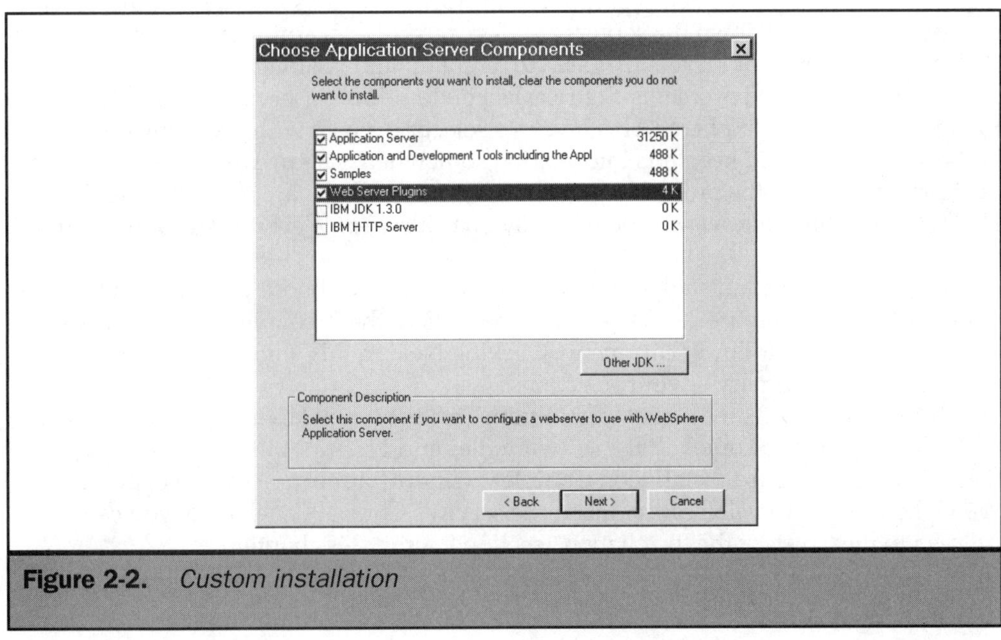

Figure 2-2. *Custom installation*

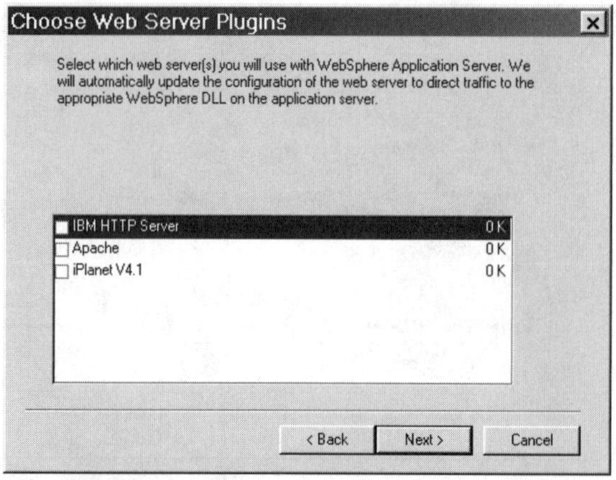

Figure 2-3. *Web Server Plug-ins*

If you don't intend to use IBM HTTP Server, deselect this option in the dialog. If you select Web Server Plugins, WebSphere prompts you to select which plug-ins you want, as shown in Figure 2-3.

If you've selected an installation directory where you already have WebSphere working and running, the Setup program will warn you that some files are in use, and that you should shut down the server. You'll get a similar warning if you are installing Web server plug-ins for servers that are currently up and running.

If there are no such problems, Setup asks you to select a user name and a password for administering WebSphere. (This involves selecting a user with "Administrator" authority.) You should keep this information somewhere safe in case you forget it. The next step is selecting the product installation directory. If you are not installing IBM HTTP Server, this window will include only one entry (for WebSphere Application Server itself).

After specifying the installation directory, you need to choose the program file folder, as shown in Figure 2-4. This determines where the WebSphere programs will appear under the Windows Start menu. Clicking Next in this window presents a window with a summary of your selections.

The next step starts the actual installation. This process takes a couple of minutes as the Setup program copies all the software files and generates the required setup files. Finally, a standard Installation Complete window appears. You can open the WebSphere administration server using the services Control Panel. Now you can proceed to the "Testing the Installation" section later in this chapter.

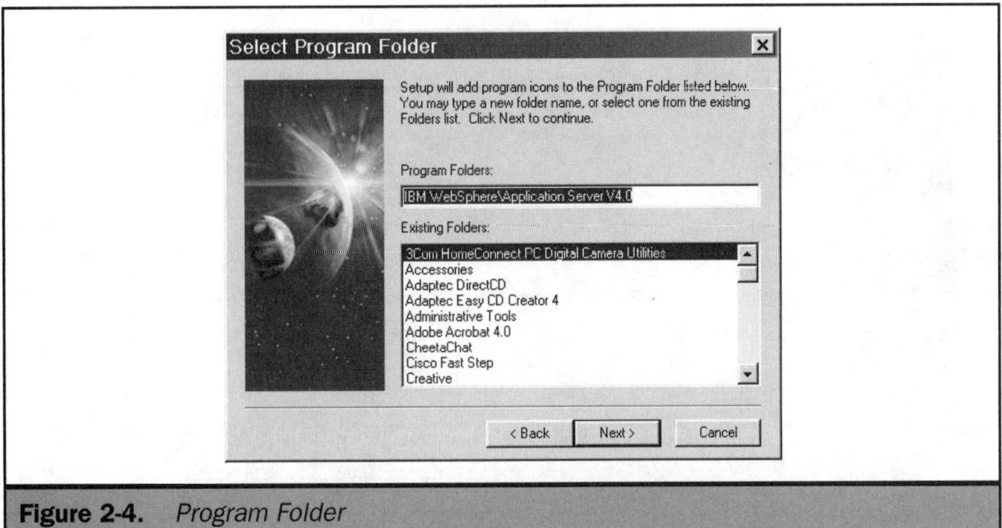

Figure 2-4. *Program Folder*

Linux Installation

WebSphere 4.0 is available for IBM AIX, Sun Solaris, HP-UX, and Linux. For all UNIX installations, you need to run the *install.sh* script from the respective directory on the WebSphere installation CD. If you've downloaded the program, you first need to extract the installation files from the *tar* archive.

All UNIX versions sport a graphical user interface (GUI) that takes you through a procedure similar to the one detailed in the preceding section on Windows installation. The only difference is the look and feel of the interface and the fact that pathnames are delimited by a slash (/) and not a backslash (\).

Here we focus on the Linux version, due to its wide availability. The installation process is similar on all platforms. An important consideration that is critical for a UNIX installation is to check which operating system patches are required in order for WebSphere to work correctly. This is especially true for Solaris and HP-UX, or for Linux variants other than Red Hat Linux 7.0. An updated list of the required patches, along with any special caveats regarding the installation, can be found in the product release notes from IBM. The installation program usually indicates any operating system inadequacies or discrepancies.

Once you run the *install.sh* script, you will see a welcome window, prompting you to click Next to continue the setup. Just as in the Windows installation, the Setup program detects any previous installations of WebSphere and offers to migrate them, as shown in Figure 2-5.

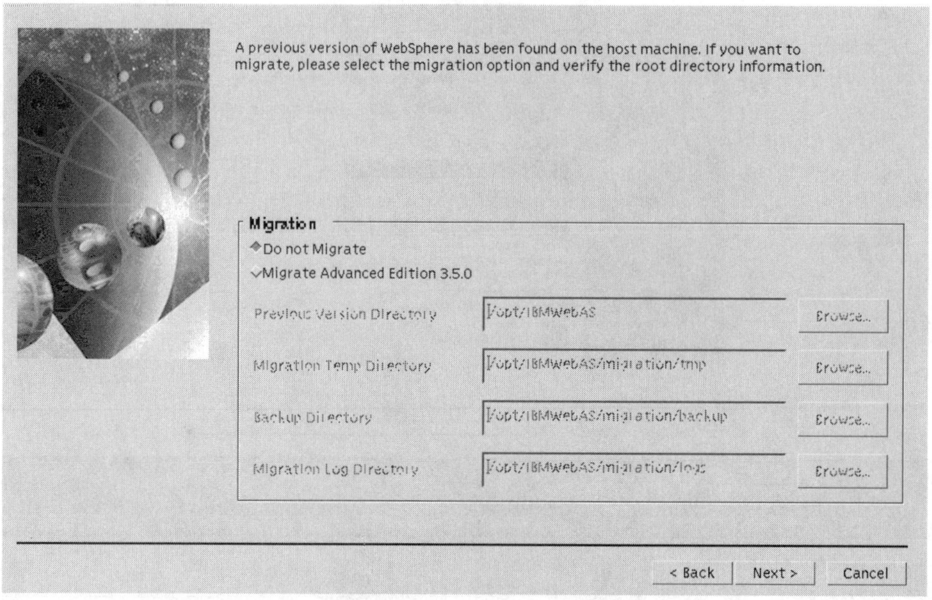

Figure 2-5. *Previous installation detected*

In the next step, you select whether you want to have a typical installation or a custom installation. As explained in the Windows installation section, the typical installation uses IBM's JDK 1.3.0, as well as IBM HTTP Server. If you want to use a different JDK or Web server, you must select the custom installation. Specifically, this is the case if you have Apache installed and running and you intend to continue using it.

If you select the custom installation, Setup will prompt you to select the installation components, as shown in Figure 2-6. If you select the Web Server Plugins option, Setup will prompt you to select which plug-ins you want, as shown in Figure 2-7.

The next step is to select the installation directory. If you are not installing IBM HTTP Server, only one entry (the one for the WebSphere server) will appear on your screen. After you select the directories, Setup prompts you with a window summarizing your selections, as shown in Figure 2-8. Clicking Install will initiate the installation process.

Finally, the window indicating Setup has finished appears. This concludes the installation, and we can proceed to testing the installation.

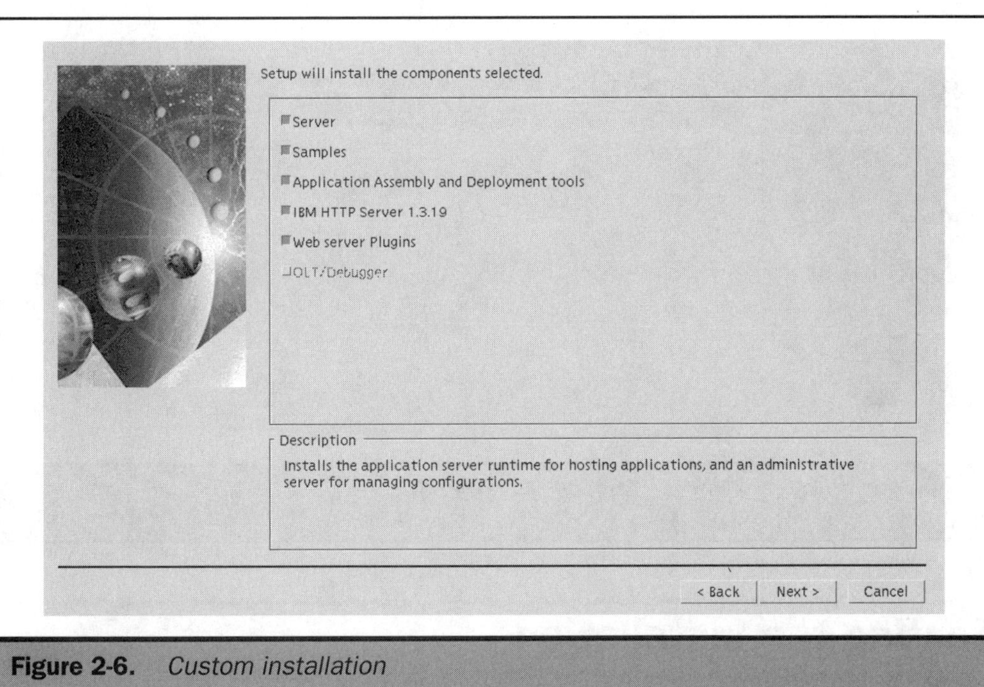

Figure 2-6. *Custom installation*

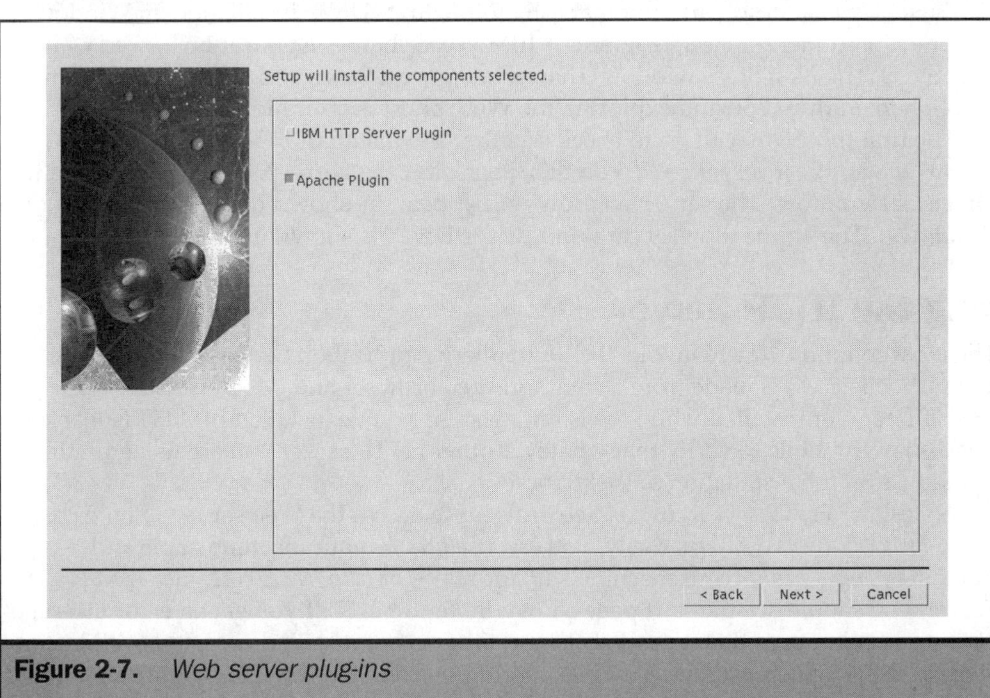

Figure 2-7. *Web server plug-ins*

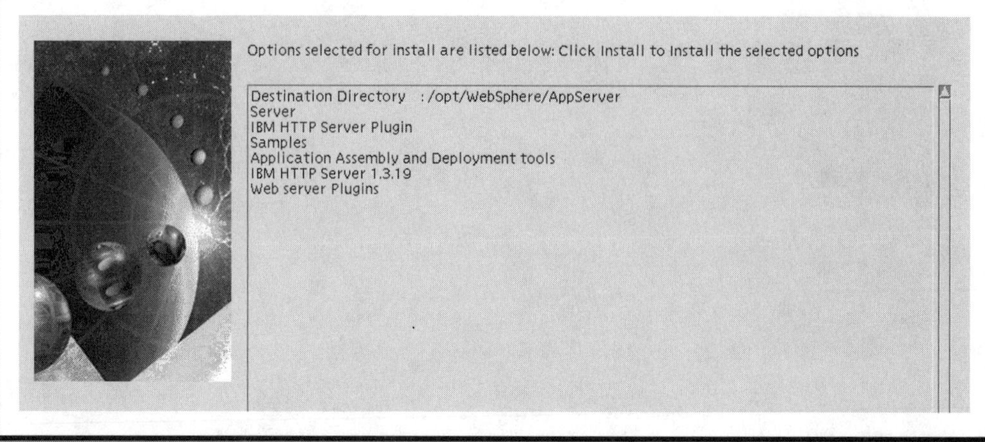

Figure 2-8. *Summary of selected installation options*

Testing the Installation

To test your installation, you must first start the application server. WebSphere 4.0 includes a new feature called First Steps, which introduces new users to WebSphere. The First Steps window starts automatically following a UNIX installation. In Windows, under the Start menu, select Programs | IBM WebSphere | Application Server V4.0 | First Steps. The First Steps window, shown in Figure 2-9, is a one-stop shop for getting WebSphere information and exploring the WebSphere Application Server.

The first thing you can do to check whether the installation was successful is to start the application server. To do this, just select the corresponding entry from the First Steps window. The server window will appear, as shown in Figure 2-10 (for Windows). The application server window for UNIX is shown in Figure 2-11.

Testing the HTTP Server

The most common way to invoke the WebSphere Application Server is via HTTP access. Such access is made from a common Web browser and depends heavily on the HTTP server installed. This step is important if you've installed IBM HTTP Server. It is also worthwhile to verify that whatever other HTTP server you are using is still working after the installation of WebSphere.

To test the HTTP server, use a Web browser to access the Web server's home page using *http://localhost.* (Alternatively, you can use *http://*<your machine name and domain name>, *http://*<your machine's IP address>, or *http://127.0.0.1.*) For IBM HTTP Server, you should see the start page shown in Figure 2-12. If you get an error message at this point, it means that your Web server either is not installed correctly or did not start. In this case, refer to the "Troubleshooting" section later in this chapter.

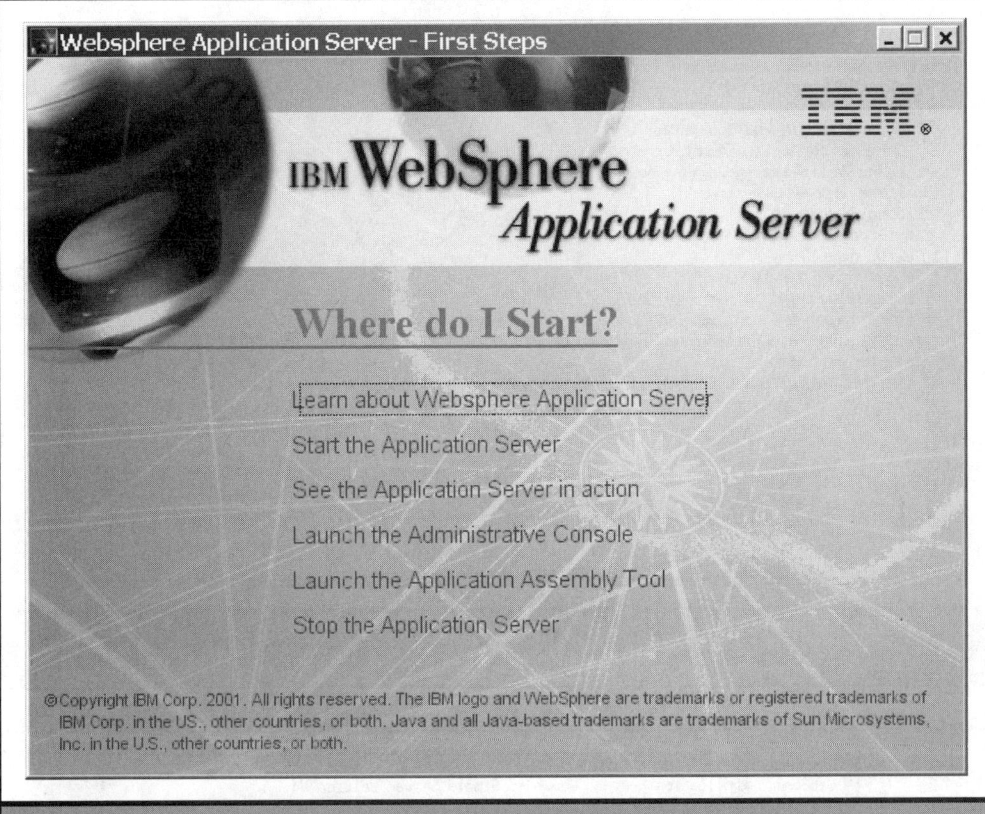

Figure 2-9. *First Steps window*

Testing the Application Server

So far, you have made sure that the HTTP server is up and running. Now it's time to verify that WebSphere is running. To do this, you need to invoke the *snoop* servlet. A servlet is a piece of Java code running on the server side. (Servlets are discussed in detail later in Part V.) A servlet can generate dynamic content, and that is the main difference between the WebSphere Application Server and the underlying HTTP server. In other words, the Web server can return only "static" content, whereas the application server can invoke servlets and other mechanisms to generate dynamic content. Note that this is not always the case with the HTTP server—you can configure the Web server to use Common Gateway Interface (CGI) scripts or other techniques to generate dynamic content. Generally speaking, however, these techniques have become obsolete since servlets were introduced.

```
Start the Application Server

IBM WebSphere Application Server'
'Application Server Launcher'
'Copyright (C) IBM Corporation, 2001'
'The configuration file was defaulted to:'
'   C:\WebSphere\AppServer\config\server-cfg.xml'
'Using the single available node or the localhost node.'
'Using the single available server.'
'Initiating server launch.'
'Loaded domain "WebSphere Administrative Domain".'
'Selected node "THINKPAD".'
'Selected server "Default Server".'
'The server launch was successfully initiated.'
'To test if the server launch completed successfully, examine'
'the logs configured for the server which was launched.  The'
'configured log files are:'
'   Standard Output: "C:\WebSphere\AppServer/logs/default_server_stdout.log"'
'   Standard Error: "C:\WebSphere\AppServer/logs/default_server_stderr.log"'
'
```

Figure 2-10. *Starting the WebSphere Application Server (Windows)*

```
WebSphere Application Server, Advanced Single Server Edition V4.0
Application Server Launcher
Copyright (C) IBM Corporation, 2001

The configuration file was defaulted to:
    /opt/WebSphere/AppServer/config/server-cfg.xml
Using the single available node or the localhost node.
Using the single available server.
Will pause after displaying results.
Initiating server launch.
Loaded domain "WebSphere Administrative Domain".
Selected node "localhost.localdomain".
Selected server "Default Server".
WSPL0065I: Initiated server launch with process id 4289.
Time mark: Saturday, November 3, 2001 11:16:14 AM GMT+02:00
Waiting for the server to be initialized.
Time mark: Saturday, November 3, 2001 11:16:21 AM GMT+02:00
Initialized server.
Waiting for applications to be started.
Time mark: Saturday, November 3, 2001 11:16:51 AM GMT+02:00
Started applications.
WSPL0057I: The server Default Server is open for e-business.
Please review the server log files for additional information.
Standard output: /opt/WebSphere/AppServer/logs/default_server_stdout.log
Standard error: /opt/WebSphere/AppServer/logs/default_server_stderr.log
Pausing; press the enter key to continue.
```

Figure 2-11. *Starting the WebSphere Application Server (UNIX)*

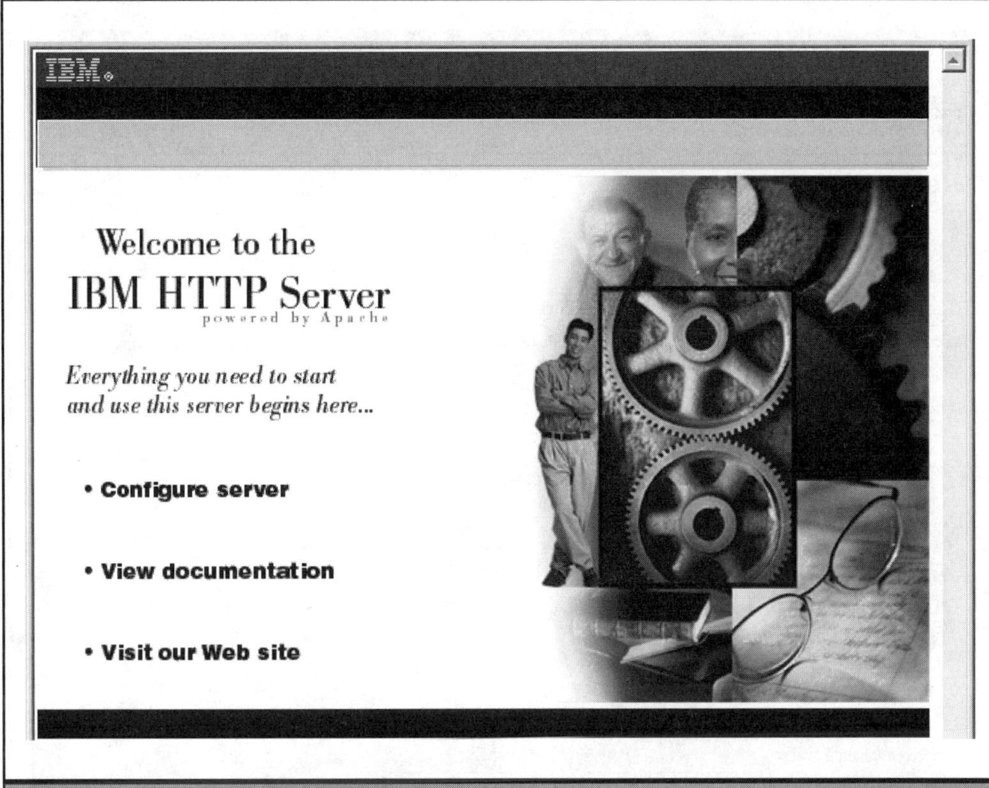

Figure 2-12. *IBM HTTP Server home page*

OK, so how do you run the servlet? Simple: you open your browser and specify the URL *http://localhost/servlet/snoop*. The result should appear as shown in Figure 2-13. Much of the output of this servlet is dynamic (meaning that it is generated at runtime), such as the Remote Address field, which appears in the list under Request Information. This field shows the IP address of the browser making the request. If another machine is handy, you can try running a browser from there (replacing *localhost* with the appropriate hostname) and observing the difference. If, for some reason, the *snoop* servlet does not start, refer to the "Troubleshooting" section later in this chapter.

If the Web server works but the *snoop* servlet does not, you should perform another test. As mentioned earlier, a built-in Web server is part of the WebSphere administrative server runtime. It runs on port 9080 by default. Once you start an application server, you can test whether it is working by pointing to *http://localhost:9080/servlet/snoop*. If this works, but *http://localhost/servet/snoop* does not, you have a problem with the communication between the Web server and the application server—usually something related to the WebSphere plug-in that needs to be loaded by the Web server.

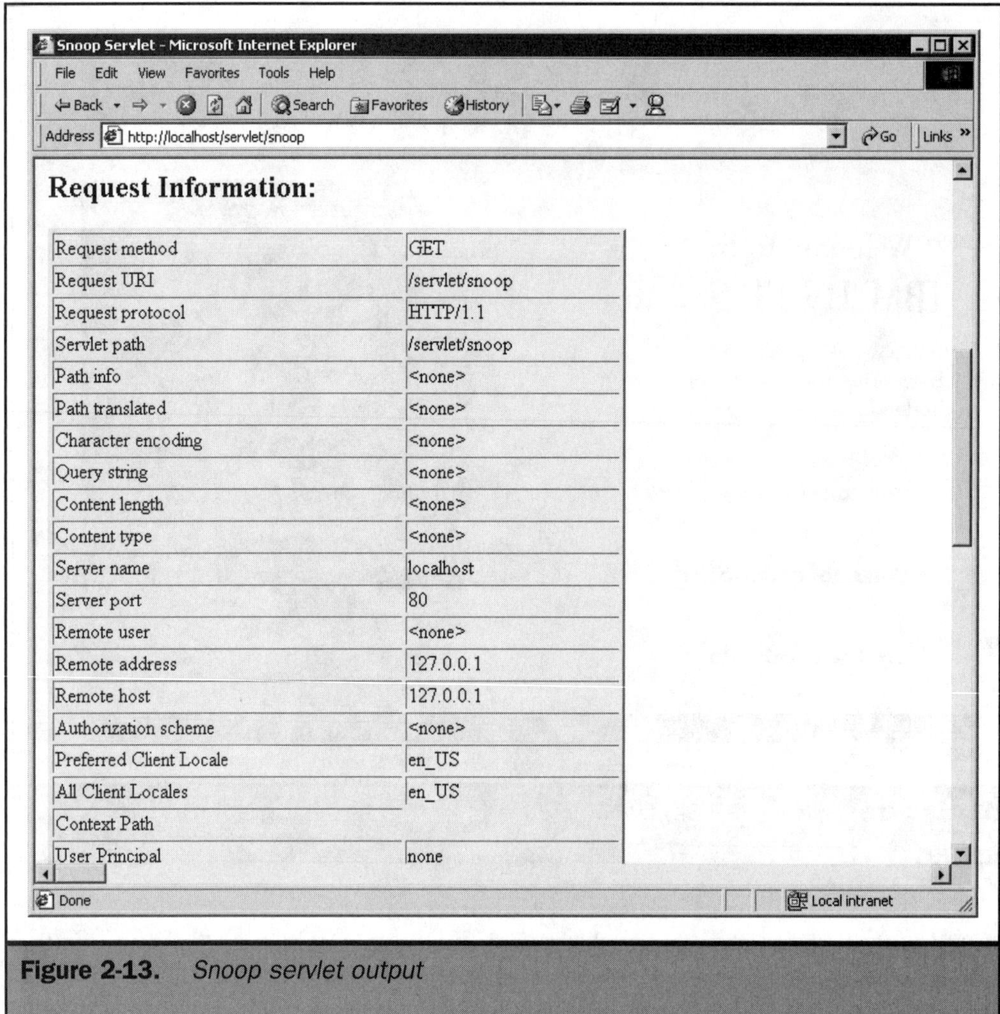

Figure 2-13. *Snoop servlet output*

WebSphere Samples

Yet another way to test your WebSphere installation is to use IBM's WebSphere samples. These samples include a variety of toy applications demonstrating the abilities of WebSphere. These samples are available only if you've chosen to install them as part of the installation process. You can start the WebSphere samples either by choosing See the Application Server in Action from the First Steps window, or simply by accessing *http://localhost/WSSamples*.

The Samples home page is shown in Figure 2-14. From this page, you can explore the various samples and explore WebSphere's technologies and features. To make sure

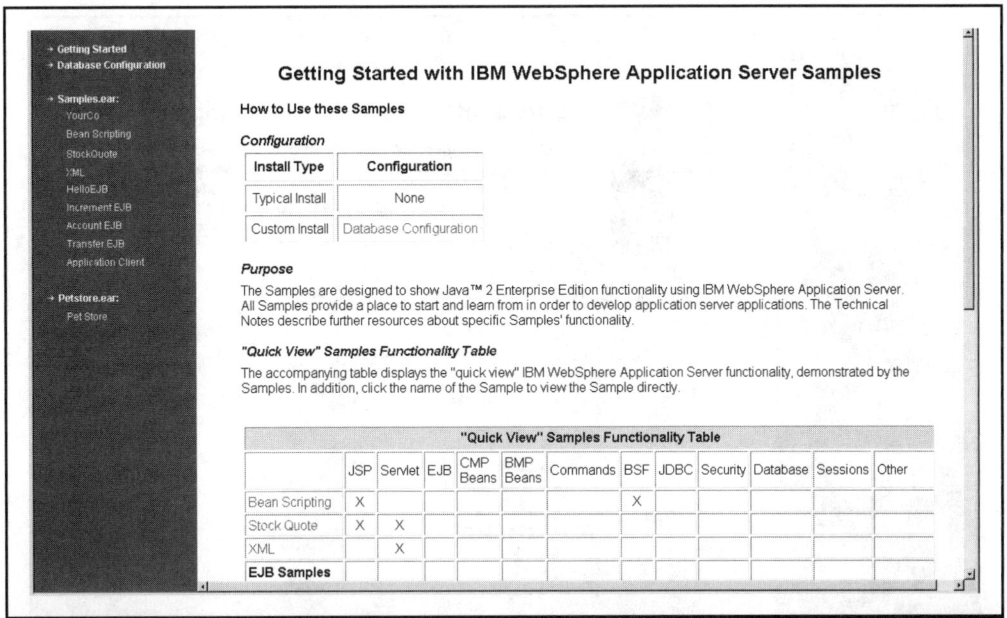

Figure 2-14. *WebSphere Samples home page*

your installation is working properly, you can try out each one of these samples. For example, you can select Whitepages from the YourCo Sample screen shown in Figure 2-15.

In the window that appears, select Run This Sample. Click the Begin Your Search button to invoke the application server. A sample result is shown in Figure 2-16. You can experiment with this example by selecting different parameters for the search.

A full description of the WebSphere samples is beyond the scope of this chapter. However, if your server is running properly, you'll find the samples well documented and easy to follow.

Troubleshooting

WebSphere is a mature product—at least as far as Java and Internet technologies are concerned. Therefore, most installation problems will typically prompt some sort of warning from the installation program. For example, during installation on UNIX, the installation script automatically detects any operating system incompatibilities.

In any case, if you have a problems, you must first double-check that your system meets the WebSphere requirements as set out in the product documentation and release notes. This is especially true if you have conducted a custom installation using a different JDK or Web server. Incompatibilities with the JDK and the server can result in various errors.

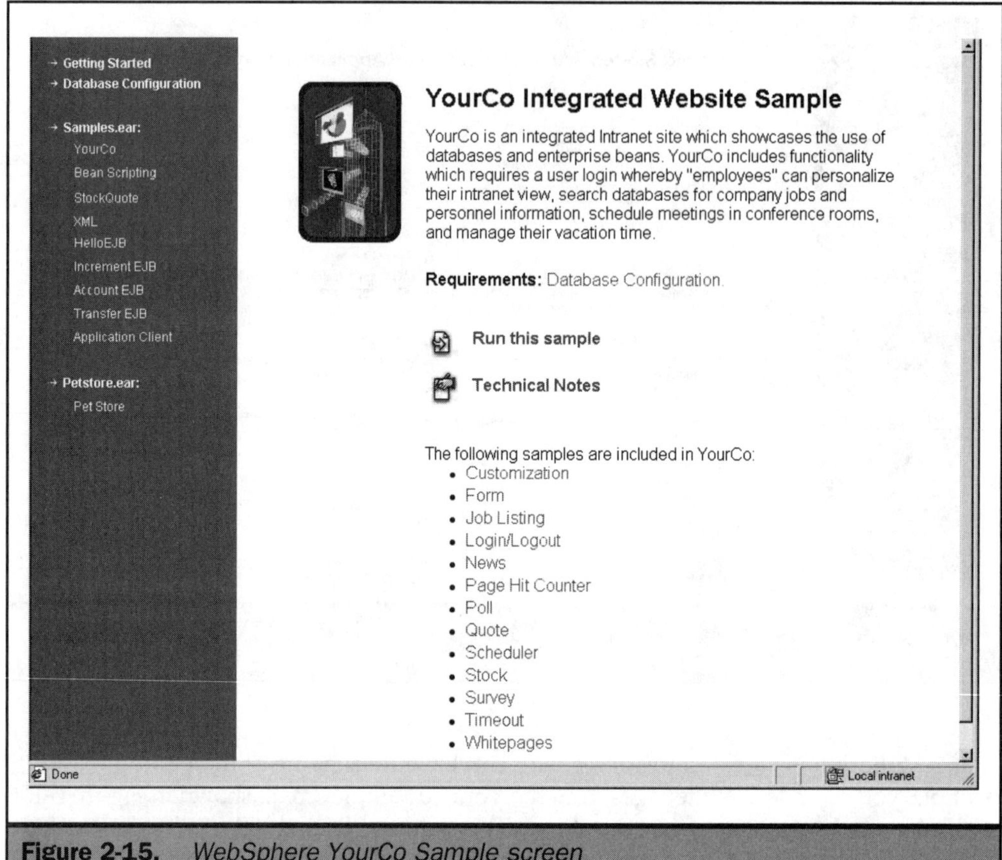

Figure 2-15. *WebSphere YourCo Sample screen*

Problems with the Web Server

If you are not able to access the HTTP server, you must first make sure that it is running.

To monitor your HTTP server (as well as any other service in Windows NT or Windows 2000), you look at the Services panel under the Windows Control Panel, as shown in Figure 2-17. The IBM Hypertext Transfer Protocol daemon (HTTPD) server should be started automatically, as shown in this figure. If for some reason it is not started, you can start it manually—although you might first want to make sure that it is running under the correct user and that the correct password is entered. In the unlikely event that manual startup also fails, you need to check the HTTP server logs for the specific problem you have. The log files appear in the *logs* directory under your IBM HTTP Server installation directory and are called *error* and *admin_error*.

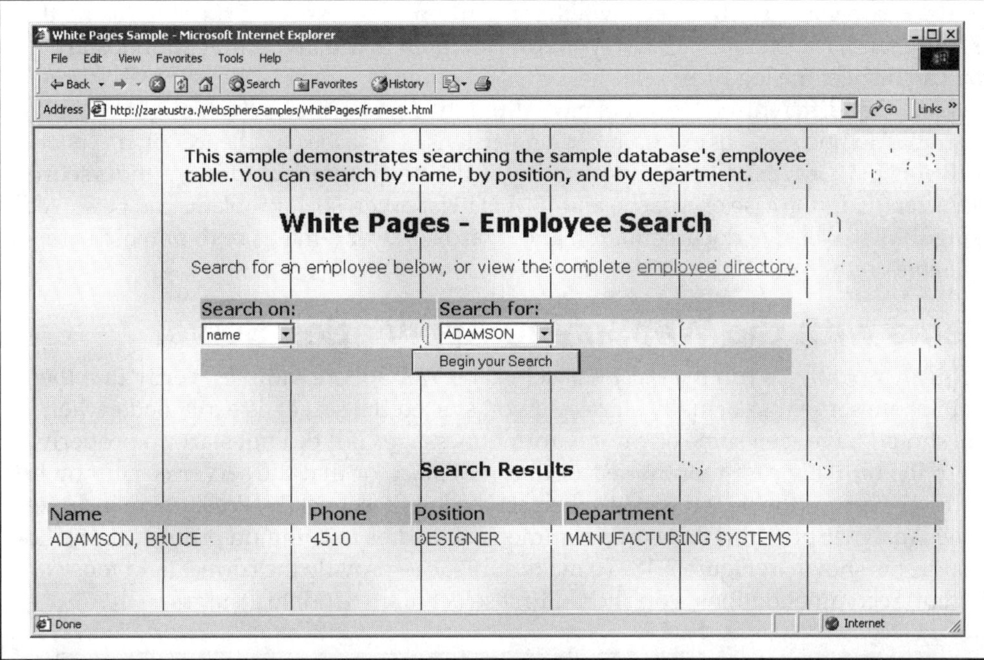

Figure 2-16. *WebSphere White Pages sample output*

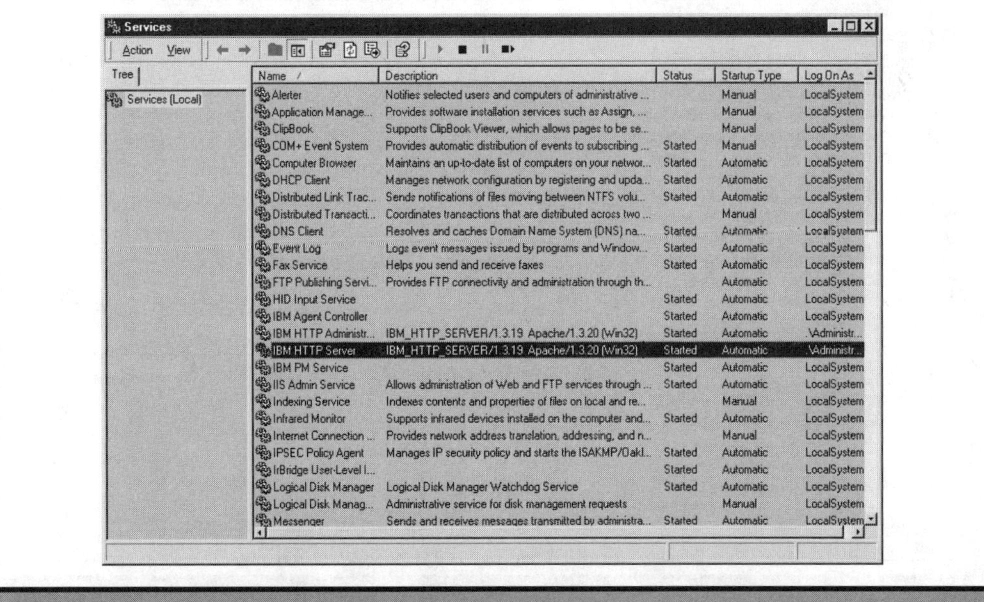

Figure 2-17. *Windows Services panel*

If you are using UNIX, check whether the `httpd` processes are running (using the `ps` command, for example). If not, you can run them manually. If they cannot start, you can inspect the log files.

Note that different Web servers have different peculiarities, which might be a little frustrating to uncover. For example, certain versions of Apache (and hence some versions of IBM HTTP Server) do not run properly if the hostname includes an underscore character (_). In the case of Apache and IBM HTTP Server, such problems can be solved using IBM's extensive documentation and hoards of user e-mails, both of which are available on the Web.

Problems with the WebSphere Application Server

If you are not able to run the *snoop* servlet or the WebSphere samples, verify that the WebSphere server has actually started. If you started the server as explained earlier, you should have seen some error or warning messages if it did not start up properly.

In the unlikely case that the server does not start, or that the server is running but with some errors, the only resort is to inspect the log files. Luckily, WebSphere includes a Log Analyzer program that can recommend remedies to common problems. The Log Analyzer is shown in Figure 2-18. To make sure it can provide the correct (and most current) recommendations, you should first select File | Update Database.

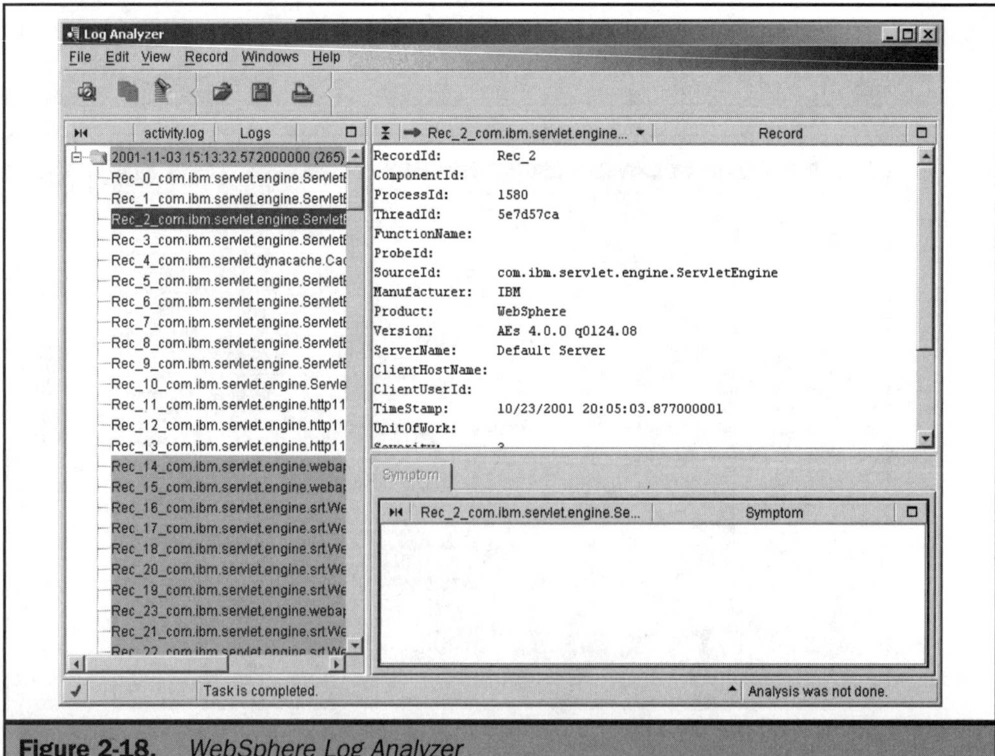

Figure 2-18. *WebSphere Log Analyzer*

Multiple WebSphere Installations

One of the questions we are often asked is whether it is possible to have more than one version of WebSphere installed. The answer is yes, and this is especially useful if you already have an older version of WebSphere, such as 3.5 or even 3.0.*x*, and you want to start experimenting with WebSphere 4.0. This question most frequently comes up in a Windows environment, because in Windows the server is usually started from the Services panel.

Each installation of WebSphere has its own classpath and does not use the definitions used by the operating system itself. It is therefore possible and easy to maintain even a WebSphere 3.0.*x* installation with a 1.1.*x* Java Runtime Environment (JRE) alongside a WebSphere 4.0 version. All you need to remember is that in the Control Panel you will see only one entry—probably for the version you first installed. This means that for the second installation, you should start the server using the *startserver.bat* file, as shown in Figure 2-19.

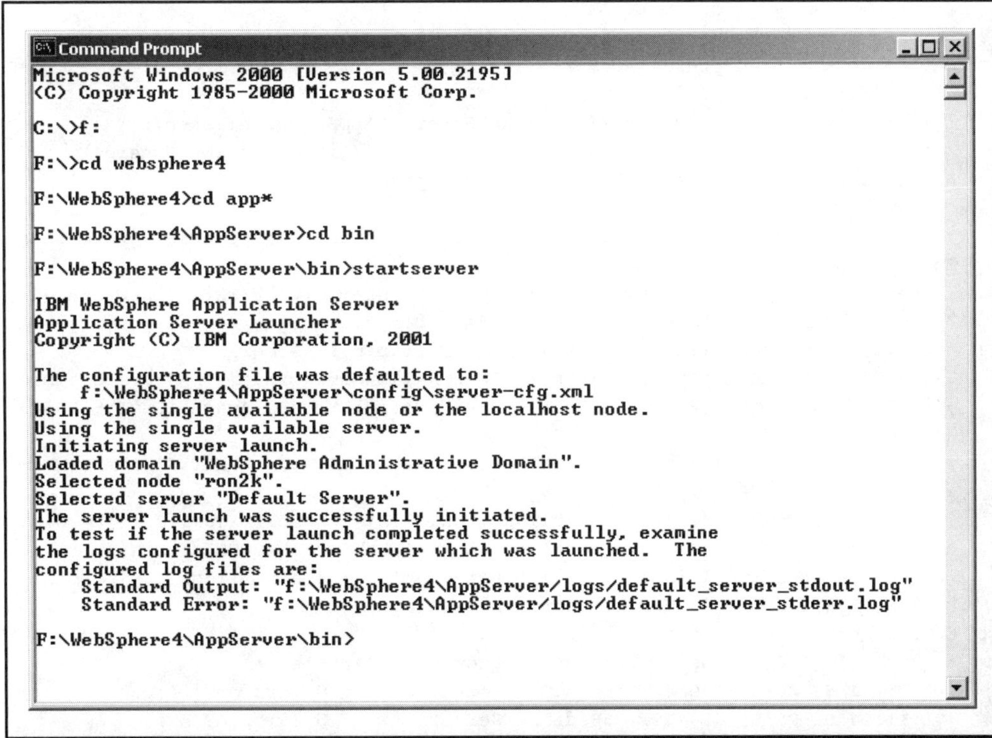

Figure 2-19. *Starting the server using* startserver.bat

When you do this, you should always look at the log files to make sure that the server has started correctly. It's important to do this, because the message on the console doesn't help much. All it says (and it always says this) is that the server launch was completed successfully. If you've forgotten to stop the other WebSphere server, for example (the most typical problem to occur), you will see the following error message in the *stdout* log file:

```
IBM WebSphere Application Server, Release 4.0.0
Advanced Single Server Edition for Multiplatforms
Copyright IBM Corp., 1997-2001

[01.11.04 02:20:28:581 EST] 566df55e Server
A WSVR0027I: Temporary product license expires on Dec 30, 2001
************ Start Display Current Environment ************
WebSphere AEs 4.0.0 q0124.08
running with process name Default Server and process id 4176
Host Operating System is Windows 2000, version 5.0
Java version = J2RE 1.3.0 IBM build cn130-20010502w (JIT enabled: jitc),
Java Compiler = jitc
server.root = f:\WebSphere4\AppServer
Java Home = f:\WebSphere4\AppServer\java\jre
ws.ext.dirs =
f:\WebSphere4\AppServer/java/lib;f:\WebSphere4\AppServer/classes;f:\
WebSphere4\AppServer/lib;f:\WebSphere4\AppServer/lib/ext;f:\WebSphere4\
AppServer/web/help;f:\WebSphere4\AppServer/properties
Classpath =
f:\WebSphere4\AppServer/lib/bootstrap.jar;f:\WebSphere4\AppServer/properties
Java Library path =
f:\WebSphere4\AppServer\java\bin;.;C:\WINNT\System32;C:\WINNT;f:\WebSphere4\
AppServer/bin;f:\WebSphere4\AppServer\java/bin;f:\WebSphere4\AppServer\java/
jre/bin;f:\Program Files\ibm\gsk5\lib;f:\Perl\bin;f:\Program
Files\IBM\GSK\lib;f:\IBMDebug\bin;f:\IBMCON~1\Encina\bin;f:\IBMVJava\hpj\bin
;f:\IBMVJava\eab\bin;F:\oracle\ora81\bin;F:\oracle\ora81\Apache\Perl\5.00503
\bin\mswin32-x86;C:\Program
Files\Oracle\jre\1.1.7\bin;C:\WINNT\system32;C:\WINNT;C:\WINNT\System32\Wbem
;f:\IMNnq_NT;f:\IBM
Connectors\CICS\BIN;f:\jdk1.2.2\bin;f:\jdk1.2.2\jre\bin;f:\jdk1.2.2\jre\bin\
classic;f:\WebSphere\AppServer\bin;f:\JDK11~1.8\bin;F:\DOCUSH~1\bin;f:\
WebSphere4\AppServer\bin;f:\jdk1.3\bin;f:\jdk1.3\jre\bin;f:\jdk1.3\jre\bin\
classic;f:\TIBCO\TIBRV\BIN;f:\vitria\bw31\bin\win32
Current trace specification =
************* End Display Current Environment *************
[01.11.04 02:20:34:600 EST] 566df55e Server       U Version : 4.0.0
[01.11.04 02:20:34:690 EST] 566df55e Server       U Edition: AEs
[01.11.04 02:20:34:820 EST] 566df55e Server       U Build date: Wed Jun 20
00:00:00 EDT 2001
[01.11.04 02:20:34:920 EST] 566df55e Server       U Build number: q0124.08
```

```
[01.11.04 02:20:51:524 EST] 566df55e NameServer     F NMSV0011E: Unable to
start Bootstrap Server. The most likely cause is that the bootstrap port is
already in use. Please ensure that no servers or other processes are already
using the bootstrap server port.
org.omg.CORBA.INTERNAL:   minor code: 8  completed: No
      at com.ibm.CORBA.iiop.GIOPImpl.createListener(GIOPImpl.java:333)
      at com.ibm.CORBA.iiop.GIOPImpl.getEndpoint(GIOPImpl.java:461)
      at com.ibm.CORBA.iiop.GIOPImpl.getEndpoint(GIOPImpl.java:524)
      at com.ibm.rmi.iiop.GIOPImpl.getBootstrapEndpoint(GIOPImpl.java:226)
      at
com.ibm.ejs.ns.CosNaming.BootstrapServer.start(BootstrapServer.java:147)
      at
com.ibm.ws.naming.bootstrap.NameServer.startBootstrapService(NameServer.java
:361)
      at com.ibm.ws.naming.bootstrap.NameServer.doInit(NameServer.java:252)
      at
com.ibm.ws.naming.bootstrap.NameServer.initialize(NameServer.java:104)
      at com.ibm.ws.runtime.Server.initializeNameService(Server.java:1433)
      at com.ibm.ws.runtime.Server.initializeRuntime0(Server.java:791)
      at
com.ibm.ws.runtime.StandardServer.initializeRuntime0(StandardServer.java:356
)
      at com.ibm.ws.runtime.Server.initializeRuntime(Server.java:728)
      at com.ibm.ws.runtime.StandardServer.main(StandardServer.java:522)
      at java.lang.reflect.Method.invoke(Native Method)
      at com.ibm.ws.bootstrap.WSLauncher.main(WSLauncher.java:63)

java.lang.Throwable
      at com.ibm.ejs.ras.TraceLogger.fatalEvent(TraceLogger.java:219)
      at
com.ibm.ejs.ras.TraceEventGeneratorImpl.fireTraceEvent(Tr.java:1331)
      at
com.ibm.ejs.ras.TraceEventGeneratorImpl.fireTraceEvent(Tr.java:1275)
      at com.ibm.ejs.ras.Tr.fatal(Tr.java:845)
      at
com.ibm.ws.naming.bootstrap.NameServer.startBootstrapService(NameServer.java
:365)
      at com.ibm.ws.naming.bootstrap.NameServer.doInit(NameServer.java:252)
      at
com.ibm.ws.naming.bootstrap.NameServer.initialize(NameServer.java:104)
      at com.ibm.ws.runtime.Server.initializeNameService(Server.java:1433)
      at com.ibm.ws.runtime.Server.initializeRuntime0(Server.java:791)
      at
com.ibm.ws.runtime.StandardServer.initializeRuntime0(StandardServer.java:356
)
      at com.ibm.ws.runtime.Server.initializeRuntime(Server.java:728)
      at com.ibm.ws.runtime.StandardServer.main(StandardServer.java:522)
```

```
      at java.lang.reflect.Method.invoke(Native Method)
      at com.ibm.ws.bootstrap.WSLauncher.main(WSLauncher.java:63)
[01.11.04 02:20:51:935 EST] 566df55e SystemOut     U NMSV0011E: Unable to
start Bootstrap Server. The most likely cause is that the bootstrap port is
already in use. Please ensure that no servers or other processes are already
using the bootstrap server port.
org.omg.CORBA.INTERNAL:   minor code: 8  completed: No
      at com.ibm.CORBA.iiop.GIOPImpl.createListener(GIOPImpl.java:333)
      at com.ibm.CORBA.iiop.GIOPImpl.getEndpoint(GIOPImpl.java:461)
      at com.ibm.CORBA.iiop.GIOPImpl.getEndpoint(GIOPImpl.java:524)
      at com.ibm.rmi.iiop.GIOPImpl.getBootstrapEndpoint(GIOPImpl.java:226)
      at
com.ibm.ejs.ns.CosNaming.BootstrapServer.start(BootstrapServer.java:147)
      at
com.ibm.ws.naming.bootstrap.NameServer.startBootstrapService(NameServer.java
:361)
      at com.ibm.ws.naming.bootstrap.NameServer.doInit(NameServer.java:252)
      at
com.ibm.ws.naming.bootstrap.NameServer.initialize(NameServer.java:104)
      at com.ibm.ws.runtime.Server.initializeNameService(Server.java:1433)
      at com.ibm.ws.runtime.Server.initializeRuntime0(Server.java:791)
      at
com.ibm.ws.runtime.StandardServer.initializeRuntime0(StandardServer.java:356
)
      at com.ibm.ws.runtime.Server.initializeRuntime(Server.java:728)
      at com.ibm.ws.runtime.StandardServer.main(StandardServer.java:522)
      at java.lang.reflect.Method.invoke(Native Method)
      at com.ibm.ws.bootstrap.WSLauncher.main(WSLauncher.java:63)
```

You will also have a file in the *logs* directory that has a filename akin to the default *ServerFatalError1004858451524.log,* with error messages of this form:

```
************ Start Display Current Environment ************
WebSphere AEs 4.0.0 q0124.08 running with process name Default Server and
process id 4176
Host Operating System is Windows 2000, version 5.0
Java version = J2RE 1.3.0 IBM build cn130-20010502w (JIT enabled: jitc),
Java Compiler = jitc
server.root = f:\WebSphere4\AppServer
Java Home = f:\WebSphere4\AppServer\java\jre
ws.ext.dirs =
f:\WebSphere4\AppServer/java/lib;f:\WebSphere4\AppServer/classes;f:\
WebSphere4\AppServer/lib;f:\WebSphere4\AppServer/lib/ext;f:\WebSphere4\
AppServer/web/help;f:\WebSphere4\AppServer/properties
Classpath =
f:\WebSphere4\AppServer/lib/bootstrap.jar;f:\WebSphere4\AppServer/properties
```

```
Java Library path =
f:\WebSphere4\AppServer\java\bin;.;C:\WINNT\System32;C:\WINNT;f:\WebSphere4\
AppServer/bin;f:\WebSphere4\AppServer\java/bin;f:\WebSphere4\AppServer\java/
jre/bin;f:\Program Files\ibm\gsk5\lib;f:\Perl\bin;f:\Program
Files\IBM\GSK\lib;f:\IBMDebug\bin;f:\IBMCON~1\Encina\bin;f:\IBMVJava\hpj\bin
;f:\IBMVJava\eab\bin;F:\oracle\ora81\bin;F:\oracle\ora81\Apache\Perl\5.00503
\bin\mswin32-x86;C:\Program
Files\Oracle\jre\1.1.7\bin;C:\WINNT\system32;C:\WINNT;C:\WINNT\System32\Wbem
;f:\IMNnq_NT;f:\IBM
Connectors\CICS\BIN;f:\jdk1.2.2\bin;f:\jdk1.2.2\jre\bin;f:\jdk1.2.2\jre\bin\
classic;f:\WebSphere\AppServer\bin;f:\JDK11~1.8\bin;F:\DOCUSH~1\bin;f:\
WebSphere4\AppServer\bin;f:\jdk1.3\bin;f:\jdk1.3\jre\bin;f:\jdk1.3\jre\bin\
classic;f:\TIBCO\TIBRV\BIN;f:\vitria\bw31\bin\win32
Current trace specification =
************* End Display Current Environment *************
[01.11.04 02:20:28:581 EST] 566df55e Server        A WSVR0027I: Temporary
product license expires on Dec 30, 2001
[01.11.04 02:20:34:600 EST] 566df55e Server        U Version : 4.0.0
[01.11.04 02:20:34:690 EST] 566df55e Server        U Edition: AEs
[01.11.04 02:20:34:820 EST] 566df55e Server        U Build date: Wed Jun 20
00:00:00 EDT 2001
[01.11.04 02:20:34:920 EST] 566df55e Server        U Build number: q0124.08
[01.11.04 02:20:51:524 EST] 566df55e NameServer    F NMSV0011E: Unable to
start Bootstrap Server. The most likely cause is that the bootstrap port is
already in use. Please ensure that no servers or other processes are already
using the bootstrap server port.
org.omg.CORBA.INTERNAL:   minor code: 8  completed: No
      at com.ibm.CORBA.iiop.GIOPImpl.createListener(GIOPImpl.java:333)
      at com.ibm.CORBA.iiop.GIOPImpl.getEndpoint(GIOPImpl.java:461)
      at com.ibm.CORBA.iiop.GIOPImpl.getEndpoint(GIOPImpl.java:524)
      at com.ibm.rmi.iiop.GIOPImpl.getBootstrapEndpoint(GIOPImpl.java:226)
      at
com.ibm.ejs.ns.CosNaming.BootstrapServer.start(BootstrapServer.java:147)
      at
com.ibm.ws.naming.bootstrap.NameServer.startBootstrapService(NameServer.java
:361)
      at com.ibm.ws.naming.bootstrap.NameServer.doInit(NameServer.java:252)
      at
com.ibm.ws.naming.bootstrap.NameServer.initialize(NameServer.java:104)
      at com.ibm.ws.runtime.Server.initializeNameService(Server.java:1433)
      at com.ibm.ws.runtime.Server.initializeRuntime0(Server.java:791)
      at
com.ibm.ws.runtime.StandardServer.initializeRuntime0(StandardServer.java:356
)
      at com.ibm.ws.runtime.Server.initializeRuntime(Server.java:728)
      at com.ibm.ws.runtime.StandardServer.main(StandardServer.java:522)
```

```
        at java.lang.reflect.Method.invoke(Native Method)
        at com.ibm.ws.bootstrap.WSLauncher.main(WSLauncher.java:63)
```

After stopping the old WebSphere server, you may need to wait until the socket is released, but you should then be able to restart the 4.0 server successfully. Once it is started, you will see the following log file. The sentence to look for is "Default Server open for e-business," which in this case is the last line shown.

```
IBM WebSphere Application Server, Release 4.0.0
Advanced Single Server Edition for Multiplatforms
Copyright IBM Corp., 1997-2001

[01.11.04 02:45:26:078 EST] 566e784c Server       A WSVR0027I: Temporary
product license expires on Dec 30, 2001
************ Start Display Current Environment ************
WebSphere AEs 4.0.0 q0124.08 running with process name Default Server and
process id 3104
Host Operating System is Windows 2000, version 5.0
Java version = J2RE 1.3.0 IBM build cn130-20010502w (JIT enabled: jitc),
Java Compiler = jitc
server.root = f:\WebSphere4\AppServer
Java Home = f:\WebSphere4\AppServer\java\jre
ws.ext.dirs =
f:\WebSphere4\AppServer/java/lib;f:\WebSphere4\AppServer/classes;f:\
WebSphere4\AppServer/lib;f:\WebSphere4\AppServer/lib/ext;f:\WebSphere4\
AppServer/web/help;f:\WebSphere4\AppServer/properties
Classpath =
f:\WebSphere4\AppServer/lib/bootstrap.jar;f:\WebSphere4\AppServer/properties
Java Library path =
f:\WebSphere4\AppServer\java\bin;.;C:\WINNT\System32;C:\WINNT;f:\WebSphere4\
AppServer/bin;f:\WebSphere4\AppServer\java/bin;f:\WebSphere4\AppServer\java/
jre/bin;f:\Program Files\ibm\gsk5\lib;f:\Perl\bin;f:\Program
Files\IBM\GSK\lib;f:\IBMDebug\bin;f:\IBMCON~1\Encina\bin;f:\IBMVJava\hpj\bin
;f:\IBMVJava\eab\bin;F:\oracle\ora81\bin;F:\oracle\ora81\Apache\Perl\5.00503
\bin\mswin32-x86;C:\Program
Files\Oracle\jre\1.1.7\bin;C:\WINNT\system32;C:\WINNT;C:\WINNT\System32\Wbem
;f:\IMNnq_NT;f:\IBM
Connectors\CICS\BIN;f:\jdk1.2.2\bin;f:\jdk1.2.2\jre\bin;f:\jdk1.2.2\jre\bin\
classic;f:\WebSphere\AppServer\bin;f:\JDK11~1.8\bin;F:\DOCUSH~1\bin;f:\
WebSphere4\AppServer\bin;f:\jdk1.3\bin;f:\jdk1.3\jre\bin;f:\jdk1.3\jre\bin\
classic;f:\TIBCO\TIBRV\BIN;f:\vitria\bw31\bin\win32
Current trace specification =
************* End Display Current Environment *************
[01.11.04 02:45:27:720 EST] 566e784c Server       U Version : 4.0.0
[01.11.04 02:45:27:720 EST] 566e784c Server       U Edition: AEs
[01.11.04 02:45:27:720 EST] 566e784c Server       U Build date: Wed Jun 20
```

```
00:00:00 EDT 2001
[01.11.04 02:45:27:720 EST] 566e784c Server        U Build number: q0124.08
[01.11.04 02:45:33:038 EST] 566e784c DrAdminServer I WSVR0053I: DrAdmin
available on port 7070
[01.11.04 02:45:33:428 EST] 566e784c ResourceBinde I WSVR0049I: Binding
Session Persistence datasource as jdbc/Session
[01.11.04 02:45:33:588 EST] 566e784c ResourceBinde I WSVR0049I: Binding
Increment Bean Datasource as jdbc/SampleDataSource
[01.11.04 02:45:33:659 EST] 566e784c ResourceBinde I WSVR0049I: Binding
Samples IDB Datasource as jdbc/sample
[01.11.04 02:45:38:165 EST] 566e784c EJBEngine     I WSVR0037I: Starting EJB
jar: Increment Bean Jar
[01.11.04 02:45:39:237 EST] 566e784c SystemOut     U Enhydra InstantDB -
Version 3.26
[01.11.04 02:45:39:247 EST] 566e784c SystemOut     U
[01.11.04 02:45:39:247 EST] 566e784c SystemOut     U The Initial Developer
of the Original Code is Lutris Technologies Inc.
Portions created by Lutris are Copyright (C) 1997-2001 Lutris Technologies,
Inc.
All Rights Reserved.
[01.11.04 02:45:41:860 EST] 566e784c EJBEngine     I WSVR0037I: Starting EJB
jar: f:\WebSphere4\AppServer/installedApps\Samples.ear/TimeoutEJBean.jar
[01.11.04 02:45:43:092 EST] 566e784c EJBEngine     I WSVR0037I: Starting EJB
jar: Increment EJB Module
[01.11.04 02:45:44:584 EST] 566e784c EJBEngine     I WSVR0037I: Starting EJB
jar: Hello EJB Module
[01.11.04 02:45:45:496 EST] 566e784c EJBEngine     I WSVR0037I: Starting EJB
jar: Account And Transfer EJB Module
[01.11.04 02:45:46:908 EST] 566e784c ServletEngine A SRVE0161I: IBM
WebSphere Application Server - Web Container.  Copyright IBM Corp. 1998-2001
[01.11.04 02:45:46:958 EST] 566e784c ServletEngine A SRVE0162I: Servlet
Specification Level: 2.2
[01.11.04 02:45:46:968 EST] 566e784c ServletEngine A SRVE0163I: Supported
JSP Specification Level: 1.1
[01.11.04 02:45:47:148 EST] 566e784c ServletEngine A Session Manager is
Configured - Initializing...
[01.11.04 02:45:47:789 EST] 566e784c CacheManager  A DYNA0011E: Servlet
cache file dynacache.xml not found; caching is disabled
[01.11.04 02:45:47:909 EST] 566e784c ServletEngine A Loading Web Module:
Default Application
[01.11.04 02:45:48:300 EST] 566e784c WebGroup      I SRVE0091I: [Servlet
LOG]: JSP 1.1 Processor: init
[01.11.04 02:45:48:380 EST] 566e784c WebGroup      I SRVE0091I: [Servlet
LOG]: InvokerServlet: init
[01.11.04 02:45:48:850 EST] 566e784c ServletEngine A Loading Web Module:
Examples Application
[01.11.04 02:45:48:971 EST] 566e784c WebGroup      I SRVE0091I: [Servlet
```

```
LOG]: JSP 1.1 Processor: init
[01.11.04 02:45:48:991 EST] 566e784c WebGroup      I SRVE0091I: [Servlet
LOG]: SimpleFileServlet: init
[01.11.04 02:45:49:511 EST] 566e784c ServletEngine A Loading Web Module:
admin
[01.11.04 02:45:49:952 EST] 566e784c WebGroup      I SRVE0091I: [Servlet
LOG]: JSP 1.1 Processor: init
[01.11.04 02:45:49:982 EST] 566e784c WebGroup      I SRVE0091I: [Servlet
LOG]: SimpleFileServlet: init
[01.11.04 02:45:50:112 EST] 566e784c WebGroup      I SRVE0091I: [Servlet
LOG]: action: init
[01.11.04 02:45:51:154 EST] 566e784c ServletEngine A Loading Web Module:
YourCo Web Application
[01.11.04 02:45:51:424 EST] 566e784c WebGroup      I SRVE0091I: [Servlet
LOG]: JSP 1.1 Processor: init
[01.11.04 02:45:51:434 EST] 566e784c WebGroup      I SRVE0091I: [Servlet
LOG]: SimpleFileServlet: init
[01.11.04 02:45:51:444 EST] 566e784c WebGroup      I SRVE0091I: [Servlet
LOG]: InvokerServlet: init
[01.11.04 02:45:51:544 EST] 566e784c ServletEngine A Loading Web Module:
Samples Web Application
[01.11.04 02:45:51:614 EST] 566e784c WebGroup      I SRVE0091I: [Servlet
LOG]: JSP 1.1 Processor: init
[01.11.04 02:45:51:634 EST] 566e784c WebGroup      I SRVE0091I: [Servlet
LOG]: SimpleFileServlet: init
[01.11.04 02:45:51:644 EST] 566e784c WebGroup      I SRVE0091I: [Servlet
LOG]: InvokerServlet: init
[01.11.04 02:45:51:694 EST] 566e784c ServletEngine A Loading Web Module:
theme Web Application
[01.11.04 02:45:51:765 EST] 566e784c WebGroup      I SRVE0091I: [Servlet
LOG]: JSP 1.1 Processor: init
[01.11.04 02:45:51:845 EST] 566e784c WebGroup      I SRVE0091I: [Servlet
LOG]: SimpleFileServlet: init
[01.11.04 02:45:51:855 EST] 566e784c WebGroup      I SRVE0091I: [Servlet
LOG]: InvokerServlet: init
[01.11.04 02:45:51:955 EST] 566e784c HttpTransport A Transport http is
listening on port 9080
[01.11.04 02:45:55:220 EST] 566e784c HttpTransport A Transport https is
listening on port 9443
[01.11.04 02:45:55:230 EST] 566e784c HttpTransport A Transport http is
listening on port 9090
[01.11.04 02:45:55:240 EST] 566e784c Server        I WSVR0023I: Server
Default Server open for e-business
```

Summary

This chapter covered a typical WebSphere installation process, which installs all the components—including the Web server, the application server, and the admin server on a single machine. In a production installation, these will not necessarily be installed on a single machine—but we are jumping ahead. At the moment, a typical installation is all you need in order to start using WebSphere and to start building applications. Now that you have both the Web server and the application server installed, and you have tested to ensure that they are working correctly, you are ready for some "Hello World" programs, which are presented in Chapters 3, 4, and 5.

The Complete Reference

Chapter 3

Hello World (Wide Web)

This chapter begins our exploration of WebSphere. The first stop is the Web server that underlies the WebSphere Java Application Server. As you will see in Chapter 6, WebSphere can be used with any one of a large number of Web servers such as the Apache Server, IBM's HTTP Server, Microsoft's Internet Information Server (IIS), Sun's iPlanet, and the Domino server. This chapter will focus on the IBM HTTP Server (IHS), which comes bundled with the WebSphere distribution. Because bringing up the HTTP Server to view files is a trivial task, we will do a bit more in this chapter; we will also bring up a secure server—one that delivers Web pages over a secure connection using the Secure Socket Layer (SSL) protocol, which is discussed in Chapter 13.

HTTP

Before we begin discussing applications on the Web, you must understand the underlying protocol and delivery mechanism used on the Web. All Web pages delivered to browsers on end-user machines are a result of a complete request/response cycle in which the browser communicates with the Web server designed to fulfill such requests. The communication protocol used by Web servers and browsers to converse with each other and pass data (in the form of requests and responses on the other) is called the Hypertext Transfer Protocol (HTTP) and is the foundation of the Web.

Because all languages, scripting mechanisms, and applications used on the Web are ultimately packaged into messages as defined by the HTTP specification, the attributes of this protocol inherently enforce certain limitations and characteristics on any information passed over the Web. These limitations are important to understand before beginning to design applications and services that will be deployed on the Web.

HTTP is an application-level protocol originally designed for delivering hypertext elements over the Internet, and it has been in use as the Web protocol since 1990. While HTTP is now used for much more than just Hypertext Markup Language (HTML) pages, its characteristics as an Internet Protocol (IP) are still valid. They include the lightness and speed necessary to provide the base for distributed collaborative hypermedia information systems. HTTP is a *state-less* protocol, meaning that each request-response session is independent and does not contain any historical information regarding previous sessions. state-less protocols are much faster than state-full protocols because less information has to be delivered. state-less protocols are also relatively simple and straightforward to implement, and this naturally simplifies the software required to support them. Finally, HTTP relies on the negotiation of data representation, which allows systems to be built independently of the development of new data representations.

HTTP is based on a request/response paradigm. Each transaction is ended once the server provides a response, thus ensuring a state-less operation. An HTTP transaction consists of the following stages:

- **Connection** The connection from the client to the server is established.
- **Request** The client sends a request message to the server.

- **Response** The server sends a response to the client.
- **Close** The server closes the connection.

A client request includes a method, a uniform resource identifier (URI), a protocol version, and a Multipurpose Internet Mail Extensions (MIME) message. The server response includes the protocol version, a status code, and a MIME message.

The HTTP version, sent both as part of the request and part of the response, is given as

<major version number>.<minor version number>

Different minor numbers are used when protocol changes do not change the general message-parsing algorithm. Message format changes require a change in the major number. This version number will always be a part of the first line on an HTTP version. For example, a response message sent from a server to a client may begin with the following line:

```
HTTP/1.0 200 OK
```

This means that the response is of protocol version 1.0 and that it is returning a status of 200 (successful completion).

HTTP defines the standard character set to be ISO-8859-1. Because this character set is a superset of US-ASCII, it has no effect on messages defined using 7-bit character sets. The presence of a `charset` parameter in the content type header overrides the default and is used by the message originator to specify which character set to use.

URIs, URLs, and URNs

Uniform resource identifiers (URIs) are strings that identify an Internet resource. URIs are best equated with Internet addresses for an object on the Web. Uniform resource names (URNs) also designate a resource on the Internet, but they do so using a location-independent name. Uniform resource locators (URLs), on the other hand, identify a resource on the Internet using a scheme based on the resource's location.

URIs, URNs, and URLs serve similar purposes and are therefore used interchangeably. URIs are the most abstract and generic; they are therefore usually used in technical specifications. For example, the grammatical definition of URIs provides the basis for the syntactic definition of both URNs and URLs. URNs are very general, but they rely on name look-up services and therefore depend on additional services that are not always generally available. URLs are the most commonly used, and are the basis for HTTP and Web software.

The syntax of URLs is quite simple. Because URLs reference a resource through a location, they specify the host and the pathname on that host where the resource can be found. In addition, the URL can also define the port through which the connection to the host should be made, and the protocol used for the connection. A URL therefore takes the following form:

```
<protocol> : "//" <host> [:<port>] "/" <absolute path>
```

Documents may reference resources using relative or virtual URLs. These URLs do not specify the protocol or the host; they provide only a relative path. This is a convenience offered by Web servers to reference resources based on their relative location to the resource on which this virtual URL is used. These URLs are extremely important in organizing a collection of resources in a cohesive manner so that they can be collectively referred to (for example, so they can be moved as a single element).

HTTP Transactions

A "round-trip" HTTP transaction consists of a request sent by the client to the server, processing done by the server to satisfy the request, and a response sent from the server to the client. HTTP is a state-less protocol. Therefore, each such transaction is completely autonomous, meaning that there are no relationships between successive transactions. The HTTP transaction is therefore the largest unit of work and is comprised of messages (the request and the response), each containing a header and a body entity.

HTTP Messages

An HTTP message is a stream of octets transmitted over a connection. The HTTP message is the basic component of an HTTP transaction. Each request sent from a client to a server and each response sent from a server to a client is an HTTP message. Requests and responses can either be simple or full; so, there are four message types in HTTP: simple request, simple response, full request, and full response. Simple requests and responses differ from their full counterparts in that they do not allow the use of any header information.

Message headers contain a series of definitions aimed at describing the message body and providing information pertaining to the HTTP transaction. A header consists of a series of lines having the following form:

<name> ":" *<value>*

Requests

Requests are HTTP messages that are sent from clients to servers. The request specifies the method to be applied at the server, the resource that this method should be applied to, and the protocol version being used. A typical request line takes the following form:

```
GET   http://www.entity93.com/docRoot.html   HTTP/1.0
```

This means that the resource at the URL should be fetched and returned in a server response. HTTP currently defines the following methods:

- **DELETE** This method deletes the resource at the provided URL.
- **GET** This method retrieves the resource identified by the URL. If the resource is a program that produces data, the response will contain the output produced by the program and not the program itself.
- **HEAD** This method is identical to the process occurring in the GET method except that the data body returned by the server when this method is in use is empty. In the case of headers, meta-information, and so on, these two methods are identical. This method is useful for testing the existence of a resource without actually fetching it.
- **POST** In this method, the client sends additional information in the message body. This information is used by the server when it services the request. This method gets its name from the fact that the client is posting information.
- **PUT** This method creates a resource at the specified URL containing the supplied data.

The most commonly used methods are GET, POST, and HEAD. In fact, not all HTTP servers are guaranteed to implement methods other than these three.

In addition, the HTTP definition of requests allows any other token to be placed as a method. This allows dynamic method extensions. When the message arrives at the server, the server will try to apply the method to the resource. If the method is not supported, the server will return a response with the appropriate error code. The list of methods acceptable for a given resource on a given server may therefore change dynamically.

Responses

Once the server's work is complete and the information to be returned to the client is ready, the server can construct the response. HTTP defines the format of a response to consist of a status line, a header, and a body. The status line records the protocol version, a numeric status code, and a status textual phrase. A status code has three decimal digits. HTTP categorizes the status codes and status phrases into five groups. Each group starts with a different first digit:

- **Informational** Currently not used: 100 through 199.
- **Success** Returned when the requested action is applied: 200 through 299. For example, a 200 status code, meaning OK, indicates that the requested resource is being returned in the response—for example, when the request applied the GET method.

- **Redirection** Returned when further action must be taken in order to complete the request: 300 through 399. For example, if a resource has migrated and a server-side program knows the new URL, a redirection response might be sent back to the client making the browser navigate to this new URL.
- **Client error** Returned when a syntax error or another error in structure is discovered in the request: 400 through 499. If the client has not completed sending the request when a client error status arrives from the server, it should stop the transmission of the request immediately. The server will usually include an explanation of the error as part of the response.
- **Server error** Returned when a server failure occurs: 500 through 599.

Message Entities

When a request is made and when a response is constructed, the contents of the messages are packaged as an entity. An entity consists of meta-information, which consists of entity headers and a content segment called the entity body. Entity headers are similar to other headers in that they consist of names and values. In addition, a specific entity header defines the format used for the entity body, called the *Entity-Body header field*.

Entity bodies are included in the message when information is transferred between client and server. Thus, POST requests contain an entity body, while HEAD and GET requests do not. Responses usually include an entity body because they are returning some information. Responses to HEAD requests and responses that are returning with status codes 204 and 304 do not contain an entity body.

When a message includes an entity body, a number of meta-information segments are required. First, the data type and encoding methods should be specified. For example, the entity body may be an HTML text compressed using *gzip*. A full specification of the following form defines for the message receiver how the data should be extracted from the entity body:

```
Content-Encoding ( Content-Type ( <entity data> ) )
```

This information is included as header fields. The length of the entity body is often specified in an additional header field. This is preferable to communication methods based on an end-of-file (EOF), because a communication channel may be shut down early for other reasons. For requests, content length is the only possible alternative; because if the client were to close down the connection, the server would have no way to return a response.

The HTTP Server

A Web server is simply a service that is registered with the operating system, by default listening on port 80 of the machine, to service HTTP requests. When a Web server is brought up, it defines a set of port numbers on which it will accept connections. This set of ports is defined in the server's configuration file—in our case, the file *httpd.conf*. Different Web servers can have different configuration files and methods. The IBM HTTP Server (IHS) is based on the Apache Web server, and segments of the default *httpd.conf* file available with the default WebSphere installation are shown here:

```
ServerName webspherebook.
# This is the main server configuration file.
# See URL http://www.apache.org/ for instructions.

...

# ServerRoot: The directory the server's config, error, and log files
# are kept in

ServerRoot "f:/IHS1_3_19"

...

# Port: The port the standalone listens to.
Port 80

...

# Apache always creates one child process to handle requests. If it
# dies another child process is created automatically. Within the
# child process multiple threads handle incoming requests. The next two
# directives determine the behaviour of the threads and processes.

# Don't force a server to exit after it has served some number of requests.
# If you do want server's to exit after they have run for a long time (to
# help the system clean up after the process), please set this to a pretty
# large number - like 10,000. What this will do, is, each child server will
# exit after serving 10,000 requests, and another server will take its
place.

MaxRequestsPerChild 0

# Number of concurrent threads at a time (set the value to more or less
# depending on the responsiveness you want and the resources you wish
# this server to consume).

ThreadsPerChild 50

...

# This should be changed to whatever you set DocumentRoot to.
```

```
<Directory "f:/IHS1_3_19/htdocs">

# This may also be "None", "All", or any combination of "Indexes",
# "Includes", "ExecCGI", or "MultiViews".

# Note that "MultiViews" must be named *explicitly* --- "Options All"
# doesn't give it to you.

Options Indexes

# This controls which options the .htaccess files in directories can
# override. Can also be "All", or any combination of "Options", "FileInfo",
# "AuthConfig", and "Limit"

AllowOverride None

# Controls who can get stuff from this server.

order allow,deny
allow from all

</Directory>

# f:/IHS1_3_19/cgi-bin should be changed to whatever your ScriptAliased
# CGI directory exists, if you have that configured.

<Directory "f:/IHS1_3_19/cgi-bin">
AllowOverride None
Options None
</Directory>

...

# DocumentRoot: The directory out of which you will serve your
# documents. By default, all requests are taken from this directory, but
# symbolic links and aliases may be used to point to other locations.

DocumentRoot "f:/IHS1_3_19/htdocs"

...

LoadModule ibm_app_server_http_module
f:/WebSphere4/AppServer/bin/mod_ibm_app_server_http.dll
Alias /IBMWebAS/  "f:/WebSphere4/AppServer/web/"
Alias /WSsamples  "f:/WebSphere4/AppServer/WSsamples/"
WebSpherePluginConfig f:\WebSphere4\AppServer\config\plugin-cfg.xml
```

A few of the directives from this file will be reviewed and details explained throughout the book. The server name defined in the *http.conf* file should be the hostname of the machine that will be referenced by the external world. This is often the hostname of the machine on which the Web server is installed, but that is not always the case. In most cases there is either a firewall, a router, or a node that does network address translation so that the domain name and hostname for using the application are not necessarily the domain name and hostname on which the Web server is installed. We will review this further in Chapter 41.

The `ServerRoot` directive defines the file system root directory on which the Web server is installed. The `Port` directive defines the port on which the Web server opens a socket and listens for incoming requests. The `DocumentRoot` directive defines the file system directory from which the server pulls information. This, in addition to `Alias` directives, defines the file system root points from which documents may be accessed by requests that reach the Web server. When a connection is made on one of the ports to which the Web server is listening, the operating system delegates the request to the Web server. The simplest request is one that accesses the Web server's root page (that is, just the hostname without a document name). In this case, the server replies with the default page as defined in its configuration file; normally this is the file named *index.html* that is placed in the document root directory. The reply provided by the IHS is shown in Figure 3-1.

The `MaxRequestsPerChild` directive defines a number of requests after which a serving thread should die. Apache (and thus IHS) is a multithreaded Web server, as are all modern Web servers. Multiple threads are started to serve up pages so that high throughput can be achieved. The `MaxRequestsPerChild` directive seems out of place—and in many ways it is. The only reason for this directive is the fact that software sometimes has bugs (but maybe you already know that). In fact, on some platforms there are well-known memory leaks; for example, if a thread remains up through the duration of the life of the Web server, it will eventually take up all of the host's memory and disable the machine. This behavior is well known on the Solaris platform, for example. To combat this, the directive ensures that if you set this to a positive number other than 0 the thread will be killed and another one started instead, ensuring that the memory leak is also reset. It has been our experience, for example, that when running on Solaris this value should be set to 5000.

`ThreadsPerChild` controls the number of active threads at any one time. There is, of course, a tradeoff between responsiveness through the concurrency of such handling threads and the amount of memory being used by the HTTP server. `ThreadsPerChild` is an amazingly important parameter to know about and is one of the most important parameters that you use when you tune a production system. `ThreadsPerChild` is really a gatekeeper for how the application server is utilized. System performance degrades rapidly as the threads begin waiting in the WebSphere Web container and connection pools. One tuning option is to ensure that there are not too many threads being spawned through the Web server. Increased throughput is often achieved by using multiple clones of the system.

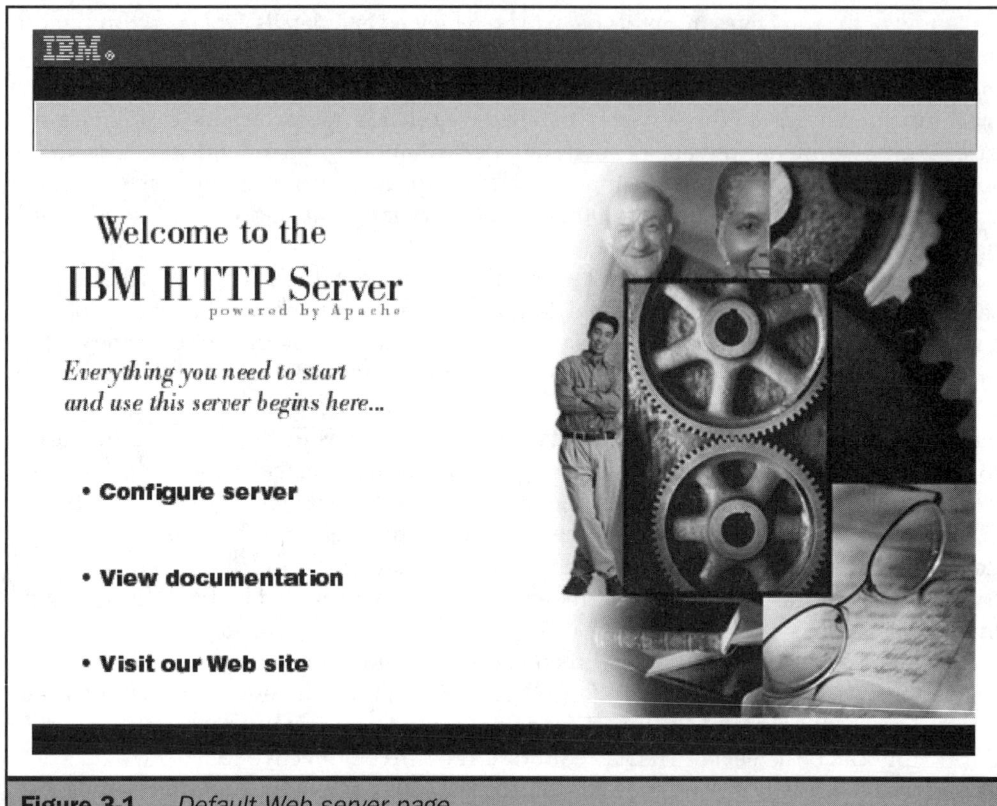

Figure 3-1. *Default Web server page*

Another parameter that is important when tuning a system is the `MaxClients` value—especially on AIX and Solaris. The `MaxClients` directive limits the number of simultaneous requests that the Web server can service. The value of the `MaxClients` parameter can significantly impact an application, particularly if it is too high. More is not always better! The optimum value depends on the application. `MaxClients` is the one HTTP parameter that is adjusted when you performance tune a configuration. It truly is the "throttle" for the application server. The lower this value is, the less work the application server will be asked to do. The flip side is, of course, that people who are trying to access the application may be turned away.

The Web server is a process managed by the operating system. Depending on the operating system, the startup sequence for the Web server within the boot of the operating system will be different. For example, in Solaris the startup may be in one of the *rc* files, whereas in Windows NT or Windows 2000 it will be defined as an operating system service. Figure 3-2 displays the Windows 2000 Service Manager showing the service under which the server is running. The initial use of the Web server is to serve up

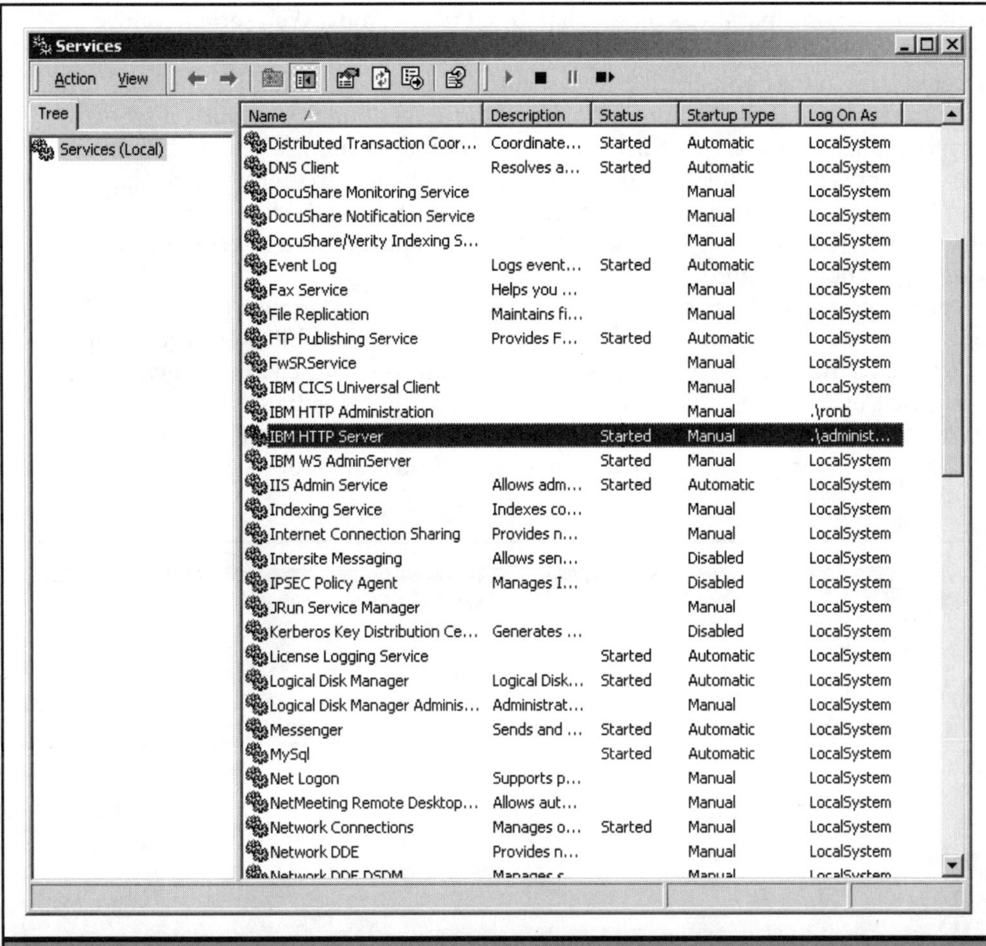

Figure 3-2. *The Web server as a Windows 2000 service*

pages that are stored within the Web server's file system; but we will describe many other uses of the Web server in building Web applications in later chapters in the book. The Web server is the gateway to the WebSphere Application Server.

Setting Up a Secure Site

While a Web server is very useful within intranets and for delivering general information to users on the Internet, once you start putting sensitive information within your Web site or you want to deliver some real applications, the Web server—

in its inherent openness—becomes a liability. Luckily, most Web servers can be configured to support secure connections using the Secure Socket Layer (SSL) protocol, covered later in the book. Setting up a secure site is not a trivial thing, because it not only involves changing the configuration of the server but also creating a set of cryptographic keys and a certificate for server authentication. We will discuss all of these concepts in Chapter 13, but at this time it is of value to guide you through a simple process for setting up a secure server using IHS. By the time we complete this process, you will have a regular server listening on port 80 and a secure server listening on port 443 (the default port for SSL).

Before you can set up the secure server, you need to generate a pair of keys. These keys are used for encrypting the session and are based on public-key cryptography, which forms the basis for all modern security protocols. These keys are generated using the Key Management utility IKeyMan. This utility can be started by choosing Start | Programs | IBM WebSphere | Application Server V4.0 | IKeyMan.

The Key Management application opens, as shown in Figure 3-3.

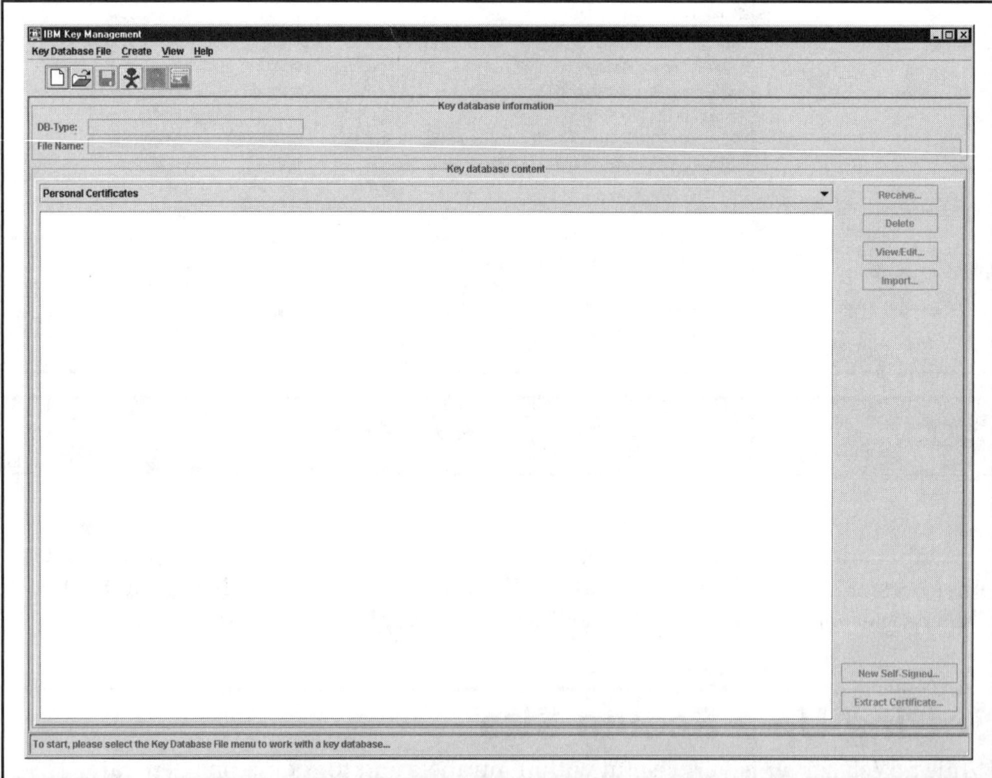

Figure 3-3. *The Key Management application window*

Select Key Database File | New to create a new database file. A dialog box opens, as shown here:

New
Key database type JKS
File Name: key.jks Browse...
Location: C:\WebSphere\AppServer\bin\
OK Cancel Help

Enter the filename and the location, and click OK. Next, enter the password as shown in Figure 3-4. (Write it down somewhere safe, so you don't forget it!) Stash the password in a *.sth* file. Note that the dialog indicates the relative strength of your password by the number of keys that are highlighted. The more keys that are highlighted, the better the password is. To improve your password, try including digits in it, and avoid English words. Click OK to finish this part of the process. The Key Management window should look similar to Figure 3-5.

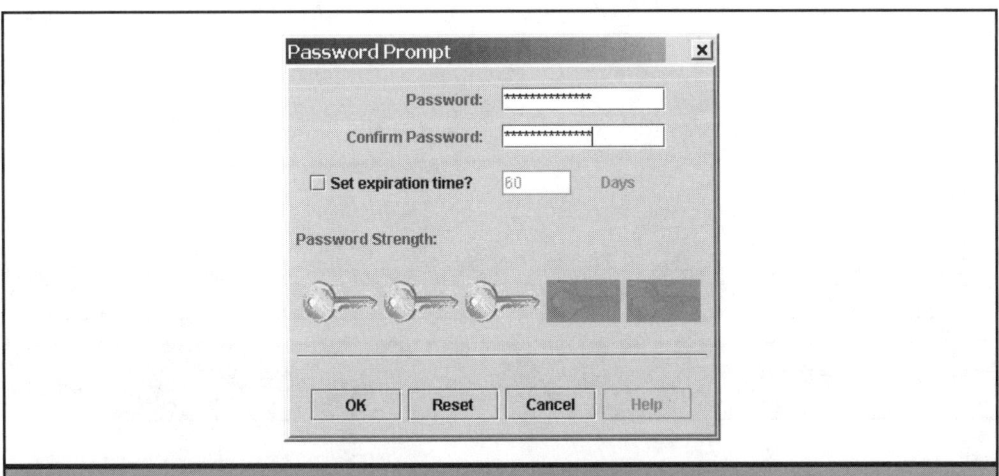

Figure 3-4. *Setting the password for the key database*

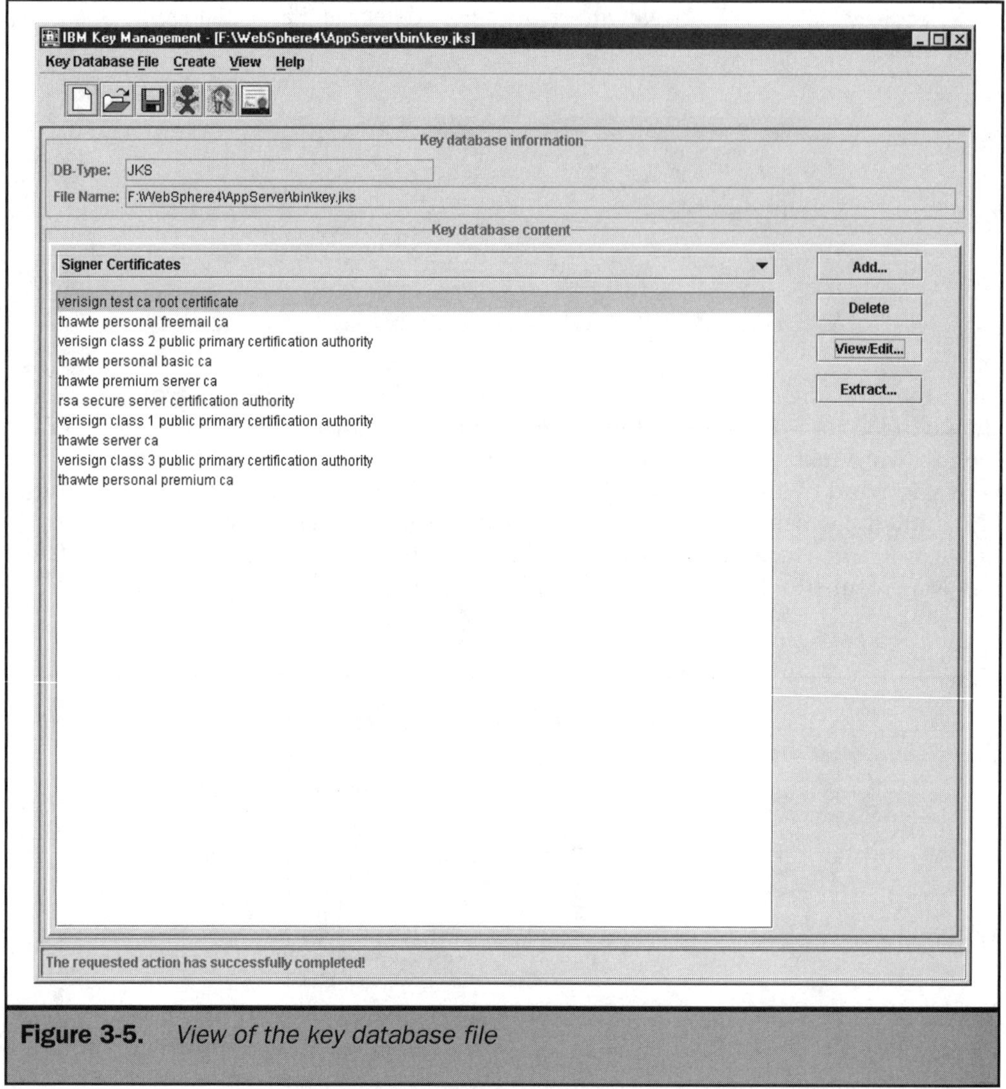

Figure 3-5. *View of the key database file*

Next, you need to update the server's configuration file (*httpd.conf* in the server's *conf* directory). To do this, add some directives to the configuration file, as shown here:

```
# Load SSL module
# This can be 40,56,128 bit encryption
# For NT
# LoadModule ibm_ssl_module modules/IBMModuleSSL128.dll
```

```
# For UNIX
# LoadModule ibm_ssl_module     libexec/mod_ibm_ssl128.so
LoadModule ibm_ssl_module modules/IBMModuleSSL128.dll

Listen 443
# A virtual host must correspond to a different IP address,
# different port number or a different host
# name for the server, in the latter case the server machine must be
# configured to accept IP packets for multiple addresses.
<VirtualHost websphere.webspherebook.com:443>
# Enter the Document "root"
DocumentRoot ":/IHS1_3_19/htdocs"
ErrorLog logs/error-ssl.log
ServerAdmin ronb@webspherebook.com
SSLEnable
SSLClientAuth none
</VirtualHost>
SSLDisable
##        Keyfile directive:
##
##        Specify the names of key files that are available, as defined
##        with the IKEYMAN utility.
##
##        Default:  <none>
##        Syntax:   Keyfile  <filename.kdb>
##        This directive is not allowed inside of a virtual host stanza

Keyfile ":/IHS1_3_19/keydb/key.kdb"

##        SSLV2Timeout and SSlV3Timeout:
##
##        Specify the timeout value for an SSL session. Once the timeout
##        expires, the client is forced to perform another SSL handshake.
##
##        Default:  SSLV2Timeout  100
##                  SSLV3Timeout  1000
##        Syntax:   SSLV2Timeout <time in seconds>  range 1-100
##                  SSLV3Timeout <time in seconds>  range 1-86400

SSLV2Timeout 100
SSLV3Timeout 1000
```

Among these configurations are the DLLs, which implements the security functionality; the port the secure server will be listening on (443); and many directives regarding the attributes of the SSL connections. Once you have updates to the configuration file, you need to restart the Web server. If for some reason the server fails to start, you should inspect your changes to the configuration file; bad values are always a cause for server failure. However, if you've managed to restart the server, you are in business. If, for example, you now access your server using *https://<your server name here>*, you will be prompted by a Security Alert dialog box:

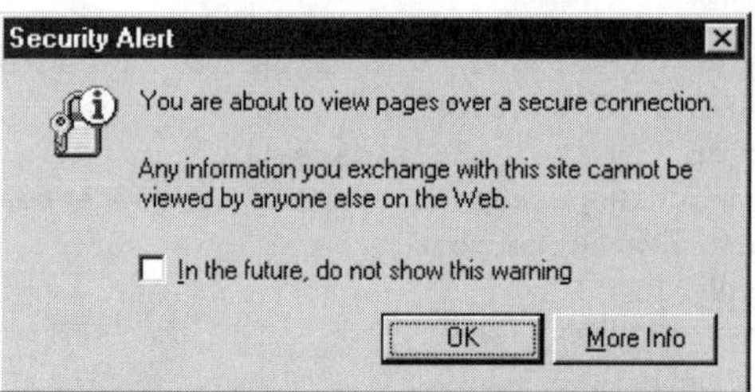

After getting an acknowledgment, you will be running over a secure connection. It's time to go out there and get some credit card numbers!

Summary

In this chapter, we described the role of the HTTP server (Web server) and showed you how to set up the Web server to serve up pages over a nonsecure and secure connection. The Web server is an important component in the overall picture, because it is the gateway or first entry point from the client (the browser) to the application components running on the WebSphere Application Server. In fact, many architectures have taken the Web server and extended it by adding various capabilities. One example is Apache Tomcat, which has taken the Apache Web server and extended it by adding support for servlets and Java Server Pages (JSP). In the WebSphere solution, packaging is different—the Web server always manages the request/response transactions but never does any of the processing unless the documents are static. This processing in WebSphere is mostly either within the Enterprise JavaBeans (EJB) container or within the Web container. We continue with an introduction to both of these topics—servlets and JSP in Chapter 4 and EJB in Chapter 5.

The Complete Reference

Chapter 4

Hello Servlets and JSPs

Most WebSphere deployments are all about Web applications. Most Web applications present HTML as the front end and have a server-based transaction system. In a Java 2 Platform Enterprise Edition (J2EE) application developed and deployed on WebSphere, the back end is comprised of a set of technologies. The two primary capabilities supported by the WebSphere Application Server that are often used to create the output to be delivered to the browser are servlets and JavaServer Pages (JSP). This chapter, as its title suggests, takes you through simple "Hello World" programs. These programs are aimed at providing some initial hands-on experience with development of servlets and JSP. While being neither very original nor complex, these examples should give you a feel for what servlets and JSP in WebSphere are all about. Part V of the book focuses on the development and deployment of servlets and JSP, and it will provide more complete examples.

Servlet Basics

Quite early on in the life of the Web, it was clear that static Web pages just won't do and that programs were required to perform some computation within a session on the Web. As a result, Common Gateway Interface (CGI) was born as a way to assign programs to certain requests coming in to the Web server. There are two main disadvantages of CGI script. One is that the scripts run as a separate process to the external server , and such a process has to be created for each request. The second is that the scripts are coded in various scripting languages such as Perl, Tcl, and Python. These scripting languages are excellent for system administration scripts and "lightweight" functionality, but they are less appropriate for serious applications and are certainly less portable than Java.

Servlets were proposed to overcome these two disadvantages. The first problem is solved by the fact that the servlet is run as a separate Java thread but under the same Java Virtual Machine (JVM) as the servlet server. This is much more efficient than creating an operating system process for servicing each request, because it requires less memory, no context switching, and very few start-up delays.

The second problem is solved by the fact that servlets are written in Java and can invoke other Java classes—sometimes in another technological category such as Enterprise JavaBeans (EJB)—to perform complex application processing such as database access, complex algorithms, document management, and so on.

Due to the fact that CGI was so common and that Java as a language is perfect for such development efforts, the servlet concept was an immediate hit and continues to be one of the more successful models in the new world of Web applications. The most consistent element in the various Java application servers on the market today is servlet support. This includes IBM WebSphere, BEA WebLogic, Oracle Application Server, iPlanet (previously Netscape Server), Apache/Tomcat, and more.

Now that you understand the motivation for having servlets, let's get down to what servlets actually are. A *servlet* is a Java code segment built to conform to JavaSoft's Servlet API standard. This API standard defines a set of methods that should be implemented by classes to be deployed as servlets. Obviously, this does not say much more than that servlet classes conform to some kind of interface or contract, but isn't that always the case with Java? In fact, the Servlet API is much more than just another set of interfaces; it defines a certain computational model that is the basis for the servlet lifecycle.

The servlet model assumes that code segments called servlets will be maintained and managed by a server that conforms to the Servlet API. This servlet server is usually coupled in some way with a Web server (an HTTP server); this coupling is the most common configuration because most servlets are HTTP servlets and are accessed over an HTTP connection, whether by a browser page or by other code fragments. This coupling with the Web server also exists in WebSphere; the WebSphere installation includes both a Web server (an iPlanet server, a Microsoft IIS server, an Apache server, or the IBM HTTP Server, which is part of the WebSphere default installation) and a server that manages the servlet lifecycle. The Web server typically forwards requests to the servlet server, which manages and invokes the servers registered with the server.

OK, you have a servlet server that can be invoked from the Web server—so what? Fundamentally, there's actually not much more than that. A servlet is simply a piece of Java code that is an entry point for allowing server-side functionality to be invoked through a servlet server. The most common type of servlet, by far, is the HTTP servlet. An *HTTP servlet* is a Java class that implements a few entry-point methods through which server-side processing can be initiated. In some cases, the servlet implements a very simple operation in which it performs something and returns; in other cases, it is only the entry point and most of the work is done in classes called by the servlet. Because an instance of a servlet is always invoked within its own thread, the servlet model inherently scales well and lends itself to being used for Web applications.

What makes the servlet model powerful is that the servlet developer is given a straightforward computational model. A request (an HTTP request, in the case of an HTTP servlet) is received, and a response should be generated. The server handles the complexities of the actual communication and transport.

"Hello World" Servlet

The servlet you will build and deploy in this chapter is probably the simplest servlet around. It merely sits there within the Web container and waits for an HTTP request (a GET request, in this case). Once such a request arrives, it writes a small HTML page with "Hello World" on it. In order to make the example slightly more interesting, we will add servlet support for French so that the servlet will print either "Hello World!!" or "Bonjour tout le monde!!"

Coding the Servlet

Since you are going to access the servlet functionality from a browser over an HTTP connection, implement the servlet as an HTTP servlet. This means that you will subclass your servlet from the `javax.servlet.http.HttpServlet` class. We will revisit this class later in the book and provide many details regarding its usage, but right now the important thing is that it has a set of methods that are invoked when HTTP requests come in. Specifically, it has a `doGet` method that is called when an HTTP GET request comes in and a `doPost` method that is called when an HTTP POST request comes in. Alternatively, one can implement the `service` method, which is called when either type of request comes in if the do methods are not implemented.

The code for the "Hello World" servlet is shown here:

```
package book.websphere.chapter4;

import javax.servlet.*;
import javax.servlet.http.*;
import java.io.*;
import java.util.*;

public class HelloServlet1 extends HttpServlet {
  Locale usEn;
  ResourceBundle usEnglishMessages;
  Locale frFr;
  ResourceBundle franceFrenchMessages;

  public void init(ServletConfig config) throws ServletException {
    super.init(config);
    Locale usEn = Locale.US;
    usEnglishMessages = ResourceBundle.getBundle(
              "HelloServletsTextMessages", usEn);
    Locale frFr = Locale.FRANCE;
    franceFrenchMessages = ResourceBundle.getBundle(
              "HelloServletsTextMessages", frFr);
  }

  public void doGet(
            HttpServletRequest request, HttpServletResponse
response)
            throws ServletException, IOException {
    response.setContentType("text/html");

    ResourceBundle aBundle;
    if (request.getHeader("Accept-Language").compareTo("FR") == 0
) {
      aBundle = franceFrenchMessages;
      response.setHeader("Content-Language", "FR");
```

```
    }
    else {
      aBundle = usEnglishMessages;
      response.setHeader("Content-Language", "EN");
    }

    PrintWriter out = new PrintWriter (response.getOutputStream());
    out.println("<html>");
    out.println("<head><title>HelloServlets1</title></head>");
    out.println("<body>");
    out.println(aBundle.getString("helloWorld"));
    out.println("</body>");
    out.println("</html>");
    out.close();
  }

  public String getServletInfo() {
    return "This is a simple servlet activated by an HTTP GET
request";
  }
}
```

The main method of interest here is the doGet method; the other is the init method. The doGet method is called when an HTTP GET method comes in to the server referencing the servlet. The init method is called when the servlet code is first loaded into the servlet server. In the example code, the init method is used to initialize the two resource bundles with the strings for the Hello World messages, while the doGet method outputs the appropriate Hello World message based on the client's locale information. Initialization simply involves reading in the two resource bundles used in this simple example. These bundles, shown next, will be maintained in memory for use while the server is up and running:

```
#Property file for HelloServlets1 text messages
#en_US
helloWorld=Hello World!!

#Property file for HelloServlets1 text messages
#fr_FR
helloWorld=Bonjour tout le monde!!
```

The processing method is activated on receipt of a GET HTTP request. Based on the URL of the request, and assuming it corresponds to your servlet, the application server invokes the servlet. Because such a URL is formed within a GET request, the `doGet` method of the HelloServlet1 servlet will be invoked. The arguments to the invocation are an `HttpServletRequest` encapsulating the request parameters and an `HttpServletResponse` encapsulating the objects pertaining to the response, the most important one being the output stream to which the reply should be written.

The first thing the processing method does is set the content type of the response stream. The content type is a MIME type that defines the type of output to be provided. Since today's browsers and other devices are based on many formats including HTML, XML, WML, and many others that will be discussed later in the book, you need to inform the requester what type of output you will be providing. In the code for your servlet, you set the content type to be HTML by informing the requester that the output would be written out as text but that the text was an encoding in HTML. This means that the text written to the output stream used later in the code will be HTML.

The next thing the code does is inspect the request object to determine what language the browser is using. This is done by accessing one of the headers within the request. While we will discuss the request header and the request object in Chapter 7, let's consider now what kind of information is available to the servlet. You already saw one of the servlets that comes with the WebSphere distribution discussed in Chapter 2. Recall the snoop servlet shown in Figure 2-13. It was invoked by opening a URL of the form *http://localhost/servlet/snoop*. Looking at the output for this servlet, you can see that the servlet contains a lot of information regarding the requesting client. The servlet not only knows such things as the request method, the language the browser is accepting, and every format the browser is accepting; it also knows what type of browser the client is using (the user-agent) and what the hostname and IP address of the client are. While it is not surprising that the HTTP and servlet models require this (for example, the output can be made to be sensitive to the user-agent), as a Web user you might want to be aware that such information is being passed around.

Referring back to the Hello World example, the determination of what language the output should be in is based on the `Content-Language` value in the request object. In your example, you will only support French and English; any language other than French will be displayed in English. Next you create the actual output. The output is written to a `PrintWriter` object that is part of the response object. This `PrintWriter` object encapsulates the output stream, and anything that is written on this stream is placed in the HTTP response body. Because you already declared your output to be an HTML output, go ahead and issue a number of `println` statements that write out the HTML source to be displayed by the browser. Most importantly, extract the correct "Hello World" string from the resource bundle selected earlier.

Web Application Assembly

Now you've written the servlet code in your favorite Java Integrated Development Environment (IDE)—WebSphere Studio Application Developer, WebSphere Studio Site Developer, or VisualAge for Java—and you are ready to deploy the servlet under WebSphere. You have one `class` file and two `properties` files. In order to get the servlet running on the server, you need to deploy it; but before that, you need to assemble an application based on this servlet. The assembly phase is aimed at providing the various parameters related to the application and its components.

First, generate a Java Archive file containing both the class file and the two resource files. Use the following command in the directory in which the files reside (all in one line):

```
jar cf HelloServlet.jar HelloServlet1.class
HelloServletsTextMessages_fr_FR.properties
HelloServletsTextMessages_en_US.properties
```

Once you have the JAR file, you can start the WebSphere Application Assembly Tool. You can start this tool from the First Steps window (see Chapter 2) or from the WebSphere entry under the Windows Start menu. Alternatively, you may run it using the *assembly.bat* script in the WebSphere Application Server *bin* directory. As the Assembly Tool loads, it displays the window shown in Figure 4-1.

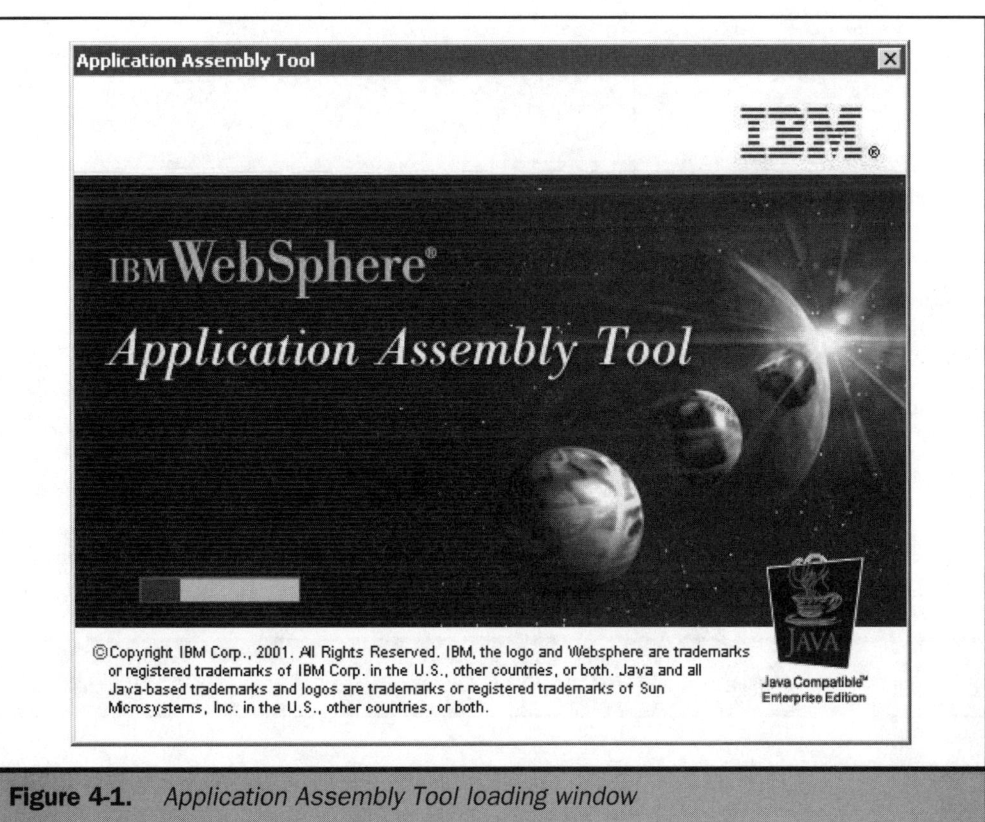

Figure 4-1. *Application Assembly Tool loading window*

Once the tool is loaded, you see a Welcome window. In this window, select Web Module and proceed to the window shown in Figure 4-2. In this window, you see the components of your Web module organized hierarchically on the left-hand side and the details for the selected object on the right. The first folder in the Web module is Web Components. Web components can be either servlets or JSP. To add the new servlet, right-click the Web Components entry and select New.

In the dialog that appears, enter the information for the new servlet. First click Browse to select the class file for the servlet. This opens the class selection window. In this window, click Browse again. A new dialog box appears; select the JAR file you prepared earlier. In the next window, select the servlet class file and click OK.

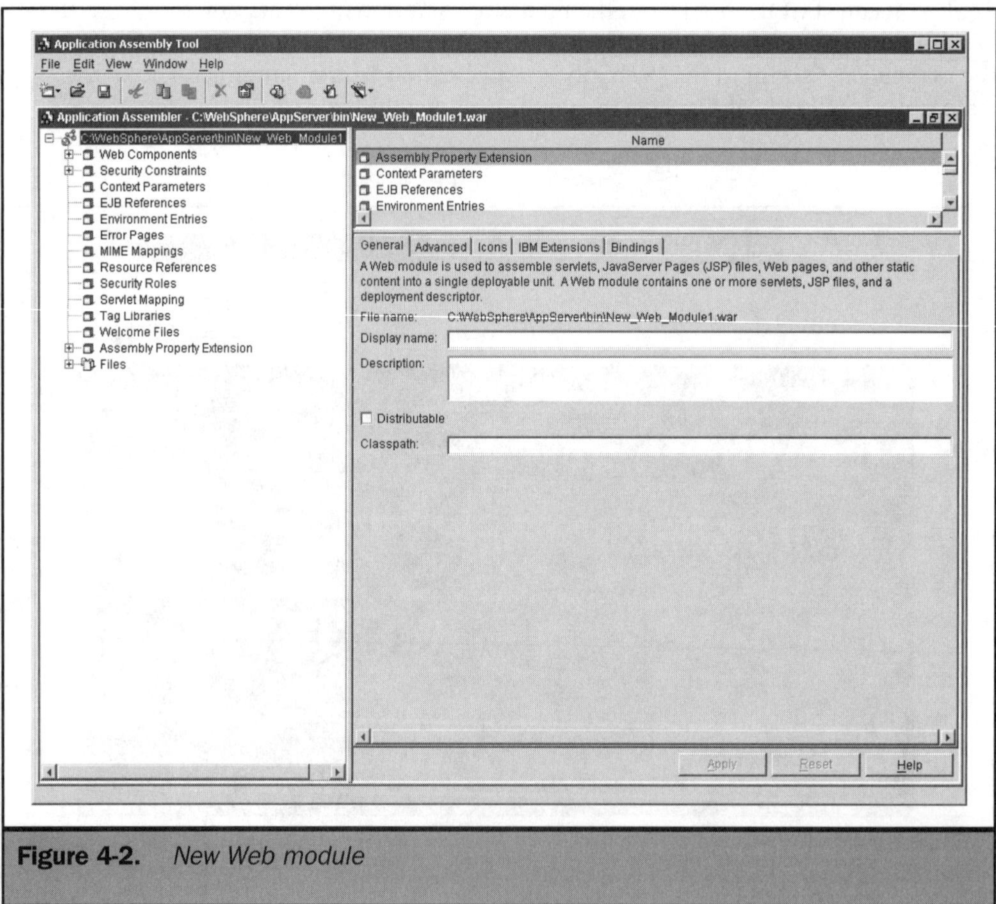

Figure 4-2. *New Web module*

Now, back in the Web component dialog box, enter the name, the display name, and the description, and check the Load on Startup box. The result is shown in Figure 4-3. Click OK.

Next, right-click the Servlet Mapping icon on the left side of the Application Assembly Tool, and select New. In the New Servlet Mapping dialog box, define a new mapping with the URL pattern */Invoke*, as well as the new servlet class, as shown in Figure 4-4. Click OK.

In the Application Assembly Tool window, under Files in the left pane, right-click JAR Files, and then select Add Files. In the Add Files dialog box, select the JAR file you prepared and the two property files, as shown in Figure 4-5.

Finally, save the newly created Web module as a Web Archive (WAR) file, with the extension *.war*. Now you are ready to create an enterprise application containing the new module.

Back in the Application Assembly Tool window, select File | New | Application. On the tree pane on the left, right-click Web Modules and select Import. In the Open dialog box, select the WAR file you just created. When you select the Web module, you

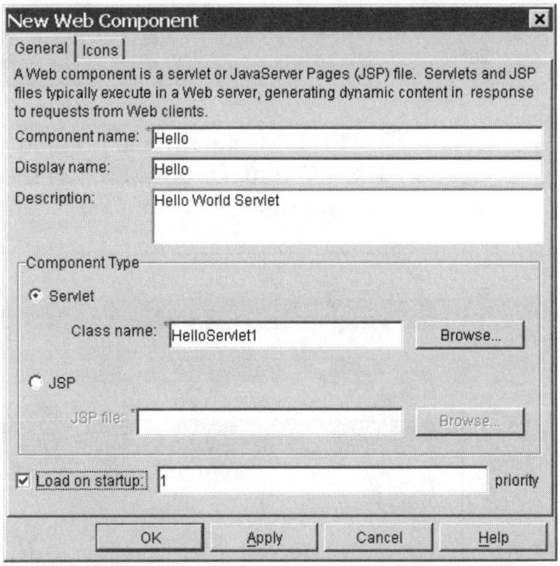

Figure 4-3. *New Web Component dialog box filled out*

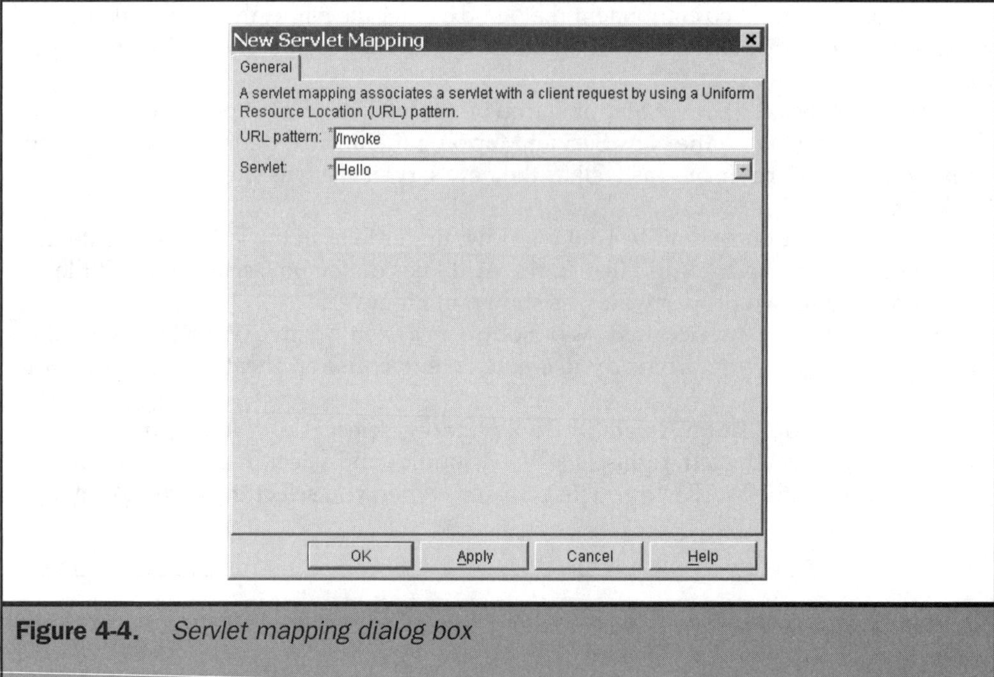

Figure 4-4. *Servlet mapping dialog box*

need to select the context root for it. This is essentially the prefix that will be used for URLs that access the application. Use the context root */Hello,* as shown in Figure 4-6. Now you are ready to save the application as a file with a *.ear* extension.

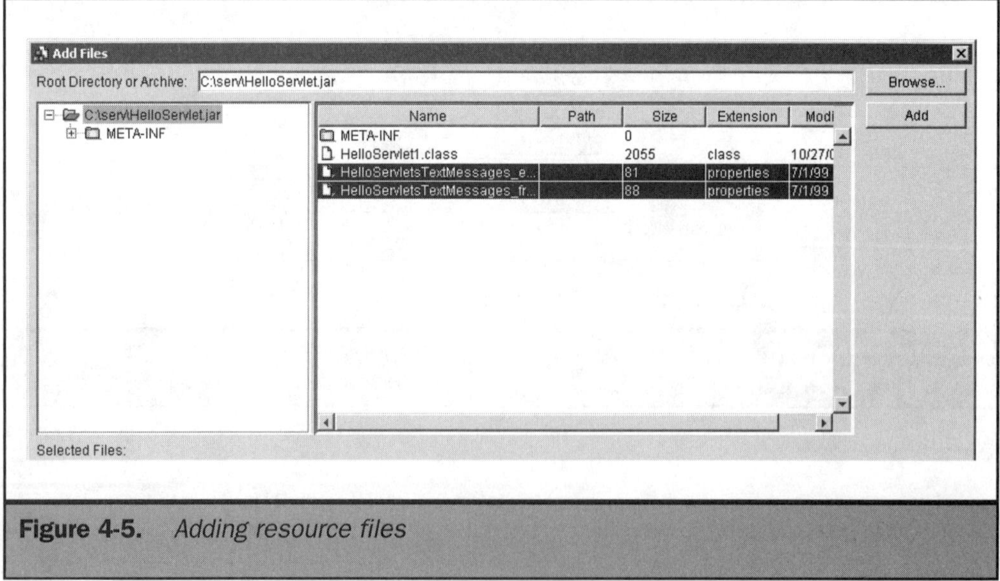

Figure 4-5. *Adding resource files*

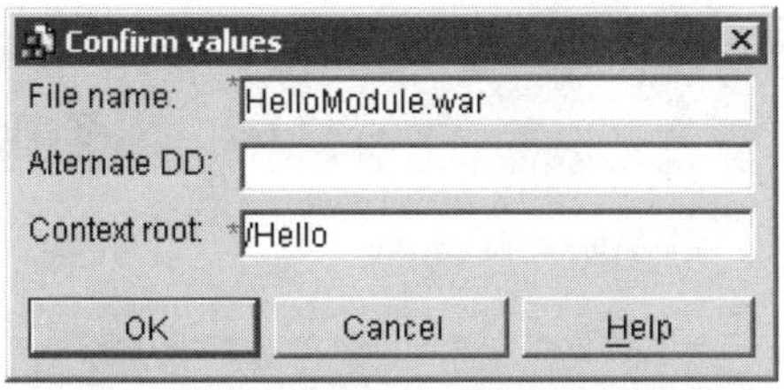

Figure 4-6. *Selecting the context root*

Web Application Deployment

Now you are ready to deploy your application (containing just the servlet) on the server. To do that, you need to invoke the Administrative Console. Note that there is a difference between the Administrative Console used in the WebSphere Application Server Advanced Edition Full Configuration and that used in the Advanced Edition Single Server Configuration. The following example uses the Single Server Configuration's Administrative Console, being the lowest common denominator.

The Administrative Console can be invoked from the Windows Start menu, or simply by accessing *http://localhost:9090/admin* on the machine where the WebSphere server is running. Note that you must start the server. (You can start it from the First Steps window, as explained in Chapter 2, from the Windows Start menu, or by using the script *startserver.bat*). The first window for the Administrative Console is shown in Figure 4-7. In this window, enter an arbitrary user name and slick Submit.

The Administrative Console opens. In the tree on the left, select Enterprise Applications. The Enterprise Applications window appears. Click Install; then, in the Path field of the next window, select the EAR file you created in the previous section, as shown in Figure 4-8. Click Next, and proceed to the second installation window. Click

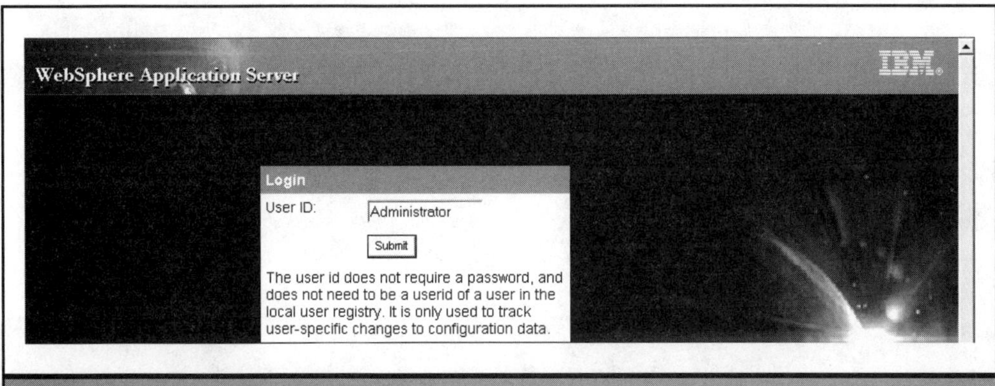

Figure 4-7. *Administrative Console Login screen*

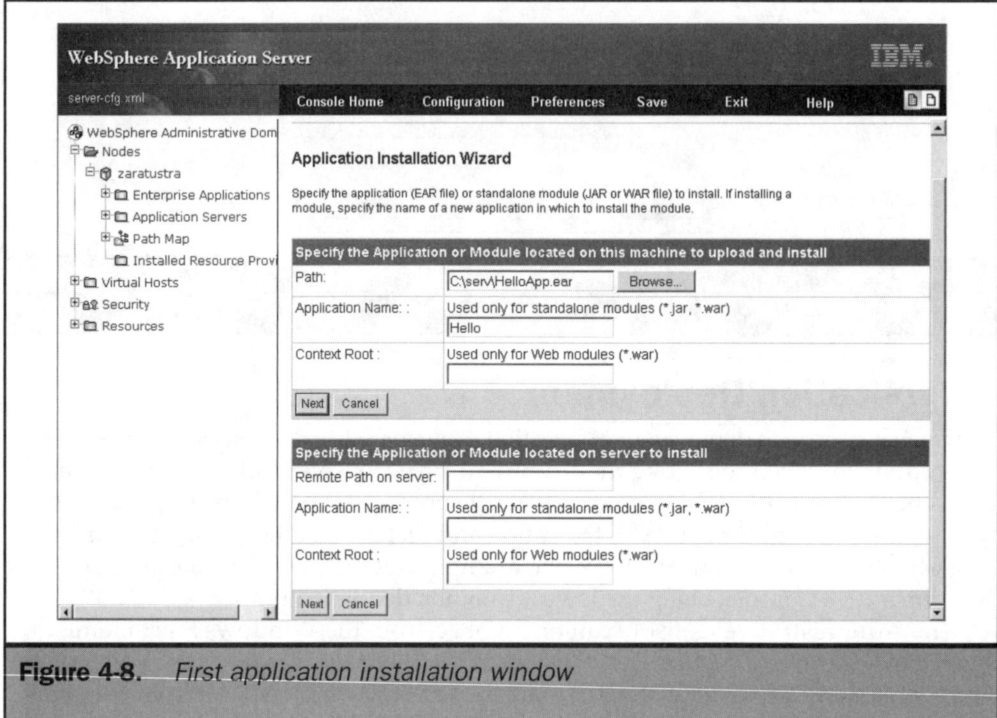

Figure 4-8. *First application installation window*

Next again, and proceed to the final window of the deployment, shown in Figure 4-9. Click Finish.

To complete the deployment of the application, you need to save the setup by clicking Save at the top of the Administrative Console. Also, the deployment requires

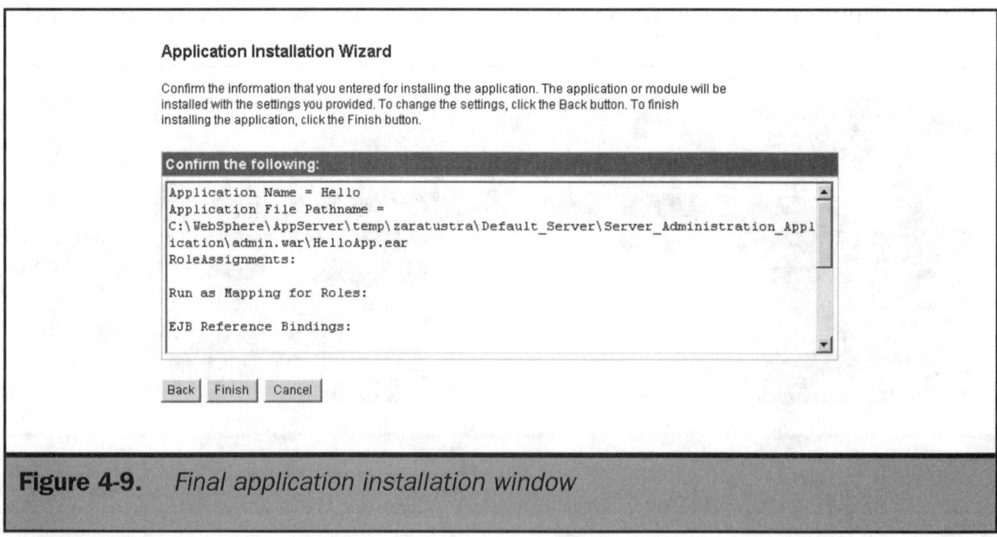

Figure 4-9. *Final application installation window*

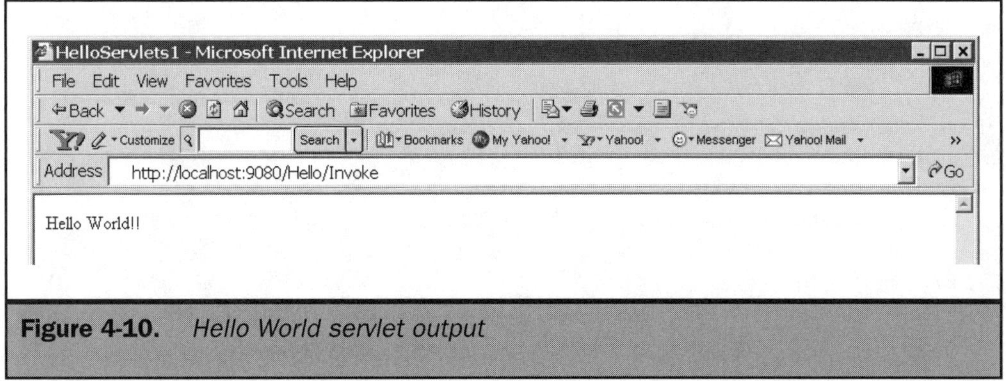

Figure 4-10. *Hello World servlet output*

that you stop and then restart the WebSphere Application Server. This can be done from the First Steps window or by using the *stopserver.bat* script.

Testing the Servlet

After all the work required to deploy the servlet, testing it is fairly simple. You just point your Web browser to the correct URL. Based on your selection of the context root and the Servlet Mapping, you need to use the URL *http://localhost/Hello/Invoke.* The result is shown in Figure 4-10.

"Hello World" JSPs

Now that you know the basics of servlets and have seen how to build and deploy a simple servlet, you can move on to a very simple JSP. JSPs follow a relatively new programming model for Java; but it is not a new model to the computing industry, because it is very similar to Microsoft's very successful Active Server Pages (ASP) model. JSPs aim to provide the same usefulness of servlets but in a way that completely separates the application processing logic from the presentation logic. They also aim to provide an environment in which it is very easy to build relatively simple e-business applications, while not sacrificing the full strength of the servlet model. We will not delve into the details of JSP and the JSP model; we will cover these later in the book. Right now, you will focus on building a very simple example and deploying it under the WebSphere server. Actually, there are a set of four examples, each showing a slightly different variant of JSP.

The Hello World JSP is shown in the following listing. It outputs "Hello World" and shows a "hit" counter—an indication of the number of times the page was accessed since the server has been up, and the current date.

```
<HTML>
<HEAD>
<TITLE>Hello World</TITLE>
</HEAD>
```

```
<BODY>
<H1>Hello World</H1>
<%! static int count = 0; %>
<H2>This servlet was accessed
<%= ++count %>
times so far. </H2>
<H3>The date is <%= new java.util.Date()%> </H3>
</BODY>
</HTML>
```

This code listing is an ordinary HTML file, with several JSP tags embedded in it. JSP tags are identified by the surrounding <% and %>. The first JSP tag defines the static variable count. Note that this tag begins with <%!, which is used when defining the variable. The other JSP tags, which begin with <%=, output expressions. The first two outputs are the counter and a Date object. When using the <%= tag, the toString() method of the expression is invoked and output to the page.

In order to deploy the example, you also need to go through an assembly phase. The assembly phase for the JSP is similar to that of the servlet; the only difference is that you must select the JSP radio button in the Web Component Properties dialog box, as shown in Figure 4-11. Once you have a Web application with the JSP inside, the deployment in WebSphere is identical to the one described in the "Web Application Assembly" section earlier in this chapter.

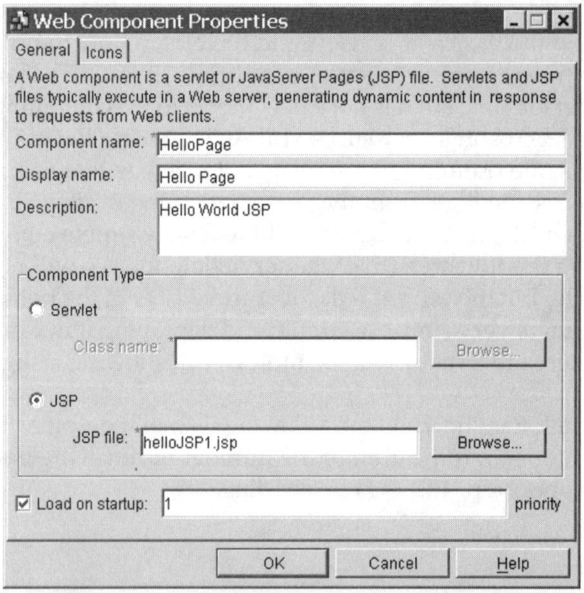

Figure 4-11. *Web Component Properties dialog box for JSP*

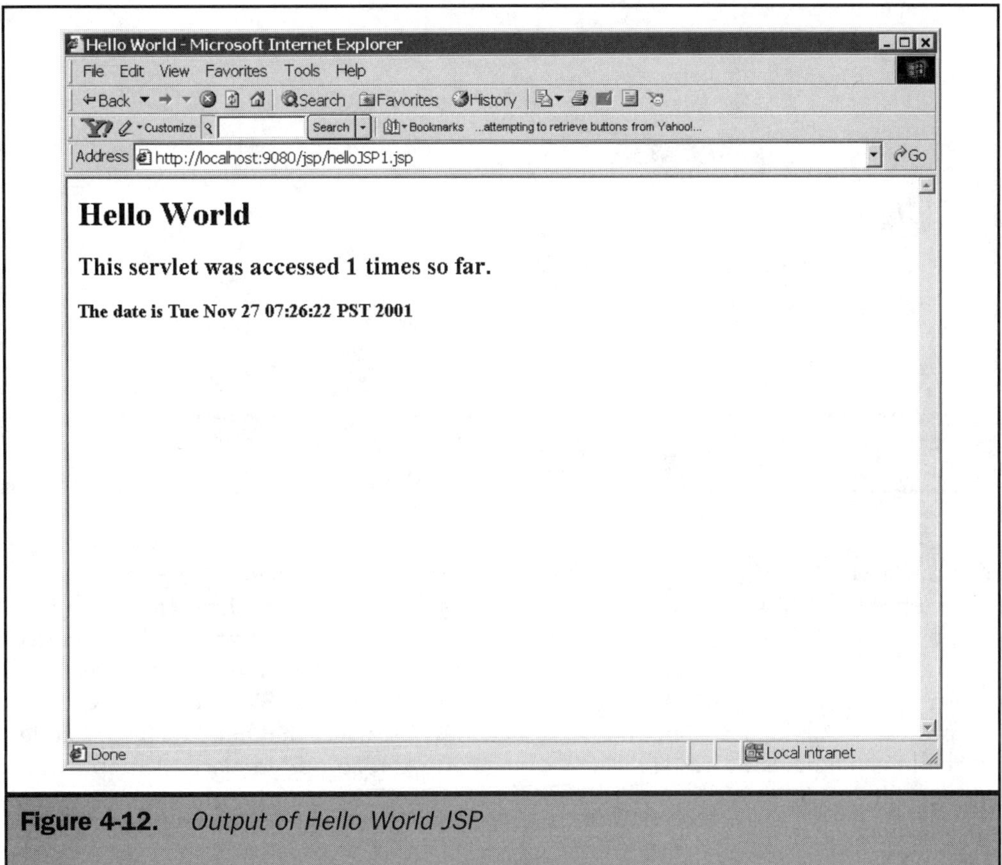

Figure 4-12. *Output of Hello World JSP*

After you have deployed the application containing the JSP (and after restarting WebSphere), you can test the JSP, as shown in Figure 4-12.

The HTML of the output page is shown here:

```
<HTML>
<HEAD>
<TITLE>Hello World</TITLE>
</HEAD>
<BODY>
<H1>Hello World</H1>
<H2>This servlet was accessed
1
times so far. </H2>
<H3>The date is Tue Nov 27 07:26:22 PST 2001 </H3>
</BODY>
</HTML>
```

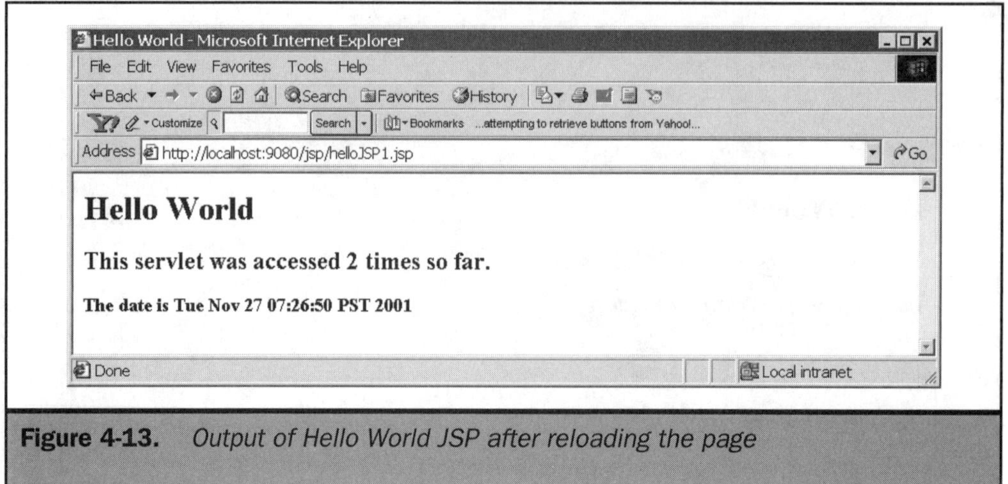

Figure 4-13. *Output of Hello World JSP after reloading the page*

You can see that this is a copy of the JSP page, with the respective JSP tags replaced by their respective output. Reloading this page increases the counter, as shown in Figure 4-13.

So what is really going on behind the scenes with this JSP? When the Web server gets a request for a URL terminating with a *.jsp* extension, it calls the WebSphere Application Server. Then the magic starts! WebSphere's JSP support takes the JSP file and goes through the process of parsing it and building a servlet (yes, a servlet!) that matches the JSP code. (It really is magic, isn't it?) The servlet Java code and compiled class file deploy as servlets on the server. This process is only performed once; additional requests will cause a quick invocation of the compiled servlet—as long as the JSP file has not changed. If the JSP file changes, the appropriate servlet is recompiled. JSP, therefore, provides a built-in version and configuration control mechanism. The Java code created for your simple JSP by is shown here:

```
import javax.servlet.*;
import javax.servlet.http.*;
import javax.servlet.jsp.*;
import javax.servlet.jsp.tagext.*;
import java.io.PrintWriter;
import java.io.IOException;
import java.io.InputStream;
import java.io.ObjectInputStream;
import java.util.Vector;
import org.apache.jasper.runtime.*;
import java.beans.*;
import org.apache.jasper.JasperException;
import java.io.ByteArrayOutputStream;
```

```
import org.apache.jasper.compiler.ibmtsx.*;
import org.apache.jasper.compiler.ibmdb.*;
import java.sql.SQLException;

public class helloJSP1_jsp_1 extends HttpJspBase {
    static char[][] _jspx_html_data = null;
    // begin
[file="C:\\WebSphere\\AppServer/installedApps\\mytt.ear/webjsp.war\\\helloJS
P1.jsp";from=(5,3);to=(5,26)]
         static int count = 0;
    // end

    static {
    }

    public helloJSP1_jsp_1( ) {
    }

    private static boolean _jspx_inited = false;

    private static boolean checkedAttributeIgnoreException = false;
    private static boolean throwException = true;

    public final void _jspx_init() throws JasperException {
        ObjectInputStream oin = null;
        int numStrings = 0;
        try {
            InputStream fin =
this.getClass().getClassLoader().getResourceAsStream("helloJSP1_jsp_1.dat");
            oin = new ObjectInputStream(fin);
            _jspx_html_data = (char[][]) oin.readObject();
        } catch (Exception ex) {
            throw new JasperException("Unable to open data file");
        } finally {
            if (oin != null)
                try { oin.close(); } catch (IOException ignore) { }
        }
    }

    public void _jspService(HttpServletRequest request, HttpServletResponse
response)
        throws IOException, ServletException {
        JspFactory _jspxFactory = null;
        PageContext pageContext = null;
        HttpSession session = null;
        ServletContext application = null;
        ServletConfig config = null;
```

```
        JspWriter out = null;
        Object page = this;
        String  _value = null;
        setBooleanIgnoreException();
        try {
            if (_jspx_inited == false) {
                _jspx_init();
                _jspx_inited = true;
            }
            _jspxFactory = JspFactory.getDefaultFactory();
            response.setContentType("text/html;charset=Cp1252");
            pageContext = _jspxFactory.getPageContext(this, request,
response"", true, 8192, true);
            application = pageContext.getServletContext();
            config = pageContext.getServletConfig();
            session = pageContext.getSession();
            out = pageContext.getOut();
            // begin
[file="C:\\WebSphere\\AppServer/installedApps\\mytt.ear/webjsp.war\\\helloJS
P1.jsp";from=(0,0);to=(5,0)]
                out.print(_jspx_html_data[0]);
            // end

            // begin
[file="C:\\WebSphere\\AppServer/installedApps\\mytt.ear/webjsp.war\\\helloJS
P1.jsp";from=(5,28);to=(6,30)]
                out.print(_jspx_html_data[1]);
            // end
            // begin
[file="C:\\WebSphere\\AppServer/installedApps\\mytt.ear/webjsp.war\\\helloJS
P1.jsp";from=(6,33);to=(6,43)]
                out.print( ++count   );
            // end

            // begin
[file="C:\\WebSphere\\AppServer/installedApps\\mytt.ear/webjsp.war\\\helloJS
P1.jsp";from=(6,45);to=(8,16)]
                out.print(_jspx_html_data[2]);
            // end

            // begin
[file="C:\\WebSphere\\AppServer/installedApps\\mytt.ear/webjsp.war\\\helloJS
P1.jsp";from=(8,19);to=(8,45)]
                out.print( new java.util.Date() );
            // end

            // begin
```

```
[file="C:\\WebSphere\\AppServer/installedApps\\mytt.ear/webjsp.war\\\helloJS
P1.jsp";from=(8,47);to=(13,0)]
                out.print(_jspx_html_data[3]);
            // end
        } catch (Exception ex) {
            if (out.getBufferSize() != 0)
                out.clearBuffer();
            pageContext.handlePageException(ex);
        } catch ( Throwable t) {
            if (out.getBufferSize() != 0)
                out.clearBuffer();
            pageContext.handlePageException(new Exception(t.getMessage()));
        } finally {
            out.flush();
            _jspxFactory.releasePageContext(pageContext);
        }
    }

    private void setBooleanIgnoreException() {
        if (checkedAttributeIgnoreException) return;
                checkedAttributeIgnoreException = true;
        String initParamIgnoreException
=(String)(getServletConfig().getInitParameter("jsp.repeatTag.ignoreException
"));
        if ((initParamIgnoreException != null) &&
(initParamIgnoreException.toLowerCase().equals("true"))){
            throwException = false;
        }
    }
}
```

By the way, if there is an error in the JSP code, output similar to that generated from a compiler will be redirected to the WebSphere error log that is stored in the *logs* directory under the WebSphere installation, as shown here:

```
org.apache.jasper.JasperException: JSPG0059E: Unable to compile class for
JSPC:\WebSphere\AppServer\installedApps\jsp1.ear\jsp1.war\WEB-
INF\classes\helloJSP1_jsp_0.java:80: Undefined variable or class name:
textProvider
                out.print( textProvider.getTextMessage() );
                           ^

1 error
      at org.apache.jasper.compiler.Compiler.compile(Compiler.java:283
      at
org.apache.jasper.compiler.ibmtools.JasperUtil.compile(JasperUtil.java:246
      at
```

```
org.apache.jasper.compiler.ibmtools.JspModC.compileDir(JspModC.java:205
        at
org.apache.jasper.compiler.ibmtools.JspModC.compileApp(JspModC.java:52
        at
com.ibm.ejs.sm.web.app.SaveAppwizAction.precompileJsps(SaveAppwizAction.java
:1058)
        at
com.ibm.ejs.sm.web.app.SaveAppwizAction.perform(SaveAppwizAction.java:236)
        at
org.apache.struts.action.ActionServlet.processActionInstance(ActionServlet
.java:960)
        at
org.apache.struts.action.ActionServlet.process(ActionServlet.java:869)
        at
org.apache.struts.action.ActionServlet.doGet(ActionServlet.java:343)
        at javax.servlet.http.HttpServlet.service(HttpServlet.java:740)
        at javax.servlet.http.HttpServlet.service(HttpServlet.java:853)
        at
com.ibm.servlet.engine.webapp.StrictServletInstance.doService(ServletManager
.java:718)
        at
com.ibm.servlet.engine.webapp.StrictLifecycleServlet._service(StrictLife
cycleServlet.java:160)
        at
com.ibm.servlet.engine.webapp.IdleServletState.service(StrictLifecycleServlet
.java:287)
        at
com.ibm.servlet.engine.webapp.StrictLifecycleServlet.service(StrictLifecycle
Servlet.java:105)
        at
com.ibm.servlet.engine.webapp.ServletInstance.service(ServletManager.java:42
8)
        at
com.ibm.servlet.engine.webapp.ValidServletReferenceState.dispatch(Servlet
Manager.java:870)
        at
com.ibm.servlet.engine.webapp.ServletInstanceReference.dispatch(Servlet
Manager.java:788)
        at
com.ibm.servlet.engine.webapp.WebAppRequestDispatcher.handleWebAppDispatch
(WebAppRequestDispatcher.java:439)
        at
com.ibm.servlet.engine.webapp.WebAppRequestDispatcher.dispatch(WebAppRequest
Dispatcher.java:239)
        at
com.ibm.servlet.engine.webapp.WebAppRequestDispatcher.forward(WebAppRequest
Dispatcher.java:104)
```

```
        at
com.ibm.servlet.engine.srt.WebAppInvoker.doForward(WebAppInvoker.java:61)
        at
com.ibm.servlet.engine.srt.WebAppInvoker.handleInvocationHook(WebAppInvoker
.java:132)
        at
com.ibm.servlet.engine.invocation.CachedInvocation.handleInvocation(Cached
Invocation.java:67)
        at
com.ibm.servlet.engine.invocation.CacheableInvocationContext.invoke(Cache
ableInvocationContext.java:106)
        at
com.ibm.servlet.engine.srp.ServletRequestProcessor.dispatchByURI(Servlet
RequestProcessor.java:125)
        at
com.ibm.servlet.engine.oselistener.OSEListenerDispatcher.service(OSEListener
.java:271)
         at
com.ibm.servlet.engine.http11.HttpConnection.handleRequest(HttpConnection
.java:49)
        at
com.ibm.ws.http.HttpConnection.readAndHandleRequest(HttpConnection.java:303)
        at com.ibm.ws.http.HttpConnection.run(HttpConnection.java:232)
        at com.ibm.ws.util.CachedThread.run(ThreadPool.java:122)
```

Summary

Servlets and JSP are two technologies that form the basis of the Web application model and, specifically, WebSphere Web applications. These technologies are easily learned and mastered, and are extremely important in every Web application—as opposed to some of the more advanced technologies that are sometimes used and sometimes not. Specifically, EJBs, which are part of the technological basis of J2EE applications, are also very heavily used; but they are used less often than servlets and JSP. We will discuss servlets and JSP further in Chapter 7 and in Chapters 22 to 28. In the meantime, flip over to the next chapter for a "Hello World" introduction to EJB.

Chapter 5

Hello EJBs

This chapter takes a quick look at one of the WebSphere Application Server capabilities, namely Enterprise JavaBeans (EJBs). The intention of this chapter is to give a quick overview of what EJBs are and what they are good for; it also provides a simple Hello World–type demonstration program. Chapter 11 looks at EJB in more detail and from a broader perspective, and Part 6 of the book discusses the aspects of developing and deploying EJBs using the WebSphere Application Server.

EJB Basics

A JavaBean is a software component conforming to a standard interface that is used for application programming, and in particular, user interface programming. (You'll find more on JavaBeans in Chapter 10.) In the same spirit, Enterprise JavaBeans (EJB) are software components for distributed systems. Just like JavaBeans, EJBs conform to a standard interface.

To capture the essence of distributed computing, EJBs are designed with a built-in notion of a client and a server. The server is an EJB container that hosts EJB objects, and the client accesses these objects to perform certain actions. To make things a little more interesting, the EJBs are not directly contained in the main EJB container, but rather in several subcontainers. An *EJB container* is essentially an execution environment for EJBs. An EJB container may well contain several more of these containers. The EJB container is, of course, part of the application server, which in this case is WebSphere.

EJB Architecture

Client access to EJB is done by means of Java Remote Method Invocation (Java RMI). However, client-side code does not directly invoke the bean code. Instead, it goes through two interfaces, called the EJB home interface and the EJB remote interface. The home interface is the initial point of contact for the client, and it acts as a factory for EJBs (that is, creating beans on request and removing them when they are no longer needed). The remote interface is a proxy for the EJB itself, used by client-side code to invoke specific methods on the EJB. To summarize, Figure 5-1 illustrates the EJB architecture.

While this architecture might be a little overwhelming with all its different components, it is quite powerful. The nice thing about it is that once you define the remote and home interfaces, you don't have to worry about implementing them, because that is the responsibility of the EJB container. When you implement an EJB, all you have to do is define the remote and home interfaces, and then the bean itself.

EJB Home

The home interface for an EJB extends the `EJBHome` interface. The methods of this interface are listed in Table 5-1. As you can see, the `EJBHome` interface provides only three mandatory methods. The first one, `getEJBMetaData()`, returns a reference to an object that contains information about the EJB. This object implements the

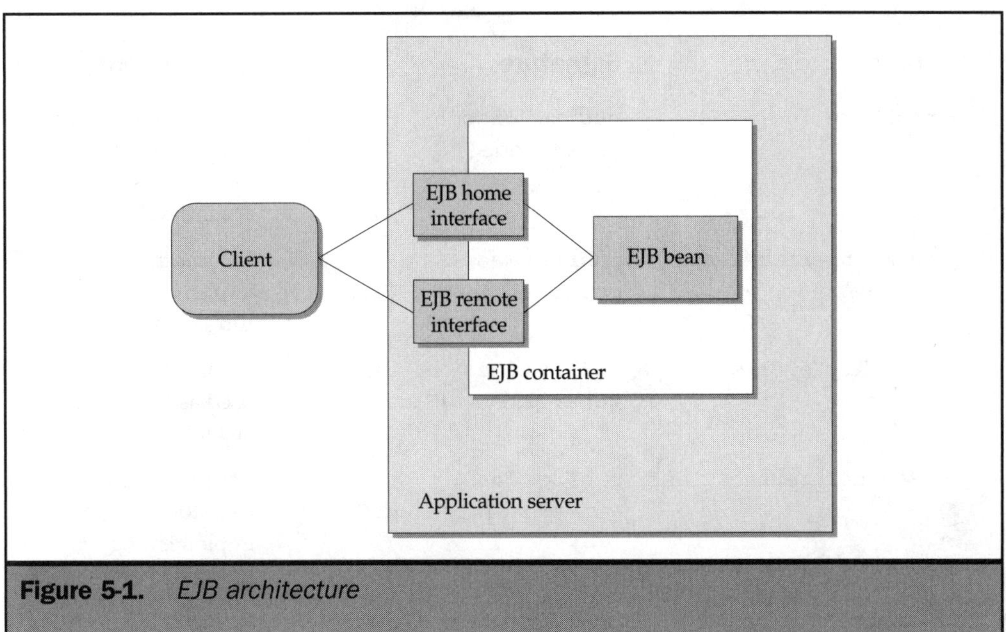

Figure 5-1. *EJB architecture*

EJBMetaData interface, and the methods of this interface are listed in Table 5-2. The two other methods of EJBHome are responsible for removing EJBs. Note that there are no methods for creating EJBs in this interface. These should be implemented in the bean-specific extension of EJBHome, as you will see in the next section.

Method	Signature	Description
getEJBMetaData	public EJBMetaData getEJBMetaData()	Returns the metadata for the bean object.
remove	public void remove(Handle handle)	Removes an EJB object given a Handle. A Handle is a reference to the bean object, which can be serialized by the client.
	public void remove(Object primaryKey)	Removes an EJB object by its primary key. (Primary keys are relevant only to entity beans.)

Table 5-1. *Methods of the EJBHome Interface*

Method	Signature	Description
`getEJBHome`	`public EJBHome getEJBHome()`	Returns a reference to an object that implements the EJB's home interface.
`getHomeInterfaceClass`	`public Class getHomeInterfaceClass()`	Returns the class implementing the EJB's home interface.
`getPrimaryKeyClass`	`public Class getPrimaryKeyClass()`	Returns the class used as the primary key for this EJB.
`getRemoteInterfaceClass`	`public Class getRemoteInterfaceClass()`	Returns the class used for implementing the EJB's remote interface.
`isSession`	`public boolean isSession()`	Returns a boolean value indicating whether this EJB is a session bean.

Table 5-2. *Methods of the EJBMetaData Interface*

The remote interface for an EJB extends the `EJBObject` interface, and the methods for this interface are listed in Table 5-3. When you write your own remote interface, you must include the signatures of all of the methods you need to invoke remotely.

The Enterprise Bean

Now that you've gone through the home and remote interfaces, you can get to the EJB itself. The top-level EJB class is called `EnterpriseBean`, and it is defined as follows:

```
public interface javax.ejb.EnterpriseBean extends java.io.Serializable
{
};
```

Method	Signature	Description
`getEJBHome`	`public EJBHome getEJBHome()`	Returns a reference to an object implementing the EJB's home interface.
`getPrimaryKey`	`public Object getPrimaryKey()`	Returns the primary key for the EJB object. This is relevant only for entity beans.
`getHandle`	`public Handle getHandle()`	Returns a Handle to the object. The Handle is a serializable reference to the object.
`isIdentical`	`public boolean isIdentical(EJBObject obj)`	Tests to see whether two EJB object references are referring to same object. This is useful mostly for entity beans. Note that two beans of the same home interface that have the same primary key are considered to be identical.
`Remove`	`public void remove()`	Removes the remote EJB object.

Table 5-3. *Methods of the EJBObject Interface*

As you can see, there's not much to this definition. When developing an EJB, you obviously do not extend this interface, since it contains nothing. Instead, you extend either one of the `SessionBean` or one of the `EntityBean` interfaces. These interfaces correspond to two different kinds of EJB. The first refers to session beans, which are usually limited to the scope of a single client session. The other refers to entity beans, which have a longer lifetime and specifically exist through several separate sessions. In the remainder of the chapter, we will limit the discussion to session beans only, since the "Hello World" EJB is a session bean.

The `SessionBean` interface is shown here:

```
public interface EntityBean extends javax.ejb.EnterpriseBean
{
                  public abstract void ejbActivate() throws
                                      java.rmi.RemoteException;
      public abstract void ejbPassivate() throws java.rmi.RemoteException;
```

```
        public abstract void ejbRemove() throws
                                          java.rmi.RemoteException,
                                         javax.ejb.RemoveException;
    public abstract void
                    setSessionContext(javax.ejb.SessionContext
                    context) throws java.rmi.RemoteException;
}
```

The invocation of these methods is event driven; that is, they are called to notify the `SessionBean` about some external event.

"Hello World" EJB

The "Hello World" EJB presented in this section is very simple. It merely provides a method to return a greeting message string. Client-side code can use this method by finding the bean's home interface, getting access to the bean, and then invoking the method.

The first step in developing the EJB is to define the remote interface. As mentioned in the previous section, this interface extends the `EJBObject` interface. The code for the remote interface is as follows:

```
package book.websphere.chapter5;
import javax.ejb.*;
import java.rmi.*;
public interface Hello extends EJBObject
{
      String getTextMessage() throws RemoteException;
}
```

In order to use the EJB, you import the EJB package *javax.ejb*. You also import the RMI package *java.rmi*, since you refer to the `RemoteException` defined there. This exception is thrown whenever there is a network problem, and the client-side code must be prepared to handle it. As a rule, all of your EJB methods in the remote interface should throw this exception.

The only method you define in the remote interface is `getTextMessage()` The signature for this method should correspond to its definition in the bean itself, the only possible difference being that in the remote interface its definition must indicate that it throws a `RemoteException`.

Once you've finished with the remote interface, you can proceed to the home interface. In the home interface, you need to define creation methods for the bean. Such methods should be named `create()`, and they can have parameters if needed. The return value type for the creation method is the type of the remote interface. As with the remote interface methods, the creation method must be declared such that it throws a `java.rmi.RemoteException`. In addition, it should also throw a `javax.ejb.CreateException`. This exception is thrown when there is a problem creating the new EJB (for example, when the EJB container is out of memory). The home interface for the EJB, called `HelloHome`, looks like this:

```
package book.websphere.chapter5;
import javax.ejb.*;
import java.rmi.*;

public interface HelloHome extends EJBHome {
      public Hello create() throws RemoteException,
                                   javax.ejb.CreateException;
}
```

Here, we have provided a `create()` method without any parameters. Note that this method must be public, as it should be visible outside of the package.

Now that you have the home and remote interfaces, you can move on to the bean implementation class. This is the cool part of writing Enterprise JavaBeans; you don't have to provide implementations for the home and remote interfaces—that's the responsibility of the container. The bean implementation class is named `HelloBean`, and it looks like this:

```
package book.websphere.chapter5;
import javax.ejb.*;
public class HelloBean implements SessionBean {
      public void ejbCreate()
      {
      }
      public void ejbRemove()
      {
      }
      public void ejbActivate()
      {
      }
      public void ejbPassivate()
      {
```

```
        }
        public void setSessionContext(SessionContext ctx)
        {
        }
        public String getTextMessage()
        {
                return "Hello World";
        }
}
```

This code implements the SessionBean interface. Since the requirements here are very simple, all the implementations of the SessionBean interface methods are empty. This means that your bean is oblivious to any calls by the container, made when it is activated or "passivated." In Part VI you will see more complicated EJB implementations. The only method that actually does anything in the HelloBean class is the getTextMessage() method, which returns the "Hello World" string. Note that its signature should match the one defined in the remote interface.

Now that you have all the code you need, the next step is to compile it and create a JAR file. To keep things as simple as possible, use the javac and jar commands. From your command-line prompt, type the following:

```
javac websphere\book\chapter5\*.java
jar cvf Hello.jar websphere\book\chapter5\*.class
```

This is assuming that you run both commands from the directory in which the source code directories reside. Before running the compilation, make sure your CLASSPATH includes the files *j2ee.jar*, *csicpi.jar*, *iwsorb.ar*, *ns.jar*, and *jts.jar*—all residing in the *lib* directory under the WebSphere installation.

Assembly and Deployment

Now you are ready to actually deploy the EJB on your application server. For this purpose, you use the Application Assembly Tool (AAT). To start it, run the *assembly.bat* script in the *bin* directory of your WebSphere installation, or click Launch the Application Assembly Tool in the First Steps window. Once the AAT starts up, a welcome window becomes visible. Select EJB Module. The AAT opens a default EJB module and names it *New_EJB_Jar1.jar*, as shown in Figure 5-2.

To proceed with deploying the sample EJB, right-click Session Beans on the left panel, and click New. The resulting window, shown in Figure 5-3, prompts you to type in the information for the new EJB. Click Browse for the home interface. In the window that appears, click Browse again, and select the *Hello.jar* file in the dialog box that appears. Once the JAR file is loaded, browse through it and select the *HelloHome.class* file.

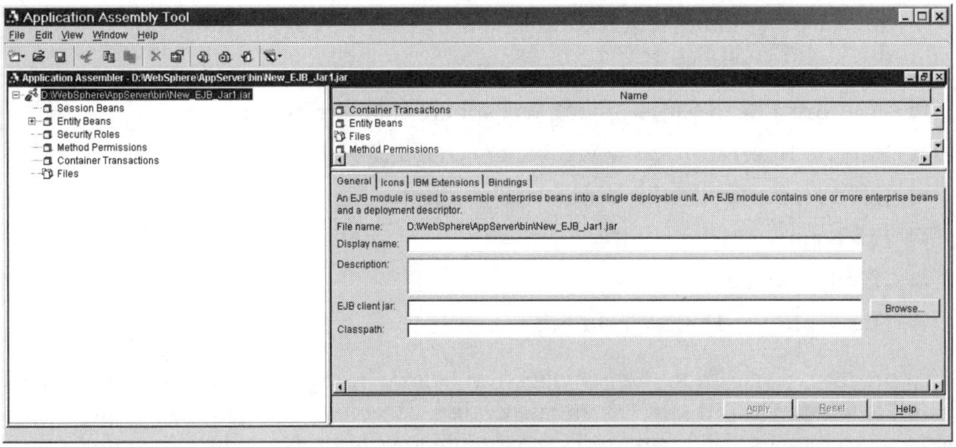

Figure 5-2. *New EJB module window*

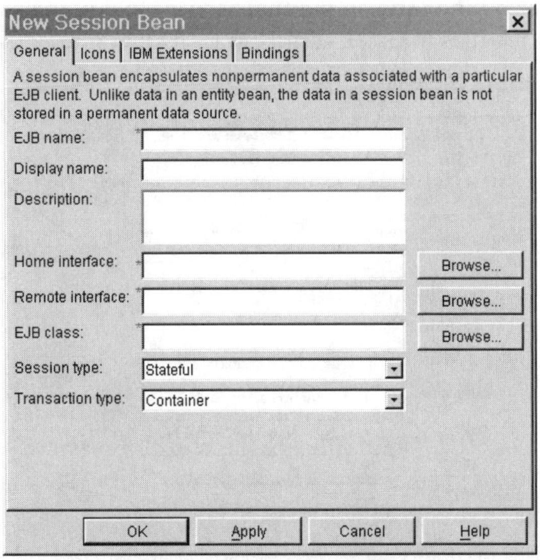

Figure 5-3. *New Session Bean window*

After going through a similar process for the remote class and the EJB bean class, you can fill out the other fields required for the EJB, as shown in the following list. The final result is shown in Figure 5-4.

- **Enterprise Bean Class** book.websphere.chapter5.HelloBean
- **Remote Interface** book.websphere.chapter5.Hello
- **JNDI Home (under Bindings)** HelloBean
- **EJB Name** Hello
- **Display Name** Hello
- **Description** Hello World EJB

To proceed, click OK in the New Session Bean window. Then right-click the JAR file on the left panel, and select Generate Code for Deployment. The AAT will prompt you to save changes. Click Yes, and save the file to *hello.jar*. Now the Generate Code for Deployment window appears. Select Generate Now, and the generation process starts. The progress of the code generation process is shown in the bottom window, as you can see in Figure 5-5. This completes the assembly phase. If you have a deployable JAR file at hand, you can proceed to the actual deployment.

Deployment takes place with either the WebSphere Administrative Console or a script called *ejbdeploy.bat*. Here we use the Administrative Console, which provides a graphic interface. If you prefer typing out commands, or want to automate deployment tasks through the use of batch files (or shell scripts in UNIX), you may use the script.

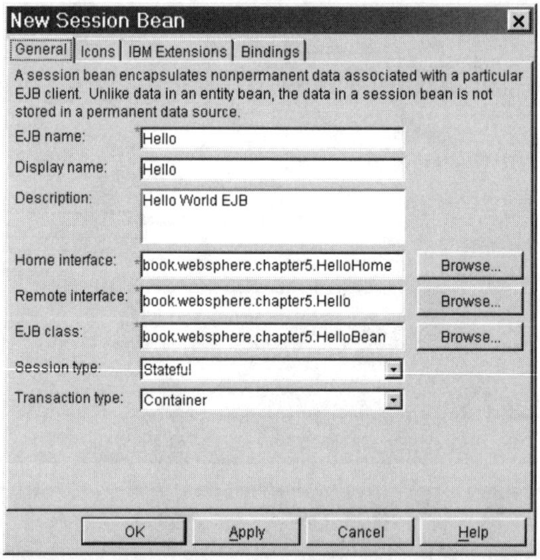

Figure 5-4. *New Session Bean window filled out*

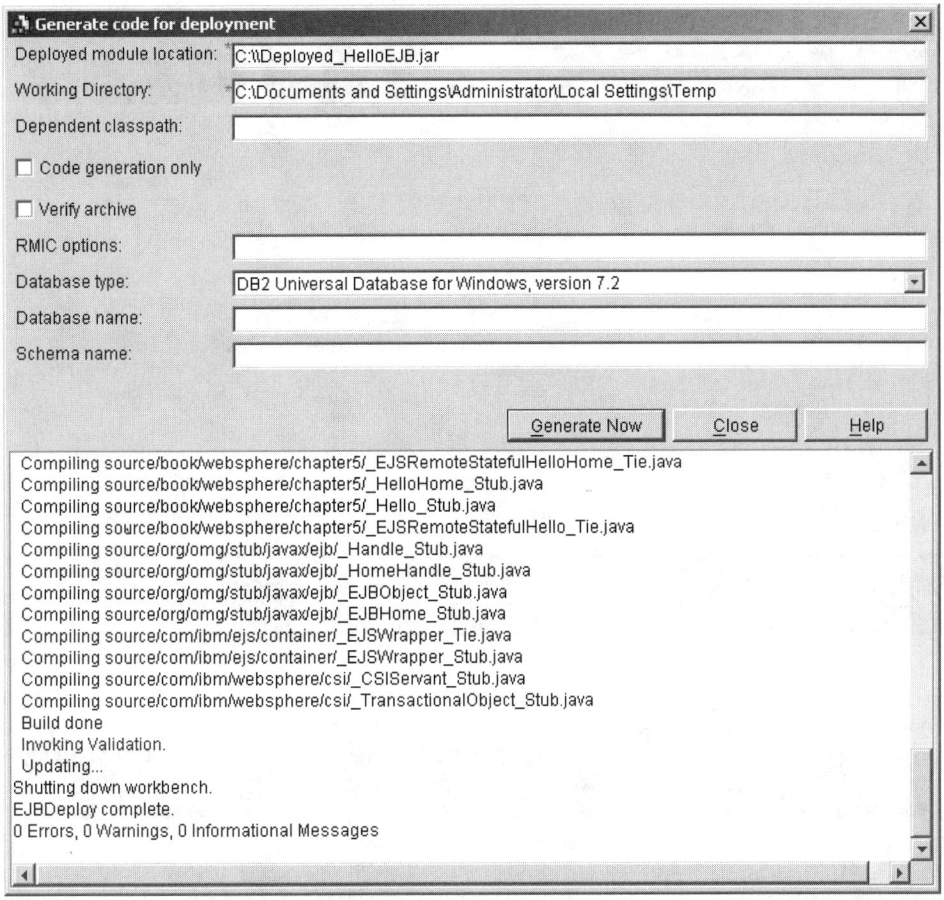

Figure 5-5. *Code generation progress*

You launch the Administrative Console from the WebSphere entry under the Windows Start menu, or from the First Steps window. First, you need to enter a user name in the browser window that appears. The main Administrative Console window appears. On the left panel, under Nodes, locate your machine name, and under it open Enterprise Applications, as shown in Figure 5-6.

Click Install to initiate the deployment. The Application Install Wizard appears. Select the JAR file created with AAT, and enter the application name.

Once you click Next, the system prompts you for the Java Naming and Directory Interface (JNDI) binding for the bean, as shown in Figure 5-7. This is the name under which it will be possible to locate the bean later on. Keep it as *HelloBean*. In the following window, click Next. This installs the application, and you can then see it in the list of enterprise applications.

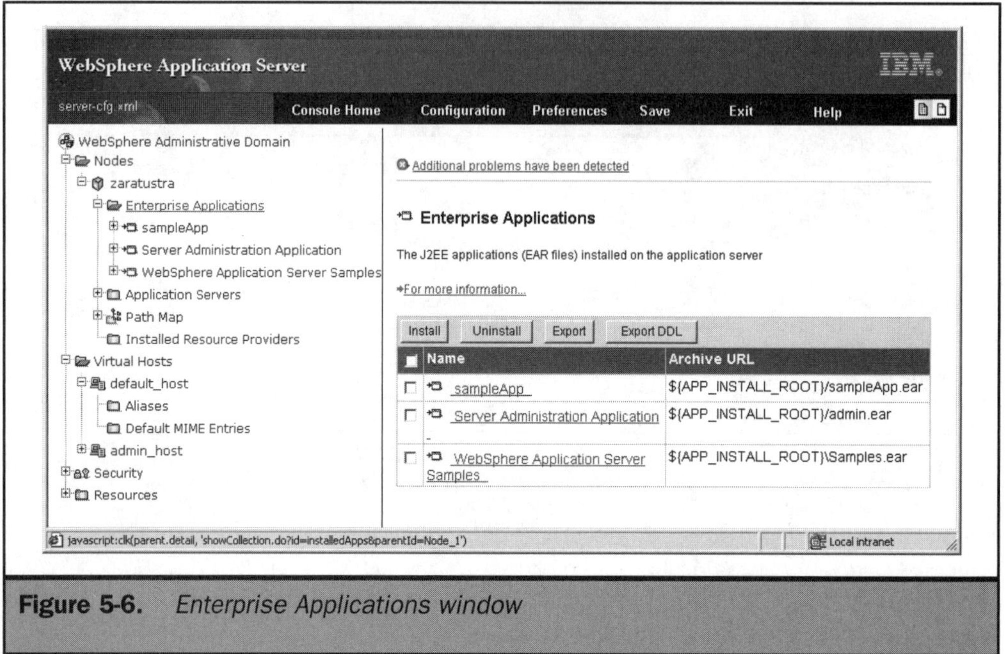

Figure 5-6. *Enterprise Applications window*

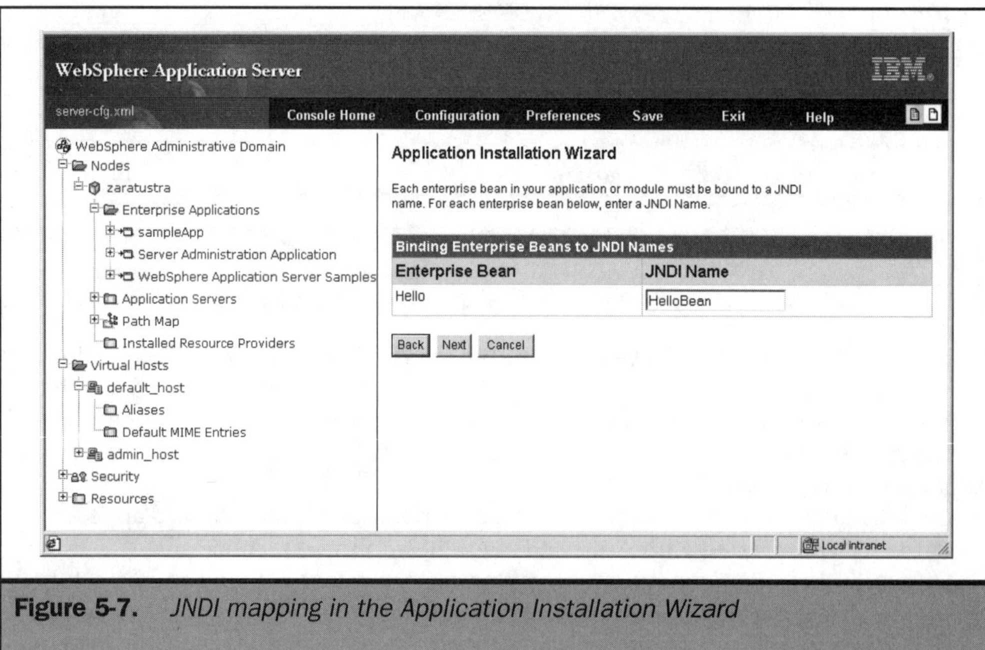

Figure 5-7. *JNDI mapping in the Application Installation Wizard*

Testing the EJB

Now that you've finished the deployment phase, what remains is to write a small client-side program, as shown here, to verify that the EJB actually works.

```
package book.websphere.chapter5;
import javax.ejb.*;
import java.rmi.*;
import java.util.*;
import javax.naming.*;

public class HelloClient {
    public static void main(String args[])
    {
      try {
        Properties env = System.getProperties();
        env.put(javax.naming.Context.INITIAL_CONTEXT_FACTORY,
               "com.ibm.websphere.naming.WsInitialContextFactory");
        env.put(javax.naming.Context.PROVIDER_
               "iiop://localhost");
        InitialContext ic = new InitialContext(env);
        HelloHome home = (HelloHome)
                  javax.rmi.PortableRemoteObject.narrow(
                  ic.lookup("HelloBean")Hello.class);
        Hello  bean = home.create();
        String ret = bean.getTextMessage();
        System.out.println("Returned Message:  " + ret);
      } catch (Exception ex) {
        System.out.println("HelloClient Runtime Error:");
        ex.printStackTrace();
      }
    }
}
```

What this program does first is to obtain an object of type `javax.naming.InitialContext`. This class provides an interface to the naming service, which is covered in more detail in Chapter 20. Once the `InitialContext` object is initialized, you use it to look up the home interface of your EJB. The initialization requires a couple of properties that point at the provider of the naming service. The provider is identified by a certain Java class (taken here from `com.ibm.websphere.naming`) and the URL of the server (in this case, the local host where WebSphere is installed).

After the lookup, you cast the home interface to the right type. This requires using `javax.rmi.PortableRemoteObject.narrow` because the object was transported over a network connection.

Finally, use the home interface to find or create a remote instance. On this remote instance, you invoke the `getTextMessage()` message.

When you look at this client-side code, you see that there is no explicit code for networking. This is all done automatically by the container-created code for the home and remote interfaces. While the code appears fairly straightforward, behind the scenes there is a lot more going on. When you call the lookup method on the `InitialContext` object, you actually perform a network-wide lookup for the specific bean. In this specific case, the network is limited to one server, but that might be different in a real-world application. Invoking the `create()` method on the `HelloHome` reference involves the EJB container, which is responsible for creating a new `HelloBean` instance and connecting it to this session. Finally, when you call `getTextMessage`, the request goes over the network and is executed in the EJB container.

All you need to do now is to compile the client-side code and run it. The result is obviously just a short message saying "Hello World," but in reality this is a distributed program running over the network.

Summary

We hope this chapter gave you a quick glimpse into developing and deploying EJBs. They are among the most important application frameworks in the world in general, and specifically in WebSphere. It is important that you master EJB development and deployment under WebSphere. This chapter is merely an introduction, so while you should be pleased with having created your first EJB-based application, you are very far from having mastered EJBs. In fact, Chapters 11, 15, and 29–34 all focus on EJBs.

The Complete Reference

Part II

WebSphere Technologies

The Complete Reference

Chapter 6

Web Servers and Java Application Servers

WebSphere is a runtime environment used for building eBusiness applications. Because an eBusiness application inherently provides access over the Web, WebSphere must be deployed over a Web server (an HTTP server). WebSphere then adds the layers forming the application server; these layers are usually accessed after the initial access over the HTTP server (apart from Java clients communicating directly with Enterprise JavaBeans).

This chapter discusses some of the Web servers (or WWW servers) with which the WebSphere product can be deployed. Because HTTP (Hypertext Transfer Protocol) servers are by now quite standard and follow a known structure, WebSphere can be deployed over a variety of HTTP servers. In fact, all major servers are supported, so you should have no problem deploying WebSphere within your environment. For those that do not have an existing HTTP server infrastructure in place, the WebSphere installation procedure includes an HTTP server called the IBM HTTP Server that you can use immediately (and with practically no configuration) after installing it from the WebSphere CD-ROM.

WebSphere supports the following Web servers:

- Apache Server
- IBM HTTP Server
- Domino
- Lotus Domino Go Webserver
- Microsoft Internet Information Server
- iPlanet Web Server

This chapter will briefly discuss Apache Server, IBM HTTP Server, and Microsoft Internet Information Server.

Apache Server

Apache Server belongs to a family of products that is a relative newcomer to the software landscape and that is both remarkable and admirable at the same time. Apache is perhaps the most well-known (or at least one of the two most well-known examples, along with Linux) piece of open-source software that was developed by a group of people scattered across the globe—and with no real money or corporate financing involved. The people doing the work did not get paid for their time, and using the server does not require that you purchase a license. The results of the Apache Server software development program are awesome.

The Apache HTTP Server Project, at *http://www.apache.org*, is a collaborative software development effort that aims to create "a robust, commercial-grade, feature full, and freely available source code implementation of an HTTP (Web) server." A group of worldwide volunteers, known as the Apache Group, manages the project using the Internet and the Web to communicate, plan, and develop the server and its related documentation. Hundreds of users have also contributed ideas, code, and documentation to the project.

Apache Server has been around since 1995, when it was developed by Rob McCool at the National Center for Supercomputing Applications, University of Illinois, Champaign-Urbana. The early version was an immediate hit, and after less than a year, with some tweaking by McCool and others, the Apache Server became the Number 1 server on the Internet.

Today, changes to the code are developed on users' local machines and then proposed by members and presented on the mailing list. Active members vote before code changes can be implemented. With about 40 messages per day flowing over the list, the group's communication is extensive and informal, though the voting process is structured and well organized.

New members of the Apache Group can be added; a frequent contributor is nominated by one member and unanimously approved by the voting members. In most cases, this "new" member has been actively contributing to the group's work for more than six months, so it's usually an easy decision.

According to the Apache Server Project Web site, the Apache Group exists to

> …provide a robust and commercial-grade reference implementation of the HTTP protocol. It must remain a platform upon which individuals and institutions can build reliable systems, both for experimental purposes and for mission-critical purposes. We believe the tools of online publishing should be in the hands of everyone, and software companies should make their money providing value-added services such as specialized modules and support, amongst other things. We realize that it is often seen as an economic advantage for one company to "own" a market—in the software industry that means to control tightly a particular conduit such that all others must pay…. To the extent that the protocols of the World Wide Web remain "unowned" by a single company, the Web will remain a level playing field for companies large and small. Thus, "ownership" of the protocol must be prevented, and the existence of a robust reference implementation of the protocol, available absolutely for free to all companies, is a tremendously good thing.

The Apache software is amazing not only because it is a free and open source, but because it is so successful. More than half the world's Web servers are based on Apache, and this number is not about to change anytime soon. Being a noncommercial piece of complex software might be synonymous with instability and partial functionality in some people's minds, but this assumption could not be further from the truth where Apache is concerned.

Apache Server is a mature and stable product with plenty of user support provided by many developers. In fact, support is much better than what we have come to expect from software vendors in general. Simply put, we recommend Apache Server to anyone who is looking for a Web server. (By the way, Tomcat, an ongoing project within the Apache organization, is building a Java application server. This successful project is being used by many organizations; in many ways, it is a competitor to WebSphere.) Another popular server discussed in this chapter, the IBM HTTP Server, is basically an Apache Server with a few add-ons.

Apache Modules

Apache Server provides a broad offering in terms of the modules that can be configured. The architecture of the server is modular in nature, provides a distribution that is probably the most comprehensive of all Web servers, and at the same time allows configurations that are slim and simple. The distribution is provided as a set of modules; each module can be compiled and loaded into the server—or not. The choice is up to you. The 1.3.*x* versions of Apache Server dynamically load modules as needed, ensuring that memory utilization is always optimized and that the image size can be small unless many services are provided.

Following is a list of some of the available modules and a brief description of each:

- **Core** Includes core Apache features that must exist in every deployment.
- **mod_access** Allows an administrator to control access to elements served by the Web server based on the accessing hosts. By using a set of *allow* and *deny* directives, the administrator can set up the access rules for directories and files based on the requesting host.
- **mod_actions** Allows an administrator to set up Common Gateway Interface (CGI) scripts to be called whenever a file of a certain Multipurpose Internet Mail Extensions (MIME) type is requested through the Web server.
- **mod_alias** Allows files that are not under the Web server root to be served up by the Web server. Allows an administrator to define a sort of symbolic link to the file to make it seem as though the file resides within the Web server directory structure while maintaining maximal flexibility for setting up the site.
- **mod_asis** Allows an administrator to specify that files of a certain MIME type are served up by the Web server as is—that is, without slapping on the HTTP response header information.
- **mod_auth** Allows an administrator to set up a text file defining authorization groups. Each line in the file names a group and specifies which users belong to this group. This information is used for authorization based on groups.
- **mod_auth_anon** Used by an administrator to set up the profile of anonymous access (similar to the anonymous user in File Transfer Protocol, or FTP).
- **mod_auth_db** Supports user authentication following the Berkeley DB file style, an embedded database system that supports keyed access to data; Apache reuses the file style used in Berkeley DB. In this case, a text file defines the groups by having a line per user in which all the groups to which the user belongs are

mentioned. An additional file maintains the password per user. These definitions are then used for authorization and authentication.

- **mod_auth_dbm** Similar to *mod_auth_db* but uses DBM files. DBM is the oldest (original) type of Berkeley DB-style databases.
- **mod_autoindex** Supports the creation and maintenance of file indexes for the Web server. Both manual index files and automatically generated index files are supported through this module.
- **mod_cern_meta** Allows the administrator to set up environment variable values based on the accessing browser. Each request received from a browser has a field called *user-agent*, whose value identifies the browser—for example, Netscape and Internet Explorer browsers will have slightly different user-agent values, and mobile phones using an HTTP connection will have a drastically different user-agent value. It is typical for software serving up responses to want to behave differently based on the user-agent—that is, based on who is making the request. This module provides built-in support for such abilities at the server level.
- **mod_cgi** Responsible for invoking CGI scripts for files that have a MIME type of *application/x-httpd-cgi*.
- **mod_digest** Allows the administrator to specify a file that contains user names and encoded passwords. The passwords are used for MD5 digest authentication. MD5 is an algorithm created in 1991 by Professor R. Rivest that is used to create digital signatures.
- **mod_dir** Supports the indexing of directories either manually or through an automated process.
- **mod_env** Allows setting environment variables for the Web server process to be passed to CGI scripts called by the server.
- **mod_example** Provides samples and examples of the Apache application programming interface (API); this module is not usually included in a production server.
- **mod_expires** Allows the administrator to set a server-wide policy regarding the *EXPIRES* value sent within the HTTP response. The *EXPIRES* value is used by the browser to determine when a page that exists in the client cache should be invalidated, causing recurring access of the file from the server. Using this module, the administrator can set the policy for all pages served by the Web server.
- **mod_headers** Allows the administrator to set server-wide policies regarding values that should be included as part of response headers. The module allows the use of directives such as *set*, *add*, and *append* for setting name-value pairs that are added to every response originating from the server.
- **mod_imap** Implements the *imagemap* facility and is part of the default setup.

- **mod_include** Handles server-side includes and is used to handle requests for .shtml files. This book does not use server-side includes because JavaServer Pages (JSP) can be used for any such required processing.
- **mod_info** Serves up configuration information regarding the installed server.
- **mod_isapi** Provides support for the Microsoft Internet Server Application Programming Interface (ISAPI). (Now, that's the true meaning of *open*—supporting another product's API in your product!)
- **mod_log_agent** Used by the administrator to log all user-agent information for all requests coming in to the server. This is a useful auditing capability.
- **mod_log_config** Used by the administrator to customize various aspects of the server log, such as where the log file is to be placed and what the format of the log file should be.
- **mod_log_referer** Used by the administrator to customize what is logged. For example, the module supports directives for specifying that requests arriving from a certain domain should not be logged.
- **mod_mime** An important module that handles attributes to be attached to MIME types (and documents conforming to such types). The module supports directives, such as *AddEncoding,* that are used to associate file extensions with MIME types; *AddHandler,* which are used to map the MIME type with a handling application; and more advanced directives.
- **mod_mime_magic** Can be used by UNIX-based servers in a system that uses UNIX magic numbers to determine the MIME type of a file.
- **mod_mmap_static** Allows a file to be brought into memory for faster request handling.
- **mod_negotiation** Supports *content selection,* which allows the server to select the best possible file based on attributes sent in the request header by the client.
- **mod_proxy** Implements proxy caching for Apache and is important for production servers. This module is relatively complex and has many features; the Web server administrator should carefully read the documentation regarding this module to derive the best possible results.
- **mod_rewrite** Another important and powerful module that allows Uniform Resource Locator (URL) rewriting based on a set of rules set up by the administrator.
- **mod_setenvif** Allows setup of rules that are evaluated for each request header, and based on the satisfaction of these rules sets values of certain environment variables.

- **mod_so** Supports loading modules (.dll on Windows; .so on Solaris; and so on) at runtime. This is how the HTTP plug-in is loaded into the Apache runtime, allowing it to communicate with the WebSphere server.
- **mod_spelling** Automatically corrects minor typos in URLs.
- **mod_status** Serves up various server statistics that are helpful for monitoring how the server is performing. The values are served up as HTML output.
- **mod_userdir** Used to set users' home directories for Web requests.
- **mod_unique_id** Creates a unique identifier for each Web request.
- **mod_usertrack** Implements tracking of user information using cookies.
- **mod_vhost_alias** Supports the notion of defining several *virtual hosts* on the same machine, a feature that allows you to set up a single server that will answer requests made using different host names.

As you can appreciate, Apache is rich in terms of server functionality. Using all the above-mentioned features, you can pretty much do anything your heart desires with Apache Server.

Apache also provides a fully functional and convenient API so that you can write applications that interface with the Web server. As we're sure you've realized by now, it is no coincidence that more than half of all Web servers deployed are Apache Servers.

IBM HTTP Server

The IBM HTTP Server is part of the WebSphere installation package and is the simplest alternative for those of you who want to be up and running as soon as possible and have no existing server in place. It is also the server with which you will get the best WebSphere support by IBM, so we urge you to use it if you can.

The IBM HTTP Server is a Web server that's basically a branding of Apache Server with the IBM name (under a licensing agreement between the Apache group and IBM). Therefore, apart from some cosmetic differences, all of what was said regarding Apache Server applies. In terms of the installation procedure, using the IBM HTTP Server is the simplest because it is part of the standard installation process (not to say that the other installation procedures are difficult—they are also pretty straightforward).

As part of the licensing agreement between IBM and the Apache group, IBM makes no effort to hide the fact that Apache Server is doing all the work. (See Figure 6-1 for a number of dynamic-link libraries that form the server code.) However, the IBM HTTP Server does include a few minor additions to Apache Server, which means that while Apache is provided with source code that can be used to port to other platforms, not all of the source code for the IBM HTTP Server is available (specifically, the few additional modules).

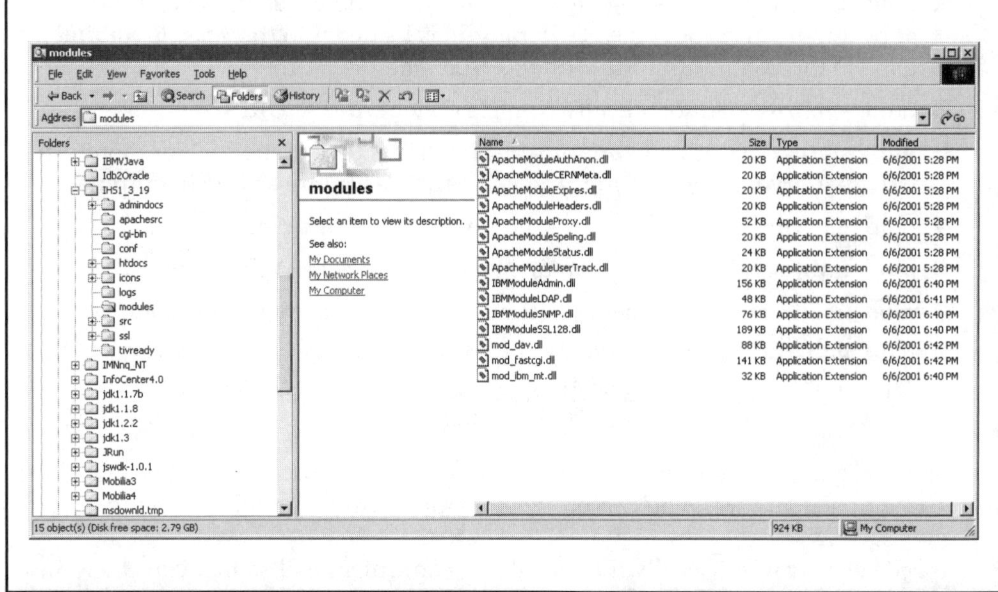

Figure 6-1. *Some of IBM's HTTP Server DLLs*

Microsoft Internet Information Server 4.0

Internet Information Server (IIS) 4.0 is a free Web server that is part of the Windows NT Server 4.0 installation. Originally it was part of Microsoft's strategy to break into the Internet product marketplace, and because use of Windows NT and Windows 2000 is quite widespread, quite a few installations of IIS exist. In fact, the many security breaks being carried out on IIS shows just how common the server is.

With the introduction of Windows 2000, Microsoft launched IIS version 5.0 with different licensing terms (specifically, it's not free, as 4.0 was). This section focuses on IIS 4.0. In addition to being free, IIS 4.0 is a simple product—both in terms of installation (you basically do nothing to install it) and in terms of using it. All this just helps in making it the default server for people who run Windows operating systems. This is, of course, also the limitation of IIS—it runs only on Windows platforms, whereas Apache Server and the IBM HTTP Server run on many platforms, including Windows and UNIX.

Another convenience in the IIS offering is that all the server's properties can be easily set using the Internet Service Manager tool, which is started from the Windows Start menu, as shown in Figure 6-2.

The services that can be managed are shown along with their status in Figure 6-3. By default, these are the HTTP service (WWW), the FTP service, and the Gopher service.

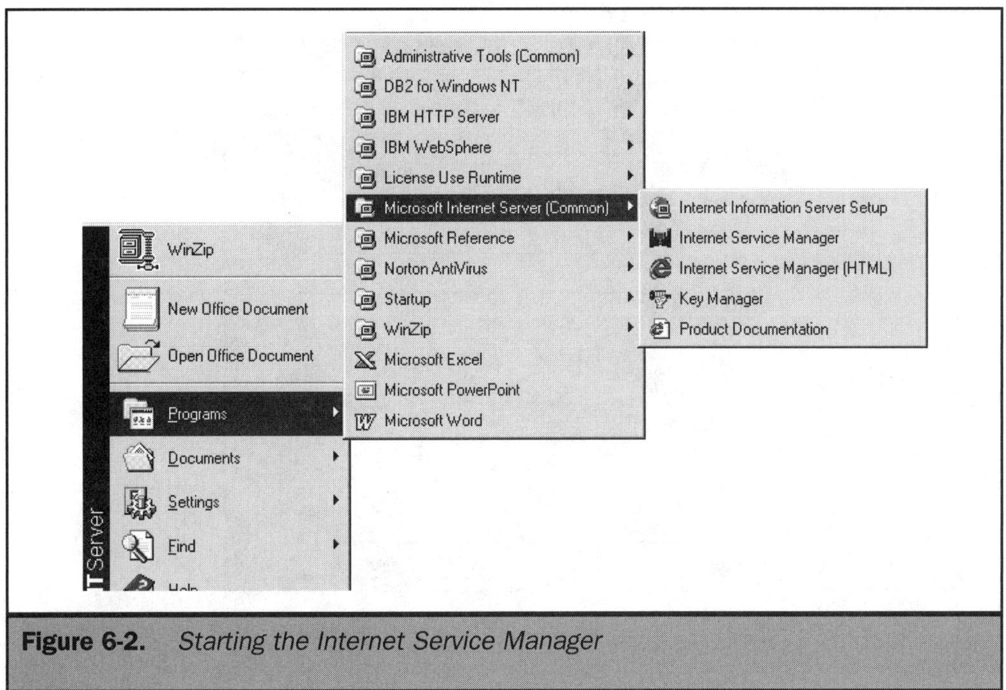

Figure 6-2. *Starting the Internet Service Manager*

Figure 6-3 shows a Windows NT server in which only the WWW service is available. Each of the services has a set of properties windows that are used to configure the characteristics of the service. Figures 6-4 through 6-7 show the windows you can use for configuring the WWW service.

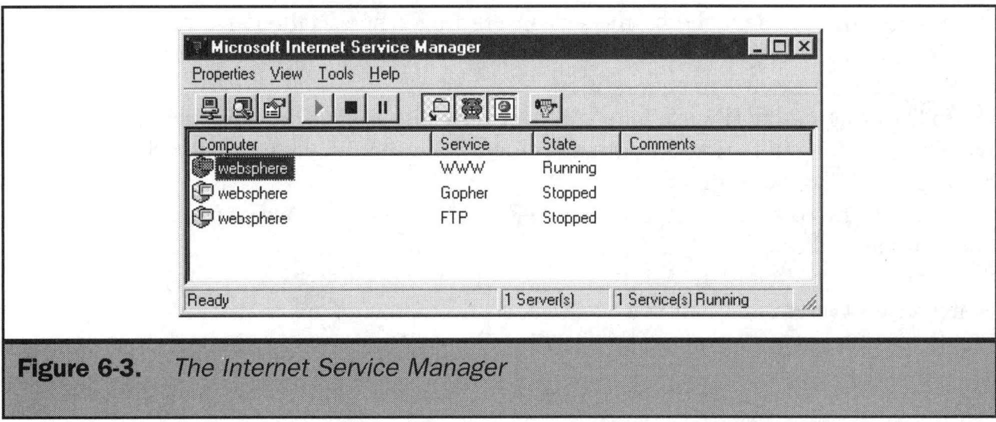

Figure 6-3. *The Internet Service Manager*

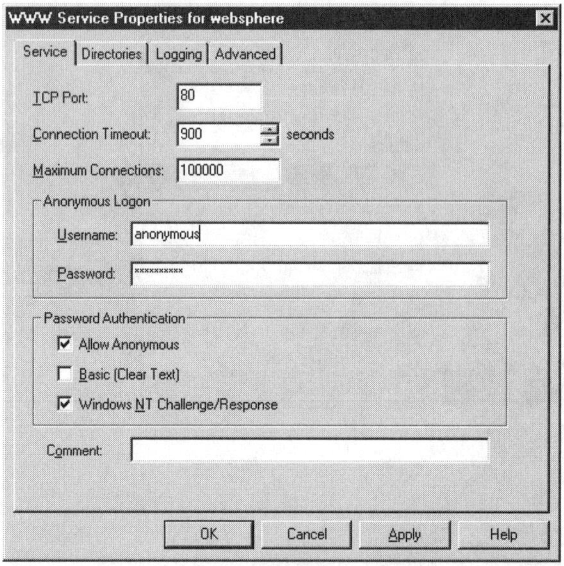

Figure 6-4. *WWW Service Properties window Service tab*

The main properties are set in the Service tab in the WWW Service Properties window shown in Figure 6-4. You can set the port on which the service is listening (80 by default; other common values include 8080 for test servers), the default timeout, the maximum number of allowed concurrent connections, anonymous account profiles, and the authentication schemes supported by the server.

In the Directories tab, you can specify the directories that participate in serving content for the site managed by the server. Figure 6-5 shows the Directory Properties window, which can be accessed from the Directories tab by double-clicking an entry for which properties are to be modified.

In the Logging tab (Figure 6-6), you set properties that affect what gets logged and where it gets logged to (including the option of logging information stored directly into an SQL/ODBC database).

The Advanced tab, shown in Figure 6-7, is used to set the access policy based on *grant* and *deny* directives.

In addition to the main tool used for setting up the service properties, the Key Manager tool (Figure 6-8) allows you to add and manage keys that are attached to certificates. You access this tool by choosing Start | Programs | Microsoft Internet

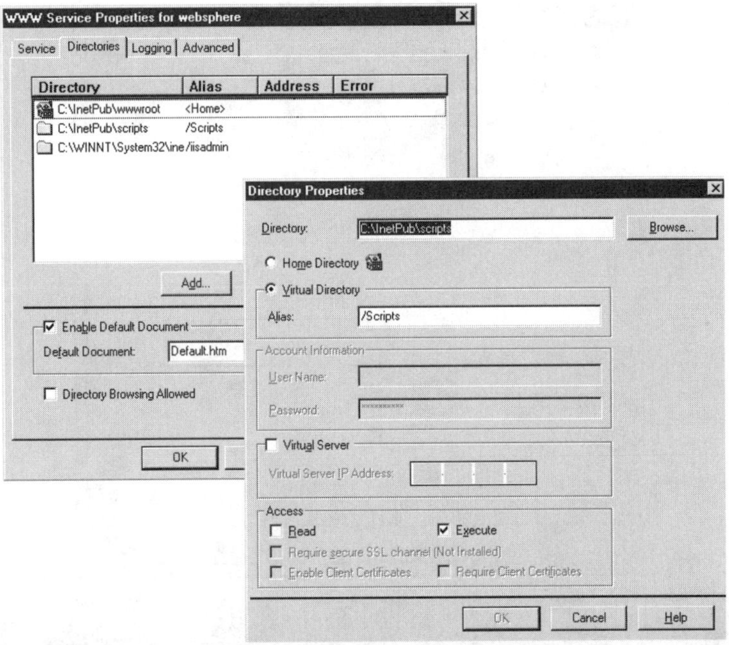

Figure 6-5. *WWW Service Properties window Directory Properties window*

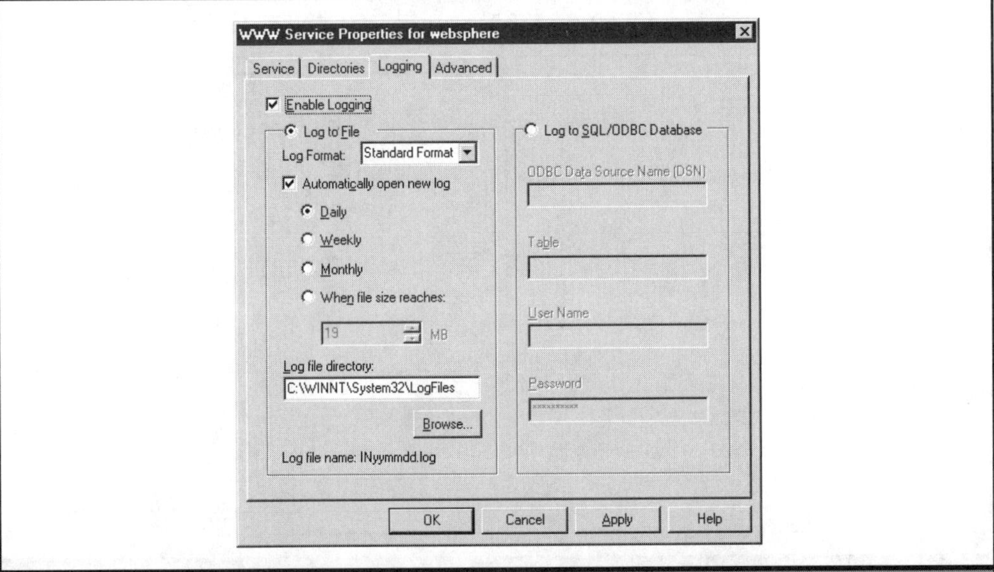

Figure 6-6. *WWW Service Properties window Logging tab*

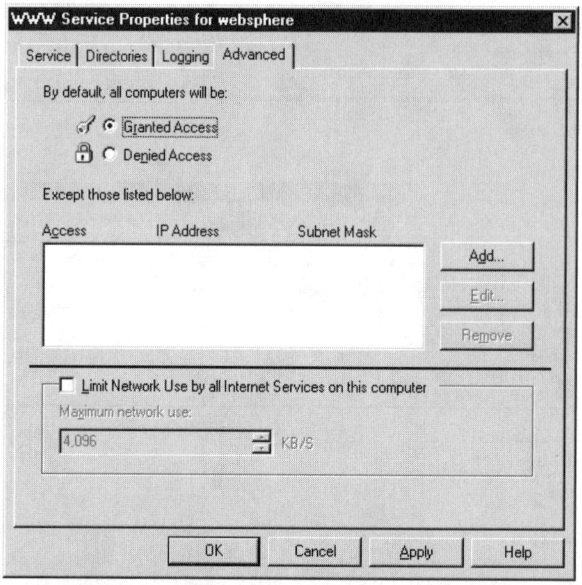

Figure 6-7. *WWW Service Properties window Advanced tab*

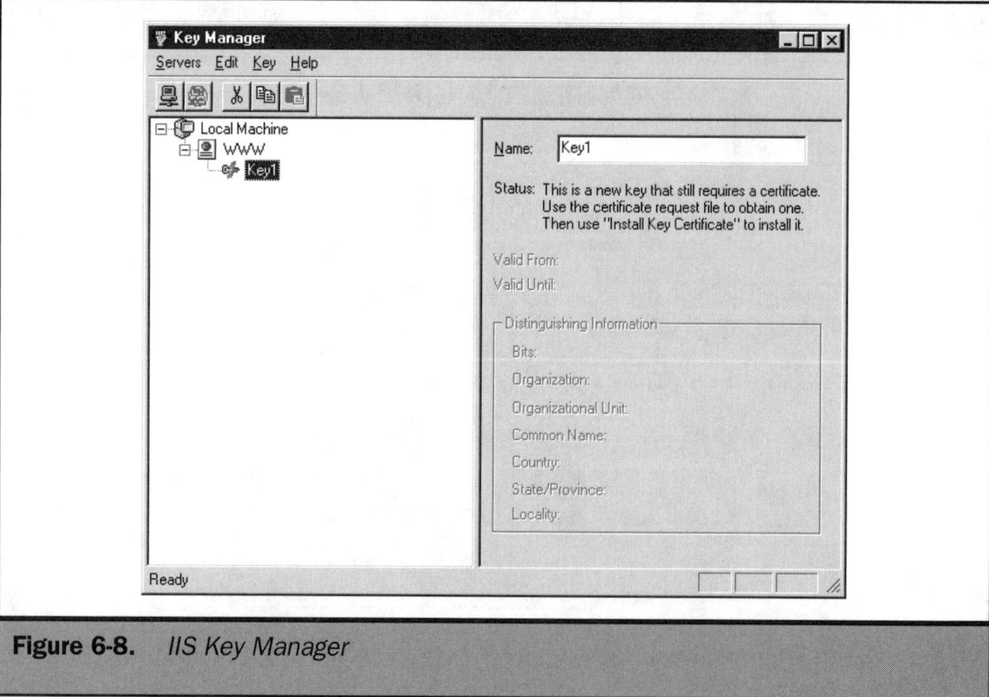

Figure 6-8. *IIS Key Manager*

Server (Common) | Key Manager. These keys are used for setting up secure servers for electronic transactions and to ensure server authentication.

Finally, because the server setup should be enabled from a remote site, and not necessarily by opening the Service Manager on the local host, all tools are also available in an HTML-based version.

Microsoft Internet Information Server 5.0

Following the footstep of IIS 4.0, IIS 5.0 offers tight integration into the host operating system, Windows 2000. Server administration is accomplished through the Administrative Tools folder on the Control Panel. The Internet Service Manager provides the user interface for administering IIS.

The Internet Information Services window provides an Explorer-style interface that allows easy navigation through the various services and their components. In Figure 6-9, the node representing the selected machine is thinkpad. A node on the network can be running more than one service, as shown in the figure, where an FTP server, a Web server, and an SMTP server are installed. You can browse files published under a server.

The Administrative Tools folder on the Control Panel also includes an item called Personal Web Manager (Figure 6-10). This tool facilitates easy management of the content and settings of the IIS Web Server.

Similar to other Web servers, the easiest way to verify the IIS installation is to access it using a Web browser. The IIS 5.0 home page is shown in Figure 6-11.

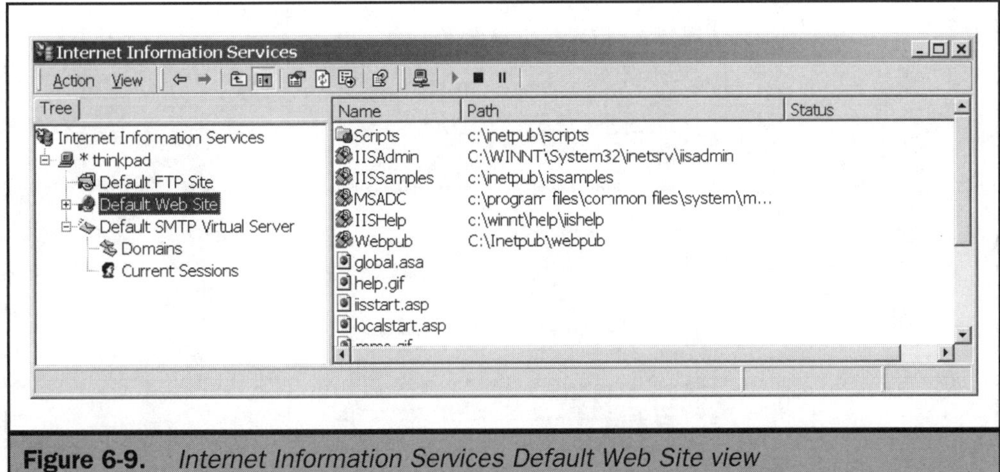

Figure 6-9. *Internet Information Services Default Web Site view*

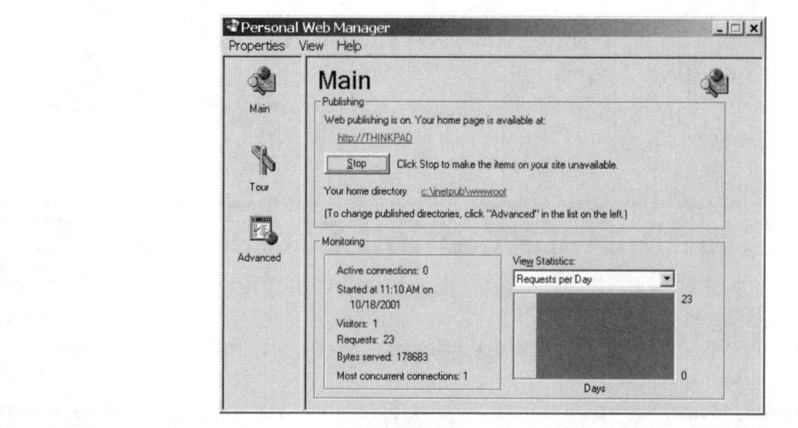

Figure 6-10. *Personal Web Manager tool*

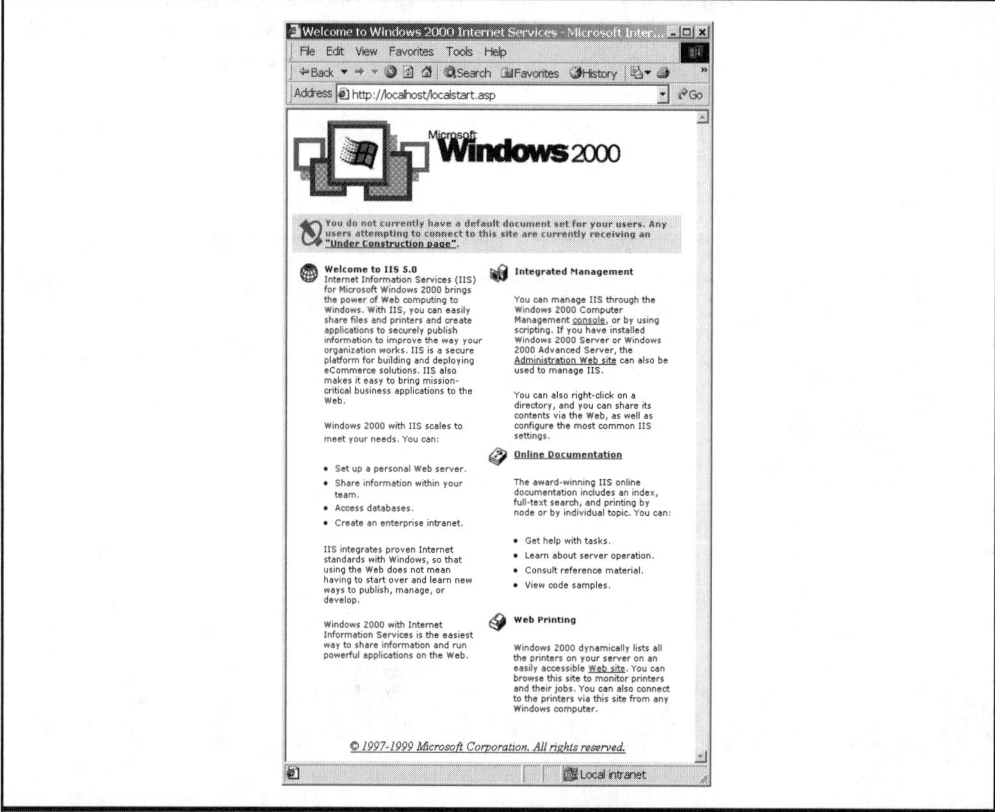

Figure 6-11. *IIS 5.0 default home page*

iPlanet Web Server

iPlanet Web Server is the successor of the Netscape server line of products, including Netscape Enterprise Server, Netscape FastTrack Server, and the Kiva application server. It is also the successor to Sun's various families of application servers starting with the Java Web Server, the Net Dynamics family, and the Forte runtime environment. Obviously, it is not a direct successor to all of these from a technical sense but rather from a marketing sense. From a technical perspective, there is no doubt that Sun and Netscape squandered their early leadership positions and have never regained it.

In March 1999, Netscape (later taken over by AOL) teamed up with Sun in an attempt to increase its share of the market for server software, as Sun is the undisputed leader in the hardware market for Internet servers. iPlanet offers a fully-fledged J2EE (Java 2 Platform Enterprise Edition) server, so it is in fact competing with IBM's WebSphere. Nonetheless, IBM provides support for the iPlanet Web Server, just as it does for Microsoft IIS.

The iPlanet Web Server is supported on various flavors of UNIX, Linux, and Windows server platforms.

iPlanet administration is Web-based. Figure 6-12 shows the main Web Server Administration Server page, from which you can manage multiple servers.

You can manage each server from the Manager Server page's Preferences tab, shown in Figure 6-13.

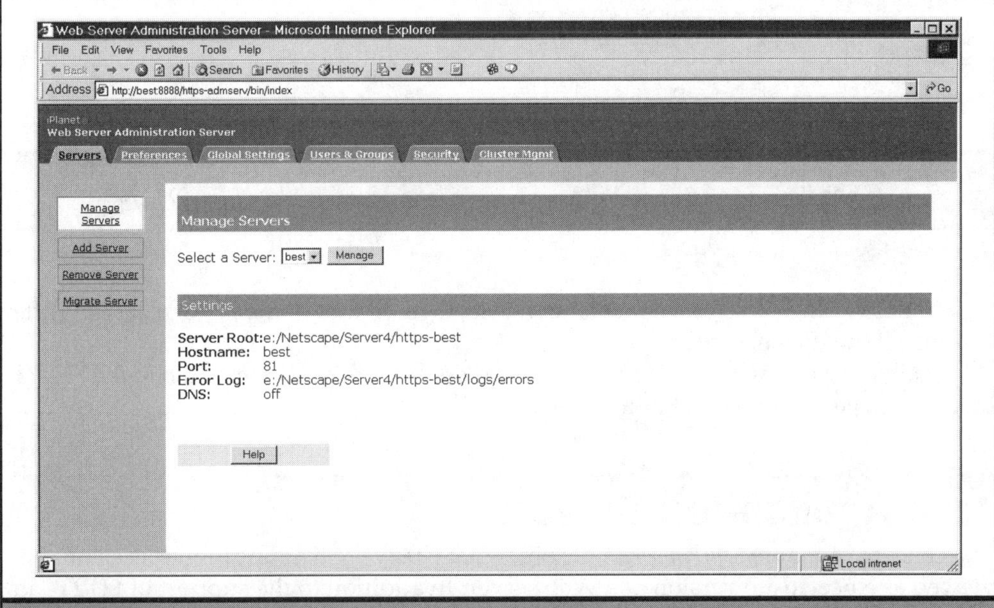

Figure 6-12. *iPlanet Administration Server page*

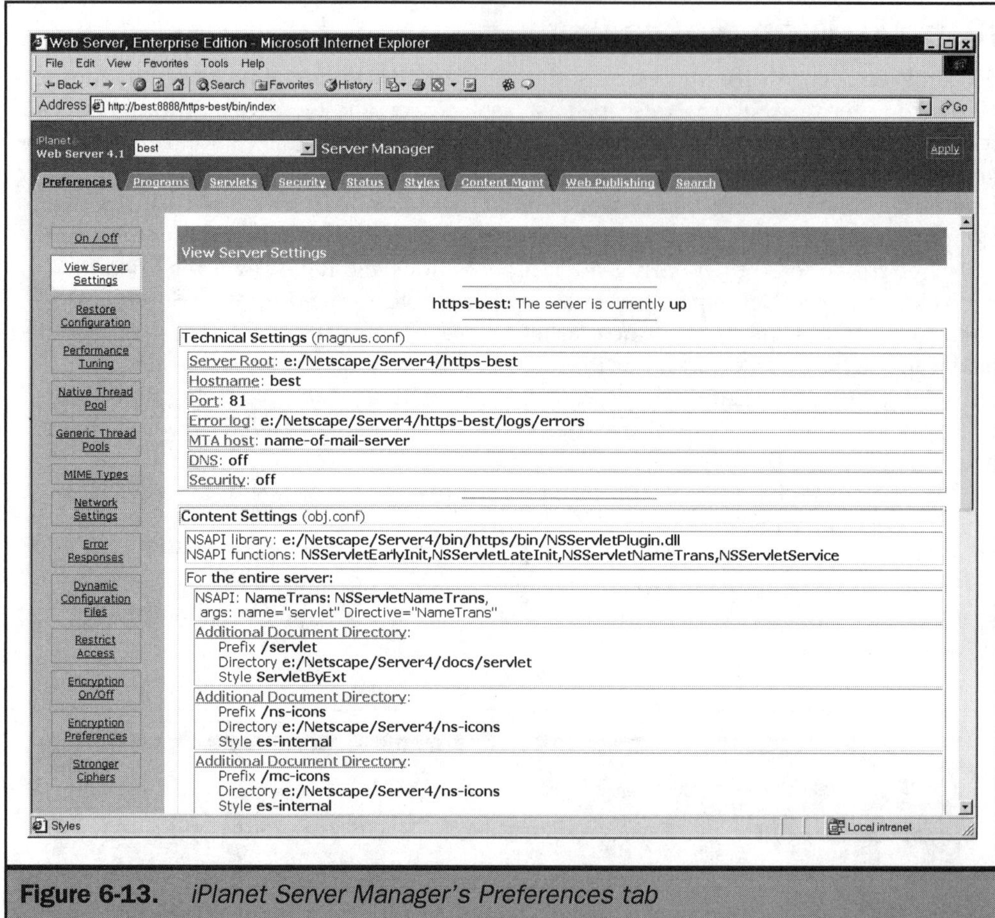

Figure 6-13. *iPlanet Server Manager's Preferences tab*

Similar to other Web servers, iPlanet has its own default home page, reachable after you install the iPlanet server.

Finally, key management in iPlanet is handled through the Security tab in the Server Manager page, as shown in Figure 6-14.

Java Application Servers

The concept of the *application server* is somewhat elusive. An application server can be viewed as a beefed-up version of a Web server. In addition to the support of HTTP, an application server provides a set of APIs and services to support developers' applications. Such APIs and services typically include support for persistence, transactions, security,

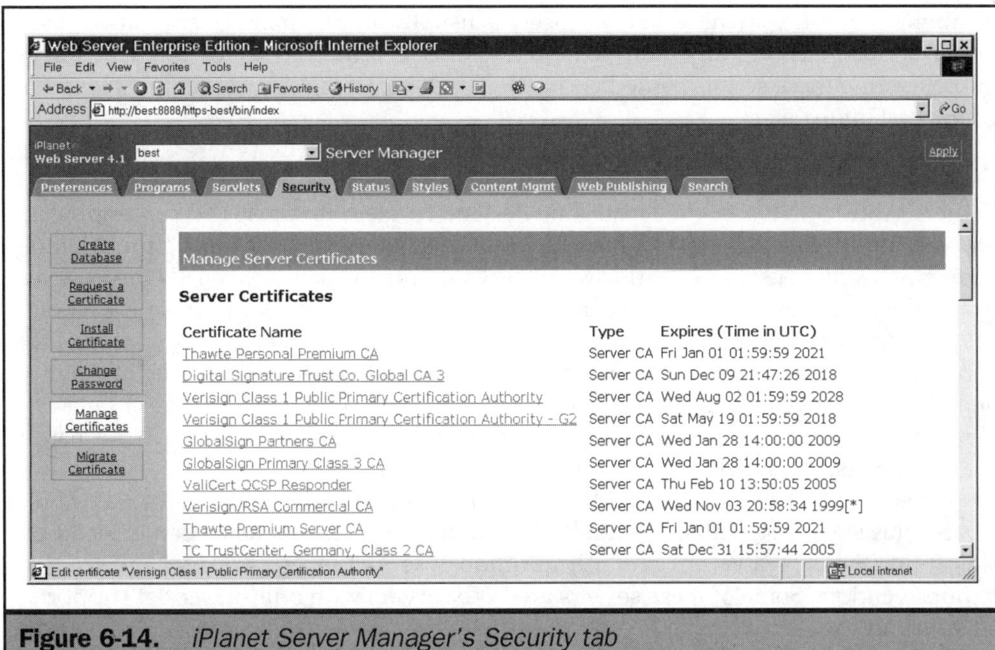

Figure 6-14. *iPlanet Server Manager's Security tab*

Extensible Markup Language (XML), and most recently Web services technologies such as Simple Object Access Protocol (SOAP) and Universal Description, Discovery, and Integration (UDDI).

WebSphere belongs to a group of application servers that are Java based. The other prominent group of such servers is based on Microsoft's .NET platform. In addition, non-aligned servers use proprietary solutions, such as Cold Fusion.

Essentially, Java application servers are extensions of Web servers that provide the ability to execute server-side Java code. The first kind of server-side Java code introduced by Sun were *servlets*, pieces of Java code that were one of the first instances of Java on the server. While servlets are a generic concept, they are most commonly invoked through an HTTP session (which is why servlets usually inherit from HTTP Servlet).

At the time servlets were first introduced, CGI scripts performed the majority of Web server-side processing. CGI was one of the first techniques used to create dynamic Web content. The importance of dynamically creating Web content is obvious, as it is the basis for most Web sites as we know them today. The concept underlying CGI is having the Web server invoke an external program that generates content, which is to be sent to the client side.

Even though CGI quickly became the de facto standard for dynamically generating content, it had severe drawbacks, especially as far as performance was concerned. Under the CGI programming model, the Web server spawns a new process to handle each incoming request. Spawning a new process is usually an expensive operation. In case of CGI scripts, it is typically more so, with the most common choice of language for implementing these scripts being Perl (so that each incoming request requires loading a new Perl interpreter).

Several different products offered a solution to this problem. Where CGI scripts are implemented in Perl, Apache Server includes a module called *mod_perl* (as mentioned in the Chapter 5). This module loads one Perl interpreter into the HTTP server process, and this interpreter takes care of handling requests. Other solutions using proprietary (and specifically nonstandard) APIs were FastCGI (from a company called OpenMarket), Active Server Pages (ASP) from Microsoft, and Server Side JavaScript from Netscape.

Servlets came into this landscape and caught on quickly because they provided the benefits of CGI and other server-side processing techniques along with the inherent benefits of Java (such as portability, safety, availability of rich collections of Java libraries, and being well known among Web programmers)—all without the performance drawbacks associated with standard CGI programming.

The servlet API specification and reference implementation were formulated by Sun's JavaSoft (as is the case with all Java-related technologies). The reference implementation was at first Sun's Java Web Server. A multitude of servlet servers are available from various vendors. Some of these servers are Web servers with built-in servlet support, such as Sun's reference implementation or Netscape's server. As mentioned, Apache also sports an extension module called JServ that provides the functionality of servlets.

The second generation of Java application servers cannot be viewed as such add-ons to Web servers. All modern Java application servers (including, obviously, IBM's WebSphere) are comprehensive runtime platforms that do much more than serve dynamic Web pages and run Java code as a result of an HTTP request. And yet, the WebSphere application server originated from just the servlet engine and was based on a previous product called ServletExpress. It has since evolved so much that little of the original kernel remains.

The next big step in the evolution of the Java application server was the introduction of the J2EE standard from Sun. J2EE was the first standardization effort for the concept of a "Java Application Server." This standard clearly defines what should comprise a J2EE server. In J2EE, execution environments called *containers* exist within the server. Such containers execute servlets, JSP (a different method for generating dynamic Web content), and Enterprise JavaBeans (EJB).

J2EE is the subject of Chapter 15. It is worthwhile to note here, however, that several J2EE implementations are available in the market today. Most notable are these:

- IBM's WebSphere
- BEA's WebLogic
- Oracle's Application Server
- Hewlet Packard's Bluestone

Many other offerings by companies such as Sybase, Silverstream, and others are also available.

Summary

While IBM offers the IBM HTTP Server as part of the WebSphere installation, you are free to select a different Web server as the deployment solution along with the WebSphere application server. Many organizations already have a Web server infrastructure in place and would not be happy with a solution that would require them to throw out an existing infrastructure. The choice is up to you, though, because all dominant Web servers are supported.

If you have no Web server in place or need a separate Web server for the applications you will deploy on WebSphere, we suggest you stick with the IBM HTTP Server. It is as good as any of the other solutions and it will be easy to install and support. It is also the combination that is used most often.

Chapter 7

Servlets and JavaServer Pages

This chapter is dedicated to a discussion of the fundamentals of the operational model of servlets and JavaServer Pages (JSPs). You have already seen how servlets and JSPs work within the WebSphere server, and servlets and JSPs will be discussed much more in Chapters 22 through 28. All of these chapters involve a set of examples that introduce the abilities of these technological elements.

This chapter provides the theory behind these examples. The model specified by the servlet and JSP specifications is introduced. This model is important for you to understand because it is the thread that unifies all of the examples involving servlets and JSPs, and as such will facilitate a better understanding of these concepts.

Servlets and JSPs—Are They the Same?

A *servlet* is a Java class that conforms to the contracts defined by the servlet specification. Servlets were introduced by Sun Microsystems as one of the first instantiations of Java on a server. At the time, the majority of Web server-side processing was performed by Common Gateway Interface (CGI) programs or by programs linked to the Web server using some proprietary application programming interface (like the Netscape Server's API, or NSAPI, and Internet Server API, or ISAPI). Servlets were introduced as a way to provide all the benefits of server-side processing while making use of the advantages inherent to Java (such as portability, access to the large number of Java libraries, and so on). In addition, servlets were faster than CGI programs and could be deployed under many Web servers. Servlets caught on quickly not only because they were far superior to the alternatives, but also because they were simple to understand. As is often the case, simple things catch on quickly.

JSPs are newer on the Java technology landscape. In many ways, JSPs can be viewed as the inverse of servlets—kind of mirror images. Servlets usually generate dynamic HTML by running some Java code that accesses databases or performs some other processing and then writes HTML to the output stream. The HTML tag elements are embedded as strings within the Java code. JSPs reverse the roles. JSPs are fundamentally HTML pages that are served up by the Web server. They differ from normal HTML pages in two ways: they have a .jsp extension and they include some additional tags that are not HTML tags—that is, JSP tags. These JSP tags allow (among other things) embedding lines of Java code inside the HTML page. So the "mirror-image" notion is that JSPs are built as HTML with embedded Java (as opposed to servlets, which have HTML strings embedded in Java code).

All this might sound unimportant, but in fact it *is* important. JSPs are better in separating the function of the application programmer from the function of the site builder or the function responsible for the presentation and the layout. Therefore, it is quite common for a development team using JSP to include people who build HTML pages with dummy static data and then pass that data on to Java programmers, who replace the dummy data with the Java code that builds the real dynamic data when it is invoked. In some cases, servlets are more appropriate, and in other cases JSPs work better; the difference involves the role that HTML plays. If most of the HTML (the *presentation layer*) is fixed and the Java code is primarily used for dynamically generating data, using JSPs is more appropriate. Until JSPs came to be, many servlet developers simulated what JSPs do by packaging "templates" of HTML pages and injected the dynamic data in between.

The Servlet Operational Model

The operational model of a servlet is shown in Figure 7-1. As the figure illustrates, the servlet interacts with the servlet server and goes through a number of stages throughout its life.

First, the servlet is registered with the server (that is, it's added to the server's configuration) as part of the abilities that must be supported by any servlet server. At some point, the server instantiates the servlet using the registered class. This is usually performed during server startup, although this may differ depending on the server itself.

Next comes the initialization phase defined contractually by the `init` method that a servlet must implement (or inherit). So after the servlet server instantiates the servlet, it calls the `init` method and passes a `ServletConfig` object that encapsulates information regarding the environment. This information may be used by the servlet in its initialization process.

Next come the actual invocations. Each servlet must implement or inherit a `service` method that is called by the servlet server upon the arrival of a request that needs to be handled by the servlet. Note that HTTP servlets can also implement the `service` method, but they can also implement the `doGet`, `doPost`, or both methods—this reflects the fact that an HTTP request uses either a *get* or a *post* method. If both the `service` method as well as one of the `doGet` or `doPost` methods are implemented, the `service` method is called first, and this calls the `doGet` and `doPost` methods. It is therefore always safer to override the `doGet` and `doPost` methods.

Finally, when the servlet server wants to reclaim the servlet, it calls the `destroy` method—another one of a servlet's contractual obligations.

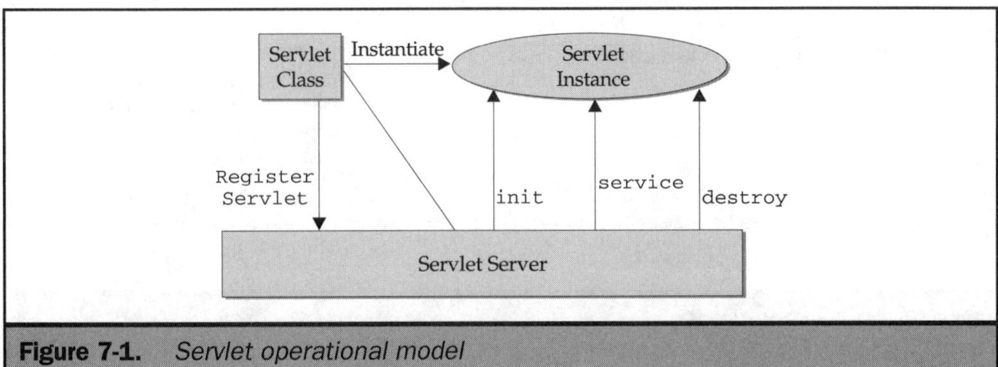

Figure 7-1. *Servlet operational model*

The Servlet API

The operational model for servlets involves the contract between them and the servlet server. This contract is defined by the `javax.servlet.Servlet` interface, whose methods are shown in Table 7-1. Essentially, three contractual obligations are required from a servlet: the initialization phase, the servicing of the request, and the finalization stage.

WebSphere Application Server 4.0 supports version 2.2 of the servlet API. The remainder of this chapter (and the book) relates to this version of the API.

Servlet Initialization

Initialization often occurs when you register the servlet with the server via the `init` method. The `init` method is the perfect place to include all startup code that is required for the correct operation of the servlet and that might take a relatively long time—such things as reading files, creating network connections, and so on. Instances are often created before the actual requests arrive, and therefore this time is saved at the critical phase when the user is awaiting a response.

Method	Signature	Description
`init`	`void init(ServletConfig config)`	Initializes the servlet. Called exactly once by the servlet engine or container. The parameter provides the servlet information about the host server.
`service`	`void service (ServletRequest request, ServletResponse response)`	Executes a single request from the client. Called each time a request is made.
`destroy`	`void destroy()`	Cleans up whatever resources are held.
`getServletInfo`	`String getServletInfo()`	Returns a string containing information about the servlet. In WebSphere, this string can be set at deployment time from the Administrative Console.
`getServletConfig`	`ServletConfig getServletConfig()`	Returns a servlet configuration object, which should be the same one passed as parameter to the init method.

Table 7-1. *Servlet Methods*

Also quite common in the real world is the model in which a pool of servlets is instantiated before requests start arriving (with the servlets in the pool often sharing the same resources). The servlet is guaranteed that the `init` method will return before any service requests are made. Furthermore, the `init` method is not called again for the same servlet instance. This basically makes the `init` method thread-safe. The `init` method can throw either the `ServletException` or `UnavailableException` exception in case any errors occur during initialization.

Servlet Processing

After the servlet has been initialized, it is ready for processing. The main method of a servlet, and the justification for its existence, is the `service` method. Through this method, the servlet implements a request and response paradigm. The `service` method takes an arriving request as a parameter in a `ServletRequest` and creates a response that is encapsulated in a `ServletResponse`. The servlet model does not require much more than this—a servlet is really a generic being that services requests and creates responses. The request object contains information about the service request, including parameters provided by the client, as shown in Table 7-2. The response object is used to return information to the client, and its methods are shown in Table 7-3.

Servlet Finalization

The last piece of the servlet contract is the finalization stage, implemented via the `destroy` method. This method is called once by the server when it unloads the servlet. After `destroy` is run, it is guaranteed that the `service` method will not be called again until the server reloads the servlet. When the server removes a servlet, it calls `destroy` after all service calls have been completed or a service-specific number of seconds have passed, whichever comes first. In the case of long-running operations, a service request could still be active when `destroy` is called.

It is the responsibility of the servlet to ensure that any threads still in the `service` stage complete. One way to achieve this is to have the `destroy` method set a flag and have the servlet check whether the flag is on at the end of each request. If the flag appears, and there are no other running requests, the servlet will clean up its resource. Such tactics are seldom required, because in most cases servlets perform relatively short operations (if for no other reason, at least for providing reasonable responsiveness to users).

Thread Safety

Thread safety is an important consideration in the programming of servlets. In addition, more than one active thread may be using the same servlet object. Therefore, unless you specifically implement the `SingleThreadModel` interface in your servlet (thus

Method	Signature	Description
`getAttribute`	`Object getAttribute (String attribute)`	Returns the value of the named attribute of the request or null if the specified attribute does not exist. Attributes are server-specific.
`getAttributeNames`	`Enumeration getAttributeNames()`	Returns enumeration object containing all the names of attributes in the request.
`getCharacterEncoding`	`String getCharacterEncoding()`	Returns the character set encoding for the input of this request.
`getContentLength`	`int getContentLength()`	Returns the size of the request data, or –1 if it is not known. Particularly useful when servicing an HTTP post request.
`getContentType`	`String getContentType()`	Returns the MIME type of the request data, or null if it is not known.
`getInputStream`	`ServletInputStream getInputStream()`	Returns an input stream for reading binary data of the request body. For textual data, the `getReader()` method should be used, since it takes into consideration the character encoding.
`getLocale`	`Locale getLocale()`	Returns the preferred locale for the client based on the "Accept-Language" header in the request.
`getLocales`	`Enumeration getLocales()`	Returns an enumeration of locale objects representing the locales that are acceptable for the client (again, based on the "Accept-Language" header). The locales are arranged in decreasing preference order.
`getParameter`	`String getParameter (String parameter)`	Returns a string containing value of the specified parameter, or null if it is not found. Can be called after the input is parsed.

Table 7-2. *ServletRequest Methods*

Method	Signature	Description
`getParameterNames`	`Enumeration getParameterNames()`	Returns the parameter names for the request as an enumeration. Can be called after the input is parsed.
`getParameterValues`	`String[] GetParameterValues (String)`	Returns an array of string with values for a parameter. Useful for parameters with multiple values.
`getProtocol`	`String getProtocol()`	Returns the protocol and version of the request.
`getReader`	`BufferedReader getReader()`	Returns a buffered reader for reading text out of the request body. Reader is initialized with the proper character encoding.
`getRemoteAddr`	`String getRemoteAddr()`	Returns IP address of client making request.
`getRemoteHost`	`String getRemoteHost()`	Returns hostname of client making request.
`getRequestDispatcher`	`RequestDispatcher getRequestDispatcher (String path)`	Returns `RequestDispatcher` object—a wrapper for the resource located in the parameter path. Wrapper can be used to forward request to resource or to include response from resource.
`getScheme`	`String getScheme()`	Returns the scheme of URL used in the request (e.g., "http").
`getServerName`	`String getServerName()`	Returns hostname of the server receiving request.
`getServerPort`	`int getServerPort()`	Returns port number on which request was received.
`isSecure`	`boolean isSecure()`	Indicates whether request is over a secure connection (e.g., HTTPS).
`removeAttribute`	`void removeAttribute (String name)`	Removes an attribute from request.
`setAttribute`	`void setAttribute(String name, Object obj)`	Stores or resets an attribute in request.

Table 7-2. *ServletRequest Methods* (continued)

Method	Signature	Description
`flushBuffer`	`void flushBuffer()`	Forces any buffered content to be written to client.
`getBufferSize`	`int getBufferSize()`	Returns the current size of the buffer used for response.
`getCharacterEncoding`	`String getCharacterEncoding()`	Returns character set encoding for response. Can be changed by changing content type.
`setContentLength`	`void setContentLength(int)`	Sets content length for response, in bytes.
`setContentType`	`String getContentType()`	Sets the MIME type of request data. If not set, default is `text/plain`.
`getLocale`	`Locale getLocale()`	Returns locale used for response.
`getOutputStream`	`ServletOutputStream getOutputStream()`	Returns output stream for writing binary data. For textual data, `getWriter()` method should be used.
`getWriter`	`PrintWriter getWriter()`	Returns print writer object used for the output of textual responses.
`isCommited`	`Boolean isCommited()`	Indicates whether response has been committed.
`reset`	`void reset()`	Clears any data stored in buffer, status codes, and headers.
`setBufferSize`	`void setBufferSize(int sz)`	Sets buffer size for response.
`setLocale`	`void setLocale(Locale loc)`	Sets locale for response. Also sets headers appropriately.

Table 7-3. *ServletResponse Methods*

indicating that you do not want your servlet to be multi-threaded), you must make sure your code is re-entrant and thread-safe. To this end, use instance variables as little as possible. When such variables are necessary, access to them must be made using synchronized methods so that you won't get errors when multiple threads start running concurrently.

HTTP Servlets

As mentioned, the most common kind of servlet is the HTTP servlet. The servlet API defines the class `javax.servlet.http.HttpServlet` (an abstract class that inherits from `javax.servlet.GenericServlet`, which is an abstract class that implements the `javax.servlet.Servlet` interface). Table 7-4 shows `HttpServlet` methods.

In an HTTP servlet, the service method is already implemented. The default implementation parses the HTTP request, invoking one of the *do* methods, according to the HTTP operation. Each of these methods takes as parameter an `HttpServletRequest` object (see Table 7-5) and an `HttpServletResponse` object (see Table 7-6).

Method	Signature	Description
`doGet`	`void doGet(HttpServletRequest request, HttpServletResponse response)`	Implements the HTTP *get* operation.
`doPost`	`void doPost(HttpServletRequest request, HttpServletResponse response)`	Implements the HTTP *put* operation.
`doPut`	`void doPut(HttpServletRequest request, HttpServletResponse response)`	Implements the HTTP *put* operation. This operation is seldom used, so the default implementation reports an HTTP *bad_request* error. Then *put* operation is similar to sending a file via FTP.
`doDelete`	`void doDelete(HttpServletRequest request, HttpServletResponse response)`	Implements the HTTP *delete* operation, which allows a client to request that a URI be removed from the server.
`doTrace`	`void doTrace(HttpServletRequest request, HttpServletResponse response)`	Implements the HTTP *trace* operation. The default implementation sends back a message with all the headers in the request. This method is seldom overridden.
`doOptions`	`void doOptions(HttpServletRequest request, HttpServletResponse response)`	Implements the HTTP *options* operation, which allows a client to determine the allowed HTTP operations. The default implementation checks the servlet class to see which of the *do* methods is implemented.

Table 7-4. *HttpServlet Methods*

Method	Signature	Description
getLastModified	long getLastModified (HttpServlet Request request)	Gets the "last modified" time in milliseconds since midnight, January 1, 1970. Used for browser caching. The default implementation returns a negative number, indicating no caching should be applied.
service	void service(ServletReqeust request, ServletResponse response)	Services a request. If not an HTTP request, an exception is thrown. Otherwise, the following *service* method is called with the parameters appropriately cast.
	void service(HttpServletReqeust request, HttpServletResponse response)	Invokes one of the *do* methods based on the operation included in the request.

Table 7-4. *HttpServlet Methods* (continued)

Method	Signature	Description
isUserInRole	boolean isUserInRole (String role)	Indicates whether the user is in the specified role.
isRequestedSession IdValid	boolean isRequestedSession IdValid()	Indicates whether the session ID associated with the request is valid.
isRequestedSession IdFromURL	boolean isRequestedSession IdFromURL()	Indicates whether the session ID associated with the request was URL encoded.
isRequestedSession IdFromCookie	boolean isRequestedSession IdFromCookie()	Indicates whether the session ID associated with the request came in as a cookie.
getSession	HttpSession getSession(boolean)	Gets the current session associated with the request. (See Chapter 22.)
	HttpSession getSession()	Equivalent to `getSession(true)`.
getServletPath	String getServletPath()	Returns part of the request URI pertaining to the invoked servlet.
getRequestURI	String getRequestURI	Returns request URI excluding any query strings.

Table 7-5. *HttpServletRequest Methods*

Method	Signature	Description
getRequested SessionId	String getRequestedSessionId()	Returns session ID associated with the request.
getRemoteUser	String getRemoteUser()	Returns name of the user making the request.
getQueryString	String getQueryString()	Returns query string included in the request URI. Query strings are indicated by question marks in the URI.
getPathTranslated	String getPathTranslated()	Returns any optional path information placed beyond the servlet path, but preceding any query parameters. Also translates this extra path information into a real path.
getPathInfo	String getPathInfo()	Returns optional path information placed beyond the servlet path, but preceding any query parameters.
getMethod	String getMethod()	Returns the HTTP operation of the request (e.g., *get*, *post*).
getIntHeader	int getIntHeader(String header)	Returns the value of an integer HTTP header.
getHeaderNames	Enumeration getHeaderNames()	Returns the HTTP header names as enumeration.
getHeader	String getHeader(String header)	Returns the value of the requested header.
getDateHeader	long getDateHeader (string name)	Returns the value of the date header field in the request. Measured in milliseconds since midnight, January 1, 1970.
getCookies	Cookie[] getCookies()	Gets the array of cookies found in the request. (See Chapter 22.)
getAuthType	String getAuthType()	Returns the authentication scheme used for this request.
getContentPath	String getContextPath()	Returns the context of the request (a prefix of the URI for the request).
getUserPrincipal	Principal getUserPrincipal()	Returns a java.security .Principal object holding the name of the currently authenticated user.

Table 7-5. *HttpServletRequest Methods* (continued)

Method	Signature	Description
addCookie	void AddCookie(Cookie)	Adds a cookie to the HTTP header of the response.
addDateHeader	void addDateHeader(String name, long date)	Adds a response header with the given name and date.
addHeader	void addHeader(String name, String value)	Adds a response header with the given name and value.
addIntHeader	void addIntHeader(String name, int val)	Adds a response header with the given name and integer value.
containsHeader	boolean ContainsHeader(String header)	Checks whether the response contains a specific header.
encodeRedirectURL	String encodeRedirectURL(String url)	Encodes the specified URL for use in the SendRedirect method. URL is unchanged if URL encoding is not required.
encodeURL	String encodeURL(String url)	Encodes the specified URL. If encoding is not needed, URL is unchanged.
sendError	void sendError(int statusCode)	Sends an error response to the client using the specified status code with default message.
	void sendError(int statusCode, String message)	Sends an error response to the client using the specified status code with specified message.
sendRedirect	void sendRedirect(String url)	Sends a temporary redirect response to the client using the specified redirect location URL.
SetDateHeader	void setDateHeader(String header, long value)	Sets a response header with the specified name and value.
setHeader	void setHeader(String header, String value)	Sets a field in the response header with specified name and value.
setIntHeader	void setIntHeader(String header, int value)	Sets a field to the response header with specified name and value.
setStatus	void setStatus(int statusCode)	Sets the status code for the response.

Table 7-6. *HttpServletResponse Methods*

`HttpServletRequest` encapsulates the HTTP request, while `HttpServlet Response` encapsulates the response. Each of the *do* methods should read any data from the request, set HTTP headers in the response, and write any response. The headers usually set include content type and also content length if the length of the response is known. The response body is written out using the output stream or the print writer. Note that many of the methods for the HTTP servlet request and response objects relate to HTTP sessions, cookies, and URL encoding. URL encoding and cookies are techniques for maintaining HTTP sessions, which themselves are mechanisms for creating a context for a servlet. These issues are treated in detail in Chapter 22; they appear in the listing of methods here for the sake of completeness. Some of the response methods relate to status codes, which are numeric codes that are part of the HTTP protocol. A value of `SC_OK` indicates that the request was successfully served, and other codes relate to errors, such as `SC_NOT_FOUND` (indicating that the requested page doesn't exist) or `SC_UNAUTHORIZED` (indicating that the request requires HTTP authentication).

An important logical distinction between the *get* operation and other operations is that the *get* operation is expected to be *safe*. In other words, it is expected not to have side effects for which users might be held responsible. Requests intended to change stored data should use some other HTTP method (such as *`post`* or *`put`*).

Java Server Pages

A JSP page is a text document that includes segments of Java code and other special JSP tags. The document itself can be in any format such as HTML, Extensible Markup Language (XML), or practically any other language. Therefore, you can use JSP pages for any application in which the response is based on some template but Java processing is required to build the actual result. As in servlets, where a generic class is provided but the majority of servlets are HTTP servlets, so in JSP is the vast majority of JSPs HTML pages that include dynamic generation of Java. As time goes on, we envision that JSP will also be used quite extensively to create XML output.

The JSP Operational Model

The JSP operational model is based on the servlet model. As you already saw, the servlet model defines how a request is processed to create a response and what are the available main objects (the request, the response, the output stream, content type, and so on). JSPs are exactly the same. They, too, define a paradigm by which requests are processed into responses, and the JSP model has precisely the same set of main objects as servlets.

Activating a JSP means pointing the Web server at the text file (but using a .jsp extension); as of JSP 1.1 (which is the JSP version supported by WebSphere Application

Server 4.0), this can be an XML file. The HTTP request is inspected and is the source from which the request object (and everything it encapsulates) is created. Requests may arrive from a Web client, from other servlets, or from other Java applications. The core JSP API defines a method called `sendRedirect` from which other servlets can cause a request for a JSP to be issued. Before doing so, they can create or change the request object to make sure the right input parameters are placed in the request (using the `setAttributes` method). When the JSP later looks for certain named parameters, it can find them in the request.

Once the request is received, the processing begins. The process picks up the text file and starts going through the tags. Its role is to create the response stream—hence, the JSP model and the servlet model are quite the same. It does this by traversing the file and looking for JSP tags. Anything that is not a JSP tag is copied as is to the output stream. Anything that is a JSP tag is processed by the engine and usually produces output that is written to the output stream. Some of these tags do not directly write to the output stream but affect how the output stream looks—for example, the content type of the output stream can be set using a JSP directive.

Most uses of JSPs employ embedded Java code in the text file to generate dynamic data. The process by which the JSP engine can take this Java code and produce the data is quite extraordinary (at least when you first come across the concept). The JSP engine generates (code-wise) a servlet for each JSP file. It generates a .java file that is a real servlet and then compiles it into a .class file. Then it invokes the servlet and thus generates the output stream. The HTML gets to the output stream because the servlet reads the .jsp file (as text) and copies certain segments from it to the servlet output stream. We will delve into more details regarding how this is done and how the generated servlets look in Chapters 22 through 28. At the moment, it is important that you know this fact, since it fully explains why the JSP model and the servlet model are so similar—they are actually one and the same.

Figure 7-2 illustrates the main process that occurs in the JSP engine. Obviously, this generation and compilation phase takes quite a long time, and it would be unfortunate if one would have to accumulate this overhead every time a .jsp file is accessed. Luckily, this phase happens only once; after that, the compiled servlet is picked up immediately (or at least as long as the .jsp file has not changed since the time it was last compiled).

In general, having a large amount of Java code in JSP pages is not good practice. If a JSP page is well written, it will use beans that encapsulate behavior (or custom tag libraries, which we will discuss in Chapter 27) but will not embed the Java code directly into the JSP page.

Because the models are identical and the JSP is actually converted into a servlet, anything that is appropriate for a servlet is appropriate for a JSP. For example, you can implement a method called `jspInit()` in your text file. If you do this, when the first request for a JSP is received (and after the servlet is generated, compiled, and instantiated), your method will be called just like the `init` method in a servlet is called after the servlet is instantiated. Note that any Java code that is not specifically placed in a method by default belongs to the servlet's `service` method.

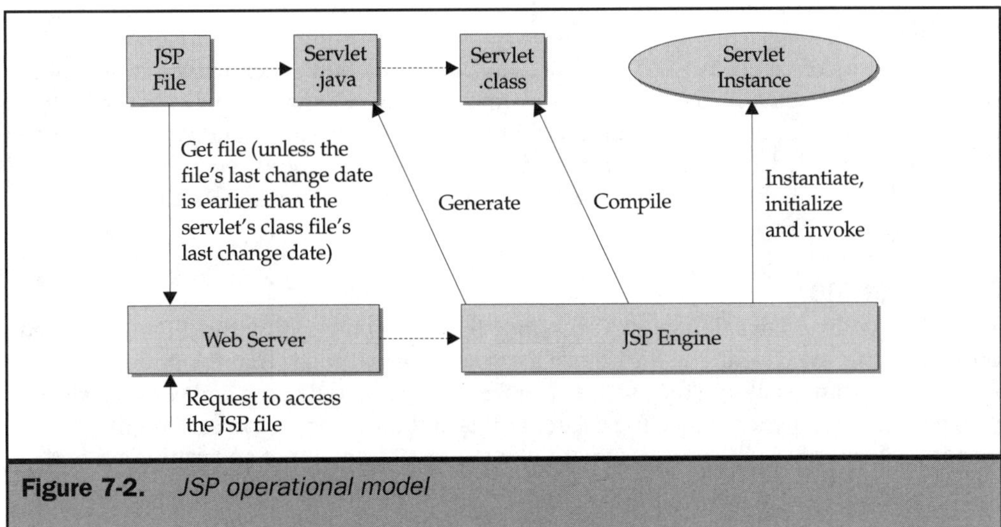

Figure 7-2. *JSP operational model*

Overview of JSP Syntax

.jsp files are text files in some format that include JSP elements. The JSP syntax defines a number of possible elements. Anything that does not fall into one of these categories is not processed by the JSP engine and passes unchanged to the resulting page. The categories of JSP elements are as follows:

- Scriptlets
- Expressions
- Comments
- Declarations
- Actions
- Directives
- Implicit objects

Two different formats are available for most elements. The first type is called the *JSP syntax.* Similar to other scripting languages, in this format scripting elements are enclosed within the bounds of the symbols `<%` and `%>`. The other format, *standardized XML format*, is slightly more cumbersome; scripting elements are enclosed within the bounds of the symbols < > and </ >, like so: `<jsp:element>` and `</jsp:element>`.

Scriptlets

JSPs include a convenient syntax in which Java code can be written in elements called *scriptlets*. By enclosing Java code within `<%` and `%>`, you tell the JSP engine to copy the code into the servlet processing method (that is, into the service method when no method directive is included, or into the method defined by the method directive).

In XML format, the code is enclosed like this: `<jsp:scriptlet>` and `</jsp:scriptlet>`.

Expressions

A similar syntax allows defining expressions that are evaluated by the JSP and written out to the output stream. The difference from scriptlet syntax is that the opening tag is followed by an equal sign (like so: `<%=opening tag>`) and that the embedded code is viewed as an expression. Since the expression is embedded in a Java statement performing a write to the output stream, the expression must not be terminated with a semicolon (`;`).

In XML format, the code for the expression is enclosed in this way: `<jsp:expression>` and `</jsp:expression>`.

Comments

Comments in the JSP file follow the general pattern of comments in HTML. By embedding a line of the form `<!-- comment -->`, you can pass a comment all the way to the browser page. Another kind of comments are *hidden comments* that appear in the JSP but are not passed to the resulting page. You can embed such a comment using the syntax `<%-- comment --%>`. Notice that the same syntax is used for HTML and XML JSPs.

Declarations

A declaration element declares a variable or a method. The syntax of declaration elements begins with the standard JSP open tag followed by an exclamation point: `<%!`. In XML format, the declaration is surrounded by something like this: `<jsp:declaration>` and `</jsp:declaration>`.

All such variables and methods enclosed in declarations are added to the servlet class generated from the JSP and thus are available anywhere within the class.

Actions

Actions are predefined functions available from the JSP engine. An action element can modify the output stream as well as create and use objects. Only one syntax is used for JSP actions, and it conforms to the XML syntax. This format is `<jsp:`*`action_name`*` />`. Following the XML conventions, actions can also have attributes, which are placed after the action name in the format `attribute="value"`.

Action elements are quite powerful, and among other things they facilitate access to JavaBeans and inclusion of other URLs. The various kinds of actions are detailed in Chapter 25.

Directives

Directives are instructions passed to the JSP engine. The format for directives is `<%@ directive_name %>`. The corresponding XML syntax is `<jsp:directive.`*`directive_name`*` />`. Further discussion of directives is deferred to Chapter 25.

Implicit Objects

The process by which JSPs are translated in servlets defines several objects that can be referenced without being explicitly declared. These objects form the "environment" one would expect in a servlet. Some of the implicit objects are shown here:

- **out** The output stream; an instance of javax.servlet.jsp.JspWriter
- **request** The HTTP request; an instance of javax.servlet.http.HttpServletRequest
- **response** The HTTP response; an instance of javax.servlet.http.HttpServletResponse
- **config** The servlet configuration; an instance of javax.servlet.ServletConfig

Summary

Servlets and JSPs form the backbone of any Web application developed and deployed on WebSphere. They are by far the most commonly used constructs and are easy to understand and simple to work with. And yet their ease of use does not compromise their value—they are powerful methods and should be mastered by all Web developers. The other important component category in building Web applications is Enterprise JavaBeans; we will build up to a detailed description of EJBs and their communication infrastructure in Chapters 8 through 11.

The Complete Reference

Chapter 8

Common Object Request Broker Architecture

This chapter outlines the fundamentals of the Common Object Request Broker Architecture (CORBA). This includes a description of the common components interacting in a CORBA-based system and their roles. The next chapter will describe CORBA 2.0 with a focus on Object Request Broker (ORB) interoperability in general and the Internet Inter-ORB Protocol (IIOP) specifically.

CORBA and IIOP are relevant to Enterprise JavaBeans (EJBs) in several ways. For one, as of its version 1.1, the EJB specification requires EJB servers to support Remote Method Invocation-IIOP (RMI-IIOP, Java RMI implemented over IIOP). By using RMI-IIOP (as opposed to plain Java RMI, which was the mechanism used for version 1.0 of the EJB specification), the specification opens the door for interoperability with legacy systems. Using CORBA, it is possible to leverage investments in non-Java software developed in languages such as COBOL or C++. The design of CORBA has influenced the design of EJB, and a lot of ideas in the EJB and the Java 2 Platform Enterprise Edition (J2EE) specification originate from CORBA. Finally, WebSphere implements EJB communication over IIOP, and the WebSphere Application Server Enterprise Edition is based (among other things) on CORBA.

The Object Management Group

During the second half of the 1980s and throughout the 1990s, distributed objects became a turnkey technology in most IT organizations. The need for distributed objects has its root in three developments: the reliance on networks for connectivity as well as computation, the need for remote access to services and collaboration, and the Internet/Web revolution. While each of these developments emerged at different times and from different technology-clients, they all required distributed access to objects, data, and services to enable powerful applications to be constructed.

While the quest for distributed objects was magnified by the need for integrating disparate applications and services over the Web, it did not start there. In fact, when the Web phenomenon was finally recognized as the primary area of growth in IT and solutions geared toward solving Web application problems, the solution to distributed objects was ready. CORBA, an industry-wide standard for distributed object-oriented architectures developed by the Object Management Group (OMG), already fully defined how applications running on different platforms and using different development environments and programming models can interoperate. CORBA is in many respects the global object middleware—perfect for the requirements of Internet applications.

The OMG was founded to work within the software industry to provide an open architecture to support multi-vendor, global, heterogeneous networks of object-based software components. The *Object Management Architecture (OMA) Guide* was published to serve as the foundation for the development of detailed specifications and infrastructure that would form the future of object-based systems. The OMA defines many components that together enable the implementation of the OMG's vision. The most important architectural piece defined in the OMA is the ORB. This component is the main mechanism facilitating the workings of the OMA, and it is used for sending and receiving messages between different objects and components. The ORB environment was defined in the CORBA Specification.

The CORBA Specification (revision 1.1) was adopted from a joint proposal produced by Digital Equipment Corporation, Hewlett-Packard Company, HyperDesk Corporation, NCR Corporation, Object Design Inc., and SunSoft Inc. It was published as OMG Document Number 91.12.1 and as a book published by the OMG and by X/Open, and it was the first widely available specification describing the adopted ORB technology. Revision 2.0 was published in mid-1995 and updated in mid-1996.

The Object Management Architecture

The Object Management Architecture is a general architecture and a taxonomy of necessary components enabling a portable and interoperable environment. The OMA outlines general technical guidelines that should be followed by every component within the architecture. These include the necessity for object-oriented interfaces, distribution transparency, a common object model forming a base for all components, full support for all stages of the software's life cycle, a flexible and dynamic nature, high performance, robust implementations, and conformance with existing standards within the software industry.

The OMA Reference Model

The OMG reference model for the OMA is shown in Figure 8-1. The model provides the underlying framework that guides the OMG technology adoption process. It defines the categories of necessary components to realize the OMG's goals and vision. The model is used as a road map to provide direction for components that must be developed. Once this architecture has been defined, the OMG's work can be seen as providing detailed specifications for the components identified within the model.

As Figure 8-1 shows, the model is composed of four component categories: the ORB, object services, common facilities, and application objects. Application object components represent the actual software being developed for solving domain-specific problems or for providing off-the-shelf products. These objects make use of the other three categories, providing them with a rich development environment. Using the other three categories, application developers can rapidly create portable interoperable code, which can later be reused by other application components. In this respect, the entire architecture is targeted to provide the best possible environment for objects in this category.

The architecture's heart is the ORB, which provides the capabilities that allow objects to interact and work together to achieve a common goal. Object services provide low-level system type services that are necessary for developing applications such as object persistence, transaction capabilities, and security. Object services define a collection of services that are necessary for any application to be constructed in

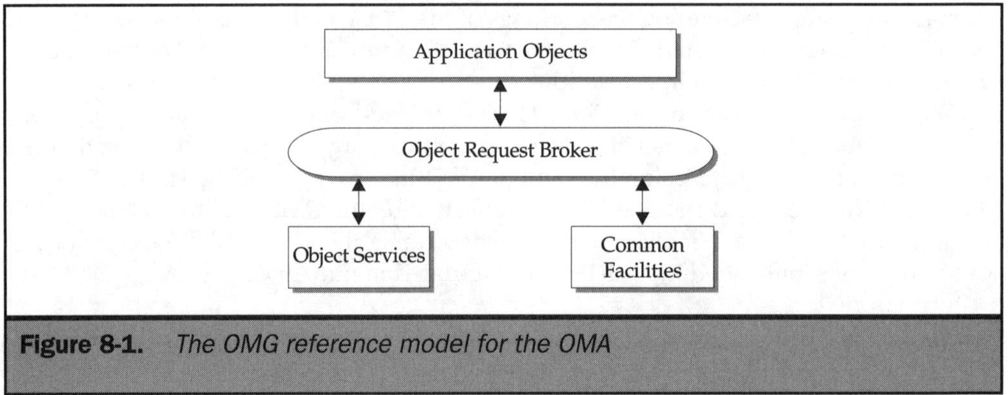

Figure 8-1. *The OMG reference model for the OMA*

a reasonably high level without requiring the application developers to "reinvent the wheel" for every application. Common facilities provide higher level services that are semantically closer to the application objects, such as mailing and printing facilities. Common facilities provide an even higher level of functionality that defines general capabilities required in many applications.

The difference between object services and common facilities might seem a little obscure; object services have a "system orientation," while common facilities have an "application orientation." Another important difference is that while object services must be supported by all ORB environments on all platforms, support for common facilities is discretionary.

The OMA is composed of objects, and every component in the architecture is defined in terms of an object-oriented interface (although it does not necessarily have to have an object-oriented implementation). Objects request services from any other object by accessing object-oriented interfaces. Any object can therefore provide services to any other object. The architecture transcends the client-server architecture because every object is potentially both a client and a server. In fact, every request invocation defines a client and server object in the context of a single invocation—the same object might be required to service a request (making it a server), while the implementation invokes a request to get some information from another object (making it a client). Any object (including application objects, object service objects, and common facilities objects) will be involved in such relationships, serving as both clients and servers.

Interactions use object-oriented interfaces. Any implementation, including non–object-oriented implementations and "legacy" software, can be made to provide object-oriented interfaces, which are often called object-oriented *wrappers* or *adapters.* In this way, the OMA can provide an underlying model for all software components, including those that were previously developed or that are not necessarily object oriented. In addition, since any non-distributed application is a special case of a distributed application (which simply uses only one machine), the architecture can represent all system architecture.

The Object Request Broker

The ORB is the central component that allows the reference model to function. It provides the basic object interaction abilities necessary for any of the components to communicate. It is therefore no wonder that this component was the first to be defined by the OMG. It allows client objects to issue requests for objects to provide required services. These service requests are issued by the client in a location-, language-, and platform-independent way. The ORB is therefore the primary vehicle delivering interoperability and portability as well as the enabler of the ability to build true distributed applications.

Requests are issued by objects using an object-oriented interface as defined by the service provider. The client constructs a request by specifying a reference to the object to which the request should be sent, an operation name, and any other information that is necessary. This will typically include the parameters to be sent but can also include such things as an environment context.

Object Services

The ORB provides basic interaction capability, but this is not sufficient for real applications to be developed. Applications need to assume certain basic services and functionality from the underlying environment; this is the role played by the object services layer. For example, the ORB provides ways for a request to be delivered to service providers, but it does not define how service providers are found.

The object services layer is of primary importance to the success of the OMG reference model. If this layer is not populated with enough functionality, the OMG's vision can not be realized—even if the ORB is fully functional and usable, this will not enable applications to be built. Too much will have to be developed by the application itself since the support provided by the ORB is at a low level. Most application developers also lack the expertise to develop such functionality on their own.

Object services are thus a primary component of the OMG reference model. In fact, once an initial ORB-based architecture was in place, the OMG (through the Object Services Task Force) began populating this layer with services. Some of these services are listed here:

- **Naming Service** Allows lookup of CORBA objects by name.
- **Event Notification Service** Facilitates asynchronous communication between CORBA objects.
- **Object Transaction Service (OTS)** Enables CORBA objects to perform transactions. This service has a lower layer implementing the mechanics of

transactions and a high-level interface for defining the scope and boundaries of transactions. OTS forms the foundation for the JavaTransaction Service (JTS), which is a critical part of JZEE.

- **Concurrency Control Service** Allows multiple clients to interact with a single resource concurrently, via locks.

Following the general concept of separation of interfaces from implementation, object services only define interfaces and provide a semantic specification of functionality. A service definition therefore supplies the developer with an application programming interface (API) set and a description of the functional behavior that is provided. This does not place any limitations regarding implementations for the service. In fact, it is assumed that many implementations will be provided for each service. This is absolutely necessary; services are generally complex and may have different characteristics. Stressing one characteristic of the service often leads to less support for another. Since users of the service will require various resolutions of such tradeoffs, a variety of implementations will be necessary. This is formulated in the Quality of Service (QOS) notion introduced by the OMG that allows different implementations stressing different attributes of the service to be provided.

In WebSphere 4.0 (as well as in version 3.5.*x*) object services are implemented by the adminServer.

Common Facilities

Common facilities also provide services, but they are typically at a higher level. They are closer to the application levels than are object services. Examples of common facilities are compound document management, electronic mail, and help systems. Such capabilities are still in the scope of the OMA; they can be used by many applications and can allow applications to be created faster in a portable and interoperable way. Like object services, they reduce the complexity of writing software within the OMG framework, thus achieving the overall goal. In fact, since common facility services are at a higher level, they will often cover more functionality of the application than will lower level services. For example, a compound document framework would be preferable than a service supporting generic object graph relationships.

The Common Object Request Broker Architecture

The ORB-based architecture supports portability and interoperability. Figure 8-2 illustrates a client making a request for a service to be provided by an object implementation. The client has an object reference and activates operations for this object. This reference is opaque, and the client has no notion as to the location of the

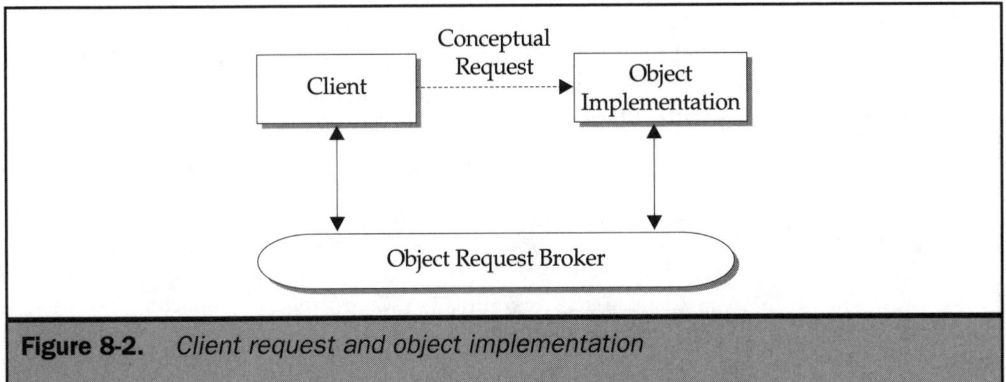

Figure 8-2. *Client request and object implementation*

object implementation, the language used to implement it, or any other detail about the implementation. It has only a specification for an operation request that is part of the interface. The client issues the request, and the ORB is responsible for delivering the request to the object implementation in a format to which the object implementation can respond.

When the client has a handle to an object implementation and wants to issue a request, two possibilities are available. If the interface was defined using the Interface Definition Language (IDL) and the client has a definition for the type of the object implementation, a static invocation can be issued. The request is made using an IDL stub specific to the interface of the target object. Otherwise, the Dynamic Invocation Interface (DII) can be used. This interface is independent of the implementation of the target object and can therefore be used even without thorough knowledge regarding the target object's implementation specifics.

The request is constructed at runtime and makes no use of IDL stubs. Instead, the request is handled by the dynamic invocation module using the information stored in the interface repository. Figure 8-3 illustrates the two possible request paths. Note that when the request is delivered to the object implementation, it is not aware of and does not care which path was taken.

Figure 8-4 shows the delivery of the request to the object implementation. After defining the interface of an object using IDL, an IDL skeleton is generated. Requests are passed from the ORB through this skeleton. An IDL skeleton will be used regardless of whether the request was issued through an IDL stub or using the DII. The object implementation is made available using information stored in the implementation repository provided at installation time.

CORBA defines a number of ORB subcomponents that interact to support this required functionality. Figure 8-5 illustrates a simple schematic view of these components. The schema does mean to imply a decomposition of the ORB. In fact, CORBA does not make any assumptions or requirements regarding ORB implementations. CORBA only defines the interfaces that must be provided by every ORB.

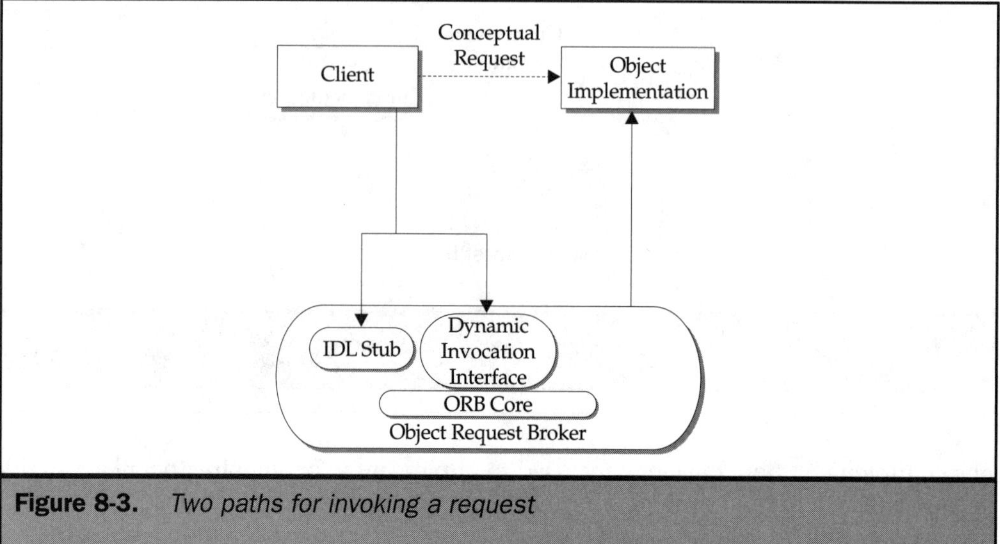

Figure 8-3. *Two paths for invoking a request*

The ORB Core

The ORB core handles the basic communication of requests to the various components. It can be seen as the underlying transport layer. CORBA is meant to support multiple systems and thus was separated into modular components so that different implementations can be used. This allows both different ORB cores to be used by

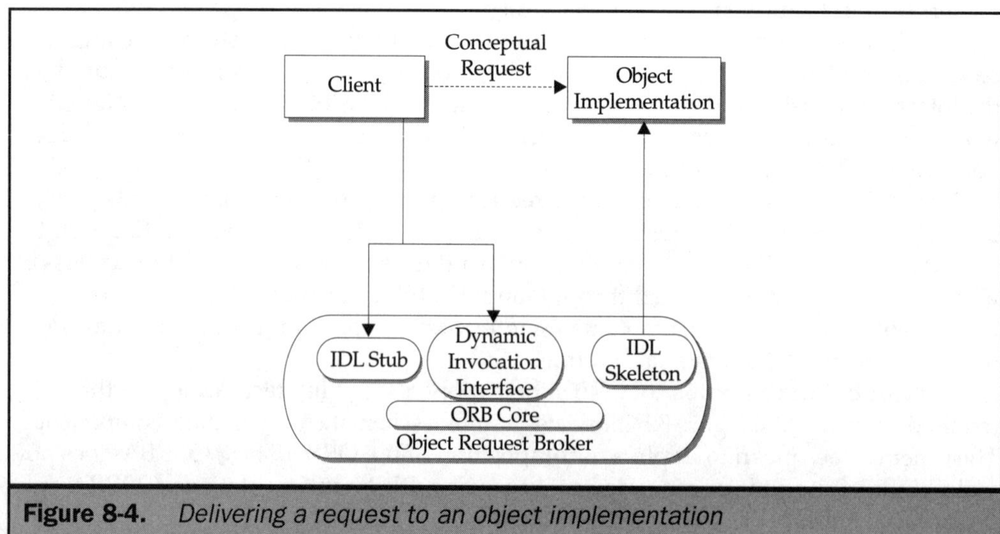

Figure 8-4. *Delivering a request to an object implementation*

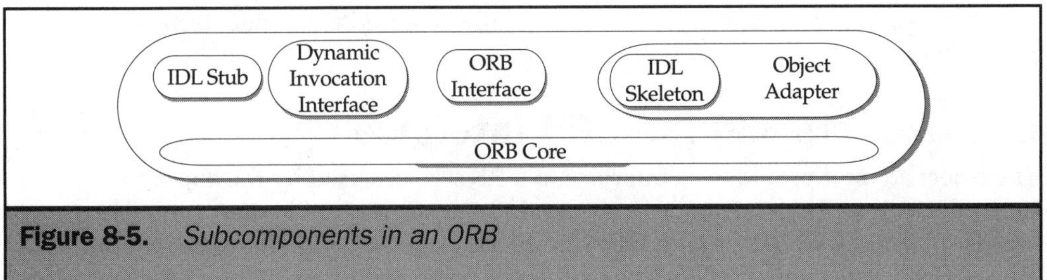

Figure 8-5. *Subcomponents in an ORB*

identical layers (while hiding the differences to external components) as well as for different layered components to use the same core. The core provides basic object representation and communication of requests.

IDL Stubs and Skeletons

IDL is used to define interfaces, types, structures, and modules. The definition of the interfaces is the method by which a client is informed which services are supported by an object implementation. Each interface defined in IDL specifies the operation signatures through which requests are made. It should be noted that the IDL source code is not necessary at runtime. The IDL definitions are used to create stubs and skeletons and are used to populate the interface repository.

Clients issue requests from within their host programming language. IDL is a definition language, and CORBA does not define a manipulation or invocation language. To allow interfaces written in IDL to be used from programming languages, *mappings* are provided. A mapping will take an IDL definition and generate a stub for each interface within the native programming language. The stubs allow the programmer to invoke operations defined as part of the target object's interface.

Implementation skeletons are generated per interface within a programming language. These structures actually invoke the methods implemented as part of the object implementation. They are called implementation *skeletons* because they are created from the IDL definitions yet include no implementation details. The developer of the object implementation must fill this skeleton with actual code that will be invoked when a request is received.

An IDL skeleton usually depends on the object adapter; multiple skeletons may exist for the same interface and the same language—per different object adapters. It is even possible to provide object adapters that do not make use of IDL skeletons but rather create implementations "on the fly" when requests come in.

The DII allows the dynamic creation of requests, which allows a client to directly specify an object, an operation, and a set of parameters and invoke this request. The interface used is common to all objects and all operations, and it does not make use of the stub routines generated for each operation in each interface. Information regarding the parameters and the operation itself is usually acquired from the interface repository.

Object Adapters and the ORB Interface

The object adapter provides an interface to ORB services used by the object implementations. It also provides services that may be required when a request is received from the ORB core and delivered to the skeleton for method invocation. Since object implementations can be extremely diverse in terms of their characteristics, many object adapters are envisioned. This allows support for diverse cases while not changing the architecture.

Other services used by object implementations are provided directly through the ORB interface. This interface is identical for all ORB implementations and does not depend on the object adapter used by the object implementations. Naturally, this interface will still be mapped to the host programming language used by the object implementation. These operations are also available to the client objects.

Repositories

The *interface repository* (IR) maintains representations of the IDL definitions. These are persistent objects that are available at runtime. The IDL information is therefore maintained as "live objects" that may be used at runtime. For example, the DII uses the information maintained in the IR to allow programs to issue requests on interfaces that were unknown when the program was compiled. The IR service is also used by the ORB. For example, the IR information is necessary for performing marshaling and unmarshaling of parameter values. The IR is also used as a persistent store for additional information pertinent to interfaces such as annotations, debugging information, and so on.

The IR maintains information needed by the ORB to locate and start up object implementations necessary to fulfill a request. It is also used for additional information associated with object implementations such as debugging information and security specifications. The IR is specific to an operating environment since it is used in the construction and activation of object implementations, and it is not standardized by CORBA.

Object References

An *object reference* is an opaque representation that is used for denoting an object in the ORB-based environment. Both clients and object implementations use object references. An ORB provides a mapping of object references to the programming language used; this mapping must not depend on the ORB representation of object references.

CORBA defines a distinguished object reference used for denoting no object. This reference is guaranteed to be different from any other object reference. In some environments, this maps to a reference of the null (or nil) object.

Clients

A *client* makes a request from within the application code. The client code uses the IDL stubs as it would use any library routine. When the stub routine is called, the object reference for the target object is mapped to the object reference as represented by the ORB. The stub then calls the ORB, which is responsible for locating the object implementation and for routing the request to the implementations, as well as delivering any results back to the client. If an error occurs during the method invocation, or if the ORB cannot complete fulfilling the request for any variety of reasons, an exception may be delivered to the client's operating context.

If the client was compiled before the target object's interface was completed, it is possible that the stubs for the target object were not available. The client code cannot therefore access the interface for this object. In this case, the client can name the type of the object and operation to be invoked and use the DII. The client can construct the call programmatically using a sequence of calls for building up the invocation and the parameters, and then invoke the request.

A client uses object references to issue requests and as values for parameters. Clients normally receive object references as output parameters of past requests, or through requests that were sent to the client from other clients. Object references can even be converted into a string format that can be made persistent by simply storing it to disk, which can later be turned back to an object reference by the same ORB that converted the reference into the string.

Object Implementations

Object *implementations* encapsulate the state and behavior of the object. These are internal to the object, but their behavior is used by the skeletons to provide services for the clients. CORBA defines only the necessary mechanisms for invoking operations. It does not define specifically how these objects are activated or stopped, how they are made to persist, or how access control is handled. However, because these object implementations must function in a real environment, all these issues must be addressed. The implementation is free to make choices regarding these issues.

Object Adapters

Object *adapters* are the primary ORB-related functionality provided to object implementations. The ORB itself also publishes an interface that may be used by the object implementation, but the object adapter provides most of the ORB-related services that are commonly used by the object implementation. Object adapters publish a public interface that is used by the object implementation as well as a private interface that is used by the interface skeleton. The adapters make use of the ORB-dependent interface.

The following are examples for services provided by object adapters:

- Method invocation used in conjunction with the skeleton
- Object implementation activation and deactivation
- Mapping of object references to object implementations, and generation of object references
- Registering object implementations so that they may be found when a request is received

CORBA does not require that all object adapters support the same functionality, nor the same interface. Object adapters may be specialized since they are a primary service provider for object implementations, as well as a major player in the request delivery mechanism. The CORBA specification defines only the Basic Object Adapter (BOA). Any CORBA-compliant implementation must provide a BOA. However, the CORBA specification does not place any limitations on definitions of additional object adapters; in fact, the specification provides some examples where additional object adapters will probably prove useful. Still, since object implementations rely on the object adapter interface, it is not recommended that a large number of object adapters exist. This is not restrictive, though, because different object adapters should be used only when different services or different quality of service is required. Thus, each object adapter will typically be able to support a large set of object implementations.

An example presented in the CORBA specification is the Library Object Adapter (LOA). The BOA starts up a processing thread per request or even a separate process per object invocation. This may be unacceptable for library implementations that may be shared by multiple clients. In addition, library objects may actually be running within the client's context so that activation and authentication are not required, thus greatly improving performance. If these object implementations were supported through the BOA, all these possible optimizations would not be possible. By providing the LOA, the improved behavior can be attained.

The Interface Definition Language

CORBA allows the development of portable and interoperable applications. It provides for systems to be built using multiple programming languages in a way that objects written in one programming language can make use of objects written in other programming languages. This is transparently handled by the ORB, and none of the participating objects are ever aware that the "other side" talks a different language; CORBA is the universal translator of the objects world.

Translating objects and invocations between different programming languages can be viewed as some sort of *bridging*—in this case, the bridging involves the translation of the object model in one programming language to the (same) object model in another language. Bridging can involve two fundamental architectures: *immediate* bridging and *mediated* bridging. In the context of programming language interoperability, immediate bridging implies translation of each relevant programming language directly into every other relevant programming language. Mediated bridging introduces a single language (and runtime format) that describes the object model and is used as the intermediate format into which every other programming language is translated.

CORBA was intended to be ubiquitously available and to support interoperability from a large set of programming languages. Already, products are available that allow CORBA interoperability in C, C++, Smalltalk, Ada, Objective-C, Java, and COBOL. Due to this large (and constantly growing) set of programming languages, the fact that a programming language may change, and the fact that different development environments may support slightly different dialects of the language, it is impossible to support programming language immediate bridging.

Mediated bridging is the only possible solution. But what is this intermediate language? The IDL is the language used to specify the interfaces that are used by clients to issue requests. Object implementations provide methods that offer the necessary services defined by the interfaces. Interfaces are defined in IDL and used by the client programs. IDL is not used for writing code; only specifications. The client will therefore not be written in IDL; it will use the IDL interface specifications while the actual call will be written in the native programming languages. These calls will be a result of a mapping of the IDL interfaces to the programming language. The object implementations are also not written in IDL but in a (possibly other) programming language. The interface operations then map to the implementation methods.

CORBA IDL Basics

Mapping from IDL involves the creation of stubs on the client side and skeletons on the server side. The stubs are programming language functions (or methods), which may be called by the client code. Calling such a stub (using a CORBA object) will cause an invocation to occur even when the real object is remote and implemented in a different programming language. All this is transparent to the client. When such a call takes place, the object implementation skeleton is invoked. This is the skeleton that was created as a result of mapping the IDL to the object implementation's programming language. Since such invocations require application-specific behavior to be performed, it is the developer's task to provide programming language implementations for each of the skeletons created as a result of the IDL mapping. All this is performed within the normal development environment used by the object-implementation developer.

As defined in the CORBA specification, any mapping of the IDL to a host programming language must include each item in the following list.

- *A mapping of all IDL data types, constants, and object references.* This includes providing a means of expressing basic data types, constructed data types, and constants in the target programming language. The mapping must also specify how an object is represented in the target programming language. Since the mapping must respect the host programming language semantics, the object representation is not dependent on the ORB's representation. The representation can either use an opaque handle to the ORB representation or as real programming language object. In the second case, the mapping must support identical object semantics of inheritance, operation signatures, and so on.
- *A mapping of operation signatures and invocations.* The mapping includes definitions for how input parameters are handled, how return values are handled, how operations map to the programming language functions, and so on. The mapping must not only define how IDL constructs are mapped but also how they are used. This involves handling memory management and lifecycle tasks.
- *A mapping of the exception model.* If the target programming language's exception-handling mechanism (when such a mechanism exists) is being used, the mapping should describe how this mechanism is used for implementing IDL exceptions. Otherwise, the mapping should describe how operations are extended to support exceptions and what management functions are required.
- *A mapping of IDL attributes.* Attributes are modeled by two accessor operations (that is, a *get* and a *set* function).
- *A mapping of the ORB interface and other pseudo interfaces.* This is necessary to allow programmers using the target programming language to access interfaces implemented by the ORB or one of the related components (the interface repository, the object adapter, the dynamic invocation interface, and so on). One approach might be to define these as a set of services packaged as a library. Another approach could involve pseudo-objects. A pseudo-object has an interface defined in IDL but is not implemented as an ORB-managed object. Operations can be invoked only using the Static Invocation Interface (SII), and the ORB may intercept such calls and handle them. In this approach, the ORB interfaces would actually be defined as IDL interfaces. These interfaces would be part of a pseudo-object. The advantage is that the ORB interfaces can then be mapped into many programming languages using the same mechanisms developed for application interfaces. Since it is just another interface, it is handled by the mapping procedures and by the case of ORB interfaces defaults to the general case.

The actual syntax of IDL is somewhat similar to that of C++. The following listing shows a simple example of an IDL file (*HelloWorld.idl*). A small caveat is that CORBA method signatures require that you specify for each parameter whether it is `in`, `out`, or `inout`. These values indicate that the parameter is input, output, or both, respectively.

These semantics are not supported in Java; hence, some slight complexity is added to the process of mapping IDL to Java, as detailed in the following section.

```
Module HelloWorld
{
        interface Hello
        {
                string getGreeting();
        };
};
```


CORBA to Java Mapping

To demonstrate how CORBA is used from within Java, consider the simple "Hello World" IDL just shown. To perform CORBA-to-Java mapping, you need to use a program called *idltojava*, which is available from the JavaSoft Web site.

After you have downloaded this program, run the following command:

```
idltojava -fno-cpp HelloWorld.idl
```

Note that the `-fno-cpp` flag is not necessary; it just avoids preprocessing the IDL using a C preprocessor, which you might not have installed.

The *idltojava* program generates five different Java files. It automatically generates a Java package of the same name as the CORBA module (in our case *HelloWorld*). Inside the package, a separate interface is created for each CORBA interface defined in the IDL. In our example, the file *Hello.java* shown in the following listing is generated.

```
package HelloWorld;
public interface Hello
    extends org.omg.CORBA.Object, org.omg.CORBA.portable.IDLEntity
{
    String getGreeting();
}
```

Other files generated for each CORBA interface are shown here.

- **Client Stub Code** For use by client code; in our example, *_HelloStub.java,* shown here:

```
package HelloWorld;
public class _HelloStub
      extends org.omg.CORBA.portable.ObjectImpl
      implements HelloWorld.Hello {

    public _HelloStub(org.omg.CORBA.portable.Delegate d) {
          super();
```

```
            _set_delegate(d);
        }

        private static final String _type_ids[] = {
            "IDL:HelloWorld/Hello:1.0"
        };

        public String[] _ids() { return (String[]) _type_ids.clone(); }

        //      IDL operations
        //          Implementation of ::HelloWorld::Hello::getGreeting
        public String getGreeting()
        {
                org.omg.CORBA.Request r = _request("getGreeting");
                r.set_return_type(org.omg.CORBA.ORB.init().get_primitive_tc(
                                     org.omg.CORBA.TCKind.tk_string));
                r.invoke();
                String __result;
                __result = r.return_value().extract_string();
                return __result;
       }

    };
```

- **Server Skeleton Code** An abstract class to be used for implementing the object; in our example, *_HelloImplBase.java,* shown next. In this example, the object developer needs to extend this class to implement the `getGreeting` method.

```
package HelloWorld;
public abstract class _HelloImplBase extends
org.omg.CORBA.DynamicImplementation implements HelloWorld.Hello {
    // Constructor
    public _HelloImplBase() {
         super();
    }
    // Type strings for this class and its superclass
    private static final String _type_ids[] = {
        "IDL:HelloWorld/Hello:1.0"
    };

    public String[] _ids() { return (String[]) _type_ids.clone(); }

    private static java.util.Dictionary _methods = new
java.util.Hashtable();
    static {
      _methods.put("getGreeting", new java.lang.Integer(0));
     }
    // DSI Dispatch call
```

```
    public void invoke(org.omg.CORBA.ServerRequest r) {
       switch (((java.lang.Integer)
_methods.get(r.op_name())).intValue()) {
           case 0: // HelloWorld.Hello.getGreeting
              {
              org.omg.CORBA.NVList _list = _orb().create_list(0);
              r.params(_list);
              String _result;
              _result = this.getGreeting();
              org.omg.CORBA.Any _result = _orb().create_any();
              _result.insert_string(_result);
              r.result(_result);
              }
              break;
            default:
              throw new org.omg.CORBA.BAD_OPERATION(0,
org.omg.CORBA.CompletionStatus.COMPLETED_MAYBE);
       }
 }
}
```

- **Helper class** A class with static methods for reading, writing, and narrowing object references. Narrowing is essentially type casting preceded by checking that the object reference is of the right type. The helper class in our example is shown here in *HelloHelper.java*:

```
package HelloWorld;
public final class HelloHolder
     implements org.omg.CORBA.portable.Streamable{
    //      instance variable
    public HelloWorld.Hello value;
    //      constructors
    public HelloHolder() {
      this(null);
    }
    public HelloHolder(HelloWorld.Hello _arg) {
      value = _arg;
    }

    public void _write(org.omg.CORBA.portable.OutputStream out) {
        HelloWorld.HelloHelper.write(out, value);
    }

    public void _read(org.omg.CORBA.portable.InputStream in) {
        value = HelloWorld.HelloHelper.read(in);
    }
```

WEBSPHERE TECHNOLOGIES

```
        public org.omg.CORBA.TypeCode _type() {
            return HelloWorld.HelloHelper.type();
        }
    }
```

- **Holder class** Implements a wrapper to a single object reference, which can be streamed. The main use of this wrapper is to implement CORBA's `out` and `inout` argument semantics, which are not easily mappable to Java. This means that if you pass a reference to your object to a method that a signature defines as `out` or `inout`, you must pass this holder instead of the actual object reference. The holder class in our example is shown in *HelloHolder.java*:

```
package HelloWorld;

class HelloImpl extends _HelloImplBase
{
    public String getGreeting()
    {
      return "Hello world!\n";
    }
}
```

To complete the implementation of this example, we need to provide a full implementation of the object. That is quite easy, because only one method is required. This implementation is shown here in *HelloImpl.java*:

```
package HelloWorld;
import org.omg.CORBA.*;
import org.omg.CosNaming.*;
import org.omg.CosNaming.NamingContextPackage.*;

public class HelloServer {

    public static void main(String args[])
    {
      ORB orb = null;
      try{
          // Create ORB and our object
          orb = ORB.init(args, null);
          HelloImpl hello = new HelloImpl();

          // Connect new object to ORB
          orb.connect(hello);
```

```
            // Access the nameserver
            org.omg.CORBA.Object nsRef =
             orb.resolve_initial_references("NameService");

            // Note the use of the helper class for narrowing
            // (the NamingContext has a helper just like the one
            // automatically created in our example).
            NamingContext ncRef = NamingContextHelper.narrow(nsRef);

            // bind the Object Reference in Naming
            NameComponent nam = new NameComponent("Hello", "");
            NameComponent path[] = {nam};
            ncRef.rebind(path, hello);

            // Wait indefinitely for invocations from clients
              java.lang.Object tmp = new java.lang.Object();
              synchronized (tmp) {
                  tmp.wait();
              }
        } catch (Exception e) {
            System.err.println("Exception Caught" + e);
            e.printStackTrace();
        }
    }
}
```

Another piece of the puzzle is a daemon process that will wait, create a copy of the object, register it, and wait for incoming requests. In general, running this server might require you to set some runtime properties that indicate the ORB server. However, when running from a machine where WebSphere Application Server is installed while WebSphere is running, no special settings are required. The code for the server is shown in *HelloServer.java*:

```
package HelloWorld;
import org.omg.CORBA.*;
import javax.naming.*;
import javax.rmi.*;
import java.util.*;

public class HelloRMITest
{
    public static void main(String args[])
```

```
    {
      InitialContext initContext = null;

      try{
          Properties props = new Properties();
          props.put(javax.naming.Context.PROVIDER_URL,
"iiop://localhost");
          props.put(javax.naming.Context.INITIAL_CONTEXT_FACTORY,
"com.ibm.webshpere.naming.WsnInitialContextFactory"
          initContext = new InitialContext(props);

            // Retrieve the object reference using the nameservice
            java.lang.Object ref = initContext.lookup("Hello");
          Hello helloRef = (Hello) PortableRemoteObject.narrow(ref,
Hello.class);
          // Invoke the Hello object and print out the result
          System.out.println(helloRef.getGreeting());

      } catch (Exception e) {
          System.out.println("Exception : " + e) ;
          e.printStackTrace();
      }
    }
}
```

Finally, the following file, *HelloTest.java,* shows a small client-side program for testing the object. This program obtains an object reference using the CORBA naming service, and then invokes the `getGreeting` method for it and prints out the result.

```
package HelloWorld;
import org.omg.CORBA.*;
import org.omg.CosNaming.*;

public class HelloTest
{
    public static void main(String args[])
    {
      ORB orb = null;
      try{
            // create and initialize the ORB
            orb = ORB.init(args, null);
```

```
            // Retrieve the object reference using the nameservice
            // We Fully qualify Object so as not to confuse
            // with java.lang.Object
            org.omg.CORBA.Object nsRef=
                  orb.resolve_initial_references("NameService");
            NamingContext ncRef =
NamingContextHelper.narrow(nsRef);
            NameComponent nc = new NameComponent("Hello", "");
            NameComponent path[] = { nc };
            Hello helloRef =
HelloHelper.narrow(ncRef.resolve(path));

          // Invoke the Hello object and print out the result
          System.out.println(helloRef.getGreeting());
      } catch (Exception e) {
          System.out.println("Exception : " + e) ;
          e.printStackTrace();
      }
    }
}
```

To test this sample, compile all eight Java files (the five created by the automatic mapping process, plus the three implemented manually). Next, run the server using this command:

```
java HelloWorld.HelloServer
```

Finally, run the test client program with this command:

```
java HelloWorld.HelloTest
```

Note that for both commands you should have the right CLASSPATH setting so that the classes can be found.

Obviously, implementing a server for each object is not realistic, and neither is manually starting and stopping it. The EJB architecture solves these problems, among others. The EJB server holds all your objects and allows clients to access them.

The Dynamic Invocation Interface

The DII allows requests to be built up and invoked dynamically by clients. The client needs only to know interface-related information at the invocation time; no prior knowledge (at compile time, for example) is necessary.

Although the structure and the process of performing requests are different, the semantics of DII requests is identical to the semantics of requests issued using mapped IDL stubs. A DII request, like a static request, is composed of an operation name, an object reference, and a parameter list. Parameters are inserted into a name-value list that is then used in the invocation. Since the DII always accepts a parameter list (as an object), it doesn't care how many parameters are there; this allows the DII to support any invocation. These structures are built and used at runtime (these may still be type checked at runtime and compared to the information in the IR).

The basic structure supporting the DII is the `NamedValue` structure (used to associate a name with a value of type *any*). This structure represents a single parameter. An `NVList` is used to hold all the parameters sent in an operation invocation. An instance of the `NamedValue` structure contains the argument name, an argument value, the length of the argument, and mode flags (which are similar to the mode specifiers `in`, `out`, and `inout` in IDL and are called `ARG_IN`, `ARG_OUT`, and `ARG_INOUT`). The value is inserted into a variable of type `any` consisting of a type code and the actual data.

A `Request` pseudo-object is used for the actual construction and invocation of requests. The operations available in the `Request` interface are shown here:

```
Interface Request {
        ORBStatus    add_arg(......);
        ORBStatus    invoke(......);
        ORBStatus    delete();
        ORBStatus    send(......);
        ORBStatus    get_response(......);
    };
```

Summary

CORBA was born out of the necessity to create interoperability between objects. It defines a remote invocation model that can be used by objects running on different platforms and forms the basis for higher level services like transaction management. When Java was born as a programming environment and runtime platform, one of its strengths was its portability. Initially this portability was valued primarily as a way to write portable user interface code. Later this was recognized as being important for writing server-side code. Java component models also evolved (more on this in Chapters 10 and 11) to the eventual domination of EJB as server-side components. These server-side components need to be accessed from many types of client applications running on many platforms. This brought back the issue of interoperability within object component models—and so was born the use of CORBA (and IIOP) within EJBs.

The Complete Reference

Chapter 9

Internet Inter-ORB Protocol

In Chapter 8, Common Object Request Broker Architecture (CORBA) was introduced as a remote invocation paradigm in a distributed object environment and higher level services. This chapter continues with a discussion of Internet Inter-ORB Protocol (IIOP), an Internet Protocol (IP)-based protocol for CORBA interactions.

Inter-ORB-ability

While CORBA 1.0 and 1.1 were successful in defining a standard architecture for distributed object-oriented systems, they did not achieve all the goals related to interoperability that their creators had envisioned. Users were reluctant in selecting Object Request Brokers (ORBs) as the central middleware component in their mission-critical systems. While this was partly due to the relative immaturity of some of the products and to nontechnical issues such as the lack of acquaintance with these products, the initial version of the CORBA specification has a fundamental flaw that also impacted ORB acceptance.

In their effort to create a flexible and open specification, the creators of CORBA 1.*x* did not address the issue of "inter-ORB-ability"—that is, the notion of interoperability among different ORBs. One of the main goals of CORBA as an architecture is to define mechanisms by which application and service objects can be constructed so that any objet can be used by any other object. The ORB is defined as the primary enabler of this architecture by delegating requests between objects. However, CORBA 1.*x* did not address issues regarding how ORBs interact with other ORBs. Therefore, the result of CORBA 1.*x* was an open architecture so long as a single ORB type was used. Systems utilizing ORBs from a single vendor could indeed accomplish what CORBA intended; unfortunately, however, if one attempted to use multiple ORB products within the system, interoperability was not achievable.

This fact was a major hurdle in the adoption of CORBA as an enterprise-wide solution by many corporations (and hence in the adoption of CORBA in general since CORBA primarily targets the corporate market). Not only was CORBA 1.*x* seen as incomplete, but because ORBs could not interoperate and an ORB-based architecture could be constructed using only a single vendor, corporations felt that they would not be achieving a vendor-independent and open solution (which, as you might recall from Chapter 8, was one of CORBA's goals). Also, because different ORB products stressed support for various programming languages and environments (for example, Iona's Orbix initially for C++ and Hewlett Packard's DST for Smalltalk—now owned by ParcPlace), it was only natural to have a mix of ORBs in most environments.

CORBA and the Web

After CORBA 2.0 was published, incorporating inter-ORB-ability, ORB vendors immediately embraced the standard and CORBA 2.0 products started appearing at an impressive rate. CORBA 2.0 was also the turning point as far as corporate (user) adoption was concerned. CORBA has taken off as a primary enabler of distributed object-oriented systems during the past couple of years. It is difficult to assess how much of this is due to CORBA 2.0 and how much is due to the simple fact that CORBA, like any technology, has matured. In addition, the phenomenal growth of the Internet and the Worldwide Web has definitely served as an important catalyst in the use of CORBA as a foundation for application-level communication.

First-generation applications offered on the Web were no more than form-based information accessors with little to no application functionality. The Web as a delivery platform, however, has quickly proved itself as having virtually infinite possibilities as far as audience and client base is concerned. This made IT organizations think of using the Web to deliver applications to a large client base. The emergence of the corporate intranet as *the* application delivery mechanism accelerated this trend and gave a tremendous boost to CORBA.

CORBA, and specifically CORBA 2.0, emerged as an obvious candidate to fill this gap. CORBA as an architecture was from the outset meant to solve precisely such interoperation problems. Luckily, the battle over CORBA 2.0 was won by the Transmission Control Protocol/Internet Protocol (TCP/IP)–Internet backers. (Certainly, had the decision been to base CORBA interoperability on the Open Software Foundation's Distributed Computing Environment (DCE), CORBA would not be where it is today. In fact, it probably would have become one more good, but unused, technology.) This positioned CORBA perfectly for being used as *the* interoperable architectural standard for Web-based systems and allowed CORBA to ride the Internet wave.

CORBA 2.0 deals with many issues ignored by CORBA 1.*x*. Among these, interoperability is not only the most important area, but the single area in which more work has been invested and more results have been produced than any other. The CORBA 2.0 specification not only defines the General Inter-ORB Protocol (GIOP) and IIOP but also addresses DCE-based interoperability and interoperation with the Microsoft Component Object Model (COM) and OLE Automation. In addition to being a concrete specification, CORBA 2.0 also addresses interoperability architectures as a design-level abstraction. By providing an in-depth discussion on what interoperability architectures should provide, how bridges should work, and what solutions should be used in different cases, CORBA 2.0 becomes central to the underlying technologies of distributed systems (no matter whether these are locally distributed systems or systems being distributed on a wide area network). The CORBA 2.0 specification is certainly one of the cornerstone documents in the field of distributed computing.

CORBA 2.0 addresses interoperability among objects running in different ORB environments (after all, even CORBA 1.*x* addressed interoperability of objects running within an ORB environment). As expressed graphically in Figure 9-1, ORB interoperability is the ability for a client on ORB A to invoke an OMG Interface Definition Language (IDL)–defined operation on an object on ORB B, where ORB A and ORB B are independently developed.

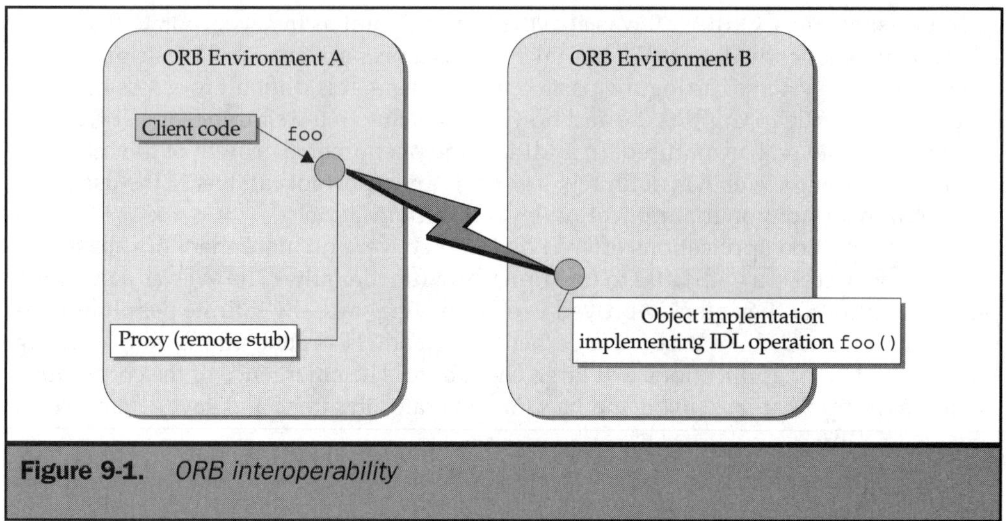

Figure 9-1. *ORB interoperability*

ORB interoperability is a difficult task (as seen by the set of solutions that were required of CORBA 2.0). The inherent complexity of ORB interoperability is the result of the following points:

- *CORBA is a specification defined at the behavioral and architectural level.* It does not enforce implementation-level properties. ORBs can therefore be very different in terms of their inner workings. Since the definition of ORB interoperability makes no assumptions on the participating ORBs, the specification ensuring interoperability must take into account any possible implementation of the specification.
- *The CORBA world (that is, the core ORB, object services, and object facilities) is a complex environment supporting a lot of functionality.* The set of properties forming the semantic context of an object and a request can therefore be large and complex. These semantics must be correctly managed and maintained when a request or object reference passes an ORB boundary. In addition, CORBA as an architecture is continuously evolving. The specifications for interoperability must ensure that future services or facilities are supported with little or no additional work—and certainly they must ensure that future additions are in no way compromised by a limited architectural view.

- *Interoperability is and must be bidirectional.* It is not enough for one ORB environment to have access to another. An invocation often includes an object reference that is passed as an argument and is then used by the object implementation to invoke another operation on the referenced object (thereby reversing the role of client and server). An invocation in which an object in one environment has access to an object in a second environment implicitly implies that every reference passed into the first environment is available to the second environment.

Since interoperability between ORBs must handle many cases, the CORBA 2.0 specification defines two distinct approaches to bridging between two environments. The first, called *mediated bridging* and shown in Figure 9-2, asserts that each internal ORB environment may adhere to its own internal representations and requires that an interoperable format be used externally to communicate between the two ORB environments. Elements that need to cross ORB boundaries are transformed into the interoperable format and then into the other ORB's representation. IIOP (for ORBs that do not use IIOP internally) is an example of a protocol used for mediated bridging.

In the second approach, called *immediate bridging* and illustrated in Figure 9-3, entities are converted directly between the two internal forms. Naturally, immediate bridging is more efficient but less flexible as transformation routines are required for each pair of differing environments.

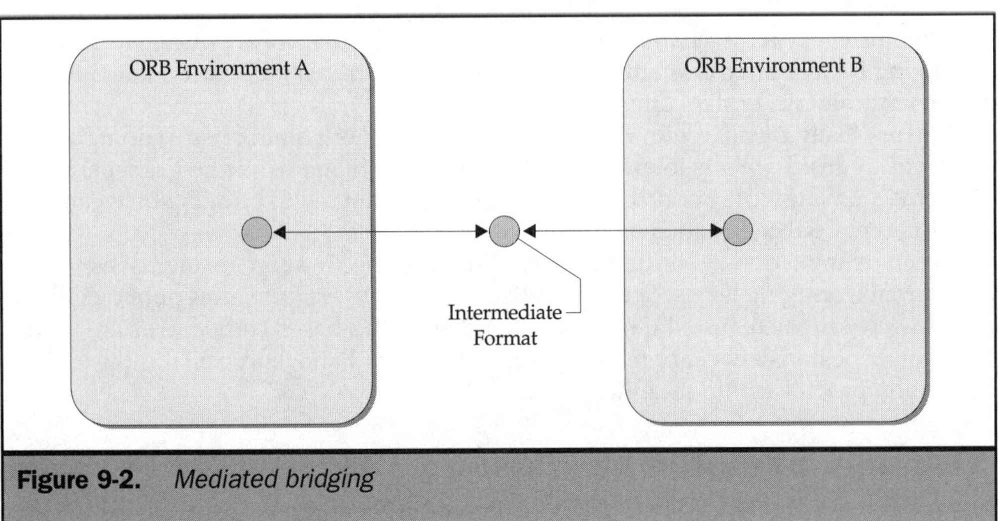

Figure 9-2. *Mediated bridging*

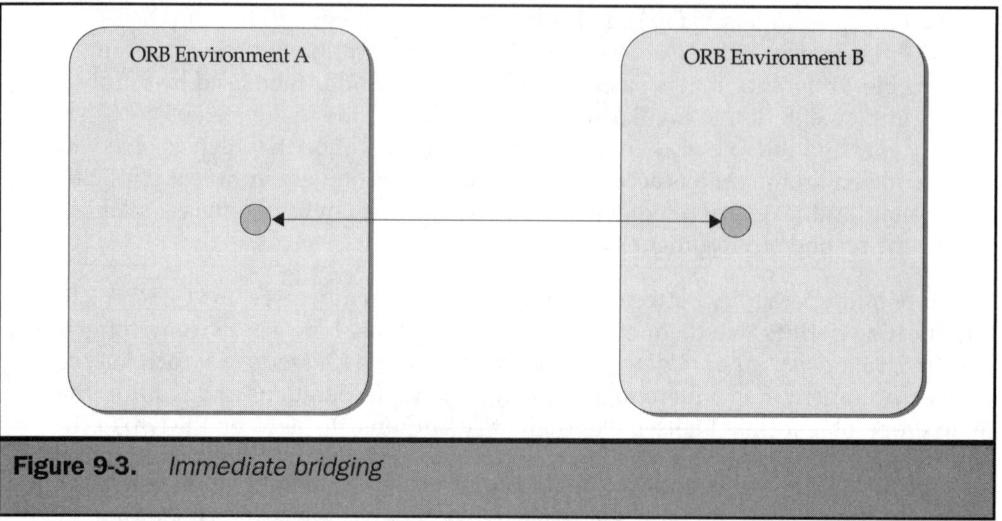

Figure 9-3. *Immediate bridging*

Domains

A *domain* is an organizational unit aggregating a set of components with similar characteristics. This is a broad term that can be used both for physical partitioning as well as for functional-related partitioning. Characteristics of domains are important when interoperability is concerned because bridging between domains requires a mapping from one set of characteristics to another. It is not always possible to define a mapping between two domains that will not lose information because some domains are semantically richer than others.

You are likely familiar with the concepts of physical or administrative domains. The focus of this chapter is interoperability between domains as defined as separate ORB environments. The notion of domain bridging is limited to bridging between two different ORB environments.

When defining domain bridging, the CORBA 2.0 specification distinguishes between two bridging levels. The first, called *request-level bridging*, uses public CORBA APIs to perform the required translations. ORB and ORB-based components are used to perform the translations. *In-line bridging*, on the other hand, encapsulates the entire translation process within the ORB.

The Dynamic Skeleton Interface

A major component defined in CORBA 2.0 for use in request-level bridging is the Dynamic Skeleton Interface (DSI). The DSI resides alongside implementation skeletons generated by IDL, as shown in Figure 9-4. Unlike an IDL-skeleton, the DSI can serve as a skeleton for any object implementation without knowing what are the actual interfaces.

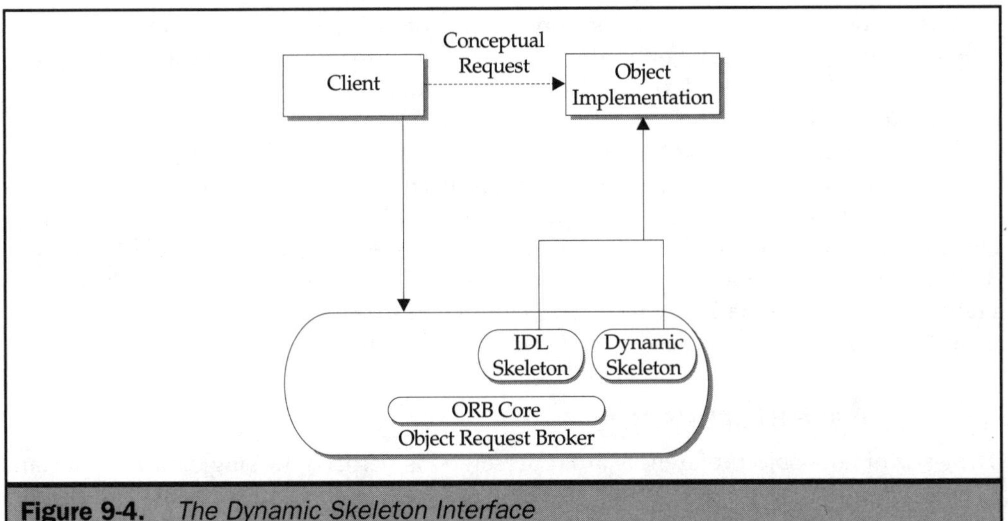

Figure 9-4. *The Dynamic Skeleton Interface*

The DSI magic is somewhat similar to the Dynamic Invocation Interface (DII) magic. The DII allows a client to create a request by specifying the target object reference, the operation name, and the parameters. It provides a mechanism by which this request can be fired off after its construction. The DSI provides the implementation-side counterpart to this process, but in reverse. No matter which request comes in, the DSI is invoked with the same method. This method is called the Dynamic Implementation Routine (DIR) and receives the same structures created within the DII that represent any operation request (that is, a structure that specifies the target object, the operations, and the parameters). The DSI is defined as a *pseudo-object* (its interface is defined using an IDL interface but not necessarily implemented as a CORBA object; for example, it can be embedded as part of the ORB). The pseudo-IDL (PIDL) representing a server request is shown by the following IDL:

```
module CORBA {
     pseudo interface ServerRequest {
          Identifier  op_name();
          Context     ctx();
          void        params(inout NVList params);
          any         result();
     };
};
```

Just as the object implementation is not aware of how a request was generated when servicing it (that is, whether the DII or an IDL stub was used), a client issuing a request (and receiving results) is oblivious to whether a request was serviced through an IDL skeleton or through the DSI.

This transparency allows the DSI to be used for request-level bridging. In such a scenario, the request (issued on an object reference managed by another ORB) is delivered to the bridge using the DSI (which can handle any request without requiring any compile-time information). On the other side of the bridge, the DII will be used to deliver the request to the real object in the second ORB environment. This is shown in Figure 9-5. The combination of these two components dealing with an abstract and generic model of a request makes such bridges relatively simple to build.

Inter-Domain Referencing

The issue of how object references are represented is perhaps the single most important issue in interoperability. As long as both the client and the object implementation reside within the same ORB environment, references are legal; but what happens if they reside in different domains and use different representations? In this case, we need to find a way to represent a reference to an object that is not dependent on the environment in which the real object lives.

The notion of *reference representation* is an important one that is crucial when the target object implementation lives in another ORB environment, but it is also relevant to additional scenarios. Observe the scenario depicted in Figure 9-6. The client invokes an operation on an object in another ORB environment. The operation call has another

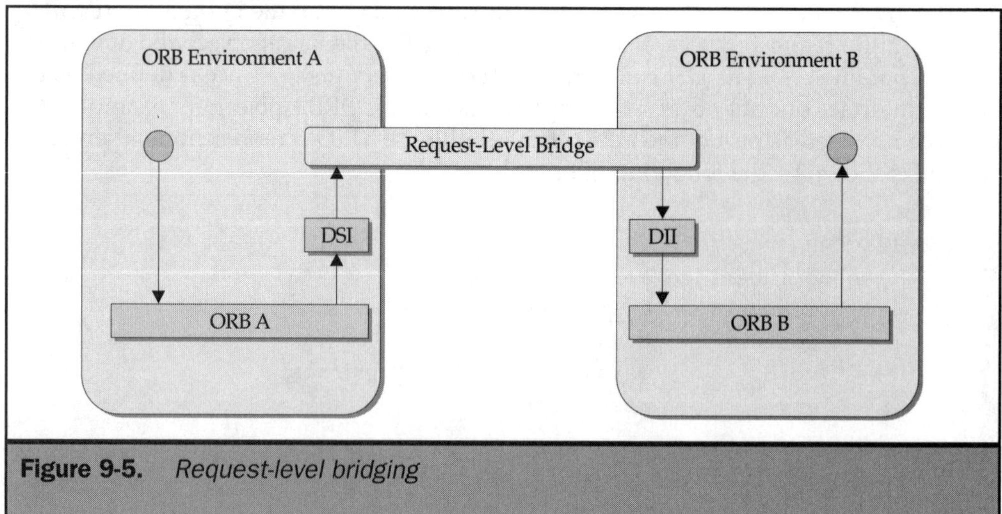

Figure 9-5. *Request-level bridging*

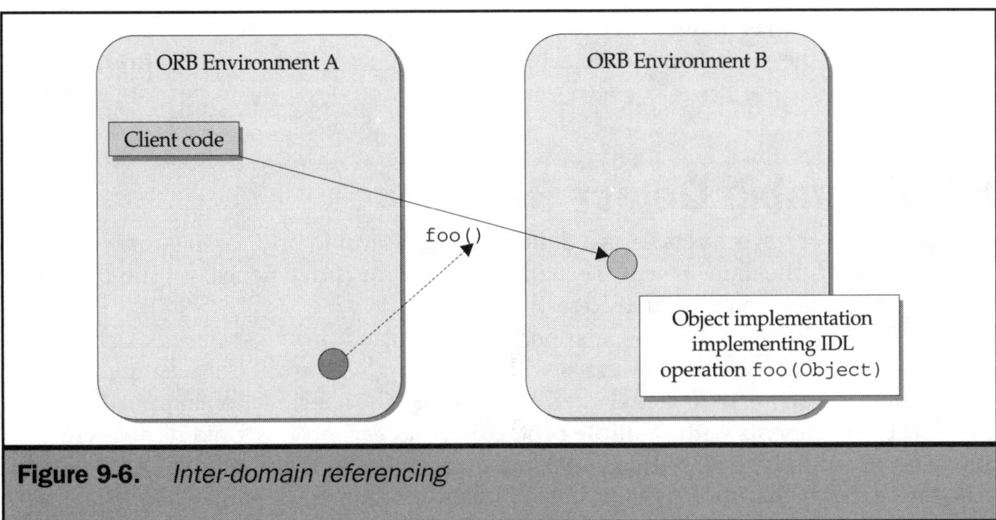

Figure 9-6. *Inter-domain referencing*

object as a parameter; the actual object used is within the client's environment. When the object implementation services the request, it may need to use the object reference passed as an argument—that is, send it a message. This implies that the inter-domain call (the first one in this example) must manage the object reference translation such that the object implementation may transparently use the argument to make additional calls. As an even more elaborate example, the object reference serving as the operation argument could reside in a third ORB environment that's different from both the client's and the object implementation's environments.

As CORBA evolved, it was clear that objects sometimes need to be passed by reference while at other times they need to be passed by value. Support for both models is important, and WebSphere supports both using the following flag:

```
-Dcom.ibm.CORBA.iiop.noLocalCopies=true
```

This flag allows objects to be passed by reference instead of by value.

The CORBA 2.0 specification identifies the following information as being necessary for object reference representation and translation:

- Is the object being referenced a *null* object?
- What is the object's type?
- What protocols are supported within the environment?
- What ORB services are available?

This data, which is required to represent an object reference correctly, comprises the structure of the Interoperable Object Reference (IOR), which is critical to ORB interoperability.

Interoperable Object References

IORs represent object references as a data structure useful to bridges to support ORB interoperability. The data structure is defined in IDL for convenience but should not be used by components other than bridges.

An IOR consists of a type specifier and a set of tagged profile specifiers, one per supported protocol. While many cases will have a single protocol (for example, ORB environments that use IIOP as the internal protocol), the specification supports multiple environments with multiple protocols. A tagged profile contains an identifier and octet streams and holds all the information required to identify the object being referenced within that particular protocol (that is, it holds the "opaque" representation of the object in the appropriate protocol). The fact that an IOR holds this identifying information for multiple protocols allows the same IOR to be passed around even when the underlying protocol changes (as long as the underlying profiles have corresponding octet streams defined within the IOR). Null objects are represented by an IOR with a special type ID as well as an empty set of profiles.

IORs may be "stringified" (that is, a string representing the IOR can be created) using the `object_to_string` operation defined in the ORB interface. This string representation can later be used to create an IOR for direct usage with the `string_to_object` call. This implies that the string representing the IOR is encoded with all the data contained in the IOR. A typical stringified representation will therefore be quite a long string similar to this:


```
IOR:000000000000002849444c3a4a4f4d6573736167696e674c617965722f4a4f4
d65737361676551756575653a312e300000000000200000001000000640000000000
0000040000000a000000107d48e77d8ceb000002500312cd0000000000000b00000
0107d48e77d8ce6000002500312cd00000008104000000000c4453543a352e363a
0113057b081040030000001038302e332e31382e3230353b333436300000000000
0002c00010000000000c38302e332e31382e323035000d840000000000107d48e7
7d8ceb000002500312cd000000
```


The stringified representation of an IOR is important for allowing systems to have a common starting point. Determining the first object reference from which others are accessed has always been problematic. While name services are already prevalent, the fact that simply passing a string in some way can create a common starting point is used extensively. For example, a string that can be embedded in an applet parameter is a convenient way to start an ORB-based interaction.

ORB Services

ORB Services is a new concept defined by the CORBA 2.0 interoperability specification and should not be confused with the term CORBA Services or object services (although they are related). ORB Services are ORB-level modules that support special interoperability transformations required to support CORBA Services.

CORBA Services provide various application-level functionalities, such as support for transactions, security, and relationships. Services can be partitioned into two groups (relevant to the discussion of ORB Services): those that require no support at the ORB level and are completely defined through a set of IDL interfaces, and those that do require ORB-level awareness. To support this second group, ORB Services were defined.

For example, the transaction service and security services both require ORB-level support. Transactions bracket code must be *atomically* performed (that is, either all code is performed or nothing is). Since a transaction may include a remote invocation, the transaction bracket may span more than one process on more than one machine. Therefore, it is necessary for the transaction context information to be passed along with the remote invocation. This management of transaction context, however, must not be visible to the application programmer and must therefore be supported by the ORB Services.

Assume now that the environment in which the application runs is different than the environment in which the object implementation resides. In such a case, the call is made in one ORB environment and must be transformed into the second ORB environment. Because this call must include appropriate transaction context information, this part of the request must also be translated into the new environment; the ORB Services created to provide interoperability support for the Transaction Services is the component responsible for performing such translations.

The Security Services are another good example for the necessity of ORB Services. Security information (such as authorization, signatures, and so on) is propagated along with a request in a secure environment. This information must be transformed when a call crosses domain boundaries—a transformation handled by the appropriate ORB Service.

Since the CORBA specification does not directly deal with CORBA Services, ORB Services are defined as architectural components. The specification does not address any particular service and how it can be supported; rather, it puts a framework in place for dealing with these services with the intent that such support can be extended later to any other service that will be added. It tries to identify the various areas in which such support may be required and what hooks are required from within the ORB layers. It also defines how negotiation between different ORBs occurs when each supports a (possibly) different set of ORB Services.

To support translation for any service-related information that might be required for various services, the interoperability specification defines an IDL type that encapsulates service-related information in a sequence of structures, each composed of a service identifier and an octet stream holding onto the service-related context information:

```
module IOP {
     // Each CORBA Service will define its own constant

     typdef unsigned long ServiceID;

     struct ServiceContext {
           ServiceIDcontext    _id;
           sequence<octet>     context_data;
     };

     typedef sequence<ServiceContext> ServiceContextList;

};
```

These additional context structures are sent by the communicating ORBs as part of the requests, thus allowing the propagation of service context.

The General Inter-ORB Protocol

The GIOP is an ORB interoperability protocol that can be mapped onto any connection-oriented transport layer. The GIOP associates a request with a connection and assumes that the connection provided by the transport layer is reliable and maintains message ordering. It also assumes that the transport layer provides some form of connection-loss notification and acknowledgment of delivery. While the GIOP is a generalized protocol and these assumptions are not limiting as far as connection-based transport protocols, the GIOP was constructed with TCP/IP as the reference transport level model; the mapping to TCP/IP, code-named IIOP, is therefore natural.

The GIOP specification consists of the Common Data Representation (CDR) and the GIOP message specifications. The CDR maps IDL types into a wire-level representation forming the GIOP transfer syntax. The GIOP also defines which set of messages may be exchanged between the participators in a session and how these messages are formatted.

The Common Data Representation

The CDR defines how IDL types are packaged into byte streams. CDR was designed to be simple, efficient, and flexible. The CDR is a wire-level transfer syntax that defines what actually goes over the wire and how IDL is packaged into these byte streams.

CDR not only maps IDL types; it maps the entire contents that will have to be passed for a request to be performed correctly. For example, CDR also defines the mapping of pseudo-objects such as typecodes as well as data types that are not fully specified by the CORBA core specification.

CDR places everything in an octet stream (a byte stream for our purposes). It deals with how these streams are created and how they may be unpacked. In doing so, it distinguishes between two types of streams: those that are used to package a GIOP message and those that package *encapsulations*. An encapsulation is a stream that packages any IDL data structure into an independent byte stream (having an IDL type of `sequence<octet>`). The encapsulation can later be used as a module for insertion into other streams, be they message streams or other encapsulations. Encapsulations are useful in creating a containment hierarchy of streams and supporting a "divide-and-conquer" approach for marshaling and unmarshaling data onto streams. CDR's approach to byte ordering is called *receiver-makes-right*. CDR does not enforce and maintain a certain byte ordering (that is, big-endian or little-endian). Instead, CDR packaging of data types may be either way. The CDR stream encodes which of the two byte orderings were used when the stream was packaged. It is the receiver's responsibility to use the bytes as they are packaged or to reverse them if the package ordering does not match its own ordering. This approach is advantageous because if the two endpoints use the same byte ordering, no conversions are necessary.

Note *Encapsulation streams also have an ordering tag, and it is quite possible for an enclosing stream to have a different byte ordering than an encapsulation stream that is embedded within it.*

In addition to IDL data types and typecodes, the CDR also defines how the following are encoded:

- **Context** A list of name-value pairs that holds information that forms the context in which a request was made. The context is passed to the object implementation by writing it to a CDR stream as a sequence of strings, which must be an even number of strings.
- **Principal** Identifies a caller and is used in security-related mechanisms. CDR merely defines that the principal is packaged as a byte stream; it does not associate any semantics with this stream at this level.
- **Exceptions** Packaged as a string identifying the exception followed by members of the exception structure.
- **Object references** Packaged using the IOR structure.

GIOP Messages

GIOP supports all functionality required by CORBA using a small set of simple messages. The core set consists of only seven messages; these support all invocation models, exception raising and propagation, context passing, and reference management.

A typical GIOP session starts out with a *Request* type message being sent from the client to the server (the client being the ORB through which the application client holding the object reference invokes the operation, and the server being the ORB through which the object implementation will be activated). If all is well, the server will respond with a *Reply* message. To close the session, the server sends a `CloseConnection`. At any time, both the client and the server may issue a `MessageError` message.

Request messages are used by clients to encode an operation invocation. The request message contains a header and a body. The header contains such information as the service, an indication of whether the request requires that a response to be sent back to the client, and the name of the operation for which the request message was issued. The body of the request message encapsulates the `in` and `inout` parameters (the parameters that are passed from the client to the object implementation) and an optional encoding of the context object.

Replies are sent in response to a request (where appropriate—for example, one-way operations do not require a response). Reply headers contain a context list, a request ID, and a reply status. The reply status can be one of the following:

- NO_EXCEPTION The request processing was completed normally. In this case, the *reply* message body encodes the return value and values for the `out` and `inout` parameters.
- USER_EXCEPTION or SYSTEM_EXCEPTION An exception occurred while processing the request. In this case, the body of the message will encode the exception that occurred.
- LOCATION_FORWARD The server is indicating to the client that the operation should be resent to a different object reference (for various possible reasons— for example, the object may have been relocated). The message body will encode the IOR that should be used for resending the message.

`CancelRequest` messages are sent by clients to servers and encode within their headers the request ID that should be canceled. `LocateRequest` and `LocateReply` are useful for querying about a particular object reference. A client can issue a `LocateRequest` for determining whether the object packaged in the message is legal, whether it is managed by the server, and so on. The server replies with a `LocateReply` message in which the locate status is either `UNKNOWN_OBJECT`, `OBJECT_HERE`, or `OBJECT_FORWARD`. If the status is `LOCATE_FORWARD`, the body of the message contains the new IOR to be used for accessing the object.

During a request session, both server and client may send `MessageError` messages to indicate inconsistencies in version number or unrecognized message structures. The last message type, `CloseConnection`, is sent by the server to indicate that it will not respond to further requests.

The Internet Inter-ORB Protocol

The IIOP is a specific version of the GIOP mapped to TCP/IP. Because TCP/IP is so ubiquitous, the name IIOP has become a code name for CORBA 2.0 and for GIOP. TCP/IP and the Internet (which is mostly composed of networks running TCP/IP) have made IIOP *the* ORB protocol.

The IIOP can serve two roles in ORB environments. The IIOP was built as an interoperability protocol in that it can be used as the common representation to which ORB environments convert when crossing ORB boundaries. Since the IIOP is a published format owned by the Object Management Group (OMG), it is a perfect candidate for the various ORB vendors to convert to.

While the IIOP's goal was to serve as the common interoperability protocol over the most common transport protocol (TCP/IP), it is being used in a far more encompassing way. IIOP is an interoperability protocol; however, it is also an ORB protocol that can represent all that is required within an ORB environment. Therefore, IIOP is not only being used as an interoperability protocol, but it is also being used as an ORB protocol for many of today's commercial ORBs. IIOP is not only being used within ORB boundaries, but it is also being used internal to an ORB's domain.

Since IIOP is merely an implementation of GIOP over TCP/IP, it requires only a specification of the IIOP profile that will serve as the "IIOP representative" in IORs. Since TCP/IP supports the abstraction in which a communication channel is formed using a host identifier and a port number, the profile body contains these identifiers along with the additional byte stream representing an opaque data structure used by the managing ORB to denote the object. This structure is placed within request messages by the ORB software; since the receiver ORB is the owner and creator of the opaque structure, it can interpret it and service the request.

RMI Over IIOP

RMI is Java's Remote Method Invocation mechanism, which came into the world to implement the notion of the Remote Procedure Call (RPC) in Java. This essentially solves the issues of communication in distributed programming, while leaving open other problems such as reliability and security (exactly the problem CORBA is tackling).

RMI and CORBA are quite similar in that both use stub code and skeleton code. RMI interfaces must be derived from `java.rmi.Remote` (and each of the methods there must throw `java.rmi.RemoteException` to have client code prepared for any kind of communication errors). Object implementations need to be derived from `java.rmi.UnicastRemoteObject`. Once you have both the interface and implementation compiled into JAVA class files, you can run the RMI stub compiler *rmic*. This compiler generates client stubs and server skeletons for your remote object.

Plain RMI runs using a protocol called Java Remote Method Protocol (JRMP). To use RMI, you need to utilize the RMI naming service to locate objects on one hand, and to register RMI objects in the RMI registry on the other. However, when using RMI over IIOP, all aspects of naming are taken care of by the CORBA Services.

The following code, *HelloRMITest.java*, shows an example of a client-side test program using RMI-IIOP, based on the example introduced in the previous chapter. Here, the Java Naming Directory Interface (JNDI) is used to perform the search. To allow the search to take place, you need to specify the underlying naming service implementation using the `Properties` object. Other than the use of JNDI, the only difference from the previous test program is that you use `javax.rmi.RemotePortableObject.narrow` instead of the CORBA narrow operation for casting. The crucial factor that differentiates between this test program and the CORBA-based one is that this one does not access the ORB at all. This also "proves" that RMI and not CORBA are used on the client side.

```
package HelloWorld;
import org.omg.CORBA.*;
import javax.naming.*;
import javax.rmi.*;
import java.util.*;

public class HelloRMITest
{
    public static void main(String args[])
    {
      InitialContext initContext = null;

      try{
           Properties props = new Properties();
           props.put(javax.naming.Context.PROVIDER_URL, "iiop://localhost");
           props.put(
                javax.naming.Context.INITIAL_CONTEXT_FACTORY,
                "com.ibm.ejs.ns.jndi.CNInitialContextFactory");
           initContext = new InitialContext(props);

             // Retrieve the object reference using the nameservice
             java.lang.Object ref = initContext.lookup("Hello");
```

```
            Hello helloRef = (Hello)
                 PortableRemoteObject.narrow(ref, Hello.class);
            // Invoke the Hello object and print out the result
           System.out.println(helloRef.getGreeting());

        } catch (Exception e) {
            System.out.println("Exception : " + e) ;
            e.printStackTrace();
        }
    }
}
```


Note that RMI-IIOP can be used in two different scenarios. One scenario is similar to that used here, in which RMI is used to access CORBA-based services and objects. This is more relevant to WebSphere development and is in line with the Enterprise JavaBeans (EJB) architecture. The other scenario involves access by CORBA clients to RMI server objects, thus allowing access to Java code from legacy code. This scenario has become less relevant following the introduction of EJB. The EJB architecture allows you to deploy Java-based components on the server and use CORBA to access them.

Summary

This chapter described IIOP, which is the way CORBA comes into play on the Web in general and in WebSphere specifically. Now that you have a good understanding of CORBA and IIOP, it is time to turn to JavaBeans and Enterprise JavaBeans. JavaBeans is a generic component model, and EJB is a component model for distributed programming. The EJB programming model is implemented on top of RMI-IIOP. As you read about the features of EJB, you should keep in mind both the principles as well as the paradigms introduced within CORBA and IIOP; these will help you understand what is going on behind the scenes when EJB are used.

The Complete Reference

Chapter 10

JavaBeans

This chapter describes the JavaBeans component model that forms the basis for most Java programs; many patterns used in Java programming are based on concepts defined in this model. You will learn what comprises a JavaBeans component and how it is described in terms of properties, methods, and events. You'll also see how to use the BeanBox tool (freely available from JavaSoft) to compose beans. The tool is used here primarily to help you understand how such beans are used within an integrated development environment (IDE) and how the beans' metadata is read and edited. This chapter also covers advanced concepts, such as event adapters and the persistence of beans.

The JavaBeans Component Model

JavaBeans is a component model that defines the structure of Java components. Software component models in general, and JavaBeans in particular, aim at defining simple yet powerful parameters that will allow for the creation of easily reusable pieces of code and their packaging. Component models aim at specifying a strict structure that is well known by both creators and users of software components. By adhering to such structures, developers can guarantee that their components well understood and compatible with common development environments, frameworks, and so on. The Java programming language is particularly suited for developing components because of its separation of interfaces and class implementations.

The purpose of any component model is to allow a component-based industry to evolve. In order for this to happen, it is not enough to create a component model; it is also necessary to achieve a certain "critical mass" in terms of IDEs, packaging tools, and third-party components. While JavaBeans is certainly not the first component model to be created (among the prestigious list of component models, consider Microsoft's highly successful Component Object Model, or COM, and Apple/IBM's not-so-successful OpenDoc), it certainly holds the record in terms of the rate at which it has been embraced. JavaBeans is currently part of Java 2 Standard Edition (J2SE), and it forms the basis for almost any Java library on the market today. (The `java.beans` package was incorporated in Java as Java Developer's Kit [JDK] 1.1) Furthermore, since the JavaBeans model lends itself to "visual" programming, the Java standard graphical user interface (GUI) components, such as the Java Foundation Classes (JFC)/Swing components, are actually JavaBeans. Most IDEs, such as IBM VisualAge for Java or Symantec VisualCafe, provide visual tools for creating and modifying instances of beans. JavaBeans also forms the base for the Enterprise JavaBeans (EJB) specification, which is the topic of Chapter 11.

The JavaBeans component model specifies the structure of Java components as a description of properties, events, and methods. In addition to this basic structure, the issues of persistence, introspection (which is akin to Java reflection), customization, and packaging will be discussed here. Readers who are already familiar with JavaBeans can skip this chapter. However, if you are not familiar with JavaBeans, we strongly urge you to take this bit of time, because Java programs often use principles and patterns defined in the core JavaBeans specification.

Definition of a JavaBean

A JavaBean (or just *bean*) is a reusable Java component with a specific structure that forms a common ground between components developed by different developers—components that do different tasks and use different resources. As such, it can be manipulated both at development time and at runtime by tools and programs that were written well before the bean was, and without any specific knowledge of the bean's particulars. These tools don't have to know anything special about the bean; instead, they can handle all beans, because all beans have the same fundamental structure. The abstraction level at which these tools and programs function is the component-abstraction level. By providing a common inheritance root, software hierarchies in object-oriented programming allow many different implementations to be viewed similarly by external users. JavaBeans does this to an even greater extent by defining a common structure. The fundamental principle behind JavaBeans (and any component model) is this: JavaBeans defines an abstraction level that unifies software entities and allows each such entity to become a component. By allowing disparate code from multiple origins to "look the same" in terms of its handling—both at the time of development and at runtime—JavaBeans elevates software reuse within the Java world.

Properties, Methods, and Events

The structure that defines the common base for all beans includes properties, methods, and events. *Properties* are the attributes of a bean. Each attribute has a name and a type, and is accessed through accessors (`get` and `set` methods). Attributes usually map to the functionality that the bean implements and much can be learned about a bean by its set of properties. Examples of properties include attributes such as size, color, and shading for visual beans as well as domain-specific attributes such as pager type, pager number, and retry policy for `PagerRequest` beans.

You may be asking why you would want to package a `PagerRequest` object as a bean. Packaging objects as beans allows tools that are being used within your system to be used with all these objects. For example, property editors can be written (or even bought) that edit any bean to allow use of the editor for creating pager requests, part orders, or almost any other domain object. What this means is that you can often create extremely generic software by doing little else but following the standard.

Methods are an object's main functional interface. A bean's public methods comprise its normal application programming interface (API), which reflects what the object knows to do. A bean developer may decide to export only a partial set of the public methods as the bean's API, in which case the developer will have to build a special "descriptor" for the bean.

Events are the actions that a bean can raise. Events are the preferred mechanism by which one software component notifies another; they support component interaction by allowing one component to react to events created by another component. The JDK 1.1 (and later) relies heavily on the notion of components raising events and other components being registered on those events through listeners. JavaBeans stresses this architecture by requesting that each bean define the set of events it can raise by a set of subscription methods through which other components can be notified of the bean's events.

Lifecycle Issues

A bean's life is slightly more complicated than the life of an "ordinary" piece of reusable Java code. This complication arises from the fact that a bean is built to be reusable. A bean knows how to behave within an IDE during development time. It must, therefore, not only provide a set of APIs for use at runtime, but also provide APIs and structures that are useful during development. For example, it must work along with the IDE so that the IDE will be aware of the bean's properties, methods, and events. It must also provide enough information about itself so that it can plug into the tools available within an IDE (for example, property editors and visual connection managers). It must allow developers the opportunity to customize and set its attributes, and it must provide the mechanisms for saving itself once it has been customized. All these additional complexities are necessary in order for a component to be a true bean. Once this complexity has been managed, the bean's value as a reusable component grows because the effort involved in using it in one's own program is much smaller.

A bean developer must be aware of the following issues in order for the bean to behave correctly at development time as well as at runtime.

Persistence

Unlike ordinary Java objects, a bean must provide the functionality required so that it can be serialized and deserialized. This is necessary because a bean user will typically set some of the bean's properties and then want to save those settings until runtime. The mechanisms afforded to beans under the JavaBeans model are those of serialization; that is, a bean should provide methods for writing itself to a stream and reading itself from a stream. These methods are then used by IDEs and programs using the bean.

Introspection

A bean must provide enough information about itself so that an IDE can help a developer understand what the bean can do and define how it interacts with other code segments in the system. JavaBeans defines two ways in which this can be done. The first relies on a set of conventions, and the second requires that the developer build helper classes. For example, in the conventions-based method, if a `PagerRequest` bean has a property called `TelephoneNumber` of type `String`, the bean developer should provide two methods of the following form:


```
String getTelephoneNumber()
void setTelephoneNumber(String aString)
```

These are the canonical accessors for a property. Often, a bean developer will not need to do much more than follow these conventions to ensure that the bean performs correctly within an IDE. However, this is not true with complex beans. For example, the naming conventions imply that all public methods are viewed as the JavaBean methods of the component. If a bean developer wants to shield some of these methods, but cannot change the access category to anything except public, then the developer will have to work a little harder. In this case, a `BeanInfo` object must be defined and implemented. A `BeanInfo` object describes the bean structure and is used by the IDE in the introspection process; it is a metadata object.

Customization

Beans can define customizers—specialized editors that are tailored to allow a bean to be more easily used within an IDE. Customizers often include wizards and attractive user interfaces that guide a bean user through the process of customizing and using a bean.

Packaging

Because beans are components written by one party and used by another, the JavaBeans specification defines how beans should be packaged by bean developers so that users of a bean are not faced with unnecessary difficulties when trying to use the bean within their own development environments.

The Juggler Example

Before describing some of the more advanced features in JavaBeans, let's look at a simple example. Here, we will look at a simple "juggler" bean, and a simple button bean and at how they look inside Sun's BeanBox. (The BeanBox is part of the Bean Developer Kit (BDK) available at *http://java.sun.com/products/javabeans/software/bdk_download.html*). You will create a simple application involving two buttons that control the juggler: one starts the juggling and one stops it. We will do all of the "programming" within the BeanBox by visually hooking events. Both of the beans used here are part of the BeanBox distribution and are provided as examples of bean development.

The BeanBox is composed of three tools: the canvas, the BeanBox toolbox, and the canvas, shown in Figure 10-1, is the work area in which beans are placed.

The ToolBox is the palette from which beans can be dragged off. On startup, the BeanBox startup procedure analyzes a set of Java Archive (JAR) files (the package

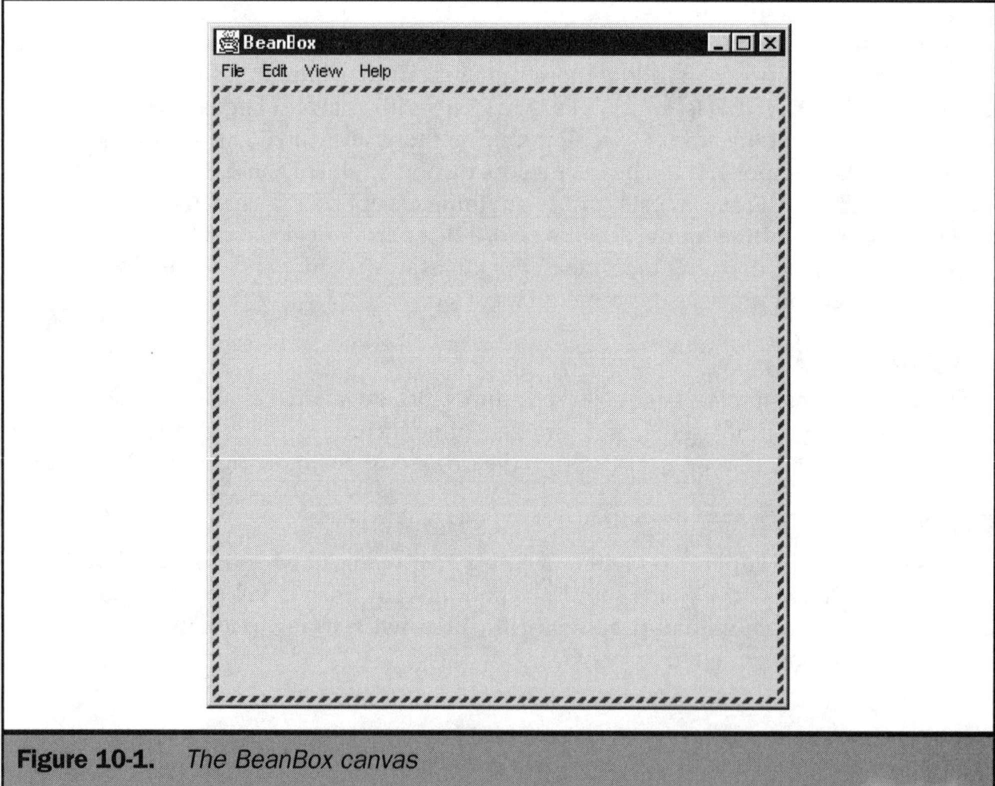

Figure 10-1. *The BeanBox canvas*

format for beans) and places all available beans in the ToolBox as shown here. All you have to do in order to add a new bean to your palette is to place the JAR file in the right directory (*%BDK_HOME%/jars*, by default).

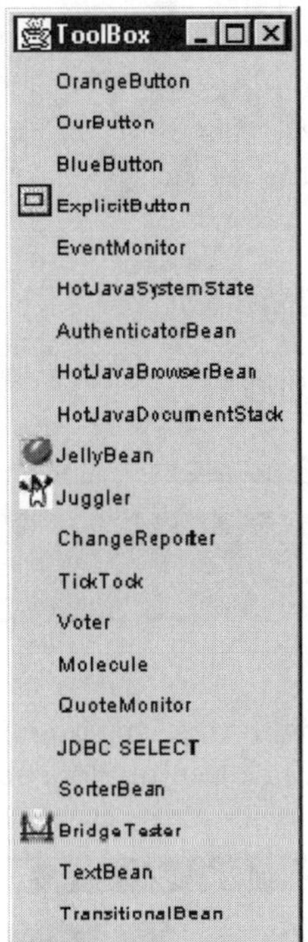

The property editor allows you to set the values of a bean's properties. The editor will always reflect the properties of the current selection; here the editor shows the property of the default container that is also part of the BDK distribution.

Properties - BeanBox
foreground
background
font Abcde...
name panel1

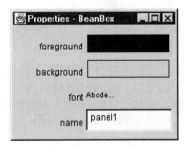

First, you drop three beans on the canvas, as shown in Figure 10-2.

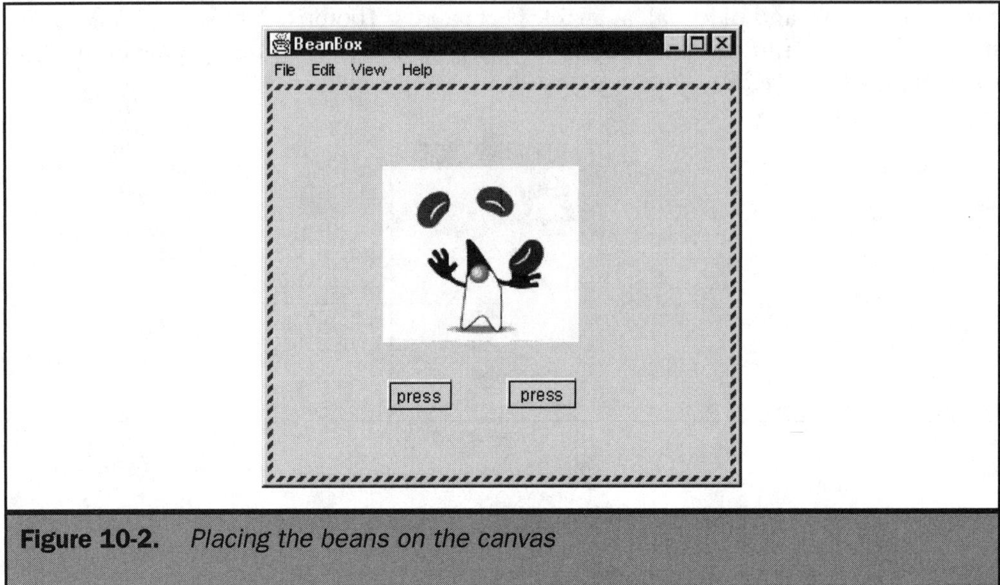

Figure 10-2. *Placing the beans on the canvas*

Notice that the juggler is juggling too fast, so you might want to change the rate at which the juggling is performed. Click the Juggler bean and look at the property editor:

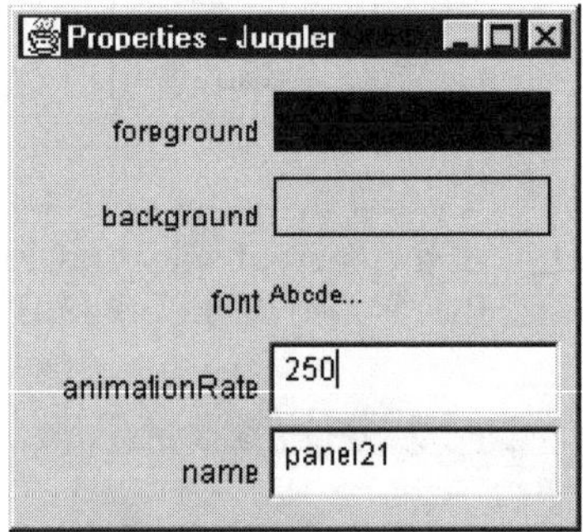

One of the juggler's properties is the juggling rate. The introspection mechanism allows the BeanBox to know this and place this property in the editor. To slow the rate down, change 250 to 125. Next, you need to set the labels of the buttons to "Stop" and "Start" respectively; one of the button bean's properties is its label, so we use the property editor for setting the right labels.

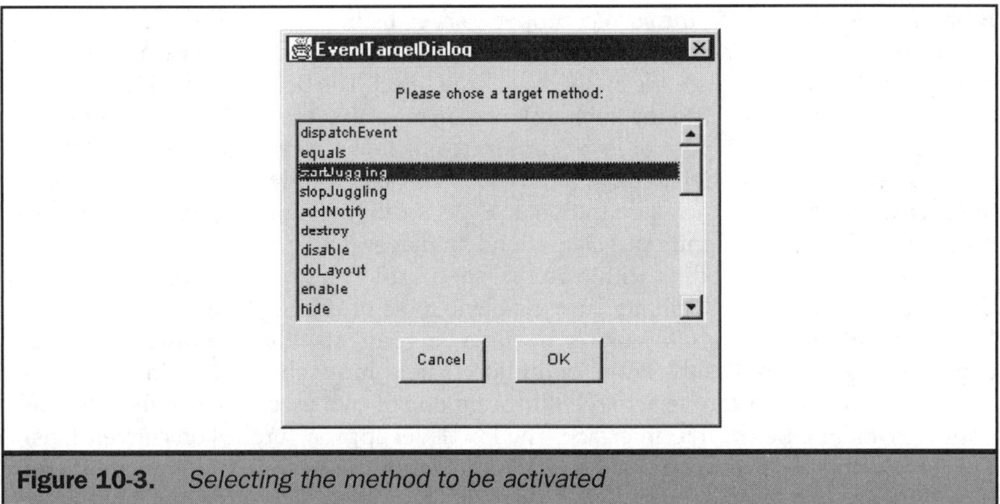

Figure 10-3. *Selecting the method to be activated*

When a button is clicked, an action event is generated. Now you'll hook up the events generated when the two buttons are clicked to call methods in the juggler—`startJuggling` and `stopJuggling`. The BeanBox allows you to do all this visually, as do many other modern IDEs. Behind the scenes, what occurs is that an adapter is placed between the juggler and each button. The adapter is added as a listener on the action-performed event (generated by the button); when the event is fired, it calls the appropriate juggler method, which is part of the API defined by the juggler.

For you, the job is much simpler. The BeanBox allows you to do all of this without writing a line of code. First, select the button you have designated to be the Start button. Then choose Edit | Events | button click | actionPerformed. This defines the event you are interested in.

Next drag the line to the Juggler bean. A list of methods forming the juggler's public interface pops up, as shown in Figure 10-3. Select `startJuggling`, and the adapter is created and compiled. The process is repeated for the Stop button. That concludes this little experiment. You now have a small working application that you can save and run; isn't technology wonderful?

Introspection

Introspection is the process through which a development environment discovers what properties, events, and methods a bean supports. In the example in the preceding section, you saw the effect of this discovery process. By knowing about a bean's properties, the

BeanBox is able to provide the correct property sheet, listing the events controlling the actions that the bean can perform. This list of events allows you to choose an action to be registered on, and to know the methods you can select. The BeanBox uses introspection, both for the button bean and for the Juggler bean, to enable this visual programming.

The fundamental purpose of JavaBeans introspection is to provide a means through which a bean's capabilities can be inspected. This is not a totally new concept; there are many environments in which a definition or a specification language is used for defining capabilities. For example, Interface Definition Language (IDL) is a specification language, and the information embodied within an IDL specification is stored as live objects within the interface repository (IR) that are accessible to tools providing browsing capabilities. JavaBeans introspection makes use of the Java language itself so as not to introduce a new language; this allows the entire definition to be completely phrased in Java.

Java introspection can be achieved through one of two mechanisms: the *low-level* approach and the `BeanInfo` interface. The low-level approach relies on conventions. The JavaBeans specification defines a set of conventions used for naming methods that provide access to properties, events, and methods. The low-level introspection mechanism uses Java reflection to access these names. Based on the set of conventions, the runtime can determine what properties, events, and methods a bean supports.

The default low-level mechanism is useful for most simple beans. For more complex beans, it is often not enough, because a complex bean may have been built to provide different services in different environments, or may contain too rich an interface to be useful for simple programming tasks. JavaBean introspection defines a second mechanism—a `BeanInfo` interface—that, while requiring more work from a bean developer, provides fine control over what a bean will show to the outside world.

The `BeanInfo` interface provides methods for describing the properties, events, and methods of a bean. A bean developer can create a class that implements the `BeanInfo` interface for describing the capabilities of a bean. The following listing shows a simple class that implements the `BeanInfo` interface for the `PagerRequest` bean. The `PagerRequestBeanInfo` class extends `SimpleBeanInfo`, a utility class in the `java.beans` package that has a null implementation for each of the required methods. The bean you create will have three simple properties (Telephone Number, PIN, and Message), a method for paging the number, and an event that will be raised when the pager gets the message. Note that we did not explicitly define the methods, thus showing that you can use an explicit `BeanInfo` definition for some aspects of the bean while relying on the default naming conventions for others.

```
import java.beans.*;



public class PagerRequestBeanInfo extends SimpleBeanInfo {
```

```
public BeanDescriptor getBeanDescriptor() {
        BeanDescriptor _descriptor =
              new BeanDescriptor(PagerRequest.class);
        return _descriptor;
}

public PropertyDescriptor[] getPropertyDescriptors() {
       try {
             PropertyDescriptor _propertyDescriptors[] = {
                   new PropertyDescriptor(
                         "Telephone Number" ,
                         String.class),
                   new PropertyDescriptor(
                         "PIN" ,
                         String.class),
                   new PropertyDescriptor(
                         "Message" ,
                         String.class)
             };
             return _propertyDescriptors;
       } catch (IntrospectionException e) {
       e.printStackTrace();
             return null;
    }
}

public int getDefaultPropertyIndex() {
      return 0;
}

public EventSetDescriptor[] getEventSetDescriptors() {
       try {
             EventSetDescriptor _eventDescriptors[] = {
             new EventSetDescriptor(
                   PagerRequest.class,
                   "Acknowledge Received",
                   java.awt.event.ActionEvent.class,
                   "acknowledgeReceived"
```

```
                    )};
                return _eventDescriptors;
            } catch (IntrospectionException e) {
            e.printStackTrace();
                return null;
        }
    }


    public int getDefaultEventIndex() {
            return 0;
    }


    public java.awt.Image getIcon(int iconKind) {
          java.awt.Image img = loadImage("PagerRequest.gif");
          return img;
    }


}
```

Because beans take the form of classes, and since a class can inherit from another class, introspection is a multiphased process that walks up the inheritance tree. For every superclass of a bean, JavaBeans introspection will try to determine if a `BeanInfo` object can be retrieved. If so, it will merge this information into the bean's complete description. If not, it will activate the low-level reflection mechanism and add the convention-based definitions to the bean-merged description.

Properties

Properties are named attributes of beans. A property has a name and a type, and is defined by accessor methods provided in a bean. If the property is read/write, two accessors (a `get` and a `set` method) will be implemented. Read-only properties require only a `get` method. Just as in Common Object Request Broker Architecture (CORBA) IDL attributes, a property does not necessarily imply that the bean has a data member, although typically it does; a property can be derived (or computed) and can involve complex business logic.

The convention regarding properties for low-level introspection is that, for a property by the name of `<PropertyName>` of type `<PropertyType>`, two accessors should be defined:

```
public <PropertyType> get<PropertyName>()
public void set<PropertyName>(<PropertyType> arg)
```

If the property is read-only, then only the `get` accessor should be defined. When a `BeanInfo` class is not provided and the low-level introspection mechanism discovers a pair of public methods as described here, it will know about the bean's property.

Special handling is defined for a number of common cases. If a property is of a boolean type, which is very common, the `get` method should be defined as follows:

```
public boolean is<PropertyName>()
```

If a property has an array type (that is, `<PropertyType>[]`), the pattern to be followed is this:

```
public <PropertyType> get<PropertyName>(int index)
public void set<PropertyName> (int index, <PropertyType> arg)
```

JavaBeans defines two more categories of properties called bound and constrained properties. *Bound properties* support automated notification upon a property value change; *constrained properties* allow subscribers to perform validation upon a property value change. Bound and constrained properties will be fully discussed later because to use them you need an understanding of events.

WEBSPHERE TECHNOLOGIES

Methods and Events

By default, all public methods of a bean are exposed as the bean's API. These include all property accessors and event listener subscription methods; therefore, it is usually wise to define the method signatures within a `BeanInfo`.

The JavaBeans event model follows the JDK event model and defines a framework for propagating notifications from a source object to a set of listeners. *Propagation* is the activation of Java methods defined in the listener objects that follow a set of naming conventions. The Java methods that handle the events are grouped in interfaces called *event listener interfaces*, whose signatures correspond to the naming conventions.

Hooking up an event subscriber to an event producer requires that both the source (the producer) and the listener (the subscriber) follow the JavaBeans event pattern. The source must provide methods that the subscriber can use to register interest in a certain event. These are the `add` and the `remove` methods. For example, if an object wishes to support publishing an `ActionEvent`, then that object should implement an `addActionListener` and a `removeActionListener` method. Using these methods, subscribers can register their interest in this event type on the source object. In order to complete the cycle, the subscribers must implement a method defined in the appropriate listener interface (the argument to the `addActionListener` method); this is the method that will be called by the source object when the event is fired.

The specifics of how an event is raised and how it is propagated to the listeners is less important and is not limited by the JavaBeans specification to one implementation method. For example, most implementations of beans will maintain a collection of dependents (subscribers) and use the `add` and `remove` methods to manage this collection; firing an event in this case implies iterating over this collection and calling each subscriber. However, nothing in the JavaBeans specification requires such a collection to be managed, and many alternative implementations are possible. The only truly important specification is the protocol between the publisher and the subscriber.

Firing an event by a source object means creating an event object (an instance of a class inheriting from `java.util.EventObject`), inserting information about the state change into this event object, and invoking a method in every one of the interested listeners. Event objects are immutable and should not be changed by individual listener objects. Since the same event object will be passed to all listeners, any such change may affect correct processing in other listeners.

As in properties and methods, low-level JavaBean introspection uses reflection and naming conventions to determine which events can be fired by a source object. A pair of methods of the following form implies that the bean creates `<EventType>` events that notify listeners implementing the `<EventListenerType>` interface:

```
public void add<EventListenerType>(<EventListenerType> ev)
public void remove<EventListenerType>(<EventListenerType> ev)
```

A special case supported in JavaBeans defines the naming convention to be used for unicast event sources. The default event-handling paradigm allows handling multiple subscribers on a single event source. If the event source model should only support a single listener, then the method definition should be of the following form:

```
public void add<EventListenerType>(<EventListenerType> ev)
              throws java.util.TooManyListenersException
```

Finally, when an event source raises an event, it iterates over all the subscribed listeners, and for each one it calls a method of the following form:

```
Public void <EventOccurenceMethodsName>(<EventStateObjectType> ev)
```

The event object encapsulates the information regarding the state change.

The event delivery semantics defined in the JavaBeans model is one of synchronous delivery with respect to the event source. The call made by the source object on the subscriber is performed within the caller's thread. If one listener fails (in a way that causes the thread to fail), the subsequent listeners will not get notification.

The synchronous event delivery semantics are fundamental to the notion of constrained properties. *Constrained properties* are an enhancement on bound properties—both being constructs that couple properties with events, and so common that they receive special status in JavaBeans. A *bound property* is a property that is of interest to another object—usually the container of the bean. This feature is useful for "binding" customized behavior to a change of a property value. Constrained properties are similar to bound properties in that an object may be interested in a property change, but the former go even further in supporting validation by allowing the interested object to reject the change if it determines the change inappropriate. Synchronous semantics are important for implementing constrained properties, because a listener may reject a change by simply raising an exception, thereby stopping normal processing of the event handler thread.

Bound Properties

As mentioned, bound properties allow coupling a property with an `onChanged` notification type. In order to provide a bound property, a bean supports a pair of multicast listener registration methods for the `PropertyChangeListener` type:

```
public void addPropertyChangeListener(PropertyChangeListener l)
public void removePropertyChangeListener(PropertyChangeListener l)
```

When a change occurs, the bean calls the listener's `propertyChange` method, passing it a `PropertyChangeEvent` object. The `PropertyChangeEvent` object includes the property name that has changed, its old value, and its new value.

If you want to register precisely on a single named property, the following methods are also supported by JavaBeans:

```
public void addPropertyChangeListener(
     String propertyName, PropertyChangeListener l)
public void removePropertyChangeListener(
     String propertyName, PropertyChangeListener l)
```

The call to the listeners' `propertyChange` methods is performed only after the change has been made; the subscribers have no say regarding the change. The following example uses a bound property of internal frame from the Swing (JFC) library (`com.sun.java.swing.JInternalFrame`). When an internal frame is maximized, the property will change and you will be notified of the change.

```
//
// When the screen is opened, set up the listener to be
// notified when the internal frame's properties change.
// One of these properties is the isMaximized property, which
// is of interest.
//

public void postOpenWindow(com.sun.java.swing.JInternalFrame win) {

      OnMaximizeOrMinimize aListener = new OnMaximizeOrMinimize();
      win.addPropertyChangeListener(aListener);

}



//
// When called, check whether this is the property of
// interest to us and, if so, call the handling routine
// (not shown here).
//

class OnMaximizeOrMinimize implements
      java.beans.PropertyChangeListener {

      public void propertyChange(java.beans.PropertyChangeEvent ev)
      {
         if (ev.getPropertyName().compareTo(
         com.sun.java.swing.JInternalFrame.IS_MAXIMUM_PROPERTY) ==
             0) {
            boolean aBoolean =
                  ((Boolean)ev.getNewValue()).booleanValue();
                        setBasedOn(aBoolean);
            }
      }
```

```
        public void setBasedOn(boolean aBoolean) {
              // ...
        }
}
```

Constrained Properties

Constrained properties extend bound properties with support for validation. Instead of being called after the property changes, subscribers are called before the change is made and are given a chance to veto the change. A subscriber can stop the change from being made by raising a `PropertyVetoException`. Due to the synchronous event semantics, it is possible for the bean to ensure that the change will not be performed until all listeners have been called and given a chance to veto the change. The naming conventions used for constrained properties include `add` and `remove` methods of the following form:

```
public void addVetoableChangeListener(VetoableChangeListener l)
public void removeVetoableChangeListener(VetoableChangeListener l)

public void removeVetoableChangeListener(
      String propertyName, VetoableChangeListener l)
public void addVetoableChangeListener(
      String propertyName, VetoableChangeListener l)
```

Notice that the handling method in the listener interface is defined to throw a `PropertyVetoException`.

One of the complexities involved with a constrained property is the fact that if one subscriber vetoes the change, it may be possible that other subscribers have been notified of the change and have already taken some actions accordingly. Since this may cause incorrect application behavior, when a veto occurs, the subscribers must be notified when the property is being changed back to the old value. Therefore, when a bean handles a veto exception raised by one of its subscribers, it must fire another "veto-able" change event for reverting back to the old value.

Event Adapters

An event adapters is an object that interposes between a source object and a subscriber (or between an event producer and an event consumer). Event adapters are not necessary for the correct propagation of events, but they are often very convenient to use. This convenience can be attributed to two issues:

First, event adapters allow decoupling the subscriber from the source. Instead of forcing the subscriber to implement the correct set of methods necessary for the event to be passed from the source, the adapter can form a "translator" of sorts, allowing the source and subscribers to remain unaware of each other. Because the different components often are developed by third parties, it is even possible that such a coupling will not be possible; in this case, event adapters are a must. The top part of Figure 10-4 shows the basic setup of an event adapter, and the bottom shows what happens at runtime. In this example, the paging system is a subscriber that has been purchased by a third party. It has an API for paging using a phone number and a PIN. Our source is a dispatch queue that raises an event whenever a dispatch request should be issued. The event adapter implements the listener API required in order for it to be added as a listener, and calls the API translation for the paging system.

Second, event adapters may perform additional operations required by the application, such as filtering events, implementing security policies, and implementing queuing. (For example, the CORBA Event Service has a notion called the Event Channel, which can be partially implemented within an application as an event adapter.) Another example of the usefulness of adapters involves transactions. Suppose you have multiple subscribers on the same node that must all perform some operation when the source fires an event. Also, suppose that all of these operations need to occur within the same transaction bracket (that is, either they all complete successfully or none are performed).

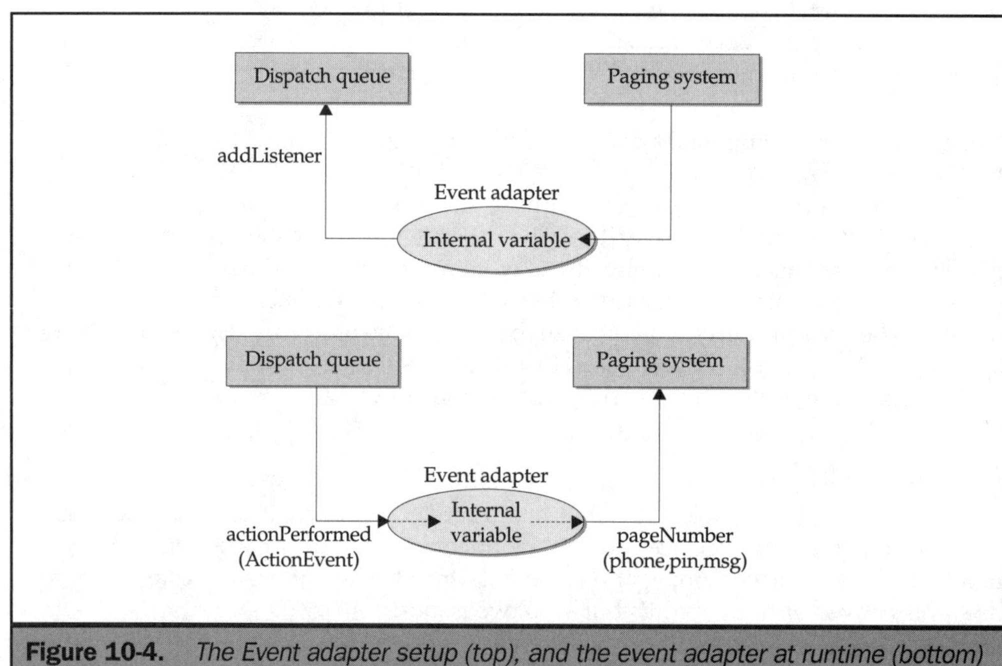

Figure 10-4. *The Event adapter setup (top), and the event adapter at runtime (bottom)*

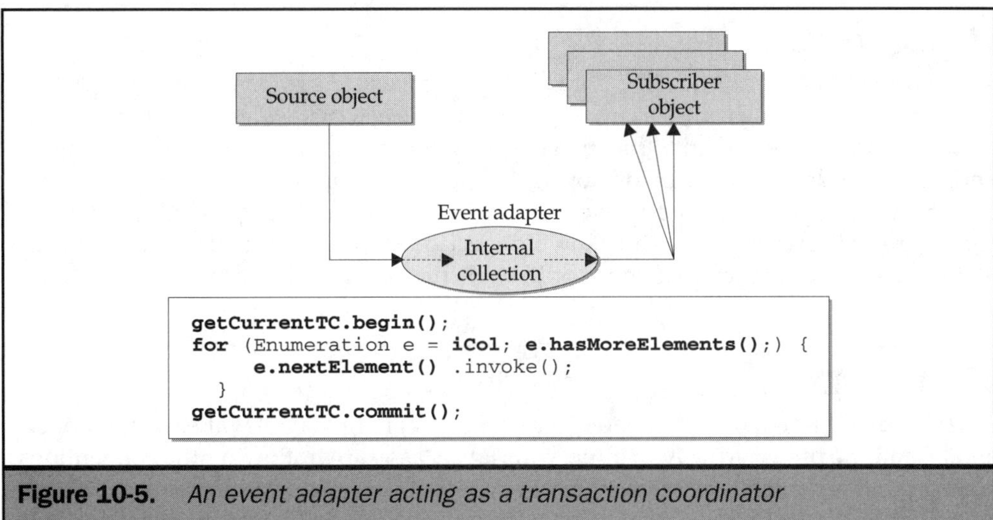

Figure 10-5. *An event adapter acting as a transaction coordinator*

Someone must coordinate this transaction. The coordinator will usually not be the source object—either because it has not been developed internally (that is, its source cannot be changed) or because other users of the same component care nothing about transactions. It certainly can't be one of the subscribers, because we can't rely on notification ordering. (Any implementation trying to make use of one of the subscribers for this coordination will almost surely be messy and nonreentrant.) This obviously is a job for an adapter. As Figure 10-5 shows, the adapter can manage the transaction for its subscribers.

Customization

Property editors are useful for simple beans. For complex beans, or for beans with complex data types as properties, the default property editors may not be enough. For such cases, JavaBeans defines the notion of a customizer. A *customizer* is a class that provides a way for a user of a bean to provide values for the properties of the bean at design time. A customizer can be a wizard, a specialized user interface, or an editor that allows complex data types to be entered.

A customizer needs to inherit (directly or indirectly) from `java.awt.Component` because it is used by the bean IDE as a GUI. It must also implement the `java.beans.Customizer` interface. The methods in this interface are used for managing the interaction, with the rest of the IDE using property change events.

Attaching a customizer to a certain bean involves going through the `BeanInfo` object. The customizer for a bean is retrieved by a call to the `getCustomizerClass()` method, by the `getBeanDescriptor()` method after the bean description is retrieved from the `BeanInfo` object.

Persistence

When using a bean within an IDE, the user typically customizes it by setting properties, attaching events, and so on. This information must be externalized to some persistent store in order for the system to function correctly at runtime. JavaBeans use Java object serialization as the mechanism for storing out and reading in beans. While the specification defines other alternatives for making a bean persistent, including allowing the tool to control the process and allowing specialized formats to be used, the current state of the market is such that you should use serialization and externalization only.

Summary

After reading this chapter, you should have a good grasp of the JavaBeans component model and the preferred way to build your Java classes. By following the conventions defined in this model, you will ensure not only that your code and metadata can be used within the context of other tools and frameworks, but also (and probably this is more important) that your code can be easily read and understood. Following the conventions defined in the JavaBeans model is especially important when you are writing visual components and components that are to be used in a visual composition IDE; still, our opinion is that it is always important. In the next chapter, we will go one step further and describe the Enterprise JavaBeans (EJB) component model. This model is much more sophisticated and provides many more services.

Chapter 11

Enterprise JavaBeans

Now that you have a pretty good handle on JavaBeans, let's move on to the most important component model for building server-side functionality in the Java world: Enterprise JavaBeans (EJB). This chapter describes the EJB architecture and the many components that comprise this architecture. It describes what code needs to be built, as well as who builds it. The bean, container, and server work together in supporting the client; this chapter provides details on the lifecycle of both entity beans and session beans. You should not underestimate the difficulty of mastering EJBs. The model is complex, and it takes time for you to understand how to make everything work together. This chapter is dedicated to describing the EJB model from the ground up, and the following chapters will provide examples of EJBs running within WebSphere.

Server-Side Components

EJB is a server-side component architecture that enables and simplifies the process of building enterprise-level distributed applications in Java. What this long definition means is that EJB provides a framework that allows you to implement a distributed Java application without writing code to handle the complex issues of distributed programming, such as communication and synchronization. The EJB architecture also manages scalability, security, and reliability issues well. All in all, EJB allows enterprise programmers to focus on the specifics of their applications, without worrying about the infrastructure of the application. The EJB server provides all the infrastructure you will need. You can choose to use any vendor's EJB server, and the architecture code is portable between servers. This book focuses on the WebSphere Application Server, but it is important for you to keep in mind that one of the advantages of EJBs is their portability. This portability, of course, stems from the fact that Java is portable and is shared by all Java 2 Platform Enterprise Edition (J2EE) mechanisms, such as JavaServer Pages (JSP) and servlets.

The EJB architecture was introduced by Sun Microsystems as the cornerstone of its strategy of pushing Java onto the server side. The EJB architecture aims at separating system-level issues such as communication, distribution, transactions, and security from actual business logic and domain-specific issues. EJB is all about letting developers focus on building domain functionality. The use of a standard application programming interface (API) and architecture allows developers to rely on off-the-shelf solutions for system and architecture problems, without being tied to a specific vendor.

The goals of the EJB architecture, as defined in the EJB specification, are as follows:

- To define a component architecture for the development of Java-based distributed business applications.
- To enable the mixing of components built by different vendors in providing an enterprise-level solution.
- To facilitate scenarios in which experts provide solutions for transactions, security, distribution, multithreading, and other system-level issues in a way that they can be used easily by domain experts building business applications.

- To address the entire software lifecycle and provide definitions by which EJB components can be used within tools during development time (much like JavaBeans address both the runtime and the design time issues).
- To define aspects of interoperability. Specifically, EJB relies on the Common Object Request Broker Architecture (CORBA) for distributed object interoperability; this does not mean that EJB interoperability is only related to CORBA, as many other API mappings and transports are also possible.

Enterprise JavaBeans Architecture

The EJB architecture attempts to take the idea of JavaBeans, discussed in the last chapter, one step further. Instead of simply providing a framework for building reusable software components, it provides a framework for building distributed, transaction-oriented components. This distinction has immense consequences. One of them is that while JavaBeans are merely development components for programmers, EJBs are *deployable* components that are ready for use. In a real-world distributed setting, the placement of objects on physical machines is usually determined at deployment time, not at development time. Furthermore, because this placement can change over time, it obviously is preferable that the placement can be modified easily without making software modifications.

Being deployable objects, EJBs must have a standard and well-defined deployment environment. To this end, the EJB architecture defines the concepts of containers and servers. *Containers* hold (or contain) EJB instances. The specification defines the mutual responsibilities of containers and EJB components, as well as their interactions. EJB containers are, in turn, contained in EJB servers. The original EJB specification did not determine the contract between the EJB server and the EJB container; this was left to the discretion of the vendors. As a result, it was not quite clear where the container ended and where the server began. In fact, if the server has only one container, there is no real difference between the server and the container. This problem was resolved with the introduction of the J2EE platform, discussed in Chapter 15. With J2EE, the concept of a container was extended, and the distinction between containers and servers was clarified.

An interesting note about containers: WebSphere 3.5.*x* allows multiple containers to be created, but this is not advised. The best practice in WebSphere 3.5.*x* is to have one container per application server. WebSphere 4.0 ends this limitation, thereby providing for more robust application deployments.

An enterprise bean can exist only within a container. The enterprise bean is never accessed directly, nor does instance creation take place directly. The container manages access to enterprise bean functionality, as well as instance creation and destruction. Because EJBs are distributed objects that are accessed remotely, the actual access is made via special proxy objects called *remote EJB objects*. These allow the bean developer to delegate the responsibility of managing transactions, persistence, communication, and security to the container. Figure 11-1 provides a schematic depiction of the EJB architecture.

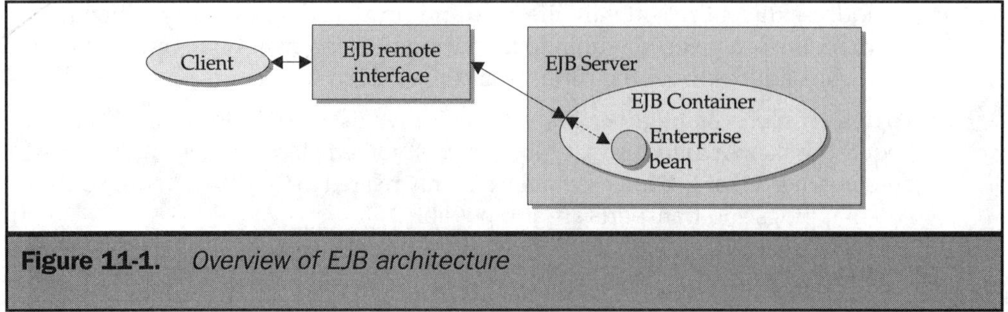

Figure 11-1. *Overview of EJB architecture*

While the relationship between an enterprise bean and the container holding it is a close one, the EJB specification requires that EJBs be portable among different containers. In other words, EJBs and containers are required to be fully decoupled. This means that all services provided to the enterprise bean by the container are well defined in the EJB specification.

In its quest to define a framework for distributed object-oriented systems, the EJB architecture must create the right balance between various contradictory requirements. On one hand, the framework must be simple so that it is easy to understand and use. On the other hand, EJBs target enterprise-level systems—very large, typically mission-critical, systems. Specifically, enterprise systems have strict performance and failure-resilience requirements, as well as other specialized requirements.

To achieve the correct balance between the various requirements and manage the inherent complexities of the issues at hand, the EJB specification takes a "divide-and-conquer" approach. The tasks and responsibilities relating to the EJB lifecycle are divided between several parties. Unlike JavaBeans, where only two parties (the bean developer and the bean user) are involved, in EJB there are six (!) different parties: the bean provider (or developer), the container provider, the server provider, the application developer, the application deployer, and the system administrator. These parties are referred to as *roles,* and some of the roles might be combined. As examples, the application deployer and the system administrator are sometimes the same person; and the same vendor usually provides the EJB container and the EJB server. The next section details the responsibilities of each role.

To allow the different parties to communicate with each other, an enterprise bean defines sets of properties that affect its runtime behavior. EJB properties are separated as metadata, or *descriptors,* to allow customization at setup and deployment time, similar to the way in which JavaBeans define the `BeanInfo` object and provide customization. However, there are differences in the nature of the properties. JavaBeans properties typically are related to user interfaces, whereas EJB properties involve control over issues related to distribution, such as transactions, security, and persistence.

EJB Roles

The EJB specification provides a clear-cut definition of the responsibilities of each role. By clearly defining the roles of each party, EJB facilitates the development of distributed and highly scalable applications in which products from different vendors can interoperate. The remainder of this section explains the different EJB roles.

The Bean Provider

The bean provider's role is to develop the EJB. This provider could be an in-house developer or a vendor of reusable software components. The most important role of the bean provider is to design the bean in a reusable manner. While the EJB architecture is designed to promote reusability, that is not to say that any EJB is reusable by definition. EJBs are truly reusable if they are designed properly. The main design choice for the bean developer is in the definition of "business" methods (methods in the application domain, as opposed to methods involving more prosaic issues such as persistence, transactions, and so on). EJB methods form the contract between the enterprise bean and users of the bean. The methods are grouped into an interface published by the EJB developer, and this interface must be applied by the bean implementation.

The bean developer must provide yet another interface called the *home interface,* which is defined for every EJB type. EJB home interfaces implement the commonly used "factory" design pattern. The factory is responsible for instantiating and destroying objects—in this case EJB objects. Another responsibility of the home interface is *bean lookup.* Bean lookup is used for acquiring a reference to a bean. This is not possible for all types of beans, only for *entity beans*—persistent beans that have an application-level identity. From the perspective of client code, object lookup involves two stages: locating the home interface and then using it to locate a specific object.

As part of the inherent support for distributed programming, client software never makes direct use of the enterprise bean. Instead of using object references, it holds references to remote "proxies" or "stubs" that, in turn, communicate with the container. The container provides the execution environment for the EJB. Because the container is responsible for managing system-level issues, it must be aware of any method invocations.

EJB Server Provider and EJB Container Provider

Theoretically, the roles of providing the server and the container are distinct, but in practice, the server is provided with the container implementation. However, the J2EE architecture allows for the introduction of new containers into a J2EE server.

The EJB container provides the execution environment for EJB. It provides all the required services for large, distributed applications such as security services, transaction services, communication services, and so on. The container handles all aspects of the bean lifecycle, as well as method invocation. From the application developer's standpoint, the fact that all these services are provided by the container has immense benefits. When relying on these services, EJB developers can ignore issues of security, transactions, resource management, lifecycle management, persistence, and multithreading. The container handles everything, and it is supposed to do so in an efficient manner.

To grant vendors some flexibility, the EJB specification allows "extended services" to be provided by the server or the container; these services are beyond the EJB specification. Such services might be aimed at advanced performance and reliability via load balancing and transparent failover, or support for legacy systems via EJB connectors. WebSphere offers connectors to IBM legacy systems such as Customer Information Control System (CICS), Encina, Information Management System (IMS), DB2, and MQSeries. Obviously, EJBs that rely on such extended services might be limited in the range of EJB containers and servers in which they can run. Note that some of these services were replaced by J2EE Connectors (see Chapter 15).

The Application Developer

The application developer is a person who utilizes available EJBs to construct an enterprise application. The available EJBs might be taken out of Java libraries provided by commercial vendors or developed in-house. While the available EJBs provide some functionality, they are usually implemented in a generic fashion, and if EJBs are taken from multiple sources, they might not be immediately interoperable. The application developer should provide the "glue" for connecting the different components. As EJBs are middle-tier software, they do not provide any user interface. The application developer should implement some user interface, which could be any Java interface such as JFC/Swing; in the J2EE model, it would typically be implemented using JSP and servlets. User interface code would invoke the EJBs. In addition, the application developer might be required to develop some EJBs that are needed for solving domain-specific problems or for connecting the different components.

The Application Deployer

The application deployer bridges the gap between the container and server provider and the application developer. The application deployer physically places the EJBs onto servers and containers. The deployer has the freedom to deploy the beans in any manner so that he or she can customize the installation to fit the available resources and their configuration. Typical considerations would be performance issues. The deployer attempts to place the beans so that there is some "locality of reference" (in other words, so that the clients invoking the beans will be as close as possible to the beans), but at the same time attempts to balance the load among different servers. Other considerations might be technical concerns, such as communication bandwidth between nodes or the existence of firewalls.

Another important responsibility of the deployer is security settings. The deployer can assign access rights to different EJB methods, as well as to Web resources. These rights should be assigned in a way that complies with the security policy of the organization and does not compromise the safety of the data stored in the system.

The System Administrator

The system administrator is in charge of troubleshooting any problems when the deployed application is being used. Various monitoring tools are at the administrator's disposal; in WebSphere, the Administrative Console provides such tools. Problems in execution could arise in various areas, such as in the hardware, the operating system, the Web server, the application server, and of course the application itself. The system administrator should be able to pinpoint the problem as much as possible, and then fix it or forward it back to the deployer or the application developer as required.

EJB Components

The EJB architecture provides a framework for building distributed transaction-oriented components. Like JavaBeans, EJB is a component model; as such, it defines the structure of an EJB component and describes the world in which it lives—an extremely important concept. A well-known thesis in philosophy is that to fully describe an entity, one must describe its surroundings and how it interacts with its environment. This is the approach taken by the EJB architecture. An EJB component is a Java component that implements business logic. As a component living within the EJB world, the EJB component must assume a well-defined environment and a set of interactions in which to participate. For example, the EJB specification defines the responsibilities of containers and the responsibilities of EJB components being managed by a container. It also fully defines the interaction between the container and the EJB component, thereby defining a structured world upon which an EJB builder can rely. This brings the task of building EJB components and EJB-based systems a little closer to being an engineering discipline than an art; that is the ultimate purpose of the computer science field known as software engineering.

The fundamentals of an EJB component's environment are defined as follows:

- An enterprise bean is developed to implement business functionality.
- Session beans typically handle the domain information and perform business functions, whereas entity beans store the information.
- An enterprise bean is not an island of its own. It lies within a container deployed within a server. It is never accessed directly; the container manages access to its functionality. This allows the responsibility of managing things like transactions and security to be moved from the enterprise bean to the container and the server. For example, the container exclusively performs instance creation of the enterprise bean type. This allows the container to manage lifecycle and transaction issues for the class.
- Enterprise beans and containers are fully *decoupled*, which means that multiple EJB-compliant containers can be used to manage instances of an enterprise bean. All services provided to the enterprise bean by the container are well defined in the EJB specification.
- An enterprise bean defines sets of properties that affect its runtime behavior. These properties are captured in a *deployment descriptor*.

For an EJB component to be used by client software, it must provide support in the following implementation areas:

- **Object identity** A unique identifier that can be used to identify an object. (Not all enterprise beans have an object identity visible at the application level.)
- **Method invocation** Business methods form the contract between the enterprise bean and, ultimately, the client. The methods are grouped into an interface that forms the contract the bean developer must satisfy.
- **Home interface** An interface that is defined for each EJB type. Within a home, each bean can be identified using the primary key, as long as the bean has an application-level identity. Object lookup, therefore, involves two stages: locating the home interface and using the primary key to locate a specific object. The home interface is stored by a naming service, and the client can access it using the standard Java Naming and Directory Interface (JNDI). An enterprise bean's home interface extends the javax.ejb.EJBHome interface.

Client software never actually uses the enterprise bean directly and never accesses the bean's functionality without first going through an intermediate container that manages most of the system-level issues and, therefore, must constantly be aware of what is happening to the enterprise bean. The effect is that each container of an enterprise bean must also support the interfaces defined by the EJB specification. This support usually requires some work of the container. For example, the container determines the transaction bracket and possibly changes it, and then delegates to the appropriate method in the enterprise bean.

A client using an enterprise bean can rely on the fact that the enterprise bean has a unique *identifier*. Creating this identifier is sometimes the responsibility of the enterprise bean and sometimes the responsibility of the container. For example, if the bean represents a *persistent* domain object, it will provide the object identifier, and the container will simply propagate this identifier to the clients when asked. On the other hand, a bean can be a *transient* object that is used by the client for performing certain tasks. Such an enterprise bean may be an extension of the client on the application server and may expire when the client is no longer using it. In this case, the bean's lifetime is cohesive with the client's, and its identity is not defined as a property of the bean itself; instead, the container may generate the object identity for use by the client—usually when it constructs the bean for the client.

Home interfaces define one or more `create` methods and zero or more `find` methods. Creation methods allow clients to create new instances of EJB components, and finder methods allow clients to look up a specific EJB. Both types of methods obviously must be supported by the enterprise bean itself; for example, an enterprise bean developer must provide an `ejbCreate` method for each of the `create` methods and must provide an `ejbFind` method for each of the `find` methods defined by the home interface. In addition, the container provides system-level functionality that is accessed by the client; some of this functionality requires that work be done by the enterprise bean developer.

Since an enterprise bean lives within an EJB container, the EJB specification also precisely defines the APIs used by the container when it manages the enterprise bean. The container is an important part of EJB because it allows an enterprise bean developer to rely on standard services handled by the container. The most important of these services is lifecycle management. Although lifecycle management is the container's responsibility, the container cannot manage the lifecycle without the full cooperation of the enterprise bean. This cooperation, or contract, between the enterprise bean and its container is defined in a set of interfaces that must be implemented by the enterprise bean. Specifically, an enterprise bean must implement a set of state management callbacks that are called by the container to notify the enterprise bean of important changes made as part of lifecycle operations. The interfaces are either `javax.ejb.SessionSynchronization` or `javax.ejb.EntityBean` interfaces, depending on whether the enterprise bean is a session bean or an entity bean. Other elements of this contract between an enterprise bean and its container include APIs through which a container can inform a bean of its current context and environment.

Finally, because EJB aims at the high-end market for component development, a standard mapping of enterprise bean interfaces to CORBA exists. This opens up the EJB architecture, making it truly a multivendor, multilanguage, and multiplatform architecture. The mapping for EJB to CORBA includes a number of important categories: the mapping of interfaces to CORBA Interface Definition Language (IDL), the propagation of an EJB transaction bracket as an Object Transaction Service (OTS) transaction context, support for the CORBA naming service, and the propagation of security information within a security context. By defining the mapping in terms of these categories, EJB elevates itself to full semantic as well as wire-level interoperability.

Session Enterprise Beans

Enterprise beans are categorized into two groups: session enterprise beans and entity enterprise beans. The major distinguishing feature between these two groups is persistence. Session beans represent server-side components that implement business logic but are not persistent, while entity beans guarantee full persistence of their state. This section focuses on session beans; the next section discusses entity beans at length.

A session bean implements business logic on behalf of a client. The session bean is not persistent and is not shared by multiple clients; in this respect it is a convenience mechanism for providing correct application partitioning. Application partitioning is an important concept in distributed computing that recognizes the need for business logic to be performed often at differing locations while continuing to support location transparency to the client software. A primary example of this is application partitioning as a facilitator of improved performance. Assume, for example, that a certain business function receives a small set of inputs and produces an output but is database intensive. Obviously, the application partition shown in Figure 11-3 will perform better than the partition shown in Figure 11-2. Session beans allow an application developer to partition the application so that some of the business logic processing occurs on the server on behalf of the client; the session bean is, therefore, a logical extension of the client process.

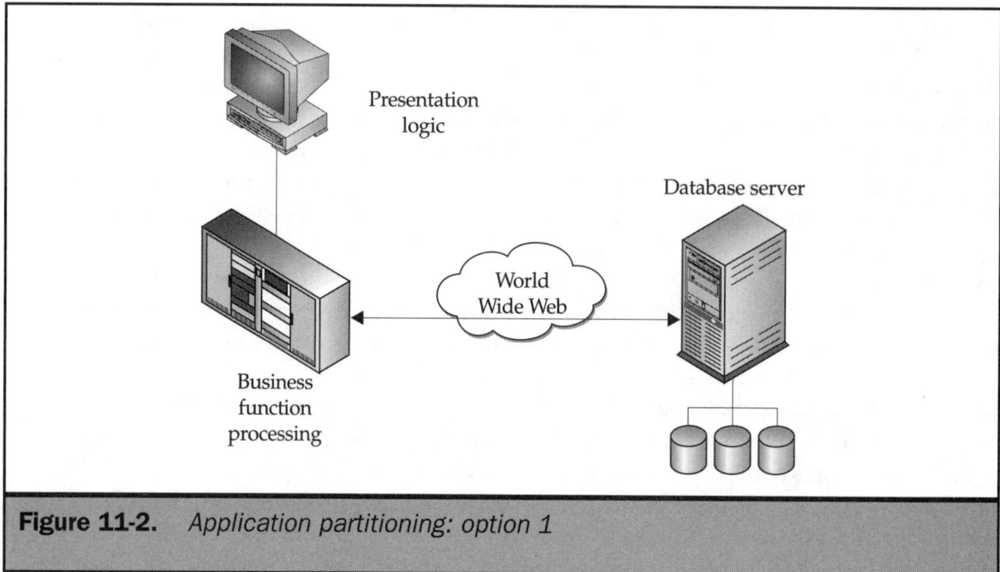

Figure 11-2. *Application partitioning: option 1*

A session bean does have an object identity; but as a nonpersistent entity, its object identity is also nonpersistent. Therefore, a session bean might live for a while, providing service to some client, and later be reborn with a different identity. So the object identity of a session bean is never an application-meaningful descriptor; at best, it might be used by the client for temporary convenience functions, such as placing it

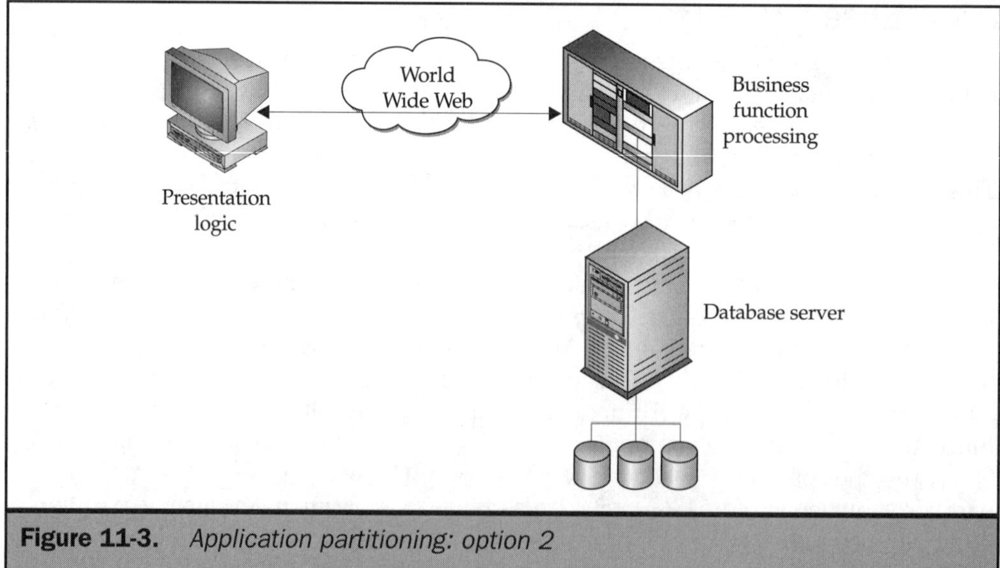

Figure 11-3. *Application partitioning: option 2*

within a hash table managed by the application. Note that while the session bean logically may be reborn to provide services to the same client, it is, in fact, a different object with a different identity and should not be confused with an entity object that can support a complex lifecycle. The session bean's identity cannot be used as a key and should, in principle, not be exposed to the client.

Access to a session bean's functionality is always through an *EJB object*, which exposes a session bean's interface as a remote interface using Java's Remote Method Invocation (RMI), layered over CORBA's Internet Inter-ORB Protocol (IIOP). All calls made on the EJB object are delegated to the enterprise bean. The user of a session bean's functionality does not have to be concerned about the precise location of the bean, as RMI and CORBA will make the remote nature of the invocations transparent. In addition to delegating the domain-level method calls to the enterprise bean, an EJB object provides a few methods for managing the EJB object itself, such as object comparison.

Like all enterprise beans, a session bean lives within an EJB container. The container manages the bean's lifecycle, access to the bean's methods, security, transactions, and more.

Using a container's lookup function, a client can access the home interface of the enterprise bean. The home interface, similar to the `BeanInfo` object, provides functions for creating new EJB objects, for removing an EJB object, and for accessing metadata information (implementing the `javax.ejb.EJBMetaData` interface) of the enterprise bean, which is useful for tools during design time. For example, the code fragment required to create a new `PartOrder` object is shown below. Note that the actual creation method (the constructor) is specific to the part order, but all creation methods are called using the home interface; the actual creation is always managed by the EJB container.

```
Context clientContext = new InitialContext();

PartOrderHome partOrderHome = javax.rmi.PortableRemoteObject.narrow(
      clientContext.lookup("applications/services/parts/orders"),
      PartOrderHome.class);

PartOrder aPartOrder = partOrderHome.create(
      new Date(),              // creation date
      "AT&T",                  // company name
      "Jane Doe",              // person ordering
      ...);
```

Figure 11-4 depicts a schematic view of the states a session bean typically goes through during its lifetime. A session bean is created when one of the home interface's creation methods is invoked. The enterprise bean is created on the server, and an object reference (possibly a remote reference) is returned to the caller (the EJB object). The client can then start invoking methods using the bean's handle.

When the client has finished using the bean and wants to release it, one of the removal methods should be called to destroy the bean. Removal methods can be called using either the EJB object or the home interface. In both cases, the result is the state in which the enterprise bean no longer exists but is still referenced by the client; the client

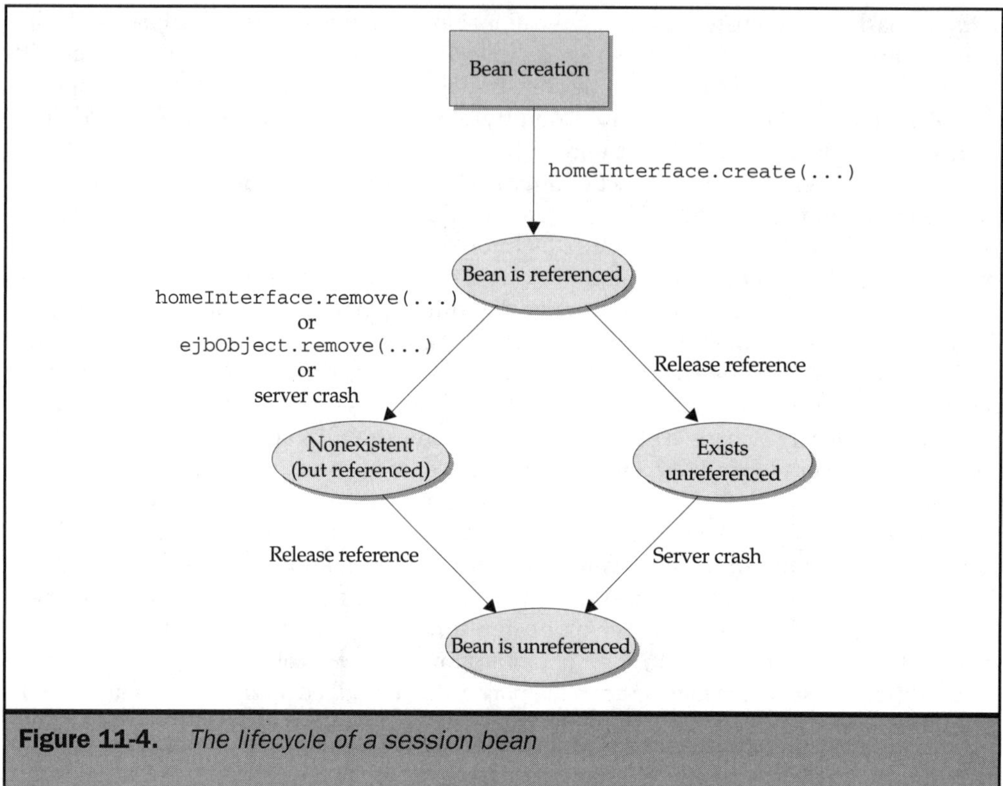

Figure 11-4. *The lifecycle of a session bean*

should then release the reference. If the client uses the handle when the enterprise bean no longer exists, a `NoSuchObjectException` will be raised. If the client releases the reference before it calls one of the removal methods, the enterprise bean will continue to exist until the server exits—either through a normal shutdown or a system crash. During that time, the client can reclaim the handle using a `getEJBObject` call to the EJB object (the handle), which returns the state machine to the state in which the enterprise bean exists and is referenced.

Calls made through the EJB object and through the container ultimately reach the enterprise bean. A session enterprise bean should implement the following methods defined in the `SessionBean` Java interface:

- **setSessionContext** Used by the container to set a bean's context; the context is managed by the container. The SessionContext object provides the following functions that are used by the enterprise bean:
  - **getEJBObject** Returns the handle object.
  - **getHome** Returns the home interface.
  - **getEnvironment** Returns the environment properties.

- **getCallerPrincipal** Returns the identity of the invoking client. This is a convenient function that allows the bean to configure its reply based on the identity of the calling object. For example, pricing information may differ based on whether the ordering entity is an internal or an external customer. A price book bean may therefore wish to know details regarding the object that requested pricing information.
- **isCallerInRole** Provides a bean with a testing method for matching a caller with a certain role.
- **setRollbackOnly** Allows the bean to guarantee that the current transaction may not be committed and that any changes made within this transaction bracket must eventually be discarded by a rollback.
- **getRollbackOnly** Returns a boolean value indicating whether or not the transaction is marked as rollback only.
- **getUserTransaction** Returns the javax.jts.UserTransaction, which provides direct access to the transaction and allows for manual handling of transaction bracketing.

- **ejbRemove** Allows the bean to perform any cleanup or finalization procedures. Because a session bean is not a persistent entity, such cleanup is usually simple. The container is responsible for managing the lifecycle for a bean; therefore, when the container removes a bean, it calls the ejbRemove method.
- **ejbPassivate** Called by the container when it intends to passivate a bean, allowing it to close resources or perform miscellaneous preparations so that, after reactivation, its state will be correct.
- **ejbActivate** Called by the container when a bean is activated. The bean can then perform any inverse operations required to prepare its state.

A session bean can also implement additional methods defined in the `SessionSynchronization` interface. These methods provide synchronization hooks allowing a session bean to tune its behavior in the context of a transaction.

- **afterBegin** Called when a transaction begins.
- **beforeCompletion** Called before the commit stage begins but after the client has completed its work. This allows the bean to make any preparations before the commit.
- **afterCompletion** Called after the transaction completes, whether by rollback or by successful commit. (A flag is passed as an argument.)

While a session bean is not a persistent entity, it can still manage state on behalf of its client; its nonpersistent nature simply implies that this state will not persist after the bean is destroyed. Distributed object applications generally can be classified as conforming to one of two models: the state-less model and the state-ful model. In a state-less model, the server does not maintain state on behalf of the client; during each invocation, the client must pass enough information to the server for the server to perform the operation successfully on behalf of the client. The HTTP Web model is state-less—that is, each request made by a browser for information from a Web server is independent and does not rely on previous requests. In a state-ful model, the server maintains a session for the client and is aware of some state parameters regarding that client. Both models of distributed interaction are legitimate, each being more appropriate in different cases. EJBs therefore supports both models.

When a session bean is deployed, it defines how it should be managed by its container. By specifying that the bean is state-less, the container is told that no conversational state needs to be maintained and that it is possible for the same bean to be used by multiple clients. (None of the clients need be aware of this fact because no state is managed within the server.) Alternatively, the container may be told that the bean is state-ful, in which case the container will manage the bean's conversational state on behalf of the client. The *conversational state* is defined as the bean's field values and every object that is reachable from one of the fields. Obviously, because object-based applications manage quite complex object graphs, this definition of the conversational state can easily include a large number of objects. Therefore, the conversational state is not coupled with transaction support. A session bean's conversational state is not transactional and is not rolled back when a bean's transaction is rolled back. The bean developer is responsible for correctly managing the conversational state in the context of transactions.

Note that while session beans are not persistent, they may be transactional in the sense of operations being atomic; the only difference is that the transaction outcome is not guaranteed to be persistent—or durable, a form of the fourth word in the transaction-defining acronym Atomicity, Consistency, Isolation, and Durability (ACID).

State-less beans should be viewed as workers belonging to a pool of service providers. The assignment of workers to clients is arbitrary, and creating a new instance of a state-less bean simply adds to the pool. The only allowed creation method in the home interface for a state-less session bean is a creation method that takes no arguments. The size of the worker pool is controlled by the container and is based on load parameters and availability times.

State-ful session beans have a much more elaborate lifecycle, as shown in Figure 11-5. A bean is created when a client invokes a `create` method on the home interface. The container then calls `newInstance` to create the bean and sets the context using `setSessionContext`. Finally, `ejbCreate` is called and an EJB object is returned to the client. The bean is then ready for use by the client.

As long as the client makes nontransactional calls, the bean stays in a nontransactional state. When a transactional method is called, the bean is included in a transaction; `afterBegin` is called, allowing the bean to perform any bean-specific handling. As long as other transactional methods are called, the bean stays in the transactional state. If a nontransactional method is called while the bean is in the transactional state, an error is flagged.

If the transaction is about to commit, the container makes the `beforeCompletion` call, which is guaranteed to be delivered before the actual commit. The same is true when the transaction is about to be rolled back. The end transaction status is passed as an argument to the `afterCompletion` call.

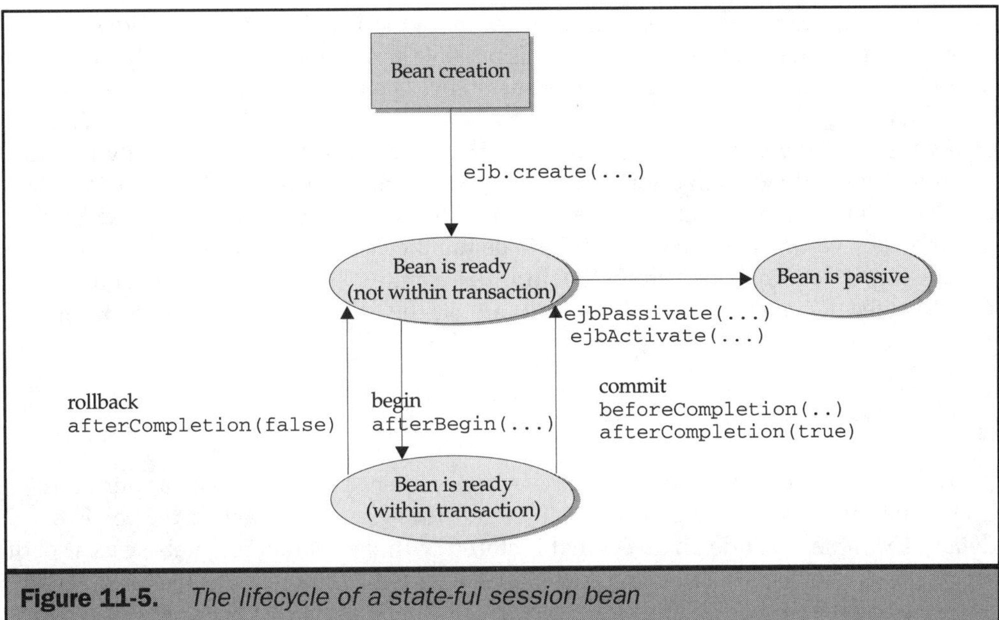

Figure 11-5. *The lifecycle of a state-ful session bean*

While the bean is in a nontransactional state, the container may decide to evict the bean from memory. In this case, it will call `ejbPassivate` to allow the bean to free up any resources it may currently be holding and prepare for its eviction. When the client later requests a service to be provided by this bean (recall that we are talking about state-ful beans), the container will reactivate the bean and call the `ejbActivate` method, giving the bean a chance to prepare itself.

Entity Enterprise Beans

Entity enterprise beans represent objects stored in some form of persistent storage. Entity beans include state information that can be saved between different uses of the object. As a persistent object, an entity bean has an object identity that is created at the same time the object is created and is fixed throughout the object's lifetime. The identity can be used to look up the object, and it serves as a primary key through which objects can be identified and compared.

Entity beans live within EJB containers that manage lifecycle, transactions, and security. In addition, containers manage the entity beans' persistence. Multiple clients can use the same entity bean concurrently. Synchronization is managed by the container in which the entity bean lives. A client accesses the entity bean by using the home interface, which returns an EJB object that serves as the handle to the bean. In this respect, the framework for entity beans is identical to session beans.

As with session beans, an entity bean requires a home interface that provides access to creation and finder methods. Unlike session beans, the home interface of an entity bean must implement the `findByPrimaryKey` method. This method provides access to entity beans using a primary key, which is possible because an entity bean is a persistent object that is uniquely identified by the primary key. Typical examples include an account number, a part order number, and a country name. A key is itself an object and can be of any type, as long as it is serializable. Note that a primary key is unique only within a home interface. The combination of a home interface and a primary key value is what uniquely identifies an object; in fact, if two objects have the same home interface and the same key value, they are considered to be identical.

The key is accessible by calling the `getPrimaryKey()` method implemented by the EJB object. Given two EJB objects, you can use the following to determine whether they are identical:

```
obj1.isIdentical(obj2)
```

As mentioned, an entity bean represents a persistent entity and is an application extension to an object residing in another system—the system that handles the persistence details. Examples include an object that is stored within a relational database as a set of records and an object that interfaces with a legacy application responsible for the persistence details.

Entity bean persistence comes in two forms: Bean-Managed Persistence (BMP) and Container-Managed Persistence (CMP). In the case of BMP, the bean itself is responsible for implementing object persistence. For example, the bean developer may use Java Database Connectivity (JDBC) or Java Structured Query Language (JSQL) calls to implement load and save capabilities directly into the bean. In CMP, the container performs database access on behalf of the bean. For the container to construct the appropriate data access calls, it requires descriptive metadata from the bean. The EJB specification calls for a `containerManagedFields` deployment descriptor to be provided by the entity bean.

There are advantages and disadvantages to each of the persistence mechanisms. BMP is sometimes necessary for specialized behavior; however, you have to do all the hard work yourself. BMP also means that a lot is hard coded into the bean and cannot remain persistence neutral. CMP delays the coupling with the data store until the bean is deployed in some container, thus making the entity bean inherently more reusable.

Figure 11-6 illustrates the lifecycle of an entity enterprise bean. An entity enterprise bean is created when the container calls the `newInstance` method, after which the context is set by calling the `setEntityContext` method. At this point, the instance is part of a pool; it has been created but has not been associated with an EJB object, nor does it have any distinguishing data. All instances in the pool are equivalent. The next transition is to the ready state; this can be performed either by using an `ejbCreate` method or by calling an `ejbActivate` method following an `ejbFind` method invocation. Immediately after calling an `ejbCreate` method, the container calls the `ejbPostCreate` method. At the time the `ejbPostCreate` method is called, the object identity is already available; the call allows the bean to take further action that may require the object identity. The first case discussed creates a new object to service

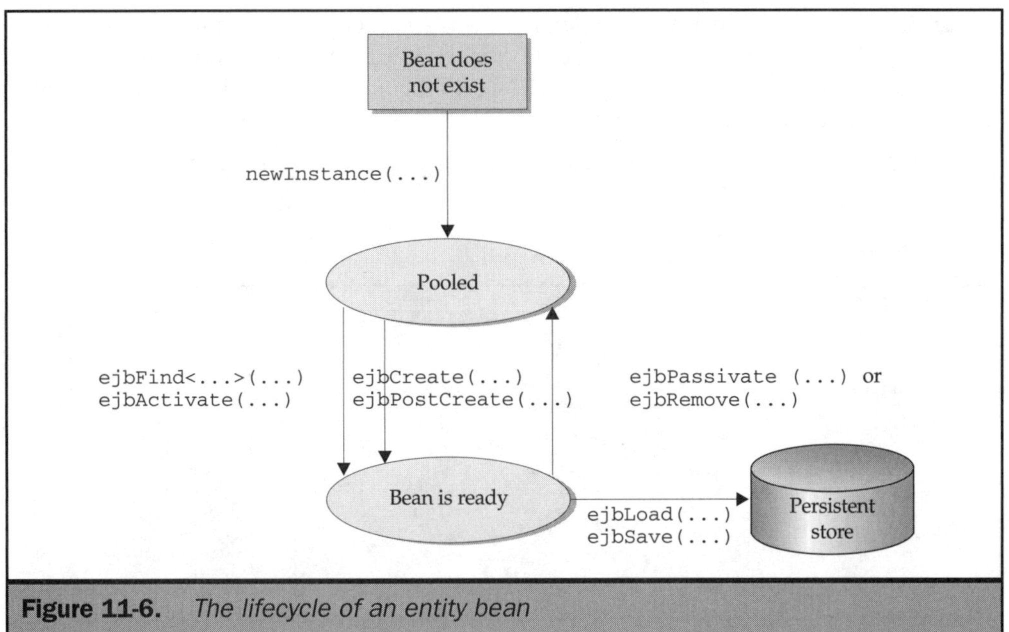

Figure 11-6. *The lifecycle of an entity bean*

the client, while the second allows for using an existing object. Once it enters the ready state, the container will activate the `ejbLoad` method to retrieve the bean's data from its persistent store; after that, the container may periodically save the data using `ejbStore` or refresh the data using `ejbLoad`. When the work is complete, the bean will transition back to the pooled state using either `ejbPassivate` or `ejbRemove`. Once back in the pool, the entity bean no longer has the object identity, and it may be assigned to a new object the next time around.

Since entity beans represent domain objects, an entity bean may be accessed by two concurrent clients. Synchronization of concurrent access is one of the services provided to the bean user and the bean developer by the container. It is the responsibility of the container to ensure correct synchronization between concurrent clients using the same entity bean. Figure 11-7 illustrates the two possible management strategies. In the case at the top of the figure, the container manages two entity beans accessed via the same EJB object. Each of the two beans lives within a different transaction context—that is, each transaction belongs to a different client. Ultimate synchronization is performed by the data store when calling the `ejbLoad` and `ejbStore` methods. In the lower case, the container manages exclusive access to the bean through the EJB object. Only one bean exists, and access to its functionality through the EJB object is serialized. In most cases, the first scenario is preferable for the following reasons:

- Better performance can be achieved.
- Database synchronization is usually more robust and has more features than container synchronization.

- In complex applications, the database is often used by many parts in the system such as the reporting module, data extraction procedures, and so on. It is much safer, therefore, to rely on transaction and locking management at the database level than within the EJB world.
- Containers do not need to incorporate complex locking and serialization code.

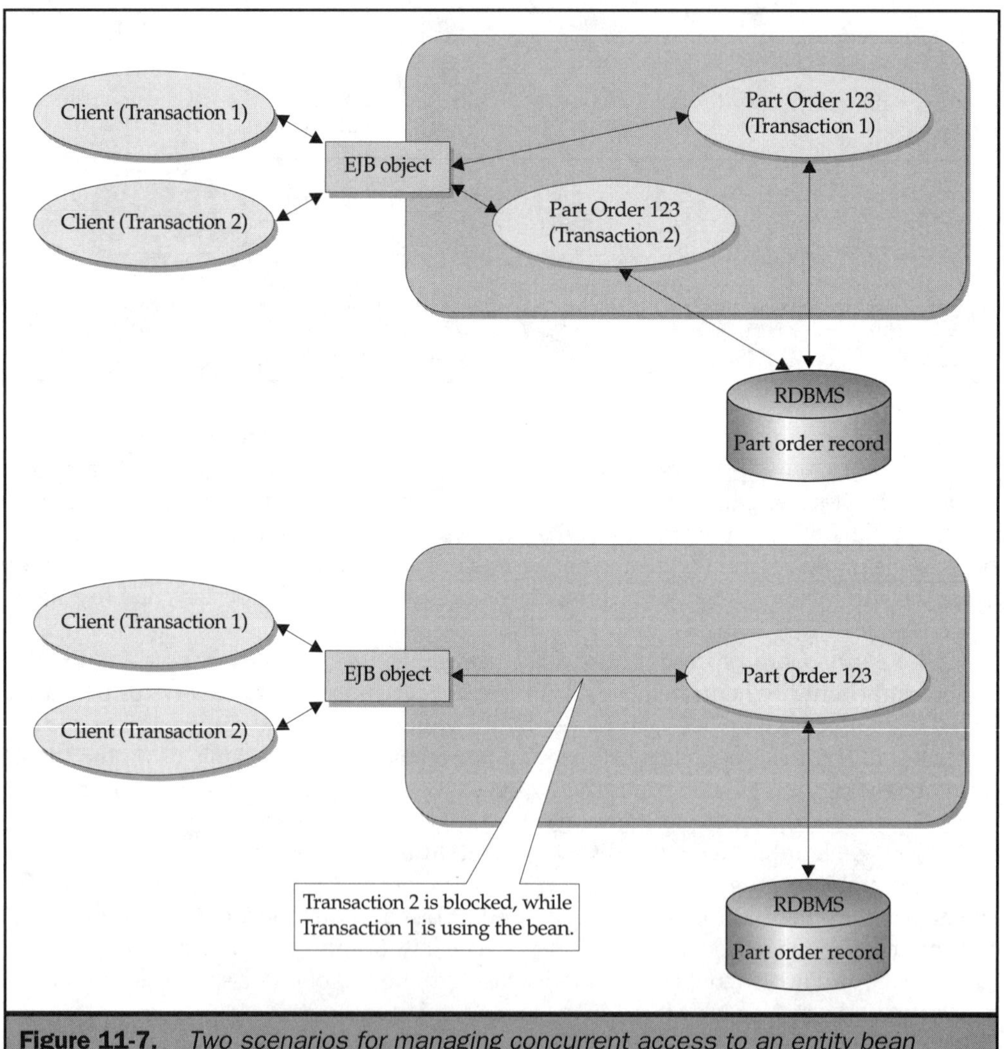

Figure 11-7. *Two scenarios for managing concurrent access to an entity bean*

The EJB Transaction Model

Support for distributed transactions is perhaps the primary feature making EJB attractive to enterprise software developers. Building support for distributed transactions into an application is a difficult task that is alleviated by using EJB. By moving the responsibility for managing transactions from the bean developer to the container and server provider, EJB simplifies application development and ensures that the difficult issues involving transactions are handled by experts.

EJB transaction support mirrors the CORBA Object Transaction Service (OTS) and supports the flat transaction model. OTS defines required support for a flat transaction model and optional support for *nested* transactions, which allow for transactions to be started within the context of another transaction. Each transaction manages its own change set. When a nested transaction is rolled back, all changes made within that nested transactions are discarded. If the nested transaction is committed, the changes made within it become part of the enclosing transaction's change set, to be committed or rolled back by the enclosing transaction. In a nested model, the top-level transactions often correspond to the database transactions. In this case, the nested transactions are limited in that often they are not durable (that is, persistent) because right up to the moment in which a top-level commit occurs, the information is not stored in the database. EJB transaction support stays with the flat transaction model; this decision is based on the fact that today's database systems and transaction monitors support the flat transaction model.

EJB uses the Java Transaction Service (JTS), and specifically the Java Transaction API (JTA). JTS maps the OTS API to the Java programming language; that is, it maps the OTS IDL definitions to Java using the IDL-to-Java language mapping. In addition, JTS is a Java mapping for the X/Open XA interface standard. The JTA provides a convenient set of Java interfaces to be used for transaction processing. Such conformance to standards ensures that JTS will remain the standard for transaction handling in Java.

The JTS `javax.transaction` package defines the application-level demarcation APIs that allow transaction bracketing to be defined by the application developer. EJB relies on this interface and, more specifically, on the `javax.transaction.UserTransaction` interface. (The EJB container provider needs to implement only this interface.) Bean developers and clients make demarcation calls using APIs in this package.

Transaction demarcation can be performed by the client, the bean, or the container. Demarcation performed by the container is the simplest because both client and bean are oblivious to transactions. Obviously, the container must use policy information defined by the bean because the container is a generic entity that must adapt its behavior to the bean. In the case of transactions, the bean defines a demarcation policy using the transaction attribute. The container uses the fact that access to bean functionality must go through the container to manage transaction demarcation. The actual decision about what to do is based on the transaction attribute defined by the bean. Note that the policy may be defined globally for the entire bean or for one bean method at a time; it is therefore possible for different transactional behaviors to occur for different methods. For example, a bean can set its transaction attribute so that every method invocation must reside within its own transaction. In this case, the container will start a new transaction for every call made on the bean and manage the propagation of that transaction context if the bean makes additional calls during the processing of the original invocation. This scenario is shown in Figure 11-8.

Possible transaction attribute values are as follows:

- **TX_NOT_SUPPORTED** By using this value, the bean notifies the container that it does not support transactions. Invocations coming through the container will not be within a transaction. The container guarantees this by suspending any transaction that is active during calls made on the bean.
- **TX_BEAN_MANAGED** This attribute is used by the bean when it intends to use explicit demarcation and wants to notify the container that it should not manage transactions on its behalf.
- **TX_REQUIRED** This attribute is used by beans that want to ensure that any processing is performed within a transaction. If the call is made within a transaction started by a client, the bean invocation is performed within the transaction. Otherwise, the container is responsible for starting a transaction before handing control over to the bean. The container is also responsible for committing the transaction before returning control to the caller.
- **TX_SUPPORTS** Used by beans that want to be invoked within the same scope as the client. If the client has a transaction open when it calls the bean, the bean will perform within the transaction of the caller; otherwise, it will perform without an active transaction.

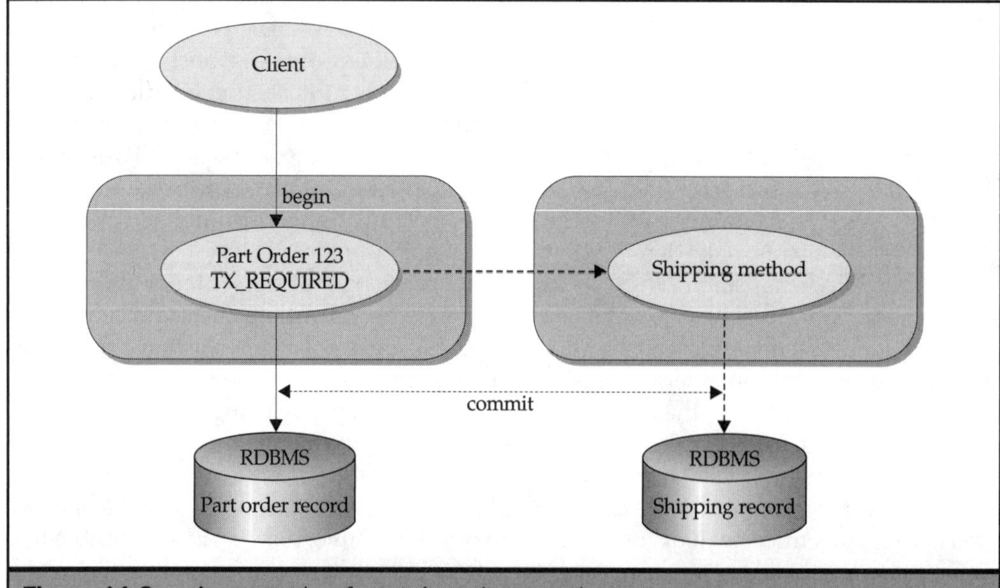

Figure 11-8. *An example of container demarcation*

- **TX_REQUIRES_NEW** Beans using this value inform their container that they need to be invoked within the scope of a new transaction. No matter what the transaction state of the client, the container always opens a new transaction that is active throughout the operation of the bean. When the bean completes, the container commits the transaction and resumes the suspended client transaction.
- **TX_MANDATORY** This attribute is similar to TX_SUPPORTS in that the bean is activated within the transaction of the client. However, if a client without an open transaction tries to make the call, a TransactionRequired exception is raised. This attribute is used by beans that need to be invoked within the context of the client transaction but want to guarantee that they cannot be invoked without a transaction.

Another attribute that must be defined by beans for the container to manage transactions on its behalf is the transaction isolation level that controls the locking options for reads. These values mirror the options available in the `java.sql.Connection` interface. Possible values for transaction isolation levels are

- **TRANSACTION_READ_UNCOMMITTED** It is possible to read data that is marked as dirty (dirty reads); uncommitted data can be read.
- **TRANSACTION_READ_COMMITTED** Dirty reads are prevented; only committed data can be read.
- **TRANSACTION_REPEATABLE_READ** Dirty reads and nonrepeatable reads are prevented.
- **TRANSACTION_SERIALIZABLE** Transactions are serialized; one transaction must complete for another to proceed.
- **TRANSACTION_NONE** No transaction is used.

Although container demarcation is certainly the simplest model for the client and for bean developers, sometimes the set of possible values allowed as transaction attributes does not provide fine enough control over transaction demarcation. Both bean-managed and client-managed demarcation are allowed under the EJB transaction model. For bean-managed demarcation, the bean will be defined using the `TX_BEAN_MANAGED` transaction attribute, which informs the container that it should not manage transactions on behalf of the bean. The bean can then use the `javax.transaction.UserTransaction` interface. Beans that do not define `TX_BEAN_MANAGED` as their transaction attribute are not allowed to make direct calls to the underlying transaction manager. Alternatively, the client itself can use the `javax.transaction.UserTransaction` interface to begin, commit, and roll back transactions.

Because the container and the server can manage transactions, transaction-related exceptions (specifically, `TransactionRolledbackException`, `Transaction RequiredException`, and `InvalidTransactionException`) can be raised. Any exception-handling mechanism is generally a mechanism designed for situations in which the error *detector* (the object that raises the exception) can be a different object than the error *handler* (the object that catches the exception and tries to take corrective measures). Therefore, raising an exception within the context of a container-managed transaction cannot automatically mean that the transaction must be marked for rollback only. It is quite possible that the client having caught the exception can fix the problem and continue with a follow-up call to the business method. The only case in which the client can assume that the current transaction has been marked for rollback is when the `TransactionRolledbackException` exception is raised. Alternatively, the exception handler can use the explicit test of `getRollbackOnly()` to verify the status of the active transaction. Beans that manage their own transaction processing (that is, those that use `TX_BEAN_MANAGED`) should use the `setRollbackOnly()` call before raising the exception, depending on whether the error they have discovered is such that it should not allow the changes made thus far to commit.

The EJB Distribution Model

EJB targets large-scale, distributed object applications. Distribution is therefore fundamental to the definition of EJB. Application programming in the EJB world involves building the enterprise beans and the clients using the business functionality implemented by the beans. The containers, servers, and other EJB infrastructure objects are provided by vendors and are used to simplify the building of distributed applications. Therefore, the EJB distribution model must be simple enough so that applications programmers can use it, yet powerful enough to build mission-critical and large-scale applications.

To accomplish this, the EJB distribution model uses a proven distribution technology based on *proxies* and object *stubs*. The EJB distribution model is not a new model; it uses standard Java RMI based on the CORBA distribution model. Distribution transparency is complete from both sides. Enterprise bean functionality may be accessed locally or remotely, and clients can access enterprise beans with no regard to their actual physical location. Neither the client nor the enterprise bean is aware of its peer's location.

The Java RMI stubs created involve the EJB object and the home interface object. Since the EJB object is the interface object through which functionality is accessed, it is only natural for it to be the object for which a Java RMI stub is created. In addition, the home interface gets its own RMI stub; this is necessary to initiate the connection with the enterprise bean, either through creation or through a finder process. Using Java RMI as the stubs and interfaces for supporting distribution in EJB does not infer the underlying wire-level protocol. In fact, the preferred solution for EJB in terms of the network protocol is CORBA IIOP. By using IIOP, EJB ensures that its distribution model remains interoperable and open to interfacing with non-Java objects and legacy systems. The basing of EJB on CORBA IIOP is quite natural; after all, the distribution model is identical, EJB transactions are based on the CORBA OTS model, and both use the same object model. Even the naming issue is resolved by mapping the CORBA naming service, which is part of Common Object Services (COS), to the JNDI API. Finally, EJB security, discussed in the following section, is mapped to CORBA security using `CORBA::Principal` for mapping the user ID, IIOP over the Secure Socket Layer (SSL) for client authentication and encryption, and Secure IIOP (SECIIOP) for mapping to a specific security mechanism such as GSSKerberos.

EJB Security

As in transactions, the primary goal of EJB in terms of its security infrastructure is to provide a set of interfaces that allow the responsibility for implementing security to be moved from the enterprise bean developer to the container and server implementer. This does not mean that an enterprise bean cannot control security; it means that mechanisms are provided so that the typical enterprise bean can declaratively define what its security attributes are, allowing the implementation details to be handled by the server and container. As in transactions, this is achieved through a set of security attributes used at deployment time.

The security attributes in the EJB deployment descriptor define a list of authorized users, each authorized entry being of type `java.security.Principal`—the standard interface in Java used for access control identification and authorization.

Additional deployment attributes related to security include the `RunAsMode` and `RunAsIdentity` attributes. The `RunAsMode` attribute defines the security identity that will be propagated when the bean makes additional calls while servicing a client request. Possible values that may be assumed by this attribute are as follows:

- **CLIENT_IDENTITY** This value is used when the call made by the bean should assume the security information of the client making the original call; the bean servicing the second call will think that the original client made the call (in terms of security). This is shown in Figure 11-9.
- **SYSTEM_IDENTITY** The call will use the identity of a privileged system account.
- **SPECIFIED_IDENTITY** The call will be made using a specific user account.

The `RunAsIdentity` attribute is relevant only when the `RunAsMode` attribute has a `SPECIFIED_IDENTITY` value; in this case, the `RunAsIdentity` attribute defines the actual user identity to be used when making the second call.

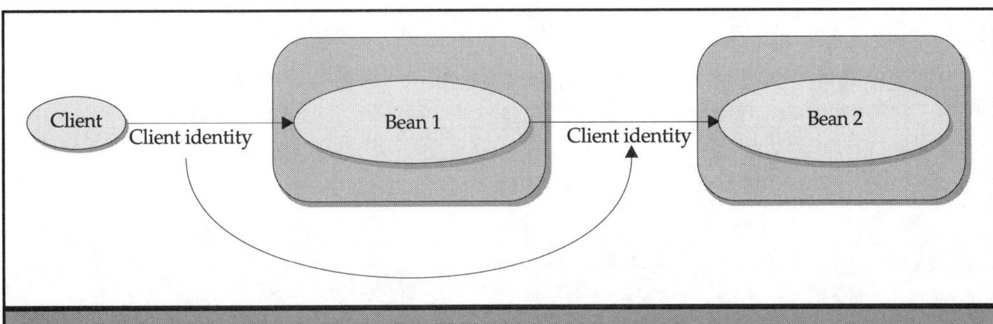

Figure 11-9. *How the CLIENT_IDENTITY attribute is used*

Summary

The EJB component model is the main programming model used in server-side applications. It brings structure and consistency to the most complex aspect of enterprise applications—server-side processing, which includes transaction management and persistence management. We have described the lifecycle of entity beans and session beans and have outlined when you should use each type. We have also described the architecture in terms of the EJB container, the EJB server, the client, and the developer roles. More detailed discussions on the development and usage of EJBs within WebSphere are covered in Chapters 29 through 34.

Chapter 12

Extensible Markup Language (XML)

Extensible Markup Language (XML) is one of the newer members of WebSphere's technology foundation. Starting with version 3.*x*, all WebSphere Application Servers include many of the XML libraries and maintain a lot of their own metadata in XML. Version 4.0 has taken this to a new level; it uses XML throughout the product, both by supporting XML parsing and generating and by using XML as the basis for more advanced technologies, such as Web services.

This chapter provides information on the various libraries with which you should be familiar when working with XML. Later chapters will delve into the uses of XML for building and deploying applications and will discuss the use of the Document Object Model (DOM), the Simple API for XML (SAX), and XSL Transformations (XSLT). While working with XML within WebSphere means working with Java libraries that create or process XML documents, the topics discussed in this chapter hold true for all XML processing, regardless of the programming language being used.

The New "Silver Bullet"

XML is the new "silver bullet" of the information technology (IT) world—that is, it is the solution for many difficult IT problems. XML is being used today as the basis for integration and automation—two keys to efficient deployment of complex information systems. In addition, XML is perhaps the single most important infrastructure component for e-business applications, because it is the key to allowing systems created by different vendors to talk to one another and share data. It is also the basis for Enterprise Application Integration (EAI) systems such as Vitria, TIBCO, MQSeries, Web Methods, Cross Worlds, and more.

Everywhere you look, you see vendors and developers scurrying to XML—and for good reason. XML is a standard that was developed by the World Wide Web Consortium (W3C) to improve data sharing and formatting over the Web; in general, it supports the notion of tagged data in a way that preserves the semantics of the domain. XML is an application (that is, a subset) of the Standard Generalized Markup Language (SGML), but it is much simpler to use. It is more powerful than Hypertext Markup Language (HTML); in fact, HTML is a subset of XML. Therefore, XML is just the right combination of SGML's powerful expression options and HTML's simplicity, and it is already slated to become the lingua franca of the Web. In addition, it promises advances in other areas, such as business-to-business applications, Electronic Data Interchange (EDI), and document management.

XML is the center of intensive research and development, both within the W3C and throughout the industry. As a standard, it is the basis for many other standards that are being developed by the W3C—such as the Extensible Linking Language (XLL), the DOM, SAX, and XSLT. All of these specifications can be found on the W3C site at *http://www.w3.org*, as well as on other sites—such as those for OASIS and most major vendors, including IBM, Microsoft, Sun, and Oracle.

XML is already an important technology used for e-business applications, and we are sure this trend will accelerate quickly to the point where XML and e-business are almost synonymous. A huge number of applications use XML today, and the sources for these applications include more than the W3C and commercial vendors. For example, the Financial Products Markup Language (FpML) is an application of XML that describes financial products such as derivatives and swaps. It is being developed by JPMorgan and PricewaterhouseCoopers and is being distributed under the Mozilla license; an example of an FpML document is shown in Listing 12-1.

Note *An obvious question is "Why would JPMorgan publish source code in which it has invested, which could then be used by its competitors to a technological advantage?" The answer is, obviously, not simply that the people at JPMorgan are "nice." It is because companies such as JPMorgan understand that they exist in a new Web and e-business paradigm in which open standards enable services and systems that were never possible before. XML is leading this charge.*

Listing 12-1 FpML example

```
<?xml version="1.0" standalone="no"?>
<!-- Copyright (c) 1999 by J.P.Morgan and PricewaterhouseCoopers.
PricewaterhouseCoopers refers to the individual member firms of the world
wide PricewaterhouseCoopers organization. All rights reserved.
-->
<!-- version 1.0b2 : August 6, 1999 -->
<fpml:FpML xmlns:fpml="urn:fpml-FpML"
 xmlns:t="urn:fpml-type"
 xmlns:d="urn:fpml-date"
 xmlns:m="urn:fpml-money"
 xmlns:r="urn:fpml-rate">

<fpml:Trade>
 <fpml:tradeIDs>
  <tid:TradeIDs xmlns:tid="urn:fpml-TradeID">
   <tid:TradeID>
    <tid:partyReference>ABC Trust</tid:partyReference>
    <tid:transactionReferenceNumber>237732</tid:transactionReferenceNumber>
   </tid:TradeID>
   <tid:TradeID>
    <tid:partyReference>XYZ Group</tid:partyReference>
    <tid:transactionReferenceNumber>1230</tid:transactionReferenceNumber>
   </tid:TradeID>
   <tid:TradeID>
    <tid:partyReference>CDF Inc.</tid:partyReference>
    <tid:transactionReferenceNumber>237732</tid:transactionReferenceNumber>
   </tid:TradeID>
   <tid:TradeID>
    <tid:partyReference>TUV Ltd.</tid:partyReference>
```

```
      <tid:transactionReferenceNumber>1230</tid:transactionReferenceNumber>
    </tid:TradeID>
    <tid:TradeID>
      <tid:partyReference>MNO LLC</tid:partyReference>
      <tid:transactionReferenceNumber>237732</tid:transactionReferenceNumber>
    </tid:TradeID>
    <tid:TradeID>
      <tid:partyReference>HIJ.com</tid:partyReference>
      <tid:transactionReferenceNumber>1230</tid:transactionReferenceNumber>
    </tid:TradeID>
   </tid:TradeIDs>
  </fpml:tradeIDs>
 </fpml:Trade>

 </fpml:FpML>
```

Extensible Markup Language

The beginning of XML was back in 1996, with a working group chaired by Jon Bosak of Sun Microsystems. XML was designed as a subset of SGML, with the following goals in mind:

- XML should be simple to use on the Internet.
- XML should support a wide variety of applications.
- XML should make it simple for application developers to build software that processes XML documents.
- XML documents must be readable to humans in native XML form.
- Creating an XML document should be a simple task.

One could say that the design goal of XML was for it to be a subset of SGML—thereby maintaining SGML's powerful feature set—while being simple to use.

XML is a format that allows documents to be structured. Therefore, the XML standard primarily describes the XML document. An XML document has a physical structure that is composed of entities. Each XML document has exactly one entity, called the *root entity*; all other entities must belong to the root entity. You define XML entities with a start tag and an end tag, in much the same way that you define many elements in HTML. When one entity is embedded in another, the start and end tags of the embedded entity must both reside within the start and end tags of the embedding entity. For example, if you want to describe a contact that has a phone number, you might embed the entities as follows:

```
<contact>
   <name>Jane Doe</name>
```

```
        <phone>201-861-7533</phone>
    </contact>
```

An empty tag—that is, an element containing no data—can be specified with start and end tags that have nothing in between, or with a simple *self-closing* start tag. For example, a contact may have two alternative phone numbers; if these tags are empty, you can use the following XML entity:

```
<contact>
        <name>Jane Doe</name>
        <phone>201-861-7533</phone>
        <altPhone1></altPhone1>
        <altPhone2/>
   </contact>
```


XML documents include entities of many types. Most entities reflect the information embedded within the XML document and the semantics of the domain being described by the document. Many other constructs, in addition to elements, comprise a typical XML document. For example, comments can be embedded into XML documents using syntax familiar to HTML developers, as shown here:

```
<!-- note that the <contact> here is not really a tag;
  it is part of the comment and will be ignored by
  applications, parsers, and other XML tools (except
  to view it as a comment).
  -->
```

XML Example: API Integration

Before moving on, let's look at some more complete examples, beginning with an example of application programming interface (API) integration. (After all, nothing beats real-world code.) Figure 12-1 shows a message that contains XML in the body; it is being sent to the ViryaNet Integration Server as an HTTP request. The XML represents the data required to activate an API that is defined in the ViryaNet system. In this example, an application is sending a message to the ViryaNet service hub to create a call. The application sending the message could be a call-center application, a trouble-ticketing application, or a provisioning system. By allowing messages to be phrased as XML, the ViryaNet Integration Server is open to any XML-enabled platform.

As Figure 12-1 shows, the message has two main parts—the *header* and the *body* of the message. These should not be confused with the HTTP header and body; all the XML code resides as part of the HTTP body. The *header* includes information about the message itself that is meaningful to the transport level of the ViryaNet Integration

Server (for example, what the message is and when it was sent). The second part, embedded within the `<input>` tag, is the arguments being sent as part of the message.

One important thing for you to note in Figure 12-1 is that all data in the file is encapsulated in a CDATA element. This element indicates that the content should be read as raw data and not interpreted. This means that you can include all forms of control codes and invisible characters that may have special meaning to various parsers. If you want your content to be read as data, and you do not control what the sender will package up, the safest thing to do is to encapsulate the content in CDATA elements.

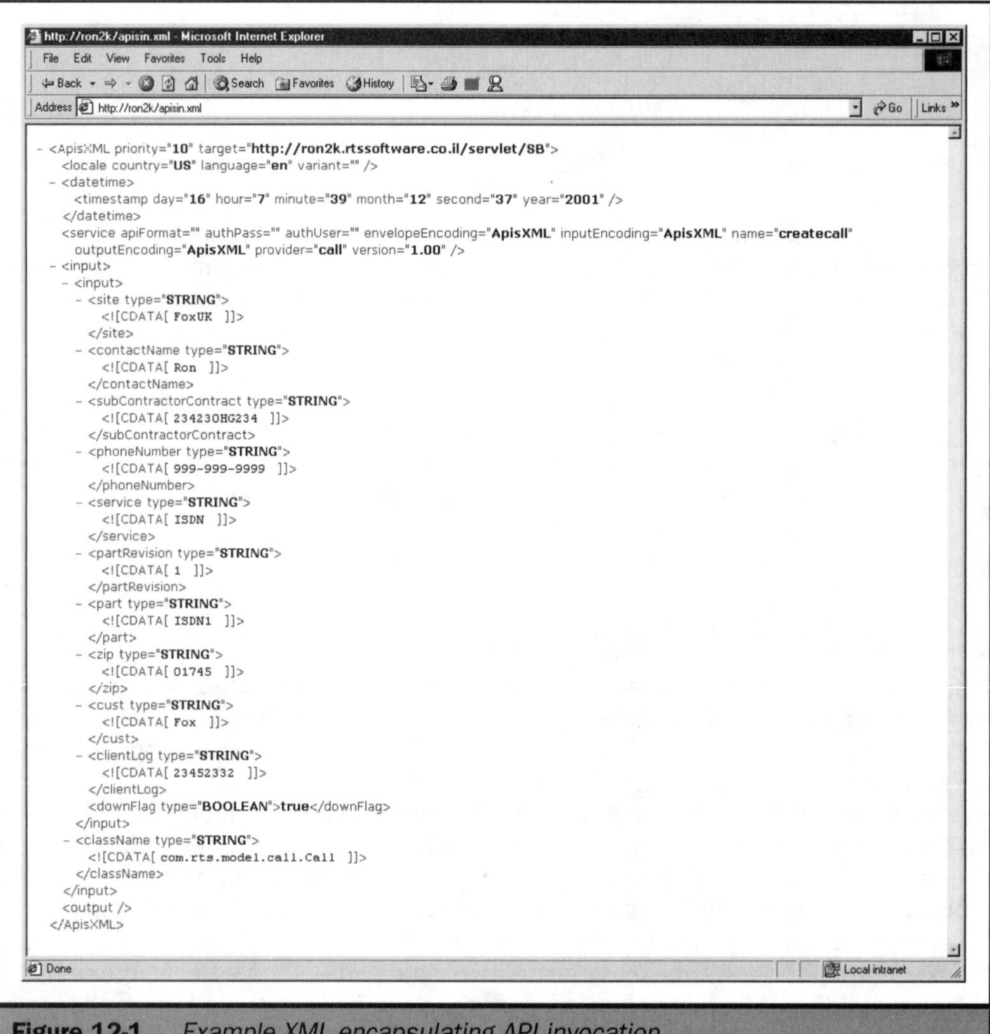


```
- <ApisXML priority="10" target="http://ron2k.rtssoftware.co.il/servlet/SB">
    <locale country="US" language="en" variant="" />
  - <datetime>
      <timestamp day="16" hour="7" minute="39" month="12" second="37" year="2001" />
    </datetime>
    <service apiFormat="" authPass="" authUser="" envelopeEncoding="ApisXML" inputEncoding="ApisXML" name="createcall"
      outputEncoding="ApisXML" provider="call" version="1.00" />
  - <input>
    - <input>
      - <site type="STRING">
          <![CDATA[ FoxUK ]]>
        </site>
      - <contactName type="STRING">
          <![CDATA[ Ron ]]>
        </contactName>
      - <subContractorContract type="STRING">
          <![CDATA[ 234230HG234 ]]>
        </subContractorContract>
      - <phoneNumber type="STRING">
          <![CDATA[ 999-999-9999 ]]>
        </phoneNumber>
      - <service type="STRING">
          <![CDATA[ ISDN ]]>
        </service>
      - <partRevision type="STRING">
          <![CDATA[ 1 ]]>
        </partRevision>
      - <part type="STRING">
          <![CDATA[ ISDN1 ]]>
        </part>
      - <zip type="STRING">
          <![CDATA[ 01745 ]]>
        </zip>
      - <cust type="STRING">
          <![CDATA[ Fox ]]>
        </cust>
      - <clientLog type="STRING">
          <![CDATA[ 23452332 ]]>
        </clientLog>
        <downFlag type="BOOLEAN">true</downFlag>
      </input>
    - <className type="STRING">
        <![CDATA[ com.rts.model.call.Call ]]>
      </className>
    </input>
    <output />
  </ApisXML>
```

Figure 12-1. *Example XML encapsulating API invocation*

XML Example: Data Files

The second example, shown in Figure 12-2, is a message file. All messages of the ViryaNet service hub are stored within an XML file and are used by the server when it needs to display a message to the user on the Web browser. An important point to note here is that the file is called *PortalMessages_en,* meaning that it is the XML file used for message requests coming in with an English locale. Whenever a request comes in from a Web browser or through the ViryaNet Integration Server, it includes a locale value. (Note that the header of the request, shown in Figure 12-1, has a locale parameter.) When something

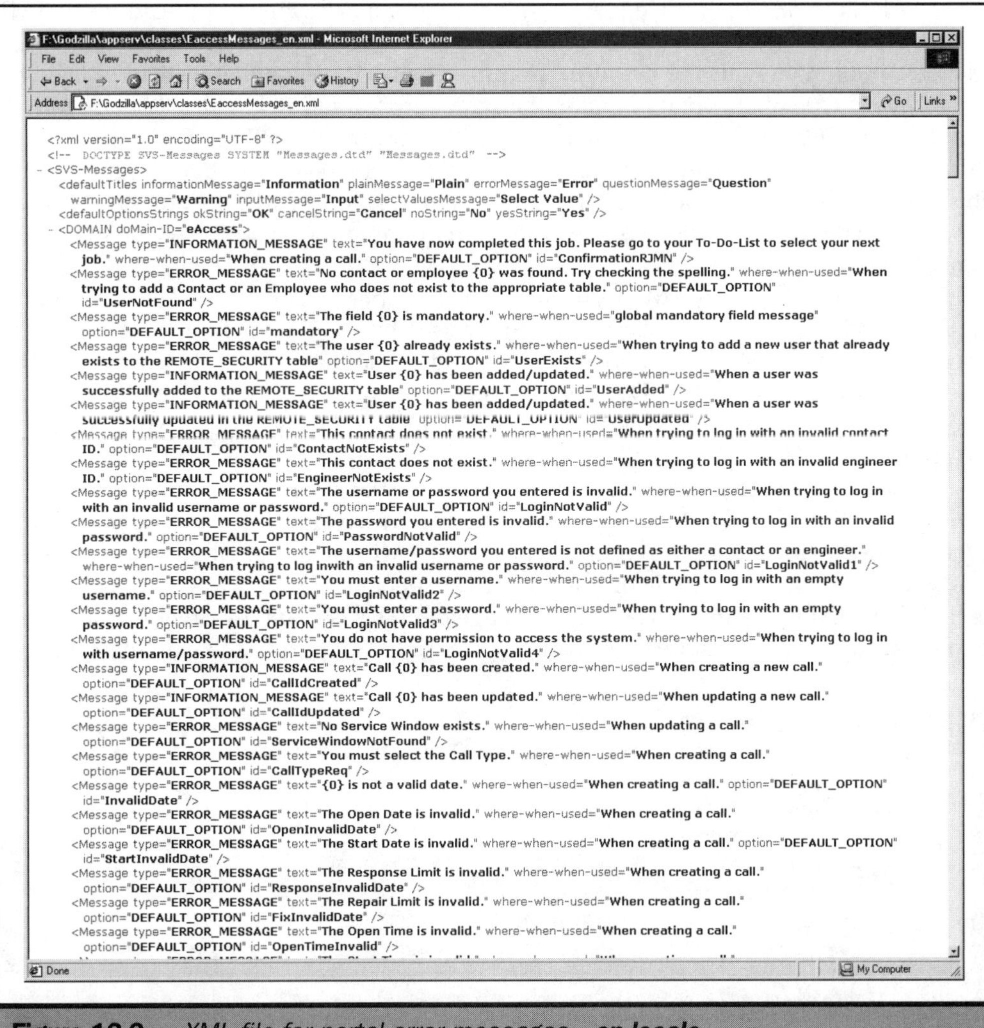


```
<?xml version="1.0" encoding="UTF-8" ?>
<!-- DOCTYPE SVS-Messages SYSTEM "Messages.dtd" "Messages.dtd" -->
- <SVS-Messages>
   <defaultTitles informationMessage="Information" plainMessage="Plain" errorMessage="Error" questionMessage="Question"
     warningMessage="Warning" inputMessage="Input" selectValuesMessage="Select Value" />
   <defaultOptionsStrings okString="OK" cancelString="Cancel" noString="No" yesString="Yes" />
 - <DOMAIN doMain-ID="eAccess">
     <Message type="INFORMATION_MESSAGE" text="You have now completed this job. Please go to your To-Do-List to select your next
       job." where-when-used="When creating a call." option="DEFAULT_OPTION" id="ConfirmationRJMN" />
     <Message type="ERROR_MESSAGE" text="No contact or employee {0} was found. Try checking the spelling." where-when-used="When
       trying to add a Contact or an Employee who does not exist to the appropriate table." option="DEFAULT_OPTION"
       id="UserNotFound" />
     <Message type="ERROR_MESSAGE" text="The field {0} is mandatory." where-when-used="global mandatory field message"
       option="DEFAULT_OPTION" id="mandatory" />
     <Message type="ERROR_MESSAGE" text="The user {0} already exists." where-when-used="When trying to add a new user that already
       exists to the REMOTE_SECURITY table" option="DEFAULT_OPTION" id="UserExists" />
     <Message type="INFORMATION_MESSAGE" text="User {0} has been added/updated." where-when-used="When a user was
       successfully added to the REMOTE_SECURITY table" option="DEFAULT_OPTION" id="UserAdded" />
     <Message type="INFORMATION_MESSAGE" text="User {0} has been added/updated." where-when-used="When a user was
       successfully updated in the REMOTE_SECURITY table" option="DEFAULT_OPTION" id="UserUpdated" />
     <Message type="ERROR_MESSAGE" text="This contact does not exist." where-when-used="When trying to log in with an invalid contact
       ID." option="DEFAULT_OPTION" id="ContactNotExists" />
     <Message type="ERROR_MESSAGE" text="This contact does not exist." where-when-used="When trying to log in with an invalid engineer
       ID." option="DEFAULT_OPTION" id="EngineerNotExists" />
     <Message type="ERROR_MESSAGE" text="The username or password you entered is invalid." where-when-used="When trying to log in
       with an invalid username or password." option="DEFAULT_OPTION" id="LoginNotValid" />
     <Message type="ERROR_MESSAGE" text="The password you entered is invalid." where-when-used="When trying to log in with an invalid
       password." option="DEFAULT_OPTION" id="PasswordNotValid" />
     <Message type="ERROR_MESSAGE" text="The username/password you entered is not defined as either a contact or an engineer."
       where-when-used="When trying to log inwith an invalid username or password." option="DEFAULT_OPTION" id="LoginNotValid1" />
     <Message type="ERROR_MESSAGE" text="You must enter a username." where-when-used="When trying to log in with an empty
       username." option="DEFAULT_OPTION" id="LoginNotValid2" />
     <Message type="ERROR_MESSAGE" text="You must enter a password." where-when-used="When trying to log in with an empty
       password." option="DEFAULT_OPTION" id="LoginNotValid3" />
     <Message type="ERROR_MESSAGE" text="You do not have permission to access the system." where-when-used="When trying to log in
       with username/password." option="DEFAULT_OPTION" id="LoginNotValid4" />
     <Message type="INFORMATION_MESSAGE" text="Call {0} has been created." where-when-used="When creating a new call."
       option="DEFAULT_OPTION" id="CallIdCreated" />
     <Message type="INFORMATION_MESSAGE" text="Call {0} has been updated." where-when-used="When updating a new call."
       option="DEFAULT_OPTION" id="CallIdUpdated" />
     <Message type="ERROR_MESSAGE" text="No Service Window exists." where-when-used="When updating a call."
       option="DEFAULT_OPTION" id="ServiceWindowNotFound" />
     <Message type="ERROR_MESSAGE" text="You must select the Call Type." where-when-used="When creating a call."
       option="DEFAULT_OPTION" id="CallTypeReq" />
     <Message type="ERROR_MESSAGE" text="{0} is not a valid date." where-when-used="When creating a call." option="DEFAULT_OPTION"
       id="InvalidDate" />
     <Message type="ERROR_MESSAGE" text="The Open Date is invalid." where-when-used="When creating a call."
       option="DEFAULT_OPTION" id="OpenInvalidDate" />
     <Message type="ERROR_MESSAGE" text="The Start Date is invalid." where-when-used="When creating a call." option="DEFAULT_OPTION"
       id="StartInvalidDate" />
     <Message type="ERROR_MESSAGE" text="The Response Limit is invalid." where-when-used="When creating a call."
       option="DEFAULT_OPTION" id="ResponseInvalidDate" />
     <Message type="ERROR_MESSAGE" text="The Repair Limit is invalid." where-when-used="When creating a call."
       option="DEFAULT_OPTION" id="FixInvalidDate" />
     <Message type="ERROR_MESSAGE" text="The Open Time is invalid." where-when-used="When creating a call."
       option="DEFAULT_OPTION" id="OpenTimeInvalid" />
```

Figure 12-2. *XML file for portal error messages—**en locale***

goes wrong and an error message needs to be displayed, the error message is taken from the file based on the locale. Figure 12-2 shows the XML file for the *en* locale.

If you want to support portal error messages in Japanese, for example, you need to create another file, called *PortalMessages_jp*, in which the error messages appear in Japanese. Then, if a request comes in over the Web from a browser in which the chosen locale is Japanese (*jp_JP*), *_jp* will reference the messages from the appropriate file.

Document Type Definitions

The most fundamental concept of XML—and where the *X* comes from—is that the tag set in XML is *extensible*, not fixed. What this means is that different applications in XML define their own tag sets and, in effect, create a new language for describing elements in a certain domain. This is a powerful notion, because it means that instead of trying to box every type of information using the same set of descriptive rules, you are free to build "languages" that are well suited to a particular domain. Still, if you were to "invent" a new language every time, you would have to make sure that the rules of this language were well known to anyone trying to use your XML document. (This is similar to the way in which you need to learn grammar and vocabulary before you can speak a language properly.)

To publish these rules, XML introduces the concept of a Document Type Definition (DTD), which describes the rules of the tag set used by an XML document. A DTD specifies the available tags and how they can and cannot be combined. A typical XML document will include the DTD so that readers of the document know how to interpret and validate the document. Note that DTDs are not mandatory; many XML documents do not include DTDs.

The following listing shows an example DTD for the message file shown in the previous section. This DTD defines rules outlining which elements can be embedded in other elements (indicating the recursive nature of XML), which attributes each element has, which attributes are mandatory, and which are default. The advantage of using DTDs is that they are fairly simple. The disadvantage of DTDs is that they do not provide enough information about the XML structure to make XML truly self explanatory.

```
<?xml encoding="UTF-8"?>
<!ELEMENT SVS-Messages (defaultTitles?, defaultOptionsStrings?, (DOMAIN)*)>
<!ATTLIST SVS-Messages >
<!ELEMENT defaultTitles EMPTY>
<!ATTLIST defaultTitles
      errorMessage              CDATA      #REQUIRED
      informationMessage        CDATA      #REQUIRED
      warningMessage            CDATA      #REQUIRED
      questionMessage           CDATA      #REQUIRED
      plainMessage              CDATA      #REQUIRED
      inputMessage              CDATA      #REQUIRED
      selectValuesMessage     CDATA        #REQUIRED>
```

```
<!ELEMENT defaultOptionsStrings EMPTY>
<!ATTLIST defaultOptionsStrings
      okString                CDATA      #REQUIRED
      cancelString            CDATA      #REQUIRED
      yesString               CDATA      #REQUIRED
      noString                CDATA      #REQUIRED>
<!ELEMENT DOMAIN (Message*)>
<!ATTLIST DOMAIN doMain-ID
      (contacts|customers|general|installedBase|products|policy|pricing|
       security|serviceOrganization|services|billing|calculation|
       contractAdministration|standard|attachments|notification|eAccess)
      'standard'>
<!ELEMENT Message
      (selectValuesDocumentation?,(
      parametersDocumentation?)*,
      (buttonTitles?)*)>
<!ATTLIST Message
      id                      ID          #REQUIRED
      text                    CDATA       #REQUIRED
      where-when-used         CDATA       #IMPLIED
      title                   CDATA       #IMPLIED
      type                    (ERROR_MESSAGE|INFORMATION_MESSAGE|
                               WARNING_MESSAGE|QUESTION_MESSAGE|
                               PLAIN_MESSAGE|INPUT_MESSAGE|
                               SELECT_VALUES_MESSAGE)
                                          #REQUIRED
      option                  (CANCEL_OPTION|NO_OPTION|YES_OPTION|
                               YES_NO_OPTION|YES_NO_CANCEL_OPTION|
                               OK_OPTION|OK_CANCEL_OPTION|DEFAULT_OPTION)
                                          'DEFAULT_OPTION'
      confirm-key             CDATA       #IMPLIED>
<!ELEMENT buttonTitles EMPTY>
<!ATTLIST buttonTitles
      id                      (okString|cancelString|yesString|noString)
                                          #REQUIRED
      text                    CDATA       #REQUIRED>
<!ELEMENT parametersDocumentation EMPTY>
<!ATTLIST parametersDocumentation
      id                      CDATA       #REQUIRED
      text                    CDATA       #REQUIRED>
<!ELEMENT selectValuesDocumentation EMPTY>
<!ATTLIST selectValuesDocumentation
      text                    CDATA       #REQUIRED>
```

XML Schemas

The new trend in the computer industry for defining XML is the use of XML *schemas*. An XML schema is an XML file that describes the XML code. An XML schema is a metadata element that uses the flexibility of XML to provide a complete description of the XML from which it is being referenced. Because XML schemas are advanced concepts, and because we do not use schemas in this book, we will not delve very far into them. In general, you can think of XML schemas as describing elements that are similar to, but much more robust and full featured than, DTDs. XML schemas are being standardized by the W3C and supported by all major vendors such as Microsoft and IBM.

Elements have attribute sets, which you use to describe those elements—that is, to define their inherent properties. You associate an attribute with an element by adding the attributes and their values as part of the start tag. These attributes are sometimes mistaken for additional tags embedded in the entity. It is easy to understand the difference between the two if you view the XML code as similar to the description of an object model. In this case, the difference is equivalent to the difference between the properties of an object and other objects it references. You define attributes as part of the DTD, and you can define them to be mandatory, to have default values, and so on. For example, if you need to add an attribute to the contact entity specifying a "VIP level," you could use the following XML code:

```
<contact vipLevel="6">
     <name>Jane Doe</name>
     <phone>201-861-7533</phone>
     <altPhone1></altPhone1>
     <altPhone2/>
</contact>
```

Document Object Model

The DOM is an API for HTML and XML documents that provides a programmatic paradigm for getting access to the objects represented by the document. DOM provides interfaces for building documents, for navigating documents and entities within the documents, for viewing and editing attributes, and for practically anything else that you might require to work with a document. The DOM standard is defined and supported by the W3C. By promoting it as a standard, the W3C is attempting to ensure that a standard API for managing XML and HTML documents will allow developers to build portable code and, in turn, further promote XML.

DOM breaks down and parses each XML (and HTML) document into a hierarchical structure of objects. It defines how forests (sets of trees) are created from XML documents (and vice versa). Since the tree structures are objects defined by DOM, DOM also provides an API for manipulating those trees and thereby for manipulating the document itself. Since DOM is composed primarily of this API for manipulating objects, it is phrased in the Common Object Request Broker Architecture's Interface Definition Language (CORBA IDL). Because IDL is a specification language that you can map to multiple programming languages, you can process DOM APIs to create sets of libraries in many programming languages, all the while maintaining a single consistent API.

DOM for XML

DOM originated from HTML. It was built to provide an object model that could be used for developing client-side applications (for example, JavaScript applications) for browsers. It has since evolved considerably, but it still contains extensive definitions for HTML objects, as well as for objects that are common in the browser. Therefore, the DOM specification has two main parts—the definition of a set of core interfaces that match XML and the definition of a set of interfaces specifically for HTML objects. Following are some of the main interfaces provided by DOM for XML:

- **Document** The entire XML or HTML document. This interface has attributes such as docType, implementation, and documentElement, and it has methods such as createElement, createDocumentFragment, createTextNode, createComment, createCDATASection, createAttribute, and createEntityReference.
- **Node** The primary object for the entire DOM. Recall that the DOM is fundamentally a tree, so each element is, therefore, a node. A node has attributes such as nodeType, parentNode, childNodes, firstChild, lastChild, previousSibling, nextSibling, and ownerDocument, and it has methods such as insertBefore, replaceChild, removeChild, appendChild, and hasChildNodes.
- **Element** A node that represents a tagged object in the document. Elements are by far the most common types of nodes encountered when traversing the tree structure. The element interface inherits from the node interface and adds methods such as getAttribute, setAttribute, removeAttribute, getAttributeNode, setAttributeNode, removeAttributeNode, and getElementsByTagName.
- **Attr** An attribute in an element (that is, one of the things inserted into the start tag when building the XML). Attributes in DOM are also nodes, so the tree that is created in DOM includes both the elements and the attributes. Therefore, an element having attributes and embedded elements will be mapped into a node in the DOM tree that has child nodes for the embedded elements; but it will have an additional relationship with nodes that represent the attributes.
- **Comment** A comment in the document.

DOM for HTML

A set of interfaces specific to HTML objects, including the following:

- **HTMLDocument** Adds attributes such as title, URL, body, images, applets, links, forms, anchors, and cookie; adds methods such as open, close, getElementById, and getElementsByName.
- **HTMLElement** Inherits from Element (the first category); adds attributes such as id, title, lang, dir, and className.

- **HTMLHeadElement** Inherits from HTMLElement; represents the head of the HTML document.
- **HTMLLinkElement** Adds attributes such as href, rel, rev, target, and type.
- **HTMLTitleElement** Inherits from HTMLElement; represents the title element in an HTML document.
- **HTMLStyleElement** Represents a style reference such as that used to define cascading style sheets or style directives.
- **HTMLBodyElement** Adds attributes such as aLink, background, bgColor, link, text, and vLink.
- **HTMLFormElement** Adds attributes such as action, method, and target; adds methods such as submit and reset.
- **HTMLSelectElement** Adds attributes such as selectedIndex, value, form, options, disabled, and name; adds methods such as add, remove, blur, and focus.
- **HTMLInputElement** Adds attributes such as defaultValue, defaultChecked, form, accept, align, checked, disabled, and value; adds methods such as blur, focus, select, and click.
- **HTMLTextElement** Adds attributes such as form, disabled, rows, tabIndex, type, and value; adds methods such as blur, focus, and select.
- **HTMLButtonElement** Adds attributes such as form, name, disable, and value.
- **HTMLLabelElement** Adds attributes such as form and htmlForm.
- **HTMLUListElement** Used for creating an unordered list (UL tags).
- **TMLOListElement** Used for creating an ordered list (OL tags).
- **HTMLLIElement** Used for creating elements in a list (LI tags).
- **HTMLHeadingElement** Used for creating header elements (H1 to H6 tags).
- **HTMLBRElement** Used to create line break elements (BR tags).
- **HTMLAnchorElement** Used for inserting an anchor element (A tags); adds attributes such as href and target.
- **HTMLImageElement** Used for inserting image elements (IMG tags); adds attributes such as name, align, alt, height, isMap, src, and width.
- **HTMLAppletElement** Used for inserting applets (APPLET tags); adds attributes such as archive, code, codebase, height, object, and width.

- **HTMLScriptElement** Used for inserting a script, both by a file reference as well as inline code; represents for SCRIPT elements in HTML 4.0; adds attributes such as event, src, and type.
- **HTMLTableElement** Adds attributes such as tHead, tFoot, rows, align, bgColor, border, and frame; adds methods such as createTHead, deleteTHead, createTFoot, deleteTFoot, createCaption, insertRow, and deleteRow.

In addition to this list of elements, DOM for HTML provides many other elements, including `HTMLTableCaptionElement`, `HTMLTableColElement`, `HTMLTableSectionElement`, and `HTMLTableRowElement`—to name a few.

The following listing illustrates the use of DOM. The example shows two forms of usage of the DOM parser. The first takes an XML string—which can be read from a file, received over the Internet, or extracted from a database—and extracts nodes, elements, and attributes from it. The second takes a DOM tree constructed using the DOM APIs and outputs an XML string that includes the elements and attributes.


```
// Assume xml is a variable holding an XML string.
// Create a reader with the string so that you can send
// it to the parser.
// create an input source - used by the parser API.
      java.io.StringReader xmlStringReader =
new java.io.StringReader (xml);
      org.xml.sax.InputSource xmlInputSource =
new org.xml.sax.InputSource(xmlStringReader);

// Create a parser. Use the Simple API for XML, but
// ask for a DOM parser to be created.
      org.xml.sax.Parser parser =
org.xml.sax.helpers.ParserFactory.makeParser(
"com.ibm.xml.parsers.TXDOMParser");

// Give the parser the input source.
      parser.parse(xmlInputSource);

      // Cast the parser object so you can directly access
      // the document object. This is not the conventional
      // way of accessing things, because usually a higher-
      // level API is used.
      com.ibm.xml.parsers.TXDOMParser actualParser =
```

```
(com.ibm.xml.parsers.TXDOMParser) parser;

// Get the document object. This is the most important
// object when you work with DOM, because from it you can
// access all nodes, elements, and attributes that are
// anywhere in the DOM tree (the XML).
      TXDocument doc =
(TXDocument)(actualParser.getDocument());

      // Now assume that path is a variable holding a string[]
      // with the path inside the XML file you are looking for.
      // The following code searches and returns the node
      // within the DOM that is in that path.
      int len = path.length;
      if (len < 1)
            return null;

      Node node = doc;

      for ( int i = 0; i < len; i++)
      {
            if (node == null)
                        break;
            NodeList childNodesList = node.getChildNodes();
            node = null;
            if (childNodesList == null)
                        break;
            {for ( int j = 0; j < childNodesList.getLength(); j++)
            if (childNodesList.item(j).getNodeName().
                                          trim().equals(path[i].trim()))
                        {
                              node = childNodesList.item(j);
                              break;
                        }
            }

      }
      // The variable node now holds the desired element.



      //-----------------------------------------------
```

```
// This part shows the flip. Given a document object
// that is created by composing elements, attributes, and
// nodes, you can write out the XML as a file or a string.

// You start with a hash table with name-value pairs.
// You then create a set of elements that encapsulate these values.
Iterator keys = hashtable.keySet().iterator();
Element child;
while (keys.hasNext())
      {
            String nextElementName = (String)keys.next();
            Object nextElement = hashtable.get(nextElementName);
            Element child =
                new TXDocument().createElement(nextElementName);
            doc.appendChild(child);
            fillDomData(child, nextElement);
      }


StringWriter stWriter = new StringWriter();
doc.printWithFormat(stWriter);
xml = stWriter.toString();
```

The next listing shows the `Domable` class (actually, a simplified version of it), a utility class used within the ViryaNet XML infrastructure, and demonstrates how to perform XML manipulation using DOM.

```
package com.rts.apis.common;

import com.sun.java.util.collections.Map;
import com.sun.java.util.collections.HashMap;
import com.sun.java.util.collections.Iterator;
import java.io.FileInputStream;
import java.net.URL;
import java.util.Calendar;
import java.util.Date;
import java.util.Locale;
import java.util.ResourceBundle;
import java.util.Vector;
import java.io.*;
import org.w3c.dom.*;
import com.ibm.xml.parser.*;
import com.ibm.xml.parsers.*;
```

```
import java.sql.SQLException;
import java.sql.ResultSet;
import java.sql.Connection;
import java.sql.PreparedStatement;
import java.sql.Statement;
import java.sql.Types;
import java.text.SimpleDateFormat;
import java.util.Enumeration;
import java.net.MalformedURLException;


public class Domable
{
      // Many definitions omitted - not important for these examples.

      // The DOM document object is most central to this class.
      TXDocument selfDoc = null;




/**
 * Parse the string into a DOM document.
 * @param xml java.lang.String
 */
public Domable(String xml) throws IOException , org.xml.sax.SAXException{
 try{
      xml = "<?xml version=\"1.0\" encoding=\"UTF-8\"?>" + xml;
            java.io.StringReader xmlStringReader = new java.io.StringReader (xml);
            org.xml.sax.InputSource xmlInputSource = new org.xml.sax. InputSource
                                                    (xmlStringReader);
            org.xml.sax.Parser parser = org.xml.sax.helpers.ParserFactory.makeParser
                                    ("com.ibm.xml.parsers.TXDOMParser");
            parser.parse(xmlInputSource);
            com.ibm.xml.parsers.TXDOMParser actualParser = (com.ibm.xml.parsers.
                                                          TXDOMParser) parser;
          setSelfDoc((TXDocument)actualParser.getDocument());
      } catch (Exception ex) {
            Log.debug("MessageFormat",ex);
      }

}
```

```
/**
 * Create an element to be added into the document with the appropriate tag.
 * @return org.w3c.dom.Element
 * @param aNode org.w3c.dom.Node
 * @param aTag java.lang.String
 */
public static Element createElement(TXDocument aDoc, String aTag) {
      Element childFirst = aDoc.createElement(aTag);
      aDoc.appendChild(childFirst);
      return childFirst;
}



/**
 * Create an element to be added as a child node.
 * @return org.w3c.dom.Element
 * @param aNode org.w3c.dom.Node
 * @param aTag java.lang.String
 */
public static Element createElement(Node aNode, String aTag) {
      Element childFirst = new TXDocument().createElement(aTag);
      aNode.appendChild(childFirst);
      return childFirst;
}



 /**
      * This method is used to get the value of an attribute of a specific
      * node that is pointed to by a path.
      * @param path the path to the node.
      * @param attributeName the name of the attribute.
      * @return the value of the required attribute.
      */
      public String getAttributeValue(String[] path, String attributeName)
            throws Exception
      {
            Node node = getNode(path);

            if (node == null)
                  throw new Exception("Not found path.");

            String result = getAttributeValue(node, attributeName);
            if (result == null)
```

```
                throw new Exception("Not found attribute " + attributeName);
            return result;
        }



    /**
        * This method is used to get the value of an attribute of a specific
        * node.
        * @param node the node.
        * @param attributeName the name of the attribute.
        * @return the value of the required attribute.
        */
        public static String getAttributeValue(Node node, String attributeName)
        {
            NamedNodeMap nodeMap = node.getAttributes();
            if (nodeMap == null)
                return null;
            Node attributeNode;

            for (int i = 0; i < nodeMap.getLength(); i++){
                attributeNode = nodeMap.item(i);
                if (attributeNode.getNodeName().equalsIgnoreCase(attributeName))
                    return attributeNode.getNodeValue();
            }

            return null;
        }



    /**
     * Parse the string into a DOM document.
     * @param xml java.lang.String
     */
    public static TXDocument getDocument(String xml) throws IOException,
    org.xml.sax.SAXException
    {
        TXDocument retDoc = null;
        try
        {
            xml = "<?xml version=\"1.0\" encoding=\"UTF-8\"?>" + xml;
            java.io.StringReader xmlStringReader = new
            java.io.StringReader(xml);
```

```
    org.xml.sax.InputSource xmlInputSource = new
    org.xml.sax.InputSource(xmlStringReader);
    org.xml.sax.Parser parser = org.xml.sax.helpers.ParserFactory.
                              makeParser("com.ibm.xml.parsers.TXDOMParser");
    parser.parse(xmlInputSource);
    com.ibm.xml.parsers.TXDOMParser actualParser =
    (com.ibm.xml.parsers.TXDOMParser) parser;
            retDoc = ((TXDocument) actualParser.getDocument());
      }
      catch (Exception ex)
      {
            Log.debug("MessageFormat",ex);
      }
      return retDoc;
}


 /**
      * Used to get a node according to the path from the root to the node.
      * @param path the path to the node.
      * @return returns the node or null if not found.
      */
      public Node getNode(String[] path)
      {
            int len = path.length;
            if (len < 1)
                  return null;

            Node node = this.getSelfDoc();

            if (node == null)
                  return null;

            for ( int i = 0; i < len; i++)
            {
                  if (node == null)
                        break;
                  NodeList childNodesList = node.getChildNodes();
                  node = null;
                  if (childNodesList == null)
                        break;
                  for ( int j = 0; j < childNodesList.getLength(); j++){ if
```

```
(childNodesList.item(j).getNodeName().trim().equals(path[i].trim()))
                        {
                                node = childNodesList.item(j);
                                break;
                        }
                }

        }

        return node;
    }
```

Simple API for XML

DOM provides the capabilities necessary for processing any XML document. As the programmer, you can use the DOM APIs to build the tree structures for the XML document and then traverse the trees to manipulate the elements, extract information, or perform any other kind of processing. While using DOMs in this way is quite easy to do, it can sometimes be highly inefficient. For example, if the XML document represents all of the contacts the company has, the XML code will certainly make for a large document. If you need to parse this document, build the trees, and then traverse them, you might be in for a long wait. If you really need to go through all the elements in the XML document, you have no choice; the solution provided by DOM is probably as efficient as any. However, if all you need to do is some processing for a subset of the elements (and potentially a much smaller set), another, better, alternative is available.

The Simple API for XML (SAX) is an event-based API for processing XML documents. Being event based means that SAX provides a way for an application developer to express interest in certain elements without requiring that all the elements be prebuilt before beginning the application-level processing. This has the benefit that unnecessary structures will not be built; instead, a callback into the application code will be made whenever any interesting event occurs. Note that SAX is not only much more efficient than DOM when you need to process a subset of the elements, but it can be a useful tool if you need to process large XML documents (for example tens or even hundreds of elements). When you use DOM, even if you need to process all the elements, you may run into memory problems because building so many objects can be memory intensive. SAX, on the other hand, does not require you to build anything; the processing is done in real time, rather than in a building-and-processing paradigm.

Using SAX is simple. It involves two stages. First, you need to use the SAX APIs to define which elements you are interested in. For example, you may be interested in the contact names only, or, in a larger context, in the contacts for the contracts that should be renewed in a given month. Once you've defined your interests, you can go ahead and fire up the parser, which will parse the XML document. As the parser goes through the XML document, it will come across the element tags and generate events (for example,

START ELEMENT CONTRACT, END ELEMENT CONTRACT, START ELEMENT CONTACT). Some of these events will be of no interest to you, so nothing will happen—that is, the parser will continue its job. When an event occurs in which you have expressed interest, the event will cause the application callback to be invoked, and processing of that particular element will begin.

Obviously, using SAX is possible only if you use a SAX-enabled parser. The parser is the component that needs to traverse the tree and generate events; therefore, it needs to know how to do this. SAX defines a package called `org.xml.sax`, which has a number of interfaces such as `Parser`, `AttributeList`, and `Locator`. A SAX-enabled XML tool needs to implement these interfaces in order to support SAX processing.

SAX defines another set of interfaces in the `org.xml.sax` package that must be implemented by the application developer. These include the following:

- **DocumentHandler** An interface that defines the methods the parser uses to notify the application of events that have occurred. This is the most important interface from the point of view of the application developer.
- **ErrorHandler** An interface that is used for calling application-level code when some error occurs while the document is being processed.

XSL Transformations

XSL Transformations (XSLT) is a subset of the Extensible Stylesheet Language (XSL) that defines a language for transforming XML documents into other XML documents. (Actually, XSLT is one half of XSL; the second half is the formatting language.) XSLT is important in the "grand scheme" of XML. An XML document is based on a tag set that is defined by the creator of the document. It is often the case that two parties want to exchange data in the form of XML documents, but do not completely agree on the tag set. In such cases, it is often feasible to perform a mapping between the two XML tag sets via XSLT.

XSLT is an application of XML that causes a tag set to allow the definition of transformation rules. These rules define how a source tree constructed from an XML document is processed into a result tree that can then be used to generate the resulting XML document. Each transformation rule has a pattern and a template. The *pattern* is matched up with the source tree to identify the constructs identified by the *rule*, the basis for the transformation. After the pattern has been matched, the *template* is applied to the source tree to create an element of the result tree. Obviously, all this is performed recursively so that, while the template is applied, other transformation rules can also be involved.

Templates can be quite complicated, and XSLT has a lot of expressive power when it comes to the templates. Tree elements can be created either independently or from the source tree; apart from the large number of element types that XSLT defines, you can also use processing instructions that are supported by XSLT.

Each rule has a pattern that defines when the rule is valid and can therefore be applied to the source tree to create the result tree. Patterns have expressions that are based on the XPath specification. These expressions select the appropriate node for processing. For example, an expression can include conditions on nodes (such as the type of node), attributes of nodes, ancestors of nodes, descendants of nodes, and any combination of the above.

Once an expression has been evaluated, causing the template to be matched, processing of the template begins. When the expression is matched, a current node is always identified; this node is the one matched by the pattern. All processing of the template is based on this node. For example, if you include a directive to traverse all subnodes, that directive will apply to the node matched by the expression.

XSLT is a complex language that takes a long time to learn and understand. We will not go over all features of this language; XSLT truly deserves a book of its own. Interested readers can refer to *http://www.w3.org/TR/WD-xslt* for more details on XSLT. We will conclude this chapter with two simple examples. The first example transforms an XML document describing trade counterparts to an HTML table. (You will recognize this document, based on FpML, from Listing 12-1.) The XSLT stylesheet is shown in the first listing, and the resulting HTML source code is shown in the second listing. The resulting HTML page is shown in Figure 12-3.

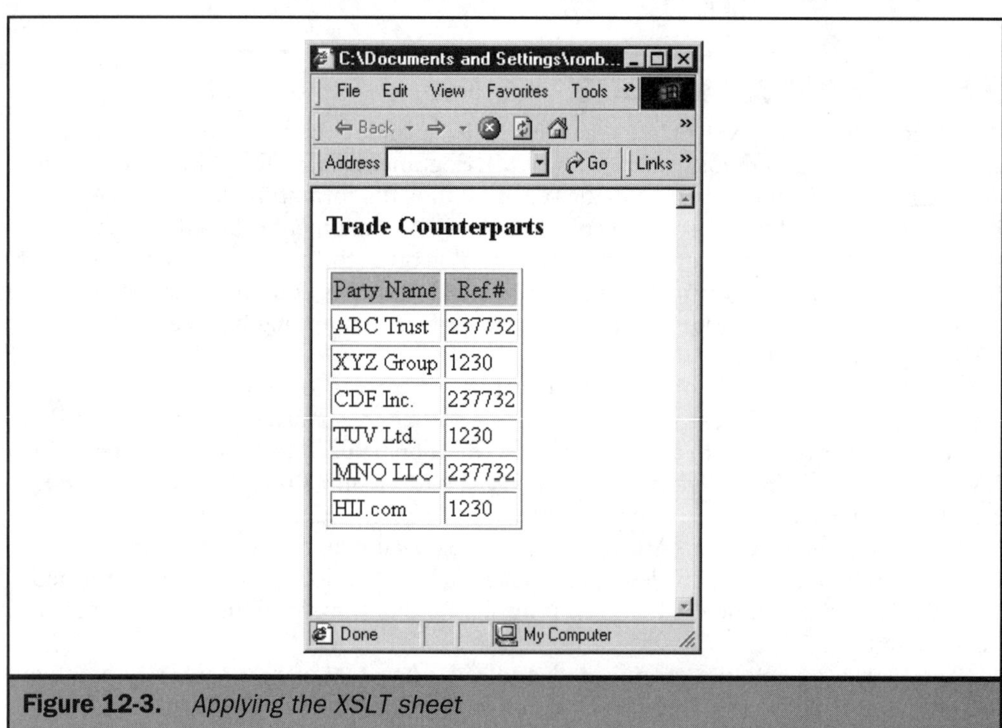

Figure 12-3. *Applying the XSLT sheet*

```
<?xml version="1.0"?>

<xsl:stylesheet
      xmlns:xsl="http://www.w3.org/XSL/Transform/1.0"
        xmlns="http://www.w3.org/TR/REC-html40"
      xmlns:fpml="urn:fpml-FpML"
      xmlns:tid="urn:fpml-TradeID"
      result-ns=""
        indent-result="yes">


<xsl:template match="fpml:Trade">
  <HTML><BODY>
  <H3>Trade Counterparts</H3>
  <TABLE BORDER="1">
   <TR align="center" bgcolor="CCCCCC">
    <TD>Party Name</TD>
    <TD>Ref.#</TD>
   </TR>
    <xsl:apply-templates/>
  </TABLE>
  </BODY></HTML>
</xsl:template>

<xsl:template match="fpml:TradeIDs">
   <xsl:apply-templates/>
</xsl:template>

<xsl:template match="tid:TradeID">
  <TR>
   <xsl:apply-templates/>
  </TR>
</xsl:template>

<xsl:template match="tid:transactionReferenceNumber">
  <TD>
   <xsl:apply-templates/>
  </TD>
</xsl:template>

<xsl:template match="tid:partyReference">
  <TD>
```

```
    <xsl:apply-templates/>
  </TD>
</xsl:template>

</xsl:stylesheet>
```

Here's the resulting HTML page:

```
<!DOCTYPE html PUBLIC "-//W3C//DTD HTML 4.0 Transitional//EN">



<HTML>
<BODY>
<H3>Trade Counterparts</H3>
<TABLE BORDER="1">
<TR align="center" bgcolor="CCCCCC">
<TD>Party Name</TD>
<TD>Ref.#</TD>
</TR>



   <TR>
    <TD>ABC Trust</TD>
    <TD>237732</TD>
   </TR>
   <TR>
    <TD>XYZ Group</TD>
    <TD>1230</TD>
   </TR>
   <TR>
    <TD>CDF Inc.</TD>
    <TD>237732</TD>
   </TR>
   <TR>
    <TD>TUV Ltd.</TD>
    <TD>1230</TD>
   </TR>
   <TR>
    <TD>MNO LLC</TD>
    <TD>237732</TD>
   </TR>
```

```
    <TR>
     <TD>HIJ.com</TD>
     <TD>1230</TD>
    </TR>


</TABLE>
</BODY>
</HTML>
```


The second example shows more detailed application integration using XML. As stated, and as is clear from the trade press, XML is being touted as the silver bullet for application integration. Most of today's applications have an XML-based interface. Unfortunately, each application uses a different "dialect" of XML. In Chapter 38, you will be introduced to Web services, a new set of technologies used for standardizing the integration efforts that use XML.

Because we are still at the start of the s-curve for Web services and its standards—Simple Object Access Protocol (SOAP), Web Services Definition Language (WSDL), and Universal Description, Discovery and Integration (UDDI)—the current solution often used to bridge different XML dialects is XSLT converters. When one application creates an XML document, an XSLT converter is used to transform it into an XML document that another application can understand. The following listings provide one such example. The first listing shows an XML document in a dialect called Service Exchange Protocol (SXP). This document is transformed by means of the XSLT sheet shown in the second listing to the XML document shown in the last listing.

Here's the SXP document generated by application A:

```
<AssignmentAdd Destination="ViryanetTest">
     <Assignment>
          <Key>290819</Key>
          <Start>2001-08-07 06:30</Start>
          <Finish>2001-08-07 09:30</Finish>
     </Assignment>
     <Task>
          <Key>33892352</Key>
          <CallID>te435</CallID>
          <Number>1</Number>
          <Status>
               <Name>Open</Name>
          </Status>
     </Task>
```

```
    <Engineers>
        <Engineer>
            <ID>JP3</ID>
            <Name>jp tEST TERMINATE</Name>
        </Engineer>
    </Engineers>
</AssignmentAdd>
```

Here's the XSLT sheet:

```
<?xml version='1.0'?>
<xsl:stylesheet xmlns:xsl="http://www.w3.org/TR/WD-xsl" language="VBScript">
    <xsl:template match="/">
            <SXPcreateGeneralEvent Revision="1.00">
                  <input>
<xsl:choose>
<xsl:when
test="AssignmentAdd"><eventDefinition>ALDMST</eventDefinition></xsl:when>
<xsl:when
test="AssignmentUpdate"><eventDefinition>ALDMST</eventDefinition></xsl:when>
<xsl:when
test="AssignmentDelete"><eventDefinition>REJNA</eventDefinition></xsl:when>

<xsl:if test="*/Task/CallID"><call><xsl:value-of select="*/Task/CallID"/>
             </ call></xsl:if>
<xsl:if test="*/Task/Number"><action><xsl:value-of select=
             "*/Task/Number"/ ></action></xsl:if>
<xsl:if test="*/Engineers/Engineer/ID"><employee><xsl:value-of select=
             "*/ Engineers/Engineer/ID"/></employee></xsl:if>
<xsl:if test="*/Assignment/Start"><dateFrom><xsl:value-of select=
             "*/ Assignment/Start"/></dateFrom></xsl:if>
<xsl:if test="*/Assignment/Finish"><dateTo><xsl:value-of select=
             "*/ Assignment/Finish"/></dateTo></xsl:if>
                        <allocator>
                              CLICK
                        </allocator>
                        <userId>
                              CLICK
                        </userId>

                  </input>
            </SXPcreateGeneralEvent>
    </xsl:template>
</xsl:stylesheet>
```

Finally, here's the XML document used by application B:

```
<SXPcreateGeneralEvent Revision="1.00">
      <input>
            <eventDefinition>
                  ALDMST
            </eventDefinition>
            <call>
                  te435
            </call>
            <action>
                  1
            </action>
            <employee>
                  JP3
            </employee>
            <dateFrom>
                  2001-08-07 06:30
            </dateFrom>
            <dateTo>
                  2001-08-07 09:30
            </dateTo>
            <allocator>
                  CLICK
            </allocator>
            <userId>
                  CLICK
            </userId>
      </input>
</SXPcreateGeneralEvent>
```

Summary

This chapter described the use of XML and other related packages and technologies, such as DOM, SAX, and XSLT. At this point, you should have a good understanding of what XML documents are, how they are used, how they are created, how they are parsed, and the different kinds of processing that can be applied to them. You will need this know-how when we discuss how XML is used to build and deploy applications within WebSphere—the topics covered in Chapters 35 through 38.

Chapter 13

Java Security

This chapter is meant to be a high-level introduction to Java security and other security schemes common in e-business applications. The issue of security is a broad one that is central to the existence of Web applications. This chapter will familiarize you with some of the concepts that should be applied when you're developing and deploying applications on WebSphere. If this topic sparks your interest, an abundance of good books dealing exclusively with this matter are available.

Java has been defined as being a portable and interpreted, distributed, reliable, robust and *secure*, high-performance and threaded, simple, dynamic, and object-oriented programming language that supports runtime environments. The first part of this chapter is a discussion of the security features that are built into the Java programming language.

Java was designed from scratch to be secure. As a language that was intended to be used for building robust distributed systems and that could be deployed over the Web, it had to be designed with security in mind—anything else would have rendered Java useless for real over-the-Web systems. Java supports security from the ground up, and coupled with an extensive set of security-related services provided by newer releases of either the Java Developer's Kit (JDK) or support packages, Java is uniquely capable in terms of making distributed Web objects a reality.

Java security is made up of many things. First off, Java as a programming language is defined in a way that eliminates the ability to use language features to break into systems written in Java. Java eliminates the notion of pointers and hides the physical layout of memory and constructs from the programmer. As a result, programmers may not use the language itself to break the runtime. Java is type-safe and casting exceptions are flagged, thus eliminating hacking within the type system. Such properties of the Java programming language are not only important in eliminating bugs and making the programming model simpler to use, but they also help to make Java safer from hackers.

While such language features help make the language more secure, they certainly cannot ensure security on their own. In fact, the truth is probably that no set of features, services, and abilities can guarantee security in a Web environment—hackers are ingenious, innovative, and motivated. However, as you shall see in this chapter, Java supplies extremely useful and all-encompassing security features that, together with sets of conventions and human intervention, can certainly make safe Web applications a reality.

The Java Security Model

Security is an inherent part of the Java programming environment, and that's why security features were incorporated into the first release of the Java JDK. Apart from the type-safety enforcement of the Java compilers and the decoupling of the logical structure from the physical implementation, the basic Java model enforces security through four primary enablers:

- The sandbox model
- The class loader

- The byte code verifier
- The security manager

The Java Sandbox

The *sandbox* model is perhaps the most well-known part of the Java security model—and certainly one of the most important parts. Java takes an approach that is different from conventional operating environments. In most operating systems, for example, applications have access to all resources in the systems, including files, printers, and the network. In Java, untrusted code that is downloaded from the Web runs within a confined environment called the *sandbox*. By confining untrusted code and severely limiting the resources to which it has access, any malicious behavior can be contained to doing harm only within this sandbox. Note that the ability to support such a model is made possible by the fact that Java uses a *virtual-machine* approach (i.e., a runtime architecture in which applications are compiled according to instructions read by another program—the Java Virtual Machine (JVM)—that converts them to native machine code instructions).

The Java sandbox could be called the "playground for untrusted code." It defines the environment in which untrusted code runs and ensures that the code (for example, a downloaded applet) cannot break out of this confined space and do harm to the client machine. It gives the applet or other downloaded code all the abilities it might require without allowing it to access external components in the system. This sandbox metaphor makes the JVM (technically only parts of the JVM) the entire world of the applet.

The sandbox model is enforced by the class loader, the bytecode verifier, and the security manager. It defines the invariants and assertions that must always exist within the JVM-state machine. Any state that might be reached when handing control over to untrusted code must remain within the confines of the Java sandbox model.

The Java sandbox model defines the following transitions of the JVM-state machine as fundamental to Java security:

1. When a class loader's constructor is called, the security manager object is called to verify that the thread can create a class loader. This ensures that untrusted code cannot create additional class loaders (even if bytecodes were tampered with).
2. The next state is entered when the JVM calls the `class loaders` method to load a class. First, any system classes are found using the class loader's `findSystemClass` method, thereby ensuring that untrusted code cannot masquerade as system code.
3. Once the code is loaded, the verifier is called to validate the code. The verifier makes sure that the code conforms to syntactic and structural rules. Static members are initialized with default values.
4. The class loader then maps the loaded class into the namespace it is maintaining.

The notion of the sandbox (assuming no bugs and security holes exist in the implementation of the sandbox) is an excellent idea. It allows you as a user to download untrusted applets and run them on your client with no worries. This is drastically different than other models in which you must rely on the creator of the downloaded code and its digital signature. (In all fairness, it is important to mention that the sandbox model is sometimes overly restrictive. In these cases, digital signatures are used to allow some code to be "more trusted" than other code.)

There are drawbacks to the sandbox model. The original sandbox as defined in JDK1.0*x* is extremely restrictive. For example, applets downloaded from untrusted sources do not have access to system resources, system properties, and so on, and such restrictions may render such programs useless. Hence, developers and users will be faced with the option of either bypassing the sandbox model, thus making their system insecure, or depriving applications of necessary functionality.

Luckily, a solution to this dilemma was introduced in JDK1.1 and expanded in Java 2 Platform Standard Edition (J2SE). The idea is to refine the level of control provided. Specifically, a notion of several levels of trust is defined. Such levels can be defined at the client side based on digital signatures, thus allowing signed, downloaded code to run within various virtual sandboxes, each with a different set of available resources and permissions.

The Class Loader

Java dynamically loads class files as required by a running program. When working on the Web, these class files are downloaded from the originating Web site and dynamically added to the working environment (similar in some respects to dynamic loading of dynamic-linked libraries, or DLLs). This loading is performed by a specific object: the *class loader*. This object forms the first line of defense, in that it controls and limits what is being loaded, from where, and when. Class loaders enforce namespace rules and ensure that inappropriate classes are not loaded. (For example, class loaders do not allow other class loaders that may incorporate security breaches in them to be loaded.)

Class loaders are responsible for mapping class names to Java bytecodes, loading the appropriate bytecodes from the class files, and calling the verifier if necessary. These responsibilities are crucial to maintaining the security invariants, thus making class loaders part of Java's first line of defense. For example, the class loader will never attempt to load any classes from `java.*` packages over the network, so that the JVM is not tricked into using unsafe representations of the Java core classes.

Java 2 starts with three class loaders in addition to any the programmer defines. The default class loaders provided are the bootstrap class loader, extension class loader and the application class loader. The application class loader is the only one that uses the `CLASSPATH` environment variable. The `CLASSPATH` environment variable can itself be overridden by the `-classpath` java command-line option.

The JDK defines the class loader as an abstract class (that is, it cannot be instantiated); subclasses define the concrete manner in which classes are dynamically loaded. The default behavior is that of loading from the CLASSPATH in a platform-dependent manner in addition to the network access allowing bytecodes to be downloaded and instantiated.

The Verifier

The *verifier* is used before the code is actually executed. Untrusted code that is loaded by the class loader must go through a verification process that "proves" that the bytecodes loaded represent Java code that adheres to all rules of the language. Because bytecodes are the "machine language" of the JVM, and because the party loading the code does not know who created the bytecodes (or how they were created), the security model must make sure that the bytecodes do not hide a dangerous breach of the internal Java type enforcement. The verifier ensures that access restrictions are maintained, that illegal casting is not performed, and that memory access is not forged.

Clearly, the verifier works at a low level and makes sure only that the bytecodes conform to the Java rules; it does not perform any application-level analysis or heuristic security validation.

If we could know that Java bytecodes were always created with a legal Java compiler, the verifier would not be necessary. Bytecodes created by legal Java compilers (such as the compiler that is part of the JDK or J2SE distribution) always adhere to the Java language rules. While it is true that the vast majority of Java bytecodes out there are created using such compilers, we cannot rely on this fact. (Unfortunately, such deceit seems to be a flaw deeply rooted in mankind.) The verifier is used specifically to block the possibility that bytecodes were created in a malicious way to break the JVM. For example, bytecodes can be artificially formed in a way that if run, they will cause a stack underflow in the JVM, thus crashing the JVM. The verifier is the security component responsible for blocking such behavior before it is allowed to run.

The Security Manager

The final component in the Java security model is the security manager, which, as the sandbox's watchdog, is the most important component of Java technology security. It is responsible for limiting what untrusted code can do. In simple terms, it is the component responsible for enforcing that untrusted code does not leave the sandbox at runtime. The security manager controls runtime access to resources including the internal objects that form the security framework in Java. For example, the security manager will not allow untrusted code to create class loaders that may potentially be used to circumvent the security provided by that layer. Access to physical resources such as sockets and files must all be okayed by the security manager.

The security manager is both active and passive. It performs runtime validation on certain methods and is also used by other security-related components that ask the security manager to approve an operation that was requested. If the security manager does not want to okay the operation, it raises a security exception, thereby disallowing the operation to occur.

Among other tests, the security manager limits

- Access to the operating system
- Access to sockets
- Access to the file system
- Access to Java packages
- Access to the security model; for example, the security manager makes sure that new class loaders are not installed
- Access to threads and thread groups
- Access to the clipboard
- Access to printers and spoolers

Applet Security

Security restrictions imposed on applets are fairly extensive, which is clearly necessary because downloaded applets may incorporate malicious code. The sandbox must be, therefore, by default, as restrictive as possible. However, supporting enterprise applications on the Web often implies that downloaded code requires a less restricted runtime environment; JDK 1.1 and JDK 1.2 introduce a richer model that provides more selective control based on digital signatures.

Applets are prevented from reading and writing files on the local (or for that matter, on any) file system. They cannot check for the existence of a file, rename a file, create a directory, or check file attributes. This eliminates the dangers of having a downloaded applet deleting the contents of your hard drive or reading confidential information and broadcasting it over the Internet. In more advanced versions of the JDK, this restriction is relaxed and includes more advanced features. For example, Sun's *appletviewer* in JDK 1.1 uses access-control lists as a mechanism with which finer control can be provided in limiting file access (using the `acl.read` property in the properties file).

Applets are also restricted in the network connections they may create. An applet can make a network connection only to the host from which it was downloaded. For example, a socket may be opened only to the host on which the Web server that supplied the applet resides.

Applets are also restricted as to which system properties they can access. System properties provide information about the environment in which a piece of Java code runs and include the name of the operating system, the host, and other environment attributes. Access to system properties is provided through the `getProperty`, `getProperties`, and `setProperties` methods, which are all implemented by the `System` class.

J2SE Security

JDK 1.0 defined the basic security model used by early Java applets but was far from adequate as far as real-world applications deployed over the Web were concerned. As explained earlier, the harsh restrictions made it difficult to implement some tasks and applications.

JDK 1.1 introduced digital signatures into the Java world. Signatures, keys, certificates, providers, and algorithms are all formulated in Java, allowing applets to be signed by their creators. Clients running this Java code can then decide to relax security restrictions for code signed by a certain party.

JDK 1.1 also introduced the notion of Java Archive (JAR) files. JAR files are archive files that can package together class files, images, locale-specific data, and other components. These JAR files can be used to form a stand-alone representation of all that is required from a download site to run an application. In terms of security, JDK 1.1 provides for signing of a JAR file with a digital signature and using this signature to uniquely identify the source of the JAR file and eliminate "man-in-the-middle" attacks.

The following features were also introduced in JDK1.1:

- **Access control** Access control lists (ACLs) are used as a mechanism for managing principals and their permissions.
- **Message digests** Support is provided for creating message digests as a digital fingerprint.
- **Key management** Initial support is provided for allowing management of keys and certificates in a security database.

J2SE has an even richer and more complete security architecture. The J2SE security model not only has more features, but it is a more consistent, well-organized model that uses a small number of primitive concepts to define a reference model. As for features, the J2SE security model improves the JDK 1.1 model in the following areas:

- **Fine-grained access control** While applications may define and implement their own class loaders and security managers, this is hard work. Java 2 provides a much easier way for an application to modify security-related control mechanisms.
- **Configurable security policies** In Java 2, security policies can be configured.
- **Extensible access control** It is possible to provide extensions to the access control model without requiring *check* methods to be added to the SecurityManager class.
- **Consistency in terms of checking** Trusted and untrusted code (applets and applications) move closer to one another and are managed in similar ways—different security attributes are implemented by using corresponding security domains. These domains are the primitive security enablers that determine what kind of sandbox (if any) is used.

The central concept in the J2SE security architecture is the notion of a *protection domain*. A protection domain aggregates code and has a set of permissions associated with it (see Figure 13-1). Every segment of code is contained within a protection domain and assumes the security attributes from the permissions associated with that domain. A single thread of execution may be completely embedded in a single protection domain, or it may have different segments each belonging to different domains. Naturally, moving from one domain to another (especially if the second has more permissions) involves some security restrictions that alter the permissions available to the caller.

Protection domains in general can be either system domains (which include system code that has more permission associated with it) or various application domains. Naturally, the system domain will be accessible to application code only under limiting restrictions.

J2SE Security APIs

The Java security APIs are mostly concentrated in the `java.security` and `java.security.*` packages.

Permissions

The most fundamental abstraction in J2SE security is a permission represented by a base class called `java.security.Permission`. Instances of classes derived from this class represent permission to perform certain operations. Subclasses of the `java.security.Permission` class are used in various packages to represent access permissions in the respective context. For example, `java.net.SocketPermission` represents access permissions to a network via sockets, and `java.io.FilePermission` represents access permissions to a file.

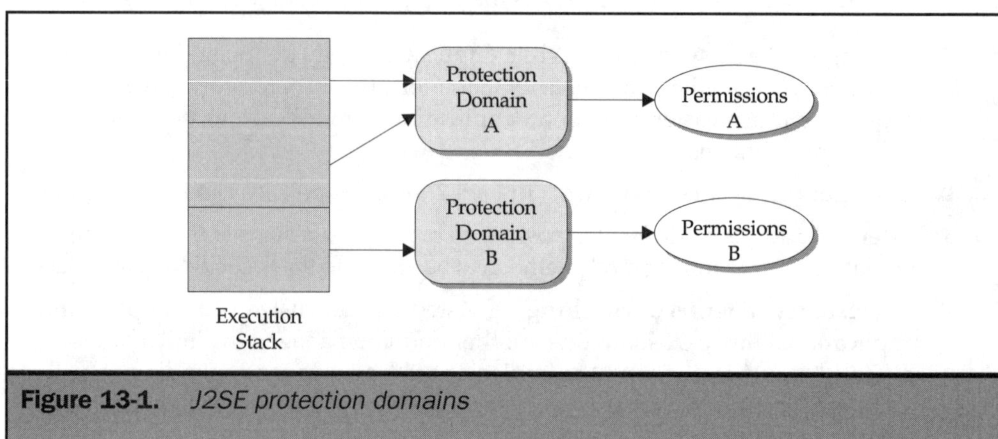

Figure 13-1. *J2SE protection domains*

Instantiations of the permission class are typically created with a constructor taking two `String` arguments. The first argument defines the object to which the permission relates and the other holds a list of comma-separated operations for which permission is granted. Let's look at a couple of examples corresponding to the two aforementioned permissions classes. The following line creates a permission object that allows a connection to port 80 of the server *www.viryanet.com*:

```
Permission p1 = new SocketPermission("www.viryanet.com:80",
"connect");
```

To grant permission to read and write the file */tmp/x*, the following line of code can be used:

```
Permission p2 = new FilePermission("/tmp/x", "read,write");
```

Permissions on their own do not suffice for actually obtaining access to system resources and objects. The permissions should be granted in a database, and the entries of this database are called *policies*. The default database is the file `java.policy` typically under the *jre\lib\security* directory in the JDK installation (its location is defined by a property file named `java.security` residing in the same directory).

The default file in the JDK distribution is shown here:

```
// Standard extensions get all permissions by default
grant codeBase "file:${java.home}/lib/ext/*" {
     permission java.security.AllPermission;
};

// default permissions granted to all domains
grant {
     // Allows any thread to stop itself using the
java.lang.Thread.stop()
     // method that takes no argument.
     // Note that this permission is granted by default only to
remain
     // backwards compatible.
     // It is strongly recommended that you either remove this
permission
     // from this policy file or further restrict it to code
sources
     // that you specify, because Thread.stop() is potentially
unsafe.
```

```
        // See "http://java.sun.com/notes" for more information.
        permission java.lang.RuntimePermission "stopThread";

        // allows anyone to listen on un-privileged ports
        permission java.net.SocketPermission "localhost:1024-",
"listen";


        // "standard" properies that can be read by anyone
        permission java.util.PropertyPermission "java.version",
"read";
        permission java.util.PropertyPermission "java.vendor",
"read";
        permission java.util.PropertyPermission "java.vendor.url",
"read";
        permission java.util.PropertyPermission "java.class.version",
"read";
        permission java.util.PropertyPermission "os.name", "read";
        permission java.util.PropertyPermission "os.version", "read";
        permission java.util.PropertyPermission "os.arch", "read";
        permission java.util.PropertyPermission "file.separator",
"read";
        permission java.util.PropertyPermission "path.separator",
"read";
        permission java.util.PropertyPermission "line.separator",
"read";
        permission java.util.PropertyPermission
"java.specification.version", "read";
        permission java.util.PropertyPermission
"java.specification.vendor", "read";
        permission java.util.PropertyPermission
"java.specification.name", "read";

        permission java.util.PropertyPermission
"java.vm.specification.version", "read";
        permission java.util.PropertyPermission
"java.vm.specification.vendor", "read";
        permission java.util.PropertyPermission
"java.vm.specification.name", "read";
        permission java.util.PropertyPermission "java.vm.version",
"read";
        permission java.util.PropertyPermission "java.vm.vendor",
```

```
"read";
      permission java.util.PropertyPermission "java.vm.name",
"read";
};
```

The file contains a set of grant statements. The general form of a grant statement contains a *signed-by* entry (not seen in this example) and a *codebase* entry (shown in the first grant statement). Classes that share the same codebase and signed by the same entity are considered to be in the same protection domain. For example, the following grants read/write permission for the files under */tmp/viryanet* to all code signed by *"viryanet"* residing at *http://viryanet.com.*


```
grant signedBy "viryanet", codeBase "http://viryanet.com/" {
    permission java.io.FilePermission "/tmp/viryanet/*",
"read,write";
};
```

Of course, for code to be "signed," you need something more than the name of the signatory (*"viryanet"* in this case). This something extra is a *digital signature.*

Note that the default permissions file shown provides unlimited access only to code residing in the *lib\ext* directory under the JDK installation, and that untrusted code can only read system properties.

While policies can be edited manually, the standard JDK distribution includes a *Policy Tool* for editing policies. Figure 13-2 shows this tool applied to the default `java.policy` file.

Keys used for digital signatures are managed using the keytool utility, a command-line utility that is also part of the JDK standard distribution. The keytool utility is used to create key pairs (either public or private) or for storing certificates from other parties. All keys and certificates are stored in a database called the *keystore*. The keystore itself is password protected to maintain the security of its content.

The Access Control List

The ACL API provides a framework through which you can express whether access to certain resources should be granted to a given user. A user or group of users are represented by the `java.security.Principal` interface.

The ACL API is defined in the `java.security.acl` package. This package defines the following interfaces:

- **Acl** The list of access permissions for a single resource.
- **Permission** A kind of permission granted to a user relating to a specific resource. Note that this java.security.acl.Permission is different than java.security.Permission described previously.

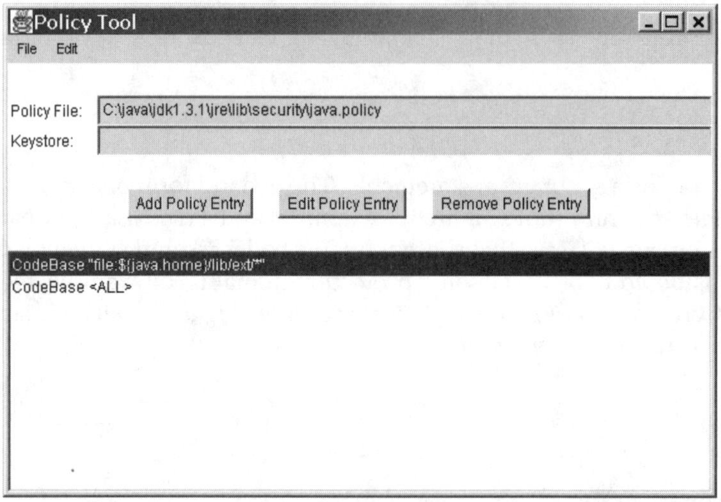

Figure 13-2. *Java Policy Tool main window*

- **Group** Encapsulates a list of principals.
- **Owner** Represents an owner of an ACL list (the Acl interface is derived from this interface), which is one or more principals.
- **AclEntry** Describes access permissions for a single Prinicpal. The entry is composed of polarity (grant or deny), Principal (to whom the specific entry relates), and Permission representing an action.

Given an `Acl` object, it is possible for you to check whether permissions are granted or denied for certain operations by certain principals.

More Security APIs: JAAS, JCE, JSSE

This section focuses on some additional security-related API that were originally offered only as optional Java packages; as of J2SE 1.4, they have become standard components. The following components offer even more security to Java:

- **Java Authentication and Authorization Service (JAAS)** Provides a framework for user-authentication
- **Java Secure Socket Extension (JSSE)** Provides Secure Socket Layer (SSL) and Transport Layer Security (TLS) support
- **Java Cryptology Extension (JCE)** Provides a framework for cryptography

While both JSSE and JCE are essentially cryptographic APIs, they were separated due to U.S. export controls.

Java Authentication and Authorization Service JAAS is a Java package that provides a framework for authenticating and enforcing access control upon users. JAAS authentication is done in a "pluggable" fashion that allows Java applications to be insulated from the underlying authentication technologies. JAAS authorization extends the Java security architecture and provides a way to grant access control not only based on what code is running (that is, based on its origin and who it was signed by) but also based on who is running the code.

Java Secure Socket Extension JSSE provides implementation of SSL of TLS. Most of the JSSE classes are concentrated in the package `javax.net.ssl`, but some are included in `javax.security.cert` and `javax.net`.

JSSE provides the classes `SSLSocket` and `SSLServerSocket`, which correspond to the non-secure `Socket` and `ServerSocket` classes. To minimize the need for code-changes, JSSE provides *socket factories* (which are `SocketFactory`, `ServerSocketFactory`, `SSLSocketFactory`, and `SSLServerSocketFactory`).

SSL is described in more detail in a later section.

Java Cryptography Extension JCE enhances Java security by catering for encryption, key generation, and key agreement, as well as Message Authentication Code (MAC) algorithms.

JCE was created to extend the Java Cryptography Architecture (JCA) APIs that are part of the Java 2 platform. It was provided separately to conform with U.S. export controls. Later on, an export-free variant of JCE was developed and integrated into J2SE v1.4.

JCE classes are located in the packages `java.security`, `javax.crypto`, `javax.crypto.interface`, and `javax.crypto.spec`.

JCE is used to encrypt streams of data using different encryption algorithms, given the desired keys, and to decrypt such streams of data subject to the availability of keys.

Secure Multipurpose Internet Mail Extensions

The Secure Multipurpose Internet MIME Extensions (S/MIME) is a specification for secure electronic mail that introduces security options to e-mail messages in Multipurpose Internet Mail Extensions (MIME) format. S/MIME is an RSA Data Security initiative that offers authentication using digital signatures and privacy using encryption. S/MIME has been submitted to the Internet Engineering Taskforce (IETF) and is the de facto standard for secure e-mail. Like most other protocols, S/MIME uses a public-key algorithm for setting up a symmetric key, after which encryption is performed using this symmetric key. X.509 digital certificates are used for authentication and certification.

RSA stands for Rivest, Shamir, and Adleman—the original inventors of public key encryption technology.

The Secure Electronic Transactions Specification

The Secure Electronic Transactions (SET) specification is an open industry standard developed by MasterCard International, Visa International, GTE, Microsoft, Netscape, SAIC, Terisa Systems, and VeriSign. SET was conceived to allow consumers and merchants to make secure bank card purchases on the Web.

SET is a technical specification for securing payment card transactions over open networks and specifically the Internet. SET's goal is to allow bank card transactions to be as simple and secure on the Internet as they are in retail stores today. Because currently more than 60 million people use the Web (most having good income), SET is of great interest to everyone. Three parts comprise the specification: a business requirements document, a developer information document, and a protocol specification document. The SET core is a payment protocol designed to protect consumers' bank card information when they choose to use bank cards to pay for goods and services on the Internet.

The SET initiative is designed to form an open specification that will ensure both a correct security model and an open interoperable standard. SET uses cryptographic concepts to ensure payment integrity and to authenticate both the buyer and the merchant. In terms of standardization, the forming of a standard specification is designed to ensure that applications developed by one vendor will interoperate with applications developed by other vendors. SET therefore not only defines the semantics of operations, but it also defines the wire-level protocol to be used.

The business requirements addressed by SET and defined in the SET Business Description (Book 1):

- Provide confidentiality of payment and order information
- Ensure data integrity
- Authenticate that a cardholder is a legitimate user of the account
- Authenticate that a merchant has the financial relationship with the card brand company
- Secure the transaction information in transit
- Ensure flexibility and extensibility for security mechanisms
- Ensure interoperability

It is interesting to note that a system supporting SET transactions is not a digital cash system. The cardholder communicates card information to the merchant. This information is used by the merchant to communicate with the financial institution and get an authorization for the transaction. The payment itself is not within the scope of SET.

Certificates are heavily used by SET both for certifying a cardholder (effectively the certificate is the electronic replacement for the piece of plastic we have gotten so used to) and for certifying that the merchant has a relationship with the financial institution (similar to that sticker on a merchant's window informing us which cards we can use there). SET certificates are verified through a hierarchy of trust. Each certificate is linked to the certification organization allowing the trust tree to be traversed in a hierarchical manner.

The Secure Socket Layer

SSL is a security protocol that supports private, authenticated communication over the Web. The protocol is layered between application-level protocols such as Hypertext Transfer Protocol (HTTP) or Common Object Request Broker Architecture (CORBA) invocations and between Transmission Control Protocol/Internet Protocol (TCP/IP) and is designed to prevent eavesdropping, tampering, or message forgery. The SSL protocol provides data encryption, authentication abilities, and data integrity verification. Because the protocol is layered under application-level protocols, it may be used for any TCP/IP-based application level protocols (such as File Transfer Protocol, Internet Inter-ORB Protocol, and so on). In addition, SSL is transparent to the application level, a property that makes it easy to integrate and add SSL into presently available Web software. SSL is the de facto industry standard.

SSL is designed primarily to provide privacy and reliability for application-level communication over the Internet. SSL is designed as two interacting layers: The low level, which is layered on top of TCP/IP, is the *SSL Record Protocol* that provides low-level services to the second layer, called the *SSL Handshake Protocol*. This protocol provides the application-level protocols with the access to required security mechanisms. The SSL Handshake Protocol allows the two interacting applications to authenticate each other (if necessary) and to negotiate an encryption algorithm and cryptographic keys.

SSL Security Features

SSL has three main security-related features:

- **Privacy** An application session using an SSL connection is private. The SSL initiation phase allows the two parties to negotiate a secret key that is used for encrypting the data stream. SSL data encryption uses algorithms such as Data Encryption Standard (DES) and RC4 (for Ron's Code 4); RC4 is a variable key size encryption algorithm invented by Ron Rivest.
- **Authentication** Each party in an SSL connection can authenticate the counterpart's identity using public key algorithms.
- **Reliability** An SSL connection is assured to be reliable and includes integrity checks countering malicious tampering attacks.

In addition, SSL is designed to be efficient and extensible. SSL includes a caching mechanism that allows a number of sessions to use the same connection, thus saving the initial setup time. Extensibility is provided by designing SSL as a framework into which additional encryption algorithms can be integrated (as long as both sides support them).

Naturally, for an SSL transaction to occur, both sides of the session must be using it. In a Web session, this means that both the browser and the Web server must be SSL-aware for a secure HTTP session over SSL to occur. In a distributed CORBA-based system, this implies that both Object Request Brokers (ORBs) must be SSL enabled.

SSL operations in a session consist of two main stages: the initiation and the data transfer. In addition, various alert handlers ensure that security attacks do not disrupt the session or compromise the participants' security. Initiation of a TCP/IP connection involves a security handshake process in which the client and the server agree on the security attributes of the session and in which authentication (both of the client to the server and of the server to the client) may occur. During the data transfer itself, one of a number of possible symmetric key encryption algorithms are used. In addition, data integrity mechanisms are used to ensure that data is not corrupted either by a mishap or due to a malicious attack.

SSL provides data encryption security for message transfer as well as client and server authentication. The technology used in SSL for data encryption is mostly RSA data security technology. For transactions occurring with one endpoint being external to the U.S., the RC4 stream encryption algorithm with a 40-bit key is used. A message encrypted with this algorithm will take a typical workstation approximately a year of "brute-force computation" to crack. Within the U.S., a 128-bit key is used, which effectively cannot be broken using brute-force computation. SSL authentication is based on digital certificates issued by trusted certificate authorities using a public key to perform a cryptographic test.

SSL supports four encryption operations:

- **Digital signatures** SSL uses either RSA signing in, with which a 36-byte structure is encrypted with a private key (that is, digitally signed); or the Defense Security System (DSS), which activates a digital signing algorithm on a 20-byte structure.
- **Block cipher encryption** In this mode, every block of data (plaintext) is encrypted into a block of ciphertext.
- **Stream cipher encryption** The data stream is exclusive OR'd (XOR-ed) with a cipher stream that is generated from a cryptographically-secure generator.
- **Public key encryption** A one-way function with a "trap door" is used to encrypt a data segment. The public key is not private to the connection (that is,

it is available to all), but the decryption of the delivered segment requires the private information.

The SSL Connection

The first phase of an SSL connection involves setting up an SSL session. SSL is not a stateless protocol and information is maintained throughout a connection and even between multiple connections (allowing SSL to provide improved performance). Session state includes:

- Session identifier
- Peer certificate
- Compression method
- Cipher spec that specifies the data encryption algorithm used
- Master (symmetric) secret key used between the parties
- Flag that indicates whether the session can be used to support multiple connections

Connection state includes:

- Random byte sequences, each chosen by one party of the connection
- Server secret key used for MAC operations
- Key used for data encrypted by the server
- Client secret key used for MAC operations
- Key used for data encrypted by the client
- A set of initialization vectors
- Sequence numbers used for ensuring correct order of messages

The first and most important phase in an SSL connection is the *handshake* phase. In this phase, the client and the server communicate to set up the session and connection state; if the two parties cannot come to an agreement regarding encryption and authentication, no transfer of data will occur. The handshake defines the protocol version used and the encryption algorithms to be used. In addition, any one of the participating parties may require the counter party to authenticate itself as part of the handshake. Finally, the handshake phase creates a set of shared secret keys using public-key encryption techniques. Once the handshake is complete, the session will usually involve only direct data communication (other than handling of exceptional events).

The handshake phase begins with the client sending a `CLIENT_HELLO` message to the server. The server responds with a `SERVER_HELLO` message. Each of these messages includes a random value generated by one party and delivered to the other. In addition, a public key algorithm is negotiated using these two messages. The next part of the handshake involves the optional authentication of each party. Assuming authentication has been successfully performed (or assuming that it is not required in the first place), the server sends the `SERVER_HELLO_DONE` message. The client then sends the `CLIENT_KEY_EXCHANGE` message using the public key that has been chosen previously.

Finally, the client selects a ciphering algorithm and sends the `CHANGE_CIPHER_SPEC` message to the server, thereby installing the new encryption algorithm in place of the (until now) NULL algorithm. Note that this message may also be used later to replace one encryption method with another. Before actually replacing the cipher spec, the server will send a `CHANGE_CIPHER_SPEC` to the client; only then will it replace the spec. When the server has successfully replaced the old spec with the new one, it sends a `FINISHED` message to the client, this time using the new cipher spec. This is done to coordinate the precise moment at which the new spec should be used in both the client and the server.

SSL Compression

Apart from encryption, SSL compresses all data passing over the wire. SSL records are compressed using an algorithm that is part of the session definition. The default algorithm does not change the stream (that is, no compression is performed), but any compression and the matching decompression algorithm to which both the client and the server agree can be used. In terms of structures, `SSLPlainText` structures are replaced by `SSLCompressed` structures.

The compressed structures are then converted into `SSLCiphertext` structures using the encryption functions and message authentication codes. This is possible since keys have already been negotiated in the handshake phase. These structures are then transmitted over the wire along with a sequence number used to monitor packets that do not arrive or that arrive in the wrong order. Note that encryption is performed after compression and not vice versa. On the receiving side, the order is reversed: first, decryption is performed, and then decompression.

Advanced Features

The SSL protocol defines some advanced features, making it suitable for Web transactions and as a basis for IIOP sessions. SSL supports a cipher change protocol that allows the client and the server to renegotiate a cipher spec. This could be used when either one of the communicating parties believes that security might have been compromised. A special SSL message is then used by one of the parties to notify the other party of the cipher change.

Another example of an advanced SSL message is the Alert Protocol. Alert messages can be used to inform a communicating party of an exceptional condition. In some cases (such as when the alert level is `fatal`), this will cause a termination of the communication session.

Other exception conditions include:

- Unexpected message
- Record contains an incorrect message authentication code
- Decompression function failure
- Handshake failure
- No certificate is available to fulfill a certification request
- Corrupt certificate
- Expired certificate

Summary

This chapter reviewed both the Java security model as well as the SSL that form the foundation for secure applications deployed on WebSphere. The Java security APIs allow you to define ACLs and protect the runtime from intrusions. SSL is the technology upon which most people rely for encryption and authentication for Web applications. Chapters 19 and 44 will introduce the WebSphere security model and discuss how application security should be implemented and administered using the WebSphere Application Server.

Chapter 14

Java Messaging Service

Distributed software systems manage a plethora of complexities that involve issues of reliability, security, fault tolerance, throughput, and networking. One of the ways to tackle these complexities is to use loosely coupled, asynchronous interactions between system components. This stands in stark contrast to the concepts of Remote Method Invocation (RMI) and Common Object Request Broker Architecture (CORBA), in which interactions are mostly synchronous—although CORBA has developed quite a few asynchronous paradigms. The critical difference between synchronous and asynchronous interactions is that the latter are more resilient in the face of network delays and malfunctions.

Enterprise messaging systems have been part of the enterprise computing system landscape for quite a while. Messaging systems such as IBM's MQSeries have gained quite a lot of popularity and are the backbone of a large number of corporate distributed software systems. Messaging is essentially a technique for achieving *loosely coupled* peer-to-peer communication. In other words, the sender and the receiver of a message do not need to synchronize the communication, and specifically, they do not need to be available at the same time. Furthermore, both parties do not need to know anything about each other; they only need to use the same message format.

To provide Java enterprise developers with the tools they need to hook into legacy systems using MQSeries or to build new systems that make use of MQSeries, IBM provides Java *connectors* for MQSeries. These are essentially *wrappers* that provide a Java interface to MQSeries.

While such an interface is definitely useful, it is not in line with the approach used to build Java application programming interfaces (APIs). This is where Java Messaging Service (JMS) comes in. JMS is a Java extension API that aims to simplify the task of integrating message-oriented middleware and Java applications. JMS is an interface-based API that allows different vendors to provide their own implementation of a JMS service similar to Java Database Connectivity (JDBC) or Java Naming and Directory Interface (JNDI). By separating the API from the implementation, JMS allows developers to make use of messaging systems, such as MQSeries, while they write generic code that is portable between messaging systems. Another advantage is that a standardized API shortens the learning curve.

The JMS standard was introduced by Sun's JavaSoft, but it is similar to other Java 2 Platform Enterprise Edition (J2EE) components, the standard which other vendors—most notably IBM—took part in defining and refining.

JMS Architecture

The backbone of any JMS-based application is the underlying messaging system, the medium through which messages are transmitted. This messaging system is referred to as the *JMS provider*. JMS itself is defined in a platform-neutral way, meaning that code written for one messaging system should work (possibly with some minor modifications) with any other JMS-compliant messaging system. The JMS API abstracts away the differences between messaging systems.

The application-level components of a JMS application are called *JMS clients.* JMS clients are pieces of Java code that generate and consume messages using the JMS API. Clients that are not implemented in Java are called *native clients.* Such clients make direct use of the underlying messaging system.

Two other components of the JMS architecture are *messages*—the objects that communicate information between clients, and *administered objects*—preconfigured objects typically created and maintained with administrative tools rather than the JMS API. There are two kinds of administered objects: destinations and connection factories.

JMS supports two messaging paradigms: point-to-point messaging and publish/subscribe messaging. Each of these paradigms is called a *domain* in JMS lingo. Point-to-point messaging implies that each message has only one consumer and that the messaging is truly asynchronous (that is, that the receiver can fetch the message regardless of the state it is in when the message is received). Point-to-point messaging is analogous to having a mailbox; the recipient chooses when to open the mailbox and retrieve the messages. Figure 14-1 shows a typical scenario for point-to- point messaging with one sender and one receiver. In general, it is possible to have several senders and several receivers.

Publish/subscribe messaging allows a single message to be sent to multiple clients. This is achieved by clients subscribing to a messaging topic. Clients receive messages that are published under a topic to which they subscribe, as shown in Figure 14-2. A messaging topic is analogous to the channels of a radio or television broadcast; once you tune in, you receive whatever is transmitted, and anybody who tunes in gets the same transmission.

The fact that clients receive messages only on topics to which they subscribe implies that clients cannot receive messages sent before they have subscribed to a topic. However, this drawback is overcome using *durable subscriptions,* which allow clients to receive messages that were sent prior to their subscriptions.

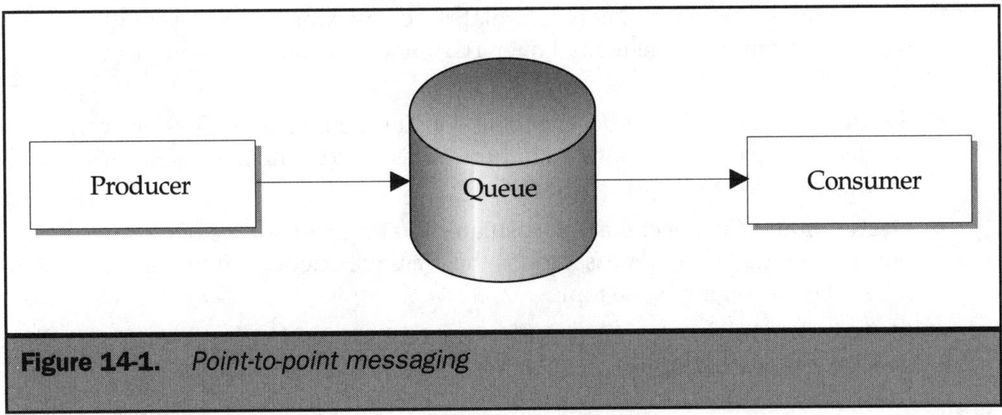

Figure 14-1. *Point-to-point messaging*

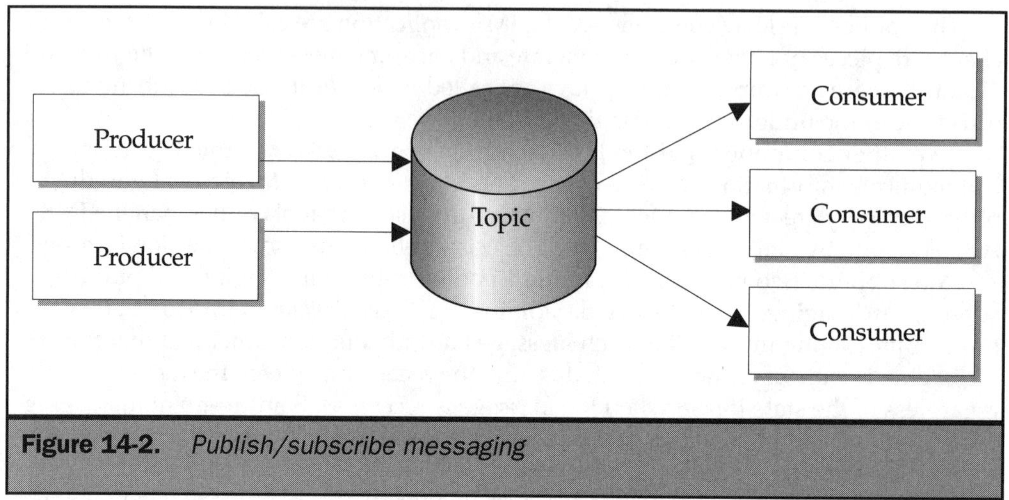

Figure 14-2. *Publish/subscribe messaging*

JMS supports two ways of consuming messages: Messages can be consumed synchronously by calling a `receive` method, which blocks the caller until a message is available (or until a certain time limit expires). Messages can be also be consumed asynchronously by defining *message listeners*. Message listeners are similar in nature to event listeners in that they both register interest in an event; their `onMessage` method is invoked when a message is received.

JMS Programming Model

The JMS programming model introduces the following abstractions:

- **Connection factory** A class used by clients to connect to a JMS provider.
- **Connection** An object that encapsulates a connection to a JMS provider. The connection can be implemented over TCP/IP or any other communication medium.
- **Session** A context for producing and consuming messages. Sessions can be created on top of connections, and they are used to create messages, message producers, and message consumers.
- **Destination** An object that encapsulates the target or source of messages, which in point-to-point messaging is the message queue, and in publish/subscribe messaging is the topic.
- **Message producer** An object that is created for a session and used for sending a message to a destination.

- **Message consumer** An object that is created for a session and used for retrieving a message from a destination.
- **Message** An object composed of a header, an optional set of properties, and an optional body. The actual purpose of JMS is to transport message objects.

Each of these abstractions has a JMS interface representing it. With the exception of messages, each of these interfaces has two interfaces extending it, one for each of the domains. For example, JMS defines a `Session` interface for sessions. The `TopicSession` interface extends it for publish/subscribe messaging, and the `QueueSession` interface extends it for point-to-point messaging. Table 14-1 summarizes the interfaces for each of the abstractions.

Connection Factories

The connection factory implements the well-known factory pattern. It is used by client code to generate connections. Connection factories are administered objects, which means that you need to generate them using the administration tools in the WebSphere Administrative Console.

In order to access the connection factory, you need to perform a JNDI lookup. Recall that in Chapter 5 a similar lookup was performed for the "Hello World" bean home interface. In Chapter 20, we will discuss JNDI in more detail.

JMS Parent	Point-to-Point Domain	Publish/Subscribe Domain
`ConnectionFactory`	`QueueConnectionFactory`	`TopicConnection Factory`
`Connection`	`QueueConnection`	`TopicConnection`
`Session`	`QueueSession`	`TopicSession`
`Destination`	`Topic`	`Queue`
`MessageProducer`	`TopicPublisher`	`QueueSender`
`MessageConsumer`	`TopicSubscriber`	`QueueReceiver` `QueueBrowser`
`Message`		

Table 14-1. *Point-to-Point and Publish/Subscribe Interfaces*

So how do you perform the lookup? You need to instantiate an initial context object, as follows:

```
        Properties env = System.getProperties();
        /* Possibly set the naming context URL and factory */
        InitialContext ic = new InitialContext(env);
```

Now you can access the specific connection factory objects. Two default connection factory objects are preconfigured in the J2EE software development kit (SDK), so you can access them immediately. The first of the two connection factories is the queue connection factory, which is instantiated as follows:

```
QueueConnectionFactory qFactory = (QueueConnectionFactory)
                         ic.lookup("QueueConnectionFactory");
```

The second connection factory is the topic connection factory, which is instantiated as follows:

```
TopicConnectionFactory topicFactory = (TopicConnectionFactory)
                         ic.lookup("TopicConnectionFactory");
```

Connections

A Connections object encapsulates a communication link to the JMS provider. This link is a connection to the messaging system, not to the message destination. The message-based communication paradigm is connectionless; there is no peer-to-peer connection at any time.

So how do you get a connection? Given a connection factory of the kind we just mentioned in the preceding subsection, you can create a connection. The name of the method used depends on whether you want a queue connection or a topic connection. For a queue connection use

```
QueueConnection qConn = qFactory.createQueueConnection();
```

For a topic connection use

```
TopicConnection tConn = topicFactory.createTopicConnection();
```

Using these connections, you can create session objects, as explained in the next subsection.

When you open the connection, the JMS provider on the other side of the connection allocates some resources. Since this is typically in a separate Java Virtual Machine (JVM), possibly on a separate machine, the garbage collector will not be able to take care of deallocating these resources. You must do that explicitly, using the `close` method. For example:

```
/* Close Queue Connection */
qConn.close();

/* Close Topic Connection */
tConn.close();
```

Sessions

A session object is used for producing and consuming messages. It is important to note that a session is a single-threaded context for messaging, so in a multithreaded application you might want to create several such objects—one for each thread.

As shown in Table 14-1, sessions come in two flavors based on the domain to which they correspond. You can create a topic session from a topic connection, as follows:

```
TopicSession tSession = tConnection.createTopicSession(false,
                                     Session.AUTO_ACKNOWLEDGE);
```

The first parameter indicates whether transactions are to be used; `false` means that you don't want transactions. The second parameter indicates the required behavior for message acknowledgment. It is only relevant for sessions that don't have transactions. For transacted sessions, acknowledgment takes place automatically upon committing the transactions (more on that later in the section "JMS and Transactions"). Following are the possible acknowledgment values and what they mean:

- **Session.AUTO_ACKNOWLEDGE** The session automatically acknowledges the receipt of a message on the client side once the client retrieves the message.
- **Session.CLIENT_ACKNOWLEDGE** The client must explicitly acknowledge messages using the acknowledge method of the message. Any such acknowledge method is applied by the session to all other messages consumed prior to the acknowledgment.
- **Session.DUPS_OK_ACKNOWLEDGE** The session is allowed to acknowledge messages lazily, thus possibly creating duplicated messages. This option can improve performance in some cases, but it can only be used by clients that can tolerate duplicate messages.

Creating queue sessions is quite similar, and the parameters are the same. Here's an example:

```
QueueSession qSession = qConnection.createQueueSession(false,
                                                   Session.AUTO_ACKNOWLEDGE);
```

Destinations

A destination is the target of messages sent and the source of messages received. As shown in Table 14-1, `Queue` objects represent destinations in point-to-point messaging, whereas `Topic` objects represent destinations in publish/subscribe messaging.

You must look up destination objects using JNDI, similar to the way you look up connections. For example, using the naming context that we defined in the code snippet for connections, you would look up a queue called `Queue1` using the following line of code:

```
Queue queue1 = (Queue) ic.lookup("Queue1");
```

Similarly, you can look up a topic as follows:

```
Topic topic = (Topic) ic.lookup("ImportantTopic");
```

Message Producers and Consumers

Message producers and consumers are objects created by the session for the purpose of sending and receiving messages. These objects serve as proxies of the messaging queue, or topics on the client side.

In point-to-point messaging, `QueueSender` and `QueueReceiver` represent message producers and consumers, respectively. You create them using the session object. Here's an example:

```
QueueSender qSender = qSession.createSender(queue1);
QueueReceiver qReceiver = qSession.createReceiver(queue2);
```

You can send a message simply by invoking the `send` method:

```
qSender.send(message)
```

Of course, you must have the message object first. You receive a message using the `receive` method as follows:

```
"message = /"qReceiver.receive();"
```

This method implements synchronous message consumption. You can also consume messages asynchronously using message listeners. A *message listener* is an object that implements the `MessageListener` interface. This object can be registered with the message consumer (or the `QueueReceiver` in point-to-point messaging); then, whenever a message is received, the `onMessage` method of the listener is invoked.

When creating a message consumer, you can optionally specify the type of messages you are interested in. You specify the messages of interest using a subset of Structured Query Language (SQL) expressional syntax, as explained later in this chapter, in the section titled "Message Selectors."

JMS defines similar producers and consumers for publish/subscribe messaging (see Table 14-1). The concept of message listeners applies to that messaging paradigm as well.

Messages

Messages are the most basic abstraction in JMS, and they are the purpose of the whole architecture. A JMS message is composed of a header, optional properties, and an optional body.

Message Header

The message header contains a set of fixed fields that are used to identify the message and to help in routing it. Each message has a unique message ID represented by the `JMSMessageID` header field and a destination (either a queue or a topic) indicated by the `JMSDestination` field. Other fields include:

- **JMSPriority** The message priority.
- **JMSTimestamp** A time stamp placed when the message is sent.
- **JMSExpiration** The expiration time for the message.
- **JMSDeliveryMode** The delivery mode—either DeliveryMode.PERSISTENT or DeliveryMode.NON_PERSISTENT. The former incurs more overhead, but it guarantees message delivery even when messaging system failures occur.
- **JMSCorrelationID** An application-level value that links the message to other messages.
- **JMSReplyTo** A destination object to which replies to the message should be addressed.
- **JMSType** A string that indicates the type of message; it is typically dependent on the JMS provider.
- **JMSRedelivered** A boolean used by the JMS provider to indicate that the message is being delivered for the second time.

Message Properties

Message properties are essentially application-level header fields. Property names are Java `String` objects, and their values are Java primitive types, such as `boolean`, `byte`, `short`, `int`, `long`, `float`, `double`, and `String`.

Property values can be set only on the sending side. Message properties are read-only for the message recipient.

Message properties are set using the `setObjectPropertyMethod` method and retrieved using the `getObjectProperty` method.

Message Body

The message body is optional, and can take six different forms. For each of these forms, JMS defines a message type, which is an interface extending the Message interface. For each such interface, corresponding set and get methods are provided. Following are the message types:

- **Message** Message with empty body
- **TextMessage** The message body is comprised of a `java.lang.String` object
- **BytesMessage** The message body is comprised of a stream of bytes
- **StreamMessage** The message body is comprised of a stream of Java primitive values
- **ObjectMessage** The message body is comprised of a serializable object
- **MapMessage** The message body is comprised of an associative array composed of name-value pairs in which the names are Java strings and the values are Java primitive objects

Coding a JMS Client

A typical JMS client follows these steps:

1. Obtains the `ConnectionFactory` object using JNDI lookup.
2. Establishes a JMS connection object.
3. Creates a JMS session object.
4. Finds the JMS destination object using JNDI lookup.
5. Creates a JMS message producer, message consumer, or both.
6. Sends or receives messages.

Point-to-Point Messaging Client

To illustrate these steps, consider the simplest possible JMS client, which sends a text message. For simplicity, the message in the following example is limited to a single word.

```
import javax.naming.*;
import javax.jms.*;

public class HelloQueueSender
{
    public static void main(String[] args)
    {
        Context                           ic = null;
        QueueConnectionFactory            qConnFactory = null;
        QueueConnection                   qConn = null;
        Queue                             queue = null;
        QueueSession                      qSession = null;
        QueueSender                       qSender = null;
        TextMessage                       message = null;
        if (args.length != 2) {
            System.out.println("Usage: java HelloQueueSender " +
                               "<queue-name> <message>");
            System.exit(1);
        }
        String qName = new String(args[0]);
        String fName = "QueueConnectionFactory";
        try {
             /* Lookup connection factory and queue */
             ic = new InitialContext();
             qConnFactory = (QueueConnectionFactory)
                                                  ic.lookup(fName);
             queue = (Queue) ic.lookup(qName);
         } catch (Exception e) {
             System.err.println("JNDI Lookup failed" + e);
             System.exit(1);
         }
        try {
            /* Create connection, session, sender, message */
            qConn = qConnFactory.createQueueConnection();
            qSession = qConn.createQueueSession(false,
                       Session.AUTO_ACKNOWLEDGE);
            qSender = qSession.createSender(queue);
            message = qSession.createTextMessage();
            /* Set message text */
            message.setText(new String(args[1]));
            /* Send message */
            qSender.send(message);
            /* Close connection */
```

```
            qConn.close();
         } catch (Exception e) {
            System.err.println("Error on Sending Message" + e);
         }
   }
}
```

Now consider such a message for the receiver side. The majority of the code is identical; the only code that is different implements the actual receive operation.

```
import javax.naming.*;
import javax.jms.*;

public class HelloQueueReceiver
{
    public static void main(String[] args)
    {
        Context                                 ic = null;
        QueueConnectionFactory                  qConnFactory = null;
        QueueConnection                         qConn = null;
        Queue                                   queue = null;
        QueueSession                            qSession = null;
        QueueReceiver                           qReceiver = null;
        if (args.length != 1) {
            System.out.println("Usage: java HelloQueueReceiver " +
                                   <queue-name>");
            System.exit(1);
        }
        String qName = new String(args[0]);
        String fName = "QueueConnectionFactory";
        try {
             /* Lookup connection factory and queue */
             ic = new InitialContext();
             qConnFactory = (QueueConnectionFactory)
                                                   ic.lookup(fName);
             queue = (Queue) ic.lookup(qName);
         } catch (Exception e) {
             System.err.println("JNDI Lookup failed" + e);
             System.exit(1);
         }
```

```
        try {
            /* Create connection, session, receiver */
            qConn = qConnFactory.createQueueConnection();
            qSession = qConn.createQueueSession(false,
                            Session.AUTO_ACKNOWLEDGE);
            qReceiver = qSession.createReceiver(queue);
            /* Receive message */
            qConn.start();
            TextMessage m = (TextMessage)queueReceiver.receive(1);
            if (m != null) {
                System.out.println("Read message: " + m.getText());
            }
            /* Close connection */
            qConn.close();
        } catch (Exception e) {
            System.err.println("Error on Sending Message" + e);
        }
    }
}
```


Publish/Subscribe Messaging Client

To demonstrate publish/subscribe messaging, here's a simple example that involves text messages. In the spirit of the example from the previous subsection, two classes are used—one for sending messages and one for receiving them. The sender class is shown in the following listing. The `main` method loops over user input and sends each line as a message on the topic specified in the command line. An empty string indicates the end of the sending process.

```
import java.io.*;
import java.util.*;
import javax.naming.*;
import javax.jms.*;

public class HelloTopicSender
{
  private TopicSession tSession;
  private TopicPublisher publisher;
  private TopicConnection conn;
  private InitialContext ic;

  public HelloTopicSender(String topicName)
  {
```

```
        try {
            /* Lookup connection factory and queue */
            ic = new InitialContext();
            String tName = "TopicConnectionFactory";
            tConnFactory = (TopicConnectionFactory) ic.lookup(tName);
         } catch (Exception e) {
            System.err.println("JNDI Lookup failed" + e);
            System.exit(1);
         }
        /* Create connection, sessions */
           try {
              conn = tConnFactory.createTopicConnection();
              tSession = conn.createTopicSession(false,
                                            Session.AUTO_ACKNOWLEDGE);
              Topic topic = (Topic)jndi.lookup(topicName);
              publisher = tSession.createPublisher(topic);
         } catch (Exception e) {
            System.err.println("Message topic initialization failed" + e);
            System.exit(1);
         }
    }

    /* Create and send message using topic publisher */
    protected void send(String text)
    {
        TextMessage message = session.createTextMessage( );
        message.setText(text);
        publisher.publish(message);
    }

    /* Close the JMS connection */
    public void shutdown()
    {
       try {
          conn.close( );
       }
       catch (Exception e) {
                /* Report error */
       }
    }

    public static void main(String [] args) {
        try {
            if (args.length != 1) {
                System.err.println("Usage: java HelloTopicSender " +
                                   "<topic>");
```

```
                System.exit(1);
            }
            HelloTopicSender sender = new HelloTopicSender(args[0],
                                                args[1],args[2]);
            BufferedReader userInput =
                    new BufferedReader(new InputStreamReader(System.in));

           // Loop until an empty line is entered
            while(true){
                String s = commandLine.readLine( );
                if (s.equals("")){
                    sender.shutdown();
                    System.exit(0);
                } else
                    sender.send(s);
            }
        } catch (Exception e) {
                  e.printStackTrace();
      }
    }
}
```


The second part of this example is a piece of code that subscribes to a message. To illustrate the use of message listeners, we derive our class from `MessageListener`. In this specific case, we implement a polling loop that is idling and waiting for messages, but in other cases an event-based handler would be used.

```
import java.io.*;
import java.util.*;
import javax.naming.*;
import javax.jms.*;

public class HelloTopicReceiver implements javax.jms.MessageListener
{
private TopicSession tSession;
private TopicSubscriber subscriber;
private TopicConnection conn;
private InitialContext ic;

public HelloTopicReceiver(String topicName)
{
        try {
             /* Lookup connection factory and queue */
             ic = new InitialContext();
             String tName = "TopicConnectionFactory";
             tConnFactory = (TopicConnectionFactory) ic.lookup(tName);
```

```
        } catch (Exception e) {
            System.err.println("JNDI Lookup failed" + e);
            System.exit(1);
        }
       /* Create connection, sessions */
         try {
             conn = tConnFactory.createTopicConnection();
             tSession = conn.createTopicSession(false,
                           Session.AUTO_ACKNOWLEDGE);
             Topic topic = (Topic)jndi.lookup(topicName);
             subscriber = tSession.createSubscriber(topic);
             subscriber.setMessageListener(this);
             conn.start();
        } catch (Exception e) {
            System.err.println("Message topic initialization failed" + e);
            System.exit(1);
        }
    }

    /* Recive message */
    public void onMessage(Message msg)
      {
            try {
                   TextMessage message = (TextMessage) msg;
                   System.out.println(msg.getText());
            }
    }


    public static void main(String [] args) {
        try{
            if (args.length != 1) {
                System.err.println("Usage: java HelloTopicReceiver " +
                                   "<topic>");
                System.exit(1);
            }
            HelloTopicSender sender = new HelloTopicSender(args[0]);
            /* Idle waiting for messages */
            while(true){
            }
        } catch (Exception e) {
                  e.printStackTrace( );
            }
    }
}
```

Advanced JMS Features

The send and publish methods, which are used to send messages, have a verbose mode in which you specify three parameters in addition to the message itself: the delivery mode, the priority level, and the expiration time (in that order).

As mentioned earlier in the chapter, the JMS message header includes a delivery mode field that can take one of the two values defined in the DeliveryMode interface: PERSISTENT and NON_PERSISTENT. Persistent delivery, which is the default, guarantees that messages are never lost; it does this by storing the messages onto stable storage. You can set the delivery mode using the setDeliveryMode method (defined for the message producer) or using the aforementioned verbose form of the send method.

The message priority level determines the order of message delivery, and it allows you to indicate that some messages are more urgent than others. The level of priority is an integer between 0 and 9, 0 being the lowest priority and 9 being the highest. The default level is 4. You can specify the priority either when creating the session, by using the setPriority method of the MessageProducer interface, or when sending the message.

Message expiration is useful for any message that might become obsolete at a certain point in time. By default, messages never expire. Therefore, if you specify an expiration time (measured in milliseconds) by using the send method or the setTimeToLive method of the message producer, the message will be destroyed if it is not delivered before the specified time interval elapses.

Consider the following example:

```
qSender.send(message, DeliveryMode.NON_PERSISTENT, 9, 1000);
```

This code sends a message as nonpersistent with the highest priority; however if it is not delivered within one second, it will be destroyed and will not be delivered at a later time.

Durable Subscriptions

Using the persistent delivery mode guarantees that messages sent by the publisher in publish/subscribe mode are not lost. However, the subscriber will receive these messages only if he or she is active at the time the message is received. To illustrate this situation, consider cell phone Short Message Service (SMS) messages. Requiring the subscriber to be active means that messages that arrive when the phone is off are lost.

While this behavior might be acceptable in some cases, it obviously is not adequate in all cases. The solution is to define durable subscriptions. A *durable subscription* has a unique identity, and once one is subscribed, the JMS provider maintains the subscription even if the requesting party is no longer active (that is, if the connection is closed). It goes without saying that this comes with a price—namely, added overhead on the messaging system. The advantage is that once registered, a subscriber—who specifies an ID of a previously registered durable subscription—will receive all the messages that have been published on the topic.

To establish a durable subscription, you need to define a connection ID for the connection and a subscription name for the subscriber. The combination of these two identifies the subscriber.

The connection ID is set with administrative tools; that is, you need to add a new connection factory with the desired client ID. Then, using a connection that has the ID, you can create the subscription. Here is an example:

```
TopicSubscriber durableSubscriber =
                tSession.createDurableSubscriber(importantTopic, "Sub1");
```

Since durable subscriptions incur some overhead on the messaging system, and since the messaging system is unable to determine when a durable subscription is no longer needed, you must explicitly unsubscribe. You do so by using the `unsubscribe` method of the session, but only after closing the subscriber. Here is an example for the durable subscription created in the preceding code line:

```
durableSubscriber.close();
tSession.unsubscribe("Sub1");
```

Message Selectors

In many cases, recipients of messages are not interested in all messages that are addressed to them (just as you probably are not interested in all the junk mail you receive at home). JMS provides a mechanism for filtering messages using SQL-like expressions for selecting messages. You define this mechanism when you create the message consumer. Each of the session methods for creating a message consumer has a full form in which you can specify the message selector. For example, you use the following code when creating a durable subscription:

```
TopicSubscriber durableSub =
                 tSession.createDurableSubscriber(topic,
                    "Sub2", "dollarAmount > 100", true);
```

The first two parameters are the topic object and the subscription name (the same as in the preceding durable subscription example). The third parameter is the message selector, and the last parameter indicates whether the subscriber wants to ignore locally published messages. (The `true` value indicates that messages published locally will be ignored.)

The message selector is a string that can specify an expression defined in terms of the message headers and properties. If you are familiar with SQL, you can imagine that you have a table of all the messages, in which the columns are the message headers and properties, and you are specifying the `WHERE` clause for a `SELECT` statement.

JMS and Transactions

Transactions provide a way to perform operations in a reliable way. That's why they play a major role in virtually every enterprise application. Several of the J2EE technologies address the issue of transactions—for example, JDBC `Connection` objects, Enterprise JavaBeans (EJB), the Java Transaction Service (JTS), and the Java Transaction API (JTA).

The importance of transactions in messaging systems is that in some cases it is important that several messages be delivered together while providing *atomicity*. That is, either they are all delivered or none are delivered. The sender has the option to roll back the operation in case of failure.

In general, transactions support the notions of atomic updates, which are either completely done or not done at all but are never half-way done; guaranteed consistency, in which failed transactions never affect data; durability, in which changes are really persistent; and isolation, in which changes made by a transaction are unknown to other transactions until they are committed.

JMS supports two different kinds of transactions: local and distributed. *Local* transactions are limited in scope to a single client, and they provide the ability to group several messages together. Local transactions are managed through the `Session` interface. When creating the session, you need to specify the first parameter as `true` (thus specifying that the session is transacted). Later on, you can use the `Session.commit` and `Session.rollback` methods. It is important to emphasize that such transactions are limited in scope to a single client; therefore, the transaction in which a message is sent has nothing to do with a transaction in which some other client receives the same message. In fact, using local transactions has serious drawbacks if you are not careful. For example, if you send a message and then wait for a reply, all within the same transaction, nothing will happen. In other words, your program will hang. The reason is that the message does not get sent until you commit, so the other party will not reply.

If you need to implement *distributed* transactions, the best way to do it is by using the EJB architecture. Chapter 32 focuses on the use of special EJBs called *message beans*, which essentially blend EJB capabilities with JMS functionality.

Summary

Messaging systems have become the most widely used infrastructure for building distributed systems. There are many such products on the market that claim to be the best. These products fall into categories called middleware or Enterprise Application

Integration (EAI). These systems come with APIs for multiple programming languages, including Java.

Initially, all such products had their own proprietary APIs. As the industry matured and the messaging model became very well defined, JMS evolved to become a standard API through which any such system can be accessed. This standardization makes it much easier to build distributed applications that make use of the messaging model, and it makes those applications more portable. It is therefore no wonder that this is now an inherent part of WebSphere Application Server.

In this chapter, we focused on JMS as a technology. In Chapter 32, we will discuss JMS further in the context of message beans and EJB, and in the context of deploying applications that make use of JMS. In terms of the technologies that form the basis of WebSphere, we still need to discuss the J2EE model; that is the topic of Chapter 15.

Chapter 15

Java 2 Enterprise Edition

Java made its first steps as a mainstream programming language with a push toward a balanced thin client. This occurred mainly via the introduction of *applets,* small programs embedded in HTML pages. However, Java's characteristics as a programming language make it an ideal candidate for developing server-side code as well as Web-based clients. Java's strengths are as important to the server side of applications as they are to the client side. As the language matures, we find it used more and more on the server rather than the client. Its strengths as a good object-oriented language, as well as security capabilities, portability, and networking features, have made it an important player in the enterprise software market (on the server). However, due to Java's relative immaturity, application server developers were at first hesitant to use Java in this central role. During 1997, it became clear that unless some structure was put in place for supporting issues such as transactions, security, and distribution, Java was going to become a language for writing applets (which would probably be the first step toward its extinction).

Enter Enterprise JavaBeans (EJB). Just as building client software requires frameworks and standards to ensure that one can make use of tools and services developed by others, so does building server-side components. Business logic on the server should focus on building domain functionality and not on system-level features such as transaction management and coordination, security, and naming. Because no serious application can do without a solution to each of these issues, a standard application programming interface (API) set was required to ensure that application components on the server can select solutions for system and architecture problems without limitations and without being locked into a single solution. This set of APIs is the EJB specification.

Later on, when Java 2 was announced, Sun Microsystems defined the Java 2 Platform Enterprise Edition (J2EE). This platform is an architecture for developing, deploying, and executing applications in a distributed environment. The platform provides applications with system-level services, such as transaction management, security, client connectivity, and database access. Although Sun's JavaSoft published the J2EE specification, the software has been developed with close cooperation with other vendors, most notably IBM. The J2EE specification was influenced by the practical experience accumulated with various application servers such as IBM's WebSphere.

The importance of J2EE stems from the fact that when building real (and especially large-scale) systems, the work of developers can be broadly partitioned into two primary categories: domain-level application programming and system-level issues. This partitioning is reflected in the fact that almost any large programming project has two types of programmers: developers faced with the need to implement business logic and domain-specific functionality and developers who build "infrastructure" that deals with issues such as distribution, communication, transactions, security, naming and so on. EJB tries to separate these two categories and provides a framework in which application developers can focus on the domain functionality while using servers and containers built by specialists to solve their needs at the system level. Thus, not only can enterprise software developers save a lot of time, they can also benefit from solutions that are potentially far superior to those they would have built themselves in-house. The J2EE platform allows infrastructure developed by infrastructure vendors to have a standard API and standard framework so that it can be used by multiple domain-level applications. The bottom line for users is improved scalability and performance.

It is important to note that while Sun's EJB and J2EE definition was the first step toward having a standardized mechanism for defining infrastructure for Java server-side code, it was not the first step in defining infrastructure software for Java. J2EE is an industry-wide standard, and other companies have contributed greatly to J2EE. Among these, IBM has had arguably the most influence on the J2EE standard. For example, IBM developed a product called SanFrancisco, which was essentially a huge package of infrastructure software. It dealt with a lot of the issues detailed in the EJB specification, and many of the ideas that make up the foundation of J2EE come from project SanFrancisco.

WebSphere 4.0 implements the J2EE specification version 1.2 dated August 2001. J2EE is still an evolving standard, with version 1.3 already finalized.

The remainder of this chapter offers an overview of what J2EE is all about. Chapters 18–38 cover in more detail the specific technologies that comprise J2EE.

J2EE Component Technologies

The J2EE specification defines a set of related APIs that provide a platform for developing and deploying Web-enabled applications including EJBs, servlets, and JavaServer Pages (JSPs). These three technologies are covered in Parts V and VI. The Java 2 Enterprise Edition Software Development Kit (J2EE SDK) is a reference implementation provided from Sun. It is important to note from a chronological standpoint that J2EE came to the world a long time (years!) after EJBs, servlets, and JSPs were introduced. So, while the J2EE SDK provides a reference implementation, IBM's WebSphere (and other products from other vendors) implemented a majority of the J2EE specification before it was ever written.

This is not to say that the definition of J2EE has no merit. It provides integration among a set of previously disparate APIs. Typically, the different Java APIs were developed and delivered independently. With J2EE, Sun shows more "maturity" by offering a set of tightly integrated APIs. The list of APIs comprising J2EE is shown in Table 15-1. All these APIs are, of course, defined on top of and in addition to the Java 2 Standard Edition (J2SE).

In addition to the APIs, J2EE includes a set of tests for verifying API compliance. The set of J2EE technologies can be broadly partitioned into three different categories:

- **Components** Application-level software building blocks, such as EJB, servlets, JSPs, or client-side applets and applications.

- **Services** Provide the ability to integrate with other systems. Services include Java Database Connectivity (JDBC), JNDI, and JTA.
- **Communication** Technologies for providing communication such as Remote Method Invocation-IIOP (RMI-IIOP), JMS, and JavaMail. Hypertext Transfer Protocol (HTTP) can also be considered one of these technologies, but it is not part of the J2EE specification.

J2EE Applications

A J2EE application is built from three different kinds of building blocks: EJBs, Web components, and J2EE application clients. One of the advantages of the J2EE as a server-side technology is that, like any Java technology, it promotes portability and reusability of code.

A J2EE application may contain zero or more enterprise beans, Web components, or J2EE application client components. An enterprise bean is composed of three class files: the EJB class, the remote interface, and the home interface. A Web component may contain files of the following types: servlet class, JSP, HTML page, or a Graphics Interchange Format (GIF) image. A J2EE application client is a Java application that runs in an environment that allows it to access J2EE services.

The J2EE application, as well as each Web component, EJB, or J2EE application client, has a deployment descriptor. The deployment descriptor is an XML file that describes the component and its deployment-time behavior. For example, as briefly mentioned, a deployment descriptor for an EJB declares transaction attributes and security authorizations. Because this information is declarative, it can be changed without requiring modifications to source code or requiring recompilation. Instead, the J2EE server reads this information at runtime and acts upon the bean accordingly.

One of the main advantages of the J2EE architecture is that it provides a clear separation between middleware (or middle-tier software), which are essentially EJBs, and the client-side software, which are generally Web components. Non-programmers such as Web designers might carry out the preparation of the latter. Another important distinction is made between actual components such as EJB and their deployment descriptors. This way, the server administrator can make modifications to issues such as object placement or security policies without any need to change the actual Java class files.

In the most general setting, client-side code can reside in applets or applications, clients both of which execute in a Java Virtual Machine (JVM) local to the client machine. When using a Web browser on the client side, Web components on the server side are invoked. Dynamic Web components (namely servlets and JSP) generate HTML and XML pages. When doing so, they typically access EJB or other J2EE server-side APIs, such as JDBC, Remote Method Invocation (RMI), JavaMail, or JMS.

Even though the J2EE framework imposes a distinction between server-side and client-side component technologies, it still facilitates true n-tier architectures. The enabling technology here is EJB. With EJB it is possible to partition software in a variety of ways. While EJBs are basically server-side entities, they can act as clients of other EJBs.

API	Description
Enterprise JavaBeans (EJB)	Framework for building server-side business objects.
Java Database Connectivity (JDBC)	Uniform API for database-independent access to relational database management systems (RDBMSs).
Java Messaging Service (JMS)	Used for distributed asynchronous messaging.
JavaMail	Framework for building mail and messaging applications independent of specific protocols and platforms.
Java Naming and Directory Interface (JNDI)	Distributed naming and directory service that provides uniform access to location-transparent repositories of data.
JavaServer Pages (JSP)	A framework for implementing dynamic HTML or XML pages usually used for Web clients.
Java Servlet	Server-side code for generating responses for requests coming in over HTTP.
Transactions	*Java Transaction Server (JTA)*—API for managing distributed transactions. *Java Transaction Service (JTS)*—Specification for the implementation of a Transaction Manager complying with the JTA specification.
Extensible Markup Language (XML)	As part of the support for Web Services, J2EE places emphasis on XML. It includes Java API for XML Processing (JAXP).
Common Object Request Broker Architecture (CORBA)	*Java IDL*—Supports CORBA interoperability, and includes a downsized Object Request Broker supporting Internet Inter-ORB Protocol. *Remote Method Interface (RMI) over IIOP*—For distributed object communication. Also, JTS is based on the CORBA Object Transaction Service (OTS).
Connector	Standard API and architecture for integrating legacy information systems (typically not implemented in Java). Connectors are not part of J2EE 1.2 but are part of J2EE 1.3.

Table 15-1. *J2EE Technologies*

J2EE Application Deployment

Packaging and deployment are important considerations for any application development, but they are even more critical for large-scale enterprise applications. Quite early in the evolution of the Java programming language the need for packaging together several Java class files emerged. The first solution was to use ZIP files (based on the standard ZIP compression format introduced by Phillip Katz). Using ZIP files, it was possible to deploy a Java applet or application without the need to copy directories of files—they were all packaged in a single ZIP file.

While ZIP files provided a reasonable solution for small applications and applets, still something was missing—the ability to provide some metadata about the files, making the package file truly self-describing. Enter the Java Archive (JAR) file format. In this format, files are still packaged and compressed into a single file with *.jar* extension and support hierarchical directories in a platform-independent manner (the compression and packaging actually still use the ZIP format). However, the directory structure for the JAR file includes a *META-INF* directory with a file called *manifest.mf*. This file defines the metadata. JAR files are manipulated using the `jar` command, which is part of the JDK distribution and whose parameters are similar to the UNIX `tar` command.

The manifest file is formatted as a sequence of lines, each with the following form:

Attribute: value

For example, JAR files holding JavaBeans could have the attribute `Java-Bean: true`. Another example is the `Sealed` attribute, which can be specified to prevent classes from other files to access the classes in the JAR file.

Using the `Main-Class` attribute, it is possible to specify a class whose main method will be invoked when providing the JAR file as a parameter to the `jre` or `java` commands.

It is also possible to restrict a certain set of attributes to a single package using the `Name` attribute. For example, if a JAR file contains several packages and we want to seal a single package, `com.viryanet.package`, the manifest file would have a couple of lines reading like so:

```
Name: com/viryanet/package/
Sealed: true
```

Web Archives

The next phase in the evolution of Java application packaging came in the form of the WAR (Web Archive) file. WAR files are JAR files with a *.war* extension. WAR files were introduced as part of the servlet API specification and were created for deploying Web-based applications. WAR files typically contain servlets, JSPs, and associated resources, as well as static HTML or XML files.

WAR files have a directory called *WEB-INF,* in addition to the *META-INF* directory inherited from the JAR format. The *WEB-INF* directory may contain a directory named *classes* in which Java class files are stored (with the appropriate directory structure), and a directory named *lib* in which JAR files and ZIP files with Java classes are stored. The *WEB-INF* directory also contains a file named *web.xml,* which holds the metadata for the Web application.

To illustrate the structure of a WAR file, consider the simplest Web application consisting of a single JSP file called *test.jsp.* The WAR file can be generated using the Application Assembly Tool (AAT) described in Chapter 4. (Note that the same chapter describes how to create a WAR file containing servlets and JSPs as well as resource files.)

Given the WAR file, you can check its contents using this command:

```
jar tf <filename>
```

For example, in the case of a small WAR file, here is the content:

```
test.jsp
META-INF/MANIFEST.MF
WEB-INF/web.xml
WEB-INF/ibm-web-bnd.xmi
WEB-INF/ibm-web-ext.xmi
```

Here, the archive includes the JSP file (since it should be deployed as part of the application) as well as a bunch of metadata files. The *manifest.mf* file is quite dull here:

```
Manifest-Version: 1.0
Main-Class: null
Class-Path:  ./
```

The reason is that most of the interesting data is placed in the *web.xml* file.

The *web.xml* file is more interesting:

```
<?xml version="1.0" encoding="UTF-8"?>
<!DOCTYPE web-app PUBLIC "-//Sun Microsystems, Inc.//DTD Web
Application 2.2//EN"
"http://java.sun.com/j2ee/dtds/web-app_2_2.dtd">
   <web-app id="WebApp_1">
      <display-name>test-app</display-name>
      <servlet id="Servlet_1">
         <servlet-name>test</servlet-name>
         <jsp-file>test.jsp</jsp-file>
```

```
        <load-on-startup>1</load-on-startup>
    </servlet>
    <servlet-mapping id="ServletMapping_1">
        <servlet-name>test</servlet-name>
        <url-pattern>test</url-pattern>
    </servlet-mapping>
</web-app>
```

This file includes most of the parameters you specify in the AAT when assembling your Web application. The DOCTYPE tag includes a reference to JavaSoft's Data Type Definition (DTD) for Web applications. Conforming to this DTD ensures that all WAR files are indeed standard and can be used in each and every J2EE-compliant server.

The final components of this example WAR file are two files that include IBM's extensions to the WAR format. Some of the parameters and settings appearing in these files are discussed later in the book in Chapter 28.

Enterprise Archives

While JSP and servlets are important components in J2EE applications, another technology has yet to be mentioned: Enterprise JavaBeans (EJBs). When EJBs were introduced, their deployment and packaging was based on JAR files that included some special manifest attributes. This mechanism was not flexible enough and was certainly not as flexible as WAR files, where metadata is expressed using XML.

To provide a comprehensive solution to the issues of enterprise application deployment, the J2EE standard introduced Enterprise Archive (EAR) files—JAR files that serve as containers for multiple WAR and JAR files.

Following the concept of WAR files, the EAR file includes a *META-INF* file called *application.xml*, which includes the application-level metadata. For example, consider a simple application that includes the WAR file detailed in the previous section. The *application.xml* file for this application follows:

```
<?xml version="1.0" encoding="UTF-8"?>
<!DOCTYPE application PUBLIC "-//Sun Microsystems, Inc.//DTD
J2EEZApplication 1.2//EN"
"http://java.sun.com/j2ee/dtds/application_1_2.dtd">
    <application id="Application_ID">
        <display-name>test.ear</display-name>
        <module id="WebModule_1">
            <web>
                <web-uri>test.war</web-uri>
                <context-root>/test</context-root>
```

```
            </web>
        </module>
    </application>
```

The DTD reference in the DOCTYPE tag is once again what ensures that the structure of the file conforms to the J2EE specification. The *application.xml* file for a larger application can be quite intricate (as you will see in Chapter 34), and that is why the AAT is a critical component of the WebSphere environment. It is worthwhile to mention that JavaSoft's J2EE SDK includes a program called *deploytool* for creating and manipulating JAR, WAR, and EAR files. However, this tool is not as powerful or as convenient as WebSphere's AAT.

The J2EE Architecture

Unlike other Java objects, a J2EE component (be it a servlet, EJB, or JSP) cannot be executed on its own or simply using a JVM. It needs a certain execution environment. J2EE containers provide this execution environment and containers themselves execute within J2EE servers.

The concepts of servers and containers were introduced in the EJB specification. Servers correspond to application servers, such as WebSphere. Containers are execution environments for J2EE components and exist within a J2EE server. The container provides various services to the J2EE component, such as lifecycle services and communication services. Prior to the introduction of J2EE, the distinction between container and server in the EJB specification was somewhat unclear.

In the J2EE architecture, more than one kind of container is specified. In addition to EJB containers are servlet engines, JSP engines, and Web containers, which are containers for Web components. Such containers provide the necessary support for HTTP as well as any other API required.

J2EE servers provide a complete set of APIs as well as component implementations. The J2EE specification also opens the door for mixing and matching containers and servers. For example, you can install a servlet engine by vendor X into an application server of vendor Y. In many ways, the use of many Apache elements within WebSphere is based on these capabilities.

Figure 15-1 shows the major components of the J2EE architecture and their roles in a typical J2EE application.

The J2EE Server

The J2EE server provides the following services:

- **HTTP** Enables Web browsers to access servlets and JSP files
- **EJB** Allows clients to invoke methods on enterprise beans

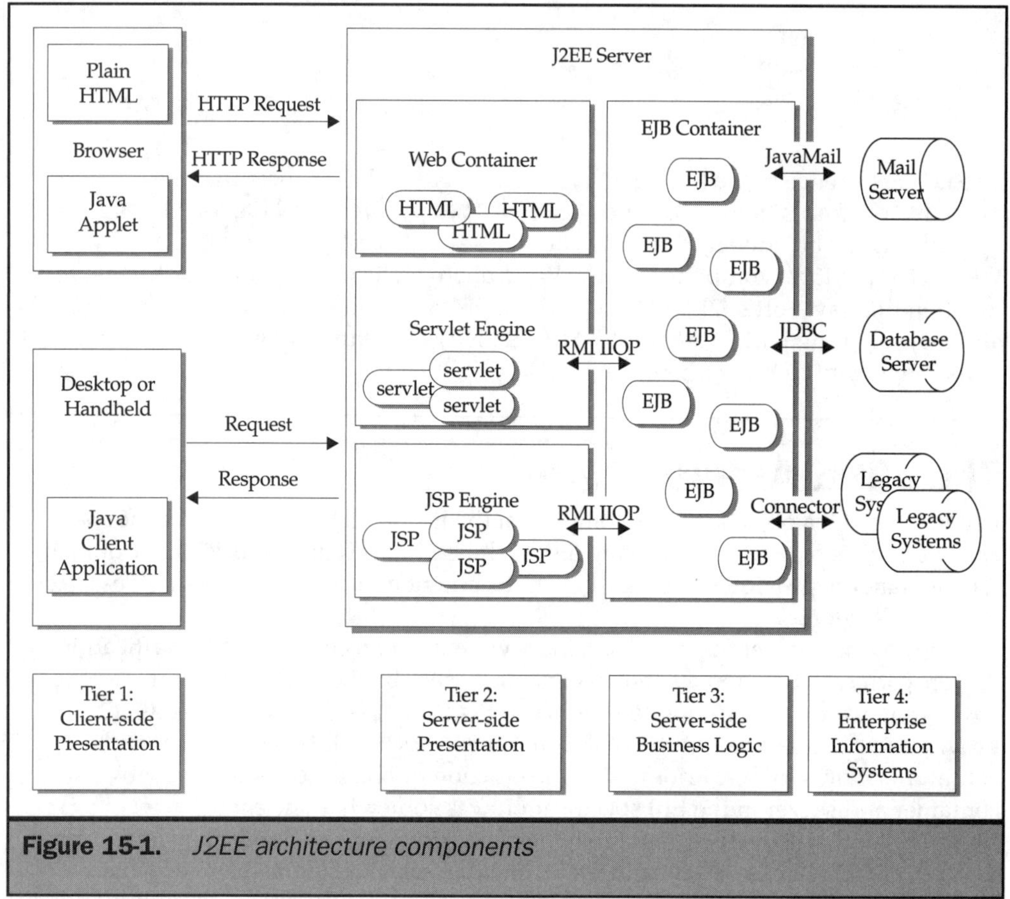

Figure 15-1. *J2EE architecture components*

- **Naming and Directory** Allows programs to locate services and components (typically EJBs) through the JNDI API
- **Authentication** Enforces security by requiring users to log in
- **Other APIs** CORBA, JavaMail, Transactions, JMS, and Connector

Web Component Container

Web components exist and execute in Web component containers. A Web container could be simply a repository for HTML, XML, and GIF files. However, for dynamic Web pages, more sophisticated containers are available, namely servlet engines and JSP engines.

A servlet container provides network services for the servlets, such as support for HTTP (or other request-response protocols, if applicable). It takes care of lifecycle management (such as the creation and destruction of servlet instances) and provides access to J2EE APIs such as Remote Method Invocation (RMI).

JSP containers are servlet containers that are also capable of converting JSP pages into servlets (via compilation).

The EJB Container

EJB instances run within an EJB container, a runtime environment that controls the enterprise beans and provides important system-level services. The container provides the following services to enterprise beans:

- Lifecycle management
- Transaction management
- Security
- Remote client connectivity
- Database connection pooling

Lifecycle Management

The container has total control over the management of the bean lifecycle but performs lifecycle-related operations as a response to client requests. An EJB passes through several states during its lifetime. The container creates the enterprise bean, moves it between a pool of available instances and the active state, and finally removes it.

Transaction Management

Whenever a client invokes an EJB method in an enterprise bean, the container intervenes to guarantee the transactional consistency of the bean. Because the container manages the transaction, developers are not required to implement code for transaction boundaries in the enterprise bean. Instead, the transactional behavior of the bean is provided in an external file called the *deployment descriptor*.

Security

Security is an obvious consideration for distributed applications and specifically Web-based applications. The container permits only authorized clients to invoke an enterprise bean's methods. Similar to transactional behavior, security definitions are not part of the code but are rather defined at deployment time.

Remote Client Connectivity

The container manages the low-level communications between clients and enterprise beans, based on Java Remote Method Invocation (RMI). After an enterprise bean has been created, a client invokes methods on it as if it were in the same virtual machine.

Database Connection Pooling

In any realistic setting, a database connection is a costly resource. Obtaining a database connection is time-consuming and the number of connections may be limited. Since database access is required in any application that is not a toy application, the container tries to limit the consequences. To this end, the container manages a pool of database connections. An enterprise bean can quickly obtain a connection from the pool. After the bean releases the connection, it may be reused by another bean.

Servlets and JSPs

Servlets provide a simple yet powerful API for generating dynamic Web content. While servlets are designed as a generic mechanism for supporting request-response protocols, their most common use is to process HTTP requests for Web content. JSPs provide a different mechanism for generating dynamic Web content. With JSPs, the Java code does not contain ordinary Java classes; instead, the code is embedded inside an HTML (or other content) page, similar to a scripting language.

Enterprise JavaBeans

EJBs are server-side reusable components written in the Java programming language. Enterprise beans contain the business logic for your application. EJBs come in two flavors:

- Session beans
- Entity beans

A session bean operates on the behalf of a client in the J2EE server. A client communicates with the J2EE server by invoking the methods that belong to an enterprise bean. A session bean converses with the client and can be thought of as an extension of the client. Session beans can be state-less or state-ful. State-less session beans can have many different clients and can be pooled. State-ful session beans have only one client. When the client terminates, its corresponding session bean also terminates. In any case, a session bean is transient, or non-persistent.

An entity bean represents a business object that is persistent. An entity bean's information is usually stored in a relational database, but this is not always the case—it could be stored in an object database, a legacy application, a file, or any other storage mechanism. The type of storage mechanism used depends on the particular implementation of EJB technology. The reference implementation (J2EE SDK) uses a relational database and so does IBM WebSphere.

J2EE Connectors

J2EE Connector architecture aims at providing a solution for integrating legacy systems or any non–Java-based enterprise systems with Java-based code. Examples of such systems include mainframe transaction processing, enterprise resource planning (ERP), and database systems. Prior to the introduction of the J2EE Connector architecture, the Java platform did not include any component addressing the issue of integrating legacy systems. This led to the evolution of a plethora of different vendor-specific products providing connectivity to their own non-Java systems. For example, IBM provided its own connectors to a Customer Information Control System (CICS).

The J2EE Connector architecture provides a framework in which the provider of an Enterprise Information System (EIS) can implement a resource adapter for its EIS. The resource adapter plugs into a J2EE server, which provides connectivity between the enterprise application and the EIS through the J2EE server. Any adapter that is properly implemented is guaranteed to provide seamless communication among applications running within the J2EE server and the respective EIS. This architecture is scalable, and multiple resource adapters can be plugged into the J2EE concurrently.

The resource adapter plays a role similar to that of a JDBC driver. It is a system-level software driver used to connect to a specific EIS. The J2EE server and an EIS collaborate in implementing transactions, security, and communication, all in a seamless and transparent manner. To that end, several contracts define the relationship between the J2EE server and EIS:

- **Connection Management contract** Provides connectivity to an underlying EIS and takes care of pooling of EIS connections
- **Transaction Management contract** Allows correctly executing transaction across multiple resource managers
- **Security Contract** Facilitates secure access to an EIS in conjunction to the underlying security mechanisms

JavaMail

JavaMail is a Java API for handling mail messaging. The JavaMail API provides a set of abstract classes that model a mail system. Using this API, mail can be accessed in a manner that is both platform- and protocol-independent. Chapter 22 features an example using JavaMail.

The JavaMail API is a specification for an open framework for e-mail messaging. As such, it provides a common API that can be implemented by different vendors. This uniformity substantially reduces the learning curve for developers and cuts down on the design dilemmas of vendors.

The Java Mail API is provided in the `javax.mail` package. The top-level entry to the API is the `Session` class, which is used to manage the configuration options and user authentication used for accessing mailing systems. Specifically, it is used to control and access the classes that represent the vendor-specific implementations of mail services. Providers of such services implement several classes.

The `Store` class allows for accessing, reading, writing, monitoring, and searching mail. The `Store` object contains a database of mail folder objects that can be retrieved from it. `Store` implements the specific access protocol (such as Internet Message

Access Protocol [IMAP] or Post Office Protocol 3 [POP3]) and also has methods for establishing and closing a connection.

The `Folder` class provides a hierarchical structure of mail messages and access to individual messages encapsulated in `Message` objects.

The `Message` class models the details of a single e-mail message, including the subject line, sender, reply-to address, recipients, and date. This class implements "lazy" fetching of messages (that is, delaying the retrieval as much as possible) to boost network performance. JavaMail supports multipart `Message` objects, where each part could have its own attributes and content types (this is useful for implementation messages with mail attachments).

The `Transport` class is used for sending messages over a specific protocol. The main method here is `Transport.send`, which implements the sending of a message.

Java Messaging Service

JMS facilitates *distributed asynchronous messaging*, a time-proven technique for building distributed applications. One of the leading products in this field is IBM's own MQSeries. JMS provides a product-independent API for such systems in Java, thus allowing developers to build applications that reply on messaging middleware without being tied to a single implementation. JMS is described in detail in Chapter 14.

Java Naming and Directory Interface

The Java Naming and Directory Interface (JNDI) provides a Java-based API to naming and directory services and is mostly used to access Lightweight Directory Access Protocol (LDAP) directories. It is described in detail in Chapter 20.

Java Database Connectivity

The Java Database Connectivity (JDBC) API provides Java developers with the ability to connect to relational database systems in a platform-independent manner. JDBC could itself be the topic of a book, so the purpose of this section is merely to make you familiar with it in case you haven't had a chance to use it in the past.

JDBC defines a standard API that is nevertheless open-ended. Vendors can provide their own "JDBC drivers" that implement access to their databases. The JDBC standard allows the vendor to make choices as to the implementation and the capabilities of the JDBC driver so long as the basic semantics are maintained. The implementation could be based on open database connectivity (ODBC) (in fact, Sun Microsystems provides a JDBC-ODBC bridge so that any ODBC-compliant database can be used with JDBC), it could be implemented using proprietary native code, or it could be implemented using proprietary code that connects to the database over a network.

The underlying implementation of the driver is usually of no interest to developers, apart from configuration and possibly performance issues. For example, ODBC-based drivers are typically slower than native ones and are not used in the mainstream.

Using JDBC

The JDBC API is contained in the package `java.sql`. To perform a database operation, the following sequence of actions is required:

1. Load the JDBC driver.
2. Establish a database connection.
3. Construct an SQL query or update statement.
4. Perform the statement.
5. Close the connection.

Other actions include querying the database for schema information or for other metadata.

Loading the JDBC Driver

JDBC drivers are managed by the class `DriverManager` in the `java.sql` package. The JDBC driver can be loaded in one of two ways: by instantiating the driver or by explicitly loading the class. For example, to instantiate an Oracle driver use

```
DriverManager.registerDriver(new
oracle.jdbc.driver.OracleDriver());
```

To load the class explicitly use

```
Class.forName("oracle.jdbc.driver.OracleDriver");
```

Connecting to Database

The database connection is achieved using the `DriverManager.getConnection` method. This method takes as parameters the database URL, user name, and password. For example, here's how it looks if you have an Oracle database called *testdb* placed on a machine called *dbhost*:

```
Connection conn = DriverManager.getConnection(
    "jdbc:oracle:thin@dbhost:1521:testdb", "dba", "dbaspass");
```

Establishing the connection might involve establishing a network connection in case the database is on a different machine.

Performing Queries

The next step is constructing an SQL statement using the connection object in the following manner:

```
Statement statement = con.createStatement();
```

The statement object can be used to perform an SQL query, using the `executeQuery` method. For example,

```
ResultSet rs = statement.executeQuery("SELECT * from MYTABLE");
```

The object returned from `executeQuery` is of type `ResultSet`. A `ResultSet` is essentially a collection of database table rows. You may iterate over the rows using the `ResultSet.next` method. For each row, the values of the various columns can be retrieved using *get* methods of the `ResultSet` object. The *get* methods can either use column ordinals or column names. For example, if the first column is called "COLUMN1" and holds integer values, you may retrieve such values in either one of the following ways:

```
int way1 = rs.getInt("COLUMN1"); // By column name
```

or

```
int way2 = rs.getInt(1);          // By ordinal
```

Similar to the `getInt` method, you have `getString`, `getObject`, and other *get* methods.

Performing Updates

Performing updates is similar to performing queries, except a different method of the `fix-width` object is used. Here's an example:

```
Statement statement = con.createStatement();
statement.executeUpdate("INSERT MYTABLE VALUES (1,2,3)");
```

Closing the Connection

Closing the connection is simple—you just invoke the `close` method of the connection object:

```
conn.close();
```

While this is only one line of code, it is an important thing to do since keeping the connection open will load the database and your JVM. If you repeatedly open new connections and forget to close them, you could run into performance and even availability problems.

More JDBC Capabilities

You now are familiar with the basic outline of how to use a database from within a Java application using JDBC. This section continues to more advanced options of JDBC.

Prepared Statements

To improve the performance of your application, JDBC lets you write statements in a way that is identical—apart from different arguments to the same parameters—using *prepared statements*. For example, consider selecting out of a table all the rows in which the first column has a certain value, `val`. You can achieve this in the following way:

```
ResultSet rs = statement.executeQuery("SELECT * from MYTABLE WHERE" +
"COLUMN1 = " + val);
```

However, this might not be efficient, because the SQL query must be generated from scratch over and over. The alternative approach is constructing a prepared statement, as follows:

```
PreparedStatement ps = conn.prepareStatement("SELECT * from MYTABLE
WHERE COLUMN1 = ?";
```

Later on, when you have the value `val` you want to use (in a loop or whatever), you could perform the query in this way:

```
ps.setInt(1, val);
ResultSet rs = ps.executeQuery();
```

JDBC 2 ResultSet

The `ResultSet` interface in JDBC 2 (which is the standard used in J2SE) provides some new capabilities, including scrolling. In addition to the `next()` method, you can use `previous()` to go back, or `first()` and `last()` to go to the first or last rows, respectively.

Another new feature of the `ResultSet` is the *update* methods. Recall that the `ResultSet` supports methods such as `getInt` for retrieving values. It also provides respective *update* methods so that you can perform updates immediately on the result set withoutf using a separate *update* statement. For example,

```
int val = rs.getInt(1);
rs.updateInt(1, val+1);
```

JDBC Transactions

JDBC supports the notion of *transactions*. Only one transaction can exist at any given time for each connection, and multiple nested transactions are not allowed. However, clients may use multiple connections.

EJB transactions are briefly discussed in Chapter 11, and a more detailed discussion of JDBC (and other) transaction management is part of Chapter 31.

Summary

Java has come a long way since its inception in terms of its maturity and readiness for building applications in general, and specifically in enterprise-level applications. Java has three tracks today, two of which are relevant to applications running over WebSphere: the standards edition (J2SE) and the enterprise edition (J2EE).

WebSphere as an application server targets primarily the enterprise market. It is used for building high-end systems that are most often accessed by multiple users. It is therefore no wonder that WebSphere as a server uses the J2EE set of APIs. As described in this chapter, J2EE is a set of packages that define a certain API set. J2EE is usually called a *standard*, because the combination of these APIs defines an environment that any application developer can rely on—in terms of API as well as semantics. This means that the application developer can reuse a lot of infrastructure services and needs to write less of his or her own code while being sure that it will work on any J2EE-conforming server. This is a new level of portability that has never been achieved before in the software industry.

Version 4 of WebSphere is the first version to fully comply with the J2EE specification—and this step is an important one in the life of WebSphere.

This chapter concludes Part II, which covers the technological basis of WebSphere. The remaining chapters of the book describe how to develop applications that run on a J2EE server (WebSphere in our case) and how to deploy these applications on the server, and they provide an overview of the development tools used by an application developer in a WebSphere-centric environment. This latter category is the subject of the next two chapters in Part III.

Part III

Development Environments for WebSphere Applications

Chapter 16

WebSphere Studio Application Developer

The WebSphere Studio family of products provides a set of integrated tools that can be used for developing Web sites. It simplifies the tasks of site design, development, and maintenance.

The most recent member of the WebSphere Studio product family is the WebSphere Studio Application Developer (WSAD). WSAD is an Integrated Development Environment (IDE) for Java 2 Platform Enterprise Edition (J2EE) applications. It covers the entire lifecycle of building, testing, and deploying J2EE applications. The appeal of the WSAD is that it combines the ease of use of Web-design tools with the power of a Java IDE (such as VisualAge for Java). To top it off, WSAD also offers a full test environment for the WebSphere Application Server.

WSAD represents a convergence of VisualAge for Java with earlier products in the WebSphere Studio family. Before WSAD was introduced, serious development work was underway with VisualAge for Java, whereas lightweight development (such as gluing together existing components) and Web site design were accomplished using WebSphere Studio. WSAD provides a single development environment for the full range of server-side components: Hypertext Markup Language (HTML) files, Extensible Markup Language (XML) files, JavaServer Pages (JSP), servlets, Enterprise JavaBeans (EJB), and Web services. WSAD provides wide functionality that appeals to the full spectrum of developer roles involved in creating a J2EE application, ranging from Web designers and Java developers to people involved in deploying and administering applications. By providing means of customization, WSAD can insulate a user involved in a single role from the functionality that is of no interest to him or her. Furthermore, while the product covers a lot of ground in terms of functionality, there is no compromise in terms of its power as a tool.

It is worth mentioning that WSAD is based on an open-source software platform called Eclipse, whose development was led by IBM. You can find more information about the Eclipse project at *http://www.eclipse.org*.

Installation

The WSAD, as well as other WebSphere Studio products, can be downloaded directly from the IBM Web site at *http://www.software.ibm.com/websphere/studio*. It is also available on the CD accompanying this book. Similar to other members of the WebSphere family, it supports multiple platforms—Windows (98/Me/2000/XP) and Linux, at the time of this writing.

The installation process is simple and easy. If you've downloaded the installation from the Internet, you should first unzip it. Then run the *setup.exe* program, which takes you through the installation. If you are installing from the CD, you can run the Setup program directly.

The installation process is quite standard. The first window for the Setup program is a welcome screen, followed by a license agreement. You need to select the product installation directory, the primary user role, and your version-control software. The primary user role is one of the following: J2EE developer, Web developer, Java developer, or Web services developer. The primary user role setting does not have any irreversible effect, but it determines what you'll see when you start WSAD. The version-control software setting allows you to integrate WSAD into your existing version control software, such as Concurrent Versions System (CVS) or Rational ClearCase. After you make these selections, you can start the installation process, which takes a few minutes.

When you start up WSAD you will see a window similiar to that shown in Figure 16-1.

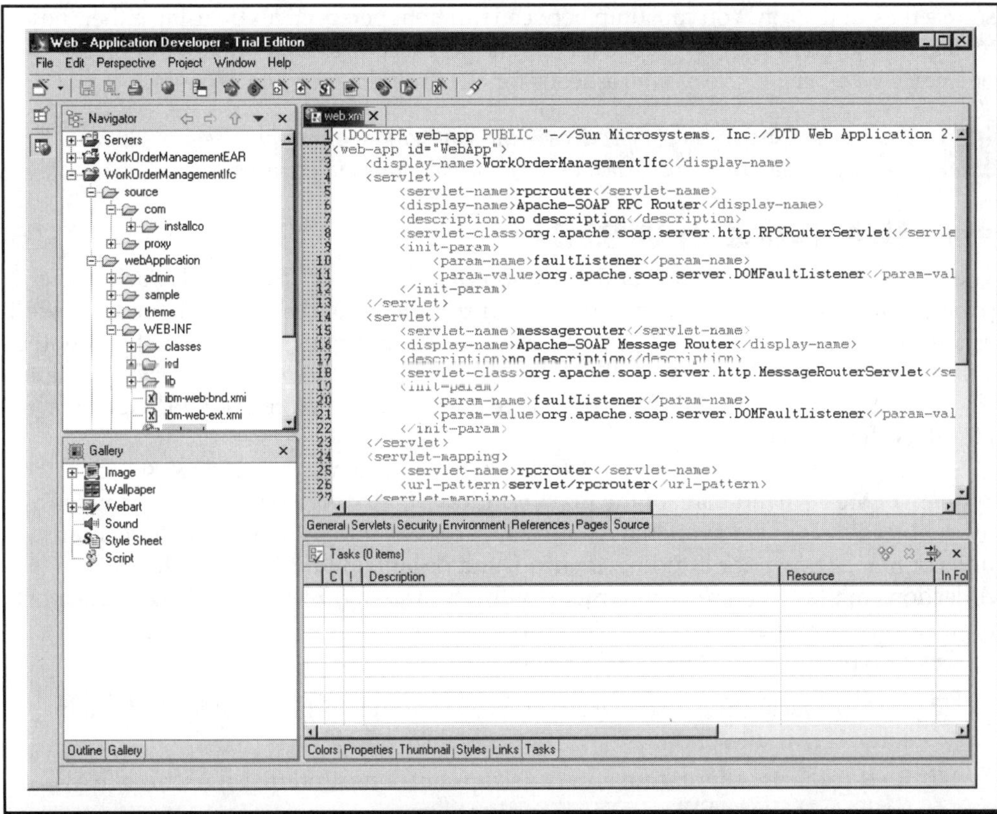

Figure 16-1. *WSAD's Welcome page*

WebSphere Studio Application Developer: A First Look

The primary user interface for WSAD is called the Workbench. The Workbench introduces a novel concept of a *perspective*, a role-based customization of the displays and editors available in a certain point in time. You can jump between perspectives as you progress in the work cycle—for example, using one perspective for coding and another for debugging.

Perspectives combine a set of interrelated views and editors. *Views* are ways of looking at a certain resource, whereas *editors* are used to create and modify code. WSAD includes a variety of editors that are suitable for specific file types, such as HTML files, XML files, Java source files, and so on. You can jump between different perspectives by using either the toolbar on the left or the Perspective menu. The perspective toolbar offers a button for opening a new perspective as well as icons for all currently open perspectives.

Note *You can have two open perspectives of the same kind. For example, you might have two Java perspectives open, each of them focusing on a different package.*

Perspective Types in WSAD

The perspectives, their icons, and descriptions are detailed in Table 16-1. Each of the perspectives is customizable, and you can control the set of displayed elements as well as their layout. Furthermore, if you access a specific resource (such as a file) you will be able to edit it using the corresponding editor, regardless of the perspective. For example, if you double-click an HTML file from the resource view or from the J2EE view, the HTML editor will appear.

An important component of the Workbench is the navigator window, which appears in the lefthand pane of the main window. The navigator window provides a hierarchical view of the available resources—projects, folders, and files. Projects are units of management for building, sharing, and organizing resources. Folders are collections of files, and are synonymous with file system directories. Files are the most basic resources in the underlying file system.

Seven types of projects exist in WSAD:

- **Web projects** Represent Web applications. Such projects typically contain static HTML files, images, Java files, servlets, and JSPs.
- **EAR projects** Represent enterprise applications. Enterprise Archive (EAR) projects combine EJB with Web applications.
- **J2EE application client projects** Represent J2EE application client programs.
- **Java projects** Represent Java applications, and are similar to projects in VisualAge for Java.
- **EJB projects** Represent collections of EJB components.
- **Server projects** Used to capture server configuration information.
- **Plug-in projects** Represent WebSphere Studio Workbench plug-ins.

Icon	Perspective	Description
	J2EE	Develop J2EE applications and EJB modules
	Web	Develop Web applications or Web services and design static and dynamic Web pages
	Server	Built-in WebSphere Application Server test environment that can be used for testing components developed in the other perspectives
	Help	Access WSAD's integrated Help facility, which provides tutorials and reference material
	Resource	Access files and folders
	Team	Access built-in support for teamwork—integrated support for configuration management systems, such as CVS and Rational ClearCase
	Java	Develop Java code
	Debug	Debug Java code (including servlets and JSP)
	Data	Explore databases, import data from them, and perform SQL queries against them
	Scripts	Author and review scripts
	XML	Design and view XML files as well as schema files and document type definitions
	Java type hierarchy	Browse through the Java type hierarchy and review methods and member variables
	Trace	Profile applications and specific classes
	Plug-in development	Develop WebSphere Studio Workbench plug-ins used to extend WSAD

Table 16-1. *WSAD Perspectives*

Another kind of project type provided is Example Projects. WSAD includes an extensive set of examples that demonstrate the concept of a J2EE application or Web application.

Another important feature of WSAD is that it contains a large number of wizards that guide you through the creation of a new resource or entity. The wizards are available by selecting File | New. The list of wizards depends on the perspective you are working in, but the list always contains the entry Other; choosing this option will take you to the full list.

The combination of wizards and the powerful editors and debugging environment make WSAD a great tool for development. With all these features, you might feel a little overwhelmed at first. The remainder of this chapter will help you become familiar with some of the features used to develop JSP, Java classes, and EJBs.

Getting Started with Web Development

As mentioned, WSAD uses a project to organize files. This is a pretty standard concept for development tools—used in tools ranging from Microsoft Visual Studio to any Java IDE. A project may represent a Web site or an enterprise application.

1. To start a new project, select File | New Project. You'll see a dialog box, which is the first window of the new project wizard. In this dialog box, you select the type of project you want to create.
2. Select Web in the lefthand pane, and then click Next.
3. Select the project name and the location where you want to place the project files. You can specify an enterprise application that is associated with the project. You can either use the default EAR (that is, the default enterprise application archive) or define your own archive. In this example, we create a new project called *Ch16* and place it in a new EAR file called *Ch16Ear*. Click Next.
4. In the window shown in Figure 16-2, select some of the Java build settings, which are organized under four different tabs: Source, the source files location; Project, dependent projects; Libraries; and Order, controlling the ordering of classpath libraries. Click Finish when you're done.

After you finish creating the new project, it appears on the left side of the Navigator pane, as shown here. The EAR file created is also shown in the Navigator pane.

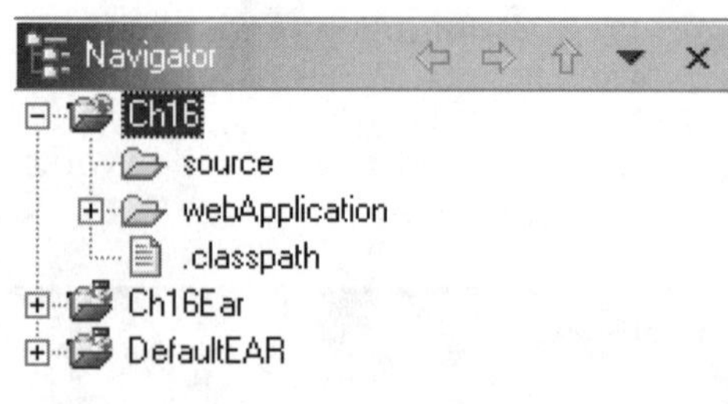

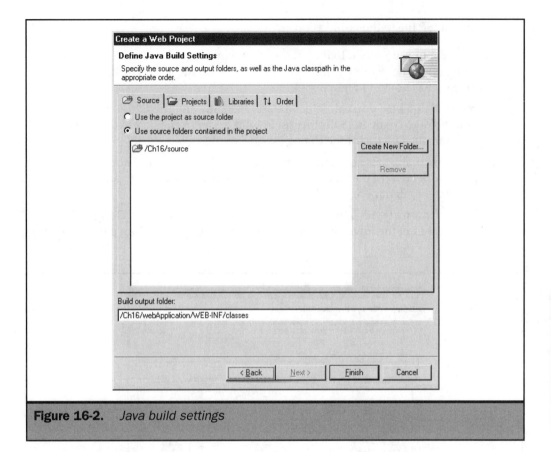

Figure 16-2. *Java build settings*

In the Navigator pane, you can right-click the *Ch16* folder (or the *source* folder below it), and add new elements (such as a JSP File, an HTML file, or a Web project) from the pop-up menu:

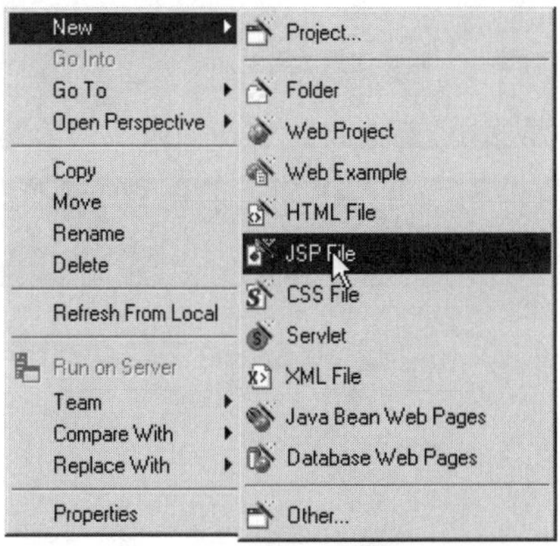

Let's add a JSP file to the application.

1. From the pop-up menu that appears when you right-click a folder icon in the Navigator pane, select the JSP File option. The Create a JSP File dialog box appears, as shown in Figure 16-3.
2. In this dialog box, you can select the JSP filename and the folder in which you would like to create it. (Selecting an invalid folder immediately prompts an error message on top of the dialog box.)
3. After you make these selections and click Finish, the new JSP appears in the main work area (to the right of the Navigator pane) with the caption "Place test1.jsp's content here," as shown in Figure 16-4.
4. Replace this text with **This is a test**. Note that this display is a Design display, as indicated in the lower-left corner of the main work area. Move to the Source

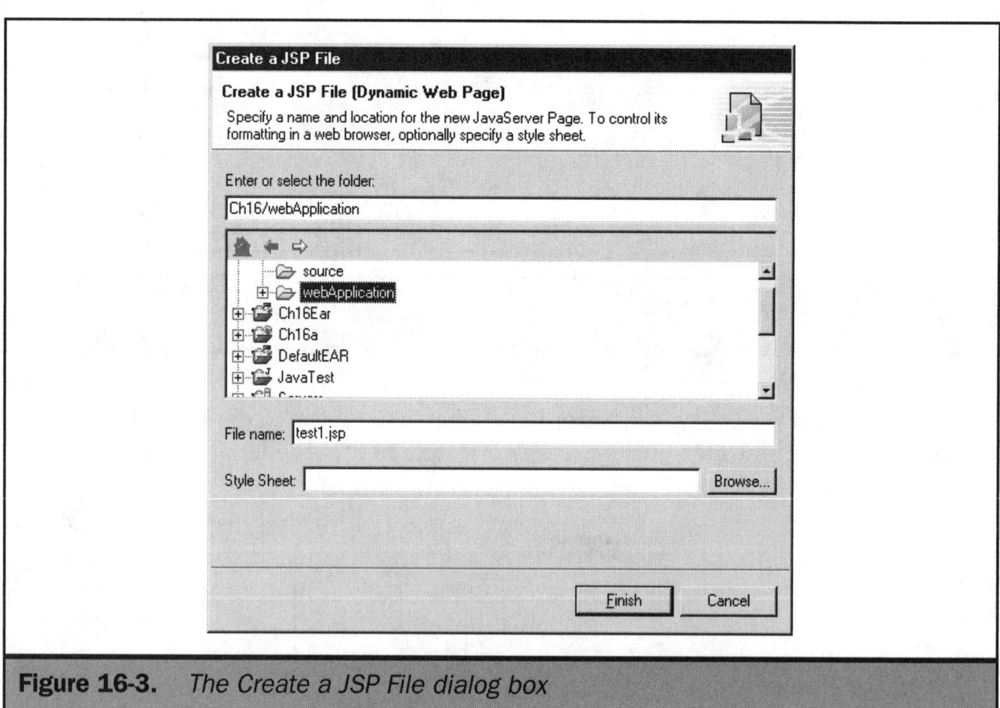

Figure 16-3. *The Create a JSP File dialog box*

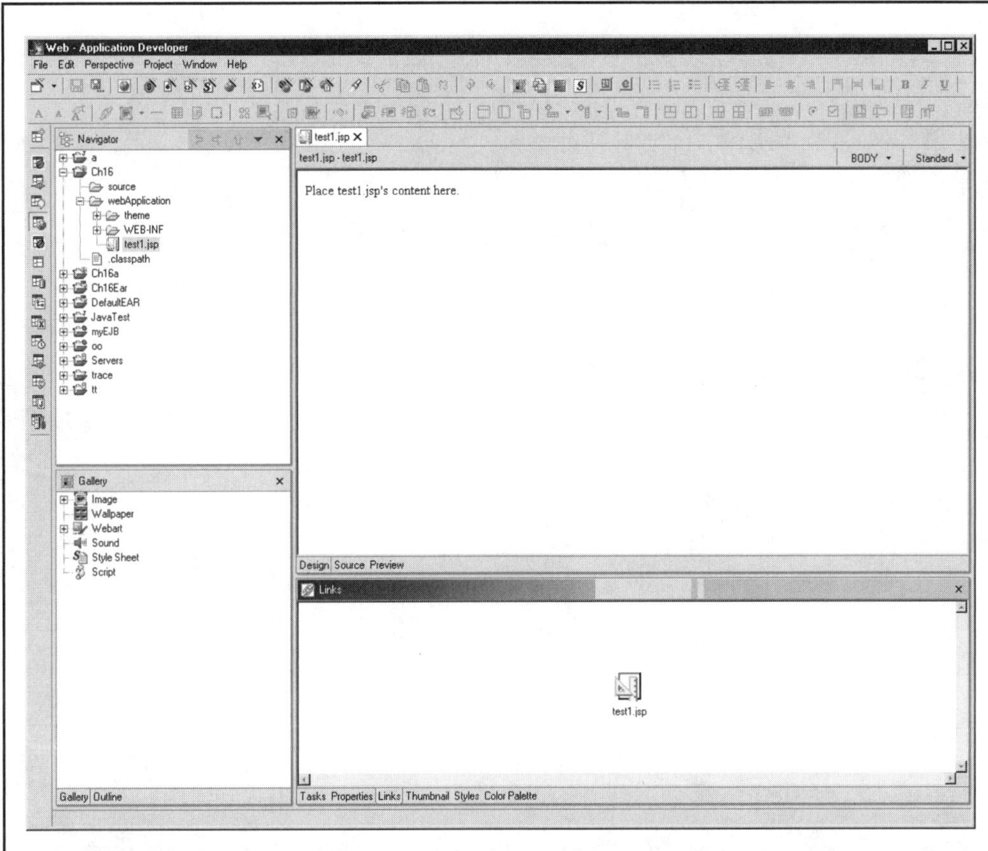

Figure 16-4. *The new JSP appears in the main work area.*

display, shown in Figure 16-5, and you'll see the JSP source. The Design display is used for a high-level view of a page. You can use this display to add various elements (such as scripts, images, form elements, frames, and so on). The Source display shows you the underlying source code, and you can modify that directly. The Preview display shows how the page will look. However, it does not execute server-side code (for JSPs) or scripts, so their effect is not shown.

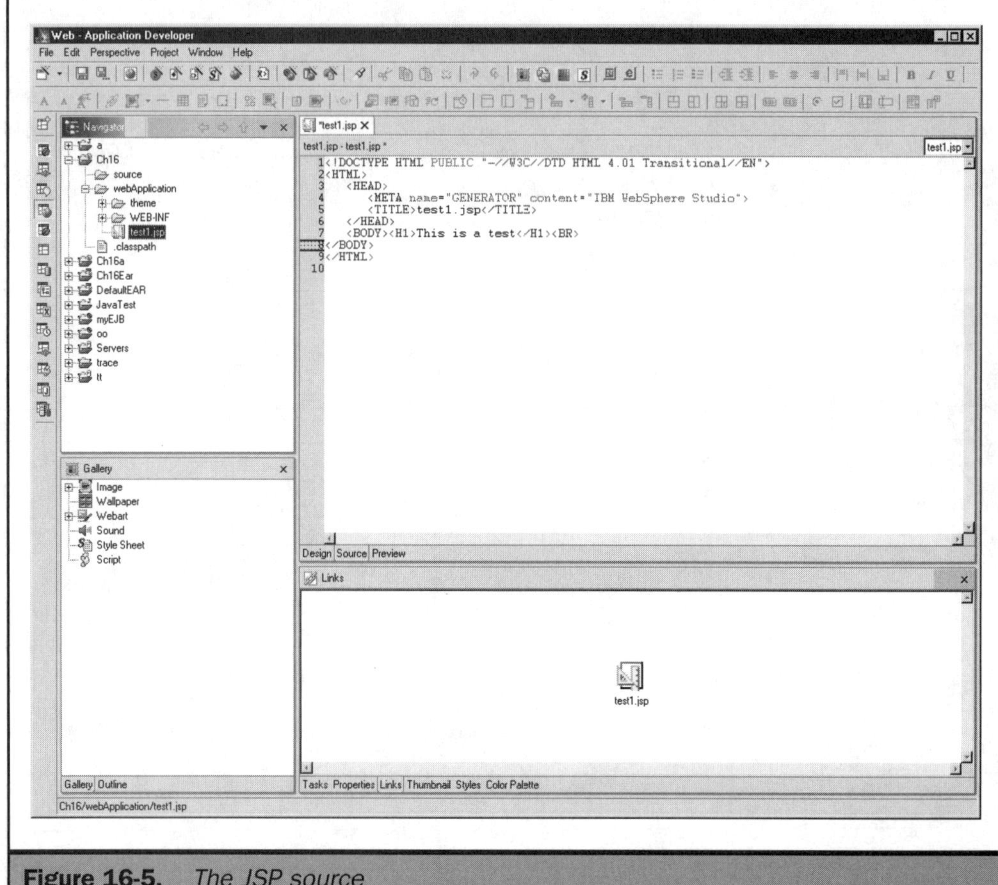

Figure 16-5. *The JSP source*

To make this page a little more interesting, we can beef it up by adding a small *for* loop, as shown here:

```
*test1.jsp
test1.jsp - test1.jsp *
<!DOCTYPE HTML PUBLIC "-//W3C//DTD HTML 4.01 Transitional//EN">
<HTML>
  <HEAD>
    <META name="GENERATOR" content="IBM WebSphere Studio">
    <TITLE>test1.jsp</TITLE>
  </HEAD>
  <BODY><H1>This is a test</H1><BR>
  <% for (int i = 0; i < 10; i++) { %>
  Counting... <%=i%><BR>
  <% } %>
</BODY>
</HTML>
```

After adding this JSP, you can execute the code. Right-click the test1.jsp icon and select Run From Server from the pop-up menu. The display changes to the test environment display, called the Server perspective. It shows a console window containing the WebSphere server messages. After the server is up (you may have to wait a few seconds), you can see the JSP. The Server perspective includes a browser window that shows the result of running your JSP, as shown in Figure 16-6.

To demonstrate the ease with which you can modify the page and review it again, lets revert back to the previous display, the Web perspective, where we edited the JSP. You can open the display either by using the toolbar on the far left or by choosing Perspective | Open | Web.

In the Web perspective, select the Design view by clicking the Design tab in the test1.jsp window, or by choosing Page | Design. Place the cursor on the bottom of the page and select Insert | Image File | From Gallery.

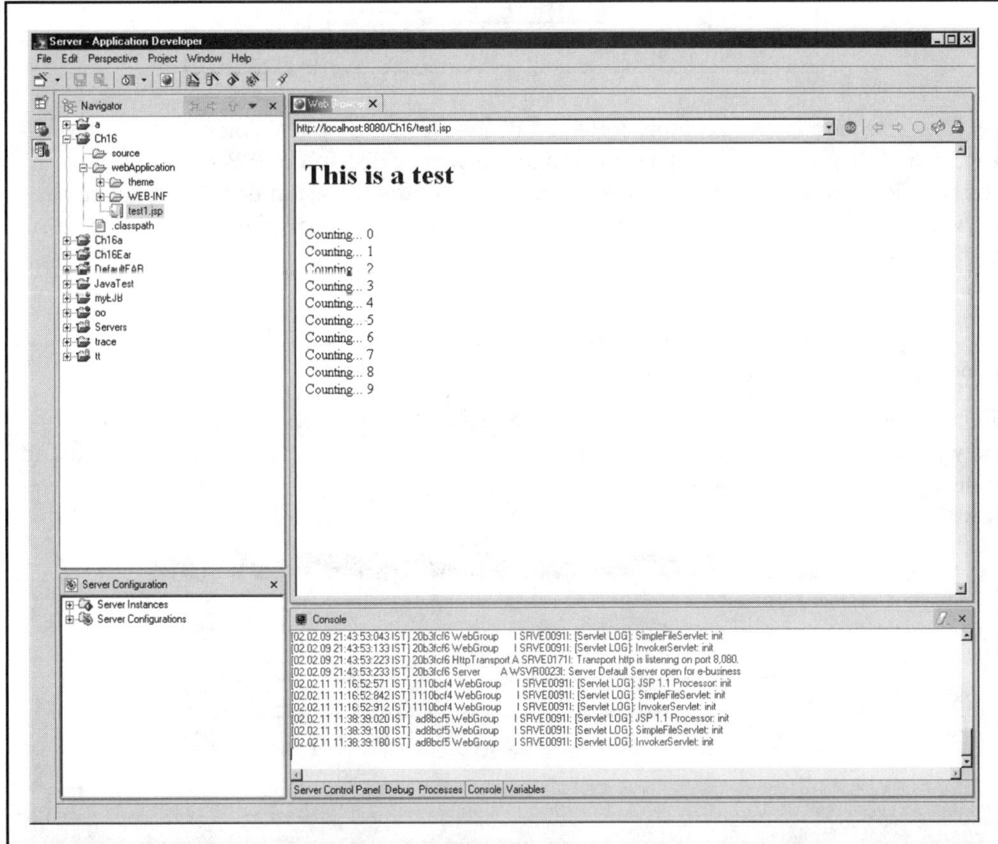

Figure 16-6. *The result of running your JSP*

WebSphere Studio Application Developer includes a large collection of images, style sheets, and other forms of Web art organized in a "gallery." To add an image to the JSP source, you select one of the images from the gallery. For example, here we select a sun icon:

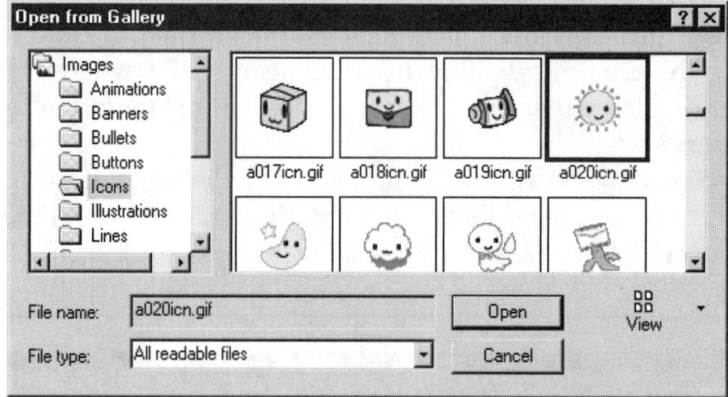

The selection is immediately reflected in the Design display. You can also open the Source display to see that a new image tag was added in the JSP source. To see the new icon in the test environment, you need to save the JSP file and go back to the Server perspective, where the new version of the page can be displayed (after refreshing the browser).

Java Development

Java development is managed mainly through the Java perspective. After you create a new Java project, you can start adding Java components to it. For example, you can add a new package, as shown here:

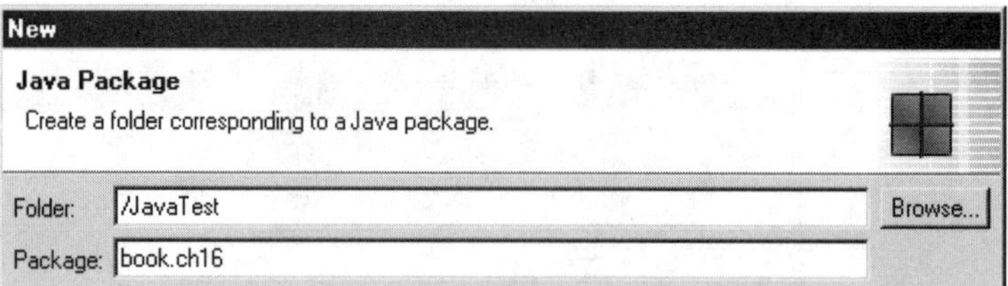

After you have added a package, you can add a Java class, as shown in Figure 16-7.

After the class is added, an editor appears in the Application Developer, where you can modify the Java code for the class. For example, you can add a simple "Hello World" print statement, as shown in Figure 16-8.

In the lower-right pane of the Application Developer is an outline of the class and the method it includes. Small icons indicate member modifiers. For example, the *S* attached to the *main* icon indicates that the member is static, and the small running figure attached to the *Hello* icon indicates that this is a runnable class. Member visibility is coded by colored shapes—a green circle indicates public, a yellow diamond indicates protected, and a red square indicates private. The letter *F* attached to a member indicates the *final* modifier.

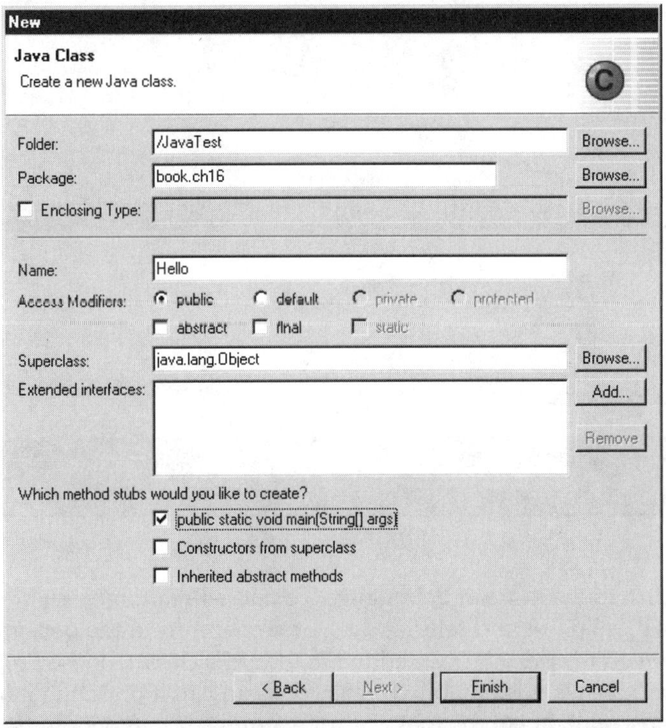

Figure 16-7. *Adding a Java class*

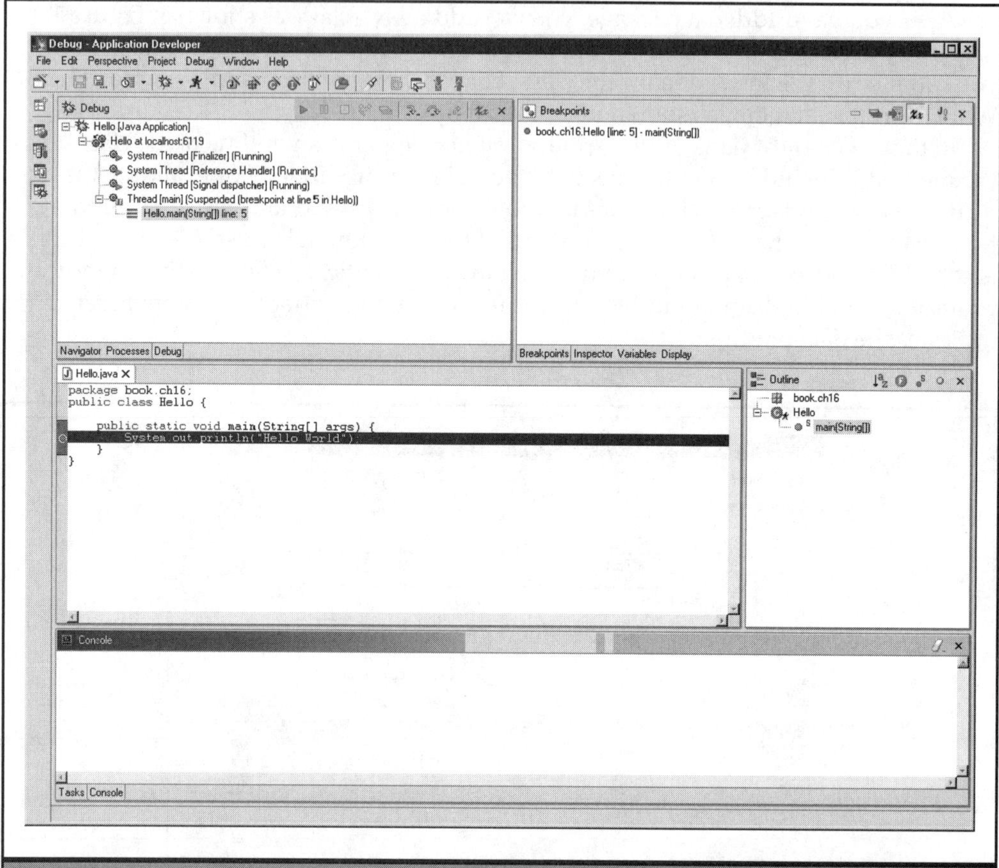

Figure 16-8. *Adding a "Hello World" statement*

Now let's turn to the issue of debugging. To add a breakpoint, right-click the location for the breakpoint and select Add | Breakpoint from the pop-up menu. Let's add a breakpoint on the print line we added in the *Hello* class. Choose Project | Build All (to make sure the class is compiled); then you can run it or debug it using the respective menus available in the toolbar. For example, if you debug the *Hello* class, it will stop at the requested breakpoint.

Note that while debugging, you immediately jump to the Debug perspective, where you can inspect variables and expressions, and view and edit the debugged code. You can also view the set of running processes.

In terms of functionality, VisualAge for Java and WSAD provide roughly the same feature set. One crucial difference is that the latter provides powerful tools for Web design and authoring. From a usability point of view, the main difference is that VisualAge for Java opens new windows for various purposes (such as the Console, Debugger, and so on), whereas WSAD has one main window and you shift between perspectives. While it might take a while for you to get accustomed to this mode of working, WSAD provides a better user interface metaphor—especially when you need to handle a lot of different components concurrently.

Note *In WSAD, debugging abilities can be invoked in conjunction with the Server perspective. In other words, you can place a breakpoint in code being executed on the built-in server, and you can then debug it in the same way you would debug any other code.*

EJB Development

EJB development is accomplished using the J2EE perspective. To add a new EJB, you can invoke the New EJB wizard by choosing File | New.

In the Create EJB dialog box, shown in Figure 16-9, select between two options: creating a new EJB or adding beans from the repository. To create a new EJB, you first need to specify the bean name. Then you need to select the bean type—Session, Entity with BMP (Bean Managed Persistence), or Entity with CMP (Container Managed Persistence). Other parameters are the EJB project to which the new bean belongs, the package for the bean class, the home interface and remote interface, the actual name for the bean class, and the optional bean superclass and supertype.

After clicking the Next button, you'll see a window that allows you to select the name of the home interface, remote interface, and key interface (only applicable to entity beans). You can also select what interfaces the remote interface extends and what import statements you want in the bean implementation. For CMP beans, you also select the persistent fields.

Click the Finish button, and the new EJB is created—an example is shown in Figure 16-10. The wizard automatically creates all the required classes and, within them,

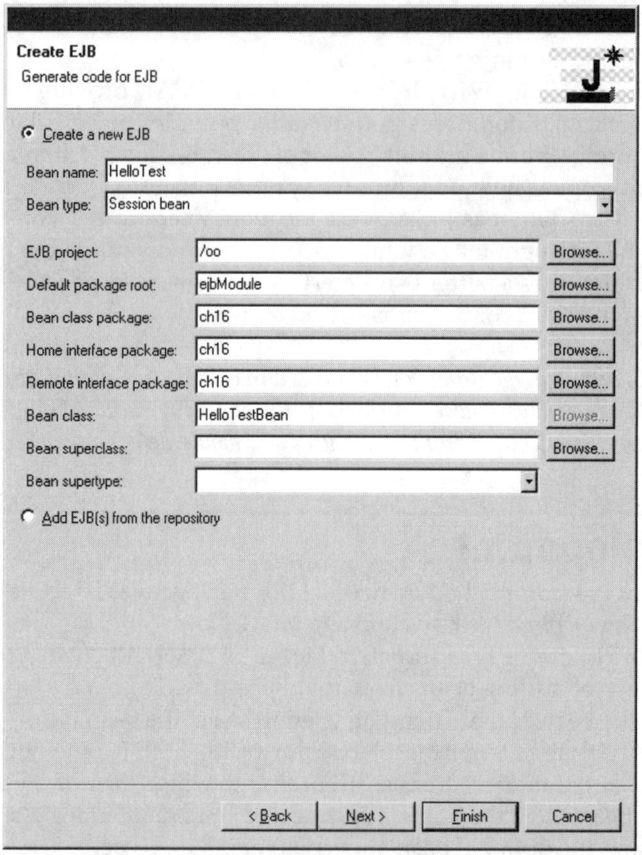

Figure 16-9. *Creating a new EJB*

all the required methods. For example, the bean implementation class defines all the EJB-required methods, as well as a member variable holding the EJB context and methods for setting and getting these variables.

As you add new EJBs using the Application Developer, the *ejb-jar.xml* file under your EJB module grows and includes all the required definitions for your EJB module. On the Bean tab in the Application Developer, you can review the beans you have defined, as shown in Figure 16-11. You can also modify the beans' attributes using the property editor; this builds the deployment descriptor XML.

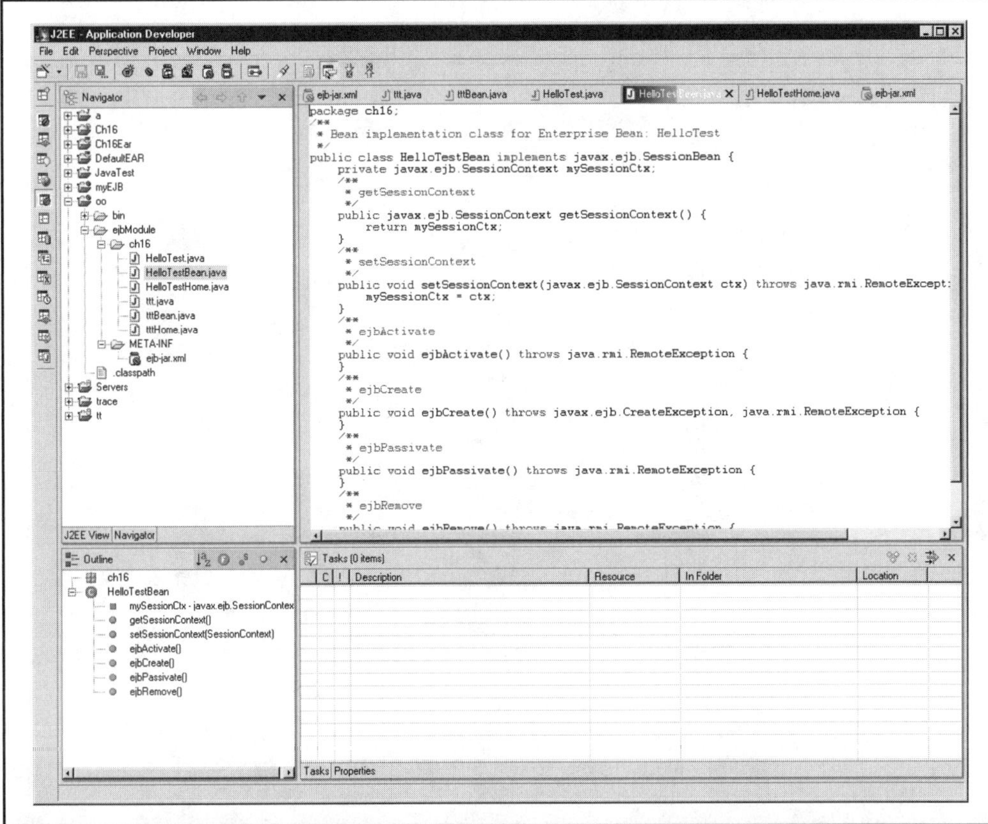

Figure 16-10. *A new EJB is ready for use.*

On the Security and Transaction tabs, you can specify the required transactional and security behavior for your beans. This behavior can be specified in the level of a single method. This functionality is equivalent to that offered by the Application Assembly Tool (AAT), but it is integrated into the Application Developer tool and is thus easy to use. EJB transactions and security are discussed in detail in Chapter 31.

Note that under the J2EE perspective, you can also look at the *application.xml* file, which defines a J2EE application. For the application, you can define the EJB and Web modules that are part of the application, and you can define the security roles for the application.

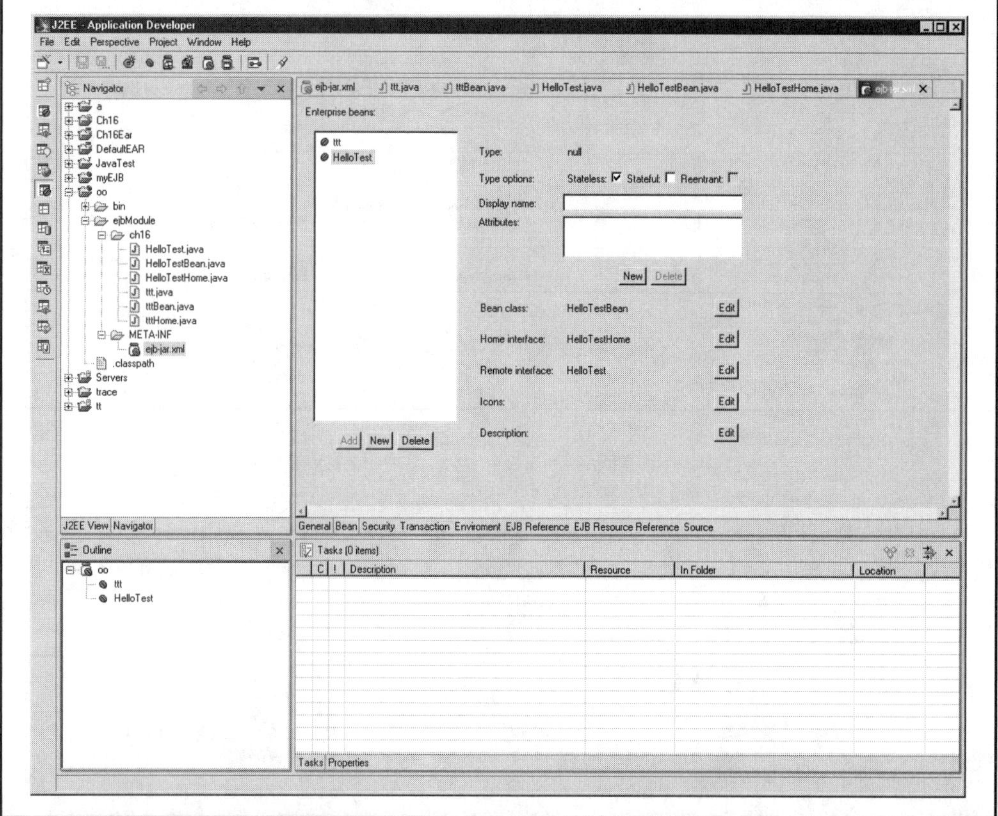

Figure 16-11. *Reviewing the beans you've defined*

Summary

This chapter includes a high-level overview of the WebSphere Studio Application Developer. The WSAD is a new tool on the WebSphere tool landscape and will eventually replace VisualAge for Java and WebSphere Studio. It is a "one-stop shop" for all developers of sites and applications deployed on the WebSphere Application Server.

As you saw here, the WSAD is based on the concept of perspectives that map to roles in the life of an application. You have seen a few of the perspectives through the examples of this chapter, and you have seen a few of the types of modules that can be developed using the tool.

WSAD as a tool covers two dimensions in the development lifecycle. By covering both of these dimensions, WSAD provides a uniquely integrated tool for making development teams building applications highly productive. The first dimension is that of team roles, and the second is that of activities. Web applications and enterprise applications can be quite complex in terms of the components they contain and the different people that come together to build them. Site designers, Java developers, and application deployers are all part of the development lifecycle of a J2EE application. Their roles comprise one dimension of the development lifecycle that is completely covered by WSAD. The activities in the cycle include development, assembly, debugging, and packaging—these form the second dimension supported by the WSAD.

Although WSAD is the flagship development tool in the WebSphere family, many developers still use (and will continue to use) VisualAge for Java. This is the topic of Chapter 17.

Chapter 17

VisualAge for Java

VisualAge for Java is IBM's Integrated Development Environment (IDE) for developing Java software. The purpose of this chapter is to acquaint you with the VisualAge for Java environment. In addition to being a powerful tool for Java development in general, VisualAge for Java has numerous advantages when used to develop WebSphere server-side code such as servlets, JavaServer Pages (JSP), and Enterprise JavaBeans (EJB). These advantages are the result of the tight integration between WebSphere and VisualAge for Java, which provides a special "WebSphere Test Environment." This environment allows you to test your software without going through the tedious process of deploying it on the application server. Therefore, the develop-compile-debug cycle becomes significantly shorter. VisualAge for Java offers additional benefits, such as built-in configuration management and a variety of wizards for adding different components.

Installing VisualAge for Java

VisualAge for Java comes in three different flavors: Entry Edition, Professional Edition, and Enterprise Edition. For the purpose of developing WebSphere servlets and JSP, the Professional Edition or Enterprise Edition are required. For developing EJBs (the subject of Part VI of the book), the Enterprise Edition must be used. The Enterprise Edition is also the only edition of VisualAge that incorporates the version and configuration control features and the shared code repository. The Entry Edition is available for free from the IBM Web site at *http://www.software.ibm.com/ad/vajava*, whereas the other editions are available for purchase and download.

After you obtain the VisualAge for Java installation, either on CD or by downloading it from the Web, you start the installation by running the *setup.exe* program. The Setup program is standard fare and takes you through the installation process. The only nontrivial issue you need to tackle during the installation process is to modify the proxy settings for your Web browser. This is required to allow your Web browser to access servlets and JSPs running within the WebSphere Test Environment. The required modification takes place automatically, and manual intervention is required only if proxy settings are automatic in your machine (for instance, if they were centrally set by a system administrator).

Once installation is completed, you can test it by starting VisualAge for Java from the windows Start menu. You should see the splash screen. A few seconds later, the splash screen is replaced by the Welcome screen, as shown next.

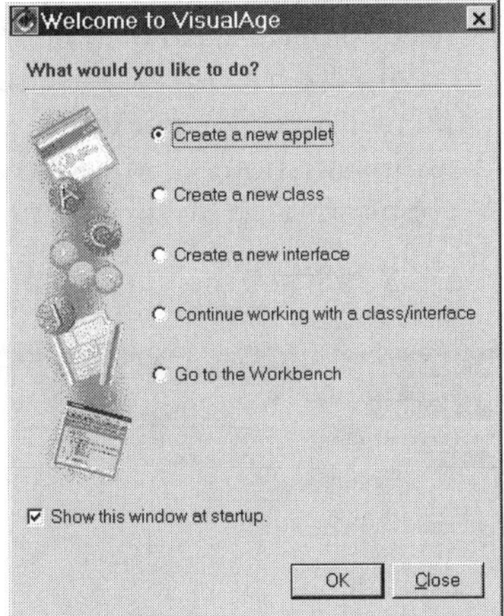

In this window, you can start creating a software component immediately. For now, click the Close button, or select Go to the Workbench, to visit the VisualAge for Java Workbench, shown in Figure 17-1.

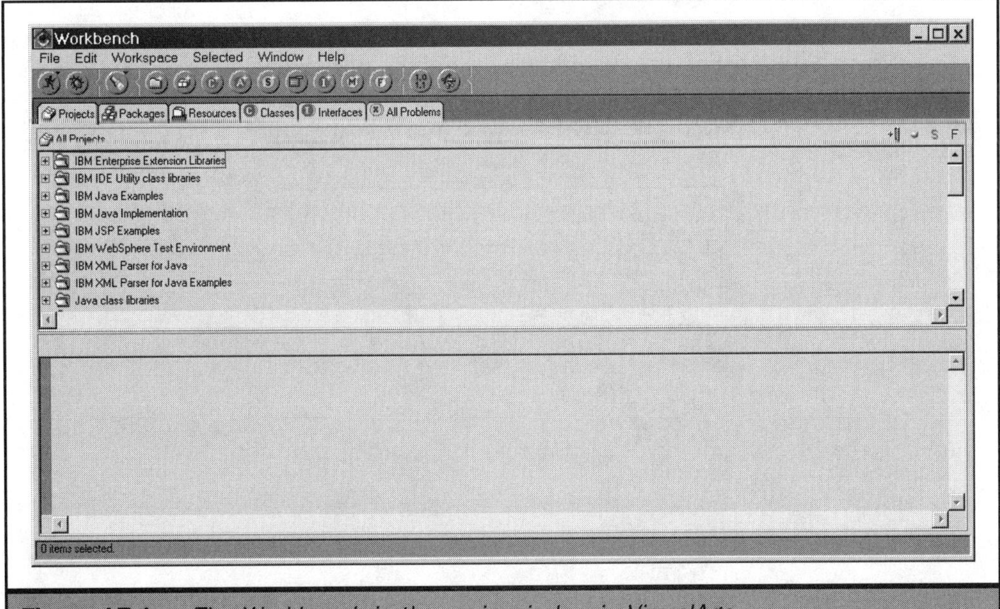

Figure 17-1. *The Workbench is the main window in VisualAge.*

One of the first actions you need to perform in the Workbench is adding new features into your system. This is a prerequisite for developing servlets, JSPs, and EJBs with VisualAge (the subjects of Chapters 28 and 34). For example, to include the WebSphere Test Environment feature in your installation, you need to add that feature.

Here's how you add the WebSphere Text Environment features to VisualAge:

1. Choose File | Quick Start. You'll see the Quick Start window:

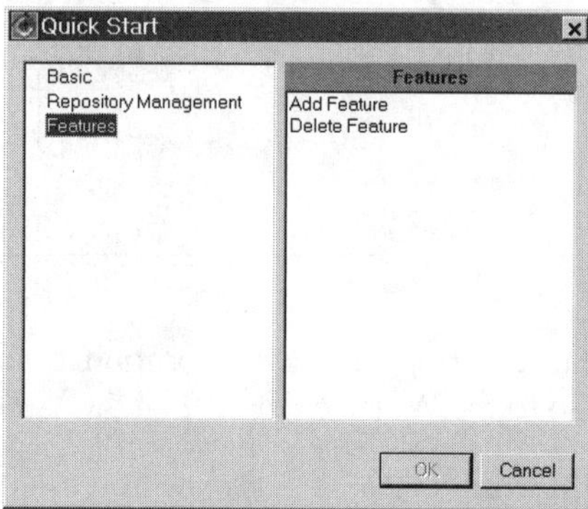

2. Select Features from the list on the left and Add Feature from the list on the right. You will see a list of features in the Selection Required dialog box:

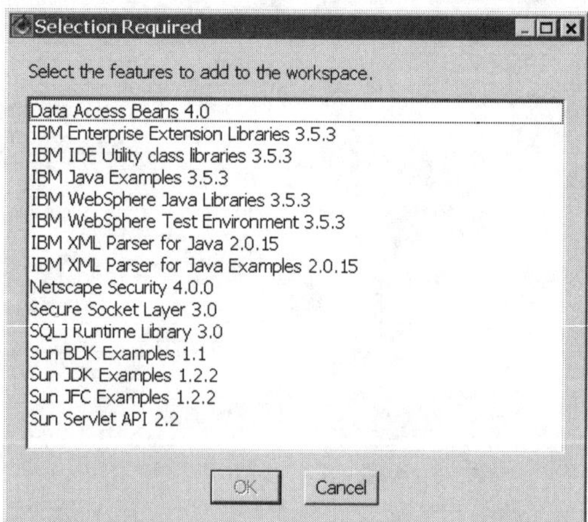

3. Select IBM WebSphere Test Environment 3.5.3 (in this case, you can add any or all of the other features as well). Alternatively, you can press the F2 button to add the feature. Then click OK.

VisualAge comes with quite a few useful components. Recently, for example we had to interface to a Service Advertising Protocol (SAP) system and we were thrilled to discover that the Enterprise Edition of VisualAge has a feature called Access Builder for SAP R/3—we were done with our interface to SAP in less than a week!

VisualAge for Java stores all programming data in two files: the repository and the workspace. The *repository* is the central data store for all classes used by you or any member of the programming group that shares a code repository. If you are working alone, this file is local to your machine—but in a typical project, the repository resides on a shared server that is backed up often. Once a class is loaded into the repository, it is not deleted unless you explicitly request a *purge*. You can do this from the Repository Explorer, which you can access by choosing Window | Repository Explorer. (In fact, even then the repository is not *really* purged and can be recovered—unless you have chosen to compact the repository.)

The *workspace* contains all the classes you are currently working with in your VisualAge environment. When you add new features to VisualAge, you also load some projects and classes into the workspace. Normally, you will want to load all classes you are using into the workspace, so it's convenient to think of the workspace as your CLASSPATH environment. However, VisualAge for Java also has a workspace classpath that you can set from an Options dialog box, accessed by choosing Window | Options. This classpath allows you to refer to classes that are not loaded into the workspace.

Creating a "Hello World" Applet with VisualAge for Java

To get you acquainted with VisualAge for Java, let's look at adding a simple "Hello World" applet. While not directly related to the main theme of this book, creating this applet demonstrates the ease of working with VisualAge.

VisualAge for Java facilitates accelerated development via a collection of wizards that are used for adding new components. While this process might seem a little lengthy, it is a real time-saver because it automatically implements code for the most common features required in applets.

1. Choose File | Quick Start.
2. In the Quick Start window, select Basic from the list on the left.
3. At the right is a list of components that you can add. Select Create Applet.
4. VisualAge will guide you through the creation of the applet in a detailed manner. From the SmartGuide dialog box, select the project name (click Browse to search for it, or type the name in the text box), the package name, and the applet's class name as shown in Figure 17-2.
5. On the same screen, select whether you want to browse the applet when you're finished or compose the class visually. Click Next.
6. In the Applet Properties screen, select whether the applet should implement a `main()` method and whether it should run in a thread. Click Next.
7. In the Events screen, select which listeners you want to implement. Click Next.

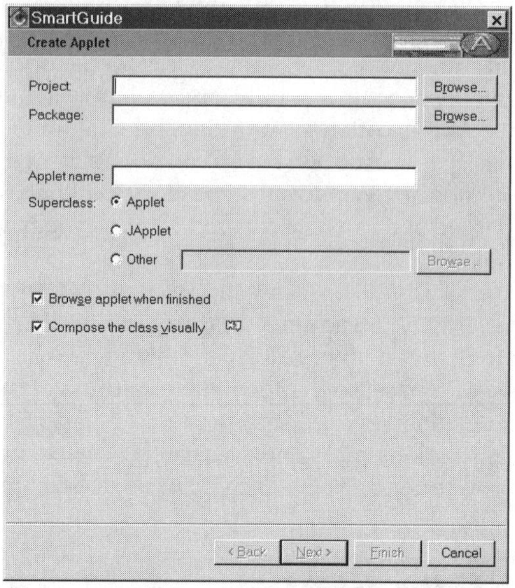

Figure 17-2. *Add the applet information to the SmartGuide dialog box.*

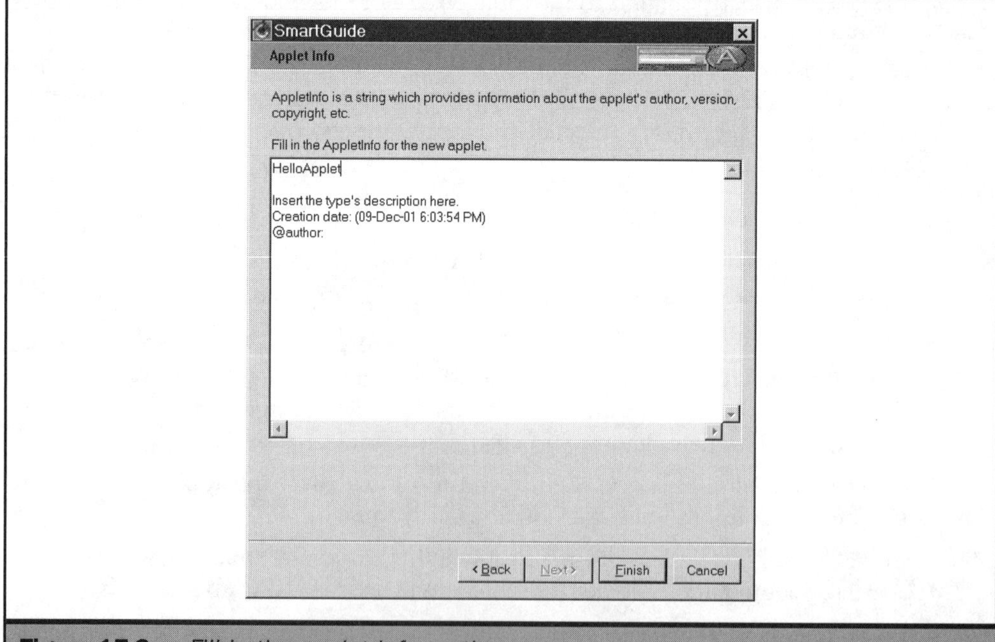

Figure 17-3. *Fill in the applet information.*

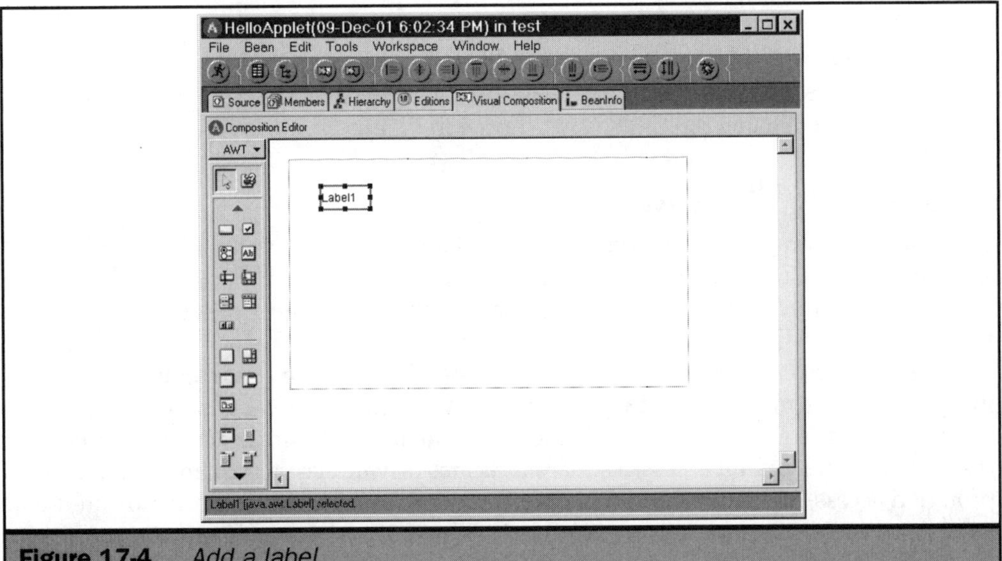

Figure 17-4. *Add a label.*

8. In the Code Writer screen, select whether you want sample code in your applet, and select any other methods to be implemented. Click Next.
9. In the Parameters screen, define applet parameters. Click Next.
10. In the final screen, Applet Info, shown in Figure 17-3, edit the string value for the `getAppletInfo` method. Then click the Finish button.

The applet is now ready, and you can "visually compose" it (as promised in the first screen).

1. From the toolbar on the left side of the HelloApplet window, you can add a label, as shown in Figure 17-4.

   You can double-click the label to see its properties, as shown here:

2. Add the text to the label string: **HelloWorld**. Make the font size larger, and the display updates to show the new font size.
3. Finally, because you're using the graphical interface of the IDE, you can "stretch" the label to show the full text, as shown in Figure 17-5.

The VisualAge Window

The VisualAge composition window includes several tabs: Source, Members, Hierarchy, Editions, Visual Composition, and BeanInfo.

Click the Source tab to review the source code for the new applet, as shown in Figure 17-6.

The Elements list on the left side of the Source tab shows the class elements. Notice that each class member is coded with a letter *M*, which indicates a method, a letter *F*, which indicates a field. The shapes attached to the letters indicate access modifiers: a triangle indicates default access, a square indicates private access, a diamond indicates protected access, and a circle indicates public access. Other modifiers are indicated with letters as well (though these aren't visible in Figure 17-6). *A* stands for `abstract`, *F* for `final`, *N* for `native`, *S* for `static`, *T* for `transient`, and *V* for `volatile`. Other visual cues include a folder symbol for a project, a package icon for a package, a circled *A* for an applet, a circled C for a class, and a circled *I* for an interface.

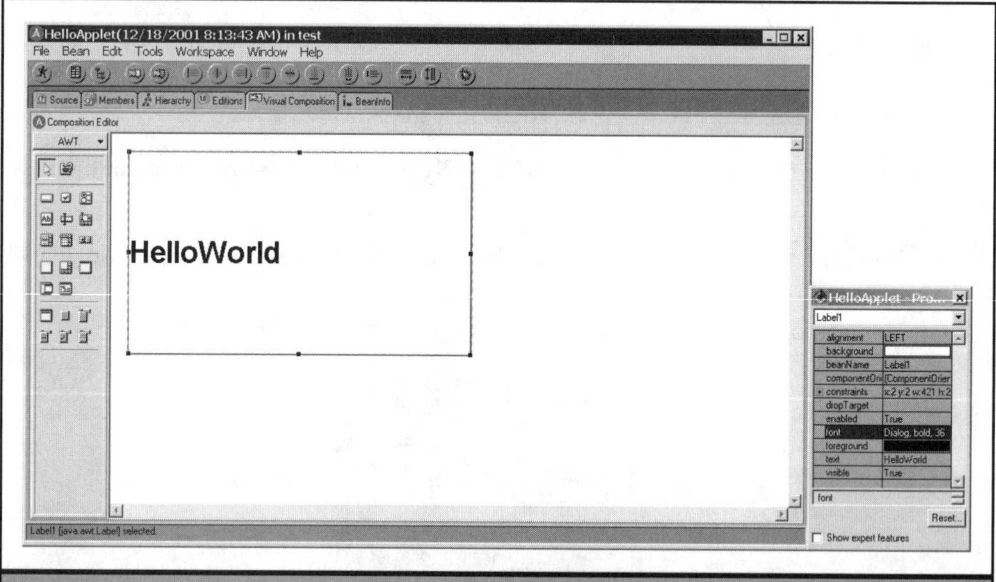

Figure 17-5. *Stretch the label to show the entire phrase.*

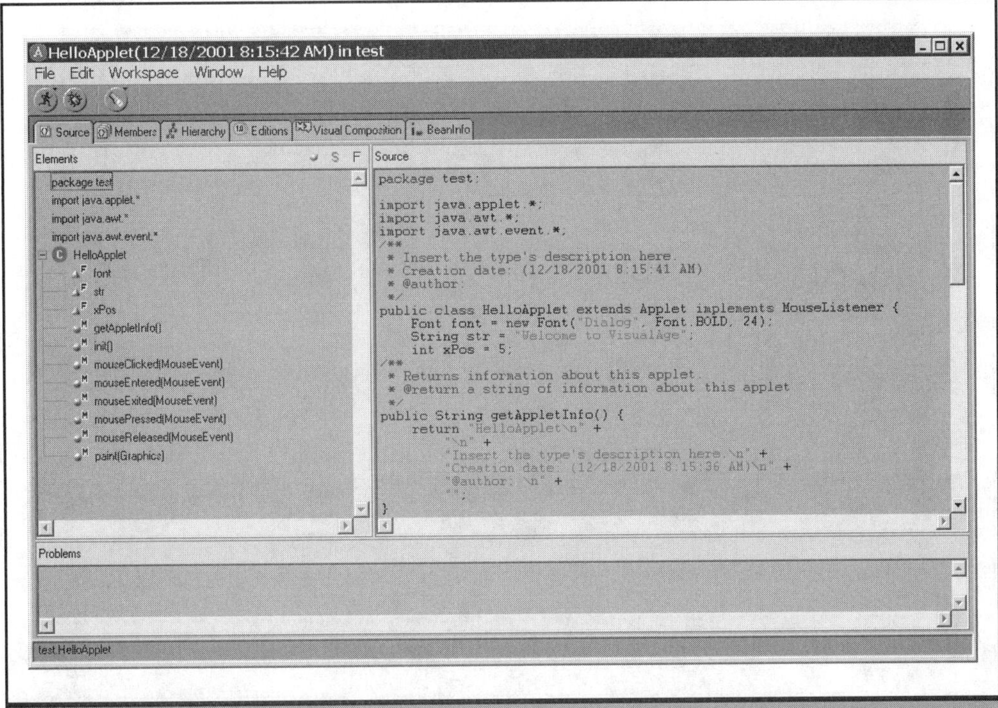

Figure 17-6. *Review the source code for the new applet.*

The Members view (on the Members tab) focuses on the class members, as shown in Figure 17-7.

The Hierarchy tab focuses on the class hierarchy, as shown in Figure 17-8. On all these tabs, you can use different entry points for browsing and reviewing the code. On the Source tab, you can edit the code.

A neat feature of the VisualAge editing mode is called *automated completion*. If you type in the name of an instance variable followed by a dot (.), you can see a listing of all possible methods that can be applied based on the object type, simply by pressing CTRL-SPACEBAR.

The Editions tab, shown in Figure 17-9, provides configuration management (although in this case, it is a new applet, so not many editions are shown), and the visual composition is the same one we just used.

Finally, the BeanInfo tab, shown in Figure 17-10, allows you to edit JavaBeans. Chapter 10 provided a quick introduction to JavaBeans. In this tab, a Features list appears at the left; each feature is either a method or a property (indicated by *P* or *M*). For each property, *R* indicates it can be *Get* and *W* indicates that it can be *Set*.

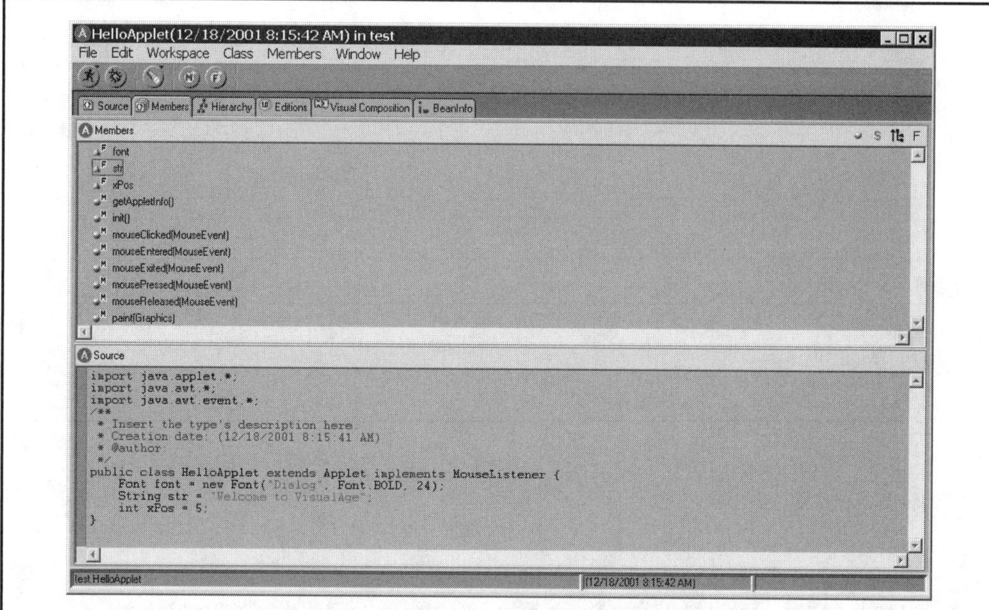

Figure 17-7. *The Members tab*

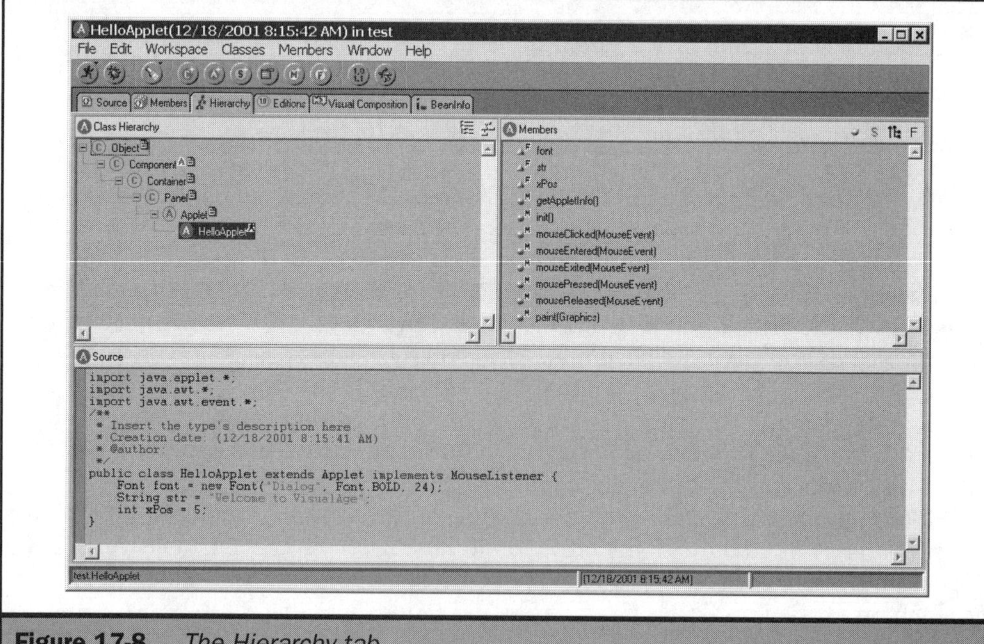

Figure 17-8. *The Hierarchy tab*

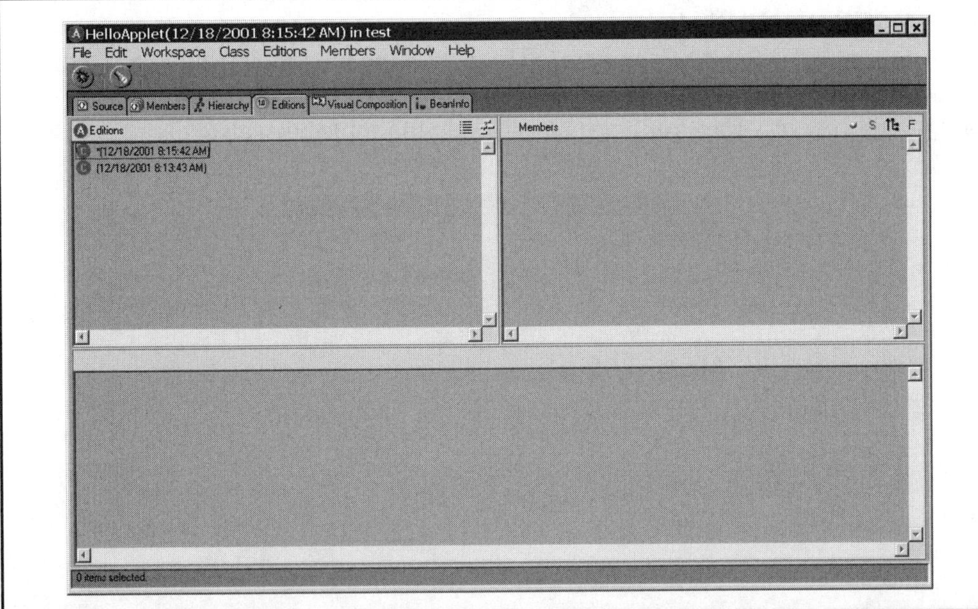

Figure 17-9. *The Editions tab*

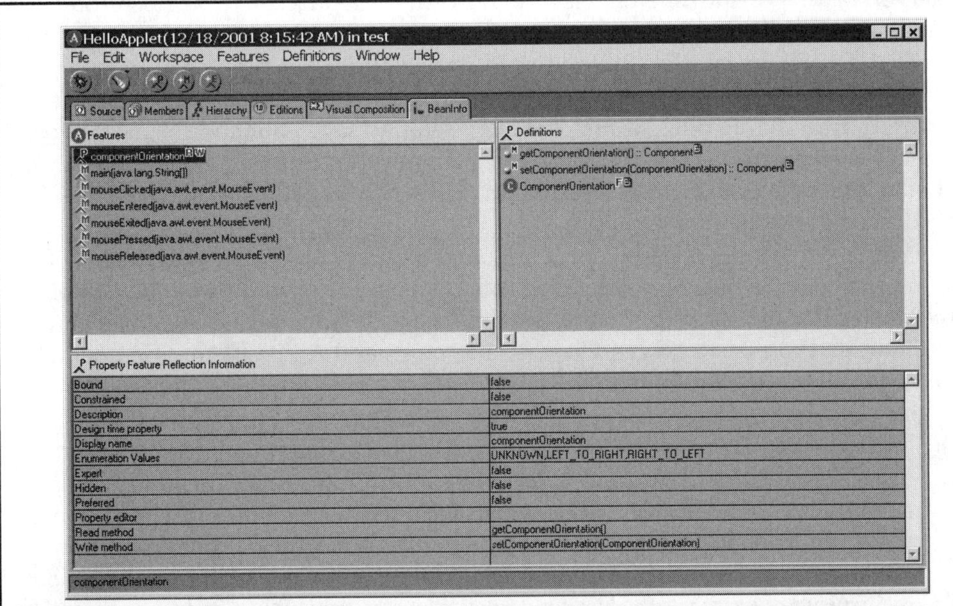

Figure 17-10. *The BeanInfo tab*

Running the Applet

On the left side of the toolbar in the Workbench is a button with a small running figure; this is the Run button. Click it to execute the applet. You'll see a prompt telling you that the applet is running. Then you'll see the applet in the applet viewer:

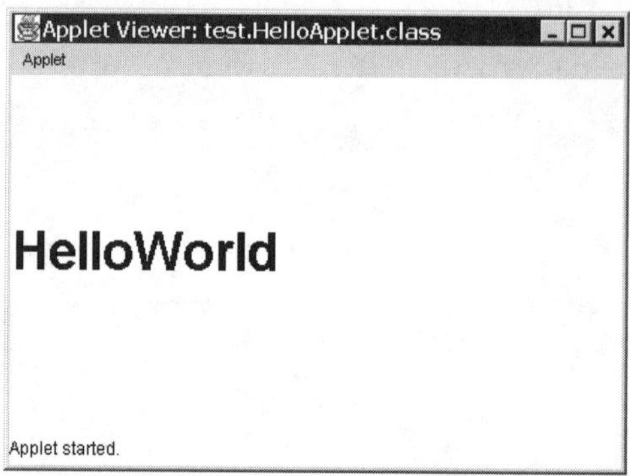

VisualAge for Java Workbench

The Workbench, shown in Figure 17-11, is the center of VisualAge development. The tabs in the Workbench provide different views of the code—via projects, packages, resources, classes, and interfaces.

The All Problems tab allows you to see syntax and other types of errors that are currently related to the code (although theoretically, you should always ensure that no errors appear in the code). VisualAge allows you to save your code even if it does not compile, and will flag this as a problem with an icon featuring a red *X* on the method, class, or Workbench tab. Incompatibilities between libraries will also be flagged as errors in the Workbench.

As with most Windows-based applications, a menu bar appears across the top of the window, a toolbar below it; a work area takes up most of the window, and a couple of status bars are located at the bottom. Inside the work area are tabs that allows you to move between Projects, Packages, Classes, Interfaces, and All Problems. The menu bar changes as you make a selection in the tab control.

Note

The Enterprise Edition of VisualAge for Java has two additional tabs, Managing for managing code ownership (that is, for configuration management in a team), and EJB for Enterprise JavaBeans. The various tabs and menus in the Workbench allow you to browse through the code looking for references of methods, members, or classes. You can also add new classes, methods, and fields. Generally speaking, the menus are self-explanatory. It is worthwhile noting that a lot of operations can be done in more than one way using the different tabs.

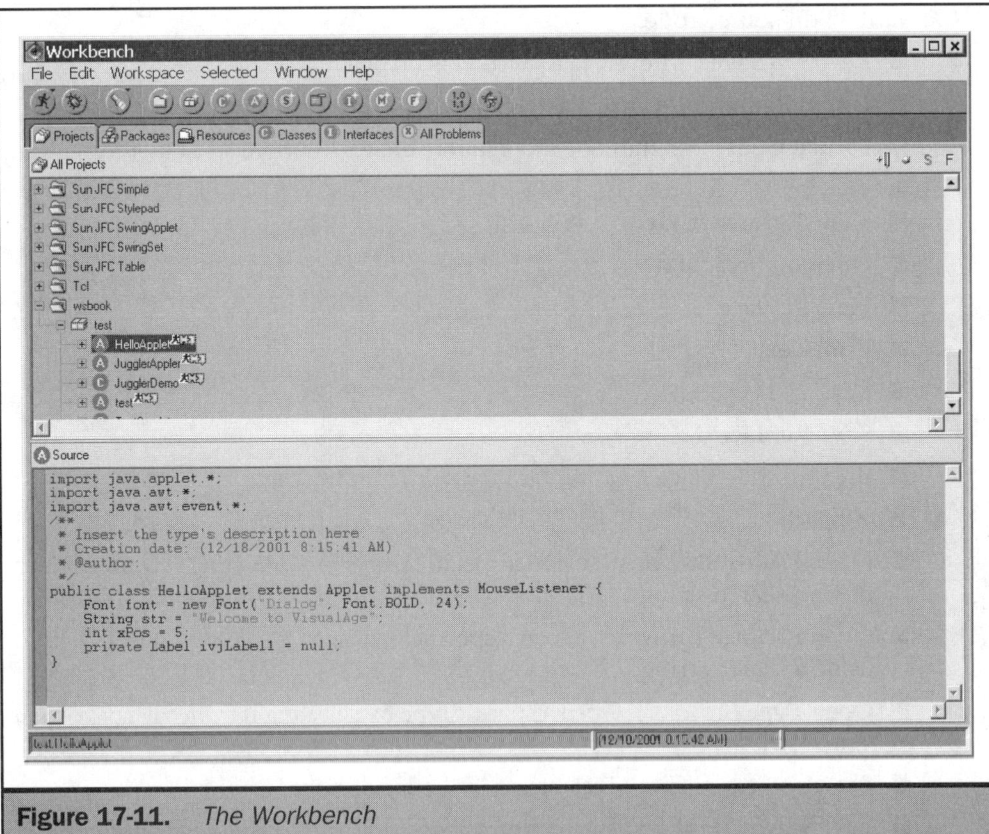

Figure 17-11. *The Workbench*

The following menus are fixed for all selections.

- **File** File creation, loading, saving, and quitting.
  - **Quick Start** Access different creation wizards, and add/remove features for VisualAge for Java.
  - **Import** Insert code from a directory, JAR file, or repository into a VisualAge project.
  - **Export** Save a VisualAge project or package to a directory, JAR file, or repository.
  - **Print Setup** Set up page options options for printing.
  - **Quick Access to Recent Files** List names of recently accessed classes, packages, and projects.
  - **Save Workspace**
  - **Exit VisualAge**

- **Edit** Edit source code.
  - **Revert to Saved** Revert to a saved version of a file.
  - **Undo, Redo, Cut, Copy, Paste, Select All** Perform clipboard operations.
  - **Format Code** Fix the code indentation, braces location, and other formatting issues.
  - **View Reference Help**
  - **Open on Selection**
  - **Find/Replace**
  - **Print Text**
  - **Save**
  - **Save Replace**
  - **Breakpoint** Place a breakpoint for debugger tracing.
- **Workspace**
  - **Open Project Browser** Open a specific project by selecting it from a list or using a search string.
  - **Open Package Browser** Open a specific package by selecting it from a list or using a search string.
  - **Open Type Browser** Open a specific type by selecting it from a list or using a search string
  - **Search** Search for a given string in the workspace.
  - **Text Search/Replace** Search for and replace a string in the workspace.
  - **Search Again** Access previously made searches.
  - **Search Results** Show the search results window.
  - **Tools** Invoke workspace tools such as Fix Manager or SQLJ tool. The set of tools appearing on this submenu depends on which features are installed in Visual Age. For example, if the SAP Access Builder is installed, the Tool menu will also include this feature.
- **Window** Window manipulation.
  - **Clone** Create a duplicate of the current active window.
  - **Switch to** Make a different window active.
  - **Refresh** Refresh the current window.
  - **Lock Window** Make sure the window remains open; useful to prevent you from closing it by accident.
  - **Maximize Pane** Maximize the selected pane to take up all the work area. (Once selected, this entry changes to **Restore Pane**.)

- **Flip Orientation** Flip the alignment of components in the work area from vertical to horizontal or vice versa.
- **Show Edition Names** Show the version names for components (projects, packages, classes).
- **Workbench** Make the Workbench the active window.
- **Scrapbook** Open the Scrapbook to review and edit code fragments, including imported code.
- **Repository Explorer** Browse through the class repository in an Explorer-like fashion.
- **Console** Show the Java console for programs using text I/O
- **Log** Show the execution log and error log window.
- **Debug** Access debugger, breakpoints, and exceptions.
- **Options** Customize the display and behavior of VisualAge through a multitude of options.

- **Help** Online help

In addition to these menus, which are fixed and available in all VisualAge for Java windows, is a set of menus specific to on the tab selected.

Projects Tab

The Projects tab work area shows the project hierarchy, which allows you to expand and contract each folder. When this tab is selected, the following menu appears between the Workspace and Window menus:

- **Selected** Manipulation of the currently selected project.
  - **Open** Open the selected project.
  - **Open To** Open the selected project and go to a specific tab—Packages, Classes, Interfaces, Editions, Resources, or Problems.
  - **Go To** Jump to a Project, Package, or Type by selecting it from a list or using a search string; add or manipulate bookmarks.
  - **Add** Add a new element: Project, Package, Class, Applet, Application, Interface, Method, or Field. This submenu is used in different contexts, and not all entries are applicable in all instances. For example, under the Selected menu for Projects, the last two entries are grayed out because you cannot add methods or fields to a project.
  - **Attribute Filters** Select the qualifications of elements on display—classes, methods, and members. You can filter by visibility (public, protected, private) or other modifiers (final, static, and so on).

- **Import** Import code into the selected project.
- **Export** Export code out of the selected project.
- **Replace With** Replace the current version of the project with the previous edition or a different edition.
- **Delete** Remove the selected project.
- **Reorganize** Copy, move, or rename the selected project.
- **Manage** Control the way version names are assigned.
- **Compare With** Compare the selected project with a previous or different edition.
- **Run** Execute the selected project; entries are available for running in Applet Viewer where applicable. Run the "main" method where applicable, and check the CLASSPATH environment (to make sure it is set correctly so that everything can indeed run).
- **Document** Print out source code or create a JavaDoc.
- **Tools** Access external tools as mentioned above.
- **Properties** Show properties of the selected project, including its name, status, creation time, and version.

Packages Tab

On the Packages tab, the upper half of the work area is split into three parts: Packages, Types, and Members, as shown in Figure 17-12. If you select a package, all the types (interfaces and classes) contained in it are shown on the middle pane. If you select a specific type, its members will appear on a third pane, and the code will appear on the lower half of the work area.

The Types area indicates whether the type is an interface (marked with an *I*) or a class (marked with a *C*). Also, graphical icons next to the name indicate whether the class is runnable (the running figure) and whether it can be visually composed (the puzzle icon). Similarly, in the Members area, a small *M* indicates a method, an *F* indicates a field, and a graphical icon at the end of the name shows the access mode (if it is not public).

When the Packages tab is selected, the menu bar shows the Packages, Types, and Members menus between the Workspace and Window menus. These menus offer commands that are similar to those on the Selected menu for projects, so we will just focus on the differences here. One difference is that each of the menus on the Packages tab has a Go To entry (for example, Go To Member on the Members tab) that is specific to the kind of object manipulated from the menu. The Packages tab menu has a Layout entry that allows you to switch between a tree or a list layout view for packages. The Attribute Filters entry appears only on the Members tab menu.

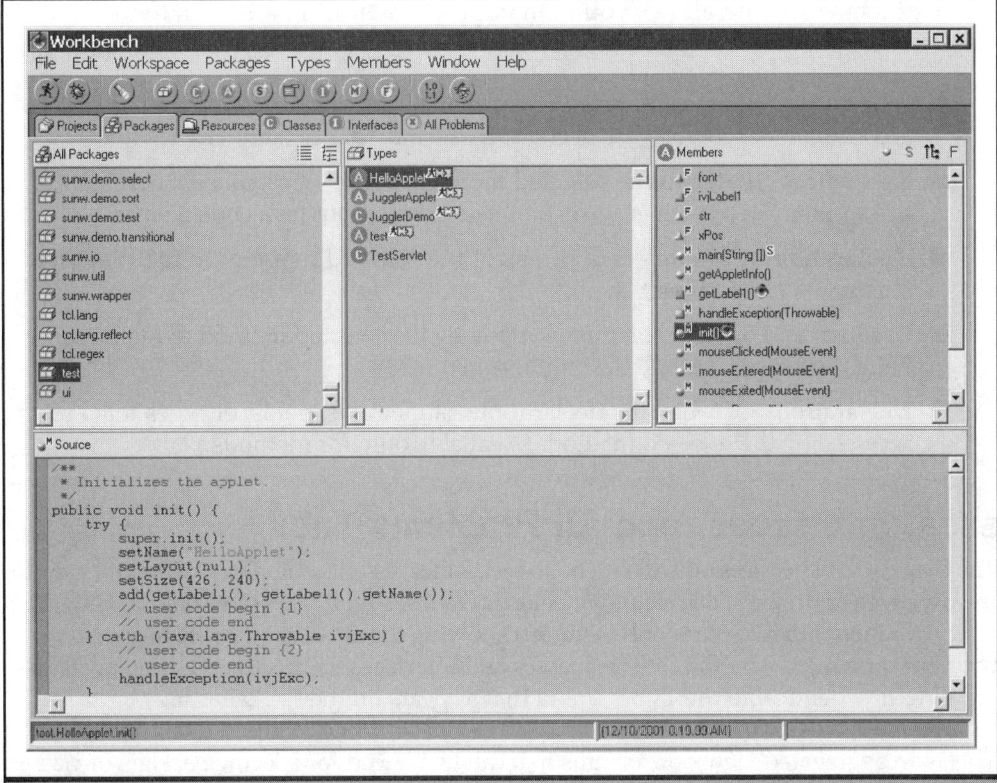

Figure 17-12. *Three parts of the Packages tab*

The Types menu allows you to manipulate types. It differs from the Selected menu for projects in the specific support it provides for types. The Types menu on the Packages tab includes the following special entries:

- **Generate** Generate automatic code for accessors or required methods.
- **Method Template** Create a new method.
- **References To** Find references to the type, or to a specific field in the type.
- **Externalize Strings** Take strings that are hard-coded or are JavaBean properties in the class and externalize them into resource bundles. (This is useful for localization and internationalization, and for externally customizing the titles and captions on controls.)
- **Tools** This submenu includes more items, such as Generate RMI for generating remote method invocation stubs.

The Members menu allows you to manipulate menus. In addition to the standard commands, the following commands are provided on this menu:

- **Inheritance Filters** Filter the display of inherited members and methods according to where they are declared in the inheritance hierarchy.
- **References** Refer to the selected member in the Workspace, Hierarchy, or Working Set (which is a user-defined collection of Java code elements).
- **Declarations** Create declarations of the selected member in the Workspace, Hierarchy, or Working Set.
- **References To** List references made by the selected method to methods, fields, and types. (Available only for methods.)
- **Declarations Of** List the declarations of methods, fields, or types that are accessed by the selected method. (Available only for methods.)

Classes, Interfaces, and All Problems Tabs

The Classes and Interfaces tabs allow you to see all the classes or interfaces without regard to the packages or projects to which they belong. On these tabs, the upper half of the work area is divided into two parts only—the left showing the class or interface hierarchy, and the right showing the methods. The Classes and Interfaces menus that become available are virtually identical to the Types menu that appears on the Packages tab.

The All Problems tab allows quick access to all errors encountered in all components. This is an aggregated view of problems that can be viewed for specific package or classes.

Using the Debugger

The VisualAge debugger is easy and intuitive to use. Right-click the source code on the Source tab to open a pop-up menu that includes the Breakpoint option. If you choose this option, a breakpoint is added to your code. A breakpoint tells the debugger that execution should be suspended when that point is reached; control is given to the programmer to decide whether he or she wants to inspect variable values, step into a method, step over a method, or perform other solutions.

When you choose the Breakpoint option, the following window opens:

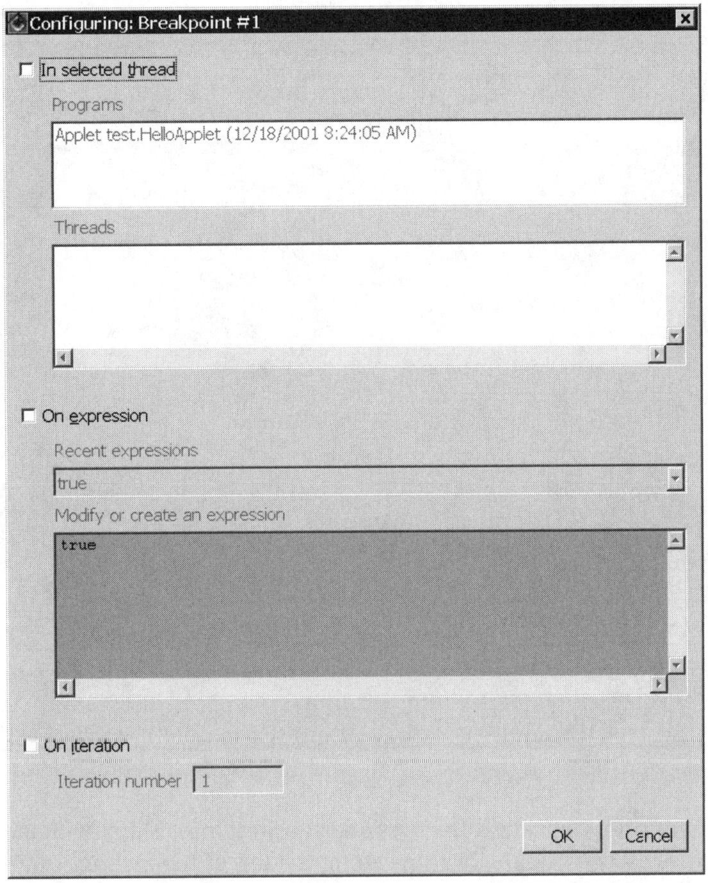

In this window, you can limit the breakpoint to a specific thread or program, or condition it upon a certain expression. You can even request that the breakpoint becomes effective after a certain number of iterations on the selected line of code.

After you set a breakpoint and run the code, the debugger is automatically invoked if a valid breakpoint is met. The Debugger window shows the source code on the lower half of the window, and the method calls stack for each of the active threads (and the thread where the breakpoint is open) on the upper half of the window, along with the variables and the values of the selected variables, as shown in Figure 17-13.

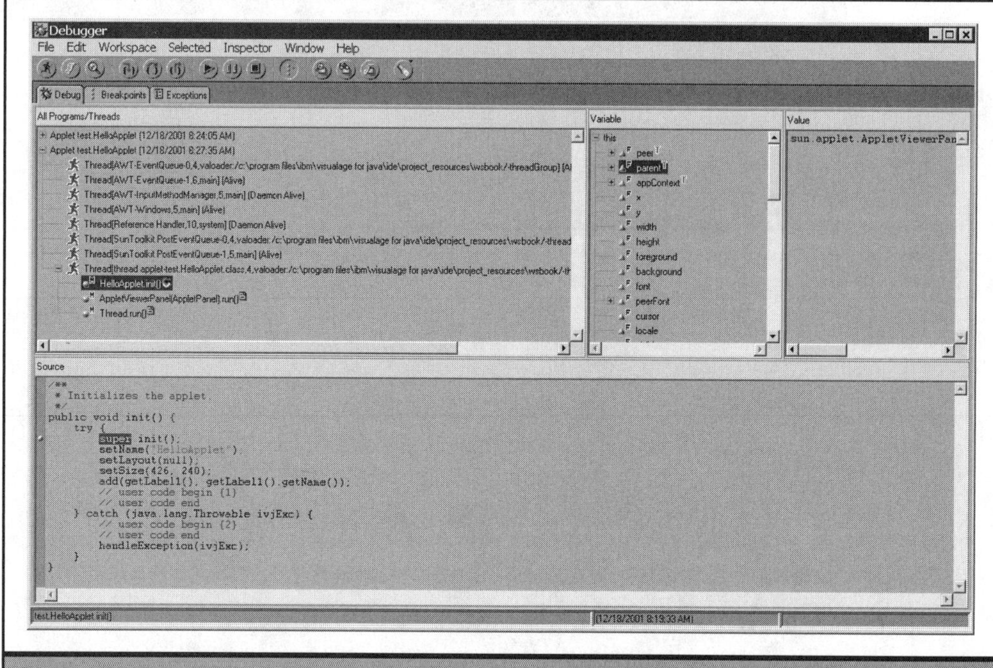

Figure 17-13. *The Debugger window*

The debugger offers standard features such as Step Into, Step Over and Step Out, which you access by clicking the buttons along the top of the Debugger window. You can also resume execution, suspend it, or terminate a thread by using these buttons. As you step through the code, the next line to be executed is highlighted.

Summary

VisualAge for Java is a great development environment. We have been using VisualAge since it was released. Since its first release, it has been one level above all other IDEs in terms of its configuration management environment. In the past few years, VisualAge for Java has gained a lot of maturity and remains, in our opinion, the best Java IDE for large-scale Java development. It is interesting to note (for those of you "square-bracket people"coming from a Smalltalk background) that VisualAge is based on the original Envy environment created by OTI (which was acquired by IBM).

The Complete Reference

Part IV

Core Services

The Complete Reference

Chapter 18

Connection Pooling and Data Access Beans

Database access is a mandatory issue for any business application. The database server is perhaps the most important component of any business application and is responsible for the persistent storage of data. Interaction with databases is also a central theme in Web-based applications. Whether the application is a search engine, an online-shopping site (an *e-tailer*), or just a plain old business application holding records of customers and suppliers, it almost always requires that large amounts of information be handled.

This chapter focuses on issues of database connectivity management. Database connectivity in Java applications is almost synonymous with Java Database Connectivity (JDBC), a Java extension application programming interface (API) that provides programmers with data access abilities based on Structured Query Language (SQL) queries. JDBC is an open API, which means that different vendors provide their own implementations of it—and which implies that code based on JDBC is portable between databases.

Note *Chapter 15 gave you a glimpse into what JDBC is all about. Providing a detailed introduction to JDBC is beyond the scope of this book, but it has been the subject of several books. A good place find out more about JDBC is Sun's JDBC Web page at http://java.sun.com/products/jdbc.*

The ability to access the database server over a JDBC connection, however, is not sufficient for production-level applications. Database connections are expensive resources that must be managed by the application server infrastructure. Connection pooling, the first subject covered in this chapter, is aimed at improving the performance and reliability of database-reliant Java server-side code (such as servlets). The second topic discussed here targets programmer productivity by providing an alternative to the JDBC API in an attempt to simplify the work of developers engaged in building developing database-reliant server-side code. This is done with a set of JavaBeans called *data access beans*.

Connection Pooling

One of the most common paradigms for developing WebSphere applications (or Web-based applications in general), and a recurring theme in this book, is that of three-tier applications:

- The first tier is responsible for user interaction and for presentation and is actually a Web browser.
- The second (or middle) tier is the Web server (or application server), which takes care of the business logic of the application.
- The third tier is responsible for managing the data used by the application. This tier can be a relational database system (such as Oracle or DB2) or some other system capable of managing data.

Before the three-tier was introduced, the dominant application architecture was the client-server architecture, in which a client controls the user interface and most of the application logic. The client usually opens a connection to the database server and maintains it in an open state throughout the life of the client. In this model, one database connection is allocated to each concurrent user of the application. In addition, if something happens to the client (as a result of a bug, for example), no serious results ensue, because the user usually kills the application, and the database connection is closed. (It's reopened when the user restarts the application.)

In a three-tier model, and especially in a Web application model, database connections must be managed. The database is accessed from the application server. The application server is used by many users, and there is no direct mapping between a user and a database connection. In fact, one of the main differences between a client-server architecture and an application-server architecture is the difference in the way that the database is accessed. A Web application can easily serve many thousands of users, and some applications serve tens and even hundreds of thousands of users.

Clearly, then, a database connection cannot be associated with every user; a more scalable model is necessary. The model is one in which database connections are reused among users and are centrally managed within the application server. Connections do not belong to the client, as in the client-server model. When a client needs data access, it asks and receives a connection, uses it for a short while, and then gives it back to the connection pool.

One of the main issues that comes up in this three-tier architecture is the communication overhead between the middle tier and the third tier. The problem is that "connecting" to a database is a relatively expensive operation. In a non Web based environment, this doesn't pose much of a problem, because a typical user logs onto the system to do his work and is willing to wait a second for the connection. This usually happens only once, because the connection stays open as long as the client is running. In contrast, Web-based applications are expected to handle large volumes of users whose access patterns are much less predictable, and access is usually composed of very short interactions. It would be unfortunate if a new database connection had to be created for every operation.

Furthermore, Web-based applications are often stateless. Even though a Transmission Control Protocol/Internet Protocol (TCP/IP) connection is established for making a Hypertext Transfer Protocol (HTTP) request, it is closed after the response is received. This means that the server side has no way of knowing whether the end user will initiate the next interaction in one second, one hour, or never. If the middle tier initiates a connection for each HTTP request, it is possible that the time spent connecting and disconnecting to the database will exceed the time spent on the actual act of retrieving data.

Because performance and scalability are critical for Web applications (since the patience of users easily wanes), WebSphere includes a built-in ability for connection pooling. *Pooling* is essentially a form of sharing resources. Instead of having each user's request incur the overhead of a connect operation, a pool of connections is prepared in advance (or created dynamically on demand) and is managed by a container (be it a Web container or an EJB container). The pool of connections is shared by all elements in the container. For example, servlets processing requests in a Web container can all share a certain pool of connections. This way, the servlets do not have to wait for a database connection. If a connection is available, it can be readily used. If no connection is available, a new connection can be created. This will add some overhead for the connection, but in subsequent requests, one more connection will be pooled. In the worst case, which occurs when the maximum allowed size for the connection pool is reached, the requesting servlet needs to wait for a connection to be freed by the servlet using it and returned to the pool. Because most database interactions are short, this waiting period shouldn't amount to much. The overhead of disconnect operations is avoided too, since the connection is kept open.

Pooling was once thought to offer an advantage in terms of database server costs. Because pooling allows database resources to be reused, it often allows a smaller number of connections (or concurrent users). This was touted as an advantage by the application server vendors because the database servers' licensing was often based on the number of concurrent users. As the three-tier architecture became dominant, the pooling trend led to a shift in database server licensing to models based on price per CPU or price per power unit.

The connection pooling mechanism in WebSphere also caches prepared statements. Prepared statements are associated with a connection; when an application requests a prepared statement, the pooling mechanism determines whether the statement is already cached. Since the operation of creating a new prepared statement is relatively expensive, this caching can significantly improve the performance of an application that repeatedly creates the same prepared statement.

Reminder: Obtaining Connections in JDBC

The implementation of the pooling mechanism in WebSphere is transparent to the using servlet. Actually, this is part of the JDBC 2.0 Optional Package API. An abstraction called `DataSource` is provided to get connections, and this object hides the details of pooling. Essentially, `DataSource` is a factory for connections. This differs from the way connections are handled in the JDBC 2.0 Core API (and in JDBC 1.0), where a connection is established using the `getConnection` method of the JDBC driver manager (and the same connection is explicitly closed after use). The following example illustrates how a connection is established using the JDBC 2.0 Core API without any connection pooling:

```
package book.ws.ch18;

import javax.servlet.*;
import javax.servlet.http.*;
import java.io.*;
import java.util.*;
import java.sql.*;
import java.text.*;

public class JDBCServlet extends HttpServlet {

  // Other methods

  public void doGet(HttpServletRequest request,
      HttpServletResponse response) throws ServletException, IOException {
      response.setContentType("text/html");
      PrintWriter out = new PrintWriter (response.getOutputStream());
      out.println("<HTML>")
      out.println("<HEAD><TITLE> Table </TITLE></HEAD>")
      out.println("<BODY>");
      try {
            Class.forName("com.ibm.db2.jdbc.app.DBDriver");
            Connection con = DriverManager.getConnection(
                             "jdbc:db2:myDb:5001",
                             "db2admin",
                             "db2passwd");
            Statement stmt = con.createStatement();
            ResultSet rs = stmt.executeQuery("select * from Tbl")
            while (rs.next()) {
                 // Assume we have two columns in the table.
                 out.println("<P> " + rs.getString(1) + "," +
                             rs.getString(2));
            }
            con.close();
      } catch (Exception ex) {
         ex.printStackTrace();
      }
      out.close();
  }
}
```

Coding for Connection Pooling

The JDBC 2.0 Optional Package API is an extension of the JDBC 2.0 Core API. This extension is aimed at supporting some of the more recent Java extensions, such as the Java Naming and Directory Interface (JNDI—the subject of Chapter 20) and EJB. The JDBC 2.0 Optional Package also provides support for connection pooling via the `DataSource` interface. The best way to see how this interface is used is through an example. We'll return to the same example shown earlier, here using `DataSource` (which implies support for connection pooling):

```
package book.ws.ch18;

import javax.servlet.*;
import javax.servlet.http.*;
import java.io.*;
import java.util.*;
import java.sql.*;
import java.text.*;


public class JDBC2Servlet extends HttpServlet {

  // Other methods

  public void doGet(HttpServletRequest request, HttpServletResponse
                  response) throws ServletException, IOException {
      response.setContentType("text/html");
      PrintWriter out = new PrintWriter (response.getOutputStream());
      out.println("<HTML>")
      out.println("<HEAD><TITLE> Table </TITLE></HEAD>");
      out.println("<BODY>");
      try {
          Properties env = new Properties();
          env.put(Context.INITIAL_CONTEXT_FACTORY,
                  "com.ibm.websphere.naming.WsnInitialContextFactory");
          Context ctx = new InitialContext(env);
          DataSource ds =
             (DataSource)ctx.lookup("java:comp/env/jdbc/mydb");
          java.sql.Connection con = ds.getConnection();
          Statement stmt = con.createStatement();
          ResultSet rs = stmt.executeQuery("select * from Tbl")
          while (rs.next()) {
                  // Assume we have two columns in the table.
                  out.println("<P> " + rs.getString(1) + "," +
                        rs.getString(2));
          }
          con.close();
      } catch (Exception ex) {
        ex.printStackTrace();
```

```
        }
        out.close();
    }
}
```

To use connection pooling, the DataSource object is looked up using JNDI. (This is the same technique used to lookup EJB in the "Hello World" example in Chapter 5. See Chapter 20 for more on JNDI.) The name of the datasource in this example is *mydb*, and it is qualified with *java:comp/env/jdbc/*. Note that you can also look up the datasource as *jdbc/mydb*, but this method is supported for backward compatibility only, and is not in compliance with Java 2 Platform Enterprise Edition (J2EE) 1.2. Note that there is no direct naming of the database server; this is handled by the connection pool.

The code executed in the `init` method takes care of looking up the `DataSource` object. For this to work, the `DataSource` object should have been created in advance by the Web administrator and stored in the naming service using the WebSphere Administrative Console (discussed in Chapter 42). For the lookup, we need to create a JNDI naming context whose parameters are provided via a properties container. Keep in mind that the `init` method is the best place to perform the JNDI lookup, since it is not likely that the datasource will change during the lifetime of a servlet instance. Thus, we perform this operation only once and save time when serving HTTP requests.

As part of the `doGet` method, the connection is retrieved from the datasource and not from the driver manager. While it may seem that getting a connection from the datasource and from the driver manager are similar, the two options have different implications on the application. If the `DataSource` object has the correct settings, it will implement connection pooling in a transparent manner and improve performance, scalability, and reliability. Although we invoke the `close` method on the connection, the datasource doesn't actually disconnect from the database, because it might need to use the database later on. To summarize, the idea is to access the `DataSource` object in the `init` method and to subsequently use it to get the connections, implicitly making use of pooling.

When using the connection obtained from the datasource, you might want to handle two possible exceptions:

- **ConnectionPreemptedException** Occurs if the servlet doesn't use a connection for a long period of time. In this case, the underlying mechanism grabs the connection to make better use of it.
- **ConnectionTimeoutException** Occurs if the pool is empty when a getConnection request is made—that is, no connections are available at the time of the call, nor are any made available during the specified timeout.

Because database connections are reusable resources central to the smooth operation of the application server, WebSphere cannot rely on application code to function correctly. If application code misbehaves and does not return the connection to the pool, the connection must be taken "forcefully." In a client-server environment, a misbehaving client affects only a single user. In a three-tier architecture, however, where database resources are among the most important shared resources, misbehaving application code might theoretically cause the entire server to run out of resources. The server must therefore protect itself by reclaiming connections that it judges have been freed from the application code, even if the application code has not surrendered the connections gracefully. In such cases, `ConnectionPreemptedException` is thrown. WebSphere implementation of pooling has a few exceptions of its own, which are described in the next section.

An important note is that `DataSource` doesn't support pooling as part of the standard; this support is implementation dependent. So when using other implementations of JDBC 2.0, you cannot count on this feature being available. And while we're on the subject of different implementations, you should note that older versions of WebSphere implemented their own mechanisms for connection pooling through the "connection manager," implemented in the `com.ibm.servlet.connmgr` package. The connection manager is no longer supported in version 4.0. If you have some old WebSphere applications implemented using the connection manager, it shouldn't be difficult to upgrade them to use `DataSource` objects, because the underlying design model is similar, and what was previously called `IBMConnSpec` can now be replaced with a `DataSource` object.

As discussed, one of the main motivations for connection pooling is performance. Setting the size of the connection pool is very important. Having a large connection pool can improve response time and availability because it increases the chances of a servlet getting a free connection from the pool upon request. On the other hand, maintaining a large connection pool takes up large amounts of memory, and might degrade performance.

WebSphere Connection Pooling

WebSphere's implementation of the JDBC 2.0 `DataSource` interface provides several properties that can be used for fine-tuning the performance of connection pooling. These properties are WebSphere-specific and are associated with `com.ibm.websphere.advanced.cm.factory.DataSourceFactory`. They are listed, along with their meanings, in Table 18-1.

Property	Meaning
CONN_TIMEOUT	The maximum time (in seconds) for an application to wait for a connection before timing out and throwing a ConnectionWaitTimeoutException. The default is 180 seconds. Setting this value to 0 disables connection timeout exceptions.
DATASOURCE_CLASS_NAME	The vendor-specific DataSource object used by WebSphere to connect to the database. This class should implement javax.sql. ConnectionPoolDataSource or javax.sql.XADataSource.
DISABLE_AUTO_CONN_CLEANUP	Indicates whether connections are to be closed at the end of each transaction. The default is *false,* which means that upon the completion of a transaction the connection is returned to the pool (and any attempt to use the connection will cause a StaleConnectionException). Setting this value to *true* implies that connections are not returned to the pool at the end a transaction and that the application must explicitly return the connection to the pool by calling close().
ERROR_MAP	This property is used for mapping SQLException objects to WebSphere exceptions; it is rarely of interest to application developers.
IDLE_TIMEOUT	The duration of time (in seconds) during which a connection can remain free in the pool without being used. After this time elapses, the connection is closed and removed from the pool. The default value is 1800. Setting this value to 0 disables this timeout. Note that a connection idle for this length of time is not removed if doing so would reduce the total number of connections in the pool below MIN_POOL_SIZE.

Table 18-1. *Connection Pooling Properties*

Property	Meaning
MAX_POOL_SIZE	The maximum number of connections to be kept in the connection pool. The default is 10. The pool size has a direct impact on the effectiveness of pooling. Using a small pool size can cause longer wait times for code requesting a connection, while using a large pool size increases the overhead since more connections are maintained. The setting for this value should correspond to the capabilities of the datasource (e.g., if the number of connections supported by the database is limited to 5, this value must be 5 or less).
MIN_POOL_SIZE	The minimum number of connections to be held in the pool. The default value is 1. The minimum pool size can affect performance. A small pool requires less overhead, but when the first requests for connections are made, the response is slow. The pool does not start with the minimum number of connections. Connections are pooled once they are created for requesting applications.
ORPHAN_TIMEOUT	The duration of time (in seconds) during which a connection can be owned by an application that is not using it. Once a connection is not used for this amount of time, it is marked for orphaning. If still not used after this timeout elapses again, it is returned to the pool. Any subsequent use of it throws a `StaleConnectionException`. The default value is 1800.
STATEMENT_CACHE_SIZE	The size of the prepared cache statement for all connections in the pool. The default value is 100.

Table 18-1. *Connection Pooling Properties* (continued)

As noted in Table 18-1, WebSphere's connection pooling throws two exceptions:

- **com.ibm.ibm.websphere.ce.cm.StaleConnectionException** Thrown when a connection is not usable because the database has failed, the application has closed the connection, or the connection has been orphaned.
- **com.ibm.ejs.cm.pool.ConnectionWaitTimeOutException** Thrown when a connection is not obtained after the defined number of seconds. (This timeout is defined by the property CONN_TIMEOUT.)

Both exceptions extend JDBC's SQLException, so a *catch* statement addressing that exception will also handle WebSphere's connection pooling exceptions.

Connection Lifecycle

As in any connection pooling scheme (and particularly in WebSphere's connection pooling), a connection can have one of three states: nonexistent, pooled, and in use. The connection lifecycle is illustrated in Figure 18-1.

Limitations of Connection Pooling

While connection pooling is useful for boosting the performance of database-reliant applications, it does not relieve you of the need to manage connections carefully. Specifically, you must remember to close any connection you obtain as soon as you are finished using it. Do not delay this to the finalize method, as there is no guarantee as to the amount of time that elapses until the garbage collector realizes that an object is no longer needed. In fact, the best practice is to close the connection in the same method that opened it, once the database access is complete.

Note *Do not forget to close connections as part of the exception handling you may be performing within your application code.*

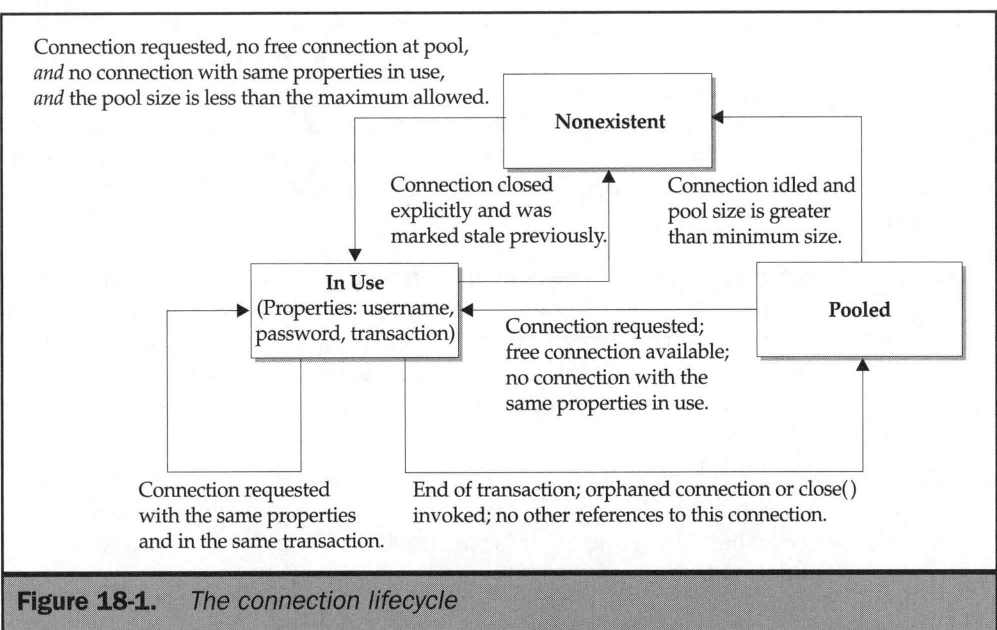

Figure 18-1. *The connection lifecycle*

It is also important to avoid the use of connections as static member variables. If you use a connection this way, it might happen that two different threads use the same connection, which might lead to undesired results. The same applies to servlet instance variables, since a single servlet instance is used by more than one thread. Recall that the same servlet instance is used for multiple client requests; thus, using a connection as an instance variable in a servlet is essentially the same as having a static member in any other class.

Administering Connection Pooling

Connection pooling is administered from the WebSphere Administrative Console. While a detailed description of this console is deferred to Chapter 42, note that connection pooling settings are associated with a datasource. For each JDBC datasource, you can set the connection pooling properties on the Connection Pooling tab.

Data Access Beans

The remainder of this chapter focuses on a different aspect of the relationship between the middle tier (business logic of the Web/application server) and the third-tier (data case server). To access the datasource, the middle-tier application code typically uses the JDBC API (assuming that the datasource is JDBC-compliant). Data access beans are a possible alternative to JDBC (which is also known as a *java.sql* package).

The idea of not using JDBC may seem surprising, since it has already gained stature as the de facto standard for Java database connectivity. The motivation for replacing JDBC is implied by the name of IBM's data access beans. The JavaBeans programming model provides numerous benefits, not the least of which is the ability to use beans in Integrated Development Environments (IDEs—such as VisualAge for Java) in a process of visual composition. Visual composition reduces the amount of code that needs to be written, thereby increasing developer productivity. Other features of data access beans include the following:

- **Caching of query results** The results of an SQL query are retrieved all at once and placed in a cache. This allows the servlet (or application) to move freely forward and backward through the cache or to jump to arbitrary rows in the cache. When SQL queries are made in JDBC, results are sometimes retrieved one at a time, and only forward iteration is allowed (although this is no longer true in JDBC 2).
- **Updates through cache** The cache-holding query results can be manipulated to add, remove, or modify rows. These changes can then be written back to the relational database. When using this feature, there is no need for you to use SQL to update the database.

- **Parameterized query** In many situations, the SQL query submitted to the database includes some parameters that are available only at runtime. Instead of explicitly composing the string at runtime, data access beans allow the definition of a base SQL query string that has variables in place of some of the actual values. Before the query is executed, these variables are replaced with the values. The base query is an ordinary SQL query with the variable elements indicated by question marks.
- **Metadata** Taking the idea of the parameterized query one step further, consider having parameters that are not necessarily strings, but arbitrary Java objects. Metadata specifications define how you convert Java objects into SQL data types, and vice versa; the same specifications take care of converting SQL data types to Java types. Metadata prevents you from having to spend time and code performing type conversions and string construction when manipulating database information.

Data access beans have been a part of WebSphere for a while now. Starting with version 4.0, these beans are implemented using JDBC 2.0 and can leverage the advantages of the datasource interface and connection pooling.

A simple servlet, which will be used to introduce the different data access beans, is shown here. This example uses the same technique for initializing the datasource that was shown in the preceding servlet. To enjoy the benefits of connection pooling, we make use of the `DataSource` object. The data access JavaBeans are contained in the `com.ibm.db` package, so we need to import it. You should also make sure that your classpath includes the *databeans.jar* file in which the relevant classes are packaged. (This file is located in the *lib* directory under your WebSphere installation root.)

```
package book.ws.ch18;

import javax.servlet.*;
import javax.servlet.http.*;
import java.io.*;
import java.util.*;
import java.sql.*;
import java.text.*;
import javax.naming;
import com.ibm.db.*;
import com.ibm.ejs.dbm.jdbcext.*;

public class DataBeanServlet extends HttpServlet {

      private static DataSource ds = null;
```

```
// Other methods

public void init(ServletConfig js) throws ServletException {
    super.init(js);
    Properties env = new Properties();
    env.put(Context.INITIAL_CONTEXT_FACTORY,
            "com.ibm.websphere.naming.WsnInitialContextFactory");
    Context ctx = new InitialContext(env);
    ds = (DataSource) ctx.lookup("java:comp/env/jdbc/mydb"
}
public void doGet(HttpServletRequest request, HttpServletResponse
                  response) throws ServletException, IOException {
        response.setContentType("text/html");
    PrintWriter out = new PrintWriter (response.getOutputStream());

    out.println("<HTML>")
    out.println("<HEAD><TITLE> Table </TITLE></HEAD>");
    out.println("<BODY>");
    try {
          Connection con = ds.getConnection();
          DatabaseConnection dconn = new DatabaseConnection(conn);
          String query = "select PRODUCT, QTY, PRICE from Tbl"+
                        "where PRICE >= ?";
          metaData = new StatementMetaData();
          metaData.setSQL(query);
          metaData.addParameter("minPrice", Integer.class,
                                Types.SMALLINT);
          metaData.addColumn("PRODUCT", String.class,Types.VARCHAR);
          metaData.addColumn("QTY", Integer.class,Types.SMALLINT);
          metaData.addColumn("PRICE", Integer.class,Types.SMALLINT);
          metadata.addTable("Table");

          SelectStatement stmt = new SelectStatement();
          stmt.setConnection(dconn);
          stmt.setMetaData(metaData);
          // Here we set the minPrice parameter.
          // We omit the details of how the price
          // is determined. The point is that it is not fixed.
          selectStatement.setParameter("minPrice", getMinPrice());
          selectStatement.execute();
```

```
            SelectResult rs = stmt.getResult();
            while (rs.nextRow()) {
                  // Assume we have two columns in the table.
                  out.println("<H1> " + (String)rs.getColumnValue("ID")
                             + "," + (Integer) rs.getColumnValue("QTY")
                             + "</H1>");
            }
            stmt.close();
            dconn.disconnect();
            con.close()
            out.println("</BODY></HTML>");
        } catch (Exception ex) {
          ex.printStackTrace();
        }
        out.close();
    }
}
```

This example uses the `DataBaseConnection` bean called `dconn`, which establishes the link between the data access beans layer to the actual database. This bean encapsulates a JDBC connection; some of its methods allow connecting to the database, disconnecting from the database, and getting/setting the transaction isolation level.

Then we create a `StatementMetaData` bean that stores metadata information for the query. This includes the SQL query string, the database column used in the query, their respective Java data types and SQL data types, the query parameters (represented by question marks in the query itself) along with their Java and SQL data types, and the table name. In case of multiple parameters, the parameters are associated with question marks in the query string in the order in which they are introduced into the `StatementMetaData` bean. The `StatementMetaData` class allows you to add columns and parameters, using various methods.

The `SelectStatement` bean represents an actual instantiation of the parameterized query defined by the `StatementMetaData` bean. To this end, it requires the connection, the metadata bean, and an assignment of a value to the parameter. Once the execute method of the `SelectStatement` bean is invoked, a `SelectResult` bean is used to extract the results. This bean provides `nextRow` and `previousRow` (not used in this example) for traversing the result rows, as well as `getColumnValue` and `setColumnValue` for getting and setting column values. The `SelectResult` bean provides a variety of ways to retrieve column values. This bean also allows you to update rows in a manner that will affect the database later.

To summarize, data access beans provide an attractive way to program database interaction. They allow efficient traversal of the database and easy construction of queries involving parameters not known at compilation time. While on the topic of efficiency, note that caching of query results doesn't necessarily take place literally when table queries are very large. In such a case, caching is broken down into blocks that are fetched individually but in a manner transparent to the programmer using the data access beans.

It is also important for you to note that data access beans are IBM proprietary code, and therefore they are not portable across J2EE servers. Using them ties you down to WebSphere (or other IBM products) and is not recommended if migrating to other J2EE servers is even a remote possibility.

Summary

Managing shared resources is one of the most important responsibilities of any application server. Database resources are among the most valuable and important resources used by any e-business application. Managing database resources is therefore one of the core tasks of the WebSphere Application Server.

This chapter outlined the need for database connection pooling and the lifecycle of database connections. It described the APIs used with the database connection pool and the properties through which you can customize and tune connection pooling behavior. It also outlined the exceptions that you need to handle when using connections from the pool.

In addition, the chapter briefly touched upon a WebSphere proprietary technology called data access beans. These beans make database access simpler than it is with the JDBC APIs, while not sacrificing anything in terms of scalability and management. Of course, some advanced features can only occur through direct use of JDBC and the connection pool, but many application developers can benefit from using data access beans.

Database access management is one of the most important core services provided by the WebSphere Application Server. Another one—the topic of the next chapter—is that of application security.

Chapter 19

WebSphere Security Services

Chapter 15 discussed the Java 2 Platform Enterprise Edition (J2EE) and operational model. One of the main goals set forth by J2EE is to define an application model that developers can work with. This model is one that is then used by application server providers—such as IBM with its WebSphere product, on which such applications can run. The main emphasis is, of course, to build a lot of infrastructure into the server platform so that application developers can make use of this functionality by conforming to an application programming interface (API) and an application framework.

Chapter 15 dealt with many of the infrastructure categories of J2EE, but it did not address security functionality. Security is a complex topic that is getting a great deal of attention these days. Web applications have always been the focus of security problems, but there is still room to elaborate on the security model that an application developer can expect in WebSphere. Chapter 13 discussed security concepts in a general way. A lot of theoretical concepts are important as a background for you to understand some of the features available in WebSphere. This chapter outlines the security model implemented by WebSphere and what it provides for us as developers. It focuses on the application assembly stage, in which we define much of the application security profile. Chapter 44 will go on to explain how this all comes together in a deployment and will show how security is administered on the application server.

The J2EE Security Model

As of version 4.0, WebSphere conforms to the J2EE security model. This model deals primarily with aspects of authorization and authentication. Encryption is handled by using Secure Socket Layer (SSL) and Hypertext Transfer Protocol over Secure Socket Layer (HTTPS) and is not directly related to the J2EE model. Authorization is managed by the mapping of roles to method permissions in a way that is external to the application. Authentication in the J2EE model supports sessions, which require a user to log in using one of a set of login methods. WebSphere also supports single sign-on functionality and unauthenticated access.

Most of the emphasis of J2EE security is on the role-based and policy-based model through which an application assembler and the application deployer can control access to application functionality. This conforms to the model first defined for Enterprise JavaBeans (EJB). In the J2EE application model, the container manages security, just as it manages other functions. Application developers can choose to programmatically control all security using a set of J2EE APIs, or they can choose to access security information that is managed and maintained by the container. In the latter case, the actual values that affect security (for example, the access control lists) are defined at deployment time. Note the following definitions, taken from the EJB specification v1.1:

- The bean provider is responsible for declaring in the security-role-ref elements of the deployment descriptor all the security role names used in the enterprise bean code.
- The application assembler can define a security view of the enterprise beans contained in the *ejb-jar* file.

- If the bean provider has declared any security role references using the security-role-ref elements, the application assembler must link all the security role references listed in the security-role-ref elements to the security roles defined in the security-role elements.
- The application assembler defines method permissions for each security role.
- The deployer's job is to map the security view that was specified by the application assembler to the mechanisms and policies used by the security domain in the target operational environment.

WebSphere Security Model

The WebSphere security model is directly based on the J2EE security model. It addresses end-to-end application security using a number of security components that interact to provide end-to-end security services to the application. Those components are shown in Figure 19-1.

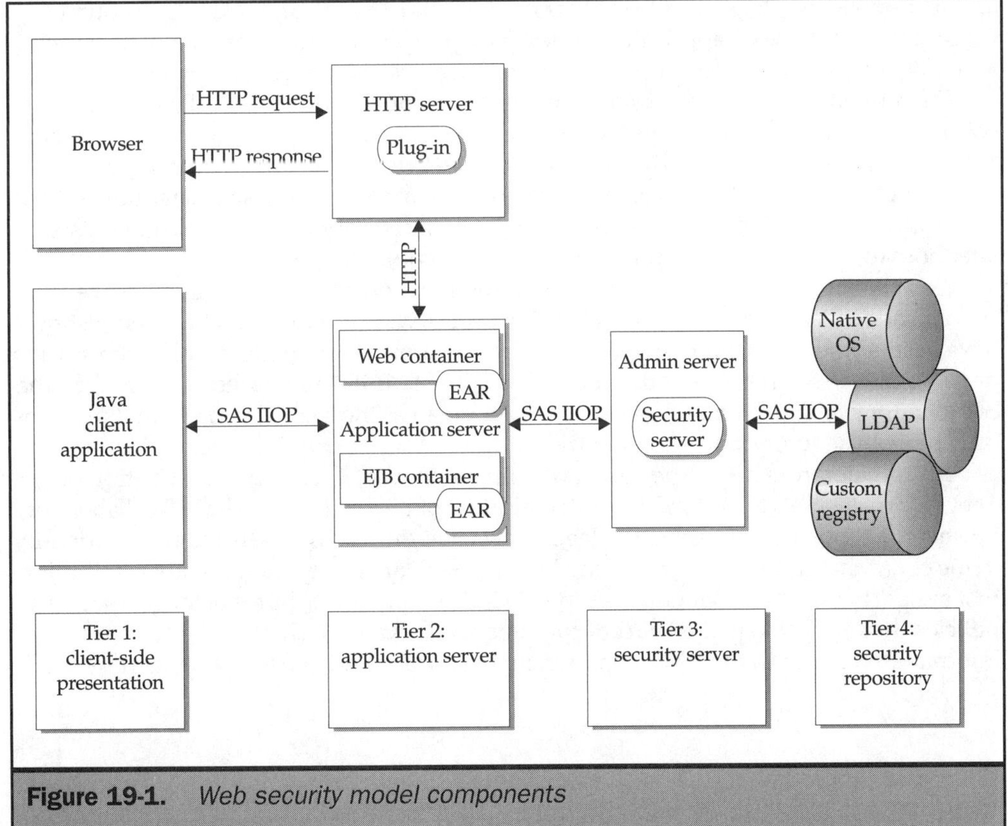

Figure 19-1. *Web security model components*

Requests come into the application server either through a Web server (if the client is a browser) or directly over Internet Inter-ORB Protocol (IIOP). The security model supports both access paths in a consistent manner. If the request comes through the Web server, it can use either HTTP or HTTPS. If it uses HTTPS, the session is encrypted under SSL, and authentication can be achieved through a mechanism built into SSL, as described in Chapter 13. In this case, the client information can be made available to the application server if the client has been authenticated.

If the client is a Java client, the requests come in directly over IIOP to the application server and the EJB container. As Figure 19-1 shows, the session runs over the Secure Association Service (SAS). The SAS runs on both the client and the server. When a client needs information from the server, it first goes through the SAS. The SAS attaches the client's security credentials to the request and adds them as part of the security context for the request before it sends that request to the server. Once in the server, the SAS extracts the security context from the incoming request, authenticates the client's credentials, and passes that information to the EJB container. The EJB handles authorization directly at this point.

Any resources can be secured through WebSphere, not only EJBs. These include resources that reside on the Web server and that are not directly managed by the application server. An example is Hypertext Markup Language (HTML) resources that are part of the Web application. A security plug-in is loaded into the Web server, and this plug-in uses the services in the security server to protect Web resources.

The container uses a component running in the application server called the security collaborator. *Security collaborators* are responsible for providing security-related services to the containers based on information they retrieve from the security server. They serve both EJB containers and Web containers, and there may be multiple collaborators on an application server. Collaborators are managed by a security policy, and you will see later how to define a security policy attached to a container.

Web collaborators are responsible for authentication and authorization, as well as some additional services, such as logging security information. A client request may have been authenticated already, either as part of a previous request within the session or using the client-side authentication feature of SSL. If it is not authenticated, then the collaborator can request that the client go through an authorization process that involves providing a user name and a password.

EJB collaborators do not perform authentication; they focus on authorization only. They rely on the SAS to perform the authentication of the Java client. The EJB collaborator, however, supports a very robust delegation security model and sets the run-as identity to the client that has been authenticated by the SAS, or sets it based on other definitions that are part of the deployment descriptor. Authorization attributes belong to security policies that are packaged as part of the Enterprise Archive (EAR). The security information resides in the XML deployment descriptor and is usually defined by the application assembler that is using the Application Assembly Tool (AAT). The EAR package includes the following security information:

- Role definitions
- Method permissions
- Run-as mode or delegation policy
- Authentication challenge types
- Data security settings

The security collaborators interact with the security server that runs on the administration server. When a collaborator needs authentication to be performed, it communicates with the security server and passes the authentication request. The security server checks a user registry to perform the authentication. WebSphere's security service supports user registries that are managed by the operating system, Lightweight Directory Access Protocol (LDAP) servers, or custom registries through an API. The result of the authentication procedure is a set of user credentials that are then used for further requests during the session.

Authentication Model

WebSphere supports multiple authentication mechanisms. The two most important ones are LDAP and native operating system authentication. The focus of these mechanisms is on eliminating the need to custom-build user registries for each application and on reusing user information in the form of both user names/passwords and more complete user profiles. This not only saves programming time, it saves on total cost of ownership by reducing the number of user profiles that must be maintained within an organization. Users are often defined in the native operating system registry (regardless of whether it is a UNIX system or a Windows system), and IT departments are usually uncomfortable with the need to replicate these definitions within the application, because it means having to manage password changes, for example. WebSphere allows this information to be used as the application authentication mechanism. Access to LDAP services for this user information, as well as for complete user profiles defined as node attributes, is steadily becoming the mainstream and is being used for enterprise applications.

WebSphere supports a number of authentication methods. These methods are the means by which users can authenticate themselves to the WebSphere server, regardless of how the server handles the authentication in terms of the user registry. They include:

- User names/passwords using basic HTTP authentication (that is, using the HTTP response codes for challenge).

- User names/passwords using an HTML form that collects user's information and delivers it to the server through a normal HTTP request.
- Digital (X.509) certificates, in which the certificate is installed or read on the user's client machine and is used to authenticate the user.

Figure 19-2 shows how the AAT is used to set the challenge type for a Web module. In this case, you use a login form that is responsible for the actual login procedure.

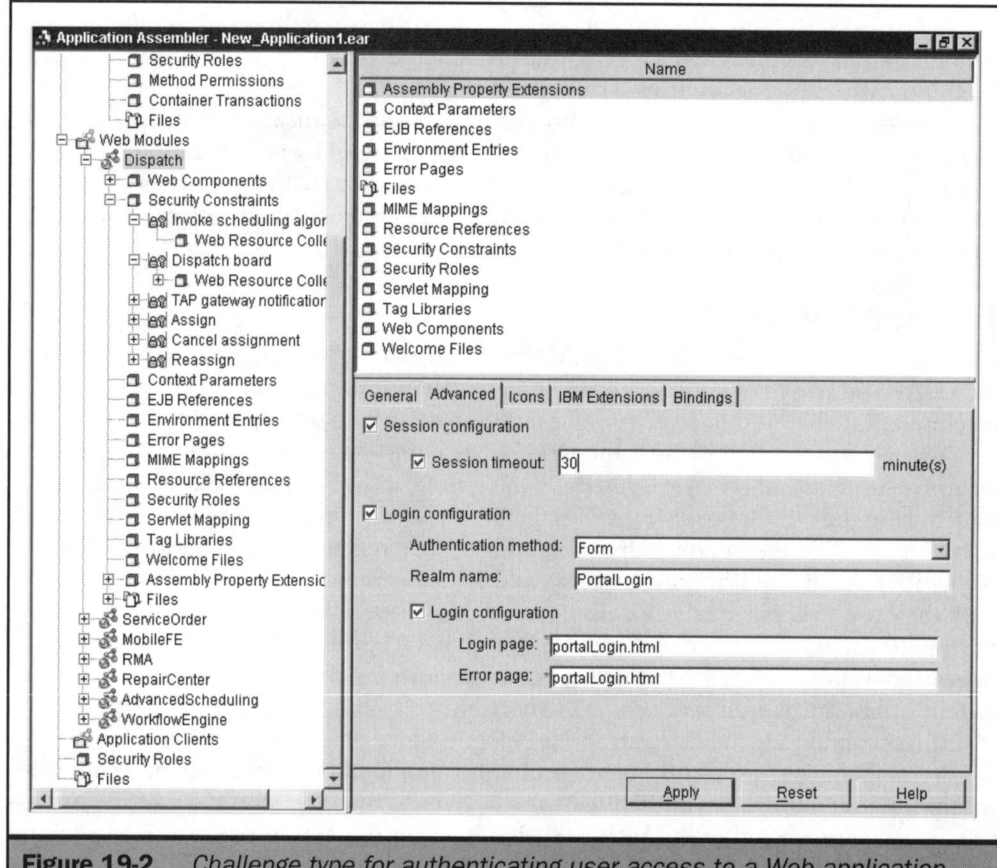

Figure 19-2. *Challenge type for authenticating user access to a Web application*

Authorization Model

Most of the WebSphere security model is devoted to managing authorization. WebSphere conforms to the J2EE authorization model in that it is based on creating security roles and permissions with the application assembler. Figure 19-3 shows an example of how security roles are defined for a Web module in a Web application.

You assign permissions to methods by defining a mapping in which roles are allowed to access resources and methods. First, you define a set of security constraints, as shown in Figure 19-4. These constraints define which security roles have access, as shown in Figure 19-5, where you provide access to a Web resource for the dispatcher, as well as service manager security roles. In each one of these constraints, you can create

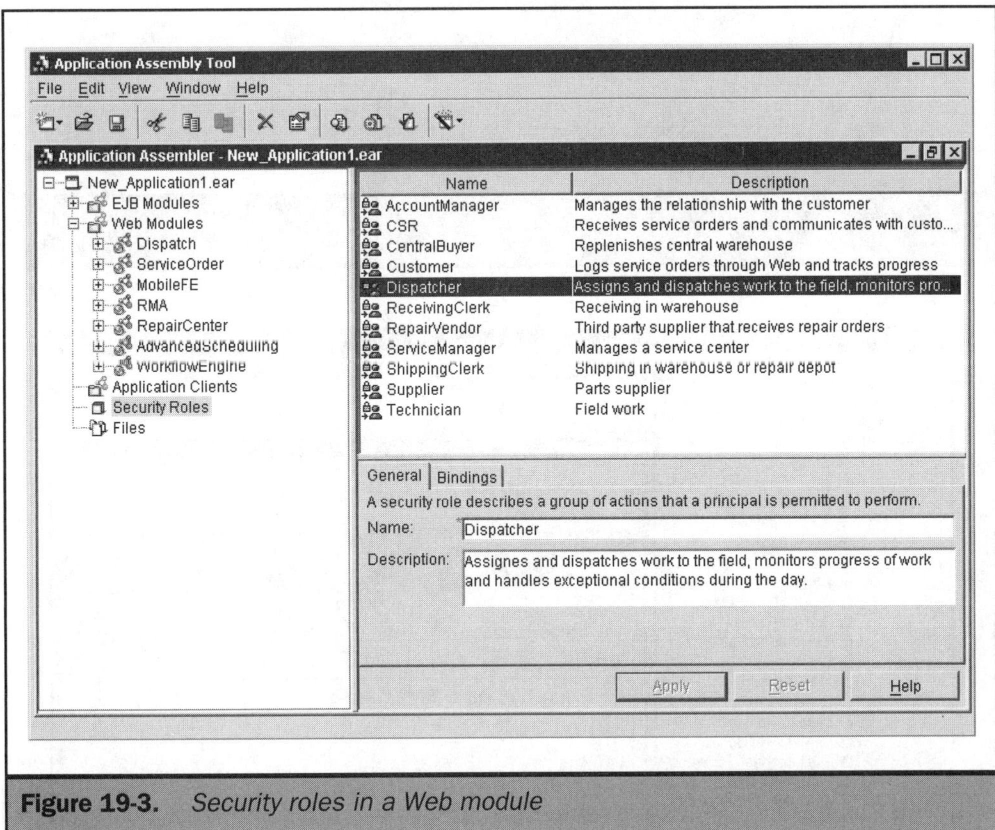

Figure 19-3. *Security roles in a Web module*

New Security Constraint

General

A security constraint describes how Web content is to be protected.

Security constraint name: Invoke scheduling algorithm

Authorization Constraints

Roles:

Role name

Dispatcher

ServiceManager

Add ...

Remove

Description: Authorized to invoke on-line scheduling

User Data Constraint

Transport guarantee: None

Description:

OK Apply Cancel Help

Figure 19-4. *Defining security constraints*

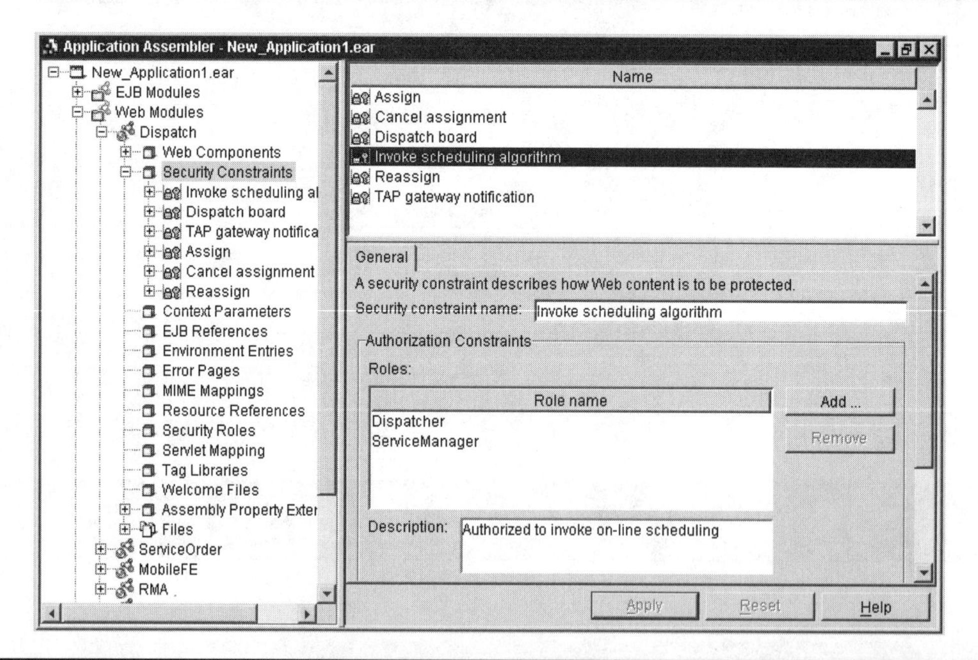

Figure 19-5. *Security role access in a security constraint*

resource groups and define exactly which resources should be managed under specific security constraints, as shown in Figure 19-6 and Figure 19-7.

When the application is deployed, an administrator defines users and user groups. These definitions are dynamic and can occur over the life of an application. The server administrator maps users and user groups to security groups using the Administration Console. This mapping can also be done with the AAT, as shown in Figure 19-8. This defines which user has access to which methods. When a request comes into the server, the server looks at the identity of the user and determines which security roles have been assigned to that user. Based on this information, the server can verify whether the user is allowed to access the called method. This scheme is shown in Figure 19-9, where the dotted lines represent mapping performed during application assembly, and the solid lines represent mappings performed by the administrator.

Delegation Model

Delegation is another important element of the J2EE security model. It allows you to define on behalf of whom a certain method invocation should be carried out. Recall that a server component like an EJB can also be a client that requests services from another component. In such a case, you can define whether a method invocation should be performed based on the authorization profile of the original request initiator or on some other criterion.

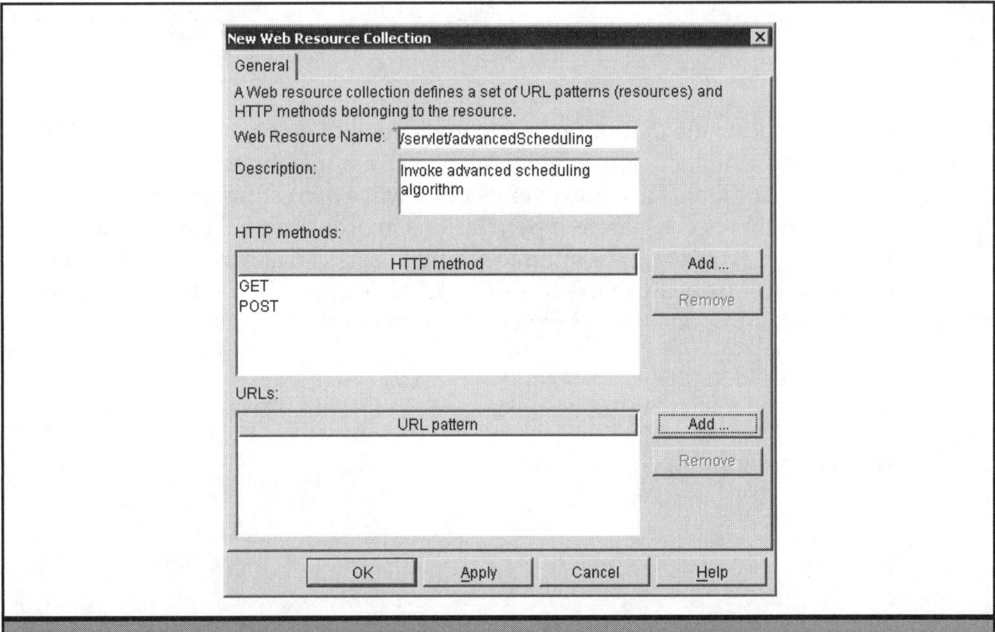

Figure 19-6. *Adding a scheduling Web resource to be managed by a security constraint*

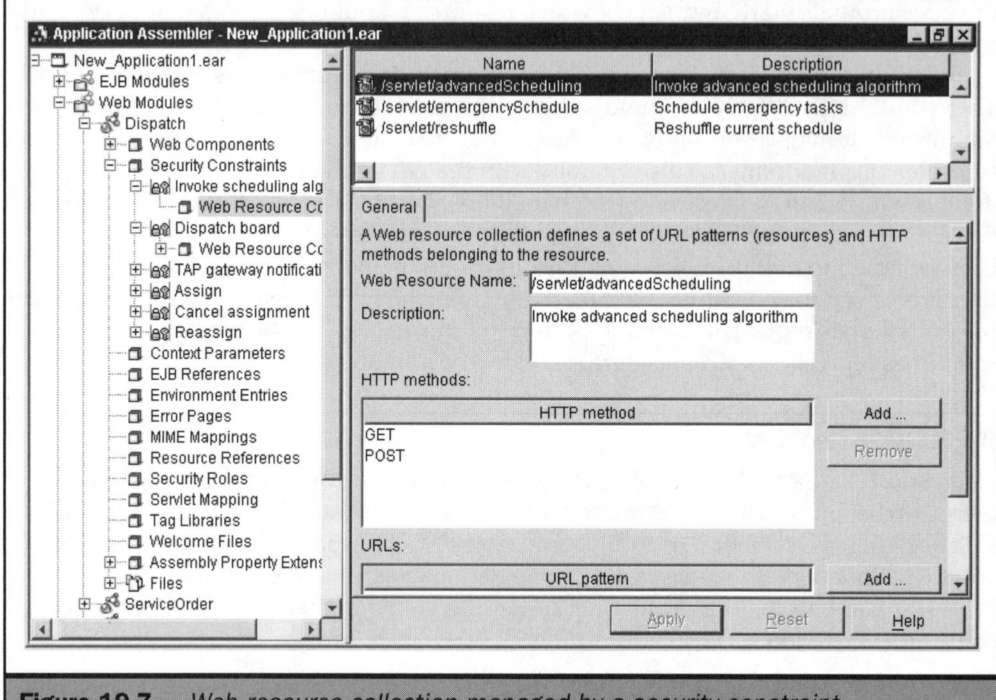

Figure 19-7. *Web resource collection managed by a security constraint*

WebSphere supports the definition and management of delegation policies. When no delegation policy is defined, the default is always to assume the security identity and profile of the original caller. This, however, is not always correct; sometimes you may build a component that needs different permissions in order to run. You will still want to expose a part of the component's interface so that users can access its functionality. You need to modify security attributes to allow such delegation, by setting the Run-As mode using the AAT. Possible values for this RA mode include:

- Run as caller (default)
- Run as system
- Run as an assigned specific identity

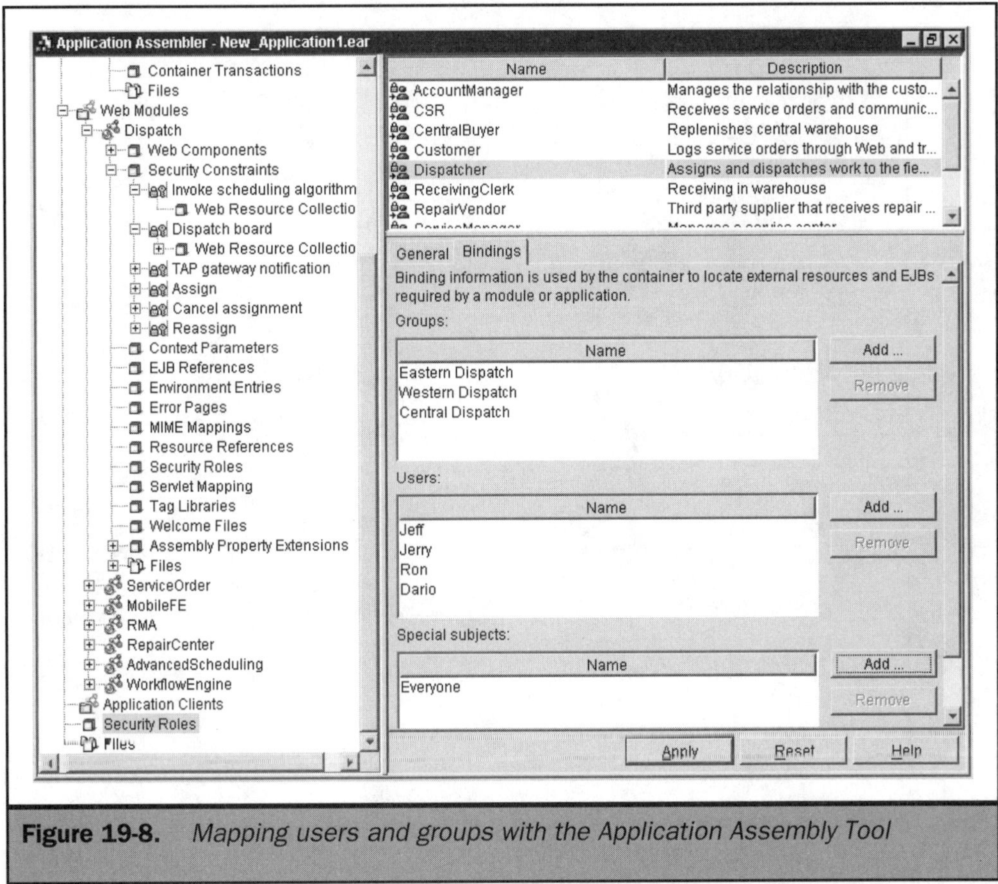

Figure 19-8. *Mapping users and groups with the Application Assembly Tool*

Figure 19-10 shows how you can set the Run-As mode for all methods in the advanced scheduling EJB to run as the Dispatcher security role.

Deployment Descriptors

Security attributes are maintained in deployment descriptors. These XML files contain security information, as well as additional properties for each of the

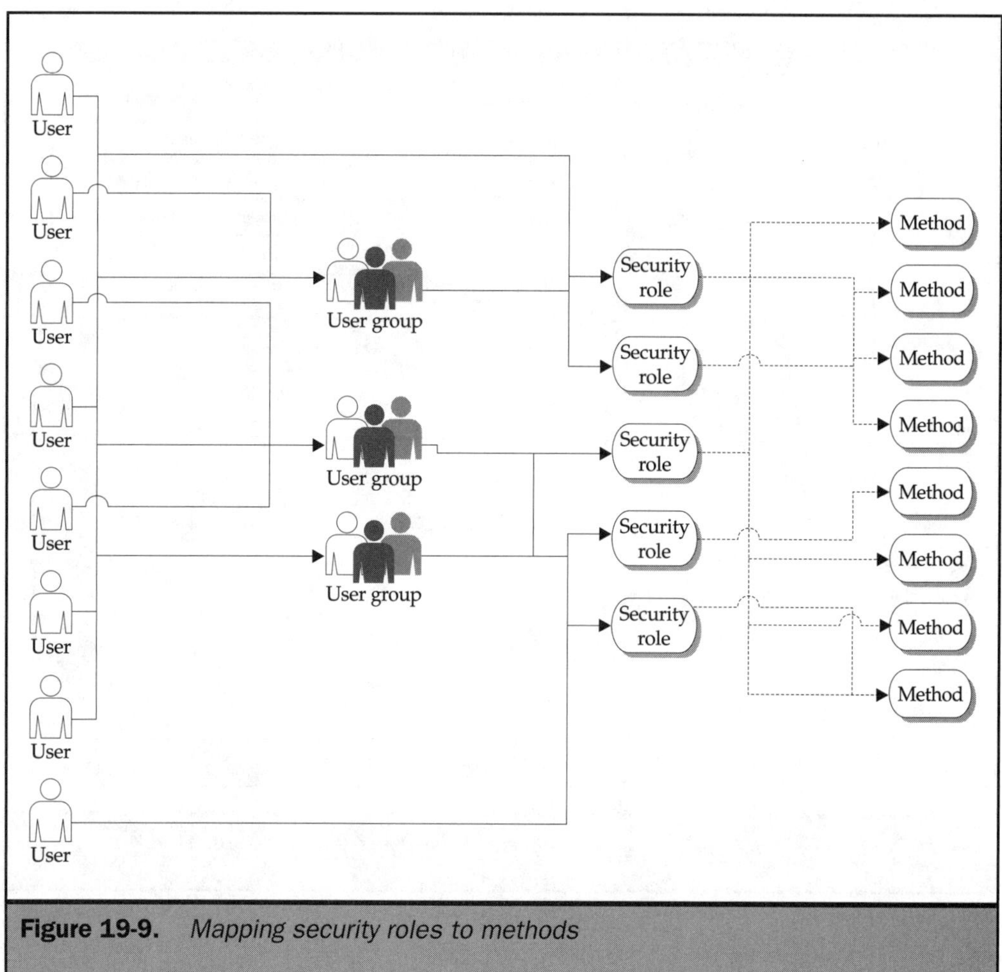

Figure 19-9. *Mapping security roles to methods*

managed resources. Security attributes maintained as part of the deployment descriptors include:

- Security roles and method permissions
- Delegation policy (that is, the Run-As mode)
- Challenge type for authentication
- Data security settings

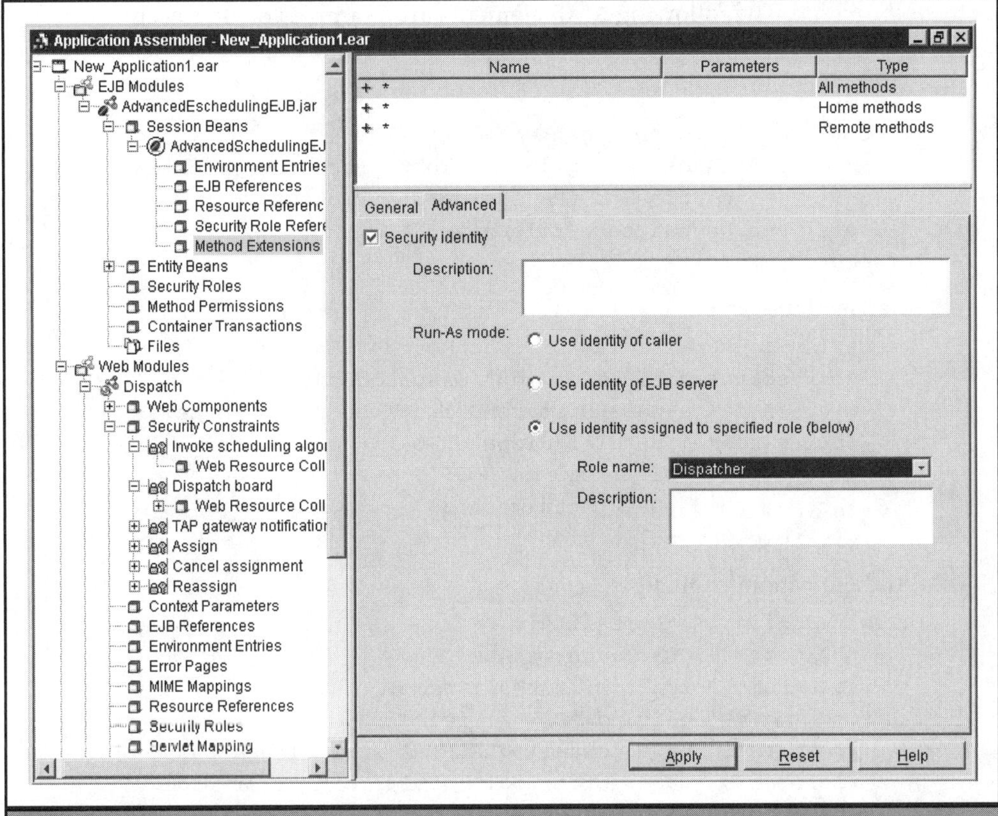

Figure 19-10. *Setting the method security delegation policy to run-as Dispatcher*

Security Profiles

WebSphere maintains global security profiles and application-specific security profiles. Application security can be defined separately for each application. This security profile overrides the global profile for that specific application. Security-related information is often maintained in Extensible Markup Language (XML) in files such as the *web.xml* file. The following XML elements are examples of such security information:

- Security roles:

```
<security-role id="Dispatcher">
  <description>Role assigning tasks to resources and dispatching
             roles to the field</description>
  <role-name>Dispatcher</role-name>
</security-role>
```

- Managed resources:

```
<security-constraint id="DispatchBoard">
  <web-resource-collection id=" DispatchBoard ">
    <web-resource-name>DispatchBoard</web-resource-name>
    <url-pattern>/servlet/dispatchBoard</url-pattern>
    <http-method>GET</http-method>
    <http-method>POST</http-method>
  </web-resource-collection>
```

- Authentication/challenge:

```
<login-config id="PortalLogin ">
  <auth-method>FORM</auth-method>
  <realm-name>PortalLogin</realm-name>
  <form-login-config id="PortalLogin">
    <form-login-page>portalLogin.html</form-login-page>
    <form-error-page>portalLogin.html</form-error-page>
  </form-login-config>
</login-config>
```

Security Administration Model

Security is administered with the Administrative Console and the Security Center tool. The security center can be opened from the Administrative Console. The same set of procedures and definitions is used to administer all resources, regardless of their types. Chapter 44 is devoted to security administration, and it focuses on the Administrative Console. Here, you merely outline what is administered and which security properties need to be set for the following resources:

- **Web resources (HTML, JSP, servlets, and so on)** Security attributes for Web resources are defined with the AAT and are maintained in the Web archive file, in the deployment descriptors for the application, and in the *web.xml* file. The security profile for Web resources includes the security role definitions, the role reference, and the security constraints.
- **EJBs** The EJB security model is quite elaborate, and WebSphere supports its administration based on the J2EE security model. The information is

maintained in the EAR, in the application deployment descriptors, in the security server's repository, and in various XML and XMI files (specifically in *ejb-jar.xml, ibm-ejb-jar-ext.xmi,* and *ibm-application-bnd.xmi*). Setting the security information is done from either the AAT or the Administrative Console, depending on whether the person setting the property is the application assembler or the deployer. A security profile for EJB includes information about roles, role reference, method permissions, Run-As identities, and Run-As mappings.

- **Global security settings** These are the security properties for all applications and components deployed on the server.
- **SSL settings** Figure 19-11 and Figure 19-12 show how the Security Center is used to set the timeout and SSL key file parameters.
- **Authentication settings** Figure 19-13 and Figure 19-14 show how the Security Center is used to set the user registry source—whether authentication is done through the operating system's user registry or through an LDAP source.
- **Security roles** These are reused when setting the profiles for Web resources and EJBs.

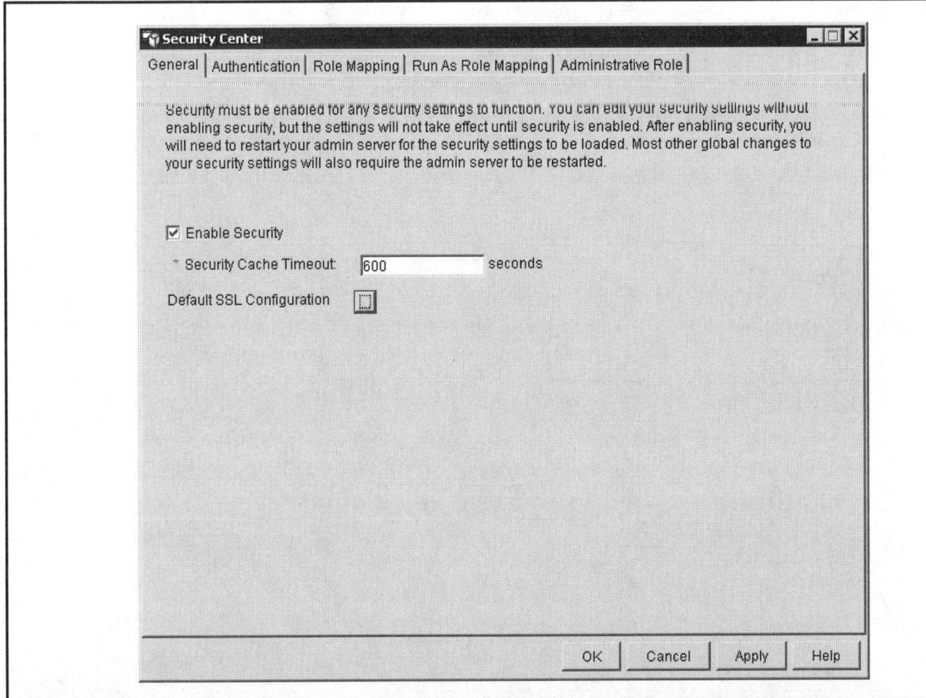

Figure 19-11. *Enabling security and setting the timeout in the Security Center*

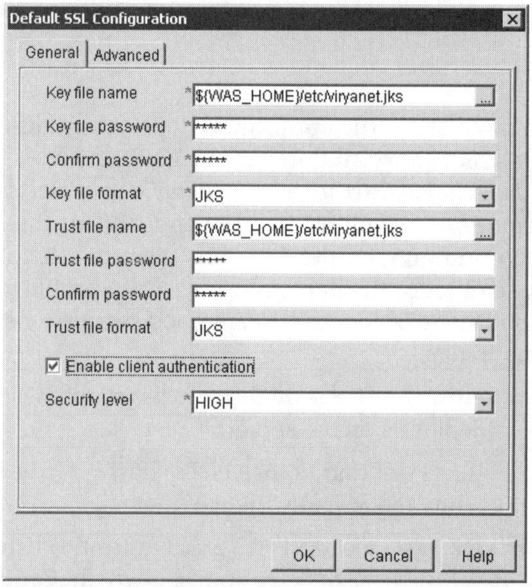

Figure 19-12. *Setting SSL key file values in the Security Center*

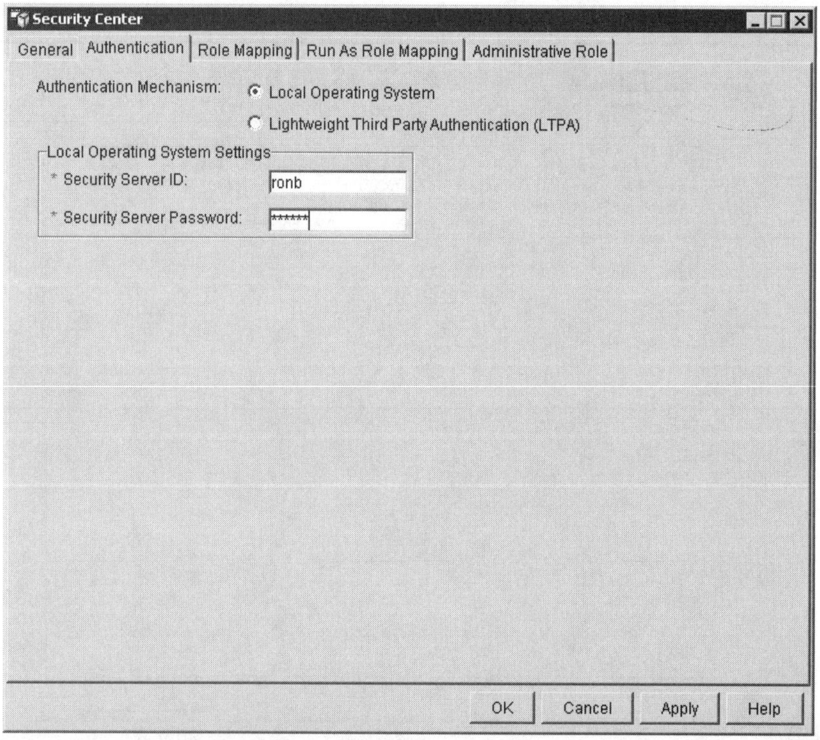

Figure 19-13. *Setting local operating system authentication in the Security Center*

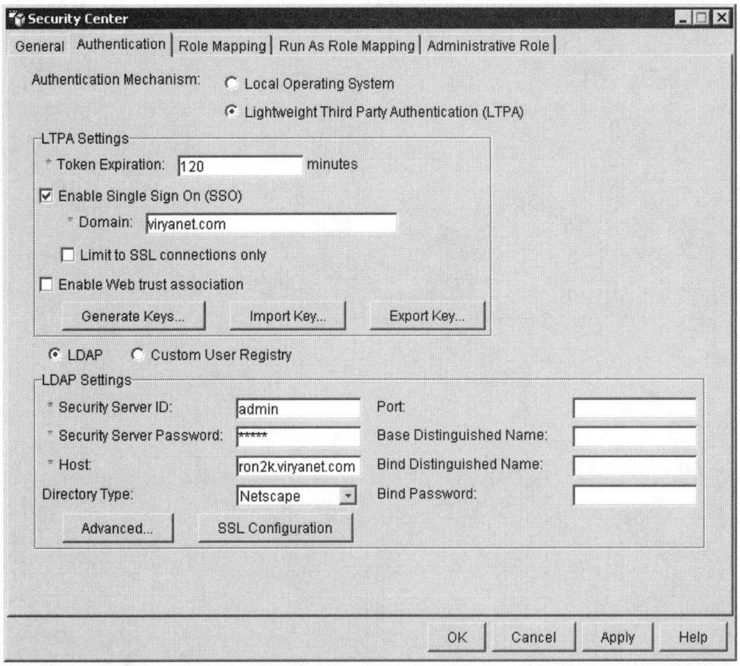

Figure 19-14. *Configuring SSL in the Security Center*

Summary

This chapter gave a brief description of the WebSphere security model and described how WebSphere implements the J2EE security model. It detailed the authentication as well as the authorization models, and described the delegation model. The focus here has been on the definitions that need to occur during application assembly. (Chapter 44 focuses on the administration of security at runtime and on the use of the Administrative Console for security-related activities.)

While describing authentication, we mentioned that one of the possible authentication methods is to use an LDAP server, where the actual authentication is done using Lightweight Third Party Authentication (LTPA). The LDAP protocol is used to access information in a directory server, and it is becoming the method of choice for storing user information and authenticating users. LDAP is the topic of Chapter 20.

Chapter 20

Lightweight Directory Access Protocol Support

Any mention of security today must include a discussion of the Lightweight Directory Access Protocol (LDAP). Security is necessary for identifying a user (for example, by a user name and password), authenticating the user credentials, and extracting the permissions and profiles associated with this user. Among other things, the user groups (or roles) to which a user belongs must be extracted.

This type of information needs to be maintained in nearly all applications, and this is precisely where things become complicated. Every application that maintains such information needs to be able to access it to function correctly. Users, however, do not want to have to enter such security information again and again; a better way to maintain security information and mapping between security information on multiple applications is necessary to enable such conveniences as single sign-on. Central to this are directory services that allow you to maintain information in a way that all applications can access.

Directory Services

A *directory* is a collection of information about objects arranged in some order. Examples from everyday life include telephone directories and library catalogs. From a software perspective, directories are databases or data repositories that list information for keyed objects. The main difference between a generic database and a directory is that directories tend to have a great number of lookup requests but relatively few update requests as compared with a generic database. This type of usage creates an opportunity to specialize and optimize, and this is precisely what directory servers do.

Directories allow users or applications to find resources with the characteristics needed for a particular task. For example, a directory of users can be accessed to look up a person's e-mail address or fax number. A directory can be searched to find a user group to which a user belongs and then queried to determine the attributes possessed by this user group or this individual.

Directory services are normally used to access information, including services for looking up information attributed to a managed entity (for example, the profile maintained for a user), updating that information (which occurs much less often), and finding an entity given some selection criteria. Directory services are provided by directory servers, software components that manage the directories and implement the services. Applications access directory services using a directory client, as shown in Figure 20-1.

Naming Services

A critical issue in distributed programming of any kind is the issue of *naming*. When clients need to gain access to a resource, they must have a way to translate a "logical" name to an actual object reference, and they must be able to do so transparently in case the object is on a remote machine. Java Naming and Directory Interface (JNDI) is the

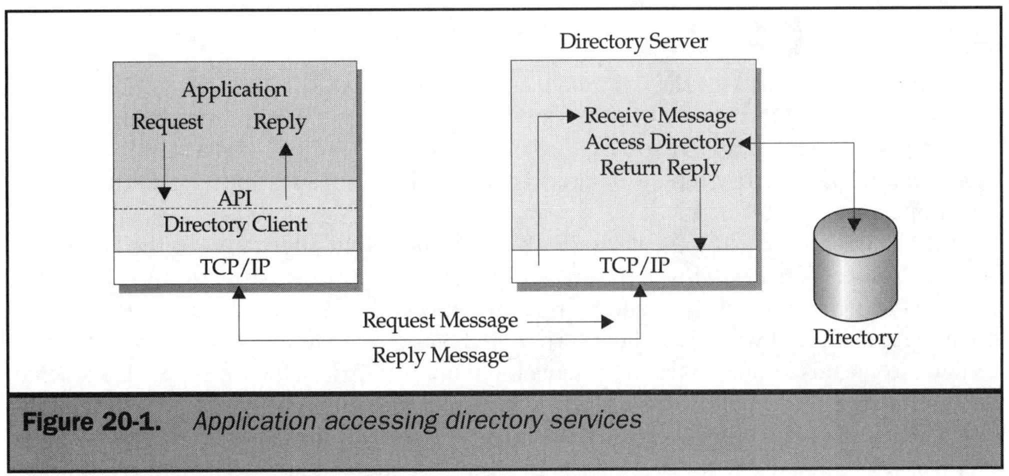

Figure 20-1. *Application accessing directory services*

Java application programming interface (API) used for accessing naming and directory services. JNDI was discussed and used in Chapter 5 for accessing Enterprise JavaBeans (EJBs) on the WebSphere server, where the actual naming services are provided by the respective Common Object Request Broker Architecture (CORBA) Services. Details about the underlying implementation of the naming service are masked through the use of JNDI. An underlying naming service implementation of independent interest is LDAP.

LDAP is an open industry standard that aims at providing a way to manage information pertaining to files, users, printers, and other resources that can be dispersed over several different networks. LDAP is an example of the kind of directory service accessed through JNDI.

Naming services are used for tagging any entity with a common name that can later be used to look up the resource. In the context of security, the entity you need to tag is the entity representing the user who is trying to get access to a set of applications managed within your WebSphere environment.

The WebSphere Application Server Advanced Edition allows the user registry (for WebSphere's own authentication purposes) to be stored on an LDAP server (or servers). This kind of environment is highly recommended because it eases user and security management and provides an environment that is ready for application integration at the security level (using the LDAP directory). However, to use LDAP, you need to install an LDAP server, which is not part of the WebSphere Application Server distribution. You can use the IBM SecureWay directory server, which includes a full implementation of LDAP. You can also use a third-party provider for an LDAP server alongside the WebSphere Application Server. Note that this feature is not available in the Advanced Single Server Edition.

What Is LDAP?

The growing popularity of the computer as a tool for supporting business, along with the advent of the Internet as a business vehicle, give rise to the requirement of having a directory service from which you can look up people or resources on a certain network. The way such a directory would be used is not unlike the way a library catalog or a telephone directory is used.

LDAP was born during the early 1990s as a lightweight alternative to the Directory Access Protocol (DAP) that was part of the specification for the X.500 protocol. X.500 was developed as part of the standardization efforts initiated by several international organizations (notably the ISO, the International Standards Organization). These efforts resulted in what is knows as Open Systems Interconnect (OSI), which was once considered an alternative to Internet protocols. The OSI model is a reference model that defines seven layers of data communication that starts with the physical layer as the lowest layer and works its way up to application protocols as the highest layer. The OSI reference model and subsequent protocols were developed from scratch, and using these protocols usually results in a cleaner application design. However, the relatively slow development and even slower deployment and installation process doomed the OSI protocols to failure, especially with the rapid development of the Internet, which is based on Transmission Control Protocol/Internet Protocol (TCP/IP).

Similar to other Internet standards, LDAP went through several stages of evolution before reaching its current state. On the way, it became an industry-wide standard, and most vendors support it. In fact, all vendors that focus on infrastructure software offer an LDAP product and numerous public domain servers can be used to store and retrieve labeled information. Although it was once thought that LDAP would become the central registry on the Internet, competing standards have emerged and this war is far from being won by any one of these standards. (As many like to say, "The nice thing about standards is that there are so many of them.")

LDAP is based on the client-server paradigm. Although it seems at first that LDAP is a "directory" protocol, it actually defines the protocol of communication between LDAP clients and LDAP servers. Through this protocol, and the structure of the messages involved, a directory model is induced. In other words, the communication protocol implies certain restrictions imposed on designers of LDAP servers, and these restrictions define what an LDAP directory is, in abstract terms.

LDAP is implemented on top of TCP/IP, and as such, the way clients interact with servers resembles other TCP/IP-based protocols such as HTTP or FTP. A session is initiated by the client that "binds" to the server (this corresponds to a TCP/IP operation that requires specifying the host IP address and TCP/IP port number for the LDAP server). Following an optional authentication procedure based on user name and password, the actual session commences. Without authentication, the client can assume "anonymous" identity with default access rights. The session itself consists of a series of operations on directory data—namely search and update operations. Operations are conducted by the client issuing a request and the server responding. When the client is done, the session is closed.

Distinguished Names and Relatively Distinguished Names

All search and update operations requested by the LDAP client revolve around the basic data structure in which the LDAP server stores information, referred to as *directory entries*. A single directory entry describes a real-world object such as a person, printer, or computer. The entry is identified by a name called a *distinguished name (DN)*, which is composed of smaller parts called *relatively distinguished names (RDNs)*. This situation is strikingly similar to the way files are organized in a hierarchy of directories in most modern operating systems (such as UNIX or Windows).

Consider, for example, a file named *E:\WebSphere\AppServer\readme.txt*. This name is composed of four smaller names delimited by backslashes. Each of these smaller names that refer to drive, directory, or filenames are the equivalents of RDNs. In addition to the entry name, each entry contains one or more attributes that make up the entry description. For example, a directory entry for a computer could include its type, operating system, IP address, physical location, and other information. The list of attributes, along with the type of each attribute and possible syntax restrictions, are described in a *schema*. The relationship between the schema and a directory entry is identical to the relationship between a class and an object in an object-oriented language—that is, the directory entry can be thought of as an *instance* of the *schema*. New schemas can be derived from existing ones, just like class inheritance is used in an object-oriented language. A special attribute called `objectClass` exists in each directory entry and identifies the schema to which it belongs. This attribute is defined in the "top" object class, which essentially is a root class from which all schemas are derived.

Attributes

In a specific directory entry, zero or more values are associated with each *attribute*. Zero values indicate that nothing is associated with the attribute, and this is possible for optional attribute (the fact that an attribute is optional is part of the schema definition). The most common case is one value, but it is possible for one attribute to have several values. Multiple values are useful for attributes such as phone numbers, where several values are associated with one object (a person, in the case of phones).

Attribute types or syntaxes are used to define what kind of values an attribute takes. The typing system is flexible enough to allow general purpose binary data as well as printable strings that can be either case sensitive or insensitive. It is possible to define new types of attribute syntaxes, limiting the length of the value or its content.

Attribute names and values are used to specify RDNs. Recall that entry names (DNs) are composed of smaller names called RDNs. These are usually of the form *<attribute name>=<value>*, but in general you can specify an RDN as a set of plus-sign delimited pairs of attribute and value. Here's an example of syntax for two pairs:

<attribute1 name>=<value1>+<attribute2 name>=<value>

Directory Information Tree

Directory entries are organized in a tree-like structure called the *Directory Information Tree (DIT)*, starting from a virtual root node. For a given entry, the RDNs composing a DN correspond to the path from the virtual root to the node of the entry on the tree. The DN is a list of comma-separated RDNs, but unlike file system pathnames, the order in which the RDNs are specified is from the node up to the root.

Figure 20-2 shows an example of a simple DIT. In this example, a directory is composed of people who belong to departments and organizations. So, for example, the DN for Ed Lopez in the sales department of Akitami is `cn=Ed Lopez,ou=Sales,o=Akitami`. The directory root shown in the figure is virtual, and there is no corresponding directory entry.

Inside the DIT, it is possible to create *aliases*, which can be thought of as links between nodes. These aliases are the reason why the DIT is a tree-*like* structure and not really a tree. Aliases can be used to represent cases in which a certain entity belongs to two categories (such as a person belonging to two departments). Another motivation to using aliases is to ensure backward compatibility—that is, while we make changes in the DIT, we may want old DNs to remain valid (at least temporarily). This can be achieved easily by moving the directory entry to its new location but leaving behind an alias with the old DN.

Referrals

Considering the kinds of applications for which LDAP is intended, *scalability* is an important issue. Specifically, this means that a single server is not sufficient for maintaining the entire DIT, and to support scalability, the DIT can include *referrals* to

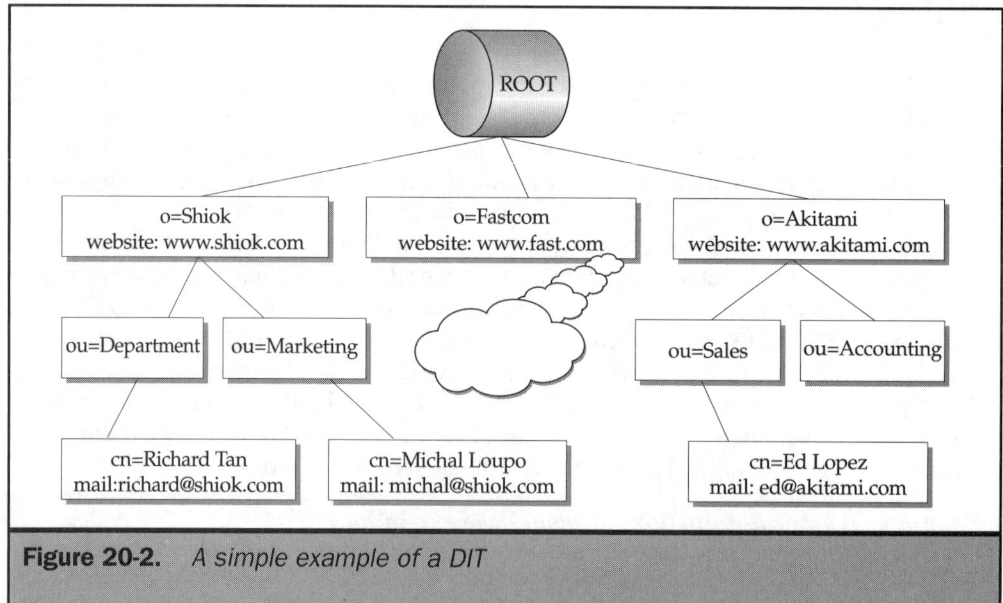

Figure 20-2. *A simple example of a DIT*

other servers, allowing creation of a distributed DIT with multiple servers. The topmost node in a server is called the server *suffix*—the longest common suffix for all DNs in this server. Actually, a single server can have several suffixes that correspond to several sub-trees of the DIT. Referrals to other servers are represented by a special kind of entry and can be handled in one of two ways: the requesting client can receive the referral and can access the referred server, or server *chaining* can take place. In the latter case, the server originally contacted by the client makes a request to the referred server.

Operations

Now let's look at how operations are performed on the DIT. The most important operation supported in the LDAP is the *search* operation. LDAP is designed under the (reasonable) assumption that most operations performed are search operations. Only a small minority of requests are updates. If that is not the case, any standard database system might do better than an LDAP server. The search operation allows a client to perform a search on a certain part of the DIT looking for certain entries.

The parameters for a search operation are as follows:

- **Base** A node in the DIT from which the search shall commence.
- **Scope** How deep within the DIT the search should go. There are three options here:
  - **BaseObject** Only the base node will be searched.
  - **SingleLevel** Only the immediate sub-nodes of the base node are to be searched.
  - **WholeSubTree** All descendants of the base node are to be searched.
- **Search Filter** A search criteria to be met by returned entries. The search criteria is composed of a series of assertions relating to an attribute, of the form attribute operator value. Operators include =, >=, <=, =*, and ~=. The first three comparison operators have the obvious meaning, the =* operator is used without a value and returns all entries that have a value set for the attribute, and the ~= operator provides an approximate match. If more than one assertion is provided, they should be accompanied by a Boolean operator, which can be &, |, or !, meaning AND, OR, or NOT, respectively. The operators are specified in *prefix* notation—that is, the operator precedes the arguments. For example, *"&(cn=Ed Lopez)(website=www.akitami.com)"*.
- **Returned Attributes** List of attributes to return.
- **Alias Dereferencing** Whether or not aliases should be followed. (If they are not followed, the "alias" itself is examined and might be returned; if they are followed, the search continues at wherever the link is pointing.)
- **Size and Time Limit** Maximal number of entries to be returned and maximal search time. These can be specified to limit the amount of load imposed by the search.

Update operations include adding a new entry to the directory, deleting entries (which must be leaf nodes), and modifying existing entries. A special variant of modifying entries is modifying DNs, which could mean either changing the first (least significant) component of the DN or changing the location of the node to a different sub-tree.

All operations, especially update operations, might require authorization. LDAP has support for various levels of user authentication (corresponding to the desired level of security), ranging from no authorization through basic authorization (similar to the one used in HTTP), to a more powerful authentication scheme, possibly using the Secure Socket Layer (SSL) and similar security mechanisms.

Java Naming and Directory Interface

This section focuses on the Java-based API called JNDI, a generic API that is not specific to LDAP and also applies to other naming and directory services such as DNS (Domain Naming Service). JNDI was developed to create a consistent model for accessing different resources maintained in different directory servers. This sounds a little like the motivation for creating LDAP. JNDI, however, can accommodate other ways of managing resources such as CORBA or DNS, but it does not contain the logic for directory management.

JNDI is a part of J2EE and is contained in the following packages:

- **javax.naming** The basic API used to look up objects and values in a naming service.
- **javax.naming.directory** A more sophisticated API used for filtered searching and updates.
- **javax.naming.spi** Interfaces for use by service provider developers. These are rarely of any interest for application developers, because they are intended for developing support for specific services (such as LDAP).

WebSphere includes a built-in implementation of a JNDI server for the purpose of providing a naming service for EJBs. The "Hello EJB" example in Chapter 5 made use (albeit basic use) of JNDI. In version 4.0 Advanced Edition, this functionality is provided by the adminServer, and in the Advanced Single Server Edition this is implemented by the application server itself.

The Naming Package

The `javax.naming` package provides a set of interfaces and classes aimed at representing a generic naming service. The most basic abstraction in the naming package is a *context*. A context can be viewed as the namespace in which your operations will take place.

Examples of a context are an LDAP node (along with the associated sub-tree) or a file system directory (and all directories inside it). An important attribute of contexts is that they can contain other contexts—that is, they can form a *recursive* construct. For example, in the domain of file systems, directories can contain other directories. When working with JNDI, *initial context* is considered the root of all naming operations that use it. So, for example, if the initial context in a file system were set to be *E:\WebSphere\AppServer*, the path to the file *E:\WebSphere\AppServer\readme.txt* would be *\readme.txt*.

To work with JNDI, you first create a context upon which operations are based. Contexts are represented in the naming package by the `Context` interface. To create a context, you need to set up the environment variables for JNDI. Table 20-1 lists some of the properties used by JNDI that are relevant when creating a context for use by a WebSphere client. JNDI supports numerous other environment variables defining security, internationalization, and service-related parameters. For all those properties not set explicitly, the system default is used. To set properties, you may either read them from a file (using the `load` method of the `Properties` object, providing an `InputStream` opened on the property file) or you can specify them during runtime using the `properties` object's `put` method.

The class `javax.naming.InitialContext` implements the `Context` interface and is used to create context objects. With the context at hand, you can retrieve naming information. The retrieval methods of the `Context` interface all take as a parameter either a `String` or a `Name`. `Name` is an interface that represents an ordered sequence of zero or more elements and is useful for cases in which multiple namespaces are required. The `Context` interface supports four retrieval methods (each with two variants, one for a `String` and one for a `Name`):

- **list** Returns a NamingEnumeration (an extension of Enumeration) of the names and the class names of the objects bound to them in the context passed as parameter (the *parameter* is a name of a context within the current context). The returned collection consists of NameClassPair objects, from which the name and class name can be retrieved.
- **listBindings** Returns a NamingEnumeration of names and the actual objects bound to them in the parameter context. The returned collection consists of Binding objects, from which the name and object can be retrieved.
- **lookup** Returns the named object.
- **lookupLink** Returns the named object, following links.

Management of the objects inside the context is done using binding objects. The `Context` interface provides the following bind-related methods:

- **bind** Binds the name to the object in the context (an exception occurs if the name is already in use).

- **createSubcontext** Creates and binds a new context to the name (the equivalent of mkdir in a file system such as MS-DOS)
- **destroySubContext** Destroys the context and removes it from the namespace (the equivalent of rmdir in a file system such as MS-DOS)
- **rebind** Binds the name to the object, overwriting any existing bind
- **rename** Takes the object bound to one name and binds it to a new name
- **unbind** Unbinds the named object from the namespace (the equivalent of a delete operation)

The Directory Package

The `javax.naming.directory` extends the naming package to provide functionality of accessing and managing directory services. The main feature supported by it is object attributes, which can be used as the basis for search operations. The directory package draws its notion of a directory search concept from the LDAP specification.

To search for objects in a directory, you need to create an object implementing the `javax.naming.directory.DirContext` interface. This interface extends the `Context` interface so all naming package operations are applicable here, too. The class `InitialDirContext` is an implementation of the `DirContext` interface.

The directory package introduces the following two interfaces to represent attributes:

- **Attribute** Represents an attribute associated with a named object. The attribute itself is a sequence of zero or more objects. The attribute can provide a schema in the form of a DirContext to describe the structure of the attribute. Yet another DirContext can be provided, holding the syntax of the values in the attribute (the syntax definitions are provider-dependent—that is, they might just be strings whose meaning depends on the underlying service).
- **Attributes** Represents a collection of Attribute objects associated with a named object.

These two interfaces provide methods for adding and removing values and attributes, respectively.

The `DirContext` interface provides four flavors of the search method. The simple one takes a name along with an `Attributes` object. It searches for objects that contain the provided set of attributes. The result of the search is a `NamingEnumeration`, just like in the naming package. The elements inside the `NamingEnumeration` are of a subclass of Binding class `SearchResult`, which provides access to search attributes.

Environment Property	Definition Constant	Description
`java.naming.factory.initial`	`Context.INITIAL_CONTEXT_FACTORY`	Class name of the initial context factory. In the WebSphere Server Advanced Edition, should be set to `com.ibm.websphere.naming.WsnInitialContextFactory`.
`java.naming.provider.url`	`Context.PROVIDER_URL`	Specifies configuration information for the provider to use. With WebSphere AE, should be `iiop://`*`servername:portnum`*. The port number can be determined using the WebSphere Administration Client, and is 900 by default.
`java.naming.dns.url`	`Context.DNS_URL`	Specifies the DNS host and domain names to use for the JNDI URL context.

Table 20-1. *JDNI Environment*

Following is a sketch of how a directory search can be accomplished using the classes `BasicAttribute` and `BasicAttributes`, which implement the respective interfaces.

```
Properties props = new Properties;
props.put(Context.INITIAL_CONTEXT_FACTORY,
          "com.ibm.jndi.LDAPCtxFactory");
props.put(Context.PROVIDER_URL, "ldap://host");
try {
      // Create Search Context
      DirContext ctx = new InitialDirContext(props);

      // Define attributes
      Attributes attrs = new BasicAttributes(true);
      attrs.put(new BasicAttribute("cn"));
      attrs.put(new BasicAttribute("website"));

      // Perform search
      Naming Enumeration result = ctx.search("ou=shiok", attrs);

      // Iterate over results
      while (result.hasMore()) {
      ...
      }
}
catch (NamingException ex) {
...
}
```

A more efficient search method allows you to specify in advance which attributes to fetch. (For example, if you are searching a directory of people, you might be looking just for their phone numbers.)

The last two search methods allow you to search with filtering and with search controls. Both ideas were described in the preceding section as part of the description of LDAP. For the purpose of filtering, the search method is provided with a filter string with the same format as LDAP search filters.

Search controls are represented by a `SearchControls` object that defines the following:

- **Search scope** OBJECT_SCOPE, ONELEVEL_SCOPE, or SUBTREE_SCOPE (corresponding to base object, single level, or whole sub-tree)
- **Maximum number of entries** A limit on the number of returned entries
- **Maximum time** Time limit in milliseconds for the search

- **Dereference flag** Indicates whether links should be de-referenced during the search
- **Returned attributes** Indicate what attributes to return (again, promoting efficiency when only part of the attributes are needed)
- **Return object values** Flag indicates whether object values should be returned or only name and class

Here is a schematic example of a search using filtering and search controls:

```
Properties props = new Properties;
props.put(Context.INITIAL_CONTEXT_FACTORY,
        "com.ibm.jndi.LDAPCtxFactory");
props.put(Context.PROVIDER_URL, "ldap://host");
try {
      // Create Search Context
      DirContext ctx = new InitialDirContext(props);

      String[] attrs = { "email" };
      String filter = "(&(cn=E*)(website=www.shiok.com))"

      // Define Search Controls
      SearchControls sc = new SearchControls(SUBTREE SCOPE, 1000,
                              0, attrs, false, false);
      // Perform search
      NamingEnumeration result = ctx.search("ou=shiok", filter, sc);
      // Return results
      while (result.hasMore()) {
      ...
      }
}
catch (NamingException ex) {
...
}
```

The directory package allows modifying attributes through the `DirContext` interface, which is important to place the attributes on objects, so that the search methods have something to work with. This is done with the `modifyAttributes` method, which takes a name, an attributes array, and the operation to perform. The operation can be one of the following:

- DirContext.ADD_ATTRIBUTE
- DirContext.REPLACE_ATTRIBUTE
- DirContext.REMOTE_ATTRIBUTE

Alternatively, it is possible to call `modifyAttributes` with a name and an array of `ModificationItem` objects, which are just pairings of such an operation with an `Attributes` object.

One last feature of the JNDI directory package is that it allows retrieving the schema of a directory using the `getSchema` and `getSchemaClassDefinition` methods, both returning `DirContext` objects (similar to the schema methods in `Attribute` mentioned previously).

LDAP in WebSphere

As explained in the beginning of this chapter, to use LDAP with WebSphere, an LDAP server is required. One option is the IBM SecureWay Directory, which has the advantage of being an IBM product, thus providing better integration with WebSphere.

One possible use of LDAP in the context of WebSphere is for maintaining the user registry, which is the basis for the authentication procedure. In other words, the WebSphere security services are capable of using an LDAP-based user database. Because WebSphere is an application server, it needs to maintain authorization and access control information. At the most basic level, it needs to maintain user names and passwords.

WebSphere supports three alternatives for the issue of maintaining the user registry. One is using the local registry—that is, the registry maintained by the underlying operating system (such as Windows 2000 or UNIX). The second is a custom-defined registry that can be implemented using an API provided by IBM. The third (which is our focus here) is to perform user ID and password-based authentication against an LDAP user registry.

IBM SecureWay Directory

IBM's SecureWay product implements LDAP and provides an LDAP-conforming directory server. The underlying data store is DB2 (remember that fundamentally a directory server is a database where most of the activities are lookups). From this perspective, SecureWay does not offer increased performance by specialization. However, DB2 is certainly one of the fastest relational databases around, and you should have no performance problems with SecureWay. In addition, IBM provides the SecureWay Directory Client SDK that provides the APIs needed to interact with the directory server. These APIs are in turn used by the WebSphere directory server to access the directory server, as shown in Figure 20-3.

To use SecureWay to manage the WebSphere user registry, you will have to do a little bit of setup on SecureWay. First you must set up a root from which all users will be managed on the directory server. Typically, this will represent the organization to which you or the application belongs. You can do this using the Directory Administration Tool, as shown in Figure 20-4.

WebSphere
Request
Reply
API
SecureWay Client
TCP/IP
SecureWay
Receive Message
Access Directory
Return Reply
TCP/IP
DB2
Directory
Request Message
Reply Message

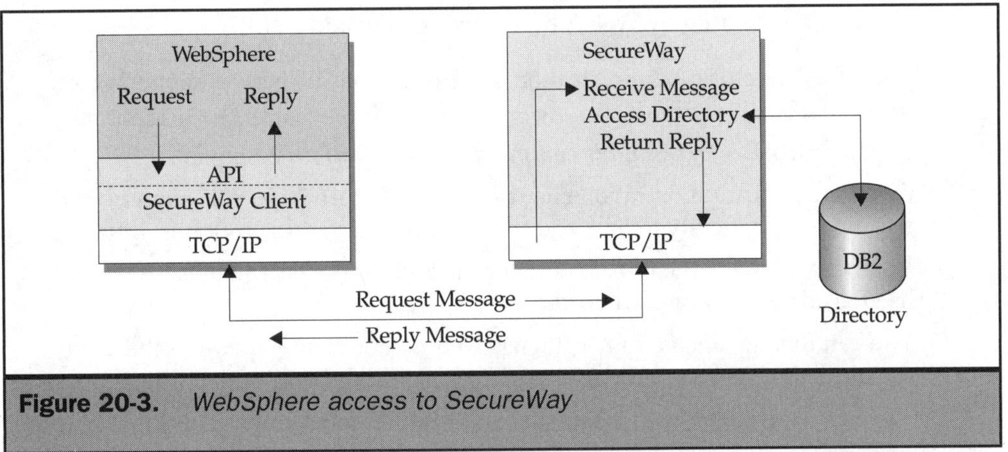

Figure 20-3. *WebSphere access to SecureWay*

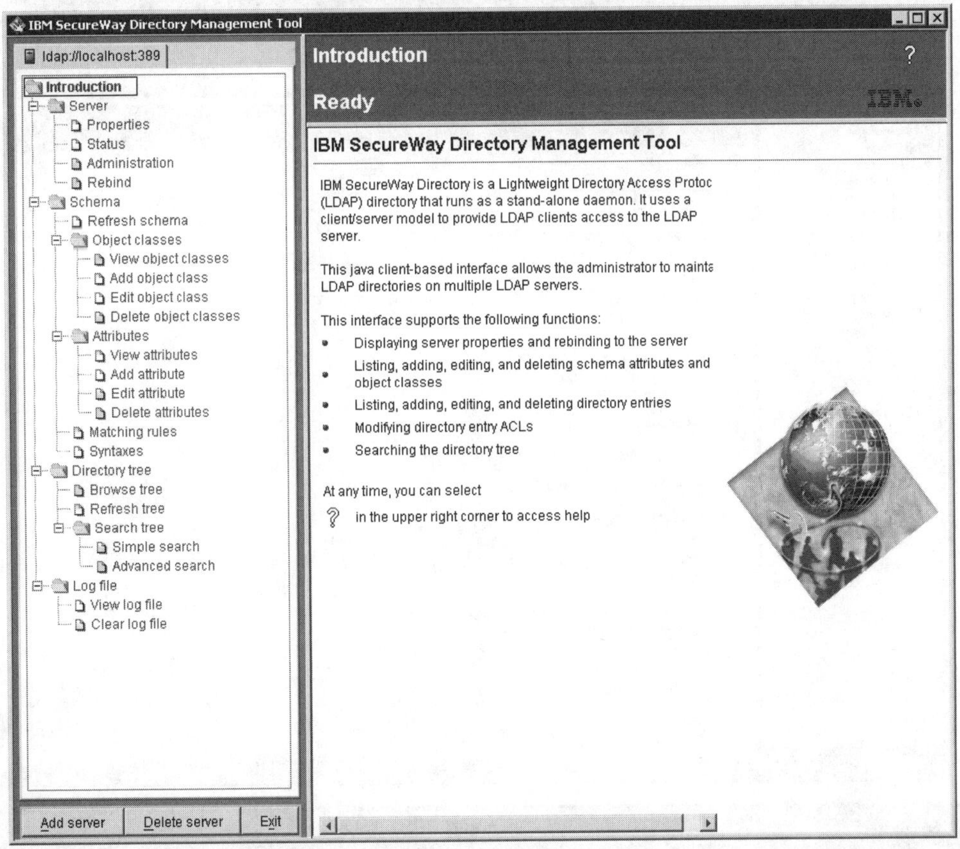

IBM SecureWay Directory Management Tool
ldap://localhost:389
Introduction
Server
Properties
Status
Administration
Rebind
Schema
Refresh schema
Object classes
View object classes
Add object class
Edit object class
Delete object classes
Attributes
View attributes
Add attribute
Edit attribute
Delete attributes
Matching rules
Syntaxes
Directory tree
Browse tree
Refresh tree
Search tree
Simple search
Advanced search
Log file
View log file
Clear log file
Add server
Delete server
Exit
Introduction
?
Ready
IBM.
IBM SecureWay Directory Management Tool
IBM SecureWay Directory is a Lightweight Directory Access Protoc
(LDAP) directory that runs as a stand-alone daemon. It uses a
client/server model to provide LDAP clients access to the LDAP
server.
This java client-based interface allows the administrator to maint
LDAP directories on multiple LDAP servers.
This interface supports the following functions:
Displaying server properties and rebinding to the server
Listing, adding, editing, and deleting schema attributes and object classes
Listing, adding, editing, and deleting directory entries
Modifying directory entry ACLs
Searching the directory tree
At any time, you can select
in the upper right corner to access help

Figure 20-4. *SecureWay Directory Administration Tool*

To add a root to be used by WebSphere, you need to add a suffix:

1. From the Directory Administration Tool, open the Suffixes folder and select the Add a Suffix option.
2. Set the suffix DN to **o=<*your company name*>,c=<*your country*>**.
3. Open the Java administration client shown in Figure 20-5. You can ignore the warning—it is merely telling you that the *dtree* under this root is empty.
4. You need to *rebind* the tree. You will be asked for the user name and password; use the administrator password.
5. You can then go ahead and add users to this root. Remember that these are the users that will form the user registry for WebSphere.

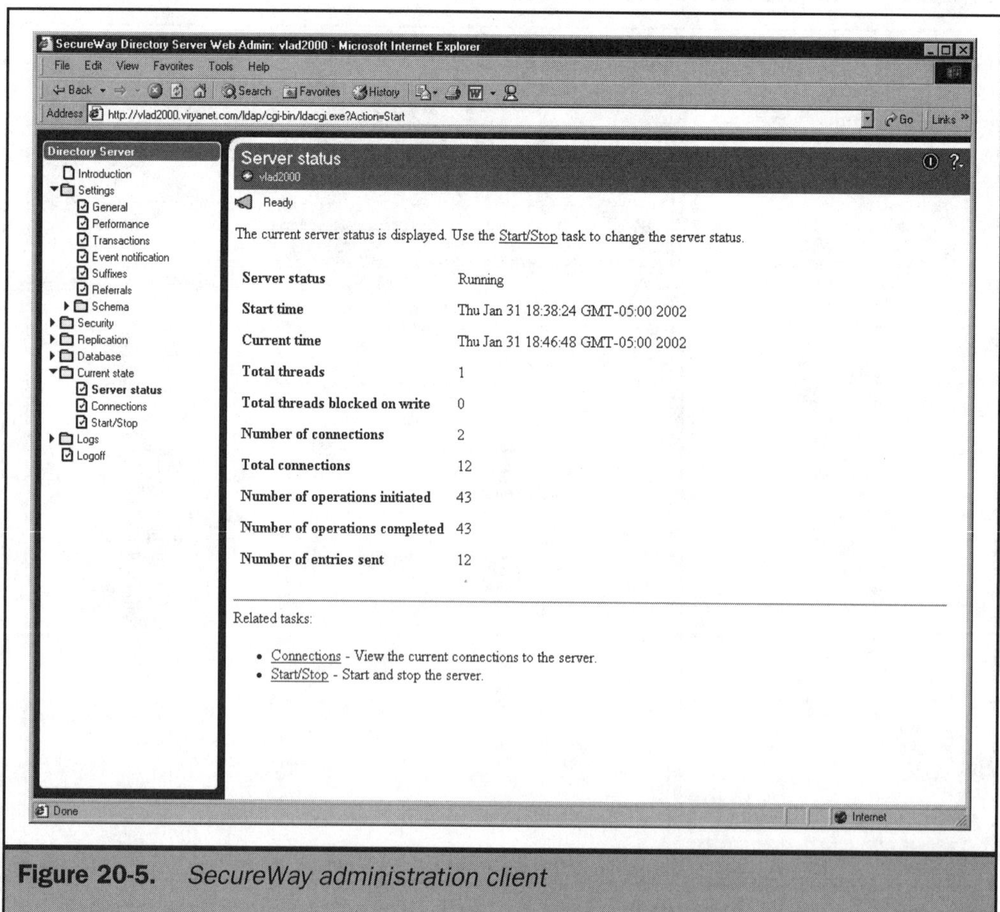

Figure 20-5. *SecureWay administration client*

WebSphere User Registry

Your goal is to make sure that all users that you set up in the previous section will be accessible as WebSphere users. The only thing left for you to do is inform WebSphere that it should be using a SecureWay server for its user registry. For this, you need to inform WebSphere that it will be using LDAP for its authentication.

1. In the Directory Management Tool, go to the Security Center and select the Authentication tab, as shown in Figure 20-6.
2. Set the Authentication Mechanism to the Lightweight Third Party Authentication (LTPA) option.

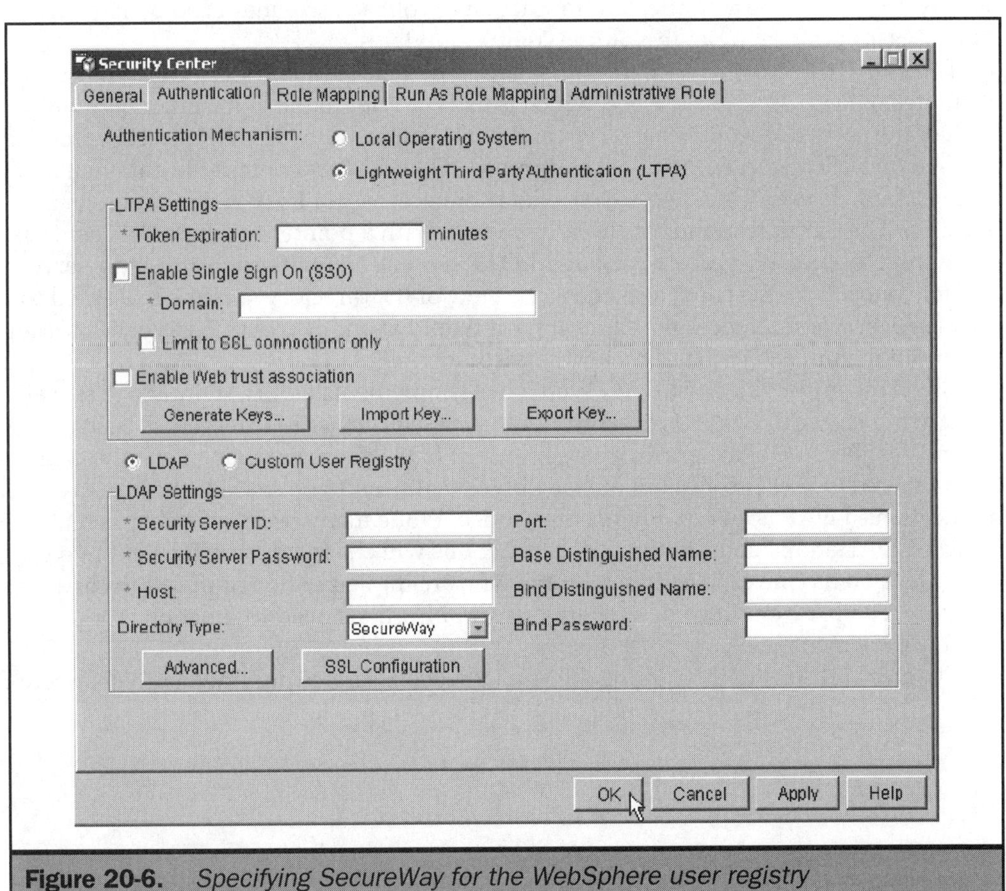

Figure 20-6. *Specifying SecureWay for the WebSphere user registry*

3. Then check the LDAP option, set the Directory Type to SecureWay, and fill out the settings including the SecureWay host name, Port (default is 389), and the suffix that you have set up in the previous section.

Summary

LDAP is used for accessing online directory services. It runs directly over TCP and can be used to access a stand-alone LDAP directory service or to access a directory service that is back-ended by X.500. A directory is like a database, but the directory tends to contain more descriptive, attribute-based information. The information in a directory is generally read much more often than it is written. As a consequence, directories don't usually implement the complicated transaction or rollback schemes used by regular databases for performing high-volume complex updates.

The LDAP directory service model is based on *entries*. An entry is a collection of attributes with a *distinguished name,* which is used to refer to the entry unambiguously. Each of the entry's attributes has a *type* and one or more values. LDAP directory service is based on a client-server model. One or more LDAP servers contain the data making up the LDAP directory tree. An LDAP client connects to an LDAP server and asks it a question. The server responds with the answer or with a pointer to where the client can get more information (typically, another LDAP server). No matter which LDAP server a client connects to, the client sees the same view of the directory: a name presented to one LDAP server references the same entry it would at another LDAP server. This is an important feature of a global directory service, such as LDAP.

Given the importance of LDAP, WebSphere implements an LDAP interface as well as allowing its use of LDAP for security (as discussed further in Chapter 19) using SecureWay. Because of the growing importance of LDAP for maintaining not only security information and user profiles but any attributes that need to be shared across many applications, LDAP is a WebSphere core service. While many users of WebSphere do not use LDAP at this point in time, we predict this will change during the next two years. This holds true especially for people who are implementing applications in a complex enterprise environment where many applications need to function in a collaborative manner.

Chapter 21 discusses the logging API—another core service provided by WebSphere.

The Complete Reference

Chapter 21

WebSphere Application Logging

Software development revolves around a well-known code-test-debug cycle. When developing Web and enterprise applications with WebSphere, you can shorten this cycle somewhat by using tools such as WebSphere Studio Application Developer and VisualAge for Java.

The built-in debugger is of tremendous value in testing and debugging code. Unfortunately, some bugs are detected only after deployment. At that stage, it is typically difficult to use a tool such as VisualAge for Java. Reasons for this may be that the tool is not always available at the deployment site, that the problem cannot be replicated using VisualAge for Java (for example, a problem that occurs only in a clustered environment), or that you need to debug a remote application. The bottom line is that some debugging tool is necessary when you are working with the actual WebSphere Application Server and not just with the development environment.

The easiest and probably the most commonly used way to debug is simply to place print statements in your code. When you write server-side code, this approach doesn't scale well (what an understatement!), because several applications run concurrently and all print to the same log file.

A more systematic approach can be provided by a logging facility. IBM addresses this need with its Logging Toolkit for Java, available as part of alphaWorks at *www.alphaworks.ibm.com/tech/loggingtoolkit4j*. The Logging Toolkit for Java provides a comprehensive architecture that includes loggers, handlers, filters, and formatters. *Loggers* generate the data to be logged, and there can be two different kinds: message loggers and trace loggers. *Message loggers* are used by end users or system administrators, whereas *trace loggers* are used by developers from within code. *Handlers* receive data to be logged and can be attached either to a logger, to a file, or to a socket. *Filters* control what data is displayed, and this allows you to focus on the data that is of interest at any point in time. *Formatters* are responsible for presenting data in a specific format.

WebSphere includes a special version of this logging toolkit, which is called JRas. It is important to point out that IBM doesn't support the use of the non-WebSphere version of the toolkit in WebSphere.

JRas Message Logging and Trace Facility

JRas distinguishes between two categories of textual information that can be generated by code: messages and traces. *Messages* are generated by default and are intended for end users and system administrators. Such messages can be localized so that the language of the message matches the locale of the user. *Traces* are intended for use by developers. Traces include detailed technical information about the current state of the application or about certain runtime errors. Trace information normally is not generated by applications and is enabled only during the debugging process.

The JRas package implements loggers, handlers, and formatters. It also provides objects called *managers,* which essentially contain configurations of loggers, handlers, and formatters.

Message and trace texts are all recorded in log files. All messages are logged to a single file that is shared by both the WebSphere server and any applications. The WebSphere log is recorded in the *default_server_stdout* file, which resides in the *logs* directory under your WebSphere installation root. A sample of such a log file is shown here:

```
IBM WebSphere Application Server, Release 4.0.1
Advanced Single Server Edition for Multiplatforms
Copyright IBM Corp., 1997-2001

[02.01.15 19:11:29:961 PST] 5dd676de Server       A WSVR0027I: Temporary
product license expires on Jul 13, 2002
************ Start Display Current Environment ************
WebSphere AEs 4.0.1 a0131.07 running with process name THINKPAD/Default
Server and process id 2432
Host Operating System is Windows 2000, version 5.0
Java version = J2RE 1.3.0 IBM build cn130-20010609 (JIT enabled: jitc), Java
Compiler = jitc
server.root = C:\WebSphere\AppServer
Java Home = C:\WebSphere\AppServer\java\jre
ws.ext.dirs =
C:\WebSphere\AppServer\java\lib;C:\WebSphere\AppServer\classes;C:\WebSphere\
AppServer\lib;C:\WebSphere\AppServer\lib\ext;C:\WebSphere\AppServer\web\help
;.\lib\ifxjdbcx.jar;.\lib\ifxjdbc.jar
Classpath =
C:\WebSphere\AppServer\properties;C:\WebSphere\AppServer\lib\bootstrap.jar
Java Library path =
C:\WebSphere\AppServer\java\bin;.;C:\WINNT\System32;C:\WINNT;C:\WebSphere\
AppServer/bin;
Current trace specification =
************* End Display Current Environment *************
[02.01.15 19:11:32:304 PST] 5dd676de Server       U Version : 4.0.1
[02.01.15 19:11:32:304 PST] 5dd676de Server       U Edition: Advanced
Single Server Edition for Multiplatforms
[02.01.15 19:11:32:304 PST] 5dd676de Server       U Build date: Thu Aug 09
00:00:00 PDT 2001
[02.01.15 19:11:32:304 PST] 5dd676de Server       U Build number: a0131.07
[02.01.15 19:11:42:459 PST] 5dd676de DrAdminServer I WSVR0053I: DrAdmin
available on port 7000
[02.01.15 19:11:43:059 PST] 5dd676de ResourceBinde I WSVR0049I: Binding
Session Persistence datasource as jdbc/Session
[02.01.15 19:11:44:121 PST] 5dd676de ResourceBinde I WSVR0049I: Binding
Increment Bean Datasource as jdbc/SampleDataSource
[02.01.15 19:11:44:191 PST] 5dd676de ResourceBinde I WSVR0049I: Binding
Samples IDB Datasource as jdbc/sample
[02.01.15 19:11:44:251 PST] 5dd676de ResourceBinde I WSVR0049I: Binding
Petstore IDB Datasource as ps/PetStoreDatasource
```

```
[02.01.15 19:11:48:517 PST] 5dd676de EJBEngine     I WSVR0037I: Starting EJB
jar: Increment Bean Jar
[02.01.15 19:11:52:783 PST] 5dd676de SystemOut     U Enhydra InstantDB -
Version 3.26
[02.01.15 19:11:52:783 PST] 5dd676de SystemOut     U
[02.01.15 19:11:52:783 PST] 5dd676de SystemOut     U The Initial Developer
of the Original Code is Lutris Technologies Inc.
Portions created by Lutris are Copyright (C) 1997-2001 Lutris Technologies,
Inc.
All Rights Reserved.
[02.01.15 19:11:54:616 PST] 5dd676de EJBEngine     I WSVR0037I: Starting EJB
jar: C:\WebSphere\AppServer/installedApps\Samples.ear/TimeoutEJBean.jar
[02.01.15 19:11:57:440 PST] 5dd676de EJBEngine     I WSVR0037I: Starting EJB
jar: Increment EJB Module
[02.01.15 19:11:57:610 PST] 5dd676de EJBEngine     I WSVR0037I: Starting EJB
jar: Hello EJB Module
[02.01.15 19:12:03:299 PST] 5dd676de ServletEngine A SRVE0161I: IBM
WebSphere Application Server - Web Container.  Copyright IBM Corp. 1998-2001
[02.01.15 19:12:03:359 PST] 5dd676de ServletEngine A SRVE0162I: Servlet
Specification Level: 2.2
[02.01.15 19:12:03:359 PST] 5dd676de ServletEngine A SRVE0163I: Supported
JSP Specification Level: 1.1
[02.01.15 19:12:03:569 PST] 5dd676de ServletEngine A SRVE0167I: Session
Manager is Configured - Initializing...
[02.01.15 19:12:04:220 PST] 5dd676de CacheManager  A DYNA0011E: Servlet
cache file dynacache.xml not found; caching is disabled
[02.01.15 19:12:04:370 PST] 5dd676de ServletEngine A SRVE0169I: Loading Web
Module: Default Application.
[02.01.15 19:12:05:011 PST] 5dd676de WebGroup      I SRVE0091I: [Servlet
LOG]: JSP 1.1 Processor: init
[02.01.15 19:12:05:091 PST] 5dd676de WebGroup      I SRVE0091I: [Servlet
LOG]: InvokerServlet: init
[02.01.15 19:12:05:191 PST] 5dd676de ServletEngine A SRVE0169I: Loading Web
Module: Examples Application.
[02.01.15 19:12:05:442 PST] 5dd676de WebGroup      I SRVE0091I: [Servlet
LOG]: JSP 1.1 Processor: init
[02.01.15 19:12:05:462 PST] 5dd676de WebGroup      I SRVE0091I: [Servlet
LOG]: SimpleFileServlet: init
[02.01.15 19:12:05:482 PST] 5dd676de WebGroup      I SRVE0091I: [Servlet
LOG]: DirectoryBrowsingServlet: init
[02.01.15 19:12:05:782 PST] 5dd676de ServletEngine A SRVE0169I: Loading Web
Module: admin.
[02.01.15 19:12:06:333 PST] 5dd676de WebGroup      I SRVE0091I: [Servlet
LOG]: JSP 1.1 Processor: init
[02.01.15 19:12:06:343 PST] 5dd676de WebGroup      I SRVE0091I: [Servlet
LOG]: SimpleFileServlet: init
```

```
[02.01.15 19:12:06:403 PST] 5dd676de WebGroup      I SRVE0091I: [Servlet
LOG]: action: init
 [02.01.15 19:12:09:457 PST] 5dd676de HttpTransport A SRVE0171I: Transport
http is listening on port 9,080.
[02.01.15 19:12:12:722 PST] 5dd676de HttpTransport A SRVE0171I: Transport
https is listening on port 9,443.
[02.01.15 19:12:12:732 PST] 5dd676de HttpTransport A SRVE0171I: Transport
http is listening on port 9,090.
[02.01.15 19:12:12:752 PST] 5dd676de Server        A WSVR0023I: Server
Default Server open for e-business
```

Similarly, all traces are logged to a single file, whether they originate from the server or from applications. Both files can be inspected using the WebSphere Log Analyzer. This tool was mentioned briefly in Chapter 2 and is described in more detail later in this chapter in the "Log Analyzer"section.

JRas Manager

The point of entry for JRas code in WebSphere is the `com.ibm.websphere.ras.Manager` class. This class is in charge of creating and maintaining loggers, and it provides a static method called `getManager()` for retrieving the singleton instance of this class. Using this instance, it is possible to create a message logger or a trace logger. The manager maintains the created loggers and it a request is made for a logger that has been previously created, it will return that logger instead of creating a new one.

Loggers are named objects whose names are composed of four different subcomponent strings: an organization, a product, a component, and a logger name. The manager also supports a simpler namespace composed of a component and a logger name only, but this namespace is reserved for internal IBM use. Given the four component strings, you can create a message logger by using the following method:

```
com.ibm.ras.RASMessageLogger createRASMessageLogger(String organization,
                          String product, String component, String name);
```

A trace logger can be created with this method:

```
com.ibm.ras.RASTraceLogger createRASTraceLogger(String organization,
                     String product, String component, String name);
```

It goes without saying that you need to be careful when assigning names so that namespace conflicts are avoided. It is recommended that you use only one logger for each class and that you associate the class name with the logger name.

Trace loggers can be grouped together into logical groups. The manager provides the following method:

```
void addLoggerToGroup(com.ibm.ras.RASTraceLogger logger, String groupName);
```

Such grouping allows you to trace several related components together. Group names must be unique to the application and must not conflict with groups associated with other applications.

JRas Loggers

Both message loggers and trace loggers are derived from the `RASILogger` interface. This interface provides the basic functionality of a logger and inherits the following methods for retrieving and setting the logger name:

```
public String getName();
public void setName(String name);
```

It also defines the method `isLoggable`, which is used to determine whether the logger is enabled for a certain type of event. The method signature is:

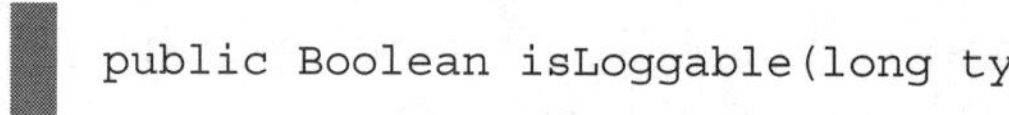

```
public Boolean isLoggable(long type)
```

The parameter type holds a valid message or trace event type. JRas supports three message types, defined by the `RASIMessageEvent` interface. These types are listed in Table 21-1, along with their mappings to WebSphere message types.

JRas Message Type	Corresponding Websphere Message Type		
Full Name	**Abbreviation**	**Advanced Edition**	**Enterprise Edition**
`TYPE_INFORMATION`	`TYPE_INFO`	Audit	Informational
`TYPE_WARNING`	`TYPE_WAN`	Warning	Warning
`TYP_ERROR`	`TYPE_ERR`	Error	Error

Table 21-1. *JRas Message Types in WebSphere*

JRas trace types are provided by the RASITraceInterface. This interface provides two kinds of trace types: leveled and nonleveled. There are three leveled trace types: level 1, level 2, and level 3. Nonleveled trace events correspond to specific kinds of trace events. Table 21-2 lists both kinds of trace events, along with the corresponding trace types in WebSphere.

Message Loggers

Message loggers differ from trace loggers in their support for message text localization. The RASIMessageLogger interface provides the methods that enable localizable message logging. Localizable message logging is based on standard Java resource bundles, which are described in detail in Chapter 39. Resource bundles are catalogs of messages that can be provided for different locales. Each message has a key that

JRas Trace Type	Corresponding WebSphere Trace Type
TYPE_LEVEL1	Event
TYPE_LEVEL2	Entry/Exit
TYPE_LEVEL3	Debug
TYPE_ERROR_EXC	Event
TYPE_OBJ_CREATE	Event
TYPE_OBJ_DELETE	Event
TYPE_SVC	Event
TYPE_API	Entry/Exit
TYPE_CALLBACK	Entry/Exit
TYPE_ENTRY_EXIT	Entry/Exit
TYPE_PRIVATE	Entry/Exit
TYPE_PUBLIC	Entry/Exit
TYPE_STATIC	Entry/Exit
TYPE_MISC_DATA	Debug

Table 21-2. *JRas Trace Types in WebSphere*

identifies it, and each can have optional objects embedded into the message text. Following are the `RASIMessageLogger` interface methods:

- **String getMessageFile( )** Returns the filename for the currently used resource bundle.
- **void setMessageFile(String)** Sets the message text resource bundle.
- **void message(long type, Object obj, String methodName, String key, Object[ ] params)** Issues a message. The parameters for this method are as follows:
  - type is one of the types shown in Table 21-1.
  - obj represents a class name. (The logger invokes obj.getClass() .getName() unless you pass a string there in the first place.)
  - methodName is a method name.
  - key is the message key for the localizable message, and it is used in conjunction with the message file specified in the setMessageFile method.
  - `param` represents objects that are to be substituted into the message text.
- **void msg(long type, Object obj, String methodName, String key, String file, Object params[ ])** Issues a message. The parameters are identical to those of the preceding method, except that you can specify the resource bundle using the parameter file.
- **void textMessage(long type, Object obj, String methodName, String text, Object[ ] params)** Issues a message whose text is specified as a parameter and not via the resource bundle, using the parameter text. This, of course, implies that no localization is provided. The meaning of the other parameters is the same as for the message method.

Note that, for convenience, the methods `message`, `msg`, and `textMessage` are provided in a variety of flavors that differ in the `params` parameter. The API defines variants of each method with no parameters, one parameter, two parameters, or an array of parameters. The latter form is the one described in the preceding list for each of these three methods.

Trace Loggers

Trace loggers are represented by the `RASITraceLogger` interface. This interface provides several methods for generating different types of traces: `entry`, `exit`, `exception`, and `trace`.

The parameters for the `entry` and `exit` methods are quite similar to those of the `RASIMessageLogger.textMessage` method. The parameters include the trace type (one of the types shown in Table 21-2), the class name or object on which getClass().getName() is to be invoked, the method name, and additional optional parameters (either none, one, two, or an array of those).

The trace method writes text messages as trace events. The parameters are similar to entry and exit, except that a text string parameter is added before the optional parameters.

The exception method takes as parameters the trace type, the class name string (or a corresponding object), the method name, and an exception object. This method then records the exception to the trace log.

The RASITraceLogger interface supports the notion of trace filtering by having an internal mask that indicates which trace events are to be logged. This mask can be gotten and set using the getTraceMask and setTraceMask methods, respectively. The latter method is invoked by the WebSphere Application Server based on the specified trace settings.

Trace Settings in WebSphere

While messages are continuously logged, traces are not logged by default. To control the logging of traces, the WebSphere Administrative Console provides the Trace Service entry under the application server. This entry allows you to control the behavior of the trace mechanism, as shown in Figure 21-1.

Following are the parameters that can be set

- **Trace String** This string determines what traces are logged. The strings are of the format *component=type=action,* where *component* is the component name, type is the type of messages (debug, entry/exit, or event), and action is either enable, disable, or inherit. For example, to log all debug traces related to IBM's servlet personalization, you can add the line com.ibm.servlet.personalization.*=debug=enabled. While you can edit this string directly, the console provides a friendly user interface for editing it.
- **Trace File** Determines the file to which the trace information will be written. You can select the standard output, the standard error, or any other file.
- **Trace Host Name** The hostname on which the application server is running.
- **Trace Port** A port to be used for tracing. The default is 7000, but you can change this if any other application is using that port.

To simplify the task of designating the desired trace levels for different components, the Administrative Console provides a special interface, as shown in Figure 21-2. You invoke this interface by clicking the Edit button under the Trace String field (see Figure 21-1).

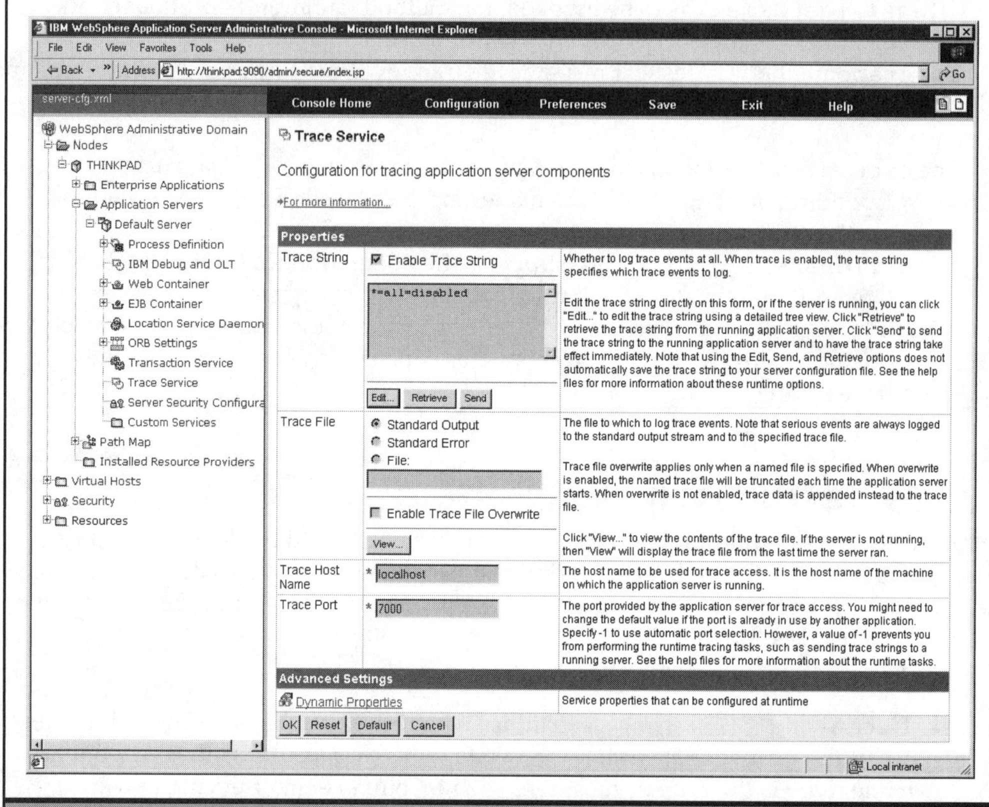

Figure 21-1. *Trace Service in the WebSphere Administrative Console*

As you edit the trace string, the Administrative Console provides a tree for browsing the various components that can be traced. Once you select such a component, you can enable, disable, or "inherit" three different levels of messages (corresponding to those shown previously in Table 21-2). Selecting Inherit means that the component follows the behavior of its direct parent in the hierarchy of components (for example, the associated package, in the case of a class), or that of the group to which it belongs.

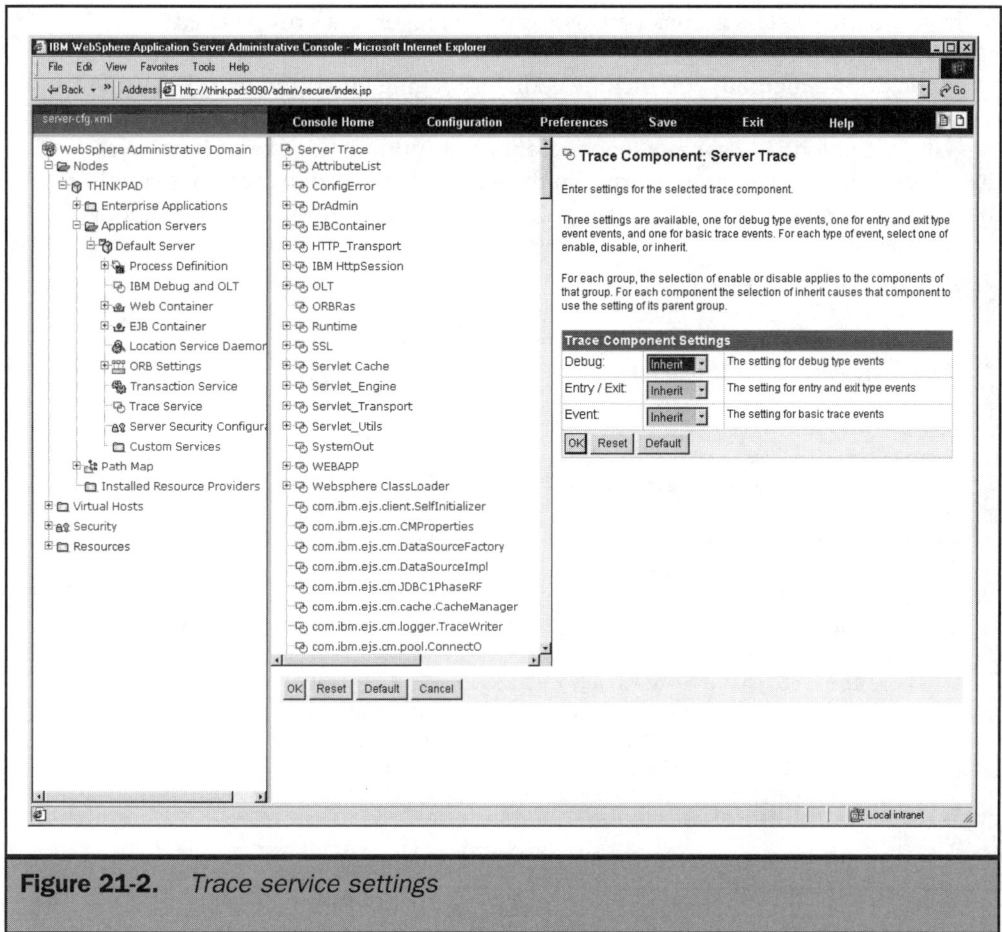

Figure 21-2. *Trace service settings*

Web Application Logging Example

To illustrate the way Web application logging is utilized, let's look at a simple example of a servlet that uses traces. This servlet recognizes two parameters in its HTTP request: `enum` and `denom`. It outputs the ratio of `enum` divided by `denom`.

You create the trace logger in the servlet `init` method, qualifying it with the organization name, the product name, the component name, and the fully package-qualified class name. You also add the logger to a group called "CompleteReferenceBooks."

In the doGet method, you include code for logging entry and exit. This code is enclosed in an if statement that checks to see if entry/exit traces should be logged. This potentially saves a few operations at runtime (for example, it saves the construction of the params array in the entry trace). If an exception is caught in the doGet method, you record it using the exception method of the trace logger.

```
package book.websphere.ch21;

import javax.servlet.*;
import javax.servlet.http.*;
import java.io.*;
import java.util.*;
import com.ibm.ras.*;
import com.ibm.Websphere.ras.*;

public class TracerServlet extends HttpServlet {
  RASITraceLogger traceLog;

  public void init(ServletConfig config) throws ServletException {
    super.init(config);
    com.ibm.websphere.ras.Manager manager =
            com.ibm.websphere.ras.Manager.getManager();
    traceLog = mgr.createRASITraceLogger("Osborne", "CompleteReference",
                      "websphere", "book.websphere.ch21.TracerServlet");
    manager.addLoggerToGroup(traceLog, "CompleteReferenceBooks");
  }

  public void doGet(
            HttpServletRequest request, HttpServletResponse response)
            throws ServletException, IOException {

    try {
       String enum = request.getParameter("enum");
       String denom = request.getParameter("denom");
       if (traceLog.isLoggable(RASITraceEvent.TYPE_ENTRY_EXIT)) {
          Object[] parms = { enum, denom };
          traceLog.entry(RASITraceEvent.TYPE_ENTRY_EXIT, this, "doGet",
                       parms);
       }
       response.setContentType("text/html");
       int enumInt = (new Integer(enum)).toInt();
```

```
            int denomInt = (new Integer(denom)).toInt();
            PrintWriter out = new PrintWriter (response.getOutputStream());
            out.println("<html>");
            out.println("<head><title>TracerServlet</title></head>");
            out.println("<body>");
            out.println("<H1>"+enum+" divided by "+denom+" is: <BR>");
            out.println((enum / denom) + "</H1>");
            out.println("</body>");
            out.println("</html>");
            out.close();
        }
        catch (Exception ex) {
            traceLog.exception(RASITraceEvent.TYPE_ERROR_EXC, this,
                              "doGet", ex);
        }
        if (traceLog.isLoggable(RASITraceEvent.TYPE_ENTRY_EXIT)) {
              traceLog.exit(RASITraceEvent.TYPE_ENTRY_EXIT, this, "doGet");
        }
    }
}
```

Log Analyzer

While the logs and traces generated by JRas are readable by humans, WebSphere also provides a graphical log-analyzing tool. The Log Analyzer, shown in Figure 21-3, takes one or more activity or trace logs, merges all the traces, and then displays all entries grouped under UnitOfWork (UOW) elements. It is important to note that the Log Analyzer cannot parse message logs; these logs can have arbitrary formats, as their content is controlled by resource bundles and is subject to localization.

The main Log Analyzer window includes three panes in addition to the standard status bar, toolbar, and menu bar. On the left side of the window, the sorting pane shows the list of log records, which by default are grouped according to their Units of Work. Each UOW has a folder icon, under which all trace records associated with it are shown. Records without UOW identification are grouped under a single folder in this tree. The UOW folders are sorted according to their timestamps, the most recent appearing at the top of the tree. Similarly, entries within a UOW are shown in reverse order. Note that the time ordering is done after the Log Analyzer merges entries from several files (if several files are loaded). You can sort your log records on a field other than UOW by making a different selection in the Analyzer Preferences dialog box (see Figure 21-4). Here you can choose to group your files by process ID, thread ID, server name, or function name, among other options.

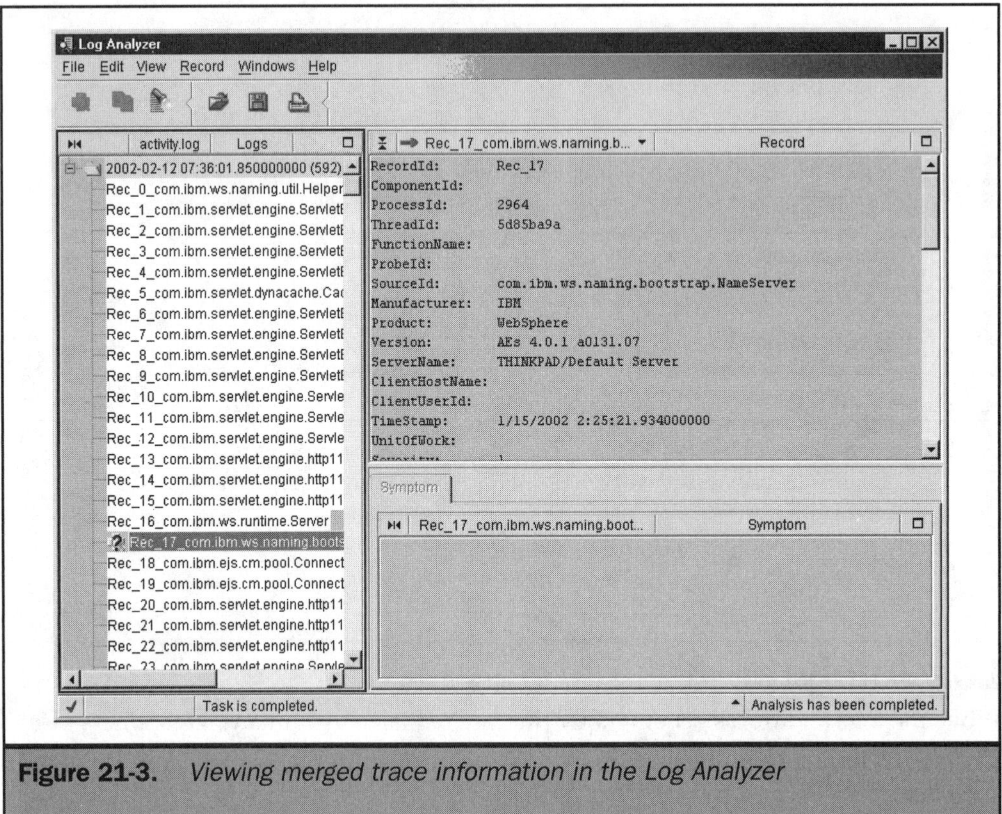

Figure 21-3. *Viewing merged trace information in the Log Analyzer*

Trace records are color coded for quick identification, as summarized in the following table. You can modify these colors in the Analyzer Preferences dialog box by selecting the General option in the left pane and setting the appearance values.

Severity Level	Selected	Nonselected
1	Pink	Red
2	Yellow	Green
3	White	Blue

The other two panes in the main Log Analyzer window are the record pane and the analysis pane. The record pane shows a detailed description of the selected record, providing all information recorded. The analysis window shows additional information in case you invoke the Analyze function (under the Record menu) and

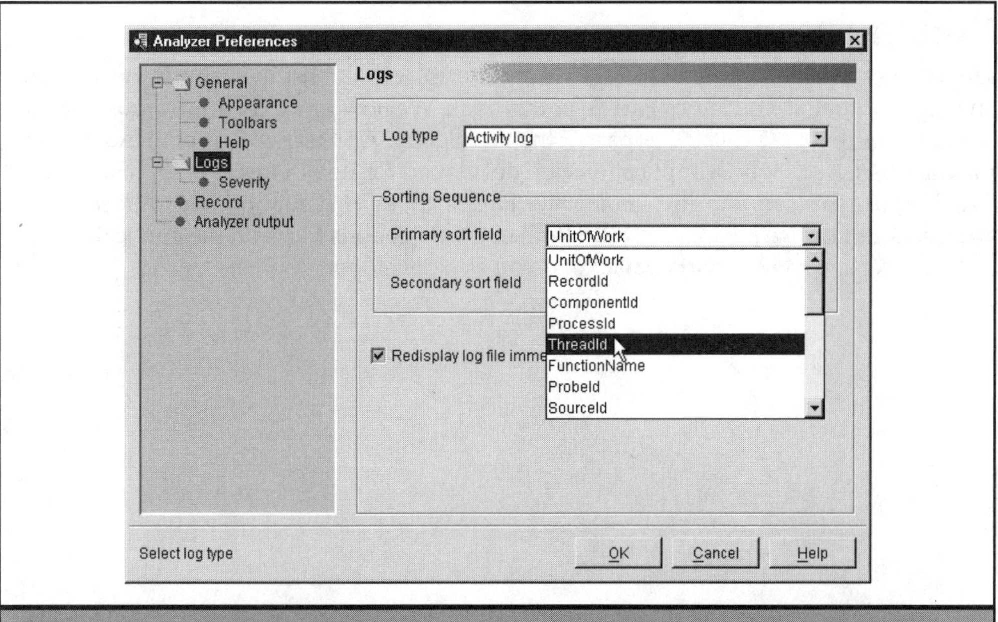

Figure 21-4. *Setting sorting sequence using the Analyzer Preference dialog box*

there exists some additional information to display. Such additional information can be symptoms identified by the Log Analyzer from a database of common WebSphere errors.

Note that after the Analyze function is applied, each analyzed record entry on the tree has a small indicator icon attached to it. The meaning of each icon follows:

Icon	Meaning
	Some analysis information is available in the Analysis window.
	Some analysis information is available in the Analysis window, but this entry is related to a problem that has occurred previously. You might want to consult previous log files to diagnose the problem.
	The entry is of severity 1 or 2, but it has no analysis information.
	The entry is of severity 3, but it has no analysis information.

Summary

This chapter, which described the logging and tracing capabilities available in WebSphere and the JRas toolkit, concludes Part IV of this book. We now move on from discussing the core services that are available as part of the WebSphere Application Server to examining the constructs with which applications are developed for deployment on WebSphere. Part V addresses servlets and JavaServer Pages (JSPs) in WebSphere, and Part VI addresses Enterprise JavaBeans (EJB). Both of these sections focus on the application frameworks and the support available to you as a developer.

Part V

Developing Servlets and JavaServer Pages

The Complete Reference

Chapter 22

HTTP Servlets

Now that you are familiar with servlets and how they work (having gone over servlet lifecycle and seen a simple "Hello World" example), you are ready to tackle the next stage. This chapter presents three examples of the most common servlets, Hypertext Transfer Protocol servlets, which are accessed through an HTTP connection. The purpose of this chapter is twofold: to show you some real-world examples of how servlets are usually used and to give you experience using WebSphere servlets. Each example illustrates an end-to-end process, including the generation of some form of user interface and access to data stored in a mail server or relational database management system (RDBMS).

The Mail Reading Servlet

The first example in this chapter is an implementation of a real-world Web-based service that allows users to read e-mail over the Web, using a Web browser (as opposed to using an e-mail program such as Microsoft Outlook). Such services are available for free on the Web—for example, at *www.mail2web.com.*

To allow our sample mail reading service to be available from any Web browser, we build an HTTP servlet to service mail requests. Our HTTP servlet will receive the e-mail request, access a Post Office Protocol 3 (POP3) mail server to check for mail, and return some user interface for viewing the mail. This servlet makes use of the JavaMail application programming interface (API), which is part of the Java 2 Platform Enterprise Edition (J2EE) and was introduced in Chapter 15.

Our servlet uses four different parameters for the e-mail user name, POP3 server, POP3 password, and operation (which is used by the servlet to identify the requested operation). The operation parameter can either be absent or take the value `detail` for retrieving the message body. Servlet parameters appear in the servlet uniform resource locator (URL), and can be accessed through the `HttpServletRequest` object. Here is the servlet code:

```
package book.websphere.chapter22;

import javax.mail.*;
import javax.servlet.*;
import javax.servlet.http.*;
import java.util.*;
import java.io.*;

public class MailReader extends HttpServlet {
      public void doGet(HttpServletRequest request,
                        HttpServletResponse response)
              throws ServletException, IOException {
```

```
        performTask(request, response);
    }

    public void doGetMail(HttpServletRequest req,
                          HttpServletResponse resp)
    {
        PrintWriter pw = null;
        try {
            pw = resp.getWriter();
        }
        catch (Exception ex) {
            return;
        }
        try {
            String userName = req.getParameter("username");
            String pop3 = req.getParameter("pop3");
            String password = req.getParameter("password");

            session = Session.getInstance
(System.getProperties(),null);
            store = session.getStore("pop3");
            store.connect(pop3, userName, password);
            folder = store.getFolder("INBOX");
            folder.open(Folder.READ_ONLY);
            messages = folder.getMessages();

            resp.setContentType("text/html");
            pw.println("<HTML><HEAD><TITLE>Your" +
            "Mail</TITLE></HEAD><BODY><TABLE>" +
            "BORDER=\"1\"><TR>");

            pw.println("<TH>From</TH><TH>Date</TH><TH>Subject</TH>");
            for (int i = 0; i < messages.length; i++) {
                pw.println("<TR><TD>" +
                        messages[i].getFrom()[0] + "</TD>");
                pw.println("<TD>" + messages[i].getSentDate()
                        + "</TD>");
                pw.println("<TD><A HREF='" +
                        req.getRequestURI() +
                        "?operation=detail&msgnum=" + i +
                        "'>" +
```

```
                        messages[i].getSubject() +
                        "</A></TD></TR>");
            }
            pw.println("</TABLE><P><A HREF='" +
                      HttpUtils.getRequestURL(req) +
                      "?operation=logoff'>" +
                      "Log-Off</A></P></BODY></HTML>");
           pw.close();
       }
       catch (Exception ex) {
           ex.printStackTrace(pw);
       }
 }

 public void doPost(HttpServletRequest request,
                   HttpServletResponse response)
                throws ServletException, IOException {
     performTask(request, response);
}

public void performTask(HttpServletRequest request,
                       HttpServletResponse response) {
    try {
        String operation = request.getParameter("operation");
        String userName = request.getParameter("username");

        if (operation == null) {
            if (userName == null)
                sendOutPage(response.getWriter());
           else
                doGetMail(request, response);
        }
        else if (operation.equals("detail")) {
            doGetDetail(request, response);
        }
        else if (operation.equals("logoff")) {
            doLogoff(request, response);
        }
}
```

```
     catch(Exception ex)
     {
         ex.printStackTrace();
     }
    }

    public void sendOutPage(PrintWriter pw)
    {
         pw.println("<HTML><HEAD><TITLE>Mail Reading " +
                    "Servlet</TITLE></HEAD>");
         pw.println("<BODY><H1>Welcome to the Mail"+
                    " Reading Servlet</H1>");
         pw.println("<FORM ACTION=" +
                    "'http://yourhost/ch22/MailReader'"+
                    "METHOD='GET'>");
         pw.println("<B>Username: </B><INPUT TYPE='TEXT'" +
                    "NAME='username'><BR>");
         pw.println("<B>POP3 Server: </B> " +
                    "<INPUT TYPE='TEXT' NAME='pop3'><BR>");
         pw.println("<B>Password: </B><INPUT TYPE='TEXT'" +
                    "NAME='password'><BR>");
         pw.println("<INPUT TYPE='SUBMIT'><INPUT" +
                    "TYPE='RESET'></FORM></BODY></HTML>");
    }

    private Folder folder;
    private Message[] messages;
    private Session session;
    private Store store;

    public void doGetDetail(HttpServletRequest req,
                            HttpServletResponse resp)
    {
         PrintWriter pw = null;

         try {
             pw = resp.getWriter();
         }
         catch (Exception ex) {
             return;
```

```
        }
        try {
            int num = Integer.parseInt(
                      req.getParameter("msgnum"));
            String s;
            Message msg = messages[num];
            resp.setContentType("text/html");
             pw.println("<HTML><HEAD><TITLE>Reading Message:" +
                        msg.getSubject() + "</TITLE>");
             pw.println("</HEAD><BODY><B>From:</B>" +
                        msg.getFrom()[0]);
           pw.println("<B>To:</B>" +

           msg.getRecipients(Message.RecipientType.TO)[0]);
           pw.println("<B>Date:</B>" + msg.getSentDate());
           pw.println("<P>");
           BufferedReader rd = new BufferedReader(new
                  InputStreamReader(msg.getInputStream()));
           while ((s = rd.readLine()) != null)
               pw.println(s);
           pw.println("</P></BODY></HTML>");
           pw.close();
      }
      catch (Exception ex) {
          ex.printStackTrace(pw);
      }
   }

   public void doLogoff(HttpServletRequest req,
                        HttpServletResponse resp)
   {
      try {
          folder.close(false);
          store.close();
      }
     catch (Exception ex)
     {
     }
   }
}
```

When no operation parameter and no user name are provided, the program assumes this is the first access to the servlet and sends out an initial login page. The login page, shown here, is a simple Hypertext Markup Language (HTML) form into which the parameters can be keyed in.

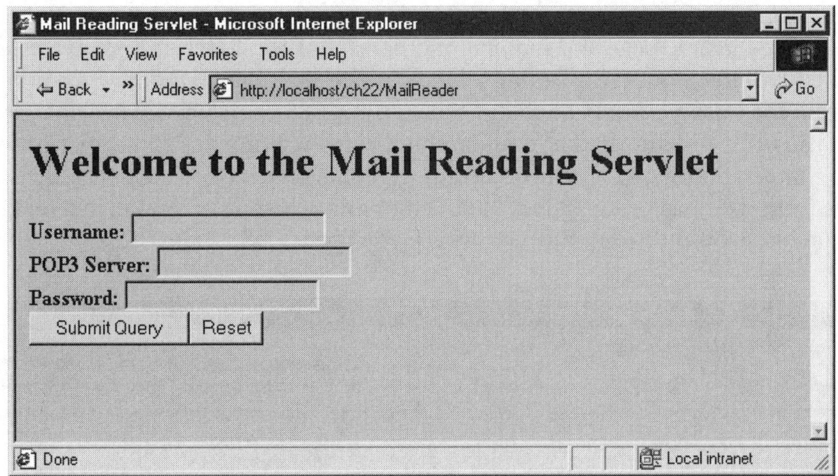

Once the Submit Query button is clicked, the same servlet is invoked again. On this second invocation, the servlet already has a user name (provided as a request parameter). Using the JavaMail API, the servlet connects to the POP3 server and downloads the user's e-mail.

Using the Session Object

The Session object is accessed using the `Session.getInstance` method. Note that it is possible to provide this method with a Properties parameter. This parameter can be used for specifying the protocols or implementations you are interested in. This example opts for the default properties, which are fine as long as no special settings exist on your system; the files in which such settings reside are `javamail.providers`, `javamail.default.providers`, `javamail.address.map`, and `javamail.default.address.map`.

Note that the `getInstance` method has another parameter not used in this example—an *authenticator*. This parameter can be used for advanced authentication schemes intended to improve e-mail security. The Session interface also provides the method `getDefaultInstance`, which provides access to a default (and shared) session instance.

With the `Session` object at hand, the program retrieves a `Store` object for the POP3 protocol. Invoking the connect method of the store with the appropriate parameters (the server, user name, and password) allows the servlet to retrieve the INBOX folder from the store. After the Folder object has been opened, the e-mail messages are retrieved using the getMessages method.

The incoming e-mail is shown in a table, where each incoming message takes one row. The information for each row is based on a single Message object. The message accessor methods are used to retrieve the e-mail sender, date, and subject. An HTML link is provided from the message subject to the message body. This link is used to obtain the details of the e-mail message and requires another round-trip to the server. To construct the original URL of the request (including all the parameters), the method getRequestURL, taken from the class javax.servlet.http.HttpUtils, is used. This class provides some static utility methods that come in handy for writing HTTP servlet code. The following illustration shows a table of incoming e-mail, provided as output by the server after the form data has been posted. Notice that this is just an example; in a real mail reader, no one would display the user's password on a URL.

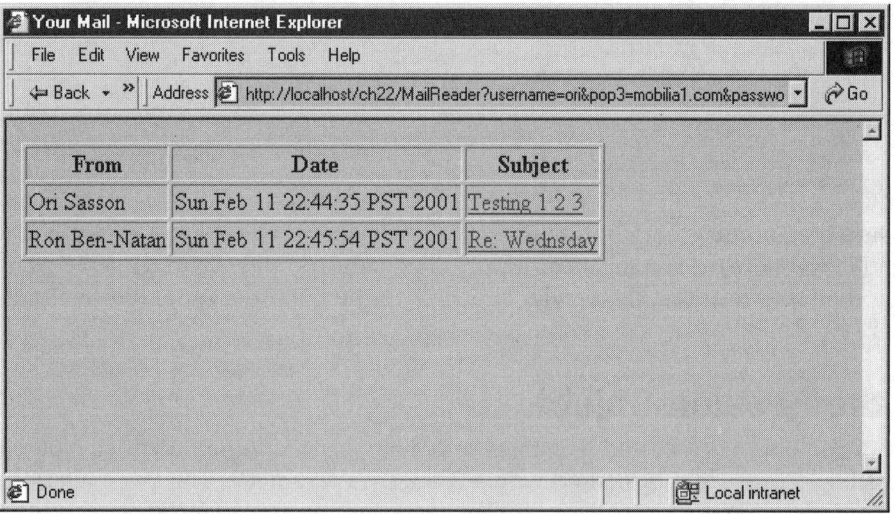

The Configuration Servlet

The second example is taken from the world of hierarchical parts configurations. This example displays a configuration of a complex piece of machinery. This machinery is composed according to a hierarchical structure, in which each part may be broken down into a set of smaller parts, which themselves may be broken down into yet smaller parts. Since most people can see only so many details at a time, almost all objects in the real world are broken down into such hierarchical structures. Each level is manageable in its own right, and the observer can decide at which level the part(s) should be viewed.

For example, computer hardware is composed of the motherboard, the network card, the disk, and so on. The motherboard is further broken down into the CPU, the memory chips, the controller, and so on. Just like computer hardware, software is also composed of parts: modules, procedures, and functions. Such a hierarchical view is not limited to information technology (IT)-related issues. Everything from projects, to power plants, to aircraft, to cities—practically everything—is maintained in some hierarchical structure.

Such a breakdown is usually maintained in a database of some sort, and we, as programmers, are asked to provide a view of this configuration. Obviously, we want to display this information as a hierarchy—and the best way to do this is to use a *tree widget*.

Given some data model representing a hierarchical structure, we are asked to build a Web-enabled interface that will display the hierarchies as trees in a browser. This will allow anyone having access to our Web site (and authorized to do so) to view the configurations in a convenient manner. Since we need to provide this service from any browser, we will build an HTTP servlet to service these requests. The HTTP servlet will receive the request, access the data in the database, and return some user interface to display the hierarchical information.

Before we begin, a couple of decisions need to be made. What will the server model be? This part is quite simple (especially after we've seen the title of this chapter). The best fit is an HTTP servlet (surprise, surprise). In this example, we will build a servlet that will accept GET requests. Upon receiving such a request (along with a set of parameters required to identify the root of the configuration), the servlet will access the database and get the information regarding the entire tree. It will then write this information to the output stream.

Next question: How should we write the information? Should we write it as straight HTML? That would be pretty ugly. Maybe we can put it in an HTML table and indent the lines based on the depth in the tree? That would be slightly better—but not by much. Actually, since we were asked to provide a dynamic user interface, we need some code to be passed to the browser so that the tree can be displayed and manipulated (that is, its nodes collapsed, opened, and so on). Our selection is therefore much narrower: we can either go with a combination of JavaScript and Dynamic HTML (DHTML) or with a Java applet. Since the subject of this book is tightly coupled with Java technology, we'll opt for the latter.

Then comes the fun part. Being lazy in nature, whenever we need to write some code, we always spend a little time on the Web looking for examples we can borrow from—or even for code to buy. After spending half an hour (isn't the Web great?), we come up with a list of 10 applets that perform precisely the tasks we need. After spending a little more time comparing the available packages, we zoom in on a package called Advanced Tree Explorer, available at *http://www.jpowered.com/tree*. This is a superb applet that is small, fast, pleasant to look at, and easy to use. So we download it (or a 30-day evaluation version) and read the instructions, which takes less than 15 minutes, and we are ready to go.

Initializing the Servlet

First, we build the servlet class and the `init` method of the servlet, as shown here:

```
package book.websphere.chapter22;

import javax.servlet.*;
import javax.servlet.http.*;
import java.io.*;
import java.util.*;
import java.sql.*;
import java.text.*;

public class ConfigServlet extends HttpServlet {
  static ResourceBundle aBundle = null;
  static String serialFormat;
  static String nonSerialRootFormat;
  static String serialRootFormat;
  static String nonSerialFormat;
  static String bgImage = "";
  static String codebase;
  static String fontString;

  public void init(ServletConfig config) throws ServletException {
      super.init(config);
      aBundle = ResourceBundle.getBundle("ConfigServlet");
      serialFormat = aBundle.getString("serialFormat");
      nonSerialFormat = aBundle.getString("nonSerialFormat");
      serialRootFormat = aBundle.getString("serialRootFormat");
      nonSerialRootFormat =
                       aBundle.getString("nonSerialRootFormat");
      codebase = aBundle.getString("codebase");
      fontString = aBundle.getString("font");
      bgImage = aBundle.getString("bgImage");
      DBConnection.init(
        aBundle.getString("dburl"),
        aBundle.getString("dbuser"),
        aBundle.getString("dbpass"));
      try {
        Connection conn = DBConnection.getConnection();
        CallableStatement stmt = conn.prepareCall(
              "alter session set NLS_DATE_FORMAT = 'DD MON YYYY'"
```

```
);
        stmt.execute();
        stmt.close();
      } catch (Throwable ex) {
        ex.printStackTrace();
      }
  }
```

The `init` method will be called whenever the servlet is loaded—that is, when the application server is started. Because our servlet accesses the database, we need to create a connection to the database. Given the fact that creating a connection takes time (it is actually one of the operations that consumes the longest amount of time to perform), it makes sense that we open the connection during servlet startup (when no users are waiting on this operation). We also do other things that need to happen only once, such as reading the property files and setting all constants to be used later in the actual processing. Note that the database connection is performed through a simplistic connection class, which is shown next. Normally, when using WebSphere, you use a connection retrieved from a connection pool, as opposed to having the servlet manage the connections. This functionality is covered at length in Chapter 18.

```
package book.websphere.chapter22;

import java.sql.*;

public class DBConnection {
  static Connection conn = null;
  static String aURL;
  static String aUserName;
  static String aPassword;

  public static void init(String url, String userName, String
                          password) {
    // Load the JDBC driver.
    if (conn == null) {
      try {
        DriverManager.registerDriver(new
                                oracle.jdbc.driver.OracleDriver());
      } catch (Exception e) {
        System.err.println("Could not load driver ");
        e.printStackTrace();
```

```
            }
            aURL = url;
            aUserName = userName;
            aPassword = password;
        }
    }

    public static Connection createConnection() {
        try {
          // Establish the connection to the database.
          conn = DriverManager.getConnection(aURL, aUserName,
                                                        aPassword);
        } catch (Exception e) {
          System.err.println("Could not create connection " +
                                                  e.getMessage());
          e.printStackTrace();
          conn = null;
        }
        return conn;
    }

    public static Connection getConnection() {
      Connection toRet = null;
      if (conn == null)
        toRet = createConnection();
      else toRet = conn;
      return toRet;
    }
}
```

This example uses the Java Database Connectivity (JDBC) *thin driver* from Oracle; make sure your WebSphere server has access to this class either by having the JDBC driver registered as a JDBC Resource in the Administrator console or by updating the classpath of the Web module you are using for deploying this servlet. If you don't perform either of these actions, you will get an exception while trying to register the servlet with the application server. Of course, if you're using a different database, the respective JDBC driver should be used.

Servicing the Request

The next step is to build the method that will do all the work. Since we want the service to be available in the most flexible way, we implement the `doGet` method of the servlet.

This method accepts a number of arguments from the request object and proceeds to build the configuration tree. The code for the method is shown here:

```
public void doGet(
                HttpServletRequest request,
                HttpServletResponse response)
             throws ServletException, IOException {
    response.setContentType("text/html");
    PrintWriter out = new PrintWriter (response.getOutputStream());
    String nodeKey = request.getParameter("nodeKey");
    String rootSerialId = request.getParameter("serialsT");
    String rootPartId = request.getParameter("partId");
    String rootPartDesc = request.getParameter("partDesc");
    String rootRevision = request.getParameter("rev");
    String quantity = request.getParameter("qty");

    out.println("<html>");
    out.println("<head><title>Configuration View</title></head>");
    out.println("<body>");
    out.println("<applet code=\"TreeApplet\" width=\"250\"
                height=\"300\"" +
                 "archive=\"Treemenu.jar\">"
    out.println("<param name=\"nodeOffset\" value=\"25\">");
    out.println("<param name=\"image1\"" +
              "value=\"closed|./IconImages/closedfolder.gif\">");
    out.println("<param name=\"image2\" +
               "value=\"open|./IconImages/openfolder.gif\">");
    out.println("<param name=\"image3\" +
             "value=\"document|./IconImages/document.gif\">");
    Stack displayStringStack = new Stack();
    Stack levelStack = new Stack();

    String rootName = formatRootBySerial(
       rootPartId,rootPartDesc, rootRevision, rootSerialId);
    out.println("<param name=\"node1\" value=\"conf|root|" +
               rootName + "|Helvetica|N|10|0|0|0|true|closed
                         |open");
    displayStringStack.push(rootName);
    levelStack.push(new Integer(1));

    // … Build the tree in the database and read it in
    // rs is the result set object returned from the
```

```
// database query - holding the nodes that need to
// go into the tree structure

while (rs.next()) {
    // read in the data per row and place it in variables
    // to be used in the following code
    // then, based on the level and the values on the stack
    // decide where in the tree the node belongs
    if (configLevel == atTop) {
        String itemString = "item" +
                            Integer.toString(itemNum++);
        String dispString = ((String)displayStringStack.peek())
                            + "/" + dString;
        out.println("<param name=\"" + itemString +
                        "\" value=\"" +
                         dispString);
    } else if (configLevel < atTop) {
        while (configLevel <
                ((Integer)levelStack.peek()).intValue()) {
          displayStringStack.pop();
          levelStack.pop();
        }
        String itemString = "item" +
                            Integer.toString(itemNum++);
        String dispString = ((String)displayStringStack.peek())
                          + "/" + dString;
        out.println("<param name=\"" + itemString +
                    "\" value=\"" +
                     dispString);
    } else {    // configLevel > atop
        String itemString = "item" +
                            Integer.toString(itemNum++);
        String dispString = ((String)displayStringStack.peek())
                          + "/" + dString;
        out.println("<param name=\"" + itemString +
                      "\" value=\"" +
                      dispString);
        displayStringStack.push(dispString);
        levelStack.push(new Integer(configLevel));
      }
  }
```

```
      stmt.close();
    } catch (Throwable ex) {
      ex.printStackTrace();
    }

    out.println("</applet>");
    out.println("</body></html>");
    out.close();
  }
```

Note *Some of the database access code is omitted because it is not of much interest here; it is sufficient that you understand that the arguments passed in through the request object are used to invoke a database operation that builds the tree. The tree is then read from the database and used to produce the arguments to the applet.*

The method starts by reading in the arguments sent to the servlet to determine what node forms the root of the configuration tree. The servlet then proceeds to set the output stream's content type (an HTML page) and write out the applet tag. The Advanced Tree Explorer applet receives the parameters affecting its display through a set of `PARAM` tags. It also receives the data forming the tree using `PARAM` tags. The servlet therefore needs to write to the output stream both the general display parameters (accomplished in the first part of the method) and the parameters encapsulating the data (the rest of the method).

After the general parameters have been written, the database is accessed to get the nodes. The database call returns the nodes in the order in which they should be displayed, as opposed to a tree ordering (such as a depth-first search or a breadth-first search). A stack object is used to build the tree structure, based on a config-level value marked in each of the rows returning from the database. Then, a `PARAM` tag is added to the applet with a name of `nodeX`, where `X` is incremented by 1 in each row. The tree structure is attained by concatenating the complete path to each node name. (The prefix is managed by the stack.) The resulting HTML source for the example is as follows:

```
<html>
<head>
<title>Install Base Configuration</title>
</head>
<body>
<applet code="TreeApplet" width="250" height="300" archive="Treemenu.jar">
<param name="nodeOffset" value="25">
<param name="image1" value="closed|./IconImages/closedfolder.gif">
<param name="image2" value="open|./IconImages/openfolder.gif">
<param name="image3" value="document|./IconImages/document.gif">
<param name="node1" value="conf|root|Root Configuration|Helvetica|
                           N|10|0|0|0|true|closed|open">
```

```
<param name="node2" value="serialeee|conf|Serial #EEE|Helvetica|
                           N|10|0|0|0|true|closed|open">
<param name="node3" value="pentium|serialeee|Pentium IV 2000|Helvetica|
                           N|10|0|0|0|true|closed|document">
<param name="node4" value="modem|pentium|ADSL Modem|Helvetica|
                           N|10|0|0|0|true|closed|document">
<param name="node5" value="printer|serialeee|Printer for MF Systems|
                           Helvetica|N|10|0|0|0|false|document">
<param name="node6" value="powersup|serialeee|110AC Power supply|
                           Helvetica|N|10|0|0|0|false|document">
</applet>
</body>
</html>
```

The corresponding Web page is shown here:

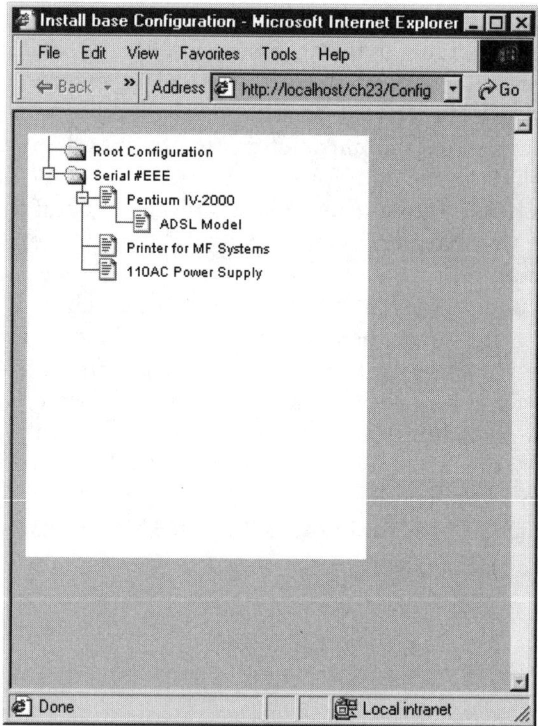

The FastTicker Servlet

We now move on to our third (and final, for this chapter) servlet. In fact, this example is a little more elaborate and includes a servlet forming the front-end and back-end server processes. The example is taken from a completely different domain—that of financial services.

The example involves a hypothetical company called FastTicker.com (at least it was hypothetical when we wrote this chapter) that provides an online stock notification service. Many examples of such services exist; in this chapter, you will see just how simple it is to build such software (and maybe realize why Internet companies that were successful on Wall Street went bust later on). Obviously, our implementation won't have any fancy bells and whistles, but it will be fully functional.

The service allows users to define a profile that consists of a set of stock symbols that the user wants to track, along with a definition of a set of thresholds. For each stock symbol that the user wants to track, a lower boundary and an upper boundary can be defined. If a lower boundary is defined and the stock price drops below that threshold, the user should be notified. If an upper boundary is defined and the stock price goes over that threshold, the user should be notified. Notification is based on sending e-mail to the user, which is also part of the profile.

Because today's pager and cellular companies allow you to send a message to a pager device or a phone (through Short Message Service, or SMS) using e-mail, e-mail notification is useful for reaching almost anyone at any time. The final part of the profile is an interval that the user sets up for checking stock prices and notification. The implementation shown here is limited—for example, if the user specifies an interval of 5 minutes, and the stock price never changes but is above the upper limit, a notification is sent every 5 minutes. It is true that there is no apparent reason to keep sending a message if the stock doesn't move, but, hey, no one is making money off of this implementation.

The maintenance of the user profiles and the processes of checking stock values and performing the notification comprise the implementation. We start with the description of the profile maintenance part.

Profile Maintenance

Because user profiles will be updated on the Web, we need a servlet to generate and manage the user profiles. We will keep this servlet simple—as a result, the user interface will be fairly ugly. The first access to the system is through a login form:

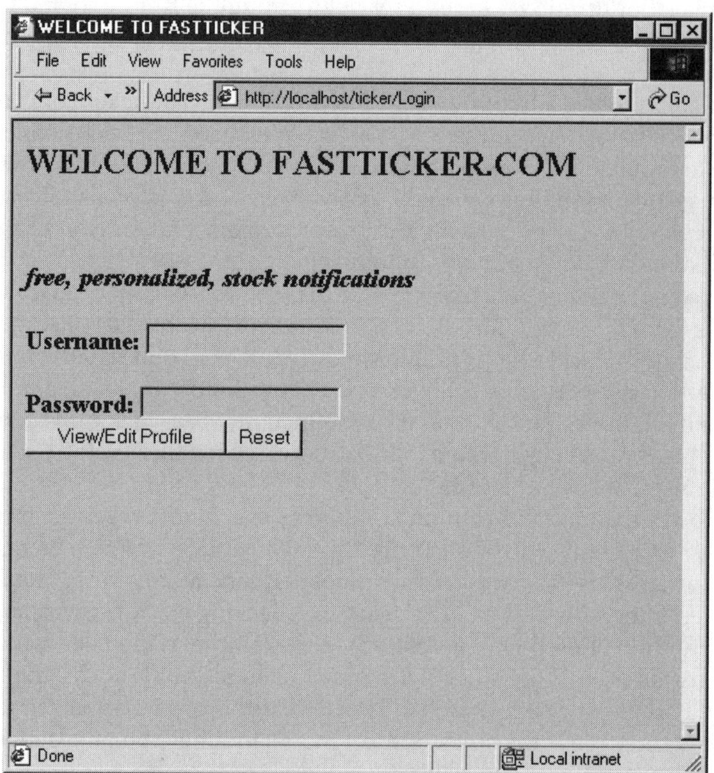

This form connects to the servlet using a *GET* request. The `doGet` method proceeds to look up the user in the database; if the user is found (and the password is correct), it proceeds to read the user's profile and creates an HTML form with the values of the user. This is written out to the servlet output stream. An example form created by this servlet is shown in Figure 22-1.

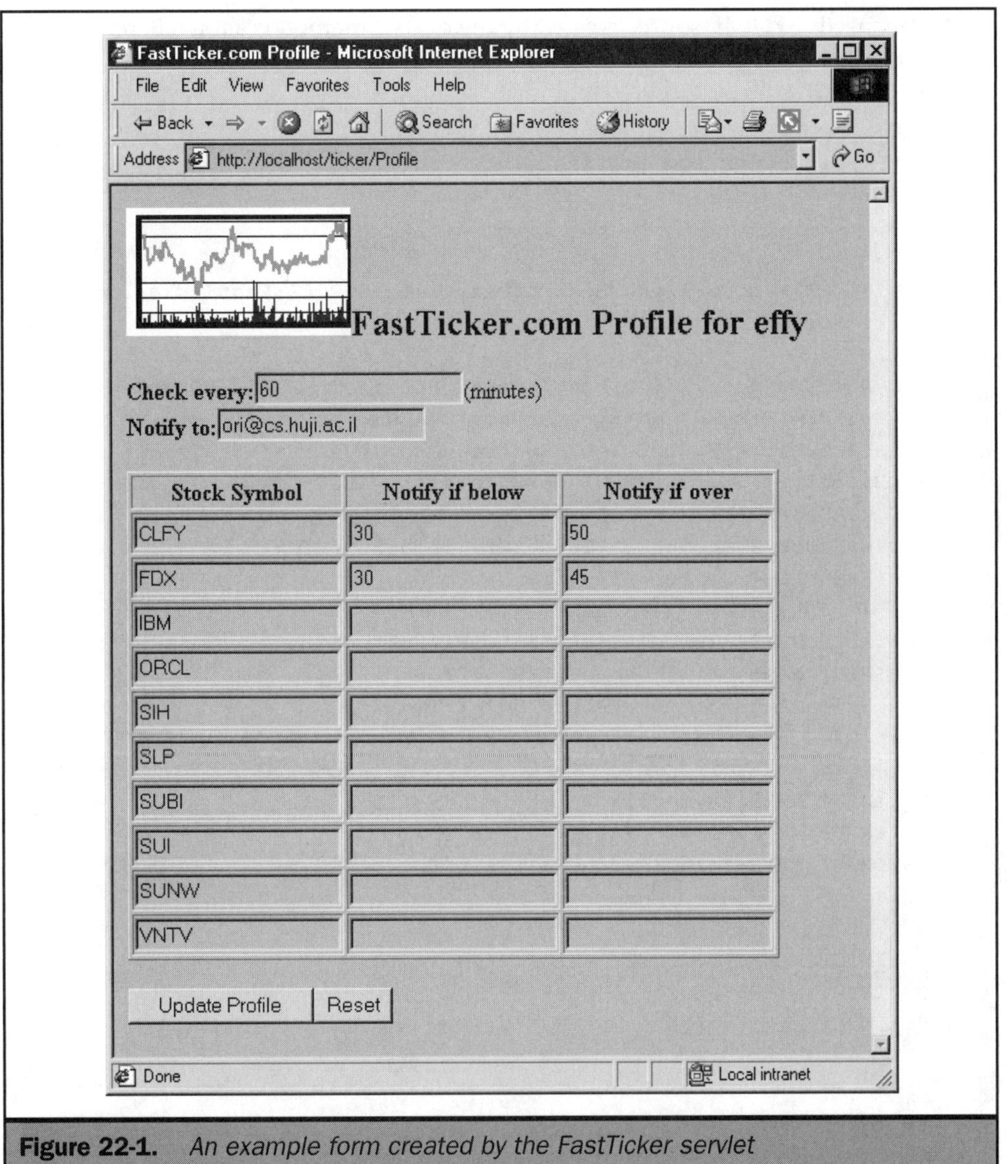

Figure 22-1. *An example form created by the FastTicker servlet*

The respective HTML source created by the doGet method is shown here:

```
<HTML>
<HEAD>
<TITLE>FastTicker.com Profile
</TITLE>
</HEAD>
<BODY>
<H2><IMG SRC="http://yourhost/ticker.gif" BORDER>FastTicker.com
Profile for
effy</H2>
<FORM ACTION="http://yourhost/ticker/Profile" METHOD=POST>
<INPUT TYPE="HIDDEN" NAME="userName" VALUE="effy">
<B>Check every:</B><INPUT NAME="frequency" VALUE="60">(minutes)
<BR><B>Notify to:</B><INPUT NAME="email" VALUE="ori@cs.huji.ac.il">
<P><P><TABLE BORDER>
<TR><TH>Stock Symbol</TH><TH>Notify if below</TH>
    <TH>Notify if over</TH></TR>
<TR>
<TD><INPUT NAME="symbol0" VALUE="CLFY"></TD>
<TD><INPUT NAME="low0" VALUE="30"></TD>
<TD><INPUT NAME="high0" VALUE="50"></TD>
</TR>
<TR>
<TD><INPUT NAME="symbol1" VALUE="FDX"></TD>
<TD><INPUT NAME="low1" VALUE="30"></TD>
<TD><INPUT NAME="high1" VALUE="45"></TD>
</TR>
<TR>
<TD><INPUT NAME="symbol2" VALUE="IBM"></TD>
<TD><INPUT NAME="low2" VALUE=""></TD>
<TD><INPUT NAME="high2" VALUE=""></TD>
</TR>
<TR>
<TD><INPUT NAME="symbol3" VALUE="ORCL"></TD>
<TD><INPUT NAME="low3" VALUE=""></TD>
<TD><INPUT NAME="high3" VALUE=""></TD>
</TR>
<TR>
<TD><INPUT NAME="symbol4" VALUE="SIH"></TD>
```

```
<TD><INPUT NAME="low4" VALUE=""></TD>
<TD><INPUT NAME="high4" VALUE=""></TD>
</TR>
<TR>
<TD><INPUT NAME="symbol5" VALUE="SLP"></TD>
<TD><INPUT NAME="low5" VALUE=""></TD>
<TD><INPUT NAME="high5" VALUE=""></TD>
</TR>
<TR>
<TD><INPUT NAME="symbol6" VALUE="SUBI"></TD>
<TD><INPUT NAME="low6" VALUE=""></TD>
<TD><INPUT NAME="high6" VALUE=""></TD>
</TR>
<TR>
<TD><INPUT NAME="symbol7" VALUE="SUI"></TD>
<TD><INPUT NAME="low7" VALUE=""></TD>
<TD><INPUT NAME="high7" VALUE=""></TD>
</TR>
<TR>
<TD><INPUT NAME="symbol8" VALUE="SUNW"></TD>
<TD><INPUT NAME="low8" VALUE=""></TD>
<TD><INPUT NAME="high8" VALUE=""></TD>
</TR>
<TR>
<TD><INPUT NAME="symbol9" VALUE="VNTV"></TD>
<TD><INPUT NAME="low9" VALUE=""></TD>
<TD><INPUT NAME="high9" VALUE=""></TD>
</TR>
</TABLE><BR>
<INPUT TYPE="SUBMIT" VALUE="Update Profile"><INPUT TYPE="RESET">
</FORM>
</BODY>
</HTML>
```

Note that the form's action accesses the same servlet but uses the POST method. This is because in this example, the servlet is used for two purposes: the GET method is used to retrieve the user profile, while the POST method is used for updating the user profile. The implementation of the doGet method itself is as follows:

```
public void doGet(
            HttpServletRequest request, HttpServletResponse
response)
```

```
    throws ServletException, IOException {
  try {
    String loginName = request.getParameter("loginName");
    String passwd= request.getParameter("passwd");

    PrintWriter out = response.getWriter();
    response.setContentType("text/html");
    out.println("<HTML><HEAD><TITLE>Ticker.com"
                + "Profile</TITLE></HEAD>");
    out.println("<BODY>");
    out.println("<H2><IMG SRC=\"http://yourhost/ticker.gif\"" +
              "BORDER>FastTicker.com Profile for " + loginName +
              "</H2>");
    Statement stmt = null;
    try {
        Connection conn = DBConnection.getConnection();
        stmt = conn.createStatement();
        ResultSet rs = stmt.executeQuery(
            "select passwd__t, frequency_c, "+
            "email_c from monitor_users where user__t = '" +
            loginName + "'");
        if (rs.next()) {
          String p = rs.getString(1);
          int f = rs.getInt(2);
          String email = rs.getString(3);
          if (email == null)
            email = "";
          if (p.compareTo(passwd) != 0)
            out.println("<H3>Incorrect password. " +
                      "Please back up and try again</H3>");
          else {
            stmt.close();
            stmt = conn.createStatement();
            rs = stmt.executeQuery("select symbol__t, low_c,
                          + "high_c " +
                           "from monitors where user__t= '" +
                           loginName + "' order by symbol__t");
            String[][] profileValues = new String[10][3];
            for (int i = 0; i < 10 ; i++)
              for (int j = 0 ; j < 3; j++)
                profileValues[i][j] = "";
```

```
int i = 0;
while ((i < 10) && rs.next()) {
  profileValues[i][0] = rs.getString(1);
  profileValues[i][1] = rs.getString(2);
  profileValues[i][2] = rs.getString(3);
  if (profileValues[i][1] == null)
    profileValues[i][1] = "";
  if (profileValues[i][2] == null)
    profileValues[i][2] = "";
  i++;
}
out.println("<FORM ACTION=" +
   "\"http://yourhost/servlet/Ticker\"METHOD=POST>");
out.println("<INPUT TYPE=\"HIDDEN\" " +
            "NAME=\"userName\"VALUE=\"" + loginName +
            "\">");
out.println("<B>Check every:</B><INPUT
           + "NAME=\"frequency\""+
             "VALUE=\"" + f + "\">(minutes)");
out.println("<BR><B>Notify to:</B><INPUT"
             + "NAME=\"email\" +
             "VALUE=\"" + email + "\">");
out.println("<P><P><TABLE BORDER>");
out.println("<TR><TH>Stock Symbol</TH><TH>Notify " +
             " if below</TH><TH>Notify if
+ "over</TH></TR>");
for (int k = 0 ; k < 10 ; k++) {
  out.println("<TR>");
  out.println("<TD><INPUT NAME=\"symbol" + k +
              "\"VALUE=\"" +
               profileValues[k][0] + "\"></TD>");
  out.println("<TD><INPUT NAME=\"low" + k +
              "\"VALUE=\"" +
              profileValues[k][1] + "\"></TD>");
  out.println("<TD><INPUT NAME=\"high" + k +
              "\"VALUE=\"" +
              profileValues[k][2] + "\"></TD>");
  out.println("</TR>");
}
out.println("</TABLE><BR>");
out.println("<INPUT TYPE=\"SUBMIT\" VALUE=\"Update" +
```

```
                              "Profile\"><INPUT TYPE=\"RESET\">");
              out.println("</FORM>");
            }
          }
          else
            out.println("<H3>No user named " + loginName +
                        ". Please back up and try again</H3>");
        } catch (Throwable ex) {
          out.println("<H3>Server error; please try again
                           later</H3>");
          ex.printStackTrace();
        }
        if (stmt != null)
          stmt.close();

        out.println("</BODY></HTML>");
        out.close();

      } catch (Exception e) {
        e.printStackTrace();
      }
    }
```

After a user name and password have been verified, the servlet proceeds to read all the rows for that user. For each row, a set of fields in the HTML form is generated with the appropriate values as initial values. The form itself is built in such a way that the servlet's `doPost` method is called when the Submit button is clicked. The `doPost` method updates the user profile in the database:

```
public void doPost(
            HttpServletRequest request, HttpServletResponse
                                                          response)
      throws ServletException, IOException
      response.setContentType("text/html");
      PrintWriter out = response.getWriter();
      out.println("<HTML><HEAD><TITLE>Ticker Profile
                                    Updated</TITLE></HEAD>");
      out.println("<BODY>");

      String[] symbols = new String[10];
```

```
String[] lows = new String[10];
String[] highs = new String[10];
String frequencyS = request.getParameter("frequency");
String emailS = request.getParameter("email");
String userName = request.getParameter("userName");
for (int i = 0 ; i < 10 ; i++) {
  symbols[i] = request.getParameter("symbol" + i);
  lows[i] = request.getParameter("low" + i);
  highs[i] = request.getParameter("high" + i);
}
Statement stmt = null;
try {
    Connection conn = DBConnection.getConnection();
    stmt = conn.createStatement();
    ResultSet rs = stmt.executeQuery(
        "update monitor_users set email_c = '" + emailS +
        "',frequency_c = " + frequencyS + "where user__t = '"
        + userName + "'");
    rs.next();
    stmt.close();
    System.out.println("delete from monitors ");
    stmt = conn.createStatement();
    stmt.executeUpdate(
        "delete from monitors where user__t = '" +
        userName + "'");
    stmt = null;
    for (int i = 0 ; i < 10 ; i++)
      if (symbols[i].trim().length() > 0) {
        System.out.println("Inserting for symbol " +
                                   symbols[i]);
        stmt = conn.createStatement();
        StringBuffer sqlString = new StringBuffer(100);
        sqlString.append(
          "insert into monitors(user__t, symbol__t");
        if (lows[i].trim().length() > 0)
          sqlString.append(", low_c");
        if (highs[i].trim().length() > 0)
          sqlString.append(", high_c");
        sqlString.append(") values ('" + userName +
          "','" + symbols[i].trim() + "'");
        if (lows[i].trim().length() > 0)
```

```
                sqlString.append("," + lows[i]);
              if (highs[i].trim().length() > 0)
                sqlString.append("," + highs[i]);
              sqlString.append(")");
              String sqlS = sqlString.toString();
              System.out.println(sqlS);
              stmt.executeUpdate(sqlS);
              stmt.close();
              stmt = null;
            }
        out.println("<H3>Profile successfully updated</H3>");
      } catch (Throwable ex) {
        out.println("<H3>Error while updating profile</H3>");
        ex.printStackTrace();
      }

      out.println("</BODY></HTML>");
      out.close();
  }
```

Notifications

The second part of the system is the process performing the actual stock lookup and notifications:

```
package book.websphere.chapter22;

import java.util.*;
import java.sql.*;
import java.net.*;
import java.io.*;
import javax.mail.*;
import javax.mail.internet.*;

public class TickerDaemon implements Runnable {

  final static int dbPollingInterval = 30000; // 30 seconds

  Hashtable workerThreads;

  void updateWorkerThreads() {
```

```
    Statement stmt = null;
    try {
      Connection conn = DBConnection.getConnection();
      stmt = conn.createStatement();
      ResultSet rs = stmt.executeQuery(
        "select user__t, frequency_c, email_c from monitor_users");
      while (rs.next()) {
        String uName = rs.getString(1);
        int f = rs.getInt(2);
        String email = rs.getString(3);
        if (email != null) {
          if (!workerThreads.contains(uName)) {
            System.out.println("Adding worker thread for " +
                               uName);
            WorkerThread nt = new WorkerThread(uName, f, email);
            workerThreads.put(uName, nt);
            (new Thread(nt)).start();
          }
        }
      }
    } catch (Throwable ex) {
      ex.printStackTrace();
    }
  }

  public TickerDaemon() {
    workerThreads = new Hashtable(100);
  }

  public void run() {
    updateWorkerThreads();
    try {
      Thread.currentThread().sleep(dbPollingInterval);
    } catch (Throwable ex) {
      ex.printStackTrace();
    }
  }

  public static void main(String[] args) {
    DBConnection.init("jdbc:oracle:thin:@websphere:1521:ORCL",
                      "ws", "ws");
    Thread t = new Thread(new TickerDaemon());
```

```
    t.start();
  }
}

class WorkerThread implements Runnable {

  String userName;
  String email;
  int frequency;

  public WorkerThread(String uName, int f, String e) {
    userName = uName;
    frequency = f;
    email = e;
  }

  void updateBaseData() {
    try {
      Connection conn = DBConnection.getConnection();
      Statement stmt = conn.createStatement();
      ResultSet rs = stmt.executeQuery(
        "select frequency_c, email_c from monitor_users where
        user__t = '" +
        userName + "'");
      rs.next();
      frequency = rs.getInt(1);
      email = rs.getString(2);
      stmt.close();
    } catch (Throwable ex) {
      ex.printStackTrace();
    }
  }

  void checkQuoteData() {
    updateBaseData();
    StringBuffer urlBuf = new StringBuffer(1000);
    urlBuf.append("http://quotes.nasdaq.com/Quote.dll?mode=stock");
    Vector values = new Vector(10);
    try {
      Connection conn = DBConnection.getConnection();
      Statement stmt = conn.createStatement();
```

```
    ResultSet rs = stmt.executeQuery(
      "select symbol__t, low_c, high_c from monitors where"
                + "user__t = '" +
                 userName + "' order by symbol__t");
    while (rs.next()) {
      String[] aValue = new String[3];
      aValue[0] = rs.getString(1);
      aValue[1] = rs.getString(2);
      aValue[2] = rs.getString(3);
      values.addElement(aValue);
      urlBuf.append("&symbol=");
      urlBuf.append(aValue[0]);
    }
  } catch (Throwable ex) {
    ex.printStackTrace();
  }
  urlBuf.append("&x=0&y=0");
  String urlString = urlBuf.toString();
  String urlResponse = getHTMLFor(urlString);
  if (urlResponse != null)
    parseAndNotify(urlResponse, values);
}

String getHTMLFor(String url) {
 try {
  URLConnection aConnection = (new URL(url)).openConnection();
  aConnection.setDoInput(true);
  aConnection.setDoOutput(true);
  aConnection.setUseCaches(false);
  InputStream inS = aConnection.getInputStream();
  StringBuffer buffer = new StringBuffer(4096);
  boolean atEnd = false;
  while(!atEnd) {
    int len = inS.available();
    byte[] buf = new byte[len];
    if (inS.read(buf, 0, len) == -1)
    atEnd = true;
    if (len > 0)
      buffer.append(new String(buf));
    Thread.sleep(10);
  }
```

```
      String retString = buffer.toString();
      return retString;
    } catch (Throwable ex) {
      ex.printStackTrace();
    }
    return null;
  }

  void notifyQuote(String messageText) {
    Vector messagesToSend = new Vector(5);
    int beginAt = 0;
    while (beginAt < messageText.length()) {
      int endAt = beginAt + 150;
      if (endAt > messageText.length())
        endAt = messageText.length();
      messagesToSend.addElement(messageText.substring(beginAt,
                                                       endAt));
      beginAt = endAt + 1;
    }
    for (int i = 0; i < messagesToSend.size() ; i++) {
      String partS = (new Integer(i + 1)).toString() + "/" +
                     (new
                         Integer(messagesToSend.size())).toString();
      sendEmail((String)(messagesToSend.elementAt(i)), partS);
    }
  }

  void sendEmail(String messageText, String part) {
    Properties props = new Properties();
    props.put("mail.smtp.host", "mail.fastticker.com");
    try {
      Message msg = new
                      MimeMessage(Session.getDefaultInstance(props,
                                                             null));
      InternetAddress from = new InternetAddress("fastticker.com");
      msg.setFrom(from);
      InternetAddress[] to = { new InternetAddress(email) };
      msg.setRecipients(Message.RecipientType.TO, to);
      msg.setSubject("Stock quote from FastTicker.com for " +
                     userName + " " + part);
```

```
      msg.setContent(messageText, "text/plain");
      Transport.send(msg);
      System.out.println("Sent email to " + email);
    } catch (MessagingException ex) {
      ex.printStackTrace();
    }
  }

  void parseAndNotify(String urlResponse, Vector values) {
    Hashtable prices = new Hashtable(values.size());
    Vector symbolLocations = new Vector(50);
    Vector symbols = new Vector(50);
    int beginAt = 0;
    int endAt = 0;
    int dollarAt = 0;

    for (int i = 0 ; i < values.size() ; i++ ) {
      String[] aValue = (String[])values.elementAt(i);
      String symbol = aValue[0];
      beginAt = urlResponse.indexOf(symbol, endAt);
      dollarAt = urlResponse.indexOf("$", beginAt);
      endAt = urlResponse.indexOf("\"", dollarAt);
      prices.put(symbol, urlResponse.substring(dollarAt+5, endAt));
    }
    StringBuffer messageText = new StringBuffer(200);
    for (int i = 0 ; i < values.size() ; i++ ) {
      String[] aValue = (String[])values.elementAt(i);
      boolean sendQuote = ((aValue[1] == null) && (aValue[2] ==
                                                                null));
      double aPrice = (new
           Double((String)(prices.get(aValue[0])))).doubleValue();
      if (aValue[1] != null)
        if ((new Double(aValue[1])).doubleValue() >= aPrice)
          sendQuote = true;
      if (aValue[2] != null)
        if ((new Double(aValue[2])).doubleValue() <= aPrice)
          sendQuote = true;
      if (sendQuote) {
        messageText.append(aValue[0]);
        messageText.append("=");
        messageText.append(prices.get(aValue[0]));
```

```
          messageText.append(" ");
        }
      }
      String text = messageText.toString();
      if (text.length() > 0)
        notifyQuote(text);
    }


    public void run() {
      while(true) {
        checkQuoteData();
        try {
          Thread.currentThread().sleep(frequency*60*1000);
        } catch (Throwable ex) {
          ex.printStackTrace();
        }
      }
    }
  }
```

The process is implemented as a `Runnable` class. It is invoked from the `init` method of a second servlet—merely a convenience allowing us to register this process for startup once the WebSphere Application Server starts up. The process manages a worker thread pool so that it can handle many users for which profiles need to be tracked. For each such user, the database information is constantly read. We need to re-read the information because it is possible that while the worker thread is running, the user has logged into the system and changed the threshold values. Then, the stock prices need to be retrieved. The servlet accesses the NASDAQ Web site at *www.nasdaq.com* to provide the actual stock quotes. The site is convenient in that the actual price lookup is performed with a URL. It is simple for us to build this URL based on the user's profile.

After hitting the NASDAQ Web site using a `URLConnection`, we read in the returning HTML page and extract the pricing values based on crude parsing. Obviously, any real application would need to perform this in a much better way. (A significant drawback of the approach taken here is that it is very sensitive to changes in the Web design of the NASDAQ site.) Then we compare the prices with the threshold values, and if need be, we create and send an e-mail message using the JavaMail package. We think it's phenomenal that the entire example, which performs a service of real value, took less than one day to build and deploy!

Summary

This chapter introduced code for three servlets, each performing a bit of function and then creating a Web page with which the application can display information to a user. The examples are fairly simply and are meant merely to make you comfortable enough to start building servlets and deploying them on WebSphere. Since the Web application model is one that is based on independent Web request/reply round-trips, application context is not natively supported by the core servlet. And yet, any application maintains some application state. So for anything but the most trivial applications (and even the simple servlets introduced in this chapter cannot manage without some application state), we need to describe how this state is managed within the servlet model; this is the topic of Chapter 23.

Chapter 23

Servlet Sessions

This chapter continues the discussion of servlets and focuses on the issue of session management within servlets. WebSphere as an application server supports two primary application models: that of servlets (and as an extension, JavaServer Pages) and that of Enterprise JavaBeans (EJBs). While it is true that EJBs are more appropriate for complex applications, and that servlets are more appropriate for Web-deployed, short-lived, transaction-oriented applications, servlets are certainly also used in scenarios in which managing application state is mandatory. Servlets form the basis for many of today's Web-enabled applications, and consequently, most development projects using servlets need to manage application state in some way.

Sessions and State

A servlet sits within a WebSphere Application Server and waits for HTTP requests (or requests arriving via some other protocol). Since the HTTP servlet model is inherently related to the Web server model, each request will usually have no associated history. This is usually called the *statelessness* of the Web model—the Web is inherently stateless. The fact that the Web model is stateless is an important factor that has allowed the Web to become a multidimensional medium. A stateless model performs better than a model that is required to manage state. Software performing in a stateless model is also simpler to build, because it does not need to address such issues as how many sessions one can manage, how to know that someone has broken off communication, and how multiple servers are used for load balancing. Hence, the stateless model fits well with the basic requirements of the Web.

However, an application often *does* need to manage state on behalf of the clients using its services. Consider the simple e-business scenario in which a customer is shopping on the Web for items and adding them to his or her shopping cart. Obviously, it is in the best interest of all parties involved to be able to store the cart, update it as the shopping progresses, and recall it when the user intends to check out.

It is not uncommon for a connectionless technology to form the basis for a connection-oriented technology. Transmission Control Protocol/Internet Protocol (TCP/IP) is an example of such a collaboration. IP and the User Datagram Protocol (UDP) do not support a notion of a connection; they merely implement a packet-oriented communication protocol. TCP, on the other hand, has the notion of a connection, and manages packets running on a lower-level protocol in a way that provides a connection-oriented view to the application. In the same way, a state-less model can be used as the foundation for a model that must maintain state. It is possible (and even simple) to add some application-level handling that uses the state-less model in a way that application state can be maintained. In fact, because this is such a fundamental need of all applications, this additional layer has been added in all application servers, and WebSphere is no exception.

This chapter describes a number of schemes for managing state on behalf of an application, and it provides examples for the use of each scheme. It focuses on the session management application programming interface (API) introduced into the servlet specification because it is the most appropriate solution for servlets. The next chapter will present more examples related to the management of sessions and will review WebSphere servlet support with more detail.

HTTP Cookies

Before delving into servlet session management, you need to understand what *cookies* are. HTTP cookies are state objects created by a server and passed to a client (typically a browser). These state-encapsulating entities were first supported by Netscape Navigator and have since become common in all browsers. As such, cookies are now the most common way in which state information created by a server program can be passed back to the client so that future invocations from the client can include this information. Cookies allows sessions to be *demarcated*—that is, a session can be defined by the existence of the cookie, and all interactions between client and server involving a certain cookie can be identified as part of a single session.

Cookies have a number of attributes:

- **A name and a value** The value is a sequence of characters that is most commonly used as an opaque structure (such as an identity).
- **An expiration date** Defines a timeout after which the cookie's value is no longer meaningful.
- **A domain and a path** Defines the cookie's scope. The domain defines the Internet domain for which the cookie is relevant. The default domain value is the server name on which the cookie was created (from whence the cookie arrived to the client), but the server can specify a broader domain if need be.
- **A path attribute** Is useful when the scope should be narrowed.

Finally, a cookie can be marked as a *secure cookie* (by an additional attribute), which means that the cookie should be transmitted between the client and the server only via a secure connection. This is an important feature without which the existence of most e-business applications would be impossible. Consider, for example, an online trading application. If the application is simple and involves only one screen, perhaps secure cookies are unnecessary. However, the typical online trading application is complex and involves system logon before the user can continue within the secure application. One possible scheme for managing the application state is a cookie, which in a sense encapsulates the identity of the user. The application can be built so that anyone holding onto the cookie can proceed with a session and, for example, perform trades. Obviously, in this case the application must protect the cookie value as fanatically as it protects the user name and password.

While cookies are used almost ubiquitously these days, they have had their share of controversy, which revolves around two issues: privacy and security. Cookies allow applications to track state. However, they can be used to perform many other tasks.

For example, they provide a mechanism by which a Web site can track users who visit the site again and again. With time, an advanced Web site may customize the information it provides to different users based on this tracking information. While, in our opinion, this is a good thing, it is apparent that such tracking can be misused and is certainly a mechanism that works against the basic anonymity that used to characterize the Web.

As an example, consider the following cookie file that we found on our hard drive:

```
SITESERVER
ID=da4fcbc400eeb9b3d9190a88570eb57a
barnesandnoble.com/
0
642859008
31887777
3660024432
29271958
*
userid
3MMN8PH9NX
barnesandnoble.com/
0
358989312
29785928
3660324432
29271958
*
browserid
BITS=2&OS=3&VERSION=5%2E0&AOLVER=0&BROWSER=2
barnesandnoble.com/
0
1841121280
29308070
3660724432
29271958
*
```

This cookie file apparently originated from *barnesandnoble.com*. (By the way, cookie files on Windows 2000 are placed in a folder called Cookies under the user's profile folder.) The second cookie—called `userid`, was placed there by the Web site; this is not an ID created explicitly by the user—that is, us. From now on, whenever we visit this site, we will be identified using that ID, and it is quite possible that this information may be used for purposes that we are not aware of (nor have given consent to). To allow "private people" to use the Web without compromising their comfort (or their company's policies), all browsers have the ability to disallow cookies. The Security Settings dialog box for Microsoft Internet Explorer 5.0 is shown next. This dialog box is accessed from Internet Explorer by choosing Tools | Internet Options. Open the Security tab, and then click the Custom Level button. As you can see, cookie support can be disabled from this dialog box.

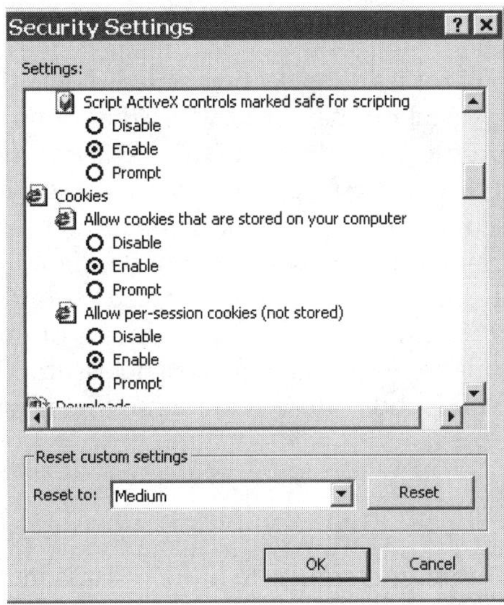

Disabling cookie support may affect your ability to use many of today's Web applications.

Another objection that has been voiced regarding cookies has to do with the fact that cookies are stored on disk so that they can be used in later visits to a Web site. This kind of use of cookies is slightly different than those used for managing an application's session or state—it is often used to identify returning users and to maintain a user's state. Therefore, it is meaningful to distinguish between cookies used within a session and cookies stored on disk. Coming back to the Security Settings dialog box, notice that you can allow cookies that are used for session management (that is, within a browser session) while disallowing persistent cookies.

"Conventional" Session Management

Because session management is fundamental to the nature of an application, it has been around since the first applications on the Web—long before the existence of servlets. Many methods of maintaining sessions have evolved.

However, we are not providing a complete overview of all such methods, because such a discussion is not within the scope of this book. In addition, we do not wish to encourage "bad habits." We believe it's best for people writing servlets to use the session management abilities that are built into the servlet API. For completeness, some of the "conventional" session management mechanisms are discussed here before a "mainstream" discussion.

Hidden Fields

Probably the oldest method for tracking session state involves hiding fields within forms. Hidden fields were used in Chapter 22 when the user's name was embedded into the FastTicker.com profile update screen. This field was inserted by the servlet's GET processing and used by the POST update. In a typical scenario, the session and state information is passed around by a set of fields hidden within forms. Since all fields, whether hidden or not, are propagated from the client to the servlet in any submit operation, this information is effectively passed around from one request-handling thread to the next. The primary benefits of this method are that it is simple, it is supported by all browsers, and it makes no assumptions regarding the operating environment (and is thus safest in the sense that it will always function correctly).

URL Rewriting

Another method, URL rewriting, is similar to hidden fields in that it piggybacks state information using a mechanism originally designed for something else. With this method, the state information is appended to the servlet path and is later retrieved using the `getPathInfo` method of the `request` object.

Cookies for Maintaining Information

The final method worthy of mention (before we move on to the built-in support for session management provided by servlets) is the use of cookies. Servlets provide a way to create and use cookies manually through the `javax.servlet.http.Cookie` class, the `addCookie` method in `HttpServletResponse`, and the `getCookies` method in `HttpServletRequest`. This API provides an approach that is simple to use and quite elegant (certainly more elegant than hidden fields, but still less so than the approach we'll learn about in the next session).

Following is a simple cookie example that provides a testing service on the Web. The user is presented with a question and asked for an answer. Each time the user submits an answer, it is compared with the correct answer. If an incorrect answer is received, the question is returned to the user, along with a cookie value maintaining the number of incorrect answers received and cookies for all incorrect answers. This session information is used to score the question (since the grade is inversely proportional to the number of attempts) and to produce the final output. (This code will omit the actual scoring of the test.) Figure 23-1 shows the screen presented to the user.

The Question screen is created by the servlet's GET handling method. In the `doGet` method, in addition to generating the HTML, a cookie named `FAILED_ATTEMPTS` is added with a value of 0. If the user enters the answer 5, for example, the `doPost` method increments the value of the cookie and resets the value for the failed attempts. It also adds an additional cookie with the incorrect answer.

For example, after the user makes one mistake, the output appears as shown in Figure 23-2. After one more mistake, the output appears as shown in Figure 23-3.

Notice that each such output writes out the number of attempts; this is possible because the cookie information comprising the application state always includes the number of failed attempts. When the user finally gets the answer correct, the output appears as shown in Figure 23-4.

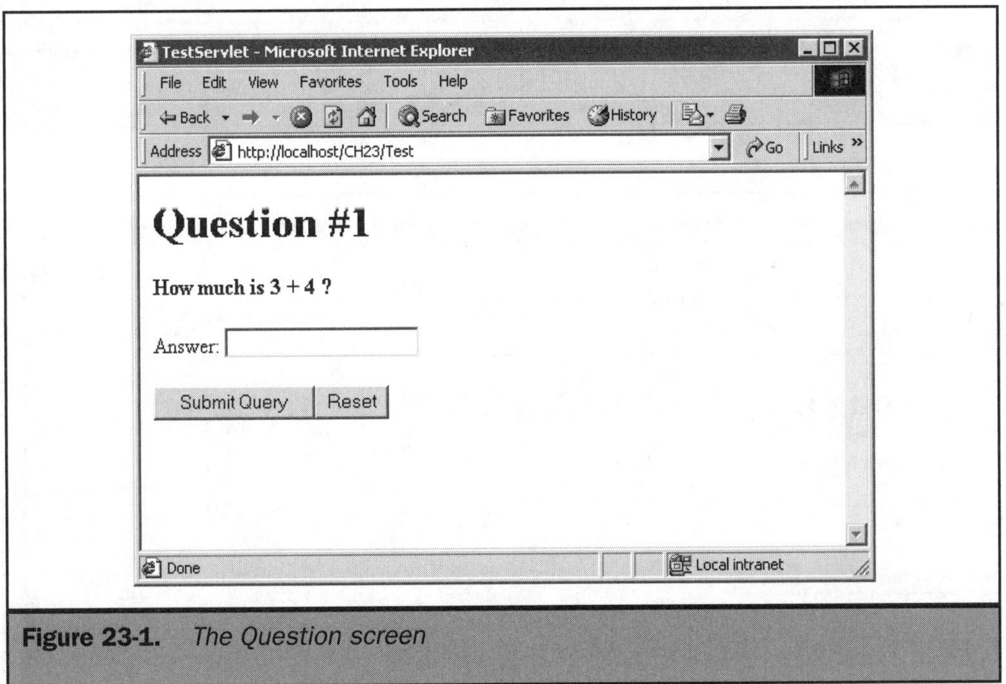

Figure 23-1. *The Question screen*

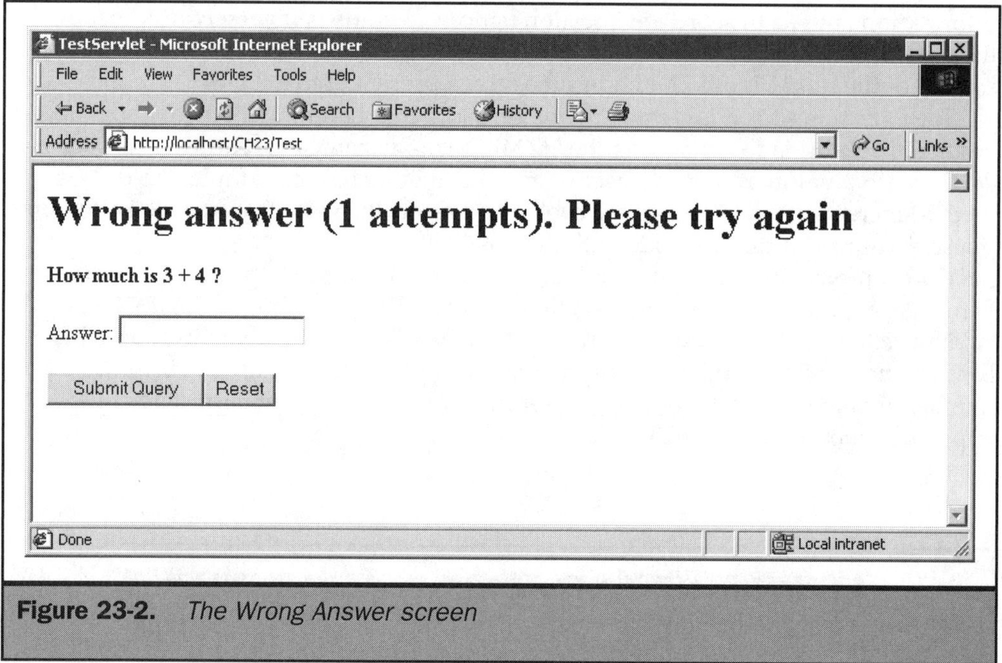

Figure 23-2. *The Wrong Answer screen*

Figure 23-3. *A second Wrong Answer screen*

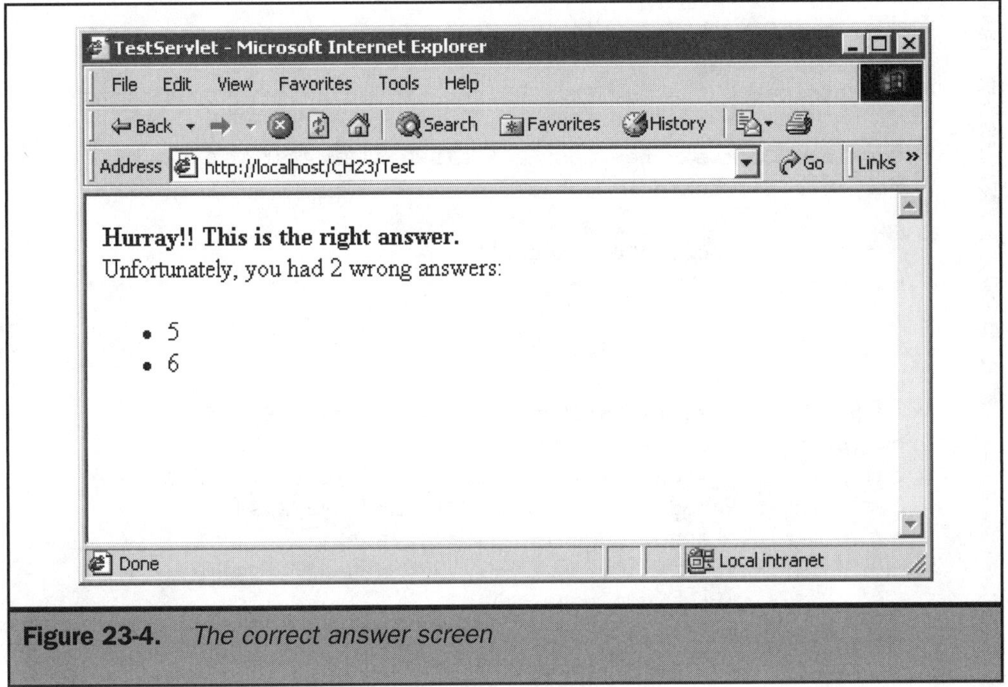

Figure 23-4. *The correct answer screen*

All the erroneous answers can be displayed because they are part of the session's *state*. Following is the servlet code for this example:

```
package book.websphere.chapter23;

import javax.servlet.*;
import javax.servlet.http.*;
import java.io.*;
import java.util.*;

public class TestServlet extends HttpServlet {
    public void init(ServletConfig config) throws ServletException
  {
    super.init(config);
  }

  public void doGet(
      HttpServletRequest request,
      HttpServletResponse response)
```

```
      throws ServletException, IOException {
    response.setContentType("text/html");
    PrintWriter out = new PrintWriter (response.getOutputStream());

    Cookie myCookie = new Cookie("FAILED_ATTEMPTS", "0");
    response.addCookie(myCookie);

    printOutForm(out, "Question #1");
    out.close();
  }


  void printOutForm(PrintWriter out, String extraString) {
    out.println("<html>");
    out.println("<head><title>TestServlet</title></head>");
    out.println("<body><H1>" + extraString + "</H1>");
    out.println("<B>How much is 3 + 4 ?</B>");
    out.println("<FORM ACTION=\"http://yourhost/ch23/Test" +
                "\"METHOD=POST>");
    out.println("Answer: <INPUT TYPE=\"TEXT\""
                 + "NAME=\"answer\"><P>");
    out.println("<INPUT TYPE=\"SUBMIT\"><INPUT
                 + "TYPE=\"RESET\"</FORM>");
    out.println("</body></html>");
  }

  public void doPost(
      HttpServletRequest request,
      HttpServletResponse response)
      throws ServletException, IOException {
    response.setContentType("text/html");
    PrintWriter out = new PrintWriter (response.getOutputStream());

    int currentNumberOfWrongAnswers = 0;
    Vector wrongAnswers = new Vector();
    Cookie[] myCookies = request.getCookies();
    for (int i = 0 ; i < myCookies.length; i++) {
      String name = myCookies[i].getName();
      String value = myCookies[i].getValue();
      System.err.println("Cookie named " + name + " has value " +
                         value);
      if (name.compareTo("FAILED_ATTEMPTS") == 0)
```

```
      currentNumberOfWrongAnswers = Integer.parseInt(value);
    else
      wrongAnswers.addElement(value);
  }
  System.err.println("Finished reading cookies");
  int currentAnswer =
      Integer.parseInt(request.getParameter("answer"));
  if (currentAnswer != 7) {
    currentNumberOfWrongAnswers++;
    Cookie anotherWrongAnswer = new Cookie(
      "WRONG_ANSWER_" + currentNumberOfWrongAnswers,
      request.getParameter("answer"));
    response.addCookie(anotherWrongAnswer);
    Cookie myCookie = new Cookie(
      "FAILED_ATTEMPTS",
      Integer.toString(currentNumberOfWrongAnswers));
    response.addCookie(myCookie);
    printOutForm(out,
      "Wrong answer (" + currentNumberOfWrongAnswers +
                    " attempts). Please try again");
  } else {
    out.println("<html>");
    out.println("<head><title>TestServlet</title></head>");
    out.println("<body>");
    out.println("<B>Hurray!! This is the right answer.</B><BR>");
    if (currentNumberOfWrongAnswers > 0) {
      out.println("Unfortunately, you had " +
                  currentNumberOfWrongAnswers +
                  " wrong answers:<BR>");
      out.println("<UL>");
      for (Enumeration e = wrongAnswers.elements() ;
           e.hasMoreElements() ; ) {
        out.println("<LI>");
        out.println(e.nextElement());
      }
      out.println("</UL>");
      out.println("</body></html>");
    }
  }
  out.close();
}
```

```
    public String getServletInfo() {
      return "book.websphere.chapter23.TestServlet Information";
    }
  }
```

Here's an interesting point of note: If you run this example in your browser and open an additional browser window (by choosing it from the File menu—not by opening an additional instance of the application), both browser windows will share the same session context, so the number of attempts will be counted as the sum of all attempts made in *both* windows. If, on the other hand, you open a new instance of the browser, the two resulting windows will not share a session, and two separate series of attempts will be tracked.

The Session Tracking API: "Preferred" Session Management

Now let's move on to the preferred way of tracking and managing session state in servlet-based application: the session-tracking API. Our discussion of cookies was important not only because of their common use in Web applications, but also because cookies form the underlying foundations for servlet session tracking. The difference between the servlet session-tracking mechanism and cookies is that in the session-tracking mechanism, the cookie is used to point to a structure maintained on the server, which in turn manages the information forming the application state. This is superior to having the state information itself flowing over the network in the form of cookies.

Cookies allow a server to attach a *dictionary* of values (a set of name-value pairs) to the messages passed between the server and the browser. The servlet session-tracking API maintains this dictionary only on the server and provides a unique identifier that can be used to retrieve this dictionary; this identifier is placed in a cookie that is sent off to the browser. This arrangement provides the best of both worlds: the supported capabilities are similar to the full power of cookies, but there is less communication, more privacy, simpler maintenance, and better encapsulation.

Testing the Servlet with the Session-Tracking API

Let's take the small test servlet that we used in the previous section and try to rewrite it with servlet sessions. The result would look like this. (All new code is indicated in boldface.)

```
package book.websphere.chapter23;

import javax.servlet.*;
```

```
import javax.servlet.http.*;
import java.io.*;
import java.util.*;

public class TestServlet2 extends HttpServlet {

  public void init(ServletConfig config) throws ServletException {
    super.init(config);
  }

  public void doGet(
      HttpServletRequest request,
      HttpServletResponse response)
      throws ServletException, IOException {
    response.setContentType("text/html");
    PrintWriter out = new PrintWriter (response.getOutputStream());

    HttpSession aSession= request.getSession(true);
    aSession.setAttribute("FAILED_ATTEMPTS", new Integer(0));

    printOutForm(out, "Question #1");
    out.close();
  }


  void printOutForm(PrintWriter out, String extraString) {
    out.println("<html>");
    out.println("<head><title>TestServlet</title></head>");
    out.println("<body><H1>" + extraString + "</H1>");
    out.println("<B>How much is 3 + 4 ?</B>");
    out.println("<FORM ACTION=\"http://yourhost/ch23/Test2" +
             "\"METHOD=POST>");
    out.println("Answer: <INPUT TYPE=\"TEXT\" "+
            "NAME=\"answer\"><P>");
    out.println("<INPUT TYPE=\"SUBMIT\"><INPUT" +
            "TYPE=\"RESET\"</FORM>");
    out.println("</body></html>");
  }

  public void doPost(
      HttpServletRequest request,
      HttpServletResponse response)
```

```
  throws ServletException, IOException {
response.setContentType("text/html");
PrintWriter out = new PrintWriter (response.getOutputStream());

int currentNumberOfWrongAnswers = 0;
Vector wrongAnswers;

HttpSession aSession = request.getSession(true);

if (aSession.getAttribute("WRONG_ANSWERS") == null)
  wrongAnswers = new Vector();
else {
  wrongAnswers =Vector)(aSession.getAttribute("WRONG_ANSWERS"));
  currentNumberOfWrongAnswers =
  ((Integer)(aSession.getAttribute("FAILED_ATTEMPTS"))).intValue();
}
int currentAnswer =
  Integer.parseInt(request.getParameter("answer"));
if (currentAnswer != 7) {
  currentNumberOfWrongAnswers++;
  wrongAnswers.addElement(request.getParameter("answer"));
  aSession.setAttribute(
   "FAILED_ATTEMPTS", newInteger(currentNumberOfWrongAnswers));
  aSession.setAttribute(
    "WRONG_ANSWERS", wrongAnswers);
  printOutForm(out,
    "Wrong answer (" + currentNumberOfWrongAnswers +
    " attempts). Please try again");
} else {
  out.println("<html>");
  out.println("<head><title>TestServlet</title></head>");
  out.println("<body>");
  out.println("<B>Hurray!! This is the right answer.</B><BR>");
  if (currentNumberOfWrongAnswers > 0) {
    out.println("Unfortunately, you had " +
      currentNumberOfWrongAnswers +
      " wrong answers:<BR>");
    out.println("<UL>");
    for (Enumeration e = wrongAnswers.elements() ;
      e.hasMoreElements() ; ) {
      out.println("<LI>");
      out.println(e.nextElement());
    }
```

```
            out.println("</UL>");
            out.println("</body></html>");
        }
      }
      out.close();
    }

    public String getServletInfo() {
      return "book.websphere.chapter23.TestServlet Information";
    }
}
```

This code provides the same functionality as the previous example and aims only at demonstrating how the code changes when you want to use session tracking.

This example uses the session-tracking API, in which the session object is used to hold onto a set of data structures. Because the objects are maintained within the WebSphere Application Server, any object can be stored within the session.

Note that you should store only serializable objects in the session. Otherwise, you will not be able to use the persistent session option. When this option is employed, the objects stored in the session object can be saved to disk and rebuilt when needed. This requires that each object placed in the session be serializable; we strongly encourage you to place only such objects in the session (even if you do not have any immediate plans to use persistent sessions). Therefore, while in the old cookie example each wrong answer was stored in a string, in the new code all wrong answers can be stored in a vector, which can be stored in the session as a single entity. This eliminates the need for using artificial names for the information to be tracked—as we had to do when by means of cookies.

The code using the session-tracking API is simple. First, the session object is retrieved using the request's `getSession` method. The argument passed to this method specifies (in this case) that if a session object has not yet been created, one should be created as a result of the call. The session object is then used as an associative array using the `getAttribute` and `setAttribute` methods.

The session-tracking API is obviously more functional than that shown in this example. Most important is the fact that the session object can be used to maintain the objects on the server; a single cookie passed to the browser is used to provide an index into this structure.

An easy way to see the cookie used for the session is to invoke the *snoop* servlet after using the test servlet (the second variant). This will work only if the snoop servlet and the test servlet are packaged together in the same Web application, because the session is maintained only within application boundaries. The session ID can be easily spotted under Client Cookies, as shown in Figure 23-5.

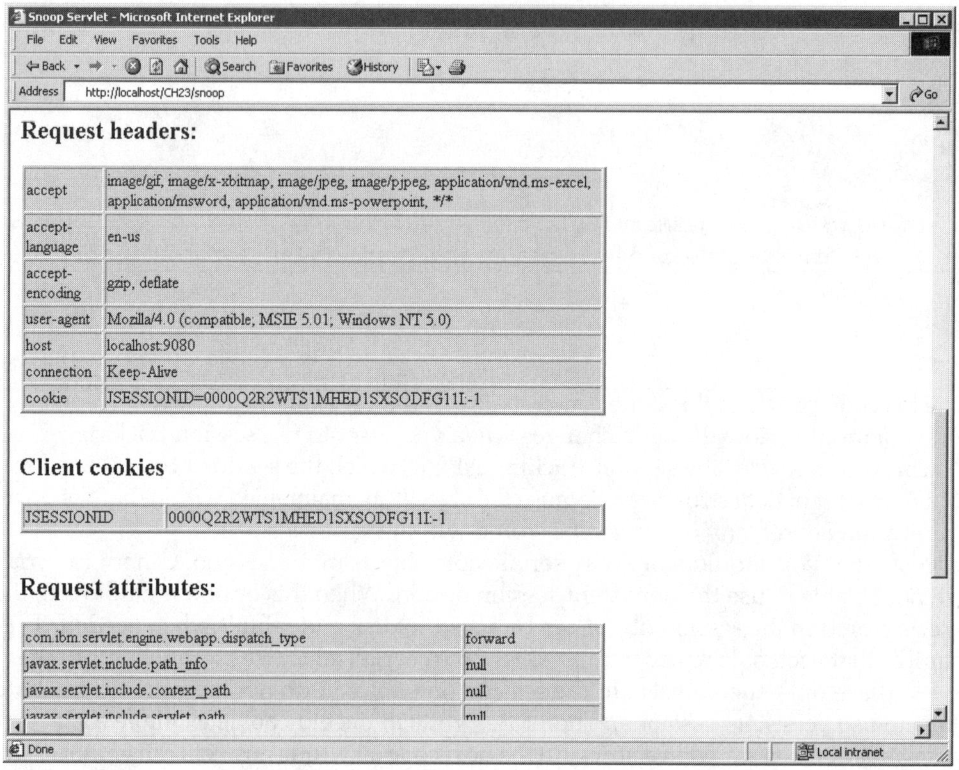

Snoop Servlet - Microsoft Internet Explorer

Address http://localhost/CH23/snoop

Request headers:

accept	image/gif, image/x-xbitmap, image/jpeg, image/pjpeg, application/vnd.ms-excel, application/msword, application/vnd.ms-powerpoint, */*
accept-language	en-us
accept-encoding	gzip, deflate
user-agent	Mozilla/4.0 (compatible; MSIE 5.01; Windows NT 5.0)
host	localhost:9080
connection	Keep-Alive
cookie	JSESSIONID=0000Q2R2WTS1MHED1SXSODFG11I:-1

Client cookies

JSESSIONID	0000Q2R2WTS1MHED1SXSODFG11I:-1

Request attributes:

com.ibm.servlet.engine.webapp.dispatch_type	forward
javax.servlet.include.path_info	null
javax.servlet.include.context_path	null
javax.servlet.include.servlet_path	null

Done | Local intranet

Figure 23-5. *The session ID is located under Client Cookies*

Because cookies are maintained by the browser using the `jsesessionid` cookie, this cookie still exists even after the test servlet has completed. This is why we can view it by activating the snoop servlet.

Obviously, there is more to sessions than just maintaining a dictionary of objects. Additional methods supported by the `HttpSession` object in the Servlet API 2.2 are listed here:

- **getCreationTime** Retrieves the time at which the session was created.
- **getId** Retrieves the identifier that is assigned to each session. This identifier is unique within WebSphere and is precisely the identifier that is passed along in the cookie to the browser.

- **getLastAccessTime** Returns the last time that the client sent a request carrying the identifier assigned to the session.
- **getSessionContext** Returns the context for the session.
- **getAttributeNames** Returns all keys of the objects associated with the session.
- **getMaxInactiveInterval** Returns the maximum time interval (measured in seconds) for which the Web container will keep the session between client requests.
- **setMaxInactiveInterval** Sets the maximum time interval (measured in seconds) for which the Web container will keep the session between client requests.
- **invalidate** Tells WebSphere that a session should no longer be maintained. (See the discussion that follows.)
- **isNew** Identifies a session as *new* if it has been created by the server but the client has not yet acknowledged joining the session.
- **removeAttribute** Removes an object from the session.

Once the `invalidate()` method is invoked, all objects maintained for that session are discarded and the session should no longer be used. This method is important given the working model of the Web, which is such that a browser uses the server and at some point "goes away." This can happen for many reasons—for example, the user may close the browser and perform another task, or the connection may be lost. In the meantime, we may still be holding on to objects maintained for that browser session. Unless we want our server's memory footprint to grow constantly (until we're out of space, or until our performance degrades so much that a reboot is necessary), this information needs to be discarded at appropriate intervals. One way is through a logoff routine that, among other things, invalidates the session. Another way is a background process that periodically invalidates sessions that have not been used for a while. (In Chapter 24, you will see yet another way to manage such cleanup.)

Summary

Application state is among the most important aspects of servlet programming. Other than the most trivial servlets, all application servlets need to manage the state information that is communicated between the many request/response pairs that make up a user session. Because it is so central to the Web application model in general, and to servlets in particular, application state has become an important part of the core servlet API. It is also the most important common aspect of all servlet programming.

The Complete Reference

Chapter 24

WebSphere-Specific Servlet Issues

This chapter continues the discussion of servlets and focuses on WebSphere-specific servlet support. WebSphere extends the Java servlet application programming interface (API) and provides some nonstandard features. The IBM extensions include support for easier session management, personalization, error reporting, and servlet chaining.

WebSphere Session Tracking

Recall from the preceding chapter that session tracking in servlets is based on the `HttpSession` interface. The WebSphere distribution extends the standard `HttpSession` with its own interface, `com.ibm.servlet.session.IBMSession`. This interface enhances "normal" session tracking with support for multiple WebSphere servers, security, and persistence.

Administrative Console Settings for Session Tracking

Chapter 23 discussed the way session management is used. Obviously, session management is available to Java servlets using the session-tracking API . However, the way sessions are actually used depends on the configuration defined with the WebSphere administration tool. Figure 24-1 shows the Session Manager page that is available under each application server. (This figure shows only one server: the default application server.)

The Session Manager tool includes a number of attributes that can be modified. You can enable or disable session management via URL rewriting and cookie support. (Recall from Chapter 23 that these are two ways to maintain sessions.) If you disable session management via URL rewriting or cookie support, session tracking will not occur—but you can always perform your own session management with hidden fields or through other self-built means. The advantage of URL rewriting is that it works even if the user disables cookies in the Web browser. However, a significant drawback of URL rewriting is that static Hypertext Markup Language (HTML) files might not work correctly, and in these cases your JavaServer Pages (JSPs) and servlets must be manually encoded with the URL data. This means a lot of extra work for you, so URL rewriting is worthwhile only if you want to support browsers without cookies.

If you enable both URL rewriting and cookies, the way session management takes place depends on the way your servlets are coded. If a servlet includes logic for encoding URLs, all session management is based on URL rewriting, regardless of the Enable Cookies setting. If you do not include code for explicit URL rewriting in your servlet, and you select Enable Cookies, then cookies are used as long as the client Web browser is willing to accept them. If the Web browser has cookies disabled, and you have not implemented URL rewriting code in the servlets, then both Enable Cookies and Enable URL Rewriting are ignored, as neither can be utilized.

IBM WebSphere Application Server Administrative Console - Microsoft Internet Explorer

File Edit View Favorites Tools Help

Address http://localhost:9090/admin/secure/logon.do

WebSphere Application Server

server-cfg.xml | Console Home | Configuration | Preferences | Save | Exit | Help

- WebSphere Administrative Domain
  - Nodes
    - zaratustra
      - Enterprise Applications
      - Application Servers
        - Default Server
          - Process Definition
          - IBM Debug and OLT
          - Web Container
            - HTTP Transports
            - Session Manager
            - Installed Web Modules
            - Thread Pool
            - Dynamic Cache
          - EJB Container
          - Location Service Daemon
          - ORB Settings
          - Transaction Service
          - Trace Service
          - Naming Service Settings
          - Server Security Configuration
          - Custom Services
      - Path Map
      - Installed Resource Providers
  - Virtual Hosts
  - Security
  - Resources

Session Manager

Configuration for session support in the Web container. When configuring the Session Manager, you can specify: ·Whether to enable sessions ·How to convey session IDs to servlets (cookies or URL rewriting) ·AE: Whether to save session data in a database during execution (persistent sessions) ·Whether to add session IDs to URLs in transition from HTTP to HTTPS and back (protocol switch rewriting)

For more information...

Properties	
☐ Enable URL Rewriting	Specifies whether the Session Manager uses rewritten URLs to carry the session IDs. If URL rewriting is enabled, the Session Manager recognizes session IDs that arrive in the URL and, if necessary, rewrites the URL to send the session IDs.
☑ Enable Cookies	Whether session tracking will use cookies to carry session IDs. If cookies are enabled, session tracking will recognize session IDs that arrive as cookies and try to use cookies for sending session IDs. If cookies are not enabled, session tracking will use URL rewriting instead of cookies (if URL rewriting is enabled). Enabling cookies takes precedence over URL rewriting.
☐ Enable SSL Tracking	Whether session tracking uses SSL to carry session IDs. Enabling SSL tracking takes precedence over cookie-based session tracking.
☐ Enable Protocol Switch Rewriting	Whether the session ID is added to a URL when the URL requires a switch from HTTP to HTTPS or from HTTPS to HTTP. If rewriting is enabled, the session ID is required in order to go between HTTP and HTTPS.
☐ Enable Persistent Sessions	When persistent sessions are enabled, the Session Manager will persist session information into the data source specified by the data source connection settings. Otherwise, the Session Manager will discard the session data when the server shuts down.
☐ Enable Security Integration	When security integration is enabled, the Session Manager will associate the identity of users with their HTTP sessions.

Advanced Settings

Local intranet

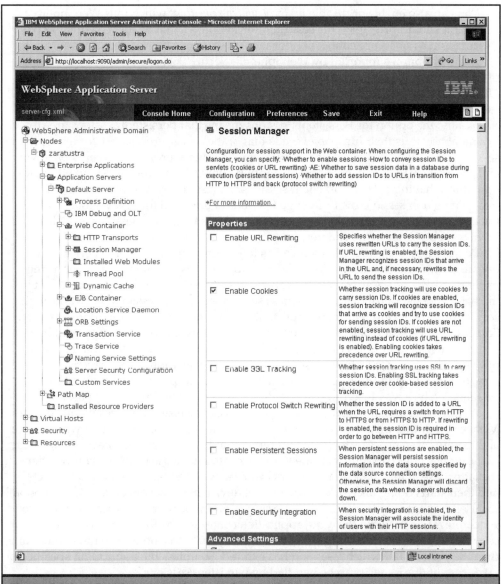

Figure 24-1. *Administrative Console Session Manager page*

You can also enable or disable *protocol switch rewriting*, which tells WebSphere whether it should propagate the session information when it needs to switch between a secure and a nonsecure connection (or vice versa).

Another option supported by WebSphere is Secure Socket Layer (SSL) session management, in which session information is transported over an SSL connection. This method has the added benefit or *security integration*; authenticated users are associated with their session information.

Finally, the option for Persistent Sessions means that persistent sessions are stored in a database; thus their lifespan exceeds that of the server process. So, for example, sessions can still persist in case of a shutdown. In other words, if a server goes down and comes back up again, enabling this option allows the server to resume where it left off without having to break off client sessions. Persistent sessions are also useful for maintaining user sessions over prolonged periods of time, and they play a role in session tracking in a clustered environment, as explained in the section "Sessions in a Clustered Environment," later in the chapter.

Persistent sessions are often viewed as inferior because of possible performance degradation during a session. After all, instead of all session management occuring in memory, disk accesses are required. Nevertheless, persistent sessions are important in many business applications and business scenarios because sessions persist through server shutdowns; this feature is important when user session information is critical. Sometimes the session object maintains only the context in which the application is serving a user. Other times the session information also includes data that has been built up in a long application session or between a few application screens. In this case, unless the application specifically takes care of this persistence, using persistent sessions can be a way to avoid slowing down the system and frustrating users.

Another scenario in which persistent sessions can be useful involves mobile devices. Mobile computing platforms typically have two modes: applications that work online and require constant access to the central servers, and applications that have enough logic in the mobile device to communicate with the central database using synchronizations. In the latter case, it may be that a user synchronizes with the central server at 9:00 A.M. and then starts doing his work on the mobile device in a disconnected mode. At noon, the user may again synchronize with the server. From the user's perspective, this second synchronization is within the same application context as the first one. Most application servers, however, will be configured in such a way that three hours is actually more time than the period after which a session has expired. So unless the application specifically takes care of this issue, it can be handled by persistent sessions.

Finally, another scenario that may favor persistent mode instead of a complete in-memory mode has to do with the expiration value. Most Web applications deployed on WebSphere and other application servers are configured with a session expiration value of 15 to 45 minutes. Because in the Web application model a user may simply close the browser without logging off the system, and because session objects are expensive resources that can consume large amounts of server memory, most Web applications assume that if a user is not actively using the system for a relatively short period of time, he can be kicked off. This is usually true for e-business applications. However, Web applications are now being used for all types of service, including those that serve internal as well as external users. In some cases, system administrators are asked to make sure that users are not kicked off the system even if they are idle for a long time. (In fact, we have had cases in which nine hours was requested!) In such a scenario, maintaining all session objects purely in memory can lead to thrashing or other problems in the server.

Let's go back to discuss cookies as a method for identifying a session. Under the Session Manager page entry, you'll find the Default Cookie Settings page, which is shown in Figure 24-2.

On this page, you can set the defaults pertaining to the cookie holding the session identifier. In contrast to previous releases of WebSphere, in version 4.0 you cannot set the cookie name because it is now part of the Java 2 Platform Enterprise Edition (J2EE) specification—but then, that didn't seem to be such a useful feature anyway. What is often useful, though, is the ability to restrict the number of domains that such a cookie will be sent to (for example, if you know that your application server supports the application only on your intranet). The Maximum Age field holds an integer value, in seconds, that defines the duration after which the cookie will be invalidated by the browser. Do not confuse this with session invalidation that may occur on the server; this cookie value goes into the response header as part of the cookie information (as was described in Chapter 23), and invalidation is performed by the browser. Finally, the Path field allows you enter information that will restrict the paths on the server to which the session cookie will be sent.

The next page, Persistent Sessions, shown in Figure 24-3, is used to configure the data source that the Session Manager will use to obtain database connections . The settings on this page determine how session information will be made persistent by the server. This is applicable only if you enable persistent sessions. You can also set the Java Database Connectivity (JDBC) datasource, as well as the user name and password to be used when connecting to the database for the purpose of storing session information. If you are using IBM DB2, you need to specify the size of your sessions. (When using Oracle, though, you can use 32K sessions without any special settings.) If you are using DB2 and need more than 4K of tablespace, you need to specify the tablespace to be used for the sessions table (using the `CREATE TABLESPACE` command in DB2).

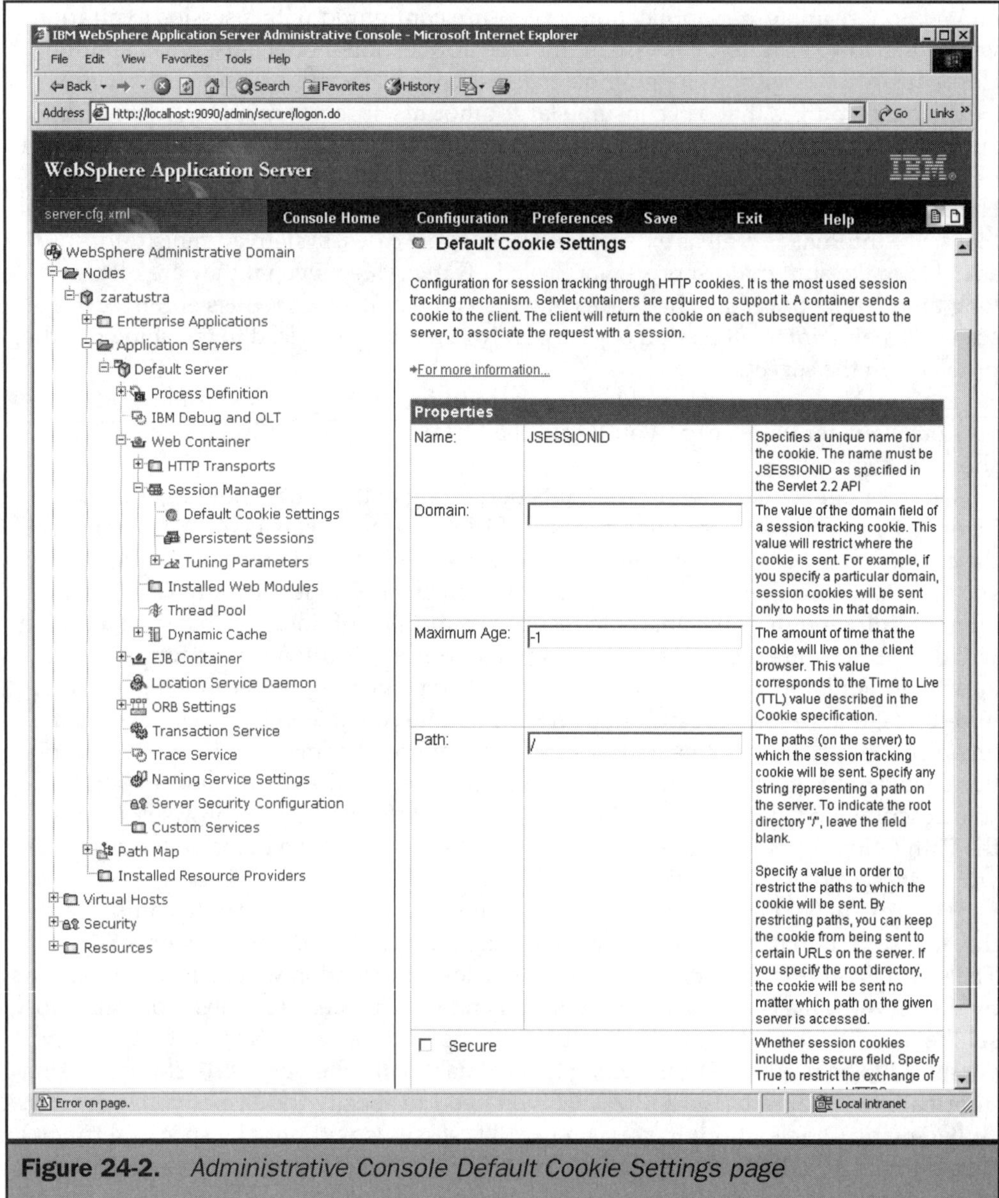

Figure 24-2. *Administrative Console Default Cookie Settings page*

Finally, the Administrative Console provides a couple of pages where you can tune session management behavior. From the Tuning Parameters page (shown in Figure 24-4),

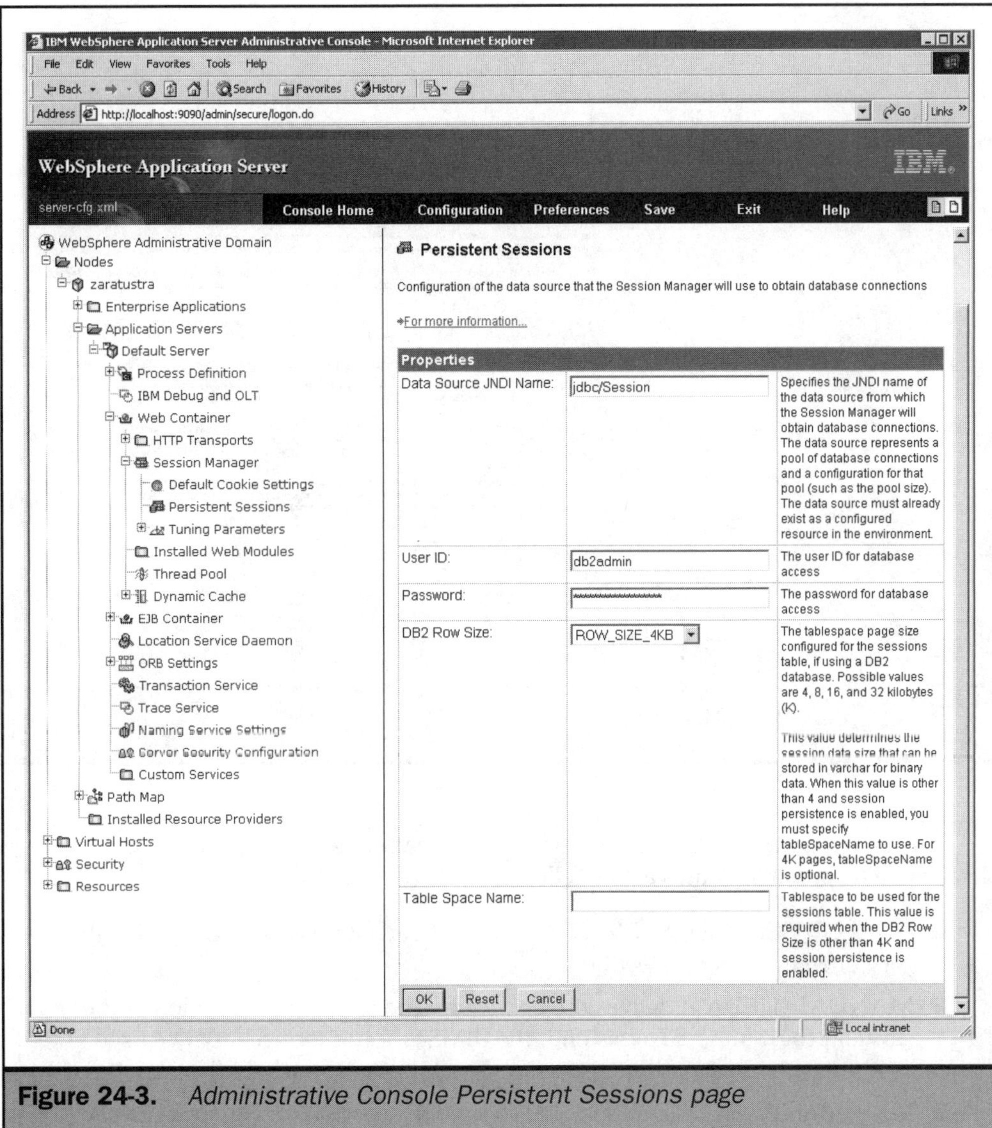

Figure 24-3. *Administrative Console Persistent Sessions page*

you can control the maximum number of sessions stored in memory and the lifetime of an unused session (how long a session should exist after its most recent use). The Allow Overflow setting indicates whether you will allow the number of session objects in memory to temporarily exceed the value you've specified as the maximum number of sessions.

Tuning Parameters

Tuning parameters for session support

For more information...

Properties		
☐ Using Multirow Schema		Whether to place each instance of application data in a separate row in the database, allowing larger amounts of data to be stored for each session. This can yield better performance in certain usage scenarios. If using multirow schema is not enabled, instances of application data can be placed in the same row.
Max In Memory Session Count:	1000	Specifies the maximum number of sessions to maintain in memory. The meaning differs depending on whether you are using in-memory or persistent sessions. For in-memory sessions, this value specifies the number of sessions in the base session table. Use the Allow Overflow property to specify whether to limit sessions to this number for the entire Session Manager, or to allow additional sessions to be stored in secondary tables. For persistent sessions, this value specifies the size of the general cache. If the Cache property is enabled, this value specifies how many session updates will be cached before the Session Manager reverts to reading session updates from the database automatically. This value holds when you are using in-memory sessions, persistent sessions with caching, or persistent sessions with manual updates. (The manual update cache keeps the last n time stamps representing "last access" times, with n being the Max In Memory Session Count value).
☑ Allow Overflow		Whether to allow the number of sessions in memory to exceed the value specified by Max In Memory Session Count property
☐ Schedule Invalidation		Enables the scheduled invalidation process for cleaning up the invalidated HttpSessions from the sessions database. When enabled, this setting specifies the two hours of a day in which the invalidator process cleans up the invalidated persistent sessions in the database.
Write Frequency:	END_OF_SERVLET_SERVICE	When the session is written to the database. If you specify END_OF_ SERVLET_SERVICE, a session is written to the database after the servlet completes execution. If you specify MANUAL_UPDATE, programmatic sync on the IBMSession object is required in order to write the session data to the database. If you specify TIME_BASED_WRITE, session data is written to the database based on the specified Write Interval value.
Write Interval:	120	If the Write Frequency is specified as TIME_BASED_WRITE, this value specifies how often the session data will be written to the database. The value must be a number of seconds, specified as a positive integer in the range from 5 to 9999. At minimum, a configured Invalidation Timeout should be twice as large as the configured write interval.
Write Contents:	ONLY_UPDATED_ATTRIBUTES	Whether only updated attributes should be written to the database. Otherwise, all of the session attributes will be written to the database, whether or not they have changed.
Invalidation Timeout:	30	Specifies how long a session is allowed to go unused before it will be considered valid no longer. The value is in minutes. Use a -1 to specify that the session will not be invalidated. The value of this setting is used as a default when the session timeout is not specified in a Web module deployment descriptor. Note, to preserve performance, the invalidation timer is not accurate "to the second." It is safe to assume that the timer is accurate to within two minutes. When the Write Frequency is time based, this value should be at least twice as large as the write interval.

OK Reset Cancel

Figure 24-4. *Administrative Console Tuning Parameters page*

You can specify when persistent session information is actually written out to the database. The possible values are as follows:

- END_OF_SERVLET_SERVICE means that persisting takes place when the servlet completes its execution.
- MANUAL_UPDATE leaves the update frequency to the discretion of the servlet programmer. To this end, the IBMSession interface must be used (see the section "WebSphere Session-Tracking API," later in this chapter).
- TIME_BASED_WRITE allows you to save the session at fixed intervals. The interval is selected using the Write Interval parameter.

You can also control the actual content to be written—the whole session object or only attributes that were modified.

One final option allows you to schedule invalidations. Using this option, you can have a garbage collection process remove invalidated sessions from the persistent store in the database. You can specify at what time such invalidation takes place on the Invalidation Schedule page, shown in Figure 24-5, which is located under Tuning Parameters.

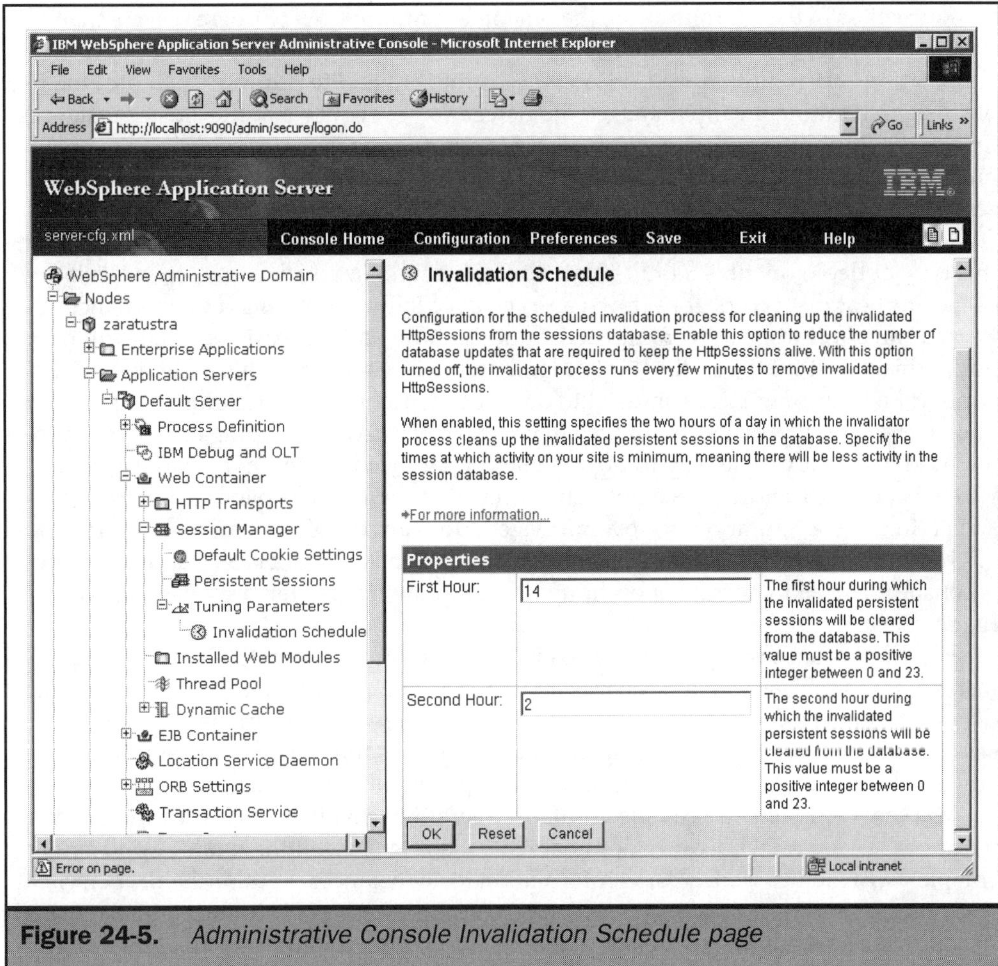

Figure 24-5. *Administrative Console Invalidation Schedule page*

The session invalidation process takes place twice daily, and on this page you can select the hours at which it takes place; hours are specified as integers between 0 and 23.

Sessions in a Clustered Environment

In a typical e-business scenario that supports a large number of users, no single processor can ever be powerful enough to support a theoretically unlimited number of users. Therefore, to support high-performance sites that scale well, the typical installation will include multiple application server instances, which together provide the illusion of a single-server instance. This can be configured on a multiple-processor machine, with each processor running a server, or on multiple machines, each possibly running a number of servers.

Regardless of the configuration, the outcome is multiple WebSphere servers that behave as one logical server. Such a logical scheme is called a *cluster*. WebSphere Application Server Advanced Edition (versus the Single-Site Edition) facilitates the use of clusters. It automatically manages the delegation of requests to the cluster instances. One of the implications of the one-logical-server scenario is that session management must be conceptually centralized. Therefore, all sessions must to be available to all servers in the cluster.

Clustering using WebSphere Advanced Edition provides a number of benefits. First, this type of deployment is a fault-tolerant architecture, in which a backup exists if one of the application servers goes down as a result of failure or planned maintenance. Because all application servers can accommodate any and all sessions, users will not notice this (apart from possible higher load on the live servers). This architecture also support *high availability*, a term used to describe an architecture that not only provides fault tolerance, but provides it in a way in which all resources (including backup resources) are used constantly. One way to provide fault tolerance is to set up a primary server with a backup server that becomes active only if something happens to the primary server. In this configuration, the overall system does not benefit in terms of performance. High availability is used to describe a system with a backup in place, but this backup is constantly used in normal operation, thereby allowing shorter response times and higher throughput.

WebSphere supports both scenarios in which session information between cluster instances is shared, as well as scenarios in which it is not. In the first scheme, no sharing of session information occurs—that is, each WebSphere instance manages its own session information and no sharing is available. This is obviously not useful if sessions are heavily used and if users will be serviced by potentially more than one server.

The second scheme is scalable and fault tolerant in that it supports the distributed nature of session tracking and does not create a bottleneck, all the while supporting complete availability of all session information to all instances. In this scheme, persistent sessions are used. When an instance needs to access a session, it contacts the database to access the session information. It is interesting to note that, ultimately, whenever something needs to have advanced capabilities, a database is always involved. Another interesting point is that using persistent sessions merely passes the "hot potato." In such a case, the hard work to the database is offloaded, and you need to make sure that the database server(s) also have some high availability solution—something like Oracle Parallel Server or IBM's HACMP.

WebSphere Session-Tracking API

As mentioned, the interface `com.ibm.servlet.session.IBMSession` presents the programmatic interface to the IBM extension to servlet sessions. This interface provides only three methods:

- **getUserName** Returns the name of the user authenticated in conjunction with the session. The value *anonymous* is returned if no user is associated with the session.
- **isOverflow** Indicates whether the memory required for session management has overflowed (that is, whether you've exceeded the limit on the number of sessions in memory).
- **sync** Synchronizes to the database (relevant only for persistent sessions).

While this programmatic interface doesn't seem very rich, a lot more action goes on behind the scenes with the IBM implementation class for this interface. This class implements the required persistence behavior as defined in the Administrative Console settings. It also enforces some security, in the sense that a servlet cannot access a session that is associated with an authenticated user unless the servlet is operating under the same credentials (that is, unless it has been authenticated for the same user).

Personalizing WebSphere

Personalization is the process of customizing the content and behavior provided by a Web application to a specific user. Customization can be based on explicitly chosen preferences or on previous interactions with the application. The former method of customization is widely available with Web portals such as Yahoo!, whereas the latter is used by e-tailers such as Amazon.com.

The basis for both methods of personalization is collecting and maintaining information regarding users. The collection of all the pieces of information relating to one user is called a *user profile*. WebSphere provides support for maintaining user profiles. A user profile is represented by the `com.ibm.websphere.userprofile.UserProfile` interface. The base implementation for this interface includes the following data items: Address, Name, Phones, City, Nation, Employer, Fax number, Language, E-mail address, State/Province, and Postal Code. These data items represent commonly used demographic information that can be read by accessor methods such as `getCity` or `getEmail`.

Obviously, these basic data items are not sufficient for all cases. To add more fields, you can have a class extend the `UserProfile` interface and implement the `UserProfileExtender` interface. The latter interface requires that you implement the getNewColumns method, which provides an array of strings holding the names of new columns. Another way to implement your own version of user profile information is to extend the UserProfileProperties interface. This is essentially a hash table that stores pairs of names and values, similar to the way java.util.Dictionary does.

Yet another way of implementing your own user profiling is to leverage the underlying implementation. WebSphere implements the user profile as an entity EJB, and you can extend this entity bean. We won't go into detail regarding this approach now, since Enterprise JavaBeans (EJB) are explained in detail later in the book. It is worth mentioning, though, that an important advantage of extending the user profile bean is that you can import legacy data stored in a relational database into the user profiles managed on the WebSphere Application Server.

In version 4.0, you can administer user profiles manually using an XML configuration file. (This is a step backward compared to version 3.5, in which user profiles were administered from the WebSphere Administrative Console, in a fashion similar to the one in which session tracking is administered.) To enable user profile support, you need to add the file *userprofile.xml* to the *properties* directory of your WebSphere installation:

```
<?xml version="1.0"?>
<userprofile>
 <userprofile-enabled>true</userprofile-enabled>
 <userprofile-wrapper-class>
  <classname>
   com.ibm.servlet.personalization.userprofile.UserProfile
  </classname>
 </userprofile-wrapper-class>
 <userprofile-manager-name>
  User Profile Manager
 </userprofile-manager-name>
 <userprofile-bean>
  <readonly-interface>
   com.ibm.servlet.personalization.userprofile.UP_ReadOnly
  </readonly-interface>
  <readwrite-interface>
   com.ibm.servlet.personalization.userprofile.UP_ReadWrite
  </readwrite-interface>
  <readonlyhome-interface>
   com.ibm.servlet.personalization.userprofile.UP_ReadOnlyHome
  </readonlyhome-interface>
```

```
    <readwritehome-interface>
     com.ibm.servlet.personalization.userprofile.UP_ReadWriteHome
    </readwritehome-interface>
    <readonly-JNDI-lookupName>UP_ReadOnlyHome</readonly-JNDI-lookupName>
    <readwrite-JNDI-lookupName>UP_ReadWriteHome</readwrite-JNDI-lookupName>
   </userprofile-bean>
   <userprofile-store>
    <database-userid>db2admin</database-userid>
    <database-password>db2passwd</database-password>
    <database-datasource>jdbc/Profiles</database-datasource>
   </userprofile-store>
  </userprofile>
```

This file is easy to follow and includes the definition of a data wrapper class, which is `UserProfile` by default, but could be any other extension alternative that we've mentioned. In addition, you can choose the underlying EJB implementation. In fact, two separate implementations are provided: one for read-only access and another for read/write access. For each of these, you can specify the home interface, remote interface, and Java Naming Directory Interface (JNDI) name. (These terms are all related to EJB deployment, and are explained in Chapter 11 and in Part VI of the book.) Finally, you are required to provide the database user, ID, passwords, and JDBC datasource used for user-profile persistence.

After you have installed the *userprofile.xml* file, you can access user profiles fro within your enterprise applications. Note that such applications should use the default (or your own) beans for representing the user profiles. The default EJBs for profiles are located in *lib/userprofile.jar* under you WebSphere installation root.

Other IBM Servlet Extensions

When building servlets, you should be aware of some additional support provided by the WebSphere Application Server. This additional functionality is not part of the servlet specification, but it saves you from doing a lot of repetitive work.

Error Handling

Servlet errors are reported when a servlet throws an uncaught exception or when it explicitly invokes `ServletResponse.sendError`. By default, WebSphere shows an error that indicates the thread stack where the error occurred. While this information is valuable for developers, it is no help to users. (In fact, it might be a little confusing or even intimidating for a typical user to confront these error pages.)

To solve this problem, WebSphere provides the `com.ibm.websphere.servlet.error.ServletErrorReporter` class, which takes care of error handling. As a developer, you do not need to interact directly with this class. Instead, you specify a New Error Page from the Application Assembly Tool, as shown here, when assembling an application.

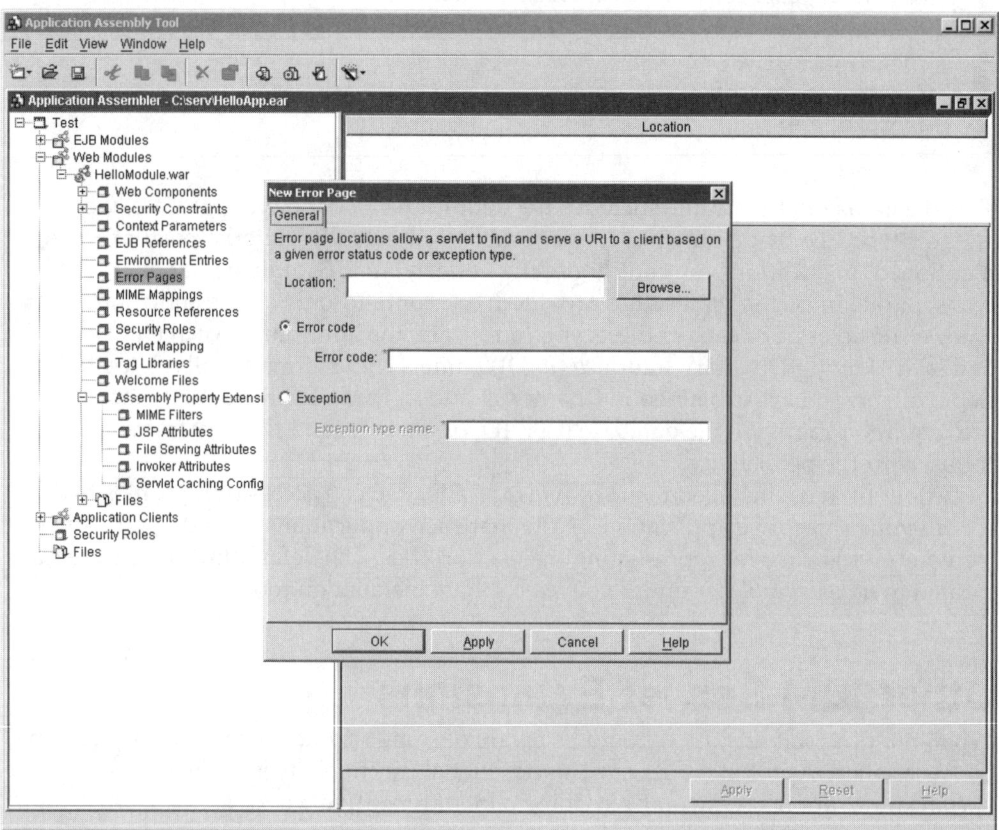

Filtering and Chaining Servlets

Multipurpose Internet Mail Extensions (MIME)-based filtering involves configuring the Web container to forward HTTP responses with a specific MIME type to a designated servlet for further processing. The servlet is designated with the Application Assembly Tool's New MIME Filter dialog box:

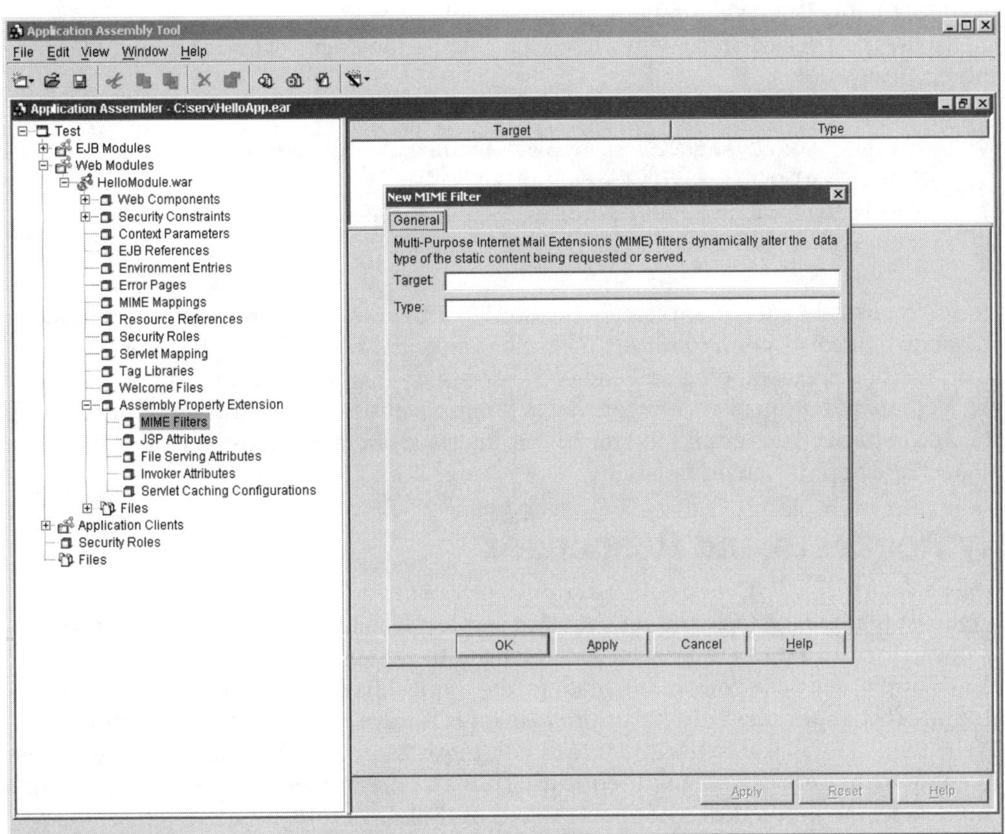

Servlet chaining is a process in which servlets forward their output and responses to other servlets for processing. This obviously promotes modularity. The mechanics of servlet chains are such that the output of one servlet is the input for the next servlet, and the last servlet in the chain returns its response to the client. To use servlet chaining, your application needs to use WebSphere's built-in servlet `com.ibm.websphere.servlet.filter.ChainerServlet`. In the initialization parameters for this servlet, you need to specify a list of URLs to be invoked under the parameter `chainer.pathlist`.

Servlet Events

The package com.ibm.websphere.servlet.event allows you to track servlet-related events—mainly those stemming from the servlet lifecycle.

To use this package from within a servlet, you use the ServletContextEventSource interface, as follows:

```
ServletContextEventSource source = (ServletContextEventSource)
    getServletContext().getAttribute(
    ServletContextEventSource.ATTRIBUTE_NAME);
source.addServletErrorListener(listener);
```

The object listener should implement the ServletListener interface, which provides methods that correspond to servlet lifecycle events: the beginning and end of the init method, the beginning and end of the destroy method, loading, and unloading.

Note that you can also define listeners for application-level events by implementing the ApplicationListener interface. This interface offers methods that allow listeners to track the application's availability.

Proxy Requests and Responses

The package com.ibm.websphere.servlet.request allows a servlet to generate a request that will be forwarded to another servlet. This is useful when a request is to be forwarded to a different servlet but you need to change something in the request. For example, suppose you want to change the request from GET to POST. Because HttpServletRequest does not provide an interface for modifying the request, WebSphere allows you to use HttpSerlvetRequestProxy. You can extend this class in any way to define your own requests. To make the request a POST request, you implement the method getMethod() so that it always returns POST. The same package also provides the class ServletInputStreamAdapter, which allows you to wrap any Java stream so that it will be used as the input stream for the servlet that takes your request.

Similarly, the package com.ibm.websphere.servlet.response supports proxies using invocations to the underlying HttpServletResponse. This is not as useful as the request proxy, but it can cache servlet responses that are not expected to change frequently. To use this package, you need to implement a response object extending the HttpServletResponseProxy. This proxy can provide an output stream using the ServletOutputStreamAdapter class to capture the output. Subsequent requests can then use the cached output.

Invoking Servlets by Name and Serving Files

WebSphere includes two built-in servlets that provide optional functionality for Web applications. The first servlet lets you access a servlet using its classname (for example,

SnoopServlet). To enable this feature, you need to enable the corresponding attribute in the Application Assembly Tool entry for Web module IBM extensions, as shown in Figure 24-6. This is not recommended, however, because it exposes what we consider to be the internals of the application and provides information that may be useful to potential hackers.

Another convenience is provided by the file-serving servlet. To enable this feature, click the File Serving Enabled checkbox in the Application Assembly Tool, shown in Figure 24-6. The effect of file serving is that files under the Web application's document root are served automatically; no additional configuration steps are required. This reduces the amount of work you must do when setting up the application in the Application Assembly Tool, since you need not explicitly configure servlets and HTML pages in the application (as long as they reside under the application document root).

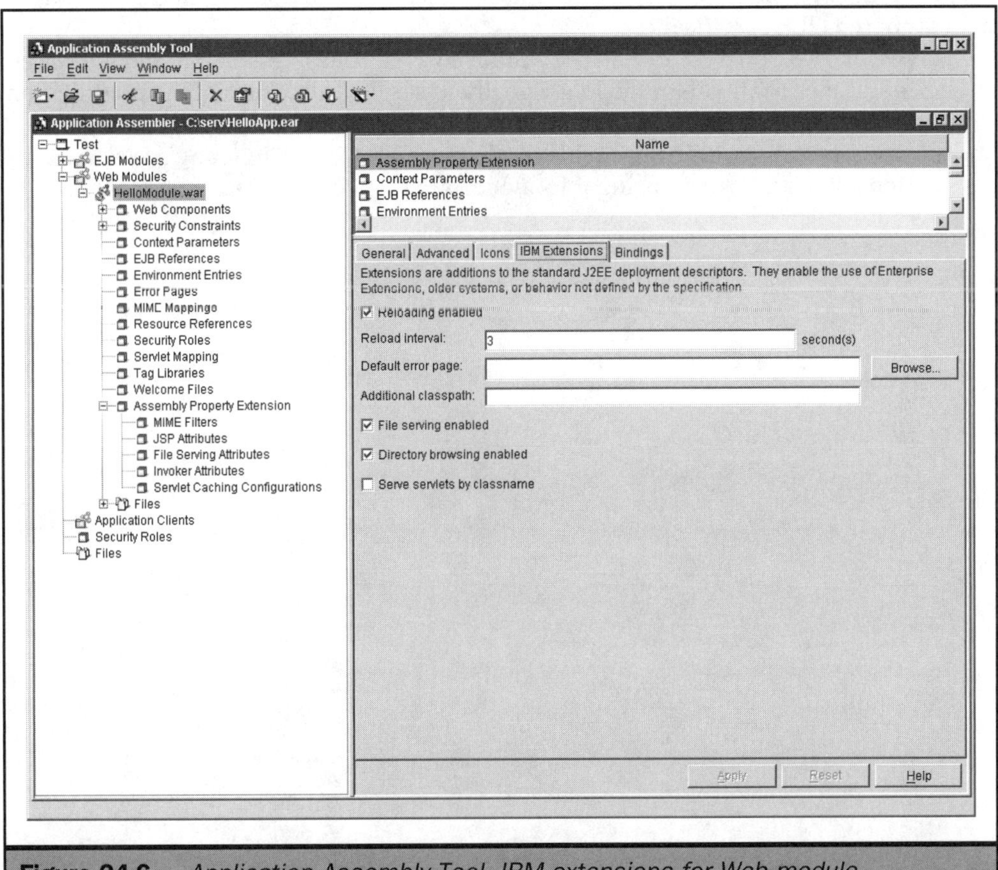

Figure 24-6. *Application Assembly Tool, IBM extensions for Web module*

Not only does the File Serving Enabled option provide great ease of use for serving out static pages, but it also may be a security risk, because any files dropped into the document root will be served out. Security measures (appropriate operating system file/directory permissions, and so on) should be taken to ensure that only the appropriate files are stored in the document root.

Summary

Servlets are among the most important constructs supported by WebSphere Application Server and the J2EE framework. They provide the entry point to practically all Web applications. It is no wonder then that so much in WebSphere helps developers management application content and session information within the context of servlets. This chapter covered these features—some of which are IBM-specific, and some that are part of the J2EE specification.

Servlets in WebSphere 4 are usually employed as central access points and interfaces to back-end functionality. Not too long ago, these servlets also formed the presentation layer in a Web application—the layer that would dynamically create the HTML to be served up to the browser. This is no longer the norm, however; in today's WebSphere applications this task is done using JSPs, which are the focus of Chapters 26 and 27.

The Complete Reference

Chapter 25

JSP Elements

JSP is the Java technology best suited for building dynamic user interfaces for Web-based applications. Such applications use presentation technologies such as Hypertext Markup Language (HTML), Dynamic HTML (DHTML), Extensible Markup Language (XML), and Java applets, while using Java server-side code for business processing. Java Server Pages (JSP) is specifically designed to support a convenient and smooth integration between these technologies by allowing dynamic content to be generated using Java server code. We have already covered the functional model and processing foundations of JSP in previous chapters; in this chapter and the next, we will delve into the details about how JSP are written and how they are deployed in WebSphere. We will start with a detailed discussion and examples illustrating the JSP tag set and functional capabilities, all the while discussing how the JSP engine performs its feats of magic. The next chapter continues with some examples of JSP.

JSP Syntax

JSP files are text files that include HTML (or XML) tags, scripts, and any other tag sets, in addition to a set of elements that conform to the JSP syntax. The syntax described here conforms to the JSP 1.1 specification. The JSP specification used in WebSphere 4.0 is JSP 1.1. The JSP specification defines two syntaxes—the standard syntax, which is based on an Active Server Pages (ASP)–like tag directive, and one that defines the tag set as an application of XML and uses XML namespaces. In XML syntax, tags imply what they are, as opposed to the standard syntax that just switches between HTML code and Java code. For example, a tag for the `include` directive following the JSP standard syntax looks like this:

```
<%@ include file="…" %>
```

The JSP XML syntax, in this case, will look like this:

```
<jsp:directive.include file="…" />
```

While it is generally better to express the JSP files as XML documents and use tags, there are also a number of disadvantages. For example, an XML document must have a single root element, while JSP pages do not have such a natural root; such a node can be defined, but it is somewhat artificial. In addition, the XML syntax is more cumbersome to use, and because one of the fundamental reasons for JSP is the fast and easy coding of Web presentations, this formalism can be a serious drawback.

The advantages of the XML syntax of JSP pages include the fact that the documents are well formatted and that they are similar to the notion of tags and attributes. This becomes crucial when you start using tag libraries, which is the direction in which the industry is going. We will talk more about tag libraries in Chapter 27. While the XML syntax may be more useful for tools and programs, the standard syntax, which we will call the *JSP syntax* throughout the rest of this chapter, is easier to use for simple programs and has become the norm for many of us who have been writing JSP pages for a long time. The specification, therefore, does not abandon the JSP syntax and neither will we.

The JSP syntax defines a number of possible elements. Anything that does not fall into one of these categories is not processed by the JSP engine and passes unchanged to the resulting page. These elements are normally called *template elements* because they usually form the presentation code into which dynamic content is injected. Each JSP element falls into one of the following categories:

- Comments
- Standard implicit objects
- Actions
- Directives
- Declarations
- Scriptlets
- Expressions
- Bean references

Comments

Comments in the JSP file follow the general pattern of comments in HTML. By embedding a line of the following form, we can pass a comment all the way to the browser page.

```
<!-- put comment here -->
```

If we require the comments to appear in the JSP but not be passed to the resulting page, we can embed a comment that follows Java conventions in a scriptlet, writing the code as follows:

```
<%-- put comment here --%>
```

Note that this does not mean the comment is passed into the Java file that is created on your behalf by the JSP engine.

Yet another way of placing comments is to use ordinary Java comments inside scriptlet elements, like this:

```
<% // put comment here %>
```

Or you can do this:

```
<% /* put comment here */ %>
```

Standard Objects

Because the JSP model follows the servlet model (and because JSPs are actually compiled into servlet code), a standard set of objects are always available. These objects can be referenced without being explicitly declared, and they form the "environment" one would expect in a servlet.

In Chapter 4, you encountered several implicitly defined JSP objects, such as `out`, `request`, and `response`. For the sake of completeness, we will briefly describe these objects again.

The `request` object is an object of type `javax.servlet.HttpServletRequest` (assuming the JSP is accessed through HTTP). The object referenced by `out` is defined by the specification to be of type `javax.servlet.jsp.JspWriter` and is similar to a servlet's print writer object. The following example uses both of these objects—in fact, it is probably the simplest possible example using them:

```
<HTML>
<BODY>
The query string passed into this URL is:<BR><B>
<%
      out.println(request.getQueryString());
%>
</B>
</BODY>
</HTML>
```

The result of accessing this JSP is shown here:

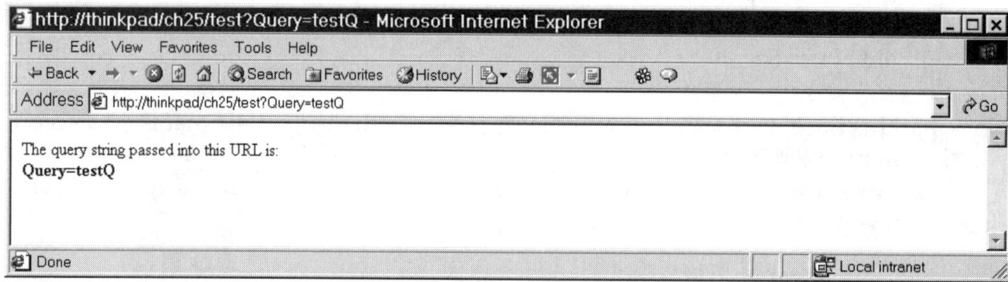

The response object is of type `javax.servlet.ServletResponse`. An equally simple example that redirects the client to another uniform resource locator (URL) is shown here:

```
<HTML>
<BODY>
<%
        response.sendRedirect("http://www.ibm.com/websphere");
%>
</BODY>
</HTML>
```

The types mentioned above are interfaces defined in the JSP specification. Because WebSphere is an implementation of the JSP standard, the actual classes used are different. To check that out, we can use a JSP:

```
<HTML>
<BODY>
<% out.println("Request is of type " + request.getClass()); %>
<BR>
<% out.println("Response is of type " + response.getClass()); %>
<BR><% out.println("Out is of type " + out.getClass()); %>
</BODY>
</HTML>
```

The output is shown here:

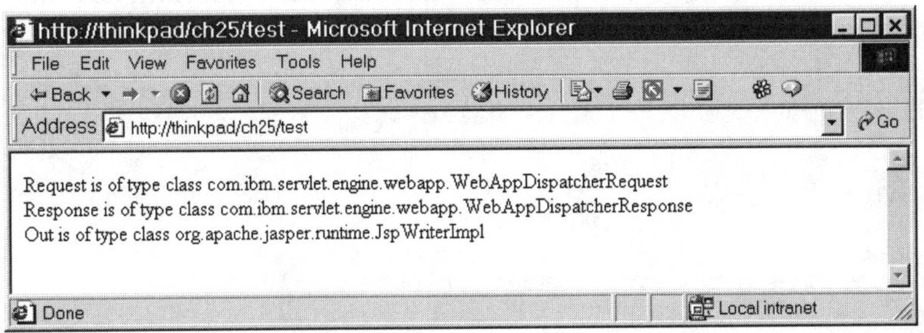

You can see that the `request` and `response` are implemented as part of the `com.ibm.servlet.engine.webapp` package, which is also used for servlets. The `out` object is taken from the `org.apache.jasper.runtime` class, which indicates that WebSphere's JSP engine is derived from the Apache/Tomcat implementation of JSP.

The JSP model provides the following other implicit objects, which essentially are derived from the underlying servlet model:

- **page** The page object can be viewed as the local this object. The page object is indeed equal to the this object when the page is instantiated. During the JSP lifecycle, the this object might not refer to the page (for example, it could refer to a subpage included within it). The page object is guaranteed to refer to the entire JSP.
- **session** The session object is an instance of HttpServletSession, which is used for session tracking and for storing objects shared throughout the session.
- **application** The application object is the ServletContext object of the generated servlet.
- **config** The config object is an instance for ServletConfig that provides access for the initialization parameters for the JSP.
- **exception** The exception object is a Java object that is available only in pages that were designated as error pages (using the errorPage directive explained in the next section). For such pages, the exception object holds the exception thrown from the previous page.
- **pageContext** The pageContext object is a container holding the request, response, application, config, session, and out objects. The page context provides an updated view of the current execution context for the page.

JSP Directives

JSP directives are instructions to the JSP engine. They comprise a set of specifications that tell the JSP engine what to compile into the generated servlet and how to compile it. Directives can take a JSP syntax or an XML syntax. The JSP syntax is

```
<%@ directive_name attribute="value" %>
```

The XML syntax is

```
<jsp:directive.directive_name attribute="value" />
```

The most important is the page directive, which allows you to set attributes that are page specific. The `language` attribute specifies which language is being used for the scripting. For JSP, the only legal value of the `language` attribute is `java`; anything else will cause the JSP engine to fail. This is also the default value; so until other languages are supported, this tag is of little practical use. The rest of the attributes for this directive define how the generated servlet class will look and how it will behave. The general syntax for the page directive is as follows:

```
<%@ page
language=<scriptingLanguage>
   extends=<className>
   import=<importList>
   session=<true|false>
   buffer=<none|sizekb>
   autoFlush=<true|false>
   isThreadSafe=<true|false>
   info=<info_text>
   errorPage=<error_url>
   isErrorPage=<true|false>
   contentType=<ctinfo>
%>
```

The import attribute tells the JSP engine what import statements to include in the generated code. Because the JSP engine first processes the JSP file and creates a Java class for the servlet and only then compiles it, import statements are useful in that they allow code inserted later in the JSP file to use shorthand when it references Java classes. By default, the java.lang.*, java.servlet.*, javax.servlet.http.*, and javax.servlet.jsp.* are imported. For example, the following directive allows you to use the IBM XML parser classes and the DOM classes within your JSP:

```
<%@ page import="com.ibm.xml.parser.*,org.w3c.dom.*" %>
```

Note that, just as with Java code, import statements should refer to classes and packages that can be found in the classpath.

Similarly, the extends attribute tells the JSP engine which class whether it should be the superclass of the generated servlet class. The use of this attribute is generally discouraged because it limits the Web container in the way it implements the servlet that corresponds to the JSP.

The contentType attribute informs the JSP engine what content type to use for the response stream. Setting the latter is equivalent to invoking response.setContentType.

Other attributes of the page directive are as follows:

- **autoFlush** Determines the behavior of the page when the buffer is full or exceeded. This is by default set to true, meaning that content is flushed once the buffer is exceeded. If it is set to false, an exception is raised once the buffer is exceeded.

- **buffer** Determines whether the page is buffered and, if so, what the buffer size is. If it is set to none, the page is not buffered. Sizes can be specified in kilobytes—for example, 32k.
- **errorPage** Specifies a URL to be invoked in case of uncaught exceptions.
- **info** Defines a string that is returned by the getServletInfo method of the generated servlet.
- **isErrorPage** Set to false by default. Setting it to true means the page is used as an error page. In this case, the page can use the implicit exception object for accessing the error information.
- **isThreadSafe** Informs the JSP compiler about the page's thread safety. This is set by default to true. If it is set to false, multiple invocations of the same page will be handled in a serial fashion, based on the order of their arrival.
- **session** Indicates whether the current page participates in a session. It is set by default to true. If it is set to false, the session implicit object is not defined.

One special directive that was introduced in the JSP 1.1 specification is the `taglib` directive, which allows you to extend the set of JSP tags. This directive has two attributes: `uri` and `prefix`. The former is a uniform resource identifier (URI) pointing to a Java Archive (JAR) file that holds a tag library descriptor describing the new tags. The `prefix` attribute indicates the keyword that is used to represent the new tags in the page. For example, the following directive allows using a special set of tags with the prefix `viryanet`:

```
<% taglib uri="http://www.viryanet.com/taglib/viryatags.jar"
prefix="viryanet" %>
```

If we had a tag named `serviceCall` defined in the tag library descriptor, we could use it as follows:

```
<viryanet:serviceCall>Call 911</viryanet:serviceCall>
```

Note *Tag libraries and the `taglib` directive are the subject of Chapter 27, and they will be discussed in detail there.*

Declarations

Java *declarations*—variables and methods—can be added to the JSP file. Declarations can take a JSP syntax or an XML syntax. These are

```
<%! java code %>
```

The XML syntax is

```
<jsp:declaration> code </jsp:declaration>
```

All such code will be added to the servlet class generated from the JSP and is, therefore, available anywhere within the class. Contrary to scriptlets and expressions, the code is not placed in the service method of the servlet but rather as part of the class definition. This allows you to add methods and class member variables to the generated servlet class.

Scriptlets and Expressions

JSP include a convenient syntax in which Java code can be written. By enclosing Java code within `<%` and `%>` tags, we tell the JSP engine to copy this code into the servlet processing method. Such code segments are called *scriptlets*. In addition, a similar syntax allows you to define expressions that are evaluated by the servlet and written to the output stream. Expressions differ from scriptlets in that the opening tag uses `<%=`, and the embedded code is viewed as an expression that produces a value. Since the expression is embedded in Java code, writing the expression to the output stream should not be terminated with a semicolon (`;`).

For example, consider the following JSP:

```
<HTML><BODY>
<% int i = 6; %>
<% i = i + 1; %>
The value of <B>i</B> is
<%= i %>
</BODY>
</HTML>
```

This JSP uses simple Java code to set the variable `i` and increment it. It uses an expression to output its value. The output for this JSP is shown here:

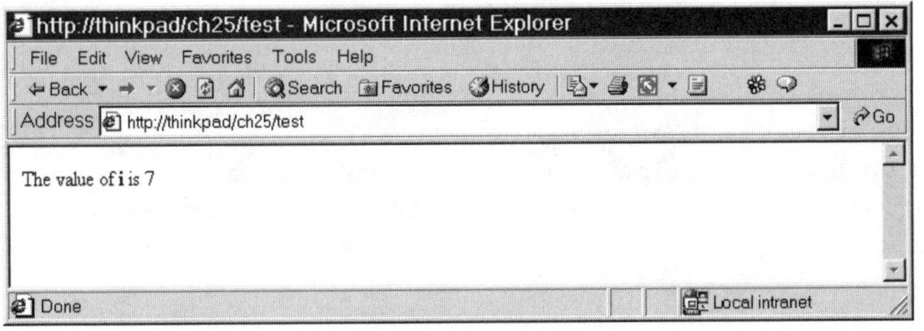

One interesting thing to note regarding scriptlets is that you can truly mix HTML output and Java source together—to a level that is slightly surprising. For example, consider the following page:

```
<HTML>
<BODY>
This is an example of what happens to a scriptlet in the output.
Notice how the line will be missing when we observe the resulting
HTML's
source.
<% int i = 1; %>
<BR/>
This is an even better example.
Based on how the scriptlet code segments evaluate
we get different lines that are really part of the HTML:
<BR/>
<% if (i == 1) { %>
i really does equal 1
<% } else { %>
i does not equal 1
<% } %>
</BODY>
</HTML>
```

In the following simple JSP file, you should notice two things. The first is that when you compare the JSP to the resulting HTML page, the lines almost completely match, but there are blank lines where the scriptlets appeared originally:

```
<HTML>
<BODY>
This is an example of what happens to a scriptlet in the output.
Notice how the line will be missing when we observe the resulting
HTML's
source.

<BR/>
This is an even better example.
Based on how the scriptlet code segments evaluate
we get different lines that are really part of the HTML:
<BR/>
```

```
i really does equal 1

</BODY>
</HTML>
```

The second interesting thing is that the "if" clause is actually written using a set of scriptlets, but the actual output of both the `then` and the `else` are in HTML. Therefore, we are writing one piece of code that combines not only programming languages but also two completely different processing models in one clause. The output of this JSP is shown here:

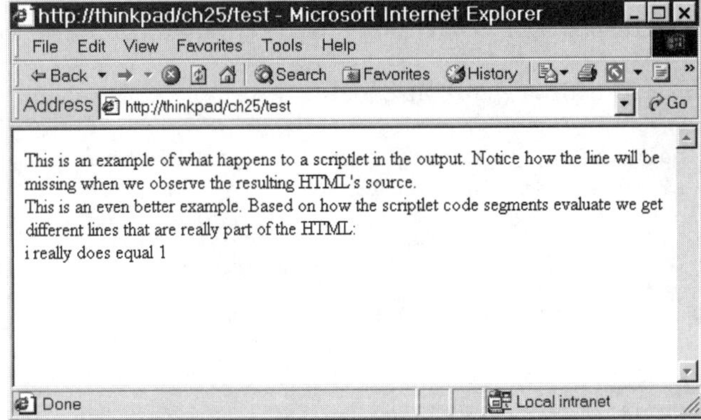

The key to understanding how such a thing works is in the generated Java servlet code shown here:

```
import javax.servlet.*;
import javax.servlet.http.*;
import javax.servlet.jsp.*;
import javax.servlet.jsp.tagext.*;
import java.io.PrintWriter;
import java.io.IOException;
import java.io.InputStream;
import java.io.ObjectInputStream;
import java.util.Vector;
import org.apache.jasper.runtime.*;
import java.beans.*;
import org.apache.jasper.JasperException;
import java.io.ByteArrayOutputStream;
import org.apache.jasper.compiler.ibmtsx.*;
import org.apache.jasper.compiler.ibmdb.*;
```

```
import java.sql.SQLException;


public class test_jsp_10 extends HttpJspBase {

    static char[][] _jspx_html_data = null;

    static {
    }
    public test_jsp_10( ) {
    }

    private static boolean _jspx_inited = false;

    private static boolean checkedAttributeIgnoreException = false;

    private static boolean throwException = true;

    public final void _jspx_init() throws JasperException {
        ObjectInputStream oin = null;
        int numStrings = 0;
        try {
            InputStream fin =
this.getClass().getClassLoader().getResourceAsStream("test_jsp_10.dat");
            oin = new ObjectInputStream(fin);
            _jspx_html_data = (char[][]) oin.readObject();
        } catch (Exception ex) {
            throw new JasperException("Unable to open data file");
        } finally {
            if (oin != null)
                try { oin.close(); } catch (IOException ignore) { }
        }
    }

    public void _jspService(HttpServletRequest request, HttpServletResponse
response)
        throws IOException, ServletException {

        JspFactory _jspxFactory = null;
        PageContext pageContext = null;
        HttpSession session = null;
        ServletContext application = null;
        ServletConfig config = null;
        JspWriter out = null;
        Object page = this;
        String  _value = null;
```

```
        setBooleanIgnoreException();
        try {

            if (_jspx_inited == false) {
                _jspx_init();
                _jspx_inited = true;
            }
            _jspxFactory = JspFactory.getDefaultFactory();
            response.setContentType("text/html;charset=Cp1252");
            pageContext = _jspxFactory.getPageContext(this,
              request, response,
                  "", true, 8192, true);
            application = pageContext.getServletContext();
            config = pageContext.getServletConfig();
            session = pageContext.getSession();
            out = pageContext.getOut();

            // begin
[file="C:\\WebSphere\\AppServer/installedApps\\ch25.ear/ch25.war\\\test.jsp"
;from=(0,0);to=(5,0)]
                out.print(_jspx_html_data[0]);
            // end
            // begin
[file="C:\\WebSphere\\AppServer/installedApps\\ch25.ear/ch25.war\\\test.jsp"
;from=(5,2);to=(5,14)]
                 int i = 1;
            // end
            // begin
[file="C:\\WebSphere\\AppServer/installedApps\\ch25.ear/ch25.war\\\test.jsp"
;from=(5,16);to=(11,0)]
                out.print(_jspx_html_data[1]);
            // end
            // begin
[file="C:\\WebSphere\\AppServer/installedApps\\ch25.ear/ch25.war\\\test.jsp
;from=(11,2);to=(11,17)]
                 if (i == 1) {
            // end
            // begin
[file="C:\\WebSphere\\AppServer/installedApps\\ch25.ear/ch25.war\\\test.jsp
;from=(11,19);to=(13,0)]
                out.print(_jspx_html_data[2]);
            // end
            // begin
[file="C:\\WebSphere\\AppServer/installedApps\\ch25.ear/ch25.war\\\test.jsp
;from=(13,2);to=(13,12)]
                 } else {
```

```
            // end
            // begin
[file="C:\\WebSphere\\AppServer/installedApps\\ch25.ear/ch25.war\\\test.jsp
;from=(13,14);to=(15,0)]
                out.print(_jspx_html_data[3]);
            // end
            // begin
[file="C:\\WebSphere\\AppServer/installedApps\\ch25.ear/ch25.war\\\test.jsp
;from=(15,2);to=(15,5)]
                  }
            // end
            // begin
[file="C:\\WebSphere\\AppServer/installedApps\\ch25.ear/ch25.war\\\test.jsp
;from=(15,7);to=(18,0)]
                out.print(_jspx_html_data[4]);
            // end

        } catch (Exception ex) {
            if (out.getBufferSize() != 0)
                out.clearBuffer();
            pageContext.handlePageException(ex);
        } catch ( Throwable t) {
            if (out.getBufferSize() != 0)
                out.clearBuffer();
            pageContext.handlePageException(new Exception(t.getMessage()));
        } finally {
            out.flush();
            _jspxFactory.releasePageContext(pageContext);
        }
    }
    private void setBooleanIgnoreException() {
        if (checkedAttributeIgnoreException) return;
        checkedAttributeIgnoreException = true;
        String initParamIgnoreException =
          (String)(getServletConfig().getInitParameter
                ("jsp.repeatTag.ignoreException"));
        if ((initParamIgnoreException != null) &&
   (initParamIgnoreException.toLowerCase().equals("true"))){
            throwException = false;
        }
    }
}
```

Let's look at the implementation of the `_jspService` method—the method that performs the action on behalf of the JSP and writes the output. This method calls `out.print` to print out the HTML data, which is stored in a special data array called _jspx_html_data that is initialized in the _jspx_init method. Effectively, what we have in this method is a series of commands that are a mix of Java commands (the code within the scriptlets in the JSP) and calls to out.print. The latter calls effectively write the HTML from the JSP source file to the output stream of the servlet. This combination of Java code and copy code is the most important aspect of the code generation process performed by the servlet engine. It is interesting to note that the Java servlet code generated for the JSP is in many ways a mirror image of the JSP. In the JSP, the scriptlets embed the Java code that is an "outsider" to the HTML code. In the generated servlet, the Java code from the scriptlets forms the "native" code, while the HTML code is copied in from the JSP source.

JSP Actions

JSP actions are used only in the XML-based syntax, as shown here:

```
<jsp:action-name attribute="value" />.
```

While different actions have different attributes, all actions share two common attributes: id and scope. The id attribute allows the JSP developer to uniquely name the action element, thus providing a way to reference it from within the page. The scope attribute determines the lifetime of the action element. It can take four different values: page, request, session, and application. As you can imagine, these values all correspond to implicit objects in the JSP. When the scope attribute is set to page, the object created by the action tag is accessible only as part of the page in which it was created. Objects with request scope are shared by pages serving the same request, and are released only upon completion of the request. Objects declared with session scope are associated with the session of the page in which they were created, so they are shared by all pages that are processing a request in the same session. Such objects are released once the session is done. Objects with application scope are available throughout all the pages that belong to the same Web application.

JSP actions provide a way to instantiate and use JavaBeans. JavaBeans are reusable Java components and are covered in Chapter 10. If you are not familiar with the concept of JavaBeans, for the purpose of the discussion here, consider them to be Java objects that have a set of attributes. Each of these attributes can be retrieved using a get method and set using a set method. The useBean action is used to find or create a new JavaBean instance. Note that this action does not simply instantiate a bean; it first looks to see whether there is another bean already defined with the same scope, based on the specified attributes. This provides a simple yet powerful mechanism for sharing objects within a session or a Web application. The useBean action creates a new scripting variable with the name specified in the id attribute. This variable can later be used in the page.

In addition to the common id and scope attributes, the useBean action has three attributes:

- **class** The Java implementation class for the bean
- **type** A Java type to which the bean should conform (that is, the class, a superclass, or an interface that it implements)
- **beanName** Chosen by the bean developer, the name of the bean, which is part of the JavaBean model and loosely corresponds to the notion of the implementation class

Either the type attribute or the class attribute must be specified. If both are specified, the class provided must conform to the type provided. When you use the beanName, the class attribute cannot be used, but the type attribute must be used. That is, it is not allowed to specify just the beanName without any type attribute.

Two additional actions allow you to set and get properties of beans. These are the setProperty and getProperty actions, respectively. The setProperty action can be used with a name attribute to indicate the bean, a property attribute to indicate the property to be modified, and a value attribute to indicate the value to be used. Note that the value itself could be a JSP expression such as the following:

```
<%= "Today is " + new Date() %>
```

Another way is to use the setProperty action with the param attribute instead of the value attribute. This way, the value is taken from the request (the HttpServletRequest object) parameter of the respective name. When you want to set a bean property to a request parameter that happens to have the same name as the bean property, the property attribute can be omitted from the setProperty action. That is, only the name and param need to be specified. A nice feature of the setProperty action is that it allows an asterisk (*) to be used as a wildcard, which means that all properties whose names match a request parameter shall be assigned the value of the parameter.

The getProperty action is simpler and has only one form. It takes two parameters, both mandatory. These are the bean name and the property name. The action translates into a string: if the attribute is not of string type, the toString method is implicitly used to convert the object to a string.

Another kind of action is the include action. This action is used to insert the output of other pages into the current page. Such pages might be static like HTML pages, or dynamic like JSP pages. When this action is encountered, the execution of the JSP is paused and the included page takes over. The include directive has two required attributes: page and flush. The first defines the page to be included (which must be a relative URL on the same server); the second indicates whether or not the included page and its buffer must be flushed before they are included. In JSP 1.0, this value must be true due to some limitations in the underlying servlet model. In the earlier section "JSP Syntax," we discussed the include directive, which is very much different from the include action. The include directive takes the specified page and inserts it into the JSP prior to compilation.

To illustrate these actions, consider the following JSP:

```
<HTML>
<HEAD><TITLE>JSP Session Date</TITLE></HEAD>
<BODY><H1>Date Example</H1>
<jsp:useBean id="mydate" scope="session" class="java.util.Date" />
<jsp:useBean id="pagedate" scope="page" class="java.util.Date" />
<H2>Date (Session scope): </H2>
<I>Day:</I>
<jsp:getProperty name="mydate" property="date" />
<I>Month:</I>
<jsp:getProperty name="mydate" property="month" />
<I>Year: </I>
<jsp:getProperty name="mydate" property="year" />
<I>Hours:</I>
<jsp:getProperty name="mydate" property="hours" />
<I>Minutes:</I>
<jsp:getProperty name="mydate" property="minutes" />
<H2>Date: </H2>
<%= pagedate.toString() %>
</BODY>
</HTML>
```

This JSP declares a JavaBean object that instantiates the class java.util.Date, which uses session scope. Then it declares another date object with page scope and outputs both. The effect is that we are able to capture the date when the session began, as well as the current date. The output of this JSP is shown here:

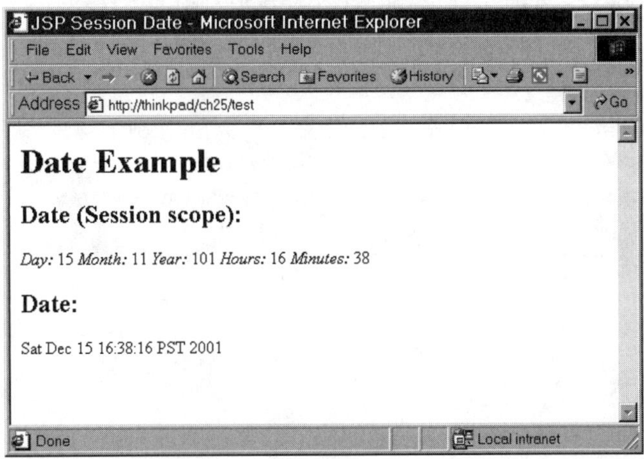

If you click the browser's Refresh button, you'll see a similar output; but the first time remains the same, whereas the latter one changes to the current time.

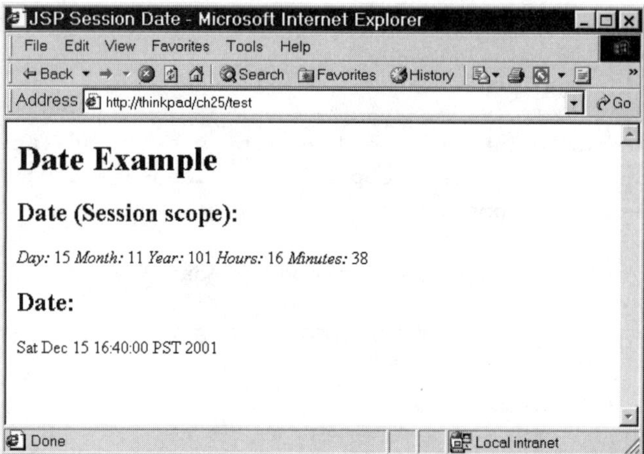

Now consider splitting this JSP into two parts. The first part is shown in a revised version of the *SessionDate.jsp* page, from Chapter 7, which uses the `include` action:

```
<HTML>
<HEAD><TITLE>JSP Session Date</TITLE></HEAD>
<BODY><H1>Date Example</H1>
<jsp:include page="/PrintDate.jsp" />
<H2>Date (Session scope): </H2>
<I>Day:</I>
<jsp:getProperty name="mydate" property="date" />
<I>Month:</I>
<jsp:getProperty name="mydate" property="month" />
<I>Year: </I>
<jsp:getProperty name="mydate" property="year" />
<I>Hours:</I>
<jsp:getProperty name="mydate" property="hours" />
<I>Minutes:</I>
<jsp:getProperty name="mydate" property="minutes" />
<H2>Date: </H2>
<%= pagedate.toString() %>
</BODY>
</HTML>
```

The *PrintDate.jsp* page is used to retrieve the date:

```
<HTML><BODY>
<jsp:useBean id="mydate" scope="session" class="java.util.Date" />
</BODY>
</HTML>
```

The latter page makes use of the `useBean` and `getProperty` actions in order to retrieve the bean called `mydate` and the date from it. The second page is able to retrieve the information because it shares the session with the first page. The output for this page is identical, but what goes on behind the scenes is completely different. The *PrintDate.jsp* page is executed and then embedded into the output for the whole page. This specific example on the `include` action doesn't seem that useful; but in general, it and the `include` directive are useful for promoting reusability of pages and page fragments.

Two other actions are the `forward` action and the `plugin` action. The `forward` action can be used to forward a request to a different page. It has one parameter, called `page`, which contains the URL to which the request is to be forwarded. Again, this must be a relative URL on the same server. The `plugin` action is used to insert Java components (either JavaBeans or applets) into the page. These components are embedded into the page and executed on the client side in the client Java Runtime Environment (JRE), typically of the browser. The `plugin` action is analogous to embedding applets into HTML pages. Since some components behave slightly differently under different browsers, this action actually has support for browser-specific definitions. The `plugin` action takes the following attributes:

- **type** The type is either an applet or a JavaBean.
- **jrerevision** Minimal revision of JRE is required on client side (the default is 1.1).
- **iepluginurl** The URL where a version of the component compatible with Microsoft Internet Explorer is found. (If it is not available in the client cache, it is downloaded.)
- **nspluginurl** The URL where a corresponding version of Netscape Navigator can be found.
- **code, align, archive, height, hspace, name, vspace, title, width** These correspond to the HTML parameters used with the `codebase` tag for applets.

IBM JSP Support

In contrast to previous versions of the WebSphere Application Server, version 4.0 does not include a lot of IBM-specific JSP features. This is probably due to the fact that with

Java 2 Platform Enterprise Edition (J2EE) compliance, all aspects of the application server moved toward some standardization.

This is not to say there are no special features provided by IBM, but that there are only a few. For starters, all the special servlet features provided in WebSphere (and detailed in Chapter 24) apply to JSP as well, because all JSP pages are converted into servlets.

IBM JSP Tags

In WebSphere Application Server 3.5, IBM introduced a special family of tags that can be used for variable data. These are essentially extensions of the standard JSP bean actions that allow data retrieved from a database to be used easily. The prefix for these tags is `tsx`. These tags are supported in version 4.0. Although WebSphere 3.5 is using a different JSP specification, namely 1.0, the JSP 1.1 specification requires backward compatibility with JSP 1.0; so these work with no changes in version 4.0.

The `tsx:dbconnect` tag is used for establishing the database connection, and its attributes are as follows:

- **id** The id of the bean representing the connection
- **userid** The database user id, which can also be specified using the tsx:userid tag
- **passwd** The database user password, which can be also specified using the tsx:userid tag
- **url** The Java Database Connectivity (JDBC) URL for the database
- **driver** The JDBC driver for the database

The `tsx:dbquery` tag is used to perform a Structured Query Language (SQL) query using a given connection. Its attributes are `id`, which is the id of the bean representing the output `ResultSet`; `connection`, which provides the id of the connection bean; and an optional attribute `limit`, which indicates the maximal number of rows to be returned. The body of the `tsx:dbquery` tag includes the SQL query to be performed.

The following JSP fragment demonstrates the use of these two tags:

```
<tsx:dbconnect id="con", userid="db2admin", passwd="db2admin"
 url="jdbc:db2:database", driver="com.ibm.db2.jdbc.app.DB2Driver"/>
<tsx:dbquery id="query" conncetion="con">
select name,phone from phonetable
</tsx:dbquery>
```

So now you have a connection and a query. What next? Well, you can use the `tsx:repeat` tag and the `tsx:getProperty` tag to actually retrieve the information from the query. The `tsx:repeat` tag iterates over each of the rows in the query result, and the `tsx:getProperty` tag allows you to retrieve a certain column out of the current row.

The tsx.repeat tag takes three optional parameters: index, which identifies the index (or the current row) inside the repeat block; start, which indicates the starting index value for the block (the default is 0); and end, an optional ending value of the index, which must be higher than start. The tsx:getProperty tag has a name attribute that indicates the query to which it relates and a property name.

Continuing with the preceding JSP fragment, we can use the query to show a list of names and phone numbers:

```
<tsx:repeat index=ind>
<B>Name:</B>
<tsx:getProperty name="query" property="name" />
<B>Phone:</B>
<tsx:getProperty name="query" property="phone" />
</tsx:repeat>
```

This set of tags essentially provides syntactic sugar for avoiding the explicit use of JDBC for database access. It is quite powerful in the sense that you can nest repeat tags and modify the database using the tsx:modify tag, which is similar to tsx:dbquery only in that it updates the database. It is also has the same format and usage as taglibs, which will be discussed in Chapter 27.

Deployment Issues

The IBM JSP processor creates and compiles a servlet for each JSP file. The Java source file corresponding to a JSP is placed in the following directory:

```
<WebSphere Installation
Dir>\temp\<hostname>\<servername>\<webmodulename>
```

The associated *.class* and *.dat* files are placed in the same directory. (The *.dat* file holds the static parts of the JSP—the same ones that are stored in the _jspx_html_data array, mentioned previously.)

Using the Application Assembly Tool, you can set the following attributes for each JSP. These attributes are stored in the IBM extensions XML file for the Web module, ibm-web-ext.xmi:

- **keepgenerated** Indicates whether the generated Java file is to be kept (possible values are true or false). Note that even when specifying false, the Java file is generated and placed in the ibm-web-ext.xmi directory. If you're quick enough, you will see it appear and disappear.
- **scratchdir** Allows you to specify a different directory for placing the *.class*, *.java*, and *.dat* files than the *temp* directory under the WebSphere installation directory.

- **defaultEncoding** The default encoding used in the absence of a *contentType* directive. If this element does not exist, the system property file.encoding is used.
- **jsp.repeatTag.ignoreException** Allows you to control some peculiar behavior exhibited in previous releases by the <tsx:repeat> tag. The implementation of this tag caught various exceptions and did not throw them, thus causing unexpected results. The default for this tag is false, but you can set it to true in order to provide backward compatibility for pages developed under older versions of WebSphere.

An interesting caveat to note is that once a Web application is deployed, you can modify the JSP pages under the Web module directory. This would cause the JSP engine to generate the servlets again and compile them. This might come in very handy during the development process and when you have to debug your code. It is, however, a dangerous thing to have in a production environment.

One more nonstandard feature offered by IBM is the batch compiling of JSP files. The idea here is to provide faster response in the first access made to your JSP pages; this is desirable because by default, the initial request would trigger the process of generating the servlet and compiling it. This feature is enabled when setting the Load on Startup feature in the Application Assembly Tool.

Summary

Among all WebSphere technologies, JSP is probably the one most heavily used by developers. JSP pages are used as the user interface layer in most Web applications; and therefore, they are used frequently. Most projects create a large number of JSP pages. Mastering JSP is therefore an important part of WebSphere development. This chapter provided more information on JSP pages and specifically focused on their tag set.

JSPs are continuously evolving, and it is important to keep up with the latest JSP technologies. To this end, we will continue working with JSP pages throughout the next two chapters. The next chapter discusses some more complex examples of JSP programming and deployment; and Chapter 27 discusses the next "great thing"—tag libraries.

The Complete Reference

Chapter 26

JSP Examples

The previous chapters discussed in detail various aspects of JavaServer Page (JSP) programming. This chapter provides a number of examples for JSP-based applications. The "Hello World" example from Chapter 4 and the examples from Chapter 25 gave you an idea of how to develop JSPs. This chapter aims to deepen your understanding.

Number Factoring JSP

The first example looks at a simple arithmetic problem: factoring integer numbers. The JSP we will build prompts the user to enter an integer number and factors all the integers from 2 up to that number.

This example shows how Java control-flow constructs can be combined neatly with JSP tags. We can close scriptlets in the middle of a `for` or `while` statement, place some HTML text, and continue the scriptlet after that to complete the loop statement. This was the preferred method for writing JSPs until the advent of taglibs, which are discussed in Chapter 27, and we recommend that you separate your Java scriptlets from the HTML elements as much as possible, as long as the code does not become completely unreadable.

```
<HTML>
<HEAD><TITLE>Number Factoring</TITLE></HEAD>
<BODY>
<%
      String param = request.getParameter("number");
      if (param == null) {
%>
            <H1>Enter a number:</H1>
            <FORM action="factor.jsp">
            Number:<INPUT type="text" name="number" title="Number:">
            </FORM>
<%
      }
      else {
            int number;

            try {
                  number = new Integer(param).intValue();
            }
            catch (Exception ex) {
                  number = 0;
            }
```

```
            if (number <= 0) {
%>
            <H1><FONT color="0x0000ff">Please Enter a Positive
                                       Number</FONT></H1>
            <FORM action="factor.jsp">
            Number:<INPUT type="text" name="number" title="Number:">
            </FORM>
<%

            }
            else {
%>
            <H1>Factors of numbers up to <%= number %> are:</H1>
            <TABLE cellpadding="0" border="1">
<%
                  for (int i = 2; i < number; i++) {
                        boolean isPrime = true;
%>
            <TR><TD>Factors of <%= i %></TD>
<%
                        for (int j = 2; j <= i / 2; j++) {
                              if (((i / j) * j) == i) {
                                    isPrime = false;
%>
                        <TD><%= j %></TD>
<%
                              }
                        }
                        if (isPrime) {
%>
                              <TD><FONT color="0xff0000">Prime</FONT></TD>
<%
                        }
%>
            </TR>
<%
                  }
            }
      }
%>
</BODY>
</HTML>
```

When this JSP is invoked, the output consists of a form with a single field, as shown here:

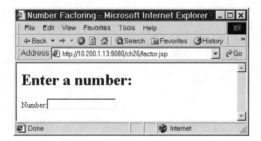

After the user enters the number **26** in the text field, the JSP provides the output shown in Figure 26-1. As you can see, the label "Prime" is shown for each prime number, and the integer factors are shown for the rest of the numbers.

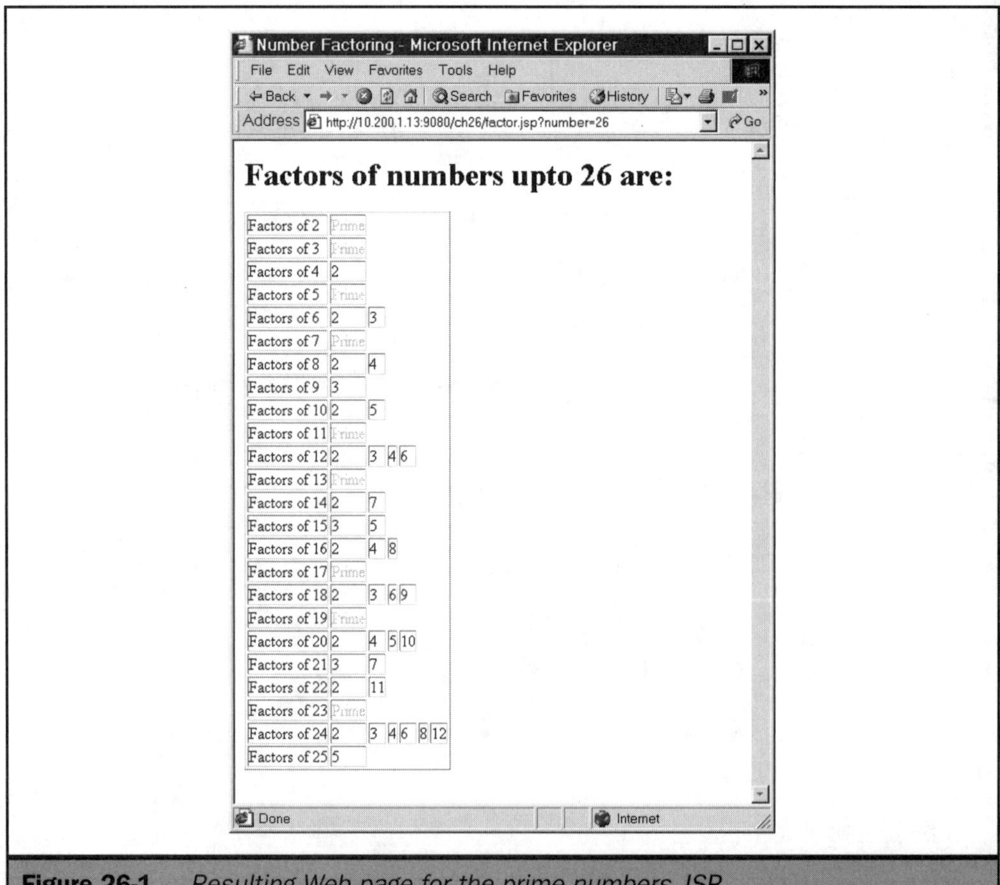

Figure 26-1. *Resulting Web page for the prime numbers JSP*

Biological Sequence Alignment JSP

Our next JSP example is from the domain of bioinformatics. *Bioinformatics* is a scientific discipline that combines biology, computer science, and mathematics in a quest to analyze the vast amounts of biological data collected in recent years.

This example focuses on proteins. Proteins are polymers. In other words, they are built from smaller building blocks, called amino acids. The standard way to represent a protein is as a sequence of letters, each of which represents an amino acid.

Consider a database table in which we store a collection of proteins. The columns of the table are as follows:

- **ID** The integer ID number for the protein, which is internal to our own database
- **LEN** The length of the sequence
- **SEQ** The sequence (a string of length LEN)
- **NAME** The full name of the protein
- **IDINSOURCE** The code name of the protein in the source database (that is, the database from which we will extract the information.

The source database we use is called *SWISSPROT*, and it is available at *http://www.expasy.ch/sprot*.

The first JSP in this section retrieves information from the database table using Java Database Connectivity (JDBC) and shows it in HTML format. When the page is invoked, it outputs a form into which a protein ID can be typed. When the form is submitted, the same JSP is invoked with the protein to be shown, and a database search is performed to retrieve the data.

```
<%@ page import="java.sql.*" %>
<%@ page import="java.net.URL" %>
<%@ page import="java.io.*" %>

<HTML>
<HEAD><TITLE>Protein Data</TITLE></HEAD>
<BODY>
<%
      Connection con;
      java.sql.Statement state = null;
      String param = request.getParameter("proteinid");
      if (param == null) {
%>
      <H1>Enter Protein ID:</H1>
      <FORM action="protein.jsp">
      ID:<INPUT type="text" name="proteinid">
      <BR>
      <INPUT type="submit">
      </FORM>
```

```
<%
      }
      else {
            int number;

            try {
                  number = new Integer(param).intValue();
            }
            catch (Exception ex) {
                  number = 0;
            }

            if (number <= 0) {
%>
      <H1>Enter Protein ID:</H1>
      <FORM action="protein.jsp">
      ID:<INPUT type="text" name="proteinid">
      <BR>
      <INPUT type="submit">
      </FORM>
<%
            }
            else {
                  int protein=number;

                   try {
                      String url = "jdbc:oracle:thin@dbhost:1521:proteindb";

                      // Load Oracle driver
                      Class.forName("oracle.jdbc.driver.OracleDriver");

                      // Perform DB connection
                      con = DriverManager.getConnection(url,"protuser","");

                       // Create a statement
                      state = con.createStatement();
                  }
                  catch (SQLException ex) {
                        return;
                  }
                  ResultSet rs = state.executeQuery(
                      "select * from proteins where id =" + number + ";")
                  if (!rs.next() ) {
%>
            <FONT color="#FF2020">Error: this protein does not exist</FONT>
```

```
            <%
                  }
                  else {
                       String protIDinSource = rs.getString("idinsource");
                      String protName =  rs.getString("name");
                      int protLen = rs.getInt("len");
                     String sequence = rs.getString("seq");
%>
                  <BODY bgcolor="# E9F800" topmargin="0" leftmargin="8"
                        rightmargin="8" marginheight="0" marginwidth="8">
                  <BR>
                  <TABLE  cellpadding="0" cellspacing="0" width="100%"
                          border="0">
                    <TR><TD bgcolor="#418A76">
                        <TABLE cellpadding="4" cellspacing="1"
                               width="100%" border="0">
                              <TR bgcolor="#DCF0E4">
                                    <TD colspan="2">
                                    <B></H2>Protein ID <%= protein%></H2>
                                    </B></TD>
                              </TR>
                              <TR bgcolor="# E9F800">
                                    <TD><B>Swissprot ID</B></TD>
                                    <TD><%= protIDinSource%></TD>
                              </TR>
                              </TR>
                              <TR bgcolor="# E9F800">
                                    <TD><B>Name</B></TD>
                                    <TD><%= protName%></TD>
                              </TR>
                              <TR bgcolor="#E9F800">
                                    <TD><B>Length in amino acids</B></TD>
                                    <TD><%= protLen%></TD>
                              </TR>
                        </TABLE>
                     </TD></TR>
                  </TABLE>
<%
                        }
            }
      }
%>
</BODY>
</HTML>
```

The form for this JSP is as follows:

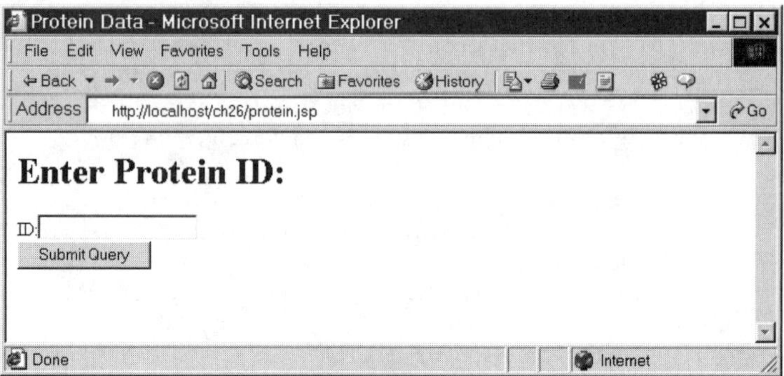

This is quite similar to the form used in the earlier number sampling.

Here is a sample output for this JSP:

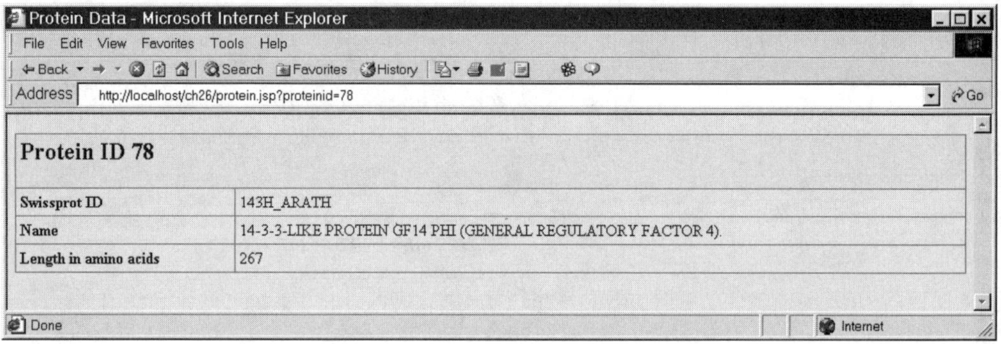

The next JSP in this example uses the same database to perform sequence alignment. *Sequence alignment* is a process in which two sequences are compared and an attempt is made to find similarities between them. Sequence alignment requires intricate algorithms, and in our case we rely on BLAST, which is a software package commonly used for this purpose, among other things. BLAST can be downloaded from *http://www.ncbi.nlm.gov/BLAST*.

BLAST is implemented in C/C++, so we need to devise a way to combine this C/C++ code into our JSP example. For the sake of simplicity, let's use the BLAST executables as they are, without making any changes. We will write a simple Java program that accepts TCP/IP connections and invokes BLAST based on the request. This program uses the runtime's `exec` command to invoke a BLAST shell program.

Two Java classes comprise this server component. One sets up a listener on a socket; the other accepts requests coming in over a socket and then invokes the BLAST program:

```
::::::::::::::
Blastd.java
::::::::::::::
import java.net.*;
import java.io.*;
import java.util.*;

class Blastd
{
      private static final int daemonPort = 4004;
      private static ServerSocket MainSocket = null;
      static void main(String args[]) {
      try {
                  MainSocket = new ServerSocket(daemonPort);
                  while (true)
                  {
                        Socket ClientSocket = MainSocket.accept();
                        Blaster thd = new Blaster(ClientSocket);
                        thd.start();
                  }

            }

            catch (Exception e)
            {}

            finally
            {
                  try
                  {
                        MainSocket.close();
                  }
                  catch (Exception exc)
                  {
                  }
            }
      }
}
```

```
::::::::::::::
Blaster.java
::::::::::::::
import java.net.*;
import java.io.*;
import java.util.*;

public class Blaster extends Thread
{
      Socket socket = null;              // Socket to client

      public Blaster(Socket clientSocket)
      {
            socket = clientSocket;
      }

      public void run()
      {
            BufferedReader input =  null;
            PrintWriter output =  null;

            try {
                  input = new BufferedReader(new InputStreamReader
                                           (socket.getInputStream()));
                  output = new PrintWriter(socket.getOutputStream(), true);
                  String seq1 = input.readLine();
                  String seq2 = input.readLine();


                  long pid = System.currentTimeMillis();
                  String fn1 = "/tmp/s1_" + pid;
                  String fn2 = "/tmp/s2_" + pid;
                  String fn3 = "/tmp/oo_" + pid;
                  PrintWriter pw = new PrintWriter(new FileOutputStream
                                                 (fn1));
                  pw.println(seq1);
                  pw.close();
                  pw = new PrintWriter(new FileOutputStream (fn2));
                  pw.println(seq2);
                  pw.close();
                  String cmd = "./bl2seq -i " + fn1 + " -j " + fn2 +
                              " -p blastp -T -o " + fn3;
                  System.out.println(cmd);
                  Process p = Runtime.getRuntime().exec(cmd);
                  p.waitFor();

                  BufferedReader fileReader = new BufferedReader(new
                              InputStreamReader(new FileInputStream(fn3)));
```

```
                    while (true) {
                          String res = fileReader.readLine();
                          if (res == null)
                                break;
                          output.println(res);
                    }
                    output.close();
                    socket.close();


              }
              catch (Exception ex) {
                    System.out.println("Exception " +ex );
              }

        }
  }
```

After compiling and running this program, we implement the following Java class, which will invoke the program. This class uses Java sockets to connect and transmit the sequences to it. What we are doing here is essentially implementing a very crude remote procedure call (RPC).

```
import java.net.*;
import java.io.*;

public class Blast {
    public String doIt(String seq1, String seq2) {
      String ret = "";
      int port = 4004;
      String server = "proteinhost";
      Socket socket = null;
      String lineToBeSent;
      BufferedReader input;
      PrintWriter output;
      int ERROR = 1;

      // connect to server
      try {
          socket = new Socket(server, port);
      }
      catch (UnknownHostException e) {
```

```
            System.err.println(e);
        }
        catch (IOException e) {
            System.err.println(e);
        }
        try {
            output = new PrintWriter(socket.getOutputStream(),true);
            input = new BufferedReader(new
                        InputStreamReader(socket.getInputStream()));

            output.println(seq1);
            output.println(seq2);
            output.flush();

            boolean done = false;
            while (!done) {
                  try {
                    String instr = input.readLine();
                    if (instr == null) {
                          done=true;
                        break;
                    }
                    System.out.println("In = "+instr);
                    ret = ret + instr;
              }
              catch (Exception ex)
              {
                    ret = ret + "Exception" + ex;
                    done =  true;
              }
            }

        }
        catch (IOException e) {
            System.out.println(e);
        }
        try {
            socket.close();
        }
        catch (IOException e) {
```

```
            System.out.println(e);
        }
        return ret;
    }
}
```

Finally, we can get to our JSP, which takes two protein IDs as parameters and outputs the sequence alignment for them. The JSP retrieves the protein sequences from the database and invokes the `Blast` class, which in turn connects to the small Java program mentioned previously.

```
<%@ page import="java.util.*" %>
<%@ page import="java.sql.*" %>
<HTML>
<HEAD>
<TITLE>Sequence Alignment</TITLE>
</HEAD>
<%
  String prot1 = request.getParameter("protein1").toString();
  String prot2 = request.getParameter("protein2").toString();
  if (prot1==null)
      prot1="";
  if (prot2==null)
      prot1="";
  int protein1=0;
  int protein2=0;

  try {
      protein1 = new Integer(prot1).intValue();
      protein2 = new Integer(prot2).intValue();
  }
  catch (Exception ex) {
     // Handle Error...
  }
%>
<BODY bgcolor="#E8F7EE" topmargin="0" leftmargin="7" rightmargin="7"
marginheight="0" marginwidth="7">
<FONT color="#6FB5A2"><H3>Sequence Alignment for Proteins
<%= protein1%>, <%=protein2%></H3></FONT>
<%
 int protLen1 = 0;
 String sequence1 = null;
 int protLen2 = 0;
 String sequence2=null;
```

```
 Connection con ;
 java.sql.Statement state ;
       try {
          String url = "jdbc:oracle:thin@dbhost:1521:proteindb";
          Class.forName("oracle.jdbc.driver.OracleDriver");
          con = DriverManager.getConnection(url,"protuser","");
          state = con.createStatement();
          ResultSet rs = state.executeQuery(
            "select * from proteins where id =" + protein1 + ";") ;
          if (!rs.next() ) {
%>
<FONT color="#FF2020">Error: this protein does not exit</FONT>
<%
      }
      else {
              protLen1 = rs.getInt("len");
            sequence1 = rs.getString("seq");
      }
      rs = state.executeQuery(
          "select * from proteins where id =" + protein2 + ";") ;
        if (!rs.next() ) {
%>
<FONT color="#FF2020">Error: this protein does not exit</FONT>
<%
      }
      else {
              protLen2 = rs.getInt("len");
            sequence2 = rs.getString("seq");
      }
      state.close();
      con.close();
   }
    catch (Exception ex) {
        ex.printStackTrace();
    }
%>
<%
  Blast b = new Blast();
  String str = b.doIt(sequence1, sequence2);
%>
<FONT face='courier'>
<%=str%>
</FONT>
</BODY>
</HTML>
```

Figure 26-2 shows sample output for this JSP.

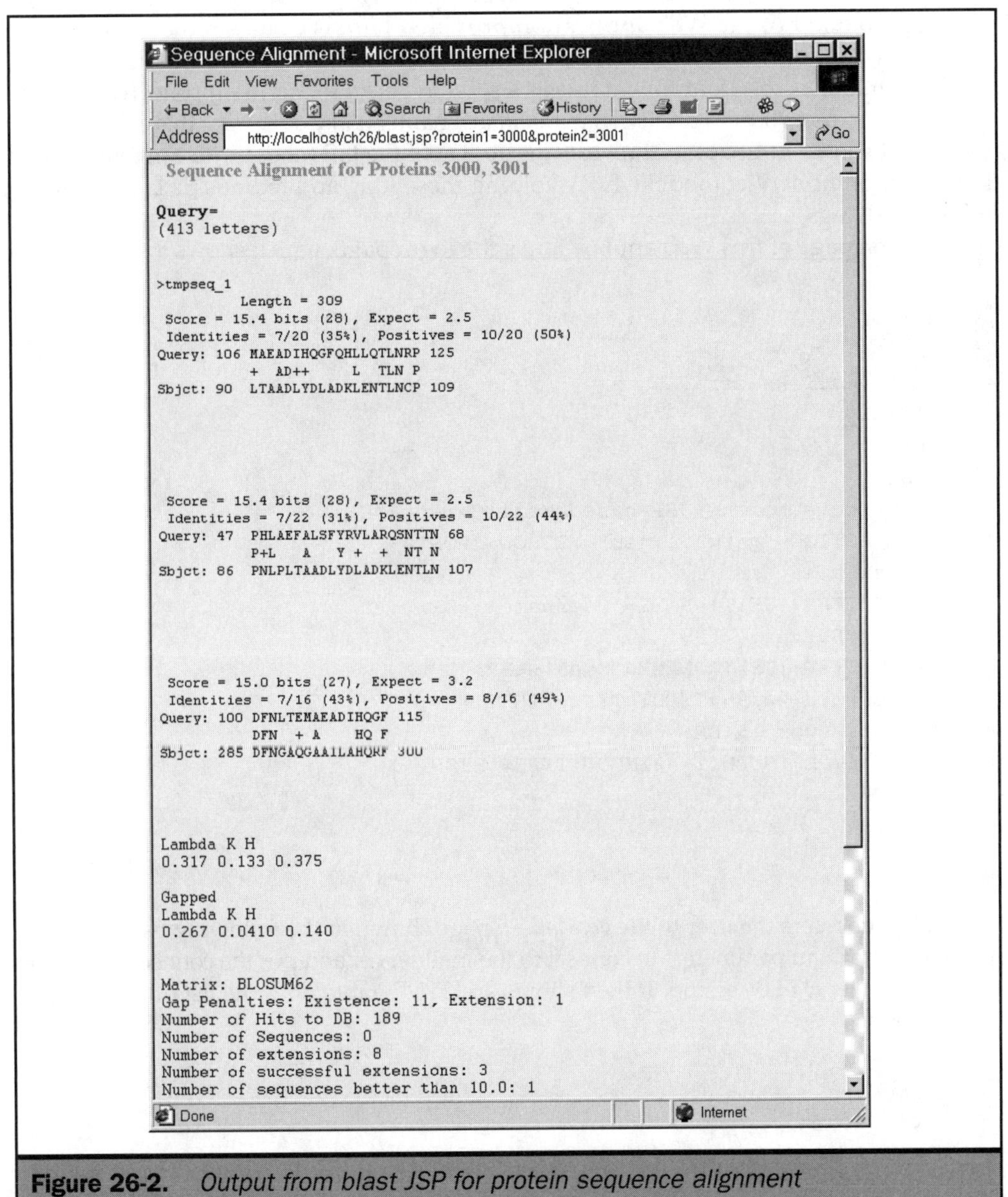

Figure 26-2. *Output from blast JSP for protein sequence alignment*

Mail Reading JSP

In the final example, we revisit the mail reading servlet example from Chapter 22. The functionality of the Web application provided here is quite similar to that provided by the servlet in Chapter 22, but the implementation is based on JSP. The implementation is different in that it uses a session object to maintain state. (Recall that HTTP session objects were discussed in detail in Chapter 23.) Comparing this example to the servlet shown in Chapter 22 reveals the appeal of the JSP model: you can maintain all the power of the servlet model while avoiding those long and tedious `println` calls with HTML tags.

The first page of this Web application is the login page, which shows a simple form.

```
<HTML>
<HEAD>
<TITLE>Mail Reader JSP
</TITLE>
</HEAD>
<BODY>
<H1>Welcome to the JSP-based Mail Client</H1>
<FORM ACTION="getMail.jsp" METHOD="POST">
<B>Username: </B>
<INPUT TYPE='TEXT' NAME='username'><BR>
<B>POP3 Server: </B>
<INPUT TYPE='TEXT' NAME='pop3'><BR>
<B>Password: </B><INPUT TYPE='TEXT'
NAME='password'><BR>
<INPUT TYPE='SUBMIT'><INPUT TYPE='RESET'>
</FORM>
</BODY>
</HTML>
```

This page refers the user to the *getMail.jsp* page shown in the following listing. This page uses the login parameters to connect to the mail server and put the connection object into the servlet HTTP session. It then shows an HTML table with the list of mail messages.

```
<% page import="java.util.*" %>
<% page import="java.io.*" %>
<% page import="javax.mail.*" %>
<% page session="true" %>
<%
    Folder folder = null;
    Message[] messages = null;
```

```
    Session mailsession = null;
    Store store = null;
    String userName = null;

            if (session.getAttribute("username") == null) {
                  userName = req.getParameter("username");
                  String pop3 = req.getParameter("pop3");
                  String password = req.getParameter("password");
                  mailsession = Session.getInstance(System.getProperties()null);
                  store = mailsession.getStore("pop3");
                  store.connect(pop3, userName, password);
                  folder = store.getFolder("INBOX");
                  folder.open(Folder.READ_ONLY);
                  messages = folder.getMessages();
                  session.setAttribute("username", username);
                  session.setAttribute("folder", folder);
                  session.setAttribute("messages", messages);
                  session.setAttribute("store", store);
                  session.setAttribute("session", mailsession);
            }
            else {
                  username = (String) session.getAttribute("username");
                  folder = (Folder) session.getAttribute("folder");
                  messages = (Message []) session.getAttribute("messages");
                  mailsession = (Session) session.getAttribute("session");
                  store = (Store) session.getAttrbute("store");
            }
%>
<HTML>
<HEAD>
<TITLE>
Welcome <%=username %>! Your Mail
</TITLE>
</HEAD>
<BODY>
<TABLE BORDER="1">
<TR>
<TH>From</TH>
<TH>Date</TH>
<TH>Subject</TH>
<%
                for (int i = 0; i < messages.length; i++) {
%>
<TR><TD>
<%= messages[i].getFrom()[0] %>
</TD>
<TD><%= messages[i].getSentDate() %>
```

```
</TD>
<TD><A HREF="getDetail.jsp?msgnum=<%=i%>">"
<%= messages[i].getSubject() %>
</A>
</TD>
</TR>
<%          } %>
</TABLE><P><A HREF="doLogout.jsp">
Log-Off</A>
</P>
</BODY>
</HTML>
```

The next page includes links to two other pages. The first one is the *doLogout.jsp* page, which is quite straightforward. It displays a quick message, invalidates the session, and closes the *JavaMail* folder and store objects.

```
<% page import="java.util.*" %>
<% page import="java.io.*" %>
<% page import="javax.mail.*" %>
<% page session="true" %>
<%
    Folder folder = null;
    Message[] messages = null;
    Session mailsession = null;
    Store store = null;
    String userName = null;

      username = (String) session.getAttribute("username");
      folder = (Folder) session.getAttribute("folder");
      messages = (Message []) session.getAttribute("messages");
      mailsession = (Session) session.getAttribute("session");
      store = (Store) session.getAttribute("store");
%>
<HTML>
<HEAD>
<TITLE>
Mail Reader JSP Logout
</TITLE>
</HEAD>
<BODY>
<H1>
Thank you for using the JSP mail reader
</H1>
</BODY>
</HTML>
```

```
<%
      try {
           folder.close(false);
           store.close();
             session.invalidate();
      }
      catch (Exception ex)
      {
      }
%>
```

The final page is *getDetail.jsp*, and it retrieves and shows the actual content of an e-mail message.

```
<% page import="java.util.*" %>
<% page import="java.io.*" %>
<% page import="javax.mail.*" %>
<% page session="true" %>
<%
      Folder folder = null;
      Message[] messages = null;
      Session mailsession = null;
      Store store = null;
      String userName = null;
      username = (String) session.getAttribute("username");
      folder = (Folder) session.getAttribute("folder");
      messages = (Message []) session.getAttribute("messages");
      mailsession = (Session) session.getAttribute("session");
      store = (Store) session.getAttribute("store");
      int num = Integer.parseInt(req.getParameter("msgnum"));
      String s;
      Message msg = messages[num];
%>
<HTML>
<HEAD>
<TITLE>
Reading Message Number <%= num %>
</TITLE>
</HEAD>
<BODY>
</H1><Reading Message: <%= msg.getSubject() %>
<B>From:</B>
<%= msg.getFrom()[0] %>
<B>To:</B>
<%= msg.getRecipients(Message.RecipientType.TO)[0] %>
<B>Date:</B>
```

```
<%=  msg.getSentDate() %>
<P>
<%
                BufferedReader rd = new BufferedReader(new
                 InputStreamReader(msg.getInputStream()));
          while ((s = rd.readLine()) != null)
              out.println(s);
%>
</P>
</BODY>
</HTML>
```

Summary

This chapter went through a few simple JSP examples. There is nothing difficult about JSPs, which is one of their major strengths; yet JSPs are used for building fairly heavy-duty applications. Simple programming paradigms and complex applications have a tendency to become misaligned; as the order of complexity rises, the complications increase and the simple model falls apart. JSPs have had these symptoms. Luckily, the JSP model is continuously evolving; just when it seems like the applications it is being used for don't fit the model, JSP is improved, and complexity is abstracted away.

The latest such development is the use of custom tag libraries to encapsulate and abstract complex behavior used on JSPs. This is the topic of Chapter 27.

The Complete Reference

Chapter 27

Custom Tag Libraries

Servlets and JavaServer Pages (JSPs) are the primary tools used by every developer of Web applications on a WebSphere platform. JSPs and servlets are really one and the same, since every JSP is transformed by the JSP engine into a servlet. The JSP lifecycle and the servlet lifecycle are identical for the most part, and you are free to use either servlets or JSPs in your applications, depending on your application's focus and needs.

Whether you use JSPs or servlets (or both) almost always depends on your role in the development organization. If you are building back-end functionality, you will be using a servlet to expose your functionality to the outside world. If you are working on the presentation layer of an application, building dynamic Web screens that access some back-end data and expose them to a browser, you will most probably be using a JSP. In terms of roles, back-end programmers usually write servlets, and page designers always use JSPs. The tools for writing JSPs are mature and follow the same paradigm as Web page development tools. Servlets, as constructs, do not include any development tools apart from templates and debuggers, which are usually part of a Java Integrated Development Environment (IDE).

While JSPs are certainly the preferred method to use for building user interfaces, they can grow to be complex. Some of the inherent problems and complexities are reviewed early in this chapter.

Later in the chapter, custom tag libraries are introduced. The use of these libraries is expanding in the industry in general, and in WebSphere—a technology that promises to revolutionize the use of JSPs and make building JSPs far easier. Using the libraries also promises to better distinguish the roles of the different people who work on Web application development projects. The topic of tag libraries deserves a book to itself; although this chapter will not cover all the options, lifecycle intricacies, and application programming interface (API) sets for custom tag libraries, you will be introduced to this important subject and will learn how to use tag libraries in a WebSphere deployment.

The JSP Complexity Problem

As reviewed in Chapter 7, the history of servlets and JSPs is based on continuous improvement. Here's a quick recap: Servlets were the greatest thing since cherry pie when they first emerged as a better way of writing Common Gateway Interface (CGI) scripts. Then they became very complex as the amount of Hypertext Markup Language (HTML) embedded as strings in Java print commands became uncontrollable. Tools could not be used because as strings, the elements lost all semantics and structure. Then JSPs emerged and reversed the roles, letting the pages be built as "normal" HTML pages with a few *scriptlets* embedded to extract dynamic data or to perform some server-side processing. JSPs were the best thing since cherry pie topped with vanilla ice cream. Unfortunately, as time progressed and JSPs became widely used for complex business applications, the next "complexity curve" emerged. JSPs, as programming constructs, have grown into monolithic monsters. In many business applications, the pages are huge and hard to read. Even more problematic is that they have become a continuous mix of HTML and Java, which means that a clear separation no longer exists between the page designer (an HTML developer) and the Java developer. As a result, building complex Web user interfaces now requires Java developers, and they are expensive.

Encapsulation and Abstraction

Almost every problem in computer science eventually can be categorized as a problem involving *lack of encapsulation* or *lack of abstraction*. As it turns out, the problems with JSPs are a bit of both. When people first start writing JSPs, they are often overwhelmed by the simplicity of the model. They simply build a Web page and then start filling in the dynamic content using Java code. This approach begs for simple use, but developers do not always think of their pages as programming constructs. They therefore often leave behind all that they have been taught about modularity and encapsulation, and the code becomes one big, unmanageable mess. Remember that a Web page itself is compiled into a servlet and, in the process, generates the servicing method.

The best way for you to understand where the JSP model has taken us is to look at a complex page. Figure 27-1 shows a fairly simple Web screen that depends on a nontrivial amount of dynamic behavior to control the work that can be done using the screen, based on a set of business rules managed by a workflow engine. We will not list the contents of this JSP, because it would fill up the rest of the chapter, with more than 2000 lines of code—a mix of HTML and Java (and more than 25 pages of code printout). Even more troublesome is the size of the service method in the generated servlet, with more than 1100 lines of code! When was the last time you wrote a single method that was this big?

While considering only the size of the generated method is misleading (after all, that's the work of code generators), it does help you to understand the seriousness of the complexity problems with JSPs. This lack of abstraction and modularity is something that most Java developers have worked hard to reverse.

The solution has been easy and natural both for the HTML and the Java code. HTML code for repetitive parts can be encapsulated as separate JSPs and embedded into other pages. Not only does encapsulation reduce the code size, but it also allows reusability and enhances maintenance, because changes can now occur in one place and be replicated elsewhere. Other than this, we don't need to do much on the HTML side, because HTML is often generated with editing tools.

As for the dynamic parts (the Java code), the solution is even easier and more natural. Because Java is an object-oriented language, the way to make a JSP more modular is to encapsulate the Java code that would normally be embedded into the JSP as methods in Java objects. These classes and methods can then be used in multiple JSPs, which allows us to diminish the size of the code and streamline its maintenance.

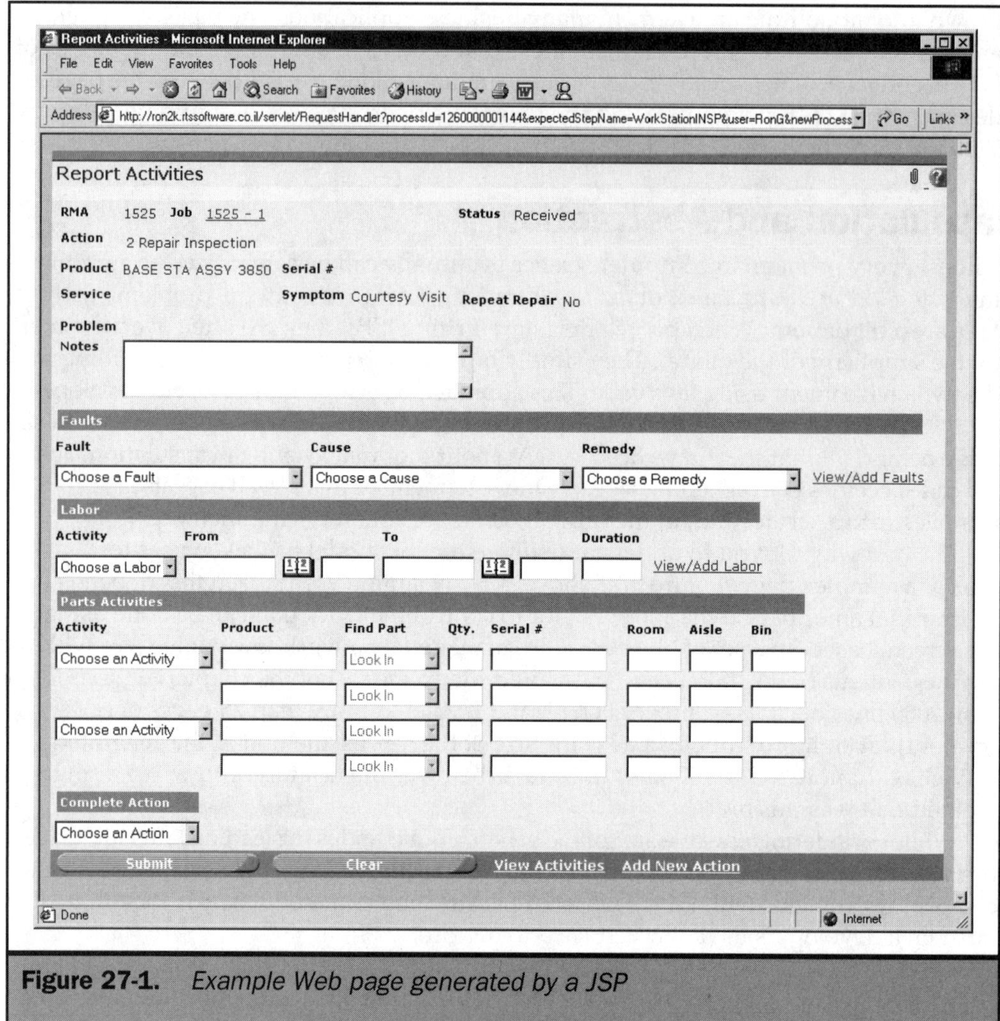

Figure 27-1. *Example Web page generated by a JSP*

The Attachments Example

Let's look at an example of how such code might look before and after encapsulation. This example is related to document attachments. In Figure 27-1, you can see a small paper clip icon at the upper-right corner of the screen. If a user clicks this clip, the following screen appears:

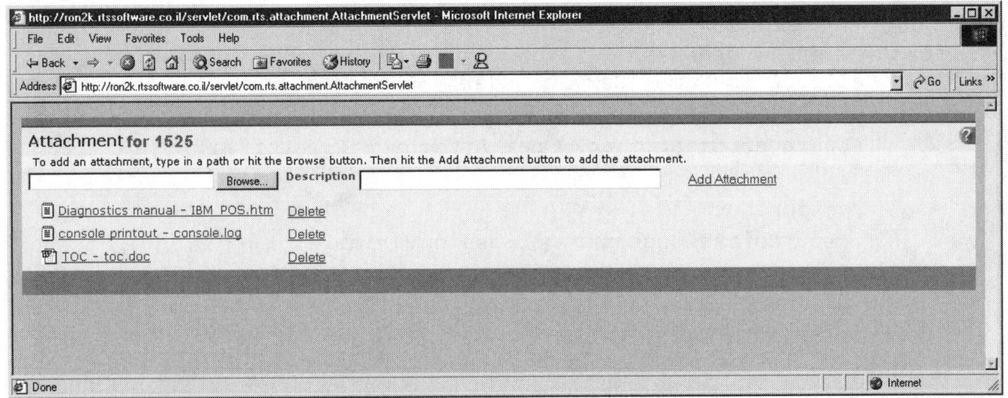

This screen shows all attachments appended to the job shown in Figure 27-1. Each document can be viewed, and an attachment can be added to the object (in our case, to a job). This mechanism is generic because you may need to add an attachment to any object being managed within the system. The mechanism, therefore, needs to be included in many different JSPs.

As is often the case with development, we get smarter with time by learning from our mistakes. So, for example, the first time you developed an attachment feature, you probably embedded the code directly into the JSP that first implemented the feature.

In your next attempt at developing this feature, you can create a new class that encapsulates the attachment functionality. As a result, it will be easy to add the attachment functionality for any entity and any JSP. This creates a new abstraction in your system, in which everything is neatly packaged; you can make use of this new abstraction to add functionality to your JSPs. From a maintenance perspective, this is great news, because now you can modify the Java class implementing the attachment functionality without touching the JSPs that make use of that functionality.

Every JSP that needs to have the attachment feature embedded will include the following code:

```
...

<%@ import = "com.rts.attachment.*" %>
...
<%
      HttpSession session = request.getSession(true);
```

```
        AttachmentInfo ai = new AttachmentInfo();
        Map keysAndValues1 = new HashMap(3);
        keysAndValues1.put("id", 1234);
        ai.setKeysAndValues(keysAndValues1);
        ai.setAccessLevel("1");
        ai.setClassName("ServiceOrder");

        AttachmentCreator ac = new AttachmentCreator(ai);

        session.putValue(
              PortalConstants.getSessionVariable(
                    "RTS_Attachment_Creator"), ac);

      // *** ATTACHMENT END ***
      %>
...
<!-- Start Attachment Link -->
<A class="WinletLinkFont" href="Attachment.jsp">
   <IMG BORDER="0" ALT="Attachment" SRC=attachment.gif/>
</A>
<!-- End Attachment Link -->
```

This code has two parts that are of interest. The first part is the creation of the attachment creator object. An attachment creator gets one or more attachment information objects. We can then add attachments to one of the entities or modify attachments belonging to one of the entities. These entities need to be referenced by the attachment information objects.

The attachments JSP makes use of the attachment creator object to display the attachments and to add or remove attachments, as follows:

```
...
<%
      HttpSession session = getSession(request);
      noCacheResponse(response);

      String root = Attachment.getRootURLLocation();

      AttachmentCreator attachCreator = (AttachmentCreator)
                 session.getValue("RTS_Attachment_Creator");

      String errorMessage = null;
      String prompt = "";
      String title = "";
```

```
        String objectInd = "";
        String description = (String) request.getAttribute
                                                ("description");
        AttachmentInfo[] attachInfo = null;

        if (attachCreator == null)
        {
              errorMessage = "Error";
        }
        else
        {
              attachInfo = attachCreator.getInfo();
              errorMessage = (String) request.getAttribute
                                               ("errorMessage");

              if (attachCreator.hasSingleObject())
              {
                    title = " for ";
                    objectInd = "0";
              }
              else
              {
                    prompt = " select the object,";
              }
        }
        }
        ...
%>
...
<!-- Begin title -->
 <tr>
  <td>
   <table width="100%" border="0" cellspacing="0"
                cellpadding="0" class="WidgetsBackground">
    <tr>
     <td>
      <table>
       <tr>
        <td class="WindowHeading">
         Attachment
        </td>
        <td class="WindowHeadingDynamicData">
```

```
          <%= title + attachCreator.getTitle() %>
        </td>
      </tr>
    </table>
  </td>
</tr>
<!-- End title -->
...
```

This is truly a good encapsulation of an attachment mechanism.

Tag Libraries

The solution described in the preceding section works well. It encapsulates behavior and creates a new abstraction. The problem, however, is that the new abstraction is *still* a Java abstraction. While this example may look simple enough for Java programmers, it might be of no help to page designers who want to stay within the realm of HTML (or maybe DHTML). After all, the page is supposed to belong to the page designer, not the Java programmer, and this is not the case with the solution presented in the preceding code.

What you really need to create is an abstraction that encapsulates the desired behavior and that can be used by the page designer. This is where custom tag libraries come into the picture. The HTML paradigm is all about tags that mark up content. The tags used are normally defined by the HTML specification. Custom tag libraries allow you to define new tags and associate Java classes to implement behavior. These new tags can then be used by the page builder to invoke the functionality encapsulated and abstracted into each tag.

Just as a page designer can use an HTML `TABLE` tag to build a table and an `ANCHOR` tag (with an `HREF` attribute) to build a link, a page designer working in a JSP editor needs to be able add an attachment button that will bring with it all of the necessary functionality. By using tag libraries, Java developers can build Java classes that expose functionality in a simple “HTML-like” way.

In the attachment project, these classes allow the page designer to incorporate the attachment link (along with the image, as well as the handlers behind the scenes) by using a simple element such as this:

```
...
< vn_attachment:attach_to_single_object
    entity="ServiceOrder"
    key="id"
```

```
    value="1234"
/>
```

Custom tag libraries allow you to extend the basic JSP tag set with your own code, thereby providing additional abstractions that can be used by the page designer. Tag libraries allow JSP development to reach a new level of productivity, reuse, and maintainability.

Using Tags in JSPs

Tag libraries are part of the JSP specification as of version 1.1, and any implementation of application servers supporting JSP needs to support them in the same way—at least as far as the usage model is concerned. This provides standardization, which ensures that many libraries can be created and reused.

To use the tags implemented within a tag library, you need to do the following:

1. Reference the tag library from your JSP.
2. Use the tags in your JSP.

To make the JSP work properly at runtime, you need to deploy the tag library to your WebSphere server. This requires you to do the following:

1. Build a tag library descriptor (TLD) file.
2. Deploy the TLD in the context of the Web application.
3. Make sure the Java classes implementing the custom tags are accessible to the JVM (that is, make sure they are included in the classpath).

Here's an example using our custom attachment tag:

```
<!DOCTYPE HTML PUBLIC "-//W3C//DTD HTML 4.0 Transitional//EN">
<HEAD>
...
<%@ taglib
   uri="http://www.viryanet.com/taglibs/attachment-taglib"
   prefix=vn_attachment %>
</HEAD>
...
<vn_attachment:attach_to_single_object
    entity="ServiceOrder"
    key="id"
    value="1234"
/>
...
```

In this example, you can proceed to reference the tags defined in the library only after you have declared the location of the taglib itself.

As you can see, using tag libraries is simple and natural. But you need to do a little bit of setup before the server can associate the correct code with the tags. (Coding aspects will be discussed in the next section, "Implementing Custom Tags," and a detailed discussion of deployment aspects will be presented later in the section, "Deploying Tag Libraries in WebSphere.")

The first thing you need to do as part of the deployment is to put the classes in the server's classpath (or package them as a Web module). Then you need to build a TLD, which holds the metadata about the tag library and is used by the server for validation, among other things. The TLD describes each tag in the library along with its structure, attributes, and other information. For example, the attachment taglib TLD looks like this:

```
<?xml version="1.0" encoding "iso-8859-1" ?>
<!DOCTYPE taglib
   PUBLIC "-//Sun Microsystems, Inc.//DTD JSP Tag Library 1.1//EN"
   "http://java.sun.com/j2ee/dtds/web-jsptaglibrary_1_1.dtd">

<taglib>
   <tlibversion>1.0</tlibversion>
   <jspversion>1.1</jspversion>
   <shortname>vn_attachment</shortname>
   <uri>http://www.viryanet.com/taglibs/attachment-taglib</uri>
   <info>
      A tag library that defines the tag elements for the
attachment framework
   </info>

   <tag>
      <name> attach_to_single_object</name>

<tagclass>com.rts.attachments.SingleObjectAttachment</tagclass>
      <bodycontent>empty</bodycontent>
      <info>
          Encapsulates attachments associated with a single entity.
          The entity is referenced by a key and the value of the
key.
      </info>

      <attribute>
         <name>entity</name>
         <required>true</required>
```

```
        </attribute>

        <attribute>
           <name>key</name>
           <required>true</required>
        </attribute>

        <attribute>
           <name>value</name>
           <required>true</required>
          <rtexprvalue>true</rtexprvalue>
        </attribute>

     </tag>

     ...

  </taglib>
```

The only element in the TLD that is not self-explanatory is the `rtexprvalue` element. This is by default *false*, and in the `attach_to_single_object` tag, both entity and key have this value set to *false*. When this value is set to *true*, it means that the value that this attribute takes at runtime may itself be a runtime expression that needs to be computed by the engine. In this example, the value for the key is the job number and is certainly not fixed; every page delivered to the user may have a different job, and you need to get the attachments for each job and not for a job with a fixed value.

In terms of the use of the tag in the JSP, we might expect the JSP to look like this:

```
...
<vn_attachment:attach_to_single_object
    entity="ServiceOrder"
    key="id"
    value="<%= jobBean.getId() %>"
/>
```

After the TLD is ready, you need to deploy it in the context of your Web application. You can do this from the administration console or by ensuring that it is referenced by the Web descriptor file. If using the Web descriptor file, (*web.xml*) you need to add a taglib element, as follows:

```
<taglib>
     <taglib-uri> http://
       www.viryanet.com/taglibs/attachment-taglib </taglib-uri>
     <taglib-location>WEB-INF/
attachment-taglib.tld</taglib-location>
</taglib>
```

Implementing Custom Tags

You can probably guess by now how the custom tags are handled by the JSP engine. A tag is an element that is processed by the JSP engine. It uses the TLD to look up the class that implements the behavior that the tag represents. The class needs to implement a certain interface—but we will get to that later. After the engine finds the class matching the tag, it invokes the methods in the class. The methods typically inject data back into the page, so the context of the page must be accessible to the class implementing the tag. The tag implementation then tells the JSP engine how to proceed with the processing of the page, based on a certain protocol that is defined by the taglib API.

A Simple Tag with No Body

Here's a basic implementation of the attachment tag shown previously:

```
package com.rts.attachments;

import java.io.IOException;
import javax.servlet.jsp.PageContext;
import javax.servlet.jsp.JspException;
import javax.servlet.jsp.JspTagException;
import javax.servlet.jsp.tagext.TagSupport;
import javax.servlet.http.*;
import com.rts.infrastructure.EntityMapper;

public class SingleObjectAttachment
    extends TagSupport {

    String key;
    String entity;
    String value;

    public void setKey(String key) {
            this.key = key;
      }

    public void setEntity(String entity) {
            this.entity = entity;
      }

    public void setValue(String value) {
            this.value = value;
```

```
        }

    public int doStartTag()
        throws JspException
    {
        try {

                AttachmentInfo ai = new AttachmentInfo();
                Map keysAndValues1 = new HashMap(3);
                keysAndValues1.put("id", key);
                ai.setKeysAndValues(keysAndValues1);
                ai.setAccessLevel("1");
                ai.setClassName(EntityMapper.mapToClass(entity));

                AttachmentCreator ac = new AttachmentCreator(ai);

                pageContext.setAttribute("RTS_Attachment_Creator",
ac, PageContext.SESSION_SCOPE);

                pageContext.getOut().println("<A " +
              "class=\"WinletLinkFont\" href=\"Attachment.jsp\">");
                pageContext.getOut().println("<IMG BORDER=\"0\"" +
                        "ALT=\"Attachment\" SRC=attachment.gif/>");
                pageContext.getOut().println("</A>");


        } catch(Throwable ex) {
            throw new JspTagException("Exception: " + ex);
        }
        return SKIP_BODY;
    }
}
```

This class is quite straightforward. It inherits from *TagSupport*, thus inheriting many methods that are part of the taglib framework and conforming to the taglib API set. This class also gives us access to a number of objects that we require.

Next come the attributes. The *entity* attribute helps us know the type of object and the key and value attributes that are needed to instantiate the object. The attributes need to be passed into the tag class. The passing of values into the tag class uses the conventions defined by JavaBeans. Every attribute that appears in the tag should have a set method. These set methods are called *before* the doStartTag method is invoked, so that the attribute values are set into the instance variables when the processing method is invoked.

Then the `doStartTag` method is called. The attachment creator object is generated and saved, in the context of the session, to be used by another JSP that will be called on to display the actual attachments. Finally, the output to the page is created in the form of the hyperlink. The method returns `SKIP_BODY`, which in our case is not important since there is no body.

Tags with a Body

In the preceding section, a class that inherits from the *TagSupport* class was implemented. This is one of the two tag base classes that are part of the specification—the other one being *BodyTagSupport*. *TagSupport* implements the *Tag* interface and *BodyTagSupport* implements the *BodyTag* interface. The main difference between them is that the *BodyTagSupport* is concerned with the body of the element, whereas the *TagSupport* is not. This affects lifecycle and abilities of the custom tag as well as its complexity.

Generally speaking, a tag that invokes a single back-end operation usually has no body. It has a set of tag attributes that are used as arguments passed to the back-end operation. The classic example you will often see in text books on tag libraries is the `send_email` example. This tag allows the page designer to indicate that an e-mail should be sent based on some dynamic properties that are usually extracted from the same dynamic objects used in the JSP.

The second major use of a tag is to provide application markup features while the page is processed. When a JSP is built, the HTML elements provide directives to the browser on how to present information to the user. This information often needs to be dynamically generated; thus, JSPs are used. Many pages do quite a bit of dynamic content generation, and it is often the case that the processing of the body of a page depends on dynamic properties. These properties often can (and should) be placed in the attributes of a custom tag, thus ensuring that the entire page can be void of scriptlets.

A tag with a body usually extracts some values from the attributes of the tag (or from previously defined context) and uses these to read the body of the tag and generate content. Examples can include *translations*, in which a tag attribute is used to replace certain words in the body; *stripping*, in which the user's identity can be used to strip out information that the user is not entitled to see; and many other useful features.

Body tags can be categorized into two groups: The first category performs an action when the tag begins and sets some variables in the page context that are then used by other tags within the tag body. These tags control the flow, but they do not actually use the body content; the body content uses information that the tag has prepared. The second category reads in the body content, applies some processing to it, and then writes it back as the new body content.

A classic example of a body tag is the *iteration* tag. (In fact, in JSP 1.2, it is part of the core specification.) Many JSPs follow a pattern in which they need to display a collection of objects. Figure 27-2 shows an HTML page that displays a collection of service calls;

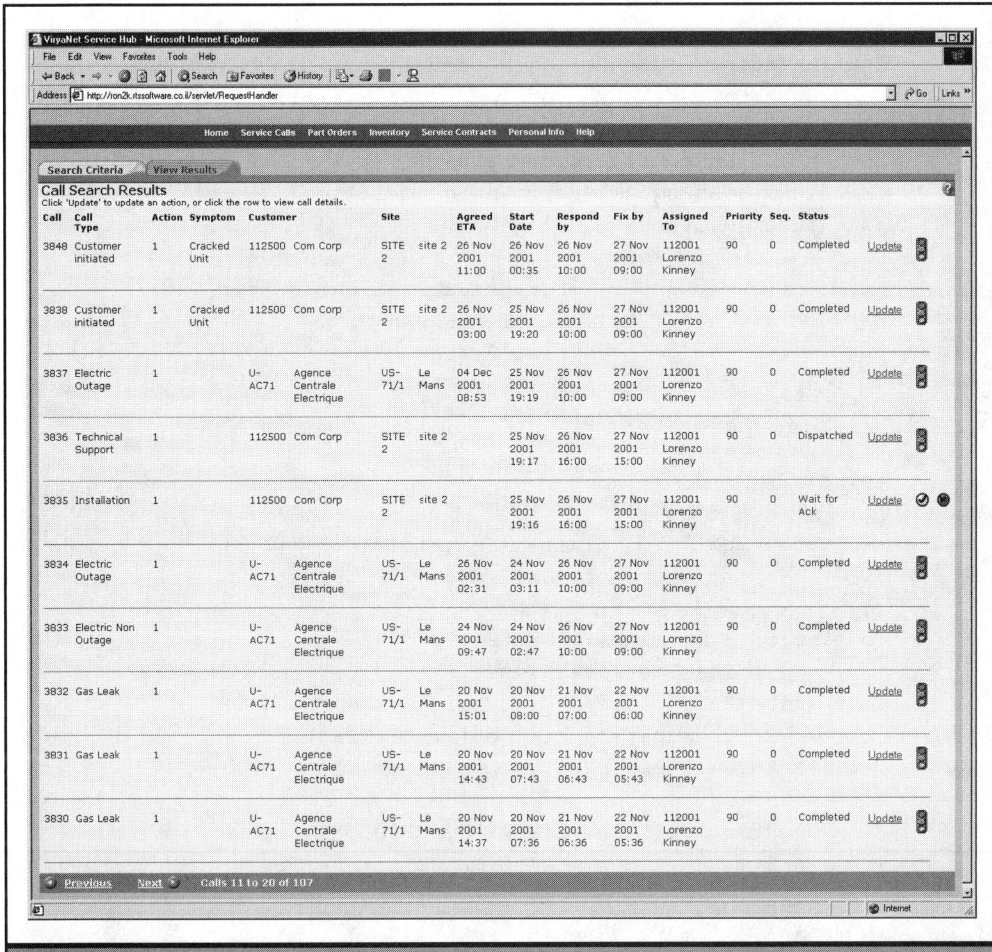

Call Search Results

Click 'Update' to update an action, or click the row to view call details.

Call	Call Type	Action	Symptom	Customer		Site		Agreed ETA	Start Date	Respond by	Fix by	Assigned To	Priority	Seq.	Status	
3848	Customer initiated	1	Cracked Unit	112500	Com Corp	SITE 2	site 2	26 Nov 2001 11:00	26 Nov 2001 00:35	26 Nov 2001 10:00	27 Nov 2001 09:00	112001 Lorenzo Kinney	90	0	Completed	Update
3838	Customer initiated	1	Cracked Unit	112500	Com Corp	SITE 2	site 2	26 Nov 2001 03:00	25 Nov 2001 19:20	26 Nov 2001 10:00	27 Nov 2001 09:00	112001 Lorenzo Kinney	90	0	Completed	Update
3837	Electric Outage	1		U-AC71	Agence Centrale Electrique	US-71/1	Le Mans	04 Dec 2001 08:53	25 Nov 2001 19:19	26 Nov 2001 10:00	27 Nov 2001 09:00	112001 Lorenzo Kinney	90	0	Completed	Update
3836	Technical Support	1		112500	Com Corp	SITE 2	site 2		25 Nov 2001 19:17	26 Nov 2001 16:00	27 Nov 2001 15:00	112001 Lorenzo Kinney	90	0	Dispatched	Update
3835	Installation	1		112500	Com Corp	SITE 2	site 2		25 Nov 2001 19:16	26 Nov 2001 16:00	27 Nov 2001 15:00	112001 Lorenzo Kinney	90	0	Wait for Ack	Update
3834	Electric Outage	1		U-AC71	Agence Centrale Electrique	US-71/1	Le Mans	26 Nov 2001 02:31	24 Nov 2001 03:11	26 Nov 2001 10:00	27 Nov 2001 09:00	112001 Lorenzo Kinney	90	0	Completed	Update
3833	Electric Non Outage	1		U-AC71	Agence Centrale Electrique	US-71/1	Le Mans	24 Nov 2001 09:47	24 Nov 2001 02:47	26 Nov 2001 10:00	27 Nov 2001 09:00	112001 Lorenzo Kinney	90	0	Completed	Update
3832	Gas Leak	1		U-AC71	Agence Centrale Electrique	US-71/1	Le Mans	20 Nov 2001 15:01	20 Nov 2001 08:00	21 Nov 2001 07:00	22 Nov 2001 06:00	112001 Lorenzo Kinney	90	0	Completed	Update
3831	Gas Leak	1		U-AC71	Agence Centrale Electrique	US-71/1	Le Mans	20 Nov 2001 14:43	20 Nov 2001 07:43	21 Nov 2001 06:43	22 Nov 2001 05:43	112001 Lorenzo Kinney	90	0	Completed	Update
3830	Gas Leak	1		U-AC71	Agence Centrale Electrique	US-71/1	Le Mans	20 Nov 2001 14:37	20 Nov 2001 07:36	21 Nov 2001 06:36	22 Nov 2001 05:36	112001 Lorenzo Kinney	90	0	Completed	Update

Figure 27-2. *Viewing details for a collection of objects*

for each call, information such as status, customer, location, and appointment times is displayed.

The JSP generating the content shown in Figure 27-2 creates a collection object and then iterates over this collection, writing out the data required for each of the calls. It might, for example, look like this:

```
...

<%
```

```
for (int i = 0;
     i < (BnEngCallSearchRes.getBottom() -
          BnEngCallSearchRes.getTop() + 1); ++ i)
{
      int top = BnEngCallSearchRes.getTop()-1;
      Map item = BnEngCallSearchRes.getCallItem(i + top);
      int index = i+top;

      if (CallParam.getObject().getExternalCallNumberFlag()){
         out.write("<TD class=\"TextField\">" +
               item.get("externalSystemId") + "</TD>");
         out.write("<TD class=\"TextField\">" +
               item.get("callId") + "</TD>");
      }
      else
      {
         out.write("<TD  class=\"TextField\">" +
                   item.get("callId") + "</TD>");
      }
      out.write("<TD class=\"TextField\">" +
                item.get("callType") + "</TD>");
      out.write("<TD class=\"TextField\">" +
                item.get("actionNo") + "</TD>");
      if (!BnEngCallSearchRes.isAppointment())
      {
            out.write("<TD class=\"TextField\">" +
                      item.get("symptom") + "</TD>");
      }
      out.write("<TD class=\"TextField\">" +
                item.get("customerId") + "</TD>");
      out.write("<TD class=\"TextField\">" +
                item.get("customerName") + "</TD>");
      out.write("<TD class=\"TextField\">" +
                item.get("siteId") + "</TD>");
      out.write("<TD class=\"TextField\">" +
                item.get("siteName") + "</TD>");


      ...
}
%>

...
```

While we can certainly improve this specific code example (yes, it is pretty bad), it is a typical example of the way people write JSPs. One could claim that the internals of the body should be written in HTML with scriptlets, where you really need dynamic code. But experience shows that this just makes things worse. Mixing tiny snippets of HTML for the TD and the TR HTML elements with many small scriptlets makes the page completely unreadable; at least in its current form it can be read by a Java developer, even if it is not readable by a page designer.

Before giving the page back to the page designer, you need to encapsulate the code that writes out the specifics for a call to allow an object to be written out using a simple tag, and you need to be able to do the iteration using a tag. The first part can be done with a *bodyless* tag. This is not our focus, so we will not elaborate on it. The big benefit is that the page designer can now use a tag of this form:

```
<vn:call object="currentCall" format="CALL_VIEW"/>
```

Here, the format specifies how the object should be displayed. Different screens may present the same object in different ways, and you want to encapsulate everything in the class implementing the call entity.

Next, you need to add an iteration tag to get rid of the *for* loop, which will also allow you to prepare the call ID for the displaying tag. Here's how the JSP should look:

```
 ...



<vn:iterate
   collection="BnEngCallSearchRes"
   object="currentCall"
   >
      <vn:call object=<%= currentCall %>" format="CALL_VIEW"/>
</vn:iterate>

...
```

In this case, the iteration tag does not actually do any processing on the body. It merely needs to perform the iteration itself and make sure that the *object* attribute is continuously updated for use by the inner tag. Note that the *from* and *to* functionality has been dropped—it serves no purpose in explaining the iteration tag, and unnecessarily complicates the code.

Let's look at the code for the tag:

```
package com.rts.infrastructure;

...
```

```
import javax.servlet.jsp.*;

public class SimpleIterator extends BodyTagSupport {

    Iterator elementsList = null;

    String collection = null;
    String object = null;

    public void setCollection(String collection)
    {
        this.collection = collection;
    }

    public void setObject(String object)
      {
              this.object = object;
    }

    public int doStartTag()
        throws JspException
    {
        Iterator elementsList =
                 (Iterator)pageContext.getAttribute("collection");
        if(elementsList.hasNext()) {
            return EVAL_BODY_TAG;
        }
        return SKIP_BODY;
    }

    public void doInitBody()
        throws JspException
    {
        pageContext.setAttribute(object, elementsList.next());
    }

    public int doAfterBody()
        throws JspException
    {
        if(elementsList.hasNext()) {
```

```
                pageContext.setAttribute(object, elementsList.next());
                return EVAL_BODY_TAG;
            }

            return SKIP_BODY;
        }
    }
```

The first thing to notice here is that the tag now inherits from *BodyTagSupport*.

Next come the tag attributes that are used to access the iterator object from the page context and the name under which you save the object that will be used for processing the body of the tag.

The `doStartTag` method is called when the tag is first entered. It gets the iterator from the context of the page and gets the first element in the collection. If the collection is empty, it returns `SKIP_BODY` to instruct the JSP engine not to process the body. This is the behavior you would expect from an iteration loop, and it is required because the body may also have static HTML that should not be written out in case the collection is empty.

After the start of the tag, the JSP engine will process the body of the tag; this is defined by the JSP specification as part of the lifecycle of the `BodyTag`. It then calls `doInitBody`, and you insert the current object into the page context. This object will be later used by the `vn:call` tag. After the JSP has finished processing the body, it calls the `doAfterBody` method. Here you again test whether there are any more objects to iterate on in the collection—if so, `EVAL_BODY_TAG` is returned, telling the JSP engine to go once again through the body. Before doing so, you again prepare the object to be used by the internal tag. If no more elements need to be processed, `SKIP_BODY` is returned and the JSP engine completes the processing of the tag.

To deploy this tag on a WebSphere node, you also need the TLD. The tag descriptor for `vn:iterate` looks slightly different, because it is a body tag:

```
<tag>
        <name>iterate</name>
        <tagclass>com.rts.infrastructure.SimpleIterator</tagclass>
         <teiclass>
         com.rts.infrastructure.SimpleIteratorExtraInfo
         </teiclass>
        <bodycontent>JSP</bodycontent>
        <info>
            Iterates over a collection
        </info>
```

```
        <attribute>
            <name>collection</name>
            <required>true</required>
            <rtexprvalue>false</rtexprvalue>
        </attribute>
        <attribute>
            <name>object</name>
            <required>true</required>
            <rtexprvalue>false</rtexprvalue>
        </attribute>
    </tag>
```

Two interesting things appear in this TLD snippet. The first is the `bodycontent` value. Since this is a tag with a body, you need to specify that a body exists and indicate what type it is. Possible values for this are `JSP` and `tagdependent`. `JSP` is the default, and it means that the content of the body should be processed by the JSP engine as just described; `tagdependent` is used when the content of the body should be read by the tag and processed by the tag—that is, when the body is really a part of the enclosing tag and not part of the page. This is a useful option when the use of attributes would create messy code. For example, in the attachment example, we mentioned that sometimes you may want to present all attachments associated with *multiple* objects (for example, with the job, the user, and the organization responsible for the work). Because the number of objects you would like to extract attachments from is dynamic, it is better to use an XML-like embedding of elements, as follows:

```
<vn_attachment:attach_to_multiple_objects>
    <attach_to
        entity="ServiceOrder"
        key="id"
        value="1234"/>
    <attach_to
        entity="User"
        key="id"
        value="100222"/>
    <attach_to
        entity="Department"
        key="id"
        value="QA"/>

/>
```

In this example, the internal elements are not custom tags; instead, they are merely content that is used by the enclosing tag to extract attachments dynamically from multiple objects. The JSP engine should not be given an opportunity to process the body, because it will fault; instead, the tag processing method reads the body content using `getBodyContent()`, which returns a `BodyContent` object.

The other novelty in this TLD snippet is the `teiclass` element. This stands for *tag extra info,* and is a class that can be added for each tag that describes metadata properties about the tag implementation. The metadata class is required in this case, because this tag dynamically creates new attributes and inserts them into the page context. The tag *extra info class,* in this case, defines the data type and scope of the attribute inserted:

```
package com.rts.infrastructure;

import javax.servlet.jsp.tagext.TagData;
import javax.servlet.jsp.tagext.TagExtraInfo;
import javax.servlet.jsp.tagext.VariableInfo;
...

public class SimpleIteratorExtraInfo
    extends TagExtraInfo {

    public VariableInfo[] getVariableInfo(TagData data)
    {
        VariableInfo[] rc = new VariableInfo[1];

        rc[0] =  new VariableInfo("currentCall",
                                  com.rts.call.Call,
                                  true,
                                  VariableInfo.NESTED);
        return rc;
    }
}
```

The `NESTED` scope means that this variable is available only between the start and end of the custom tag. This is the main use of the metadata here. In most cases, the `TagExtraInfo` object is also used for validating the usage of the tag. A tag implementer can implement the `isValid` method and insert all the validation code there (instead of in the `doStart` or `doInit` methods), ensuring that before processing of the tag begins, it is determined to be valid.

Deploying Tag Libraries in WebSphere

Deploying a taglib under WebSphere is simple and, more importantly, conforms to the standards defined by the JSP1.1 and the Java 2 Platform Enterprise Edition (J2EE) specifications. The elements involved in the deployment of a taglib are the JSP, the class implementing the tag, the TLD, and the Web application. You can either choose to manage all of these entities separately or you can package them all into a Web Archive (WAR) file. While manual deployment simply involves getting the files to the right place and updating the *web.xml* file, we strongly encourage you to deploy your taglibs inside Web modules.

The advantages of using a WAR are that the Web application can be managed in one piece, and that a WAR affords much simpler administration and configuration control. You can create a WAR and publish it to the application server as a Web module. In this example, the WAR will have to be housed in an Enterprise Archive (EAR) file and then loaded into the server.

To create the WAR, we use the Application Assembly Tool (AAT). We can either start the tool from the Administration Console or directly from the command line Programs menu.

1. From the WebSphere Administrative Console, choose Tools | Application Assembly Tool.
2. In the Application Assembly Tool window, select a wizard that will guide you along the assembly process. In this case, click the Create Web Module Wizard icon:

3. In the wizard, fill in the WAR information, as shown in Figure 27-3. The display will be used later when we add the Web module to an enterprise application. You can set a containing application (assuming you already have one) by using the pull-down list. The enterprise application will be created later in this procedure. Click the Next button to move on to the next stage.
4. Add the class resources. Select the appropriate JARs to add all the files to the WAR. To add a JAR file, click Add Jar Files and then select the file. Each JAR file adds a set of classes, as shown in Figure 27-4. The tag implementation classes must be included as a resource. When you are done adding the resources client, click the Next button.

   A number of additional steps are required for creating the Web module; these are no different from those of other assembly processes. Our focus right now is to add tag libraries, as shown in Figures 27-5 and 27-6. We'll use this step of the wizard to add our TLD. You can add any number of TLDs to your WAR. Since the TLD includes all the metadata pointing to the JSPs, Java classes, and so on, you need to add only the TLD to the WAR.
5. Add your TLDs. (In our case, only one is added.)
6. Now you can complete the assembly of the WAR and save it.

Create Web Module Wizard

Specifying Web Module Properties

Enter a display name and the file name for your Web module. The display name is used to identify the Web module.

Select a parent application from the list, or leave blank to create a stand-alone module. Enter the file name of your Web module. Web modules have a .war extension.

Containing application: Browse...

Context root:

Display name: ServiceOrderWithAttachments

File name: ServiceOrderWithAttachments.war

Description:

Help < Back Next > Finish Cancel

Figure 27-3. *Specifying the WAR info*

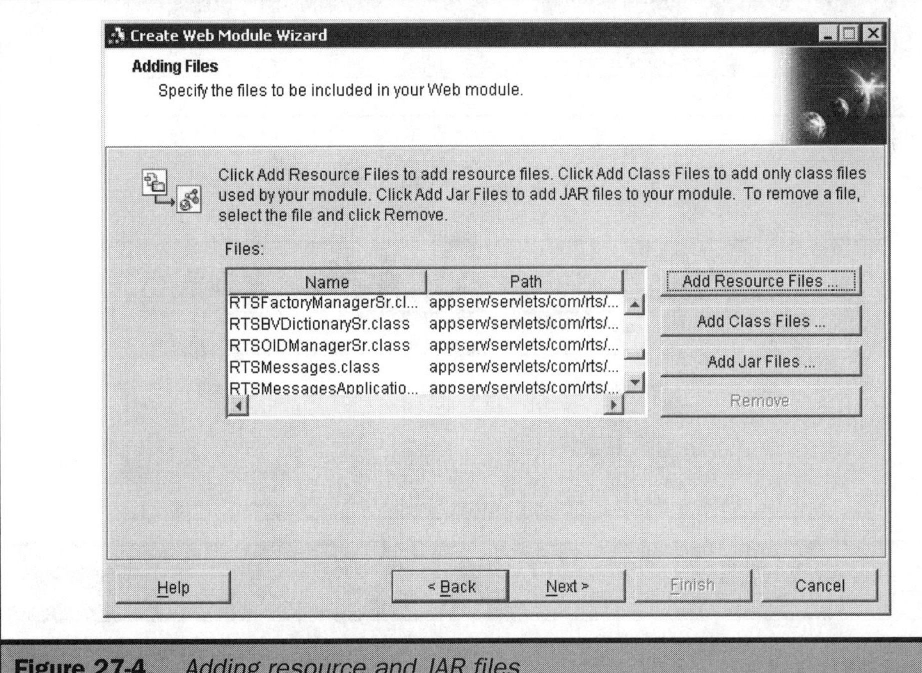

Figure 27-4. *Adding resource and JAR files*

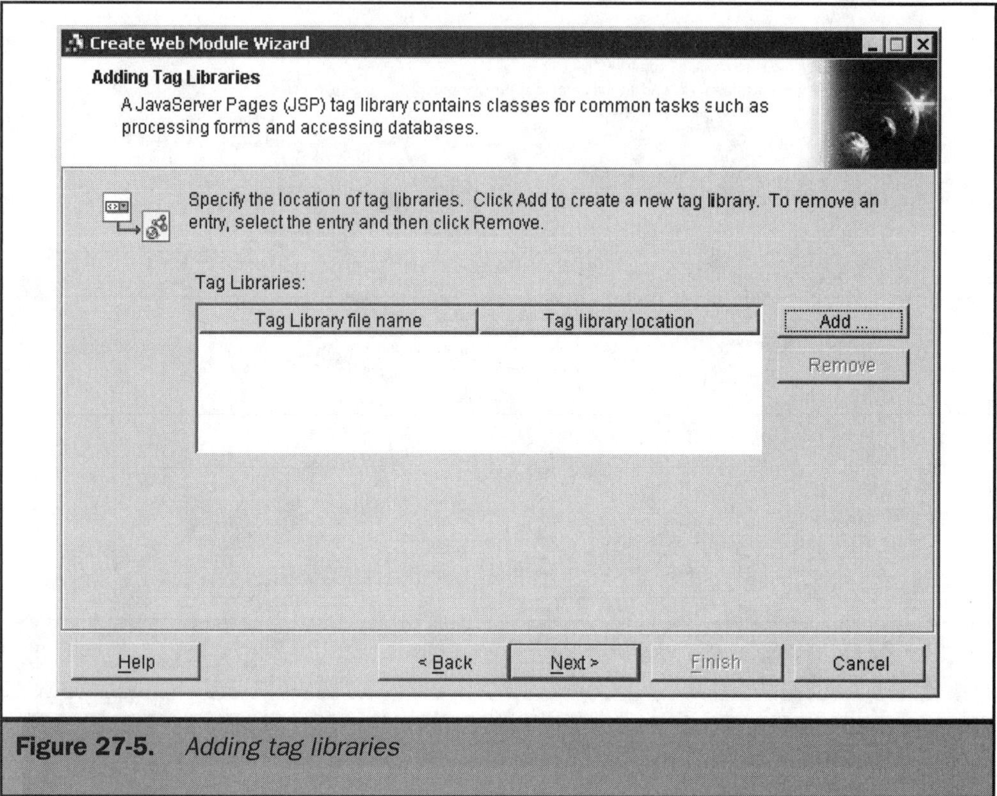

Figure 27-5. *Adding tag libraries*

Add Tag Libraries

Tag Library file name: attachments.tld

Tag library location:

OK | Apply | Cancel | Help

Figure 27-6. *Adding the TLD*

7. Next, you'll create the EAR, which again can be done using an appropriate wizard started from the assembly tool.
8. We will not go through all the steps of creating the EAR; the important thing for you to remember is that the WAR needs to be loaded into the EAR in the "Adding Web Modules" step of the Wizard, shown in Figure 27-7.
9. After you have saved the EAR, exit the Application Assembly Tool and return to the Administration Console. Here, you need to install the enterprise application. You do this by right-clicking the Enterprise Application folder in the tree pane, and selecting the Install Enterprise Application option.
10. Regenerate the Web server plug-in from within the Administration Console by right-clicking the node you are deploying on, and then selecting the Regen Webserver Plugin option. This is the last step in the procedure.

Now the tag library, as well as the application itself, are installed on the WebSphere server and ready to go.

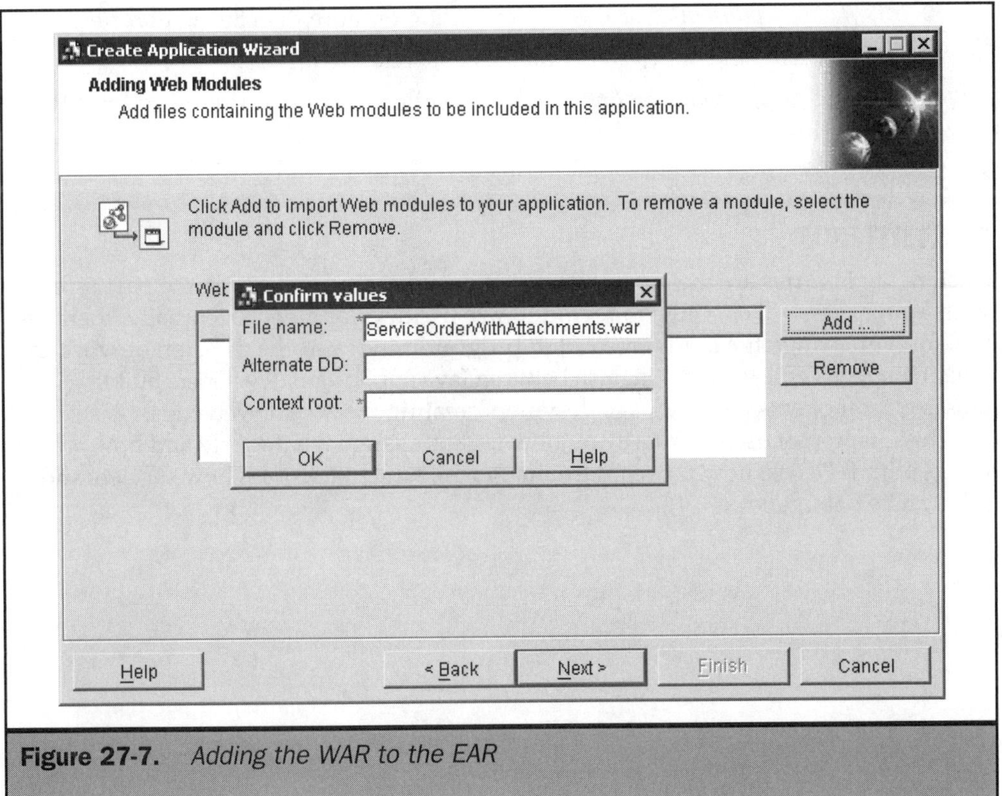

Figure 27-7. *Adding the WAR to the EAR*

Tag Library Resources

Tag libraries are relatively new on the Web application landscape, and we believe that their use will revolutionize the way we build JSPs. In an ideal programming world, all JSPs will return to being what they should be—just Web pages. As tag library use grows among the Java development community, it will emerge as a mainstream technique—and not only for internal development schemes. Hopefully, developers will start using commercially available tag libraries that they buy instead of build.

To this end, you should be familiar with a few resources on the Web that provide good starting points for staying current on tag libraries. Among them are the following sites:

- *http://jakarta.apache.org/taglibs/* The Jakarta taglib project site is one you *must* be aware of. One of the projects is the standard tag library (JSTL, at *http://jakarta.apache.org/taglibs/doc/standard-doc/intro.html*), which promises to be at least as important as the Standard Template Library is to C++.
- *http://jsptags.com/tags/* A large collection of taglibs and pointers to other sites.
- *http://www.taglib.com* Resources and news for JSP developers.
- *http://www.jspin.com/home/tags* A collection of more than 80 tag libraries.
- *http://www.javaskyline.com/dev.html* A collection of taglibs.
- *http://www.jspinsider.com/index.view* A collection of good resource on JSPs and taglibs.

Summary

Custom tag libraries are the *most important evolution of the JSP model* in the past three years—and they will continue to revolutionize JSP development. Eventually, their use will forever change the landscape of JSP programming, and the division of work in building screens will again distinguish between Java application developers building reusable components and JSP page designers creating the actual Web pages.

This chapter focused primarily on how taglibs change what we do and how we do things with JSPs. We now move on to Chapter 28, which discusses how servlets and JSPs can be debugged.

The Complete Reference

Chapter 28

Debugging Servlets and JSPs Using VisualAge

The WebSphere runtime platform supports servlets and JavaServer Pages (JSPs) as a core technology. You have already seen quite a few examples of how servlets and JSPs are deployed under WebSphere. However, developing and debugging servlets and JSPs has been saved for this chapter.

While you can develop servlets and JSPs using any development environment, even using the plain old Java Developer's Kit (JDK)—with TextPad or another good text editor), IBM's VisualAge for Java offers a better environment for developing servlets and JSPs. VisualAge for Java has a built-in WebSphere test environment that can be activated from within VisualAge so that the program-test-debug cycle is all done from within the VisualAge Integrated Development Environment (IDE). The alternative is to build the servlets in some other Java IDE using a text editor (or build the JSP pages using a site builder), and then install them in the WebSphere environment and view the results (or *try* to view the results).

Using VisualAge for Java, development productivity can be significantly improved. The reasons for this are VisualAge's unified environment and debugging tools. As you shall see, when using VisualAge for Java's WebSphere test environment, coding, running, and testing can all be completed from the IDE without ever starting up the WebSphere server or the administration tool. When using WebSphere, the test-debug process is lengthy and difficult, especially if you go through the whole process of assembly and deployment for each change in your code. In addition, if you are using the Enterprise Edition of VisualAge for Java, the whole issue of version control and configuration management is automatically part of the development cycle for the servlets.

The second advantage to using the WebSphere test environment is access to its debugging tools. If you were to use another environment or editor, the only way to know what was going on would be to use a series of print commands that would need to be inspected to see what code was reached, what the variables' values were, and to compile other information. When using the VisualAge IDE with the WebSphere test environment, the entire set of debugging tools are available to the servlet and JSP developer. This means, for example, that you can insert breakpoints in the servlet code and have the WebSphere test environment stop at this breakpoint to allow you to perform any action that you used to do when building a plain, old Java application.

While today's tight coupling between WebSphere and VisualAge has a lot going for it, the trend of standardization in Java-based servers means that other IDEs will eventually become viable alternatives to using VisualAge for Java.

Developing Servlets in VisualAge

VisualAge for Java offers a servlet creation wizard that's similar to the applet-creating wizard you used in Chapter 17. To invoke the Create Servlet Wizard, right-click the workspace and select Add | Servlet from the pop-up menu. The wizard opens, as shown in Figure 28-1.

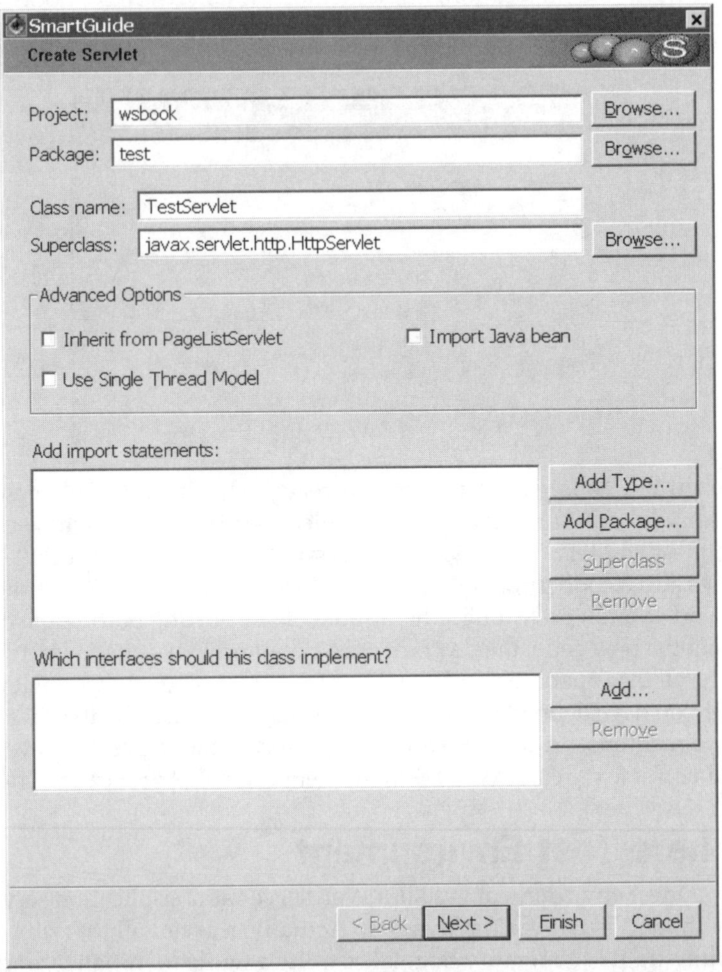

Figure 28-1. *The Create Servlet Wizard opening screen*

Here, you indicate the project name, package name, and class name. The new servlet is derived by default from `HttpServlet`, but you can change that if you need to use a different superclass. You can also add import statements and specify what interfaces (other than the `Servlet` interface) the servlet should implement.

After you click Next, the wizard screen asks you to specify the Java modifiers for the new class and indicate which methods you want to implement. The default selections (shown in the illustration) implement the methods `init`, `doGet`, `doPost`, and `getServletInfo`.

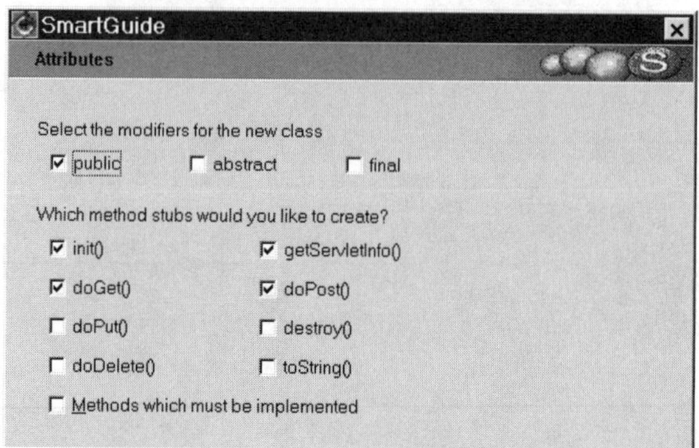

Click Finish, and voilà! The new servlet is ready. The default implementation for both `doGet` and `doPost` calls a method called `performTask`, which receives the HTTP request and response objects. In the spirit of our "Hello World" servlet from Chapter 4, let's add a code snippet that will produce a "Hello World" message. However, in this case, you will not go through the trouble of supporting both English and French. Upon inserting the new code, the `performTask` method looks as shown in Figure 28-2.

Obviously, all the capabilities of VisualAge for Java can be applied to developing servlets. After you have defined the servlet (either manually or using the wizards), you can add or remove methods, browse the code, and perform other tasks. However, the most powerful and useful feature for servlet development is the WebSphere test environment.

The WebSphere Test Environment

The WebSphere test environment is a slim Web server and application server that is integrated with the Visual Age for Java IDE. Actually, it is not all that slim, which is our major criticism. It is a memory hog, takes quite a while to initialize, and is quite slow in running. However, it is superior to anything else available in terms of the code-test-debug cycle.

The WebSphere test environment allows you to deploy servlets under a Web server, serve up Hypertext Markup Language (HTML) pages, and process JSP pages creating HTML pages that are propagated to the browser. It includes precisely all the components that are necessary to make sure your servlet/JSP e-business application works correctly before you deploy it under WebSphere. The tools are conveniently packaged into the IDE so that their activation is simple.

Here's how you use it:

1. To start up the WebSphere test environment from the Workbench, choose Workspace | Tools, and select the name of the servlet.

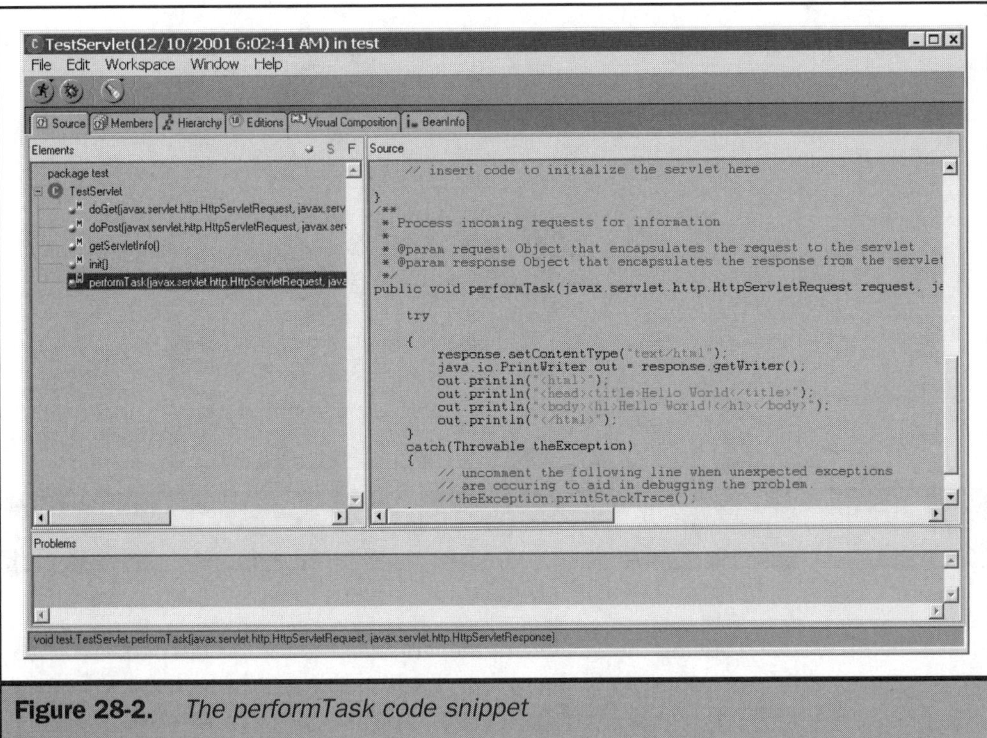

Figure 28-2. *The performTask code snippet*

2. The test environment start up process takes a few seconds, at the end of which, the WebSphere Test Environment Control Center window appears, as shown next.

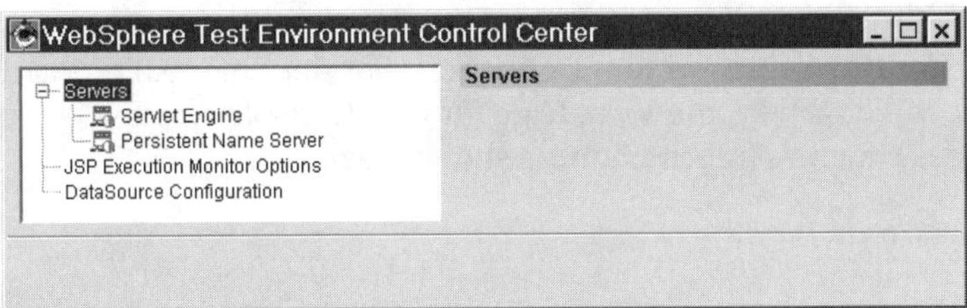

This window serves as the "Administrative Console" for the test environment. IBM uses the same color codes for the servers that are used in the WebSphere Administrative Console (blue for running and red for stopped).

3. Click the Servlet Engine item on the left side of the window. You'll see a window similar to that shown in Figure 28-3.

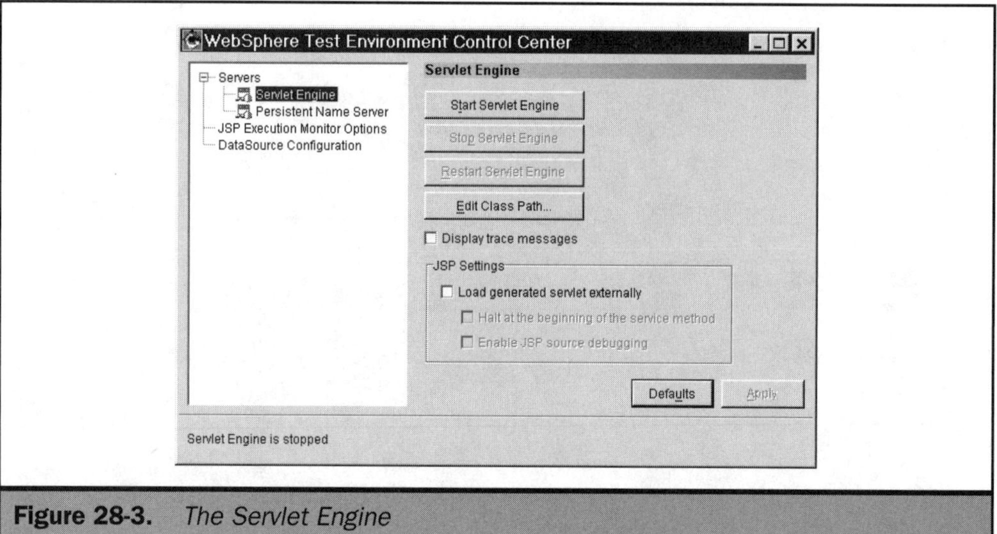

Figure 28-3. *The Servlet Engine*

4. Before you start using the servlet engine, you need to set its classpath. To open the Servlet Engine ClassPath dialog box shown in Figure 28-4, click the Edit Class Path button on the Test Environment Control Center window.
5. Select the project in which you placed your new servlet. This is a useful feature that allows you to set the classpath in terms of a set of VisualAge projects instead of directories and files. (After all, this is your environment when developing and debugging your code.) In this dialog box, you can also add any classpath that's external to VisualAge.
6. When you're finished, click OK to return to the Test Environment Control Center window.
7. In the Control Center window, click Start Servlet Engine. During the servlet engine initialization, the VisualAge for Java Console window appears and provides progress information, as shown next.

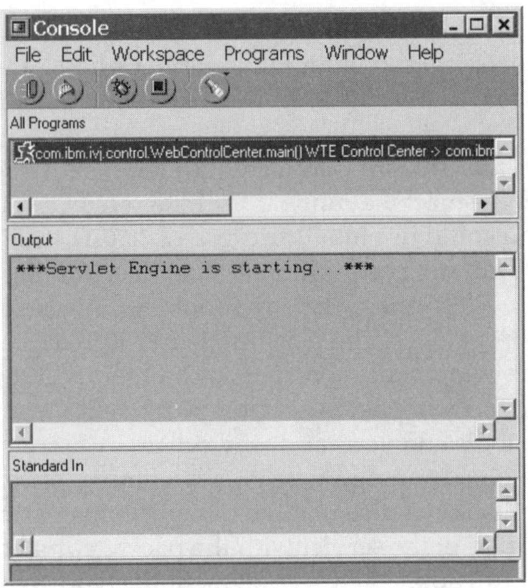

After the initialization is complete, the display is updated to reflect that the servlet engine is running.

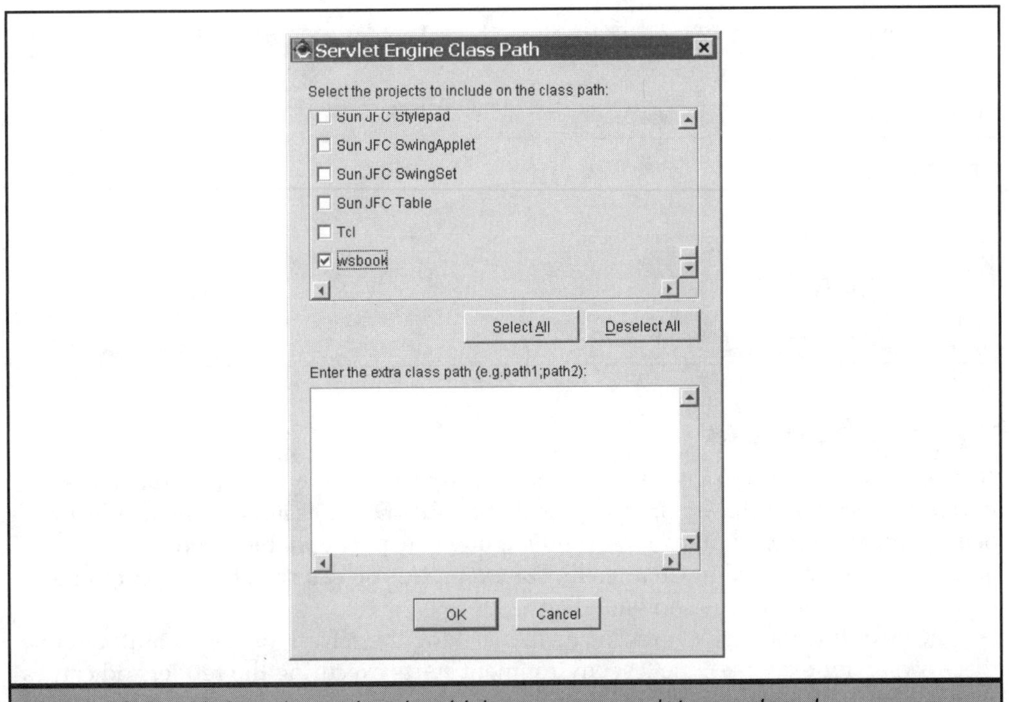

Figure 28-4. *Select the project in which your new servlet was placed*

Now that the servlet engine is running, you can invoke the small test servlet. To do that, open any Web browser and point it to the servlet's URL. This URL includes the fully qualified servlet name. For example, for our TestServlet it is *http://localhost:8080/servlet/test.TestServlet*.

Three points about this URL are worth mentioning here. First, note the hostname used is *localhost*—this is the machine running the Integrated Development Environment (IDE) (equivalently, you could use the IP address *127.0.0.1*). This does not preclude remote access to an IDE running on a different machine, but this would not be the typical case, because the WebSphere test environment is normally used as a small personal server for the developer. The port number is 8080 by default, because this is the convention for a "development server." You can modify it through the VisualAge for Java Options window. WebSphere uses port 80 by default, so clashes do not usually occur between the two tools and you can easily run an instance of the WebSphere server on the same machine running VisualAge (assuming, of course, that you have a whole lot of memory). Finally, notice that the naming convention for the URL path is based on the concatenation of the servlet with the package-qualified servlet name. You are not able to perform full application deployment like you are with WebSphere. On the upside, there is no hassle related to registering or deploying the servlet. Once the servlet is coded and compiled, you can access it here.

The following illustration shows the output for our servlet:

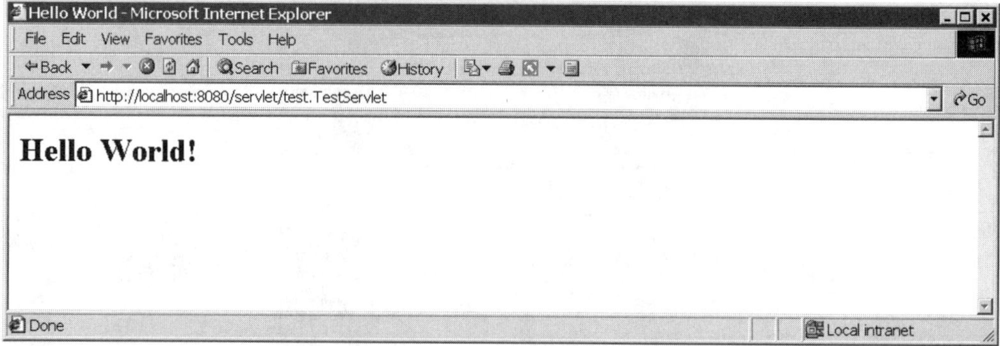

Debugging Servlets

After you've managed to install, load, and start up the test environment, the rest is trivial. The beauty of this environment is that all the IDE tools are now available for debugging the servlet. You can insert breakpoints, inspect variables, and perform other tasks, as explained in Chapter 17. For example, you can set a breakpoint in the `performTask` method, as shown in Figure 28-5.

The next time the servlet is accessed (by clicking the refresh or reload button on the browser, for example), the test environment starts executing the servlet and comes across the breakpoint, immediately bringing up the debugger shown in Figure 28-6.

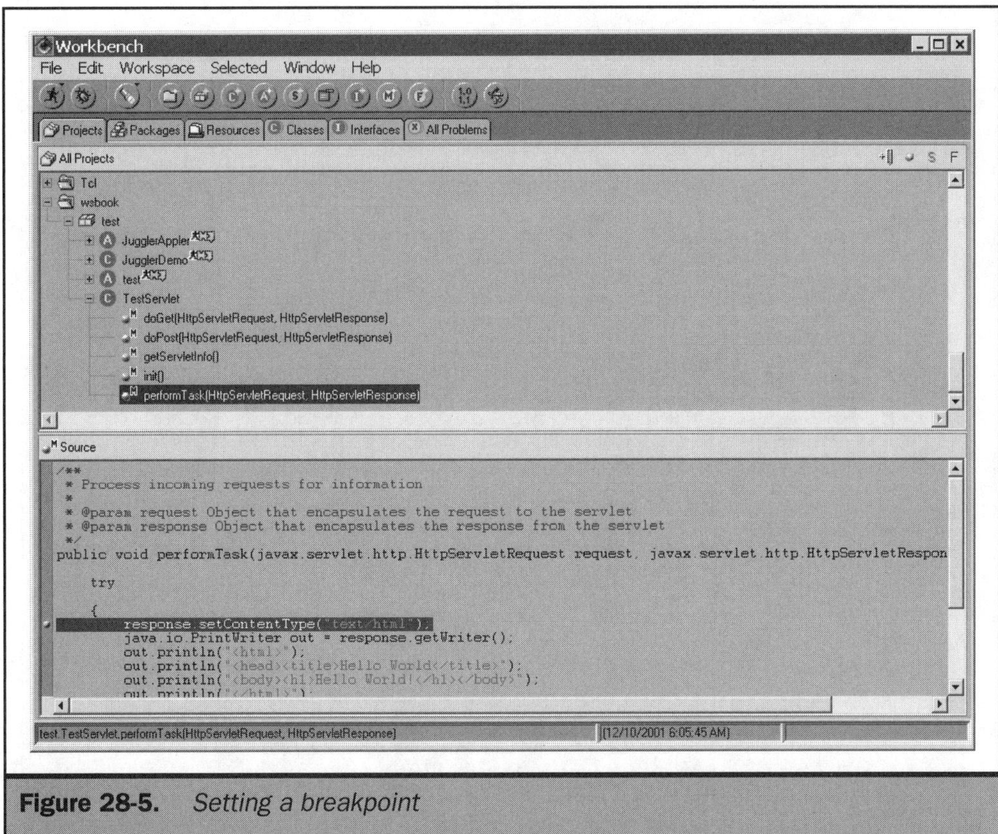

Figure 28-5. *Setting a breakpoint*

In the debugger, you are free to do anything you usually do in the IDE—you can inspect any object reachable from the debugger. For example, you can inspect the request object uniform resource indicator (URI), as shown in Figure 28-7.

These debugging abilities can save you hours of work, compared to using the real WebSphere installation for testing and debugging software. Not only is the deployment cycle significantly shorter, but the debugging tools make all the difference.

Debugging JSPs

This chapter concludes with the tools available for JSP development and debugging. Unlike the servlet development and execution environment, JSP requires some minimal deployment. As mentioned, the VisualAge for Java WebSphere Test Environment runs a miniature Web server that has a "document root" just like the actual IBM HTTP server. This root is located by default in the directory *ide\project_resources\IBM WebSphere Test*

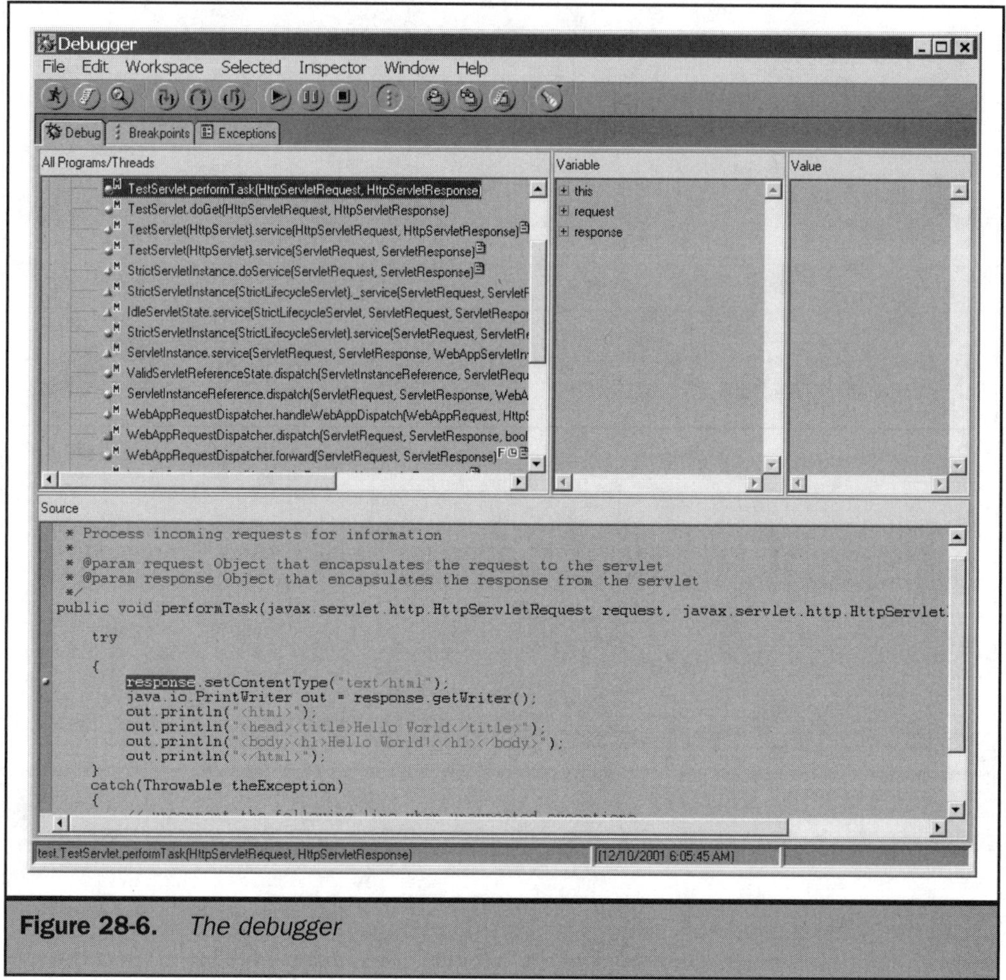

Figure 28-6. *The debugger*

Environment\hosts\default_host\default_app\web under the VisualAge for Java installation. The default content of this directory is shown next.

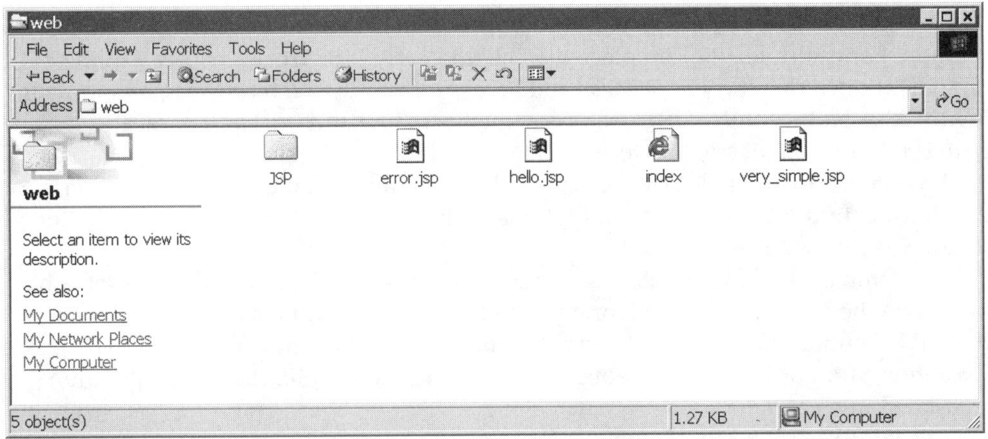

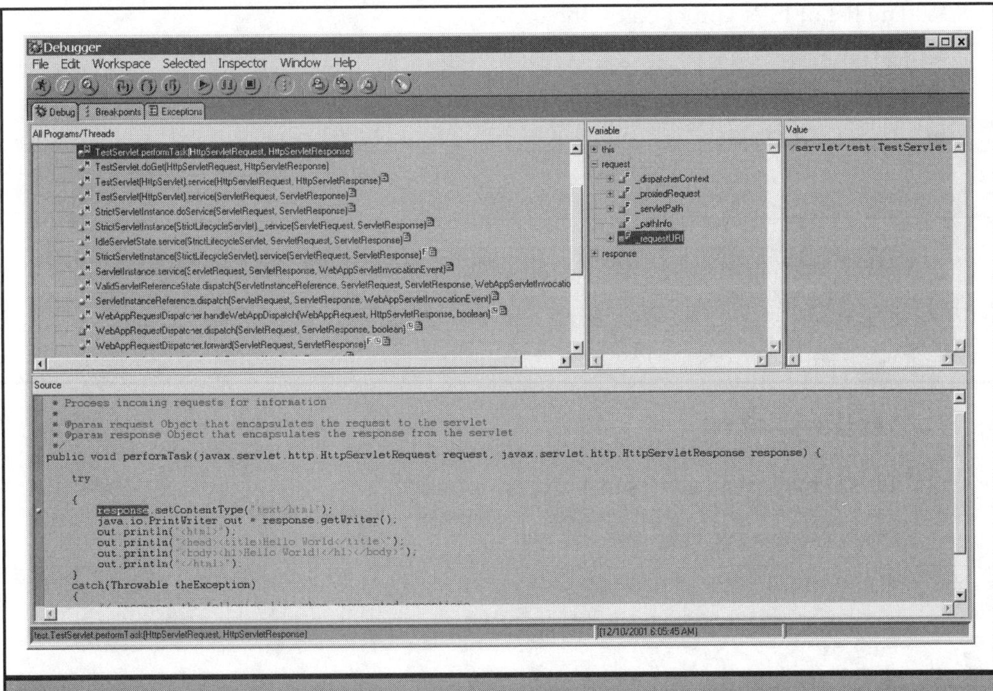

Figure 28-7. *Inspecting the request object URI*

To run JSPs from within VisualAge for Java, you first need to place them in this location. For example, you can place the "Hello World" JSP from Chapter 4 in the aforementioned directory as *hello.jsp* and access it from the Web browser, as shown in Figure 28-8. Note that the URL uses the same hostname and port as before, and the path is relative to the *web* directory.

If you need to debug JSPs (which is likely), you must enable the JSP execution monitoring, under the JSP Monitor Options in the Test Environment Control Center window, as shown in Figure 28-9.

After you enable JSP monitoring, when you invoke a JSP (by clicking the refresh button on the browser window, for example), VisualAge for Java automatically starts the JSP Execution Monitor window with your JSP, as shown in Figure 28-10. The JSP Execution Monitor is a special debugging environment for JSP. Recall that JSP are translated into servlets.

The JSP Execution Monitor shows four subwindows:

- The list of JSPs launched by the browser
- JSP source
- Servlet Java source
- Generated HTML

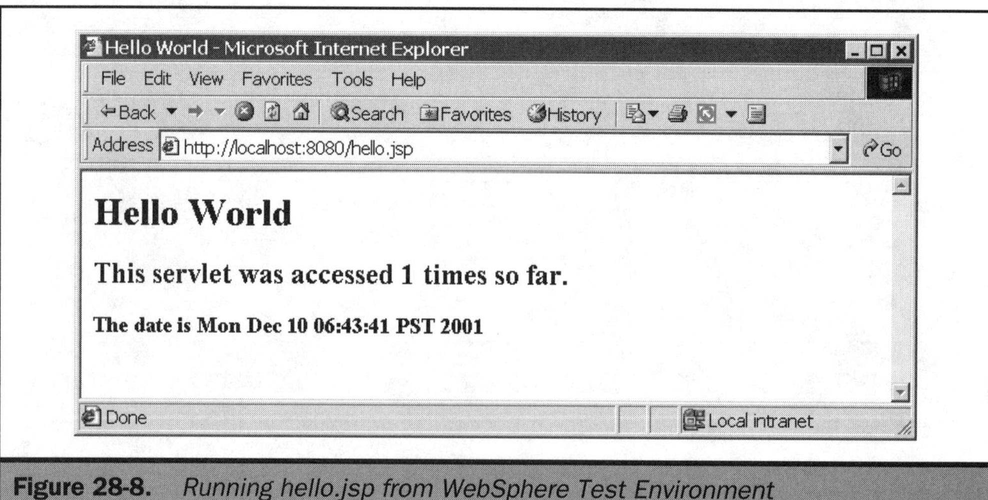

Figure 28-8. *Running hello.jsp from WebSphere Test Environment*

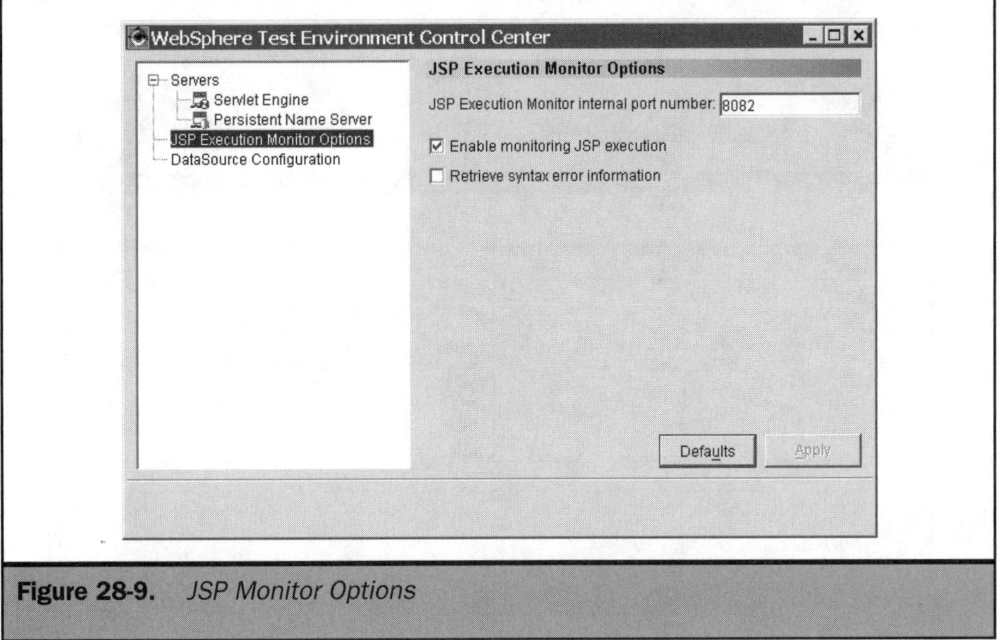

Figure 28-9. *JSP Monitor Options*

The JSP Monitor allows you to step through the Java code and see the HTML content generated dynamically. It does not provide all the functionality of the VisualAge for Java debugger but is still useful for debugging JSP. To get the JSP running, you must click the Step, Run, or Fast-Forward buttons on the JSP monitor toolbar.

You can control the JSP Monitor settings via the JSP Execution Monitor Options. You can enable or disable JSP monitoring and syntax error retrieval, as well as set the port used for JSP monitoring. (Note that this is for internal communication within VisualAge for Java and is not related to the port 8080 used for the HTTP connection from your browser.)

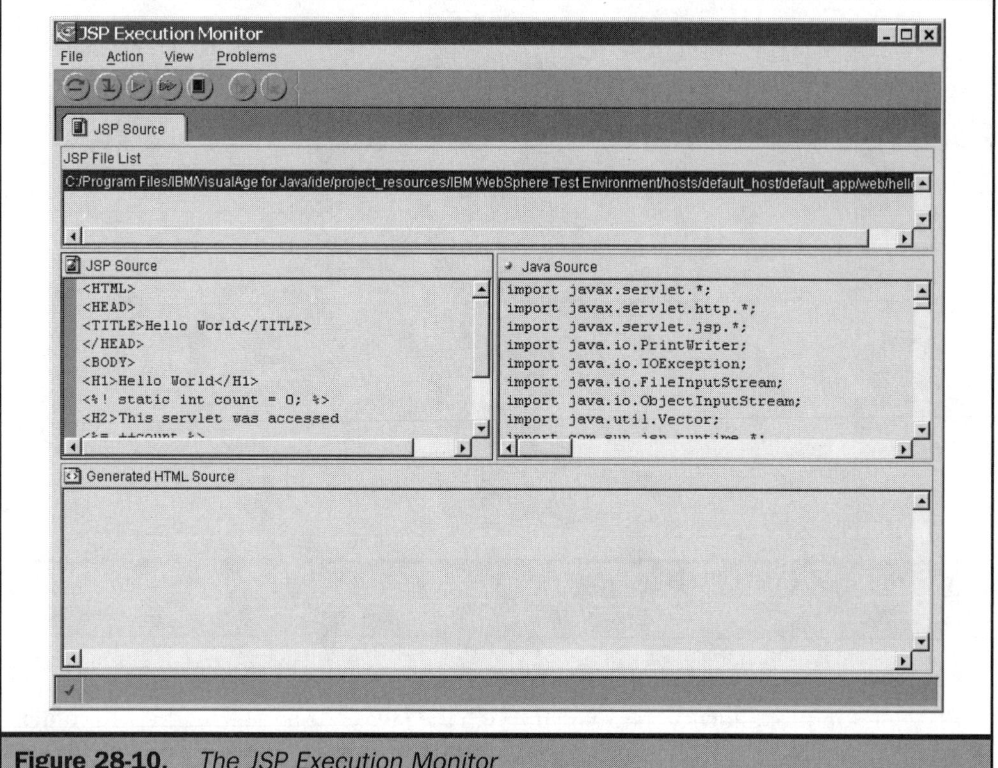

Figure 28-10. *The JSP Execution Monitor*

Summary

IBM is considered one of the premier vendors in the space for Java, Java application servers, and e-business. The strength of the integration between VisualAge for Java (which has the best support for multiple-person development teams using the Enterprise Edition) and the WebSphere application server, in the form of the WebSphere Test Environment, is of utmost importance to the WebSphere application developer. If you plan to use the WebSphere Application Server for deploying your applications, we strongly recommend that you use VisualAge for development and make use of the tools described in this chapter.

This chapter concludes the discussion of servlets and JSPs. On to Enterprise JavaBeans!

The Complete Reference

Part VI

Developing EJB

Chapter 29

Session Beans

This chapter begins an in-depth discussion of Enterprise JavaBeans (EJB), a server-side component architecture that enables and simplifies the process of building enterprise-level distributed applications in Java. As mentioned in Chapter 11, EJBs are categorized into two groups: session beans and entity beans. The major distinguishing feature between these two groups is the notion of *persistence*. Session beans represent server-side components that implement business logic but are not persistent, while entity beans are used when the beans' state needs to be persisted beyond a single user's session.

In Chapter 5, you saw a simple state-less "Hello World" session bean. Chapter 11 elaborated on EJB, the EJB architecture, roles, and framework. It described session beans and covered their lifecycles. This chapter looks at some examples of session EJBs. Through these examples, you will explore how session beans are built and how they are deployed in a WebSphere Application Server. The discussion here includes state-less as well as state-ful session beans and covers all aspects of EJBs, including building them, assembling them, and deploying them.

PageFetch: A State-less Session Bean

A *state-less* session bean does not maintain a conversational state—in other words, when invoked, a state-less bean does not maintain any context that is used for subsequent calls. One consequence of this is that EJB containers can pool and reuse state-less sessions. For example, they can use the same instance for different invocations by different clients. This is possible because instances of a state-less session bean are expected to be identical. Note that although the bean does not maintain a conversational state, this does not necessarily imply that it does not have any member variable. Such variables are, however, of limited use because the client must not rely on their existence (that is, the client must not assume that consecutive method invocations actually use the same bean instance). If a state-less session bean does have state (that is, it contains member variables), these member variables should be declared as final. If they're not declared as final, you can run into race condition scenarios if two or more clients of the bean simultaneously access the state of the state-less session bean.

The state-less session bean example in this section is the `PageFetch` bean. Recall from Chapter 11 that one of the motivations for using session EJB is to promote application partitioning. Our bean does just that. This bean acts on the behalf of the client and retrieves a Web page. It then compresses the Web page content and returns it to the client. This kind of bean can be useful for retrieving "busy" Web pages, assuming that the EJB server in which the bean is deployed is located in the vicinity of the Web server holding the content (for example, both are on the same LAN).

PageFetch Remote Interface

The first step in developing a new enterprise bean is defining the remote interface, which defines the contract with the user of the bean. In our case, the bean provides one "business" method called `getPage`. This method takes as parameter a Hyptertext

Transfer Protocol (HTTP) uniform resource locator (URL), retrieves the page, and returns the page in compressed form. The interface is shown here:

```
import javax.ejb.*;
import java.rmi.*;
import java.io.*;

public interface PageFetch extends EJBObject
{
      byte[] getPage(String url) throws RemoteException, IOException;
}
```

The remote interface extends the `EJBObject` interface that is part of the *javax.ejb* package. The class implementing this interface is generated by the EJB container. Each method defined in the remote interface must throw the `RemoteException` exception to deal with cases in which some communication or other problem prevents the method from being invoked. This requirement stems from the fact that an EJB method is called using Java Remote Method Invocation (RMI). In addition, each of the parameters and returned values for the method must either be Java primitive types or must implement the `Serializable` interface.

Our `getPage` method also throws an `IOException`. When it accesses the Web page designated by the parameter `url`, some network failure might occur. The reasons for such a failure could range from the URL being malformed to the server or network being down. Such an occurrence is indicated by throwing the exception.

PageFetch Home Interface

The next step is to define the home interface for our EJB. The home interface is used to create and destroy EJB instances. The EJB home interface extends the `EJBHome` interface defined in the *javax.ejb* package.

```
import javax.ejb.*;
import java.rmi.*;
import java.io.*;

public interface PageFetchHome extends EJBHome
{
      PageFetch create() throws RemoteException, CreateException;
}
```

The `create` method returns the remote interface just defined and does not require any parameters. In general, the `create` method for a home interface can take whatever parameters are required for constructing the bean object. In the case of state-less beans, there are usually no such parameters. The `create` method can throw either a `RemoteException` (due to RMI problems) or `CreateException`, which indicates that while no problems have been encountered with the communication, the server is still unable to create the bean instance (for example, due to memory limitations).

PageFetch Bean Implementation

After defining these two interfaces, we can turn to the implementation of our bean. The first thing to note is that the bean implements the `javax.ejb.SessionBean` interface. It does *not* implement the `PageFetch` interface (our remote interface) because that interface is implemented by a stub class generated by the EJB container.

Our bean implementation can still implement other interfaces or extend a class. To be able to describe a state-ful bean in the next section, we need to separate the implementation of the bean into two parts. First, we define the class `PageBean`, which implements the `SessionBean` interface. This class has two auxiliary methods that allow loading a Web page and compressing a string:

```
import javax.ejb.*;
import java.rmi.*;
import java.io.*;
import java.util.*;
import java.net.*;
import java.util.zip.*;

public class PageBean implements SessionBean
{
      // Implementation of "business" method
      public byte[] getPage(String url) throws IOException
      {
            // Get the page content.
            StringBuffer buf = loadPage(url);
            // Compress the page.
            return pack(buf);
      }

      // EJB methods
      public void ejbCreate()
      {
      }

      public void ejbRemove()
      {
      }

      public void ejbActivate()
      {
      }
```

```
public void ejbPassivate()
{
}

public void setSessionContext(SessionContext context)
{
}

// Given a URL, access the page and return it in a string buffer.
protected StringBuffer loadPage(String urlString) throws IOException
{
      URL finalUrl = new URL(urlString);
      StringBuffer stringBuffer = new StringBuffer();
      URLConnection urlconnection = finalUrl.openConnection();
      urlconnection.setDoInput(true);
      urlconnection.setRequestProperty("User-Agent",
              "Mozilla/4.0(compatible; MSIE 5.5; Windows 98)");
      InputStreamReader reader = new InputStreamReader
                               (urlconnection.getInputStream());
      int  i = urlconnection.getContentLength();
      int j;
      char[] inbuf = new char[4096];
      for (; (j = reader.read(inbuf)) != -1; ) {
            stringBuffer.append(inbuf, 0, j);
            int k = stringBuffer.length();
            if (i <= 0) {
                  continue;
            }
            if (i <= k) {
                  break;
            }
      }
      return stringBuffer;
}

/*
 * Compress the byte stream before sending it. It is worth doing
 * a bit of extra work because the bytes are normally sent over
 * a slow wireless line.
 */
protected byte[] pack(StringBuffer stringBuffer) throws IOException
{
      String pageStr = stringBuffer.toString();
      ByteArrayOutputStream s = new ByteArrayOutputStream();
      ByteArrayOutputStream st2 = new ByteArrayOutputStream();
      ObjectOutputStream out = new ObjectOutputStream(s);
```

```
            out.writeBytes(pageStr);
            out.flush();
            byte[] full = s.toByteArray();
            int fullsz = s.size();

            Deflater def = new Deflater();
            def.setStrategy(Deflater.DEFAULT_STRATEGY);
            def.setLevel(Deflater.BEST_COMPRESSION);
            def.setInput(full);
            DeflaterOutputStream os = new DeflaterOutputStream(st2, def);
            int len = fullsz;
            int st = 0;
            int jump = 1024;
            byte[] buf = new byte[1024];

            while (st < len) {
                  if (len - st < 1024)
                        jump = len - st;
                  System.arraycopy(full, st, buf, 0, jump);
                  os.write(buf, 0, jump);
                  st += 1024;
            }
            os.close();
            return st2.toByteArray();
      }
}
```

The implementation of the EJB methods is empty, mainly because our bean is state-less, so there is not a whole lot to do when it is created, removed, activated, or passivated. We implement two protected auxiliary methods that are to be used by subclasses of the class. These auxiliary methods account for most of this class.

The `loadPage` method loads a Web page whose URL is given and returns a `StringBuffer` holding the content. This method establishes a URL connection and reads the page over this connection. The `pack` method uses the *java.util.zip* package to compress a `StringBuffer`.

The next class is the actual implementation of our session bean. It extends `PageBean` and implements our business method `getPage`. By implementing this method, as well as the required methods of the `SessionBean` interface, our `PageFetchBean` complies with what the EJB container expects from the bean implementation. Note that this method must be declared public and must match the signature defined for it in the remote interface. The only allowed difference in terms of the signature is that the bean implementation method need not throw a `RemoteException`. It may want to do so if its own logic requires performing RMI, in which case the method's signatures will be identical. However, that is not the case here.

```
import javax.ejb.*;
import java.rmi.*;

public class PageFetchBean extends PageBean
{
      // Implementation of "business" method
      public byte[] getPage(String url) throws IOException
      {
            // Get the page content.
            StringBuffer buf = loadPage(url);
            // Compress the page.
            return pack(buf);
      }
}
```

As noted earlier, the bean's superclass implements two protected auxiliary methods that are used by the single method defined in this class. This is allowed because the bean class is an ordinary Java class. However, some restrictions stem from the EJB model:

- The bean cannot start new threads or use the synchronized keyword.
- The bean must not be abstract.
- Static variables can be used only if they are declared final (that is, all static variables are actually constant).

These restrictions are not enforced by the compiler, the assembly tools, or the EJB container. The developer has the freedom to make mistakes; as in most cases, EJB applications still require careful design.

PageFetch Bean Assembly and Deployment

Bean assembly and deployment is performed using the Application Assembly Tool (AAT) and the Administrative Console, respectively.

When adding the new bean (as part of a new EJB module), we use the AAT to set the bean parameters. You can use the General tab in the New Session Bean dialog box, shown in Figure 29-1, to indicate the EJB name, display name, and description. These three are used to assist in the task of deploying the beans. Remember that the person deploying the EJB module can be someone other than the application assembler (possibly even someone from a different organization). Other parameters are the remote interface, home interface, and bean class. Finally, you can select whether the bean is state-less or state-ful; in our case, it is state-less. We also set the transaction attributes for the bean. Transaction attributes are discussed in Chapter 31. It is worthwhile to note that the AAT is not able to determine automatically whether the bean is state-ful or state-less because being state-less does not necessarily mean that there are no member variables.

You can use the icons tab (not shown) to associate an icon with the bean. This icon will be shown at assembly and deployment time. The IBM Extensions tab shown in

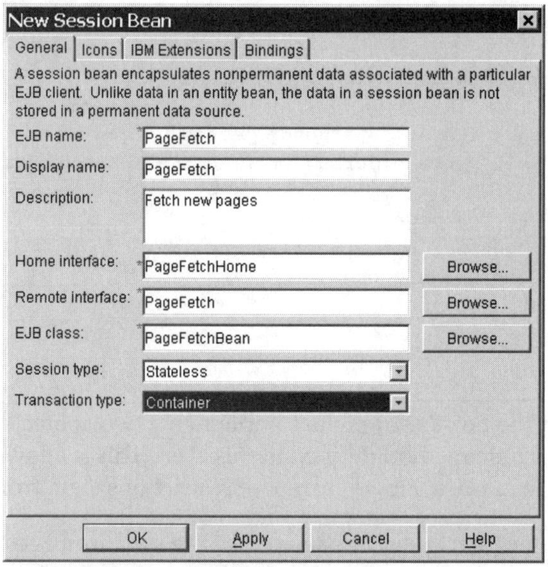

Figure 29-1. *New Session Bean General tab*

Figure 29-2 is used to define some WebSphere-specific attributes, such as timeout, caching, and local transactions. These are discussed in detail in Chapter 33.

The Bindings tab, shown in Figure 29-3 is used to determine the Java Naming Directory Interface (JNDI) name of the bean. This name is important because it is the key by which client-side code can access the bean.

Deploying this bean to the WebSphere Application Server is straightforward once you've packaged it in an EJB module (repeating the procedure described in Chapter 5). The next section presents a small JavaServer Pages (JSP) page that uses the `PageFetch` bean, so it makes sense to package the EJB and JSP together in one Enterprise Archive (EAR) file. An EAR file holds zero or more Web Archive (WAR) files as well as zero or more EJB modules.

Creating an EAR File

To create a new EAR file, choose File | New | Application. Then, in the lefthand pane of the Application Assembly Tool, you can import EJB modules into the EAR file by right-clicking the EJB Modules icon and selecting Import. Later on, you can also import Web modules (by right-clicking the Web Modules icon and selecting Import). After adding both an EJB module and a WAR module, the AAT should look like the one shown in Figure 29-4.

Notice that the Web module contains a single JSP. It is described in the next section, "PageFetch in Action."

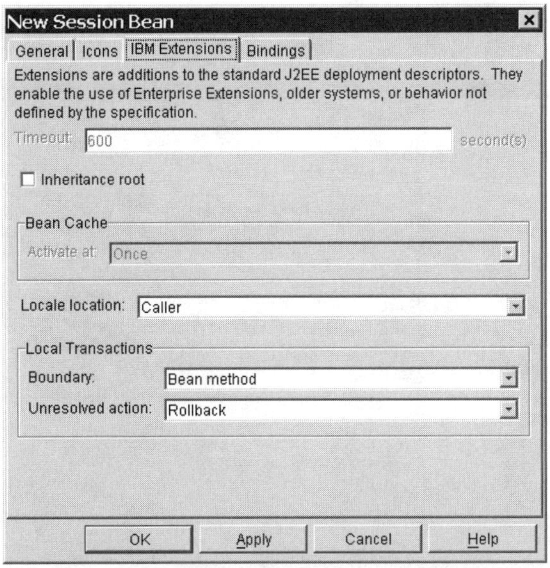

Figure 29-2. *New Session Bean IBM Extensions tab*

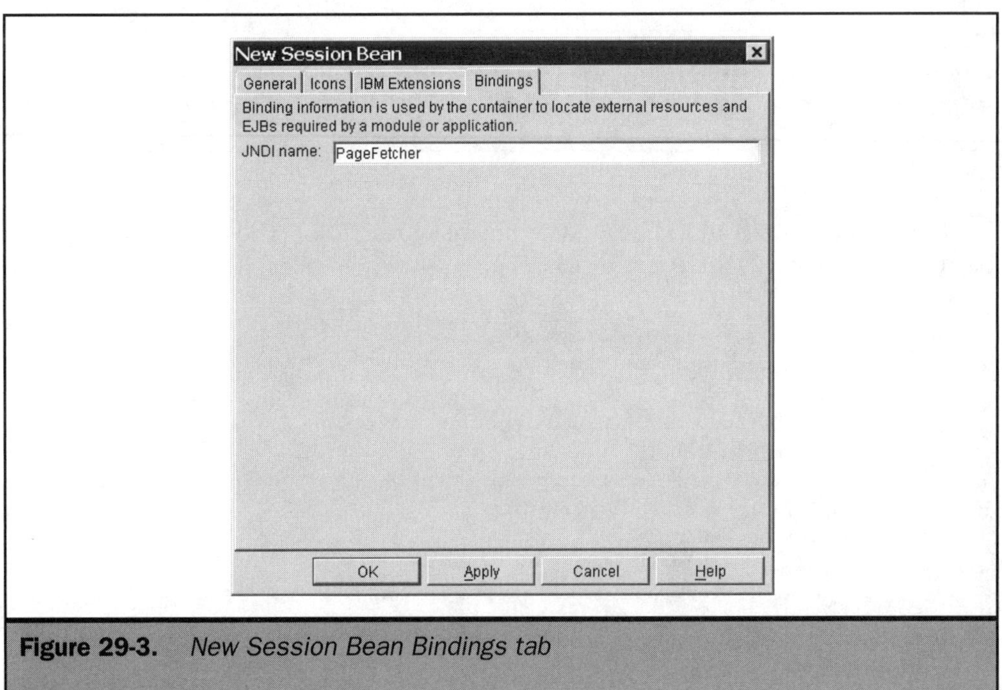

Figure 29-3. *New Session Bean Bindings tab*

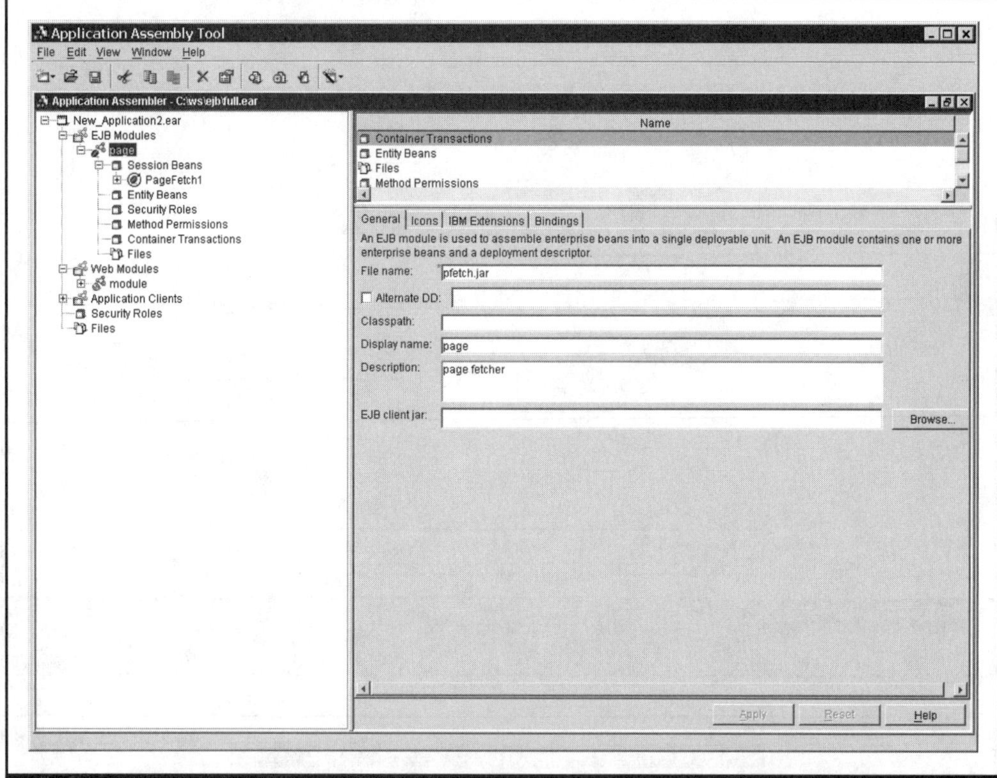

Figure 29-4. *AAT with an enterprise application containing a PageFetch EJB and a Web module*

The AAT generates an XML-based deployment descriptor. The descriptor for our bean is as follows:

```
<?xml version="1.0" encoding="UTF-8"?>
<!DOCTYPE ejb-jar PUBLIC
    "-//Sun Microsystems, Inc.//DTD Enterprise JavaBeans 1.1//EN"
    "http://java.sun.com/j2ee/dtds/ejb-jar_1_1.dtd">
   <ejb-jar id="ejb-jar_ID">
      <description>page fetcher</description>
      <display-name>page</display-name>
      <enterprise-beans>
         <session id="Session_1">
          <description>Page Fetch1</description>
            <display-name>PageFetch1</display-name>
            <ejb-name>PageFetch1</ejb-name>
            <home>PageFetchHome</home>
            <remote>PageFetch</remote>
```

```
            <ejb-class>PageFetchBean</ejb-class>
            <session-type>Stateless</session-type>
            <transaction-type>Container</transaction-type>
         </session>
      </enterprise-beans>
      <assembly-descriptor id="AssemblyDescriptor_1">
      </assembly-descriptor>
</ejb-jar>
```

In this XML file, you can clearly see the bean attributes we selected in the AAT: the bean description, display name, remote and home interface, bean implementation class, state-less session type, and transaction type.

PageFetch in Action

To demonstrate our PageFetch bean, we will implement a simple JSP in which a specific page is accessed and the data is decompressed and shown to the user:

```
<%@page import="javax.ejb.*" %>
<%@page import="javax.naming.*" %>
<%@page import="java.util.*" %>
<%@page import="java.rmi.*" %>
<%@page import="java.util.zip.*" %>
<%
      String str = null;
      byte[] ret = null;
      byte[] full = null;
      try {
        Properties env = System.getProperties();
        env.put(javax.naming.Context.INITIAL_CONTEXT_FACTORY,
                "com.ibm.websphere.naming.WsnInitialContextFactory");

        env.put(javax.naming.Context.PROVIDER_URL, "iiop://localhost");
        InitialContext ic = new InitialContext(env);
        PageFetchHome home = (PageFetchHome)
                      javax.rmi.PortableRemoteObject.narrow(
                             ic.lookup("PageFetcher"),
                             PageFetchHome.class);
        PageFetch bean = home.create();
        ret = bean.getPage("http://www.viryanet.com");
        Inflater inf = new Inflater();
        inf.setInput(ret);
        full = new byte[2000000];
        len = inf.inflate(full);
        str = new String(full, 0, len);
      } catch (Exception ex) {
        %>
        Error <%= ex %>
```

```
    <%
  }
    %>
  <%= str %>
```

The implementation of this JSP is quite straightforward, and the output here is the page as it looks after the content is decompressed and returned from the bean. We've chosen to have the JSP access a single constant URL, which is, of course, not practical—but it is sufficient for demonstrating the use of our EJB.

DiffPageFetch: A State-ful Session Bean

Next we turn to state-ful session beans. A *state-ful* session bean holds a conversational state that spans multiple method invocations. This implies that the bean has some member variables holding the state, and that the container must typically keep a separate instance for each client because the bean instances are no longer interchangeable. For state-less beans, the container can use the same instance for all clients, but for state-ful beans, this management is mandatory. What the container typically does is resort to *passivating* beans—placing them in persistent storage and using the same instance for different clients.

Our example of a state-ful session bean will be similar to the state-less example earlier in the chapter. Suppose we are again interested in accessing a Web page, except we expect it to change marginally from one access to another. The bean must be able to send back to the client just the changes, thus reducing the amount of network traffic. To do that, the bean must maintain a state that is the recent copy of the page itself. The only way to implement this functionality with a state-less bean is to send the bean the previous page content as a method parameter at each invocation. This is obviously wasteful in network traffic, however, and it defies the purpose of calculating differences and compressing the data.

The state of a state-ful session bean is determined by the values of its nontransient member variables. These variables must be primitive Java types or they must implement the `Serializable` interface so that the container can place them in external memory. State-ful session beans, however, save design work and make for a simpler program. State-less session beans produce systems that perform better and are inherently scalable. State-less session beans are managed within a pool and are reused by multiple clients. They create an environment well suited for enterprise applications in which scalability and performance are the most important factors. State-ful session beans, on the other hand, do not support high volumes and are therefore seldom used for production applications.

DiffPageFetch Remote Interface

As with the PageFetch bean, our first step is defining the remote interface. Our bean provides two business methods: This first is called getPage, and it retrieves the page and returns it in compressed form. This method is used for a full refresh of the page or for obtaining the initial copy of the page. Note that the method does not take any parameters. An instance of this bean corresponds to a single URL, so the URL is passed to the bean at construction time. The second method is getDiff, which returns the difference in the page from the most previous invocation of either getPage or getDiff.

```
import javax.ejb.*;
import java.rmi.*;
import java.io.*;

public interface DiffPageFetch extends EJBObject
{
      byte[] getPage() throws RemoteException, IOException;
      byte[] getDiff() throws RemoteException, IOException;
}
```

One thing you should note about state-ful session beans is that the data stored in them is not really persistent, in the sense that it can withstand a server failure. This stands in stark contrast to entity beans, which are guaranteed to be fully persistent using an external data store such as a database. You should, therefore, not use state-ful session beans if the state is of any long-term applicative importance. For example, if the bean holds some data relating to a financial transaction, you might not want to risk losing your data. In our case, a loss will not be too critical, because if the bean state is lost, we can just call getPage again to reload the Web page.

DiffPageFetch Home Interface

Now let's turn to the home interface, which defines the create method. In our case, the create method takes one parameter—the page URL, which is used for subsequent invocations of getPage and getDiff.

```
import javax.ejb.*;
import java.rmi.*;
import java.io.*;

public interface DiffPageFetchHome extends EJBHome
{
      PageFetch create(String url) throws RemoteException, CreateException;
}
```

DiffPageFetch Bean Implementation

Our class still implements the `javax.ejb.SessionBean` interface because this bean, too, is a session bean. We implement the `SessionBean` interface indirectly by extending the class `PageBean`.

This bean has two member variables that hold its state. One variable holds the HTTP URL that the bean retrieves, and the other holds the most recent copy of the page retrieved.

For the sake of completeness, we implement all the methods of the `SessionBean` interface. Note that while the `ejbActivate` and `ejbPassivate` methods still remain empty (as we are not holding any resources that need to be freed), the `ejbCreate` method now takes a parameter that is the URL and stores it in the respective member variable. The `ejbRemove` method clears this variable.

```
import javax.ejb.*;
import java.rmi.*;

public class PageFetchBean extends PageBean
{
      // Conversational State
      StringBuffer content;
      String url;

      // Implementation of "business" method
      public byte[] getPage() throws IOException
      {
            StringBuffer buf = loadPage(url);
            content = buf;
            return pack(buf);
      }

      public byte[] getDiff() throws IOException
      {
            if (content == null)
                 return null;
            StringBuffer buf = loadPage(url);
            StringBuffer diff = doDiff(content, buf);
            content = buf;
            return pack(diff);
      }

      // EJB methods
      public void ejbCreate(String theUrl)
      {
          url = theUrl;
          content = null;
```

```
    }

    public void ejbRemove()
    {
        content = null;
    }

    public void ejbActivate()
    {
    }

    public void ejbPassivate()
    {
    }

    public void setSessionContext(SessionContext context)
    {
    }

    // Auxiliary Method
    protected String doDiff(String orig, String next)
    {
            int ind1 = 0;
            int origLen = orig.length();
            int nextLen = next.length();
            String diff = "";

            while (orig.charAt(ind1) == next.charAt(ind1) &&
                   ind1 < nextLen && ind1 < origLen)
                ind1++;
            if (ind1 == origLen)

            {
                if (ind1 == nextLen)
                    return diff;
                return "start " + ind1 + " end 0%%" +
                               next.subString(origLen);
            }
            int ind2 = 0;
            while (orig.charAt(origLen - ind2 - 1) == next.charAt(nextLen -
                  ind2 - 1) && ind2 < (origLen - ind1) &&
                  ind2 < (nextLen - ind1))
               ind2++;
            return "start" + ind1 + " end " + ind2 + "%%" +
                   next.SubString(ind1, nextLen-ind2);
     }
     }
```

This bean has two business methods. The first is the getPage method, which loads the page and behaves pretty much like the getPage method of the PageFetch bean. The difference is that it doesn't take a parameter and instead uses its state variable to determine the target URL.

The second method is getDiff. This method loads the current version of the page and compares it to the old version, sending the differences back to the client. For the sake of simplicity, we implement a crude method of calculating the difference. We look for the longest common prefix and longest common suffix of the two versions of the page and consider changed whatever is in the middle. This is, of course, not generally useful, but it is useful for pages in which only one field changes (such as a status). In any case, this difference calculation method satisfies the bare minimum requirement, making sure that if no changes occur, the difference is empty. Note that the getDiff method returns null in case it is called without calling the getPage method first.

Application assembly and deployment for this bean are quite similar, except that the bean should be designated as state-ful on the General tab of the New Session Beans dialog box.

Client-side code can make use of this bean by invoking the getPage method and then repeatedly invoking the getDiff method to find out whether any updates have been made to the page. After receiving the method's returned value, client-side code needs to uncompress it and do some simple parsing of the prefix and suffix lengths.

Understanding the Session Bean Lifecycle

Chapter 11 discussed the session bean lifecycle. This section inspects the session bean lifecycle using the "Hello World" bean from Chapter 5, adding debug prints in the various EJB methods. Later, we'll look at a state-ful variant of this bean to highlight the differences between the lifecycles of state-less and state-ful session beans.

State-less Debug Hello World Bean

The remote interface for our state-less bean is as follows:

```
import javax.ejb.*;
import java.rmi.*;
public interface HelloDbg extends EJBObject
{
      String getTextMessage() throws RemoteException;
}
```

The home interface is shown here:

```
import javax.ejb.*;
```

```
import java.rmi.*;

public interface HelloDbgHome extends EJBHome
{
      HelloDbg create() throws RemoteException, CreateException;
}
```

These two interfaces are similar to those of the state-less session bean described in Chapter 5. The bean implementation is also similar, except printouts have been added:

```
import javax.ejb.*;
import java.rmi.*;

public class HelloDbgBean implements SessionBean
{
      // Implementation of "business" method
      public String getTextMessage()
      {
            return "Hello World";
      }

      // EJB methods

      public void ejbCreate()
      {
            System.out.println("ejbCreate");
      }

      public void ejbRemove()
      {
            System.out.println("ejbRemove");
      }

      public void ejbActivate()
      {
            System.out.println("ejbActivate");
      }

      public void ejbPassivate()
      {
            System.out.println("ejbPassivate");
```

```
        }

        public void setSessionContext(SessionContext context)
        {
              System.out.println("setSessionContext");
        }
}
```

We use the following simple client program to invoke this bean, adding an infinite loop to the end so that the program will not exit. This way, we can guarantee that resources are not freed (at least not until timeout intervals elapse).

```
import javax.ejb.*;
import java.rmi.*;
import java.util.*;
import javax.naming.*;

public class HelloClient {
    public static void main(String args[])
    {
      try {
        Properties env = System.getProperties();
        env.put(javax.naming.Context.INITIAL_CONTEXT_FACTORY,
                "com.ibm.websphere.naming.WsnInitialContextFactory");
        env.put(javax.naming.Context.PROVIDER_URL, "iiop://localhost");
        InitialContext ic = new InitialContext(env);
        HelloDbgHome home = (HelloDbgHome)
                          javax.rmi.PortableRemoteObject.narrow(
                          ic.lookup("HelloDbgHome"), HelloDbgHome.class);
        HelloDbg  bean = home.create();
        System.out.println(bean.getTextMessage());
        for (;;);
      } catch (Exception ex) {
        System.out.println("HelloClient Runtime Error:");
        ex.printStackTrace();
      }
  }
}
```

After you deploy this bean and run the client program, go to the WebSphere log files located in the *logs* directory under your WebSphere installation root. If everything goes smoothly (and the client-side program prints out the "Hello World" message), the WebSphere *stdout* log should show something similar to this:

default_server_stdout - Notepad
File Edit Format Help
[02.01.14 19:34:42:603 PST] 5d8750c1 WebGroup I SRVE0091I: [Servlet LOG]: JSP 1.1 Processor: init
[02.01.14 19:34:42:613 PST] 5d8750c1 WebGroup I SRVE0091I: [Servlet LOG]: SimpleFileServlet: init
[02.01.14 19:34:42:623 PST] 5d8750c1 WebGroup I SRVE0091I: [Servlet LOG]: DirectoryBrowsingServlet: init
[02.01.14 19:34:42:713 PST] 5d8750c1 HttpTransport A SRVE0171I: Transport http is listening on port 9,080.
[02.01.14 19:34:48:171 PST] 5d8750c1 HttpTransport A SRVE0171I: Transport https is listening on port 9,443.
[02.01.14 19:34:48:181 PST] 5d8750c1 HttpTransport A SRVE0171I: Transport http is listening on port 9,090.
[02.01.14 19:34:48:201 PST] 5d8750c1 Server A WSVR0023I: Server Default Server open for e-business
[02.01.14 19:38:08:709 PST] 6f7510c3 SystemOut U setSessionContext
[02.01.14 19:38:08:719 PST] 6f7510c3 SystemOut U ejbCreate

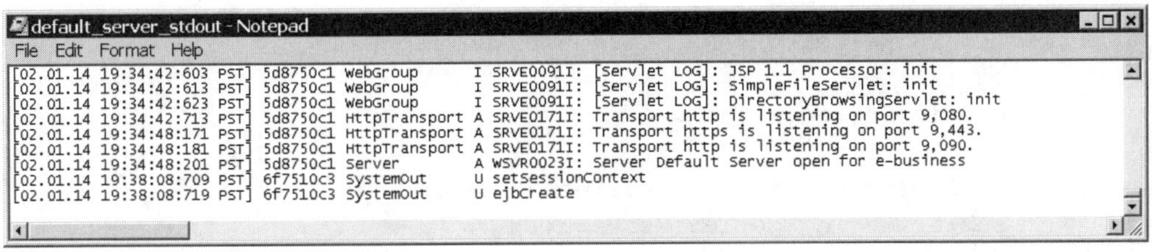

Now repeatedly invoke the same program using different windows. This creates many concurrent clients that do not die. Look at the log file again and notice that it hasn't changed. This implies that WebSphere is implementing instance pooling. Because the bean is state-less, the same instance can serve any number of clients.

State-ful Debug Hello World Bean

Now we'll take the previous bean and augment it in the following way: we pass it a message string at construction time, and this string is returned when invoking the `getMessageText` method.

The remote interface for this bean is shown here:

```
import javax.ejb.*;
import java.rmi.*;
public interface HelloDbg2 extends EJBObject
{
      String getTextMessage() throws RemoteException;
}
```

The home interface is as follows:

```
import javax.ejb.*;
import java.rmi.*;
public interface HelloDbgHome2 extends EJBHome
{
      HelloDbg2 create(String m) throws RemoteException, CreateException;
}
```

The bean implementation prints out messages in a unique way:

```
import javax.ejb.*;
import java.rmi.*;
```

```
public class HelloDbgBean2 implements SessionBean
{
	public String msg;

	// Implementation of "business" method
	public String getTextMessage()
	{
		return msg;
	}

	// EJB methods

	public void ejbCreate(String m)
	{
		msg = m;
		System.out.println("ejbCreate" + msg);
	}

	public void ejbRemove()
	{
		System.out.println("ejbRemove 2");
	}

	public void ejbActivate()
	{
		System.out.println("ejbActivate 2");
	}

	public void ejbPassivate()
	{
		System.out.println("ejbPassivate 2");
	}

	public void setSessionContext(SessionContext context)
	{
		System.out.println("setSessionContext 2");
	}
}
```

The client code for testing this bean is shown next. It takes the string used to initialize the bean from the command-line arguments.

```
import javax.ejb.*;
import java.rmi.*;
import java.util.*;
import javax.naming.*;

public class HelloClient2 {
    public static void main(String args[])
    {
      try {
        Properties env = System.getProperties();
        env.put(Context.INITIAL_CONTEXT_FACTORY,
                  "com.ibm.websphere.naming.WsnInitialContextFactory"); ");
        env.put(javax.naming.Context.PROVIDER_URL, "iiop://localhost");
        InitialContext ic = new InitialContext(env);
        HelloDbgHome2 home = (HelloDbgHome2)
                    javax.rmi.PortableRemoteObject.narrow(
                    ic.lookup("HelloDbgHome2"), HelloDbgHome2.class);
        HelloDbg2  bean = home.create(args[0]);
        System.out.println(bean.getTextMessage());
         for (;;);
      } catch (Exception ex) {
        System.out.println("HelloClient Runtime Error:");
        ex.printStackTrace();
      }
   }
}
```

After compiling all the code and deploying the bean, we are ready for repeating the test—running several clients and checking the logs.

We run the client-side program three times with the parameters *Test*, *Another Test*, and *Yet Another Test*. The results in the log are shown in the following illustration. Notice that the output of the previous execution is still shown in the log, but you can distinguish the new output by the number 2 that follows the `setSessionContext` invocations and the message string following the `ejbCreate` invocations. As you can see in the log, each client gets its own bean instance, and the container cannot share the same instance among all three beans.

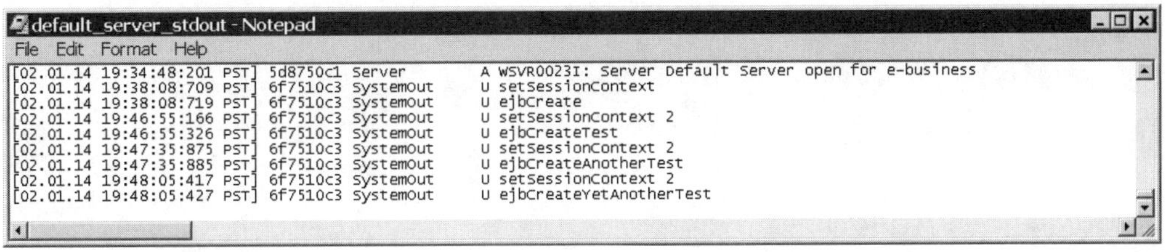

```
default_server_stdout - Notepad
File  Edit  Format  Help
[02.01.14 19:34:48:201 PST] 5d8750c1 Server       A WSVR0023I: Server Default Server open for e-business
[02.01.14 19:38:08:709 PST] 6f7510c3 SystemOut    U setSessionContext
[02.01.14 19:38:08:719 PST] 6f7510c3 SystemOut    U ejbCreate
[02.01.14 19:46:55:166 PST] 6f7510c3 SystemOut    U setSessionContext 2
[02.01.14 19:46:55:326 PST] 6f7510c3 SystemOut    U ejbCreateTest
[02.01.14 19:47:35:875 PST] 6f7510c3 SystemOut    U setSessionContext 2
[02.01.14 19:47:35:885 PST] 6f7510c3 SystemOut    U ejbCreateAnotherTest
[02.01.14 19:48:05:417 PST] 6f7510c3 SystemOut    U setSessionContext 2
[02.01.14 19:48:05:427 PST] 6f7510c3 SystemOut    U ejbCreateYetAnotherTest
```

Summary

This chapter provided further details on session beans, which are important constructs used to implement server-side code that is either an extension of a client (state-ful beans) or reusable pool-managed components used by multiple clients (state-less beans). In both cases, the client communicates with the bean over RMI, and the EJB container manages access to the bean.

The chapter presented examples for both state-less and state-ful session beans and described the differences in terms of their lifecycles and how WebSphere manages them. Classes and methods built when implementing session beans were discussed, as well as the assembly process and the deployment descriptor.

Session beans are often used for coding server-side processes. Session beans do not normally represent business objects, because they are linked to sessions (hence, their name) and not to persistent data. Chapter 30 deals with entity beans, which are usually used for implementing persistent business objects.

The Complete Reference

Chapter 30

Entity Beans

Chapter 29 discussed Enterprise JavaBeans (EJB) session beans. In the original EJB specification, the other half of the EJB realm deals with *entity* beans. Entity beans differ from session beans in that they are persistent objects. *Persistent* objects are stored in external storage such as a disk or a database. This chapter will discuss what entity beans are and how they are built, assembled, and deployed. It focuses on the persistence of data encapsulated within entity beans. Entity beans and session beans are compared to help you ensure that you choose the right bean type for your future projects, and a few examples of how to use entity beans are discussed.

Persistence

Object persistence is an important concept, and a variety of techniques can be used for implementing it. The importance of persistence stems from the fact that large software systems usually are required to handle and store large volumes of data over prolonged periods of time. Java provides object serialization as a basic method for achieving persistence. *Serialization* in Java is a mere extension of the core Java input and output mechanisms that allows these mechanisms to support objects. While serialization is useful for transmitting objects over the network, it is not very useful for storing objects in a database. Persistence in the computer industry today almost exclusively refers to the use of a relational database, which implies that the data needs to be stored in a tabular format. Object serialization is sometimes useful for storing data directly on a file system as raw data in a relational database column or in an object database, but it has not proven itself useful for large, mission-critical applications.

The most popular way to implement Java persistence—in fact, the most popular way to store data of any kind—is by using a traditional relational database, such as Oracle or IBM's DB2. However, storing objects in relational databases poses a conceptual problem of data representation: How do you map object data into the relational database? In some cases, such mappings are trivial and are obtained simply by mapping each class to a table and each member variable to a database column. In these cases, each object is represented in the database as a record in a single table. In other cases, objects might contain other object references or arrays, or they might have to be decomposed into a number of tables due to normalization constraints; then the mapping becomes more complex.

Entity beans provide support for persistence in the EJB architecture. They can implement their own persistence using Bean Managed Persistence (BMP), or they can rely on the EJB container to implement persistence for them using Container Managed Persistence (CMP). CMP in WebSphere (and in EJB in general) is implemented by means of relational databases.

As we have pointed out, relational databases are the most common way to store large amounts of data—at least in applications built in the last 15 years. By aligning itself with the relational database model, the EJB specification is ensured compatibility with legacy data. The WebSphere EJB server supports such compatibility by allowing you to use existing databases. Relational databases have been optimized to a point where their efficiency in handling queries, as well as in updating data, is greater than with other alternatives by orders of magnitude. While there will always be circumstances in which there is an advantage to another storage paradigm, relational databases are still (and probably will remain for a long time) the best alternative in terms of performance, reliability, flexibility, and industry acceptance.

While supporting relational databases, EJBs nevertheless allow any other object storage technique to be used in EJB implementations with the use of BMP. For example, it is possible to hook object database systems and Extensible Markup Language (XML) databases into your Java 2 Platform Enterprise Edition (J2EE) applications. Object databases prevent the problems associated with mapping object data to the database simply by keeping an object-based representation of data.

To illustrate the concepts associated with entity beans, we will look at a bean that can cache the contents of a Web page. This is in the spirit of the examples shown in the previous chapter, with one crucial difference: the page data is persistent. This persistence can be used to make sure that the page content on the server side is in sync with the page content on the client side.

Session Beans Versus Entity Beans

The fact that we are now accessing Web pages by using entity beans, which we did in Chapter 29 by using session beans, might seem a bit confusing. After all, session beans and entity beans are supposed to be conceptually different. This is true, but choosing the best type of bean depends on the application requirements that the EJB need to address. The session beans in Chapter 29 were used to reduce the amount of network traffic. Consider a more sophisticated application in which you would like to cache the content of the page to allow offline Web browsing on the client side. In other words, you would like the client to download the current copy of the page (actually copies of a set of pages) and later request updates from the server. In this case, the server would need to be aware of the most recent copy of the data held at the client side to determine what pages were updated. Furthermore, this process might span a prolonged period of time, much longer than a typical "session." Therefore, entity beans would be the best choice for this application.

The immediate benefit of implementing our bean as an entity bean is its persistence and, consequentially, its ability to withstand server failures. Entity beans differ from session beans in several ways. One critical difference is that with state-ful session beans, the client that created the bean is typically the sole user of the bean. With entity beans, a bean can be created by one client and used by another client. Clearly, this functionality is an important one that enables entity beans to be used as business objects representing business data stored in a database.

The entity bean model has built-in support for using beans created by other clients, in that entity beans can be "found" using a finder method. Using such a method makes it possible to look up a specific entity bean and access it. To implement this functionality, entity beans have keys associated with them. (More on keys in the next section.)

Another interesting difference between session beans and entity beans is that the latter are potentially subject to modification that is external to the EJB architecture.

Because persistence is typically achieved by means of a relational database, changes to the data stored in the database would imply that entity beans are changed when they are accessed by client-side code. In fact, you could say that entity beans provide a different "view" into the relational database. Of course, entity beans provide much more than that, as they encapsulate complex business logic.

Another difference between session beans and entity beans is in their lifecycles; and this difference is due to the fact that session beans are persistent. Session beans have a limited life span and are typically destroyed after a certain time. In contrast, entity beans have longer time spans and are destroyed only upon an explicit invocation of the `remove` method on either the remote interface or the home interface. Note that, in other ways, entity beans behave like session beans. For example, like stateless session beans, entity bean instances are pooled; the same in-memory object can be used for several bean objects.

The EJB context is different for entity beans and session beans. Recall from Chapter 11 that the EJB context object informs the bean about the surrounding environment. For entity beans, the bean context adds two new methods, `getEJBObject` and `getPrimaryKey`. The `getEJBObject` method also exists for session beans, and it allows the bean implementation to obtain a reference to a "remote" interface to itself, so in some sense it is the remote version of the `this` object in Java. The `getPrimaryKey` method allows the bean to get its own primary key. While that might not make a lot of sense at first glance, it is necessary because bean instances are pooled and reused. Whenever an entity bean needs to find out what its primary key is (especially in the `ejbLoad`, `ejbStore`, and `ejbRemove` methods), the prudent way to find it is by using `getPrimaryKey`.

CachedPage Bean Design

A single instance of the CachedPage bean represents a single Web page specified by a Hypertext Transfer Protocol (HTTP) Uniform Resource Locator (URL). By contacting the respective HTTP server, the user of the bean can ask the bean to check to see whether the page has changed. Such a bean could be useful for clients with limited network bandwidth (mobile clients, for example) who want to constantly monitor updated data. This ignores the fact that the same URL can create different page content based on the user making the invocation. In a real application, the content might change due to security constraints and user roles. This, too, can be easily implemented using the EJB security model and the `run-as` attribute, which allows the bean to take on the identity of the caller. In the rest of this example, we will assume that a URL uniquely defines the generated content no matter who is requesting the page.

The bean (and the surrounding server) takes the burden of refreshing the page, and the actual end user wastes bandwidth only if there is an update. To provide this functionality, the bean must be able to store the URL of the Web page involved, as well as its actual content. The content is required so the bean will know whether or not any changes have been made to the page.

To implement an entity bean, you need to implement all the components you already know: the remote interface, the home interface, and the bean implementation. One new component that you have not seen before is the key, which is discussed next.

CachedPage Bean Key

When designing entity beans, you must consider keys. The concept of a key in entity beans is similar to that of unique keys in relational databases—a unique key is a set of one or more columns that uniquely define a row. In other words, no two distinct rows in the same table can have the same key value. The corresponding concept for EJB is a key object that uniquely defines the EJB instance. The EJB key can be retrieved from the EJB instance, and an EJB instance can be searched for using its key.

For our example, we could simply let the key be the cached URL. To make things more interesting and more practical, consider having the key include both the URL and a user name. This allows several users to access the same Web page without interfering with each other, and it is also more useful as an extension of functionality that uses the `run-as` behavior. The combination of a user name and a URL adheres to the main requirement for a key because it is unique, meaning that there is no possibility for the same user to cache the same page more than once. The `CachedPagePK` class, representing the key for our `CachedPage` bean, is defined as follows:

```
package book.ch30;

public class CachedPagePK implements java.io.Serializable
{
      public String userName;
      public String pageURL;

      public boolean equals(Object obj) {
            if (obj instanceof CachedPagePK) {
                  CahcedPage pk = (CachedPagePK) obj;
                  return (userName.equals(pk.userName) &&
                        pageURL.equals(pk.pageURL));
            }
            return false;
      }
      public int hashCode() {
            String concat = userName + pageURL;
            return concat.hashCode();
      }
}
```

The key should implement the `Serializable` interface, because all types used as parameters to methods of the bean remote interface or as returned values of those methods must conform to the conventions of Java Remote Method Invocation (RMI). These conventions require that such types are either primitive types, types that implement either `java.io.Serializable` or `javax.rmi.Remote`, or arrays of the aforementioned types. Note that failure to adhere to these conventions might not be detected at compile time and could cause a `RemoteException` to be thrown when the involved method is invoked. WebSphere places an additional limitation on the primary key definition: The primary key must override the `equals` and `hashCode` methods of `java.lang.Object`. When you implement BMP, this is not required.

CachedPage Remote Interface

To complete our bean, we need to provide a remote interface, a home interface, and a bean implementation. The remote interface to the cached page bean, shown in the following code listing, provides standard JavaBean-like *get* methods. It is also possible to provide *set* methods for attributes to be set. Our bean does not have any *set* methods because all the attributes are either part of the key (the user name and the Web page) or are determined internally by the bean (the last modified date and the page content). *Set* methods are never defined for attributes comprising the key because modifying them changes the identity of the bean.

```
import java.util.*;
import javax.ejb.*;

public interface CachedPage extends EJBObject
{
        public Boolean     hasChanged()       throws RemoteException;
        public String      getUserName()      throws RemoteException;
        public String      getPageURL()       throws RemoteException;
        public Date        getLastModified()  throws RemoteException;
        public String      getContent()       throws RemoteException;
};
```

CachedPage Home Interface

The home interface for our bean is as follows:

```
import java.rmi.*;
import java.util.*;
import javax.ejb.*;

public interface CachedPageHome extends EJBHome
{
        public CachedPage  create(String userName, String pageURL);
```

```
      public CachedPage  findByPrimaryKey(CachedPagePK key)
                 throws RemoteException, FinderException;
      public Enumeration findByUserName(String userName)
                 throws RemoteException, FinderException;

};
```

This home interface is different from the one shown in Chapter 29 for the "Hello World" session bean, most notably due to the finder methods (`findBy`*`XXX`*). The first finder method is `findByPrimaryKey`. This method takes as parameter the primary key and finds an instance of the bean. The implementation is the responsibility of the container. The other finder method defined in our home interface is `findByUsername`. This method demonstrates how you can define finder methods that do not take a key. Such methods might find several beans that match the search criteria and return the value `java.util.Enumeration`. In our example, we are allowing lookup of all the cached pages for a single user using the user name.

With BMP, implementing the `findByPrimaryKey` method is the responsibility of the developer. With CMP, implementing the same method is the responsibility of the container. Obviously, the container cannot implement such a finder method solely by looking at its signature. With BMP, you must supply actual code for performing the search. When using CMP, the extra information takes the shape of a "finder helper" interface, which essentially provides the container with the query logic. Finder helpers are not part of the EJB specification and, therefore, are not portable. The finder helper class for our example is as follows:

```
public interface CahcedPageBeanFinderHelper
{
      String findByuserNameWhereClause = "userName = ?";
}
```

Finder logic is specified using an interface called *<bean-name>*`BeanFinderHelper`, and the query logic should be contained in a string constant called *<find-method-name>*`WhereClause`. This string contains the *Where* clause of an SQL-like query statement. In this *Where* clause, question marks represent variables that are to be replaced with the actual values of the finder method arguments (in the same order in which they are passed). The fields of the bean implementation class can be used in the *Where* clause. In our example, we use the field `userName` from the implementation class of our `CachedPage` bean. Note that in older versions of WebSphere, the finder helper interface included a full *Select* query; this is now deprecated because such queries are difficult to optimize and they allow the user to select too much or not enough to find the bean.

Using the Application Assembly Tool, you can also provide the *Where* clause in the deployment descriptor.

CachedPage Bean Implementation

An important technical detail is that the bean implementation class, which follows, must define all the persistent fields of the bean as public (actually only the fields whose persistence is managed by the container) so that the container can access them. An EJB developer can also define nonpersistent fields, and the visibility for those fields is completely at the developer's discretion.

```
import java.util.*;
import javax.ejb.*;
import java.net.*;
import java.io.*;
public class CachedPageBean implements EntityBean
{
      public String userName;
      public String pageUrl;
      public boolean changeFlag;
      public Date lastModified;
      public String content;

      private void refresh() throws IOException
      {
            StringBuffer stringBuffer = new StringBuffer();
            String urlString = pageUrl;
            URL finalUrl;
            URLConnection urlconnection;
            InputStreamReader reader;

           try {
                  finalUrl = new URL(urlString);
                  urlconnection= finalUrl.openConnection();
                  urlconnection.setDoInput(true);
                  urlconnection.setRequestProperty("User-Agent",
                   "Mozilla/4.0 (compatible; MSIE 5.5; Windows 98)");
                  reader = new InputStreamReade
                               (urlconnection.getInputStream());
            }
            catch (Exception ex) {
                   System.err.println("Cannot connect to URL " + pageUrl +
                                     " Exception " + ex);
                   return;
            }
```

```
        int  i = urlconnection.getContentLength();
        if (i == -1)
              return;
        int j;
        String s2;
        char[] inbuf = new char[4096];
        for (; (j = reader.read(inbuf)) != -1; ) {
              stringBuffer.append(inbuf, 0, j);
              int k = stringBuffer.length();
              if (i <= 0) {
                    continue;
              }
              if (i <= k) {
                    break;
              }
        }
        String newContent = stringBuffer.toString();
        if (content == null || !content.equals(newContent)) {
              changeFlag = true;
              content = newContent;
              lastModified = new Date();
        }
  }

  public boolean      hasChanged()
  {
        try {
              refresh();
        }
        catch (Exception ex) {
              System.err.println("Error reading " + pageUrl +
                    " Exception" + ex);
        }
        return changeFlag;
  }

  public String      getUserName()
  {
        return userName;
  }

  public String      getPageURL()
  {
        return pageUrl;
  }

  public Date             getLastModified()
  {
```

```
            return lastModified;
      }

      public String      getContent()
      {
      return content;
      }

      public void ejbCreate(String user, String url)
      {
            changeFlag = false;
            lastModified = new Date();
            userName = user;
            pageUrl = url;
      }

      public void setEntityContext(EntityContext c) {}
      public void unsetEntityContext() {}
      public void ejbRemove()                          {}
      public void ejbPassivate()                         {}
      public void ejbActivate()                         {}
      public void ejbLoad()                              {}
      public void ejbStore()                              {}
};
```

The bean implementation includes the method `hasChanged`, which checks to determine whether a Web page changed on the HTTP server. This is the main "business" method in our bean, and it encapsulates the main business logic for which this object was built. The business logic implemented in this bean retrieves the Web page using a `java.net.URLConnection` object and compares it to the last version of the page. If there is no change in content, `false` is returned. Otherwise, the new content is stored, the last modification date is updated, and `true` is returned. The actual content can then be accessed using the `getContent` method.

Note that the bean must implement as many `ejbCreate` signatures as were defined in the home interface. All should be `public` and have a return value of `void`.

As explained in Chapter 11, the methods `ejbCreate`, `ejbActivate`, `ejbPassivate`, `ejbRemove`, `ejbLoad`, `ejbStore`, `ejbPostCreate`, `setEntityContext`, and `unsetEntityContext` are used by the container to inform the bean about lifecycle-related events that take place. These events are creation, activation, passivation, removal, loading, storing, and post-creation. (*Post-creation* means initialization after the key is already set.) Similar to session beans, the EJB server can temporarily "swap out" entity beans using activation and passivation. Note that unlike session beans, the creation method is optional with entity beans.

In this specific case, we will leave all these methods empty. Another approach might have been to load the page automatically in the `ejbPostCreate` method so that the first invocation of `hasChanged` would have some version of the content to compare to the current page content. If a bean implements more than one *create* method, it must implement one *post-create* method per *create* method; the *post-create* method takes the same parameters as the *create* method.

CachedPage Bean Assembly and Deployment

The overall process of entity bean deployment is similar to that of session beans, as described in Chapter 29. The most significant difference is that the deployment descriptor for entity beans contains different information.

After creating a new EJB module in the Application Assembly Tool (AAT), you can add new entity EJB by right-clicking the Entity Beans entry on the left panel. Unlike session beans, you have two options—BMP or CMP:

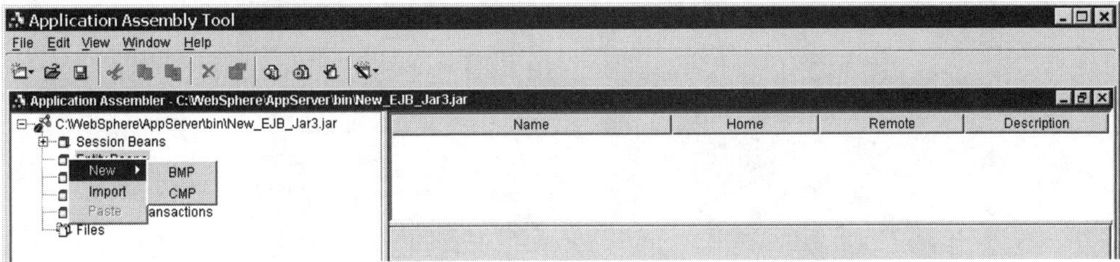

Select CMP. (BMP is the subject of the next section.)

Like the dialog box for adding a new session bean, the dialog box for adding a new entity bean has several tabs. The General tab includes fields used for specifying the primary key class and the key field, if it is a single field. In our case, the key is not a single field, so the Primary Key Field entry shows Compound key.

New Entity Bean
General | IBM Extensions | Bindings
An entity bean encapsulates permanent data, which is stored in a data source such as a database or a file system, and associated methods to manipulate that data.
EJB name: cachedpage
Display name: cachedpage
Description: cachedpage
Home interface: book.ch30.CachedPageHome Browse...
Remote interface: book.ch30.CachedPage Browse...
EJB class: book.ch30.CachedPageBean Browse...
Primary key class: book.ch30.CachedPagePK Browse...
Primary key field: Compound key
Persistency: Container managed
Reentrant
OK Apply Cancel Help

The IBM Extensions tab is identical to that for session beans, but the Timeout field is removed and caching options can be configured. The IBM EJB extensions are discussed in detail in Chapter 33.

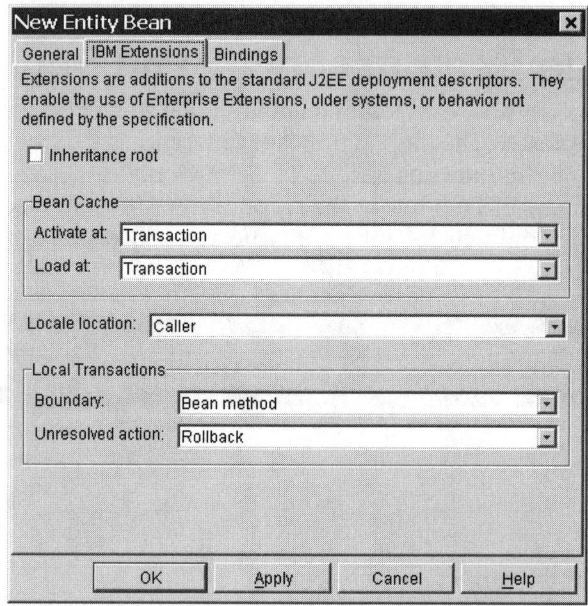

The Bindings tab includes the Java Naming and Directory Interface (JNDI) name and the data source used for storing the bean.

New Entity Bean
General | IBM Extensions | Bindings
Binding information is used by the container to locate external resources and EJBs required by a module or application.
JNDI name: CachedPageHome
Datasource
JNDI name:
Default Authorization
User ID:
Password:

To inform the container as to which fields are to be persistent, you need to specify them as CMP fields by right-clicking the CMP Field entry in the AAT and selecting New. This opens the New CMP Field dialog box, in which you select the fields that should be persistent. After selecting the fields whose persistence is to be managed by the container, the CMP Fields entry lists all of them, as shown here:

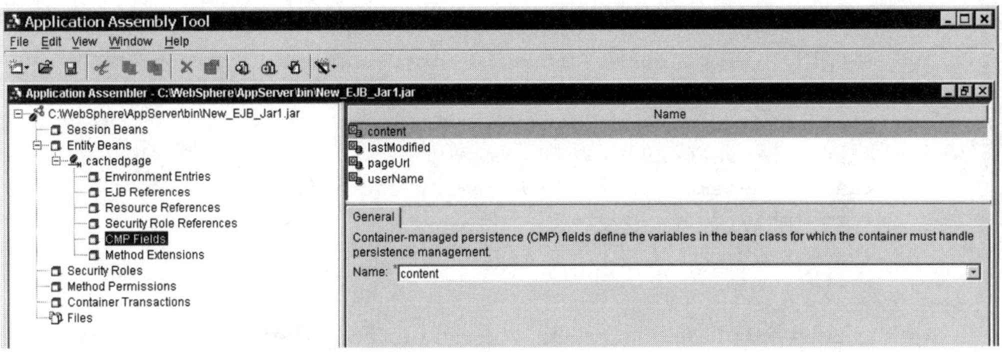

The EJB assembly descriptor provides a straightforward account of the choices we make in the AAT with regard to our bean:

```
<?xml version="1.0" encoding="UTF-8"?>
<!DOCTYPE ejb-jar PUBLIC "-//Sun Microsystems, Inc.//DTD Enterprise
 JavaBeans 1.1//EN"
"http://java.sun.com/j2ee/dtds/ejb-jar_1_1.dtd">
   <ejb-jar id="ejb-jar_ID">
      <description>cachedpage</description>
      <display-name>cachedpage</display-name>
      <enterprise-beans>
         <entity id="ContainerManagedEntity_1">
            <description>cachedpage</description>
            <display-name>cachedpage</display-name>
            <ejb-name>cachedpage</ejb-name>
            <home>book.ch30.CachedPageHome</home>
            <remote>book.ch30.CachedPage</remote>
            <ejb-class>book.ch30.CachedPageBean</ejb-class>
            <persistence-type>Container</persistence-type>
            <prim-key-class>book.ch30.CachedPagePK</prim-key-class>
            <reentrant>False</reentrant>
            <cmp-field id="cachedpage_userName">
               <field-name>userName</field-name>
            </cmp-field>
            <cmp-field id="cachedpage_lastModified">
               <field-name>lastModified</field-name>
            </cmp-field>
            <cmp-field id="cachedpage_pageUrl">
               <field-name>pageUrl</field-name>
            </cmp-field>
```

```
            <cmp-field id="cachedpage_content">
               <field-name>content</field-name>
            </cmp-field>
         </entity>
      </enterprise-beans>
      <assembly-descriptor id="AssemblyDescriptor_1">
      </assembly-descriptor>
   </ejb-jar>
```

Once the assembly phase is complete, you can proceed to bean deployment. Bean deployment is similar to that of other EJB modules. The only difference relates to the bindings and database settings. As explained, the bindings here include the data source attributes, which, in addition to the JNDI name, can be modified at deployment time. You can also select the type of database in which the bean's data will be stored.

After the bean is deployed, there is no need to perform any database setup. WebSphere automatically creates a database table called `ejb.`*`beanName`*`beantbl`, where *`beanName`* is the bean name. So, for our example, the table name will be `ejb.book.ch30.CachedPagebeantbl`. The AAT generates the SQL code for creating this table, and the code is executed at deployment time.

Remember that WebSphere 4.0 will not automatically create the tables. It simply creates a Data Definition Language (DDL) file, specific to the DB type selected, which enables the user to create the table.

Example of Bean-Managed Persistence

To illustrate BMP, consider modifying the `CachedPage` bean to be bean managed. Typical motivations for doing so are a requirement for using nonrelational data stores or the desire to improve performance using specially designed mechanisms, such as optimized queries and stored procedures.

It's not necessary to change the remote interface and the home interface to make the transition to BMP; you simply need to change the bean implementation. This makes perfect sense, because the user of a bean should be oblivious to details of the internal implementation, including persistence implementation. Note, too, that the finder helper class is not needed in this case.

The EJB specification does not place any limitations on how to implement BMP. You can use ASCII files, Java object serialization, legacy transactional systems, or any other storage mechanism at your disposal—as long as it has an implementation or some interface in Java.

In our example, we look at a Java Database Connectivity (JDBC) connection to a relational database, which is the most typical scenario for Java-based persistence. The code for the bean implementation with BMP is as follows:

```
import java.util.*;
import javax.ejb.*;
import java.sql.*;
import javax.sql.*;
import java.net.*;
import java.io.*;

public class CachedPageBean implements EntityBean
{
      public String userName;
      public String pageUrl;
      public boolean changeFlag;
      public java.util.Date lastModified;
      public String content;
      transient protected EntityContext context;

      private void refresh() throws IOException
      {
            StringBuffer stringBuffer = new StringBuffer();
            String urlString = pageUrl;
            URL finalUrl;
            URLConnection urlconnection;
            InputStreamReader reader;

            try {
                  finalUrl = new URL(urlString);
                  urlconnection= finalUrl.openConnection();
                  urlconnection.setDoInput(true);
                  urlconnection.setRequestProperty("User-Agent",
                  "Mozilla/4.0 (compatible; MSIE 5.5; Windows 98)");
                  reader = new InputStreamReader
                              (urlconnection.getInputStream());
            }
            catch (Exception ex) {
                  System.err.println("Cannot connect to URL " +
                                    pageUrl + " Exception " + ex);
                  return;
            }
            int  i = urlconnection.getContentLength();
            if (i == -1)
                  return;
            int j;
            String s2;
            char[] inbuf = new char[4096];
            for (; (j = reader.read(inbuf)) != -1; ) {
                  stringBuffer.append(inbuf, 0, j);
                  int k = stringBuffer.length();
                  if (i <= 0) {
```

```
                    continue;
                }
                if (i <= k) {
                    break;
                }
            }
            String newContent = stringBuffer.toString();
            if (content == null || !content.equals(newContent)) {
                changeFlag = true;
                content = newContent;
                lastModified = new java.util.Date();
            }
        }

        public boolean      hasChanged()
        {
            try {
                refresh();
            }
            catch (Exception ex) {
                System.err.println("Error reading " + pageUrl +
                                        " Exception " + ex);
            }
            return changeFlag;
        }

        public String      getUserName()
        {
            return userName;
        }

        public String      getPageURL()
        {
            return pageUrl;
        }

        public java.util.Date           getLastModified()
        {
            return lastModified;
        }

        public String      getContent()
        {
            return content;
        }

        public void ejbLoad()
        {
```

```
        Connection con = null;
        PreparedStatement stmt = null;
        ResultSet rs = null;
        try {
              CachedPagePK key = (CachedPagePK) context.getPrimaryKey();
              userName = key.userName;
              pageUrl = key.pageURL;

              String query =  "select * from CACHEDPAGES set " +
                          "where USER = '" + userName + "','" +
                          "PAGE = '" + pageUrl + "'";
              con = DriverManager.getConnection(
                          "jdbc:db2:myDb:5001",
                            "db2admin",
                            "db2passwd");
              stmt = con.prepareStatement();
              rs =  stmt.executeQuery(query);
              boolean more = rs.next();
              if (more) {
                    changeFlag = true;
                    content = rs.getString(3);
                    lastModified = new java.util.Date(rs.getString(4));
              }
        }
        catch (Exception ex) {
              System.err.println("Error in ejbLoad " + pageUrl +
                                    " Exception " + ex);
        }
        finally {
              rs.close();
              stmt.close();
              con.close();
        }
  }


  public void ejbStore()
  {
        Connection con = null;
        PreparedStatement stmt = null;
        try {
              String query =  "update CACHEDPAGES set " +
                    "CONTENT = " + content + ",MODIFIEDDATE = " +
                    lastModified + "where USER = '" + userName + "'," +
                    "PAGE = '" + pageUrl + "'";
              con = DriverManager.getConnection(
                          "jdbc:db2:myDb:5001",
                            "db2admin",
```

```
                              "db2passwd");
                  stmt = con.prepareStatement();
                  int count = stmt.executeUpdate(query);
            }
            catch (Exception ex) {
                  System.err.println("Error in ejbStore " + pageUrl +
                                          " Exception " + ex);
            }
            finally {
                  stmt.close();
                  con.close();
            }
      }

      public void ejbRemove()
      {
            Connection con = null;
            PreparedStatement stmt = null;
            try {
                  String query =  "delete from CACHEDPAGES where USER = '" +
                              userName + "'," + "PAGE = '" + pageUrl +
                              "'";
                  con = DriverManager.getConnection(
                            "jdbc:db2:myDb:5001",
                              "db2admin",
                              "db2passwd");
                  stmt = con.prepareStatement();
                  int count = stmt.executeUpdate(query);
            }
            catch (Exception ex) {
                  System.err.println("Error in removing " + pageUrl +
                                          " Exception " + ex);
            }
            finally {
                  stmt.close();
                  con.close();
            }
      }

      public void setEntityContext(EntityContext ctx)
      {
            context = ctx;
            try {
                  Class.forName("com.ibm.db2.jdbc.app.DBDriver");
            }
            catch (Exception ex) {
            }
      }
```

```
public void unsetEntityContext()
{
      context = null;
}

public void ejbPostCreate(String user, String url)
{
}

public CachedPagePK ejbCreate(String user, String url)
{
      userName = user;
      pageUrl = url;
      CachedPagePK key = new CachedPagePK();
      key.userName = userName;
      key.pageURL = pageUrl;
      changeFlag = false;
      lastModified = new java.util.Date();
      try {
            refresh();
      }
      catch (Exception ex) {
            System.err.println("Error in reading " + pageUrl +
                                    " Exception " + ex);
      }

      String query =  "insert into CACHEDPAGES (USER, PAGE, " +
                  "CONTENT, LASTMODIFIED)" +
                  "values ('" + userName + "','" +
                  pageUrl + "'," + content + "," +
                  lastModified + "')";

      Connection con = null;
      PreparedStatement stmt = null;
      try {
            con = DriverManager.getConnection(
                        "jdbc:db2:myDb:5001",
                          "db2admin",
                          "db2passwd");
            stmt = con.prepareStatement();
            int count = stmt.executeUpdate(query);
      }
      catch (Exception ex) {
            System.err.println("Error in creating " + pageUrl +
                                    " Exception " + ex);
      }
      finally {
            stmt.close();
```

```
            con.close();
        }
        return key;
    }

    public CachedPagePK ejbFindByPrimaryKey(CachedPagePK key) throws
                                                        FinderException
    {
        String name = key.userName;
        String url = key.pageURL;

        String query =  "select * from CACHEDPAGES set " +
                "where NAME = '" + name + "','" +
                "PAGE = '" + url + "'";
        Connection con = null;
        PreparedStatement stmt = null;
        ResultSet rs = null;
        try {
            con = DriverManager.getConnection(
                    "jdbc:db2:myDb:5001",
                     "db2admin",
                     "db2passwd");
            stmt = con.prepareStatement();
            rs =  stmt.executeQuery(query);
            boolean more = rs.next();
            boolean toomany = false;
            if (more)
                toomany = rs.next();
            if (more)
            {
                if (toomany) {
                    throw new FinderException("Too many rows");
                }
                else {
                    return key;
                }
            }
            else {
                throw new FinderException("Not found");
            }
        }
        catch (Exception ex) {
                throw new FinderException("Exception Caught: " + ex);
        }
        finally {
            rs.close();
            stmt.close();
            con.close();
        }
```

```
    }

    public Enumeration ejbFindByUserName(String name) throws
                                                   FinderException
    {
          Vector v;
          Connection con = null;
          PreparedStatement stmt = null;
          ResultSet rs = null;
          try {
                String query =  "select * from CACHEDPAGES set " +
                            "where USER = '" + name + "'";
                con = DriverManager.getConnection(
                            "jdbc:db2:myDb:5001",
                              "db2admin",
                              "db2passwd");
                stmt = con.preparedStatement();
                rs =  stmt.executeQuery(query);
                v = new Vector();
                CachedPagePK key;
                boolean more = rs.next();

                while (more) {
                      key = new CachedPagePK();
                      key.userName = name;
                      key.pageURL = rs.getString(1);
                      v.addElement(key);
                      more = rs.next();
                }
          }
          catch (Exception ex) {
                      throw new FinderException("Exception Caught: " + ex);
          }
          finally {
                rs.close();
                stmt.close();
                con.close();
          }
          return v.elements();
    }

    public void ejbPassivate()                              {}
    public void ejbActivate()                              {}
}
```

JDBC connections need to be established for the methods `ejbLoad`, `ejbStore`, `ejbRemove`, and `ejbCreate`. They are also required in finder methods, which look up rows in the database. We should throw the `FinderException` in the `findByPrimaryKey` method if nothing is found. The `findByUserName` method does not throw this exception. This might seem a little confusing; it occurs because `findByPrimaryKey` is always expected to return exactly one object (a remote reference). In contrast, the `findByUserName` method returns a Java `Enumeration` object, and this enumeration can be empty. The returned enumeration will indeed be empty if no bean instances match the parameters of the method.

The way we chose to implement database connections here might look curious at first. In general, here are four ways to approach such a problem:

- The database connection can be established in setEntityContext and released in unsetEntityContext. This approach is the easiest to implement, but it is useful only in conjunction with database connection pooling (see Chapter 34).
- We can establish the database connection in the ejbActivate and ejbCreate methods, establish and release connections in the ejbFind method, and release connections in the ejbRemove and ejbPassivate methods. This approach improves performance because only active beans have database connections, but it is slightly more difficult to implement.
- The most tedious approach, and the one we chose to use in the previous example, is to establish and later release the connection in each method that requires a database connection. That way, we know that the connections are open only when needed, thus making the code both more efficient and more scalable.
- The best approach is to acquire a reference to the data source (using JNDI) during ejbActivate, ejbCreate, and so on, and then get and release the connection for each method.

Database connection pooling is used to minimize the overhead of a database connection for a single operation by reusing a pool of existing connections. Note that the EJB server itself implements thread pooling and EJB instance pooling to improve EJB performance. Chapter 18 covers WebSphere's connection pooling, and Chapter 34 covers the implementation of BMP with connection pooling.

Let's turn to the application assembly phase. When you add a new BMP entity bean to an EJB module, the parameters are slightly different than those used for CMP. The General tab indicates that persistence is bean managed and does not include the Primary Key Field entry.

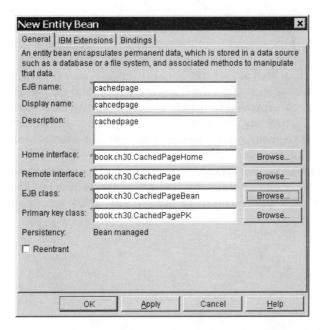

The IBM Extensions tab (not shown) is unchanged; the Bindings tab doesn't have the data source specification fields, so it is actually identical to that of session beans.

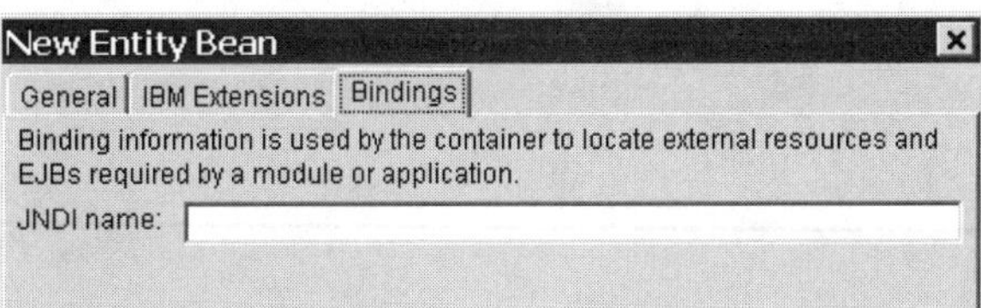

When using BMP, the difference in the bean implementation is quite evident: Much more code is needed. You should only use BMP if you have special persistence requirements.

Summary

Entity beans are central to any application architecture that uses EJB. Entity beans represent business objects and allow you to build applications in which data access and business functions are encapsulated in an object-oriented framework. You can then write your applications using good object-oriented abstractions.

Entity beans can use container-managed persistence, in which case you can delay the decision of the mapping to the repository and have the container handle the complex issue of data persistence. At other times, you might prefer to manage persistence yourself, which sometimes yields more efficient database access. In either case, you are shielded from the implementation of data persistence and you work at a high-level abstraction in which objects can be accessed easily and used by other components, which are often session bean extensions to a client application.

Database access requires queries to get data, as well as inserts and updates to store data. Inserts and updates mean that transactions need to be defined, along with transaction brackets to support Atomicity, Consistency, Isolation, and Durability (ACID) properties. we have not dealt with transaction properties and have only briefly mentioned the `run-as` feature of EJB security. These are among the subjects discussed in Chapter 31.

Chapter 31

EJB Transactions and Security

Chapters 29 and 30 paid some attention to two issues that are central to Enterprise JavaBeans (EJB) architecture: transactions and security. Both issues are of immense importance in the setting of enterprise applications.

One of the foundational points in EJB is that it is a server-side application framework that can help developers avoid some of the headache involved in building complex server-side code. Instead, developers can rely on the *container* to handle a lot of this complex code using *directives*. Transactions and security are complex issues that the bean developer does not need to handle manually if working within the container-managed EJB framework.

The EJB architecture provides a flexible and powerful solution for managing the transactional behavior and security features of EJB. Most of the attributes relating to these issues can be set at assembly (or deployment) time, thus separating the business logic and bean implementation from these issues. Of course, the EJB architecture leaves the door open for any developer interested in implementing his or her own transaction management strategy or programmatic security management.

Transactions in Java

Transactions play an important role in business applications. Consider the act of transferring funds from one account to another. Roughly speaking, such an act is composed of taking out funds from one account and putting them into another. Obviously, such an action should take place atomically—it must either be completed fully or not completed at all. If we allow such a transaction to be only partially accomplished, the consistency of our data would be damaged; in this case, funds could start "disappearing."

A transaction is a series of operations on a set of shared resources grouped as a single unit of work and maintaining ACID properties. The acronym *ACID* stands for *Atomicity*, *Consistency*, *Isolation*, and *Durability*, which are the required properties of the transaction.

- **Atomicity** The actions performed as part of the transaction are treated atomically in the sense that either all the actions are executed or none of them is executed. In case of failure, any changes performed in the scope of the transaction are completely undone.
- **Consistency** In case of failure, the system state is restored to its original state prior to the transaction.
- **Isolation** Any changes made by a transaction are not visible to other clients of the transaction system until the transaction is complete.
- **Durability** Once the transaction is complete, its effects are there for good; specifically, they withstand a system failure.

Note *A full discussion of theory behind transactions is beyond the scope of this book. Check out* Databases and Transaction Processing, *by Lewis, Bernstein, and Kifer (Addison Wesley, 2001), for example.*

In distributed systems, the chance of a possible failure is higher especially due to local failures that could affect part of the actions. For instance, when performing funds transfer, three parties could be involved: the originator of the transfer, the source account, and the destination account. Each of these parties may fail independently of the others. It is possible that the receiving account is online but that the source account is not available for whatever reason. Performing the transfer in this case would cause unexpected results (for example, creation of new funds).

Distributed transaction processing systems have been part of the IT landscape for several decades. Proprietary solutions, such as IBM's own Customer Information Control System (CICS), dominated this market until the 1980s, when the trend shifted toward open UNIX-based solutions with organizations such as the X/Open group that drafted standards for transaction processing. This is not to say that proprietary systems have lost their market share, as products such as CICS still hold a significant market share today.

As part of the standardization efforts for transaction processing, the Object Management Group (OMG) defined an object-oriented framework for distributed transaction processing, which was incorporated into Common Object Request Broker Architecture (CORBA). This framework is the *Object Transaction Service* (OTS) that was mentioned briefly in Chapter 8.

When introducing transactions into the Java programming language, the issues in transaction management were separated into two distinct parts. The first part is the Java *Transaction Service* (JTS). JTS essentially provides OTS capabilities through the Interface Definition Language/Java mapping detailed in Chapter 8. The other part is the *Java Transaction API* (JTA).

JTA provides a high-level API for managing transactions and is provided in the package `javax.transaction`. This package defines several interfaces for managing transactions. The `javax.transaction.UserTransaction` package provides the basic functionality primitives for use by code initiating a transaction as methods:

- **begin** Creates a new transaction and associates it with the current thread.
- **commit** Completes the transaction associated with the current thread.
- **getStatus** Returns the status of the transaction associated with the current thread (the list of possible statuses is part of the javax.transaction.Status interface).
- **rollback** Rolls back the transaction associated with the current thread.
- **setRollbackOnly** Makes the transaction associated with the current thread one that can only be rolled back.
- **setTransactionTimeout** Sets a timeout (in seconds) for the transaction associated with the current thread. After this time, the transaction will automatically roll back.

For most purposes, application-level code is not interested in JTS and the implementation of transaction management. Application-level code is interested only in manipulating transactions in which it participates; the `UserTransaction` interface provides exactly that.

The `UserTransaction` object is typically obtained via Java Naming and Directory Interface (JNDI) lookup. For example, in the WebSphere environment, the transaction service of the server is accessed using the JNDI name `jta/usertransaction`. After a transaction context is obtained, the client code can initiate a transaction using the `begin` method followed by the actions to be performed in the scope of the transaction. Finally, the `commit` method is invoked to complete the transaction. Here's an example:

```
import javax.transaction.*;
class ClientCode {
        // ...
        void transactionMethod() {
        // ...
             Context initialContext = new InitialContext();
             UserTransaction tcon =
                     (UserTransaction) initialContext.lookup(
                                       "jta/usertransaction");
              tcon.begin();
              // Use resources within the transaction scope
              tcon.commit();
        }
}
```

Obviously, managing transactions programmatically in this way is a little tedious. The EJB specification allows you to manage transactions declaratively while still allowing you to write code for managing transactions, if that is your desire.

Enabling Transaction Support

Similar to EJB persistence, the transactional behavior of EJB can be managed either by the container or the developer. The EJB specification defines two deployment attributes in the EJB deployment descriptor that define the transactional behavior of the bean. As discussed in Chapter 11, these are the *transaction attribute* and the *isolation attribute*. The former informs the container of which transactional behavior applies to method invocation. This can be defined for the whole bean but also for individual methods. The isolation attribute indicates how transactions should be isolated from each other inside the container, and it can also be defined for the whole bean as well as for individual methods. Recall from Chapter 11 that the possible transaction settings are `TX_NOT_SUPPORTED`, `TX_BEAN_MANAGED`, `TX_REQUIRED`, `TX_SUPPORTS`, `TX_REQUIRES_NEW`, and `TX_MANDATORY`.

When using Container Managed Persistence (CMP) for entity beans, you cannot use `TX_NOT_SUPPORTED` because the container requires transactions to persist data.

Both transaction attributes can be defined at the time of deployment either for the bean as a whole or for individual methods. The only exception is that the `TX_BEAN_MANAGED` specification cannot be applied to an individual method but only to the bean as a whole. When the `TX_BEAN_MANAGED` setting is used, the bean is able to obtain the transaction from the `SessionContext` or `EntityContext` object provided to it in the `setSessionContext` method or `setEntityContext` method, respectively. This is done using the `getUserTransaction` method of the entity context. The returned value of this method is `javax.transaction.UserTransaction` used for transaction demarcation as explained. Note that unless specified as `TX_BEAN_MANAGED`, beans should not directly access the transaction services.

Similar to the transaction attribute, isolation levels were discussed in detail in Chapter 11. The possible isolation levels are `TRANSACTION_READ_UNCOMMITTED`, `TRANSACTION_READ_COMMITTED`, `TRANSACTION_REPEATABLE_READ`, `TRANSACTION_SERIALIZABLE`, and `TRANSACTION_NONE`. Isolation levels control the way transactions are isolated from each other in terms of the way they view the database. If no special precautions are taken, three common problems can occur when several transactions access a database: dirty read, unrepeatable read, and phantom read.

A *dirty read* takes place when a transaction reads from the database data that was written by another transaction that has not committed yet. In case the latter transaction rolls back, the former transaction is actually using the wrong data. An *unrepeatable read* takes place if a transaction reads data from the database, and then at a later time, it reads the same data but that data already has changed. This could happen due to the actions of another transaction. A *phantom read* occurs when a transaction queries the database and retrieves a certain data set, another transaction updates the database, and at a later time the former transactions performs the same query and gets new records (the new records are phantom records).

The more "relaxed" isolation level for EJB is the `TRANSACTION_READ_UNCOMMITTED`; this level imposes no isolation guarantees, but it provides the best performance. Using this isolation level makes your system susceptible to all three types of problems (dirty reads, unrepeatable reads, and phantom reads). The `TRANSACTION_READ_COMMITTED` level solves the dirty read problem and guarantees that it does not occur. The `TRANSACTION_REPEATABLE_READ` prevents both the dirty read problem as well as the unrepeatable read problems. The `TRANSACTION_SERIALIZABLE` level provides the best guarantees, and specifically none of the dirty read, unrepeatable read, and the phantom read problems can occur in this level.

Since isolation is related to database access, it applies differently to beans with CMP. For session beans or entity beans with Bean-Managed Persistence (BMP), the container sets the transaction isolation level for each database connection used by the bean at the beginning of a transaction. For beans with CMP, the persisted object implements the database access code in a manner that conforms to the specific isolation level.

Your selection of which isolation level to use depends first and foremost on the isolation levels supports by the underlying database. Otherwise, there is a clear tradeoff between performance and risk to data consistency. This tradeoff results from the simple fact that the longer a lock on a certain data record is kept, risks to data consistency are lower but overall performance degrades (because concurrent transactions are kept waiting). In extreme cases, deadlocks could result. The Serializable isolation level is the most restrictive and the safest, but in some cases is not required. For example, code that never performs updates but only reads could use the ReadUncommited level.

The issue of which levels are supported by the underlying database is not theoretical, as not all levels of isolations are supported by all databases. For example, Oracle (a prominent player in the database market) supports only the ReadCommitted and Serializable levels. This means that you must choose the lesser of two evils: run a risk of phantom reads and unrepeatable read anomalies or end up with poor performance.

Controlling EJB Transactions with the AAT

The WebSphere Application Assembly Tool (AAT) provides a convenient way for setting the transactional behavior of EJB. On the General tab for a session bean, you can set the transactional behavior either as bean managed or container managed, as shown in Figure 31-1. Development tools such as the WebSphere Studio Application Developer (WSAD), described in Chapter 16, also allow you to set the EJB's transaction behavior. This selection is not needed for entity beans, because the container manages transactions for such beans.

When using container-managed transactions, the transaction attribute is set through the Container Transaction entry of the EJB module. To define the transaction attribute

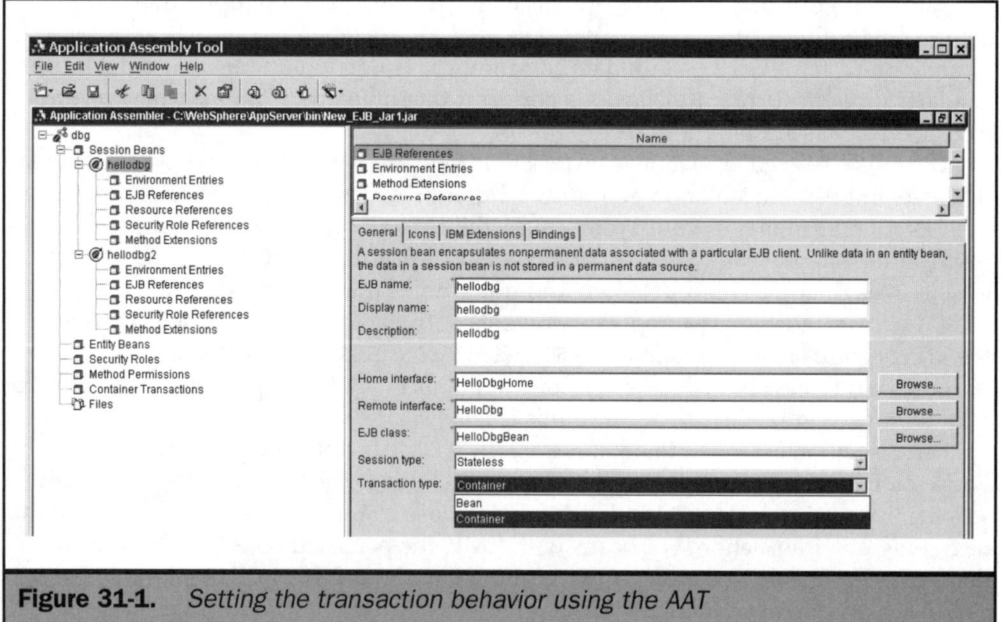

Figure 31-1. *Setting the transaction behavior using the AAT*

for one or more methods, you can right-click this entry and choose New. This dialog box opens

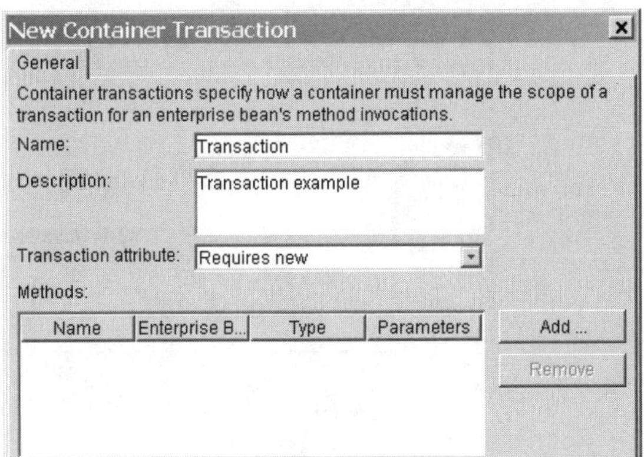

Clicking the Add button opens a new window where you can select an EJB method from any of the beans in the module for which container-managed transactions are used.

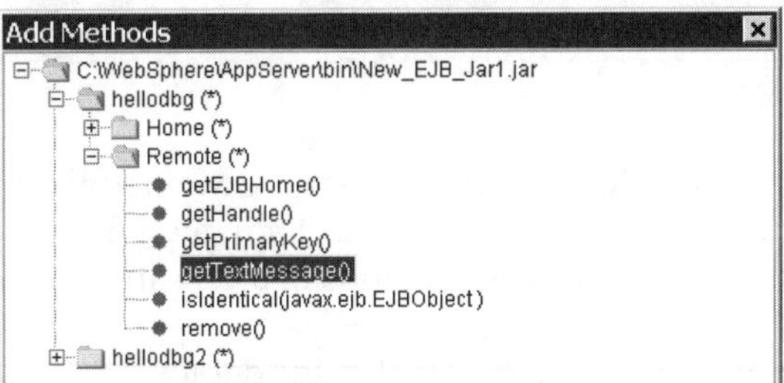

You can select as many methods as you want and select the transaction attribute desired for these methods, as shown here:

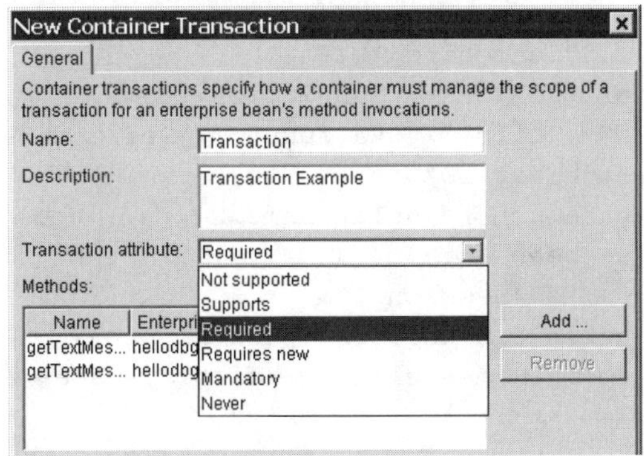

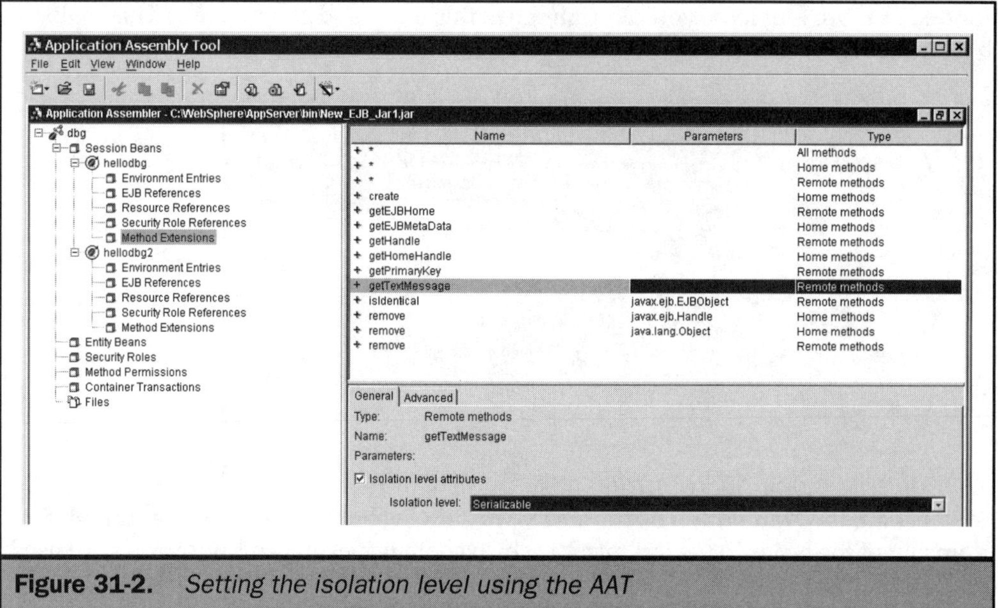

Figure 31-2. *Setting the isolation level using the AAT*

The isolation level attribute is selected under the Method Extensions entry for each EJB, as shown in Figure 31-2. Here you can select any method and set its isolation level. Wildcards are also included for all the methods of a certain interface or all the methods associated with this bean.

Whatever settings you make are reflected in the deployment descriptor. For example, after adding transaction Required for the two `getTextMessage` methods of the beans introduced in Chapter 29, the XML deployment descriptor would appear as follows (the entries relating to transactions appear in boldface font):

```
<?xml version="1.0" encoding="UTF-8"?>
<!DOCTYPE ejb-jar PUBLIC "-//Sun Microsystems, Inc.//DTD Enterprise
JavaBeans 1.1//EN" "http://java.sun.com/j2ee/dtds/ejb-jar_1_1.dtd">
   <ejb-jar id="ejb-jar_ID">
      <display-name>dbg</display-name>
      <enterprise-beans>
         <session id="Session_1">
            <description>hellodbg</description>
            <display-name>hellodbg</display-name>
```

```
          <ejb-name>hellodbg</ejb-name>
          <home>HelloDbgHome</home>
          <remote>HelloDbg</remote>
          <ejb-class>HelloDbgBean</ejb-class>
          <session-type>Stateless</session-type>
         <transaction-type>Container</transaction-type>
       </session>
       <session id="Session_2">
          <description>hellodbg2</description>
          <display-name>hellodbg2</display-name>
          <ejb-name>hellodbg2</ejb-name>
          <home>HelloDbgHome2</home>
          <remote>HelloDbg2</remote>
          <ejb-class>HelloDbgBean2</ejb-class>
          <session-type>Stateless</session-type>
          <transaction-type>Container</transaction-type>
       </session>
    </enterprise-beans>
    <assembly-descriptor id="AssemblyDescriptor_1">
      <container-transaction id="MethodTransaction_1">
         <description>Transaction:+:Example Transaction</description>
         <method id="MethodElement_1">
             <ejb-name>hellodbg</ejb-name>
             <method-intf>Remote</method-intf>
             <method-name>getPrimaryKey</method-name>
             <method-params>
       </method-params>
          </method>
          <method id="MethodElement_2">
             <ejb-name>hellodbg2</ejb-name>
             <method-intf>Remote</method-intf>
             <method-name>getTextMessage</method-name>
             <method-params>
             </method-params>
          </method>
          <trans-attribute>Required</trans-attribute>
       </container-transaction>
</assembly-descriptor>
   </ejb-jar>
```

Limitations of EJB Transactions

While transactions are very useful, it is important that you realize that they do not cover all instance variables in your EJB. In a state-ful session bean, the bean state is not transactional. In other words, if a transaction is started within a state-ful EJB and later a rollback is performed, the EJB state is unchanged. The state must be modified explicitly to reflect the state *before* the transaction started. As explained in Chapter 11, a session bean can be informed about the state of the transaction associated with it using the `SessionSynchronization` interface.

In entity beans, the bean state is transactional, but only for persistent fields (managed either by CMP or BMP). Non-persistent variables are not stored in the database. Furthermore, such variables must not be used to maintain the state associated with an EJB client between method invocations, as the values might change due to invocations by other clients or be lost when the bean is passivated.

An important restriction is that EJB declared with any sort of transactional support from the container must never use the Java Database Connectivity (JDBC) commit and rollback operations. These operations are reserved to the container.

When running under container-managed transactions, the container might roll back the transaction in case of an exception. If a system exception is caught, the transaction is rolled back before the exception is passed to the client. However, if an application exception is caught, the container assumes that the transaction is still valid. In this case, the transaction is not rolled back. In fact, if it is a new transaction whose scope is the method call throwing the exception, the transaction commits. Of course, if the application explicitly invokes `setRollbackOnly` for the transaction, it does not commit but rather rolls back.

Note that an uncaught application exception might cause a rollback. Consider the case in which a bean method declares that it throws an application exception and its transaction attribute is `TX_REQUIRES_NEW`. If this method throws the application exception, that transaction will roll back even if the calling method catches and handles it.

Even though uncaught application exceptions may cause a transaction rollback, throwing an exception is not the recommended way to roll back a transaction when using container-managed transactions. The container might not be able to tell whether the exception is "serious enough" to warrant a rollback. Instead, what you should do is invoke `setRollbackOnly` on the EJB context. A typical situation in which you invoke this method is when a call to another EJB fails and an exception is caught. In some cases, you might want to retry the EJB invocation. For example, it is possible that an exception was thrown due to some temporary network connectivity problem. After one or more such retries fail, or in case the exception caught is such that it does not leave any room for doubt—for example `TransactionRolledbackException`)—set the EJB context to be rollback only.

If your code implements lengthy transactions involving several EJB instances, there is always the risk that an EJB early in the progress of the transaction invoked `setRollbackOnly`. In such a scenario, a potential pitfall is that beans that are later in the progress of the transaction waste CPU cycles processing a transaction that is doomed to fail. To avoid this, you can use the `getRollbackOnly` method, so that your bean implementation can check whether it is executing within a transaction that is relevant at all.

Bean-Managed Transactions

Bean-managed transactions (BMTs) are to be used for cases in which a bean needs to be actively involved in transactions. As explained, bean-managed transactions are limited to session beans. Note that BMT is really targeted for expert developers, and you should have a really good reason for using it over container-managed transactions.

The bean can retrieve a transaction context (represented by a `UserTransaction` object) from the EJB context. If the bean is a stateless session bean, it cannot use the same transaction context in multiple method invocation by its EJB client. The rationale is obvious: any member variables in a stateless bean cannot be relied upon across method invocation. As you saw in Chapter 29, the container can use the same bean for different clients. For state-ful session beans, the situation is different. A state-ful session bean can reuse the same transaction context across several method invocations by making it an instance variable. In this case, it is also possible to implement the `javax.ejb.SessionSynchronization` interface to synchronize the conversational state with the transaction. (This is, of course, only a matter of convenience, as the transaction is manipulated directly from the code.)

Note *You should not have a transaction span multiple methods (that is, one in which one method starts a transaction, another method does stuff, and a third method commits the transaction).*

To implement BMTs, your bean must hold the `SessionContext` object passed to it in the `setSessionContext` method. Later on, it can retrieve the transaction context from the session context object. The following code snippet outlines the way BMTs should be implemented:

```
import javax.ejb.*;
import javax.transaction.*;

public class StatelessBeanManagingTransactions implements SessionBean
{
    private SessionContext ctx = null;

    // EJB required methods...
    public void setSessionContext(SessionContext c)
    {
        ctx = c;
    }
```

```
    // Business method implementation
    public void invoke(int a, int b, int c)
    {
        UserTransaction trans = ctx.getUserTransaction();
        // Perform non-transactional work
        ...
        try () {
          trans.begin();
          // Perform transactional work
          ...
          trans.commit();
        } catch (RollbackException ex1) {
          ...
        } catch (HeuristicRollbackException ex2) {
          ...
        } catch (HeuristicMixedException ex3) {
          ...
        } catch (NotSupportedException ex4) {
          ...
        } catch (SystemException ex5) {
          ...
        }
        // Perform non-transactional work
        ...
    }
    ...
}
```

When using BMT, you may use the `getStatus` method of the `UserTransaction` object to determine whether the current transaction is doomed to fail. In case of failures, BMT beans can invoke the `setRollbackOnly` method of the `UserTransaction` object. This method should be invoked only after any retries are attempted.

Managing Transactions from Client-Side Code

While the EJB programming model allows for clients to take part in transaction management, this complicates client-side programming. From the perspective of system design, it contradicts the notion of a thin client that focuses on presentation while using server-side services for handling issues such as transactions. In the WebSphere environment, the transaction service of the server is contacted using the JNDI name `jta/usertransaction`, as shown. After a transaction context is obtained, transaction demarcation can take place using the `begin` and `commit` methods. EJB invocations (and their effects on the bean's data) enclosed by a transaction will of course be part of this transaction. The outline of such an invocation is quite similar to that shown in the code segment earlier:

```
import javax.transaction.*;
import javax.ejb.*;

class ClientCode {
      // ...
      void transactionMethod() {
          // Obtain EJB reference
          ...
          // Perform non-transactional work
          ...
          // Lookup transaction
          Context initialContext = new InitialContext();
          UserTransaction tcon =
                (UserTransaction) initialContext.lookup(
                                  "jta/usertransaction");
           tcon.begin();
           // Perform EJB invocations that are part of the
transaction
           tcon.commit();
           // Non-transactional work
      }
}
```

Such direct activation of transactions from the client side is not recommended. A better design choice is to encapsulate all transactional management in session beans (which act on the behalf of the client by their definition). Such beans can use the transactional attributes of EJB, taking full advantage of the EJB container's transactional facilities.

EJB Security

Whenever an EJB method invocation takes place, the calling party passes to the EJB container a *user context*, which represents the caller identity as previously authenticated. (Authentication is beyond the scope of EJB security and is discussed in Chapters 19 and 44.) EJB security focuses on *authorization*.

EJB security can be enforced either programmatically or declaratively. Programmatically managing security means writing explicit code for handling security checks. This makes security hard coded into your bean and also increases the amount of code in the bean. Declarative authorization delegates authorization to the EJB container and keeps the bean implementation focused on business logic rather than on security. It is also important in maintaining the flexibility that comes with the separation of responsibility between the bean developer and the person responsible for assembly and deployment.

Declarative EJB Authorization

Declarative EJB authorization is defined using the AAT, similar to other deployment attributes. Authorization in EJB relies on *security roles*. A security relation loosely corresponds to a client identity or set of client identities. Security roles and the permissions associated with them are defined at deployment time.

Adding a new security role in the AAT is straightforward.

1. Right-click the Security Roles entry for the EJB module and select New. The following dialog appears

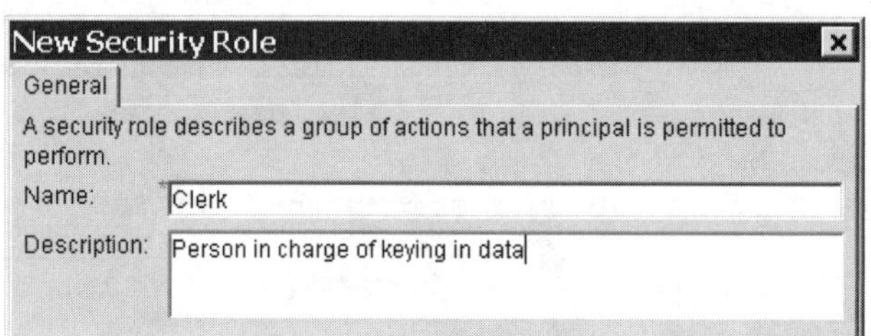

2. The AAT displays the list of roles available in the EJB module. For example, after adding two roles, the display appears as shown in Figure 31-3.
3. To define method invocation permissions, right-click the Method Permissions entry and select New to bring up the New Method Permission dialog:

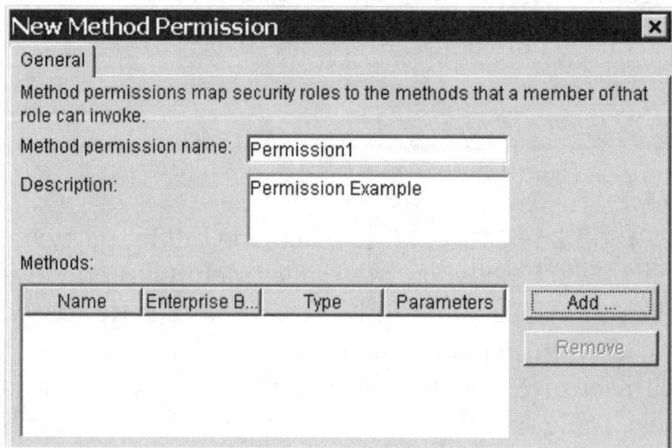

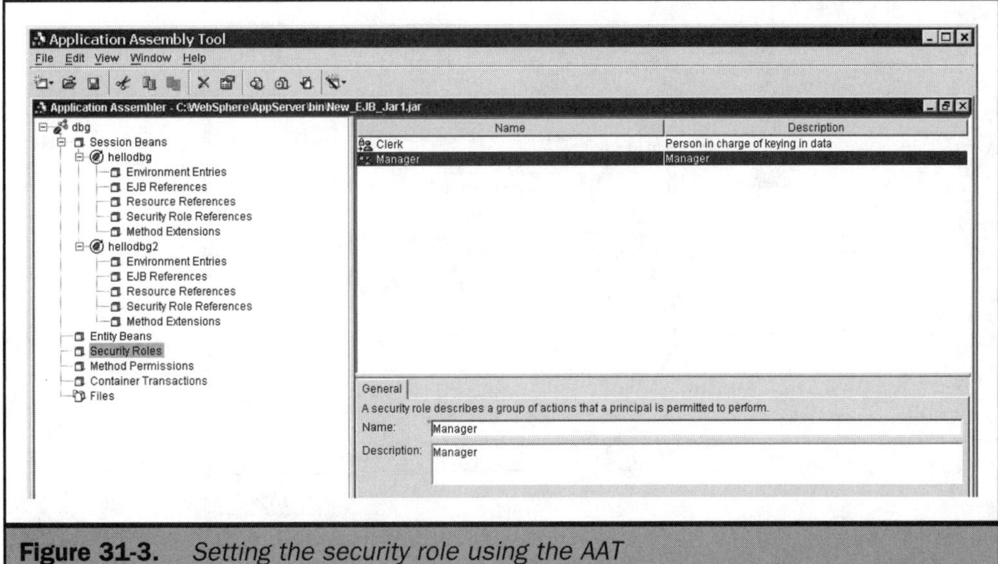

Figure 31-3. *Setting the security role using the AAT*

4. In this dialog, you can select one or more methods, and one or more security roles. To select a method, click the Add button to open the Add Method window:

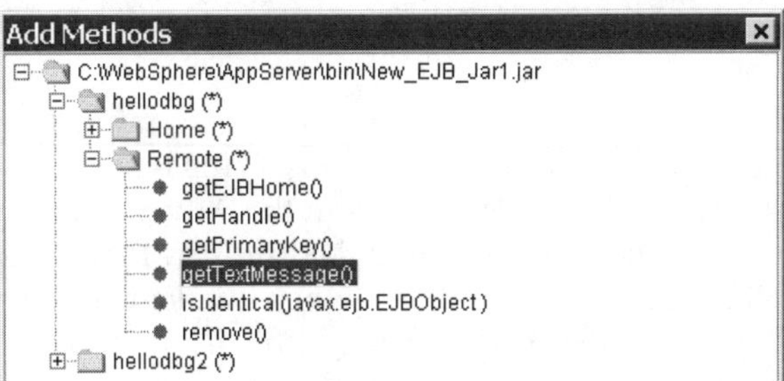

5. You can select security roles in a similar way from the list of available roles:

6. After you select from the available roles, you complete the method permission entry (composed of the selection of both method and roles), as shown in Figure 31-4. The meaning of the method permission is that all selected security roles are allowed to invoke all selected methods.

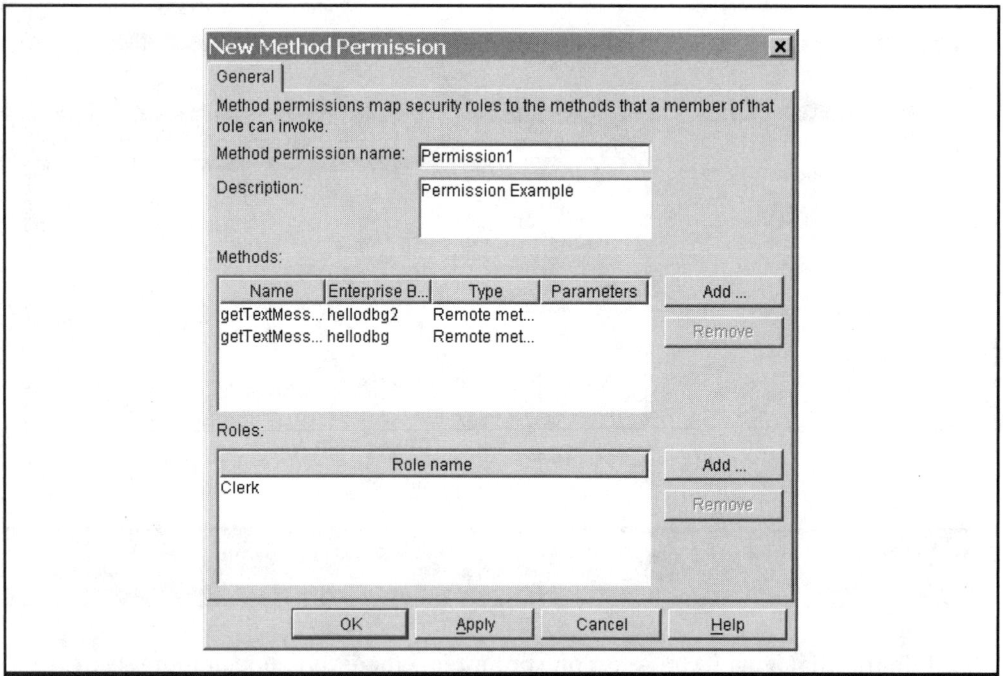

Figure 31-4. *Defining method permission*

In addition to method permissions, you may also determine the way the security identity is propagated across method invocations. (This is sometimes referred to as *security delegation*.) This is accomplished from the Advanced tab of the Method Extensions dialog box, in which you can select the Run-As Mode. This mode determines the identity under which the method will run when invoked. The method can assume the identity of the caller, the identity of SYSTEM (that is, the EJB server), or another "specified" security role. For selecting a specific role, you need to select the Run-As Identity option from the list of available security roles—the same list used in Figure 31-4.

While security roles for an EJB module are just names with descriptions, in the enterprise application level, they are bound to actual users and groups. This binding is accomplished using the Bindings tab for the Security Roles entry of the application, AAT, as shown in Figure 31-5.

Programmatic EJB Authorization

Programmatic EJB authorization relies on invoking the `isCallerInRole` and `getCallerIdentity` methods of the EJB context. The former checks whether the caller is part of a certain role, whereas the latter returns the security identity of the caller.

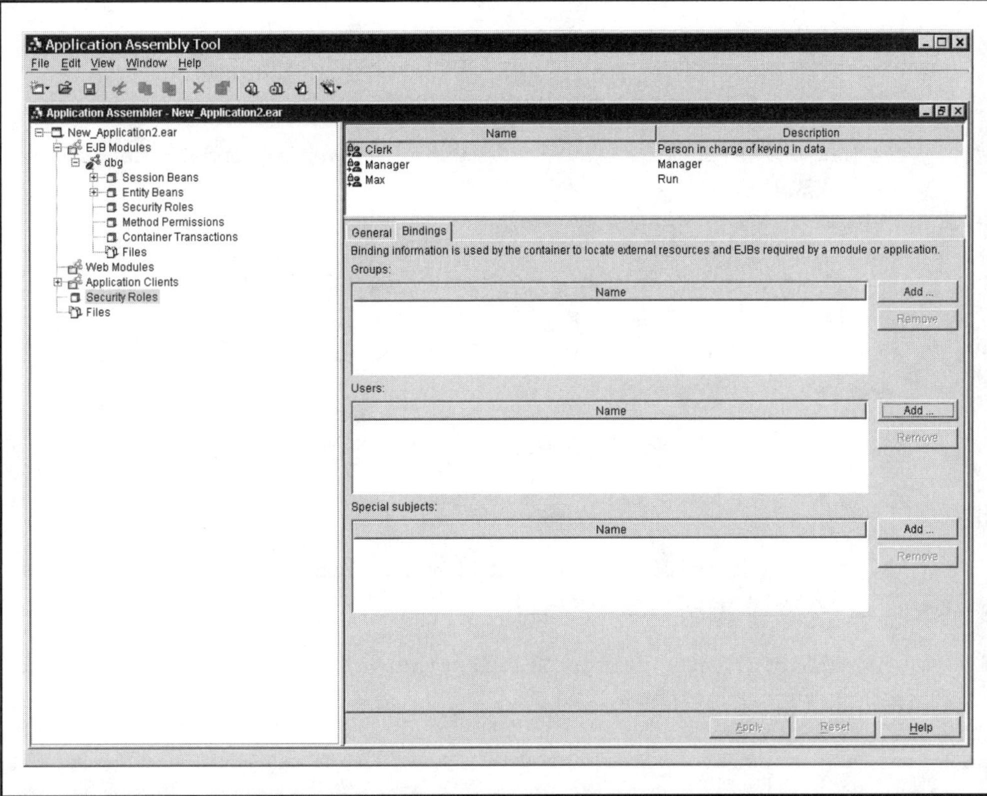

Figure 31-5. *Binding security roles using the AAT*

The following code snippet demonstrates the use of these methods:

```
import javax.ejb.*;
import java.security.Principal;

public class SecureSessionBean implements SessionBean
{
    private SessionContext ctx;

    void setSessionContext(SessionContext c)
    {
       ctx  = c;
    }
```

```
    // Other methods
    ...

    // Method which makes sure the user is running under the role
    // 'SYSOP'
    public void sensitiveMethod()
    {
       if (ctx.isCallerInRole("SYSOP")) {
           // Do important stuff
           ...
       }
       else {
           // Don't do anything or throw exception
       }
    }

    // Method which returns the caller identity
    String void getCallerIdent()
    {
        Principal p = ctx.getCallerPrincipal();
        return p.getName();
    }
}
```

An important prerequisite assumed in this code is that the deployment descriptor will include the "SYSOP" security role. When it is available in the list of security roles, the application deployer will be able to map users to this role at his or her discretion. If the developer fails to include this security role in the deployment descriptor, this code will not run properly (or at least it will never run the code enclosed in the `if` statement testing the caller role).

Security Attributes in the Deployment Descriptor

The security attributes, like all other deployment attributes, are captured in the XML deployment descriptor. The following is the XML descriptor resulting from adding the users and permissions shown in Figure 31-4. The attributes related to security are highlighted in boldface.

```
<?xml version="1.0" encoding="UTF-8"?>
<!DOCTYPE ejb-jar PUBLIC
    "-//Sun Microsystems, Inc.//DTD Enterprise JavaBeans 1.1//EN"
```

```
 "http://java.sun.com/j2ee/dtds/ejb-jar_1_1.dtd">
<ejb-jar id="ejb-jar_ID">
   <display-name>dbg</display-name>
   <enterprise-beans>
      <session id="Session_1">
         <description>hellodbg</description>
         <display-name>hellodbg</display-name>
         <ejb-name>hellodbg</ejb-name>
         <home>HelloDbgHome</home>
         <remote>HelloDbg</remote>
         <ejb-class>HelloDbgBean</ejb-class>
         <session-type>Stateless</session-type>
         <transaction-type>Container</transaction-type>
      </session>
      <session id="Session_2">
         <description>hellodbg2</description>
         <display-name>hellodbg2</display-name>
         <ejb-name>hellodbg2</ejb-name>
         <home>HelloDbgHome2</home>
         <remote>HelloDbg2</remote>
         <ejb-class>HelloDbgBean2</ejb-class>
         <session-type>Stateless</session-type>
         <transaction-type>Container</transaction-type>
      </session>
   </enterprise-beans>
   <assembly-descriptor id="AssemblyDescriptor_1">
       <security-role id="SecurityRole_1">
         <description>Manager</description>
         <role-name>Manager</role-name>
      </security-role>
      <security-role id="SecurityRole_2">
      <description>Person in charge of keying in data</description>
       <role-name>Clerk</role-name>
      </security-role>
      <method-permission id="MethodPermission_1">
         <description>Permission1:+:Permission Example</description>
          <role-name>Clerk</role-name>
         <method id="MethodElement_1">
            <ejb-name>hellodbg2</ejb-name>
            <method-intf>Remote</method-intf>
            <method-name>getTextMessage</method-name>
            <method-params>
            </method-params>
```

```
            </method>
            <method id="MethodElement_2">
               <ejb-name>hellodbg</ejb-name>
          <method-intf>Remote</method-intf>
               <method-name>getTextMessage</method-name>
               <method-params>
               </method-params>
            </method>
         </method-permission>
      </assembly-descriptor>
   </ejb-jar>
```

Summary

Transactions and security are possibly the most difficult issues faced by a developer of server-side business logic. All business applications need to handle the issues of transactions and security. These two topics are therefore handled by the EJB framework, thus creating a uniform application framework and potentially saving a lot of work for business systems developers.

Both transactions and security in the EJB model have two modes—one in which the EJB container manages these issues and one in which the developer directly handles transactions and/or security using a set of APIs. The first approach is preferable for a number of reasons. The developer needs to do less work, the container that is built by specialists (in our case by the WebSphere core development team) can handle these better, and decisions on transaction and security behavior can be flexible to the point at which the application deployer can make decisions regarding application behavior. Chapter 32 continues with the EJB model and introduces the latest addition to EJB on WebSphere—message beans.

The Complete Reference

Chapter 32

Message-Driven Beans

Given that the enterprise JavaBeans (EJB) architecture aims at playing a significant role on the server side, it is only natural that it would address the issue of messaging. Because EJBs are implemented in Java, it is possible to use the Java Messaging Service (JMS) from within EJB. However, EJB method invocations are implemented over Remote Method Invocation-Internet Inter-ORB Protocol (RMI-IIOP), which implies that communication with remote clients takes place in a *synchronous* manner. Therefore, it is not simple to blend EJB and JMS asynchronous communication. A comprehensive solution for blending EJB and JMS together must address a variety of issues that relate to EJB, such as lifecycle and transaction management. Most of the complexities begin when JMS is used for asynchronous communications. Because asynchronous invocation is central to a decoupled distributed application, a merge of the EJB model with the JMS model holds much promise for application developers.

Messaging is an important tool for enterprise software development, as discussed in Chapter 14. The developers of the EJB specification have realized that some support for messaging must be incorporated into the specification. To cater to the needs of message-based, server-side software, the EJB specification has been extended to define a special kind of EJB called *message-driven* beans. These beans partly conform to the notion of EJB while adding some specialized functionality and behavior to support messaging. Message-driven beans are new to the EJB 2.0 specification, and as such, are not part of the WebSphere Advanced Edition version 4.0. They will be available in WebSphere version 5.0.

WebSphere Enterprise Edition version 4.0 includes a nonstandard implementation of message beans. This chapter describes the standard message-driven beans. We believe that IBM will include support for such message-driven beans in an upcoming release of WebSphere as part of its commitment to the Java 2 Platform Enterprise Edition (J2EE), and to promote its own MQSeries product. The last section of this chapter describes the message-driven bean support in WebSphere Enterprise Edition version 4.0.

Introduction to Message-Driven Beans

Message-driven beans are specialized EJB components aimed at providing the capacity for consuming Java Messaging Service (JMS) messages. As explained, blending together EJB and JMS brings up some conceptual difficulties. Because JMS (and messaging in general) is based on the premise of *decoupling* the parties involved (the client and server, for example), the way clients invoke EJB (and especially state-ful beans) is unsuitable. Also, the home interface and remote interface are not relevant for beans that are invoked through JMS, because JMS itself provides the mechanism for the invocation.

Message-driven beans can be viewed as a sort of hybrid of state-less session beans and JMS listeners. A message-driven bean has no conversational state, allowing the container to manage the lifecycle of such beans based on the needs of clients. Such beans have only one business method, called `onMessage`, which has a single `Message` object as a parameter and a `void` return value. It is worthwhile for you to note that this message is weakly typed, just like the respective method for JMS listeners. The `onMessage` method must carefully inspect the message using the `instanceof` predicate to determine the actual type of the message. This stands in stark contrast to entity beans and session beans, which can be used to define several business methods, each of which can take strongly typed parameters. Furthermore, entity beans and session beans can have a return value, whereas the asynchronous messaging paradigm forbids the message-driven bean from having a return value. Instead, the message-driven bean can respond by sending a message encapsulating the response.

The `onMessage()` method in message-driven beans cannot throw application-level exceptions because of the nature of asynchronous communication in general and messaging in particular. Of course, system exceptions might be thrown, and these are caught and handled by the EJB container.

Developing Message-Driven Beans

Message-driven beans need to implement two separate interfaces: `javax.ejb.MessageBean` and `javax.jms.MessageListener`. This shows us that message-driven beans are a hybrid of EJB and JMS listeners.

From the EJB side, a message-driven bean class should implement the following methods. All three methods are mandatory:

- **void ejbCreate( )** A creation method declared public but not static, and with void return value—similar to session and entity beans. However, no arguments to the creation method are used. This method is the place to look up other EJB references or create JMS connections (other than one receiving the messages forwarded to the onMessage method).
- **void ejbRemove( )** A removal method invoked by the container before it destroys the bean. Any database or JMS connections created in the creation method should be closed in this method.
- **void setMessageDrivenContext(MessageDrivenContext ctx)** Provides the bean with an EJB context with information about the surrounding environment. The MessageDrivenContext extends EJBContext and offers the programmer a way to access transactional information, as described in Chapter 31. Other methods of the EJBContext interface cannot be used, because the bean has no home interface or remote interface. Security-related methods are meaningless because the onMessage method is not invoked using EJB method invocation.

In addition to these methods, the `MessageListener` interface requires that we implement the `onMessage` interface described earlier in the chapter.

As explained earlier, you don't need to provide a home interface or a remote interface for a message-driven bean. The bean implementation itself is all the container needs. The implementation is therefore simpler than the implementation required for entity or session beans.

Just like its implementation, the lifecycle of a message-driven bean is quite straightforward. The bean lifecycle begins when the bean is instantiated by the container, which then invokes the `ejbCreate` method. The bean is then ready to receive messages and is repeatedly invoked using the `onMessage` method. Finally, when the container decides the bean is no longer needed (upon container shutdown, for example), it invokes the `ejbRemove` method to deactivate it. The following illustration shows the lifecycle of a message driven bean.

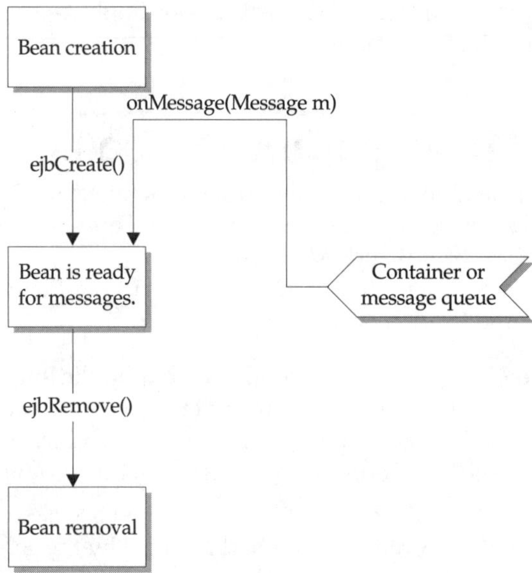

Advantages of Using Message-Driven Beans

One of the main benefits of the EJB architecture is that the EJB container vendor implements the infrastructure for your application, so you deal only with the application-level details, such as your specialized business logic. This approach is also reflected in the way message-driven beans are implemented.

The container automatically performs several actions on behalf of the bean: It creates a message consumer to receive messages, based on the settings configured at deployment time. It registers the message listeners (in fact, you must not call `setMessageListener` yourself). The container also specifies a message acknowledgement mode, based on the bean deployment parameters.

Most important, the container takes care of pooling bean instances. In other words, it creates a single bean instance for handling messages, and if the message load is high, it can create several such instances that serve incoming message concurrently.

The container also provides support for container-managed transactions. It is important that you realize that these are not nearly as powerful as container-managed transactions for session beans or for entity beans. The main difference here is that the message handler cannot expect to execute as part of the same distributed transaction as the party that sends the message. The rationale for this is, of course, that asynchronous message processing is all about decoupling the sender and the receiver, so using the same transaction pretty much brings us back to synchronous communication. The practical implication of a single transaction context is that if you allow one transaction to include both the sender and the recipient of a message, the application may run into a deadlock because the sender will not actually place the message at the destination (such as the queue) until the transaction commits. The receiver will not commit until the message appears in the destination, and this might cause the whole application to hang.

So what does the container do when you ask for container-managed transactions? It uses a single transaction scope for both reading the message and performing the `onMessage` business logic. In case of failures of any kind, the transaction is rolled back, and in particular, an acknowledgement is *not* sent to the sending party. Container-managed transactions for message-driven beans are similar to transactions for other EJBs in the sense that you do not need to include explicit calls to `rollback` and `commit` in your code.

In addition to container-managed transactions, you can use either bean-managed transactions or no transactions at all. With bean-managed transactions, the container lets you implement your own transaction bracketing. The transaction begins after the message-driven bean has received the message, and you can choose the acknowledgement mode in the deployment descriptor. The transaction begins when you explicitly invoke the `begin` method of the `UserTransaction` object, which can be obtained from the bean context. Because the transaction can begin only after the message is received, rolling back the transaction does not cause the message to be redelivered. This is in contrast to the situation with container-managed transactions, in which an invocation of `setRollbackOnly` in the `MessageDrivenContext` method (or a rollback due to any external reason) causes the message to be redelivered.

When asking for no transactional support, the behavior of the container with respect to message acknowledgement is undefined. The EJB specification does guarantee that the container will issue a message acknowledgement. However, the container acknowledges the message at its own discretion; it does not provide any timing guarantees. (That is, the acknowledgment may or may not be sent after the bean's `onMessage` method returns.)

Message-Driven Bean Example

The following simple example illustrates the concepts of message-driven beans. This bean receives text messages and prints out the message, preceded by the message provided by the "Hello World" EJB from Chapter 5.

The bean implements each of the required methods for message-driven beans:

- The ejbCreate method looks up the home interface of the Hello bean and creates one remote reference to that bean.
- The ejbRemove method removes the session bean.
- The setMessageDrivenContext method stores the context in the member variable ctx.
- The onMessage method receives the message. If the message is not a text message, an error message is printed. Otherwise, the remote method is invoked to retrieve its text message, and a concatenation of that text message and the text of the input message is printed out.

The following example is somewhat artificial in that the remote bean provides a constant message, but it illustrates the idea of a message bean that invokes a session bean. This is a common combination in that the session bean often serves as an entry point into the application logic, whereas the message-driven bean provides a managed way to expose this functionality in an asynchronous messaging environment.

```
import javax.jms.*;
import javax.ejb.*;
import book.websphere.chapter5;

public class HelloMsgBean implements MessageDrivenBean, MessageListener {

 private MessageDrivenContext ctx;
 private Hello helloBean;

 public void ejbCreate()
 {
    try {
        Properties env = System.getProperties();
        env.put(javax.naming.Context.INITIAL_CONTEXT_FACTORY,
                "com.ibm.ejs.ns.jndi.CNInitialContextFactory");
        env.put(javax.naming.Context.PROVIDER_URL, "iiop://localhost");
        InitialContext ic = new InitialContext(env);
        HelloHome home =
                            (HelloHome) javax.rmi.PortableRemoteObject.narrow
                                                    (ic.lookup("HelloBean"));
        helloBean = home.create();
```

```
        }
        catch (Exception ex) {
            ex.printStackTrace();
        }
    }

    public void ejbRemove()
    {
        try {
            Properties env = System.getProperties();
            env.put(javax.naming.Context.INITIAL_CONTEXT_FACTORY,
                    "com.ibm.ejs.ns.jndi.CNInitialContextFactory");
            env.put(javax.naming.Context.PROVIDER_URL, "iiop://localhost");
            InitialContext ic = new InitialContext(env);
            HelloHome home = (HelloHome) javax.rmi.PortableRemoteObject.narrow(
                                                 ic.lookup("HelloBean"));
            home.remove(helloBean);
        }
        catch (Exception ex) {
            ex.printStackTrace();
        }
    }

    public void setMessageDrivenContext(MessageDrivenContext c)
    {
        ctx = c;
    }

    public void onMessage(Message msg)
    {
        if (!(msg instanceOf TextMessage)) {
            System.out.println("HelloMsgBean received wrong message type" +
                            msg.getClass().getName());
            return;
        }
        try {
            TextMessage textMsg = (TextMessage) msg;
            String msgText = msg.getText();
            String helloText = null;
            helloText = helloBean.getTextMessage();
            System.out.println(helloText + textMsg);
        }
        catch (Exception ex) {
            ex.printStackTrace();
        }
    }
```

Deployment Descriptors for Message-Driven Beans

Similar to session beans and entity beans, an Extensible Markup Language (XML)-based deployment descriptor is used to specify deployment parameters.

The following example provides a deployment descriptor for our sample message-driven bean. The tags for message-driven beans appear in boldface .

```
<?xml version="1.0" encoding="UTF-8"?>
<!DOCTYPE ejb-jar PUBLIC
   "-//Sun Microsystems, Inc.//DTD Enterprise JavaBeans 2.0/EN"
   "http://java.sun.com/j2ee/dtds/ejb-jar_2_0.dtd">
   <ejb-jar id="ejb-jar_ID">
      <description>Hello Message Bean Module</description>
      <display-name>HelloMsgBeanModule</display-name>
      <enterprise-beans>
         <message-driven id="MessageDriven_1">
          <description>Hello Message Bean</description>
            <display-name>HelloMsgBean</display-name>
            <ejb-name>HelloMsgBean</ejb-name>
            <ejb-class>book.websphere.chapter32.HelloMsgBean</ejb-class>
            <transaction-type>Container</transaction-type>
            <message-driven-destination>
            <destination-type>javax.jms.Queue</destination-type>
            <subscription-durability>nondurable</subscription-durability>
            </message-driven-destination>
         </message-driven>
      </enterprise-beans>
      <assembly-descriptor id="AssemblyDescriptor_1">
      </assembly-descriptor>
</ejb-jar>
```

The `destination-type` descriptor defines how the messages are delivered over JMS—for example, by use of a queue or a topic. The `subscription-durability` tag controls the bean's durability property; the bean can be durable only if it is a topic bean. The `transaction-type` takes on a different meaning for message-driven beans. The optional `<acknowledgement-mode>` tag can be used to specify how the messages are to be acknowledged when bean-managed transaction demarcation is used. Another tag supported for message-driven beans and not shown is the `<message-selector>` tag. This tag implements the concept of message selectors detailed in section 14.4.3 of the EJB specification. Using this tag, you can specify SQL-like statements that can refer to message types and properties. Additional tags need to be used to attach the deployed bean to a specific message queue, but such tags are not provided as part of the EJB specification and can be addressed by vendor-specific extensions.

Message-Driven Beans in WebSphere 4.0 with Enterprise Extensions

WebSphere Application Server version 4.0 includes an enterprise extension called Extended Messaging Support that provides a nonstandard form of message-driven beans.

To introduce message-driven beans into WebSphere quickly, its designers made a small shortcut. Instead of extending the EJB container to support the notion of three kinds of beans, they implemented message-driven beans as session beans.

This might seem a little confusing, considering the EJB 2.0 specification for message-driven beans as described. However, it provides a reasonable compromise for practical purposes: Any EJB 2.0 implementation on the market today is probably no match for WebSphere 4.0 in terms of stability and reliability. The shortcut taken in introducing message beans provides most of the convenience of these beans, albeit in a nonstandard way.

WebSphere Extended Messaging Service plays the same role that the EJB container plays with message-driven beans. It sets up the connections and message queues (or topics), and invokes the message bean upon receiving a message. To use this service, you need to follow two steps.

First, you need to develop your message bean—an ordinary session bean with a home interface and remote interface. The bean defines and implements the `onMessage(javax.jms.Message)` method. Similar to the requirements in the "real" EJB 2.0 message-driven beans, this method should be public and non-static, contain a `void` return value, and should not throw any application exceptions.

The next step is to configure the messaging service. To that end, you need to provide an XML file detailing the configuration. You can introduce this file to WebSphere via the Administrative Console (described in detail in Chapter 42) by editing the Extended Messaging Support Service entry under the Custom tab for the application server. This option is available only while you're using enterprise extensions.

The XML file details the parameters for pooling the JMS connections (and associated beans) and the parameters for the message beans. The pooling parameters include an idle timeout (in milliseconds) after which a connection is discarded after the maximum number of unused connections in the pool.

The bean (or *listener*) parameters include the following:

- Java Naming Directory Interface (JNDI) name of the bean home interface
- JMS connection factory
- JMS destination name
- JMS destination type (queue or topic)
- Durability (durable or nondurable)
- Subscription name (for durable topic subscriptions)

- JMS selector
- JMS acknowledge mode
- Maximum number of retries for attempting to retrieve a message
- Maximum number of sessions the listener has with a destination it is monitoring
- Transactional flag

An example of such a configuration is provided here:

```
<Config>
  <Pooling>
    <Timeout>30000</Timeout>
    <Threshold>10</Threshold>
  </Pooling>
  <Listener>
    <HomeJNDIName>msgBeanHome</HomeJNDIName>
    <JMSConnectionFactory>ivtQCF<JMSConnectionFactory>
    <JMSDestination>MessageQueue</JMSDestination>
    <JMSDestinationType>javax.jms.Queue</JMSDestinationType>
    <JMSSubscriptionDurability>nondurable</JMSSubscriptionDurability>
    <JMSAcknowledgeMode>auto-acknowledge</JMSAcknowledgeMode>
    <MaxRetries>0</MaxRetries>
    <MaxSessions>1</MaxSessions>
    <Transactional>True</Transactional>
   </Listener>
  </Config>
```

Summary

Messaging and asynchronous communication are quickly becoming the preferred architecture for building decoupled, distributed systems. Messaging paradigms are therefore central to e-business and to applications deployed over WebSphere. Recognizing this fact, the EJB definition process has introduced message-driven beans into the EJB 2.0 specification. WebSphere 4.0 still does not fully implement this feature, but given IBM's adherence to standards, it will undoubtedly be included in a future version—perhaps WebSphere 5.0, or possibly a version within the 4.*x* line. In the interim, WebSphere includes an implementation for JMS-ready session beans that provides similar benefits. We chose to introduce both in this chapter because we believe this metaphor to be useful for many WebSphere applications.

This concludes the discussion of different types of EJB supported within WebSphere. Chapter 33 will outline some proprietary features that are available for EJB developers within WebSphere; we will then move on to a summary chapter that uses many of the concepts we've covered in an example that illustrates the use of ETB in multitiered applications.

Chapter 33

IBM EJB Extensions

While the Java 2 Platform Enterprise Edition (J2EE) is an emerging standard for server-side development, WebSphere does provide some Enterprise JavaBeans (EJB) capabilities that are not part of the EJB 1.1 specification. But this is a two-edged sword: These features are often useful and save quite a bit of work; however, this makes your code non-portable. Obviously, the more mature a standard, the fewer products that need to diverge from it. Previous versions of the WebSphere Application Server offered more features that diverged from the standard.

In previous chapters, you have encountered several deployment parameters in the Application Assembly Tool (AAT) that were designated as related to IBM EJB extensions. This chapter describes these parameters, as well as other features that are *not* part of the EJB 1.1 standard.

IBM WebSphere-Specific Deployment Parameters

During the assembly phase of an EJB module, when you're adding a new bean (either a session bean or entity bean), the dialog box for the new bean includes a tab for IBM Extensions. In these dialog boxes, extensions are additions to the standards J2EE deployment descriptors. They enable the use of Enterprise Extensions, older systems, or behavior not defined by the specification. Some of these extensions are common to both session beans and entity beans (as shown in Figures 33-1 and 33-2. Some parameters are relevant only to one bean category (as shown in Figure 33-2).

Both session beans and entity beans can refer to a local transaction. A *local* transaction context is created when an EJB method executes in a context that the EJB specification refers to as an *unspecified* context. The unspecified transaction context can be active during bean creation, removal, passivation, or activation, or during the `setSessionContext` method. Similarly, for cases in which the bean does not support transactions or does support transactions while the client is not within a transaction context, the transaction context is that of a local transaction. While these cases do not appear to be the most important ones (that is, typical code will not initiate a transaction from within `setSessionContext`), WebSphere addresses these cases using local transactions. This ensures that in every possible case, transactions can be used to ensure correct business behavior. The actions that can be activated are rollback and commit, with rollback always being the default.

Session Bean IBM Extensions Deployment Parameters

The IBM-specific deployment parameters for session beans are as follows:

- **Timeout** Timeout duration for a session bean. When this timeout occurs, the bean instance is removed from the system.
- **Inheritance Root** Indicates whether the enterprise bean is a root of an inheritance hierarchy.
- **Activate at** Specifies the point at which a bean is activated and placed in the bean cache. Possible values include the following:
  - **Once** (This is the default value.) The bean is activated once it is accessed in the server process, and is passivated (paged out) at the sole discretion of the container. This is sometimes called *lazy* activation.
  - **Transaction** The bean is activated at the start of a transaction and is passivated only after this transaction has ended. This parameter is relevant only for state-ful session beans. (It is irrelevant for state-less beans because the container can share these among different clients.)
- **Locale Location** Specifies the locale settings for the bean. When retrieving message catalogs, the language used could be based either on the locale of the invoking client or on the locale of the server. The possible values are Server and Caller.

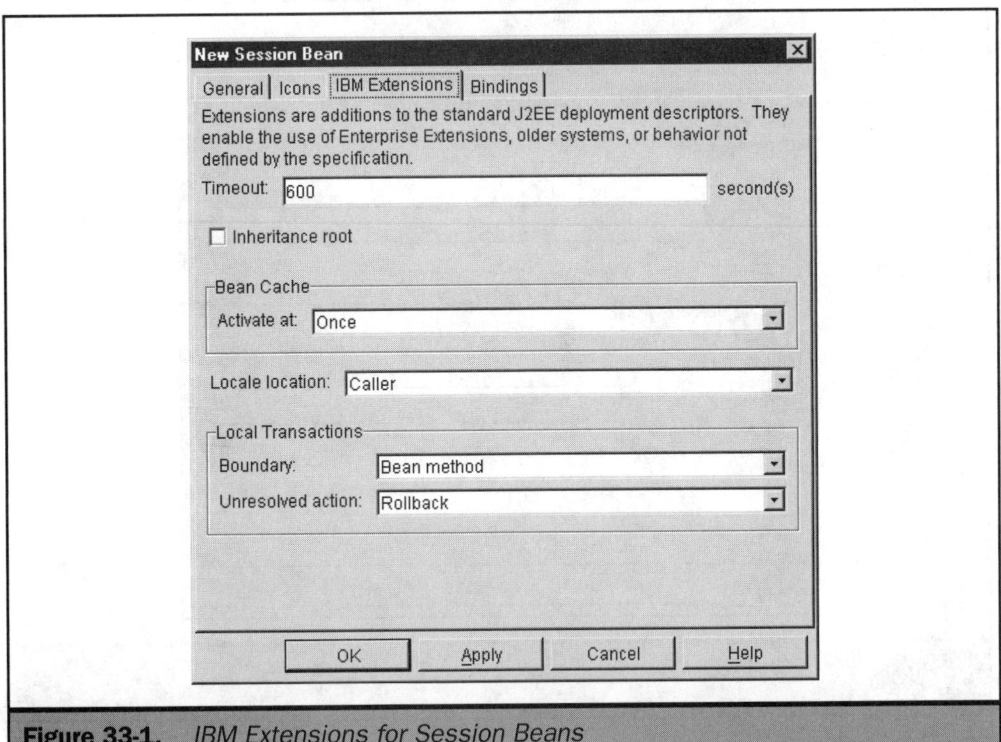

Figure 33-1. *IBM Extensions for Session Beans*

- **Local Transactions** Include the following:
  - **Boundary** Specifies where a local transaction begins. This property is not applicable to session beans, even though the AAT allows it to be set.
  - **Unresolved Action** Specifies the action to be taken by the container if an application "uncommits" resources in a local transaction. The values here are Rollback (the default) and Commit.

Entity Bean IBM Extensions Deployment Parameters

For entity beans, the following parameters have the same meaning as they do with session beans:

- Inheritance Root
- Locale Location
- Local Transactions—Boundary and Unresolved Action

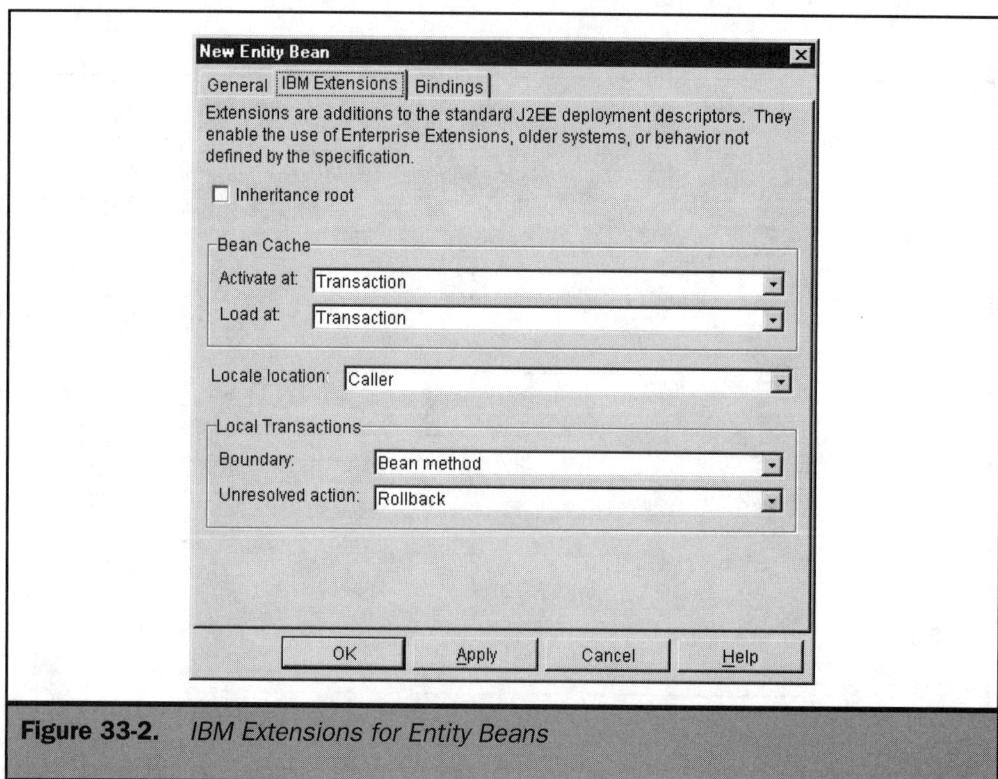

Figure 33-2. *IBM Extensions for Entity Beans*

The Bean Cache attribute of Activate At is similar to that of state-ful session beans. The Load at attribute specifies when a bean is to load its state from the database. Valid values are Activation and Transaction. The former indicates that the bean is loaded upon activation, and the latter indicates that the bean is loaded upon a transaction. The value of the Load At attribute indicates whether the EJB container is expected to have exclusive or shared database access. (Activation implies exclusive access, whereas Transaction implies shared access.)

The setting of the Activate and Load at properties for entity beans determine the commit options that are used. Commit options are part of the EJB 1.1 specification, and these two attributes allow the application assembler to decide which option to use. Table 33-1 shows EJB 1.1 commit options and the corresponding bean cache settings.

Commit Option	Implied Mode of DB Access	Bean Cache Settings	Comment
A	Exclusive	Activate at = Once Load at = Activation	Effectively minimizes database I/O by avoiding the need for `ejbLoad` calls. The downside is that all transactions accessing the bean instance are serialized in the database as opposed to in the container, which could cause poor performance if bean instances are concurrently accessed by multiple transactions. Also, you can have only one container (no clones/WLM, other containers or any other DB applications) can access those tables.
B	Shared	Activate at = Once Load at = Transaction	Increases memory requirement since it has more objects populating the cache. It is possible that a single bean instance would have several copies in the cache (one per transaction). This option is preferable to option A only in cases where the bean is continuously accessed throughout the transaction (which translates into multiple `ejbActivate` calls, which are free since the bean is already in the cache).
C	Shared	Activate at = Transaction Load at = Transaction	Reduces memory requirements by minimizing the number of cached entity beans. However, it allows for multiple copies of the same instance of memory (one per transaction, as with option B). Beneficial if bean instances that are accessed concurrently are seldom updated.

Table 33-1. *EJB 1.1 Commit Options and Corresponding Bean Cache Settings*

Managing Database Connections

When implementing Bean-Managed Persistence (BMP), most of the EJB methods interact with the underlying database. To facilitate connection pooling, EJB code that is interested in establishing a database connection should use the `DataSource` interface described in Chapter 18.

The administrator of a WebSphere node can create a set of special entity beans that encapsulate the information about the database and the database driver. It is possible to obtain a `DataSource` object using these beans. The `DataSource` interface provides transparent access to the WebSphere server connection pooling, providing a boost to application performance.

To access the datasource set up by the administrator, your code needs to use simple Java Naming and Directory Interface (JNDI) lookup. For example, if the datasource name is `DataSourceName`, you can use the following code fragment:

```
InitialContext ic = new InitialContext();
DataSource ds =
      (DataSource) ic.lookup("java:comp/env/jdbc/DataSourceName");
```

Notice that the application deployer must map the local JNDI reference (`"java:comp/env/jdbc/DataSourceName"`) to the global resource (`"DataSourceName"`).

After the `DataSource` object is obtained, it can be used to establish a database connection:

```
Connection con = ds.getConnection();
```

When using the `DataSource` to establish a connection, you may still use either one of the approaches mentioned in Chapter 30 to establish the connection. The easiest approach to implement is that of establishing the connection at the `setEntityContext` method and releasing it in the `unsetEntityContext`. This becomes a viable alternative when using a connection manager, because you don't need to worry about using too many connections, as the manager pools the connections anyway.

To illustrate this, let's revisit the BMP bean example from Chapter 30 and modify its implementation to use this technique. The changes required are as follows:

1. Create a new `import` statement for JNDI and for the `DataSource` interface:

   ```
   import javax.naming.*;
   import javax.sql.DataSource;
   ```

2. Add the datasource as a member of the class:

   ```
   public class CachedPageBean implements EntityBean
   {
         public String userName;
         public String pageUrl;
   ```

```
        public boolean changeFlag;
        public Date lastModified;
        public String content;
        transient protected EntityContext context;
        private DataSource ds = null;
        ...
}
```

3. The `setEntityContext` method sets the ds member:

```
        public void setEntityContext (EntityContext ctx)
        {
                context = ctx;
                try {
                        InitialContext ic = new InitialContext();
                        DataSource ds = (DataSource)
                          ic.lookup("java:comp/env/jdbc/CachedPageDataSource");
                }
                catch (Exception ex) {
                }
        }
```

4. The `unsetEntityContext` clears it:

```
        public void unsetEntityContext()
        {
                context = null;
                ds = null;
        }
```

5. Finally, each method that establishes a connection can use `ds` :

```
public void ejbLoad
        {
                try {
                        CachedPagePK key = (CachedPagePK)context.getPrimaryKey();
                        userName = key.userName;
                        pageUrl = key.pageURL;

                        String query =  "select * from CACHEDPAGES set " +
                                        "where USER = '" + userName + "','" +
                                        "PAGE = '" + pageUrl + "'";
                        Connection con = ds.getConnection();
                        PreparedStatement stmt = con.prepareStatement();
                        ResultSet rs =  stmt.executeQuery(query);
                        boolean more = rs.next();
                        if (more) {
                              changeFlag = true;
```

```
                    content = rs.getString(3);
                    lastModified = new java.util.Date(rs.getString(4));
                }
                rs.close();
                stmt.close();
                con.close();
            }
            catch (Exception ex) {
                System.err.println("Error in ejbLoad " + pageUrl +
                                        " Exception " + ex);
            }
        }
```

Summary

This has been a brief chapter, which is a good sign; WebSphere 4 is truly a standards-based server and provides complete coverage of the EJB 1.1 specification. The few extensions provided are used in extreme cases and most developers will not come across such instances. This chapter almost concludes our coverage of EJB in WebSphere. The next chapters summarizes a lot of what you have learned in Chapters 29–33 by using a set of examples to show how all of this comes together in patterns common in multitiered distributed applications.

Chapter 34

Using EJB in a Multitiered Application

The advent of distributed objects and the opportunities of Web applications have fueled an important paradigm shift in the world of enterprise computing. The commonly used client-server paradigm has been taken over by the three-tier or multitier approach.

In a multitiered architecture, components are layered in such a manner that each layer can be physically separated from the other layers, and each layer uses the layers below it. Specifically, the topmost layer concentrates on the user interface or presentation, a middle layer takes care of business logic, and the lowest layer (or *back end*) is a data store layer that is most often a database and sometimes a wrapper for a legacy system. Because the different layers may or may not be co-located in the same memory space, they need to communicate using mechanisms such as Common Object Request Broker Architecture/Internet Inter-ORB Protocol (CORBA/IIOP—described in Chapters 8 and 9).

The crucial difference between a multitiered architecture and a client-server approach is the separation of business logic from the user interface layer, which usually gives rise to a thin client approach (although clients may be thin, fat, or anything in between). A multitiered architecture provides several distinct advantages over the client-server approach. First and foremost, the multitiered approach promotes *modularity*, which in an architecture imposes a clear separation between user interface, business logic, and data processing. This in turn means that each of these components can be modified at lower cost. Changing the user interface component or modifying business logic is obviously easier in a modular structure than it would be with a monolithic application.

Other advantages of the multitiered approach relate to network traffic and deployment. The volume of communication between the user interface and business logic is typically much lower than the volume of communication between the business logic and the database. By separating the business logic from the user interface, the business logic can be placed in a location near the server, removing the high cost of network communications on longer, slower lines. This, of course, makes the user experience better. Multitiered architectures scale better than client-server systems. They reduce the amount of elements that the server side needs to serve. Instead of being contacted by each and every client, the server is contacted only by the elements of the tier above it.

Multitiering and J2EE

Java 2 Platform Enterprise Edition (J2EE) in general and the Enterprise JavaBeans (EJB) architecture in particular inherently support a multitiered architecture. This is accomplished by the well-defined separation between presentation, business logic, and data repository. The presentation logic is based on Web applications composed of static content (such as HTML pages, images, and PDFs), JavaServer Pages (JSPs), and servlets. Business logic is captured by EJB, and database logic is usually based on a relational database. The ability to have container-managed bean persistence means that it is possible for you to develop applications without doing any coding for the database logic.

The separation between Web applications and EJB does not necessarily imply that there are no business rules encapsulated in the presentation layer. This is not something that is explicitly prevented. The presentation layer can be implemented in a variety of ways, including some that capture all business logic. However, to make an application scalable as well as more robust, the use of EJB as a middle tier is recommended. Some business logic will always occur at the presentation layer (such as input field validation).

By offering clear separation between presentation logic, business logic, and the database, J2EE provides a three-tiered architecture by definition. The nature of EJB opens the door for more intricate architectures involving multiple tiers. EJBs that serve requests from their clients (for example, presentation logic) can themselves be clients of other EJBs.

In a true multitiered architecture (with more than three tiers), several layers of EJBs are used to provide the middle tier. This is suitable for complex applications, where multiple layers are required either for modularity, reliability, or performance. In the case of complex business logic, it is better for you to promote modularity and break up the code into several EJBs than to build a single monolithic EJB. Using several EJBs doesn't imply multiple layers, but to simplify client-side programming it is convenient to provide a well-defined entry point—one (or a small number of) EJB providing the interface to the middle tier.

J2EE provides further support for multitiered architectures using the EJB *connectors* construct. As mentioned in Chapter 15, EJB connectors are special components that allow existing systems to hook into the EJB platform. Such connectors allow legacy system to plug-and-play with any J2EE-compliant application server. Such legacy systems could be mainframe-based transactional systems, such as a Customer Information Control System (CICS), or back-end applications such as enterprise resource planning (ERP) or customer relationship management (CRM) systems. Such connectors were made available by IBM with previous releases of WebSphere, providing connectivity with Information Management System (IMS), CICS, Encina, and MQSeries. At the time of this writing, these are not yet available as EJB connectors, but they will probably be available in the near future. The main advantage of the EJB connector architecture is that it standardizes the methodology for connecting with external systems, hence making both EJB code and connectors more portable between J2EE systems.

The remainder of the chapter provides a detailed example of a multitiered application built with WebSphere.

An Example: Onamix Online Food Store

To demonstrate a multitiered architecture in WebSphere, we will develop a simple e-commerce application. Many e-commerce applications capture the essence of the multitiered paradigm. Such applications require the scalability of a multitiered architecture because a virtually endless pool of users (Web surfers) can access a Web application. The actions of these users are propagated via a middle tier to the application database. Our example will focus on an online shop for Japanese food, which we will call "Onamix."

Onamix Components

Figure 34-1 shows a high-level view of the components in the Onamix application. The topmost layer, responsible for the presentation, or user interface, is composed of servlets and JSPs. These servlets interact with the middle tier, which is made up of EJBs that are used to represent dishes (food), customers, orders, and the shopping cart. Some of the EJBs are session EJBs used to capture session-related data as well as to encapsulate business logic. In our case, such business logic could be used for providing discounts or delivery charges. Other beans capture persistent data and are implemented using entity beans.

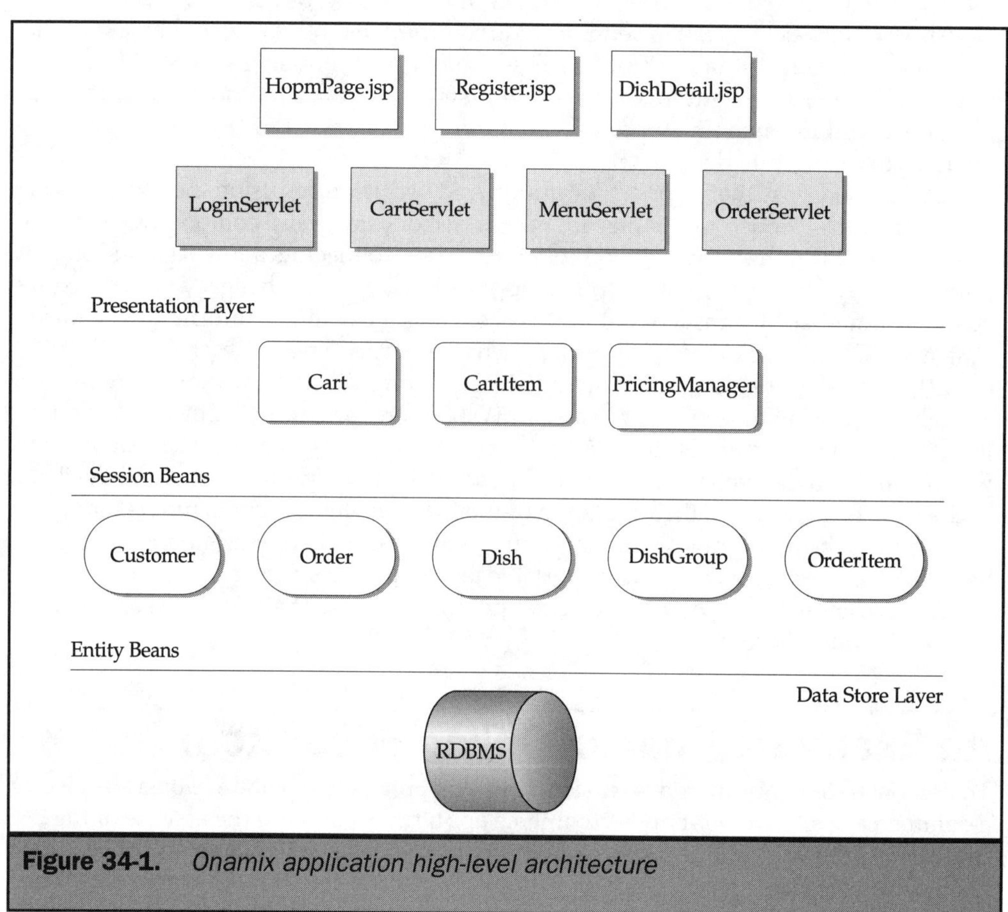

Figure 34-1. *Onamix application high-level architecture*

The presentation layer consists of the following elements:

- **HomePage.jsp** JSP providing the "front window" of the store, showing (among other things) today's specials.
- **LoginServlet** Servlet taking care of customer login.
- **Register.jsp** JSP allowing new customers to register.
- **MenuServlet** Servlet allowing customers to browse through the menu.
- **DishDetail.jsp** JSP showing details of a specific dish.
- **CartServlet** Servlet showing the current shopping cart.
- **OrderServlet** Servlet for carrying out an actual order.

The session EJB used in our example consist of the following:

- **Cart** Shopping cart, composed of CartItem elements.
- **CartItem** Single item in a shopping cart.
- **PricingManager** Encapsulates logic for delivery charges and for discounts.

Both the `Cart` and `CartItem` beans are state-ful because they maintain a user session.

Entity beans, shown next, are used to represent objects in the application domain such as customers, dishes, and orders. All the entity beans in this examples will use container managed persistence.

- **Customer** A user of the system to which dishes are to be delivered.
- **Dish** A single dish available on the menu.
- **DishGroup** A group of dishes. The menu is made up of DishGroup objects.
- **Order** An order made by a customer consisting of OrderItem elements.
- **OrderItem** A single item in an order.

It is important to note that to have a functional online store, you need to provide some additional service programs. For example, a set of functions, often called *online catalog management,* can be used for setting up (in our case) the database of dishes. We omit such service programs from this example for the sake of brevity, and because the implementation of such features often involves reusable off-the-shelf classes libraries.

Onamix User Perspective

The user experience for this application starts with *Onamix* home page, which shows the current date and time, as well as today's specials:

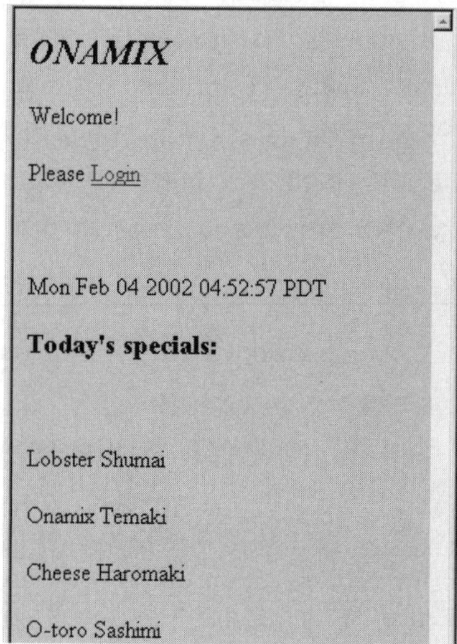

A customer needs to log in prior to ordering anything or browsing through the menu.

A new user needs to register as a user before entering the system:

ONAMIX REGISTRATION

ID Nr. (used for Login)

Name:

Password:

Address:

Delivery Instructions:

Phone:

Submit

Once registered, the user can browse through the menu:

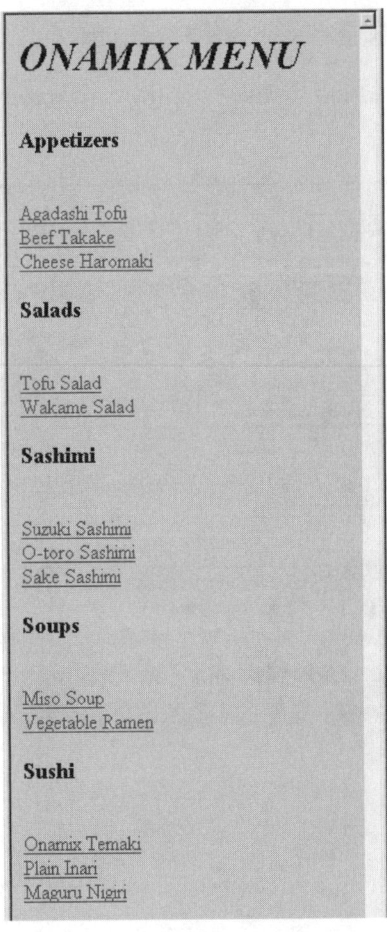

The user is also able to select specific dishes:

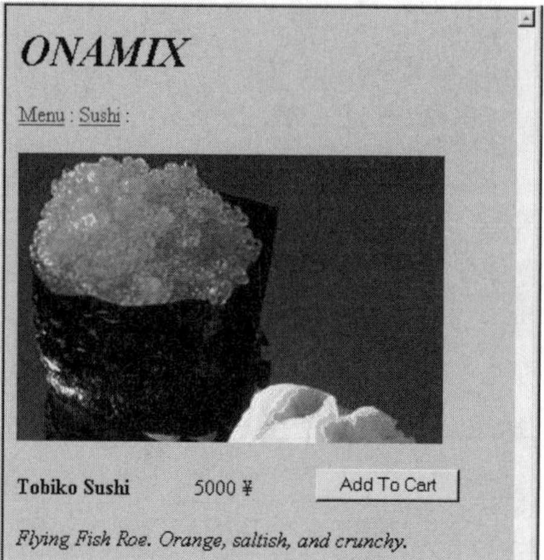

Specific dishes can be added to the shopping cart, which shows the total of all selected items:

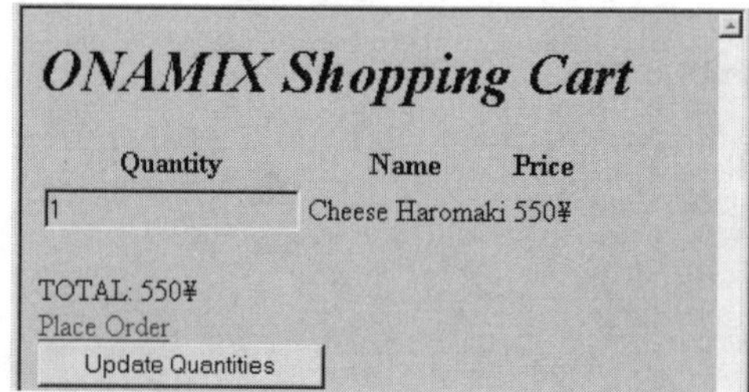

After an order is placed, a confirmation message appears indicating that the order has been processed by the application:

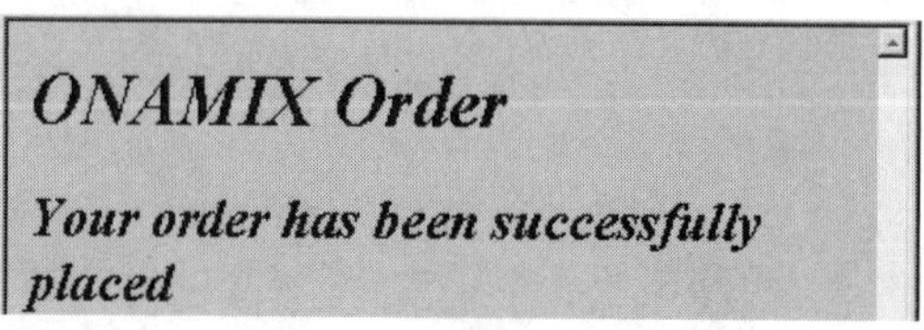

Onamix Application Implementation

The implementation for the Onamix application is presented in a bottom-up fashion, starting with the entity EJBs, which hold the actual data for the application, followed by the session beans implementing the business logic and the session-related information (the shopping cart), and finally the user interface components.

Onamix Entity Beans

The entity beans used in the Onamix application relate directly to the real-world application domain entities: Dish, Customer, and Order.

The Dish Entity Bean

The `Dish` entity bean represents a single dish on the menu. Each dish has a name, which will be used as primary key, a description, and an integer price (because we assume Yen-denominated prices). Each dish also has three `boolean` attributes indicating whether it is warm or cold, whether it is one of the day's specials, and whether it is out of stock. Finally, the bean can include an optional image, specified as a string holding the uniform resource locator (URL) for the image. The remote interface for this bean is as follows:

```
package com.onamix;

import javax.ejb.*;
import java.rmi.RemoteException;

public interface Dish extends EJBObject {
      public String getName() throws RemoteException;
      public String getDescription() throws RemoteException;
      public void setDescription(String description) throws
RemoteException;
      public int getPrice() throws RemoteException;
      public void setPrice(int price) throws RemoteException;
      public String getPicture() throws RemoteException;
      public void setPicture(String pic) throws RemoteException;
      public boolean getIsWarm() throws RemoteException;
      public void setIsWarm(boolean isWarm) throws RemoteException
      public boolean getIsOutOfStock() throws RemoteException;
      public void setIsOutOfStock(boolean isOut) throws RemoteException;
      public boolean getIsSpecial() throws RemoteException;
      public void setIsSpecial(boolean isSpec) throws RemoteException;
}
```

The primary key for the `Dish` bean is based on the dish name, as shown by the implementation of the class for the primary key objects:

```
package com.onamix;
public class DishPK implements java.io.Serializable {
      public String name;
      public DishPK(String nm)
      {
            name = nm;
      }
      public String toString() {
            return name;
      }
      public boolean equals(Object d)
      {
             return ((DishPK) d).name.equals(name);
      }
      public int hashCode()
      {
             return name.hashCode();
      }
```

The home interface provides a variety of finder methods that allow us to retrieve dishes by name, price, description, and warm or cold, and also allows us to retrieve the day's specials. Even though all these finder methods are not actually used in our sample application, providing interfaces that are as extensive as possible is useful. Doing so makes your EJB open ended and much more reusable. If this extensibility is built in from the start, EJBs can be reused, sometimes in ways that the original developer did not foresee.

```
package com.onamix;
import javax.ejb.*;
import java.rmi.RemoteException;
import java.util.*;

public interface DishHome extends EJBHome {
      Dish create(String name, String description, int price,
                        String picture,
                        boolean warm, boolean outOfStock, boolean special)
                        throws CreateException, RemoteException;

      public Dish findByPrimaryKey(DishPK key)
                        throws FinderException, RemoteException;
```

```
      public Dish findByName(String name)
                      throws FinderException, RemoteException;
      public Enumeration findBySpecial()
                      throws FinderException, RemoteException;
      public Enumeration findAllDishes()
                      throws FinderException, RemoteException;
}
```

The bean implementation is straightforward. We rely on container-managed persistence. This approach is simple and hassle-free, because all data elements in the bean are primitive elements. Because we let the container manage everything, the implementation becomes not much more than simple *get* and *set* methods, as shown here:

```
package com.onamix;
import javax.ejb.*;

public class DishBean implements EntityBean {
      private EntityContext ctx;
      private String name;
      private String description;
      private boolean isOutOfStock;
      private boolean isWarm;
      private boolean isSpecial;
      private String picture;
      private int price;

      public String getName()
      {
            return name;
      }

         public String getDescription()
      {
            return description;
      }
         public void setDescription(String desc)
      {
            description = desc;
      }
         public boolean getIsOutOfStock()
      {
            return isOutOfStock;
```

```
}

    public void setIsOutOfStock(boolean b)
{
      isOutOfStock = b;
}

    public boolean getIsWarm()
{
      return isWarm;
}

    public void setIsWarm(boolean b)
{
      isWarm = b;
}

    public boolean getIsSpecial()
{
      return isSpecial;
}

    public void setIsSpecial(boolean b)
{
       isSpecial = b;
}

    public String getPicture()
{
      return picture;
}
    public void setPicture(String pic)
{
      picture = pic;
}
    public int getPrice()
{
      return price;
}
    public void setPrice(int pr)
{
      price = pr;
```

```
    }

    public void setEntityContext(EntityContext ct)
    {
          ctx = ct;
    }

    public void unsetEntityContext() {
          ctx = null;
    }

    public void ejbActivate() {}
    public void ejbPassivate() {}
    public void ejbStore() {}
    public void ejbLoad() {}
    public void ejbRemove() {}

    public void ejbCreate(String nm, String desc, int pr, boolean warm)
    {
          name = nm;
          description = desc;
          price = pr;
          isWarm = warm;
    }

    public void ejbPostCreate(String nm, String desc, int pr,
                              boolean warm) {}
}
```

We still need to specify the finder logic class for the Dish bean so that the container can implement the finder methods. We define the strings that will be used as the WHERE clauses in the SELECT statements used by the container to query the database—one for every way in which dishes can be queried, as shown here:

```
package com.onamix;
public interface DishBeanFinderHelper
{
      String findByNameWhereClause = "name = ?";
      String findBySpecialWhereClause = "isSpecial = TRUE";
      String findAllDishesWhereClause = "TRUE";
}
```

The Customer Entity Bean

The `Customer` bean is used to represent a single customer. For simplicity, we assume customers have a special ID number (such as a driver's license number or passport number) that is used to identify them in our application. The information stored for a single customer includes a name, address, phone number, and special delivery instructions. The bean remote interface is as follows:

```
package com.onamix;
import javax.ejb.*;
import java.rmi.RemoteException;

public interface Customer extends EJBObject
{
      public String getID() throws RemoteException;
      public void setID(String id) throws RemoteException;
      public String getPassword() throws RemoteException;
      public void setPassword(String password) throws RemoteException;
      public String getName() throws RemoteException;
      public void setName(String name) throws RemoteException;
      public String getPhone() throws RemoteException;
      public void setPhone(String phone) throws RemoteException;
      public String getAddress() throws RemoteException;
      public void setAddress(String address) throws RemoteException;
      public String getDeliveryInstruction() throws RemoteException;
      public void setDeliveryInstruction(String inst)
                                            throws RemoteException;
}
```

The primary key is based on the ID and provides a simple way to key our customers in the database:

```
package com.onamix;
import java.io.Serializable;

public class CustomerPK implements java.io.Serializable {
      public String ID;
      public CustomerPK(String id) {
            this.ID = id;
      }
      public CustomerPK() {
      }
```

```
        public String toString() {
              return ID;
        }

        public int hashCode() {
              return ID.hashCode();
        }

        public boolean equals(Object c) {
              return ((CustomerPK)c).ID.equals(ID);
        }
}
```

The home interface provides the ability to create new customers (this is used by the registration page) and to look up customer by name or ID:

```
package com.onamix;
import javax.ejb.*;
import java.rmi.RemoteException;
import java.util.*;

public interface CustomerHome extends EJBHome {
      Customer create(String ID, String name,
                        String passwd, String address,
                        String deliveryInst, String phone)
                       throws CreateException, RemoteException;
      public Customer findByPrimaryKey(CustomerPK key)
                       throws FinderException, RemoteException;
      public Enumeration findByName(String name)
                       throws FinderException, RemoteException;
      public Enumeration findAllCustomers()
                       throws FinderException, RemoteException;
}
```

The bean implementation is again straightforward, and here we omit some of the *set/get* methods.

```
package com.onamix;

import javax.ejb.*;
```

```
public class CustomerBean implements EntityBean {
      private EntityContext ctx;
      private String ID;
      private String name;
      private String password;
      private String address;
      private String deliveryInstructions;
      private String phone;

      public String getName() {
            return name;
      }
      public void setName(String nm) {
            name = nm;
      }

      ...

      public void ejbActivate()       {}
      public void ejbPassivate()       {}
      public void ejbLoad()             {}
      public void ejbStore()             {}
      public void ejbRemove()        {}

      public void ejbCreate(String id, String nm, String passwd,
                        String addr, String deliveryInst, String ph)
      {
            ID = id;
            name = nm;
            password = passwd;
            address = addr;
            deliveryInstructions = deliveryInst;
            phone = ph;
      }

      public void ejbPostCreate(String id, String nm, String passwd,
                        String addr, String deliveryInst, String ph)
       {}
}
```

Here, too, we rely on container-managed persistence for simplicity. This requires that we implement a finder helper class for creating the appropriate WHERE clauses:

```
package com.onamix;

public interface CustomerBeanFinderHelper
{
      String findByNameWhereClause = "name = ?";
      String findByIDWhereClause = "id = ?";
      String findAllCustomersWhereClause = "TRUE";
}
```

The DishGroup Entity Bean

A DishGroup aggregates several dishes and is slightly more complex than the previous beans. Dishes are assigned to groups to provide a hierarchical structure in the menu. The DishGroup EJB provides an excellent example of entity EJB containment. A single DishGroup contains one or more Dish beans, and it provides the functionality of a *container*. This means that you can add or remove elements. The remote interface defines methods for adding and removing elements as well as accessing elements:

```
package com.onamix;
import javax.ejb.*;
import java.rmi.RemoteException;
import java.util.*;

public interface DishGroup extends EJBObject {
      public String getName() throws RemoteException;
      public Enumeration getElements() throws RemoteException;
      public void addElement(Dish aDish) throws RemoteException;
      public void removeElement(Dish aDish) throws RemoteException;
}
```

The primary key class is based on the group name—the same name that will be used to build the hierarchy in the menu:

```
package com.onamix;

public class DishGroupPK implements java.io.Serializable
{
      public String name;
```

```
        public DishGroupPK(String nm)
        {
              name = nm;
          }

        public String toString()
        {
              return name;
        }

        public boolean equals(Object dish)
          {
                 return ((DishPK) dish).name.equals(name);
          }

          public int hashCode()
          {
              return name.hashCode();
          }
}
```

The home interface for a Dish group includes only a finder method based on the group name:

```
package com.onamix;
import javax.ejb.*;
import java.rmi.RemoteException;
import java.util.*;

public interface DishGroupHome extends EJBHome
{
      DishGroup create(String name)
            throws CreateException, RemoteException;
      public DishGroup findByPrimaryKey(DishGroupPK key)
                        throws FinderException, RemoteException;
      public Enumeration findAllGroups()
                        throws FinderException, RemoteException;
}
```

The bean implementation for a Dish group maintains a vector of Dish group instances and implements the methods for adding and removing elements from this vector. The ejbLoad method ensures that the vector is populated when the bean is loaded into the container:

```
package com.onamix;
import javax.ejb.*;
import java.util.*;
import java.io.*;
import java.naming.*;
import java.rmi.RemoteException;
public class DishGroupBean implements EntityBean
{
      private EntityContext ctx;
      private String name;
      private Vector dishesPK;
      private Vector dishes;
      public void setEntityContext(EntityContext ct)
      {
            ctx = ct;
      }
      public void unsetEntityContext()
      {
            ctx = null;
      }

      public void ejbActivate() {}
      public void ejbPassivate() {}
      public void ejbStore() {}
      public void ejbRemove() {}
      public void ejbLoad() throws RemoteException;
      {
            try {
                    Properties p = new Properties();
                    p.put(Context.INITIAL_CONTEXT_FACTORY,
                        "com.ibm.websphere.naming.WsnInitialContextFactory");
                    p.put(Context.PROVIDER_URL, "iiop://localhost");
                    InitialContext ic = new InitialContext(p);
                      Object homObj = ic.lookup("DishHome");
                    DishHome dishHome = (DishHome)
                                        javax.rmi.PortableRemoteObject.narrow(
                              homObj, DishHome.class);
                  Enumeration e = dishesPK.elements();
                  while (e.hasMoreElements()) {
```

```
                DishPK pk = (DishPK) e.nextElement();
                    dishes.addElement(dishHome.findByPrimaryKey(pk));
            }
        }
        catch (Exception ex) {
            throw new RemoteException(ex.toString);
        }
    }

    public void ejbCreate(String nm)
    {
        name = nm;
        dishesPK = new Vector();
        dishes = new Vector();
    }

    public void ejbPostCreate(String nm) {}

    public String getName()
    {
        return name;
    }

    public Enumeration getElements()
    {
        return dishes.elements();
    }

    public void addElement(Dish dish)
    {
        dishes.addElement(dish);
        dishesPK.addElement((DishPK) dish.getPrimaryKey());
    }

    public void removeElement(Dish dish)
    {
        DishPK pk = (DishPK) dish.getPrimaryKey();
        for (int i = 0; i < dishesPK.size(); i++) {
                if (dishesPK[i].equals(pk)) {
                    dishesPK.removeAt(i);
                    dishes.removeAt(i);
                    i--;
```

```
                        }
                }
        }
}
```

The OrderItem Entity Bean

An order item corresponds to a single line in an order, and is represented by the `OrderItem` bean. This bean holds the product and its quantity as well as an optional discount. The key for the order item is a number that is the concatenation of the order number and the line number. The remote interface for the order item bean is as follows:

```
package com.onamix;
import javax.ejb.*;
import java.rmi.RemoteException;

public interface OrderItem extends EJBObject
{
      public Dish getDish() throws RemoteException;
      public void setDish(Dish dish) throws RemoteException;
      public int getPrice() throws RemoteException;
      public int getQuantity() throws RemoteException;
      public void setQuantity(int quantity) throws RemoteException;
      public int getDiscount() throws RemoteException;
      public void setDiscount(int discount) throws RemoteException;
}
```

The class `OrderItemPK` implements a primary key for the order item based on a unique order item ID (similar to the `GroupDishPK` class). The home interface for the order item bean is as follows:

```
package com.onamix;
import javax.ejb.*;
import java.rmi.RemoteException;
import java.util.*;

public interface OrderItemHome extends EJBHome {
      public OrderItem create(String orderItemId, Order order,
                        Dish dish, int quantity, int discount)
                        throws CreateException, RemoteException;
      public OrderItem findByPrimaryKey(OrderItemPK key)
```

```
                        throws FinderException, RemoteException;
        public Enumeration findByOrderID(String orderID)
                        throws FinderException, RemoteException;
  }
```

The bean implementation for `OrderItem` beans is again fairly simple, and we omit some of the *set/get* methods:

```
package com.onamix;
import javax.ejb.*;
import java.util.*;
import java.rmi.RemoteException;
import javax.naming.*;

public class OrderItemBean implements EntityBean {
      private EntityContext ctx;
      private String orderItemID;
      private DishPK dishPK;
      private OrderPK orderPK;
      private Dish dish;
      private Order order;
      private int quantity;
      private int discount;

      public void ejbActivate() {}
      public void ejbPassivate() {}
      public void ejbRemove() {}
      public void ejbStore() {}
      public void setEntityContext(EntityContext ct)
      {
            ctx = ct;
      }

      public void unsetEntityContext()
      {
            ctx = null;
      }

      public void ejbLoad() throws RemoteException
      {
```

```
        try {
              Properties p = new Properties();
                p.put(Context.INITIAL_CONTEXT_FACTORY,

                 "com.ibm.websphere.naming.WsnInitialContextFactory");
                     p.put(Context.PROVIDER_URL, "iiop://localhost");
                InitialContext ic = new InitialContext(p);
                  Object homObj = ic.lookup("OrderHome");
              OrderHome orderHome = (OrderHome)

                                 javax.rmi.PortableRemoteObject.narrow(
                           homObj, OrderHome.class);
              order = orderHome.findByPrimaryKey(orderPK);
        }
        catch (Exception e) {
              throw new RemoteException(e.toString());
        }
  }

  public void ejbCreate(String oiid, Order ord, Dish aDish,
                  int qty, int disc) throws RemoteException
  {
        orderItemID = orderItemID;
        quantity = qty;
        discount = disc;
        order  = ord;
        dish = aDish;
        orderPK = (OrderPK) order.getPrimaryKey();
        dishPK = (DishPK) dish.getPrimaryKey();
  }

  public void ejbPostCreate(String oiid, Order ord, Dish aDish,
                              int qty, int disc) {}

  ...
  public int getPrice() throws RemoteException
  {
        return (100 - discount) * quantity * dish.getPrice() / 100;
  }

}
```

We again rely on CMP and use the following finder helper class:

```
package com.onamix;
public interface OrderItemBeanFinderHelper
{
      String findByOrderIDWhereClause = "orderPK = ?";
}
```

The Order Entity Bean

Orders relate a customer with one or more order items. An order consists of order items, a reference to a customer, and a date. An order records the discount and the delivery charges. The primary key for the order is a serial number identifying the order. The remote interface for the `Order` bean is as follows:

```
package com.onamix;
import javax.ejb.*;
import java.util.*;
import java.rmi.RemoteException;

public interface Order extends EJBObject
{
      public Enumeration getItems() throws RemoteException;
      public Customer getCustomer() throws RemoteException;
      public int getTotal() throws RemoteException;
      public int getDeliveryCharges() throws RemoteException;
      public void setDeliveryCharges(int delivery) throws RemoteException;
      public Date getDate() throws RemoteException;
}
```

The public key for an order is based on a unique order ID, as shown in the primary key class implementation:

```
package com.onamix;
public class OrderPK implements java.io.Serializable
{
  public String orderID;
  public OrderPK(String oid)
  {
      orderID = oid;
  }
  public String toString()
```

```
    {
        return orderID.toString();
    }
    public boolean equals(Object order)
    {
       return ((OrderPK)order).orderID.equals(orderID);
    }

    public int hashCode()
    {
       return orderID.hashCode();
    }
}
```

The home interface for the `Order` bean defines finder methods based on the primary key and on the customer, so that we may look up the orders related to a certain customer.

```
package com.onamix;
import java.rmi.RemoteException;
import javax.ejb.*;
import java.util.*;

public interface OrderHome extends EJBHome {
      public Order create(String orderID, Customer cust)
            throws CreateException, RemoteException;
      public Order findByPrimaryKey(OrderPK orderKey)
            throws FinderException, RemoteException;
      public Enumeration findByCustomer(CustomerPK customer)
            throws FinderException, RemoteException;
      public Enumeration findAllOrders()
            throws FinderException, RemoteException;
}
```

The bean implementation includes the *get/set* methods (which we again omit for lack of interest), the framework methods for loading, creating, and removing, and a business method for calculating the total price of an order:

```
package com.onamix;
import java.util.*;
import java.io.*;
```

```
import java.rmi.RemoteException;
import javax.naming.Context;
import javax.naming.InitialContext;
import javax.ejb.*;

public class OrderBean implements EntityBean {
      private EntityContext ctx;
      private Customer customer;
      private Vector items;
      private String orderID;
      private CustomerPK customerPK;
      private Date date;
      private int deliveryCharges;

      public Enumeration getItems() throws RemoteException
      {
            OrderItemHome home = null;
            try {
                    Properties p = new Properties();
                    p.put(Context.INITIAL_CONTEXT_FACTORY,
                     "com.ibm.websphere.naming.WsnInitialContextFactory");
                         p.put(Context.PROVIDER_URL, "iiop://localhost");
                    InitialContext ic = new InitialContext(p);
                      Object homObj = ic.lookup("OrderItemHome");
                  home = (OrderItemHome)
                                    javax.rmi.PortableRemoteObject.narrow(
                             homObj, OrderItemHome.class);
                   return home.findByOrderID(orderID);
            } catch (Exception e) {
                  throw new RemoteException(e.toString());
            }
      }
      ...
      public int getTotalPrice() throws RemoteException
      {
            int total = 0;
            for (int i = 0; i < items.size(); i++) {
                  try {
                        OrderItem item = (OrderItem) items.elementAt(i);
                        total += item.getPrice();
                  }
```

```
            catch (Exception ex) {
                 throw new RemoteException(ex.toString());
            }
       }
       total += deliveryCharges;
       return total;
}

public void setEntityContext(EntityContext ct)
{
       ctx = ct;
}

public void unsetEntityContext()
{
       ctx = null;
}

public void ejbActivate()       {}
public void ejbPassivate()       {}
public void ejbStore()            {}
public void ejbLoad() throws RemoteException
{
       try {
              Properties p = new Properties();
              p.put(Context.INITIAL_CONTEXT_FACTORY,
                  "com.ibm.ejs.ns.jndi.CNInitialContextFactory");
              p.put(Context.PROVIDER_URL, "iiop://localhost");
              InitialContext ic = new InitialContext(p);
                Object hom1Obj = ic.lookup("CustomerHome");
                Object hom2Obj = ic.lookup("OrderItemHome");
              CustomerHome customerHome = (CustomerHome)

                        javax.rmi.PortableRemoteObject.narrow(
                                 hom1Obj, CustomerHome.class);
              OrderItemHome orderItemHome = (OrderItemHome)

                        javax.rmi.PortableRemoteObject.narrow(
                                     hom1Obj, OrderItemHome.class);
            customer = customerHome.findByPrimaryKey(customerPK);
            Enumeration e = orderItemHome.findByOrderId(orderID);
               items = new Vector();
```

```
                while (e.hasMoreElements()) {
                    items.addElement((OrderItem) e.nextElement());
                }
            }
            catch (Exception e) {
                throw new RemoteException(e.toString());
            }
        }

        public void ejbCreate(String oid, Customer c) throws RemoteException
        {
            orderID = oid;
            customer = c;
            customerPK = (CustomerPK)customer.getPrimaryKey();
            date = new Date();
            items = new Vector();
        }

        public void ejbPostCreate(String orderItemID, Customer c)
                    throws CreateException, RemoteException {
        }

        public void ejbRemove() throws RemoteException, RemoveException
        {
            Enumeration e = getItems();
            while (e.hasMoreElements()) {
                OrderItem item = (OrderItem) e.nextElement();
                item.remove();
            }
        }
}
```

The finder helper class is similar to those shown earlier:

```
package com.onamix;

public interface OrderBeanFinderHelper
{
    String findByCustomerWhereClause = "customerPK = ?";
    String findAllOrderssWhereClause = "TRUE";
}
```

Deployment Parameters

Now that we have written the code for the entity beans, we need to determine the deployment parameters that go into the deployment descriptor. For all the beans in this application, we assume that the security *run-as* mode is set to CLIENT_IDENTITY. This is sufficient because we don't expect any of our beans to perform any secured or privileged operations. It means that all authorization is based on the client that initiated the operation.

The transactional behavior is a bit more complex, and different beans have different transaction modes. The Customer bean, which is typically created only once and is not modified frequently (and even if it is, it is only by one user), can be set to have a transaction mode of TX_SUPPORTS with the lowest level of isolation—TRANSACTION_READ_UNCOMITTED. Similar settings can be applied to dishes and dish groups.

For orders and order items, on the other hand, we set a transaction mode of TX_REQUIRES and the highest isolation level—TRANSACTION_SERIALIZABLE. This avoids some concurrency issues in the application (but you need to watch for deadlocks).

Onamix Session Beans

The Onamix application uses session beans to encapsulate business logic as well as session-specific data.

The Cart Session Bean

In this application, the shopping cart maintains all session-specific data. The shopping cart is represented by the Cart bean, whose remote interface includes methods specific to the cart, such as clear and getTotalPrice, as well as methods for managing the context of the shopping session, such as getCustomer:

```
package com.onamix;
import javax.ejb.*;
import java.util.*;
import java.rmi.RemoteException;
public interface Cart extends EJBObject
{
      public int getCount() throws RemoteException;
      public Enumeration getItems() throws RemoteException;
      public void addDish(Dish dish) throws RemoteException;
      public void setDishQuantity(Dish dish, int quantity)
             throws RemoteException;
      public void clear() throws RemoteException;
      public Customer getCustomer() throws RemoteException;
```

```
        public int getTotalPrice() throws RemoteException;
        public Order placeOrder() throws RemoteException;
        public void setDiscount(int disc) throws RemoteException;
}
```

The shopping cart contains an array of `CartItem` objects. In addition, it contains a reference to the customer to which the cart belongs. The `Cart` bean provides methods for setting the delivery costs and discount amount; these are determined externally by the `PricingManager` bean. The `Cart` bean also provides a method for creating an order out of the items in the cart. This involves creating a new `Order` bean with an `OrderItem` bean for each of the `CartItem` beans in the shopping cart.

The home interface for the `Cart` bean is simply the creation method:

```
package com.onamix;
import javax.ejb.*;
import java.rmi.RemoteException;

public interface CartHome extends EJBHome {
      public Cart create(Customer customer)
                  throws CreateException, RemoteException;
}
```

The bean implementation is shown next. An interesting implementation detail is that the `ejbRemove` method of the shopping cart bean removes the cart item beans. Technically, it is possible to rely on the timeout mechanism for session beans to let the container free up unused session beans. Relying on such services is a bad practice, though, and should never be done, as it makes for very non-scalable and buggy applications. You should always explicitly deallocate objects held by your beans (unless, of course, you can reuse them between client invocations). In contrast to the cart items, the `Customer` bean referenced from the shopping cart is not removed, because this is a persistent entity whose existence does not depend on the session or on the shopping cart.

```
package com.onamix;
import javax.naming.*;
import javax.ejb.*;
import java.util.*;
import java.io.*;
import javax.naming.*;
import java.rmi.*;

public class CartBean implements SessionBean
```

```
{
    private SessionContext ctx;
    private Customer customer;
    private Vector items;

    public void setSessionContext(SessionContext ctx)
    {
        this.ctx = ctx;
    }

    public void ejbActivate()        {}
    public void ejbPassivate()       {}
    public void ejbCreate(Customer cust)
    {
        customer = cust;
        items = new Vector();
    }

    public void ejbRemove()
    {
        Enumeration e = items.elements();
        while (e.hasMoreElements()) {
            try {
                CartItem item = (CartItem) e.nextElement();
                item.remove();
            }
            catch (Exception ex) {
            }
        }
    }

    public void setDiscount(int d) throws RemoteException
    {
        Enumeration e = items.elements();
        while (e.hasMoreElements()) {
            try {
                CartItem item = (CartItem) e.nextElement();
                item.setDiscount(d);
            }
            catch (Exception ex)
            {
                throw new RemoteException(ex.toString());
```

```
                }
            }
        }

        private CartItem getItem(Dish dish)
        {
            Enumeration e = items.elements();
            while (e.hasMoreElements()) {
                try {
                    CartItem item = (CartItem) e.nextElement();
                    Dish otherDish = item.getDish();
                    if (dish.isIdentical(otherDish)) {
                        return item;
                    }
                }
                catch (Exception ex)
                {
                }
            }
            return null;
        }

        public Customer getCustomer()
        {
            return customer;
        }

        public Enumeration getItems()
        {
            return items.elements();
        }

        public int getCount()
        {
            return items.size();
        }

        public void addDish(Dish dish, int qty) throws RemoteException
        {
            try {
                CartItem item = getItem(dish);
                if (item != null) {
```

```
                item.setQuantity(item.getQuantity() + qty);
                return;
            }
              Properties p = new Properties();
              p.put(Context.INITIAL_CONTEXT_FACTORY,
               "com.ibm.websphere.naming.WsnInitialContextFactory");
              p.put(Context.PROVIDER_URL, "iiop://localhost");
              InitialContext ic = new InitialContext(p);
                Object homObj = ic.lookup("CartItemHome");
              CartItemHome cartItemHome = (CartItemHome)
                        javax.rmi.PortableRemoteObject.narrow(
                        homObj, CartItemHome.class);
            item = cartItemHome.create(dish, qty);
            items.addElement(item);
      }
      catch (Exception e) {
            throw new RemoteException(e.toString());
      }
}

public void setDishQuantity(Dish dish, int quantity)
                                          throws RemoteException
{
      CartItem item = getItem(dish);
      if (item != null)
            item.setQuantity(quantity);
}

public void clear()
{
      for (int i=0; i < items.size(); i++) {
            CartItem item = (CartItem) items.elementAt(i);
            try {
                  item.remove();
            }
            catch (Exception e) {
                  e.printStackTrace();
            }
      }
      items = new Vector();
}
```

```
public int getTotalPrice() throws RemoteException
{
      int total = 0;
      for (int i = 0; i < items.size(); i++) {
            try {
                  CartItem item = (CartItem) items.elementAt(i);
                  total += item.getPrice();
            }
            catch (Exception ex) {
                  throw new RemoteException(ex.toString());
            }
      }
      return total;
}

public Order placeOrder() throws RemoteException
{
      Order order = null;
      try {
              Properties p = new Properties();
                     p.put(Context.INITIAL_CONTEXT_FACTORY,
                    "com.ibm.websphere.naming.WsnInitialContextFactory");
                     p.put(Context.PROVIDER_URL, "iiop://localhost");
                     InitialContext ic = new InitialContext(p);
                       Object homObj1 = ic.lookup("OrderItemHome");
                       Object homObj2 = ic.lookup("OrderHome");
                       Object homObj3 = ic.lookup("PricingManagerHome");
                     OrderItemHome orderItemHome = (OrderItemHome)
                               javax.rmi.PortableRemoteObject.narrow(
                               homObj1, OrderItemHome.class);
                     OrderHome orderHome = (OrderHome)
                               javax.rmi.PortableRemoteObject.narrow(
                               homObj2, OrderHome.class);
                     PricingManagerHome pricingManagerHome =
                              (PricingManagerHome)
                               javax.rmi.PortableRemoteObject.narrow(
                               homObj3, PricingManagerHome.class);
                   PricingManager pm = pricingManagerHome.create();
                   String oid = Long.toString(System.currentTimeMillis())
  +
                                     customer.getPrimaryKey().toString();
                   order = orderHome.create(oid, customer);
```

```
            order.setDeliveryCost(
                pm.getDeliveryCost(customer.getAddress());
            Vector orderItems = new Vector();
            for (int i=0; i < items.size(); i++) {
                  CartItem item = (CartItem) items.elementAt(i);
                  Dish dish = item.getDish();
                  String id = oid + dish.getPrimaryKey().toString();
                  OrderItem oitem = orderItemHome.create(id,
                              order, dish,
                              item.getQuantity(), item.getDiscount());
            }
      }
      catch (Exception ex) {
            throw new RemoteException(ex.toString());
      }
      return order;
   }
}
```

The CartItem Session Bean

The cart bean makes used of the `CartItem` bean that represents a single item in the cart. This bean holds the relevant data for a single entry in the shopping cart. This data is the relevant dish and its quantity. The bean provides a method for retrieving the dish price, which is implemented by delegating the method invocation to the `Dish` bean. The remote interface and home interface for the `CartItem` bean is as follows:

```
package com.onamix;
import javax.ejb.*;
import java.rmi.RemoteException;

public interface CartItem extends EJBObject
{
      public Dish getDish() throws RemoteException;
      public int getPrice() throws RemoteException;
      public int getDiscount() throws RemoteException;
      public void setDiscount() throws RemoteException;
      public int getQuantity() throws RemoteException;
      public void setQuantity(int quantity) throws RemoteException;
}
```

```
package com.onamix;
import javax.ejb.*;
import java.rmi.RemoteException;

public interface CartItemHome extends EJBHome {
      public CartItem create(Dish dish, int qty)
                  throws CreateException, RemoteException;
}
```

The bean implementation is not very interesting and has little more than *get/set* methods and EJB framework methods; we'll skip it for lack of interest.

The PricingManager Session Bean

The `PricingManager` bean is an example of a session bean that provides only business logic. In our case, this bean is responsible for calculating total order prices (applying any discounts available) and for calculating delivery charges. The business logic implemented in this bean is very simplistic. A five percent discount is applied to orders above 100,000 Yen, and there are no shipping charges inside Tokyo (there is a shipping charge of 1000 Yen outside Tokyo). These "business rules" are just an illustration of what can be done in session beans like `PricingManager`. Obviously, the rules implemented in a real-world application would be more complex. The `PricingManager` remote interface is as follows:

```
package com.onamix;
import javax.ejb.*;
import java.util.*;
import java.rmi.RemoteException;

public interface PricingManager extends EJBObject
{
      public int getDeliveryCost(String address) throws RemoteException;
      public void determinePrice(Cart order) throws RemoteException;
}
```

The home interface for this bean includes only the `create` method:

```
package com.onamix;
import javax.ejb.*;
import java.rmi.RemoteException;

public interface PricingManagerHome extends EJBHome
```

```
{
        public PricingManager create()
                throws CreateException, RemoteException;
}
```

The bean implementation implements the logic for calculating costs:

```
package com.onamix;

import javax.naming.*;
import javax.ejb.*;
import java.util.*;
import java.io.*;
import javax.naming.*;
import java.rmi.*;

public class PricingManagerBean implements SessionBean
{
        public void setSessionContext(SessionContext ctx) {}
        public void ejbActivate()       {}
        public void ejbPassivate()      {}
        public void ejbCreate()             {}
        public void ejbRemove()         {}
        public int getDeliveryCost(String address)
        {
                if (address.indexOf("Tokyo") >= 0)
                        return 0;
                return 1000;
        }

        public void determinePrice(Cart order) throws RemoteException
        {
                try {
                        int price =  order.getTotalPrice();
                        if (price > 100000)
                                order.setDiscount(10);
                        else
                                order.setDiscount(0);
```

```
                }
                catch (Exception ex) {
                      throw new RemoteException(ex.toString());
                }
          }
    }
```

One alternative to the "if blocks" used in the `determinePrice()` method would be to use business rule beans that ship with enterprise extensions. This way, the business rules can be changed at runtime based on business requirements.

The transactional behavior for the session beans is simple because it is session-related. Therefore, we do not expect any issues of concurrency to surface. The transactional behavior can be set to `TX_SUPPORTS` with the lowest level of isolation—`TRANSACTION_READ_UNCOMITTED`.

The Onamix Presentation Layer

The Onamix presentation layer is a Web application that provides customers a user interface through which they can browse the menu and place an order. All the elements of the presentation layer are packaged together in a module under the root */onamixapp*. We have chosen to use a mix of JSP and servlets—for the purpose of using all elements covered in Parts V and VI. The mix is somewhat arbitrary, and some of our servlets include embedded HTML. Generally, you should avoid this and break the login into a servlet and a JSP, as discussed in the chapters in Part V.

The Home Page

The home page is implemented as a JSP using the `DishHome` bean to retrieve and show all the day's specials:

```
<%@ page import="java.util.*" %>
<%@ page import="javax.ejb.*" %>
<%@ page import="javax.naming.*" %>
<%@ page import="com.onamix.*" %>
<html>
<head>
<title>ONAMIX</title>
</head>
<body>
<p><b><H2><i>ONAMIX</i></H2></b> </p>
<p>Welcome!</p>
<p>Please <a
```

```
href="http://onamix.com/onamixapp/LoginServlet">Login</a></p>
<br><br>
<%= new Date() %><br>
<H3>Today's specials: </H3><br>
<br>
<%
try{
      Properties p = new Properties();
      p.put(Context.INITIAL_CONTEXT_FACTORY,
            "com.ibm.websphere.naming.WsnInitialContextFactory");
           p.put(Context.PROVIDER_URL, "iiop://localhost");
        InitialContext ic = new InitialContext(p);
       Object homObj = ic.lookup("DishHome");
      DishHome dishHome = (DishHome)
            javax.rmi.PortableRemoteObject.narrow(
            homObj, DishHome.class);
      Enumeration e = dishHome.findBySpecials();
      while (e.hasMoreElements()) {
            Dish d = (Dish) e.nextElement();
            out.println("<p>" + d.getName() + "</p>");
      }
}
catch (Exception ex) {
      out.println("Error " + ex.toString());
}
%>
</body>
</html>
```

The LoginServlet Servlet

The `LoginServlet` servlet is used for user login. This servlet prompts the user to provide a user name and password. After the user has been authenticated, a new shopping cart session bean is created and associated with the current HTTP session. Note that in all the servlets, we build the required home object within the `init` methods. This method is called only once and should contain only code that is relevant for all threads of the servlet. By storing the home objects, we save processing time per request coming into the servlet.

```
package com.onamix;
import java.io.*;
import java.util.*;
```

```
import javax.servlet.*;
import javax.servlet.http.*;
import javax.naming.*;

public class LoginServlet extends HttpServlet {
  private CustomerHome customerHome;
private CartHome cartHome;
  public void init(ServletConfig config) throws ServletException {
     super.init(config);
     try {
                    Properties p = new Properties();
                    p.put(Context.INITIAL_CONTEXT_FACTORY,
                          "com.ibm.websphere.naming." +
                          "WsnInitialContextFactory");

                     p.put(Context.PROVIDER_URL, "iiop://localhost");
                    InitialContext ic = new InitialContext(p);
                      Object homObj = ic.lookup("CustomerHome");
                    customerHome = (CustomerHome)
                              javax.rmi.PortableRemoteObject.narrow(
                              homObj, CustomerHome.class);
                  Object homObj2 = ic.lookup("CartHome");
                    cartHome = (CartHome)
                              javax.rmi.PortableRemoteObject.narrow(
                              homObj2, CartHome.class);
      }
      catch (Exception e) {
            throw new ServletException(e.toString());
      }
  }

  private void sendOutForm(HttpServletResponse response) throws IOException
{
      response.setContentType("text/html");
      PrintWriter out = response.getWriter();
      out.println("<HTML><HEAD><TITLE>ONAMIX</TITLE></HEAD>" +
            "<BODY><H1><I>ONAMIX Login</I><BR></H1>");
      out.println("<P><B>Enter Usename and Password</B><P><BR>");
      out.println("<form action=onamix.com/onamixapp/LoginServlet" +
            "\" method=\"get\">" +
            "<BR><B>Name:</B><input type=\"text\" name=\"login\"" +
            "value=\"\" size=\"30\"><BR><B>Password:</B>" +
            "<input type=\"text\" name=\"password\" " +
```

```
            "value=\"\" size=\"30\"><BR><input type=\"submit\"" +
            "value=\"Login\"></form>");
        out.println("</BODY></HTML>");
        out.close();
    }

    public void doPost (HttpServletRequest request,
                            HttpServletResponse response)
                        throws ServletException
        {
            HttpSession session = request.getSession(true);
            String ID = request.getParameter("id");
            String name = request.getParameter("name");
            String passwd = request.getParameter("password");
            String address = request.getParameter("address");
            String deliveryInst = request.getParameter("deliveryInst");
            String phone = request.getParameter("phone");
            try {
                Customer c = customerHome.create(ID, name, passwd, address,
                    deliveryInst, phone);
                Cart cart = cartHome.create(c);
                session.putValue("cart", cart);
                response.sendRedirect(response.encodeUrl("/MenuServlet"));
                sendOutForm(response);
            }
            catch (Exception e) {
                throw new ServletException(e.toString());
            }
        }
        public void doGet (HttpServletRequest request,
                        HttpServletResponse response)
                        throws ServletException
        {
            HttpSession session = request.getSession(true);
            String login = request.getParameter("login");
            String password = request.getParameter("password");

            try {
                Enumeration customers = null;
                Customer c = customerHome.findByPrimaryKey(new
CustomerPK(login));
                String realPassword = c.getPassword();
                if (realPassword.equals(password)) {
```

```
                    Cart cart = cartHome.create(c);
                    session.putValue("cart", cart);
                  response.sendRedirect(response.encodeUrl("/MenuServlet"));
                    return;
                 }
               sendOutForm(response);
          }
          catch (Exception e) {
               throw new ServletException(e.toString());
          }
     }
}
```

The Registration Page

The registration page allows new customers to register. After registering, the user is automatically logged into the site—the registration page makes a call to the login servlet.

```
<HTML><HEAD><TITLE>ONAMIX</TITLE></HEAD>
<BODY><H1><I>ONAMIX REGISTRATION</I><BR></H1>
<form action=onamix.com/onamixapp/LoginServlet" method="post">
<BR><B>ID Nr. (used for Login)</B>
<input type=\"text\" name="id" value="" size="30">
<BR><B>Name:</B>
<input type=\"text\" name="name" value="" size="30">
<BR><B>Password:</B>
<input type=\"text\" name="password" value="" size="30">
<BR><B>Address:</B>
<input type=\"text\" name="address" value="" size="30">
<BR><B>Delivery Instructions:</B>
<input type=\"text\" name="deliveryinst" value="" size="30">
<BR><B>Phone:</B>
<input type=\"text\" name="phone" value="" size="30">
<BR><input type="submit" value="Submit"></form>
</BODY></HTML>
```

The MenuServlet Servlet

`MenuServlet` allows users to browse through the menu and review items. This servlet uses the `DishGroup` beans to show menu sections.

```
package com.onamix;
import java.io.*;
```

```
import java.util.*;
import javax.servlet.*;
import javax.servlet.http.*;
import javax.naming.*;

public class MenuServlet extends HttpServlet
{
  private DishGroupHome dishGroupHome;
  public void init(ServletConfig config) throws ServletException {
      try {
                  super.init(config);
                    Properties p = new Properties();
                    p.put(Context.INITIAL_CONTEXT_FACTORY,
           "com.ibm.websphere.naming.WsnInitialContextFactory");
                     p.put(Context.PROVIDER_URL, "iiop://localhost");
                    InitialContext ic = new InitialContext(p);
                      Object homObj = ic.lookup("DishGroupHome");
                    dishGroupHome = (DishGroupHome)
                              javax.rmi.PortableRemoteObject.narrow
                              homObj, DishGroupHome.class);
      }
      catch (Exception e) {
            throw new ServletException(e.toString());
      }
  }
       public void doGet (HttpServletRequest request,
                        HttpServletResponse response)
                        throws ServletException, IOException
       {
            response.setContentType("text/html");
            PrintWriter out = response.getWriter();
            String groupName = request.getParameter("group");
            out.println("<HTML><HEAD><TITLE>ONAMIX</TITLE></HEAD>" +
                  "<BODY><H1><I>ONAMIX MENU</I><BR></H1>");
            try {
                  if (groupName == null) {
                        Enumeration groups = dishGroupHome.findAllGroups();
                        while (groups.hasMoreElements()) {
                              DishGroup group = (DishGroup)
                                  groups.nextElement();
                              printOutGroup(group, out);
                        }
                  }
```

```
              else {
                    DishGroup group =
                            dishGroupHome.findByPrimaryKey(new
                                            DishGroupPK(groupName));
                    printOutGroup(group,out);
              }
        }
        catch (Exception e) {
              throw new ServletException(e.toString());
        }
         out.println("</BODY></HTML>");
         out.close();
  }
   public void printOutGroup(DishGroup group, PrintWriter out)
                    throws  IOException
  {
                    out.println("<BR><H3>"+ group.getName()
                                + "</H3>");
                    Enumeration items = group.getElements();
                    while (items.hasMoreElements()) {
                          Dish dish = (Dish) items.nextElement();
                          out.println("<BR><a href=\"" +
                          "http://onamix.com/onamixapp/DishDetail?" +
                          "dish=" + dish.getName() +
                          "\">" + dish.getName() + "</a>");
                    }
  }
}
```

The Dish Page

The following JSP shows the details of a specific dish. It is invoked by the menu servlet for a selected dish. The JSP retrieves all information using the bean and adds an image of the dish.

```
<%@ page import="java.util.*" %>
<%@ page import="javax.ejb.*" %>
<%@ page import="javax.naming.*" %>
<%@ page import="com.onamix.*" %>
<html>
<head>
```

```
<title>ONAMIX</title>
</head>
<body>
<%
try{
      Properties p = new Properties();
      p.put(Context.INITIAL_CONTEXT_FACTORY,
            "com.ibm.websphere.naming.WsnInitialContextFactory ");
           p.put(Context.PROVIDER_URL, "iiop://localhost");

        InitialContext ic = new InitialContext(p);
       Object homObj = ic.lookup("DishHome");
      DishHome dishHome = (DishHome)
            javax.rmi.PortableRemoteObject.narrow(
            homObj, DishHome.class);
      String dishName = request.getParameter("dish");
      String dishGroupName = request.getParameter("dishgroup");
      Dish dish = dishHome.getPrimaryKey(new DishPK(dishName));
}
catch (Exception ex) {
      out.println("Error " + ex.toString());
}
%>
<form action="onamix.com/onamixapp/CartServlet?operation=add+dish="
<%= dish.getName() %>
 method="get">
<p><b><font size="6"><i>ONAMIX</i></font></b> </p>
<p><a href="http://onamix.com/onamixapp/MenuServlet">Menu</a> :
<a href="http://onamix.com/onamixapp/MenuServlet?group=<%= dishGroupName
%>"><%= dishGroupName %></a>
: </p>
<p><img border="0" src="<%= dish.getPicture()%>" width="322"
height="212"></p>
<p><b><%= dish.getName()%>
</b>  
<%= dish.getPrice() %>¥
<input type="button" value="Add To Cart" name="B1"></p>
<p><i><%= dish.getDescription()%></i></p>
</body>
</html>
```

The CartServlet Servlet

CartServlet displays the shopping cart using the CartItem bean. It also uses the pricing manager to calculate prices for display.

```
package com.onamix;
import java.io.*;
import java.util.*;
import java.text.*;
import javax.servlet.*;
import javax.servlet.http.*;
import javax.naming.*;

public class CartServlet extends HttpServlet
{
        private PricingManagerHome pricingManagerHome;
            private DishHome dishHome;
        public void init(ServletConfig config) throws ServletException {
            super.init(config);

            try {
                          Properties p = new Properties();
                          p.put(Context.INITIAL_CONTEXT_FACTORY,
                              "com.ibm.websphere.naming." +
                              "WsnInitialContextFactory");
                           p.put(Context.PROVIDER_URL, "iiop://localhost");
                          InitialContext ic = new InitialContext(p);
                            Object homObj = ic.lookup("PricingManager");
                          pricingManagerHome = (PricingManagerHome)
                                   javax.rmi.PortableRemoteObject.narrow(
                                   homObj, PricingManagerHome.class);
                            Object homObj1 = ic.lookup("PricingManager");
                          dishHome = (DishHome)
                                   javax.rmi.PortableRemoteObject.narrow(
                                   homObj1, DishHome.class);
            }
            catch (Exception e) {
                  throw new ServletException(e.toString());
            }
        }
      public void doPost (HttpServletRequest request, HttpServletResponse response)
              throws ServletException, IOException {
              try {
            PrintWriter out = response.getWriter();
            HttpSession session = request.getSession(false);
            Cart cart = (Cart) session.getValue("quote");
            Enumeration e = request.getParameterNames();
            while (e.hasMoreElements()) {
```

```
                String paramName = (String) e.nextElement();
                if (paramName.startsWith("updateqty")) {
                      int ind = Integer.parseInt(paramName.substring(8));
                      int val =
                        Integer.parseInt(request.getParameter(paramName));
                      Enumeration items = cart.getItems();
                      int count = 0;
                      while (items.hasMoreElements()) {
                            CartItem cartItem = (CartItem)
                                                  items.nextElement();
                            if (count == ind)
                                  cartItem.setQuantity(val);
                            count++;
                      }
                }
          }
          PricingManager pm = pricingManagerHome.create();
          pm.determinePrice(cart);
          response.sendRedirect(response.encodeURL("/CartServlet"));
            }
            catch (Exception ex) {
                throw new ServletException(ex.toString());
          }
    }

        public void doGet (HttpServletRequest request, HttpServletResponse
response)
              throws ServletException, IOException {
          response.setContentType("text/html");
          PrintWriter out = response.getWriter();
    try {
          HttpSession session = request.getSession(false);
          if (session == null || session.getValue("cart") == null) {
                response.sendRedirect(
                   response.encodeURL("/LoginServlet"));
                return;
          }
          Cart cart = (Cart) session.getValue("quote");
          out.println("<HTML><HEAD><TITLE>ONAMIX</TITLE></HEAD>" +
                      "<BODY><H1><I>ONAMIX Shopping" +
                            " Cart</I><BR></H1>");
          String operation = request.getParameter("operation");
          String dishName = request.getParameter("dish");
          if (operation == null) {
                      out.println(
                            "<form action=\"" +
                            response.encodeURL("/CartServlet") +
```

```
                        "\" method=\"put\">" +
                        "<TABLE><TR><TH> Quantity </TH>" +
                        "<TH> Name </TH><TH> Price </TH></TR>");
                Enumeration items = cart.getItems();
                int i = 0;
                while (items.hasMoreElements()) {
                        CartItem cartItem = (CartItem)
                            items.nextElement();
                        Dish dish  = cartItem.getDish();
                        out.println(
                                "<TR>" +
                                "<TD><input type=\"text\" name=\"" +
                                "updateqty" + i +
                                "\" value=\"" +
                                 cartItem.getQuantity() +
                                "\">" +
                                "</TD>" + dish.getName() + "</TD>" +
                                "</TD>" + dish.getPrice() +
                                 "¥</TD></TR>");
                        i++;
                }
                out.println("</TABLE><BR>TOTAL:" +
                        cart.getTotalPrice() + "¥");
                out.println(
                     "<BR><a href="
                    "\http://onamix.com/onamixapp +
                    "/OrderServlet\">" +
                        "Place Order</A>" +
                        "<BR><input type=\"submit\" " +
                        "value=\"Update " +
                        " Quantities\">");
        }
        else if (operation.equals("empty")) {
                cart.clear();
                out.println("<H2><I>Your cart is now empty</I></H2>");
        }
        else if (operation.equals("add")) {
                Dish dish = dishHome.findByPrimaryKey(new
DishPK(dishName));
                cart.addDish(dish);
                PricingManager pm = pricingManagerHome.create();
                pm.determinePrice(cart);
                response.sendRedirect(
                        response.encodeURL("/CartServlet"));
        }
    }
    catch (Exception e) {
            throw new ServletException(e.toString());
```

```
        }
      out.println("</body> </html>");
      out.close();
      }
}
```

The OrderServlet Servlet

`OrderServlet` takes care of the ordering process. It creates a persistent order out of the current shopping cart.

```
package com.onamix;
import java.io.*;
import java.util.*;
import java.text.*;
import javax.servlet.*;
import javax.servlet.http.*;
import javax.naming.*;

public class OrderServlet extends HttpServlet
{
        public void doGet (HttpServletRequest request,
                          HttpServletResponse response)
              throws ServletException, IOException {
            response.setContentType("text/html");
            PrintWriter out = response.getWriter();
      try {
            HttpSession session = request.getSession(false);
            if (session == null || session.getValue("cart") == null) {

response.sendRedirect(response.encodeURL("/LoginServlet"));
                  return;
            }
            Cart cart = (Cart) session.getValue("quote");
            cart.placeOrder();
            out.println("<HTML><HEAD><TITLE>ONAMIX</TITLE></HEAD>" +
                       "<BODY><H1><I>ONAMIX Order</I><BR></H1>");
            out.println("<H2><I>Your order has been successfully" +
                   "placed</I></H2>");
        }
        catch (Exception e) {
                throw new ServletException(e.toString());
        }
```

```
        out.println("</body> </html>");
        out.close();
        }
}
```

Summary

This chapter presented a complete example for a simple e-commerce application that makes use of servlets, JSPs, session beans, and entity beans. The code fragments have been fairly lengthy but simple. We hope that you appreciate the fact that using this technology is actually fairly straightforward, and while complications always result from complex business logic, the technical framework implemented by WebSphere is clear, clean, and useful.

This chapter completes Part VI of the book and is in many ways a "summary project" for Parts V and VI.

Part VII

Using XML

Chapter 35

Writing XML E-Business Applications

Welcome to Part VII. Part VI was devoted to Enterprise JavaBeans (EJBs)—an important technological foundation for WebSphere applications. This part of the book is devoted to the Extensible Markup Language (XML), another important technology dominating Web applications. For an introduction to XML, please refer back to Chapter 12.

XML and XML-rated technologies will be demonstrated through a set of examples, starting with a few examples that use XML within applications. Chapter 36 uses XSL Transformations (XSLT) for transforming data packaged in XML documents. Chapters 37 and 38 are devoted to a relatively new technology, Web services, which are based on XML and promise to change fundamentally the way we use business systems.

As mentioned in Chapter 12, XML is viewed by many software experts as one of the most important technologies for developing e-business applications, both in the consumer space and in the business-to-business markets. XML is a fairly young technology, and as such all possible applications of the technology have yet to be seen; the industry hasn't yet managed to define in which precise category (or categories) this technology fits. Still, some application themes are already dominated by XML, including integration, data exchange and storage, and more. The industry has developed a set of common tools for using XML, including the XML parser, Document Object Model (DOM) structures, and Simple API for XML (SAX).

In this chapter we develop a complete application that will exhibit the use of these themes and will illustrate how to use the XML tools that come bundled with WebSphere. We also provide an example from a bigger business application that makes use of XML to do presentation-level transcoding.

The Insider Trading Application

We start with an application built to satisfy our newfound hobby of losing money on the stock market. As have many others, we have fallen for the fallacy that we can figure out what stock to purchase based on what the "insiders" do. Because of the seemingly unlimited number of stock symbols, it is difficult for us to check manually which stocks are being purchased by insiders. Therefore, our application performs an automated scan to determine in which companies insiders have decided to purchase company stock. Our assumption is that if insiders have decided to purchase stock using their own money, they must know something that we don't—and we should also purchase this stock.

The application works for companies listed on the NASDAQ exchange and makes use of two primary information sources. The first source is from the NASDAQ Web site and is used to determine all stock symbols on the exchange. Figure 35-1 shows an example of a typical Web page listing NASDAQ companies. So the first thing our application needs to do is access the NASDAQ Web site, look up all the pages in this range, and extract from it the stock symbols.

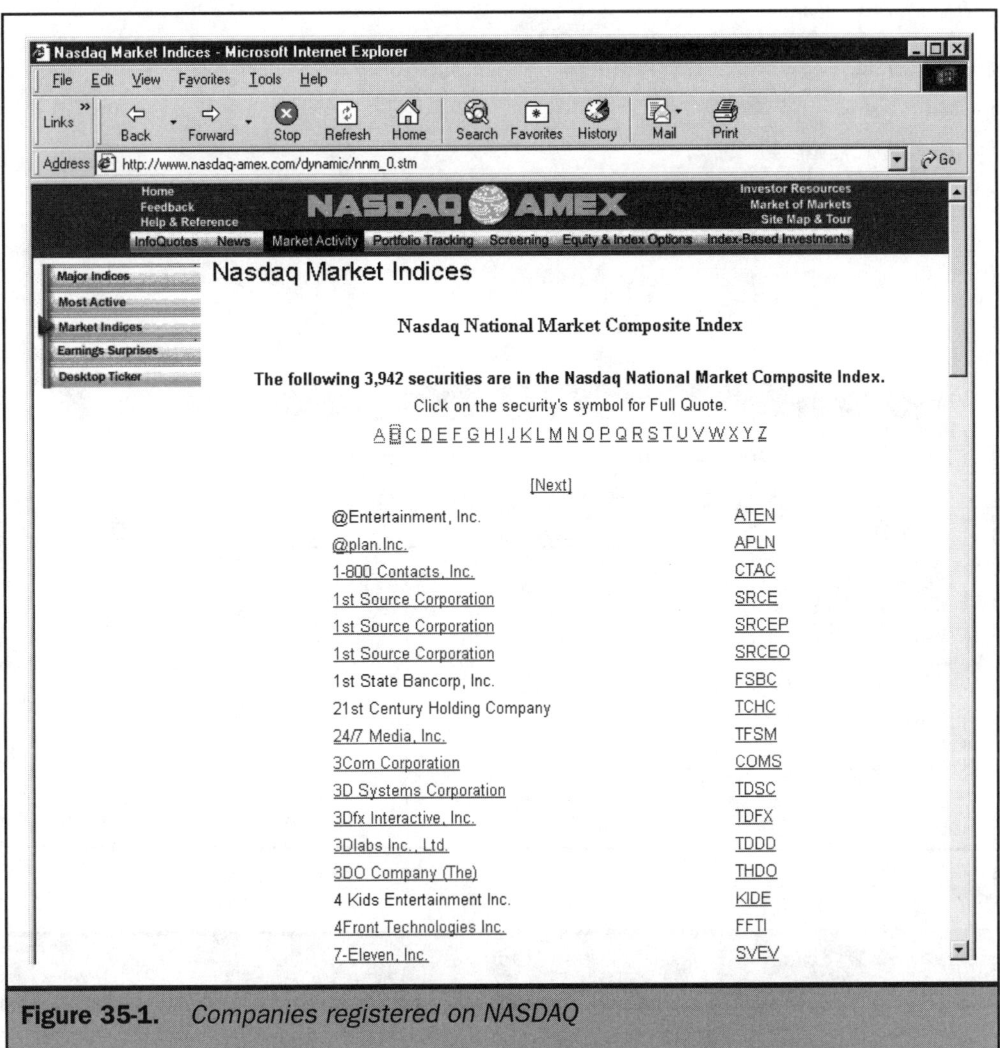

Figure 35-1. *Companies registered on NASDAQ*

With all stock symbols in hand, we will access another data source. The Yahoo! Finance section lists insider trading information for any stock symbol. Figure 35-2 shows an example of the page we want to find. The Yahoo! data sources list all insider trades per stock symbol (the page we have chosen shows a number of insider buys). As you can tell from the URL (*http://biz.yahoo.com/t/i/IACO.html*), given a stock symbol such

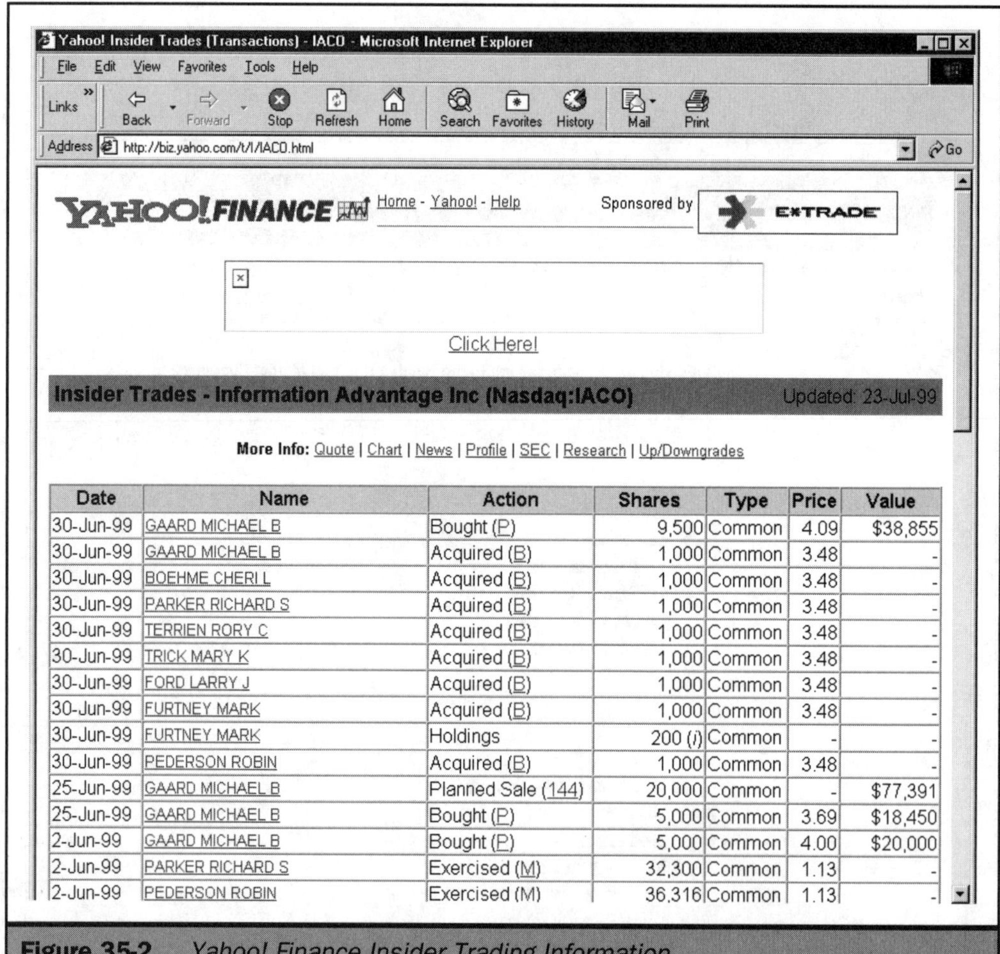

Figure 35-2. *Yahoo! Finance Insider Trading Information*

as MSFT (for Microsoft), the URL we will need to access is *http://biz.yahoo.com/t/m/MSFT.html*. Therefore, with all the stock symbols at hand (from the first stage), we can get access to all these pages.

We need to parse these pages and look for entries in the Bought or Acquired section, and then extract the date when this occurred and the price at which the stock was purchased. Then, all the results can be packaged and written out as an XML document that we can later view or use from within another application. The generated file is an

XML document, making it especially simple to use from another application; this is one of the primary benefits of XML over conventional formats.

All parts of the application are written to be autonomous. Thus, the first module accesses the NASDAQ pages and outputs the symbols as an XML document. The second application module parses this document to find all symbols. Apart from the fact that this is a good software engineering practice, separating these two processes in two applications gives us more opportunities to illustrate the use of the XML tools.

We use IBM's Java XML Parser, which is part of WebSphere, to parse XML documents, build DOM trees, and access information. In our first example, we also use the package to build DOM structures and output them as XML. The TreeViewer (Figure 35-3) application allows us to view XML documents for debugging purposes.

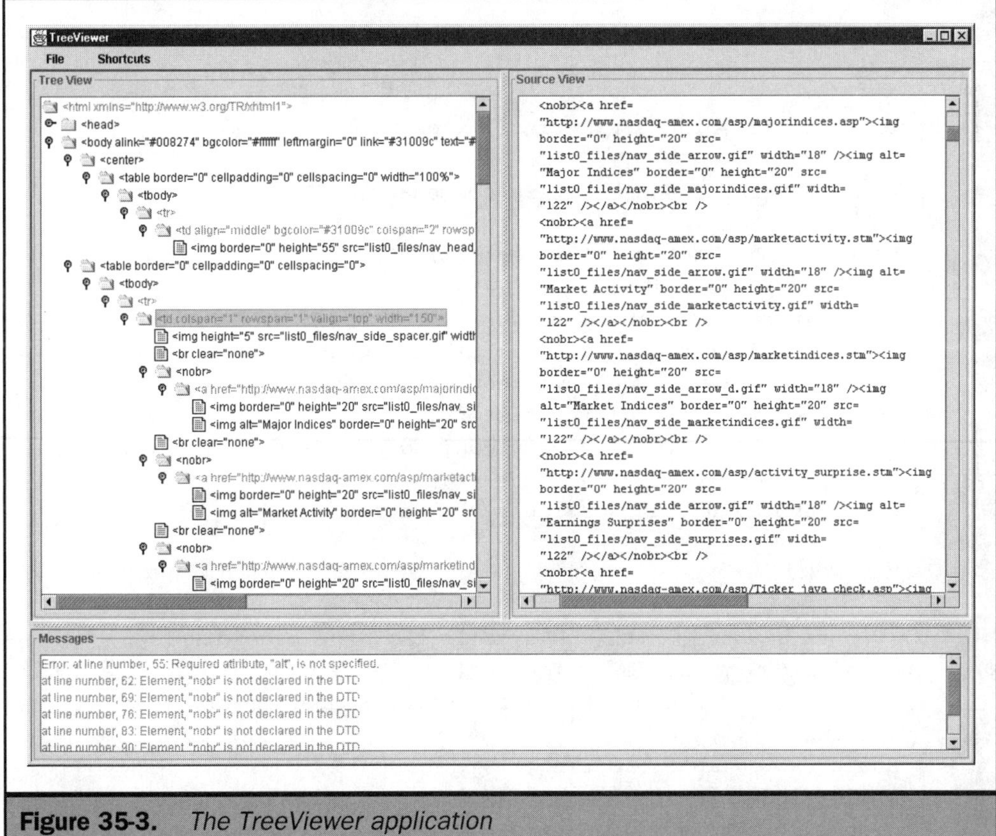

Figure 35-3. *The TreeViewer application*

Generating the Stock Symbols

The first part of the application is simple enough:

```
import java.util.*;
import java.io.*;
import org.w3c.dom.*;
import org.xml.sax.helpers.ParserFactory;
import com.ibm.xml.parsers.*;
import org.xml.sax.*;

public class SymbolGenerator {

  public SymbolGenerator() {
  }

  public static void main(String[] args) {

    SymbolGenerator gen = new SymbolGenerator();

    Vector symbolVector = new Vector(1000);
    for (int i = 0 ; i <= 50 ; i++) {
      // Get the HTML and process it
      StringBuffer htmlText = HTMLFetcher.getHTMLFor(
        "http://www.nasdaq-amex.com/dynamic/nnm_" +
        Integer.toString(i) + ".stm");
        gen.extractSymbolInformationInto(htmlText, symbolVector);
    }
    gen.outputSymbolInformation(symbolVector);
  }


  // Return a vector with the symbols that the page displays
  void extractSymbolInformationInto(
                StringBuffer aBuf, Vector symbolVector) {
    int index = 0;
    String str = aBuf.toString();
    while (index != -1) {
      index = str.indexOf("symbol=", index);
      if (index != -1) {
        int nextIndex = str.indexOf(">", index);
        String aSymbol = str.substring(index+7, nextIndex);
```

```
          symbolVector.addElement(aSymbol);
          index = nextIndex + 1;
        }
      }
    }

    // Write an XML document by building an element per symbol
    void outputSymbolInformation(Vector symbolVector) {
      com.ibm.xml.parser.TXDocument myDocument =
        new com.ibm.xml.parser.TXDocument();

      try {
        ProcessingInstruction pi = myDocument.
          createProcessingInstruction("xml","version=\"1.0\"");
        myDocument.appendChild(pi);

        Element root = myDocument.createElement("stockSymbols");
        root.setAttribute("exchange", "NASDAQ");
        myDocument.appendChild(root);

        for (Enumeration e = symbolVector.elements();
                     e.hasMoreElements(); ) {
          String aSymbol = (String)e.nextElement();
          Element child = myDocument.createElement("symbol");
          Text t = myDocument.createTextNode(aSymbol);
          child.appendChild(t);
          root.appendChild(child);
        }

        FileWriter fw = new FileWriter("symbols.xml");
        myDocument.toXMLString(fw);
        fw.close();

      } catch (Exception e) {
          e.printStackTrace();
      }
    }
  }
```

We iterate through the 50 pages that list all symbols on NASDAQ, and get the HTML page for each one. We then look through the HTML for the place where the "symbol" string occurs and extract the stock symbol. To do this, we use a utility class called `HTMLFetcher`, which we will reuse in other code samples throughout this chapter. The code for this class is shown here:

```
import java.net.*;
import java.io.*;

public class HTMLFetcher {

// Given a URL get the HTML page. If there is an exception
// the method returns null. Use the net package to open a
URLConnection
  // to get the HTML response
  static public StringBuffer getHTMLFor(String url) {
   try {
    URLConnection aConnection = (new URL(url)).openConnection();
    aConnection.setDoInput(true);
    aConnection.setDoOutput(true);
    aConnection.setUseCaches(false);
    InputStream inS = aConnection.getInputStream();
    StringBuffer buffer = new StringBuffer(4096);
    boolean atEnd = false;
    while(!atEnd) {
      int len = inS.available();
      byte[] buf = new byte[len];
      if (inS.read(buf, 0, len) == -1)
      atEnd = true;
      if (len > 0)
        buffer.append(new String(buf));
      Thread.sleep(10);
    }
    return buffer;
   } catch (Throwable ex) {
    ex.printStackTrace();
   }
   return null;
  }

}
```

The next step is to iterate through all the symbols in the vector and construct the XML file. We use the DOM classes to build a document, and then dump it to an XML file. Building the document is simple enough—instantiate the nodes and create the relationships between them. Once the document has been created, we simply use the `toXMLString` method to create the XML string and write it out to a file. Figure 35-4 shows a segment of the resulting XML file.

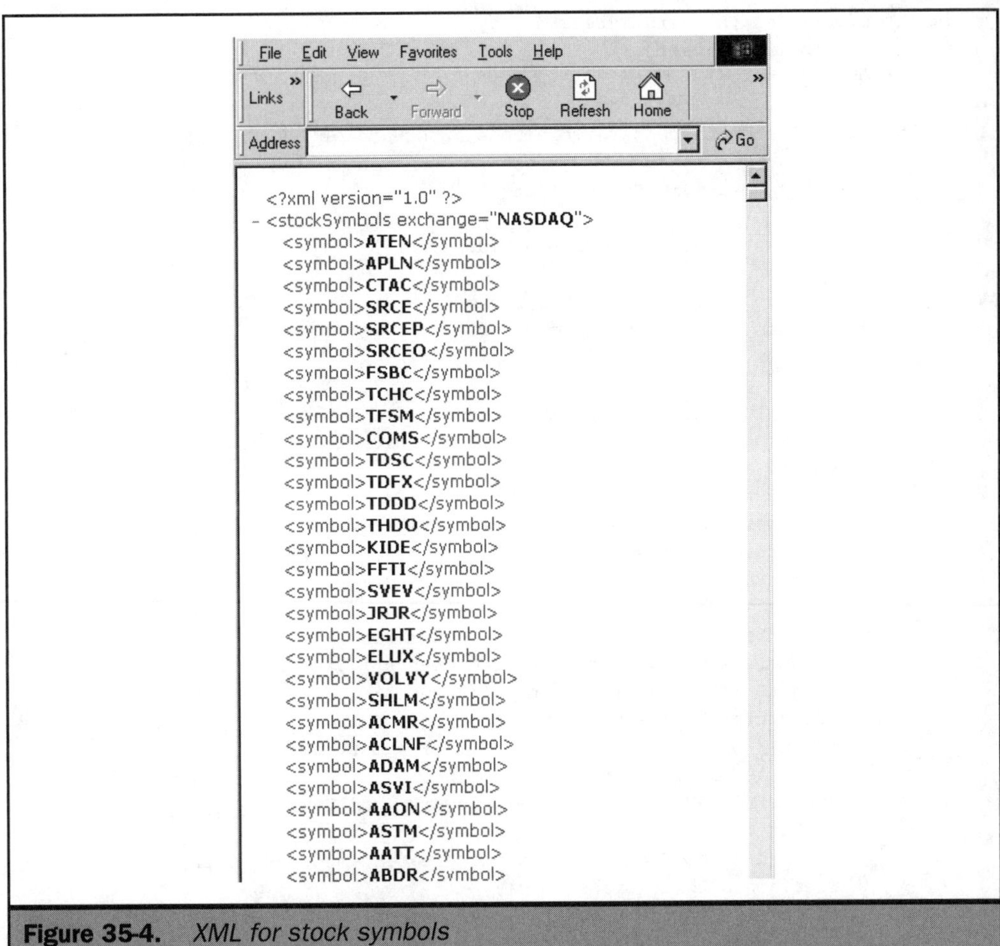

Figure 35-4. *XML for stock symbols*

Getting the Insider Information

The second module is a bit more complex; the code is shown here:

```
import java.util.*;
import java.io.*;

import org.w3c.dom.*;
import org.xml.sax.helpers.ParserFactory;
import com.ibm.xml.parsers.*;
import org.xml.sax.*;

public class InsiderInspector implements ErrorHandler{

  public static void main(String[] args) {

    InsiderInspector gen = new InsiderInspector();

    com.ibm.xml.parser.TXDocument myDocument =
      new com.ibm.xml.parser.TXDocument();

    try {
      ProcessingInstruction pi = myDocument.
        createProcessingInstruction("xml","version=\"1.0\"");
      myDocument.appendChild(pi);

      Element root = myDocument.createElement("insiderTrading");
      root.setAttribute("asOf", (new Date()).toString());
      myDocument.appendChild(root);

      Vector symbolVector = gen.retrieveAllSymbols();
      for (Enumeration e = symbolVector.elements() ; e.hasMoreElements() ; ) {
        String aSymbol = (String)e.nextElement();
        StringBuffer htmlText = HTMLFetcher.getHTMLFor(
          "http://biz.yahoo.com/t/" + aSymbol.substring(0,1) +
          "/" + aSymbol + ".html");
        StringBuffer aBuf = HTMLTidier.tidyHTML(htmlText);
        if (aBuf != null) {
          Element symbolRoot = myDocument.createElement(aSymbol);
          root.appendChild(symbolRoot);
          gen.extractInsiderInfo(aBuf, myDocument, symbolRoot);
        }
      }

      FileWriter fw = new FileWriter("insiderTrading.xml");
      myDocument.toXMLString(fw);
      fw.close();
    } catch (Exception ex) {
      ex.printStackTrace();
```

```
    }
  }

  Vector retrieveAllSymbols() {
    Vector symbols = new Vector(4096);
    BufferedReader br = null;
    try {
      br = new BufferedReader(new FileReader("symbols.xml"));
    } catch (Exception ex) {
      ex.printStackTrace();
      return null;
    }
    Parser parser = null;
    try {
      parser =
ParserFactory.makeParser("com.ibm.xml.parsers.NonValidatingDOMParser");
      parser.setErrorHandler(this);
    } catch (Exception ex) {
      ex.printStackTrace();
      return null;
    }

    try
    {
      parser.parse(new org.xml.sax.InputSource(br));

      org.w3c.dom.Document d = ((NonValidatingDOMParser)parser).getDocument();

      org.w3c.dom.Element rootElement = d.getDocumentElement();
      NodeList nodes = rootElement.getChildNodes();
      for (int i = 0 ; i < nodes.getLength() ; i++)
      {
        org.w3c.dom.Node aNode = nodes.item(i);
        if ((aNode instanceof org.w3c.dom.Element) &&
            aNode.getNodeName().equalsIgnoreCase("symbol")) {
          org.w3c.dom.Element aSymbolElement = (org.w3c.dom.Element)aNode;
          String symbolName =
              ((org.w3c.dom.Text)aSymbolElement.getFirstChild()).getData();
          symbols.addElement(symbolName);
        }
      }
    } catch (Throwable ex) {
      ex.printStackTrace();
    }
    return symbols;
  }

  void extractInsiderInfo(
      StringBuffer aBuf,
```

```
      com.ibm.xml.parser.TXDocument myDocument,
      Element symbolRoot) {
    Parser parser = null;
    try {
      parser = ParserFactory.makeParser(
        "com.ibm.xml.parsers.NonValidatingDOMParser");
      parser.setErrorHandler(this);
    } catch (Exception ex) {
      ex.printStackTrace();
    }

    try {
      parser.parse(new org.xml.sax.InputSource(
        new ByteArrayInputStream(aBuf.toString().getBytes())));
      org.w3c.dom.Document d = ((NonValidatingDOMParser)parser).getDocument();
      org.w3c.dom.Element inputElement = d.getDocumentElement();
      recursivelyDescend(inputElement, myDocument, symbolRoot);
    } catch (Exception ex) {
      ex.printStackTrace();
    }
  }

  void recursivelyDescend(
      org.w3c.dom.Node aNode,
      com.ibm.xml.parser.TXDocument myDocument,
      Element symbolRoot) {
    if (aNode instanceof org.w3c.dom.Text) {
      String theText = ((org.w3c.dom.Text)aNode).getData().trim();
      if (theText.length() >= 6) {
        String subS = theText.substring(0,6);
        if ((subS.compareTo("Bought") == 0) ||
            (subS.compareTo("Acquir") == 0)) {
          Node aParent = aNode.getParentNode().getParentNode();
          Element newElement = myDocument.createElement("insiderPurchase");

          // This processing is very tightly coupled with the XML
          // structure and normally a more flexible pattern would
          // be used - but it serves the purpose of illustrating the
          // relationship between the XML document and the Java APIs
          try {
            Node dateNode = aParent.getFirstChild().getNextSibling().
                            getFirstChild();
            newElement.setAttribute(
              "date",
              ((Text)dateNode).getData().trim());
            Node priceNode = aParent.getFirstChild().getNextSibling().
              getNextSibling().getNextSibling().getNextSibling().
              getNextSibling().getNextSibling().getNextSibling().
              getNextSibling().getNextSibling().
              getNextSibling().getNextSibling().getFirstChild();
```

```
            newElement.setAttribute(
              "price",
              ((Text)priceNode).getData().trim());
          } catch (Throwable ex) {
              newElement.setAttribute(
                "error",
                "There was an inside trade that could not be parsed");
          }

          symbolRoot.appendChild(newElement);
        }
      }
    }
    NodeList nodes = aNode.getChildNodes();
    for (int i = 0 ; i < nodes.getLength() ; i++) {
        org.w3c.dom.Node subNode = nodes.item(i);
        recursivelyDescend(subNode, myDocument, symbolRoot);
    }
  }

  public void warning(SAXParseException exception) throws SAXException {
    // In our case we can ignore any parsing exception since it is
    // not part of the elements we need to process
  }

  public void error(SAXParseException exception) throws SAXException {
    // In our case we can ignore any parsing exception since it is
    // not part of the elements we need to process
  }

  public void fatalError(SAXParseException exception) throws SAXException {
    // In our case we can ignore any parsing exception since it is
    // not part of the elements we need to process
  }


}
```


First, we read in the XML file with the symbol information. This is fairly straightforward because we know the structure of the XML file, so we simply can't go wrong. Once we have the symbols, we iterate through all symbols, and for each we open a connection to the Yahoo! site and get the HTML using the `HTMLFetcher` class.

The next step is the interesting part. Instead of traversing the HTML source as we did in the previous section, we want to view the HTML file as an XML document and traverse the XML document using the document nodes. In time, processing HTML pages as well-formed XML documents will be more commonly used—at the moment, processing these pages as though they were XML documents is difficult to do because most HTML pages on the Web are not well formed.

Therefore, we start out by converting the HTML page into a page that conforms to XML rules. We use a program called TIDY (created by Dave Raggett of Hewlett Packard), which can be downloaded from *http://www.w3.org/People/Raggett/tidy*. Among other things, the application can fix HTML documents so that they can be parsed by an XML parser. The following code shows our utility class for performing this—it's not a sophisticated way to do it, but it gets the job done.

```
import java.io.*;

public class HTMLTidier {

  public HTMLTidier() {
  }

  public static StringBuffer tidyHTML(StringBuffer inBuf) {

    try {
      File outputFile = new File("insiders.html");
      FileWriter out = new FileWriter(outputFile);
      out.write(inBuf.toString());
      out.close();
    } catch (Throwable ex) {
       ex.printStackTrace();
       return new StringBuffer(32);
    }

    String[] cmdLine = {
      "tidy.exe", "-f", "errs.txt", "-im", "-asxml", "insiders.html"};
    try {
       Runtime.getRuntime().exec(cmdLine);
       // Yes - it is ugly to wait a few seconds
       // but it's just a demo after all
       Thread.sleep(5000);
    } catch (Throwable ex) {
       ex.printStackTrace();
       return new StringBuffer(32);
    }

    try {
      File inputFile = new File("insiders.html");
      FileReader in = new FileReader(inputFile);
      int justRead = 0;
      int index = 0;
      StringBuffer aBuf = new StringBuffer(4096);
      while(justRead != -1) {
        char[] buf = new char[1024];
        justRead = in.read(buf, index, 1024);
        aBuf.append(buf);
```

```
            }
            in.close();
            return aBuf;
        } catch (Throwable ex) {
            ex.printStackTrace();
        }
        return null;
    }
}
```


After we have created a well-formed XML document, we can run it through our parser and look for Text nodes that have the word *Bought* or *Acquired* in them. At this point, we look for the siblings that hold the date and the price information (remember that each such node will have the structure as shown by the highlighted nodes in Figure 35-5), and append it to the XML document.

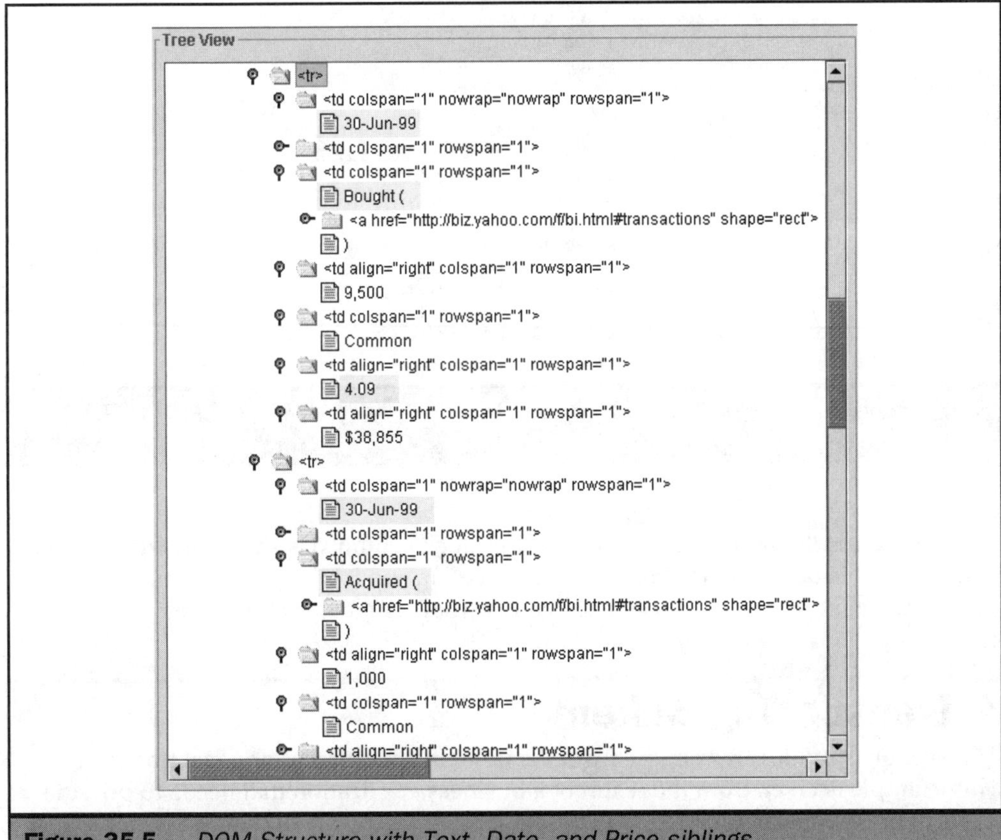

Figure 35-5. *DOM Structure with Text, Date, and Price siblings*

```
- <insiderTrading example="1">
  - <ATEN>
      <insiderPurchase date="27-Jan-99" price="-" />
      <insiderPurchase date="27-Jan-99" price="-" />
      <insiderPurchase date="27-Jan-99" price="-" />
      <insiderPurchase date="4-Nov-98" price="7.25 - 9.00" />
      <insiderPurchase date="2-Nov-98" price="7.25" />
      <insiderPurchase date="2-Nov-98" price="7.25" />
      <insiderPurchase date="22-Oct-98" price="3.94" />
      <insiderPurchase date="22-Oct-98" price="4.00" />
      <insiderPurchase date="21-Oct-98" price="4.25" />
      <insiderPurchase date="20-Oct-98" price="4.31 - 4.38" />
      <insiderPurchase date="19-Oct-98" price="4.63" />
      <insiderPurchase date="14-Oct-98" price="4.75" />
      <insiderPurchase date="15-Sep-98" price="10.38" />
      <insiderPurchase date="14-Sep-98" price="9.88" />
      <insiderPurchase date="4-Sep-98" price="9.19" />
      <insiderPurchase date="31-Aug-98" price="8.80" />
      <insiderPurchase date="31-Aug-98" price="8.63 - 8.75" />
      <insiderPurchase date="4-Aug-98" price="-" />
      <insiderPurchase date="4-Aug-98" price="-" />
      <insiderPurchase date="4-Aug-98" price="-" />
      <insiderPurchase date="4-Aug-98" price="-" />
      <insiderPurchase date="4-Aug-98" price="-" />
      <insiderPurchase date="4-Aug-98" price="-" />
    </ATEN>
    <APLN />
  - <CTAC>
      <insiderPurchase date="17-Mar-99" price="12.50 - 12.63" />
      <insiderPurchase date="30-Sep-98" price="5.94" />
      <insiderPurchase date="29-Sep-98" price="6.00" />
      <insiderPurchase date="9-Sep-98" price="6.50" />
      <insiderPurchase date="9-Sep-98" price="6.50" />
      <insiderPurchase date="26-Aug-98" price="5.75" />
      <insiderPurchase date="18-Aug-98" price="6.06" />
      <insiderPurchase date="14-Aug-98" price="6.00" />
      <insiderPurchase date="13-Aug-98" price="6.06" />
    </CTAC>
```


Figure 35-6. *Insider trading XML*

The end result (after checking all possible stock symbols) is shown in Figure 35-6. Obviously, this takes a long time to run, but we can run it all night and be ready for trading the next morning. Yahoo! Let's go lose (oops, I mean *make*) money!

A Transcoding Scheme

This section provides an example from the domain of presentation-level transcoding. This example is taken from the realm of a business application that needs to provide application screens to multiple devices, including PCs, personal digital assistants (PDAs), and phones. Each such device has a browser (or microbrowser) that receives information packaged in some dialect of XML—HTML, Wireless Markup Language (WML) and Compact HTML (CHTML) all fall under the XML umbrella.

In this example, our assumption is that the application generates well-formed XML that can be generated by servlets, JSPs, or any other component. The transcoder is a filter that parses the XML and applies some simple rules to create another XML, which is ultimately delivered to the device. The use of the transcoder could be to filter out images, delete white spaces, replace one element with another, and perform other such presentation-level modifications. As an example, when delivering content over a local or wide area network (LAN or WAN), we might prefer to leave white spaces as follows:

```
<html>


  <head>


    <meta content="text/html"http-equiv="Content-Type">
    <title class="MultiLingual">
My Calls
    </title>
  </head>
  <body>



    <table>

      <tr>
        <td>
          <b>

                Call:

          </b>
          <a
href="/servlet/RequestHandler;jsessionid=GVYTQ2IAAAAAC5YAAAARGUQ?task=
ActionDetails&action=runQuery&skipLogin=yes&callId=3529&actionId=1&formBean
=MobileMainMenu">
  3529

                /


  1
          </a>
        </td>
        <td>
```

```
            <b>

                  Resp:

            </b>
Aug 08,2001 15:00
        </td>
      </tr>
      ...
  </body>
</html>
```

On slow wireless connections in which every byte counts, we might choose to remove all white spaces, as follows:

```
<html><head><meta content="text/html"http-equiv="Content-Type"><title
class="MultiLingual"> My Calls</title></head><body><div align="right"><a
href="/RTS_HTML_Pages/RTS_General/OnLineHelp/en_US/MobileHelp/MyCallsPage.
jsp"name="Help"> ?</a></div><table><tr><td><b> Call:</b><a href="/servlet/
RequestHandler;jsessionid=GVYTQ2IAAAAAC5YAAAARGUQ?task=ActionDetails&action=
runQuery&skipLogin=yes&callId=3529&actionId=1&formBean=MobileMainMenu">
3529/1</a></td><td><b> Resp:</b> Aug 08,2001 15:00</td></tr><tr><td><b>
 Sched. From:</b> Aug 03,2001 10:00</td><td><b> Sched. To:</b> Aug 03,2001
10:29</td></tr><tr><td><b> Status:</b> Acknowledged Appointment</td></tr>
<tr><td><b> Priority:</b> 90</td><td><b> Site:</b> site 2</td></tr><tr>
<td><b> Product:</b> ISDN2</td></tr><tr><td><hr color="black"></td></tr>
<tr><td><b> Call:</b><a href="/servlet/RequestHandler;jsessionid=
GVYTQ2IAAAAAC5YAAAARGUQ?task=ActionDetails&action=runQuery&skipLogin=yes&
callId=3695&actionId=1&formBean=MobileMainMenu"> 3695/1</a></td><td><b>
Resp:</b> Sep 21,2001 13:00</td></tr><tr><td><b> Sched. From:</b>
Sep 27,2001 12:00</td><td><b> Sched. To:</b> Sep 27,2001 13:00</td></tr>
<tr><td><b> Status:</b> Wait for Ack</td></tr><tr><td><b> Priority:</b>
90</td><td><b> Site:</b> site 2</td></tr><tr><td><b> Product:</b> ISDN</td>
</tr><tr><td><hr color="black"></td></tr><tr><td><b> Call:</b><a href="/
servlet/RequestHandler;jsessionid=GVYTQ2IAAAAAC5YAAAARGUQ?task=ActionDetails
&action=runQuery&skipLogin=yes&callId=3721&actionId=1&formBean=MobileMain
Menu"> 3721/1</a></td><td><b> Resp:</b> Oct 16,2001 11:00</td></tr>
<tr><td><b> Sched. From:</b> Oct 16,2001 06:30</td><td><b> Sched. To:</b>
Oct 16,2001 06:59</td></tr><tr><td><b> Status:</b> In work</td></tr>
<tr><td><b> Priority:</b> 90</td><td><b> Site:</b> site 2</td></tr>
<tr><td><b> Product:</b> ISDN</td></tr><tr><td><hr color="black"></td>
</tr><tr><td><b> Call:</b><a href="/servlet/RequestHandler;jsessionid=
GVYTQ2IAAAAAC5YAAAARGUQ?task=ActionDetails&action=runQuery&skipLogin=yes&
callId=3809&actionId=1&formBean=MobileMainMenu"> 3809/1</a></td><td><b>
Resp:</b> Nov 12,2001 10:53</td></tr><tr><td><b> Sched. From:</b> Nov 12,
2001 02:53</td><td><b> Sched. To:</b> Nov 12,2001 03:23</td></tr><tr><td><b>
```

```
Status:</b> In work</td></tr><tr><td><b> Priority:</b> 90</td><td><b>
Site:</b> Le Mans</td></tr><tr><td><b> Product:</b> U-187-A</td></tr>
<tr><td><hr color="black"></td></tr></table><div align="left"> Calls: 1 to 4
of 4<br></div><table><tr><td><div align="center"><a href="/servlet/
RequestHandler;jsessionid=GVYTQ2IAAAAAC5YAAAARGUQ?task=SearchCalls&action=
runQuery&skipLogin=true&login=true&formBean=MobileMainMenu"name="Search
Calls"><b> Search for Calls</b></a></div></td></tr><tr><td><div
align="center"><a href="/servlet/RequestHandler;jsessionid=
GVYTQ2IAAAAAC5YAAAARGUQ?task=OtherCalls&action=runQuery&skipLogin=yes"><b>
Activity - Other Calls</b></a></div></td></tr><tr><td><div align="center">
<a href="/servlet/RequestHandler;jsessionid=GVYTQ2IAAAAAC5YAAAARGUQ?task=
MobileMainMenu&action=runQuery&skipLogin=true"><b> Main Menu</b></a>
</div></td></tr></table><hr color="black"></body></html>
```

In the first example above the generated HTML includes 7,442 characters, while the second page includes only 3,125 characters.

The Transcoder

We start with the `Transcoder` class, although much of the work is done by assisting classes. The code for the transcoder is shown in the next example. The important method is the `parse` method. The first thing that happens in this method is that a handler object is created based on from what device the request came. Sets of property files are used by the transcoder and they allow it to identify which handler should be created—based on the user-agent value in the HTTP request. An example is that for regular browsers on PDAs, an HTML handler is created; while for Wireless Application Protocol (WAP) phones, a WML handler is created. Handlers are required to manage the transcoding based on how the output should be formed. The handlers are the most important elements because they do most of the work. Handlers within the transcoding framework even perform additional tasks such as providing support for multilingual capabilities and security features.

```
public class Transcoder {
      public final static String SUPPORTED_TAGS = "supportedTagList";
      public final static String HANDLER_CLASS  = "handlerClass";
      public final static String PAGE_HEADER    = "pageHeader";
      public final static String PARSER_CLASS   = "transcoder.parser";

      public final static java.util.Stack transcoders =
                           new java.util.Stack();
      public final static String ERROR_MESSAGE_PREFIX = "Html filter: ";

      protected PrintWriter          writer;
      protected TranscoderHandler    handler;
```

```
      protected TranscoderParser      parser;
      protected Map                   deviceProfile;
      protected String                deviceName;
      protected InputStream           inputStream;
      protected String                pageName;
      protected List                  modificators = new ArrayList();
      protected boolean               disableTagRemoving;
      protected boolean               isMobileApplication = true;
      protected Locale                locale;

      protected HttpServletRequest    servletRequest;
      protected HttpServletResponse   servletResponse;
      protected HttpServlet           servlet;

      // ....



      public void parse() {
      try {
            String handlerClass = (String)deviceProfile.get(HANDLER_CLASS);
            if(handlerClass == null) {
                  handlerClass = HtmlTranscoderHandler.class.getName();
            }

            try {
                  handler =
(TranscoderHandler)RTSFactoryManager.getInstanceForAbstract(handlerClass);
            } catch(Exception e) {
                  RTSTracker.handleException(ERROR_MESSAGE_PREFIX,e);
                  copyStreams();
                  return;
            }

            handler.setWriter(writer);
            handler.modificators = modificators;

            String supportedTagList = (String)deviceProfile.get(SUPPORTED_TAGS);
            if(supportedTagList == null) {
                  RTSTracker.displayString(ERROR_MESSAGE_PREFIX +
                      "Failed to get " + SUPPORTED_TAGS +
                      " property for " + deviceName);
                  copyStreams();
                  return;
            }
```

```
            Map tagList = TagListLoader.getTagList(supportedTagList);
            if(tagList == null) {
                  copyStreams();
                  return;
            }

            handler.setTagList(tagList);
            handler.setDeviceProfile(deviceProfile);
            handler.setPageName(pageName);
            handler.setTagRemovingDisabled(disableTagRemoving);
            handler.setIsMobileAppliction(isMobileApplication);
            handler.setLocale(locale);
            handler.setTranscoder(this);

            parser.setDocumentHandler(handler);
            parser.setErrorHandler(handler);
            parser.setCommentHandler(handler);
            parser.setXmlTags(handler.isXml());

            parser.parse(inputStream);
            return;
      }
      catch(SAXNotRecognizedException e) {
                RTSTracker.handleException(ERROR_MESSAGE_PREFIX +
                              "Unrecognized SAX2 feature",e);
      }
      catch(SAXException e) {
            RTSTracker.handleException(ERROR_MESSAGE_PREFIX +
                              "SAX exception",e);
      }
      catch(IOException e) {
            RTSTracker.handleException(ERROR_MESSAGE_PREFIX +
                              "IO Exception",e);
      }
      catch(Throwable e) {
            RTSTracker.handleException(ERROR_MESSAGE_PREFIX,e);
      }
      }

      // ...
}
```

After a handler is created, several other objects are instantiated and held by the handler. Modificators are created and stored within the handler as is a list of the available tags. All this is done based on a set of XML files that represent metadata on how elements should be manipulated by the transcoder. These files define the legal tags as well as changes that may possibly be required to create the correct form of presentation. Even the metadata that forms the base of how the transcoder works is based on XML.

The following two XML files show two samples of such metadata—the first for HTML and the second for WML. Here's the first example:

```
<ROOT>
    <tag name="A" attributes="accesskey,charset,coords,href,hreflang,
name,onblur,onfocus,rel,rev,shape,tabindex,target,type"/>
    <tag name="ABBR,ACRONYM,ADDRESS"/>
    <tag name="APPLET"
attributes="height,width,align,alt,archive,code,hspace,name,vspace"/>
    <tag name="AREA"
attributes="alt,accesskey,coords,href,$nohref,onblur,onfocus,shape,
tabindex,target"/>
    <tag name="B"/>
    <tag name="BASE" attributes="href,target"/>
    <tag name="BASEFONT" attributes="size,color,face,id"/>
    <tag name="BDO" attributes="dir,id,style,title"/>
    <tag name="BIG"/>
    <tag name="BLOCKQUOTE" attributes="cite"/>
    <tag name="BODY"
attributes="bgcolor,background,text,link,vlink,alink,onload,onunload"/>
    <tag name="BR" attributes="clear" properties="empty"/>
    <tag name="BUTTON"
attributes="accesskey,$disabled,name,onblur,onfocus,tabindex,type,value"/>
    <tag name="CAPTION" attributes="align"/>
    <tag name="CENTER,CITE,CODE"/>
    <tag name="COL" attributes="align,char,charoff,span,valign,width"/>
    <tag name="COLGROUP"
            attributes="align,char,charoff,span,valign,width"/>
    <tag name="DD"/>
    <tag name="DEL" attributes="cite,datetime"/>
    <tag name="DFN"/>
    <tag name="DIR" attributes="$compact"/>
    <tag name="DIV" attributes="align"/>
    <tag name="DL" attributes="$compact"/>
    <tag name="DT,EM,FIELDSET"/>
    <tag name="FONT" attributes="size,color,face"/>
    <tag name="FORM" attributes="action,method,enctype,accept-charset,
onreset,onsubmit,target,name,id"/>
    <tag name="FRAME"
attributes="frameborder,longdesc,marginheight,marginwidth,$noresize,
scrolling,src"/>
    <tag name="FRAMESET" attributes="cols,onload,onunload,rows"/>
    <tag name="HEAD" attributes="profile"/>
    <tag name="H1,H2,H3,H4,H5,H6" attributes="align"/>
```

```
    <tag name="HR" attributes="align,size,width,$noshade,color"/>
    <tag name="HTML" attributes="version"/>
    <tag name="I"/>"
    <tag name="IFRAME"
attributes="align,frameborder,height,longdesc,marginheight,marginwidth,
name,scrolling,src,width"/>
    <tag name="IMG"
attributes="src,align,hspace,vspace,alt,border,usemap,ismap,width,height"/>
    <tag name="INPUT" attributes="accept,accesskey,align,alt,$checked,
$disabled,maxlength,name,onblur,onchange,onfocus,onselect,$readonly,size,
src,tabindex,type,usemap,value"/>
    <tag name="INS" attributes="cite,datatime"/>
    <tag name="ISINDEX" attributes="prompt"/>
    <tag name="KBD"/>
    <tag name="LABEL" attributes="accesskey,for,onblur,onfocus"/>
    <tag name="LEGEND" attributes="accesskey,align"/>
    <tag name="LI" attributes="type,value"/>
    <tag name="LINK" attributes="href,rel,rev,urn,methods,title,id"/>
    <tag name="LISTING" properties="preformatted"/>
    <tag name="MAP" attributes="name"/>
    <tag name="MENU" attributes="$compact"/>
    <tag name="META" attributes="name,http-equiv,content"/>
    <tag name="NEXTID" attributes="n"/>
    <tag name="NOFRAMES,NOSCRIPT"/>
    <tag name="OBJECT"
attributes="align,archive,border,classid,codebase,codetype,data,$declare,
height,hspace,name,standby,tabindex,type,usemap,vspace,width"/>
    <tag name="OL" attributes="type,start,$compact"/>
    <tag name="OPTGROUP" attributes="label,$disabled"/>
    <tag name="OPTION" attributes="$selected,value,$disabled,label"/>
    <tag name="P" attributes="align"/>
    <tag name="PARAM" attributes="name,id,type,value,valuetype"/>
    <tag name="PLAINTEXT,XMP" properties="preformatted"/>
    <tag name="PRE" attributes="width" properties="preformatted"/>
    <tag name="Q" attributes="cite"/>
    <tag name="S,SAMP"/>
    <tag name="SCRIPT" attributes="type,charset,$defer,language,src,
title"/>
    <tag name="SELECT"
attributes="name,size,$multiple,$disabled,onblur,onchange,onfocus,
tabindex"/>
    <tag name="SMALL,STRIKE,STRONG"/>
    <tag name="STYLE" attributes="type,media,title"/>
    <tag name="SUB,SUP"/>
<!--    <tag name="SPAN" attributes="class,id"/> -->
    <tag name="TABLE"
attributes="align,border,width,cellspacing,cellpadding,frame,summary,
```

```
bgcolor"/>
    <tag name="TBODY" attributes="align,char,charoff,valign"/>
    <tag name="TD" attributes="abbr,align,axis,bgcolor,char,charoff,
colspan,headers,height,$nowrap,rowspan,scope,valign,width"/>
    <tag name="TEXTAREA" attributes="cols,rows,accesskey,
$disables,name,onblur,onchange,onfocus,onselect,$readonly,tabindex"
properties="alwaysClosed"/>
    <tag name="TFOOT" attributes="align,char,charoff,valign"/>
    <tag name="TH"
attributes="abbr,align,axis,bgcolor,char,charoff,colspan,headers,height,
$nowrap,rowspan,scope,valign,width"/>
    <tag name="THEAD" attributes="align,char,charoff,valign"/>
    <tag name="TITLE"/>
    <tag name="TR" attributes="align,bgcolor,char,charoff,valign"/>
    <tag name="TT,U"/>
    <tag name="UL" attributes="type,$compact"/>
    <tag name="VAR"/>
</ROOT>
```

Here's the second example:

```
<ROOT>
    <tag name="WML" attributes="xml:lang"/>
    <tag name="HEAD"/>
    <tag name="ACCESS" attributes="domain,path"/>
    <tag name="META" attributes="http-equiv,name,forua,content,scheme"/>
    <tag name="TEMPLATE"
              attributes="onenterforward,onenterbackward,ontimer"/>
    <tag name="CARD"
attributes="onenterforward,onenterbackward,ontimer,title,newcontext,
ordered,xml:lang,id"/>
    <tag name="SELECT" attributes="multiple,name,value,iname,ivalue,
title,tabindex,xml:lang"/>
    <tag name="OPTION" attributes="value,title,onpick,xml:lang"/>
    <tag name="OPTGROUP" attributes="title,xml:lang"/>
    <tag name="INPUT" attributes="name,value,type,format,emptyok,size,
maxlength,title,xml:lang,tabindex,accesskey" properties="empty"/>
    <tag name="FIELDSET" attributes="title,xml:lang"/>
    <tag name="TIMER" attributes="name,value"/>
    <tag name="EM,STRONG,I,B,U,BIG,SMALL" attributes="xml:lang"/>
    <tag name="P" attributes="align,mode,xml:lang"/>
    <tag name="BR" properties="empty"/>
    <tag name="TABLE" attributes="title,align,columns,xml:lang"/>
    <tag name="TR"/>
    <tag name="TD" attributes="xml:lang"/>
    <tag name="PRE" attributes="xml:space" properties="preformatted"/>
```

```
    <tag name="IMG" attributes="alt,src,localsrc,vspace,hspace,
align,height,width,xml:lang"/>
    <tag name="POSTFIELD,SETVAR"
      attributes="name,value"  properties="empty"/>
    <tag name="GO"
      attributes="href,sendreferer,method,enctype,accept-charset"/>
    <tag name="PREV,REFRESH,NOOP"/>
    <tag name="DO" attributes="type,label,name,optional,xml:lang"/>
    <tag name="ANCHOR" attributes="title,accesskey,xml:lang"/>
    <tag name="A" attributes="href,title,accesskey,xml:lang"/>
    <tag name="ONEVENT" attributes="type"/>
</ROOT>
```


After the handler is ready, it is set into an instance variable of the parser. Then the `parse` method is called and the parser starts doing its job. An example of a parser is shown here:

```
public class SimpleParser extends TranscoderParserImpl {
      protected SimpleLexer lexer  = new SimpleLexer();
public void parse (InputStream stream) throws Exception {
      lexer.reset(stream);

      documentHandler.startDocument();
      while (lexer.nextToken() != lexer.TOKEN_EOF) {
            int type = lexer.getTokenType();
            if(lexer.mWhiteSpace.count != 0) {
                  documentHandler.characters(
                  lexer.mWhiteSpace.data,0,lexer.mWhiteSpace.count);
            }

            switch(type) {
                  case lexer.TOKEN_TAG:
                        TagInfo tag = lexer.mCurrentTag;
                        if(tag.isEndTag()) {
                        documentHandler.endElement(tag.mName);
                        break;
                        }
                        attributeList.clear();
                        for(int i = 0; i < tag.parameterCount(); i++) {
                              attributeList.addAttribute(
                                    tag.getParameterName(i),
                                    null,tag.getParameterValue(i));
                        }
                        documentHandler.startElement(tag.mName,attributeList);
                        if(tag.isStartEndTag()) {
                        documentHandler.endElement(tag.mName);
```

```
                    }
                    break;

                case lexer.TOKEN_SCRIPT:
                case lexer.TOKEN_TEXT:
                    if(lexer.mBuffer.count != 0) {
                        documentHandler.characters(lexer.mBuffer.data,0,
                                                   lexer.mBuffer.count);
                    }
                    break;

                case lexer.TOKEN_COMMENT:
                    if(lexer.mBuffer.count != 0) {
                        commentHandler.comment(lexer.mBuffer.toString());
                    }
            }

        }
        documentHandler.endDocument();
}
public void setXmlTags(boolean flag) {
}
}
```

SimpleParser class that inherits from the class TrancoderParserImpl shown here:

```
public abstract class TranscoderParserImpl implements TranscoderParser {
      protected DocumentHandler   documentHandler;
      protected ErrorHandler      errorHandler;
      protected AttributeListImpl attributeList;
      protected CommentHandler    commentHandler;
public TranscoderParserImpl() {
      attributeList = new AttributeListImpl();
}
public void parse (String systemId) throws SAXException, IOException {
      try {
            parse(new FileInputStream(systemId));
      } catch (Exception e) {
            if(e instanceof IOException) {
                  throw (IOException)e;
            }
      }
```

```
}
public void parse (InputSource src) throws SAXException, IOException {
      try {
            parse(src.getByteStream());
      } catch (Exception e) {
            if(e instanceof IOException) {
                  throw (IOException)e;
            }
      }

}
public void setCommentHandler(CommentHandler commentHandler) {
      this.commentHandler = commentHandler;
}
public void setDocumentHandler (DocumentHandler handler) {
      documentHandler = handler;
}
public void setDTDHandler (DTDHandler handler) {
}
public void setEntityResolver (EntityResolver resolver) {
}
public void setErrorHandler (ErrorHandler handler) {
      errorHandler = handler;
}
public void setLocale(java.util.Locale locale) throws SAXException {
}
}
```

This class forms the root of the transcoder parser hierarchy but is never meant to be instantiated because, as its code shows, it will do very little. This base class implements the `TranscoderParser`, which itself extends the `org.xml.sax.Parser` interface:

```
public interface TranscoderParser extends org.xml.sax.Parser {
      public void parse (InputStream is) throws Exception;
      public void setCommentHandler(CommentHandler commentHandler);
      public void setXmlTags(boolean isXml);
}
```

Now things are starting to become clearer; the transcoder is based on the notion of parsing through events—that is, SAX. It has handlers that (through the parsers) register for events and manipulate the code. If we look at the implementation of the `parse` method in the `SimpleParser`, we can see that it uses a "lexer" object to recognize tokens. Based on whether the token recognized is a tag, script, or text, it will perform different tasks—but always through the handler object (that's where all the intelligence resides).

Summary

This chapter provided two examples on how XML can be used within applications. These examples are just a tip of the iceberg; the use of XML within applications is proving itself to be extremely valuable. The crux of its applicability is its dynamic and hierarchical nature. Most data structures in computer science are hierarchical. With time, the parsers and tolls for manipulating and using XML are becoming fast, standard, and of high quality. This brings with it the widespread use of XML for pretty much anything you can think of. This is only natural—once you get the hang of using these libraries, you will start to come back to using XML for anything that has to do with hierarchical, recursive, dynamic, or pretty much any kind of data structure manipulation.

Chapter 36

Application of XSL Transformations

The central role that the Extensible Markup Language (XML) is beginning to play in e-business applications is augmented by the capabilities of XSL Transformations (XSLT), a subset of the Extensible Stylesheet Language (XSL) that defines how transformations from one XML dialect to another can be phrased. XSLT is of fundamental importance to the success of XML in e-business applications. Because different systems and different Web sites ultimately end up with different XML structures, the ability to exchange information by bridging over semantic mismatching is perhaps the primary factor that will determine the success or failure of XML. You achieve this bridging by defining conversion rules in the form of XML transformations.

This chapter focuses on two aspects of XSLT processing. First, it shows how XSL stylesheets are used to process an XML document. Then it shows you how the Java code used in a generic XSLT processor as part of an interface layer that accepts data in any XML format converts the data into a native XML format that the application can understand.

More Insider Trading

This section continues with the insider trading example from Chapter 35 to describe how XSLT is used for processing XML documents as part of an e-business application. This example uses LotusXSL, which is included in the WebSphere libraries.

Removing Errors

In Chapter 35, we created an XML file with a listing of insider buyers. Unfortunately, the file is huge (at almost 2MB) and difficult to sift through. It is also not quite in the format most useful to a typical user. In this and the following sections, we provide a few XSLT examples that show how you can process the data until you get the format and content just right.

The first thing we'll do is strip out useless data, such as XML nodes of any stock for which the `insiderPurchase` node has an `error` attribute (see Figure 36-1). The `error` attribute is generated whenever the parsing of node traversal fails in the insider trading program. Because such nodes contain no information, we can start by removing them.

The following code shows a processing instruction, a document root, and the XSLT rules required for removing these nodes:

```
<?xml version="1.0"?>

<xsl:stylesheet xmlns:xsl="http://www.w3.org/XSL/Transform/1.0">

  <xsl:template match="/">
      <insiderTrading example="1">
      <xsl:apply-templates/>
```

```
        </insiderTrading>
    </xsl:template>

    <xsl:template match="insiderTrading/*">
        <xsl:copy>
        <xsl:apply-templates/>
        </xsl:copy>
    </xsl:template>

    <xsl:template match="insiderPurchase[not(@error)]">
        <insiderPurchase date="{@date}" price="{@price}"/>
    </xsl:template>

</xsl:stylesheet>
```


Every XSLT file is also an XML file; therefore every XSLT file contains a processing instruction defining the XML version, followed by a single document root. The *document root* is an element of type `<xsl:stylesheet>`, and all the other elements are embedded within this root element. The root element contains a namespace attribute that defines the uniform resource identifier (URI) to be used for all elements that belong to the XSL namespace.

Because the syntax and semantics of XSLT rules are nontrivial (to say the least), we will go over each rule in detail and provide explanation as much as possible along the way.

The document in our example has three rules. Each rule supplies a pattern for the XSLT processor to attempt to match and indicates the nodes to be processed once the pattern has been matched. The first rule in the file matches the root node, designated by a slash (/), of the source XML file. The second rule matches any node that is a direct descendant of the `insiderTrading` node. The syntax of the pattern-matching rules is similar to directory structures in UNIX. The third and final rule matches any `insiderPurchase` node that does not have an `error` attribute. In XSL, an attribute is designated by a preceding "at" symbol (@). Therefore, the pattern-match definition of the third rule should be read as "all `insiderPurchase` nodes such that there does not exist an attribute by the name of `error`."

The processing parts of the rules are fairly simple. For the root node, we create an XML element called `insiderTrading` with a single attribute called `example`. This element will form the root element in the resulting XML. Then we apply all rules for the rest of the document from the source file. The processing for the stock nodes is the easiest task. We simply copy the nodes over and continue processing the children. Finally, whenever we get to a purchase node that is not an error, we create an appropriate node in the output. Note that the syntax surrounds a calculated value embedded in a string with curly brackets.

```
    <insiderPurchase date="8-Oct-98" price="-" />
  </KIDE>
  <FFTI />
- <SVEV>
    <insiderPurchase error="There was an inside trade that could not be parsed" />
    <insiderPurchase error="There was an inside trade that could not be parsed" />
    <insiderPurchase error="There was an inside trade that could not be parsed" />
    <insiderPurchase error="There was an inside trade that could not be parsed" />
    <insiderPurchase error="There was an inside trade that could not be parsed" />
    <insiderPurchase error="There was an inside trade that could not be parsed" />
    <insiderPurchase error="There was an inside trade that could not be parsed" />
    <insiderPurchase error="There was an inside trade that could not be parsed" />
    <insiderPurchase error="There was an inside trade that could not be parsed" />
    <insiderPurchase error="There was an inside trade that could not be parsed" />
    <insiderPurchase error="There was an inside trade that could not be parsed" />
    <insiderPurchase error="There was an inside trade that could not be parsed" />
    <insiderPurchase error="There was an inside trade that could not be parsed" />
    <insiderPurchase error="There was an inside trade that could not be parsed" />
    <insiderPurchase error="There was an inside trade that could not be parsed" />
    <insiderPurchase error="There was an inside trade that could not be parsed" />
    <insiderPurchase error="There was an inside trade that could not be parsed" />
    <insiderPurchase error="There was an inside trade that could not be parsed" />
    <insiderPurchase error="There was an inside trade that could not be parsed" />
    <insiderPurchase error="There was an inside trade that could not be parsed" />
    <insiderPurchase error="There was an inside trade that could not be parsed" />
    <insiderPurchase error="There was an inside trade that could not be parsed" />
    <insiderPurchase error="There was an inside trade that could not be parsed" />
    <insiderPurchase error="There was an inside trade that could not be parsed" />
    <insiderPurchase error="There was an inside trade that could not be parsed" />
  </SVEV>
  <JRJR />
- <EGHT>
    <insiderPurchase date="1-Feb-99" price="3.40" />
    <insiderPurchase date="3-Aug-98" price="3.40" />
```

Figure 36-1. *The error attribute in insiderPurchase node*

Removing Symbols That Have No Insider Purchasers

Now we've managed to write our first XSLT file, and the file size is down to 1316KB from 1942KB—but we can do better. There are plenty of nodes with no inside trades at all (you know, companies that follow the rules), and we can get rid of those, too. We need only make a small change to the pattern match of the second rule by stating that the rule is satisfied only for nodes that are child nodes of the `insiderTrading` nodes and have at least one `insiderPurchase` node:

```
<?xml version="1.0"?>

<xsl:stylesheet xmlns:xsl="http://www.w3.org/XSL/Transform/1.0">
```

```
  <xsl:template match="/">
      <insiderTrading example="2">
      <xsl:apply-templates/>
      </insiderTrading>
  </xsl:template>

  <xsl:template match="insiderTrading/*[insiderPurchase]">
      <xsl:copy>
      <xsl:apply-templates/>
      </xsl:copy>
  </xsl:template>

  <xsl:template match="insiderPurchase[not(@error)]">
      <insiderPurchase date="{@date}" price="{@price}"/>
  </xsl:template>

</xsl:stylesheet>
```


Removing Nodes That Have No Prices

That worked, but it didn't help much—we're only down to 1306KB. Now let's get rid of the nodes with no prices; if we don't know at what price the insider purchased the stock, we can't really tell whether the current price is high or low. The following XSLT file brings our file size down to 1148KB:

```
<?xml version="1.0"?>

<xsl:stylesheet xmlns:xsl="http://www.w3.org/XSL/Transform/1.0">

  <xsl:template match="/">
      <insiderTrading example="3">
      <xsl:apply-templates/>
      </insiderTrading>
  </xsl:template>

  <xsl:template match="insiderTrading/*[insiderPurchase]">
      <xsl:copy>
      <xsl:apply-templates/>
      </xsl:copy>
  </xsl:template>

  <xsl:template match="insiderPurchase[not(@price='-')]">
      <insiderPurchase date="{@date}" price="{@price}"/>
```

```
    </xsl:template>

</xsl:stylesheet>
```

Sorting

That's enough for cutting down the size. The next step is to look at sorting. In the following example, we sort the values by price. For each stock symbol, we want the inside trades to be listed with the price values determining the order; after all, we want the lowest possible price, so we might as well compare the current price to the lowest price purchased by insiders. The following sheet shows the XSLT file performing the sort. Note that the `sort` element has an optional `data-type` attribute for specifying how sorting should be performed. In our case, we do not want an alphanumeric sort; otherwise, a price of 10 will appear before a price of 3.

```
<?xml version="1.0"?>

<xsl:stylesheet xmlns:xsl="http://www.w3.org/XSL/Transform/1.0">

  <xsl:template match="/">
      <insiderTrading example="4">
      <xsl:apply-templates/>
      </insiderTrading>
  </xsl:template>

  <xsl:template match="insiderTrading/*[insiderPurchase]">
      <xsl:copy>
      <xsl:apply-templates select="insiderPurchase">
            <xsl:sort select="@price" data-type="number"/>
      </xsl:apply-templates>
      </xsl:copy>
  </xsl:template>

  <xsl:template match="insiderPurchase">
      <insiderPurchase date="{@date}" price="{@price}"/>
  </xsl:template>

</xsl:stylesheet>
```

Transforming the XML Document to HTML

The next step is a useful one that will be practical for e-business applications. We want to transform the XML file into an HTML document that will display all data in a table. Sounds simple—and it should be. As things stand, however, there is a big problem. We cannot get the value of the actual tag in XSL because in XML, the stock symbols are tags instead of data. This is an important lesson, so we hope that after reading this chapter you will remember never to use data as tags.

To complete the program, we need to change the code of the servlet created in Chapter 35, as shown here:

```
public static void main(String[] args) {

    InsiderInspector gen = new InsiderInspector();

    com.ibm.xml.parser.TXDocument myDocument =
      new com.ibm.xml.parser.TXDocument();

    try {
      ProcessingInstruction pi = myDocument.
        createProcessingInstruction("xml","version=\"1.0\"");
      myDocument.appendChild(pi);

      Element root = myDocument.createElement("insiderTrading");
      root.setAttribute("asOf", (new Date()).toString());
      myDocument.appendChild(root);

      Vector symbolVector = gen.retrieveAllSymbols();
      for (Enumeration e = symbolVector.elements() ;
                               e.hasMoreElements() ; ) {
        String aSymbol = (String)e.nextElement();
        StringBuffer htmlText = HTMLFetcher.getHTMLFor(
          "http://biz.yahoo.com/t/" + aSymbol.substring(0,1) +
          "/" + aSymbol + ".html");
        StringBuffer aBuf = HTMLTidier.tidyHTML(htmlText);
        if (aBuf != null) {
          Element symbolRoot = myDocument.createElement("stock");
          symbolRoot.setAttribute("symbol",aSymbol);
          root.appendChild(symbolRoot);
          gen.extractInsiderInfo(aBuf, myDocument, symbolRoot);
          System.err.println("Finished processing " + aSymbol);
        }
      }

      FileWriter fw = new FileWriter("insiderTrading.xml");
      myDocument.toXMLString(fw);
      fw.close();
    } catch (Exception ex) {
      ex.printStackTrace();
    }
  }
```

Now when we rerun the XML generation code, we can change our XML source to look like Figure 36-2. This allows us to use the following XSLT code to produce the end result shown in Figure 36-3.

```
<?xml version="1.0"?>
<xsl:stylesheet xmlns:xsl="http://www.w3.org/XSL/Transform/1.0">

  <xsl:template match="/">
      <HTML>
        <HEAD>
          <TITLE>
            Insider Buyer patterns
          </TITLE>
        </HEAD>
        <BODY>
          <H3>
           This table lists all insider purchases for Nasdaq stock.
          </H3>
          <TABLE BORDER="1" WIDTH="100">
            <xsl:apply-templates/>
          </TABLE>
        </BODY>
      </HTML>
  </xsl:template>

  <xsl:template match="stock">
      <TR>
        <TD>
          <xsl:value-of select="@symbol"/>
        </TD>
          <xsl:apply-templates/>
      </TR>
  </xsl:template>

  <xsl:template match="insiderPurchase">
      <TD>
        <xsl:value-of select="@date"/>
        <xsl:text>
            ;
        </xsl:text>
        <xsl:value-of select="@price"/>
```

```
      </TD>
  </xsl:template>

</xsl:stylesheet>
```

```
- <insiderTrading example="4">
  - <stock symbol="ATEN">
      <insiderPurchase date="22-Oct-98" price="3.94" />
      <insiderPurchase date="22-Oct-98" price="4.00" />
      <insiderPurchase date="21-Oct-98" price="4.25" />
      <insiderPurchase date="20-Oct-98" price="4.31 - 4.38" />
      <insiderPurchase date="19-Oct-98" price="4.63" />
      <insiderPurchase date="14-Oct-98" price="4.75" />
      <insiderPurchase date="4-Nov-98" price="7.25 - 9.00" />
      <insiderPurchase date="2-Nov-98" price="7.25" />
      <insiderPurchase date="2-Nov-98" price="7.25" />
      <insiderPurchase date="31-Aug-98" price="8.63 - 8.75" />
      <insiderPurchase date="31-Aug-98" price="8.80" />
      <insiderPurchase date="4-Sep-98" price="9.19" />
      <insiderPurchase date="14-Sep-98" price="9.88" />
      <insiderPurchase date="15-Sep-98" price="10.38" />
    </stock>
  - <stock symbol="CTAC">
      <insiderPurchase date="26-Aug-98" price="5.75" />
      <insiderPurchase date="30-Sep-98" price="5.94" />
      <insiderPurchase date="29-Sep-98" price="6.00" />
      <insiderPurchase date="14-Aug-98" price="6.00" />
      <insiderPurchase date="18-Aug-98" price="6.06" />
      <insiderPurchase date="13-Aug-98" price="6.06" />
      <insiderPurchase date="9-Sep-98" price="6.50" />
      <insiderPurchase date="9-Sep-98" price="6.50" />
      <insiderPurchase date="17-Mar-99" price="12.50 - 12.63" />
    </stock>
  - <stock symbol="SRCE">
      <insiderPurchase date="28-Aug-98" price="31.56" />
      <insiderPurchase date="25-Aug-98" price="34.00" />
      <insiderPurchase date="28-Jan-99" price="35.00" />
      <insiderPurchase date="1-Feb-99" price="36.00" />
    </stock>
  - <stock symbol="FSBC">
      <insiderPurchase date="27-Apr-99" price="19.00" />
      <insiderPurchase date="29-Apr-99" price="19.25" />
      <insiderPurchase date="26-Apr-99" price="19.38" />
```

Figure 36-2. *New and improved XML*

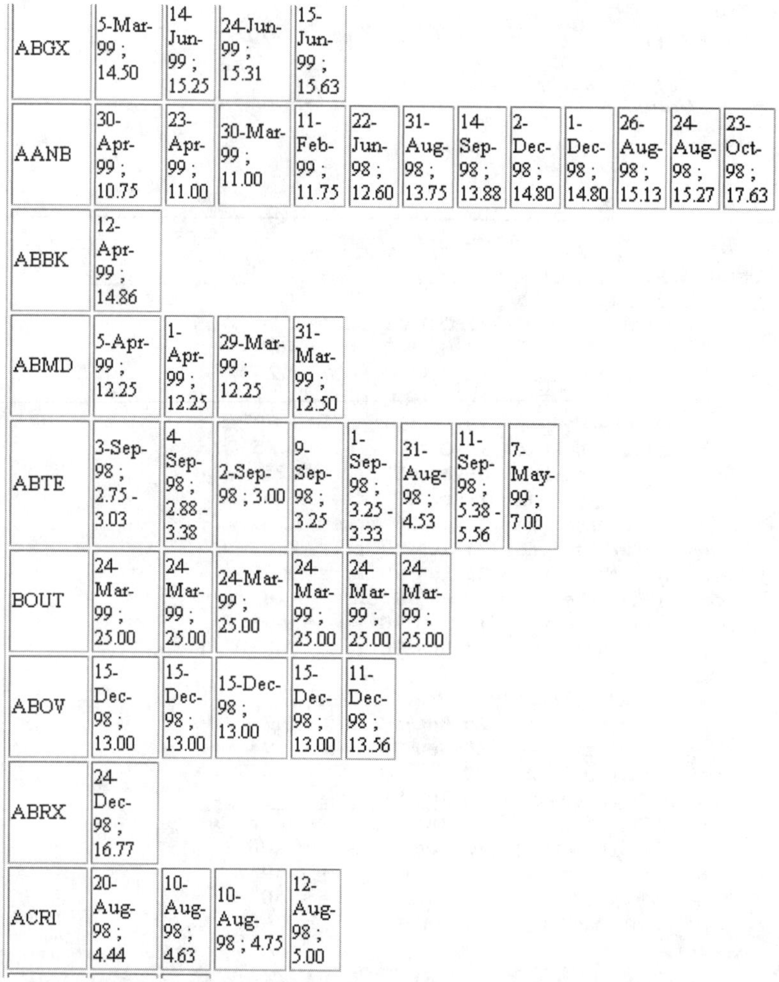

ABGX	5-Mar-99 ; 14.50	14-Jun-99 ; 15.25	24-Jun-99 ; 15.31	15-Jun-99 ; 15.63								
AANB	30-Apr-99 ; 10.75	23-Apr-99 ; 11.00	30-Mar-99 ; 11.00	11-Feb-99 ; 11.75	22-Jun-98 ; 12.60	31-Aug-98 ; 13.75	14-Sep-98 ; 13.88	2-Dec-98 ; 14.80	1-Dec-98 ; 14.80	26-Aug-98 ; 15.13	24-Aug-98 ; 15.27	23-Oct-98 ; 17.63
ABBK	12-Apr-99 ; 14.86											
ABMD	5-Apr-99 ; 12.25	1-Apr-99 ; 12.25	29-Mar-99 ; 12.25	31-Mar-99 ; 12.50								
ABTE	3-Sep-98 ; 2.75 - 3.03	4-Sep-98 ; 2.88 - 3.38	2-Sep-98 ; 3.00	9-Sep-98 ; 3.25	1-Sep-98 ; 3.25 - 3.33	31-Aug-98 ; 4.53	11-Sep-98 ; 5.38 - 5.56	7-May-99 ; 7.00				
BOUT	24-Mar-99 ; 25.00	24-Mar-99 ; 25.00	24-Mar-99 ; 25.00	24-Mar-99 ; 25.00	24-Mar-99 ; 25.00	24-Mar-99 ; 25.00						
ABOV	15-Dec-98 ; 13.00	15-Dec-98 ; 13.00	15-Dec-98 ; 13.00	15-Dec-98 ; 13.00	11-Dec-98 ; 13.56							
ABRX	24-Dec-98 ; 16.77											
ACRI	20-Aug-98 ; 4.44	10-Aug-98 ; 4.63	10-Aug-98 ; 4.75	12-Aug-98 ; 5.00								

Figure 36-3. *HTML display of insider buying patterns*

Finally, the following XSLT file can be used to transform the XML into WML, as shown in Figure 36-4.

```
<?xml version="1.0"?>
<xsl:stylesheet xmlns:xsl="http://www.w3.org/XSL/Transform/1.0">

  <xsl:template match="/">
```

```
    <xsl:pi name="xml">
      version="1.0"
    </xsl:pi>
    <wml>
      <xsl:apply-templates/>
    </wml>
</xsl:template>

<xsl:template match="stock">
    <xsl:element name="card">
      <xsl:attribute name="id">
        <xsl:text>n</xsl:text>
        <xsl:number/>
      </xsl:attribute>
      <xsl:attribute name="title">
        <xsl:value-of select="@symbol"/>
      </xsl:attribute>
              <do type="options" label="First">
              <go href="#n1"/>
              </do>
              <do type="options" label="Second">
              <go href="#n2"/>
              </do>
            <p>
              <xsl:apply-templates/>
            </p>
    </xsl:element>
</xsl:template>

<xsl:template match="insiderPurchase">
    <xsl:value-of select="@date"/>
    <xsl:text>
      ;
    </xsl:text>
    <xsl:value-of select="@price"/>
    <br/>
</xsl:template>

</xsl:stylesheet>
```

The underlying model for WML introduces the notion of cards. The display of a cellular device displays one WML card at a time and allows the user to move between

```
<?xml version="1.0" ?>
- <wml>
  - <card id="n1" title="ATEN">
    - <do type="options" label="First">
        <go href="#n1" />
      </do>
    - <do type="options" label="Second">
        <go href="#n2" />
      </do>
    - <p>
        22-Oct-98 ; 3.94
        <br />
        22-Oct-98 ; 4.00
        <br />
        21-Oct-98 ; 4.25
        <br />
        20-Oct-98 ; 4.31 - 4.38
        <br />
        19-Oct-98 ; 4.63
        <br />
        14-Oct-98 ; 4.75
        <br />
        4-Nov-98 ; 7.25 - 9.00
        <br />
        2-Nov-98 ; 7.25
        <br />
        2-Nov-98 ; 7.25
        <br />
        31-Aug-98 ; 8.63 - 8.75
        <br />
        31-Aug-98 ; 8.80
        <br />
        4-Sep-98 ; 9.19
        <br />
        14-Sep-98 ; 9.88
        <br />
        15-Sep-98 ; 10.38
        <br />
```

Figure 36-4. *Resulting WML*

cards using the phone's controls. Figure 36-5 shows the resulting display on the cellular phone: two cards surround the screen used to navigate between the cards. Note that we have cheated a bit, because the WML file has been created for only three stock symbols. Obviously, we would not want to move 1MB through a cellular connection—nor would we want thousands of cards on the device.

Figure 36-5. *WML display of insider buying patterns*

XML-to-XML Conversion

Our second example is a practical one. While it is true that most applications today can read XML and make use of it within their interface layers, it is also unfortunately true that most applications use their own XML dialects. This makes interfacing between different applications almost as difficult as it was before XML, and is where XSLT comes to the rescue. Because XSLT is all about transformations between one XML structure and another, it makes sense to use XSLT as the mediation layer.

Specifically, we can inject a translation layer that looks at the XML document through a mapping between the XML root node (of which there is only one in every XML document), selects an XSLT sheet, and applies it to the XML document. This means that before we hand the XML document to the application itself, we convert it into an XML document that the application can understand. The transformation process makes use of the `XSLProcessor` object, which is part of the *pcom.lotus.xsl* package. The real work is done in the following method, and it is amazing how simple it is

```
public Document customize(String _xslPath)
      throws SAXException
```

```
{
    XSLProcessor processor = new XSLProcessor();
    Throwable ex = null;
    // Tries to customize the Document by using XML instruction
    // with references to an XSL file
    try
    {
        outDocument = processor.process(inDocument);
    }
    catch(MalformedURLException e){ex = e;}
    catch(FileNotFoundException e){ex = e;}
    catch(IOException e){ex = e;}
    catch(SAXException e){ex = e;}

    if(ex != null)
        System.err.println("XslCustomizer" + ex);

    // if customization using XML instruction failed and _xslPath
    // has value (i.e. there is a mapping between the root node
    // and an XSL file then customize the document
    // using XSL file from '_xslPath' location
    if(_xslPath.length() > 0 && outDocument == null)
        outDocument = processor.process(inDocument,
            XmlDomGenerator.readDocument(_xslPath), null);

    //if customization failed outDocument equals inDocument
    if(outDocument == null)
        outDocument = inDocument;
    return outDocument;
}
```

Summary

XSLT is a powerful tool and, therefore, one that is important for you to be familiar with. Unfortunately, XSLT is difficult to use. It is not difficult from the point of view of the Java code required to do the processing—that is simple. What is difficult is writing XSLT sheets, a process that is based on a pattern-matching paradigm as opposed to a procedural paradigm. This inherent difficulty makes XSLT less centralized than it was once thought to be.

It was once a common belief that the way to architect applications was to build a business logic layer that generated data in XML, and to have XSLT sheets create the presentation layers for different browser types to use. The difficulty in building XSLT sheets (even with tools) has made this technique less practical than originally hoped.

Another promise that XSLT never fulfilled was the bridging between XML dialects. The code shown in the preceding section is easy, but the XSLT sheets required to perform such bridging are complex and difficult to write. The industry has instead turned to creating standards for application interoperability—the topic of Chapters 37 and 38.

Chapter 37

Web Services: SOAP, WSDL, and UDDI

Web services are the hottest thing in computing these days. Vendors and users alike are converging on this new set of technologies that promises simple, standards-based interoperability among distributed decoupled systems. It is by far the most talked about topic in the software technology space, and the investments being made in Web services technologies are considerable. In fact, Microsoft has pretty much defined its entire .NET strategy (and thus its entire strategy as a technology vendor) on Web services.

This chapter introduces you to the concepts of Web services and describes the three dominant technologies forming this new category: the Simple Object Access Protocol (SOAP), which is used for making remote calls and transferring messages; the Web Services Description Language (WSDL), which is used to describe service end points; and the Universal Description, Discover, and Integration (UDDI), which is used to publish and discover services using a common registry. We will describe these technologies, and then examine how they are supported within the WebSphere Application Server.

The Web Services Model

The shift to e-business is fundamentally changing how systems look and, even more important (for us developers), how systems are built. To support e-business, systems often evolve "from the outside in," in the sense that a Web site is put up quickly, and it slowly "reaches back" into the corporation's back-end systems. The other focus of e-business is on interconnections between partners' systems, sometimes within the enterprise and sometimes outside it. In today's e-business strategy, the concept of e-bonding is no longer far-fetched. *E-bonding* in this context is the ability of one's system to connect flexibly and quickly to the systems of customers and business partners. For example, ViryaNet's Service Hub platform supports not only internal employees, but also suppliers, third parties, and customers—all members of the service community. What this means is that the business applications of tomorrow need to interact with each other continuously and without the need for a huge investment in point-to-point integration. Obviously, some standards are required.

The notion of a new model for running business applications in a cooperative manner is not a new one. It has been discussed in theory for many years within academic circles. But today's technological world has brought us to a point where it is doable—and doable within the mainstream. These are exciting times for anyone involved in building the new world. We are actually in the midst of an inflection point in the model for delivering business features to users. This new model is called *Web services.* In fact, support for Web Services is perhaps the most important addition to WebSphere 4.0.

The Web services model revolves around functional elements (it's hard to use words such as "components" or "modules" without their being overloaded with meaning) that are accessible using standard Internet protocols. It is the marriage of the experience attained by the industry in component-based development and usage to Web-based access and invocation. The basic ideas of the model are not new; they are similar to various technologies to which we have grown accustomed over the past 10 years.

The Web services model, however, is unique in two ways: First, it is natively based on Internet protocols and, therefore, is optimally suited to make use of the ubiquitous connectivity of the Internet. It can deliver on the promise of tapping into a practically endless availability of information, functionality, and computing power. Second, it is being supported by both the Microsoft camp and the non-Microsoft camp. This is the first time we can remember such a phenomenon.

The potential of this new model is huge. For users, it promises low cost and quick deployment, highly functional systems, continuously improving systems, flexibility, and extensibility. For solution and application providers, it promises more revenue opportunities and lower development costs. And most important, for infrastructure vendors, it holds the ultimate promise of new license revenue. So everyone is on board.

Elements of the Web Services Model

The basis for what is required to support a Web services model is actually fairly simple. Web services are functional elements deployed on a node connected to any network and accessed over the Internet. For Web services, there is no restriction on the programming language the functional element can be written in or the operating platform it can be deployed on. Therefore, three elements are required for delivering on the promise of the Web services model:

- A standard way to represent data and messages or invocations that activate such functional elements
- A standard way to describe what a Web service does that is understandable to a user of a service (typically, another functional element that makes use of the Web service)
- A standard way to discover providers of Web services

Fortunately, all of these elements are very real. The three technologies that together can deliver on the promise of Web services are the SOAP, WSDL, and UDDI mechanisms. Interestingly enough, all three are applications of Extensible Markup Language (XML), proving without any room for doubt that XML is "the lingua franca of the Web." Since WebSphere is IBM's platform for e-business, it is not surprising that IBM is among the first vendors to offer a full development and deployment environment for Web Services—within WebSphere 4.0.

The reality of Web services changes not only *how* things are done but also *what* is done. XML over HTTP is merely a pattern that specifies how systems communicate with one another. But Web services cover much broader issues. Once systems can communicate, one needs to address the question of *what* they communicate and how they decide *whom* to communicate with. The Web is evolving from a fairly static model to a very dynamic and interactive one. In this model, the Web needs a way to tie many services together. This not only means supporting an ability to find these services, but also devising a way to define what services can be provided by a Web site, and how they are registered and discovered. Once all of these issues are resolved, the result can be a fully interconnected world with universal service delivery and usage—something that until now people could only dream about. It is true that all of these standards are still early in their evolutionary cycles, and that universal service is not yet a reality; however, the tools necessary for getting us there are maturing very rapidly. Anyone building systems for this brave new world should be fully aware of them.

Creating the New Standards

History is full of battles on the front of application interoperability, and it's full of failures. One needs to go back only five years to remember the battles between the Object Management Group's (OMG) Common Object Request Broker Architecture (CORBA) and Microsoft's Distributed Component Object Model (DCOM). Neither of these technologies, while good for interoperability between applications on a LAN, is really suited for interoperability on the Internet. More important, both of these technologies are more suitable for tightly coupled environments. In the Web environment, the real benefit can be achieved only with a loosely coupled model. For that reason, Internet Inter-ORB Protocol (IIOP) may be fitting for EJB communication, but not for e-bonding scenarios. In this environment, Hypertext Transfer Protocol (HTTP) must be the underlying protocol, and XML must be the language of choice.

This fact has been acknowledged by all, including IBM and Microsoft. (Yes, both companies are cooperating and are the main drivers for the standards being formed for Web services.) As atypical as it is, the fact that IBM and Microsoft are cooperating on a technological basis gives anything produced a tremendous amount of clout, and the result is widespread industry acceptance. For example, many other vendors, including Ariba, BEA, HP, Iona, SAP, and Software AG, are already buying into the IBM/Microsoft lead-initiative for Web services. A recent breakthrough in the acceptance of these standards, and in the fight against fragmentation, is Sun's announced support for SOAP and UDDI as part of the Sun Open Network Environment (ONE) initiative. Even the competing Electronic Business XML (ebXML) camp has endorsed SOAP, and hopefully will endorse WSDL and UDDI sometime in the future—bringing with it the de facto agreement on SOAP/WSDL/UDDI and the standard foundations for Web services.

Analysts, too, are in agreement. A research report issue by the Gartner Group in April, 2001 estimates that IBM and Microsoft will exert leadership in defining Web services standards with 0.8 probability. Anyone following analysts' estimates knows that for them to give a 0.8 probability means that it's practically a done deal. Such analyst reports often create the market, as opposed to just informing the business community on the state of the market.

From XML to SOAP

HTTP and XML are the foundations, but they are not enough. HTTP is mainly a facility for transferring files, and possibly requests, from one place to another; it just isn't adequate for full application interoperability. So the first step is to extend it slightly, by adding a set of HTTP headers, encapsulating the requests in a new type of HTTP POST command (called M-POST), and adding a rich XML structure in the body of the HTTP request to enable complex application-to-application communication over the Internet. This is what SOAP is all about.

SOAP uses HTTP to carry messages that are formatted in XML. It provides a standard object invocation protocol built on Internet standards, using HTTP as the transport layer and XML as the encoding layer. It is extensible in nature, due to the fact that it uses XML for the body, and to its approach to the addition of headers so that messages can evolve over time. SOAP functions at the level of HTTP clients and servers. It does not focus on operating systems, programming languages, or other such issues; therefore, it truly can serve as the foundation for interoperability. Since SOAP is built on HTTP and XML—both simple technologies—it is itself quite simple, much more so than the previous generation of interoperability invocations such as CORBA and DCOM.

Adding WSDL

Once basic communication between disparate systems is available, we can start talking about Web services. Obviously SOAP provides the ability to make the invocation, but SOAP is not sufficient for creating the fabric or the essence of Web services. The next step in the standards process has been the creation of the Web Services Description Language (WSDL) by IBM, Microsoft, and Ariba. WSDL defines an XML grammar for describing network services as collections of communication end points capable of exchanging messages. This grammar describes both document-oriented and procedure-oriented services. WSDL provides definitions both for the abstract notion of the messages and for the protocol specifics required to make the communication possible. All of this is done without limiting message types, protocols, services, or anything else. Using WSDL, one can define the end points of a system that are used for communicating, and aggregate those end points into collections that can be exported out to the world as Web services.

Adding UDDI

The last piece of the puzzle is Universal Description, Discover and Integration (UDDI), also developed by IBM, Microsoft, and Ariba. Successful e-business requires that companies be able to discover each other, make their needs and capabilities known, and integrate services using different processes. The model that UDDI is intended to support is one in which a business can connect to a registry deployed on the Internet to locate other businesses, learn about their capabilities, and continuously discover additional services. UDDI as an initiative defines what is required for supporting such business scenarios. It enables businesses to quickly, easily, and dynamically find and transact with one another. It creates a means by which a business can describe its services and processes and dynamically discover and interact with other businesses, all via the Internet. UDDI is, of course, also based on SOAP,

XML, and HTTP. The actual functions supported by UDDI are described in the UDDI Programmer's API Specification, a document that defines a set of more than 30 SOAP messages used both by publishers of Web services information and by those inquiring about the availability of various Web services. The SOAP messages defined by UDDI allow Web service providers to register themselves within UDDI registries. They also help Web service consumers find service providers that match their specific requirements. Finally, UDDI has a very practical spin. The companies working on UDDI have made a commitment to managing this process not only by creating a standard (a set of documents), but also by implementing a business registry as a central site. Furthermore, they are committed to implementing this registry inside their own core systems, as in the case of WebSphere 4.0.

Let's look at what a UDDI description actually looks like. A UDDI description has four layers to it—the `businessEntity` layer, the `businessService` layer, the `bindingTemplate` layer, and the `tModel` layer. A `businessEntity` consists of elements that provide information about the party publishing the services. Each such party may publish multiple Web services, so a `businessEntity` may be associated with multiple `businessService` entities. Each `businessEntity` describes an entire family of technical services, usually provided via a SOAP messaging interface. A `businessService` entity can be linked with multiple `bindingTemplate` elements, each providing technical information to a service provider about a certain entry point. The `bindingTemplate` elements themselves have references to `tModel` elements, which provide the descriptors and specifications for usage of the service—including various properties that describe the service and can be used for searches and qualification processes.

Figure 37-1 shows an example of the four layers that form the UDDI hierarchy. In this example, ServiceCompany provides various workforce-centric services to its customers. For the sake of this example, assume that ServiceCompany is in the business of managing a workforce of technicians that are used by cable companies, digital dish providers, and DSL providers. ServiceCompany's customers provide these services to the home, but do not themselves have technicians to do the work. Instead, they subcontract the work for the actual dispatch to the home. Since ServiceCompany deals with multiple customers each having different systems, it uses the ViryaNet Service Hub to expose its online feed capture systems as Web services. It therefore publishes a `businessEntity` element that includes all the information about the company itself. This may allow additional providers that are not yet customers of ServiceCompany to discover that ServiceCompany exists, and to ultimately become customers. ServiceCompany has three primary families of Web services, one for each of the three domains it works in (that is, each of the three lines for which it has skilled technicians and online order capturing systems). Finally, within the DSL family, three `bindingTemplates` exist, allowing ServiceCompany's customers to feed requests for DSL installations, repair orders, and cancellations. Each may involve different processes and/or data structures, and these may be defined through the separate `tModel` elements.

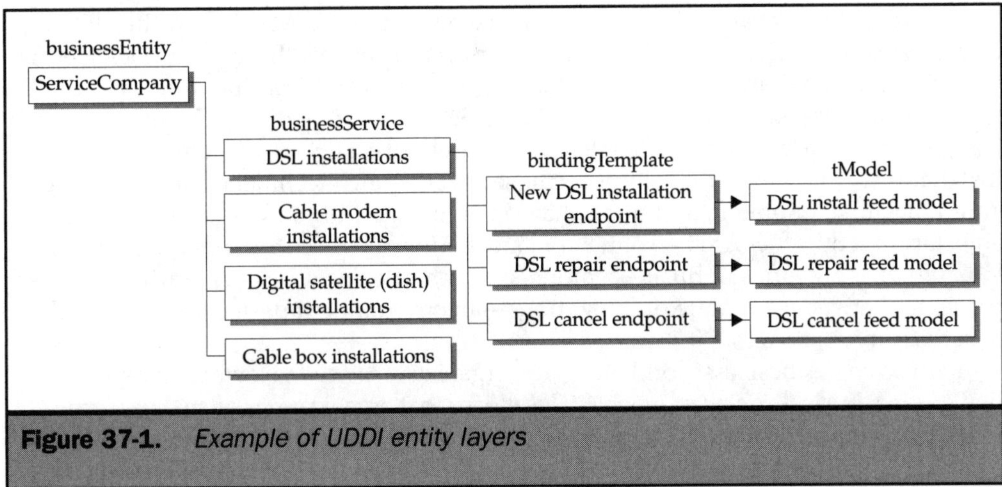

Figure 37-1. *Example of UDDI entity layers*

Support for Web Services in WebSphere

IBM is leading the progress of all three standards described in this chapter—SOAP, WSDL, and UDDI. These three form the IBM service-oriented architecture, as shown in Figure 37-2. As a vendor, IBM is committed to delivering an implementation of each one of these standards within the WebSphere product family, both in terms of development tools and in terms of the runtime system (WebSphere Application Server). Support for SOAP, WSDL and UDDI exists both in WebSphere 4.0 and in new versions of WebSphere Studio and VisualAge for Java. WebSphere is the first comprehensive XML and Web services development environment in the industry to support all three standards.

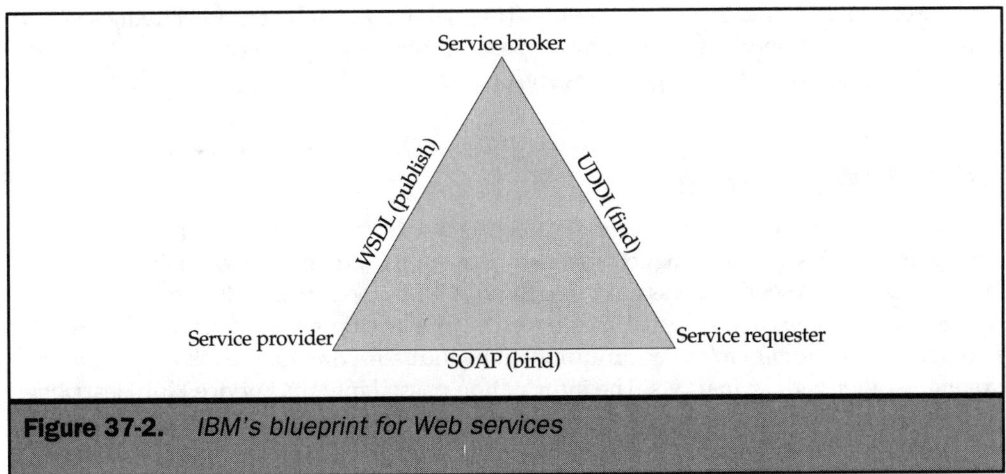

Figure 37-2. *IBM's blueprint for Web services*

The rest of this chapter includes an overview of SOAP, WSDL, and the UDDI mechanism. The goal is to provide a basic understanding of how the three technologies fit together, how they can be used, and what the structures are in each technology set.

The examples are taken from ViryaNet's Service Hub platform. They involve companies that are in the business of service delivery, such as those that perform installations in homes and businesses, those that dispatch technicians for repairing and replacing equipment, and those that manage a distributed workforce of claims adjusters and other service personnel. Businesses in such industries are constantly looking for more efficient business models, which often require cooperative business processes between disparate organizations—an environment perfect for gaining the benefits of Web services.

In the complex business world of service, organizations need to lower costs and find efficient business delivery models. This means that organizations often outsource parts of the service delivery business. For example, some companies will preserve the customer-facing personnel and the customer relationship but will outsource the actual work to other companies that manage the workforce itself. This means that the work information needs to be communicated from one organization to another. In the "old world," this would involve point-to-point integration between various systems, which would be extremely painful. It would involve a lock-in to one workforce-delivering company and would preclude, for example, such models as bidding out the work, working with multiple providers of workforce services, and the notion of workforce marketplaces. Since all of these concepts are the crux of business-to-business (B2B) interactions, and the true enablers of business efficiencies, they are of fundamental interest to the service industry. The examples shown here, therefore, involve the transmission of "service order" information. In one possible scenario, an organization captures order-related information such as the customer location, the required service to be performed, and various entitlement terms (for example, when the service should be provided). Once the company owning the customer relationship captures this information, it communicates with a workforce provider and creates a call entity. This is done by sending a SOAP request—that is, activating a Web service provided by the second company. This Web service is defined in WSDL and discovered through the use of a UDDI registry.

SOAP Messaging

Listing 37-1 shows a SOAP message for creating a service order within the ViryaNet Service Hub. The scenario in which such a document would be used is one in which an external system sends a message to the Service Hub—specifically, to the workforce management system. The external system can be a provisioning system, a trouble ticket management system in the telecommunications industry, or a help desk or call center system in other vertical markets. The information passed into the Service Hub describes the customer, the equipment, and the service that is requested. This data is sent to the workforce management system so that field engineers can be dispatched to the field to work the order.

Listing 37-1 Example SOAP message: request

```
POST /CreateCall HTTP/1.1
Host: virya.viryanet.com
Content-Type: text/xml; charset="utf-8"
Content-Length: 953
SOAPAction:
http://virya.viryanet.com/servlet/ServletBroker?provider=Call&service=createCall

<SOAP-ENV:Envelope
  xmlns:SOAP-ENV="http://schemas.xmlsoap.org/soap/envelope/"
  SOAP-ENV:encodingStyle="http://schemas.xmlsoap.org/soap/encoding/">
  <SOAP-ENV:Body>
     <viryanet:CreateCall xmlns:viryanet="http://virya.viryanet.com/servlet/
          ApiRepository">
          <problemDescription type="STRING">
            <![CDATA[BURNING SMELL]]>
          </problemDescription>
          <warrantyFlag type="BOOLEAN">false</warrantyFlag>
          <subContractorFlag type="BOOLEAN">false</subContractorFlag>
          <replacementTerm type="STRING">
            <![CDATA[123123]]>
          </replacementTerm>
          <equipmentNumber type="STRING">
            <![CDATA[1234]]>
          </equipmentNumber>
          <externalSystemId type="STRING">
            <![CDATA[2143234324]]>
          </externalSystemId>
          <contactName type="STRING">
            <![CDATA[Jane Doe]]>
          </contactName>
          <site type="STRING">
            <![CDATA[ML1]]>
          </site>
          <repeatCallFlag type="BOOLEAN">false</repeatCallFlag>
          <responseOriginalValue type="STRING">
            <![CDATA[12]]>
          </responseOriginalValue>
          <responseTerm type="STRING">
            <![CDATA[1]]>
          </responseTerm>
          <serviceWindowTerm type="STRING">
            <![CDATA[1]]>
          </serviceWindowTerm>
          <centerLogged type="STRING">
            <![CDATA[US East]]>
          </centerLogged>
          <loanOriginalValue type="STRING">
            <![CDATA[12]]>
          </loanOriginalValue>
```

```
<node type="LONG">123213</node>
<overheadPrice type="FLOAT">12.0</overheadPrice>
<contract type="STRING">
  <![CDATA[CONT1]]>
</contract>
<alertColorCode type="STRING">
  <![CDATA[RED]]>
</alertColorCode>
<subContractorContract type="STRING">
  <![CDATA[1]]>
</subContractorContract>
<phoneNumber type="STRING">
  <![CDATA[123-123-1234]]>
</phoneNumber>
<chargeFlag type="BOOLEAN">false</chargeFlag>
<quoteNumber type="INTEGER">1233123123</quoteNumber>
<preventiveMaintenanceCallFlag type="BOOLEAN">
     false
</preventiveMaintenanceCallFlag>
<acceptFlag type="INTEGER">1</acceptFlag>
<bOTag type="STRING">
  <![CDATA[1]]>
</bOTag>
<assetNumber type="STRING">
  <![CDATA[2343214]]>
</assetNumber>
<faultGrade type="STRING">
  <![CDATA[FAULT1]]>
</faultGrade>
<loanUnitOfMeasureCode type="STRING">
  <![CDATA[1]]>
</loanUnitOfMeasureCode>
<loanValue type="STRING">
  <![CDATA[12]]>
</loanValue>
<service type="STRING">
  <![CDATA[24x7]]>
</service>
<responseValue type="STRING">
  <![CDATA[12]]>
</responseValue>
<partRevision type="STRING">
  <![CDATA[1]]>
</partRevision>
<fixOriginalValue type="STRING">
  <![CDATA[12]]>
</fixOriginalValue>
<alsoCreateAction type="BOOLEAN">false</alsoCreateAction>
```

```
<serviceOrderId type="STRING">
  <![CDATA[1]]>
</serviceOrderId>
<fixUnitOfMeasureCode type="STRING">
  <![CDATA[1]]>
</fixUnitOfMeasureCode>
<downtime type="STRING">
  <![CDATA[1]]>
</downtime>
<callStatusCode type="STRING">
  <![CDATA[0]]>
</callStatusCode>
<symptomCode type="STRING">
  <![CDATA[1]]>
</symptomCode>
<quantity type="INTEGER">10</quantity>
<part type="STRING">
  <![CDATA[ROUTER1]]>
</part>
<quoteFlag type="BOOLEAN">false</quoteFlag>
<priority type="INTEGER">1</priority>
<entitlementRemarks type="STRING">
  <![CDATA[scratched]]>
</entitlementRemarks>
<purchaseOrder type="STRING">
  <![CDATA[21384098]]>
</purchaseOrder>
<zip type="STRING">
  <![CDATA[01745]]>
</zip>
<callTypeCode type="STRING">
  <![CDATA[0]]>
</callTypeCode>
<outstandingStatusCode type="BOOLEAN">false</outstandingStatusCode>
<serialNumber type="STRING">
  <![CDATA[3475987435]]>
</serialNumber>
<subContractorPo type="STRING">
  <![CDATA[1]]>
</subContractorPo>
<user type="STRING">
  <![CDATA[rbn]]>
</user>
<cust type="STRING">
  <![CDATA[ML]]>
</cust>
```

```
            <fixValue type="STRING">
              <![CDATA[12]]>
            </fixValue>
            <projectId type="STRING">
              <![CDATA[2134]]>
            </projectId>
            <actualResponseTime type="STRING">
              <![CDATA[17 Nov 2000 7:00]]>
            </actualResponseTime>
            <loanTerm type="STRING">
              <![CDATA[1]]>
            </loanTerm>
            <fixTerm type="STRING">
              <![CDATA[1]]>
            </fixTerm>
            <responseUnitOfMeasureCode type="STRING">
              <![CDATA[1]]>
            </responseUnitOfMeasureCode>
            <clientLog type="STRING">
              <![CDATA[1]]>
            </clientLog>
            <downFlag type="BOOLEAN">false</downFlag>
         </viryanet:CreateCall>
  </SOAP-ENV:Body>
</SOAP-ENV:Envelope>
```

As you can see in Listings 37-1 and 37-2, SOAP messages are usually encapsulated in HTTP requests and responses. The data itself is an XML document and is encapsulated inside an XML envelope defining the routing and messaging information.

Listing 37-2 Example SOAP message: response

```
HTTP/1.1 200 OK
Content-Type: text/xml; charset="utf-8"
Content-Length: 423

<SOAP-ENV:Envelope
  xmlns:SOAP-ENV="http://schemas.xmlsoap.org/soap/envelope/"
  SOAP-ENV:encodingStyle="http://schemas.xmlsoap.org/soap/encoding/">
  <SOAP-ENV:Body>
     <viryanet:CreateCall xmlns:viryanet="http://virya.viryanet.com/servlet/
            ApiRepository">
            <problemDescription type="STRING">
              <![CDATA[BURNING SMELL]]>
            </problemDescription>
            <warrantyFlag type="BOOLEAN">false</warrantyFlag>
            <subContractorFlag type="BOOLEAN">false</subContractorFlag>
            <replacementTerm type="STRING">
```

```
  <![CDATA[123123]]>
</replacementTerm>
<equipmentNumber type="STRING">
  <![CDATA[1234]]>
</equipmentNumber>
<externalSystemId type="STRING">
  <![CDATA[2143234324]]>
</externalSystemId>
<contactName type="STRING">
  <![CDATA[Jane Doe]]>
</contactName>
<site type="STRING">
  <![CDATA[ML1]]>
</site>
<repeatCallFlag type="BOOLEAN">false</repeatCallFlag>
<responseOriginalValue type="STRING">
  <![CDATA[12]]>
</responseOriginalValue>
<responseTerm type="STRING">
  <![CDATA[1]]>
</responseTerm>
<serviceWindowTerm type="STRING">
  <![CDATA[1]]>
</serviceWindowTerm>
<centerLogged type="STRING">
  <![CDATA[US East]]>
</centerLogged>
<loanOriginalValue type="STRING">
  <![CDATA[12]]>
</loanOriginalValue>
<node type="LONG">123213</node>
<overheadPrice type="FLOAT">12.0</overheadPrice>
<contract type="STRING">
  <![CDATA[CONT1]]>
</contract>
<alertColorCode type="STRING">
  <![CDATA[RED]]>
</alertColorCode>
<subContractorContract type="STRING">
  <![CDATA[1]]>
</subContractorContract>
<phoneNumber type="STRING">
  <![CDATA[123-123-1234]]>
</phoneNumber>
<chargeFlag type="BOOLEAN">false</chargeFlag>
<quoteNumber type="INTEGER">1233123123</quoteNumber>
<preventiveMaintenanceCallFlag
```

```
type="BOOLEAN">false</preventiveMaintenanceCallFlag>
          <acceptFlag type="INTEGER">1</acceptFlag>
          <bOTag type="STRING">
            <![CDATA[1]]>
          </bOTag>
          <assetNumber type="STRING">
            <![CDATA[2343214]]>
          </assetNumber>
          <faultGrade type="STRING">
            <![CDATA[FAULT1]]>
          </faultGrade>
          <loanUnitOfMeasureCode type="STRING">
            <![CDATA[1]]>
          </loanUnitOfMeasureCode>
          <loanValue type="STRING">
            <![CDATA[12]]>
          </loanValue>
          <service type="STRING">
            <![CDATA[24x7]]>
          </service>
          <responseValue type="STRING">
            <![CDATA[12]]>
          </responseValue>
          <partRevision type="STRING">
            <![CDATA[1]]>
          </partRevision>
          <fixOriginalValue type="STRING">
            <![CDATA[12]]>
          </fixOriginalValue>
          <alsoCreateAction type="BOOLEAN">false</alsoCreateAction>
          <serviceOrderId type="STRING">
            <![CDATA[1]]>
          </serviceOrderId>
          <fixUnitOfMeasureCode type="STRING">
            <![CDATA[1]]>
          </fixUnitOfMeasureCode>
          <downtime type="STRING">
            <![CDATA[1]]>
          </downtime>
          <callStatusCode type="STRING">
            <![CDATA[0]]>
          </callStatusCode>
          <symptomCode type="STRING">
            <![CDATA[1]]>
          </symptomCode>
          <quantity type="INTEGER">10</quantity>
          <part type="STRING">
```

```
  <![CDATA[ROUTER1]]>
</part>
<quoteFlag type="BOOLEAN">false</quoteFlag>
<priority type="INTEGER">1</priority>
<entitlementRemarks type="STRING">
  <![CDATA[scratched]]>
</entitlementRemarks>
<purchaseOrder type="STRING">
  <![CDATA[21384098]]>
</purchaseOrder>
<zip type="STRING">
  <![CDATA[01745]]>
</zip>
<callTypeCode type="STRING">
  <![CDATA[0]]>
</callTypeCode>
<outstandingStatusCode type="BOOLEAN">
     false
</outstandingStatusCode>
<serialNumber type="STRING">
  <![CDATA[3475987435]]>
</serialNumber>
<subContractorPo type="STRING">
  <![CDATA[1]]>
</subContractorPo>
<user type="STRING">
  <![CDATA[rbn]]>
</user>
<cust type="STRING">
  <![CDATA[ML]]>
</cust>
<fixValue type="STRING">
  <![CDATA[12]]>
</fixValue>
<projectId type="STRING">
  <![CDATA[2134]]>
</projectId>
<actualResponseTime type="STRING">
  <![CDATA[17 Nov 2000 7:00]]>
</actualResponseTime>
<loanTerm type="STRING">
  <![CDATA[1]]>
</loanTerm>
<fixTerm type="STRING">
  <![CDATA[1]]>
</fixTerm>
<responseUnitOfMeasureCode type="STRING">
  <![CDATA[1]]>
```

```
            </responseUnitOfMeasureCode>
            <clientLog type="STRING">
              <![CDATA[1]]>
            </clientLog>
            <downFlag type="BOOLEAN">false</downFlag>
        </viryanet:CreateCall>
        <viryanet:CreateCallResult>
            <date null="" type="NULL"/>
            <status type="STRING">
              <![CDATA[0]]>
            </status>
            <id type="STRING">
              <![CDATA[886]]>
            </id>
        </viryanet:CreateCallResult>
  </SOAP-ENV:Body>
</SOAP-ENV:Envelope>
```

A SOAP message typically has three parts: an envelope, a header, and a body. The envelope and the body are mandatory elements within the SOAP message, while the header is optional. The envelope is the root element of the XML document, and the body is the payload of the message. The body is a child element of the envelope. The header element is a generic mechanism for adding attributes and properties to the message without requiring a prior centralized agreement between communicating parties, or some form of federation for messaging patterns. Header attributes tell recipients how to process the message.

A header in a SOAP message can have various attributes. One of these is the `mustUnderstand` attribute. By tagging a header element with a value of 1 for this attribute, the sender of the message is implying a processing pattern that requires the semantics of that element to be obeyed. If the receiver of the message cannot abide by that directive, it must fail in the processing of the message. Another important attribute for header elements is the `actor` attribute. A SOAP document can be passed from a sender to an ultimate receiver in such a way that it passes through multiple parties, which may or may not do some processing based on the SOAP document. These *actors* may implement simple functions, such as routing, or they may address message semantics. The `actor` attribute allows the tagging of header elements in a way that forces an intermediary to process an element and remove it from the SOAP document.

Encoding of data within a SOAP message is fairly straightforward; it is similar to the encoding used by most information systems, such as databases and object-oriented languages. Types are either primitive or compound; compound elements can be constructed from several parts. This is a recursive structure in which the compound types are made either from other compound types or from primitive types. Eventually everything becomes one big tree, or hierarchy, where the leaf nodes are simple (primitive) types. The types themselves follow the XML Schema methodology and allow the messages to be truly self-describing. This is an assumption that SOAP is built on, but it cannot be called an inherent part of SOAP. SOAP is more focused on the messaging and routing elements. It makes use of XML and the XML Schema for the body of a message, which is often called the *message payload.* Here is an example of the generic encoding method (without the use of a Schema):

```
<SOAP-ENV:Body>
          <ServiceOrder>
               <ID>213408798</ID>
               <CustomerRef>Fleet<CustomerRef>
               <TimeWindow>
                    <From>2001:4:6:13:0:0</From>
                    <To>2001:4:6:15:0:0</To>
               </TimeWindow>
               …
          </ServiceOrder>
</SOAP-ENV:Body>
```


SOAP is not directly related to HTTP. It can be delivered on multiple transports using multiple protocols—not just HTTP. Still, HTTP plays a very central role in the life of SOAP. Remember, the main theme is that of XML over HTTP. So while SOAP messages can be sent over additional protocols (and mail protocols are certainly being used), the most common binding of SOAP to a transport is to HTTP. Therefore, a large part of the SOAP specification document is dedicated to describing how to use SOAP over HTTP.

SOAP makes use of the HTTP headers in many ways, but it adds a few additional headers that are specific to SOAP. A SOAP message in an HTTP request/response pair always uses the `text/xml` content type, as mandated by the SOAP specification. Other than that, most SOAP headers remain the same as HTTP headers. One additional header is the `SOAPAction` header field specifying a uniform resource identifier (URI) that hints at the intent of the message. A SOAP response, including the header, uses the same structure as an HTTP response.

Apart from using general HTTP requests and responses, SOAP also defines an HTTP extension framework. Messages that are sent in this way force the receiver of a SOAP message to manage the processing of the request as a SOAP operation, as opposed to letting the receiver decide what to do with the request. Basically, the difference is the use of an `M-POST` request type instead of a `POST` request type. For example, if the message shown in Listing 37-1 is invoked within the HTTP extension framework, it will appear as shown in Listing 37-3.

Listing 37-3 Service document structure in WSDL

```
M-POST /CreateCall HTTP/1.1
Man: "http://schemas.xmlsoap.org/soap/envelope/"; ns=VN
Content-Type: text/xml; charset="utf-8"
Content-Length: 953
```

```
VN-SOAPAction:
http://virya.viryanet.com/servlet/ServletBroker?provider=Call&service=createCall

<SOAP-ENV:Envelope
  xmlns:SOAP-ENV="http://schemas.xmlsoap.org/soap/envelope/"
  SOAP-ENV:encodingStyle="http://schemas.xmlsoap.org/soap/encoding/">
  <SOAP-ENV:Body>
    <viryanet:CreateCall xmlns:viryanet="http://virya.viryanet.com/servlet/
          ApiRepository">
          <problemDescription type="STRING">
            <![CDATA[BURNING SMELL]]>
          </problemDescription>
          <warrantyFlag type="BOOLEAN">false</warrantyFlag>
          <subContractorFlag type="BOOLEAN">false</subContractorFlag>
          <replacementTerm type="STRING">
            <![CDATA[123123]]>
          </replacementTerm>
          <equipmentNumber type="STRING">
            <![CDATA[1234]]>
          </equipmentNumber>
          <externalSystemId type="STRING">
            <![CDATA[2143234324]]>
          </externalSystemId>
          <contactName type="STRING">
            <![CDATA[Jane Doe]]>
          </contactName>
          <site type="STRING">
            <![CDATA[ML1]]>
          </site>
          <repeatCallFlag type="BOOLEAN">false</repeatCallFlag>
          <responseOriginalValue type="STRING">
            <![CDATA[12]]>
          </responseOriginalValue>
          <responseTerm type="STRING">
            <![CDATA[1]]>
          </responseTerm>
          <serviceWindowTerm type="STRING">
            <![CDATA[1]]>
          </serviceWindowTerm>
          <centerLogged type="STRING">
            <![CDATA[US East]]>
          </centerLogged>
          <loanOriginalValue type="STRING">
            <![CDATA[12]]>
          </loanOriginalValue>
          <node type="LONG">123213</node>
          <overheadPrice type="FLOAT">12.0</overheadPrice>
```

```
<contract type="STRING">
  <![CDATA[CONT1]]>
</contract>
<alertColorCode type="STRING">
  <![CDATA[RED]]>
</alertColorCode>
<subContractorContract type="STRING">
  <![CDATA[1]]>
</subContractorContract>
<phoneNumber type="STRING">
  <![CDATA[123-123-1234]]>
</phoneNumber>
<chargeFlag type="BOOLEAN">false</chargeFlag>
<quoteNumber type="INTEGER">1233123123</quoteNumber>
<preventiveMaintenanceCallFlag type="BOOLEAN">
     false
</preventiveMaintenanceCallFlag>
<acceptFlag type="INTEGER">1</acceptFlag>
<bOTag type="STRING">
  <![CDATA[1]]>
</bOTag>
<assetNumber type="STRING">
  <![CDATA[2343214]]>
</assetNumber>
<faultGrade type="STRING">
  <![CDATA[FAULT1]]>
</faultGrade>
<loanUnitOfMeasureCode type="STRING">
  <![CDATA[1]]>
</loanUnitOfMeasureCode>
<loanValue type="STRING">
  <![CDATA[12]]>
</loanValue>
<service type="STRING">
  <![CDATA[24x7]]>
</service>
<responseValue type="STRING">
  <![CDATA[12]]>
</responseValue>
<partRevision type="STRING">
  <![CDATA[1]]>
</partRevision>
<fixOriginalValue type="STRING">
  <![CDATA[12]]>
</fixOriginalValue>
<alsoCreateAction type="BOOLEAN">false</alsoCreateAction>
<serviceOrderId type="STRING">
  <![CDATA[1]]>
```

```
</serviceOrderId>
<fixUnitOfMeasureCode type="STRING">
  <![CDATA[1]]>
</fixUnitOfMeasureCode>
<downtime type="STRING">
  <![CDATA[1]]>
</downtime>
<callStatusCode type="STRING">
  <![CDATA[0]]>
</callStatusCode>
<symptomCode type="STRING">
  <![CDATA[1]]>
</symptomCode>
<quantity type="INTEGER">10</quantity>
<part type="STRING">
  <![CDATA[ROUTER1]]>
</part>
<quoteFlag type="BOOLEAN">false</quoteFlag>
<priority type="INTEGER">1</priority>
<entitlementRemarks type="STRING">
  <![CDATA[scratched]]>
</entitlementRemarks>
<purchaseOrder type="STRING">
  <![CDATA[21384098]]>
</purchaseOrder>
<zip type="STRING">
  <![CDATA[01745]]>
</zip>
<callTypeCode type="STRING">
  <![CDATA[0]]>
</callTypeCode>
<outstandingStatusCode type="BOOLEAN">
     false
</outstandingStatusCode>
<serialNumber type="STRING">
  <![CDATA[3475987435]]>
</serialNumber>
<subContractorPo type="STRING">
  <![CDATA[1]]>
</subContractorPo>
<user type="STRING">
  <![CDATA[rbn]]>
</user>
<cust type="STRING">
  <![CDATA[ML]]>
</cust>
<fixValue type="STRING">
  <![CDATA[12]]>
</fixValue>
<projectId type="STRING">
```

```
            <![CDATA[2134]]>
          </projectId>
          <actualResponseTime type="STRING">
            <![CDATA[17 Nov 2000 7:00]]>
          </actualResponseTime>
          <loanTerm type="STRING">
            <![CDATA[1]]>
          </loanTerm>
          <fixTerm type="STRING">
            <![CDATA[1]]>
          </fixTerm>
          <responseUnitOfMeasureCode type="STRING">
            <![CDATA[1]]>
          </responseUnitOfMeasureCode>
          <clientLog type="STRING">
            <![CDATA[1]]>
          </clientLog>
          <downFlag type="BOOLEAN">false</downFlag>
      </viryanet:CreateCall>
  </SOAP-ENV:Body>
</SOAP-ENV:Envelope>
```

WSDL

WSDL is an XML format used for describing services on the Web. It views a service as a set of end points invoked by client applications that send and receive XML documents. WSDL describes services both in an abstract manner and as concrete implementations. Since WSDL follows the same general pattern as SOAP, the WSDL specification describes how WSDL can be used in a SOAP environment. While WSDL is not limited to use with SOAP, WDSL is protocol- and platform-agnostic, so chances are that people writing software that conforms to WSDL are probably using SOAP.

Abstractions in WSDL

WSDL describes seven abstractions—types, messages, operations, port types, bindings, ports, and services. A service is the entity that is the focus of WSDL, and the purpose of a WSDL document is to describe the structure of a service. A *service* is described as a collection of ports that represent network end points—that is, routines that can communicate over the Web to request and provide the service. A *port* is defined as an address on the Web combined with a binding as the concrete protocol and data format that is supported by the end point. The binding is described by a more abstract entity—the *port type*—which is defined as a collection of operations. The data being exchanged by the end points is also described in an abstract manner by messages. Finally, the definition of the data being passed within a message is encapsulated within type definitions.

Types in WSDL are described according to the XML Schema specification. WSDL defines a set of specific bindings in addition to the general binding method. The extensions of concrete bindings are for SOAP, HTTP GET and POST requests, and Multipurpose Internet Mail Extensions (MIME).

Listing 37-4 shows the canonical service document structure as defined by the WSDL specification.

Listing 37-4 Canonical WSDL document

```
<wsdl:definitions name="nmtoken"? targetNamespace="uri"?>

    <import namespace="uri" location="uri"/>*

    <wsdl:documentation/> ?

    <wsdl:types> ?
        <wsdl:documentation/>?
        <xsd:schema/>*
        extensibility element --> *
    </wsdl:types>

    <wsdl:message name="nmtoken> *
        <wsdl:documentation/>?
        <part name="nmtoken" element="qname"? type="qname"?/> *
    </wsdl:message>

    <wsdl:portType name="nmtoken">*
        <wsdl:documentation/>?
        <wsdl:operation name="nmtoken">*
           <wsdl:documentation/> ?
           <wsdl:input name="nmtoken"? message="qname">?
               <wsdl:documentation/> ?
           </wsdl:input>
           <wsdl:output name="nmtoken"? message="qname">?
               <wsdl:documentation/> ?
           </wsdl:output>
           <wsdl:fault name="nmtoken" message="qname"> *
               <wsdl:documentation/> ?
           </wsdl:fault>
        </wsdl:operation>
    </wsdl:portType>

    <wsdl:binding name="nmtoken" type="qname">*
        <wsdl:documentation/>?
```

```
        extensibility element --> *
        <wsdl:operation name="nmtoken">*
           <wsdl:documentation/> ?
           extensibility element --> *
           <wsdl:input name="nmtoken"?> ?
               <wsdl:documentation/> ?
               extensibility element -->
           </wsdl:input>
           <wsdl:output name="nmtoken"?> ?
               <wsdl:documentation/> ?
               extensibility element --> *
           </wsdl:output>
           <wsdl:fault name="nmtoken"> *
               <wsdl:documentation/> ?
               extensibility element --> *
           </wsdl:fault>
        </wsdl:operation>
    </wsdl:binding>

    <wsdl:service name="nmtoken"> *
        <wsdl:documentation/>?
        <wsdl:port name="nmtoken" binding="qname"> *
           <wsdl:documentation/> ?
           extensibility element -->
        </wsdl:port>
        extensibility element -->
    </wsdl:service>

    extensibility element --> *

</wsdl:definitions>
```

Listing 37-5 shows an example of a WSDL document that describes the order creation service in ViryaNet's Service Hub platform. Note that services are defined using five major element categories:

- **Types** Define the data types used in the messages
- **Messages** Logically define what is transmitted between the end points
- **Port types** Specify the abstraction of the operation
- **Bindings** Define the concrete protocol and data format
- **Ports** Specify the address for the binding

Finally, there is the service definition itself, which aggregates all of the above.

Listing 37-5 WSDL definition for a createCall message

```
<?xml version="1.0"?>
<definitions name="Call"

   targetNamespace=
    "http://virya.viryanet.com/servlet/ApiRepository/call.wsdl"
   xmlns:tns=
    "http://virya.viryanet.com/servlet/ApiRepository/call.xsd"
   xmlns:xsd_vn=
    "http://virya.viryanet.com/servlet/ApiRepository/call.wsdl"
   xmlns:soap="http://schemas.xmlsoap.org/wsdl/soap/"
   xmlns="http://schemas.xmlsoap.org/wsdl/">

   <types>
       <schema targetNamespace="http://virya.viryanet.com/servlet/
           ApiRepository/call.wsdl"
              xmlns="http://www.w3.org/1999/XMLSchema">
           <element name="CallRequest">
              <complexType>
                <all>
                  <element name="problemDescription " type="string"/>
                  <element name="warrantyFlag" type="boolean"/>
                  <element name="subContractorFlag" type="boolean"/>
                  <element name="replacementTerm" type="string"/>
                  <element name="equipmentNumber" type="string"/>
                  <element name="externalSystemId" type="string"/>
                  <element name="contactName" type="string"/>
                  <element name="site" type="string"/>
                  <element name="repeatCallFlag" type="string"/>
                  <element name="responseOriginalValue" type="string"/>
                  <element name="responseTerm" type="string"/>
                  <element name="serviceWindowTerm" type="string"/>
                  <element name="centerLogged" type="string"/>
                  <element name="loanOriginalValue" type="string"/>
                  <element name="node" type="long"/>
                  <element name="overheadPrice" type="float"/>
                  <element name="contract" type="string"/>
                  <element name="alertColorCode" type="string"/>
                  <element name="subContractorContract" type="string"/>
                  <element name="phoneNumber" type="string"/>
                  <element name="chargeFlag" type="boolean"/>
                  <element name="quoteNumber" type="integer"/>
                  <element name="acceptFlag" type="integer"/>
                  <element name="bOTag" type="string"/>
                  <element name="assetNumber" type="string"/>
                  <element name="faultGrade" type="string"/>
                  <element name="loanUnitOfMeasureCode" type="string"/>
                  <element name="loanValue" type="string"/>
```

```
              <element name="service" type="string"/>
              <element name="responseValue" type="string"/>
              <element name="partRevision" type="string"/>
              <element name="fixOriginalValue" type="string"/>
              <element name="alsoCreateAction" type="boolean"/>
              <element name="serviceOrderId" type="string"/>
              <element name="fixUnitOfMeasureCode" type="string"/>
              <element name="downtime" type="string"/>
              <element name="callStatusCode" type="string"/>
              <element name="symptomCode" type="string"/>
              <element name="quantity" type="integer"/>
              <element name="part" type="string"/>
              <element name="quoteFlag" type="boolean"/>
              <element name="priority" type="integer"/>
              <element name="entitlementRemarks" type="string"/>
              <element name="purchaseOrder" type="string"/>
              <element name="purchaseOrder" type="string"/>
              <element name="zip" type="string"/>
              <element name="callTypeCode" type="string"/>
              <element name="outstandingStatusCode" type="string"/>
              <element name="serialNumber" type="string"/>
              <element name="subContractorPo" type="string"/>
              <element name="user" type="string"/>
              <element name="cust" type="string"/>
              <element name="fixValue" type="string"/>
              <element name="projectId" type="string"/>
              <element name="actualResponseTime" type="string"/>
              <element name="loanTerm" type="string"/>
              <element name="fixTerm" type="string"/>
              <element name="loanTerm" type="string"/>
              <element name="clientLog" type="string"/>
              <element name="downFlag" type="boolean"/>
            </all>
          </complexType>
        </element>
  <element name="CallResponse">
          <complexType>
            <all>
              <element name="date" type="string"/>
              <element name="status" type="string"/>
              <element name="id" type="string"/>
            </all>
          </complexType>
        </element>

    </schema>
</types>

<message name="InputCall">
```

USING XML

```
          <part name="body" element="xsd_vn:CallRequest"/>
     </message>

     <message name="OutputCall">
          <part name="body" element="xsd_vn:Response"/>
     </message>

     <portType name="CreateCallPortType">
          <operation name="CreateCall">
             <input message="InputCall"/>
             <output message="OutputCall"/>
          </operation>
     </portType>

     <portType name="UpdateCallPortType">
          <operation name="CreateCall">
             <input message="InputCall"/>
             <output message="OutputCall"/>
          </operation>
     </portType>

      <binding name="CreateCallSoapBinding" type="CreateCallType">
          <soap:binding style="document"
transport="http://schemas.xmlsoap.org/soap/http"/>
          <operation name="CreateCall">
             <soap:operation soapAction=
             "http://virya.viryanet.com/servlet/
             ServletBroker?provider=Call&service=createCall"/>
             <input>
                 <soap:body use="literal" namespace="
http://virya.viryanet.com/servlet/ApiRepository/call.xsd"

encodingStyle="http://schemas.xmlsoap.org/soap/encoding/"/>
             </input>
             <output>
                 <soap:body use="literal" namespace="
http://virya.viryanet.com/servlet/ApiRepository/call.xsd"

encodingStyle="http://schemas.xmlsoap.org/soap/encoding/"/>
             </output>
          </operation>
      </binding>

      <binding name="UpdateCallSoapBinding" type="UpdateCallType">
          <soap:binding style="document"
transport="http://schemas.xmlsoap.org/soap/http"/>
          <operation name="CreateCall">
             <soap:operation soapAction="
             http://virya.viryanet.com/servlet/
```

```
           ServletBroker?provider=Call&service=updateCall"/>
           <input>
               <soap:body use="literal" namespace="http://virya.
                viryanet.com/servlet/ApiRepository/call.xsd"

encodingStyle="http://schemas.xmlsoap.org/soap/encoding/"/>
           </input>
           <output>
               <soap:body use="literal" namespace="
http://virya.viryanet.com/servlet/ApiRepository/call.xsd"

encodingStyle="http://schemas.xmlsoap.org/soap/encoding/"/>
           </output>
        </operation>
    </binding>

    <service name="CallService">
        <documentation>Call creation/update service</documentation>
        <port name="CreateCallPort" binding="tns:CreateCallSoapBinding ">
           <soap:address location="http://virya.viryanet.com/
                 servlet/ServletBroker"/>
        </port>
        <port name="UpdateCallPort" binding="tns:UpdateCallSoapBinding ">
           <soap:address location="http://virya.viryanet.com/
                 servlet/ServletBroker"/>
        </port>

    </service>

</definitions>
```

Types in WSDL

Types in WSDL are XML Schema types. A message consists of one or more logical parts, each one having a type. Message parts have a name and an element; the `element` attribute specifies a type that is defined in the document. Messages therefore define the abstractions in terms of the data types used in communication between the two systems. Recall that a port type is a named set of abstract operations and messages. Each port type has a name and some optional attributes, such as an attribute that defines whether or not the end point can support one-way, request-response, solicit-response, or notification type communications.

If the port type defines a one-way operation, the definition will take this form:

```
<wsdl:portType>
          <wsdl:operation name="createCall">
               <wsdl:input .../>
          </wsdl:operation>
</wsdl:portType>
```

If the port type defines a request-response or a solicit-response operation, the definition will take this form:

```
<wsdl:portType>
          <wsdl:operation name="createCall">
               <wsdl:input … />
               <wsdl:output … />
               <wsdl:fault … />
          </wsdl:operation>
</wsdl:portType>
```

If the port type defines a notification operation, the definition will take this form:

```
<wsdl:portType>
          <wsdl:operation name="createCall">
               <wsdl:output …/>
          </wsdl:operation>
</wsdl:portType>
```

Bindings describe the message formats and protocol details for operations and messages defined by a particular port type. There may be numerous bindings for a single port type. Ports are the physical end point descriptors, and they specify the physical location from which the service can be received. Finally, services group a set of related ports together, and effectively define a domain where a service is provided.

The SOAP Binding in WSDL

Since WSDL is in many ways so close to SOAP, the WSDL specification has a special section describing a SOAP binding. The SOAP-specific definitions include a way to specify that an operation is bound to SOAP, a way to specify an address for a SOAP end point, a way to use a `SOAPAction` URL in an operation definition, a set of definitions for headers that are transmitted as part of a SOAP envelope, and a way of specifying SOAP roots in XSD. Each of these specifications makes use of a SOAP namespace. For example, a SOAP binding element can specify the fact that SOAP is being used as the underlying protocol. In this case, the WSDL binding section will take the following form:

```
<binding … >
          <soap:binding … />
</binding>
```

In the same way, when an operation is defined using the SOAP extension, the operation takes this form:

```
<operation … >
         <soap:operation soapAction="…" … />
</operation>
```

Another part of the WSDL specification defines an HTTP GET/POST binding, which allows for a more primitive implementation. Here, HTTP is used for the messaging transport, and the service definer can specify a binding using HTTP GET or HTTP POST, specify that the port is implemented as an HTTP end point, and specify an address for each operation relative to the HTTP end point.

UDDI

UDDI defines a way to publish and discover information about Web services. UDDI defines infrastructure that is absolutely mandatory for the development of e-commerce, collaborative marketplaces, and other online business operations. UDDI primarily is a tool for developers and designers, and it is a relatively low-level definition that helps standardize how services can be defined and discovered. UDDI is, therefore, complementary to WSDL and SOAP in the sense that it is fairly logical to see the definitions themselves defined in WSDL, activated with SOAP, but registered and discovered with UDDI.

The focus of UDDI is the registration and discovery of services. UDDI relies on the existence of a distributed registry that is implemented in XML and accessed with XML. UDDI business registration is done with an XML file that describes a business entity and its associated Web services. There are three parts to such a definition, which are equivalent to real world services provided by white pages—allowing address and contact information to be discovered, yellow pages—allowing categorizations, and green pages—exposing technical information about services that are being published. All of this information is maintained within the UDDI registry on the Web. UDDI defines XML standards that allow developers to register information within the registry, and also to discover and use information stored within the registry. In a typical scenario using UDDI, one party registers information about the Web services supported in a system. The information is added to the UDDI registry, either through a Web site or by means of tools that make use of the programmatic APIs defined by the UDDI specification. (We will discuss this further, in the context of WebSphere 4.0, in Chapter 38.) The UDDI registry is logically one database, but physically may be (and usually is) distributed through sets of physical registries; after all, it has to scale well. UDDI does not focus on the discovery stage per se, and does not mean to replace search engines and portals. It merely defines the structure through which such programs can look up information.

Structures in UDDI

Technically, UDDI consists of an XML Schema (or XSD) for SOAP messages and a definition of APIs for performing the UDDI operations themselves. The Schema definitions allow a programmer to define business information, service information, binding information, and information about specifications for services. Business information takes the form of the `businessEntity` element, which supports "yellow pages" taxonomies so that searches can be performed. Substructures of the `businessEntity` element also define the information required to support "green pages"-type functions. Service information is described by the `businessService` element. Such elements are higher-level elements—within each one of the `businessService` elements, for example, many Web service descriptors can exist. Such an element allows segmentation and categorization at a higher level. The `bindingTemplate` element allows programmers to provide information about the addresses through which a Web service can be contacted.

A `businessEntity` structure typically represents information about a business and the services it offers. This includes the business name, a unique identifier for the business, a description of the business entity, contact information, and most important, a list of supported `businessServices`. A `businessService` has a name and a description, a unique key, and most importantly, a list of `bindingTemplates`. Each `bindingTemplate` has a set of descriptors and a required element called `accessPoint`, which describes the access end point (for example, an http: URL or a mailto: URL). This element also points to the `tModel` entity, which defines the actual technical fingerprint of the service.

As for the UDDI API itself, it is a SOAP-based API, meaning that every invocation takes the form of a SOAP message. The invocation typically defines which function is requested. This request is passed to a UDDI registry provider that replies with a SOAP document. The API consists of over 30 SOAP messages, which can be partitioned into three groups:

- **Browse APIs** These APIs find elements and the information associated with entries in a UDDI registry. This category consists of find_xx APIs.
- **Drill-down APIs** These are the elements in a UDDI registry that are organized into hierarchies. Once we can find elements using the find_xx APIs, we can further navigate the hierarchy using get_xx APIs.
- **Publishing APIs** These allow programmers and systems to manage the information stored in a UDDI registry.

Summary

Now that you have an understanding of the Web services model and its underlying technologies (SOAP, WSDL, and UDDI), you are ready to go to the next chapter. It describes the set of tools available to WebSphere developers for the development, as well as the deployment of Web Services on the WebSphere Application Server.

Chapter 38

Deploying Web Services on WebSphere

IBM is one of the most dominant players in the push for Web services. It is not surprising, therefore, that much of the Web services work done by IBM has been incorporated into its flagship product, WebSphere. As of WebSphere version 4.0, support for Web services is incorporated into every level. This means that a few of the Web Services libraries come with the WebSphere Application Server—specifically, the Apache SOAP (Simple Object Access Protocol) and UDDI4J libraries, which are used for implementing Web services, servicing calls made with SOAP, making calls to other Web services, and allowing applications deployed over WebSphere to interact with Universal Description, Discovery and Integration (UDDI) registries—both for discovering as well as publishing services.

The support provided for Web services within WebSphere focuses on deployment aspects only. The focus on tools and developer productivity is part of WebSphere Studio, which includes a Web Services Description Language (WSDL) generator. These tools, which were originally packaged as Web Services Toolkit (still available through AlphaWorks), have been improved and repackaged as part of WebSphere Studio. They work with WebSphere 4.0 (actually, they also work with WebSphere 3.5), as well as with a number of UDDI repositories.

This chapter focuses on the deployment aspects of WebSphere and describes a full process in which a JAR file implementing an important business function is exposed as a Web service deployed on a WebSphere server.

The Scheduling Service

The example used as our Web service involves an important business function from the realm of workforce management. A brief description of the service is offered here because it is important that you see a real use of Web services in a real business context. We have been disappointed and frustrated by the fact that almost every example we see of Web services is some permutation of the stock-quote function. You might get the impression reading through the trade press that this is all Web services are good for, which of course is not true.

The example used in this chapter is taken from a real application called the ViryaNet Service Hub, which publishes its core capabilities as XML-enabled application programming interfaces (APIs) and Web services.

The service that will be deployed as a Web service in this example is a scheduling service. The input to the service is a set of tasks that have to be performed within a day.

(The general problem is not limited to a single day, but that simplification is used here.) Each task has a location where the service needs to be provided. Think of this as a place where something needs to be installed or something needs to be fixed. Each task also has an appointment window that includes a start and end time that define when our resource should be on site. The other input to the system is a set of resources—usually field personnel. Each resource has a home location and a set of availability constraints that define when the resource can perform work. The output of the service is a list of assignments of tasks to resources. The list also includes a sequencing telling each resource the order in which it should perform the tasks assigned to it. The goal is to find an efficient assignment that minimizes travel time while conforming to all kinds of constraints that may be applicable. Different schedules imply different costs to the business, and a good scheduling algorithm can result in huge savings.

The scheduling service is a good example of a function that should be deployed as a Web service. The problem at hand is difficult; in fact, it is really a more complex version of the traveling salesman problem, which is known to be *NP-complete*. NP-completeness is one of the central concepts in complexity theory. A problem is considered to be in the NP class of problems for which if, given a solution, a polynomial algorithm exists to determine whether it is valid. A problem is NP-complete if the algorithm can be used for any other problem in NP. Note that the polynomial algorithm is used only for verifying a solution, not for finding one. For most of us practical folks, this is not very meaningful. However, because of the "completeness," and due to the fact that thousands of the best minds working on thousands of such NP-complete problems have never been able to comeup with a fast algorithm for finding the optimal solution, we can assume that no algorithm that solves this problem probably will not provide the optimal solution in every case, but can employ heuristics to get good solutions. The algorithm is something that is therefore of great value, is difficult to build, and is worth much to a potential small business—which often would not have the resources to build such an algorithm in-house. What better way to provide value than to offer the creation of such an algorithm as a service through a central site, where customers can easily submit their problem data and get a good schedule that they can then use for the workday? This service is certainly something that would be worth paying for.

Figures 38-1 and 38-2 show two possible assignment schedules for a given day with 30 resources. Figure 38-1 shows the driving pattern of an assignment solution that does not employ smart optimization heuristics. Each shaded line represents the driving route of a single resource, and the points on the route represent the locations of the tasks. Figure 38-2 shows the same set of tasks handled by the same set of resources,

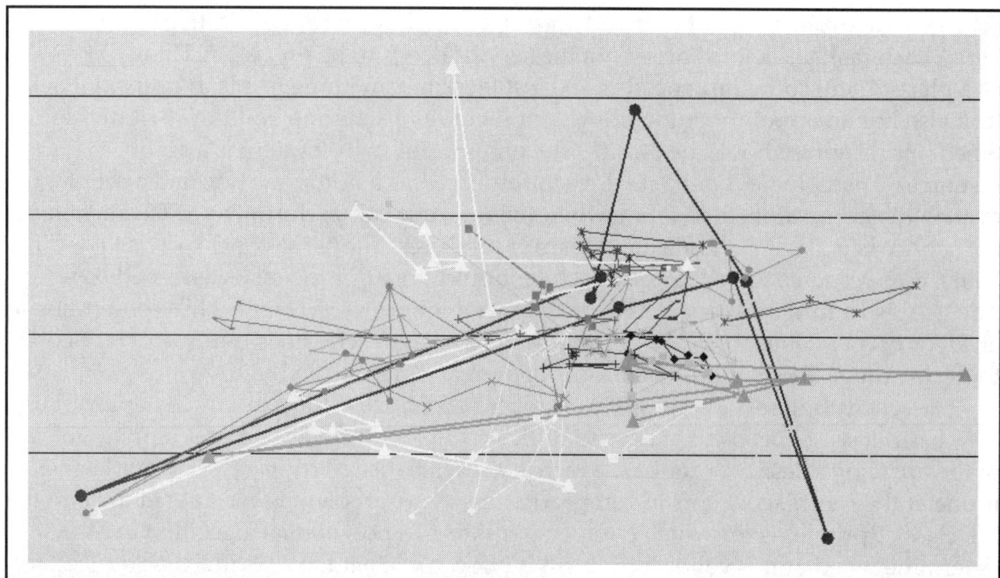

Figure 38-1. *Travel routes before applying an optimizing scheduling algorithm*

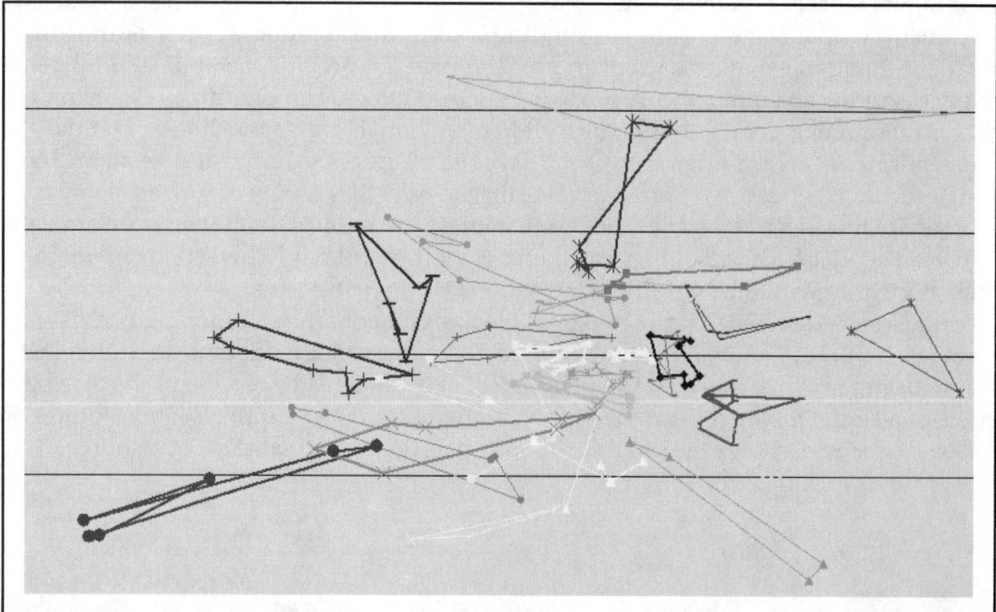

Figure 38-2. *Travel routes after applying an optimizing scheduling algorithm*

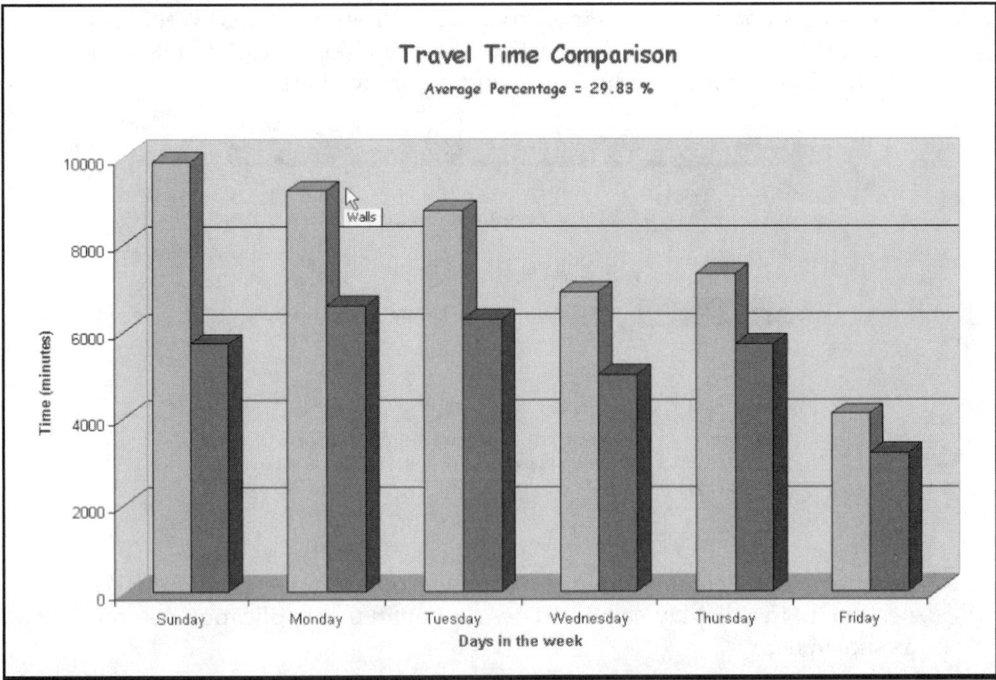

Figure 38-3. *Savings in travel time (and thus total work time) achieved with the use of an optimizing scheduling algorithm*

but here the scheduling algorithm makes use of smart heuristics. As you can see by the bar graph in Figure 38-3, the difference in productivity achieved with an optimizing scheduling algorithm can be as much as 25 percent—meaning that the business can either cut its payroll by 25 percent or do much more work using the same cost structure. In any case, this translates to a huge cost savings that would easily justify the price of using such a Web service.

Building the EAR/WAR

We will forego discussing the details of the algorithm, because it is very complex and highly proprietary. Assume that we have packaged the scheduling algorithm as a set of Java classes packaged in a Java Archive (JAR) file. The first thing we need to do in exposing this as a Web service in WebSphere is to deploy it as an application and a Web module.

1. To open the application assembly tool, select Programs | IBM WebSphere | Application Server v4.0 | Application Assembly Tool. Next, double-click the Application option from the entry window, shown here:

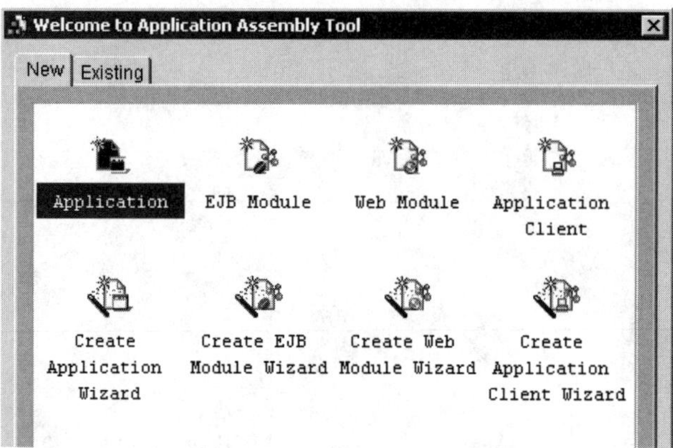

2. Because you are creating a new Enterprise Application Archive (EAR), you need to fill in a display name and description in the Application Assembly Tool, as shown here:

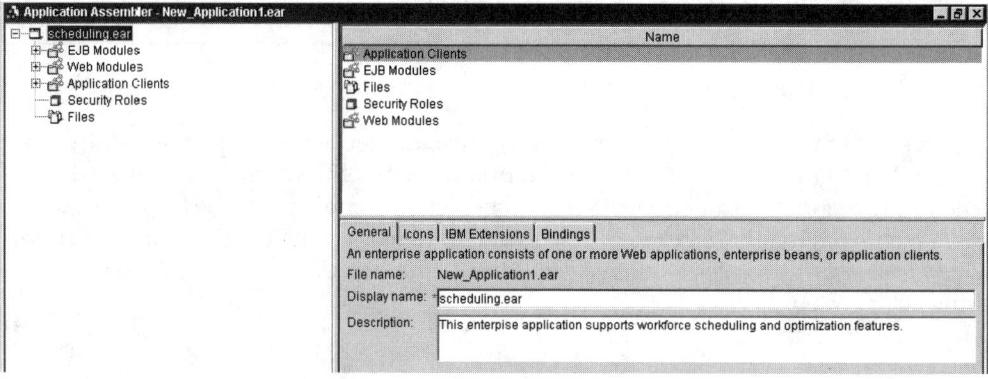

3. Within the EAR, you need to add the appropriate Java classes. You therefore need to add the right JAR file to the EAR. Right-click the Files submenu, and select Add Files:

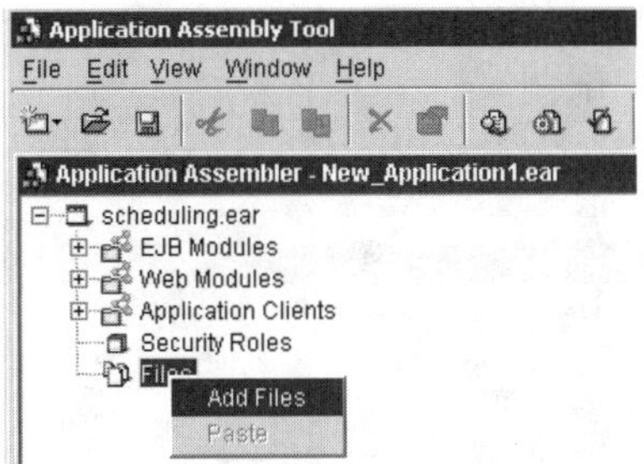

4. In the Add Files dialog box, select the *scheduling.jar* file to add. The end result of selecting the JAR file is shown in Figure 38-4.
5. Now you create a new Web module by selecting File | New | Web Module. The new Web module includes a set of servlets and JSPs. Set the classpath for this Web module by entering the path in the Classpath field.

   The Web module is not directly related to the invocation of the Web service, but a true scheduling package requires more than just the service. It will include an interface where the user can view and modify the assignments, see outstanding tasks, and view locations. Figure 38-5 shows an example of such a user interface; it includes a dispatch board that a dispatcher can use to view a Gantt chart indicating who is doing what along with maps upon which tasks and resources can be overlaid.

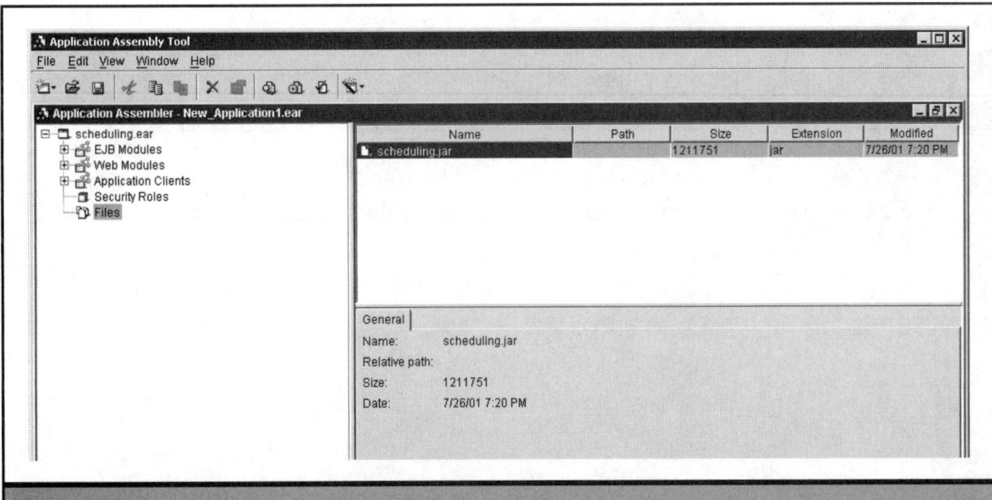

Figure 38-4. *JAR file within the EAR description*

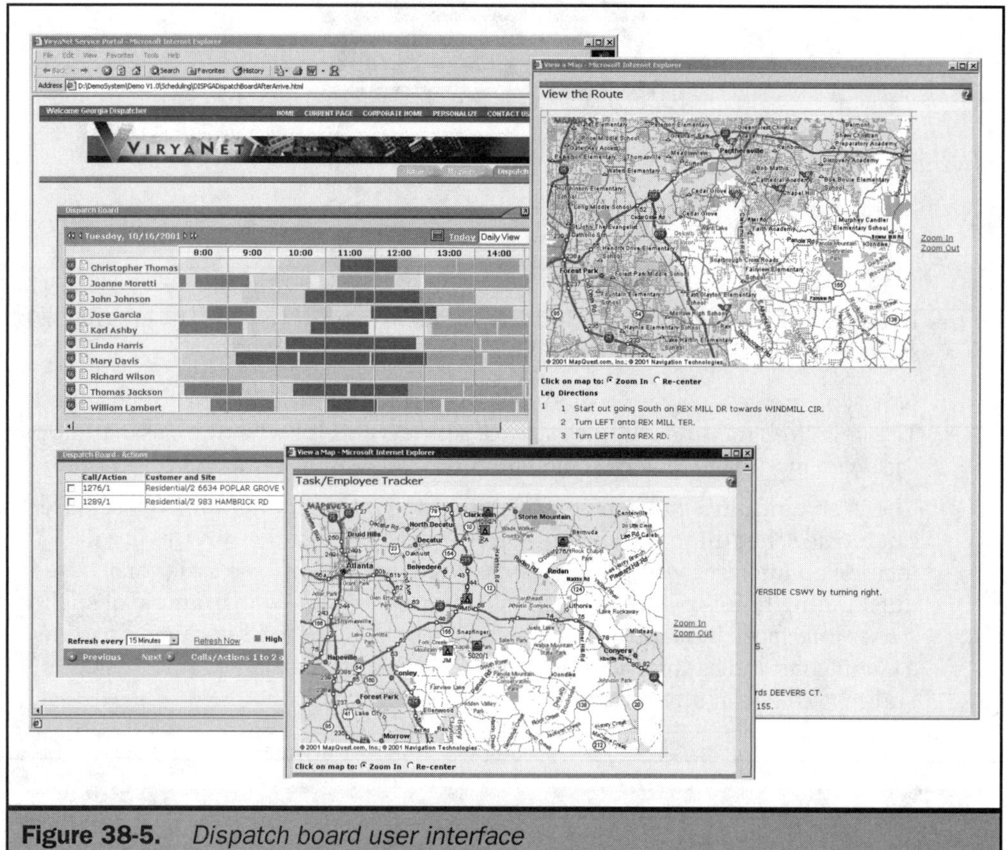

Figure 38-5. *Dispatch board user interface*

6. Next, you need to define a set of JSPs and servlets and add them as part of the Web module:

New Web Component
General | Icons
A Web component is a servlet or JavaServer Pages (JSP) file. Servlets and JSP files typically execute in a Web server, generating dynamic content in response to requests from Web clients.
Component name: DispatchBoard
Display name: Dispatch Board
Description:
Component Type
Servlet
Class name: Browse...
JSP
JSP file: DispatchBoard.jsp Browse...
Load on startup: 1 priority
OK Apply Cancel Help

7. When you have finished, you can save the newly created Web Application Archive (WAR), close it, and return to the EAR. Back in the EAR, you need to import the Web module by right-clicking Web Modules in the directory tree and selecting Import. The Confirm Values dialog box opens, as shown here:

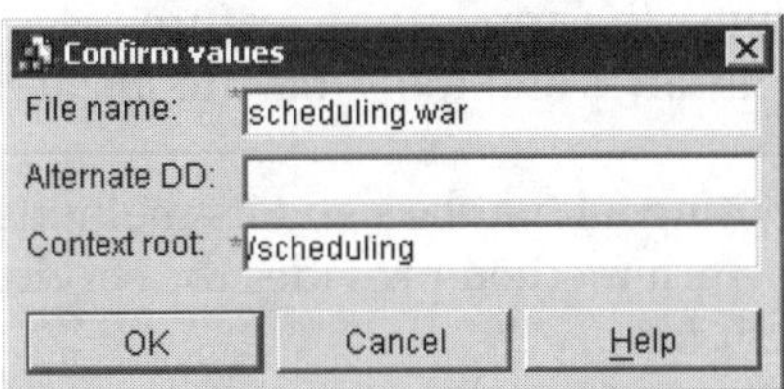

8. If all goes well, the Web module becomes part of your enterprise application, as shown in Figure 38-6, and you can save the EAR.

You're all done. You have wrapped the algorithm within an EAR (along with the user interface components), and you are ready to move on to create the SOAP wrapper and then install it on the WebSphere server for use as a Web service.

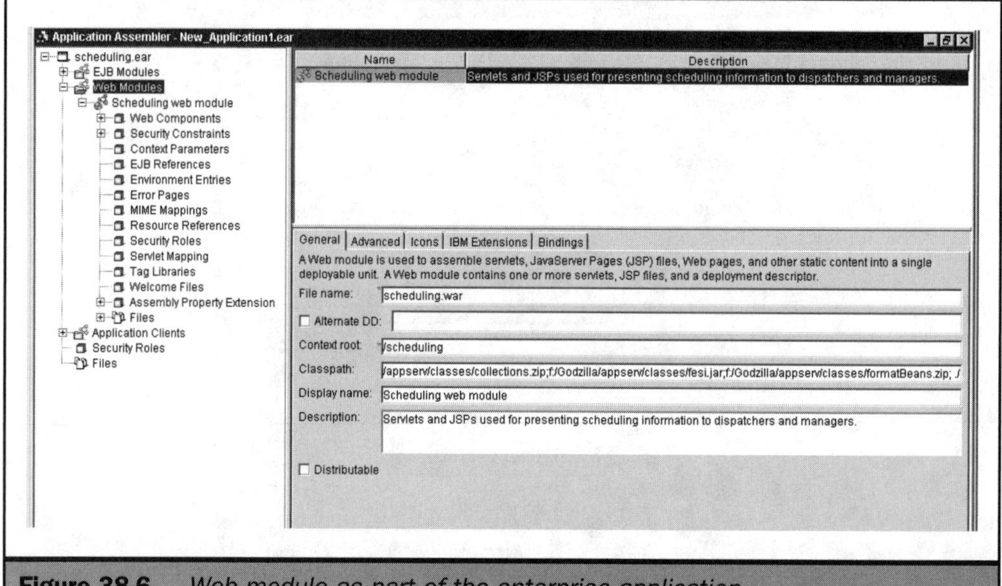

Figure 38-6. *Web module as part of the enterprise application*

Creating the SOAP Deployment Descriptor

To enable your server to expose the application features as a Web service, you need to create the SOAP layer. The libraries and tools that are installed as part of WebSphere make this easy to do.

In this case, you are exposing a Java class and its methods. Therefore, you need to specify which class and which method provides the service. You do this with the following deployment descriptor:

```
<isd:service
   xmlns:isd="http://xml.apache.org/xml-soap/deployment"
   id="urn:viryanet-advanced-scheduling">
      <isd:provider
         type="java"
         scope="application"
         methods="runAdvancedScheduling">
     <isd:java class="com.rts.scheduling.AdvancedScheduling"/>
      </isd:provider>
```

```
        <isd:faultListener>
            org.apache.soap.server.DOMFaultListener
        </isd:faultListener>
</isd:service>
```

The deployment descriptor is part of the Apache SOAP package. *Deployment descriptors* are XML documents that provide information to the SOAP runtime about the services that are available to client invocations. The exact content depends on the *artifact* that provides the service. For example, the deployment descriptor for an Enterprise JavaBeans (EJB) server providing the service will have `isd:option` elements in the `isd:provider` element. For a quick introduction to deployment descriptors, see *http://xml.apache.org/soap/docs/guide/deploy.html*.

After the deployment descriptor is ready, you need to run the *SoapEarEnabler* tool. This tool is part of the WebSphere distribution, and it exists in *WAS_HOME/AppServer/bin*. Running the tool for your EAR is simple enough, and the console session is shown here:

```
IBM WebSphere Application Server Release 4
SOAP Enterprise Archive enabler tool.
Copyright IBM Corp.,1997-2001

Please enter the name of your ear file:
f:\Godzilla\appserv\classes\scheduling.ear

***Backing up EAR file to: f:\Godzilla\appserv\classes\scheduling.ear~

How many services would you like your application to contain (1...n)?1

Now prompting for info for service 1:
Please enter the filename of the SOAP deployment descriptor xml file:
f:\Godzilla\appserv\classes\scheduling.xml
Is this service an EJB;(y =yes /n =no)?n
How many jarfiles are required for this service (0...n)?1
Classpath requirement 1:Please choose a file:([1 ]schedulings.war):1
Should this service be secured;(y =yes /n =no)?n

Please enter a context root for your non-secured services (e.g./soap):
/scheduling

Do you wish to install the administration client?
Warning,you should not install this client in a production ear unless
you intend to secure the URI to it.

Install the administration client;(y =yes /n =no)?y
```

Installing the Service

Now that you have installed the package, you can deploy it onto WebSphere—a fairly standard deployment of the package as an EAR.

You install the EAR from the Administrator Console, in the Enterprise Applications folder, as shown in Figure 38-7.

1. Click the Install button to open the Application Installation Wizard. Enter the EAR application filename:

Application Installation Wizard

Specify the application (EAR file) or standalone module (JAR or WAR file) to install. If installing a module, specify the name of a new application in which to install the module.

Specify the Application or Module located on this machine to upload and install	
Path:	F:\Godzilla\appserv\classes [Browse...]
Application Name: :	Used only for standalone modules (*.jar, *.war) Scheduling
Context Root :	Used only for Web modules (*.war) /scheduling
[Next] [Cancel]	

Specify the Application or Module located on server to install	
Remote Path on server:	
Application Name: :	Used only for standalone modules (*.jar, *.war)
Context Root :	Used only for Web modules (*.war)
[Next] [Cancel]	

2. Select the host (in this case, just leave it at its default), as shown here:

Application Installation Wizard

Each Web module in your application must be mapped to a virtual host and may have JSPs precompiled.For each Web module below, enter a virtual host name and select precompiled JSP option.

Specifying Virtual Host names and Precompiled JSP option for Web Modules

Web Module Name	Virtual Host Name	Precompile JSPs
Scheduling web module	default_host	Yes

[Back] [Next] [Cancel]

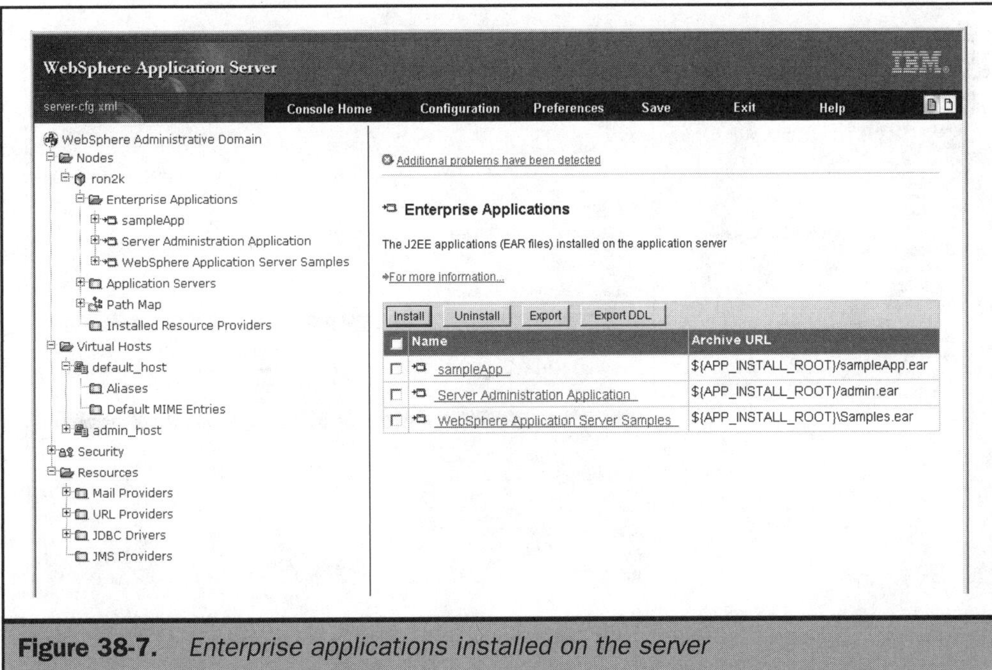

Figure 38-7. *Enterprise applications installed on the server*

3. Confirm the application details, and click the Finish button:

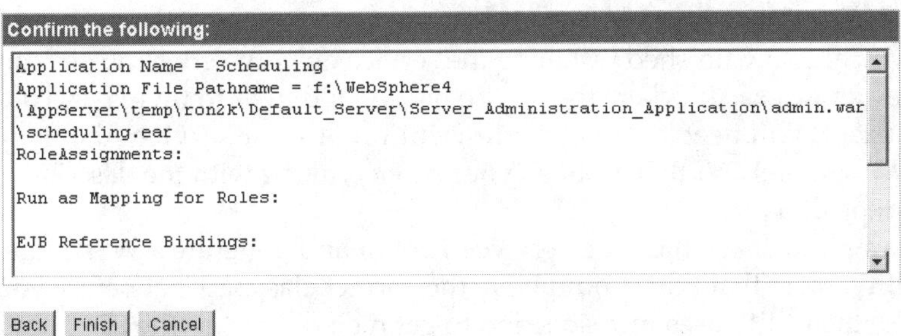

4. Now go back to the list of enterprise applications and select the newly installed enterprise application (either by clicking its name in the tree view on the left pane or by clicking a hyperlink on the right pane). Start the application as shown in Figure 38-8.

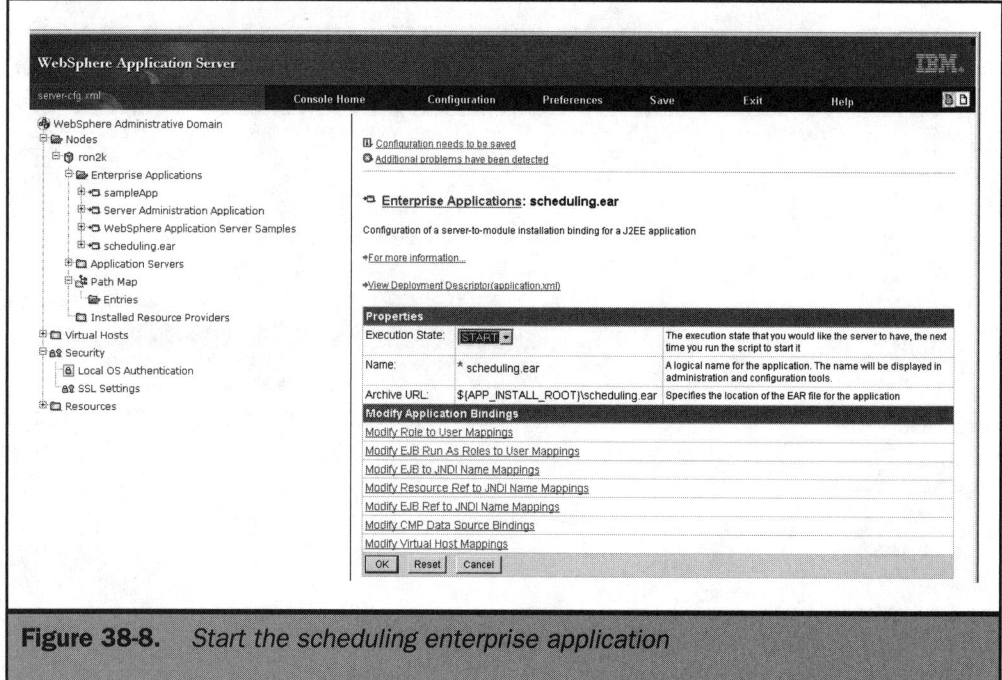

Figure 38-8. *Start the scheduling enterprise application*

5. Finally, click Generate to regenerate the Web plug-in configuration to allow for access to the enterprise application. You are now set to go—your WebSphere instance is ready to provide scheduling services using the advanced algorithms.

Creating the WSDL File

Although you are now finished installing the service on your server, no one can really use it unless they know exactly where the service resides and how to invoke it. To complete the deployment, you need to create a description of your service (that is, you must generate a WSDL file) and then publish your service, along with the describing metadata, to a UDDI repository.

This example will use the Web Services Toolkit and generate a WSDL file using the *wsdlgen* utility. Note that you should have the correct classpath set before you attempt this, because the utility uses introspection to get metadata from the class definition in order to create the appropriate typing information.

Starting the utility brings up the first screen of the WSDL Generation Tool. Fill in the class name and make changes to the uniform resource name (URN) and the service name, as shown here:

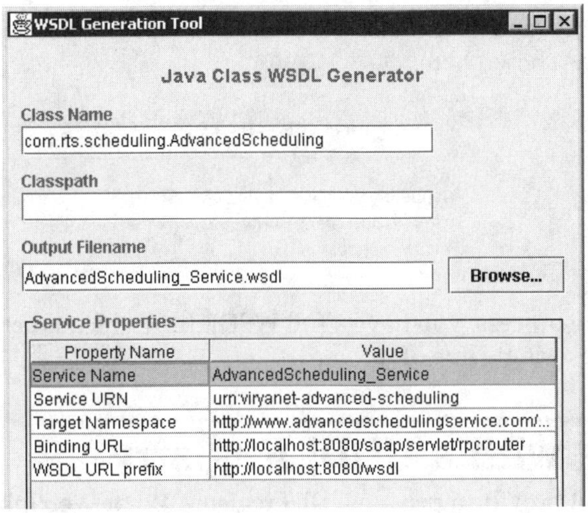

WSDL Generation Tool

Java Class WSDL Generator

Class Name

com.rts.scheduling.AdvancedScheduling

Classpath

Output Filename

AdvancedScheduling_Service.wsdl

Browse...

Service Properties

Property Name	Value
Service Name	AdvancedScheduling_Service
Service URN	urn:viryanet-advanced-scheduling
Target Namespace	http://www.advancedschedulingservice.com/...
Binding URL	http://localhost:8080/soap/servlet/rpcrouter
WSDL URL prefix	http://localhost:8080/wsdl

The utility then brings up the available methods in the class. It allows simple wrapping of the available public methods, as well as creation of the metadata for these methods in the form of a WSDL file. If the method signatures have only simple types, wrapping does not require any work on your behalf. In such a case, you can be finished in no time.

Unfortunately, real business functions do not have one *int* and one string as their arguments. Complex services typically require complex data structures. In our scheduling service, for example, the input to the service includes complex and recursive data types. In this case, the method will be marked with a red dot on its left. If you select this method, you are shown the complex types for which an additional mapping is required:

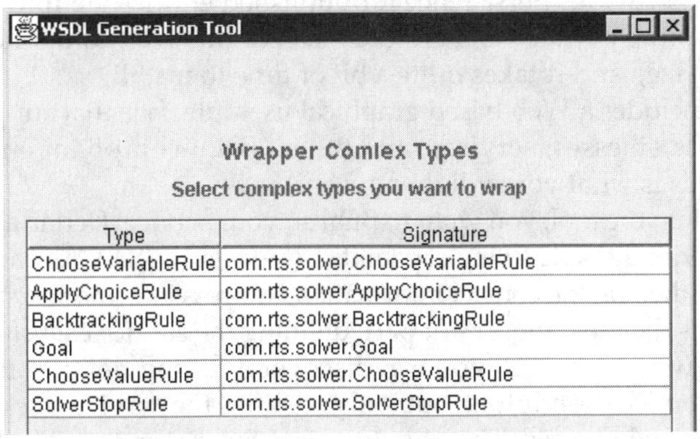

WSDL Generation Tool

Wrapper Comlex Types

Select complex types you want to wrap

Type	Signature
ChooseVariableRule	com.rts.solver.ChooseVariableRule
ApplyChoiceRule	com.rts.solver.ApplyChoiceRule
BacktrackingRule	com.rts.solver.BacktrackingRule
Goal	com.rts.solver.Goal
ChooseValueRule	com.rts.solver.ChooseValueRule
SolverStopRule	com.rts.solver.SolverStopRule

You can select any (and eventually all) of these complex types and generate a wrapper for them, as shown here:

Confirm your choices

Wrappering source: com.rts.solver.Solver
To WSDL document: Solver_Service.wsdl
Fields wrapped: 1

At the end of the process, you have a full WSDL file (which is *very* lengthy) without having had to write a single line of it.

Interacting with a UDDI Registry

WebSphere does not provide a private UDDI registry. What WebSphere does offer in terms of support for UDDI is a Java library called *UDDI4J*. This library allows Java programs to interact with a UDDI registry, both for publishing services and for discovering services. This means you can put together a simple Java program to publish your service in a private or public registry.

While this may be enough, one would hope (and believe) that future versions of WebSphere will indeed include a UDDI registry. At the moment, you are left with using a public registry, a third-party registry that you can install and manage, or a preview release of the IBM UDDI registry that can be downloaded from *http://www7b.boulder.ibm.com/wsdd/downloads/UDDIregistry.html*. Let's proceed with the third option.

The WebSphere UDDI Registry Preview runs on WebSphere Application Server version 4.0. It supports the 20 SOAP-based APIs defined by version 1.0 of the UDDI specifications, and provides persistence for published entities via IBM DB2. The download of the entire package is therefore massive (the DB2 component itself is almost 300MB in size), and it takes quite a bit of time to install.

The package includes a Web-based graphical user interface that supports publishing and querying of businesses, services, and other UDDI-compliant entities without programming. This is what you will do now.

After logging into the tool, you want to publish your service. Define a new business entity that will service the scheduling capabilities (see Figure 38-9). As part of the business entity, you should then define contact information, address information, and so on.

The next step is the most important part: defining the service *endpoint*. This not only specifies various ways by which you can discover and find details on how to invoke the service with service descriptors, but it also defines the service *access point*—that is, where this service can be found. This should define the method by which you can create a request to the WebSphere server on which you've installed the package. The service endpoint is defined by setting the access point in the Add a Service window as shown in Figure 38-10. Press the Add a new access point link and fill in the URL and the access point details.

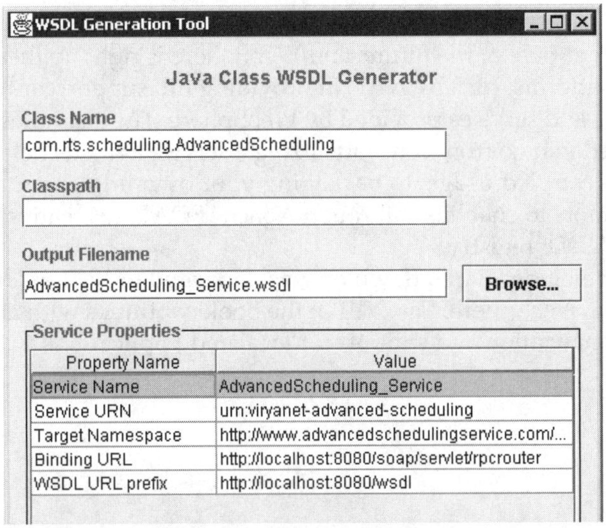

WSDL Generation Tool

Java Class WSDL Generator

Class Name

com.rts.scheduling.AdvancedScheduling

Classpath

Output Filename

AdvancedScheduling_Service.wsdl

Browse...

Service Properties

Property Name	Value
Service Name	AdvancedScheduling_Service
Service URN	urn:viryanet-advanced-scheduling
Target Namespace	http://www.advancedschedulingservice.com/...
Binding URL	http://localhost:8080/soap/servlet/rpcrouter
WSDL URL prefix	http://localhost:8080/wsdl

Figure 38-9. *Adding a new business entity*

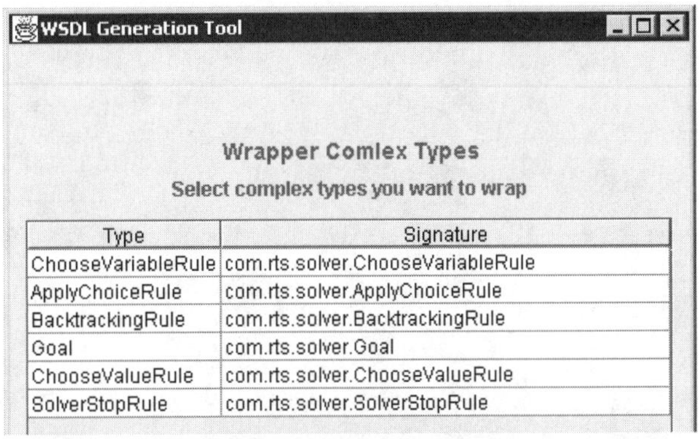

WSDL Generation Tool

Wrapper Comlex Types

Select complex types you want to wrap

Type	Signature
ChooseVariableRule	com.rts.solver.ChooseVariableRule
ApplyChoiceRule	com.rts.solver.ApplyChoiceRule
BacktrackingRule	com.rts.solver.BacktrackingRule
Goal	com.rts.solver.Goal
ChooseValueRule	com.rts.solver.ChooseValueRule
SolverStopRule	com.rts.solver.SolverStopRule

Figure 38-10. *Service details including the access point*

Summary

Web services are the wave of the future, and WebSphere is right up there (along with other dominant platforms, such as .NET) in providing full support for them. This chapter discussed the tools and services provided by WebSphere. The examples presented here should have helped you go from conceptualizing a service as a business function, useful for remote and decoupled usage, to packaging your own implementation as an enterprise application, to enabling it through Apache SOAP, to creating the WSDL and publishing it in a UDDI registry.

This chapter concludes Part VII, which was dedicated to XML-related technologies available as part of WebSphere. Part VIII of the book continues with another important feature: internationalization and support for localized applications.

The Complete Reference

Part VIII

Internationalization and Localization

The Complete Reference

Chapter 39

Java Support Features for Internationalization

This chapter discusses the support provided by Java for building internationalized applications. It describes the inherent internationalization features of Java, such as its support for the Unicode standard, its use of resource bundles, and it's use of many other such mechanisms. Examples show you how to code Java applications in WebSphere in such a way that localization is possible. The focus of this chapter is therefore a mechanism-centric one—that is, it's an explanation that is intended to introduce you to the wealth of support that is provided in Java.

All examples in this chapter and in the next chapter are extracted from ViryaNet's Service Hub offering, which is sold successfully in Japan after having been localized for the Japanese market.

Unicode

It all starts with Unicode—a standard endorsed by pretty much all players in the IT world. It is a standard created by a non-profit organization called the Unicode Consortium that targets the creation of a unified encoding method for all characters in all languages. As a standards committee, this is one of the most successful organizations; no other encoding standard can be taken as seriously today. Figure 39-1 shows the home page of the Unicode Consortium at *http://www.unicode.org*. Notice the left panel, with a set of multilingual texts.

Java is based on Unicode. In fact, character representation in Java (and all derived technology platforms such as WebSphere) uses Unicode natively (that is, the native representation of a character in the Java Virtual Machine [JVM] uses 2 bytes). This premise is the basis for the fact that Java, and hence any WebSphere application, is inherently capable of internationalized and localized applications. A thorough treatment of the subject of Unicode is beyond the scope of this book. The reader is encouraged to refer to *http://www.unicode.org/unicode/standard/principles.html* for an excellent introduction to the concept of Unicode.

Resource Bundles

Every application needs to use strings, which generally can be one of two types (depending on how the application uses these strings). One type includes strings that are part of the data that the application is managing. Examples include product descriptions in a product catalog and company names in a customer master database. The second type includes strings used by the application in prompts, error messages, informational messages, and other messages in the interface.

The first category of strings does not require application intervention, apart from being able to store the various descriptions (such as a product's description) in different persistent structures and using the correct description based on the user's language. (For example, if we are using a relational database to store data, one convenient method is to keep a number of columns—one per product description in the various languages

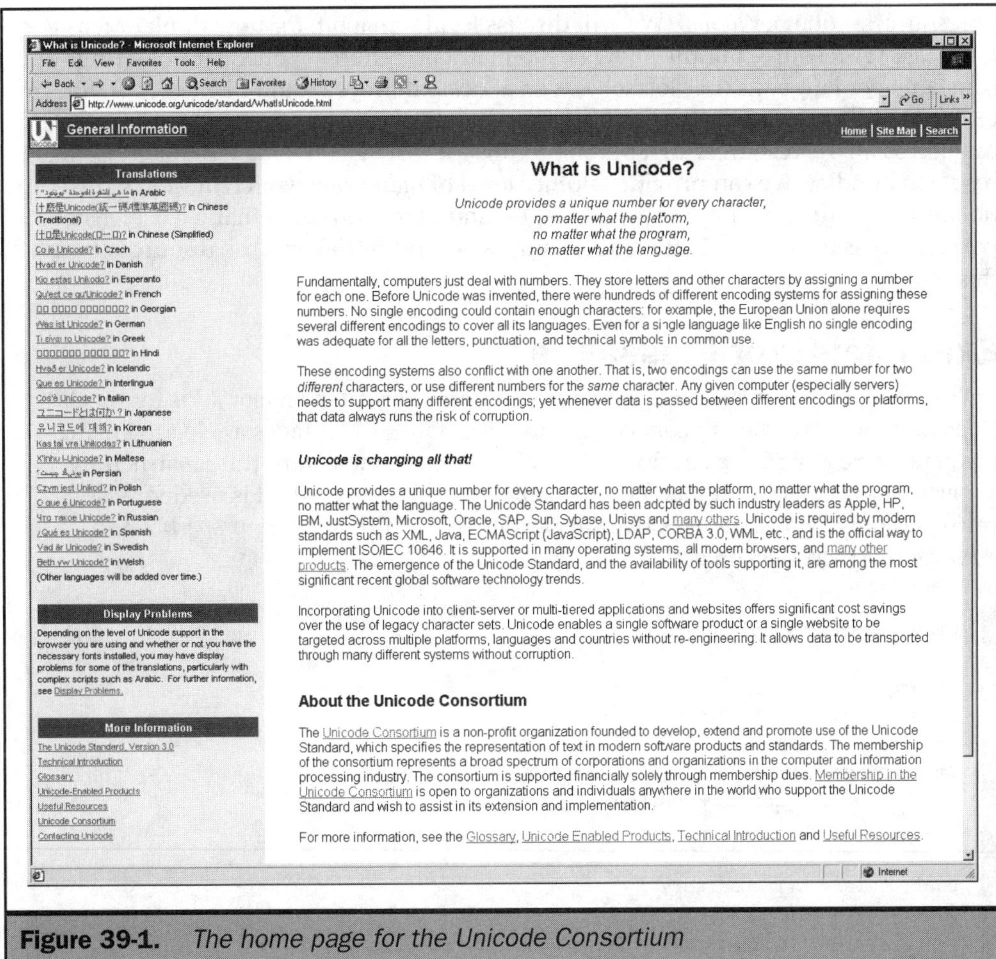

Figure 39-1. *The home page for the Unicode Consortium*

we are supporting within the application—and have the application pull (and insert/update) the appropriate column based on which language is the active language. We will discuss this type of solution further in the next chapter.)

The second category of strings includes messages, prompts, labels, and constant strings used by the application. In this case the set of strings that require support is limited—and fully controlled by the application. It is not a matter of data entry or of maintaining this in the data store. It is a simple matter of providing language-level support for such cases.

Java provides full support for internationalization and language-level support in the form of *resource bundles*. A resource bundle, as its name implies, maintains bundles of resources—one per *locale*. (We will discuss locales in a bit; for now think of it as a language.) A resource bundle allows us to maintain different collections of strings and constants per language (per locale). Given a locale that we would like to serve (for example, the user for which we are creating the display uses a certain language), we can access all the resources that pertain to this locale in a convenient manner. Using resource bundles, we can provide another level of *indirection*, which means that we do not need to hard code the strings, messages, and other constants that we use; instead, we can access the bundle that matches our locale and retrieve all the resources from this bundle.

An Example: Error Messages

Let's look at an example. The class shown next provides all the major APIs for the API Repository and handles all connections to the database. Messages are logged using the generic `com.rts.apis.core.Log` class. For the most part, the constructor is superfluous because most methods are static. The `main()` method is used for testing purposes only. The class uses two properties files: *APIRepository.properties* and *APIRepositoryMessages.properties*.

```
package com.rts.apis.common;

import java.sql.*;
import java.util.*;
import java.io.*;
import java.text.*;
import com.rts.apis.common.Log;


public class APIRepository {
  private static Locale currentLocale = null;
  private static ResourceBundle apiRepositoryMessages = null;
/** Class variable that maintains the connection to the database.
  * It is accessed via the public class method
  * getRepositoryConnection.
  *  getRepositoryConnection.*/
  private static Connection con = null;

/** Hashtable used for caching components when querying
  * during the API Server processing.
  * There is no caching when using the API Repository definition tool
  */
  public static Hashtable componentHash = new Hashtable(100);
/** Hashtable used for caching services when querying during
  * the API Server processing.
  * There is no caching when using the API Repository definition tool
```

```
  */
  public static Hashtable serviceHash = new Hashtable(100);
/** Hashtable used for caching component bindings when querying
  * during the API Server processing.
  * There is no caching when using the API Repository definition tool
  */
  public static Hashtable componentBindingHash = new Hashtable(100);
/** Hashtable used for caching argument bindings when querying
  * during the API Server processing.
  * There is no caching when using the API Repository definition tool
  */
  public static Hashtable argumentBindingHash = new Hashtable(100);

  private static ResourceBundle apiRepositoryProps = null;

      static {
            if (apiRepositoryProps == null) {
                  initProps();
            }
      }

/**
  * Closes the repository connection
  * Exceptions must be handled by caller of this method
  *
  * @exception SQLException An sql exception if one occurs
  */
  public static void closeRepositoryConnection() throws SQLException {
      //Try to disconnect.
  if (con != null)
      con.close( );
      con = null;
      }
/**
  * Get API Repository Messages Bundle for all locale sensitive messages
  * @return ResourceBundle  API Repository messages
  * @exception  FrontEndException If the message file is missing
  */
  public static ResourceBundle getApiRepositoryMessages()
                  throws FrontEndException {
      try {
        if (apiRepositoryMessages == null) {
            apiRepositoryMessages = ResourceBundle.getBundle(
                  "APIRepositoryMessages",getCurrentLocale());
        }
      }
      catch (MissingResourceException ex) {
```

```
              //do not use the resource bundle for this message
            // because clearly it will not be found
              Log.debug("APIRepository",ex);
                        throw new FrontEndException(
                "Missing Resource Exception: "+ ex.getMessage());
      }
        return apiRepositoryMessages;
  }
/**
  * Get API Repository Properties
  * @return Properties API Repository properties
  */
  public static ResourceBundle getApiRepositoryProps() {
      if (apiRepositoryProps == null) {
        initProps();
      }
      return apiRepositoryProps;
  }
/**
  * Get locale based on language, country properties in the
  * APIRepository properties file
  * @return Locale  current locale
  * @exception  FrontEndException If an error occurs
  */
  public static Locale getCurrentLocale() throws FrontEndException {
      if (currentLocale == null) {
        String lang = apiRepositoryProps.getString("language");
        String cntry = apiRepositoryProps.getString("country");
        currentLocale = new Locale(lang,cntry);
      }
      return currentLocale;
  }
/**
  * Gets the next version string based on the input argument last version
  * examples: argument: 1.00, returns 1.01
  *           argument: 1.0a, return 1.0b
  *           argument: 1, returns 2
  * @param  String last version
  * @return String next version
  */
  public static String getNextVersion(String lv) {
  //Find last period and determine if after it is numeric only...
  // if so add 1, if not increment character
   String strValue = "";
   StringTokenizer st = new StringTokenizer(lv,".");
   while (st.hasMoreTokens()) {
        strValue = st.nextToken();
```

```
    }
    if (strValue.equals(""))
         return "1.00";
    boolean allDigits = true;
    char [] c = new char[strValue.length()];
    strValue.getChars(0,strValue.length(),c,0);
    for (int i=0;i<c.length;i++) {
       allDigits = Character.isDigit(c[i]);
    }
    if (allDigits)   {
       String s = lv.substring(0,lv.length() - strValue.length()) +
                    ((new Integer(strValue)).intValue() + 1);
       return s;
    }
    else {
       char lastChar = c[c.length-1];
       int cv = Character.getNumericValue(lastChar) + 1;
       String newChar = String.valueOf(
               Character.forDigit(cv,Character.MAX_RADIX));
       return lv.substring(0,lv.length() -1) + newChar;
    }
   }
  public static Connection getPortalConnection()
                throws SQLException, FrontEndException {
        Connection con = null;
        if (con == null)
        {
                String driverClassName =
                       apiRepositoryProps.getString("dbDriver");
                String databaseURL =
                   apiRepositoryProps.getString("dbDriverType") +
                   apiRepositoryProps.getString("dbURL");
                  Properties properties = new Properties( );
                properties.put("user",
                   apiRepositoryProps.getString("portal_name"));
                properties.put("password",
                   apiRepositoryProps.getString("portal_pass"));
            try {
              String ns = apiRepositoryProps.getString(
                                  "driverNeedsServer");
                  properties.put(
                     "server",
                     apiRepositoryProps.getString("portal_env"));
            } catch (MissingResourceException ex) {}
            try {
              Class c = Class.forName(driverClassName);
              DriverManager.registerDriver((Driver)c.newInstance());
```

```
                    con = DriverManager.getConnection(
                            databaseURL, properties);
                  } catch (ClassNotFoundException ex) {
              System.err.print(
       getApiRepositoryMessages().getString("ClassNotFoundExcepti"));
             System.err.println(ex.getMessage());
                 throw new FrontEndException(
                 getApiRepositoryMessages().getString(
                                       "ClassNotFoundExcepti")+ ex.getMessage());
                 } catch (IllegalAccessException ex) {

System.err.print(getApiRepositoryMessages().getString("IllAccEx"));
             System.err.println(ex.getMessage());
                 throw new FrontEndException(
                               getApiRepositoryMessages().getString("IllAccEx")
                                  + ex.getMessage());
                 } catch (InstantiationException ex) {
             System.err.print(
               getApiRepositoryMessages().getString("InstEx"));
             System.err.println(ex.getMessage());
                 throw new FrontEndException(
               getApiRepositoryMessages().getString("InstEx")+
                                          ex.getMessage());
                 }
        }
        return con;
      }
/**
  * Get the repository connection allows a single place
  * for establishing a DB connection
  * Exceptions must be handled by those that call this method
  * The username/password/environment are taken from the properties file
  * The exception messages need to be internationalized...
  *
  * @exception SQLException An sql exception if one occurs
  * @exception  FrontEndException If another error occurs in
  * methods called from here
  * @return Returns a Connection instance*/
  public static synchronized Connection getRepositoryConnection()
                      throws SQLException, FrontEndException {
      if (con == null)
      {
              //Supply the information specific to the local system.
             //Enter your JDBC driver name and URL.
             // Using Weblogic
              String driverClassName =
                  apiRepositoryProps.getString("dbDriver");
            String databaseURL =
```

```
        apiRepositoryProps.getString("dbDriverType") +
        apiRepositoryProps.getString("dbURL");
      Properties properties = new Properties( );
    //Enter your user name and password.
   //Additional properties may be required.

      properties.put("user",
          apiRepositoryProps.getString("dbUser"));
      properties.put("password",
      apiRepositoryProps.getString("dbPassword"));
//Some drivers need the server property and others don't
//so have property to say whether needs,
//its value is irrelevant. If the driver does not need
//the server the property is commented out
try {
    String ns = apiRepositoryProps.getString("driverNeedsServer");
        properties.put("server",
            apiRepositoryProps.getString("dbEnvironment"));
} catch (MissingResourceException ex) {}

try {
    Class c = Class.forName(driverClassName);
    DriverManager.registerDriver((Driver)c.newInstance());
            //Try to connect to the database through the driver.
      con = DriverManager.getConnection(databaseURL, properties);
      } catch (ClassNotFoundException ex) {
      Log.debug("APIRepository",
  getApiRepositoryMessages().getString("ClassNotFoundExcepti"),2);
     Log.debug("APIRepository",ex.getMessage(),2);
         throw new FrontEndException(
          getApiRepositoryMessages().getString("ClassNotFoundExcepti")+
   ex.getMessage());
     } catch (IllegalAccessException ex) {
     Log.debug("APIRepository",
     getApiRepositoryMessages().getString("IllAccEx"),2);
    Log.debug("APIRepository",ex.getMessage(),2);
         throw new FrontEndException(
                    getApiRepositoryMessages().getString("IllAccEx")+
          ex.getMessage());
     }   catch (InstantiationException ex) {
     Log.debug("APIRepository",
     getApiRepositoryMessages().getString("InstEx"),2);
     Log.debug("APIRepository",ex.getMessage(),2);
         throw new FrontEndException(
          getApiRepositoryMessages().getString("InstEx")+
          ex.getMessage());
     }
```

```
      }
      try      {
            con.setAutoCommit(true);
      } catch (SQLException e)      {
            try      {
                    String driverClassName =
                    apiRepositoryProps.getString("dbDriver");
                  String databaseURL =
                    apiRepositoryProps.getString("dbURL");
                    Properties properties = new Properties( );
                    properties.put("user",
                    apiRepositoryProps.getString("dbUser"));
                    properties.put("password",
                    apiRepositoryProps.getString("dbPassword"));
                    try {
                        String ns =
                apiRepositoryProps.getString("driverNeedsServer");
                      properties.put("server",
                apiRepositoryProps.getString("dbEnvironment"));
                    } catch (MissingResourceException ex) {}
                    Class c = Class.forName(driverClassName);
                  DriverManager.registerDriver((Driver)c.newInstance());
                    //Try to connect to the database through the driver.
                    con = DriverManager.getConnection(
                      databaseURL, properties);
                    con.setAutoCommit(true);
            }      catch (Exception e1)      {
                  con = null;
            }
      }
      return con;
  }
      private static void initProps () {
            apiRepositoryProps = ResourceBundle.getBundle(
                 "ApisInits", Locale.getDefault());
  }
/**
  * main Method is used for testing purposes only
  */
  public static void main(String[] args) {



  }
/**
  * Class method to return an argument binding from the repository
  * based on the name, version
```

```
 *
 * @exception  FrontEndException propagates exceptions to caller
 * @param String service name
 * @param String service version
 * @param boolean cachingEnabled
 * @return An instance of ArgumentBinding or null if none.*/
 public static ArgumentBinding queryArgumentBinding(
            String name, String version, boolean cachingEnabled)
                    throws FrontEndException{
     return ArgumentBinding.query(name, version, cachingEnabled);
 }
/**
 * Class method to return a component from the repository based on the
 * name, version
 *
 * @exception  FrontEndException propagates exceptions to caller
 * @param String service name
 * @param String service version
 * @param boolean cachingEnabled
 * @return An instance of Component or null if none.*/
 public static Component queryComponent(
          String name, String version, boolean cachingEnabled)
                  throws FrontEndException{
     return Component.query(name, version, cachingEnabled);
 }
/**
 * Class method to return a component binding from the repository
 * based on the name, version
 *
 * @exception  FrontEndException propagates exceptions to caller
 * @param String service name
 * @param String service version
 * @param boolean cachingEnabled
 * @return An instance of ComponentBinding or null if none.*/
 public static ComponentBinding queryComponentBinding(
            String name, String version, boolean cachingEnabled)
                throws FrontEndException{
    return ComponentBinding.query(name, version, cachingEnabled);
 }
/**
 * Class method to return a service from the repository based on the
 * name, version and provider. If the version is an empty string
 * then it will bring the latest version of the service found.
 * Caching will be used based on the cachingEnabled argument
 *
 * @exception  FrontEndException propagates exceptions to caller
 * @param String service name
```

```
    * @param String service version
    * @param String service provider
    * @param boolean cachingEnabled
    * @return An instance of Service or null if none.*/
    public static RepositoryService queryService(
        String name, String version,
        String provider, boolean cachingEnabled)
              throws FrontEndException{
        return RepositoryService.query(
                name, version, provider, cachingEnabled);
    }
}
```

This example shows the usage of static error messages. A static object is maintained by the class—called `apiRepositoryMessages`. Whenever the program wants to get an error message, it does not include that constant string but rather retrieves a string from the resource bundle object. Therefore, all strings used in the `getString` calls using the resource bundles are merely keys used in the lookup process and not the string itself.

This allows us to externalize the actual message strings to a file, as shown here:

```
#Sun Mar 21 13:28:53 GMT 1999
ErrorCode=Error Code:
ClassNotFoundExcepti=Class Not Found Exception:
IllAccEx=Illegal Access Exception:
InstEx=Instantiation Exception:
DBException=DB Exception: {0}
Message=Message:
Transaction_rollback=Transaction is being rolled back...
SQLException=---------SQLException-----------
Connecting_to_the=Connecting to the database...
Service_exists=Validation Error: Service already exists for this version.
Change the version number to save this Service.
Try_to_connect_to=Trying to connect to {0}/{1}@{2}
Not_found=Not found.
This_is_the_info=This is the information retrieved.
Structures_must_be_defined=Validation Error: Input, Output, Error and
Exception Structures must be defined.
Exception_caught_due=Exception caught due to: {0}
DOM_Creation=DOM Creation Exception: {0}
SQLState=SQLState:
CB_exists=Validation Error: Component Binding already exists for this
version. Change the version number to save this Component Binding.
input_invalid=Validation Error: The input component must be a valid
component.
output_invalid=Validation Error: The output component must be a valid
component
```

```
CB_invalid=Validation Error: The component binding must be valid.
AB_exists=Validation Error: Argument Binding already exists for this
version. Change the version number to save this Argument Binding.
prim_prop=Invalid Request: The property is a primitive type.
version_not_allowed=Validation Error: This is a primitive type. It cannot
have a version number.
invalid_version=Validation Error: This is a non-primitive type. Please give
it a valid version number.
invalid_comp=Validation Error: The structure properties must be valid
components.
cond_not_allowed=Validation Error: Output and Error Structures must have
conditions. Please add one.
missing_cond=Validation Error: Input and Exception Structures cannot have
conditions.
NumberFormatException=Invalid number format for version:
type_required=Validation Error: Please enter a property type.
Comp_exists=Validation Error: A component already exists for this version.
Please change the version number to save this Component.
Only_one_default_cond=Validation Error: Only one default condition is
allowed on output/error structures.
Req_default_cond=Validation Error: One default condition is required on
output/error structures.
Name_prov_required=Validation Error: Please enter a service name and
provider.
Name_required=Validation Error: Please enter a property name.
duplicate_name=Validation Error: You cannot duplicate a property name.
default_only=Validation Error: Default conditions cannot have a reference or
match.
reference_required=Validation Error: Please enter a reference for this
condition.
match_required=Validation Error: Please enter a match for this condition.
stp_name_req=Validation Error: Please enter the stored procedure name.
db_req=Validation Error: Please enter either a database class/method or a
database driver/URL/name/password.
Invalid_DB_URL=Error: You have entered an invalid URL format to extract
database information.
Target_required=Validation Error: Please enter the target.
Source_required=Validation Error: Please enter the source.
bind_not_matching=Validation Error: The target and source should be of the
same type/version, or a component binding should be provided.
Both_must_be_array=Validation Error: The source and target must both be
arrays.
static_info_req=Validation Error: Please enter a static class name and
method for this static mechanism.
corba_info_req=Validation Error: Please enter all the mandatory information
for this corba mechanism.
corba_array_error=Validation Error: A corba service property can't be array
.
```

The file shown above provides the error messages of U.S. English. Note that the file ends with the `en_US` extension, meaning the English language for a U.S. locale (`en_UK` would be the English flavor used in the U.K.). If you wanted to localize the application for Japanese, for example, you would need to translate the strings on the right hand side of each equal sign (=) and use the file `APIRepositoryMessages_jp_JP`, as shown in Figure 39-2.

By getting the resource bundle using a different locale, the appropriate strings can be retrieved without even a single change to the application code; this is the essence of an internationalized application!

Resource bundles contain locale-specific objects. When your program needs a locale-specific resource—a `String`, for example—your program can load it from the resource bundle that is appropriate for the current user's locale. In this way, you can write program code that is largely independent of the user's locale, isolating most, if not all, of the locale-specific information in resource bundles. This allows you to write programs that can

- be easily localized, or translated, into different languages
- handle multiple locales at once
- be easily modified later to support even more locales

One resource bundle is, conceptually, a set of related classes that inherit from `ResourceBundle`. Each related subclass of `ResourceBundle` has the same base name, plus an additional component that identifies its locale. For example, suppose your resource bundle is named `MyResources`. The first class you are likely to write is the default resource bundle that simply has the same name as its family—`MyResources`. You can also provide as many related locale-specific classes as you need: for example, perhaps you would provide a German one named `MyResources_de`.

Each related subclass of `ResourceBundle` contains the same items, but the items have been translated for the locale represented by that `ResourceBundle` subclass. For example, both `MyResources` and `MyResources_de` may have a `String` that's used on a button for canceling operations. In `MyResources`, the `String` may contain `Cancel`, and in `MyResources_de` it may contain `Abbrechen`.

If there different resources are used for different countries, you can make specializations: for example, `MyResources_de_CH` is the German language (`de`) in Switzerland (`CH`). If you want to modify only some of the resources in the specialization, you can do so.

When your program needs a locale-specific object, it loads the `ResourceBundle` class using the `getBundle` method:

```
ResourceBundle myResources =
     ResourceBundle.getBundle("MyResources", currentLocale);
```

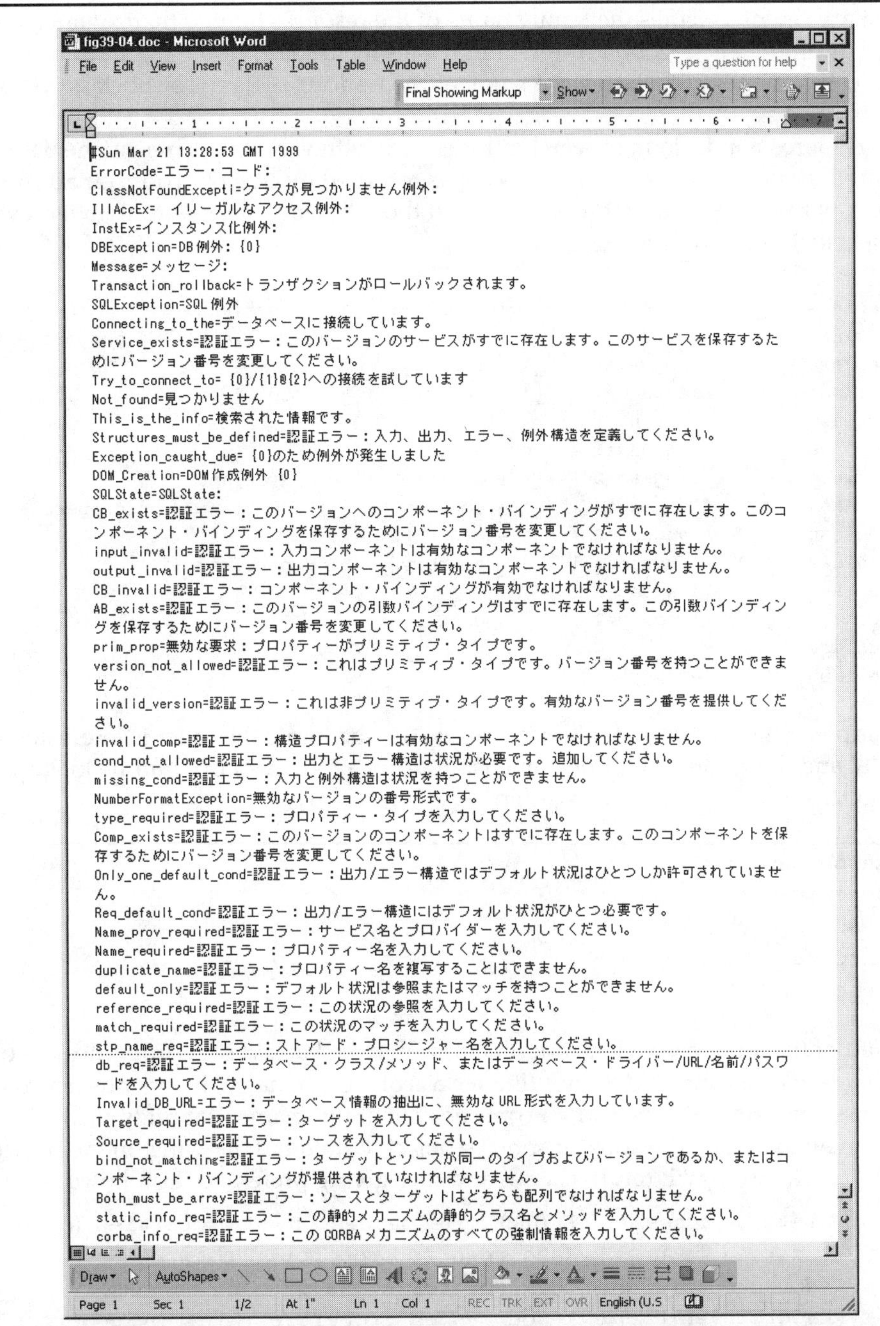

```
#Sun Mar 21 13:28:53 GMT 1999
ErrorCode=エラー・コード:
ClassNotFoundExcepti=クラスが見つかりません例外:
IllAccEx= イリーガルなアクセス例外:
InstEx=インスタンス化例外:
DBException=DB 例外: {0}
Message=メッセージ:
Transaction_rollback=トランザクションがロールバックされます。
SQLException=SQL 例外
Connecting_to_the=データベースに接続しています。
Service_exists=認証エラー：このバージョンのサービスがすでに存在します。このサービスを保存するためにバージョン番号を変更してください。
Try_to_connect_to= {0}/{1}@{2}への接続を試しています
Not_found=見つかりません
This_is_the_info=検索された情報です。
Structures_must_be_defined=認証エラー：入力、出力、エラー、例外構造を定義してください。
Exception_caught_due= {0}のため例外が発生しました
DOM_Creation=DOM 作成例外 {0}
SQLState=SQLState:
CB_exists=認証エラー：このバージョンへのコンポーネント・バインディングがすでに存在します。このコンポーネント・バインディングを保存するためにバージョン番号を変更してください。
input_invalid=認証エラー：入力コンポーネントは有効なコンポーネントでなければなりません。
output_invalid=認証エラー：出力コンポーネントは有効なコンポーネントでなければなりません。
CB_invalid=認証エラー：コンポーネント・バインディングが有効でなければなりません。
AB_exists=認証エラー：このバージョンの引数バインディングはすでに存在します。この引数バインディングを保存するためにバージョン番号を変更してください。
prim_prop=無効な要求：プロパティーがプリミティブ・タイプです。
version_not_allowed=認証エラー：これはプリミティブ・タイプです。バージョン番号を持つことができません。
invalid_version=認証エラー：これは非プリミティブ・タイプです。有効なバージョン番号を提供してください。
invalid_comp=認証エラー：構造プロパティーは有効なコンポーネントでなければなりません。
cond_not_allowed=認証エラー：出力とエラー構造は状況が必要です。追加してください。
missing_cond=認証エラー：入力と例外構造は状況を持つことができません。
NumberFormatException=無効なバージョンの番号形式です。
type_required=認証エラー：プロパティー・タイプを入力してください。
Comp_exists=認証エラー：このバージョンのコンポーネントはすでに存在します。このコンポーネントを保存するためにバージョン番号を変更してください。
Only_one_default_cond=認証エラー：出力/エラー構造ではデフォルト状況はひとつしか許可されていません。
Req_default_cond=認証エラー：出力/エラー構造にはデフォルト状況がひとつ必要です。
Name_prov_required=認証エラー：サービス名とプロバイダーを入力してください。
Name_required=認証エラー：プロパティー名を入力してください。
duplicate_name=認証エラー：プロパティー名を複写することはできません。
default_only=認証エラー：デフォルト状況は参照またはマッチを持つことができません。
reference_required=認証エラー：この状況の参照を入力してください。
match_required=認証エラー：この状況のマッチを入力してください。
stp_name_req=認証エラー：ストアード・プロシージャー名を入力してください。
db_req=認証エラー：データベース・クラス/メソッド、またはデータベース・ドライバー/URL/名前/パスワードを入力してください。
Invalid_DB_URL=エラー：データベース情報の抽出に、無効な URL 形式を入力しています。
Target_required=認証エラー：ターゲットを入力してください。
Source_required=認証エラー：ソースを入力してください。
bind_not_matching=認証エラー：ターゲットとソースが同一のタイプおよびバージョンであるか、またはコンポーネント・バインディングが提供されていなければなりません。
Both_must_be_array=認証エラー：ソースとターゲットはどちらも配列でなければなりません。
static_info_req=認証エラー：この静的メカニズムの静的クラス名とメソッドを入力してください。
corba_info_req=認証エラー：この CORBA メカニズムのすべての強制情報を入力してください。
```

Figure 39-2. *Example property file for the Japanese locale*

The first argument specifies the family name of the resource bundle that contains the object in question. The second argument indicates the desired locale .`getBundle` uses these two arguments to construct the name of the `ResourceBundle` subclass it should load as follows.

The resource bundle lookup searches for classes with various suffixes on the basis of the desired locale, the current default locale as returned by `Locale.getDefault()`, and the root resource bundle (`baseclass`), in the following order—from lower level (more specific) to parent level (less specific):

```
baseclass + "_" + language1 + "_" + country1 + "_" + variant1
baseclass + "_" + language1 + "_" + country1 + "_" + variant1 + ".properties"
baseclass + "_" + language1 + "_" + country1
baseclass + "_" + language1 + "_" + country1 + ".properties"
baseclass + "_" + language1
baseclass + "_" + language1 + ".properties"
baseclass + "_" + language2 + "_" + country2 + "_" + variant2
baseclass + "_" + language2 + "_" + country2 + "_" + variant2 + ".properties"
baseclass + "_" + language2 + "_" + country2
baseclass + "_" + language2 + "_" + country2 + ".properties"
baseclass + "_" + language2
baseclass + "_" + language2 + ".properties"
baseclass
baseclass + ".properties"
```

For example, if the current default locale is `en_US`, the locale the caller is interested in is `fr_CH`, and the resource bundle name is `MyResources`, resource bundle lookup will search for the following classes, in order:

```
MyResources_fr_CH
MyResources_fr
MyResources_en_US
MyResources_en
MyResources
```

The result of the lookup is a class, but that class may be backed by a properties file on disk. That is, if `getBundle` does not find a class of a given name, it appends *.properties* to the class name and searches for a properties file of that name. If it finds such a file, it creates a new `PropertyResourceBundle` object to hold it. Following on the previous example, `getBundle` will return classes and files giving preference as follows:

> (class) `MyResources_fr_CH` (file) `MyResources_fr_CH.properties` (class) `MyResources_fr` (file) `MyResources_fr.properties` (class) `MyResources_en_US` (file) `MyResources_en_US.properties` (class) `MyResources_en` (file) `MyResources_en.properties` (class) `MyResources` (file) `MyResources.properties`

If a lookup fails, `getBundle()` throws a `MissingResourceException`.

The baseclass *must* be fully qualified (for example, `myPackage.MyResources`, not just `MyResources`). It must also be accessible by your code; it cannot be a class that is private to the package where `ResourceBundle.getBundle` is called.

Note *`ResourceBundles` are used internally in accessing `NumberFormats`, `Collations`, and so on. The lookup strategy is the same.*

Resource bundles contain key/value pairs. The keys uniquely identify a locale-specific object in the bundle. Here's an example of a `ListResourceBundle` that contains two key/value pairs:

```
class MyResource extends ListResourceBundle {
     public Object[][] getContents() {
             return contents;
     }
     static final Object[][] contents = {
     // LOCALIZE THIS
             {"OkKey", "OK"},
             {"CancelKey", "Cancel"},
     // END OF MATERIAL TO LOCALIZE
     };
}
```

Keys are always `Strings`. In this example, the keys are `OkKey` and `CancelKey`. In the preceding example, the values are also `Strings`—`OK` and `Cancel`—but they don't *have* to be. The values can be any type of object.

You retrieve an object from resource bundle using the appropriate *get* method. Because `OkKey` and `CancelKey` are both strings, you would use `getString` to retrieve them:

```
button1 = new Button(myResourceBundle.getString("OkKey"));
button2 = new Button(myResourceBundle.getString("CancelKey"));
```

The *get* methods all require the key as an argument and return the object if found. If the object is not found, the *get* method throws a `MissingResourceException`.

In addition to `getString`, `ResourceBundle` supports a number of other methods for getting different types of objects, such as `getStringArray`. If no object matches one of these methods, you can use `getObject` and cast the result to the appropriate type. For example:

```
int[] myIntegers = (int[]) myResources.getObject("intList");
```

You should always supply a baseclass with no suffixes. This will be the class of "last resort," if a locale is requested that does not exist. In fact, you must provide all the classes in any given inheritance chain for which you provide a resource. For example, if you provide `MyResources_fr_BE`*, you must provide both* `MyResources` *and* `MyResources_fr` *or the resource bundle lookup won't work.*

The Java 2 platform provides two subclasses of `ResourceBundle`—`ListResourceBundle` and `PropertyResourceBundle`—that provide a fairly simple way to create resources. As you saw briefly in a previous example, `ListResourceBundle` manages its resource as a list of key/value pairs. `PropertyResourceBundle` uses a properties file to manage its resources.

If `ListResourceBundle` or `PropertyResourceBundle` do not suit your needs, you can write your own `ResourceBundle` subclass. Your subclasses must override two methods: `handleGetObject()` and `getKeys()`.

The following is a simple example of a `ResourceBundle` subclass, `MyResources`, that manages two resources. (For a larger number of resources you would probably use a hash table.) Notice that if the key is not found, `handleGetObject` must return `null`. If the key is `null`, a `NullPointerException` should be thrown. Notice also that you don't need to supply a value if a parent-level `ResourceBundle` handles the same key with the same value (as in German below). Also notice that because you specify an `g_GE` resource bundle, you also have to provide a default en resource bundle even though it inherits all its data from the root resource bundle. Here's an example:

```
// default (English language, United States)
 abstract class MyResources extends ResourceBundle {

    public Object handleGetObject(String key) {

         if (key.equals("okKey")) return "Ok";
         if (key.equals("cancelKey")) return "Cancel";
     return null;
     }
 }

 // German language
 public class MyResources_de extends MyResources {
     public Object handleGetObject(String key) {
         // don't need okKey, since parent level handles it.
         if (key.equals("cancelKey")) return "Abbrechen";
         return null;
     }
 }
```

You do not have to restrict yourself to using a single family of `ResourceBundles`. For example, you could have a set of bundles for exception messages, `ExceptionResources` (`ExceptionResources_fr`, `ExceptionResources_de`, and so on), and one for widgets, `WidgetResource` (`WidgetResources_fr`, `WidgetResources_de`, and so on), breaking up the resources however you like.

Of course, many other issues regarding internationalized applications need to be resolved—issues such as date formats, address formats, string concatenation, strong collation, and sorting. Fortunately, Java has built-in mechanisms for handling all these issues. Fully covering the topic of internationalization in Java requires a book in its own, and we will not attempt to cover it all here. Still, after what you've learned here and in the next chapter, you'll be able to write a multilingual application.

Summary

This chapter discussed the support provided by Java for building internationalized applications. Specifically, it presented some of the inherent internationalization features of Java, such as its support for the Unicode standard, its use of resource bundles, and many other such mechanisms. But mechanisms are not enough. All these mechanisms must be used collectively to provide a coherent framework by which multilingual applications are possible. This is the focus of Chapter 40, which makes use of many of the mechanisms discussed in this chapter to describe a fully internationalized application.

The Complete Reference

Chapter 40

Building Multilingual Applications

Chapter 39 covered a few elements that make it possible to build international applications. The fact that Java is inherently built for international use (one of the reasons it succeeded on the Internet) is of course fundamental to the ease with which multilingual applications can be built. But this is not enough, and this chapter provides a few approaches for building multilingual applications using WebSphere, along with source code examples for doing so.

Multilingual issues, though important, form only a subset of WebSphere's full internationalization and localization picture. Other elements include date formats, currency formats, and address formats—and in some languages, more advanced elements like widgets, which allow you to type from right to left or top to bottom.

This chapter focuses mostly on the multilingual aspect of WebSphere, because the date/address/currency/numeric formatting issues are relatively simple to handle and are usually handled in a way that is similar to the approaches with which multilingual support is provided. (A discussion of widgets is not within the scope of this book, as such issues are not normally resolved by application developers.)

Taxonomy for Multilingual Issues

When looking at multilingual applications, the notion of supporting multiple languages can be divided into three broad categories:

- Screen presentation
- Data
- Messages

Screens accessed by users (in browsers, client-server applications, or on wireless devices) all include formatting information such as prompts, titles, and labels. When delivering a screen that appears in different languages, the layout of the screen—or its presentation characteristics—need to adjust so that prompts and other messages to users can accommodate the particulars of the language. (For example, texts in German are usually much longer than their equivalents in English.)

In multilingual applications, the same data often needs to be provided in various languages. A company's sales representative in Japan, for example, may need access to the same sales information accessed by a representative in Argentina. That *same data* must be understandable to speakers of various languages across the globe. Multilingual data issues are not about simply translating screens of information into a number of languages; rather, they are about *maintaining* the same data in multiple languages. Maintaining data is an involved process because it often includes the necessity to be able to display multiple-language versions of the same data on one screen.

Messages are about displaying errors and other types of information, including dialog box messages, debug messages, and logging messages, in multiple languages. This is the simplest form to solve because Java resource bundles (covered in Chapter 39) are specifically built to support this natively. We will not discuss this issue further in this chapter.

Screen Presentation

Multilingual presentations differ in their approach and implementation in three ways:

- **Multiple JavaServer Pages (JSPs) Method** Appropriate for small-scale applications where application size (and later maintenance requirements) does not justify the initial investment required for the more pricey Transcoder Method approach
- **String Injection Method** Appropriate for application where ease of use by the developer is sacrificed for the ability to maintain a single code line without the large infrastructure investment.
- **Transcoder Method** Appropriate for large applications where an up-front investment in development time is well worth it because of savings to be had later in the maintenance cycles

Multiple JSP Method

During development, a WebSphere application's presentation layer consists of a JSP layer that takes the data usually created by internal servlets or EJBs and formats it to create Hypertext Markup Language (HTML), Wireless Markup Language (WML), or other markup language scripts. These scripts are then presented to the user via some kind of presentation software, such as a browser or microbrowser.

For this approach, we create multiple JSPs—one per language that needs to be supported. It is a simple, economic approach that, because of its simplicity, is highly recommended for small applications. Another advantage of this method is that the layout is never compromised; each JSP can be optimally built for the best possible presentation in each language.

Figure 40-1 shows two login screens for ViryaNet's Service Process module, in Japanese and English. Note that this HTML is generated from various JSPs (in this case, amazingly, simple JSPs).

Figure 40-1. *Login screens in Japanese and English*

The JSP script used to create these login screens follows. Remarkably, all the code within both the Japanese and English JSPs is the same (and hence it is less suitable for highly complex applications).

```
<!DOCTYPE HTML PUBLIC "-//W3C//DTD HTML 4.0//EN">
  <html>

<%@ page
extends = "com.rts.eAccess.framework.EAccessBaseServlet" %>
    <head>

      <link href="/RTS_HTML_Pages/RTS_General/Css/Customization.css"
rel="stylesheet" title="Customization style sheet" type="text/css"  />

      <meta content="text/html" http-equiv="Content-Type">
      <title>

  &#12532;&#12451;&#12522;&#12450;&#12493;&#12483;&#12488;
 &#12469;&#12540;&#12499;&#12473;&#12503;&#12525;&#12475;&#12473;
      </title>
      <link href="/RTS_HTML_Pages/RTS_General/Css/rts.css"
              rel="stylesheet"
              title="ViryaNet Style Sheet"
```

```
            type="text/css"  />
        <link href="/RTS_HTML_Pages/RTS_General/Css/rts_remote.css"
                rel="stylesheet"
                title="ViryaNet Service Process Style Sheet"
                type="text/css"  />
        <script language="JavaScript" type="TEXT/JAVASCRIPT">




  function fnTrapKD()
{
    if(event.keyCode == 13)
    {
        formLogin.submit();
    }
}
</script>
    </head>
    <body onkeydown="fnTrapKD()" onload="showMsg()"
     onresize="window.location.href = window.location.href;">
 <jsp:scriptlet> if (isExplorer(request)){ </jsp:scriptlet>
      <DIV id="images" CLASS="outerLayer">
 <jsp:scriptlet>}
 else{</jsp:scriptlet>
 <DIV align="center">
<jsp:scriptlet> } </jsp:scriptlet>

        <img alt="ViryaNet.com" border="0" height="134" width="483"
       src="/RTS_HTML_Pages/RTS_General/images/viryanet_hd.gif">
        <br />
        <img alt="ViryaNet.com" border="0" height="195" width="483"
       src="/RTS_HTML_Pages/RTS_General/images/viryanetlogin.gif">
        <br />
        <img alt="ViryaNet.com" border="0" height="34" width="483"
       src="/RTS_HTML_Pages/RTS_General/images/viryanet_ft.gif">

  <jsp:scriptlet> if(isNetscape(request)){ </ jsp:scriptlet >
        <div align="center" class="nestedLayer" id="login" name="login">
   ViryaNet Service Process
   < jsp:scriptlet> } else{ </ jsp:scriptlet >
          <div align="center" class="nestedLayer" id="login" name="login">

  &#12532;&#12451;&#12522;&#12450;&#12493;&#12483;&#12488;
```

INTERNATIONALIZATION AND LOCALIZATION

```
&#12469;&#12540;&#12499;&#12473;&#12503;&#12525;&#12475;&#12473;

  < jsp:scriptlet> } </ jsp:scriptlet >
            <form action="/servlet/RequestHandler" method="POST"
                         name="formLogin" target="_top">
              <input name="task" type="HIDDEN" value="BnLogin"  />
              <input name="action" type="HIDDEN" value="run"  />
              <table align="center" border="0">
                <tr>
                  <td class="TableBodyFontBold">
                  < jsp:scriptlet>
                          int j1 =9;
                          if (isNetscape(request))
                            for (int ii = 0; ii < j1; ii++)
                            {
                           </ jsp:scriptlet >
                                 
                           < jsp:scriptlet>
                            }
                    </jsp:scriptlet >
                    &#12518;&#12540;&#12470;&#21517;
                  </td>
                  <td>
                    <input class="TableBodyFont" name="username"
                          size="10" type="TEXT" value=""  />
                  </td>
                </tr>
                <tr>
                  <td class="TableBodyFontBold">
                    < jsp:scriptlet>
                               int j2 =9;
                             if (isNetscape(request))
                             for (int ii = 0; ii < j2; ii++)
                             {
                            </ jsp:scriptlet >
                                  
                            < jsp:scriptlet>
                             }
                    </ jsp:scriptlet >
                    &#12497;&#12473;&#12527;&#12540;&#12489;
                  </td>
                  <td>
                    <input class="TableBodyFont" name="password"
                       size="10" type="PASSWORD" value=""  />
                  </td>
                </tr>
```

```
            <tr>
              <td colspan="2">
                <div align="center">
                 < jsp:scriptlet>
                            int j22 =9;
                            if (isNetscape(request))
                            for (int ii = 0; ii < j22; ii++)
                            {
                           </ jsp:scriptlet >
                                   
                           < jsp:scriptlet>
                           }
                  </ jsp:scriptlet >
                  <input  value="&#12525;&#12464;&#12452;&#12531;"
                 class="ButtonFont" name="buttonName"
                 onclick="formLogin.submit()" type="BUTTON"   >

                    </input>
                </div>
              </td>
            </tr>
          </table>
        </form>
      </div>
    </div>
  </div>
</body>
</html>
```


Having multiple JSPs means that each will be used to build the page for a different set of users—but how does the system know which JSP to use for which user? One option (which would probably have been used a few years ago) is to maintain information about users (for example, in a user profile database or in an .ini file) and, upon logon, to start forwarding the server code to the appropriate JSPs. But in today's world of e-business, where the number of users accessing the system can grow to tens and hundreds of thousands of users, and where systems also need to support casual users who are not necessarily recorded as users in the system, a more scalable way is required.

In identifying which presentation needs to be created for the user, you can make use of the fact that browsers record information about the encoding they receive and pass it to the server. Every browser lets the user select the encoding he or she wants to see. The selected encoding is, in fact, equivalent to the user's locale. Figure 40-2 shows the encoding selection for Microsoft Internet Explorer.

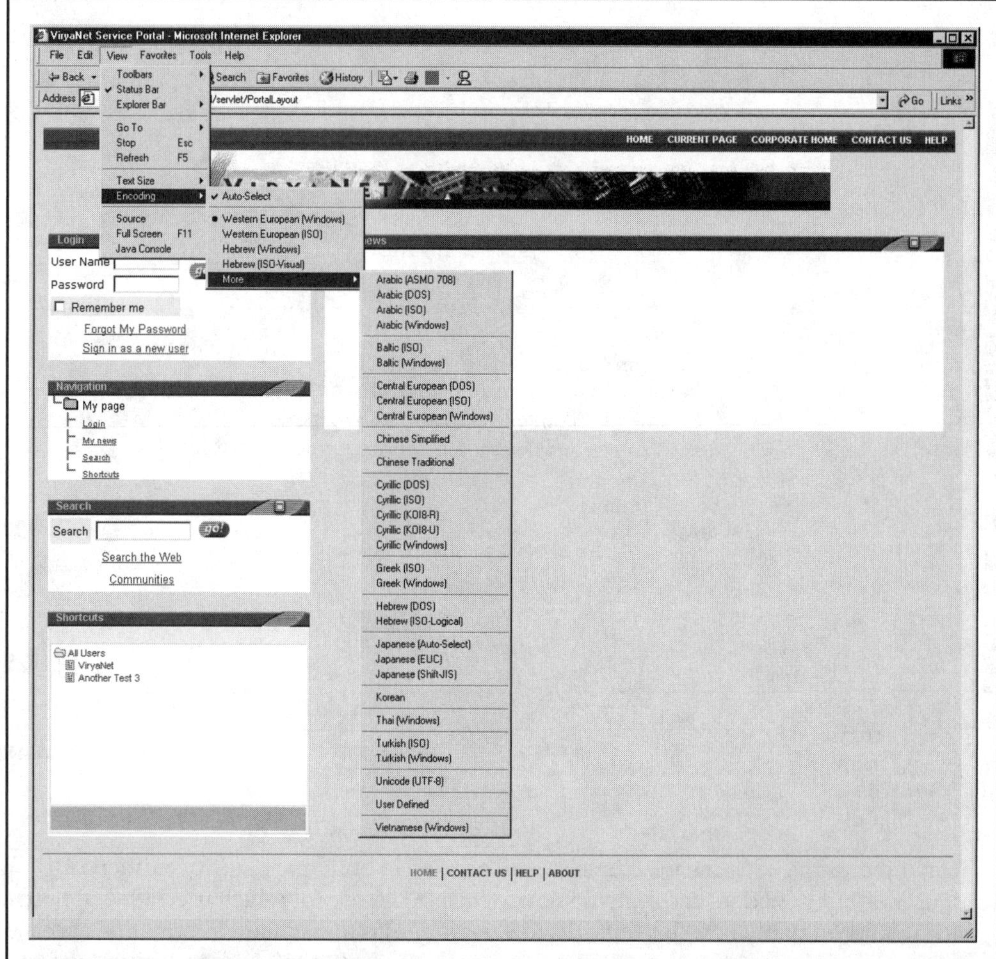

Figure 40-2. *Setting the encoding used by the browser*

Every time the browser sends an HTTP request to the server, it passes this locale information to the server within the request's HTTP header. The server can make use of this information—for example, to select the appropriate JSP. Figure 40-3 shows the output generated by WebSphere's snoop servlet, which prints out items in the HTTP request. (Note the field under Request Headers called *accept-language*.)

The following listing shows a code fragment within the ViryaNet Service hub that is responsible for forwarding the locale information to the server so it can use the correct JSP. The code uses the locale stored in the HTTP request. The method looks

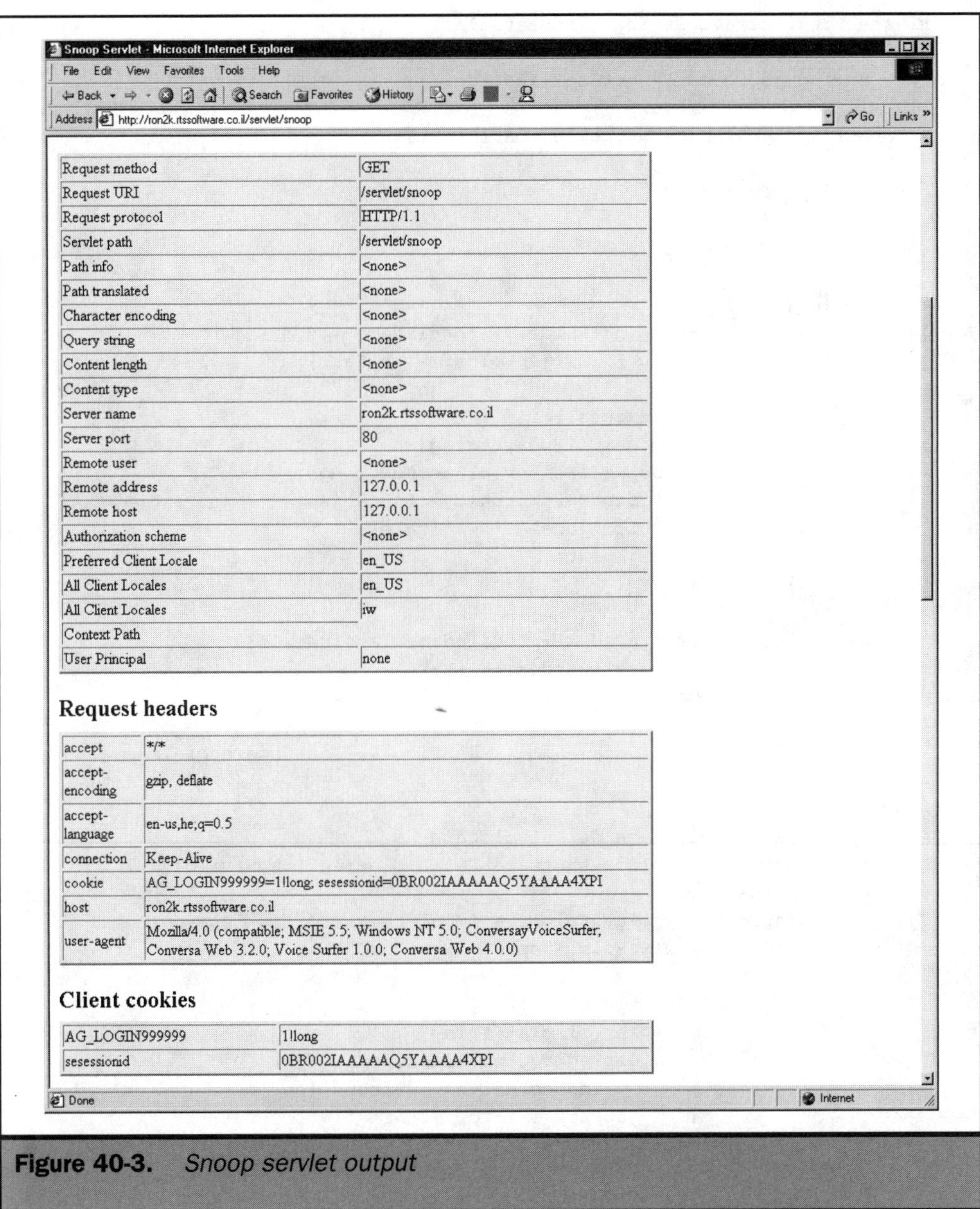

Figure 40-3. *Snoop servlet output*

for a JSP that most closely matches the locale. First it will attempt to use the full locale specification (such as *jp_JP_WIN*), but if this is unsuccessful, the method will also search for a JSP based on partial locales (such as *jp_JP*, or even simply *jp*).

```
private final static String findBestFile (
            String jspBaseFolder, String jspName, Locale locale) {
      String jspFolder = getJspFileFolder();

      String localeName = locale.toString();

      String jspPath;
      File jspFile;
      int lastUnderscoreIndex;

      while (true) {
            jspPath = jspBaseFolder + localeName + "/" + jspName;
            jspFile = new File (jspFolder + jspPath);

            if (jspFile.exists()) {
                  RTSTracker.displayString(
                        JspRedirector.class.toString() +
                        ".findBestMatch() - found jsp: " + jspPath +
                        " for locale " + locale);
                  return jspPath;
            }

            lastUnderscoreIndex = localeName.lastIndexOf("_");
            if (lastUnderscoreIndex == -1)
                  break;

            localeName = localeName.substring(0, lastUnderscoreIndex);
      }

      // try again with the default locale
      localeName = PortalConstants.getDefaultLocale().toString();
      while (true) {
            jspPath = jspBaseFolder + localeName + "/" + jspName;
            jspFile = new File (jspFolder + jspPath);

            if (jspFile.exists()) {
                  RTSTracker.displayString(
                          JspRedirector.class.toString() +
                          ".findBestMatch() - found jsp: " +
                          jspPath + " for locale " + locale);
                  return jspPath;
            }

            lastUnderscoreIndex = localeName.lastIndexOf("_");
            if (lastUnderscoreIndex == -1)
                  break;

            localeName = localeName.substring(0, lastUnderscoreIndex);
      }
```

```
        jspPath = jspBaseFolder + jspName;
        jspFile = new File (jspFolder + jspPath);

        if (jspFile.exists()) {
              RTSTracker.displayString(JspRedirector.class.toString() +
                  ".findBestMatch() - found jsp: " + jspPath +
                  " for locale " + locale);
              return jspPath;
        }

        RTSTracker.displayString(JspRedirector.class.toString() +
                 ".findBestMatch() - not found jsp file for: pagename= " +
                 jspName + ", basefolder=" + jspBaseFolder + ", locale=" +
                 locale + " & file folder=" + jspFolder);
        return null;
}
```

For this scheme to work, the JSPs need to be organized according to locales. Hence, in the ViryaNet Service hub, all JSPs are stored in directory structures that include the locale specification—as shown in Figure 40-4.

String Injection Method

This method makes use of string injection into a single JSP. The JSP is written so that it does not directly contain the string to be presented. Instead, a call to a Java routine is made to look up the actual string to be presented, based on a key. (For simplicity, the key is usually the string in the *en_US* locale-specific file.) The system maintains all

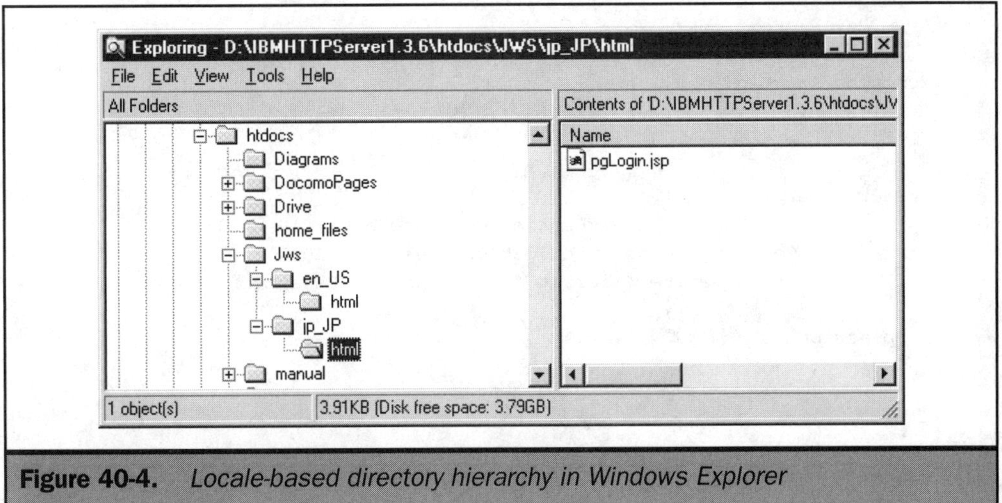

Figure 40-4. *Locale-based directory hierarchy in Windows Explorer*

strings for all supported locales in the database. The call to the Java routine uses the locale information passed in by the browser as the key to look up the correct string to be placed in the generated page delivered to the browser. An example script for the login screen is shown here:

```
<!DOCTYPE HTML PUBLIC "-//W3C//DTD HTML 4.0//EN">
  <html>

<%@ page
extends = "com.rts.eAccess.framework.EAccessBaseServlet"
import=com.rts.ml.translate.MultiLingual %>
    <head>
      <link href="/RTS_HTML_Pages/RTS_General/Css/Customization.css"
          rel="stylesheet" title="Customization style sheet"
          type="text/css"  />
      <bean create="NO" introspect="NO" name="SelfServiceException"
       scope="REQUEST" type="com.rts.selfservice.SelfServiceException">
        </bean>
      <meta content="text/html" http-equiv="Content-Type">
      <title class="MultiLingual">

  <jsp:expression>
       MultiLingual.translate("pgLogin.jsp", "TITLE", "H",
         "Login to ViryaNet Service Process", "NA", "true")
</jsp:expression>
      </title>
      <link href="/RTS_HTML_Pages/RTS_General/Css/rts.css"
        rel="stylesheet" title="ViryaNet Style Sheet" type="text/css"  />
      <link href="/RTS_HTML_Pages/RTS_General/Css/rts_remote.css"
        rel="stylesheet" title="ViryaNet Service Process Style Sheet"
        type="text/css"  />
      <script language="JavaScript" type="TEXT/JAVASCRIPT">
  function showMsg()
{


<jsp:scriptlet>
            if ((SelfServiceException.getClassName() != null) ||
            (SelfServiceException.getOverride() != null))
                out.write("alert(\"" + SelfServiceException.toString() +
                "\");");
</ jsp:scriptlet >
}



  function fnTrapKD()
```

```
{

    if (event.keyCode == 13)
    {
        formLogin.submit();
    }
}
</script>
    </head>
    <body onkeydown="fnTrapKD()" onload="showMsg()"
       onresize="window.location.href = window.location.href;">
 < jsp:scriptlet> if (isExplorer(request)){ </ jsp:scriptlet >
      <DIV id="images" CLASS="outerLayer">
 < jsp:scriptlet >}
 else{ </ jsp:scriptlet >
 <DIV align="center">
< jsp:scriptlet >} </ jsp:scriptlet >

        <img alt="ViryaNet.com" border="0" height="134" width="483"
         src="/RTS_HTML_Pages/RTS_General/images/viryanet_hd.gif">
        <br />
        <img alt="ViryaNet.com" border="0" height="195" width="483"
         src="/RTS_HTML_Pages/RTS_General/images/viryanetlogin.gif">
        <br />
        <img alt="ViryaNet.com" border="0" height="34" width="483"
         src="/RTS_HTML_Pages/RTS_General/images/viryanet_ft.gif">

  < jsp:scriptlet> if(isNetscape(request)){ </ jsp:scriptlet >
        <div align="center" class="nestedLayer" id="login" name="login">
         ViryaNet Service Process
   < jsp:scriptlet> } else{ </ jsp:scriptlet >
          <div align="center" class="nestedLayer" id="login" name="login">
            <span class="MultiLingual" id="100">

  <jsp:expression>
    MultiLingual.translate("pgLogin.jsp", "100", "T",
         "ViryaNet Service Process ", "NA", "false")
</jsp:expression>
<jsp:expression> "<!--" </jsp:expression>
ViryaNet Service Process
<jsp:expression> "-->" </jsp:expression>
            </span>

  < jsp:scriptlet> } </ jsp:scriptlet >
            <form action="/servlet/RequestHandler" method="POST"
                name="formLogin" target="_top">
              <input name="task" type="HIDDEN" value="BnLogin"  />
              <input name="action" type="HIDDEN" value="run"  />
```

```
                <table align="center" border="0">
                  <tr>
                    <td class="TableBodyFontBold">
                     < jsp:scriptlet>
                            int j1 =9;
                            if (isNetscape(request))
                              for (int ii = 0; ii < j1; ii++)
                              {
                             </ jsp:scriptlet >
                                   
                             < jsp:scriptlet>
                              }
                      </ jsp:scriptlet >
                      <span class="MultiLingual" id="200">

  <jsp:expression>
  MultiLingual.translate(
        "pgLogin.jsp", "200", "T", "User Name", "NA", "false")
</jsp:expression>
<jsp:expression> "<!--" </jsp:expression>
User Name
<jsp:expression> "-->" </jsp:expression>
                      </span>
                    </td>
                    <td>
                      <input class="TableBodyFont" name="username" size="10"
                        type="TEXT" value=""  />
                    </td>
                  </tr>
                  <tr>
                    <td class="TableBodyFontBold">
                      < jsp:scriptlet>
                               int j2 =9;
                               if (isNetscape(request))
                               for (int ii = 0; ii < j2; ii++)
                               {
                              </ jsp:scriptlet >
                                     
                              < jsp:scriptlet>
                                }
                      </ jsp:scriptlet >
                      <span class="MultiLingual" id="300">

  <jsp:expression>
MultiLingual.translate(
  "pgLogin.jsp", "300", "T", "Password", "NA", "false")
</jsp:expression>
<jsp:expression> "<!--" </jsp:expression>
```

```
Password
<jsp:expression> "-->" </jsp:expression>
                    </span>
                  </td>
                  <td>
                    <input class="TableBodyFont" name="password" size="10"
                          type="PASSWORD" value=""  />
                  </td>
                </tr>
                <tr>
                  <td colspan="2">
                    <div align="center">
                     < jsp:scriptlet>
                                 int j22 =9;
                                 if (isNetscape(request))
                                 for (int ii = 0; ii < j22; ii++)
                                 {
                                </ jsp:scriptlet >
                                       
                                < jsp:scriptlet>
                                 }
                      </ jsp:scriptlet >
                      <span class="MultiLingual" id="400">
                        <input value="<jsp:expression>
MultiLingual.translate(
"pgLogin.jsp", "400", "B", "Log in", "NA", "false")
</jsp:expression>"
class="ButtonFont" name="buttonName"
onclick="formLogin.submit()" type="BUTTON"  >

                        </input>
                      </span>
                    </div>
                  </td>
                </tr>
              </table>
            </form>
          </div>
        </div>
      </div>
    </body>
  </html>
```

The code performing the actual lookup is shown next. The advantages of this method are that a single JSP is used for all locales, and that translation of the strings is easily and centrally maintained. The disadvantage (and it's a big one) is that the JSPs are malformed—not in the sense that they are incorrect, but in the sense that all strings have been removed and, therefore, if viewed through a WYSIWYG editor, the script will not be convenient to the developer.

```
package com.rts.ml.translate;

import com.sun.java.util.collections.*;
import java.util.Locale;
import java.sql.*;
import com.rts.sql.*;
import com.rts.gen.RTSTracker;
import com.rts.gen.RTS;
import java.util.PropertyResourceBundle;
import java.util.MissingResourceException;
import com.rts.util.RTSUtil;
import com.rts.ml.RTSMLManager;

/**
 * Call stored function to translate string.
 * Reads a translation on/off switch from server.properties
 * If  switch is not found in server.properties - sets a switch to OFF
 */
public class MultiLingual {

      public static Locale TRANSLATION_NOT_NEEDED = Locale.US;
      public static final  String                NBSP = " ",

      NBSP_WRONG = " "      ;
      private static Connection _connection;

      private static Map _cache;
      private static boolean _filled = false;

      private static String _translation = null;

public MultiLingual() {
      super();
}
private static void clearCache() {
      _cache = null;
}
private static void display(String s) {
      RTSTracker.displayString(s);

}
private static void fillCacheFromDb(String jspName) {

      display("Fill cache for =" + jspName  );
```

```
com.rts.sql.RTSConnection con = null;
com.rts.sql.RTSPreparedStatement stmt = null;
String id = null,
            type = null,
               textJsp = null,
               textMlt = null;

 String sql =
 " SELECT ID,TYPE,TEXT_JSP,TEXT_MLT FROM JSP_TEXT where JSP_NAME=?";

 try {

        con = com.rts.sql.RTSDB.getSelectConnection();
        stmt = con.prepareStatement(sql);
        stmt.getStmt().setString(1, jspName);



        ResultSet res   = stmt.executeQuery();
        boolean b =  false;
        while (res.next())
        {
               id = res.getString(1);
               type = res.getString(2);
               textJsp = res.getString(3);
               textMlt = res.getString(4);
               if( id != null ) {
                      MltCacheObject o = new MltCacheObject();
                      o.setId(id);
                      o.setType(type);
                      o.setTextJsp(textJsp);
                      o.setTextMlt(textMlt);

                      setToCache(jspName , id , o);
                      b = true;
               }
        }
        if( b) {
        RTSTracker.displayString("Translation Screen Cache filled");
        }
 }
 catch (SQLException ex) {
        com.rts.gen.RTSTracker.handleException(
          "MultiLingual : fillCacheFromDb", ex);
 }
 finally {
        com.rts.gen.RTS.close(con, stmt, null);
 }
```

```
}
 private static Map getCache() {

        if( _cache == null ) {
               _cache = new Hashtable();
        }

 return _cache;

}
private static MltCacheObject getFromCache(String s) {

        return (MltCacheObject) getCache().get(s);
}
private static String getTranslationFromCache(
String jspName, String fieldId, String fieldType, String text) {

        String translated = null;

        StringBuffer sb = new StringBuffer(jspName);
        sb.append(".");
        sb.append(fieldId);
        MltCacheObject o = getFromCache(sb.toString());

        if (o != null) {
               translated = o.getTextMlt();
        }
        return translated;
}
private static String getTranslationFromDb(
String jspName, String fieldId, String fieldType, String text, String language)
{

        display(" getTranslationFromDb JspName=" + jspName + " fieldId=" +
                fieldId + " text=" +text);

        String translated = text;

        com.rts.sql.RTSConnection con = null;
        com.rts.sql.RTSCallableStatement stmt = null;
        String old = text;
        String pureText = stripNbsp(text);

        try {
               String sql = "{call JSP_TEXT_TRANS(?,?,?,?,?) }";
```

```
            con = com.rts.sql.RTSDB.getSelectConnection();
            stmt = con.prepareCall(sql);

            stmt.bindValue(1, jspName);
            stmt.bindValue(2, fieldId);
            stmt.bindValue(3, fieldType);
            stmt.bindValue(4, pureText);
            stmt.getStmt().registerOutParameter(
                 5, java.sql.Types.VARCHAR);

            stmt.execute();
            translated = stmt.getStmt().getString(5);
            RTSTracker.displayString("translation - OK");
      }
      catch (SQLException ex) {
            com.rts.gen.RTSTracker.handleException(
                "MultiLingual : translate", ex);
      }
      finally {
            com.rts.gen.RTS.close(con, stmt, null);
      }

      // if there were nbsp in the original string
      // replace in the original string the non-bnsp value
      // with the new value saving nbsp-aces
      if (!pureText.equals(old)) {
                  String str = RTSUtil.replace(
                       old, pureText, translated);
                  translated = str;
      }

      display("Translation result=" + translated);
      return translated;
}

private static boolean getTranslationSwitch() {

            boolean _switch =  true;
            if( _translation == null ) {
               PropertyResourceBundle configBundle =
                     (PropertyResourceBundle)
                     PropertyResourceBundle.getBundle("server");
               try {
                  _translation = configBundle.getString("translation");
               }
               catch(MissingResourceException ex) {
                _translation = "off" ;
```

```
                }
            }


            if( "0".equalsIgnoreCase(_translation)  ||
                    "off".equalsIgnoreCase(_translation)  ||
                    "false".equalsIgnoreCase(_translation) ||
                    "no".equalsIgnoreCase(_translation)  )
          {

                          _switch = false;
                    }

            return _switch;


}
        public static void main(String[] args) {
                    String s = MultiLingual.translate(
                      "JSpName", "1", "T","Site","NA", "true");

                    RTSTracker.displayString(s);
        }

private  static boolean  needTranslation() {
            boolean need = true;


        boolean  _switch = getTranslationSwitch();

        if(  ! _switch ) {
                            return false;

        }

        if (
TRANSLATION_NOT_NEEDED.equals(RTSMLManager.getClientLocale())){
                     need = false;
        }
        else if(
TRANSLATION_NOT_NEEDED.getDisplayLanguage().equalsIgnoreCase(
             RTSMLManager.getClientLocale().getDisplayLanguage())){
                     need = false;
        }


        return need;
```

```
}
private static String realTranslate_NEW(
String jspName, String fieldId, String fieldType, String text, String language)
{

       display("TrealTranslate_NEW =" + jspName + " fieldId=" +fieldId +
                  " text=" +text);
       String translated = getTranslationFromCache( jspName,
                  fieldId, fieldType, text );

       if( translated == null ) {

              translated = getTranslationFromDb(
                 jspName, fieldId, fieldType, text, language);
              MltCacheObject o = new MltCacheObject();
              o.setId(fieldId);
              o.setType(fieldType);
              o.setTextJsp(text);
              o.setTextMlt(translated);

              setToCache(jspName , fieldId , o);
              RTSTracker.displayString(
                 "Translation Screen Cache appended by "+ text +
                 " -  " + translated);
       }

       return translated;

}
private static void setToCache(String key, MltCacheObject o) {
       getCache().put(key, o);
}
private static void setToCache(
   String jspName, String fieldId, MltCacheObject o) {
       StringBuffer sb = new StringBuffer(jspName);
       sb.append(".");
       sb.append(fieldId);
       setToCache(sb.toString(), o);
}
/**
 * Sets a Locale for which the translation is not needed </br>
 * The default is Locale.US
 * @param Locale locale
 *
 */
public static void  setTranslationNotNeeded(Locale l) {
       TRANSLATION_NOT_NEEDED = l;
```

```
}
/**
 * Removes nbsp from the string.
 * Also removes a wrong nbsp (without ; at the end )
 * @param String string
 * @return String string stripped from nbsp
 */
private static String stripNbsp(String s) {

        String r = new String();

        String stripped = null;
        int i = s.indexOf(NBSP);
        if (i > -1) {
                stripped = RTSUtil.replace(s, NBSP, r);
        }
        else {
                stripped = s;
        }


        i = stripped.indexOf(NBSP_WRONG);
        String stripped1 = null;
        if (i > -1) {
                stripped1 = RTSUtil.replace(stripped, NBSP_WRONG, r);
                display("Wrong NBSP occured in line:" + s );
        }
        else {
                stripped1 = stripped;
        }



        return stripped1;
}
/**
 * The API method. Translates a given string into the default client
 * language if that language is not US English. </br>
 * Uses an STP JSP_TEXT_TRANS in its translation process. </br>
 *
 * @param String jsp screen name (like pgMyFavoriteLovelyScreen.jsp)
 * @param String field id - the unique identifier of the field within
 * the screen (usually a number which is built automatically)
 * @param String field type (T - text, H - title, B - botton, O - option)
 * @param String text to translate
 * @param String language - currently optional & may be null
 * @return String translated string
```

```
 *
 */
public static String translate(
          String jspName, String fieldId, String fieldType,
          String s, String language, String fillCache) {

       if ( needTranslation() ) {
              display("start translating..");
              if( fillCache.equalsIgnoreCase("true") ) {
                     display("start building a cache ..");
                     fillCacheFromDb(jspName);
              }
              return realTranslate_NEW(
                jspName, fieldId, fieldType, s, language);
        }
         else {
                return s;
         }
}
}
```


Transcoder Method

The third and final method, and one that we consider superior to the other two, maintains the "natural" form of the JSP in the sense that strings are inserted into the JSP but they are marked. The marking makes use of the `SPAN` tag to indicate that a certain string should be interpreted as one that needs to undergo a multilingual lookup. A component called the *transcoder* (not to be confused with the IBM WebSphere Transcoder) is then responsible for replacing the string inside the `SPAN` tag with another string based on the locale information. This method, therefore, has all advantages—a single JSP, translation strings in the database, and a JSP that "looks right."

The following script shows the JSP as it looks according to this method. A second script shows the transcoder code responsible for replacing the string within the `SPAN` element.

```
<% com.rts.transcoder.servlet.RTSMobileTranscoderServlet
      .preparePageForFiltering(request,response); %>
<!DOCTYPE HTML PUBLIC "-//W3C//DTD HTML 4.0//EN">
  <html>
<%@ page
extends = "com.rts.eAccess.framework.EAccessBaseServlet" %>
    <head>
      <link href="/RTS_HTML_Pages/RTS_General/Css/Customization.css"
       rel="stylesheet" title="Customization style sheet" type="text/css"
```

```
/>
 <bean create="NO" introspect="NO" name="SelfServiceException"
       scope="REQUEST" type="com.rts.selfservice.SelfServiceException">
        </bean>
      <meta content="text/html" http-equiv="Content-Type">
      <title class="MultiLingual">
  Login to ViryaNet Service Process
      </title>
      <link href="/RTS_HTML_Pages/RTS_General/Css/rts.css" rel="stylesheet"
         title="ViryaNet Style Sheet" type="text/css"  />
      <link href="/RTS_HTML_Pages/RTS_General/Css/rts_remote.css"
         rel="stylesheet" title="ViryaNet Service Process Style Sheet"
         type="text/css"  />
      <script language="JavaScript" type="TEXT/JAVASCRIPT">
  function showMsg()
{
              < jsp:scriptlet>
             /* if ((SelfServiceException.getClassName() != null) ||
               (SelfServiceException.getOverride() != null))

                out.write("alert(\"" + SelfServiceException.toString() +
                          "\");"); */
              </ jsp:scriptlet >
}
  function fnTrapKD()
{
    if (event.keyCode == 13)
    {
        formLogin.submit();
    }
}
</script>
    </head>
    <body onkeydown="fnTrapKD()" onload="showMsg()"
        onresize="window.location.href = window.location.href;">
 < jsp:scriptlet> if (isExplorer(request)){ </ jsp:scriptlet >
      <DIV id="images" CLASS="outerLayer">
 < jsp:scriptlet >}
 else{</ jsp:scriptlet >
 <DIV align="center">
< jsp:scriptlet >} </ jsp:scriptlet >
        <img alt="ViryaNet.com" border="0" height="134" width="483"
         src="/RTS_HTML_Pages/RTS_General/images/viryanet_hd.gif">
        <br />
        <img alt="ViryaNet.com" border="0" height="195" width="483"
         src="/RTS_HTML_Pages/RTS_General/images/viryanetlogin.gif">
        <br />
```

```
     <img alt="ViryaNet.com" border="0" height="34" width="483"
      src="/RTS_HTML_Pages/RTS_General/images/viryanet_ft.gif">
< jsp:scriptlet> if(isNetscape(request)){ </ jsp:scriptlet >
     <div align="center" class="nestedLayer" id="login"
           name="login">ViryaNet Service Process
 < jsp:scriptlet> } else{ </ jsp:scriptlet >
       <div align="center" class="nestedLayer" id="login" name="login">
         <span class="MultiLingual" id="100">
             ViryaNet Service Process
         </span>
< jsp:scriptlet> } </ jsp:scriptlet >
         <form action="/servlet/RequestHandler" method="POST"
             name="formLogin" target="_top">
           <input name="task" type="HIDDEN" value="BnLogin"  />
           <input name="action" type="HIDDEN" value="run"  />
           <table align="center" border="0">
             <tr>
               <td class="TableBodyFontBold">
                < jsp:scriptlet>
                       int j1 =9;
                       if (isNetscape(request))
                         for (int ii = 0; ii < j1; ii++)
                         {
                        </ jsp:scriptlet >
                               
                        < jsp:scriptlet>
                         }
                 </ jsp:scriptlet >
                 <span class="MultiLingual" id="200">
                     User Name
                 </span>
               </td>
               <td>
                 <input class="TableBodyFont" name="username" size="10"
                    type="TEXT" value=""  />
               </td>
             </tr>
             <tr>
               <td class="TableBodyFontBold">
                 < jsp:scriptlet>
                              int j2 =9;
                          if (isNetscape(request))
                          for (int ii = 0; ii < j2; ii++)
                          {
                         </ jsp:scriptlet >
                                
                         < jsp:scriptlet>
                           }
```

```
                  </ jsp:scriptlet >
                  <span class="MultiLingual" id="300">
                      Password
                  </span>
                </td>
                <td>
                  <input class="TableBodyFont" name="password" size="10"
                   type="PASSWORD" value=""  />
                </td>
              </tr>
              <tr>
                <td colspan="2">
                  <div align="center">
                   < jsp:scriptlet>
                               int j22 =9;
                               if (isNetscape(request))
                               for (int ii = 0; ii < j22; ii++)
                               {
                             </ jsp:scriptlet >
                                     
                             < jsp:scriptlet>
                             }
                    </ jsp:scriptlet >
                    <span class="MultiLingual" id="400">
                      <input value="Log in" class="ButtonFont"
                      name="buttonName" onclick="formLogin.submit()"
                      type="BUTTON"   >
                      </input>
                    </span>
                  </div>
                </td>
              </tr>
            </table>
          </form>
        </div>
      </div>
    </div>
  </body>
</html>
```

The following script shows the transcoder code responsible for replacing the string within the SPAN element.

```
package com.rts.transcoder;

/**
```

```
 * This type was created in VisualAge.
 */
import org.xml.sax.*;
import java.io.*;
import java.lang.System.*;
import com.commerceone.xdk.standards.sax.*;
import com.rts.transcoder.taglist.*;
import com.sun.java.util.collections.*;
import com.rts.gen.RTSTracker;
import java.util.ResourceBundle;
import java.util.PropertyResourceBundle;
import com.rts.ml.translate.MultiLingual;
import org.xml.sax.helpers.AttributeListImpl;
import java.util.Locale;

public class MultilingualHandler implements
                TranscoderModificator,Tags,
                com.rts.transcoder.taglist.Attributes {
      public final static int MAX_JSP_NAME_SIZE = 50;
      public final static String ML_CLASS = "MultiLingual";

      boolean translateMode;
      String translateId;
      String translateType;
      String specialId;
      int translateIndex;
      TranscoderHandler handler;
      String language;
      String jspName;

public void end(){}
public String mlTranslate(
String fieldId, String fieldType, String s, String fillCache) {
      s = s.trim();
      String src = specialId;
      if(src == null) {
            src = s;
      } else {
            fieldId = "T" + specialId.hashCode();
      }

      String dst =
MultiLingual.translate(jspName,fieldId,fieldType,src,language,fillCache);
      //System.out.println("Translate: <<" +jspName+" , "+fieldId+" ,
         "+fieldType+" , "+src+" , "+language+" , "+fillCache);
```

```
if(specialId == null) {
      return dst;
}

String s1 = specialId.trim();
String s2 = s.trim();
String s3 = dst.trim();
specialId = null;

StringBuffer sb = new StringBuffer();
for(int i = 0; i < s1.length(); i++) {
      char ch = s1.charAt(i);
      if(ch == '%') {
            i++;
            if(s1.charAt(i) != '%') {
                  ch = '\n';
            }
      }
      sb.append(ch);
}

s1 = sb.toString();
java.util.StringTokenizer st = new java.util.StringTokenizer(s1,"\n");
java.util.Vector v = new java.util.Vector();
boolean first = true;
s2=s2.trim();

while(st.hasMoreTokens()) {
      String str = st.nextToken().trim();
      int idx = s2.indexOf(str);
      if(idx >= 0) {
            if(idx != 0) {
                  v.addElement(s2.substring(0,idx).trim());
            } else
            if(first) {
                  first = false;
                  if(s1.indexOf('\n') == 0) {
                        v.addElement("");
                  }
            }
            s2 = s2.substring(idx + str.length());
      }
}
if(s2.trim().length() > 0)  {
      v.addElement(s2.trim());
}
```

```
        sb.setLength(0);
        for(int i = 0; i < s3.length(); i++) {
            char ch = s3.charAt(i);
            if(ch == '%') {
                i++;
                if(s3.charAt(i) != '%') {
                    if(v.size() > 0) {
                        String str = (String)v.elementAt(0);
                        sb.append(str);
                        v.removeElementAt(0);
                    }
                    continue;
                }
            }
            sb.append(ch);
        }
        return sb.toString();
    }
    /**
     * printing the start tag
     */
    public AttributeList modifyAttributes(AttributeList atts,TagDescription td) {
        AttributeListImpl attributes = (AttributeListImpl)atts;
        if(td == null) {
            return atts;
        }

        int id = td.getId();

        if(!translateMode) {
            if(id == t_TITLE) {
                String mlClass = atts.getValue(an_CLASS);
                if(mlClass != null &&
                   mlClass.equalsIgnoreCase(ML_CLASS)) {
                      translateMode = true;
                      translateType = "H";
                      translateId = "TITLE";
                      translateIndex = -1;
                }
                specialId = atts.getValue(an_ID);
            } else
            if(id == t_SPAN) {
                String mlClass = attributes.getValue(an_CLASS);
                translateId = attributes.getValue(an_ID);
                if(translateId != null && mlClass != null &&
                    mlClass.equalsIgnoreCase(ML_CLASS)) {
```

```
                    translateMode = true;
                    translateType = null;
                    translateIndex = -1;
                }
            }
        } else {
            if(id == t_INPUT) {
                String type  = attributes.getValue(an_TYPE);
                String value = attributes.getValue(an_VALUE);

                if(type != null && (type.equalsIgnoreCase("button") ||
                    type.equalsIgnoreCase("submit") ||
                    type.equalsIgnoreCase("reset"))) {
                    value = mlTranslate(
                      translateId, "B", value, "false");
                    attributes.removeAttribute(an_VALUE);
                    attributes.addAttribute(an_VALUE,"",value);
                }
            } else
            if(id == t_OPTION) {
                specialId = atts.getValue(an_ID);
                translateType = "O";
                translateIndex ++;
            }
        }
        return attributes;
    }
    /**
     * processing the end tag
     */
    public String modifyTag(String tagName,TagDescription td,boolean isEndTag){
        if(isEndTag && td != null) {
            if(td.getId() == t_TITLE || td.getId() == t_SPAN) {
                translateMode = false;
            }
        }
        return tagName;
    }
    public String modifyText(String s) {
        if(translateMode && s.trim().length() > 0) {
            String id = translateId;
            if(translateIndex >= 0) {
                id += "." + translateIndex;
            }
            String flag = (translateType != null && translateType.equals("H"))
                ? "true" : "false";
```

```
            s = mlTranslate(id, translateType == null
                    ? "T" : translateType, s, flag);
        }
        return s;
  }
  public void reStart(TranscoderHandler handler) {
        start(handler);
  }
  public void start(TranscoderHandler handler) {
        this.handler = handler;
        language = "NA";
        translateMode = false;
        translateId = null;
        translateType = null;
        specialId = null;
        translateIndex = -1;

        if(handler.pageName != null) {
              jspName = handler.pageName;
              if(jspName.length() > MAX_JSP_NAME_SIZE) {
                    jspName = jspName.substring(
                      jspName.length() - MAX_JSP_NAME_SIZE);
              }
        }
  }
  }
```


Multilingual Data

Supporting multiple languages for data is simpler although not trivial. Here, too, we can suggest two different approaches—one that makes use of the application server code and another that makes use of database views.

The first method, shown in the following script, is to introduce a new encapsulation called `MLString`. For a certain data string, this class maintains multiple strings, each in a different language supported by the application (and therefore by the database schema). This means that when `MLString` is read from the database, all values for all languages are read. Then when a user wants to change the locale (or even just browse the data in a different locale without making a change), the data is available in the server, and the user request can be easily accommodated.

```
package com.rts.ml;


//Title:        FW ML
```

```
//Version:
//Copyright:    Copyright (c) 2001
//Author:       ViryaNet
//Company:      ViryaNet
//Description:  FW ML



import com.sun.java.util.collections.*;
import com.rts.fw.RTSBusinessObject;
import com.rts.session.RTSEncodable;
import com.rts.session.RTSEncDec;
import com.rts.session.RTSEncoder;
import com.rts.session.RTSDecoder;
import com.rts.gen.RTS;
import com.rts.gen.RTSTracker;
//import com.rts.util.RTSUtil;
//import com.rts.util.RTSIterator;
import java.util.Locale;
import com.rts.gen.RTSResultTable;
import com.rts.dbl.*;
import com.rts.xml.schema.description.SchemaDescriptor;

abstract public class MLString implements
         Cloneable, RTSEncodable, SchemaDescriptor {

/** dictionary with all pairs of language - String
 */
      private Map _stringInLang;

/**
 * Class constructor
 */

public MLString() {
      this((String[])null, (String[])null);

}
/**
 * Class constructor
 *
 * @param languages
 *   array of language codes. The codes can be
 *   a language code with optional country code.<br>
 *   For example:<br><ul><tt>
 *   <li>enus -- US English
 *   <li>fr   -- French
```

```
 *   <li>ru   -- Russian
 *   </ul></tt><br>
 *   Language codes are taken from:
 *   <a href=
 * "http://userpage.chemie.fu-berlin.de/diverse/doc/ISO_639.html">
 * ISO 639</a>.
 *   <br>
 *   Country codes are taken from:
 *   <a
href="http://userpage.chemie.fu-berlin.de/diverse/doc/ISO_3166.html">ISO
3166</a>.
 * @param values
 *   array of values. a value for each language code
 */
public MLString(String[] languages, String[] values) {
      initialize(languages, values);
}
/**
 * Class constructor: Use the given business class and the name of
 * the business variable in that class, to get the list of supported
 * languages. String values are null.
 *
 * @param aClass a business class
 * @param bvName a business variables path
 */
public MLString(Class aClass, String path) {

      this( RTSMLManager.getSupportedLanguageCodes(aClass, path), null);
}
/**
 * adds new language + String to the dictionary
 * @param language  a language (or language + country) code
 * @param value     a value (can be null)
 */
public void add(String language,String value)
{
      getLanguagesDict().put(language,value);
}
public   Object  asXml( String vName, Object value )
{

      return null;

}
      /**
       * Clone this object. The returned object is a deep copy of this object.
       */
```

```
        public Object clone()
        {
              MLString obj;

              try
              {
                    obj = (MLString) super.clone();
              }
              catch(CloneNotSupportedException ex)
              {
                    // Ignore
                    obj = null;
              }

              obj.setLanguagesDict( new HashMap(getLanguagesDict()) );
              return obj;
        }
        /**
         * Decode the given object.
         * <br>
         * <blockquote><pre>
         * enc:
         *    [ ENC_TYPE_MLSTRING class-name languages-dictionary ]
         *
         * </pre></blockquote>
         * <br>
         *
         * @param enc encoded object
         * @return the decoded object
         */
        public Object decode(Object [] enc, RTSDecoder decoder)
        {
              _stringInLang = (Map)decoder.decode((Object[])enc[2]);
              return this;
        }
/**
 *  Answers a new empty MLString
 */

public MLString empty()
{

        String [] langs = getLanguages();

        MLString emptyML = (MLString)clone();
        for( int i = 0 ; i < langs.length ; ++i )
        {
              emptyML.setValue(langs[i], null);
```

```
        }

        return emptyML;

}
        /**
         * Encode the given object.
         */
        public Object [] encode(RTSEncoder encoder)
        {
              Object [] enc = new Object[3];

              enc[0] = RTSEncDec.ENC_TYPE_MLSTRING;
              enc[1] = getClass().getName();
              enc[2] = encoder.encode(_stringInLang);

              return enc;
        }
/**
 * Returns the default language
 */
private static String getDefaultLanguage()
{
        return "en";
}
/**
 * Returns the default languages
 */
public static String [] getDefaultLanguages()
{
        String [] langs = new String[1];
        langs[0] = getDefaultLanguage();
        return langs;
}
/**
  * Get the languages dictionary
  */

public String[]  getLanguages()
{

        Set s = getLanguagesDict().keySet();
        String[] _langs = new String[s.size()];
        Iterator it =s.iterator();
        int i = 0;
        while( it.hasNext() ) {
              _langs[i++] = (String) it.next();
        }
```

```
        return _langs;
}
/**
  * Get the languages dictionary
  */

protected Map getLanguagesDict()
{
        return _stringInLang;
}
/**
 * Returns String for the current language
 * @param language java.lang.String
 * added by Zeev 26/9/99
 */
public String getValue() {
        return (String) _stringInLang.get( getDefaultLanguage() );
}
/**
 * Returns String for the given language
 * @param language a language code, or null if not found
 */
public String getValue (String lang)
{
        return (String)getLanguagesDict().get(lang);
}
/**
* SchemaDescriptor implementation
*/
public Object getVariableValue(String vName)
{
        return getLanguagesDict().get( vName);



}
/**
 * Fills a dictionary of languages.
 * If no string given - null will be taken
 * @param String[] languages
 * @param String[] strings
 */
private void initialize(String[] langs, String[] strings)
{
        int min;
```

```
        if( langs == null )
            langs = getDefaultLanguages();

        Map dict = new HashMap(langs.length);
        setLanguagesDict(dict);

        if( strings == null )
        {
            min = 0;
        }
        else
        {
            min = langs.length;
            if( strings.length < min )
                min = strings.length;
        }

        int i = 0;

        for (i = 0; i < min; i++)
        {
            dict.put(langs[i], strings[i]);
        }

        for ( ; i < langs.length ; i++ )
        {
            dict.put(langs[i], null);
        }
    }
    /**
     * Check if this object is empty.
     * MLString object is empty if all values of all languages are empty.
     */
    public boolean isEmpty()
    {
        Iterator itr = getLanguagesDict().values().iterator();
        while(itr.hasNext())
        {
            String str = (String)itr.next();
            if( str != null && !str.equals("") )
                return false;
        }
        return true;
    }
    /**
     * Returns true if the given language is supported by the mls
```

```
 */
public boolean isLanguageIncluded(String language)
{
      return getLanguagesDict().containsKey(language);
}
/**
 * List all supported languages
 */
public String[] listLanguages()
{
      Map dict = getLanguagesDict();
      String [] langs = new String[ dict.size() ];

      int i = 0;
      Iterator itr = dict.keySet().iterator();
      while (itr.hasNext())
      {
            langs[i++] = (String)itr.next();
      }

      return langs;
}
/**
 * Set the languages dictionary
 */

protected void setLanguagesDict(Map dict)
{
      _stringInLang = dict;
}
/**
 * Set a new value for the default language
 */
public void setValue(String value)
{
      getLanguagesDict().put(getDefaultLanguage(), value);
}
/**
 * Set a new value for an existing language
 */
public void setValue(String language, String value)
{
      getLanguagesDict().put(language, value);
}
/**
 * SchemaDescriptor implementation
 */
public void setVariable (String vName, Object val)
```

```
{


            getLanguagesDict().put(vName, val);

}
 /** returns value by current locale,
  * if doesn't exist, then English version
  */
  public String toString()
  {
          return   RTSTracker.objToString(getLanguagesDict());
  }
}
```

The second approach makes use of database views. The "real" table in the database has multiple columns for each language that should be supported. In addition, for each language supported by the system, a database view exists. This view maps all columns in the "real" table that are not involved in the multilingual scheme, and also maps the column for the locale's language. A database user is created for each language that is to be supported; this database user contains all views for the appropriate locale.

Within the WebSphere application server, you create multiple connection pools, one per database user (that is, per supported locale). Whenever a request needs to be serviced, the locale is extracted. Based on the requesting locale, a database connection is requested from the appropriate pool. Since this connection maps to the database user matching the locale used by the end user, the correct data strings will be retrieved. Therefore, the same query (for example, `SELECT PART_DESC FROM PARTS WHERE ..`) will retrieve different data from the "real" table based on the locale on which the request was made. This is depicted in Figure 40-5.

Summary

Now you know how to use the mechanisms and methods by which you can build global applications for deployment in a WebSphere application server. Remember that after you open your Web application for business, you cannot know who will be using it. Therefore, if you care about localizing your application to different user communities in different locales, you will need to use these mechanisms to ensure that your data is presented correctly.

One last word before moving on to the next subject: Do not underestimate the effort involved with localization. Translation takes a long time and is expensive to implement. In addition, other issues such as date formats, address formats, conventions, colors,

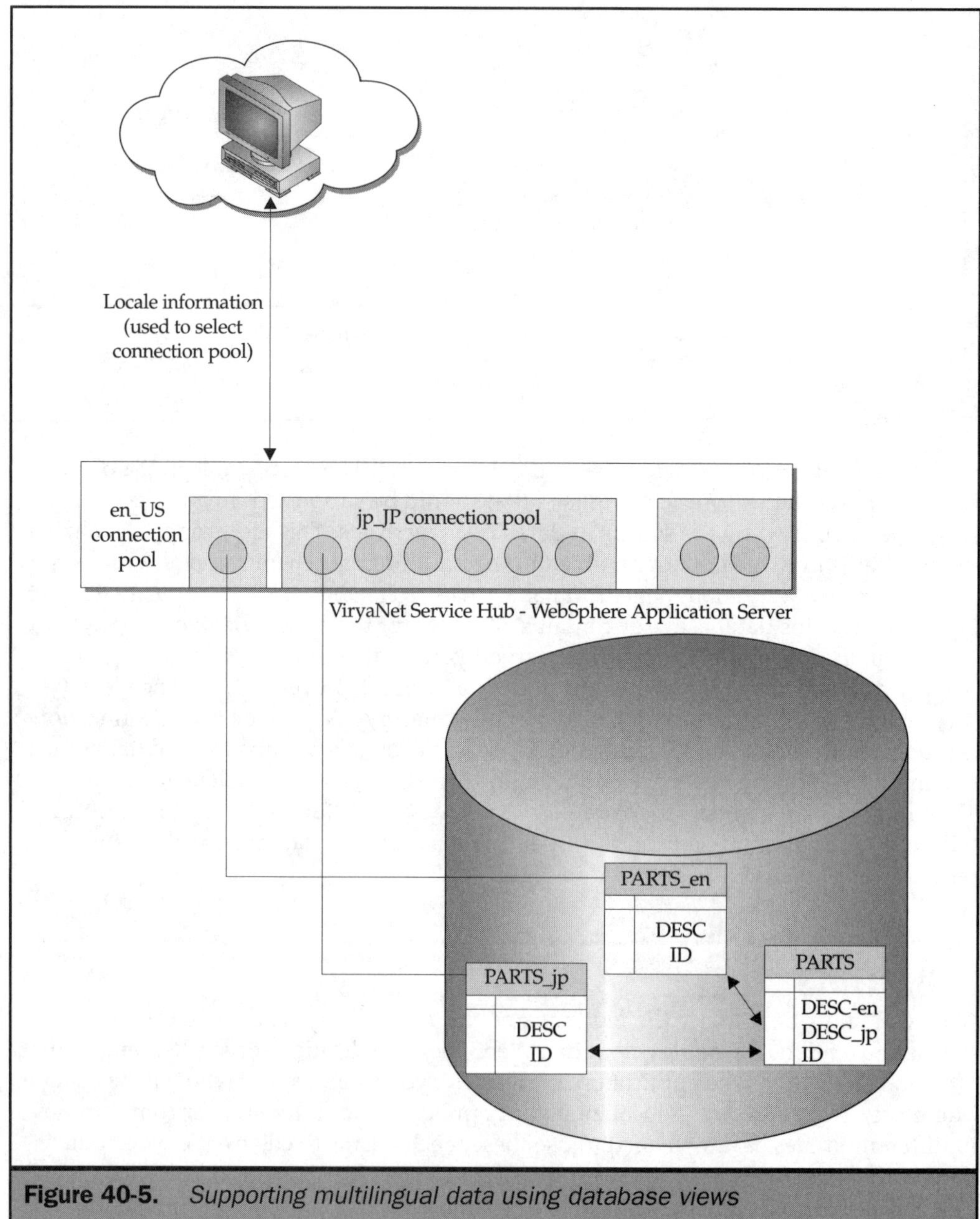

Figure 40-5. *Supporting multilingual data using database views*

cultural implications, and so on complicate the localization process and require a lot of attention, especially for applications that are not used within a controlled business environment and that may serve consumer markets.

The Complete Reference

Part IX

Administering WebSphere Sites

The Complete Reference

Chapter 41

Deploying WebSphere for Scalability and Fault Tolerance

WebSphere is an application server that is used to deploy Web applications. This book has emphasized how you should develop these Web applications. It has provided details and examples of the configuration and administration of the server and the Web applications deployed on the server, but a high-level view of the final configuration has been saved until this chapter. This chapter walks you through how a typical WebSphere deployment may look, including all the relevant components.

As you can probably appreciate, a full-scale deployment of an e-business system requires a whole set of technological components in addition to the WebSphere Application Server. These components will be discussed one at a time. The purpose of this chapter is to guarantee that you can put together all the different information that you've learned throughout the book (and in your work-related experience) to manage a full deployment scheme.

Another major goal of this chapter is to leave you with a clear view of the server topology in a full production deployment. Whenever you design a system, you must decide on the hardware that should be purchased and on the server configuration. Naturally, your hardware needs depend on the performance of the underlying applications, and we can shed little light on that aspect in this chapter (the problem obviously being that every application has its own performance requirements and characteristics). Still, regardless of the actual performance requirements, there is great commonality between most systems in terms of topology. So while one system may require a dual-CPU server with 866Mhz CPUs and a Windows2000 operating system, and another system may require a quad-CPU server with SPARC processors and a Solaris operating system, the overall system topologies tend to be similar.

This chapter describes the most common topology that is useful in the initiation phase of any project, regardless of whether it is a sale on an e-business application or an internal development project.

Server Topologies

Let's start with the obvious (always a good place to start). To run most applications, you need to have four components in place: a database server on which to store your data, an application server on which your code runs, a Worldwide Web (WWW) server (or Web server) that handles the Hypertext Transfer Protocol (HTTP) requests, and a browser that interprets the markup language and presents data to the user. The browser is owned by the user, so you don't need to worry about it, but the other three components are definitely your responsibility.

Figure 41-1 shows a server topology, illustrating which server communicates with which other server. The browser initiates it all by generating an HTTP request. Note that this scenario is the focus, as opposed to a Java client communicating directly with an Enterprise JavaBean (EJB) on the application server, because it is more widely used.

The HTTP request is served by the Web server. If it is a request for a static page, the story ends—the Web server responds with the page, and you are done—but this is not

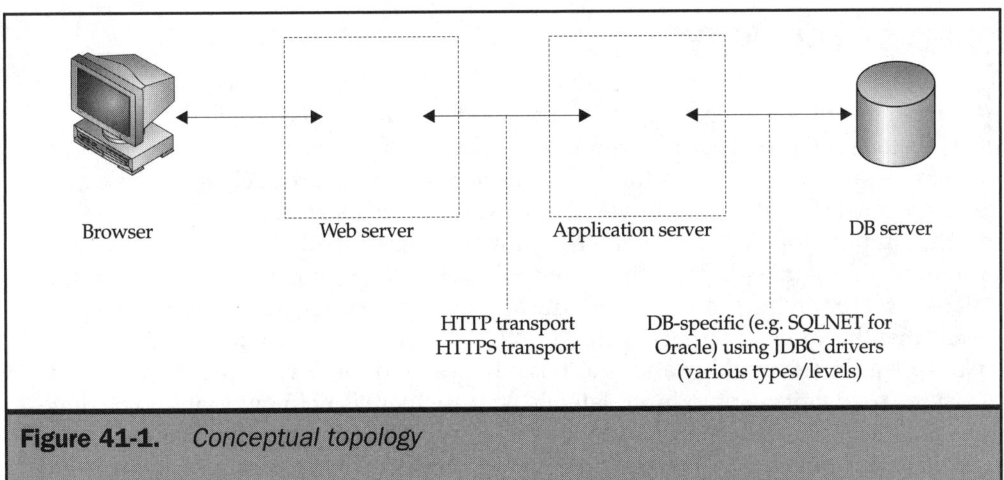

Figure 41-1. *Conceptual topology*

your everyday scenario. Most pages are dynamic in some way or another, and in that case, the request is passed to the application server. Until the release of WebSphere version 4.0, this was accomplished using a set of proprietary methods, such as local pipes or the Open Servlet Engine (OSE) proprietary protocol over sockets. In version 4.0, the request is passed via HTTP (or Hypertext Transfer Protocol, over a Secure Socket Layer [HTTPS] if an encrypted communication channel is required, even within the demilitarized zone [DMZ], which we will discuss in the section, "DMZ Configurations").

Once in the application server, the application code kicks in and performs the application logic to perform actions and transactions. The application server code typically will also create the next presentation to be delivered to the browser, using some form of markup language. To perform both tasks, the application code will need access to the database. This is accomplished by communicating with the database server. Because the vast majority of database servers are relational, a Java Database Connectivity (JDBC) driver is used, and, depending on the type of JDBC connection, the call will be handled either directly in Java through a gateway, or by means of a native library. In either case, the traffic between the application server and the database server is a proprietary one that depends on the database vendor. For example, if the database being accessed is Oracle, the traffic on the network will be SQLNET. The standard part is the fact that the application server may work directly with a JDBC driver using a standard application programming interface (API)—it is the driver's responsibility to then manage the proprietary communication with the database server.

In this context, it is worth mentioning the WebSphere Connection Manager. Another of WebSphere's advantages is that it provides transparent access to relational databases, as long as the JDBC driver is supplied. As seen in Chapter 18, the Connection Manager provides numerous performance improvements over direct-to-database calls from an application perspective.

Two-Server Topology

The topology described in Figure 41-1 is merely a conceptual one. As you will see later in the chapter, it is somewhat imprecise, because the components described can cause many threads and processes to be running simultaneously to increase throughput and decrease response time. In addition, it does not yet define precisely how these elements are distributed over physical hardware. So let's start there.

The simplest topology imaginable is shown in Figure 41-2. (In fact, you may even think of a single server with all components on it, but you should *never* put the database server on the same box with the application server!) This two-server topology means that the application server and the Web server are running on the same box. This is a legitimate topology and is almost always used for development systems. It also has the advantage of reduced latency because there is no networking to be done between the application server and the Web server. This topology has been extensively used in earlier versions of WebSphere—in fact, it was the only possible topology until version 3.0, since WebSphere did not support the separation of the Web server from the application server until then. And while this was possible in WebSphere 3.*x* by use of the proprietary OSE protocol (an IBM proprietary socket-based protocol), version 4.0 replaces this with HTTP and HTTPS connection schemes. This not only allows a secure connection, but it uses a standard protocol that (for example) firewalls understand (so no longer do we have to argue with the firewall administrator to define a new protocol called WebSphere and define special rules for it).

Three-Server Topology

While a two-server topology may be legitimate, a three-server topology is often better. This topology is shown in Figure 41-3.

In this topology, the Web server processes are running on one physical server, and the WebSphere application Java Virtual Machines (JVMs) are running on another physical server. For this topology to work, the HTTP plug-in must be loaded into the WWW runtime. In most deployments, the Web server being used is the Apache server, rebranded by IBM as the IBM HTTP Server (IHS). The WebSphere client in this case

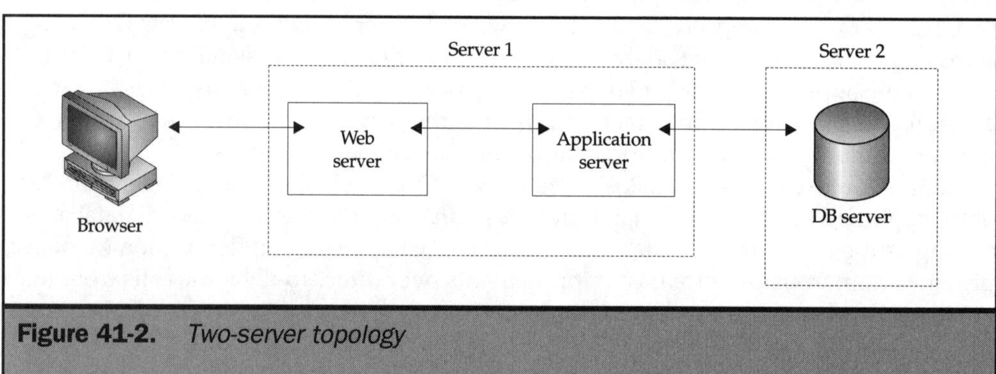

Figure 41-2. *Two-server topology*

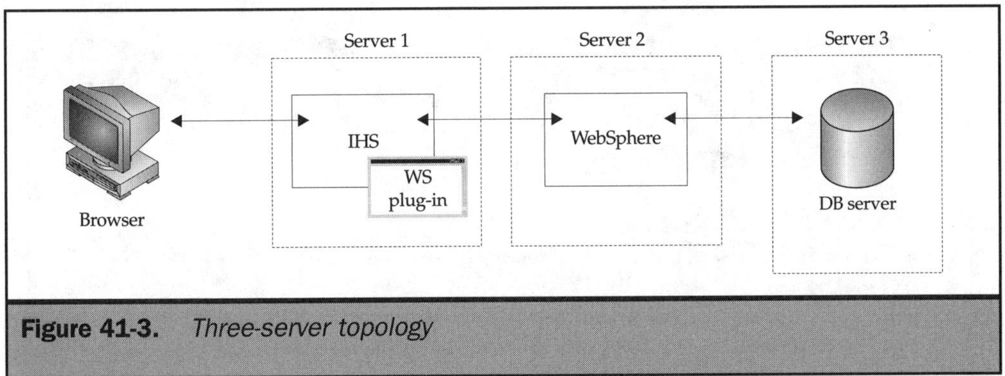

Figure 41-3. *Three-server topology*

is packaged as an Apache module and loaded into the Apache runtime, as shown in Figure 41-4, which also shows the reference to the Extensible Markup Language (XML) configuration file that will be describe at length later in the chapter, in the section "Setting Up a Three-Server Configuration."

As mentioned, a three-server topology is superior to a two-server topology. Here's why. Sometimes, especially when WebSphere is run on symmetric multiprocessing (SMP) architectures, several instances of the application server and the Web server can be running concurrently. The upside is less hardware, easier configuration, and better performance, but the downside is a possible decrease in security. The fact is, there are numerous reasons why a three-server topology is better than a two-server topology. One of them is simply that (perhaps contrary to intuition) a three-server topology performs better than a two-server topology. The communication between the Web server and the JVMs is fast, and giving the JVMs a separate physical server is important for the overall performance. (Unfortunately, the JVMs are still much slower than any of the other components.) In addition, a three-server configuration allows increased flexibility in terms of applying redundancy, as you will see in the section "High Availability," later in the chapter. But the most important differentiator between the two topologies is that the three-server topology naturally supports a DMZ configuration.

DMZ Configurations

DMZ is a concept that defines how applications are deployed in environments that include firewalls, and how security from external intruders is guaranteed. The Internet and e-business applications deployed by companies are relatively new. When such applications first emerged, it was obvious that security was a grave issue that had to be resolved immediately. By then, firewall solutions were already used to protect internal networks, and they were a good fit with the e-business deployment model.

When deploying an Internet application, a company typically placed a firewall in front of the Web server and opened up port 80 (the default port for HTTP) for access by all client machines. This enabled all users, regardless of their locations on the Internet, to access the application, and yet the internal network remained (relatively) protected.

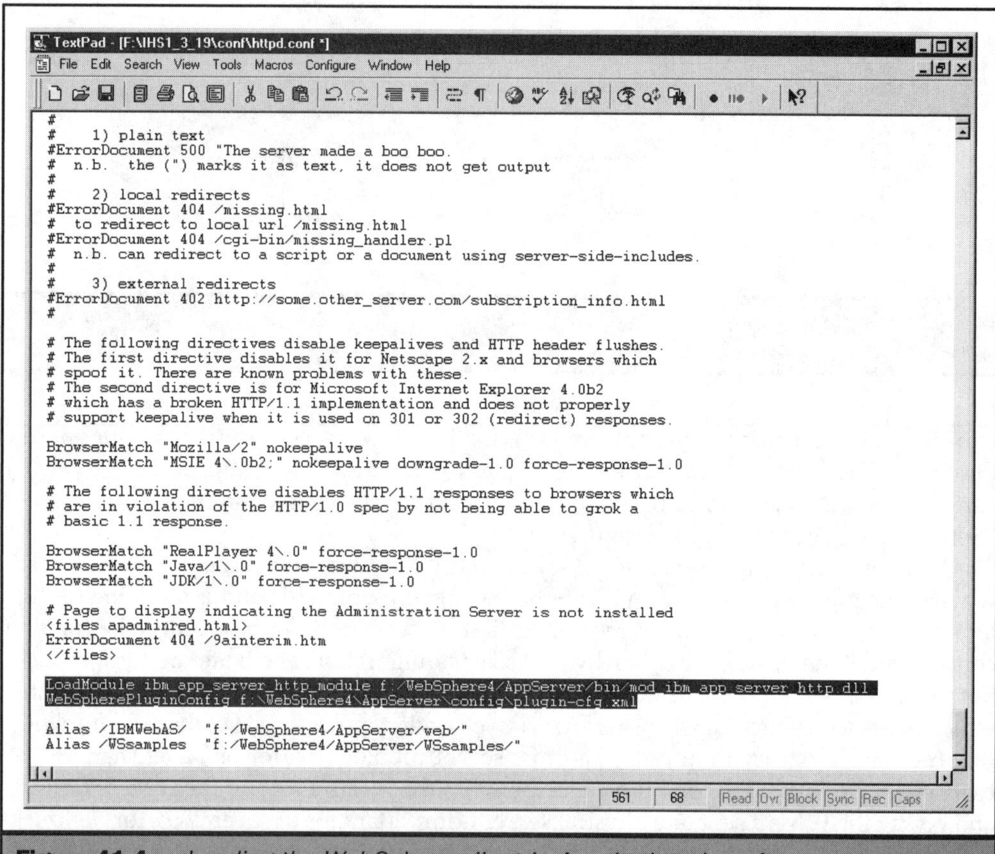


```
#
#    1) plain text
#ErrorDocument 500 "The server made a boo boo.
#  n.b.  the (") marks it as text, it does not get output
#
#    2) local redirects
#ErrorDocument 404 /missing.html
#  to redirect to local url /missing.html
#ErrorDocument 404 /cgi-bin/missing_handler.pl
#  n.b. can redirect to a script or a document using server-side-includes.
#
#    3) external redirects
#ErrorDocument 402 http://some.other_server.com/subscription_info.html
#

# The following directives disable keepalives and HTTP header flushes.
# The first directive disables it for Netscape 2.x and browsers which
# spoof it. There are known problems with these.
# The second directive is for Microsoft Internet Explorer 4.0b2
# which has a broken HTTP/1.1 implementation and does not properly
# support keepalive when it is used on 301 or 302 (redirect) responses.

BrowserMatch "Mozilla/2" nokeepalive
BrowserMatch "MSIE 4\.0b2;" nokeepalive downgrade-1.0 force-response-1.0

# The following directive disables HTTP/1.1 responses to browsers which
# are in violation of the HTTP/1.0 spec by not being able to grok a
# basic 1.1 response.

BrowserMatch "RealPlayer 4\.0" force-response-1.0
BrowserMatch "Java/1\.0" force-response-1.0
BrowserMatch "JDK/1\.0" force-response-1.0

# Page to display indicating the Administration Server is not installed
<files apadminred.html>
ErrorDocument 404 /9ainterim.htm
</files>

LoadModule ibm_app_server_http_module f:/WebSphere4/AppServer/bin/mod_ibm_app_server_http.dll
WebSpherePluginConfig f:\WebSphere4\AppServer\config\plugin-cfg.xml

Alias /IBMWebAS/   "f:/WebSphere4/AppServer/web/"
Alias /WSsamples   "f:/WebSphere4/AppServer/WSsamples/"
```


Figure 41-4. *Loading the WebSphere client in Apache httpd.conf*

Unfortunately, hackers are creative and motivated when it comes to causing damage. It was quickly discovered that, while theoretically a firewall blocking everything but port 80 should have been enough, due to bugs in the infrastructure software (such as the many bugs discovered in Microsoft's IIS) and bugs in the applications themselves, hackers could almost always find a way to break in. The consequences of such holes ranged from undamaging "I was here" type notes to destructive "format the disk" type programs—or worst of all, the theft of critical confidential business data. And so was born the concept of a second firewall and the DMZ.

To understand this concept, it is first important that you understand the purpose of a firewall, and what better way to start than to inspect the name. A firewall in the physical world (such as in a building) is placed to prevent the spread of fire. This is also the primary role of a firewall software solution for network deployment. The external firewall (the one placed between the public Internet and the Web server) prevents the "spread of fire" from the Internet, or in our case the access of unauthorized individuals. However, what happens when the fire does manage to get in? The answer is that another firewall should be placed to isolate the fire. And this is where the DMZ concept is important.

Figure 41-5 shows a DMZ scheme. A second firewall placed between the Web server and the internal network ensures that if the Web server is compromised, the "fire" of unauthorized access does not spread throughout the internal network. If such access to the Web server does occur, only that server is compromised. The second firewall usually has a very restrictive rule base. For example, while the external firewall may define that all hosts can access the Web server as long as they are coming in on port 80 or port 443 (for secure connections), the second firewall will allow access only for the Web server host and only on a specific port.

Are there any disadvantages to a three-server topology, as compared to a two-server topology? Of course, nothing in life is completely clear cut. The disadvantages are that the overall deployment is more complex and that more physical hardware needs to be procured for the project. However, since the Web server processes are so efficient, they do not require a serious investment in hardware, and in fact many network architects (including the authors) claim that a three-server topology allows you to invest less capital in the hardware, because you can get an inexpensive server for the Web server and invest only in the server running the WebSphere JVMs. So, really, the only advantage of the two-server topology is that it *seems* slightly less complex—a minor issue compared with all the advantages afforded by the three-server topology.

Setting Up a Three-Server Configuration

Figure 41-6 shows the setup required for this preferred three-server topology. The Web server is placed within the DMZ, and references the *plugin-cfg.xml* file, as shown in Figure 41-4. (The file resides in the.../*WebSphere/AppServer/config* directory.) This file tells the HTTP plug-in where the WebSphere server is located and what port it should communicate on. The port defined in the file must, of course, be the same port

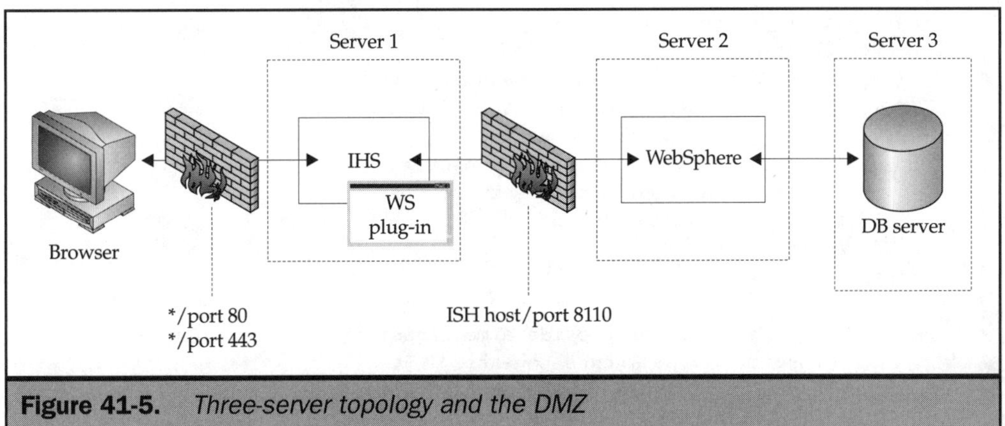

Figure 41-5. *Three-server topology and the DMZ*

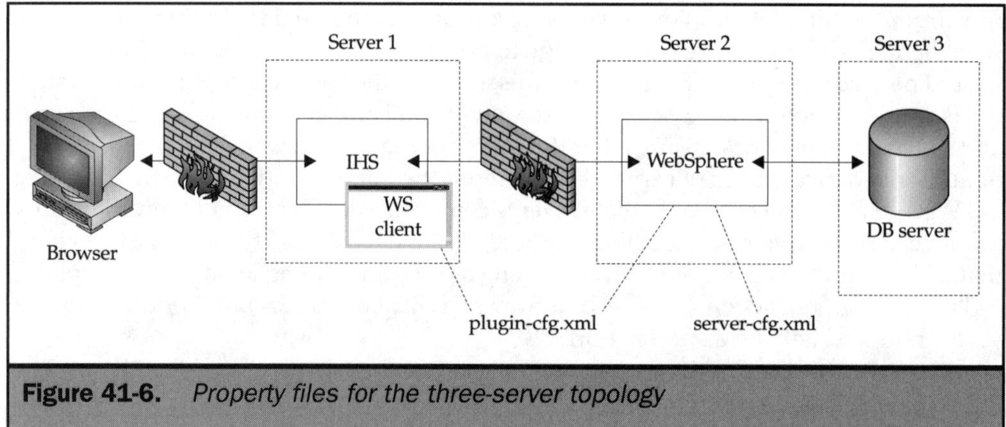

Figure 41-6. *Property files for the three-server topology*

allowed through the internal firewall. It also contains routing information and servlet uniform resource identifier (URI) mappings, which explains why you need to regenerate the plug-in information every time you install a new enterprise application. This file replaces the `queues.properties`, `vhosts.properties`, `rules.properties` files that existed in WebSphere 3.*x* (and which were strangely placed in the *WebSphere/AppServer/temp* directory). The content in this file is shown here:

```
<Config>
   <!-- The LogLevel controls the amount of information that
        is written to the plug-in log file. Possible values
        are Error, Warn, and Trace. -->
   <Log Name="f:/WebSphere4/AppServer/logs/native.log" LogLevel="Error"/>

   <!-- Server groups provide a mechanism of
        grouping servers together. -->
   <ServerGroup Name="default_group">
      <Server CloneID-="vn1" Name="default_server">
         <!-- The transport defines the hostname and port
              value that the Web server
              plug-in will use to communicate
              with the application server. -->
         <Transport Hostname="washost" Port="8110" Protocol="http"/>
      </Server>
   </ServerGroup>

   <!-- Virtual host groups provide a mechanism of
          grouping virtual hosts together. -->
   <VirtualHostGroup Name="default_host">
      <VirtualHost Name="*:*"/>
```

```
    </VirtualHostGroup>


    <!-- URI groups provide a mechanism for grouping URIs together. Only
         the context root of a Web application needs to be specified unless
         you want to restrict the request URIs that are passed to the
         application server.  -->
    <UriGroup Name="default_host_URIs">
       <Uri Name="/servlet/*"/>
       <Uri Name="/webapp/examples"/>
       <Uri Name="*.jsp"/>
       <Uri Name="/ErrorReporter"/>
       <Uri Name="/j_security_check"/>
       <Uri Name="/tradetheme"/>
       <Uri Name="/theme"/>
       <Uri Name="/WebSphereSamples/*"/>
    </UriGroup>

    <!-- A route ties together each of the above components. -->
    <Route ServerGroup="default_group" UriGroup="default_host_URIs"
       VirtualHostGroup="default_host"/>
 </Config>
```

The *plugin-cfg.xml* file is used by the Web server. The main file used by the application server itself is *server-cfg.xml;* the default file that comes with the 4.0 installation is shown in the following listing. Note that this file consistently brings together all the configuration properties in a neatly packaged, self-describing format. It includes information previously existing in the `queues.properties`, `vhosts.properties`, `rules.properties` file, and in many other property files. Finally, if you choose to set up a secure transport (HTTPS), the plug-in will contain the key and certificate information for each of the application servers.


```
<applicationserver:Domain xmi:version="2.0" xmlns:xmi="http://www.omg.org/XMI"
xmlns:applicationserver="applicationserver.xmi" xmlns:security="security.xmi"
xmlns:resources="resources.xmi" xmlns:server="server.xmi" xmi:id="Domain_1"
name="WebSphere Administrative Domain">
  <virtualHosts xmi:id="VirtualHost_1" name="default_host">
    <aliases xmi:id="HostAlias_1" hostname="*" port="8110"/>
    <aliases xmi:id="HostAlias_2" hostname="*" port="9443"/>
    <aliases xmi:id="HostAlias_3" hostname="*" port="80"/>
    <aliases xmi:id="HostAlias_4" hostname="*" port="443"/>
    <defaultMimeEntries xmi:id="MimeEntry_1" type="image">
      <extensions>gif</extensions>
    </defaultMimeEntries>
```

```
    <defaultMimeEntries xmi:id="MimeEntry_2" type="text/plain">
      <extensions>txt</extensions>
      <extensions>java</extensions>
      <extensions>wsdl</extensions>
    </defaultMimeEntries>
    <defaultMimeEntries xmi:id="MimeEntry_3" type="text/html">
      <extensions>htm</extensions>
      <extensions>html</extensions>
    </defaultMimeEntries>
    <defaultMimeEntries xmi:id="MimeEntry_4" type="x-application">
      <extensions>exe</extensions>
    </defaultMimeEntries>
    <defaultMimeEntries xmi:id="MimeEntry_5" type="x-application/zip">
      <extensions>zip</extensions>
    </defaultMimeEntries>
    <defaultMimeEntries xmi:id="MimeEntry_6" type="application/pdf">
      <extensions>pdf</extensions>
    </defaultMimeEntries>
  </virtualHosts>
  <virtualHosts xmi:id="VirtualHost_2" name="admin_host">
    <aliases xmi:id="HostAlias_5" hostname="*" port="9090"/>
  </virtualHosts>
  <security xmi:id="Security_1" cacheTimeout="30000" enabled="false"
   activeAuthMechanism="LocalOSAuthentication_1">
    <authMechanisms xmi:type="security:LocalOSAuthentication"
     xmi:id="LocalOSAuthentication_1">
      <userRegistry xmi:type="security:LocalOSUserRegistry"
       xmi:id="LocalOSUserRegistry_1" serverId="demouser"
       serverPassword="{xor}OzoyMC8+LCwoOw==" name="LOCALOS">
        <properties xmi:id="UserRegProperty_1" name="myCustomProperty"
         value="myCustomValue"/>
      </userRegistry>
    </authMechanisms>
    <defaultSSLSettings xmi:id="SecureSocketLayer_1"
     keyFileName="${WAS_ROOT}/etc/DummyKeyring.jks"
     keyFilePassword="{xor}CDo9Hgw="
     keyFileFormat="JKS" trustFileName="${WAS_ROOT}/etc/DummyKeyring.jks"
     trustFilePassword="{xor}CDo9Hgw=" clientAuthentication="false"
     securityLevel="HIGH" enableCryptoHardwareSupport="false">
      <cryptoHardware xmi:id="CryptoHardwareToken_1"
      tokenType="PKCS#11" libraryFile="" password="{xor}"/>
    </defaultSSLSettings>
  </security>
  <resourceProviders xmi:type="resources:JDBCDriver" xmi:id="JDBCDriver_1"
name="Db2JdbcDriver" description="DB2 JDBC Driver"
implementationClassName="COM.ibm.db2.jdbc.DB2ConnectionPoolDataSource"
urlPrefix="jdbc:db2">
    <factories xmi:type="resources:DataSource" xmi:id="DataSource_1" name="Session
```

```
Persistence datasource" jndiName="jdbc/Session" description="Data source for
session persistence" category="Samples" jtaEnabled="false" databaseName="Session"
minimumPoolSize="1" maximumPoolSize="30" connectionTimeout="1000"
idleTimeout="2000" orphanTimeout="3000">
      <propertySet xmi:id="DataSource_1_ps"/>
    </factories>
    <propertySet xmi:id="JDBCDriver_1_ps"/>
  </resourceProviders>
  <resourceProviders xmi:type="resources:JDBCDriver" xmi:id="JDBCDriver_2"
name="idbJdbcDriver" description="instantDB JDBC Driver"
implementationClassName="com.ibm.ejs.cm.portability.IDBConnectionPoolDataSource"
urlPrefix="jdbc:idb">
    <factories xmi:type="resources:DataSource" xmi:id="DataSource_2"
name="Increment Bean Datasource" jndiName="jdbc/SampleDataSource"
description="Increment Bean Datasource" category="Samples1" jtaEnabled="false"
minimumPoolSize="1" maximumPoolSize="10" connectionTimeout="1000"
idleTimeout="2000" orphanTimeout="3000">
      <propertySet xmi:id="DataSource_2_ps">
        <resourceProperties xmi:id="J2EEResourceProperty_1" name="url"
type="java.lang.string" value="jdbc:idb:f:\WebSphere4\AppServer/bin/sampleDB.prp"/>
      </propertySet>
    </factories>
    <factories xmi:type="resources:DataSource" xmi:id="DataSource_3" name="Samples
IDB Datasource" jndiName="jdbc/sample" description="Samples Gallery IDB Datasource"
category="Samples" jtaEnabled="false" minimumPoolSize="1" maximumPoolSize="10"
connectionTimeout="1000" idleTimeout="2000" orphanTimeout="3000">
      <propertySet xmi:id="DataSource_3_ps">
        <resourceProperties xmi:id="J2EEResourceProperty_2" name="url"
type="java.lang.string"
value="jdbc:idb:f:\WebSphere4\AppServer/installedApps/Samples.ear/IDBDatabase/
sample.prp"/>
      </propertySet>
    </factories>
    <propertySet xmi:id="JDBCDriver_2_ps"/>
  </resourceProviders>
  <resourceProviders xmi:type="resources:URLProvider" xmi:id="URLProvider_1"
name="Default URL Provider" description="The default internal URL Provider that can
be used to create URL Factories. This provider's StreamHandler class name and protocol
must be set to 'unused' in order for it to be valid"
streamHandlerClassName="unused" protocol="unused">
    <propertySet xmi:id="URLProvider_1_ps"/>
  </resourceProviders>
  <resourceProviders xmi:type="resources:MailProvider" xmi:id="MailProvider_1"
name="Default Mail Provider" description="The default internal Mail Provider that
can be used to create Mail Sessions">
    <propertySet xmi:id="MailProvider_1_ps"/>
  </resourceProviders>
```

```
    <nodes xmi:id="Node_1" name="ron2k">
      <servers xmi:type="applicationserver:ApplicationServer"
xmi:id="ApplicationServer_1" desiredExecutionState="START" name="Default Server"
id="-1" moduleVisibility="COMPATIBILITY">
        <processDefinition xmi:type="server:JavaProcessDef" xmi:id="ProcessDef_1"
executableName="${JAVA_HOME}/bin/java" commandLineArguments=""
workingDirectory="${WAS_ROOT}/bin" executableTargetKind="JAVA_CLASS"
executableTarget="com.ibm.ws.bootstrap.WSLauncher">
          <executionSettings xmi:id="ProcessExecution_1" umask="777"
runAsUser="root"/>
          <ioRedirect xmi:id="OutputRedirect_1"
stdoutFilename="${LOG_ROOT}/default_server_stdout.log"
stderrFilename="${LOG_ROOT}/default_server_stderr.log"/>
          <jvmSettings xmi:id="JavaVirtualMachine_1"
classpath="${WAS_ROOT}/lib/bootstrap.jar;${WAS_ROOT}/properties" bootClasspath=""
verboseModeClass="false" verboseModeGarbageCollection="false"
verboseModeJNI="false" initialHeapSize="4" maximumHeapSize="256" runHProf="false"
hprofArguments="" debugMode="false" debugArgs=""
genericCommandLineArgs="com.ibm.ws.runtime.StandardServer" disableJIT="false">
            <systemProperties xmi:id="SystemProperty_1" name="server.root"
value="${WAS_ROOT}"/>
            <systemProperties xmi:id="SystemProperty_2" name="ws.ext.dirs"
value="${JAVA_HOME}/lib;${WAS_ROOT}/classes;${WAS_ROOT}/lib;${WAS_ROOT}/lib/ext;
${WAS_ROOT}/web/help;${WAS_ROOT}/properties"/>
            <systemProperties xmi:id="SystemProperty_3"
name="com.ibm.CORBA.ConfigURL"
value="file:/${WAS_ROOT}/properties/sas.server.props"/>
          </jvmSettings>
        </processDefinition>
        <performanceMonitoring xmi:id="PerformanceMonitor_1" enable="false"
specification=""/>
        <objectLevelTraceSettings xmi:id="ObjectLevelTrace_1" enable="false"
hostname="localhost" port="2102" debug="false" sourcePath=""/>
        <locationServiceDaemon xmi:id="LocationServiceDaemon_1" hostname="localhost"
port="9000" mode="NONE"/>
        <transactionService xmi:id="TransactionService_1"
transactionLogFile="${TRANLOG_ROOT}/tran1.log,${TRANLOG_ROOT}/tran2.log"
totalTranLifetimeTimeout="60000" clientInactivityTimeout="30000"/>
        <traceService xmi:id="TraceServiceConfig_1" enable="true"
traceSpecification="*=all=disabled" traceOutputFilename="stdout"
diagThreadPort="7000"/>
        <namingServiceSettings xmi:id="NamingServiceProvider_1" enable="true"
providerHost="localhost" providerPort="9070"
providerClassname="com.ibm.ejs.naming.transient.NamingServiceProvider"
enablePersistentNaming="true"/>
        <orbSettings xmi:id="ORBConfig_1" enable="true" bootstrapHost="localhost"
bootstrapPort="900">
```

```
 <threadPool xmi:id="ThreadPool_2" minimumSize="10" maximumSize="50"
inactivityTimeout="3500" isGrowable="false"/>
      </orbSettings>
      <webContainer xmi:id="WebContainer_1"
installedWebModules="WebModuleRef_1 WebModuleRef_2 WebModuleRef_3
WebModuleRef_4 WebModuleRef_5 WebModuleRef_6">
        <transports xmi:type="applicationserver:HTTPTransport"
xmi:id="HttpTransport_1" hostname="*" port="9080"/>
        <transports xmi:type="applicationserver:HTTPTransport"
xmi:id="HttpTransport_2" hostname="*" port="9443" sslEnabled="true"/>
        <transports xmi:type="applicationserver:HTTPTransport"
xmi:id="HttpTransport_3" hostname="*" port="9090" external="false"/>
        <sessionManager xmi:id="SessionManager_1" enableUrlRewriting="false"
enableCookies="true" enableSSLTracking="false"
enableProtocolSwitchRewriting="false" enablePersistentSessions="false"
enableSecurityIntegration="false">
          <defaultCookieSettings xmi:id="Cookie_1" domain="" maximumAge="-1"
path="/" secure="false"/>
          <persistentSessions xmi:id="SessionPersistence_1"
datasourceJNDIName="jdbc/Session" userId="db2admin"
password="{xor}Oz1tPjsyNjF7dxoRHBAbGht2" db2RowSize="ROW_SIZE_4KB"
tableSpaceName=""/>
          <tuningParams xmi:id="TuningParams_1" usingMultiRowSchema="false"
allowOverflow="true" scheduleInvalidation="false"
writeFrequency="END_OF_SERVLET_SERVICE" writeInterval="120"
writeContents="ONLY_UPDATED_ATTRIBUTES" invalidationTimeout="30">
            <invalidationSchedule xmi:id="InvalidationSchedule_1"
firstHour="14" secondHour="2"/>
          </tuningParams>
        </sessionManager>
        <dynamicCache xmi:id="DynamicCache_1" enable="false"
cacheSize="1000" defaultPriority="1"/>
        <threadPool xmi:id="ThreadPool_1" minimumSize="10" maximumSize="50"
inactivityTimeout="10" isGrowable="false"/>
      </webContainer>
      <ejbContainer xmi:id="EJBContainer_1"
passivationDirectory="${WAS_ROOT}/temp" inactivePoolCleanupInterval="30000"
installedEJBModules="EJBModuleRef_2 EJBModuleRef_1 EJBModuleRef_3
EJBModuleRef_4 EJBModuleRef_5" defaultDatasource="DataSource_1">
        <cacheSettings xmi:id="EJBCache_1" cleanupInterval="1000"
cacheSize="2000"/>
      </ejbContainer>
      <serverSecurityConfig xmi:id="ServerSecurityConfig_1"
useDomainQualifiedUserNames="false"/>
    </servers>
    <installedResourceProviders xmi:id="ResourceProviderRef_1" classpath=""
resourceProvider="JDBCDriver_1"/>
```

```
    <installedResourceProviders xmi:id="ResourceProviderRef_2"
classpath="${WAS_ROOT}/lib/idb.jar" resourceProvider="JDBCDriver_2"/>
    <installedApps xmi:id="ApplicationRef_1" name="sampleApp"
archiveURL="${APP_INSTALL_ROOT}/sampleApp.ear">
      <modules xmi:type="applicationserver:WebModuleRef"
xmi:id="WebModuleRef_1" uri="default_app.war"/>
      <modules xmi:type="applicationserver:WebModuleRef"
xmi:id="WebModuleRef_2" uri="examples.war"/>
      <modules xmi:type="applicationserver:EJBModuleRef"
xmi:id="EJBModuleRef_2" uri="Increment.jar"/>
    </installedApps>
    <installedApps xmi:id="ApplicationRef_2" name="Server Administration
Application" archiveURL="${APP_INSTALL_ROOT}/admin.ear">
      <modules xmi:type="applicationserver:WebModuleRef"
xmi:id="WebModuleRef_3" uri="admin.war"/>
    </installedApps>
    <installedApps xmi:id="ApplicationRef_3" name="WebSphere Application
Server Samples" archiveURL="${APP_INSTALL_ROOT}\Samples.ear">
      <modules xmi:type="applicationserver:WebModuleRef"
xmi:id="WebModuleRef_4" uri="YourCo.war"/>
      <modules xmi:type="applicationserver:WebModuleRef"
xmi:id="WebModuleRef_5" uri="Samples.war"/>
      <modules xmi:type="applicationserver:WebModuleRef"
xmi:id="WebModuleRef_6" uri="theme.war"/>
      <modules xmi:type="applicationserver:EJBModuleRef"
xmi:id="EJBModuleRef_1" uri="TimeoutEJBean.jar"/>
      <modules xmi:type="applicationserver:EJBModuleRef"
xmi:id="EJBModuleRef_3" uri="IncrementEJBean.jar"/>
      <modules xmi:type="applicationserver:EJBModuleRef"
xmi:id="EJBModuleRef_4" uri="HelloEJBean.jar"/>
      <modules xmi:type="applicationserver:EJBModuleRef"
xmi:id="EJBModuleRef_5" uri="AccountAndTransferEJBean.jar"/>
    </installedApps>
    <pathMap xmi:id="PathMap_1">
      <entries xmi:id="PathMapEntry_1" symbolicName="APP_INSTALL_ROOT"
path="${WAS_ROOT}/installedApps" description="The filesystem path to
the directory that will contain installed enterprise applications."/>
      <entries xmi:id="PathMapEntry_2" symbolicName="LOG_ROOT"
path="${WAS_ROOT}/logs" description="The filesystem path to the directory
that will contain server log files."/>
      <entries xmi:id="PathMapEntry_3" symbolicName="TRANLOG_ROOT"
path="${WAS_ROOT}/tranlog" description="The filesystem path to the directory
that will transaction log files."/>
      <entries xmi:id="PathMapEntry_4" symbolicName="PRODUCT_INSTALL_ROOT"
path="${WAS_ROOT}" description="The filesystem path to the product installation
directory"/>
      <entries xmi:id="PathMapEntry_5" symbolicName="WAS_ROOT"
```

```
path="f:\WebSphere4\AppServer" description="The filesystem path to the
product installation directory"/>
      <entries xmi:id="PathMapEntry_6" symbolicName="JAVA_HOME"
path="${WAS_ROOT}/java" description="The filesystem path to the product Java
home directory"/>
     </pathMap>
  </nodes>
</applicationserver:Domain>
```

High Availability

Now you know that you probably need three physical servers on your network, but is that enough? Most probably not. Three servers are enough if you are not including an application that needs to meet high performance requirements or that does not have some form of fault tolerance requirements. If you do use such an application, you will need to make a larger investment. Java is still a relatively slow runtime environment, and the applications deployed on WebSphere are usually serving a large number of users. In addition, you may be facing requirements that you be online 24×7. Such requirements necessitate that you have *redundancy* built into your deployment, which means that you will have more hardware than you minimally need. Redundancy is used to distribute load at peak times, through the use of load balancing, over all your deployed servers, as well as for fault tolerance—if some of your servers go down, the rest are still available online to process your requests.

In terms of failover and recovery for WebSphere version 4.0, we recommend accessing the white paper at *http://www7.software.ibm.com/vadd-bin/ftpdl?1/vadc/wsdd/pdf/modjeski.pdf.*

Vertical and Horizontal Scaling

Two primary forms of scaling are shown in Figure 41-7. *Vertical scaling* is a term used for describing a configuration in which multiple JVMs are placed on a single physical server. The server may have a single CPU or multiple CPUs. JVMs support a *threading model*. Depending on the JVM, the threading model may use native operating system threads or may simulate threading within the JVM. (Simulated threads are sometimes called *green threads* or *lightweight processes*.) If operating system threads are used, even a single JVM can consume all the server's resources. In version 3.*x* (due to the scalability problems with JDK1.1), this was not always true; if you had a four-CPU box, you would have been far better off bringing up four JVMs running the same code line than bringing up one JVM. This is no longer the case in version 4.0, and as a general guideline, the fewer JVMs the better.

For example, on a four-way machine, there is never reason to have the same application running in more than two JVMs. Having two allows some process failover. If not for fault tolerance, a single JVM can fully utilize a four-way, and in most cases an eight-way. The latest JDKs, 1.3*x*, rely on a large memory model and do not have the problems experienced in earlier JVM versions.

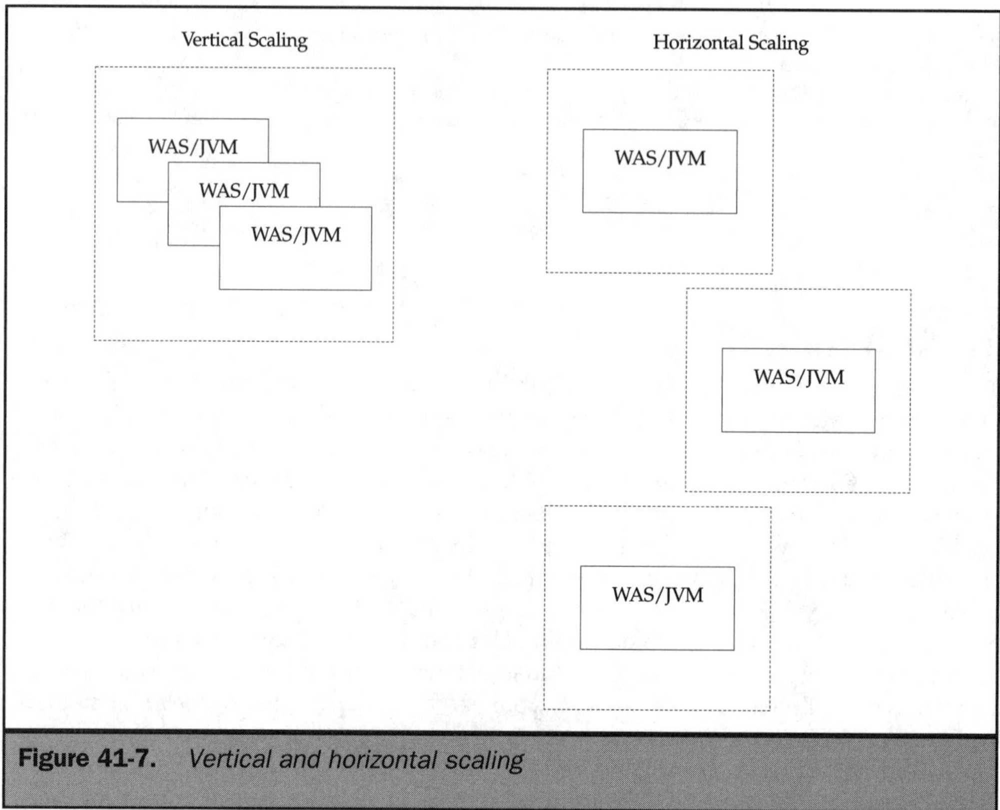

Figure 41-7. *Vertical and horizontal scaling*

In version 3.*x*, the best performance and fault tolerance was achieved in the deployment shown in Figure 41-8. In this scheme, two physical servers run two WebSphere JVMs each. The physical servers are usually two-CPU machines. As a rule of thumb, every CPU runs a JVM (this assuming that the servers are being used only for WebSphere and do not run any other intensive process).

In version 4.0, the preferred configuration is much simpler, and again, the rule of thumb is that fewer JVMs are better. You should use more than one JVM for high availability only—certainly not for performance. The good news is that this configuration is simpler to build and maintain.

Setting Up the Web Server

What about the Web server? Having multiple JVMs set up to perform EJB and JSP processing is great, but you also need a Web server to handle the HTTP sessions from browsers. The simplest deployment of multiple JVMs combined with a Web server is shown in Figure 41-9. In this figure, all clones are accessed by a single Web server.

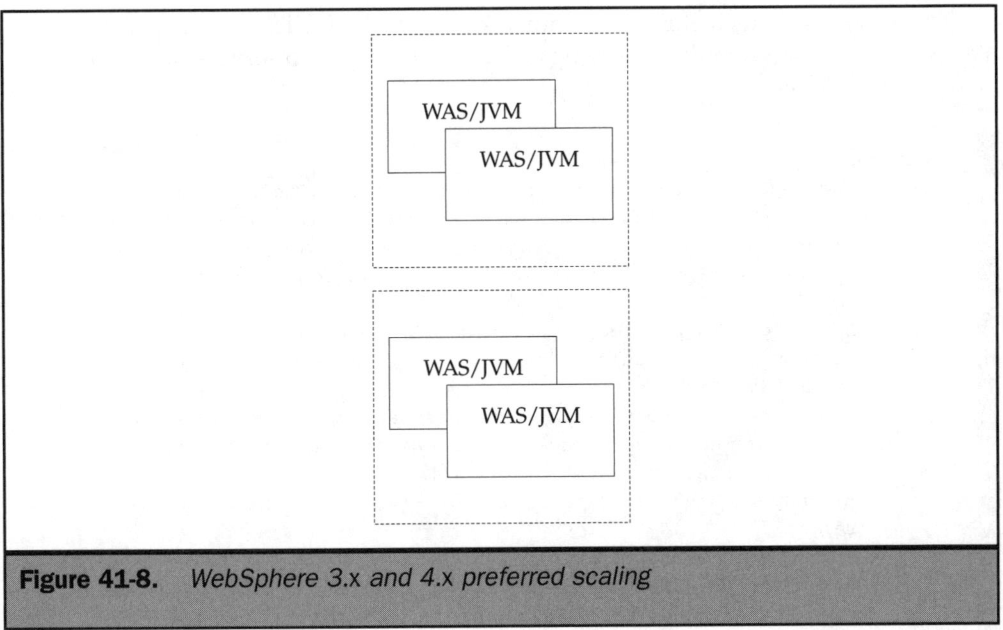

Figure 41-8. *WebSphere 3.x and 4.x preferred scaling*

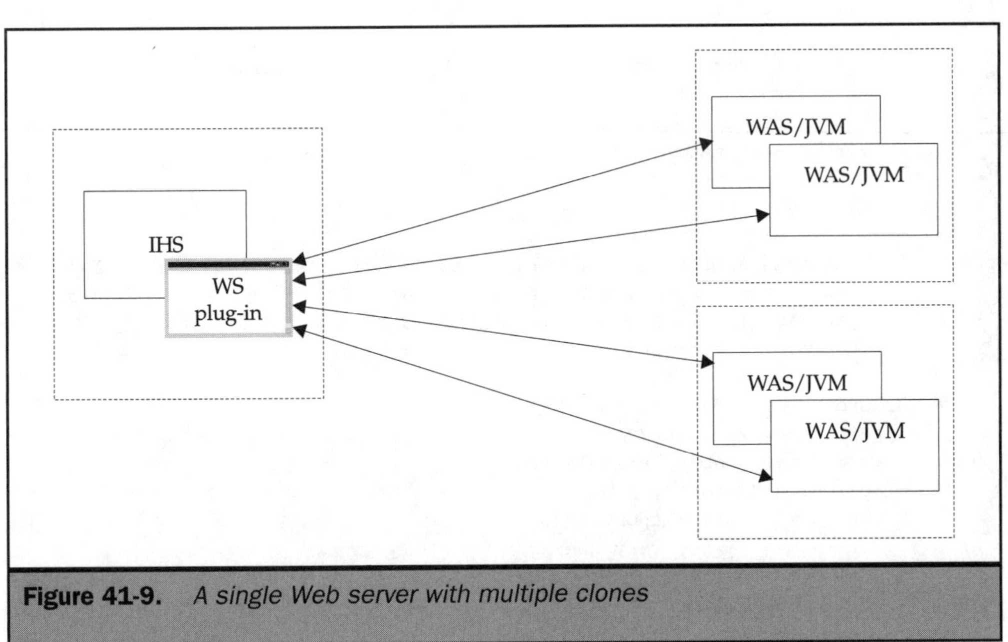

Figure 41-9. *A single Web server with multiple clones*

To support four such clones, you must configure the HTTP plug-in of the Web server, as shown in the following code. In this case, two servers each run two separate JVMs.

```
<Config>
   <!-- The LogLevel controls the amount of information that is
        written to the plug-in log file. Possible values are
        Error, Warn, and Trace. -->
   <Log Name="f:/WebSphere4/AppServer/logs/native.log" LogLevel="Error"/>

   <!-- Server groups provide a mechanism of grouping servers together. -->
   <ServerGroup Name="default_group">
      <Server Name="washost1">
         <!-- The transport defines the hostname and port value that
              the web server plug-in will use to communicate with the
              application server. -->
        <Transport Hostname="washost1" Port="8110" Protocol="http"/>
      </Server>
      <Server Name="washost2">
         <!-- The transport defines the hostname and port value that
              the web server plug-in will use to communicate with the
              application server. -->
        <Transport Hostname="washost2" Port="8120" Protocol="http"/>
      </Server>
   </ServerGroup>

   <!-- Virtual host groups provide a mechanism of grouping
           virtual hosts together. -->
   <VirtualHostGroup Name="default_host">
      <VirtualHost Name="*:*"/>
   </VirtualHostGroup>


   <!-- URI groups provide a mechanism for grouping URIs together. Only
        the context root of a Web application needs to be specified unless
        you want to restrict the request URIs that are passed to
        the application server.  -->

   <UriGroup Name="default_host_URIs">
      <Uri Name="/servlet/*"/>
      <Uri Name="/webapp/examples"/>
      <Uri Name="*.jsp"/>
      <Uri Name="/ErrorReporter"/>
      <Uri Name="/j_security_check"/>
      <Uri Name="/tradetheme"/>
      <Uri Name="/theme"/>
```

```
      <Uri Name="/WebSphereSamples/*"/>
   </UriGroup>

   <!-- A route ties together all of the above components. -->
   <Route
     ServerGroup="default_group" UriGroup="default_host_URIs"
     VirtualHostGroup="default_host"/>
</Config>
```

WebSphere 4.0 supports quite an impressive set of properties that can be added to the plug-in XML property file, including the following:

- **LoadBalance** Specifies the algorithm for dispatch to the separate servers. The supported algorithms are *round-robin* or *random*. In round-robin, the HTTP plug-in loops through available WebSphere JVMs (skipping those that cannot be reached). In a random algorithm, each request is randomly sent to one of the JVMs. This property is a part of the ServerGroup element in the XML file that also defines the retry interval, which is the length of time between the first time that the plug-in notices that a server is down and the time when the plug-in will next try that server.
- **Transport** Specifies how the plug-in communicates with the WebSphere server (HTTP or HTTPS), as well as the port number and server name used for the communication.

In addition to these new properties, the *plugin-cfg.xml* file includes all the definitions that were in the various property files in WebSphere 3.*x* (`queues.properties`, `rules.properties`, and `vhosts.properties`). The `VirtualHost` element allows us to define the virtual host names to which we want the server to respond. These can be grouped within the VirtualHostGroup element.

The plug-in information is not static and can be changed even while the server is running. The `Config` element (the root element in the XML file) has an attribute called `RefreshInterval`. This value defines the interval (in seconds) in which the plug-in re-reads the *plugin-cfg.xml* file.

One of the main problems with previous versions of WebSphere is that they did not correctly handle session affinity. Version 4.0 fixes this and provides a completely new implementation that is based on adding the cloneID into the sessionID cookie. *Session affinity* (sometimes called *session persistence* or *sticky sessions*) ensures that if a browser session has been initiated on one JVM, then all requests coming from the same browser will always be directed by the plug-in to the same server that originally served the request. Until WebSphere 3.5.2, session affinity did not exist, and even in 3.5.*x* it did not always work. Version 4.0 finally fully implements this feature and allows a deployment, as shown in the following code listing.

```
<?xml version="1.0"?>
<Config>
```

```
    ...
    <ServerGroup Name="ronhome/Default Server">
        <Server CloneID="tbajpkr1" Name="Default Server">
            <Transport Hostname="ronhome1" Port="9080" Protocol=
            "http"/></Server>
        <Server CloneID="tbajpkr2" Name="Default Server">
            <Transport Hostname="ronhome2" Port="9080" Protocol=
            "http"/></Server>
    </ServerGroup>
    ...
</Config>
```

Just to clarify things further, we strongly suggest that unless you are running WebSphere 4.0 or later, you do not rely on the WS client for load balancing or fault tolerance.

Note that while you may invest a lot in hardware for the JVMs, you need not be concerned about the Web server (assuming you are running Apache or IHS), because the Apache runtime is very fast. In addition, its configuration file allows you to tune the number of processes that will be used for serving HTTP requests.

```
##
## httpd.conf -- Apache HTTP server configuration file
##

...

# Server-pool size regulation.  Rather than making you guess how many
# server processes you need, Apache dynamically adapts to the load it
# sees --- that is, it tries to maintain enough server processes to
# handle the current load, plus a few spare servers to handle transient
# load spikes (e.g., multiple simultaneous requests from a single
# Netscape browser).

# It does this by periodically checking how many servers are waiting
# for a request.  If there are fewer than MinSpareServers, it creates
# a new spare.  If there are more than MaxSpareServers, some of the
# spares die off.  These values are probably OK for most sites ---

MinSpareServers 5
MaxSpareServers 10

# Number of servers to start --- should be a reasonable ballpark figure.
```

```
StartServers 5

# Limit on total number of servers running, i.e., limit on the number
# of clients who can simultaneously connect. If this limit is ever
# reached, clients will be LOCKED OUT, so it should NOT BE SET TOO LOW.
# It is intended mainly as a brake to keep a runaway server from taking
# Unix with it as it spirals down...

MaxClients 150

# MaxRequestsPerChild: the number of requests each child process is
#  allowed to process before the child dies.
#  The child will exit so as to prevent problems after prolonged use when
#  Apache (and maybe the libraries it uses) leaks.  On most systems, this
#  isn't really needed, but a few (such as Solaris) do have notable leaks
#  in the libraries.

MaxRequestsPerChild 500

...
```

The preceding code listing shows some of the important parameters used in IHS (and Apache) on a Solaris deployment. The `StartServers` value is the number of HTTP daemon (HTTPD) processes that will be started when the server first initializes. In this case, if you invoke

```
apachectl start
```

and then, on the command line, enter

```
ps -ef | grep http
```

you will see five such processes. The `MinSpareServers` and `MaxSpareServers` are used by the Apache runtime to maintain a pool of ready-to-go processes for peak hits.

Assuming that you are running WebSphere 4.0, you may indeed deploy your system as described here. Unfortunately, this means that your Web server becomes a single point of failure, and therefore the system is not truly fault tolerant—if that single server goes down, your entire system is down. In fact, there are many alternatives to load balancing can be accomplished using software that is part of WebSphere, and we strongly recommend choosing one of them.

Eliminating Single Points of Failure

To eliminate the single points of failure, the best approach is to create two full clones—not only of the JVM but also of the Web server. Figure 41-10 shows such a configuration using two sets of IHS+WebSphere. But this is not enough. Most of us cannot afford to let users loose with such instructions as "Use *www1.mycompany.com,* and if that doesn't work try *www2.mycompany.com.*" What we need is for all users to use *www.mycompany.com,* and have the system be smart enough to redirect to the correct clone.

The element needed in this deployment topology is the *router*. The router in this scheme implements the load-balancing and fault-tolerance features by redirecting traffic to the appropriate servers. Obviously, because session affinity must be preserved if your applications are to function correctly, you will select a "smart router"—one that can be configured to ensure correct traffic redirection. All the major router vendors have products that support these features, and we do not presume to be experts in this field, so we cannot recommend one vendor's product over another's. Still, because we need to discuss some router fundamentals, we will describe the topology shown in Figure 41-11, which uses an Alteon AD3 router running WebOS 8.*x*. We have used this router in a number of deployments, and it has worked well for us.

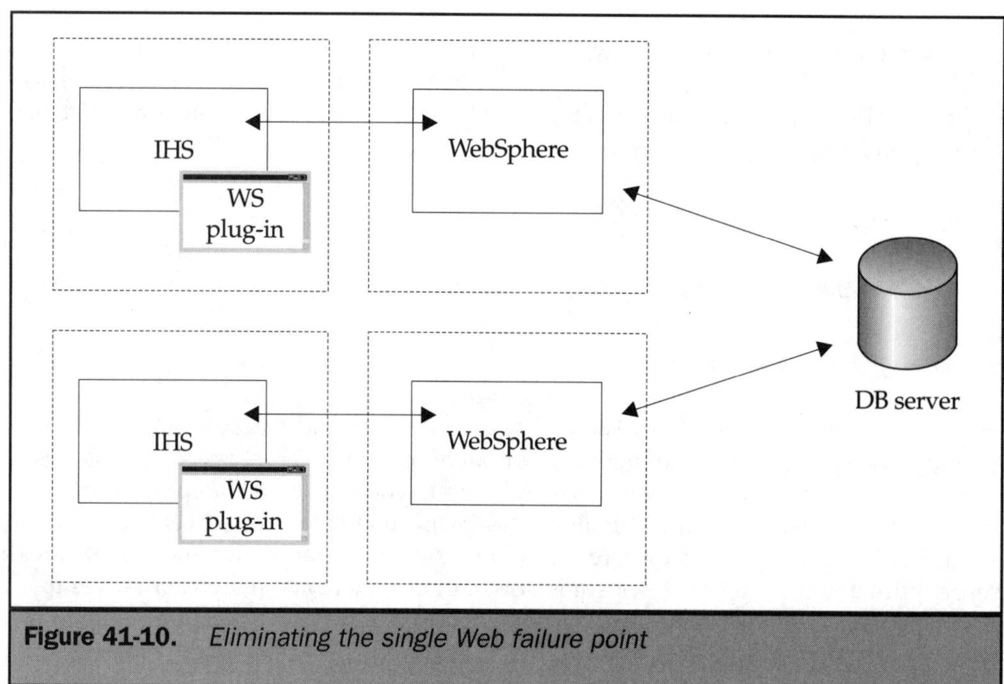

Figure 41-10. *Eliminating the single Web failure point*

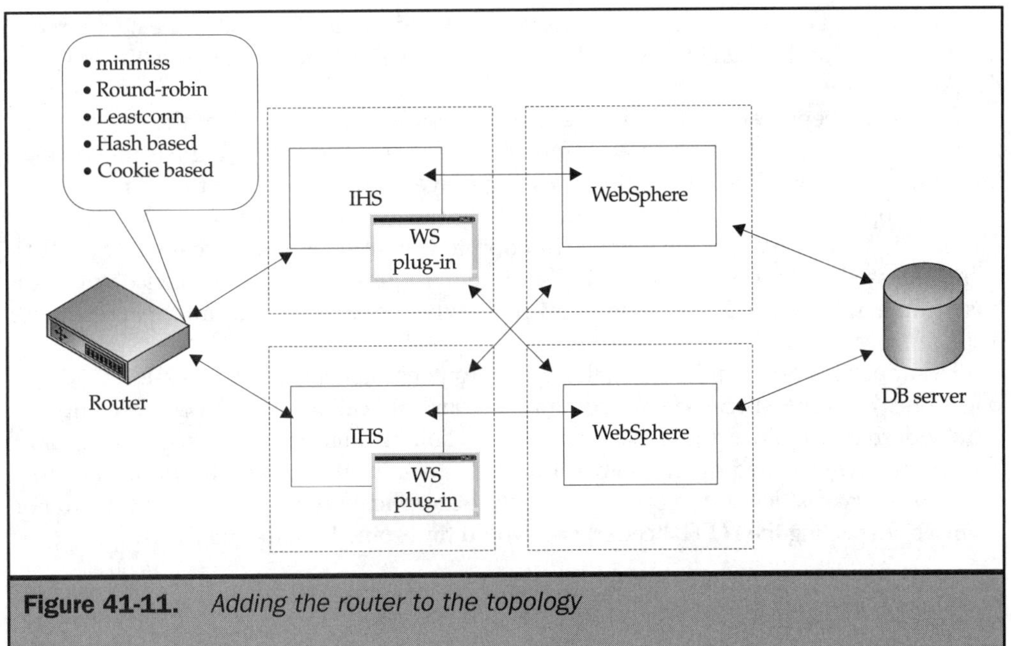

Figure 41-11. *Adding the router to the topology*

Setting Up Server Load Balancing

One (if not *the*) most important uses of Alteon routers is for server load balancing (SLB). Given that this is such an important feature, the Alteon routers support numerous deployment metrics for SLB. Among these are the following algorithms:

- *Minmiss*
- *Round-robin*
- *Leastconn*
- *Hash*

Minmiss directs all traffic coming from a certain client Internet Protocol (IP) to a single server. This algorithm guarantees that session affinity is preserved because, in fact, it guarantees something stronger: that all requests from a single client will always go to the same Web server. Therefore, even if you open a few browsers on the client machine, all requests (even those that do not share a session) will be forwarded to the same server. This algorithm tends to function well for applications that involve caching (hence the term *minmiss*), and in general works well for online applications. (It may have disadvantages for some specific applications that won't be mentioned here.)

Round-robin is a simple recurring pattern of forwarding each request to the next server in line. This algorithm can be used only if the session persistence feature is activated on the Alteon router.

Leastconn keeps track of the number of open connections on each of the servers and forwards the request to the one with fewer open connections. This algorithm works best if the two clones have similar processing power and are running the same code line. This option, too, can only be used if session persistence is turned on.

Hash is based on applying a hash function to the uniform resource locator (URL) being accessed and/or on the client IP. This option requires session persistence unless the hash function is also applied to the client IP, in which case session affinity is preserved as in *minmiss*.

To support session affinity using the Alteon router, you need to set its session persistence attributes. Because you are running your applications on WebSphere using the standard conventions, the session context is maintained using the `jsessionid` cookie. This cookie is generated by the Web application, usually at logon time, and is used to access the server-side session object in which the application context is maintained. For example, inspecting the HTTP header, you would find something like this:

```
cookie: jsessionid=LBAZ1SIAAAAAFR4LOVUAAAA
```

You need to guarantee that this same cookie name is used by the Alteon router to direct all HTTP traffic with a certain value for the cookie to the same server. This is easily done with the following WebOS command:

```
# /cfg/slb/virt 1/service 80/pbind cookie passive "cookiename"
jsessionid 1 23 disable
```

This configuration command is quite simple. It configures the server load-balancing feature for virtual system 1 (hence, `/cfg/slb`). It defines attributes for the HTTP traffic (hence, `service 80`). It tells the router that it should be using the value of a cookie named `jsessionid` between the first character and the twenty-third character. In this case, it means that the entire cookie is used for the cookie value. Any HTTP request with the same values for characters 1–23 will be forwarded to the same server.

Now let's put it all together, as shown in Figure 41-12. The router is *the* address that all requests go to; it is probably defined by the Domain Name System (DNS) naming tables as *www.mycompany.com* (or something of that form). Based on one of the server load balancing (SLB) algorithms, traffic is forwarded to one of the Web servers. Each Web server then issues request to a set of JVMs—sometimes one and sometimes many, depending on how comfortable you are with WebSphere load balancing. Finally, the database server usually has a hot backup running so that if the server goes down, its replacement comes online within a few seconds so that the system can continue to function properly.

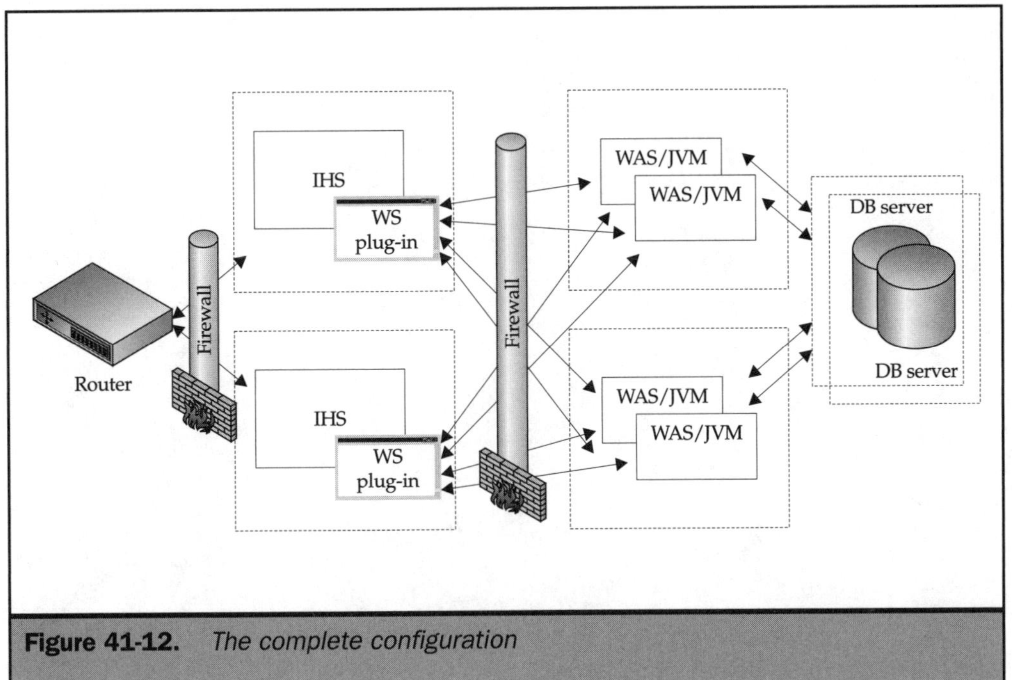

Figure 41-12. *The complete configuration*

Summary

This chapter took you on a gradual tour through various possible deployment topologies. The end results should be that you are able to architect a fully fault-tolerant solution and that you understand how to set up various servers and routers. Some of this setup will be discussed more in Chapter 42, which delves into the WebSphere administrative tools.

Chapter 42

The WebSphere Administrative Console

The WebSphere Application Server is a complex and sophisticated product. As a result, configuring and administering WebSphere are not trivial tasks. To help with these tasks, IBM provides a user-friendly interface called the WebSphere Administrative Console.

The Administrative Console is one of the features that differentiate the WebSphere Advanced Edition Single-Server (AEs) and the WebSphere Advanced Edition (AE) products. In AEs, the Administrative Console is implemented by means of a Web-based interface that is accessed through port 9090. In contrast, AE provides a Java client application that implements this console. The latter is more powerful and more interactive. (For example, the console can print error messages without the need for the user to refresh.) Another distinction is that the AE Administrative Console provides true support for managing multiple sites. From a historical perspective, it is interesting to note that "ancient" versions of WebSphere (versions 2.0 and earlier) have a Web-based interface (using applets), and later versions (versions 3.*x* and later) provide the Java-based Administrative Console.

This chapter covers both variants of the Administrative Console. The WebSphere installation provided on the CD in this book is AEs, so if you are using it, your interest will probably be limited to the first half of this chapter, which focuses on the Web-based console. However, if you are running (or plan to run) a production site, you will most probably be using AE, and will be interested more in the information in the latter half of the chapter.

The AEs Administrative Console

You have accessed the AEs Administrative Console in previous chapters, mainly for such tasks as deploying Web and enterprise applications. The AEs Administrative Console is Web-based and is accessed using the URL *http://localhost:9090/* (assuming that WebSphere is running locally). When you access this page, you are prompted to enter a user name, as shown here. This user name does not require a password and is used only for tracking the changes made to the configuration.

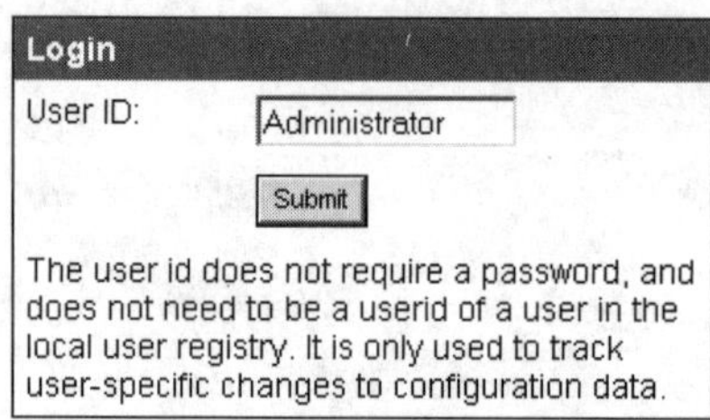

After you enter the user name, the home page for the AEs Administrative Console appears, as shown in Figure 42-1.

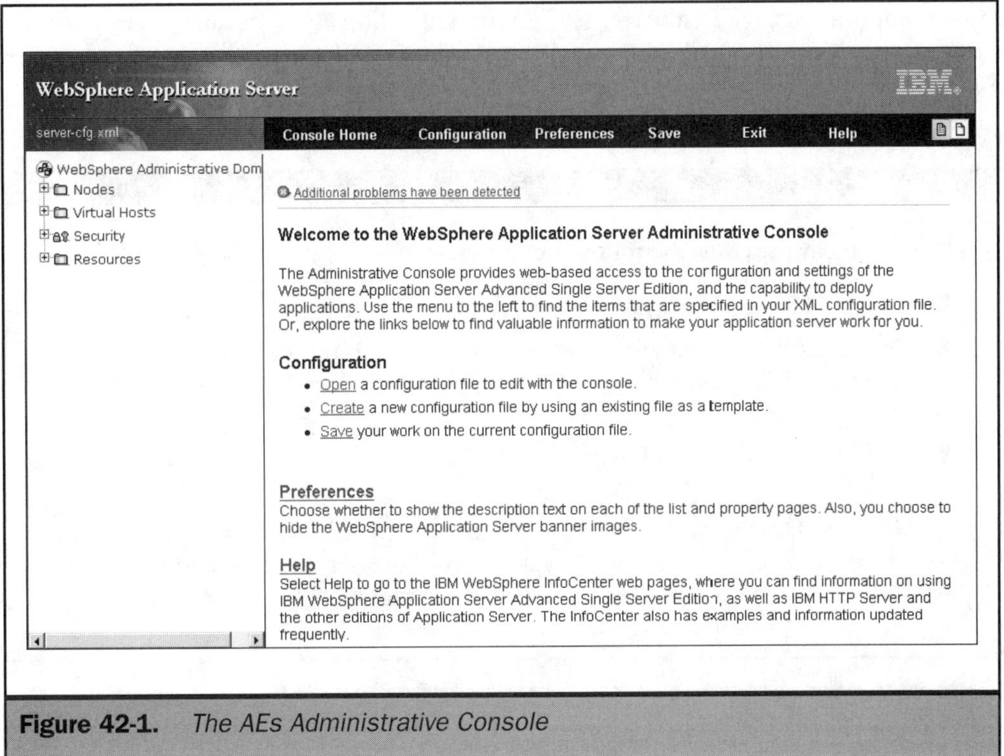

Figure 42-1. *The AEs Administrative Console*

The lefthand pane of the console contains a tree control, shown here, that allows you to navigate through the various configuration components. Above the tree control is the name of the currently active configuration file. WebSphere configuration information is stored in Extensible Markup Language (XML) files, which reside in the *config* directory under your WebSphere installation root.

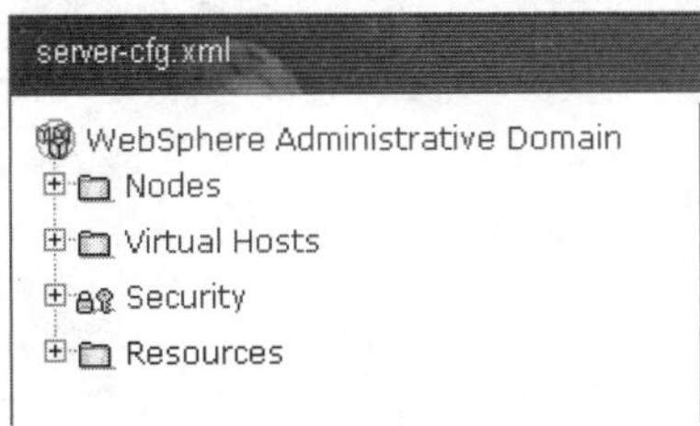

The tree control is available at all times when you're working with the AEs Administrative Console. It mimics the standard behavior of Windows Explorer and similar applications, where the tree is used for navigation and you can select a node on the tree to view its details in the main application window (which appears on the righthand pane, and is not shown here). At the top of the righthand pane, the AEs Administrative Console provides a menu bar, shown here:

The menu bar provides the following options:

- **Console Home** Returns you to the console home page.
- **Configuration** Lets you choose a configuration file for editing. By default, you are editing *config/server-cfg.xml*, but you can load other files, as shown in Figure 42-2.
- **Preferences** Controls the behavior of the console. It provides the following options:
  - **Show Descriptions** With descriptions turned on, the console provides a detailed explanation for each and every field. At the right end of the menu bar are two buttons for quickly enabling and disabling descriptions.

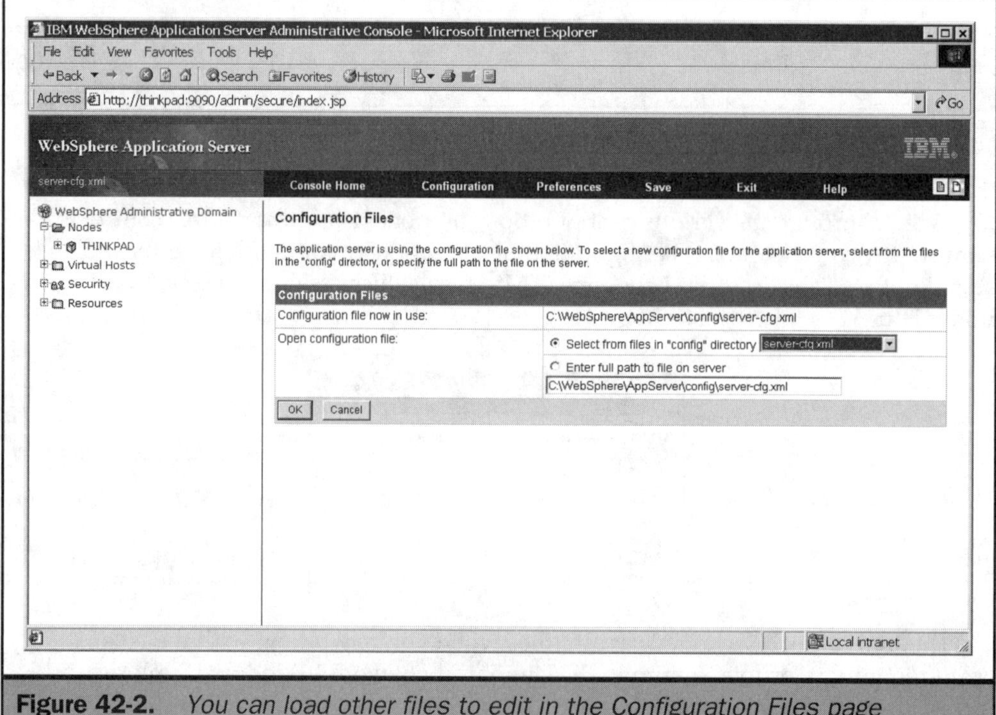

Figure 42-2. *You can load other files to edit in the Configuration Files page*

- **Show IBM Banner** Toggles the display of the blue banner at the top of the console, which displays the product name and IBM logo.
- **Enable Validation After Every Edit** Makes the console validate every action. An experienced administrator performing a batch of operations might want to turn off this feature to improve response time.
- **JavaScript or no JavaScript Tree** Allows you to select the underlying implementation of the tree control. By default, the console shows a JavaScript tree. You can choose a plain HTML tree by choosing the Load NoJavaScript Tree option. The HTML tree always appears in a fully expanded mode, as shown here. (This option is useful only for cases in which your browser does not support JavaScript all that well.)

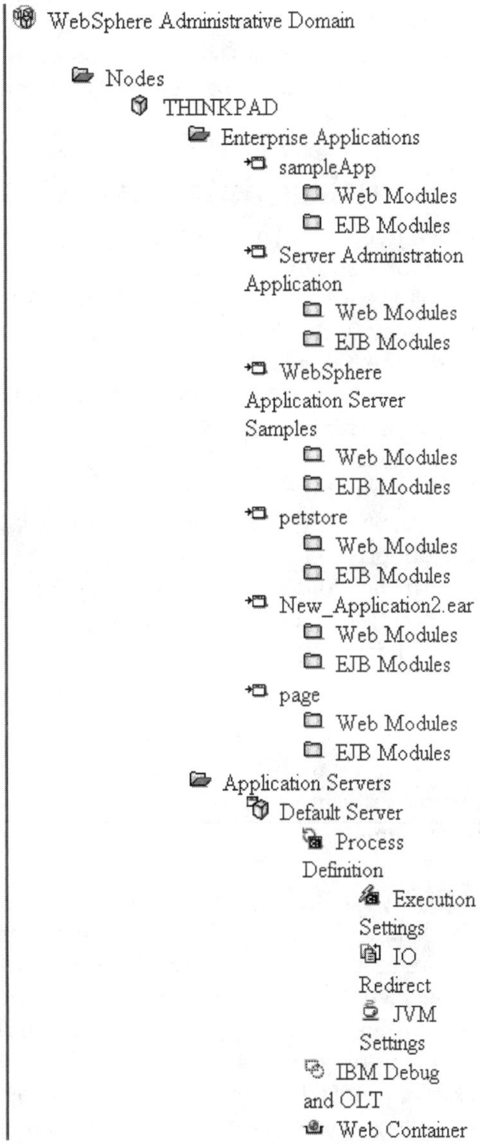

- WebSphere Administrative Domain
  - Nodes
    - THINKPAD
      - Enterprise Applications
        - sampleApp
          - Web Modules
          - EJB Modules
        - Server Administration Application
          - Web Modules
          - EJB Modules
        - WebSphere Application Server Samples
          - Web Modules
          - EJB Modules
        - petstore
          - Web Modules
          - EJB Modules
        - New_Application2.ear
          - Web Modules
          - EJB Modules
        - page
          - Web Modules
          - EJB Modules
      - Application Servers
        - Default Server
          - Process Definition
            - Execution Settings
            - IO Redirect
            - JVM Settings
          - IBM Debug and OLT
          - Web Container

- **Save** Saves your edits to the configuration file, which is quite critical, since any changes you make are lost if you do not save them. To remind you to save your changes, the console shows a message indicating that the configuration needs to be saved whenever any unsaved changes are made.
- **Exit** Allows orderly termination of an Administrative Console session. When exiting through this menu bar, you are prompted to save any changes you have made.
- **Help** Opens a browser window displaying context-related Help pages from the product online documentation.

A typical session with the Administrative Console consists of a series of edit operations followed by saving the changes. The tree control is used to navigate to the object of interest, and editing is accomplished in the main window on the righthand pane side of the console. The next section describes in detail each of the elements in the tree control.

AEs Administrative Console Topology

In the tree control on the lefthand pane of the console, four folders appear under WebSphere Administrative Domain: Nodes, Virtual Hosts, Security, and Resources.

Nodes are the physical machines, or hosts, on which WebSphere is installed. When you work with AEs, one such node always exists (after all, this is the single-site edition) under the Nodes folder.

The Virtual Hosts folder allows you to manage virtual hosts. A *virtual host* is a single machine that provides a façade of several machines, each with a different logical name (and a different Domain Name System, or DNS, alias). Virtual hosts do not share Web resources.

The Security folder contains security-related settings, such as authentication against the underlying operation system and the Secure Sockets Layer (SSL).

The last folder, Resources, is where you can manage Java 2 Platform Enterprise Edition (J2EE) resources such as JavaMail providers, Java Database Connectivity (JDBC) drivers, and Java Messaging Service (JMS) providers.

Nodes

In the Nodes folder, you can access most of the configuration settings for each host via the Enterprise Applications, Application Servers, Path Map, and Installed Resource Providers items.

Enterprise Applications

By clicking the Enterprise Applications item, you open the Enterprise Applications page, where you can access the applications installed on the server. A graphical indication shows whether they are running or not running. (In the example shown in Figure 42-3, the arrows indicate applications that are running; the application *New_application2.ear* is not running, as indicated by the little x icon.). From this window, you can start, stop, restart, uninstall, or export each of the installed applications. To perform any of these actions, you need to select one or more of the check boxes associated with the application and click the appropriate button.

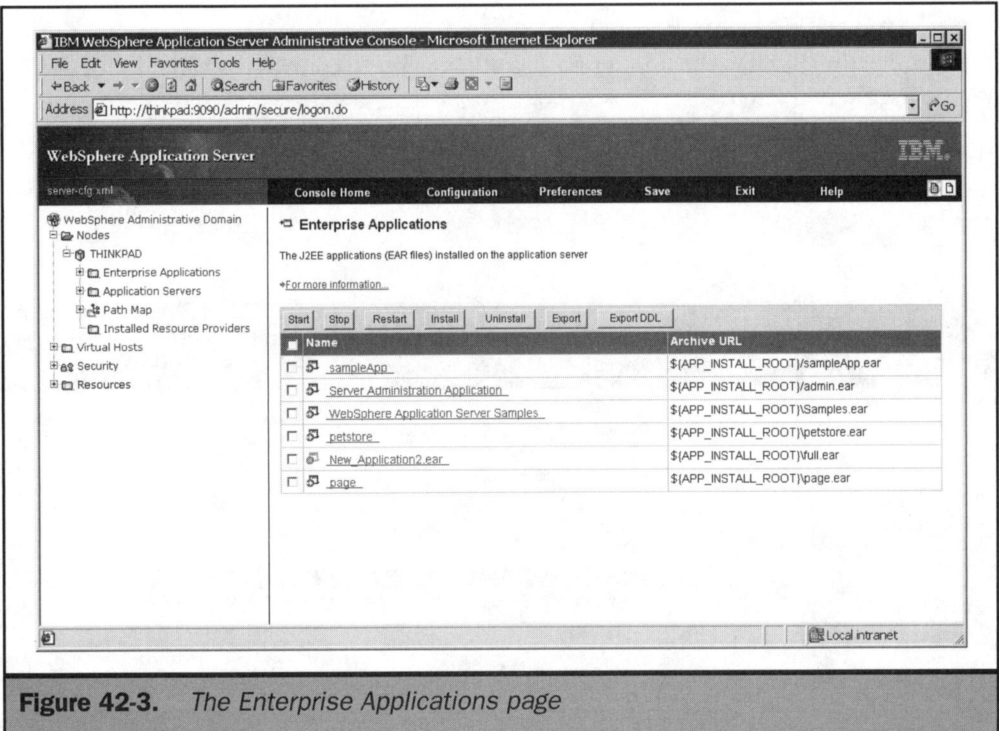

Figure 42-3. *The Enterprise Applications page*

For example, if you select two applications and click the Export button, the following page opens. Here you can click each of the Enterprise Archive (EAR) files that correspond to the selected application and export them to a file.

Export an application

Click the EAR files listed below to download them.

Exported application EAR files
Name
admin.ear
petstore.ear

OK

Installing a new application or module does not require that you choose any of the installed applications. Clicking the Install button from the Enterprise Applications page opens the Application Installation Wizard, where you can select a local or remote Web module, an EJB module, or an enterprise application. You can then deploy your selection in WebSphere. The details of this process are covered in Chapters 4 and 5. Note that for a Web or EJB module, you need to specify the application in which you want to deploy the module, because a module can run only as part of an application in WebSphere.

Application Servers

The Application Server entry under Nodes allows you to control the behavior of the WebSphere server itself.

Default Server Under the Application Servers entry are several entries, including the Default Server. From the Default Server page, you can PING, start, and stop your application server:

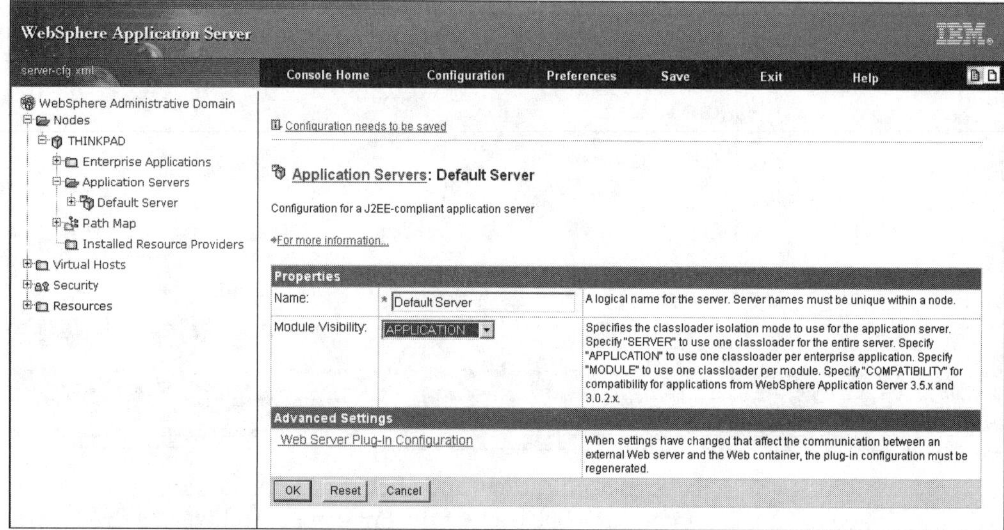

From the Default Server page, you can change the server name and control the module visibility. *Module visibility* is a technical issue; it controls the namespace in which your applications operate. The module visibility options MODULE, APPLICATION, and SERVER allow you to determine whether a Java class loader is provided for each module, for each application, or for the whole server, respectively. Another option, COMPATIBILITY, guarantees the same behavior as that of WebSphere 3.*x*. If you are running a J2EE-compliant application, it is recommended that you run MODULE, because it conforms to the J2EE specification

Under Advanced Settings, you can regenerate the Web server plug-ins, an important feature that allows users to access your application through the underlying HTTP server. After you deploy new applications, they can be accessed with a URL that points to the WebSphere server (for example, a server using port 9080). Regenerating the plug-ins will allow the HTTP server to redirect requests to WebSphere that are related to the new applications. If you skip this phase, the HTTP server will not recognize URLs that refer to new applications and will return an error message whenever one of these URLS is specified. Any time you make changes to an application that will change URI paths or virtual hosts, you need to regenerate the plug-ins.

Additional options are available under Default Server, as shown here:

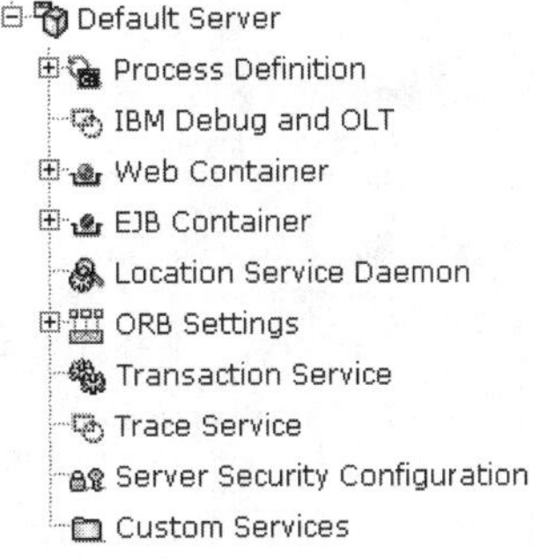

- **Process Definition** Lets you specify the executable for Java, the working directory for the application server, and the environment properties. This entry has the following subentries:
  - **Execution Settings** Controls operating system settings for the application server process: Priority, Umask (for file access permissions of created files), Run-as User, and Run-as Group. These settings pertain to UNIX systems. (This can easily be observed by examining the attributes and also the default Run-as User being root, which is not typically defined in Windows-based systems.)
  - **IO Redirect** Lets you select files to which the standard output and standard error of the application server JVM are redirected. By default, these are located in the *logs* directory under your installation root.
  - **JVM Settings** Controls technical Java Virtual Machine (JVM)–related settings, such as the CLASSPATH, verbose mode for various JVM components (class loader, Java Native Interface [JNI], and garbage collection), heap size settings, debug settings (such as requesting the use of `java_g` to enable debugging), and system properties settings.

- **IBM Debug and OLT** Starts a distributed debugger and object-level trace mechanism that can be used with WebSphere. These tools are not covered in this book, but they are bundled with WebSphere. Using this option, you can also determine the hostname and port where the object-level trace viewer is located, as shown here:

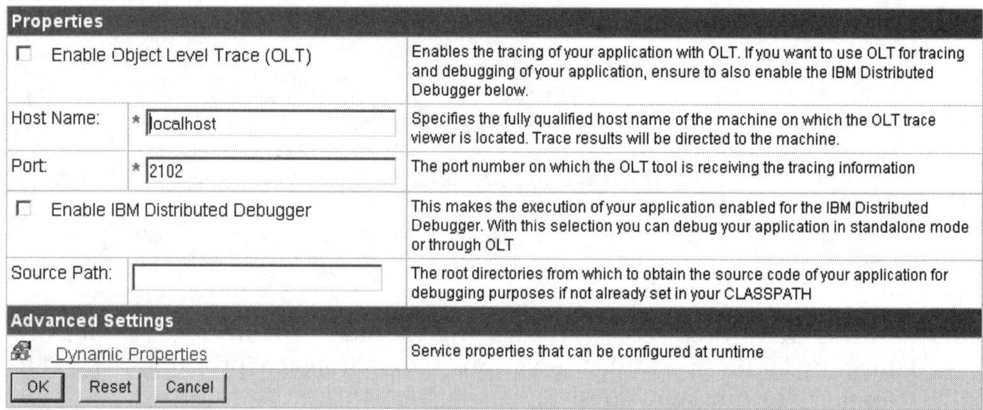

IBM Distributed Debugger and Object Level Trace Settings
Configuration for IBM Object Level Trace and IBM Distributed Debugger. Complimentary copies of these products are provided for tracing and debugging the applications running on your application server. See the InfoCenter for extensive information.
For more information...
Properties
Enable Object Level Trace (OLT)
Enables the tracing of your application with OLT. If you want to use OLT for tracing and debugging of your application, ensure to also enable the IBM Distributed Debugger below.
Host Name:
localhost
Specifies the fully qualified host name of the machine on which the OLT trace viewer is located. Trace results will be directed to the machine.
Port:
2102
The port number on which the OLT tool is receiving the tracing information
Enable IBM Distributed Debugger
This makes the execution of your application enabled for the IBM Distributed Debugger. With this selection you can debug your application in standalone mode or through OLT
Source Path:
The root directories from which to obtain the source code of your application for debugging purposes if not already set in your CLASSPATH
Advanced Settings
Dynamic Properties
Service properties that can be configured at runtime
OK
Reset
Cancel

Web Container The Web container holds and services your Web applications. Under this option are the following items: HTTP Transports, Session Manager, Installed Web Modules, and Thread Pool.

HTTP Transports control the list of ports to which the Web container binds. By default, the ports are 9080 (for accessing your Web applications), 9090 (for the Administrative Console), and 9443 (for the Web server plug-in). For each port, you can specify whether it is SSL enabled. If so, you can specify the SSL-related attributes, as shown in the following illustration. These attributes determine the cryptography-related settings, such as the key file and trust file.

SSL Settings

Configuration settings for using Secure Socket Layer (SSL)

For more information...

Properties		
Key File Name:	${WAS_ROOT}/etc/DummyServe	The fully qualified path to the key file that contains public keys and perhaps private keys
Key File Password:	******	The password for accessing the key file
Key File Format:	JKS	The format of the key file
Trust File Name:	${WAS_ROOT}/etc/DummyServe	The fully qualified path to a trust file containing the public keys
Trust File Password:	******	A password for accessing the trust file
Enable Client Authentication		Specifies that the server and client should prove their identities through an exchange of keys.
Security Level:	HIGH	One of a preconfigured set of security levels
Enable Crypto Token Support		Whether cryptographic token support is enabled
Advanced Settings		
Dynamic Properties		
Crypto Token		Specifies information about the cryptographic tokens related to SSL support

OK | Reset | Cancel

After you specify a new HTTP transport, you need to define a corresponding virtual host alias.

The HTTP transport settings are useful for changing the internal HTTP transport port used for accessing your Web applications directly (without going through the Web server) in case port 9080 is taken. For a production environment, you might want to disable this port, since the performance and scalability of the internal transport are no match for those of the Web plug-in that is used with a Web server.

The **Session Manager**, shown in the next illustration, controls the servlet sessions mechanism, as described in Chapter 23. The Session Manager properties allow you to enable both methods of session tracking: URL rewriting and cookies. You can also enable SSL tracking (that is, having sessions in SSL sessions), protocol switching (maintaining the session when switching from HTTP to HTTPS or the other way around), persistent sessions, and security integration (associating the authenticated username with the session). In addition, you have the option of adding Java properties to be used by the Web container service.

Session Manager

Configuration for session support in the Web container. When configuring the Session Manager, you can specify: ·Whether to enable sessions ·How to convey session IDs to servlets (cookies or URL rewriting) ·AE: Whether to save session data in a database during execution (persistent sessions) ·Whether to add session IDs to URLs in transition from HTTP to HTTPS and back (protocol switch rewriting)

For more information...

Properties	
☐ Enable URL Rewriting	Specifies whether the Session Manager uses rewritten URLs to carry the session IDs. If URL rewriting is enabled, the Session Manager recognizes session IDs that arrive in the URL and, if necessary, rewrites the URL to send the session IDs.
☑ Enable Cookies	Whether session tracking will use cookies to carry session IDs. If cookies are enabled, session tracking will recognize session IDs that arrive as cookies and try to use cookies for sending session IDs. If cookies are not enabled, session tracking will use URL rewriting instead of cookies (if URL rewriting is enabled). Enabling cookies takes precedence over URL rewriting.
☐ Enable SSL Tracking	Whether session tracking uses SSL to carry session IDs. Enabling SSL tracking takes precedence over cookie-based session tracking.
☐ Enable Protocol Switch Rewriting	Whether the session ID is added to a URL when the URL requires a switch from HTTP to HTTPS or from HTTPS to HTTP. If rewriting is enabled, the session ID is required in order to go between HTTP and HTTPS.
☐ Enable Persistent Sessions	When persistent sessions are enabled, the Session Manager will persist session information into the data source specified by the data source connection settings. Otherwise, the Session Manager will discard the session data when the server shuts down.
☐ Enable Security Integration	When security integration is enabled, the Session Manager will associate the identity of users with their HTTP sessions.
Advanced Settings	
Dynamic Properties	Service properties that can be configured at runtime

OK | Reset | Cancel

The Session Manager has the following subentries:

- **Default Cookie Settings** Controls the behavior of the cookie used for session tracking. The cookie name is fixed as per the J2EE specification. You can modify the domain and paths the cookie is associated with, and its time to live.
- **Persistent Sessions** Specifies the datasource and database parameters (such as the user ID, password, and tablespace name) for storing persistent sessions. (This entry is relevant only when you enable persistent sessions.)
- **Tuning Parameters** Specifies technical parameters associated with the Session Manager, including the invalidation timeout for sessions, the maximum number of sessions to maintain in memory, and the tuning parameters for persistent sessions (such as the policy used for deciding when to write the session to the database—at the end of the service method, manually by hard-coded invocations, or at fixed intervals).

Installed Web Modules show a list of installed Web modules; for each installed module, a link is provided to the enterprise application containing it, and you can review its deployment descriptor. The Web container pools the threads used by the running servlets. Using the Thread Pool subentry, you can indicate the minimum and maximum sizes, inactivity timeout (the interval after which a thread is removed), and whether the maximum size can be exceeded.

WebSphere can cache the output of dynamic servlets and JSP files, and this feature can significantly boost the performance of a Web application. (However, the data taken out of the cache might not be current.) The sophisticated caching mechanism is based on intercepting invocations of the `service` method, and it considers request parameters, uniform resource indicators (URIs), cookies, and session information.

The Dynamic Cache entry allows you to enable the cache, control the cache size, and set the default priority for a cached servlet (which represents the number of cycles through an LRU algorithm for which an entry is guaranteed to remain in the cache; the recommended value is 1).

The caching mechanism can also work with external caches that can be specified with the Cache Groups subentry. (This feature is fully supported only in the AE, so it is discussed in more detail later in this chapter.)

EJB Container The EJB container holds and invokes EJB and provides the following parameters:

- **Passivation Directory** Lets you specify a directory in which the passivated session beans will be stored—the "swap space" for the EJB container.
- **Inactive Pool Cleanup Interval** Lets you specify the time interval (in milliseconds) after which inactive bean pools will be reduced to their minimal size.
- **Default Data Source** Lets you specify a default JDBC-compliant datasource that the EJB container that will work with (for container managed persistence, for example).

Additional parameters are available under **Cache Settings**; these can be used to set the cache size and cleanup interval. This interval determines how frequently the container attempts to remove unused items from the cache.

The other subentry under the EJB container is **Installed EJB Modules**. As with the respective entry for Web modules, you can use this option to review the deployment descriptor for the module, and you add a link to the surrounding enterprise application.

ORB Settings From here, you can control the Object Request Broker (ORB). You can enable this service (it is enabled by default because it is required for EJB) and specify the host and port for bootstrapping. This host and port can be used if the ORB is used in conjunction with another ORB, but by default you use `localhost` with port 900. In addition, you can specify additional properties as defined in the `com.ibm.CORBA` package.

Under the ORB Settings entry are Thread Pool and SSL Settings. The former is identical to the option that controls the Web module thread pool, except that the parameters specified relate to a different pool. The EJB Container maintains its own thread pool. The SSL Settings entry allows you to define SSL parameters for using SSL over Internet Inter-ORB Protocol (IIOP). The parameters here are identical to those you use to set the SSL for HTTP transport ports.

These subentries follow the ORB Settings:

- **Transaction Service** Controls the behavior of the transaction service. You can enable EJB transactions here, as well as specify a log file. In addition, the container allows you to specify a maximum limit (in seconds) on the lifetime of a transaction. After this time elapses, the transaction is forced to roll back. This feature is important for preventing deadlocks. Similarly, you can specify a client inactivity timeout, against which the container measures the time since the last interaction with a client. If this inactivity timeout elapses, the transaction is aborted. The Transaction Service feature is shown here:

Configuration needs to be saved

Transaction Service

Configuration of the transaction service

For more information...

Properties		
☐ Enable		Whether the server will attempt to start the specified service
Transaction Log File:	${TRANLOG_ROOT}/tran1.log,${	The log file for transaction service logging. If specifying multiple log file names, separate them with commas. For example, specify: "W:WebSphereAppServerlogs ran1.log,W:WebSphere4_0AppServerlogs ran2.log" If this property is blank, the server will use in-memory logging. In a production environment, be sure to set a value because transaction rollback capability requires transaction logging.
Total Tran Lifetime Timeout:	120	The container will rollback transactions whose total lifetime (ie. timeperiod since beginning of transaction) exceeds the value of this setting.This value should be specified in seconds.
Client Inactivity Timeout:	60	The container uses client inactivity timeout to forcibly abort transaction if a client becomes inactive. Basically, assume that a client calls an EJBServer and invokes some method. When the call returns to client, the timer is started. If client does not come back within the client inactivity timeout interval, the transaction in the server is rolledback by the container.This value should be specified in seconds.
Advanced Settings		
Dynamic Properties		Service properties that can be configured at runtime

OK | Reset | Cancel

- **Trace Service** Controls the logging of traces, as discussed in detail in Chapter 21.
- **Server Security Configuration** The only option here is Use Domain Qualified User Names. When this is enabled, user names are always qualified with the security domain in which they reside. This would apply to user names returned from methods such as getPrincipal().
- **Custom Services** Allows you to attach your own services to the application server. Such services are essentially classes that you provide and that are invoked when the server is started (and are shut down when the server is shut down).

  Here you can define custom services, for which you need to specify names, descriptions, and class names. The classes should implement the interface com.ibm.websphere.runtime.CustomService. When specifying a custom service, you can also specify an external configuration file (specified as a URL) for the service, and the classpath where the class can be found.

  The com.ibm.websphere.runtime.CustomService is straightforward and provides only two methods . The initialize method takes as parameter a java.util.Properties object that is constructed from the external configuration you specify, and it is invoked when the application server is started. The shutdown method is invoked when the server shuts down.

Path Map

The Path Map entry is the next subsection of Nodes. It summarizes the list of logical paths used in other settings, as shown here:

Entries

A list of file system roots

For more information...

New | Delete

Symbolic Name	Path	Description
APP_INSTALL_ROOT	${WAS_ROOT}/installedApps	The filesystem path to the directory which will contain installed enterprise applications.
LOG_ROOT	${WAS_ROOT}/logs	The filesystem path to the directory which will contain server log files.
TRANLOG_ROOT	${WAS_ROOT}/tranlog	The filesystem path to the directory which will transaction log files.
PRODUCT_INSTALL_ROOT	${WAS_ROOT}	The filesystem path to the product installation directory
WAS_ROOT	C:\WebSphere\AppServer	The filesystem path to the product installation directory
JAVA_HOME	C:\WebSphere\AppServer\java	The filesystem path to the product java home directory

You can then use any of these paths when you need to specify a directory. This allows you to control the directories where files are located in one centralized place. For example, the default value for the transaction service log is specified relative to the TRANLOG_ROOT path:

```
${TRANLOG_ROOT}/tran1.log,${TRANLOG_ROOT}/tran2.log
```

Installed Resource Providers

This is the final subentry under Nodes. It lets you specify the list of J2EE resources (such as JDBC drivers) available for the application server as well as the classpath associated with them. You can add new resources using the Resources entry, which is discussed in the section, "Resources."

Virtual Hosts

The Virtual Hosts entry allows you to add and remove a virtual host, after which you can set its name, DNS aliases (including a port number to which it is bound), and default MIME entries.

By default, a *default_host* entry with ports 80 and 443 is used, while ports 9080 and 9443 are used for the Web server plug-in. The *admin_host* uses port 9090.

Note *A virtual host alias must correspond to each port being used by an HTTP transport.*

Security

Using the Security entry, you can enable security and determine a timeout for the authentication cache. Note that security is disabled by default, so for a production environment, the first thing you should do is enable it. Under the Security entry are entries for authentication against the underlying operating system, and for SSL settings. Chapter 44 is fully dedicated to security administration, and in that chapter you'll see how the Administrative Console is used for these tasks.

Resources

From the Resources entry, you can add the following J2EE resources to your application server: JDBC providers, JMS providers, URL providers, and JavaMail providers. Once a resource is selected, its entry shows a list of available providers.

For example, selecting the JDBC Drivers entry shows the list of configured drivers. You can add or delete drivers using the appropriate buttons. When adding a driver, preset options are included for Oracle, DB2, and Microsoft SQL Server, but you can add other drivers for any JDBC-compliant database.

The list of available drivers can also be accessed directly from the tree control by expanding the JDBC Drivers entry. Under each driver entry is an entry for Data Sources, as shown in the following illustration. Each entry includes specific data sources for which a JNDI name is defined, as well as a database table, a database user name and password, and connection pooling parameters.

For other resources, a similar concept is used: for example, under the Resources folder are specific providers (analogous to JDBC drivers), and under them are lists of objects (analogous to datasources). Such objects are sessions for the mail providers, URLs for the URL provider, and JMS connections for JMS providers.

JavaMail, JDBC, and JMS were discussed in Chapters 14 and 15. The URL provider is used to handle new protocols. The default provider handles protocols supported by the JDK, such as http, ftp, and file protocols. For other protocols, you can add your own provider and then specify the class handling the stream of data for each protocol.

You can define you own JavaMail session objects, in which case you need to specify the details of the mail transport and the mail store (such as protocols, hostname, username, and password).

AEs provides limited support for JMS resources. It supports only two kinds of JMS providers (MQSeries and SonicMQ). For each of them, you can define connection factories and destinations. As explained in Chapter 14, JMS-based code relies heavily on administrative settings that define connection factories and message destinations.

The AE Administrative Console

The WebSphere Application server AE Administrative Console is provided as a Java application. Furthermore, this console communicates with an administrative server, which in turn can start and stop the application server (or servers). This stands in contrast to the AEs, where the Administrative Console can interact only with the application server. The approach used with AE is more scalable in the sense that it lends itself to managing multiple application servers. Furthermore, it is easier to use when performing actions such as restarting an application server.

The AE Administrative Console, shown in Figure 42-4, can be started through WebSphere's First Steps window, or from the Start menu, or by using the script `adminclient.bat`.

When you start the console, a window appears with the IBM and WebSphere logos. The console needs to communicate with the administrative server, which must be started before you invoke the console. Failing to do so will prevent the console from starting, and the following message will appear:

```
ADGEU2008E: The Administration Client failed to connect to the
Administration Server. Start the local or remote Administration Server
service before launching the Administration Client.
```

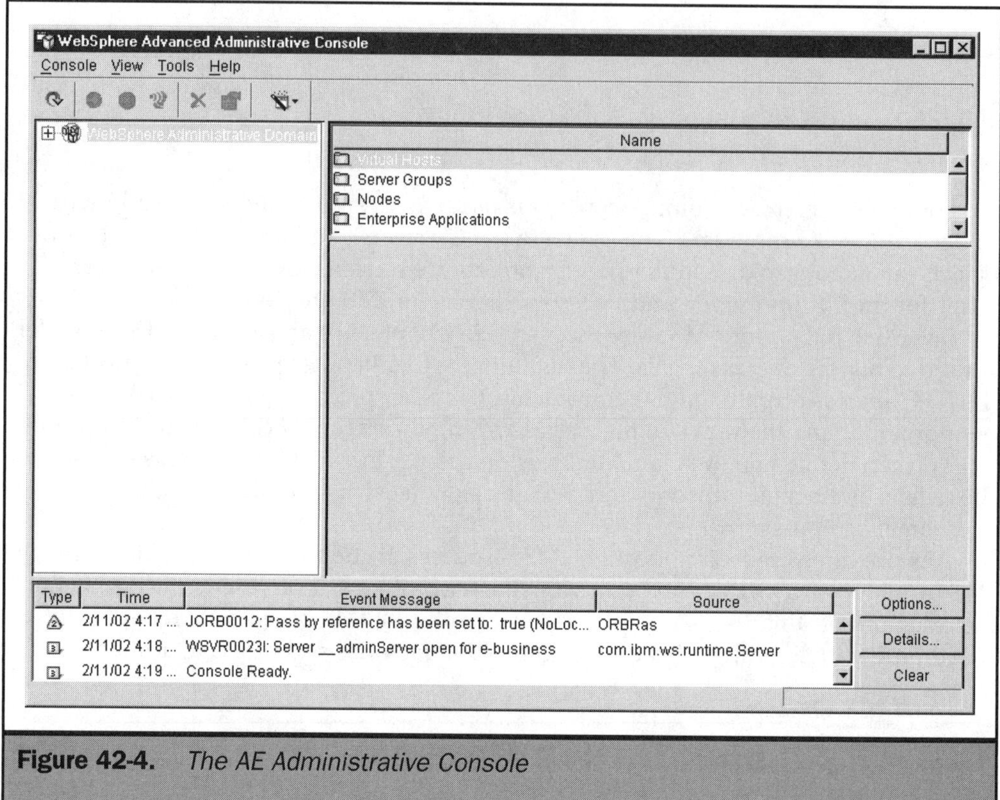

Figure 42-4. *The AE Administrative Console*

When you invoke the administration server from the command-line, the script is different and is called `adminserver.bat` (or `adminserver.sh` if running on UNIX). On Windows, the administration server can also be started as an Windows NT service.

The AE Administrative Console is a Java application. It consists of a menu bar, a toolbar, a tree control on the left, a details window on the right, and a message area on the bottom.

The tree control allows you to browse through the various servers and their components, and to review and edit properties in the details window on the right. The message area provides a significant improvement in terms of functionality compared to the Web-based interface of the AEs Administrative Console, because if notifies you immediately about any events or problems that occur.

The root of the tree control is the WebSphere Administrative Domain (as it was in AEs). Under this root are five entries. Four of them, Virtual Hosts, Nodes, Enterprise Applications, and Resources, use the same names and provide equivalent functionality as the entries in the AEs console tree control. One new entry is Server Groups. This entry is used to manage multiple WebSphere instances that cooperate to provide the façade of a single server.

If the application server is not up and running, you need to start the server. Just to avoid confusion, remember that the admin server needs to be running for the console to come up, but the application server does not. Expand the Nodes folder, and access the Application Servers folder. Here you should find the Default Server, which is automatically created during installation. Right-click the Default Server and choose Start from the pop-up menu. When the server is running, it issues its "open for e-business" message in the message area.

Using the AE Administrative Console

From the AE Administrative Console, you can browse through the tree of objects in the administrative domain, while reviewing and editing these objects—similar to the process of working with the AEs console. To alleviate the administration work, the AE console provides a collection of wizards that provides a guided walkthrough for common administrative tasks.

AE Administrative Console Menu Bar

The AE Console menu provides the following commands:

- **New** Creates new objects.
- **Wizards** Provides wizards used for common tasks.
- **Trace** Controls the trace mechanism.
- **Security Center** Opens the Security Center dialog box (shown here), which summarizes security settings. Note that by default, security is disabled, so you must remember to enable it if you are interested in security-related features. (Administering security is the subject of Chapter 44.)

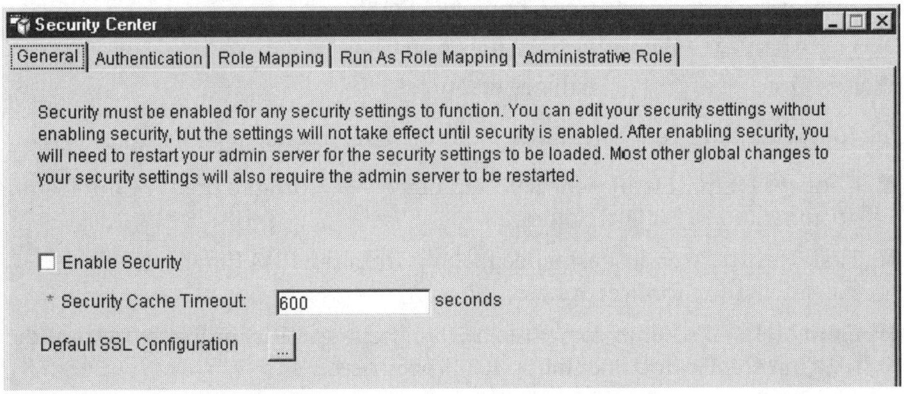

Security Center

General | Authentication | Role Mapping | Run As Role Mapping | Administrative Role

Security must be enabled for any security settings to function. You can edit your security settings without enabling security, but the settings will not take effect until security is enabled. After enabling security, you will need to restart your admin server for the security settings to be loaded. Most other global changes to your security settings will also require the admin server to be restarted.

☐ Enable Security

* Security Cache Timeout: 600 seconds

Default SSL Configuration ...

- **Import from XML** Imports an XML configuration file.
- **Export to XML** Exports configuration to an XML file.
- **Start** Starts the selected object.
- **Stop** Stops the selected object.
- **Force Stop** Forces the selected object to stop.
- **Ping** Pings the selected object (to determine whether it is working).
- **Remove** Removes the selected object.
- **Properties** Shows properties of the selected object.
- **Find** Allows you to search for an object based on type and name criteria.
- **Command History** Shows a table with all commands performed, including their status, completion time, and completion result. In case of failure, you can view the error associated with the command.
- **Exit** Exits the console.

The View menu offers the following options:

- **Show Property Pane** Allows you to turn on and off the property pane that shows the properties of the selected object
- **Show Message Pane** Allows you to turn on and off the message pane.
- **Runtime Inspector** Allows you to toggle on and off the runtime inspector. The runtime inspector is a modeless dialog box that is separate from the console's main window. It displays runtime information, such as process ID and the currently used settings.

The Tools menu invokes external tools related to administrative tasks:

- **Application Assembly Tool** Assembles Web modules, EJB modules, and enterprise applications (see Chapters 4 and 5).
- **Log Analyzer** Analyzes trace files (see Chapter 21).
- **Resource Analyzer** Analyzes resources.

The following options are available from the Help menu:

- **Concept Help** Defines the selected object according to the IBM InfoCenter documentation for WebSphere.
- **Task Help** Provides task-specific help from the IBM InfoCenter documentation for WebSphere.
- **Field Help** Provides context-sensitive (field-specific) online help from the IBM InfoCenter documentation for WebSphere.

- **Information Center** Opens the AE Administrative Console pages in the IBM InfoCenter documentation for WebSphere.
- **About** Shows product information.

AE Administrative Console Toolbar

The AE Administrative Console toolbar provides the buttons shown in Table 42-1. The functionality of each button can be achieved from the Console menu or from the pop-up menu that appears when you right-click an object.

AE Administrative Console Message Pane

Each message in the AE Administrative Console message pane includes a type, time, message text, and source. Messages can be Severe, Warning, and Audit. You can filter messages; and control the polling interval and the limit on the length of the message log

Button	Function
	Refreshes the selected object (and its subtree)
	Starts the selected object
	Stops the selected object
	Pings the selected object (to check that it is alive)
	Removes the selected object
	Shows the properties of the selected object in a new dialog box (the same properties appear in the properties pane)
	Displays the Wizards menu (identical to the Wizards entry in the Console menu)

Table 42-1. *AE Administrative Console Toolbar Buttons*

through the message pane's Event Viewer Options dialog box, shown here. You can access this box by clicking the Options button on the message pane.

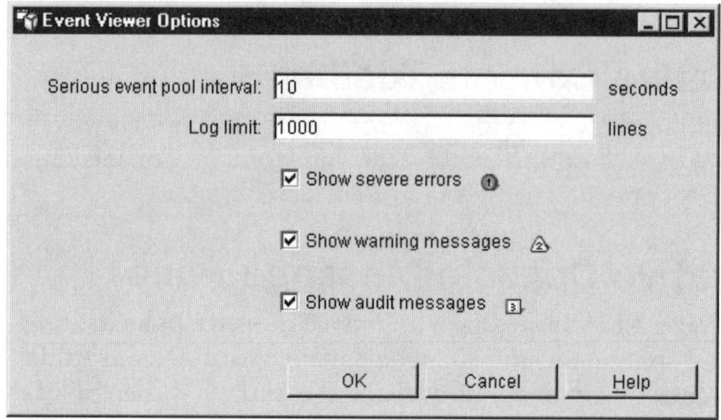

To view the full details for a specific message, select it in the console message pane and click the Details button. The event details window displays the event ID, time, type, node, server, thread ID, source, and full text. Finally, you can click the Clear button to clear the message log.

Virtual Hosts and Nodes Folders

The Virtual Hosts folder contains information similar to the information available in the AEs console's Virtual Hosts folder. You can define a list of virtual hosts here, and for each host, you can define an alias composed of a hostname and port number. Under the Advanced tab of the Virtual Hosts page, you can define MIME extensions.

As in the AEs Administrative Console, the AE console's Nodes folder contains a list of physical machines. Under Node are Application Servers and Generic Servers, described in the next two subsections. The node properties include the node name (which cannot be changed—as this is the prerogative of the underlying operating system) and the set of installed J2EE resources. Each type of resource has a tab that corresponds to the Installed Resources entry in the AE console.

Each of the tabs in the Nodes page displays a list of resources for the respective types and allows you to install new resources. If you install new providers, you can select a provider from the list of providers of the respective type in the Resources folder.

Application Servers Folder

Within each node (appearing in the Nodes folder) are two subfolders: the Application Servers Folder and the Generic Servers folder. Under the Application Servers folder you can find each of the application servers instances running on the node. Right-click an application server icon to open a pop-up menu, where you can start, stop, remove, or ping the server. (Some of the options might be grayed out—for example, you cannot start it if the server is already started.) The pop-up menu also includes a Transactions item that allows you to review a set of currently running transactions. This is useful for handing deadlocks or other transaction-related problems. In the Transactions window, you can commit or roll back each transaction, as well as review its details.

The application server properties provide seven different tabs. The General tab includes the server logical name, the node on which it resides, the working directory, and the environment. You can specify the startup state, which determines whether the server will start automatically when the node is up. By default, the WebSphere server does not start automatically. This setting determines what the application server will do when administration server starts. The last option in the General tab is Module Visibility, which offers the same options described for the AEs console.

In the Advanced tab, you can set the parameters for the ping operation (its interval and timeout). You can also set the operating system settings for the process (process priority, user ID, and group ID). The last option is to use domain qualified user names (which was under Security in AEs).

The File tab, shown next, is where you can specify the standard input, standard output, and standard error files for the server. It also provides a graphical interface for setting the umask for created files.

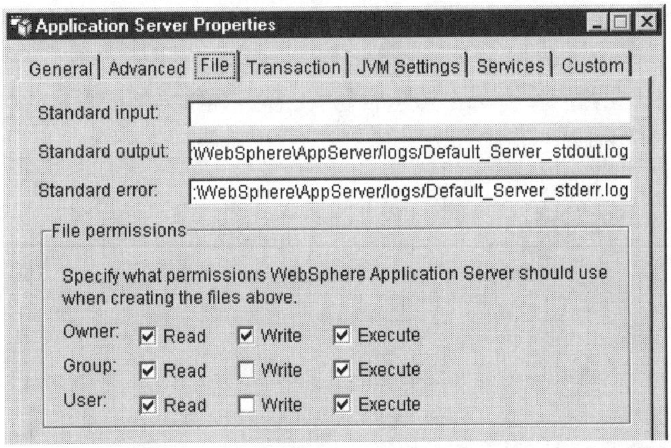

The Transaction tab is where you can set the transaction timeout and transaction inactivity timeout in seconds. The JVM Settings tab allows you to control the JVM heap sizes, class path, system properties, and other settings (such as enabling garbage collector verbose mode).

The Services tab contains a list of services, most of which were covered earlier in the chapter in the discussion of the AEs console. The only new service in the list is related to performance monitoring. Here the various service settings are separated from the other settings (such as Process Definition), and the parameters are grouped into tabs that do not reflect the subdivision of parameters in the AEs. Other subtle differences exist as well. For example, under the Web Container service, you can enable servlet caching and use external cache groups.

External cache groups are supported to a larger extent than the support provided by AEs. You can specify an adapter bean for your external group. The adapter bean bridges between WebSphere and the external cache. The Custom tab allows you to define custom services implementing the `CustomService` interface.

Another difference from AEs is in the AE Session Manager service. When using persistent sessions, the console offers a set of predefined configurations for tuning parameters, as shown in Figure 42-5.

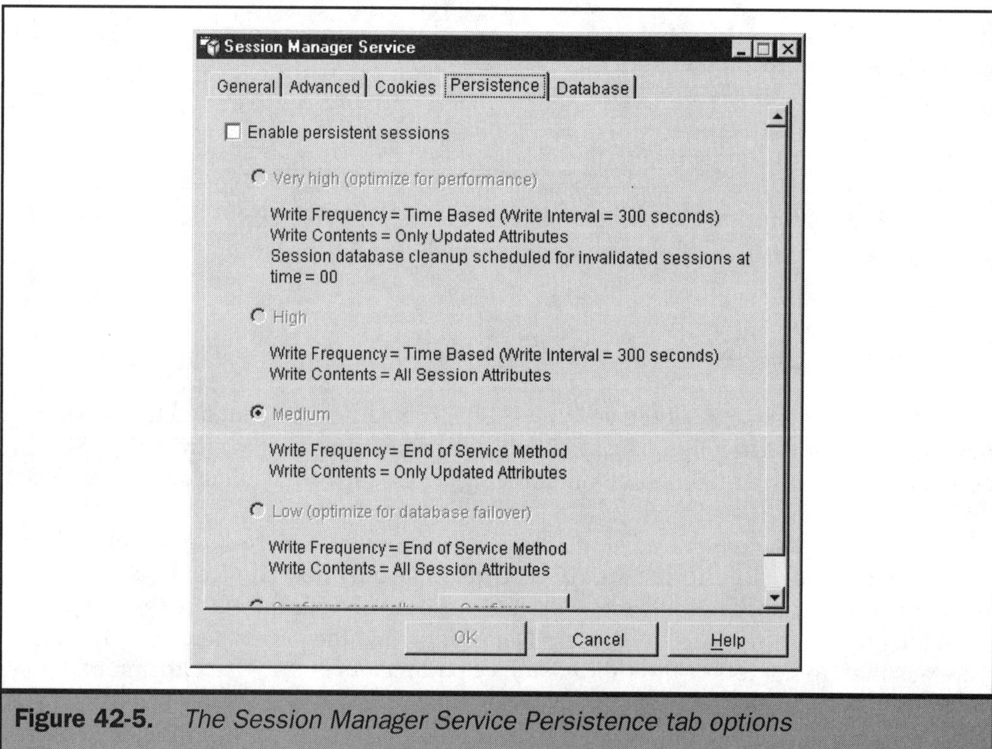

Figure 42-5. *The Session Manager Service Persistence tab options*

You can also tune parameters manually and then specify the same parameters required for this feature in the AEs console.

The settings for the EJB container, trace service, OLT service, and ORB service are identical to those described for AEs. In the Performance Monitoring Settings dialog box, shown in Figure 42-6, you can monitor the performance of various components of the server as well as your own application.

The Performance Monitoring Settings dialog box provides a hierarchical display of the application server components, via a tree control that you can use to locate and select a single servlet or EJB and then select a level of monitoring. As shown in Figure 42-6, the dialog box shows the list of counters maintained for each level of monitoring. The display of monitoring data is accomplished through the Resource Analyzer tool (which also provides the ability to define the monitoring settings). You should remember that setting a high level of monitoring will severely affect performance, and you should never run a production system with monitoring enabled.

Under the Application Server folder, two entries represent the installed Web and EJB modules. These correspond to the respective entries under the Web container and EJB container in the AEs console.

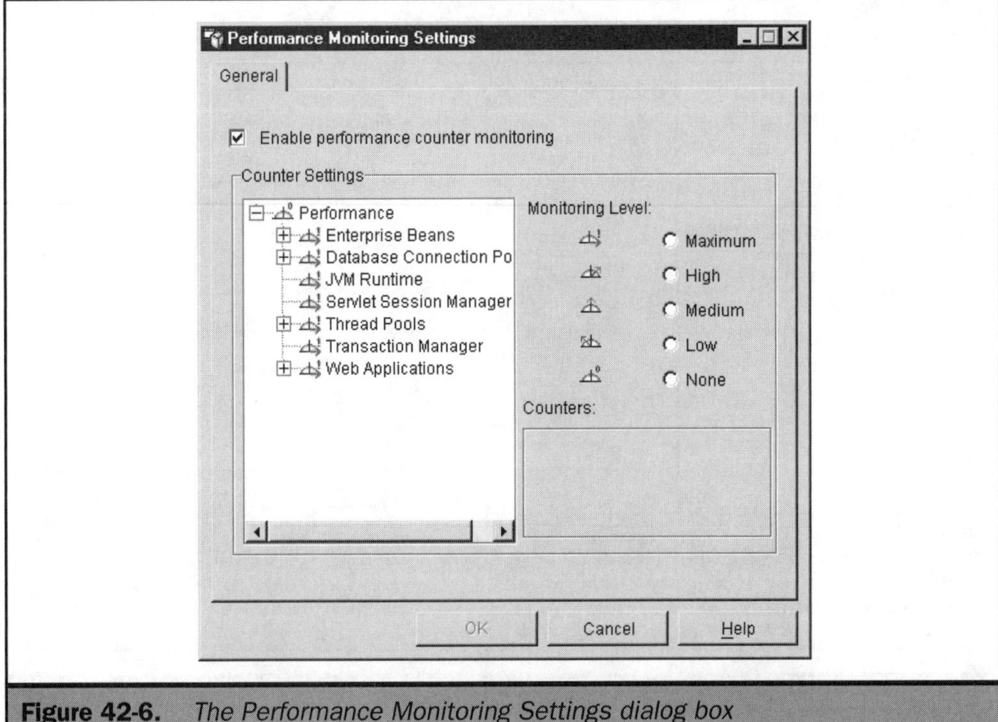

Figure 42-6. *The Performance Monitoring Settings dialog box*

The EJB Modules entry provides a list of all installed modules. By selecting a module, you can review its deployment attributes. In contrast to the AEs console, here you can actually edit the deployment attributes. Obviously, this feature provides enormous flexibility, and makes deployment of an application much easier.

Similarly, the Web Modules entry lists the available Web modules and allows you to review and edit their attributes. You cannot edit the Context Root for a Web module—this is determined by the application deployer via the Application Assembly Tool.

Note in Figure 42-7 that both Web and EJB modules are detailed under the Enterprise Application. The properties shown for each module under the Enterprise Application are identical to those under the respective module's folder, as listed under the Application Server's folder.

Generic Servers Folder

Generic servers in WebSphere are plain executables that can be binaries, scripts, or invocations of Java code accessed through the Java Runtime Environment (JRE). The ability

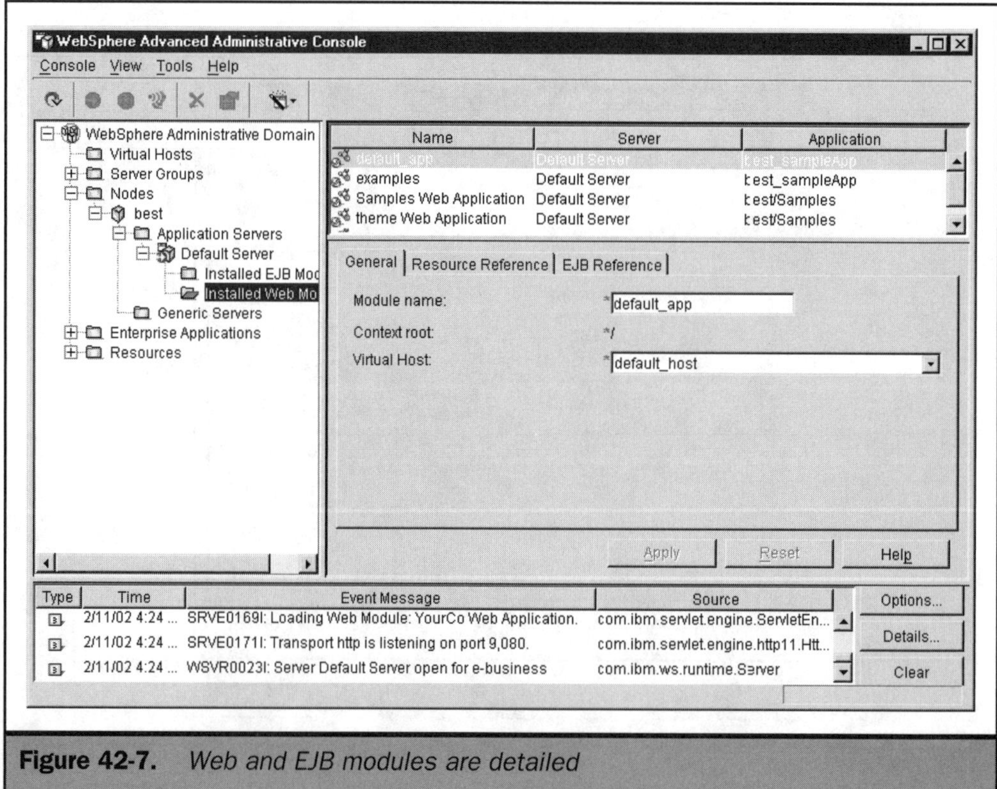

Figure 42-7. *Web and EJB modules are detailed*

to attach such generic servers complements the notion of custom services in a Java class with the `CustomService` interface.

Under Generic Servers, you can define generic servers and edit their settings. These servers are included in the Administrative Console to provide an easy way for you to define external processes that start and stop together with the application server. For example, it is common for enterprise applications to be packaged as RMI servers that can be deployed outside of the WebSphere Java Virtual Machine (JVM) but that need to be started and stopped along with the rest of the application components.

Enterprise Applications Folder

The Enterprise Applications folder contains all deployed applications. Here you can view the EJB modules and Web modules for each application.

The properties of an enterprise application are organized in three tabs:

- **General** Contains the application name.
- **User/Role Mappings** Maps application roles to specific users and groups. When specifying a user, you also need to specify a valid password
- **Run-as Mappings** Maps Run-as roles to specific users. When specifying users, you need to specify a valid password.

Right-click an enterprise application to see a pop-up menu, where you can view the deployment descriptor and export the application. Both functions behave similarly to the way they do in the AEs console. In the same menu, you can also start, stop, or remove the application.

Resources Folder

The Resources folder contains JDBC providers, JavaMail sessions, URL providers, J2EE Connector Architecture (J2C) resource adapters, and JMS providers. The AE console provides functionality similar to that of the AEs interface, but in a more technical and detailed manner. For example, when adding a JDBC driver, you select the implementation class instead of specifying the database product. Another difference is that you can easily add new resources by choosing Console | New, or by right-clicking the resource type entry and selecting New.

After adding JDBC drivers, you can define specific JDBC datasources. Each of these is identified by a JNDI name and mapped to a specific database, table, username, and password.

For JavaMail sessions, the functionality is similar to that of AEs. You can specify your own sessions, including settings for outgoing mail. URL providers, too, can be added as with AEs. Right-click the URL Providers icon and select New to open the URL Provider resource window. Here you can define specific URLs and bind them to JNDI names for use by server-side code.

Under JMS Providers you can add providers for new JMS-compliant messaging systems (and unlike AEs, you are not limited in the list of supported products). For a new JMS provider, you specify a name, description, context factory classname, and provider URL, as shown here:

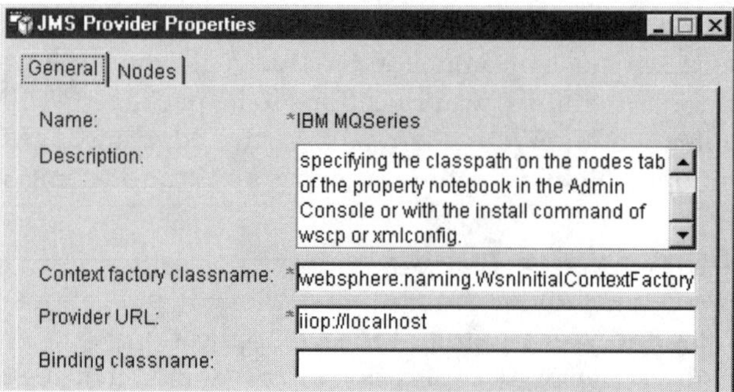

Also under JMS Providers are JMS connection factories and JMS destinations. You can add, remove, and edit these two lists. For each of these, you need to specify a display name, description, JNDI name, optional free-text category, and additional custom properties. The associated JMS provider is displayed as a read-only property. (It matches the provider under which you are creating the connection factory.) For destinations, you specify the destination type (either topic or queue), and for connections, you specify the connection type (point-to-point or publish/subscribe).

J2C resource adapters provide a way for WebSphere to interface with legacy systems or any Enterprise Information System (EIS). For a J2C adapter, you need to specify a display name and the archive in which it resides (a *.rar* file), as well as a classpath, a description, and optional vendor-specific properties.

Server Groups Folder

One of the main differentiators between AE and AEs is AE support for multiple servers. (The lowercase *s* stands for *Single-Server*, after all.) To ease administration of a large site, AE introduces the concept of a *server group*, which is a collection of application server instances that cooperate and provide the façade of a single application server. This replication boosts both performance and reliability. A server group has the same properties as a single application server, with the following additions. (These can be found on the server groups property editor, which becomes available when you click a server group.)

- **Server Group Name** Displays the name of the group.
- **Workload Management Policy** Binds clients to servers in the group. The options are as follows:
  - **Random** Each request is randomly assigned to a server.
  - **Round Robin** Application servers are ordered in some random sequence. Clients are bound to servers according to this list, and once all the servers in the list are selected, the whole list is repeated again. Of course, if a server instance in the sequence is not available, it is skipped.

- **Random Prefer Local** Specifies that assignment is based on random selection unless the request can be serviced locally, in which case a local application server is selected randomly.
- **Round Robin Prefer Locally** Organizes requests for local application servers. If no local application servers can service a given request, a remote host is selected according to the round-robin policy.

After you create a server group using these settings, it still cannot be used. It is missing the actual application servers that participate in the group. To add these application server instances, you need to right-click the server group icon and select New | Clone. Then you can select a name for the clone, and the node on which it is to be installed. The term *clone* in WebSphere refers to an application server instance that is running as part of a server group.

AE Administrative Console Wizards

The AE Administrative Console provides a set of wizards that can ease the task of managing your WebSphere installation. This section describes each of these wizards in detail.

Install Enterprise Application Wizard

The Install Enterprise Application Wizard takes you through the process of deploying a new application. The first window is similar to the one offered by AEs for installing a new application and is shown in Figure 42-8.

You can select either an Enterprise archive (EAR) file or a standalone (Web or EJB) module. If you select the standalone option, WebSphere will create an enterprise application consisting of your new module. In the next window, you can specify the mapping between logical roles in the application and the actual users.

You define the mapping by selecting a set of users and/or groups for each role. You can choose to drop the authentication requirement or allow all authenticated users to assume the specific role.

In the next window, you map EJB RunAs roles to users. RunAs roles are the roles defined for specific EJB methods (under the Advanced tab for method extensions in the EJB). You can map the RunAs role, which includes the definition of the same role that appeared in the previous window to a single user.

After you've defined the security-related configuration, the next window touches upon EJB references. In the Application Assembly Tool (AAT), a module can define EJB references that refer to beans external to the module. These references are bound to specific beans in the AAT, but in the Administrative Console you can modify these bindings. You can bind a bean reference either to an EJB installed on your server or to a free-text JNDI name.

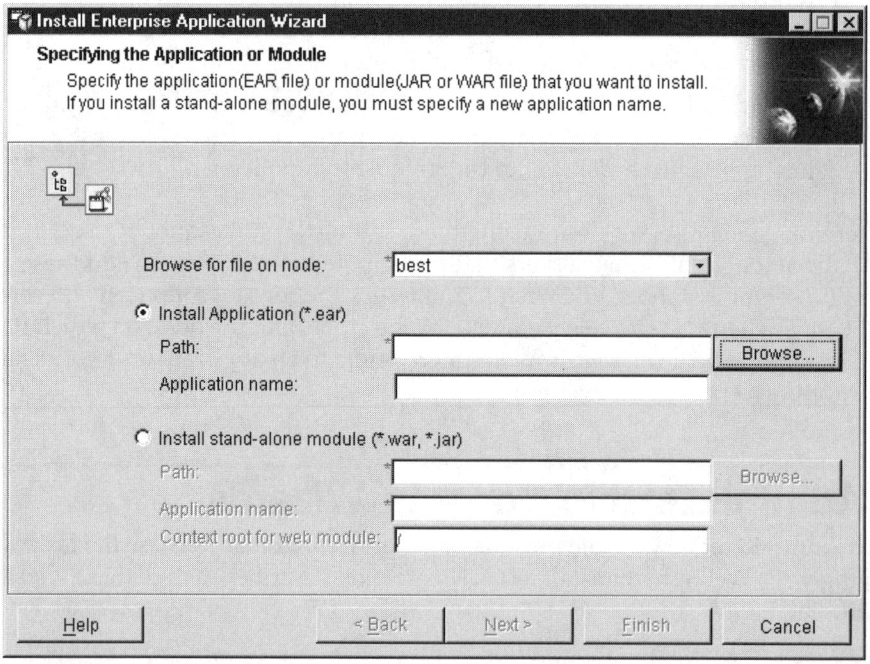

Install Enterprise Application Wizard
Specifying the Application or Module
Specify the application(EAR file) or module(JAR or WAR file) that you want to install.
If you install a stand-alone module, you must specify a new application name.
Browse for file on node: best
Install Application (*.ear)
Path:
Browse...
Application name:
Install stand-alone module (*.war, *.jar)
Path:
Browse...
Application name:
Context root for web module: /
Help
< Back
Next >
Finish
Cancel

Figure 42-8. *The Install Enterprise Application Wizard*

Much like EJB references a module can include resource references to URLs, datasources, JavaMail sessions, or JMS objects. The next step in this wizard allows you to bind such references to an installed resource of the respective type. You must bind the references prior to proceeding.

The next step involves choosing the default datasource in case you have modules that contain EJB with Container Managed Persistence (CMP). Here you can also select datasources for individual beans.

In the final two steps of the wizard, you decide where to locate your application. First, you need to choose a virtual host for each of the Web modules. Next, you need to choose the application server instance for each of the modules in the application. By default, all modules are set to run on the default server. Note that at this point you can click the Finish button, since it is no longer disabled. Clicking the Next button again will bring up a confirmation window, which is the last stage in this wizard.

Create Application Server Wizard

The Create Application Server Wizard, shown in Figure 42-9, starts with a window in which you specify the server name and the node where you want to install the application server.

In the next step, you can edit the service properties. This process is identical to editing the Services tab of the application server. The final phase here is again a confirmation window.

Datasource Wizard

The Datasource Wizard for creating a new datasource starts with the window shown in Figure 42-10, in which you specify the name and description of the datasource, as well as the name of the target database.

Next you select a JDBC provider. You can either select an existing provider (available under the Resources folder in the main window) or specify a new one.

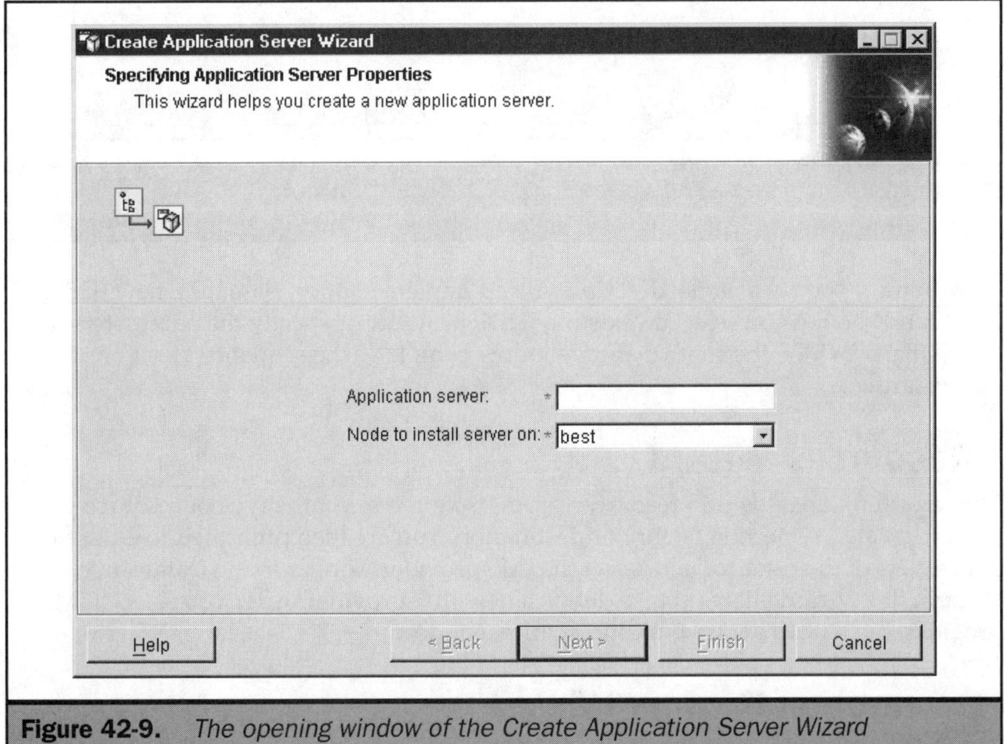

Figure 42-9. *The opening window of the Create Application Server Wizard*

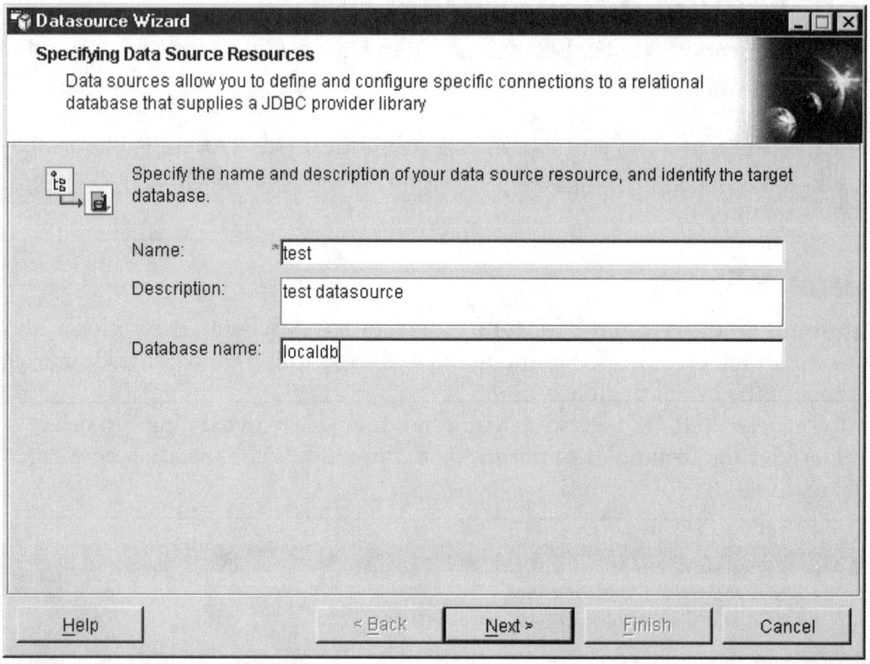

Figure 42-10. *The opening window for the Datasource Wizard*

You must specify a name, description, and implementation class for a new JDBC provider. Whether you select an existing JDBC provider or specify the parameters for a new JDBC provider, the confirmation window completes the sequence of actions for this wizard.

JMS Resources Wizard

The wizard for creating JMS resources prompts you to select the type of resource you want to create: connection factory or destination. You are then prompted to enter the parameters of the resource and select the JMS provider. Similar to the Datasource Wizard, this wizard allows you to define a new JMS provider. After you select a JMS provider, the wizard shows the confirmation window.

J2C Connection Factory Wizard

The flow of the J2C Connection Factory Wizard is similar to that of the Datasource and JMS Wizards. You start by selecting the name and description for your connection factory. Then you can select a resource adapter or define your own. When defining a new adapter, you must specify a name, description, and full path.

URL Resource Wizard

The URL Resource Wizard allows you to define a URL and attach to it a name and description, as shown in Figure 42-11.

After you click the Finish button, a new URL is created; the JNDI name for it is *url/name*, where *name* is the name you've specified for the new URL.

Performance Tuner

The Performance Tuner Wizard takes you through the important performance-related settings for the application server. Your first step in the wizard is to select the application server or server group you want to tune.

The first parameter of interest is the thread pool size for the Web container. The wizard shows a dialog box in which you specify the maximum number of threads in the pool.

The next dialog box focuses on the Object Request Broker (ORB). You can select its thread pool size here, as well as define that the objects using Remote Method Invocation-IIOP (RMI/IIOP) requests be passed by reference. This latter option should be used carefully, and only if you are sure it is suitable for your application, because it breaks

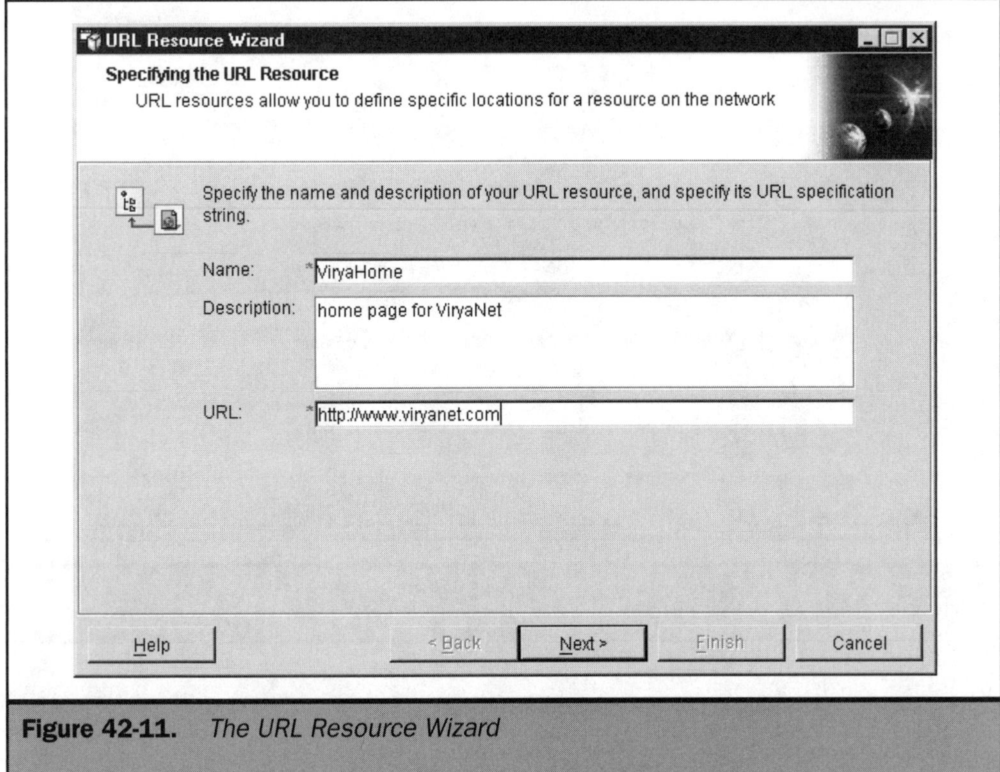

Figure 42-11. *The URL Resource Wizard*

the semantics of remote invocations. In particular, it allows an EJB method to modify objects on the caller side.

The next few steps relate to database connections. You select a datasource, and then you can tune the associated connection pool size and prepared statement cache size. After tuning the database, the final step allows you to tune the JVM heap size.

Create Server Group Wizard

This wizard helps you create a server group. It guides you through the process of specifying the server group name and workload management policy; then you choose the services properties, finally creating clones for the group. To save time, you can create a new server group, based on the settings you have for an existing application server. Alternatively, you can select the check box (as shown in Figure 42-12) and choose one of the existing application server instances.

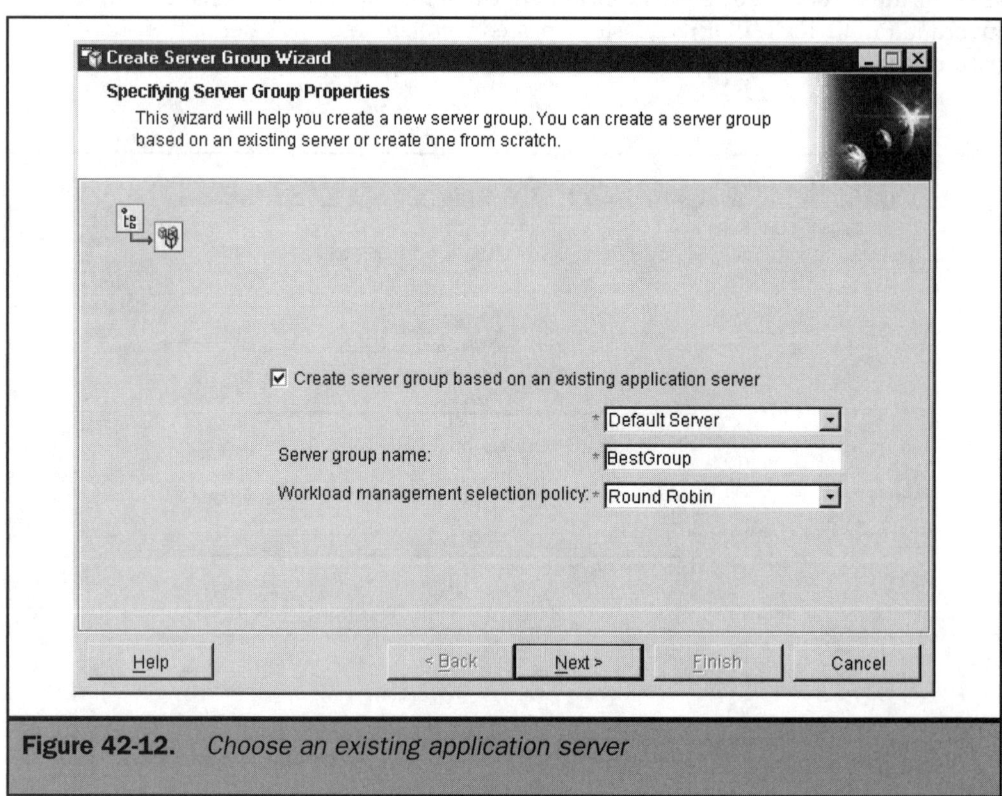

Figure 42-12. *Choose an existing application server*

The AE Resource Analyzer

WebSphere Application Server AE provides tools for monitoring the server and your applications to identify potential bottlenecks. The Resource Analyzer allows you to retrieve statistics for whatever monitoring you request. Figure 42-13 shows the Resource Analyzer window.

The Resource Analyzer continuously polls each of the monitored elements for the required counters. It then presents the readings in a tabular form. You can browse the various elements by using the tree control on the left. The entries in the tree include the server components and the individual components in your applications. A small icon showing the current level of monitoring provided it accompanies the icon for each entry.

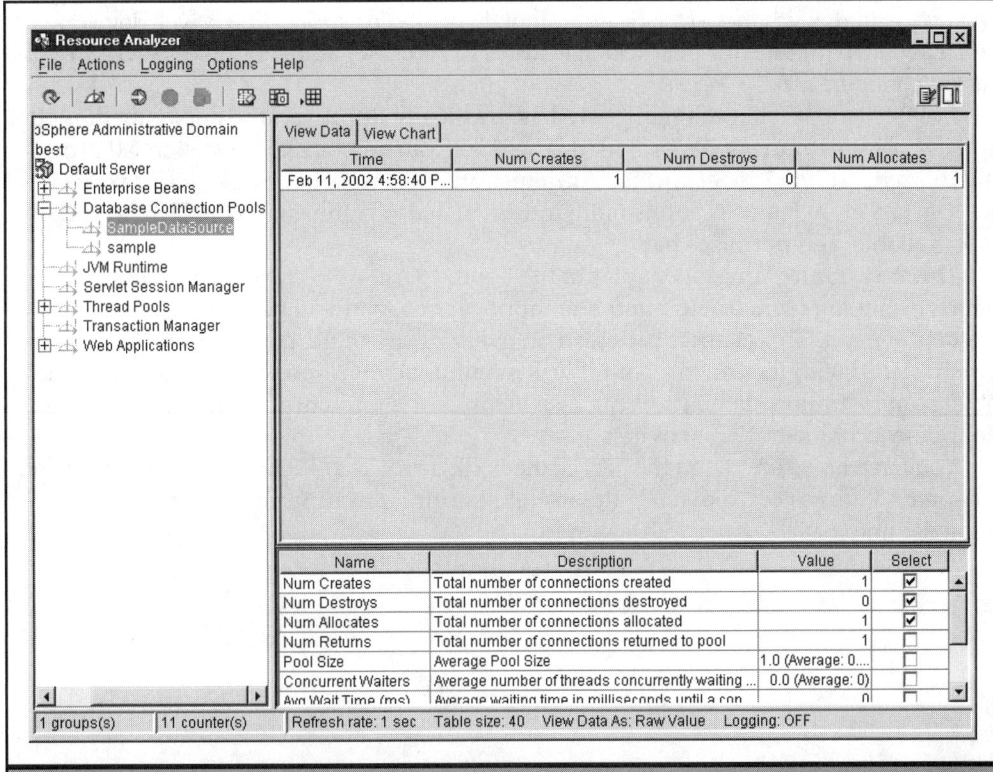

Figure 42-13. *The Resource Analyzer*

To minimize overhead while monitoring performance, you should start the Resource Analyzer on a separate machine and point it to the application server that is being monitored.

You can filter some of the information for a certain element by clicking its option in the tabular display along the bottom of the window. The Resource Analyzer can provide graphs showing the progression of the readings for the selected element. These graphs can help you identify performance problems and bottlenecks.

Summary

This chapter reviewed the tools that target the administrator community. WebSphere AE (and to a lesser extent, AEs) are used for deploying applications. To set up an application and administer the servers effectively, an administrator needs a set of tools. Understanding what you can do with these tools is important. Even if your application is well developed, you may fail to provide the application features to your user audience unless you set up the correct configuration.

Every major version of WebSphere has drastically improved the deployment model and the administrative tools provided. The leap from version 3.5 to version 4.0 proves this; both the server model and the Administrative Console have been improved. The console has more features and is more intuitive. It also conforms to the J2EE model, is more reliable, and performs better.

This is by far the longest chapter in the book—perhaps because, regardless of which technology you use to build your applications, you will need to administer the deployment. This chapter provided an overview of all the components that can be administered with the console, and it was intentionally written to provide an overview of all administration elements. It can also be used as a reference when you are doing your daily administration activities.

You have now completed the part of the book devoted to WebSphere administration. Chapter 43 moves on to discuss the use of scripting environments and security administration.

The Complete Reference

Chapter 43

WebSphere Administration Scripts

In Chapter 42, you learned how to use the administrative client to configure and administer the WebSphere server. No matter which version of WebSphere you are using—and, therefore, which version of the administration tool you are using—there are pros and cons in using this tool for daily administration tasks. An advantage is that the tool is intuitive and easy to use, and it has a good user interface. But for repetitive tasks—regardless of whether the activity you are trying to do is composed of many tasks or whether you need to perform a set of tasks repetitively (for example, once a week or once a day)—the process of bringing up the tool, navigating to the right place, and performing the work is cumbersome.

Administration Tools in the Advanced Edition

Configuration and administration tasks are often repetitive and usually mechanical. To support such configuration and administration tasks, the WebSphere distribution includes two important tools: the WebSphere Control Program (WSCP) and the XMLConfig tool. WSCP is built on the Tcl scripting environment that allows administration of WebSphere using a set of objects and actions defined in Tcl. The tool allows you to perform any configuration and administration action using a scripting language. Because Tcl is a powerful language and well known among system administrators, it is a useful tool for administering the WebSphere server. As a scripting environment, WSCP allows you to create script files that can be used over and over again for the tasks at hand, and because the WSCP program is activated from the command line, you can schedule automated administration tasks by using tools such as cron on UNIX.

The second tool, XMLConfig, has existed since the WebSphere 3.*x* product. This tool supports configuration and administration of the server using declarations inserted into an Extensible Markup Language (XML) file. The XML file defines which object should be acted on and what action should be performed. This tool is also useful for repetitive as well as complex tasks. Like WSCP, it is activated from the command line. XMLConfig provides a way to back up, restore, and replicate the admin repository that houses all the WebSphere configuration information.

Each tool is best suited for certain purposes. WSCP is a scripting environment and is therefore procedural in nature. XMLConfig follows a declarative paradigm instead, which is a little more difficult for most people to use but is useful when you need to create structures of objects in the server. And let's not forget the GUI tools. All the tools interact with the admin server and eventually manipulate the admin database (as shown in Figure 43-1), which after all is what controls the application server. This chapter will continue the general topic of configuration and administration by describing WSCP and XMLConfig. As you become proficient in WebSphere administration, you will see that you almost never use the GUI tools and will instead work with one of the tools described in this chapter.

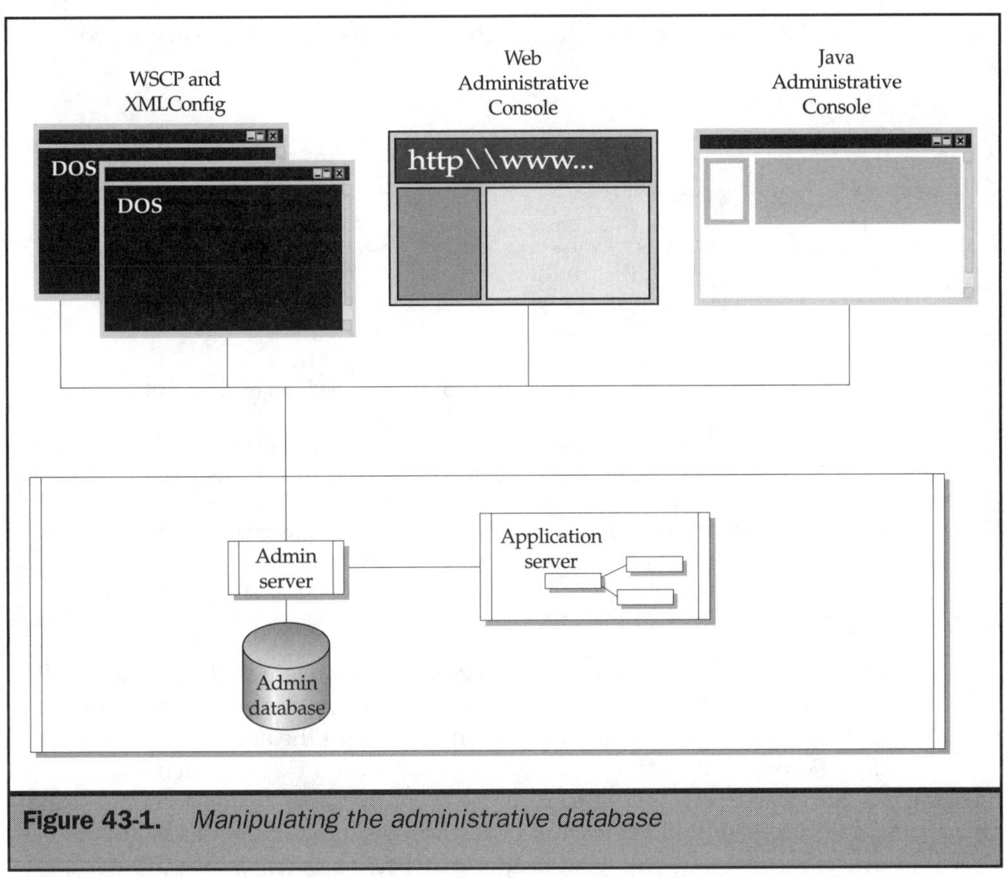

Figure 43-1. *Manipulating the administrative database*

WebSphere Control Program

The WebSphere Control Program is a Tcl program. You activate it by running the *wscp.bat* file in Windows or the *wscp.sh* file in UNIX; these files are in the *WebSphere/AppServer/bin* directory. WSCP can be invoked as an interactive program. If you type **wscp**, you will be placed into an interactive shell in which you can issue commands to configure, administer, and display the objects managed within the application server.

However, this is not the typical use of WSCP; after all, if you want to administer the server in an interactive session, you will probably prefer using the administration GUI. The more common use of the WSCP program is with a file containing the commands that should be run by the program. Such a file can be built once and used many times. This makes it efficient to perform repetitive tasks and easy to make slight modifications to procedures that you have already built. To run the WSCP program using a file, use the `wscp -f <file_name>` option. The full command line options are displayed using `wscp -h`:

```
D:\WebSphere\AppServer\bin>wscp -h

Usage: wscp [-h] [-c command] [-f file] [-p file] [-x extension] [-- options]

    -c command   : evaluate the specified Tcl command
    -h           : display this usage information
    -f file      : evaluate the specified file of Tcl commands
    -p file      : evaluate the specified properties file
    -x extension: load the specified Tcl extension class
    -- options   : Tcl argc and argv variables are set as specified

The WSCP shell evaluates Tcl commands in the order specified on the
command line, so any extensions should be loaded prior to invoking commands
dependent on those extensions. If no command-line commands or files are
specified, an interactive shell is invoked, which is terminated by the exit
command. Command-line options not supported by WSCP or specified after
-- on the command line, are used to set the Tcl argc and argv variables,
which may be interpreted by Tcl extensions or other commands.
```

The `-f` option allows you to control which commands are entered into the WSCP session. The `-p` option allows you to set properties that affect the environment of the WSCP session. The most common use of this option is to set the admin server, which will be configured by the WSCP session. By default, the admin server on the same machine is used. However, it is easy to administer another application server residing on another machine. You do this by setting the `wscp.hostname` property.

For example, assume that you need to administer two servers on two different machines (named *host1.mydomain.com* and *host2.mydomain.com*), as shown in Figure 43-2. Assume that the two servers are identical and you need to perform the same sequence on both servers. Assume also that all objects in the servers are precisely the same and the only change in the names of the objects managed internally is that of the hostname. In this case, you should put all your WSCP commands in a file called *wscp_commands1.tcl*. If this is the file with the commands for the host named *host1.mydomain.com*, let *wscp_commands2.tcl* be a copy of the same file after you have replaced every instance of `host1.mydomain.com` with `host2.mydomain.com`. Then create a file called *host2.prop*, which contains the following single line:

```
wscp.hostname=host2.mydomain.com
```

Next, run the following two WSCP sessions on *host1.mydomain.com*, as shown in Figure 43-2.

```
wscp -f wscp_commands1.tcl
wscp -f wscp_commands2.tcl -p host2.prop
```

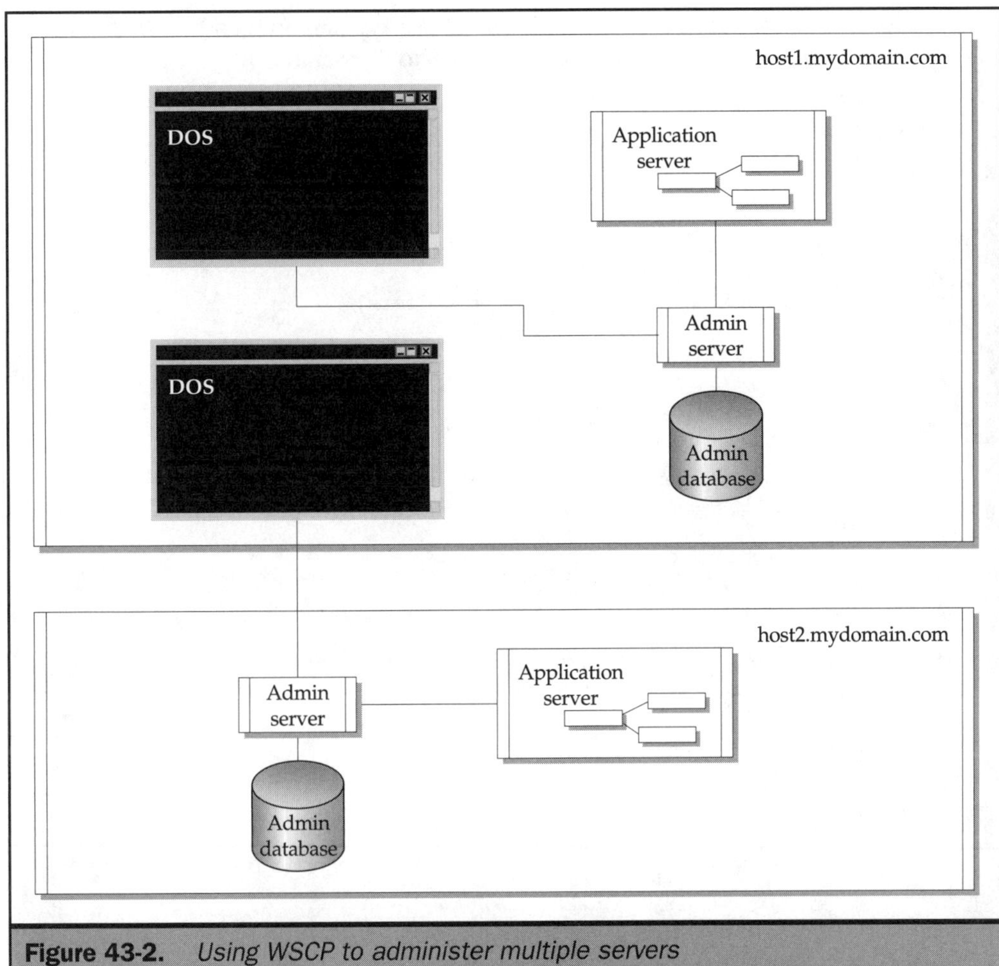

Figure 43-2. *Using WSCP to administer multiple servers*

WSCP Objects and Actions

A WebSphere server is composed of a number of objects. These include the application server, nodes, servlets, Enterprise JavaBeans (EJB), and so on. Each such object can be administered by a WSCP session by issuing commands; each command is an action applied to an object. Each object has a type, and each type has a set of objects that can be issued to an instance of that type. Every command starts with the name of the type and the name of the action. If the action is to be applied to an instance, the instance identifier goes next. If the action is to be applied to the type object (or to the extent), no instance identifier is required. The object types managed by WSCP and the format for each command within a WSCP session are as follows:

```
D:\WebSphere\AppServer\bin>wscp
wscp> Help

The general format of all WSCP actions is:
        <object-type> <action> [name] [options]

The following is a list of the supported objects:

        ApplicationServer
        Context
        DataSource
        DrAdmin
        EnterpriseApp
        GenericServer
        Help
        J2CConnectionFactory
        J2CResourceAdapter
        JDBCDriver
        JMSConnectionFactory
        JMSDestination
        JMSProvider
        MailSession
        Module
        Node
        PmiService
        Remote
        SecurityConfig
        SecurityRoleAssignment
        ServerGroup
        URL
        URLProvider
        VirtualHost
        XMLConfig

To list all actions an object supports: <object> help
To list all the options for an action:  <object> help <action>
For verbose information on an action:   <object> help <action> -verbose
```

Some actions are issued to a specific object, and some actions are issued to the extent. An *extent* is the set of all instances of a certain type. An extent and a type are actually one and the same in that you can think of the type itself as an object—some of the actions are applied to the type (or the extent) and some to an instance. One example of an action applied to a type object (or to an extent) is the command used to list all instances of a certain type. Another example of an action applied to the type object is the use of the `create` action to create a new object of a certain type. In this case, the type object (or extent object) is serving as a factory object.

If you want to perform an action on an instance, you still name the type and the action, but you also include the unique identifier of the object. For example, use the following code to view all attributes of the `host1` node:

```
wscp> Node show /Node:host1/ -all

{FullName /Node:host1/} {Name host1} {CurrentState Running} {DesiredState
Running} {StartTime 1005070676469} {DependentClasspath
{}}{DeployedJarDirectory {d:\WebSphere\AppServer\deployedEJBs}} {HostName
host1} {HostSystemType x86} {InstallRoot {d:\WebSphere\AppServer}}
{ProcessId 1756}
```

Each object type has a set of attributes. Server configuration involves assigning values to these attributes. Attributes follow a name-value paradigm, but the values can themselves be complex types. An example is the Multipurpose Internet Mail Extensions (MIME) type table, which is a value associated with an attribute of the `VirtualHost` objects. Each attribute has a default; in the case where an object of a certain type is created, the initial value of the attribute is defined by this default. To see all attributes and their defaults for a certain object type, use the following actions:

```
wscp> VirtualHost attributes

FullName Name AliasList IsDefault MimeTable


wscp> VirtualHost defaults

{IsDefault False} {MimeTable {{wk4 application/vnd.lotus-1-2-3}{wk3
application/vnd.lotus-1-2-3}{aiff audio/x-aiff}{ief image/ief}{txt
 text/plain}{wk1 application/x-123}{aifc audio/x-aiff}{xsl
 application/xml}{cc text/plain}{mpg video/mpeg}{SOL application/solids}
{mpe video/mpeg}{asm text/x-asm}{t application/x-troff}{cpio application/
x-cpio}{s text/css}{UNV application/i-deas}{htmls text/x-ssi-html}{tiff
 image/tiff}{CCAD application/clariscad}{mjpg video/x-motion-jpeg}{sh
 application/x-sh}{rtx text/richtext}{jpeg image/jpeg}{xwd image/
x-xwindowdump}{VDA application/vda}{m text/plain}{snd audio/basic}{gif
 image/gif}{h text/plain}{for text/plain}{mov video/quicktime}{xbm image/
x-xbitmap}{uil text/x-uil}{src application/x-wais-source}{STEP
 application/STEP}{dtd text/xml}{dxf application/dxf}{js application/
x-javascript}{c text/plain}{tcl application/x-tcl}{tsv text/tab-separated-
values}{set application/set}{rtf application/x-rtf}{MPG video/mpeg}{sam
 application/vnd.lotus-wordpro}{MPE video/mpeg}{IGES application/iges}
{pdf application/pdf}{ppm image/x-portable-pixmap}{zip multipart/x-zip}
```

```
{shar application/x-shar}{nc application/x-netcdf}{avi video/x-msvideo}
{mpeg video/mpeg}{au audio/basic}{list text/plain}{DXF application/dxf}
{mime www/mime}{igs application/iges}{org application/vnd.lotus-
organizer}{sv4crc application/x-sv4crc}{SET application/set}{latex
 application/x-latex}{ksh application/x-ksh}{dwg application/acad}{rgb
image/x-rgb}{gtar application/x-gtar}{C text/plain}{etx text/x-setext}
{pclapplication/x-pcl}{ms application/x-troff-ms}{ai application/
postscript}{eps application/postscript}{qt video/quicktime}{pgm image/
x-portable-graymap}{java text/plain}{conf text/plain}{vew application/
vnd.lotus-approach}{xml text/xml}{uu text/x-uuencode}{bsh application/
x-bsh}{aif audio/x-aiff}{step application/STEP}{sv4cpio application/
x-sv4cpio}{me application/x-troff-me}{stp application/STEP}{movie video/
x-sgi-movie}{123 application/vnd.lotus-1-2-3}{mar text/plain}{IGS
 application/iges}{*.* www/unknown}{tex application/x-tex}{stl
 application/SLA}{cxxtext/plain}{DWG application/acad}{man application/
x-troff-man}{cdf application/x-netcdf}{tar multipart/x-tar}{* www/
unknown}{dvi application/x-dvi}{iges application/iges}{JPEG image/jpeg}
{prz application/vnd.lotus-freelance}{pbm image/x-portable-bitmap}{ustar
 multipart/x-ustar}{sdml text/plain}{DRW application/drafting}{der
 application/x-x509-ca-cert}{jpg image/jpeg}{ps application/postscript}
{prt application/pro_eng}{xpm image/x-xpixmap}{jpe image/jpeg}{apr
 application/vnd.lotus-approach}{prs application/x-freelance}{scm
 application/vnd.lotus-screencam}{lst text/plain}{tr application/
x-troff}{ras image/cmu-raster}{hh text/plain}{pnm image/x-portable-
anymap}{tif image/tiff}{STP application/STEP}{PS application/
postscript}{shtml text/x-ssi-html}{hdf application/x-hdf}{roff
 application/x-troff}{or3 application/vnd.lotus-organizer}{bcpio
 application/x-bcpio}{lwp application/vnd.lotus-wordpro}{STL
 application/SLA}{def text/plain}{or2 application/vnd.lotus-organizer}
{wrl x-world/x-vrml}{htm text/html}{log text/plain}{class application/
octet-stream}{pre application/vnd.lotus-freelance}{f90 text/plain}{unv
 application/i-deas}{oda application/oda}{gz multipart/x-gzip}{css text/
css}{com text/plain}{texinfo application/x-texinfo}{wav audio/x-wav}{vda
 application/vda}{bin application/octet-stream}{texi application/
x-texinfo}{bmp image/bmp}{JPG image/jpeg}{PRT application/pro_eng}{JPE
image/jpeg}{csh application/x-csh}{MPEG video/mpeg}{html text/html}}}
```

Each action is part of an object type definition. Different object types may have different actions. To see which actions are available for a type, use the help command:

```
wscp> ApplicationServer help
The following actions are available for ApplicationServer

attributes          Display the attributes of the object
```

```
containment         Display the containment hierarchy for the object
create              Create the specified object
defaults            Display or set attribute defaults
help                Display this help message
list                Display all the instances of this type
modify              Modify the attributes of the specified object
operations          List all the actions available on the object type
remove              Remove the specified object
show                Display the attributes of specified object
start               Start the specified object
stop                Stop the specified object


wscp> Context help
The following actions are available for Context

bind                Bind the object to the specified name
cd                  Change directory to the specified name
create              Create the specified object
env                 List the current environment
help                Display this help message
init                Create the initial context
list                List contents of the context
operations          List all the actions available on the object type
rebind              Rebind the object to the specified name
remove              Remove the specified object
rename              Rename the object to the specified name
unbind              Unbind the specified object


wscp> JDBCDriver help
The following actions are available for JDBCDriver

attributes          Display the attributes of the object
containment         Display the containment hierarchy for the object
create              Create the specified object
defaults            Display or set attribute defaults
help                Display this help message
install             Install a JDBC driver
list                Display all the instances of this type
modify              Modify the attributes of the specified object
operations          List all the actions available on the object type
remove              Remove the specified object
show                Display the attributes of specified object
uninstall           Uninstall the JDBC driver
```

Some actions are available for all object types within WSCP. Examples include actions that operate on an individual object, such as the `remove` action, as well as actions that operate on the extent object, such as the `list` action. In addition, different object types have actions that are specific to that object. These are actions that operate on an object, such as the `start` and `stop` actions, which can be used to start and stop a certain application server.

A WSCP Example

WSCP is a powerful tool, and once you get the hang of the Tcl syntax, you can use it to manage your entire environment easily. In fact, our experience has been that administrators with some kind of Tcl background tend to do all their administration in WSCP, regardless of whether they are administering version 3.5 or 4.0. It has also been our experience that developing complex scripts saves a lot of time in administrating WebSphere in the long run. Before moving on to XMLConfig, let's run through a simple example of using WSCP.

You start by defining the virtual host for your system. You need to create a new virtual host object using the factory object, and then set its mandatory attributes. All you really need to set is the alias list for this host as follows:

```
wscp> VirtualHost create /VirtualHost:vhost/ -attribute {{AliasList {host1
host1.mydomain.com 127.0.0.1 10.10.10.40}}}
```

Next, you create the Java Database Connectivity (JDBC) driver and install it. Creating the driver makes use of the factory object once more. Installing the driver is an action that you apply to the newly created object, so you use the identifier given during the creation of the driver. Here, we will be using an Oracle thin driver, so creating and installing it looks like this:

```
wscp> JDBCDriver create /JDBCDriver:myOracleDriver/ -attribute {{ImplClass
oracle.jdbc.driver.OracleDriver} {Description "Oracle Thin Driver"}}

wscp> JDBCDriver install /JDBCDriver:myOracleDriver/ -node /Node:host1/
-jarfile "f:/WebSphere/Appserver/lib/classes111.zip"
```

Next, you create the application server instance and configure the session management properties for the application server. Note that in version 4.0, the session management properties are part of the application server; in version 3.*x*, they were part of the `SessionManager` object, which no longer exists.

```
wscp> ApplicationServer create /Node:host1/ApplicationServer:myAppServer/
-attribute {{JVMConfig {{InitialHeapSize 64} {MaxHeapSize 128}}}
```

```
{WebContainerConfig {SessionManagerConfig {{EnablePersistentSessions false}
{TuningScheduleInvalidation true} {TuningInvalidationTimeout 15}}}}}
```

Creating clones using WSCP is a simple thing. The `ServerGroup` object has an action for creating clones. For example, if you define an application server as in the preceding listing, you can create a server group object from it and then use the `clone` action on the server group. In the following sample, you will create a server group named `Clone1` and then a second clone named `Clone2`:

```
wscp> ServerGroup create /ServerGroup:Clone1/ -baseInstance
/Node:host1/ApplicationServer:myAppServer/

wscp> ServerGroup clone /ServerGroup:Clone1/ -node /Node:host1/ -cloneAttrs
{{Name Clone2}}
```

In this case, if you then list all server groups (clones), you will see the following:

```
wscp> ServerGroup list

{/Node:host1/ServerGroup:Clone1/} {/Node:host1/ServerGroup:Clone2/}
```

XMLConfig

XMLConfig is another utility that is part of the WebSphere Advanced Edition, and it was introduced as early as version 3.0. This utility is invoked from the command line, and it accepts an XML file that conforms to a document type definition (DTD) that defines the structural patterns that the utility allows. XMLConfig can be used for anything that WSCP can be used for, including creating environments, modifying attributes, and starting and stopping servers. In fact, the two utilities can be viewed as complementary because each one fits a certain type of usage more than the other. For example, it has been our experience that when an application solution is packaged as a WebSphere application and distributed as a product, its administration is easier using XMLConfig. This is because the application installation can include an XMLConfig file that can be imported into the WebSphere application server to be used for deployment. On the other hand, when a project group develops an application internally and a system administrator is responsible for administering the server, WSCP is more commonly used because it is more similar to other scripting environments. We prefer using XMLConfig, but this is simply a matter of personal preference.

To invoke XMLConfig, go to the *WebSphere/AppServer/bin* directory and use the command line program XMLConfig (*XMLConfig.bat* in Windows and *XMLConfig.sh* in UNIX). The possible arguments are as follows:

```
{ ( -import <xml data file> ) ||
[ ( -export <xml output file> [-partial <xml data file>] ) }
-adminNodeName <primary node name>
[ -nameServiceHost <host name> [ -nameServicePort <port number> ]]
[-traceString <trace spec> [-traceFile <file name>]]
[-generatePluginCfg <true || false>]
[-substitute <"key1=value1[;key2=value2[...]]">]}
In input xml file, the key(s) should appear as $key$ for substitution.
```

One of the reasons we like XMLConfig so much is that it conforms to the classic way of building anything related to software: the copy and paste metaphor. The easiest and safest way to configure and set up a server configuration is to copy something from an existing server and make appropriate modifications as required. XMLConfig supports this in a natural way, because it allows you to export an XML description file, make modifications to it, and then import it back. In this way, you are less dependent on careful debugging of the commands because you always start out from a working XML file with the correct syntax, and only the changes that you make need to be carefully reviewed.

XMLConfig Commands

Sessions of XMLConfig accept an XML file that conforms to the XMLConfig DTD in which a set of commands is issued. Each command is wrapped in an XML tag that defines the element within the WebSphere containment hierarchy that the command is issued against, as well as the command itself. The commands can be control commands, such as `start` and `stop`; structural commands, such as `create` and `update`; or an `export` command.

Here are some control commands:

- **start** Starts a resource such as the node or the application server
- **stop** Stops the resource
- **restart** Stops and starts the resource
- **disable** Suspends a Web application
- **enable** Resumes a Web application
- **stopforrestart** May stop a node for a restart

Here are some structural commands:

- **create** Creates an element in the admin server, placed within the hierarchy based on where the create command was placed in the XML file.
- **update** Updates an element already defined in the admin server, using attributes and internal elements defined in the XML structure.
- **delete** Deletes an element from the admin server.
- **locate** Identifies an element in the admin server. Used to point to an element in the containment hierarchy so that structural commands such as create and delete are executed in the appropriate context. For example, if you need to add a resource to a Web application, you first locate the Web application and then use a create command.

And here's the Export command:

- **export** Exports a subtree of the containment hierarchy into an XML export file.

The combination of the `export` command and the structural commands is what supports the copy and paste metaphor so well. If, for example, you need to create an additional enterprise bean, you can export an existing one, modify some of the attributes to conform to the new classes and arguments, and then use that file in an import mode with the structural commands (`update` most probably). This is by far the simplest and safest way to generate a new enterprise bean, and we recommend it.

An XMLConfig Example

Let's run through a similar example to the one we used for WSCP. First, let's create the virtual host with the alias list and the MIME table. Note that you use the `update` command even when the virtual host does not exist; an `update` command will create the element if it does not exist and will update the values if it does exist. Therefore, it is always the safest command to use.

```
<?xml version="1.0" encoding="UTF-8"?>
<!DOCTYPE websphere-sa-config SYSTEM
"$XMLConfigDTDLocation$$dsep$xmlconfig.dtd" >
<websphere-sa-config>
   <virtual-host action="update" name="vhost">
<mime-table>
      <mime type="application/vnd.lotus-1-2-3">
```

```
                <ext>wk4</ext>
                <ext>wk3</ext>
        </mime>
        <mime type="audio/x-aiff">
                <ext>aiff</ext>
        </mime>
        <mime type="image/ief">
                 <ext>ief</ext>
        </mime>
        <mime type="text/plain">
                 <ext>txt</ext>
        </mime>
        …
</mime-table>
<alias-list>
        <alias>host1</alias>
        <alias>host1.mydomain.com</alias>
        <alias>127.0.0.1</alias>
        <alias>10.10.10.40</alias>
</alias-list>
   </virtual-host>
</websphere-sa-config>
```

Next, create a JDBC driver, as in the WSCP example:

```
<jdbc-driver action="update" name="myOracleDriver">
      <implementation-class>
            com.oracle.jdbc.driver.OracleDriver
      </implementation-class> <description/>
      <description>Oracle Thin Driver</description>
      <install-info>
            <node-name>host1</node-name>
            <jdbc-zipfile-location>
                  f:/WebSphere/Appserver/lib/classes111.zip
             </jdbc-zipfile-location>
      </install-info>
</jdbc-driver>
```

Finally, create the application server itself and set some of the tuning parameters. Note once more that you always use the `update` command. This takes care of both the creation and updating scenarios.

```
<?xml version="1.0" encoding="UTF-8"?>
<!DOCTYPE websphere-sa-config SYSTEM
"file:///$XMLConfigDTDLocation$$dsep$xmlconfig.dtd">
<websphere-sa-config>
  <node name="host1" action="locate">
    <application-server action="update" name="Host1">
      <executable>java</executable>
      <command-line-arguments/>
      <environment/>
      <user-id/>
      <group-id/>
      <working-directory/>
      <umask>18</umask>
      <stdin/>
      <stdout>f:/WebSphere/AppServer/logs/host1_stdout.log</stdout>
      <stderr>f:/WebSphere/AppServer/logs/host1_stderr.log</stderr>
      <process-priority>20</process-priority>
      <maximum-startup-attempts>2</maximum-startup-attempts>
      <ping-interval>60</ping-interval>
      <ping-timeout>200</ping-timeout>
      <ping-initial-timeout>300</ping-initial-timeout>
      <selection-policy>roundrobinpreferlocal</selection-policy>
      <trace-specification/>
      <trace-output/>
      <transaction-log-file/>
      <olt-enabled>false</olt-enabled>
      <system-properties/>
      <debug-enabled>false</debug-enabled>
      <transaction-timeout>120</transaction-timeout>
      <transaction-inactivity-timeout>
        60000
      </transaction-inactivity-timeout>
      <thread-pool-size>20</thread-pool-size>
      <security-enabled>false</security-enabled>
      <admin-agent-ior/>
      <cache-config>
        <cache-size>4097</cache-size>
        <cache-sweep-interval>1000</cache-sweep-interval>
        <passivation-directory/>
      </cache-config>
      <log-file-spec/>
      <performance-monitor-spec>
        pmi=none:beanModule=maximum:connectionPoolModule=medium:
        j2cModule=medium:jvmRuntimeModule=none:jvmpiModule=low:
```

```
    servletSessionsModule=none:threadPoolModule=high:
    transactionModule=none:webAppModule=maximum
  </performance-monitor-spec>
  <olt-server-host>localhost</olt-server-host>
  <olt-server-port>7001</olt-server-port>
  <selection-policy>roundrobinpreferlocal</selection-policy>
  <source-path/>
  <wlm-template-ior/>
  <thread-pool-size>15</thread-pool-size>
  <jvm-config>
    <initial-heap-size>64</initial-heap-size>
    <max-heap-size>128</max-heap-size>
    <generated-command-line-arguments>
      -Xms64m -Xmx128m
    </generated-command-line-arguments>
    <system-properties/>
    <additional-command-line-arguments/>
    <debug-mode>false</debug-mode>
    <debug-string/>
    <run-hprof>false</run-hprof>
    <hprof-args/>
    <disable-jit>false</disable-jit>
    <verbose-class-loading>false</verbose-class-loading>
    <verbose-jni>false</verbose-jni>
    <verbose-gc>false</verbose-gc>
    <boot-classpath-replace/>
    <boot-classpath-append/>
    <boot-classpath-prepend/>
  </jvm-config>
  <web-container>
    <dynamic-cache-config>
      <enabled>false</enabled>
      <cache-size>0</cache-size>
      <default-priority>0</default-priority>
    </dynamic-cache-config>
    <transport name="http">
      <transport-host>*</transport-host>
      <transport-port>7007</transport-port>
      <http-transport>
        <connection-timeout>5</connection-timeout>
        <backlog-connections>50</backlog-connections>
        <keep-alive-timeout>5</keep-alive-timeout>
        <maximum-keep-alive>25</maximum-keep-alive>
```

```
      <maximum-req-keep-alive>300</maximum-req-keep-alive>
      <ssl-enabled>false</ssl-enabled>
    </http-transport>
  </transport>
  <thread-maximum-size>50</thread-maximum-size>
  <thread-minimum-size>25</thread-minimum-size>
  <thread-inactivity-timeout>10</thread-inactivity-timeout>
  <thread-is-growable>true</thread-is-growable>
  <session-manager>
    <enable-security-integration>
      false
    </enable-security-integration>
    <enable-ssl-tracking>
      false
    </enable-ssl-tracking>
    <invalidation-schedule-first-hour>
      0
    </invalidation-schedule-first-hour>
    <invalidation-schedule-second-hour>
      0
    </invalidation-schedule-second-hour>
    <persistent-db2-row-size>
      0
    </persistent-db2-row-size>
    <maximum-inmemory-session-count>
      1000
    </maximum-inmemory-session-count>
    <write-contents>0</write-contents>
    <write-frequency>0</write-frequency>
    <write-interval>0</write-interval>
    <enable-sessions>false</enable-sessions>
    <enable-url-rewriting>false</enable-url-rewriting>
    <enable-cookies>true</enable-cookies>
    <enable-protocol-switch-rewriting>
      false
    </enable-protocol-switch-rewriting>
    <cookie name="JSESSIONID">
    <domain/>
    <maximum>-1</maximum>
    <path>/</path>
    <secure>false</secure> </cookie>
    <tuning-invalidation-time>15</tuning-invalidation-time>
    <persistent-sessions>false</persistent-sessions>
```

```
          <data-source name="">
            <default-user/>
            <default-password/>
          </data-source>
          <using-multi-row>false</using-multi-row>
          <allow-overflow>true</allow-overflow>
        </session-manager>
      </web-container>
      <orb-config>
        <bootstrap-host-name/>
        <bootstrap-port>900</bootstrap-port>
        <comm-trace-enabled>false</comm-trace-enabled>
        <connection-cache-maximum>240</connection-cache-maximum>
        <connection-cache-minimum>100</connection-cache-minimum>
        <external-config-url/>
        <force-tunnel>whenrequired</force-tunnel>
        <listener-port>0</listener-port>
        <locate-request-timeout>180</locate-request-timeout>
        <local-host-name/>
        <lsd-host-name/>
        <no-local-copies>false</no-local-copies>
        <request-retries-count>1</request-retries-count>
        <request-retries-delay>0</request-retries-delay>
        <request-timeout>180</request-timeout>
        <thread-pool-size>20</thread-pool-size>
        <tunnel-agent-url/>
        <rmi-remote-code-base/>
        <ssl-listener-port>0</ssl-listener-port>
      </orb-config>
      <custom-service-config-list>
        <custom-service-config name="AutoGen">
          <description>Generated when started/description>
          <classname>
com.ibm.websphere.plugincfg.initializers.AEPluginCfgService
          </classname>
          <classpath/>
          <external-config-url/>
          <enabled>false</enabled>
        </custom-service-config>
      </custom-service-config-list>
    </application-server>
  </node>
</websphere-sa-config>
```

Summary

Most administrators do not use the GUI client for continuous, ongoing daily administration and configuration. They use tools that are repeatable, easy to learn, and easy to use. In most complex distributed environments, script-based administration is a necessity. In addition, firewalls, security, and performance issues often cause the Administrative Console to be abandoned in favor of these tools in production environments.

We highly recommend both WSCP and XMLConfig. Which one is better for you is really a matter of preference, and you can use both because they follow the same model. If you are already a Tcl master, you will probably prefer to use WSCP. If you like XML and are well versed in an XML editor, such as XML Spy, you will probably prefer using XMLConfig. You can't go wrong with either tool.

This chapter introduced both of these tools and explained the main administration model and hierarchy. One subject that was not covered is security administration. This topic is complex enough to require a chapter to itself—Chapter 44, in fact.

The Complete Reference

Chapter 44

Administering WebSphere Security

Welcome to the last chapter in the book—the last, but certainly not the least important. Application security has always been important, but Web application and server security has received a lot of focus due to the many security breaches that happen on the Internet and to the increased focus on security, in general, that is a direct result of the terrorist attacks of September 11, 2001.

After the brief introduction to security-related concepts in Chapter 13 and the description of the WebSphere Security Services in Chapter 19, this chapter continues with what is perhaps the most important chore of the WebSphere administrator—that is, administering security on the WebSphere Application Server. This chapter provides a brief account of the security features over which the administrator has control and how these tasks are performed using the Administrative Console and the Security Center tool. Note that this chapter focuses on the most common activities and is by no means a full account of security administration and configuration. In fact, IBM has published an excellent redbook called *WebSphere Advanced Edition: Security*, which provides full coverage of all security features and security administration—and it's more than 500 pages long.

The topics covered in this chapter include how to secure the server using a password, how to set up a custom user registry, how to assign users to security roles, how to encrypt traffic within the demilitarized zone (DMZ), and more. Many security topics have already been discussed in other chapters (including Chapters 3, 13, 19, and 20), and some of those topics are referenced here.

Securing the Application Server

If you don't secure your server, anyone can use the Administrative Console to bypass any security settings you create. (Here, we will not discuss security of the machine itself—either the physical security or logging as an administrator. This is obviously a prerequisite for the application server to be secure.) The first thing you need to do is open the Security Center from the Administrative Console using the Console menu. You then select the Security Center option and open the General tab. Finally, check the Enable Security check box and apply the changes.

If you try to apply only this change, you are prompted for the user registry with which the username/password verification is made, as discussed in Chapter 19. The simplest thing to do is use the operating system's registry, as shown in Figure 44-1.

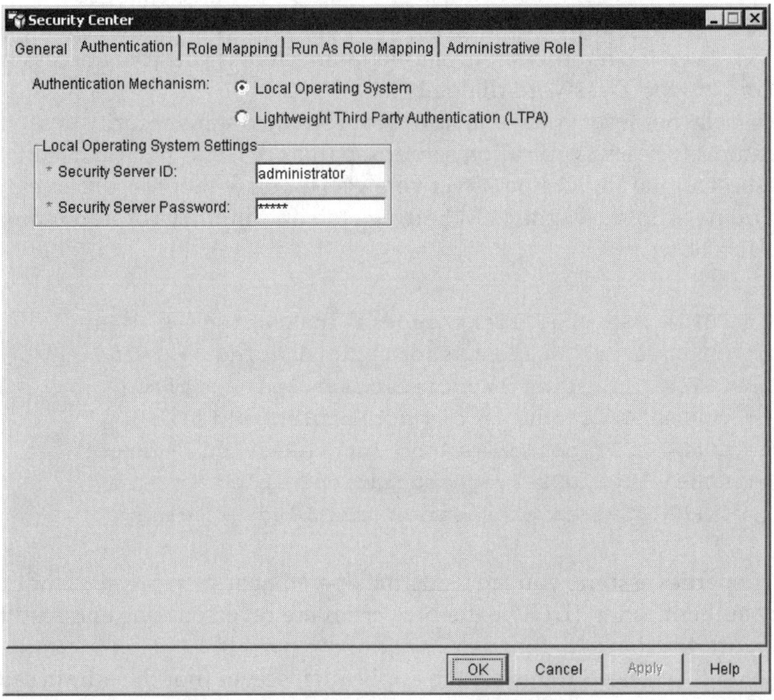

Figure 44-1. *Using the operating system's registry*

At this point, you need to restart the admin server—that's where the security server runs. After restarting the admin server, your server is secured. If you try to open the Administrative Console, you get a dialog box that asks you for a password:

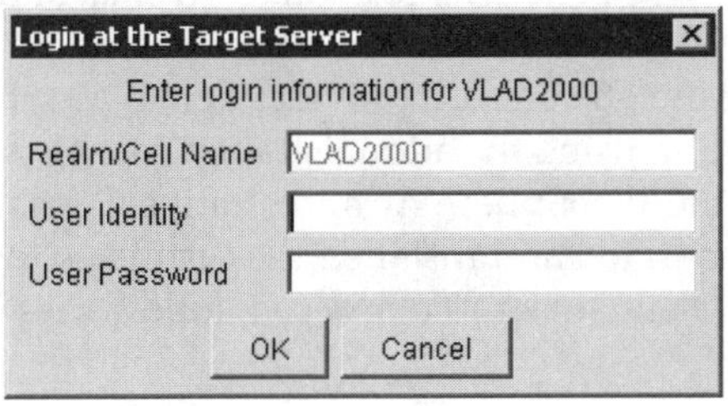

At this point, the server is securing every access. You have changed the global settings of the server, and that is affecting all application servers managed by this admin server. Even the famous snoop servlet is affected; if you try to access it, you'll get the Enter Network Password dialog box.

This is usually not what you want, however. You can disable security or set up specific security features for each application server separately. To do so, you need to open the properties sheet for the application server you wish to run without secure access.

Then you need to select the JVM Settings tab and modify (or add) some of the properties as follows:

```
com.ibm.CORBA.SSLTypeIClientAssociationEnabled → false
com.ibm.CORBA.LocalOSClientAssociationEnabled → false
com.ibm.CORBA.LTPAClientAssociationEnabled → false
com.ibm.CORBA.DCEClientAssociationEnabled → false
com.ibm.CORBA.SSLTypeIServerAssociationEnabled → true
com.ibm.CORBA.LocalOSServerAssociationEnabled → true
com.ibm.CORBA.LTPAServerAssociationEnabled → false
```

These properties assume you are using the operating system registry; for lightweight third-party authentication (LTPA), the properties are reversed. The end result should look like Figure 44-2.

At this point, you need to restart the application server (not the admin server) using the Administrative Console. Your admin server is now running in a secure mode, while the application server is running in a non-secure mode.

Administering Security for the HTTP Server

Chapter 3 explained how to set up a secure site using the IBM HTTP Server. You learned how to generate a key pair using the IKEYMAN utility and how to enable the Secure Socket Layer (SSL) setup by changing the configuration files. This will not be repeated here, so it may be beneficial for you to go back and reread the last section in Chapter 3. The focus of this chapter is on the administration tools and how they are used for configuring security. Therefore, it provides details about how to secure the HTTP server and how to set up SSL using the administration console for the IBM HTTP Server (which is different from the WebSphere Administrative Console). (We are assuming that you have already generated and installed the certificate to be used for the server authentication in the SSL handshake.) To proceed, follow these steps:

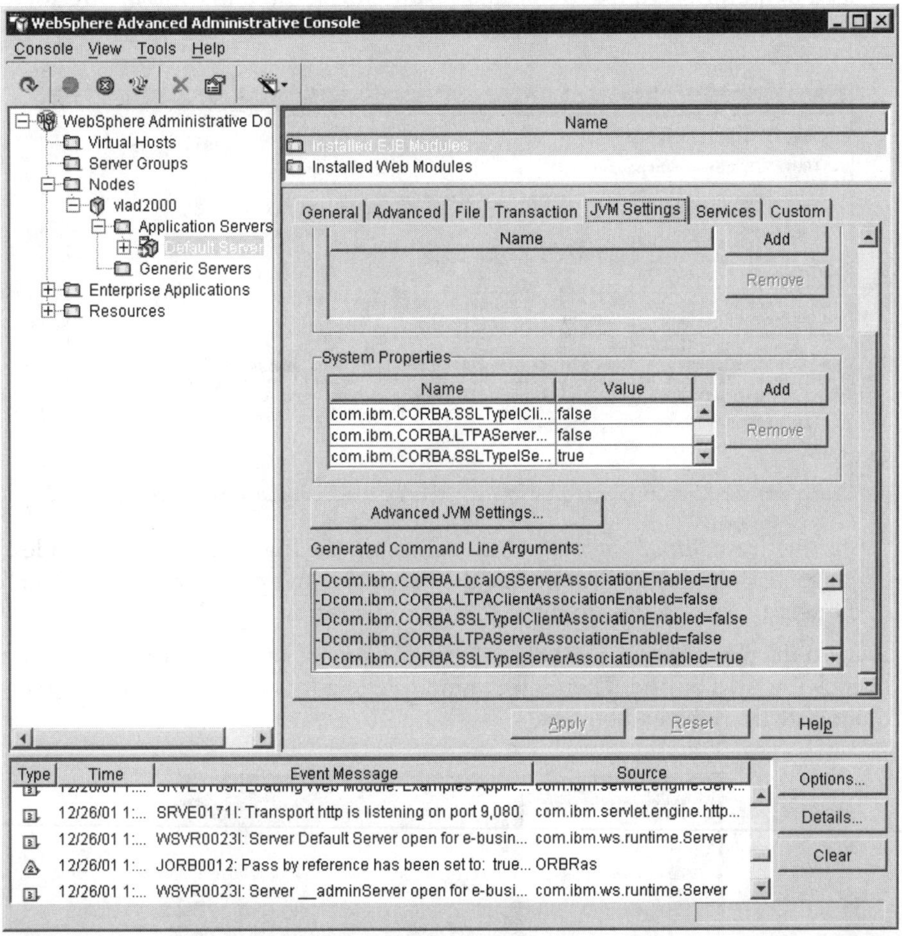

Figure 44-2. *JVM Settings for Default Server*

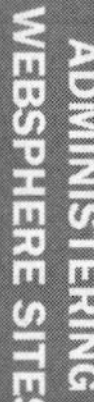

1. The first thing you need to do is set the admin password using the *htpasswd* utility in the root installation directory for the IBM HTTP Server. The file you

need to modify is called *admin.passwd*, and it is located in the *conf* directory. Possible arguments for this utility are shown here:

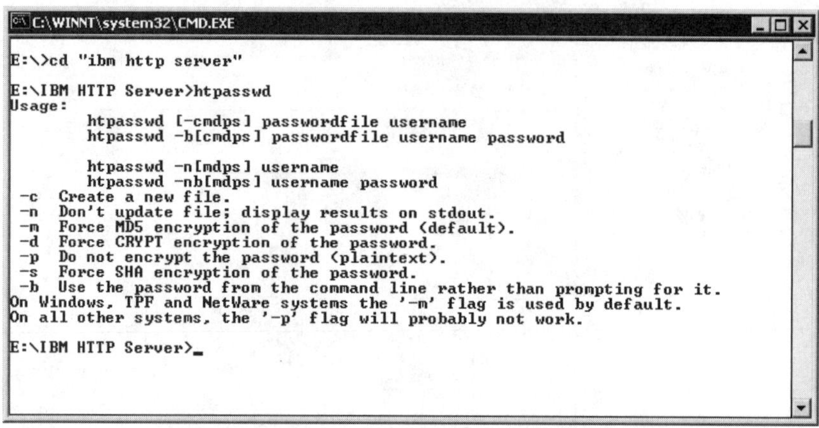

2. Starting from *http://localhost*, which brings up the IBM HTTP Server's index page, click Configure Server. Use the username and password you just set for the server. This brings up the HTTP administration console.
3. Load the SSL module. Click the Module Sequence option on the tree view, and click the Add button. Then select a module to add, and choose the *ibm_ssl* module from the combo box:

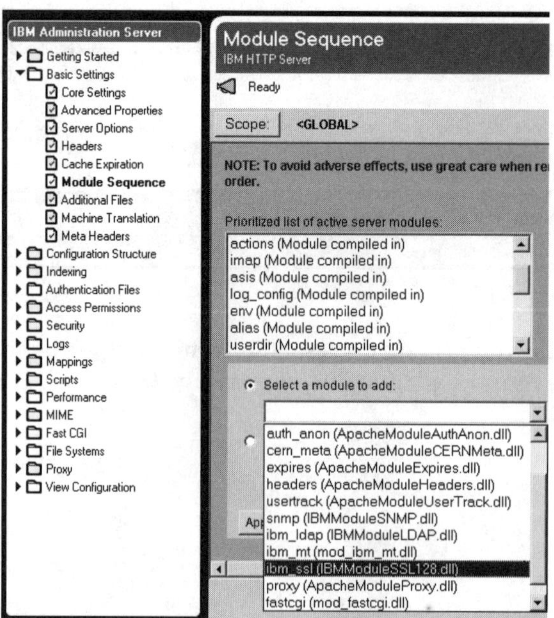

4. After you have added the module, you can modify the order in which the modules are loaded. Normally, this should not affect other modules; but just to play it safe, you can ensure that the SSL module is the last module to be loaded by using the Move Down button:

NOTE: To avoid adverse effects, use great care when removing modules or changing module order.

Prioritized list of active server modules:
negotiation (Module compiled in)
auth (Module compiled in)
access (Module compiled in)
mime (Module compiled in)
so (Module compiled in)
ibm_afpa (Module compiled in)
ibm_ssl (IBMModuleSSL128.dll)

Add | Edit | Remove
Move Up | Move Down

Submit | Reset

5. Now you need to set up the secure host port. Using the Advanced Properties option in the Basic Settings selection, click the Add button and enter the port number to be used by the secure server. In this case, you choose port 443, which is the default Hypertext Transfer Protocol over Secure Socket Layer (HTTPS) port. The result is shown here:

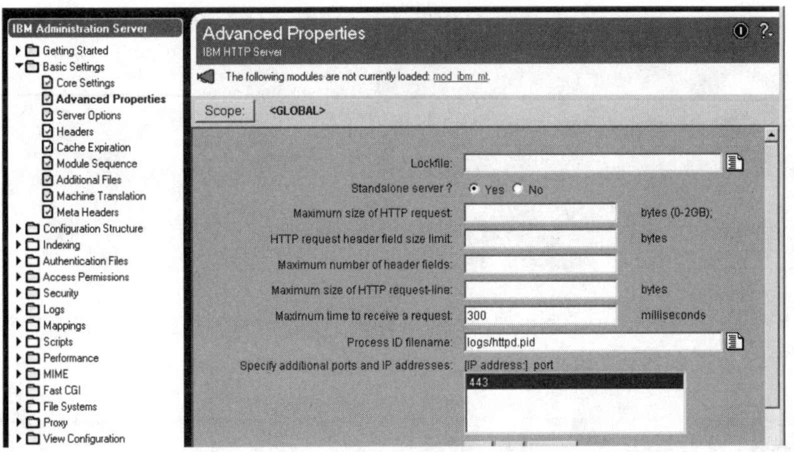

6. Now you set up a virtual server and a scope in which SSL will be activated. Choose Configuration Structure | Create Scope and enter the virtual host name, the port, and the server name. Then scroll down the middle pane and click Submit.

7. After the scope has been created, you set up the document root by choosing Basic Settings | Core Settings. (Any virtual host needs a document root; this is not directly related to the secure server.)
8. Finally, you need to activate the SSL for the newly created scope. First, make sure that SSL is disabled for the main server. Ensure that you are working on the GLOBAL scope, and make sure that SSL is disabled.
9. Then click the Scope button, and select the scope you have just created for your secure server:

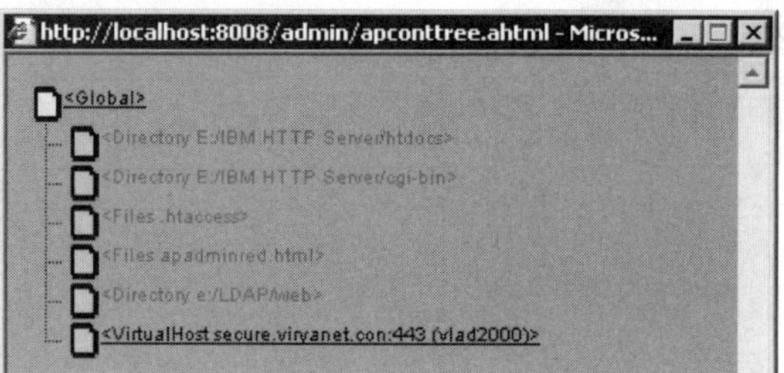

10. Every action you now perform will affect only the selected scope—that is, the secure server you are setting up. Turn on SSL, select the key file that you want to use (typically generated using IKEYMAN, as described in Chapter 3), and set the timeout values:

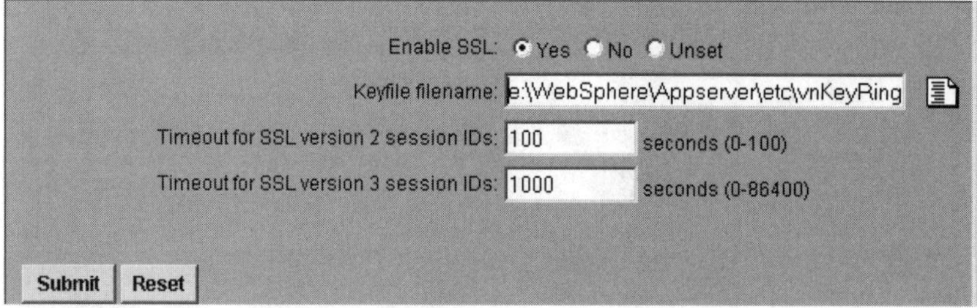

11. Finally, submit and restart the server. You now have an SSL-secured server in parallel to your normal server.

Custom User Registries

Chapter 19 discussed authentication in the context of the WebSphere security model. Two options can be used as an authentication mechanism: using the local operating system or using LTPA. If you decide to use the local operating system, you merely need to specify the user name and password to access the application with the permissions associated with that user. This was shown in Figure 44-1. If you choose to use LTPA, you need to select one of two possible sources of user information, as shown in Figure 44-3.

The most typical usage of LTPA is when your user information comes from a Lightweight Directory Access Protocol (LDAP) server. As discussed in Chapter 20, in this case, you need to set the location of the host, the port, and the base distinguished name (DN). This allows the WebSphere server to communicate with the LDAP server (a SecureWay server, for example) to authenticate users.

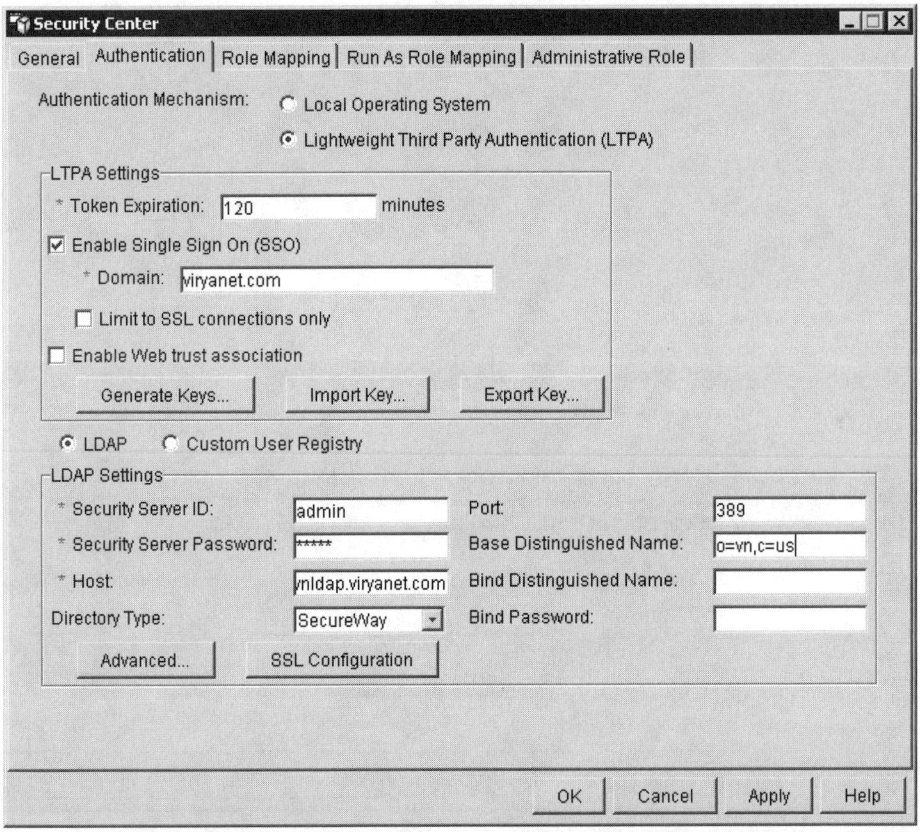

Figure 44-3. *Selecting LTPA authentication with an LDAP user registry*

Alternatively, you may need to use a custom registry, possibly because it is already in place as the corporate standard or for other internal reasons. In this case, you need to provide a class that you have programmed (or received) that implements a protocol defined by WebSphere. This class acts as an interface between the actual registry information and the WebSphere security server. You need to register this class with the Security Center, as shown in Figure 44-4. Properties that may be required by the class implementation are provided using the Special Custom Settings button, as shown in Figure 44-5.

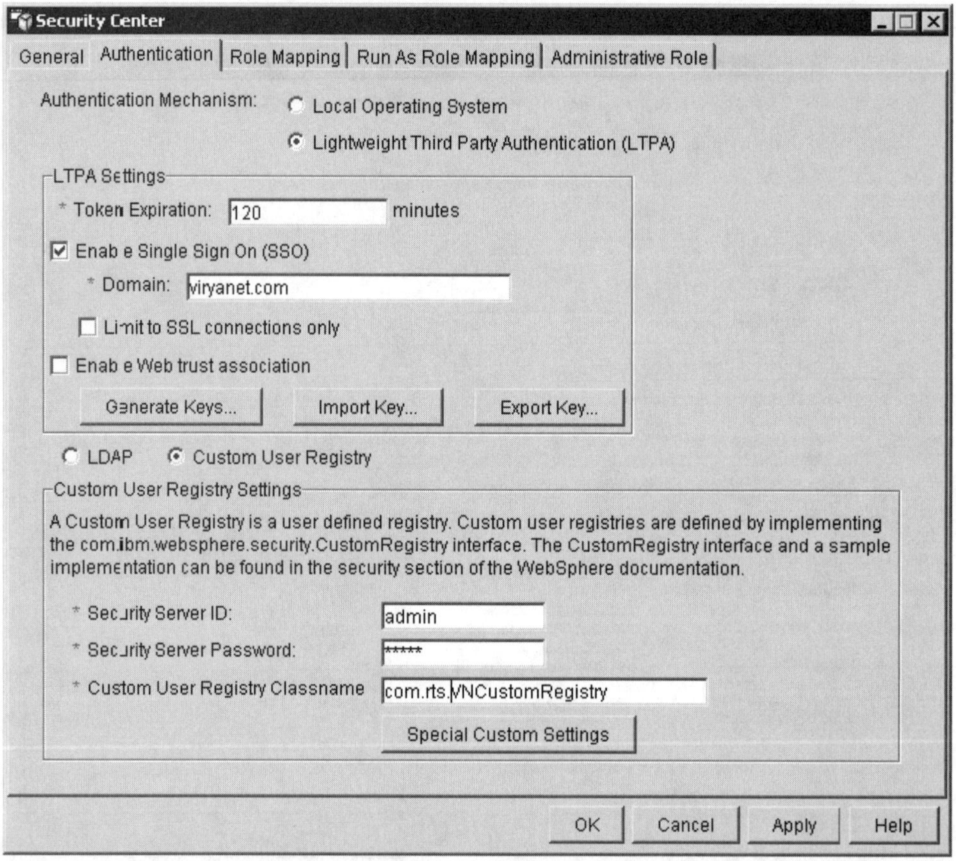

Figure 44-4. *LTPA with a custom user registry*

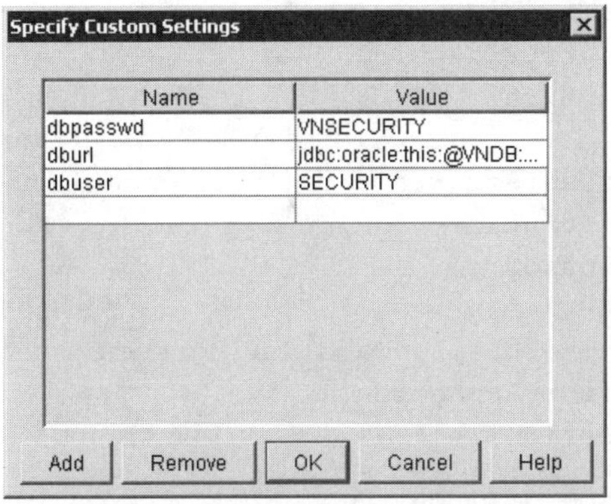

Figure 44-5. *Setting properties for the custom registry interface class*

This class is placed in WebSphere's classpath and is used by the application server to perform authentication. The protocol is defined in the `CustomRegistry` interface as follows:

```
public interface CustomRegistry
{
// General methods
public void initialize(java.util.Properties props)
throws CustomRegistryException;

public String getRealm()
throws CustomRegistryException;

// User-related methods
public boolean isValidUser(String userName)
throws CustomRegistryException;

public List getUsers()
throws CustomRegistryException;

public List getUsers(String pattern)
throws CustomRegistryException;
```

```
public String getUniqueUserId(String userName)
throws CustomRegistryException,
EntryNotFoundException;

public String getUserSecurityName(String uniqueUserId)
throws CustomRegistryException,
EntryNotFoundException;

public String getUserDisplayName(String securityName)
throws CustomRegistryException,
EntryNotFoundException;

public List getUsersForGroup(String groupName)
throws CustomRegistryException,
EntryNotFoundException;

public List getUniqueUserIds(String uniqueGroupId)
throws CustomRegistryException,
EntryNotFoundException;

// Group-related methods
public boolean isValidGroup(String groupName)
throws CustomRegistryException;

public List getGroups()
throws CustomRegistryException;

public List getGroups(String pattern)
throws CustomRegistryException;

public String getUniqueGroupId(String groupName)
throws CustomRegistryException,
EntryNotFoundException;

public String getGroupSecurityName(String uniqueGroupId)
throws CustomRegistryException,
EntryNotFoundException;
```

```
public String getGroupDisplayName(String groupName)
throws CustomRegistryException,
EntryNotFoundException;

public List getGroupsForUser(String userName)
throws CustomRegistryException,
EntryNotFoundException;

public List getUniqueGroupIds(String uniqueUserId)
throws CustomRegistryException,
EntryNotFoundException;

// Authentication methods
public String checkPassword(String userId, String password)
throws PasswordCheckFailedException,
CustomRegistryException;

public String mapCertificate(X509Certificate cert)
throws CertificateMapNotSupportedException,
CertificateMapFailedException,
CustomRegistryException;
}
```

The custom properties are passed to the `initialize` method when the class is first used. In our example, the user registry information is actually maintained in an Oracle database, and the custom properties tell the custom registry class how to access this database.

Mapping Users and Groups to Security Roles

As discussed in Chapter 19, application assembly involves the definition of security roles. These roles are then assigned permissions to invoke methods and access resources. It is then necessary to map users and user groups to these security roles to complete the authorization profile. Based on this mapping, every user that accesses the system can be associated (or not) with security roles and authorized (or not) for access. This mapping can be done while you are installing an enterprise application, as well as later using either the Administrative Console or the Security Center.

When installing an enterprise application, one of the steps in the wizard is shown here:

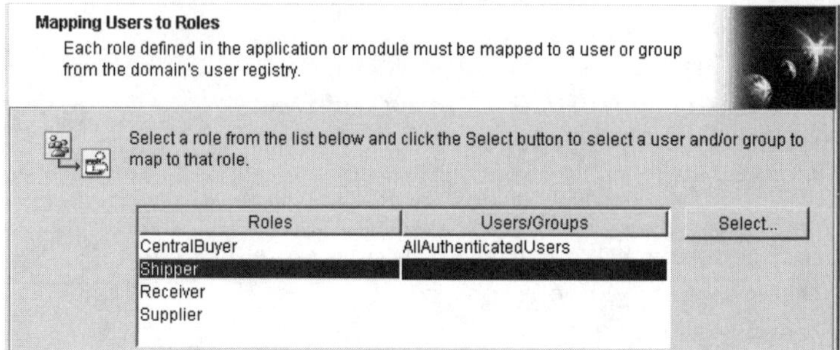

For each role, you need to select a set of users and/or groups. This is done by clicking the Select button, which allows you to select various users and groups. This needs to be done for every security role defined in the application.

After the application has been installed, you can modify this mapping directly in the Administrative Console:

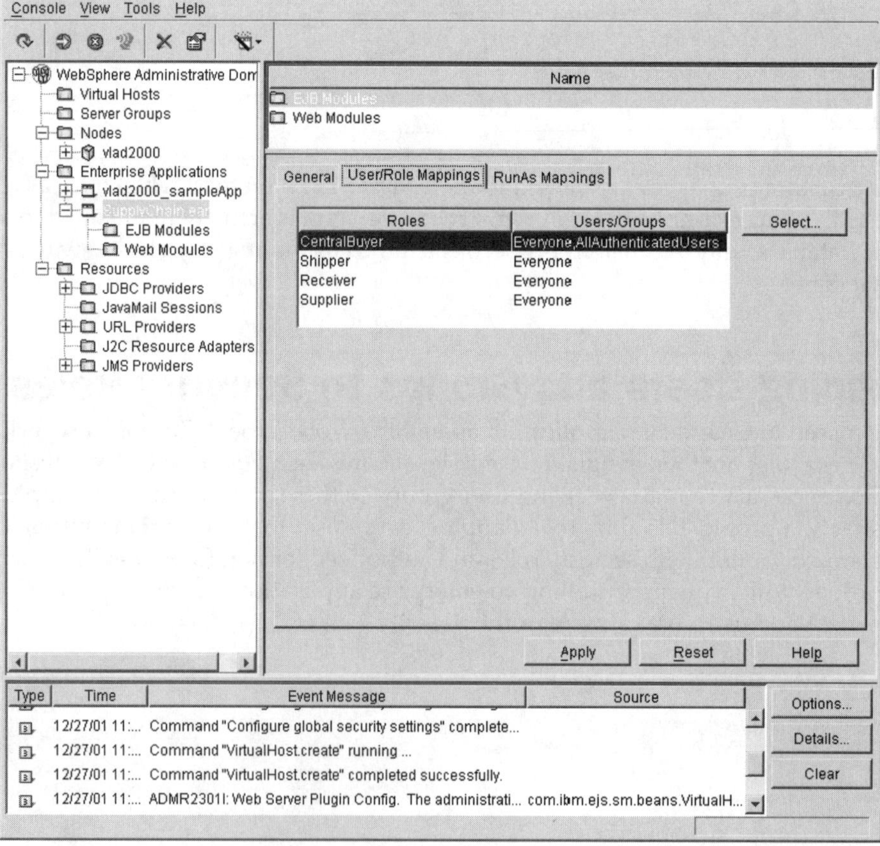

You can also modify the mapping from the Security Center, where clicking Edit Mappings opens the Role Mapping dialog box:

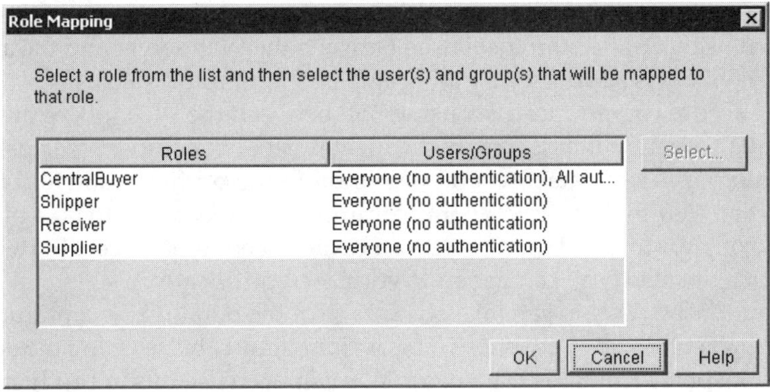

Secure Connections Between Web Server and Application Server

Chapter 41 reviewed a deployment in a DMZ environment. As Figure 44-6 shows, this scenario involves two firewalls—one between the public Internet and the Web server, and one between the Web server and the application server.

In WebSphere version 4.0, the communication between the WebSphere plug-in and the WebSphere Application Server is over the Hypertext Transfer Protocol (HTTP).

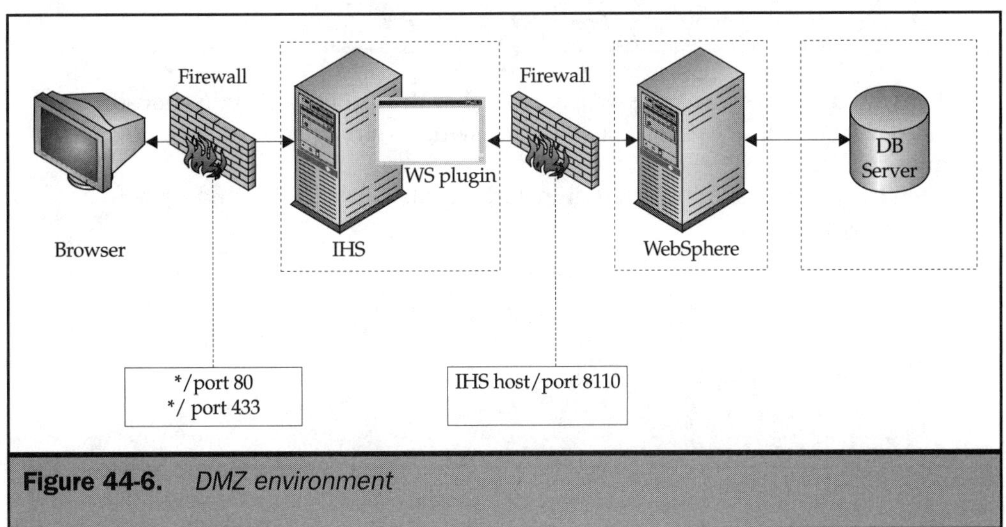

Figure 44-6. *DMZ environment*

As mentioned in Chapter 41, this is a great improvement over the Open Servlet Engine (OSE) protocol, on which WebSphere version 3.*x* was based. One of the benefits this provides is that in using SSL, the communication between the Web server and the application server can itself be encrypted, thus enhancing the security of the overall system. When using SSL, the protocol used between the Web server and the application server is HTTPS and is supported by all firewalls, routers, and so on.

To set up secure communications using SSL between the WebSphere plug-in and the application server, you must create certificates for both components, install them in each counterpart's key database, and then modify the configuration for both the plug-in and the Web container. Since this communication is going to take place only between two of your internal servers, so you do not need to use a certificate authority (CA) certificate; instead, you can generate your own certificate.

For testing purposes, you can take advantage of the default SSL configuration and dummy key that ship with WebSphere. This is done simply by selecting the appropriate box in the Transport Properties Data page. You can even use this in production if your HTTP server is not in the DMZ. In this case, you need to generate one certificate for the Web server plug-in and one certificate for the Web container in the application server.

For the Web server plug-in, you create a key file using the key management utility that comes with the IBM HTTP Server (IHS) installation. Once the utility is open, you create a new CMS key database file:

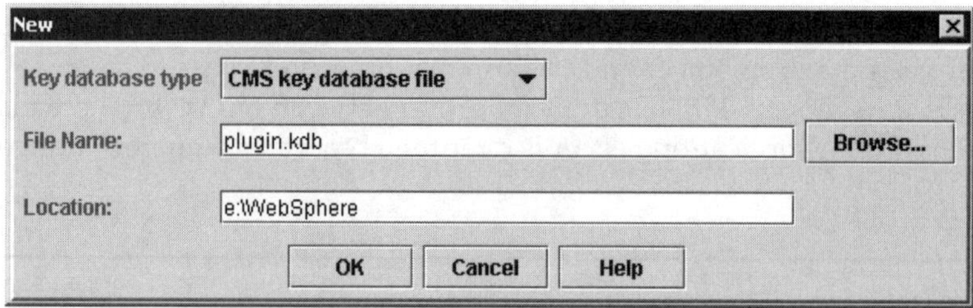

Then you need to select a password. Note that the utility helps you choose a password by marking what it thinks your password's strength is—that is, how easy it is to guess or break.

When the key file is first created, it includes quite a few CA trusted signer certificates, as shown next:

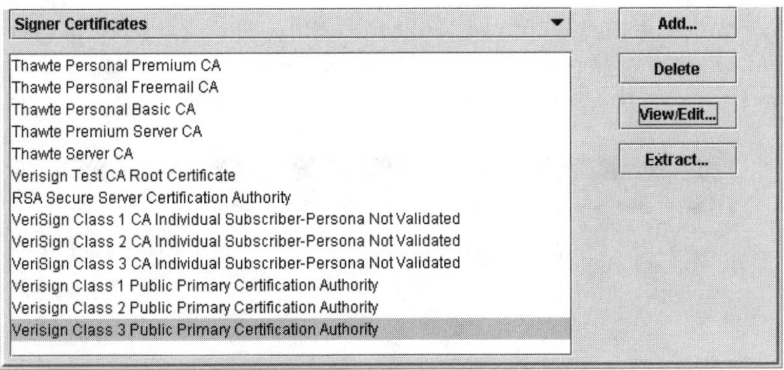

Because the plug-in needs only to certify itself to the Web container, you can delete all of those and create your own certificate. Later you will import this certificate directly into the container's key file. At this stage delete all the lines shown in the preceding illustration and instead create a new, self-signed certificate:

Create New Self-Signed Certificate

Please provide the following:

Key Label	plugin
Version	X509 V3
Key Size	1024
Common Name	vlad2000.viryanet.com
Organization	ViryaNet
Organization Unit (optional)	
Locality (optional)	
State/Province (optional)	
Zipcode (optional)	
Country	US
Validity Period	365 Days

OK Reset Cancel Help

Then you need to extract the certificate into a file that you will use later on in the process:

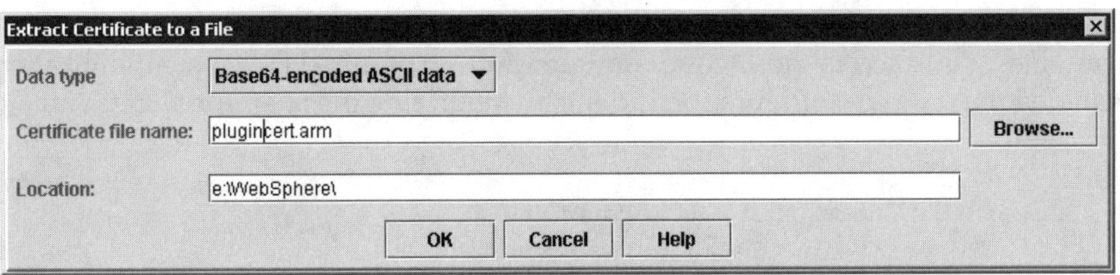

Now you can close the key file and quit the utility. The next stage is to start the key management utility that is part of the WebSphere installation. Again, you start out by creating a key file, but this time it is a Java Key Store (JKS) file:

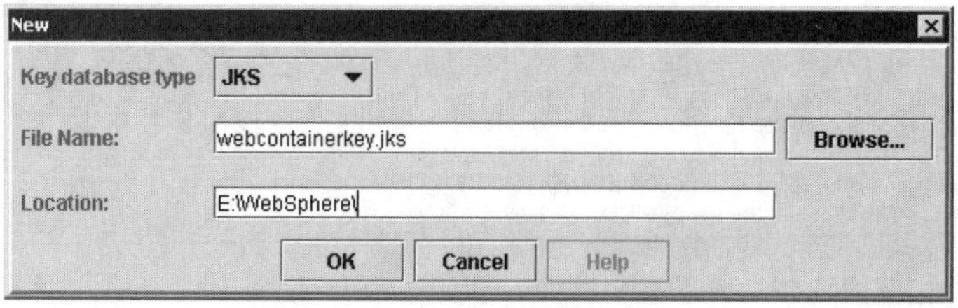

New
Key database type JKS
File Name: webcontainerkey.jks Browse...
Location: E:\WebSphere\
OK Cancel Help

After setting its password, you are again confronted with a whole set of signer certificates. Again, you can delete them all and add a new signer certificate. After you have this certificate, you again extract it out into a file.

Now you have finished the first steps and are ready to proceed to the next two steps. At this stage, you have created the two key files and have extracted each of the certificates into a *.arm* file. You need to import these into the respective key databases. What you are doing is making sure that when the Web container receives a request from the plug-in, it will have the plug-in's certificate and will be able to authenticate it.

To do this, you again open the key management utility from the IHS installation, and then open the plug-in key file. Select Signer Certificates from the pull-down menu and click the Add button. Select the *.arm* file extracted from the container, as shown here:

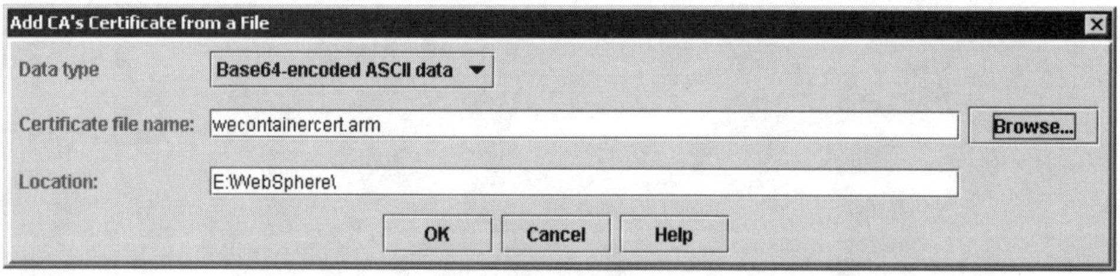

Add CA's Certificate from a File
Data type Base64-encoded ASCII data
Certificate file name: wecontainercert.arm Browse...
Location: E:\WebSphere\
OK Cancel Help

The new key database content appears in the IBM Key Management dialog box. You can close the plug-in key database and quit the utility. Invoking WebSphere's key management utility, you do the same thing with the plug-in's certificate, and you import the *plugin.arm* file into the container's key file.

The last two steps you need to perform involve the plug-in and the container themselves. You need to modify the configurations to require HTTPS communication. Changing the plug-in configuration is done by modifying the *plug-in.xml* file. You replace this

```
<ServerGroup Name="default_group">
      <Server Name="default_server">
        <Transport Hostname="ihs" Port="9080" Protocol="http"/>
```

```
      </Server>
</ServerGroup>
```

with this:

```
<ServerGroup Name="default_group">
      <Server Name="default_server">
        <Transport Hostname="ihs" Port="9080" Protocol="https"/>
            <Property name="keyring" value="e:\WebSphere\plugin.kdb"/>
            <Property name="stashfile" value="e:\WebSphere\plugin.sth"/>

        </Transport
      </Server>
</ServerGroup>
```

Changing the Web container to use HTTPS is accomplished from the Administrative Console.

1. Start the console and select the application server with which you want to set secure communication. Right-click the application server, and then select Properties.
2. From the Services tab, select the Web Container Service in the list and then click the Edit Properties button.
3. In the dialog box, select the Transport tab and click the single available transport:

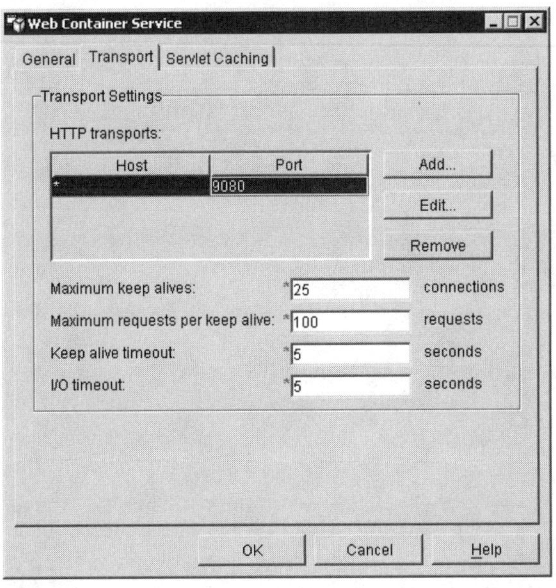

4. Click the Edit button, and then modify the transport's properties. Toggle the Enable SSL option and fill in the key filenames and the passwords.
5. After clicking OK in all the dialog boxes and restarting both servers, you are all set to go; communication between the servers will now be over HTTPS.

One final comment: Administrators can utilize both HTTP and HTTPS for the same application. Simply open two ports, and WebSphere is smart enough to direct non-secure requests via HTTP and secure requests via HTTPS.

Summary

Setting up a secure Web application involves a lot of work. The tasks described in this chapter are only part of the picture. In addition, you need to set up the firewall infrastructure and the routers—all within a security structure. All this becomes complex, and you should leave yourself plenty of time, because problems often arise due to faulty configuration.

This concludes the last chapter in the book. We hope that the text has been readable and that you have gained a lot of information that will help you develop, deploy, and administer applications running over the WebSphere Application Server. We also urge you to install and get familiar with IBM's info center because it is a useful tool for daily tasks. There are also a handful of good redbooks published by IBM that cover various aspects of WebSphere development and administration. These total up to more 5000 pages—so it is difficult to use them unless you want to go deep into a certain facet of the WebSphere Application Server; but if this is your goal, we highly recommend these reference materials.

Index

A

B

C

E

F

G

H

I

J

K

L

M

N

O

S

T

U

V

W

Y

Z

INTERNATIONAL CONTACT INFORMATION

AUSTRALIA
McGraw-Hill Book Company Australia Pty. Ltd.
TEL +61-2-9417-9899
FAX +61-2-9417-5687
http://www.mcgraw-hill.com.au
books-it_sydney@mcgraw-hill.com

CANADA
McGraw-Hill Ryerson Ltd.
TEL +905-430-5000
FAX +905-430-5020
http://www.mcgrawhill.ca

GREECE, MIDDLE EAST, NORTHERN AFRICA
McGraw-Hill Hellas
TEL +30-1-656-0990-3-4
FAX +30-1-654-5525

MEXICO (Also serving Latin America)
McGraw-Hill Interamericana Editores S.A. de C.V.
TEL +525-117-1583
FAX +525-117-1589
http://www.mcgraw-hill.com.mx
fernando_castellanos@mcgraw-hill.com

SINGAPORE (Serving Asia)
McGraw-Hill Book Company
TEL +65-863-1580
FAX +65-862-3354
http://www.mcgraw-hill.com.sg
mghasia@mcgraw-hill.com

SOUTH AFRICA
McGraw-Hill South Africa
TEL +27-11-622-7512
FAX +27-11-622-9045
robyn_swanepoel@mcgraw-hill.com

UNITED KINGDOM & EUROPE (Excluding Southern Europe)
McGraw-Hill Education Europe
TEL +44-1-628-502500
FAX +44-1-628-770224
http://www.mcgraw-hill.co.uk
computing_neurope@mcgraw-hill.com

ALL OTHER INQUIRIES Contact:
Osborne/McGraw-Hill
TEL +1-510-549-6600
FAX +1-510-883-7600
http://www.osborne.com
omg_international@mcgraw-hill.com

e-Pro magazine

About the CD

The CD-ROM contains IBM® WebSphere® Studio Application Developer, Version 4.0, for Windows NT® and Windows® 2000, Evaluation Copy, as well as IBM® WebSphere® Application Server, Advanced Single Server Edition, Version 4.0, for Windows NT® and Windows® 2000, Evaluation Copy, and IBM VisualAge® For Java™, Entry Professional Edition, Version 4.0 for Windows® 98, Windows NT 4.0, and Windows 2000, Evaluation Copy.

The software allows you to start building Web and enterprise applications making use of servlets, JSP, EJB, and more. Once you have built your applications you can deploy and run them using the WebSphere Application Server Advanced Single Server Edition Version 4.0. All software is courtesy of IBM and is provided under the end-user license agreement on the CD.

To install the WebSphere Application Server Advanced Single Server Edition Version 4.0 insert the CD, open the AS40 folder and double-click the setup program. To install WebSphere Studio Application Developer, open the Studio40 folder and double-click the setup program. To install VisualAge for Java Entry Professional Edition Version 4.0, open the VAJEP40 folder and double-click the setup program.

Hardware Requirements for the Products on the CD

IBM® WebSphere® Application Server, Advanced Single Server Edition, Version 4.0, for Windows NT® and Windows® 2000, Evaluation Copy

- 500Mhz Pentium® processor
- 384 MB RAM minimum, 512 MB recommended
- 180 MB free disk space for the base application server
- Ethernet or Token Ring card
- CD-ROM drive
- Network connectivity to the internet

IBM WebSphere Studio Application Developer, Version 4.0, for Windows NT and Windows 2000, Evaluation Copy

- A mouse or an alternative pointing device
- Pentium II processor or higher recommended
- SVGA (800x600) display or higher (1024 x 768 recommended)

- 256 MB RAM minimum
- Disk space requirements: 400 MB minimum (based on NTFS, actual disk space on FAT depends on hard [disk] drive size and partitioning)

IBM VisualAge® for Java™, Entry Professional Edition, Version 4.0, for Windows 98, Windows NT 4.0, and Windows 2000, Evaluation Copy

- Mouse or pointing device (see "Note" below)
- Pentium II processor or higher recommended. If you plan to work in the WebSphere Test Environment we recommend a minimum processor speed of 400 MHz.
- SVGA (800x600) display or higher (1024 x 768 recommended)
- 48 MB RAM minimum (96 MB recommended)
- 128 MB RAM minimum is required if you wish to work in the VisualAge for Java WebSphere Test Environment. We strongly recommend 256 MB to avoid disk thrashing.
- Disk space requirements: (based on NTFS) 350 MB minimum (400 MB or more recommended). Disk space on FAT depends on hard disk size and partitioning: If you are installing to a very large FAT drive, then the space required for VisualAge for Java is almost doubled (due to 32KB cluster overhead).

VisualAge for Java does not support the Logitech scroll mouse. Any Logitech mice with drivers that remap scrolling action to the mouse will cause a system error to occur when it is used to scroll.

LICENSE AGREEMENT

THIS PRODUCT (THE "PRODUCT") CONTAINS PROPRIETARY SOFTWARE, DATA AND INFORMATION (INCLUDING DOCUMENTATION) OWNED BY THE McGRAW-HILL COMPANIES, INC. ("McGRAW-HILL") AND ITS LICENSORS. YOUR RIGHT TO USE THE PRODUCT IS GOVERNED BY THE TERMS AND CONDITIONS OF THIS AGREEMENT.

LICENSE: Throughout this License Agreement, "you" shall mean either the individual or the entity whose agent opens this package. You are granted a non-exclusive and non-transferable license to use the Product subject to the following terms:
(i) If you have licensed a single user version of the Product, the Product may only be used on a single computer (i.e., a single CPU). If you licensed and paid the fee applicable to a local area network or wide area network version of the Product, you are subject to the terms of the following subparagraph (ii).
(ii) If you have licensed a local area network version, you may use the Product on unlimited workstations located in one single building selected by you that is served by such local area network. If you have licensed a wide area network version, you may use the Product on unlimited workstations located in multiple buildings on the same site selected by you that is served by such wide area network; provided, however, that any building will not be considered located in the same site if it is more than five (5) miles away from any building included in such site. In addition, you may only use a local area or wide area network version of the Product on one single server. If you wish to use the Product on more than one server, you must obtain written authorization from McGraw-Hill and pay additional fees.
(iii) You may make one copy of the Product for back-up purposes only and you must maintain an accurate record as to the location of the back-up at all times.

COPYRIGHT; RESTRICTIONS ON USE AND TRANSFER: All rights (including copyright) in and to the Product are owned by McGraw-Hill and its licensors. You are the owner of the enclosed disc on which the Product is recorded. You may not use, copy, decompile, disassemble, reverse engineer, modify, reproduce, create derivative works, transmit, distribute, sublicense, store in a database or retrieval system of any kind, rent or transfer the Product, or any portion thereof, in any form or by any means (including electronically or otherwise) except as expressly provided for in this License Agreement. You must reproduce the copyright notices, trademark notices, legends and logos of McGraw-Hill and its licensors that appear on the Product on the back-up copy of the Product which you are permitted to make hereunder. All rights in the Product not expressly granted herein are reserved by McGraw-Hill and its licensors.

TERM: This License Agreement is effective until terminated. It will terminate if you fail to comply with any term or condition of this License Agreement. Upon termination, you are obligated to return to McGraw-Hill the Product together with all copies thereof and to purge all copies of the Product included in any and all servers and computer facilities.

DISCLAIMER OF WARRANTY: THE PRODUCT AND THE BACK-UP COPY ARE LICENSED "AS IS." McGRAW-HILL, ITS LICENSORS AND THE AUTHORS MAKE NO WARRANTIES, EXPRESS OR IMPLIED, AS TO THE RESULTS TO BE OBTAINED BY ANY PERSON OR ENTITY FROM USE OF THE PRODUCT, ANY INFORMATION OR DATA INCLUDED THEREIN AND/OR ANY TECHNICAL SUPPORT SERVICES PROVIDED HEREUNDER, IF ANY ("TECHNICAL SUPPORT SERVICES"). McGRAW-HILL, ITS LICENSORS AND THE AUTHORS MAKE NO EXPRESS OR IMPLIED WARRANTIES OF MERCHANTABILITY OR FITNESS FOR A PARTICULAR PURPOSE OR USE WITH RESPECT TO THE PRODUCT. McGRAW-HILL, ITS LICENSORS, AND THE AUTHORS MAKE NO GUARANTEE THAT YOU WILL PASS ANY CERTIFICATION EXAM WHATSOEVER BY USING THIS PRODUCT. NEITHER McGRAW-HILL, ANY OF ITS LICENSORS NOR THE AUTHORS WARRANT THAT THE FUNCTIONS CONTAINED IN THE PRODUCT WILL MEET YOUR REQUIREMENTS OR THAT THE OPERATION OF THE PRODUCT WILL BE UNINTERRUPTED OR ERROR FREE. YOU ASSUME THE ENTIRE RISK WITH RESPECT TO THE QUALITY AND PERFORMANCE OF THE PRODUCT.

LIMITED WARRANTY FOR DISC: To the original licensee only, McGraw-Hill warrants that the enclosed disc on which the Product is recorded is free from defects in materials and workmanship under normal use and service for a period of ninety (90) days from the date of purchase. In the event of a defect in the disc covered by the foregoing warranty, McGraw-Hill will replace the disc.

LIMITATION OF LIABILITY: NEITHER McGRAW-HILL, ITS LICENSORS NOR THE AUTHORS SHALL BE LIABLE FOR ANY INDIRECT, SPECIAL OR CONSEQUENTIAL DAMAGES, SUCH AS BUT NOT LIMITED TO, LOSS OF ANTICIPATED PROFITS OR BENEFITS, RESULTING FROM THE USE OR INABILITY TO USE THE PRODUCT EVEN IF ANY OF THEM HAS BEEN ADVISED OF THE POSSIBILITY OF SUCH DAMAGES. THIS LIMITATION OF LIABILITY SHALL APPLY TO ANY CLAIM OR CAUSE WHATSOEVER WHETHER SUCH CLAIM OR CAUSE ARISES IN CONTRACT, TORT, OR OTHERWISE. Some states do not allow the exclusion or limitation of indirect, special or consequential damages, so the above limitation may not apply to you.

U.S. GOVERNMENT RESTRICTED RIGHTS: Any software included in the Product is provided with restricted rights subject to subparagraphs (c), (1) and (2) of the Commercial Computer Software-Restricted Rights clause at 48 C.F.R. 52.227-19. The terms of this Agreement applicable to the use of the data in the Product are those under which the data are generally made available to the general public by McGraw-Hill. Except as provided herein, no reproduction, use, or disclosure rights are granted with respect to the data included in the Product and no right to modify or create derivative works from any such data is hereby granted.

GENERAL: This License Agreement constitutes the entire agreement between the parties relating to the Product. The terms of any Purchase Order shall have no effect on the terms of this License Agreement. Failure of McGraw-Hill to insist at any time on strict compliance with this License Agreement shall not constitute a waiver of any rights under this License Agreement. This License Agreement shall be construed and governed in accordance with the laws of the State of New York. If any provision of this License Agreement is held to be contrary to law, that provision will be enforced to the maximum extent permissible and the remaining provisions will remain in full force and effect.